Hirohito's War

Hirohito's War

The Pacific War, 1941–1945

FRANCIS PIKE

BLOOMSBURY

LONDON · OXFORD · NEW YORK · NEW DELHI · SYDNEY

Bloomsbury Publishing Plc

An imprint of Bloomsbury Publishing Plc

50 Bedford Square   1385 Broadway
London   New York
WC1B 3DP   NY 10018
UK   USA

www.bloomsbury.com

BLOOMSBURY and the Diana logo are trademarks of Bloomsbury Publishing Plc

First published 2015

Paperback edition published 2016

© Francis Pike, 2015, 2016

British Library Cataloguing-in-Publication Data
A catalogue record for this book is available from the British Library.

ISBN: HB: 978-1-4725-9670-3
        PB: 978-1-4725-9671-0
        ePDF: 978-1-4725-9672-7
        ePub: 978-1-4725-9673-4

Library of Congress Cataloging-in-Publication Data
A catalog record for this book is available from the Library of Congress.

Cover design: Catherine Wood
Cover image © National Naval Aviation Museum

Typeset by RefineCatch Limited, Bungay, Suffolk
Printed and bound in India

For my godchildren

Alexander Johnson

Frederick Barber

Julia Colfer

Contents

Appendices

A) Submarines: America Draws Tight the Noose

[December 1941–August 1945]

*Planned Submarine Attack on the Panama Canal: The Failure of Japanese
Submarine Design: Wasteful Dissipation of Japanese Submarine Force:
Japanese Submarine Cargo Missions to Europe: Japanese Submarines'
Disappointing 'Kill' Performance: Japan's 'Long Lance' Jockeys: Newport
Torpedo Station: Rear-Admiral Charles Lockwood: US Submarine
Achievements in the Pacific War: The Failure of Japanese
Counter-Submarine Strategy*

B) Oil, Raw Materials and Logistics: 'Just Start Swinging'

[December 1941–August 1945]

*Logistics of Oil in the Pacific War: America's T-2 Tanker: Japan's Oil Tanker
Fleet: Raw Materials Issues of the US Economy: Liberty Ships 'to go': Cargo Attack
Ships, LSTs and Higgins Boats: Japan's Cargo Ship Problems: Japan's Air Force
Logistics: US Supply Logistics in the Pacific Region: Operation OLYMPIC and
Japan's Logistical Denouement*

C) Economics of the Pacific War: The 'New Deal' Mobilized

[December 1941–August 1945]

*Management of the US Wartime Economy: US Economy in 1941:
Guns and Butter: Inflation and General Max: Japan's Wartime Economy:
Productivity, Entrepreneurs, Management, Labor, Blacks, Women:
Expansion of America's Productive Capacity: US Aircraft Production:
Tanks, Artillery, Trucks, Ordnance and the Problem of Obsolescence:
Electronics, Radio, and Radar: Was the Depression a Hindrance or
Boon to US War Mobilization?*

D) The Japanese Empire: From Co-Prosperity to Tyranny

[December 1941–August 1945]

The Philosophy of Japan's Great Co-Prosperity Sphere: Old Empire: Taiwan, Korea and Manchuria: The Structures of Japan's New Empire: Slave Labor in Japan and in the Field: Cruelty and Suppression: Prisoners of war: The Psychology of Brutality: Unit 731 and the Secrets of Medical Experimentation

E) Kamikaze: Divine Winds

[October 1944–August 1945]

Halsey: After Leyte Gulf: Kamikaze: Individual Beginnings: The Formal Adoption of Kamikaze as a Strategy: Recruitment, Motivation and Training: Japanese Government Propaganda: Developments in Kamikaze Technology and the US Response: Naval Kamikaze and Yamato's Suicide Mission: US Defense Tactics: Fight to the Death and Operation KETSU (Decisive): Admiral Ugaki, The Last Kamikaze: The Cost and Effectiveness of the Kamikaze Campaign: Kamikaze: A Unique Japanese Phenomenon?

F) ULTRA: American Intelligence in the Pacific War

G) Could Japan Have Won the Pacific War?

H) The Role of Oil in the Pacific War

Oil's Early History: Development of the Oil Industry in the United States: Royal Dutch Shell: The Growth of Oil Fired Engines in the Marine Industry: The Rise of the Automobile, Tanks and Trucks Transform Battlefield Mobility: Aviation Gasoline: Interwar Development of the Aeronautical Industry: Global Oil Output: Oil and the Decision for War: Conclusion

I) Aircraft Carriers in the Pacific War

Summary: Comparison of Pacific War Aircraft Carriers: Essex Class Carrier: US Light Carriers: Japanese Fleet Carriers

J) The 'Pacific War': Sundry Tables and Lists

Ground Weapons: *i) Artillery ii) Tanks iii) Rifles and Machine Guns iv) Other Field Weapons*
Ships: *i) Aircaft Carriers, ii) Battleships, iii) Cruisers, iv) Destroyers v) Others*
Aircraft: *i) Fighters ii) Bombers*
Pacific War Casualties: *i) Military and Navy ii) Civilian*
World War II Conferences
Political Leaders: *i) America ii) Japan iii) China iv) Great Britain v) Australia*

K) Month by Month Timeline of the Pacific War

[December 1941–August 1945]

Appendices available online:
http://bloomsbury.com/hirohito/
http://francispike.org

Map, Diagram, Drawing and Chart List

Maps available online:
http://bloomsbury.com/hirohito/
http://francispike.org

Graphic Design of Maps by Amy Martin: amy_beijaflor@yahoo.co.uk

Online Resources for *Hirohito's War*

Additional resources have been provided online for *Hirohito's War: The Pacific War, 1941–1945*; please visit:

http://www.bloomsbury.com/hirohito

or

http://francispike.org

Online Resources

210+ Maps and Charts, 500+ Photographs, 11 Appendices on Thematic Subjects regarding the *Pacific War*, a Timeline: 1930–1945, Bibliography, Notes and Sundry Lists and Tables. Reviews and a contact form have also been added.

Author's Note

Printing technicalities made it possible to publish a book that was up to 1,200 pages but the addition of over 230 maps, charts, drawings and diagrams was not practical within these limitations. Neither would it have been possible to include eleven appendices adding a further 200-plus pages or the more than 500 photographs that have been collated to accompany *Hirohito's War* chapter-by-chapter. Furthermore the addition of these resources into print would have necessarily meant an unwanted increase in cover price.

Fortunately in the last five years technology has come to our rescue. Smart phones, tablets and laptop computers give us easy mobile access to online resources. This new technology is now ubiquitous and provides readers unprecedented access to written and visual information. Military history is sometimes difficult to follow without maps and for this reason, both to help me and to elucidate my readers, I have compiled over 210 maps, drawings, diagrams and charts on my website **www.francispike.org**. These are presented in a consistent color format to help readers track action in the unfamiliar geography in which the major engagements of the *Pacific War* took place. It is envisaged that readers will be able to follow the narrative of *Hirohito's War* in conjunction with these online resources.

I apologize in advance to the technologically phobic. But I have been advised that access to online resources is easier than having to flip to the back of a book to search for maps. This arrangement may be different but I believe that Bloomsbury has found an innovative solution that offers considerable advantages. In the future I believe that it may become commonplace even for history books of a more limited scale.

Francis Pike

20 January 2016

Notes on Language and Text

Maps, appendices and notes referred to in the book are available online; please visit http://bloomsbury.com/hirohito and http://francispike.org

Notes on Romanization of Chinese

The transcription of Chinese language into Romanized form began in the early seventeenth century with the Jesuit missionary and Chinese scholar Matteo Ricci. Subsequently there have been many such Romanized systems. The most important from the second half of the nineteenth century was the Wade-Giles system. Originally developed by Sir Thomas Wade, a British Ambassador to China and later the first Professor of Chinese at Cambridge University, his Romanized English-Mandarin dictionary was further developed by Herbert Giles, a diplomat in China and his son Lionel, a curator at the British Museum and translator of Sun Tzu's *The Art of War*.

The Wade-Giles system remained dominant until the 1950s when the People's Republic of China began to develop a new system of Romanization called '*Hanyu Pinyin*'. Published in 1958 the *Pinyin* system has been revised a number of times subsequently.

Hirohito's War has used both the Wade-Giles and the *pinyin* systems depending on usage and context. For example Peking (Wade-Giles) has been preferred to Beijing (*pinyin*) because that was the usage of the *époque*. Similarly Nanking has been preferred to Nanjing. Mukden (*viz* the Mukden Incident) has been favored rather than the present day Shenyang. However Chongqing (*pinyin*) has been preferred to Chung king.

Chinese names have mainly been transcribed using *pinyin* but numbers of leading people are referred to in earlier Romanized form such as Sun Yat-sen, Chiang Kai-shek, H.H. Kung, and T.V. Soong whose *pinyin* forms are virtually unknown in Western literature. *Kuomintang* (Chinese Nationalist Party) is also preferred to the less used *pinyin* form *Guomindang*.

Note on Japanese Names

Japanese names have been used with given name first and family name second as in the Western rather than the Japanese tradition. Japan's Emperor is referred to by his personal name, Hirohito, as he has been known historically outside of Japan. In Japan he is referred to by his posthumous name, Emperor Showa.

Notes on Italicization and Capitals

The author has used italics throughout the book for wars, battles, treaties, foreign words and publication titles. Italics have also been used for ship names. Less conventionally, to different land and sea locations, italics have also been used to denote the names of islands, oceans, seas, bays, gulfs, lakes, rivers, creeks etc. Capital letters have been used for radio messages, and for the names of war plans and operations as well acronyms.

Notes on Spelling, Punctuation and Capitalization

American rather than British spelling has been used. Thus 'honor' not 'honour', 'capitalization' not 'capitalisation' etc.

American punctuation for quotations has been used in preference to British usage. Thus "I will return" rather than 'I will return'. Single parentheses have been used for nicknames etc., e.g. 'Hellzapoppin Ridge', 'Betty' bomber, 'Pappy' Boyington

Capital letters have been used for abbreviations and acronyms, the verbatim quotation of messages and for the code names of Operations and Conferences, e.g. Operation NIBBLE AND CANDY; Tehran Conference [EUREKA].

Bold has only been used for titles, subtitles and indication of Maps, Charts and Diagrams. Except in quotations, distances and weights have used analogue rather than decimal descriptions – thus miles not kilometers.

Acknowledgments

In writing *Hirohito's War: The Pacific War, 1941–1945*, I have been helped by many friends in different capacities. In particular, a chance meeting with Christopher Szpilman, Professor of History at Kyushu Sangyo University, Fukuoka, in a Berlin café led to a friendship with one of the foremost experts on Japanese interwar politics. He has been an invaluable source of knowledge and advice.

Geoffrey Mann, Managing Director of Russell House Publishing, an old friend from Cambridge, has read every word of *Hirohito's War* and has been a steadfast editor who has given advice on every aspect of my work. Stephen Barber, a Managing Director of Pictet, Chairman of Prix Pictet and author of *Style and Usage*, has been an authoritative advisor on my text. Ratan Engineer, a Partner at Ernst and Young, was another volunteer reader who has read and commented on much of my work. It is a source of great and continuing sadness that this extraordinarily learned, cultured, erudite and kind giant of a man died suddenly in April 2015.

Simon May, Professor of Philosophy at King's College London and formerly a Professor at Tokyo University, has been a constant supporter of my book, giving particular advice on structure and content. Professor Mark Blum at the University of Louisville has also been a helpful reader. Other important readers have been my mother, Mrs. Elizabeth Pike and my brother John Pike. My business partner, Dr. Sir Richard Temple, a world authority on Russian and Byzantine Icons at The Temple Gallery, has also been unfailingly supportive and understanding of my long disappearances.

Historians who had a formative influence on my career and inspired my passion for history as an undergraduate at Cambridge, include Professor Blair Worden, Professor Richard Overy, Professor Vic Gatrell, Professor John Whitehead, Dr. Gordon Johnson, Professor Christopher Andrew, and the late Dr. Clive Trebilcock who introduced me to modern Japanese history. At Selwyn College, the master, the Reverend Owen Chadwick, Regius Professor of Modern History at Cambridge was also unfailingly supportive during my years as an undergraduate. He died at the age of 99 in July 2015 just as *Hirohito's War* was being published. Basil Morgan was an outstanding and inspirational teacher at Uppingham School. David Gaine was another Uppingham teacher who was a formative influence on my academic career.

I am also indebted to Bruce Anderson and the late Frank Johnson, a former editor of *The Spectator*, who encouraged me to write about Asia. Lester Crook, history editor at IB Tauris was instrumental in getting my book writing career underway with the publication of *Empires at War, A Short History of Modern Asia Since World War II* (2010). Subsequently Nigel Newton and Claire Lipscomb and their colleagues at Bloomsbury Publishing have given me tremendous support in the publication of

Hirohito's War, which, at over 1,150 pages (not including 1,000 pages of online resources), has been an enormous undertaking which few other publishers would have considered.

A number of friends have been kind enough to host me at their houses while I have worked on *Hirohito's War*. They include Howard and Veronika Covington, Marie-Christine Dokhélar and Jacques Neyton, Richard Edwards, Francois and Jacqueline Granier, Lynn Guinness, Sabina Keresztes, Katinka Langloh, Professor John Studd and Professor Margaret Johnson, and Pierre Sapin. On long visits to China I have been hugely indebted to Sun Hong and Lu Tongyan.

The building and maintenance of my website (www.francispike.org), which supports almost 1,000 pages of online resources for *Hirohito's War,* has been an enormous task and I am very grateful for Tim Sander's huge effort on this project. Likewise Amy Martin, juggling her life between Cambodia, the Welsh hills, and Portugal, has done prodigious amounts of working with me to build a resource of over 230 maps, charts, drawings and diagrams for *Hirohito's War*—a resource that will continue to expand in the year ahead. I would also like to thank Kate Vaughan Williams for her help in various research projects over the past year.

Other friends who have supported me in different ways over the five years in which I have written *Hirohito's War* include Peter and Gemma Johnson, Nicholas and Jennifer Johnson, Sylvia Wolf and Rüdiger Kuhnke, Joachim and Marie-Elisabeth Köhler, William and Dilla Daniel, Sarah Daniel, Tim and Diana Stephenson, Jasper and Abbey Morris, Rebeccah Blum, Lester Crook, Jo Elford, Elaine Moore, Daniel Walter, Anja Gröshel, Mark Bedingham, Marta Gnyp, Petek Sketcher, Hendrik Berinson, Thomas Mönius, Richard Edwards, Christopher Wood, the late Tim Gäre and Saya Mizuno. My nieces, Rebecca Pike, Helen Pike and Maximiliane Pike have also been a great support. I would like to thank my London catering manager, Kimiko Barber, who has enlivened all my trips to England with her great hospitality and kindness.

Lastly I would like to thank Peter Daniel for allowing me to use the photographs he took of Hiroshima a few months after the dropping of the atom bomb. The photographs are available in the online Appendix to *Hirohito's War*. After serving on the extraordinarily dangerous Arctic Convoys for which he has now been given a medal by the British and Russian governments, Peter then deployed to the *Pacific* as a sub-Lieutenant on the battleship HMS *Duke of York*. After they docked at Kure, the main naval base of the Japanese Imperial Fleet on the Inland Sea, Peter, ever curious, asked for and received permission to take a train the short distance along the coast to Hiroshima. A keen amateur photographer, he took photographs of the devastation. After a distinguished career as both a lecturer and practitioner of landscape architecture, Peter Daniel lived in Berwickshire in the Scottish borders until death at the age of 90 in December 2015. He is a reminder to us all of the men and women, few remaining, who fought in *World War II*. For this I would also like to thank him.

Francis Pike
21 January 2016

Introduction and Background

[Maps: 0.1, 0.2]

I saw Hirohito (the Emperor Showa) in person on two occasions—both at the Tokyo Basho, one of Sumo wrestling's six *honbasho* (main tournament). The first time I was sitting some fifty yards away as he made his entrance. He was tiny, wizened, and impassive; the deep creases falling down from the corners of his mouth giving him the appearance of permanent sadness. On the second occasion I was on the far side of the *Ryogoku Kokugikan* (sumo stadium) and this time I was struck by the roar of approval of the 13,000 capacity crowd that greeted his entrance.

I could not help but reflect on the different fate that had befallen Germany's Führer and compare it to that of his Axis partner, Hirohito. It has been a question that has intrigued me ever since. However, the title of this work, *Hirohito's War* does not mean that I believe that his role was identical to that of Hitler. Although Hirohito was never the entirely passive creature invented by the elaborate post-war propaganda of the Japanese Imperial Court and General Douglas MacArthur, neither was he the arch villain and prime mover behind Japan's expansionist foreign policy imagined by some historians. In constitutional terms, although Hirohito was, at least in theory, an absolute monarch, head of state, commander-in-chief of the armed forces and godhead, by convention he operated within a framework that allocated power to different elite interest groups. Only ever nominally democratic, Japan's constitutional checks and balances broke down in the 1930s and power shifted toward the Army and Navy.

It was a shift that the Emperor, perhaps fearing a *coup d'état*, was powerless to resist. Hirohito, weak and indecisive by nature, was frustrated by the Army's aggression in Manchuria in 1931 and then later in Mainland China, yet nevertheless enjoyed the fruits of military success and conquest after the event. He may not have been as hard line as his ultranationalist generals but there is no reason to believe that the Emperor's views differed markedly from the belief in Japanese Imperial expansion, which underlay the zeitgeist in Japan. Thus Hirohito spent most of the *Pacific War* dressed in military uniform and followed the tides of conflict in minute detail from the war room built in the basement of his palace—increasingly offering the military the benefits of his cryptic advice as Japan stumbled toward defeat. It is notable that the two most decisive interventions of his reign—the last being his acceptance of the Allies' unconditional terms of surrender in August 1945—came when the army was in a state of decision-making paralysis.

As for his responsibility for Japan's war crimes in Asia, including mass executions, the use of gas and biological weapons and human experimentation, it seems unlikely that Hirohito was totally unaware of atrocities, particularly in China. However, there is no proof that he was informed about them and certainly no evidence that he was in any way an instigator of policies that in the case of China, where an estimated twenty million civilians died, were in effect genocidal. In international war crimes law, as established at the tribunals at Nürnberg, Tokyo, Shanghai, Darwin and elsewhere after *World War II*, guilt for atrocities was determined merely by dint of responsibility. In other words ignorance of war crimes was no defense for the senior commanders on trial. On this principle, Hirohito, as Japan's commander-in-chief, would almost certainly have been found guilty and executed if he had been placed before the Tokyo Tribunal. He was saved by the arbitrary and misguided decision by General MacArthur and the Truman administration to not allow Hirohito or his family to stand trial on the misguided understanding that the Emperor was the key to the post-war stability of Japan.

Whatever the legal and constitutional position of Hirohito, there can be no denying the centrality of his person in the mythology of Japanese exceptionalism. In the post-Meiji Restoration period, the role of the Emperor was put at the heart of an all-encompassing state philosophy and in the *Pacific War*, Hirohito was the idol for which millions of Japanese soldiers died. As Prime Minister Tojo said in 1942, "The Emperor is the Godhead . . . and we, no matter how hard we strive as Ministers, are nothing more than human." Many of Japan's soldiers, in suicidal charges, uttered the last words, *Tenno Heika Banzai!* (Long live the Emperor!) Hirohito may not have been the prime mover of the *Pacific War*, but he was certainly its embodiment.

Understanding Hirohito's role was just one objective of writing a history of the *Pacific War*. In working on my previous book *Empires at War: A Short History of Modern Asia since World War II* [2010], it became evident that both the origins and conduct of the *Pacific War* were historical issues inviting further investigation. *Hirohito's War: The Pacific War, 1941–1945* is a result of this work and also serves as a prequel to my earlier publication.

In spite of the vast and growing literature of the *Pacific War*, there has been no recent comprehensive one-volume history of the conflict. Indeed since 1945, there have only been three: *The Rising Sun: The Decline and Fall of the Japanese Empire, 1936–1945* [1970] by John Toland, *The Pacific War 1941–1945* [1981] by John Costello, and *Eagle Against the Sun: The American War with Japan* [1985] by Ronald Spector. While these books have their strengths, they have all become somewhat dated. The main aim of writing *Hirohito's War* has been to present a balanced, comprehensive and readable one-volume narrative of the conflict. The book takes advantage of the new material that has become available over the last few decades. Although the written history of the *Pacific War* is abundant in thousands of narrower studies, many of them superb, I nevertheless believe that there is a point to a one-volume history that is written with a single and consistent voice. Without it, a balanced overview of the war is not possible.

The narrative structure of *Hirohito's War* is different from other histories of the *Pacific War*. The approach I have taken reflects some of its unique characteristics. First, there is the matter of geographic scale. *World War II* in Europe took place on a battlefield that was approximately 3m square miles in size (based on a 1,000 mile radius from Berlin). By comparison the *Pacific War* took place on a battlefield of approximately 28m square miles (based on a 3,000 mile radius from Tokyo). **[Map: 0.1]**

Second, whereas the war in Europe was mainly two-dimensional (land and air), the war in the *Pacific* was four-dimensional (land, air, sea and undersea). Although the maritime components were present in the war in Europe they were, apart from the first two years of the submarine *Battle of the Atlantic*, secondary elements of the conflict. There were no great set piece naval battles in the European sector of *World War II*.

Third, the war in the *Pacific*, unlike Europe, was fought throughout on multiple fronts and in multiple dimensions at the same time. In 1944 battles were raging in the *Pacific* Islands, New Guinea, the Philippines, northern, central and southern China, Northern Burma and the Burma-India borders. Although the land battles of the *Pacific War* are most closely associated with jungle and tropical conditions, important action took place in the snowy wastes of the Himalayas and Alaska, as well as Siberia, Mongolia, Northern Manchuria, *Sakhalin Island* and the *Kuril Islands*.

As a consequence of these special characteristics, the *Pacific War* was probably the most complex conflict geopolitically, geographically and militarily since the *Thirty Years War* of 1618–1648. Over the last decade new tools have been transformational in helping to understand the nature of the war. Google Maps for instance has enabled the historian to drill down onto the terrain of battles that are particularly difficult to understand without a detailed understanding of the topography. The fighting of the *Pacific War* was highly characterized by its unique geography and concomitant logistical requirements. The *South Pacific*'s geography in particular adds a complexity which may be one of the reasons that there have been so few attempts at writing a comprehensive one-volume history of the conflict.

A pure linear timeline narrative of the action of the *Pacific War*, as undertaken by others, sees the storyline constantly jump from region to region. It is a structure that makes analysis and understanding of the strategic issues of each regional campaign difficult to comprehend.

My approach has therefore been to tell timeline narratives based on individual campaigns rather than across multiple campaigns. *Hirohito's War* therefore divides up the narrative into chapters based on individual campaigns or battles. Timelines aim to be consistent within chapters if not always between the forty chapters into which the book is divided. However, as an aid to readers, an overall timeline of key events is included in the appendices. *Hirohito's War* is structured as follows:

Chapter 1 (Part I: Meiji Restoration: 1868) sets out the historical context of the *Pacific War* between 1868 and 1930.

Chapters 2–4 (Part II: Japan versus America and the World: 1931–1941) describe the events leading up to the *Pacific War* and evaluate the causes of the conflict.

Chapters 5–11 (Part III: Hirohito's Whirlwind Conquests: December 1941–June 1942) narrate Japan's riotous military conquest and expansion in the first six months of the war.

Chapters 12–20 (Part IV: 'Victory Disease': Japan's Reversal of Fortune: June 1942–December 1942) analyse the turning point battles and campaigns of the *Pacific War*.

Chapters 21–30 (Part V: Toil and Sweat: The Pacific, India, Burma, and China: January 1943–June 1944) report the hard fought battles and campaigns of the middle years of the *Pacific War*.

Chapters 31–35 (Part VI: Japan's Forces of Empire Annihilated: June 1944–February 1945) explain the reasons for the crushing Allied victories that put an end to Japan's imperial ambitions.

Chapters 36–40 (Part VII: Destruction of Japan's Homeland: February 1945–August 1945) cover the battles on and over Japanese soil as America prepared for the invasion of its four main islands—a campaign that was obviated by Hirohito's surrender after the dropping of atom bombs on Hiroshima and Nagasaki.

The subjects of economics, logistics, the submarine war, the Japanese Empire, *kamikaze*, aircraft carriers and the role of oil in the *Pacific War*, which have been interwoven in the narrative of Hirohito's War, have been expanded as special thematic studies in the online appendices. Another theme given particular emphasis is the importance of technology in tipping the balance of the war toward the United States. In 1939 the world was at the cusp of moving from a purely mechanical age to an electro-mechanic age and the onset of war speeded up the adoption of new technologies that had a significant impact on the outcome of the war as well as global prosperity in the succeeding decades. A short counterfactual history essay on the "what if" question, *Could Japan have won the Pacific War?* is also included as an appendix. This essay argues that victory for the Allies was not inevitable. History is awash with examples of Davids beating Goliaths. Athens' and Sparta's defeat of Persia in the fifth century BC is just one important example. Over 200 maps, charts, drawings and diagrams have been added to the online resources available at **www.francispike.org**.

In looking at the origins of the *Pacific War*, I have sought to place the conflict within the context of a 100-year struggle for the domination of the *Pacific* between the United States and its competitors, particularly Japan. *Hirohito's War* argues that it is pointless to look in isolation at Japan's imperial aggression as the cause of the *Pacific War*. The economic, social and political implosion of China from its pinnacle as the world's strongest nation at the beginning of the nineteenth century is central to the story of the destabilization of Asia in which the Western powers, as well as Russia (later the Soviet Union) and Japan scrambled for pieces of its former regional superpower. After *World*

War I, the establishment of a "Pax Anglo-Saxon" in the form of the Treaty of Versailles, the League of Nations and the Washington System was fatally undermined by the failure of the Western powers to underwrite their international structures with concomitant force.

Finally, in a global context, President Franklin Roosevelt's determination to prevent America from being locked out of incipient autarkic empires and their markets in Europe and Asia, led him to bring America out of its 1930s isolation to confront fascism that not only threatened America's own Asian Empire but also its opportunities for global commercial expansion. By his *de facto* embargo of oil supplies to Japan in July 1941, arguably an act of war in itself, Roosevelt forced Japan's leaders to consider a war with America—a conflict both sides had contemplated for decades. Faced with the unpalatable alternative of yielding to America's demand that it withdraw its armies from China, Japan's leaders determined on a high-risk strategy of attacking *Pearl Harbor* with the hope of battering America into accepting its imperial ambitions. The result triggered all-out war for America with both Japan and Germany.

The *Pacific War* is the most written about subject in American history and, perhaps not surprisingly, the focus of American historians tends to be very largely on the campaigns in the *Pacific*. An unscientific poll of American friends and acquaintances with no strong interest in history normally produces the recall of just five events: *Pearl Harbor*, *Midway*, *Guadalcanal*, *Iwo Jima* and Hiroshima. The importance of mainland Asia, particularly China but also Burma, is largely eviscerated from the American narrative. Yet China provided not only the *casus belli* but also the vast majority of the military casualties of the *Pacific War*—some four million dead compared to 110,000 Americans. Similarly overlooked has been the contribution of the Australians in the "turnaround" battles of the *Pacific War*; the all-conquering Japanese Armies suffered their first major defeats, not at *Guadalcanal*, but at the *Battles of the Kokoda Trail* at the hands of Australian troops. In part this neglect has been the legacy of General MacArthur whose brilliant propaganda machine wrote Australia out of the picture. Partly as a result, British and American historians in the post-war period have largely ignored the significant Australian contribution to the war effort. The campaign in the Dutch East Indies (Indonesia) has similarly been overlooked although their oil was the primary objective of the Japanese Army's sweep through South East Asia.

Readers of *Hirohito's War* will be confronted with the remarkable effect that MacArthur, the *Pacific War*'s totemic military figure, had on America's conduct of the *Pacific War* and its historiography. MacArthur was fortunate that his reputation was rescued after his bungled defense of the Philippines, his incompetence during the *Battles of the Kokoda Trail* on New Guinea and his mistakes at the *Battles of Buna and Gona*. It was rescued not only by his skills as a politician, propagandist and self-publicist but also by much more able American generals under his command such as Lieutenant-General Robert Eichelberger, Lieutenant-General Walter Krueger and US Army Air Force Lieutenant-General George Kenney—a cadre of superb army officers whose achievements were suppressed by comparison with their European counterparts such as Generals George Patton and Omar Bradley. Apart from seeking to debunk the remnants of the MacArthur myth, *Hirohito's War* also questions the role of General 'Vinegar Joe' Stilwell in the Allies' military debacle in China and its post-war loss to Chairman Mao's Red Army.

Hirohito's War puts aside the issue of atrocities to look dispassionately at the capabilities of Japanese commanders. It is argued that Japan's commanders at the start of the war were a great deal more able than their western counterparts and led troops who were among the finest of the *Pacific War*, both in terms of bravery and technique. Japan's commanders were not the unimaginative, one-dimensional soldiers as they are often portrayed. They were aggressive, resourceful, creative and technically highly proficient. Japanese Army units proved as robust in defense as they were fluid in attack—hence it took them just six months to win a new empire after *Pearl Harbor* while it took the Allies three years to win it back.

Arguably General Tomoyuki Yamashita, the conqueror of Malaya, was the finest of the Japanese generals whose ranks included exceptional soldiers such as Lieutenant-General Masaharu Homma, Lieutenant-General Shojiro Iida and General Shinroku Hata. As with many of his colleagues Yamashita had to operate on the tightest of logistical margins, which made his victories even more remarkable. These men were not the brutes often described in the post-war period and were often more cultured and accomplished than their western counterparts. The conquest of the *Pacific* and South East Asia was a stunning military achievement by a Japanese Army that was, contrary to most post-war belief, largely unprepared for a jungle campaign. With the Japanese economy already in total war mode to fight the continuing *Second Sino-Japanese War*, the conquests of Malaya, Burma, Indonesia, New Guinea and the *Pacific* were achieved on the thinnest of operating resources with hastily prepared troops brought from the temperate to cold conditions of Manchuria and northern China.

British historians, like their American counterparts, have tended to focus on the actions where their nation's troops were represented. Burma has inevitably come to be seen by the British as a central stage of the *Pacific War*, whereas it was in fact a sideshow, if not without importance. The war in Burma conducted by the British, but mainly with Indian and Chinese troops, had its strategic purpose in keeping Chiang Kai-shek's *Kuomintang* (Nationalist) forces supplied and active in the war. In absorbing the resources of the Japanese Army, the *Kuomintang* armies played in terms of human life the same sacrificial role in Asia that Soviet forces played in Europe. American and British historians have tended to ignore the centrality to the narrative of the *Pacific War* of China and the *Second Sino-Japanese War*. Many Japanese refer to *World War II* as the *Great East Asia War*, the *Asia-Pacific War* or the *Fifteen Year War*. I would argue that the Marco Polo Bridge Incident in the suburbs of Peking in July 1937 would be the more logical date for the beginning of *World War II*. That its start date is normally given as 1 September 1939, after the German invasion of Poland, merely reflects the western-centric narrative that has been dominant in the post-war period.

For the same reasons the West has tended to ignore the role of Chiang Kai-shek and the *Kuomintang* in defeating the Japanese Empire. Much of this effort was achieved in the first four years of the *Second Sino-Japanese War* starting in September 1937, in which China drew Japan into a war of attrition that ultimately debilitated its ability to fight a protracted war with the West. The war of attrition in China also undermined the *Kuomintang* armies. Contrary to the myths propagated by General Stilwell at the end of the war and by the New Deal supporters of Mao Zedong, Chiang Kai-shek's armies did not flinch from the fight; after 1942, they were simply too exhausted and under-resourced to do anything other than to try to defend the territories under their control until the issues of supply from America were finally resolved by Brigadier-General William Tunner in 1945. (He would go on to expedite the Berlin airlift in 1948.)

The conflict in Burma was important in one particular respect. At the *Battle of Imphal* in northeast India, in his complete annihilation of a 100,000 strong army led by Lieutenant-General Renya Mutaguchi, Lieutenant-General 'Bill' Slim proved himself the finest field commander of the *Pacific War* in a battle, which was unique in the conflict. It was the only occasion on which two armies met while intent on advancing into each other's territories. It was a strategic and tactical triumph for Slim who followed it up with an equally crushing victory at the *Battle of the Irrawaddy River*, the most fluid tactical military victory achieved by either side's armies during the war. Slim's innovations would also point to the future of strategic and tactical deployment.

As for the naval war, *Hirohito's War* demonstrates how it was America's inferior pre-war navy, not the one under construction in America, which brought Japan's expansion to a halt in the *Pacific* in the summer of 1942, first at the *Battle of the Coral Sea* and then at the *Battle of Midway*. Good fortune and mistakes by Japan's Admiral Yamamoto, not the paladin often portrayed, played a significant part. Particular emphasis is then placed on the often-neglected naval engagements of the *Guadalcanal* campaign that significantly degraded the formerly superb Japanese Navy. Admiral Raymond Spruance is highlighted as America's most able commander, while 'Bull' Halsey, the more famous and charismatic leader, is shown to have been increasingly reckless and unreliable as the war drew to a close.

Admiral Chester Nimitz, commander-in-chief of the US Pacific Fleet, was an able commander whose only major mistake was the invasion of the island of *Peleliu* at the end of his thrust through the *Central Pacific*. In Washington, Admiral Ernest King is shown to be the brilliant and aggressive navy leader who orchestrated the US Navy's success in the *Pacific* and America's winning strategy. On the ground the Marines deserved their reputation as the peerless shock troops of America's advance in the *Pacific*. Overlooked groups such as the American submariners and their leader, Admiral Charles Lockwood are given due prominence, as are the US intelligence officers in Washington and *Hawaii*.

Similar weight is given to the US Navy's remarkable logistical organization built by Vice-Admiral William Calhoun and to the Seabees, the Naval Construction Battalions, who made Nimitz's winning *Pacific* advance possible. It is interesting to note that in the current age, when a political union the size of Europe is barely able to field 20,000 troops outside its borders, America, in the *Pacific War*, supported an army of 1.5m troops in Asia and the *Pacific* at distances as far as 8,000 miles from the West and East Coasts of the United States. (Military components or equipment manufactured on America's West Coast might have to travel by train to the East Coast, boat across the Atlantic and round the Horn of Africa, train from Bombay to Calcutta, narrow gage to Dimapur in the Indian state of Nagaland, truck to airfields in northern Assam, flight over the Himalayan hump to Kunming, and finally by truck to Chongqing or central China—a circuitous journey of almost 15,000 miles.) At the same time that America was providing for its own troops, it was also giving critical supply and logistical support to its Allies, Great Britain, the Soviet Union, China and Australia. The *Pacific War* represented the largest logistical military exercise that the world is ever likely to witness. **[Map: 0.2]** The scale of the Pacific War meant that *World War II* was the first genuine 'World War' whereas *World War I* would be better described as a European war or the *Great War* as it was originally called.

Finally, it is shown that in the late 1930s armed forces were in the process of a dramatic shift in technology from the purely mechanical to the electro-mechanical. War hastened the process of technological change in a wide number of areas, including fire and control, servo motors, radar, decryption, manufacturing automation, mass assembly, communications, explosives, automatic weapons, engine design, aeronautics and of course the atom bomb. *Hirohito's War* explains how America won the technological war. As a result, in the course of the *Pacific War*, Japan was qualitatively as well as quantitatively outgunned.

Japan's war strategy was predicated on the mistaken belief that a rapid victory and settlement was possible. As the war dragged on, it was a conflict that Japan found was logistically and economically unsustainable in the face of an American enemy that found the will to fight for unconditional surrender. Ultimately America won the *Pacific War* because it could harness its huge under-utilized pre-war industrial capacity not only to produce more weapons but also better ones. Furthermore by mobilizing its economic and logistical resources America was able to project its firepower at distances from American shores that would have been inconceivable a generation earlier.

At the forefront of the range-extending technological war was the aircraft carrier, whose arrival on the world stage as the key weapons system of the conflict was only announced by Japan's sneak attack on *Pearl Harbor* on 8 December 1941. The battleship, until then the principal weapon of mass destruction for all of the interwar period, was instantly relegated. *Hirohito's War* shows that with its aircraft carriers, in their infancy as a weapons system, and so complex and advanced that still only nine countries have ever built and operated one, the United States made the better technological and operational choices. In addition, although the Mitsubishi Zero A6M appeared all-conquering as a fighter plane in the first few months of the war, by the summer of 1942 the Marine and US Army Air Forces had nullified its superior flying characteristics as a result of better training and tactics. Thereafter the Zero rapidly became technologically redundant as America produced better, more heavily armed and faster fighter aircraft. Not only did Japan's armed forces choose the wrong design route for its fighters—light and maneuverable rather than America's heavily armed, armored and robust aircraft—but also its designers and factories could never keep up with technological advance. In exasperation at America's fighter dominance in the air, Japan eventually had to turn to using its pilots as *Kamikaze*, not an illogical choice of tactic in the circumstances but one whose effectiveness helped make the decision to drop an atom bomb an easy one to make.

Lastly, in the writing of *Hirohito's War*, I have not forgotten that war is not just about geopolitics, technology and strategy. The *Pacific War* was fought by ordinary Allied and Japanese soldiers, sailors and aviators, most of them called-up civilian recruits, who operated in the most difficult of conditions—usually thousands of miles from home. Arguably in the sparsely populated jungles of New Guinea and the *Solomon Islands*, Japanese and Allied soldiers fought in probably the most hostile topographical environment of any war in history. The living and fighting conditions of the foot-soldiers and seamen, both American and Japanese, including food, clothing, accommodation, disease, and medical treatment, are described in detail, often using their own words. Neither are the sufferings of civilians ignored, particularly those who faced imprisonment and the barely credible scale and barbarity of atrocities committed by the Japanese armed forces. The moral issues of bombing—conventional, fire-bombing and the atom bomb—are also confronted. It was a war that posed unique questions concerning morality, justice, blame and accountability—issues that are still alive and relevant today.

Hirohito's War shows that the *Pacific War* was an astonishing triumph of arms for America at significant human cost but little economic pain. It is easy to forget that in the history of warfare, the conquest of one nation by another by invasion by sea has rarely been accomplished, let alone at a distance of 6,000 miles. By comparison it should be noted in *World War II* Germany failed to negotiate the 25 miles of the *English Channel*. Those who blithely assert that American victory was inevitable should think again. Thereafter, America's victory in the *Pacific*, over which it achieved mastery, set the stage for Asia's remarkable surge in prosperity in the post-war period. For Japan the war, under the leadership of the hapless Hirohito, was a human and economic tragedy from which it nevertheless recovered rapidly under the umbrella of American protection. For Britain the *Pacific War* brought the curtain down on it great Asian empire as it struggled to deal with its reduced circumstances at home. The United States meanwhile embarked on an époque of unprecedented economic growth and prosperity with an economy far more productive and technologically advanced than the one with which it had started *World War II*.

For China, its principal victim, the *Pacific War* was just the start and probably the major cause of a national calamity that, under the aegis of Mao Zedong, would run for a further thirty-five years. The irony for America and Japan, two nations implacably hostile to Marxist-Leninist ideology in the pre-war period, is that the *Pacific War* was significantly responsible for condemning them to a much longer drawn-out war against communism in Asia in the second half of the twentieth century.

Francis Pike
5 November 2014

Part I
Meiji Restoration: 1868

1 Empires in Conflict

[1868–1931]

[Maps: 1.1, 1.2, 1.3, 1.4, 1.5, 1.6, 1.7, 1.8, 1.9, 1.10, 1.11]

American Empire in the Ascendant [1789–1922]: **[Map: 1.1] [Map: 1.2] [Map: 1.3]**
In 1918 it may have seemed to many observers that the scramble for empire was over. *World War I* ended with crushing victory for the world's two strongest powers. Great Britain, in spite of the economic cost of the war, remained the world's largest empire; the United States, the other big winner from the war, emerged as the world's most powerful and fastest growing economy—at US$517bn it was more than 10 percent larger than Great Britain and Germany combined, and more than seven times larger than Japan.

The rise of America had been meteoric. From its sliver of land on the east coast of America, the original thirteen colonies, having liberated themselves from Great Britain in 1783, had conquered from coast to coast. The Spanish were defeated and forced to yield Florida; vast French territories, stretching from the Mexican border to Canada, comprising present day Louisiana, Arkansas, Oklahoma, Colorado, Kansas, Missouri, Wyoming, Nebraska, Iowa, Montana, North Dakota, South Dakota, and Minnesota, were gained by the *Louisiana Purchase* [1803], after Napoleon's failed bid to conquer America. At four cents an acre, US$15m in aggregate, it was the greatest land deal in history. President Thomas Jefferson proclaimed, "The world will here see such an extent of country under a free and moderate government as it has never yet seen . . ."[1]

The ethnic cleansing of Indian natives from the southeastern parts of the United States began after the passing of the *Indian Removal Act* [1830], which required the forced removal of Indian tribes such as the *Muscogee* (Creek), *Seminole, Chickasaw* and *Choctaw* to mountainous, forested land in eastern Oklahoma; in 1935 the *Cherokee* nation was coerced into ceding their lands in Georgia and three years later the entire population was rounded up and put in stockades before being deported in a death march that became known as the Trail of Tears; the defeat of President Santa Anna by the Texan Army led by General Sam Houston at the *Battle of Jacinto* [1836] won independence for Texas from Mexico. The independent nation of Texas was duly absorbed into the United States, becoming its twenty-eighth state in 1845. In 1846, President James Polk provoked a war with Mexico as an excuse to annex California; the Oregon territories were taken as part of a deal with Great Britain at the *Treaty of Ghent* [1814]; southern Arizona and parts of New Mexico were added by means of the Gadsden Purchase for US$10m, and Alaska was purchased from Russia in 1867 for US$7.2m.

America populated this vast country with land-hungry immigrants from around the world, though former British and German subjects predominated. Since independence in 1776, the population of America had risen from 3 million to 103.2 million in 1914. By comparison the populations of Great Britain, Germany and Japan respectively were 42 million, 64.5 million and 58 million. The rights of the indigenous peoples, the native Indians, were trampled underfoot. By 1918, with the late additions of Oklahoma [1907], New Mexico [1912] and Arizona [1912], the United States had expanded its original number from 13 to 48. It was, as David Reynolds has noted in *America, Empire of Liberty* [2010], an Empire, which transposed "onto the map of Europe . . . would extend from the Urals to the Pyrenees."[2]

Although America has chosen not to define this advance as Imperial, this is not how the rest of the world perceived the growth of the United States. As the historian Niall Ferguson has observed, America "is an empire, in short, that dare not speak its name. It is an empire in denial."[3] The word 'empire,' which Americans associated with Great Britain, from whom they had won their independence, has always been a dirty word in the United States. It is no coincidence that "The 'Empire' in Hollywood's *Star Wars* [1977] is the force of evil, its storm troopers modelled partly on Roman praetorian guards."[4]

In reality America's imperial storm troopers were usually missionaries who carried bibles, not 'light-sabers.' They did not stop at the *Pacific* Coast. US missionaries led by Hiram Bingham descended on *Hawaii* in 1819. It was missionaries who similarly led the way for America's commercial exploitation of China where America, like every country that could, concluded 'unequal treaties.' American ships were almost as complicit in the opium trade as those of Great Britain. In 1856 Andrew Hull Foote, commander of USS *Portsmouth*, a sloop with cannon, landed a force at *Guangzhou* (Canton) and defeated a 5,000-strong Chinese army. In *Hawaii*, within 80 years of the arrival of American missionaries, the native population of the island had fallen by 75 percent and the original inhabitants owned less than 1 percent of their land. It was said that "Hawaiians were taught to close their eyes in prayer, and when they opened them the land was gone."[5] Sugar planters, many of them from missionary families, deposed Queen Liliuokalani in a *coup d'état* in 1893 and, after the US Senate refused to ratify the annexation of *Hawaii* by formal treaty, a resolution of both governments on 7 July 1898 secured its transfer to the United States.

From the seventeenth ranked naval power in 1880, within a decade the United States rose to third. With a navy, America could extend its power internationally. To the alarm of the states of Central and South America, President Grover Cleveland's secretary of state, Richard Olney declared in 1893, "Today the United States is practically sovereign on this continent [North and South America] and its fiat is law upon the subjects to which it confines its interposition . . ."[6] America's long sought ambition to control the *Caribbean Sea* and bring *Cuba* under its power resulted in a war with Spain in 1898. The unexpected bonus from the *Spanish War* was that the US fleet sailed from its base in *Hong Kong* to *Manila Bay* where it sought out and sank the Spanish fleet. At a stroke America had acquired an Asian empire in the form of the region's second largest archipelago, after the Dutch East Indies. "The policy of isolation is dead," enthused an editorial in the *Washington Post*, "A new consciousness seems to have come upon us—the consciousness of strength, and with it a new appetite, a yearning to show our strength . . . The taste of empire is in the mouth of the people, even as the taste of blood in the jungle."[7] As in Japan and Europe, metaphors of Darwinism abounded in the pursuit of empire at the end of the nineteenth century.

President McKinley claimed not to have envisaged American occupation of the Philippines but concluded, ". . . we could not turn them over to France and Germany— our commercial rivals in the Orient—that would be bad business and discreditable," besides he added, "They were unfit for self-government."[8] The subsequent pacification of the Philippines took two years at a cost of 100,000 Filipino lives. For American businessmen, the conquest of the Philippines opened new horizons; Senator Albert Beveridge of Indiana declared, "The Philippines are ours forever" and that,

> . . . just beyond the Philippines are China's illimitable markets. We will not retreat from either . . . We will not renounce our part in the mission of our race, trustees of God, of the civilization of the world . . . God has marked us as his chosen people, henceforth to lead in the regeneration of the world . . . He has made us adept in government [so] that we [can] administer government among the savages and senile people.[9]

Senator Beveridge's justifications for empire were remarkably similar to the Japanese arguments for a pan-Asian empire that emerged thirty years later. Beveridge may have presented an extreme view—most Americans politicians were not in the market for more conquest—but the expansion of commercial interests was another matter. By 1900, the world's largest economy had built a global commercial empire. It had already become axiomatic for US Presidents, evident from Commodore Perry's forced opening of Japan, that open door economics should be pursued by military means if necessary. As Brooks Adams, great grandson of President John Adams, noted in *America's Economic Supremacy* [1900], "East Asia is the prize for which all energetic nations are grasping" and concluded that Britain was "wearing down"[10] and that the United States must inherit the role of guarantor of the 'open door' to China. With the conquest of the Philippines, as a marker to the future, it should be noted that America now became Japan's southern neighbor and regional rival.

In 1899 US Secretary of State John Hay sent notes to the European powers and Japan asking for the recognition of the rights of free trade access to China. They found a willing audience in Britain. The *Times* commented, "Even the anti-capitalists welcome an imperial policy which contemplates no conquests but commerce."[11] Joseph Chamberlain thought that Hay's project was a noble cause and thought that "the Stars and Stripes and the Union Jack should wave together over an Anglo-Saxon alliance" while Brooks Adams congratulated Hay for effectively "industrialising the Monroe Doctrine."[12]

Thus in 1903 Theodore Roosevelt encouraged a separatist revolt, and rushed a gunboat to Panama's assistance to support their separatist claims against Colombia. Roosevelt negotiated the rights to build and operate the *Panama Canal* in perpetuity in return for US$10m and US$250,000 per annum. Even a nationalist newspaper such as the afternoon daily, *Chicago American*, owned by Randolph Hearst, protested that Roosevelt had assaulted "another republic over the shattered wreckage of international law and diplomatic usage."[13] As the Panama episode illustrated, after 1900 American imperialism was aimed not principally at territorial expansion but the protection and support of rapidly expanding markets in Japan and China, not to mention its newly acquired possession of the Philippines. The *Panama Canal* was a project that was not only invaluable for trade but also enabled a much faster switch of naval assets from ocean to ocean. After one of the greatest engineering projects in history, the *Panama Canal* opened on the same day, 3 August 1914, that Germany declared war on France.

Development of Japan, Shintoism and the Imperial System [660 BC–1868]: Unification of the Japanese Archipelago seems to have evolved around the first century AD and extended at least as far as the northern island of *Hokkaido*, which until the mid-nineteenth century remained a Japanese equivalent of a Wild West occupied mainly by the *Ainu*, indigenous hunter-gatherer tribes of northeast Asian descent, who were gradually corralled into reservations. A mythical Emperor, Jimmu, who by legend came to power in 660 BC, was invented in the eighth century providing Japanese nationalists, even today, with the myth of an Imperial dynasty over 2,000 years old descending from the sun-goddess *Amaterasu*. The three holy objects of the myth, the sword (valor), the mirror (wisdom) and the jewel (benevolence) are still treasured. By repute the mirror is still held at Ise Shrine, the private place of worship of the Imperial family until it was opened up to the public at the beginning of the nineteenth century—leading to a mass pilgrimage by six million people in the first year. The myths were set out in two official chronicles, the *Kojiki* (Record of Ancient Matters) [712] and the *Nihon Shoki* (Chronicles of Japan) [720]. The word *Shinto* (Way of the Gods) was first used in this latter chronicle and became the name for Japan's state religion, which was a modern creation after the *Meiji Restoration*. The creation of a mythical past by the Yamato regime was part of an attempt to create a highly centralized bureaucratic state on the Chinese model. Dynastic capitals were built at Nara in 710 and Heian (Kyoto) in 794. Until 1185 power was usurped by the Fujiwara family, whose line extended down to Emperor Hirohito's adviser and prime minister, Prince Konoe. Fujiwara power did not survive but the cult of the Emperor did.

The introduction of Buddhism in the sixth century did not replace *Shinto*. Japan subsumed Buddhist philosophy and the two religions developed side by side with followers more often than not practicing both. A nationalist version was even created in the thirteenth century by the monk, Nichiren, the leader of one of many Buddhist sects to emerge, who is said to have introduced *hinomaru* (the Rising Sun flag) that was to become the symbol of Japan's militarist expansion in the nineteenth and twentieth centuries. Nichiren Buddhism proclaimed Japan as the 'land of the gods' and stripped Buddhism of any remaining vestiges of asceticism and mysticism. Moreover, somewhat in the manner of Martin Luther in Germany, he attacked corrupt monks who deviated from true Buddhist practice. Nichiren was prosecuted for heresy and banished to *Sado Island* in the *Sea of Japan*, but his teachings had a profound influence on the development of Japan's socio-religious culture. In essence it helped create a nation of believers that worshiped themselves and the state that they had created. The simplified Buddhism for the masses was later added to by the development of Zen Buddhism, which emphasized mental and physical asceticism as a means of training samurai for the exigencies of war. It meshed seamlessly with *Bushido* (the military scholar code) whose first tenets were established in the coastal city of Kamakura when it was the *shogun*'s capital in the twelfth century. *Bushido* was actively promoted in the Tokugawa era to instil loyalty among the samurai class. Instead of a European-style contractual obligation in its feudal system, Japan developed the concept of *giri* (moral imperative) to bind the samurai's duty to his *daimyo* (master). When trapped between their loyalty to their lord or the *shogun*, the only way out was ritual suicide—as in the much-celebrated case of the '47 Ronin' (masterless samurai).

For the next thousand years the Imperial family existed as powerless pawns, kept alive as little more than religious embodiments of the national religion of *Shinto*, for the embellishment of warlord rulers, the last of which, Yoshinobu, was overthrown in 1868.

The Meiji Restoration [1868], Growth and Expansion: [**Map: 1.4**] It would be a mistake to think that *Shinto* ultra-nationalism developed straight out of the box with the restoration of the Emperor in 1868. Whatever the peculiarities of Japanese religious beliefs and cultural practices, the Tokugawa family, based in Edo (present-day Tokyo) came to power by *realpolitik* and ruled accordingly. Confucianism guided their philosophy of government while Buddhism was used as a system of social control.

After a sixteenth century spent largely in warfare between competing domain leaders, or in effect warlords, the *Momoyama* period ended with victory for Tokugawa Ieyasu at the *Battle of Sekigahara* in 1600. The rule of the Tokugawa Shogunate began in 1603. The Japanese Emperor, Go-Yozei, remained the country's nominal ruler, but in continuation of a now long tradition, real power rested with the *shogun* (hereditary military ruler). Ieyasu died just two years after becoming *shogun* but his domain maintained its position for the next 264 years. Perhaps learning from the mistakes of his predecessor, Hideyoshi Toyotomi, whose attempt to conquer China's Ming Dynasty via an invasion of Korea from 1592–1598 had come to grief, the Tokugawa Shoguns not only spurned foreign ventures but also turned Japan in on itself. Aside from a Dutch trading post at Nagasaki on the southern island of *Kyushu*, all foreign contact was prohibited for the next quarter of a millennium. Foreigners who did arrive in Japan, even by accident, were dealt with harshly.

In 1852 President Millard Fillmore gave papers for Commodore Perry to give to the fourteenth Tokugawa Shogun, Iemochi. The following year Perry dropped anchor with four warships at Uraga Harbor near Tokyo. When he was directed to Nagasaki, Perry refused and threatened to bombard Japan. Eventually Perry left but promised to return in expectation of a favorable response. When he returned in February 1854, this time with eight warships, his demands for access were granted. Fillmore's request for 'freedom to trade,' which destabilized an ossified political system, began a rapid period of change for Japan. The Tokugawa Shogunate began to modernize. Masayoshi Hotta, Lord of Sakura, an adviser to the Tokugawas until 1858, stated the propositions that "military power always springs from national wealth" and that wealth is "principally to be found in trade and commerce."[14] Hotta's negotiations ultimately resulted in the *Harris Treaty* [1858], also known as the *Treaty of Amity and Commerce*, which brought commercial and diplomatic advantages for America. It initiated a period of liberalization of Japan's treatment of foreign trading powers.

However, the old regime's changes were too little too late. Four domains, the Satsuma (southwest *Kyushu Island*), the Saga (northwest *Kyushu Island*), Choshu (southwest *Honshu Island*) and Tosa (south *Shikoku Island*), supported by Great Britain, mounted a campaign to overthrow the *shogun*, Yoshinobu Tokugawa, supported by France. The southern clans, advancing northwards met and defeated Yoshinobu's poorly led forces at the *Battle of Toba-Fushima* on 27 January 1868. The battle mixed modern armaments and troops trained in modern techniques, with traditional samurai formations engaged in their last hurrah. The *Boshin War* continued with the rebel domains' forces, naval and military, advancing on Edo. Further battles consolidated the southern domains' control of the Tokugawa's capital and the 15-year-old Emperor, Meiji, in whose name the uprising had been given legitimacy, was moved from Kyoto to Edo, now renamed Tokyo. Yoshinobu, the last *shogun*, resigned and spent the remainder of his life in obscure retirement.

Japanese expansionism preceded the overthrow of the Tokugawa Shogunate. At the *Treaty of Shimoda* [1855] otherwise known as the *Treaty of Commerce and Navigation*, between Japan and Russia, the latter recognized the island of *Hokkaido* and the northern chain of *Kuril Islands* as Japanese territories. After 1868 the new government in Tokyo moved even more aggressively. The newly established *Hokkaido* Colonization Office, encouraged migration with the offer of cheap land and by 1889 some 2,000 samurai families had been enticed north. Foreign expertise was sought with Professor William Smith Clark, an American agricultural educationalist, recruited to set up Sapporo Agricultural College (later Hokkaido University) in 1876. In the process of colonization, as in America, *Hokkaido*'s tribal population was significantly diminished. The indigenous *Ainu* tribes were driven into reservations, forced to learn Japanese and converted to the new state religion, Shintoism. By 1908 the population of *Hokkaido* had risen to 1.45 million from tens of thousands a few decades earlier. In the south the *Ryukyu Islands*, of which *Okinawa* was the largest, were similarly annexed in 1874 after renouncing their vassal status with China.

Korea, Formosa and the First Sino-Japanese War [1894–1895]: **[Map: 1.5]** No sooner had the restoration government been established in Tokyo than the new government started to look toward Korea, which it had last tried to conquer at the end of the sixteenth century. When Korea failed to recognize Japan's Imperial rule, Takamori Saigo, the Satsuma general who had led the Imperial forces in the *Boshin War* proposed sending a punitive expedition in 1873. Over the next thirty years Japan vied for domination of Korea with China, the traditional regional power. Japan, with a growing economy, driven by centrally driven industrialization policies, became increasingly bellicose even though it was still a minnow compared with the great powers of the West. Tokichi Tarui, the political activist and adventurer, envisaged "big boned and strong Koreans learning from the advantages of our military system and together [with us] preventing a Russian threat."[15] In 1885, leading Meiji intellectual, Yukichi Fukuzawa, founder of Keio University, urged Japan, a superior Asian culture, to abandon Asia and to be more like Europe in its attitude to its Asian neighbors:

> Our nation cannot afford to wait for the enlightenment of
> our neighboring countries to happen, and to join with them
> in the effort of building Asia. Rather, we should avoid that
> situation and join in the fate of the civilized and enlightened
> West, dealing with China and Korea as Westerners do,
> without being bound by special protocols, simply because
> we are neighbors. If one keeps bad company, one cannot
> avoid being branded with a bad name. In my heart, I vow
> to sever ties with our bad friends in Asia's east.[16]

Japan's increasing sense of racial superiority crept into the national consciousness as the country's economic advance bespoke a growing sense of Darwinian success. A popular Japanese song of the 1880s went,

> There is a law of nations, it is true
> but when the moment comes, remember,
> the Strong eat up the Weak.[17]

In 1887 the political writer Soho Tokutomi founded a fiercely nationalist journal, *Kokumin No Tomo* (the nation's friend), which advocated, in imitation of the West, the creation of a Japanese empire. Soho wrote of his "scorn of white peoples."[18] For the time being however, Japan's focus remained regional domination. Hence the vying for position on the Asian mainland brought about the *First Sino-Japanese War* in 1894. Japan's defeat of China, hitherto seen as the great Asian power, came as a profound shock to the West. *Formosa*, which had only been incorporated as a Chinese province by the Qing Dynasty ten years earlier, was ceded to Japan and became her first colonial possession after the *Treaty of Shimonoseki*.

Writer Soho Tokutomi reflected after the Japanese victory in the *First Sino-Japanese War* that "civilization is not a monopoly of the white man."[19] Henry Trench, the British

Minister in Tokyo noted that "the conquest and absorption by Japan of the entire Chinese empire is now freely spoken of . . ." and he observed that some sections of the public hoped that Japan might "become the greatest Power in the world, just as she now undoubtedly is the greatest in Asia."[20] After the *First Sino-Japanese War*, diplomat Munemitsu Mutsu recalled in his memoirs that the German Ambassador feared, "Japan enjoyed advantages of cheap labor . . ." which would allow Japan "under the new treaty arrangements to establish *de facto* an impregnable position in China over trade and commerce of European nations."[21]

However, Russia, Germany and France (the so-called Triple Intervention) forced Japan to yield control of the Liaodong Peninsula, including the important harbor of Port Arthur in return for the payment of a further payment from China. In spite of diplomatic efforts by Prime Minister Hirobumi Ito, neither Britain nor America came to Japan's aid. To Japan's fury Imperial Russian forces then occupied Port Arthur—a major cause of resentment and one which was a major factor in the forthcoming war with Russia. The Triple Intervention was a humiliation at the hands of the West, which sank deep into the Japanese psyche.

The Russo-Japanese War [1904–1905] and Shock Waves in Asia and the World:

[Map: 1.6] [Map: 1.7] [Map: 1.8] In the political domain supporters of a more aggressive international policy included General Aritomo Yamagata, one of the *Meiji Restoration* oligarchs, who became the archetypal military cheerleader for the Japanese Empire. Yamagata led an increasing group of bellicose politicians who advocated an expansionist policy "to preserve our independence and enhance our national position" and that "If we wish to maintain the nation's independence among the powers of the world at the present time it is not enough to guard only the line of sovereignty, we must also defend the line of advantage."[22] To a large extent this expansionist strategy was driven by fear of the regional growth of Russian power.

To defend its interests, Japan, with its rapidly developing economy was able to establish its most important international alliance with Great Britain in 1902. Both feared Russia's construction of the Trans-Siberian railway, intended to extend Imperial Russia's influence in the Far East. Yamagata advocated a war with Russia before her power in the region became unassailable. The result was that Japan risked a war with its much larger European power and, in an engagement that transformed Japan's standing in the world, Admiral Togo annihilated the Russian fleet at the *Battle of Tsushima* [1905]. Meanwhile a Japanese expeditionary force led by Field Marshal Iwao Oyama besieged and captured Port Arthur and defeated the Russian Army in a series of engagements culminating in the *Battle of Mukden* [1905]. After the battle, Japan, economically exhausted by its efforts on land and sea, was as keen as Russia to accept President Theodore 'Teddy' Roosevelt's offer to host a peace conference. The outcome of the *Treaty of Portsmouth* [1905] proved a huge disappointment to Japanese nationalists. Outmaneuvered by Russia's wily chief negotiator, Count Sergei Witte and Roosevelt, Japan, with a much weaker hand than its nationalists understood, was forced to back down in its demand for an indemnity and was only able to extract sovereignty over the southern half of *Sakhalin Island*. The Japanese public, largely unaware of Japan's budgetary and military exhaustion, turned hostile toward the peace treaty while the ultra-nationalists blamed liberal politicians and the racist bias of America and the western powers.

Nevertheless, Japan's victory led to Korea becoming a vassal state and eventually to the effective annexation of Korea in 1910. Imperial conquest continued to be viewed in Japan as a rite of passage for a developing nation.

The outcome of the *Russo-Japanese War* did not make the United States happy as their interests lay in an 'open door' trade policy, though they recognized that there was not much that could be done about the Japanese advance into Manchuria. As ex-President 'Teddy' Roosevelt noted in 1910 with regard to Japan's advance, "we cannot stop it unless we are to go to war, and a successful war about Manchuria would require a fleet as good as that of England, plus an army as good as that of Germany."[23] Ultimately, "Japan's rise to the status of a world power in the aftermath of the *Russo-Japanese War* jeopardized American interests. As tensions increased, both militaries, especially their navies, made extensive preparations for war with each other, which, almost like a self-fulfilling prophecy, did occur."[24]

The administration of 'Teddy' Roosevelt saw a sea change in attitudes toward Japan. The plucky little nation had received America's unspoken support versus Russia, which was seen as imperial, old world and autocratic and a threat to America's own interests in East Asia. After the *Battle of Tsushima* however, this sentiment reversed. Plucky little Japan became the 'Yellow Peril' and from then until *Pearl Harbor*, the Japanese became the main theoretical enemy against which the American Navy pitted nearly all its plans. Japan's war planners returned the compliment. In 1907 Roosevelt sent the US fleet, The Great White Fleet as it became known, around the world, but particularly the *Pacific Ocean*, as an overt display of strength. With growing fears of the rise of Japan, US diplomatic efforts sought to tie down its perceived threat. Thus the *Root-Takahira Agreement* [1908] was an agreement by US Secretary of State Elihu Root, negotiated with Ambassador Kogoro Takahira, to a carve-up of Asia by their recently acquired spoils of war. In return for Japan's recognition of America's annexation of the Philippines and *Hawaii*, an 'open door' trade policy in China and the right to limit immigration to California, Root agreed to Japan's control of Korea, as well as their right to dominate southern Manchuria. Political and popular fears in America were not assuaged. Remarkably, *The Valor of Ignorance* [1909] written by geopolitical analyst and adviser to Sun Yat-sen, Homer Lea, described a surprise Japanese attack on *Hawaii* and the west coast. Such was the nascent antagonism between the countries that historians Tal Tovy and Sharon Halevi have argued that "a proto-cold war existed from the end of the *Russo-Japanese War* until the outbreak of *World War II* . . ."[25]

Victory for Japan in the *Russo-Japanese War*, the first time in the post-industrial age that an Asian power had defeated a European power, provided an inspiration to nationalists not only in Japan, but also throughout Asia. Indian independence leader

Jawaharlal Nehru recalled in *An Autobiography: With Musings on Recent Events in India* [1939],

> The next important event . . . was the Russo-Japanese War. Japanese victories stirred up my enthusiasm and I waited eagerly for the papers for fresh news daily. I invested in a large number of books on Japan and tried to read some of them . . . Nationalist ideas filled my mind. I mused on Indian freedom from the thraldom of Europe.[26]

In Europe reaction to Japanese victory was mixed. Great Britain, Japan's ally and the builder of her fleet, was initially delighted and seized on her strength in East Asia as a co-guarantor of peace in the region and as a bulwark to Germany. Some European nations were less sanguine. The Frenchman, de Lannesan, writing in *Le Siècle*, 8 February 1904, expressed the feelings of many: "Japan is a child people. Now that it has huge toys like battleships, it is not reasonable enough, not old enough not to try them. It wants to see how that works, like a 'kid' who has been given a model railway . . . Despite their borrowings from western civilization, the Japanese remain barbarians."[27]

The German imperialist cheerleader, Baron von Falkenegg, reflected the conflicted reaction of many Europeans to Japan's victory when he argued in *Japan, die neue Weltmacht: Politische Betrachtungen* [1905] (Japan the New World Power: Political Considerations) that "Even today there are thousands of Europeans, supposedly educated in historical matters, who are rejoicing wildly over the victory of Japan over Russia . . . and do not see that in Manchuria, not Russia, but Europe was beaten . . ."[28] What Falkenegg failed to point out was that Russia's weakness broke the balance of power in Europe whereby the Franco-Russian alliance kept Germany's hegemonic ambitions in check.

Although the British reaction to Japan's great victory over Russia was to sign a revised and more encompassing treaty with Japan on 12 August 1905, the motives were more self-protection than love. As British Foreign Minister, Henry Petty-Fitzmaurice, fifth Marquis of Lansdowne, admitted, Britain, in fear of Japan's emerging naval strength, had raised the wall of its "back garden to prevent an over adventurous neighbour . . . from attempting to climb it."[29] British imperialists in India were even more concerned. Indian Viceroy Lord Curzon's recently set up Department of Intelligence [1904] in Delhi noted, "A European power like the Russian being whipped by a small Asiatic nation like the Japanese. Why, that was unthinkable. It was a prelude to a revolution in Asia . . ."[30] Indeed Mahatma Gandhi observed "Our reading of this account of the Japanese War [with Russia] would be fruitful only if we emulate to some extent the example of Japan."[31] *The Spectator* magazine warned of the danger "if the government of India does not take steps to stop the dispatching of Indian students to Japan."[32] For Britain the dangers were not just internal. A few years after the *Russo-Japanese War*, a British agent in Japan warned that they were "casting covetous eyes on much of what England now holds" and that the Japanese realized "the strength of England's position in the East is closely bound up with her possession of India."[33] Thus the victory of Britain's ally in the war with Russia engendered feelings that were far from straightforward. As Sir Ernest Satow, diplomat and noted Japanologist, observed in the aftermath, "The Rise of Japan has so completely upset our equilibrium as a new planet the size of Mars would derange the solar system."[34]

Attitudes to the *Russo-Japanese War* in China were mixed. Students in China organized a 'Resist Russia' movement and some contributed to the Japanese War Fund or even asked to join the Imperial Japanese Army as volunteers. More sanguine voices in the Shanghai press warned that Japan might become as predatory as Russia. Thus the reformist leader, Liang Qichao, came to the conclusion that whoever won, China would be the loser. Above all Japan's victory showed how far the Qing Dynasty had fallen behind in the modernization race. By contrast with Liang Qichao, Sun Yat-sen saw the *Battle of Tsushima* [1905] as a victory for Asia against western imperialism. Seeing the Japanese as racial cousins, he concluded "Blood is thicker than water."[35] However, Sun did not speak to the people of Manchuria. In *The Times* [1906] Dr. George Morrison, previously a champion of the Japanese cause, on a visit to Manchuria, noted his surprise at finding that "In Manchuria the Japanese are hated with a fervor that you can hardly imagine."[36] Indeed Sun was far too optimistic. Two years after Japan and Russia concluded peace at the *Treaty of Portsmouth* [1905], Japan and Russia signed an agreement to support each other in respect of their claims on China's northeast, and formalized that with the *Russo-Japanese Treaty* [1910]. Sichuan's Governor General Xi Liang warned that while Russia was "wildly ambitious," Japan posed the greater threat because of her proximity to China compared to the western powers: "Her [Japan's] intrusions into Chinese politics in defense of her sphere of influence made her a more tangible and immediate threat to the integrity of China . . ."[37] As historian Harold Z. Schiffrin has concluded, ". . . by 1908 this 'Golden decade' of Sino-Japanese relations had ended and the two nations were on a collision course."[38]

By 1916 the racist treatment of Japanese businessmen was such that a formal complaint was sent to Britain expressing "a general feeling of regret is prevalent in the Imperial Diet [Japan's bicameral national assembly] that anti-Japanese feeling is strong in the British colonies."[39] During the Great War, Yamagata, Japan's elder statesman, warned that it was "extremely important . . . to take steps to prevent the establishment of a white alliance against the yellow people."[40] In 1893 journalist and historian, Soho Tokutomi wrote that for all the economic progress made by Japan, the West still refused to revise the unequal treaties. Even though Japan was the "most progressive, developed, civilized and powerful nation in the Orient, the Japanese could not escape 'the scorn of the white people.'"[41] Popular political and cultural commentator, Rinjiro Takayama, editor-in-chief of the bi-weekly *Taiyo*, wrote in 1898 that "Race is the greatest fact of history. Most of the cultural differences are based on racial differences."[42] In the same year Duke Konoe, whose son would become prime minister in the late 1930s, wrote, "Asia's future, in the end, lies in the ultimate struggle between different races . . . Chinese and Japanese would need to stand together against the arch-enemy of the white race."[43]

In 1916 Japan signed an agreement with Russia, which recognized Japan's special position in Manchuria and eastern Mongolia. In 1918 Billy Hughes, prime minister of Australia, referred to his Welsh ancestry when he told British Prime Minister Arthur Balfour that the industrious Japanese were moving in everywhere and that "we too must work in like fashion or retire like my ancestors from the fat plains to the lean and rugged hills."[44] In the immediate aftermath of war, Lord Curzon, British foreign minister, warned somewhat prophetically in 1921 that Japan was a "restless and aggressive power, full of energy, and somewhat like the Germans in mentality."[45]

Anti-Asian Racism in the West: In addition to tariffs, the post-war period saw increasing American discrimination against immigrants from Asia. American racial legislation traced a long history from the late eighteenth century. The *Naturalization Act* [1790] prohibited the naturalization of non-white subjects while the *Page Act* [1875] tried to stem the tide of immigration by Asian laborers and prostitutes. The legislation was largely ineffectual and the growth of mining and the building of America's transcontinental railways would have been difficult without Asian and particularly Chinese labor. President Chester Arthur's signing of the *Chinese Exclusion Act* [1882] was the first major piece of legislation limiting the import of specifically Chinese labor into the United States. In this lacuna the demand for Japanese labor grew rapidly, which in turn spawned anti-Japanese sentiment.

On 14 May 1905 the Japanese and Korean Exclusion League was formed in San Francisco with the support of sixty-seven trade unions. Rather than increasing admiration of Japan, Admiral Tojo's naval victory over the Russian fleet at the *Battle of Tsushima* [1905] increased fear of Japan and its immigrants. Andrew Furuseth of the Japanese and Korean Exclusion League asked: "What is the West [the US Pacific Region] to be, 'yellow or white'?"[46] In 1907 a similar anti-Japanese league was founded in Vancouver and led to race riots and the siege of Chinatown. A year later the California Board of Education passed legislation requiring Japanese children to attend segregated schools.

Nineteenth-century laws also discriminated against Japanese ownership of land. As Japanese immigrants were land-poor, they, unlike white immigrants, were forced to remain tenant farmers or farm workers. Land discrimination specifically legislated in the *Alien Land Law* [1914], was mainly targeted at Japanese immigrants. Nevertheless by 1915, it was estimated that as much as 75 percent of vegetables consumed in Los Angeles were grown by Japanese farmers. After *World War I*, the *California Alien Land Act* [1920] cut out many of the loopholes in the *Alien Land Law* including the ownership of stock in companies that acquired land. Further amendments and exclusions were made in 1923. In the same year Canada's Asian Exclusion League scored its greatest political victory with the passage of the *Chinese Immigration Act* [1923], which all but ended new Chinese immigration into the British dominion of Canada. In the United States, racially prejudiced land laws were not restricted to California and between 1913 and 1925, thirteen other US states passed restrictive land ownership laws including

Arizona, Arkansas, Idaho, Louisiana, Montana, Minnesota, Nebraska, New Mexico, Oregon, Texas, Utah, Washington, and Wyoming.

In Japan the observation of the media and the intellectual elite was that in the post-*World War I* period, there was a disconnection between the Anglo-Saxon call for an international system based on respect for the equal rights and sovereignty of nations and what was perceived to be the racial discrimination of the western powers—of whom the United States and Great Britain were clearly the most prominent. The combination of the Washington System and increasing recourse to tariff policies, viewed as highly discriminatory against Japanese industry, was inevitably seen by some of the more nationalist political groups to be a protective and racial response of an established elite of western countries against Asia, and Japan in particular. It is interesting to note that compared to the millions who emigrated from Europe to the United States, the number of Japanese who crossed the *Pacific* between 1901 and 1924 was just 244,483 or a little over 10,000 per year. No wonder Japan considered the California brouhaha over Japanese immigration to be profoundly racist. For an increasingly successful and powerful Japan, the entire global geopolitical structure in the first decades of the twentieth century was therefore seen as a western conspiracy against Asia.

World War I: The Rise and Fall of the German Empire [1848–1918]: **[Map: 1.9]** In 1917, following Germany's declaration that it would attack all shipping in the *Atlantic*, America dispatched to Europe an Expeditionary Force under General John 'Black Jack' Pershing, fresh from his punitive Mexican campaign to capture Pancho Villa. Although America's fighting alongside its allies Great Britain, France and Italy lasted only a year before Germany's economic collapse, which forced its effective surrender at an Armistice signed on 11 November in a railway carriage at Compiègne. The German Army withdrew to its own borders but was forced to negotiate the *Treaty of Versailles* as losers. The nature of Germany's defeat led many to believe that it had not been defeated but betrayed by Jews and Bolsheviks. In reality Germany had been overwhelmed by the combined military and economic power of Britain, France, Russia, Italy, Japan and America.

Under the leadership of President Woodrow Wilson, the United States emerged from *World War I* economically not only unscathed but also enhanced, unlike all the other combatants (Japan excepted) and as the powerful arbiter of world peace at the *Treaty of Versailles* [28 June 1919]. Germany's imperial ambitions both within Europe and in Africa and Asia appeared to have been permanently ended.

In 1860, Germany had consisted of a number of independent kingdoms connected by language and culture. King Wilhelm I of Prussia, the strongest state of northern Germany, under the guidance of his prime minister, Otto von Bismarck, set about an imperial project. In the north, Danish influence was ended in 1864 by the *Second Schleswig War*, which brought about the annexation of Schleswig-Holstein, while two years later, in the south, the Austrian Empire was defeated in the *Austro-Prussian War* [1866]. Austria was expelled from German politics and Bismarck thus extended the German Empire further to the west by the annexation of Nassau in the Rhineland and the Kingdom of Hanover in the northwest. In the same year a *Zollverein* (a customs union not dissimilar to the European Economic Community, in 1951) was established across most of the German states, enabling a 'soft' annexation by Prussia of central and southern Germany. In 1870 conflict between Germany and France erupted after Bismarck tried to place a German prince on the Spanish throne. In the ensuing *Franco-Prussian War*, France's emperor, Napoleon III, was captured and her armies routed by the Prussian Army led by General Helmuth Graf von Moltke at the *Battle of Sedan*. While occupying Versailles, on 20 January 1871, Bismarck, wearing his cuirassier's uniform, stood in the Hall of Mirrors in front of Germany's assembled princes who had just celebrated the *Te Deum*, and proclaimed the German Empire of *Kaiser* (Emperor) Wilhelm I.

It was an Empire, which extended in the east from the Baltic Coast of modern day Lithuania, with East and West Prussia occupying the coast and hinterlands of Konigsberg and Danzig (modern Kaliningrad and Gdansk respectively) to Holland in the west. Further southeast Germany occupied much of modern-day Poland to the east of Poznan and Silesia, part of the modern-day Czech Republic. In the southeast Germany extended to Alsace and Lorraine and in the south included Bavaria with borders to Switzerland and the Austro-Hungarian Empire. For the last seventeen years of his reign Wilhelm I concentrated on the consolidation of his new Empire in a period in which the German economy saw explosive economic growth with Berlin, its imperial capital, at its center. Having secured its European Empire, Germany began the construction of a global empire under Wilhelm II after he acceded to the throne in 1888.

In a bid to catch up with Britain, France, Holland, Belgium and Portugal, Wilhelm II's Germany—late in the game—made an aggressive quest for colonial expansion. German protectorates were established in German East Africa comprising modern day Tanganyika, Rwanda and Kenya, German West Africa, including Cameroon and Togoland and Southwest Africa including Namibia and parts of Botswana; a valuable trading concession was won from the Chinese government at *Kiautschau Bay*; and in the *South Pacific* German colonies were established in Kaiser-Wilhelmsland comprising 96,300 square miles of modern day east New Guinea; the *Bismarck Archipelago* including the islands of *New Pomerania* (later *New Britain*), *New Mecklenburg* (later *New Ireland*), *Buka* (an island off *Bougainville*) and various smaller islands of the *Solomon* chain. In the mid-*Pacific*, Germany snaffled the *Caroline Islands, Palau*, the *Marianas* (except *Guam*, an American spoil from the *Spanish-American War*), the *Marshall Islands, Nairu* and *Samoa*. All but the last of these islands were to be scenes of some of the heaviest fighting between the United States and Japan in the *Pacific War*.

The German quest for Empire launched her into a massive program of naval construction, which started an arms race with Great Britain, owner of the world's most powerful navy, which sought to protect its empire from the threat of German aggression. One of the results of the German threat was Great Britain's alliance with Japan. Together they could counter Germany's emerging naval power in the *Pacific*, which posed a threat to both their interests. Similarly, Britain's *entente cordiale* with France in 1904 also sought to counter Germany. The Anglo-Russian Entente of 1907 completed the diplomatic envelopment of Germany. The diplomatic maneuvering of the European powers set up a Triple Entente, of Britain, France and Russia against a German military alliance with the Austro-Hungarian Empire.

For Japan the growth of the German Empire was both a model of economic development and imperial expansion and yet another threat to Japan's hopes of regional domination of the Asian mainland.

The Demise of the Austro-Hungarian, Russian and Ottoman Empires [1918]:

[Map: 1.10] Although the underlying *casus belli* of *World War I* was the aggressive expansionist policy of Wilhelm II, the trigger to conflict came from the varying fortunes of two other empires. By the twentieth century, Turkey's Ottoman Empire was in terminal decline; the Empire, which had stood at the gates of Vienna and threatened the whole of Christian Europe as recently as 1683, was imploding and powerless to prevent the Austro-Hungarian Empire from annexing Bosnia in 1908. It was a development that did not please an Imperial Russia that pleaded solidarity with the Slavic populations of the Balkans. In Serbia, nationalists sought to lift the yoke of both the Austro-Hungarian Empire in the north and the Ottomans in the south. While an uprising by the Serbs, Bulgarians, Montenegrins and Greeks in the *First Balkan War* [1912] finally threw off the Ottoman yoke ending with the *Treaty of London* in 1913, the outcome of the peace was to increase the power of the Serbs. A *Second Balkan War* [June 1913] ended with the repulse of a Bulgarian offensive against Serbia. Bulgaria lost some of the gains of the *First Balkan War* to Serbia where a rising tide of Serb nationalism looked to unite the Slavic populations of the Balkans into a new Serbian Empire modeled on the brief Serbian Empire of the fourteenth century.

For the Austro-Hungarians, the increasing bellicosity of Serbia was a threat worse than the Ottomans that had preceded them. The Hapsburgs sought reassurance of German support if they needed to go to war to suppress the Serbs. Wilhelm II guaranteed the German Empire's support if needed. It was a guarantee that the Austro-Hungarian government sought to redeem after the assassination of the Hapsburg heir, Archduke Franz Ferdinand, on 28 June 1914. Instead of restraining the Hapsburgs from taking their revenge on Serbia, Kaiser Wilhelm gave a blank check to support them in their actions, even though it was known that Russia's Tsar Nicholas II would mobilize in defense of their fellow Slavs. When the Hapsburgs presented Serbia with an ultimatum with a 48-hour time limit, unacceptable to a sovereign nation, Europe woke up to the likelihood of war. With Kaiser Wilhelm and the German Army raring to go to war, mobilization of the European armies moved into gear. In London, Germany's ambassador worked feverishly to split the British government from the Tripartite Alliance without effect. Ultimately it was Germany's invasion of neutral Belgium, required by an update of Von Schlieffen's plan to outflank France's borders, which triggered Britain's guarantee of protection for Belgium signed in 1839 at the *Treaty of London*.

At the Paris Peace Conference [1919], Wilhelm II's Empire was dismantled. Germany lost significant lands in the East including much of East and West Prussia (but not Konigsberg and its hinterland) and Silesia as well as Lorraine and Alsace, which it had taken from France in the *Franco-Prussian War* of 1870. Germany's incipient overseas empire was lost entirely. Notably the valuable *Kiautschou Bay* concession, with its expensively built new town of Tsingtao, went to Japan along with the South Pacific mandate including Palau, the Northern Mariana Islands, the islands of Micronesia and the Marshall islands. The Bismark Archipelago, including New Guinea, were awarded by League of Nations mandate to Australia.

The German Empire was not the only global competitor to fall. Imperial Russia, which had entered the war in the popular cause of protecting fellow Slavs in Serbia, soon faced internal dissent as a result of military defeats and food shortages on the home front. Germany's control of the Baltic prevented Russian access to markets and a collapsing economy was accompanied by rising food price inflation. Revolution followed in February 1917. Tsar Nicholas II was toppled. The following year, after the *Bolsheviks* (the majority) seized power, the Tsar and his family were murdered. The Russian Soviet Federative Socialist Republic established the world's first communist state that spent the next four years in a fight for survival against counter-revolutionary 'White Russian' armies. After the Red Armies defeated the insurgents, the Soviet Union was formed comprising Russia, Ukraine, Belarus and Transcaucasia.

Two further Empires fell in the aftermath of *World War I*. The Austro-Hungarian Empire of the Hapsburgs was split up and gave life to new sovereign states. Its successor states were the Austrian Republic and the Kingdom of Hungary while former Slav subject-states were divided up into Yugoslavia in the south and Czechoslovakia in the east; other bits went to Poland. The Ottoman Empire, after a final flourish of brutality in Armenia in 1915, fell to a revolt by the Arabs in the following year, famously stirred to action by Lawrence of Arabia. Some 7 million Turkish refugees fled from former conquered territories of the Caucasus, Crimea, the Balkans and the Mediterranean islands to settle in Anatolia. A Turkish *War of Independence* under the nationalist leader Mustafa Kemal Ataturk led to the abdication of the last Sultan Mehmed VI in 1922 and the declaration of the Republic of Turkey in 1923. The Turkish caliphate was abolished the following year.

The deafening crash of empires that greeted the end of *World War I* indicated to most Western observers that the age of empires was over. Monarchic governments in Russia, Germany, Austria and Turkey had collapsed in the space of a few years. In Japan's *Taisho* court alarm bells rang as, around the world, one royal family after another was overthrown. The Soviet Union excluded, the stage seemed to be set for a new world order, one based on democratic structures, mutually agreed security and gentlemanly behavior between those great powers possessed of constitutional democracy. In 1918 it was an idea that President Wilson was preparing to bring to the world.

***Anglo-Saxons Triumphant: The Paris Peace Conference and the Treaty of Versailles
[1919]:*** When the great powers met at the Quai d'Orsay, the offices of the French
Foreign Ministry, on 18 January, the five powers represented were America, Great
Britain, France, Italy and Japan. Japan felt somewhat isolated by the 'Big Four'
consisting of Woodrow Wilson, David Lloyd George, Georges Clemenceau and Vittorio
Orlando, and was disappointed by President Wilson's refusal to countenance the
insertion of a clause on racial equality. To the rest of the world, the outcome of the *Great
War*, as they referred to it, must have seemed to be a final victory for the Anglo-Saxon
powers. Competitors, including allies, had either been weakened or were in the process
of dissolution.

Just over a century earlier President Jefferson had mused that America and Britain
were "endeavouring to establish, the one a universal dominion by sea, the other by
land."[47] By 1918, it was a mission accomplished. A golden era of 'Pax Anglo-Saxon'
beckoned. It started well. Woodrow Wilson, deciding to be the first American President
to visit Europe while still in office, heralded his arrival with a speech, which became
known as the '14-Point Declaration.' It was notable for idealistic intentions and was
enthusiastically received worldwide. Five of the key points were particularly notable for
the 'liberal' world-view that they promoted:

> 2. Absolute freedom of navigation upon the seas, outside
> territorial waters, alike in peace and in war, except as the
> seas may be closed in whole or in part by international
> action for the enforcement of international covenants.
> 3. The removal, so far as possible, of all economic barriers
> and the establishment of an equality of trade conditions
> among all the nations consenting to the peace and
> associating themselves for its maintenance.
> 4. Adequate guarantees given and taken that national
> armaments will be reduced to the lowest points consistent
> with domestic safety.
> 5. A free, open-minded, and absolutely impartial
> adjustment of all colonial claims, based upon a strict
> observance of the principle that in determining all such
> questions of sovereignty the interests of the population
> concerned must have equal weight with the equitable
> claims of the government whose title is to be determined.
> 14. A general association of nations must be formed under
> specific covenants for the purpose of affording mutual
> guarantees of political independence and territorial
> integrity to great and small states alike.

Starting on 18 January 1919, the work of the Paris Peace Conference, conducted over
145 meetings, spent most of its early months dealing with the dissolution of the German

and Austro-Hungarian Empires. The *Treaty of Versailles* was concluded on 26 June 1919. The conference continued for another six months, finally wrapping up on 21 January 1920. Wilson's lofty ideals were partially buried by the more *realpolitik* approach of Great Britain and France, which, against Wilson's wishes, insisted on the insertion of Article 231, which laid the blame for *World War I* on German aggression. Britain and France also insisted on large war indemnities. With most of the world's leaders assembled in Paris for the best part of a year, the Paris Peace Conference became a melting pot for government lobbies from around the world. Diplomats or representatives came from thirty-three governments. Non-government lobby groups also arrived, whether or not they were invited. Ho Chi Minh, wearing a borrowed tailcoat, made a highly theatrical appearance at the conference and delivered a petition calling for Vietnam's independence. In spite of Wilson's call for "political independence and territorial integrity to great and small states alike," these fine sentiments would not be applied to the Philippines or the other conquered countries of Asia. Although the Wilsonian ideals expressed in the 14 points were heavily watered down, the 'Big Four' were able to agree to the setting up of a League of Nations.

The League of Nations [1920]: The concept of a union of nations that would individually and collectively agree on the promotion of a peaceful society worldwide was an idea that had been kicking around for almost three centuries. The seventeenth-century Dutch jurist, Hugo Grotius (Huig de Groot), who wrote *De Jure Belli ac Pacis* [1625] (On the Law of War and Peace), was a significant influence on the intellectual background to the *Treaty of Westphalia* [1648], whose concept of mutual security, leaving aside Athens' Delian League of the fifth century BC, was arguably a first modern stab at collective government. The great Konigsberg philosopher, Immanuel Kant, took the philosophical underpinnings of the 'Westphalia System' even further with the publication of *Perpetual Peace: A Philosophical Sketch* [1795] in which he called for 'world government.'

These ideas were not without their impact. At the *Congress of Vienna* [1815], Prince Klemens von Metternich, Tsar Alexander I, Talleyrand, Lord Castlereagh, Prince Karl August von Hardenberg and a host of diplomats from other nations negotiated a European peace accord that settled the nation states of Europe after the disruptions of the Napoleonic era. The so-called Concert of Europe or the Vienna System of International Relations, a balance of sovereign states, kept the peace of almost 100 years. During this period other features of international law began to emerge including the Geneva Convention, which established laws on the treatment of civilians in wartime. The Hague Conventions of 1899 and 1907, signed by forty-four nations, agreed rules governing the conduct of war as well as guidelines on the peaceful resolution of international disputes. In 1914 the British political philosopher, Goldsworthy Lowes Dickinson, coined the term League of Nations and during *World War I*, the League of Nations Union gained significant public support in the Anglo-Saxon world, becoming an influential lobby group. Later the British Fabian Society developed the idea of a permanent body dedicated to the maintenance of peace.

It was an intellectual framework for a new world order that had grown in Europe side-by-side with political Darwinism and one that had seemingly vanquished this more brutal model of geopolitical development after *World War I*. However, for Japan the idea of the League of Nations was outside their historical and philosophical cultural lineage. Although there were many post-war Japanese political supporters of a new world order based on the mutually supportive structures embodied by the League of Nations, it was a philosophy not as deeply rooted or universally accepted as it was in the Anglo-Saxon countries. For Japan there was another major difference. *World War I* only touched Japan in a peripheral sense. The scale of death and destruction visited on the British, French, and later American, armies in engagements such as the *Battles of the Somme, Verdun* and *Ypres* was not a collective trauma visited on Japan and its people. The psychological necessity of the search for lasting peace and the banishment of the possibility of another war of mass carnage that so infused the post-war Anglo-Saxon nations did not correspond with sentiments in Japan—that would have to wait for the cataclysm of *World War II.*

In America, President Woodrow Wilson took up the idea of the League of Nations. Lord Robert Cecil and General Jan Smuts, the great Boer leader and international statesman, did the main drafting. The League of Nations, with fifty-eight nations as members at its peak, furthered the idea of a peace secretariat with the construct of a permanent organization for dealing with international disputes and relying on the great powers to enforce resolutions and sanctions. For the first time the concept of an agreed standard of ethical behavior introduced the idea of how a state should conduct itself in relation to others.

The League of Nations quickly suffered a setback when the US Senate rejected Woodrow Wilson's brainchild. Although Wilson would win the Nobel Peace Prize in 1919, Republican opposition in Congress, led by Henry Cabot Lodge, scuppered American ratification of the League of Nations over Article-10, which required members to come to the aid of a member under attack. In a speech in Omaha, Nebraska, Woodrow Wilson warned, "I tell you, my fellow citizens, I can predict with absolute certainty that within another generation, there will be another world war if the nations of the world do not concert the method by which to prevent it."[48] In spite of the setback of American ratification of the League of Nations, Anglo-Saxon concepts of 'mutual responsibility,' 'co-operation' and 'ethical behavior' in international relations flourished in the post-war period. However, in terms of the construct of an international system to replace the Concert of Europe, the most important event of the immediate post-war period was not the League of Nations, but the Washington System.

The Washington System [1922]: Conducted under the auspices of the League of Nations, the Washington Naval Conference organized by Woodrow Wilson's Republican successor, President Warren Harding, a former Ohio Senator, convened in Washington on 12 November 1921. In a presidency plagued by corruption involving his Ohio cronies and Navy petroleum reserves, in what became known as the Teapot Dome Scandal,

Harding, in spite of what he had said on the campaign trail, dutifully followed the mantra of international responsibility laid down by the League of Nations. Nine nations were invited to attend: the United States, Great Britain, Japan, China, France, Italy, Belgium, Holland and Portugal. Notably the Soviet Union, still a pariah nation in the West, was not invited. The intention of the meeting was to limit the growth of capital ships in the Far East. The aim was to avoid the dreadnought arms race between Great Britain and Germany in the decades before *World War I*. As such the Washington Conference was the first arms limitation treaty in history—the early twentieth century equivalent of the *SALT I & II* and *START I & II*, the ballistic missiles and nuclear weapons limitation talks that took place in Helsinki, Finland from 1969 to 2011. For the Washington Conference the main aim was to limit battleships that were the 'weapons of mass destruction' of the era. Above all America wanted to avoid a repetition of the dreadnought arms race between Great Britain and Germany [1906–1913], which many believed was one of the causes of the *Great War*.

After discussions about quality of ships, it was finally decided that limitations be put only on size of battleships and total tonnage. Thus a single battleship could weigh no more than 35,000 tons and the gross tonnage for Britain and America was limited to 525,000 tons while Japan was allowed 315,000 tons; a ratio of 5:5:3. In addition the treaty agreement allowed for a ratio of 1.75 each for France and Italy. As for aircraft carriers, a weapons system barely out of the concept stage, the major naval powers, America, Great Britain and Japan agreed on 135,000 tons, 135,000 tons and 81,000 tons respectively. The agreement resulted in the scrapping of old battleships by America and Great Britain, while new keels were converted to aircraft carriers. Cruisers were omitted from the calculations although their size was limited to 10,000 tons. Predictably perhaps, the result was a cruiser arms race. Submarines were omitted completely from the treaty that was finally registered with the League of Nations in April 1924.

A side agreement at the Washington Conference was the Japanese reversion of the Kiautschou Bay Concession to China, which came about through pressure brought to bear on Japan by the Anglo-Saxon powers. The Kiautschou Bay Concession had been awarded to Germany on a 99-year lease in 1898. Situated in Southern Shandong Province, Kiautschou Bay (also *Jiaozhou Bay*) had been scouted by the Prussian Navy as early as 1860. A decade later Baron Ferdinand von Richtofen, a geographer-geologist and uncle of the *World War I* flying ace Manfred von Richtofen, the 'Red Baron,' made a survey of the area and recommended the site as a naval base. In 1897, using the murder of two German Catholic priests in China by the Big Sword Society as an excuse, Kaiser Wilhelm overrode the caution of his Chancellor, Chlodwig von Hohenlohe and ordered Admiral Otto von Diederichs's cruiser squadron to invade *Jiaozhou Bay*. After the Chinese government was forced to grant a 99-year lease the German government invested the then vast sum of US$100m in the 213 square mile area, which included the construction of a port, the complete redevelopment of the fishing village of Tsingtao (from 1903 home of the famous Chinese beer that takes its name) into a model town and the construction of a spur of the Manchuria–Peking railway to link Germany's

Kiautschou Concession to China's capital city, Peking (Peking became known as Beijing after the triumph of Mao communists in 1949). At the outbreak of *World War I*, Japan, a British ally since 1902, invaded the German colony and took possession of it until its return to China in 1922.

The combination of the *Treaty of Versailles* and the *Washington Treaties* three years later confirmed America's arrival on the world stage as by far its most powerful participant. In the 1920s the United States was unquestionably the global superpower. Together with Britain, the Anglo-Saxon fleets easily outgunned the rest of the world. As British military historian John Keegan has concluded, the *Washington Naval Treaty* forced the scrapping of obsolete tonnage and the building of new ships and "assured the artificial dominance of the British and United States navies over all others in the world."[49] In 1922 America and Great Britain, the Anglo-Saxon powers, reigned supreme. Putative enemies, such as Germany and the Soviet Union had been brought low by *World War I*, while Japan had seemingly been brought inside the tent of global security provided by the Versailles–Washington System. At the Congress of the Toilers of the East [1922], Grigory Zinoviev gave a closing speech in which he described the Washington Conference as "one of the blackest days in the history of mankind."[50] The *Soviet Encyclopaedia* [1979] described it as "a system of the imperialist world, established by the victorious governments, mainly Great Britain, France, the USA, and Japan, after *World War I*." A Western led pacifist new world order was similarly heralded by the *Kellogg-Briand Pact* [1928]; the brainchild of US secretary of state Frank Kellogg and the French foreign minister Aristide Briand, their pact called for states to renounce the use of force as a means of settling disputes. It was another example of the ethos of the League of Nations era and after the initial signing by the US, France and Germany, most other nations, including Japan, followed.

In spite of the seeming overwhelming advantages enjoyed by the Anglo-Saxon nations in the 1920s, within twenty years, the Anglo-Saxon alliance would be put on the rack at sea and on land by a military alliance of Germany, Japan and Italy—the Axis powers. How and why did this spectacular reverse come to pass?

Tariffs and Isolationism: In part, the seeming decline of Anglo-Saxon power from the high point of the Washington Conference came from the mood of their public that swung decisively toward 'isolation' from international affairs. Americans came to the conclusion that *World War I* was a product of Europe's corrupt, undemocratic monarchies and determined to turn their back on any future involvements. In the aftermath, Republican Senator Gerald Nye fed the isolationist tendency by claiming that bankers and munitions manufacturers had pushed America to war. War profiteering became a recurrent theme of the isolationists over the course of the next decade. *Merchants of Death* [1934], a best seller, was one of many polemic publications that turned the American public toward neutrality in international affairs. The political isolationists also harked back to a long tradition of non-intervention. First President, George Washington, had warned against foreign ventures while his successor, Thomas Jefferson, in his inaugural address, advocated a foreign policy of "peace, commerce, and honest friendship with all nations, entangling alliances with none."[51]

US isolationism was also reflected in restrictions placed on immigration. The *Quota Act* [1921] put a limit of 3 percent on the total number that had emigrated from any one country in 1910, with a total cap applied of 350,000 immigrants. Three years later the quota was reduced to 2 percent and the base year put back to 1890. The *National Origins Act* [1929] limited total immigration to 150,000. In the 1920s the United States also started raising import tariffs on raw materials as well as manufactured products.

In the post-*World War II* era, the US has become so closely associated with the idea of free trade and open access to its own consumer markets that it comes as a surprise to note that America began the twentieth century as a country committed to protectionist tariffs—except those that excluded American merchants from profitable markets. When Democrats, at that time more committed to free trade, seized the Congress in 1910, and the White House two years later, the *Underwood-Simmons Tariff Act* [1913] broke with America's traditional stance of trade protectionism.

It was a short-lived moment. The return of Republicans to office with the election of Warren Harding in 1920 brought a reversion to trade protection for farmers whose markets appeared to be under threat as post-war agricultural output began to recover. The *Emergency Tariff Act* [1921] followed by the *Fordney-McCumber Tariff Act* [1922] increased tariffs to a level higher than in 1912. As global commodity prices continued to fall during the decade and after the 1929 Wall Street Crash, Republican President Herbert Hoover moved to further protect American farmers as well as industry by the passing of the infamous *Tariff Act* [1930] (generally known as the *Smoot-Hawley Act*), which arguably turned a recession into a global depression. Between 1932 and 1934, world trade fell by 66 percent. America was not the only country to row back on free trade. Great Britain, the global leader in free trade for more than three-quarters of a century since the Repeal of the Corn Laws enabled by the *Importation Act* [1846], organized an imperial tariff preference system at the Ottawa Imperial Conference [1932].

Japanese Reaction to the Treaty of Versailles and the Washington System: The rise of Japan in the world's global esteem, or at least notoriety, was not matched by feelings of greater security. *World War I* greatly expanded Japan's opportunities for trade in Asian countries that had previously been the reserve of the British. On 18 January 1915, in the aftermath of their seizure of Germany's Kiautschou Concession (Tsingtau), Japan issued the famous Twenty-one Demands that tried to force Peking's government to yield control of Manchuria and northern China. Japan's sphere of influence was to include Shatung, Fukien, South Manchuria and Inner Mongolia and in addition they were to act as 'advisers' to the Chinese government.

Even within Japan the aggressive nature of these demands was controversial. The *genro*, who had not been consulted by foreign minister Takaaki Kato, were furious. Even Prime Minister Aritomo Yamagata, although broadly supportive, was alarmed by the tone in which the demands were couched. Great Britain and the United States, both interested in a *status quo*, which guaranteed their access to China's markets, ganged up against Japan and forced it to give up its demands. It was an episode that left sour feelings on the part of Japan toward its British allies, while the Anglo-Saxon powers were alerted to Japan's intentions with regard to China. In London faith in the Japanese alliance was severely shaken. Meanwhile in China, the extortionate Twenty-one Demands gave cause for the breakdown of trust with Japan, whose rise against the imperialist western powers had previously been acclaimed by Chinese nationalists.

The *Treaty of Versailles* did nothing to assuage Japan's fears that they were still being treated as second-class world citizens. President Woodrow Wilson's instincts were wholly supportive of China. He was convinced of the need to foment the moral regeneration of a country that was seen to be in steep economic and moral decline. Wilson, whose cousin edited a Presbyterian weekly newspaper in Shanghai, observed that he wanted to stand by China as "friend and exemplar."[52] Post-war Minister to China, Jacob Schurman, gave a stark warning about Japanese intentions. He complained about their activities in bribing officials and stirring unrest. With remarkable foresight he warned:

> Should Japan be given a freer hand and should anything
> be done which could be interpreted as recognition of a
> special position of Japan, either in the form of a so-called
> Monroe Doctrine or in any other way, forces will be set in
> action, which make a huge armed conflict absolutely
> inevitable within one generation. There is no single
> problem in Europe, which equals in its importance to the
> future of peace of the world, the need of a just settlement
> of Chinese affairs.[53]

For Japan the key issue of the Versailles peace talks was the ownership of the Concession in *Kiautschau Bay*, adjacent to Peking. The US delegation sided with China, arguing that leaving Japan in control would leave a "dagger pointed at the heart of China."[54] Britain, still technically a Japanese ally, supported the US. Not surprisingly the Paris Peace Conference marked the end of Britain's special relationship with Japan, which America had treated with suspicion. In 1921 Lord Curzon viewed "the renewal of the Anglo-Japanese Alliance in any form with disquietude."[55] At a crucial 1921 Committee of Imperial Defence, Churchill stated that "no more fatal policy could be contemplated than that of basing our naval policy on a possible combination with Japan against the United States."[56] Although Prime Minister Lloyd George responded that reliance on the US was "one more fatal policy," in 1922 the alliance was allowed to lapse even though former prime minister, Arthur Balfour had asserted: ". . . it is a fact that if we had not Japan on our side we should be second or third power in the *Pacific* after a considerable number of years . . . it is, from a strategic point of view, of very great importance that the Japanese Alliance should be maintained."[57]

The Washington Conference confirmed for some in Japan that the *Treaty of Versailles* was a stitch-up by the Anglo-Saxon powers, designed to deny the position of dominance that they deserved. Japan felt vulnerable and friendless. In spite of having fought on the 'right side' in *World War I*, many in the Japanese political elite believed that they were friendless and dispossessed. Having built up their empires by force of arms, it now seemed to some Japanese observers that the Anglo-Saxon powers were trying to deny Japan the same opportunity. At first glance it is hard to disagree with Noam Chomsky when he writes that in building its empire, Japan "was simply following the precedent established by Great Britain and the United States; it was establishing its own Monroe Doctrine and realizing its manifest destiny."[58] Thus Major-General Sadao Araki, a right-wing ultra-nationalist within the Imperial Japanese Army argued that:

> We are the leading Asiatic power and we should now take matters into our own hands. We must be active, ever expanding the last portion of our national strength. We must be prepared to wage a desperate struggle. The Whites have made the countries of Asia mere objects of oppression and Imperial Japan should no longer let their impudence go unpunished.[59]

However, it would be a mistake to think that the ultra-nationalist view was dominant in post-war Japanese politics. Powerful figures such as Prince Kinmochi Saionji, two-time prime minister and *genro* and Kijuro Shidehara, who as Minister for Foreign Affairs in 1924 argued for a policy of non-intervention in China, represented a much more moderate faction within the Japanese government. In spite of the noisy ultra-nationalist faction, these figures and their liberal supporters and allies would dominate the international argument for the next decade; Japan, for the time being was not only a supporter of the Anglo-Saxons' collective security club but one of its leading lights.

The Collapse of the Qing Dynasty and the Rise of Chinese Nationalism [1911]:

[Map: 1.11] While Japan was on the rise in the late nineteenth century, China's Imperial system under the Qing Dynasty was falling into decrepitude. The eleven-year *Taiping Rebellion* in southern China, starting in 1849, in which over 20 million Chinese died, was a harbinger and a model for later revolutions. Although attempts were made by the Emperor to modernize the Chinese state after the accession of the Emperor Tongzhi in 1861, the radical reforms required by the Qing Dynasty were thwarted by his mother the Empress Dowager Cixi, who was China's effective ruler until her death in 1908. Cixi, who was brought into the imperial court as a concubine of the sixth rank, had used her rare skills in reading and writing to advance her position at court. After Tongzhi's death in 1875, Cixi, still just forty-one years of age, her lust for power unassuaged, engineered the dynastic succession of her nephew, Emperor Guangxu. However, when he embarked on an ambitious 100-day reform in June 1898, Cixi engineered a *coup d'état*. Guangxu was put under house arrest for the remainder of his reign while his closest advisers were executed—some slowly sliced in the traditional 'death by a thousand cuts.'

In June 1900 rebellious Boxer forces besieged foreign legations in Peking. Cixi, who had encouraged the Boxers' attack on foreign powers, escaped to Shanxi Province and, in a further embarrassment to the Qing Dynasty, the relief of the city was accomplished by an alliance of foreign troops including soldiers from the United States, Russia, Japan, Germany, France, Italy, and Austria. The Japanese provided the largest force but Graf von Waldersee was appointed as commander after European officers refused to serve under an Asian general. After surviving the Boxer Rebellion in 1902 Empress Dowager Cixi, previously thought to be a block on change, embarked on a radical reform program inspired by the one carried out by the *Meiji Restoration* in Japan. Chinese envoys were dispatched worldwide to gather information to enable sweeping changes to the political system, law, the army, and social programs. In 1905 the imperial examination system was abolished as the government sought to diminish the influence of Confucianism. As with the Tokugawa Shogunate, the changes were too little too late to save the Imperial system. As in Japan, and later Russia, Austria-Hungary and Turkey, the Qing Dynasty would be another *ancien regime* to succumb as it scrambled for modernity. In 1908 Cixi was poisoned with arsenic and died the day after Pu-yi was installed as China's new emperor.

Popular Chinese nationalism orchestrated by Sun Yat-sen and his followers outflanked the changes planned by the Qing government. Republican sentiments were driven by the failure of the Qing to deal with the incursions of the western nations, either in terms of the granting of concessions or with regard to the 'unequal treaties' forced upon their government. Following the *Opium Wars*, the imperial government had been forced to give in to free trade and the establishment of treaty ports that allowed western powers privileged access to the Chinese market as well as extraterritorial jurisdiction for their nationals. By far the most important of these was Shanghai; others included Hankou (Hubei Province), Changsha (Hunan Province), Ningpo and Wenzou (Zhejiang Province), Fuzhou and Amoy (Fujian Province), Guangzhou (Guangdong Province), Belhai (Guangxi Province), Tientsin (Hebei Province) and Harbin (Heilongjiang Province). Western powers who took advantage of these privileges included Great Britain, United States, Japan, Russia, Germany, France, Austro-Hungary, Italy, Belgium, and Portugal. In addition Great Britain had been ceded the island of *Hong Kong* in perpetuity after the first *Opium War* [1839–42]. The adjacent Kowloon Peninsula was ceded in 1860 and in 1898 a 99-year lease was obtained for *Lantau Island* and the 600 square miles of the New Territories up to the *Shenzhen River*.

In 1911 Imperial power finally cracked under the pressure of mounting disaffection in the provinces, which led to the *Wuchang Uprising* and the defeat of imperial forces at the *Battle of Yangxia* [October 1911]. The defeat led to a cascade of disaffection and the downfall of the boy Emperor Pu-yi.

On 1 January 1912, Sun Yat-sen was appointed President of the Provisional Government of the Republic of China. Sun declared, "On that day I saw the successful accomplishment of the great ambition for which I had struggled during thirty years, the restoration of China and the establishment of a republic."[60] However, he was soon muscled out of power by the commander of China's northern armies, General Yuan Shi-kai, who unsuccessfully attempted to have himself crowned emperor before his sudden death on 6 June 1916. By then China was already descending into political chaos with the southwestern province of Guangxi having declared independence.

Mongolia declared independence on 1 December 1911 and Tibet was liberated by an uprising led by the thirteenth Dalai Lama, who entered the capital Lhasa in January 1913, ushering a period of independence lasting until 1951. For the next decade China succumbed to the era of competing regional warlords. In Manchuria, Zhang Zuo-lin established a separate state. Yan Xi-shan ruled Shanxi Province, while Wu Pei-fu controlled Hubei Province from his base in Hankou. Yunnan was controlled by Tang Ji-yao; Hunan by Zhao Heng-ti; Fujian, Anhui, Jiangxi and Jiangsu were controlled by Zhi-li warlord, Sun Chuangfung. Sun Yat-sen and his *Kuomintang* (Nationalists) became the effective rulers of Guangzhou in the south. An attempted peace conference in 1919 failed. In July 1920 civil wars broke out between the Zhi-li and Anhui factions in northern China; and between Zhang Zuo-lin and Wu Pei-fu during the spring and summer of 1922. A 22 March conference of academics calling for the establishment of a new constitution failed to attract the support of a single warlord. In the far west, Xingjiang Province, home of the Turkic Muslim Uighurs, which had only been incorporated into China in 1884, broke free under the rule of Yang Zeng-xin who became governor in 1911. Throughout the 1920s control of China's provinces was constantly molded, broken and molded again by warlords—some more enlightened than others.

In 1917 another threat to China emerged in the form of socialism, starting with the seizure of the Chinese Eastern Railway by a Workers Soviet. Meanwhile in Peking, Chinese students, in the political chaos of the period, became a crucible of new political ideas. Political clubs abounded; the New Tide Society, the Citizens Magazine Society, the Work-Study Society, the Common Voice Society, and the Co-Operative Society were all products of new intellectual freedoms that emerged from the collapse of the Qing Dynasty. In this period of intellectual ferment it is not surprising that Marxist ideas took root, leading to the founding of the Chinese Communist Party (CCP) on 21 July 1921. In spite of the disparate political voices, all agreed on the need to throw out the 'foreigners.' Particular hatred was focused on Japan because of its Twenty-one Demands in 1915 and periodic boycotts of Japanese goods followed. After the *Treaty of Versailles*, which failed to immediately hand back the German concession to China, popular opprobrium applied to all foreigners. Wellington Koo, a member of the Chinese delegation at Versailles noted, "[if] I sign [the *Treaty of Versailles*] . . . even under orders from Peking—I shall not have what you in New York call a Chinaman's chance."[61]

It was not until 1924 that a stronger unifying force began to gather under Sun Yat-sen in the south. In part he was helped by the financial skills of financier T. V. Soong who became the *Kuomintang*'s Minister of Finance, but it was the support of the Soviet Union who wanted to build up Sun Yat-sen as a bulwark to Japanese power that was essential. Over a two-year period to 1926, T. V., as Soong became known, was able to grow *Kuomintang* revenues from US$8m to US$80m. Apart from a US$10m loan, a Soviet-financed military academy was established at *Whampoa*, an island in the *Pearl River*, on the site of a former Imperial Naval Academy to the east of Guangzhou (Canton). Here a rising young *Kuomintang* military commander, Chiang Kai-shek began to forge the officer class that he would use to reunify China. Chinese communists also enrolled at *Whampoa*, including Zhou Enlai who forged a close personal bond with Chiang. However, Chiang Kai-shek, after a visit to Moscow in September 1923, in which he had meetings with Leon Trotsky, Lev Kamenev, Grigory Zinoviev, and Joseph Stalin, came away with a very clear understanding of the Soviet interest in China: "The Russian Communist Party in its dealings with China has only one aim," Chiang wrote, "namely to make the Chinese Communist Party its chosen instrument."[62]

Sun Yat-sen died on 13 March 1925. The Comintern agent, Borodin, floundered as he sought a response from Moscow as to whom they preferred as Sun's successor. It was not a propitious moment as Stalin was in the middle of a two-year battle with Trotsky, Kamenev and Zinoviev for control of the Soviet Union. In Canton, Chiang Kai-shek, claiming that his name was on Sun's last breath, seized the moment and over the next year maneuvered to become the new *Kuomintang* leader—much to the annoyance of Sun's wife, T. V. Soong's sister, Soong Ching-ling, would become a staunch communist supporter. Two years later Chiang Kai-shek would make a dynastic match when he divorced and shunted his wife off to America, and married one of T. V.'s other sisters, Soong Meiling. Before Sun Ya-sen died, he gave his final orders: ". . . my recent declaration in favor of holding a National Convention of the People of China and abolishing the unequal treaties should be carried into effect as soon as possible. This is my last will and testament."[63] Sun's deathbed statement became a form of catechism at *Kuomintang* meetings. It contributed to Sun's deification by both the CCP and the *Kuomintang*.

In 1926 Chiang's National Revolutionary Army (NRA) joined with the Guangxi Army and marched northwards on what became known as the Great Northern Expedition. Chiang Kai-shek, who had become Chairman of the *Kuomintang*'s Military Council announced his intentions: "to protect the welfare of the people, we must overthrow all warlords and wipe-out reactionary power so that we may . . . complete the National Revolution."[64]

As the NRA moved northwards, liberating China from the warlords, Chiang Kai-shek became increasing aware of the gathering radicalization of his forces by communist ideology. On 12 April 1927, three weeks after the NRA had liberated Shanghai, Chiang launched his purge. Communists in Shanghai were massacred. In Wuhan, the heavily industrialized city inland on the *Yangtze River*, the CCP General Secretary set up a communist-led government with a left-wing cadre of the *Kuomintang* led by Wang Jingwei. On this occasion Stalin, the master plotter, who had planned to subvert the *Kuomintang* to the communist cause, was outmaneuvered by Chiang Kai-shek. The Shanghai Massacre initiated the long civil war between Chiang Kai-shek and the CCP that was to continue for the next twenty years apart from the brief respite of the anti-Japanese 'United Front' in 1936. After the expulsion of the Communists, Chiang continued the northern advance, liberating Peking in June 1928.

At the same time as consolidating his grip on northern China, Chiang began to hunt down CCP forces in southern and central China in the First Encirclement Campaign in November 1930. Over the next four years Chiang would launch four more Encirclement Campaigns. The CCP, riven by bitter factional fighting, elected Mao Ze-dong as Chairman of the Central Executive Council on 27 November 1931, while Zhu-de became Chairman of the Revolutionary Military Commission. With the destruction of the Jiangxi Soviet in the autumn of 1934, Mao Ze-dong led the First Front Army westward on 16 October in what would become known as the Long March.

Setting the Stage for a Renewed Conflict of Empires: At the end of the 1920s, the Anglo-Saxon empires, Great Britain and the United States, appeared to dominate a new global, collegiate system of responsible rule under the auspices of the League of Nations, the Washington System and the *Kellogg-Briand Pact*. At this point Japan appeared to be a fully paid-up member of this club. The age of empire creation appeared to be over.

However, there were fault lines in the new global order. In Europe, Germany saw itself as one of the losers in the new collective system, from whose inception it had been excluded. Shorn of its empire, demoralized by a banking crisis and a great inflation that destroyed middle-class wealth, blame was laid on France and the Anglo-Saxon nations, which had humiliated Germany at the *Treaty of Versailles*. Germany proved fertile ground for a new nationalism based on racial purity, Darwinian struggle, and an anti-capitalist, autarkic, economic agenda. Fascist ideology swept both Germany and Italy bringing to the fore leaders, Hitler [1933] and Mussolini [1922], who were fiercely opposed to the liberal, free trade democracy and benign collective responsibility that the Anglo-Saxon powers were now foisting on the world.

In the Far East, the Asian powers felt similarly excluded. A crumbling China, which had disintegrated into warlord fiefdoms over fifteen years since Sun Yat-sen's overthrow of the Qing Dynasty in 1911, was in the process of re-unification by Chiang Kai-shek. He sought to reunite China by appealing to a rising nationalism that was both anti-western and anti-Japanese. Meanwhile in Japan, which had fought on the winning side in *World War I*, ultra-nationalistic elements were increasingly disillusioned by an international system that had, by their interpretation, sought to stop it from assuming its rightful place as the dominant imperial power in Asia, were gathering strength. For the time being western-leaning moderates in Japan still had the whip hand in government—but for how long? Spurred on by the hubris of economic and military success following the defeat of China and Imperial Russia either side of the new century, Japanese ultra-nationalism, uniquely based on Emperor worship, was developing a fascist ideology that was as much a forerunner as a mimic of the National Socialism of the *Nazi* party in Germany.

Meanwhile the Soviet Union, also excluded from the Anglo-Saxon security system, was consolidating the territories of former Imperial Russia and through the Comintern (short for Communist International), was seeking to foment global revolution in the powers that surrounded it, including Germany, China and Japan. The Comintern was set up in Moscow in 1919 to organize and control Soviet agents sent to fund, inspire and coordinate revolutionary cells worldwide. It was committed to fight "by all available means, including armed force, for the overthrow of the international bourgeoisie and for the creation of an international Soviet republic as a transition stage to the complete abolition of the State."[65] Neither did the fall of Imperial Russia end the determination for expansion of influence in the Far East. For the Soviet Union expansionism was as much about defense as conquest. As former Soviet leader, Michael Gorbachev observed,

> Two centuries of domination by the Mogul Khans inclined Russian leaders and the Russian people to deep suspicion of predatory powers on its borders, or rather to the suspicion that any powers on its borders must be predatory, which posed potential threats. Extending the frontiers of the nation was, from this point of view, a defensive necessity, rather than an act of aggression. The wider the circle of Russian power, the wider the circle of powers which posed potential threats.[66]

Within a span of fifteen years from the *Treaty of Versailles*, Germany, Italy, the Soviet Union, and Japan were soon to embark on a vigorous, totalitarian quest to build empires. Meanwhile the Anglo-Saxon nations and France were undergoing a period of introspection and soul searching—a fact not unobserved by the emerging totalitarian nations. France, beset by a failure to fully industrialize its economy, and faced by stagnant population growth, was bereft of confidence and political direction. Great Britain, which suffered a steep economic decline for three years from 1919 to 1921 after shouldering the costs of the *Great War*, had seen a significant erosion of its global power and was coming face to face with the reality of American supremacy. The confidence of the old British political elite was being challenged by the emergence of powerful trade unions and a vigorous Labour Party. In a new intellectual climate that supported emancipation for women as well as for colonies, increasing numbers of Britain's political elite, Churchill excluded, started to face up to the realities of nationalism within its colonies and their rights to 'self-determination.' The first tentative moves to giving political power to Indians were made. By 1929, many British leaders had begun to accept the possibility of the loss of its Empire, the very thing that had symbolized the greatness of a Britain that had achieved global power during the industrial revolution, which it had inaugurated in the nineteenth century.

America did not emerge from *World War I* lacking confidence, but the American public and its political leaders, in part revolted by its entrapment in the horrors of *World War I*, became isolationist and eschewed foreign entanglements. For America, its empire posed different questions.

The mainland United States, which the original thirteen colonies had conquered in the nineteenth century, was never considered an empire; its growing population, drawn in from countries around the world, was provided with land, often free, and legal and political rights. Ideals of individualistic advancement were quickly imbued in a new immigrant population that saw America as a nation granted a special providence and a 'manifest destiny' to prosper and rule. Nevertheless for many, the brutal conquest of the Philippines at the end of a century of seemingly boundless expansion was a step too far and appeared to negate the very values on which America had been founded. There was a very real change in the expression of America's foreign policy at the beginning of the twentieth century. After the appropriation and suppression of the Philippines in 1898–1900, it began to dawn on American consciousness that the "colonial expansion of empire by conquest was neither moral, nor compatible with the ideals of America's own battle for independence."[67] President Theodore 'Teddy' Roosevelt may not have agreed but increasingly, America turned to the ideal of 'self-determination' as the framework through which international interventions would be justified. By 1929 both America and Great Britain had started to give the populations of the Philippines and India respectively, access to political power.

This change may have denoted a softer approach to international expansion, but it did not change the realities of the growth of American power and the United States' desire to expand its commercial empire or affect the need to exercise power when required. The whole process of naval limitation treaties negotiated at the Washington Conference was predicated on the understanding that America, with Britain as its clear ally, now that Japan had been levered out of that position, could, if they chose, win any arms race. Great Britain and America, unlike Germany, Italy, the Soviet Union, and Japan, may have started to give up on the idea of empire, but that did not mean that the Anglo-Saxons would give up their empires to others.

American utopianism, based on the mythological construct of its own revolution, as much a civil war as a war of independence, created an extreme disconnection between how American leaders saw the United States and how the rest of the world viewed America. Resentment of American power was an already well-established feature of global politics by the end of the 1920s. European and Asian states alike feared US expansion, not so much by conquest as by its apparent mission to proselytize the world with its commercial and democratic ideals. America had long been viewed by other nations as neither utopian nor selfless. Thus James Cambon, the French ambassador to the United States from 1897 to 1902, complained that "These people [the Americans] are ignorant and brutal and if they stick their hand in the complicated and patient game that the old world is playing it will little trouble them to set fire to the four corners of the Empire."[68] In the late nineteenth century figures as diverse as the Austrian Foreign Minister, Count Agenor von Guluchowsky, and the Italian historian, Ugo Ojetti, called for a united Europe to guard against the American advance. By 1921 that advance had happened. America had become the world's new superpower.

However, during the interwar years, the Anglo-Saxon powers fell into inward-looking complacency, artificially secure in the global security constructs that they had built and unaware that new forces were about to be unleashed to sweep them all away. Both Great Britain and America failed to sustain a level of naval and military investment concomitant with their imperial commitments or the military spending of the emerging totalitarian nations. Just as militarism was rising in Germany and Japan, pacifism was sweeping the West. Christian pacifists, and rationalist pacifists such as Bertrand Russell, joined with the more esoteric followers of Mahatma Gandhi. Establishment leaders such as the centrist British conservative politician, Lord Robert Cecil, orchestrated mass peace movements. In America, congressmen railed against bankers and 'merchants of death.' Economic depression would only heighten isolationist sentiment as voters turned inwards to worry about deflation and unemployment. As late as 1933, a League of Nations rally passed a resolution stating that "This meeting records its unaltered conviction that only through the League of Nations and the collective system can war be averted and civilization saved."[69] The Anglo-Saxons nations had forgotten that peace and security could not be secured by fine ideals and words to match. Collective security needed an enforcer and both Britain and America fell down on the job.

In Japan, as the 1920s progressed, the need to resist the Anglo-Saxon lock on Asia became the clarion call of the rising ultra-nationalist groups within the political and military elite. The idea of Pan-Asianism in Japan grew from the increasing belief that Asia would be forever dominated by the 'whites,' unless Japan led a crusade to overthrow the 'white yoke.' In the immediate aftermath of *World War I*, Japanese moderates within the political elite, who dominated the post-war decade, had played the 'white' game of international collective responsibility but all the while forces were building to reject the Anglo-Saxon rulebook, which, from a Japanese standpoint, stacked the odds against the emergence of Japan as a great Asian power. By the end of the 1920s plans for regional Japanese hegemony, with which to confront the West, were already being plotted in the ultra-nationalist factions within the Imperial Japanese Army; for them the domination of China, the fallen giant of Asia, was the key to their hegemonic Asian future. The *Great War*, far from drawing an end to the age of empires, merely set the stage for what was an even larger and far more global conflict. Thus, by 1933, when Hitler came to power in Germany, the 'have-nots' of the German and Japanese regimes were moodily resentful of the apparent dominance of the Anglo-Saxon world. Finally it would be China, weakened by economic stagnation and decades of civil war, that would provide the *casus belli* for the *Pacific War* and turn Hitler's war of aggression in Europe into *World War II*.

Part II
Japan versus America and the World: 1931–1941

2 Ultra-nationalism and the Death of Democracy

[1930–1936]

[Maps: 2.1, 2.2, 2.3, 2.4]

The London Naval Conference [1930] and the Death of Hamaguchi: Convened on 21 January 1930, the London Naval Conference aimed to renew the limitations to the building of battleships agreed by the great naval powers at the *Washington Naval Treaty* [1922]—sometimes known as the Five Powers Treaty. The 5:5:3 capital ships tonnage ratios agreed eight years earlier for the United States, Great Britain and Japan respectively, were kept in place in London. However, for light cruisers and auxiliary ships Japan achieved an improvement to 10:10:7 respectively. To add to the complexity America was allowed 18 heavy cruisers to 15 for Great Britain and 12 for Japan. A five-year ban was set on new capital ships. However, the provisions for the naval treaties of 1922 and 1930 were set to lapse in 1936. France and Italy, which had been allowed a ratio of 1.75 each in the *Washington Naval Treaty*, refused to sign up to the *Treaty of London* [1930].

It was a slight upward adjustment to Japan's quota but not one that satisfied the main opposition party, *Rikken Seiyukai* (Friends of Constitutional Government), and conservatives within the *Sumitsu-in* (Privy Council). In a sign of the Diet's hostility, parliamentarian Ichiro Hatoyama, later a Prime Minister in 1954 and one of the founders of the Liberal Democratic Party (LDP) a year later, went as far as to suggest that civilian decisions on armaments had been made which had ignored the opinions of the Navy. It was an argument that undermined both the cabinet and parliamentary democracy.

The more nationalistic senior Navy officers were hostile to the London Naval Conference and many younger ultra-nationalists were vocal in disapproval. It was quibbled that the new ratios were 0.4 percent short of their original target. Their main gripe was that Japan was forced to halt production of heavy cruisers, which had been excluded in Washington, but were now limited in a way which would allow the United States to catch up in this category. To outsiders, opposition to the *London Naval Treaty* [1930] appeared to be based more on a pro-forma opposition to Hamaguchi's firm civilian leadership, than to any substantive issues. In reality Japan's tonnage remained at 80 percent compared to the United States because America, during the depression, allowed the building of new warships to lapse. This did nothing to mollify the ultra-nationalists who were intent on not being mollified. For them the treaty would remain a touchstone issue for the next six years. Behind the scenes, Navy Chief of Staff, Admiral Kanji Kato, an outspoken critic of the naval limitation system, and Admiral Nobumasa Suetsugu, both leaders of the opposition to the *London Naval Treaty*, were supported by the opposition *Rikken Seiyukai* and advocated that Japan should withdraw from the treaty arrangements when they expired in 1936. In the meantime they wanted set in motion plans to implement a massive naval building program.

Within the Navy's middle ranks, as in the Army, there was a hard core of ultra-nationalists whose voice was becoming increasingly strident. In 1931, Lieutenant-Commander Shingo Ishikawa, a section chief in the Naval Ministry's Naval Affairs bureau, was a rising star on the general staff. Writing under a pseudonym, Ishikawa published a controversial polemic, *Japan's Crisis* [1931] in which he warned that America's foreign policy aim was to control Asia, a policy that had been in process for over eighty years. In this context the *Washington Naval Treaty* and *London Naval Treaty* were seen as attempts to bind Japan with the ultimate aim of subjugation. Naval officers, fiercely proud of their destruction of the Russian Navy at the *Battle of Tsushima* found it difficult to comprehend that they were still being treated as second-class citizens on the world stage—on the whole this was not the case but the misconception was sustained as a matter of ultra-nationalist faith. Ishikawa proposed "a great national march to ensure its right to survival."[1] Within the decade, Ishikawa's outspoken and radical analysis would become the mainstream view of both the Army and Navy and may have carried some influence within Hirohito's court circle.

In spite of Navy opposition, Hamaguchi stood his ground. He was confident of the Emperor's support: "It doesn't matter if the Privy Council opposes us. I intend to request an imperial sanction [against the council] and will take no steps toward reaching a compromise."[2] Hamaguchi, the son of a forestry official from Kochi on the fourth of Japan's major islands, *Shikoku*, won a place at the law faculty of Tokyo University (*Todai*) and graduated in 1895. From here he followed a classic bureaucratic career, entering the Ministry of Finance and moving up to become Director of the Monopoly Bureau. This was crowned when he became Vice-Minister of Finance in 1914. The following year he entered politics, joining the party that became *Kenseikai* in 1915 and later morphed into *Rikken Minseito* (Constitutional Democratic Party).

He was duly elected to the second district of Kochi, an area he served as a Diet member until his death. In 1927 he became Chairman of the new *Rikken Minseito* (Constitutional Democrat Party). A natural fiscal conservative, he was appointed as Prime Minister on the advice of Prince Saionji Kinmochi in 1929. Hamaguchi's forcing of the *London Naval Treaty*, which made sense from a fiscal and security point of view, increased his unpopularity with the ultranationalists. At the same time his unpopularity was underpinned by the support he gave to finance minister Inoue's maintenance of a Yen fixed to the Gold Standard. The policy brought deflation and depression, particularly in the agricultural sector, to an already struggling economy. The only beneficiaries were the speculators, bankers and large corporations, who drained liquidity from the domestic economy by buying specie in the certain knowledge that Japan would be forced off the

Gold Standard. Speculation by bankers and corporations increased even more rapidly after Great Britain was forced to abandon the gold standard in September 1931.

Hamaguchi's unpopularity with the Japanese ultra-nationalist fringe came to a head on 14 November 1930. Hamaguchi was shot as he entered Tokyo Station. Severely wounded he was rushed to hospital. His would-be assassin, Tomeo Sagoya, was a member of the ultra-nationalist society, *Aikokusha* (Society of Patriots), one of a rash of such groups that were springing up in Japan. In the Japanese Diet there was little sympathy for Hamaguchi among the opposition. In spite of his serious injuries, Ichiiro Hatoyama, a leading member of *Rikken Seiyukai* in the lower house, demanded the Prime Minister's attendance to answer questions of policy. The Diet turned into a bear pit with some of the most hostile and disruptive sessions of the interwar years.

A combination of a recession and the contentious *London Naval Treaty*, which was portrayed in the right-wing press as a national humiliation, combined to create a febrile political atmosphere. During sessions at which Hamaguchi was not able to attend parliament, his deputy was physically attacked. In March 1931, against medical advice, Hamaguchi attended Diet sessions to push through liberal legislation favoring labor unions, more equitable distribution of taxes, a reduction of the male voting age from 25 to 21 and giving women the right to vote in local elections. As he stumbled onto the podium barely able to speak *Rikken Seiyukai* members shouted "Speak louder" and "Get lost and die."[3]

Not surprisingly many observers, including the Emperor and the military, saw that the Diet, parliamentary party politics, and the constitution were falling into disrepute. For many in the military, there had to be a better way to govern. A month after his enfeebled performance in the Diet, Hamaguchi resigned. A few months later, on 26 August 1931, he died.

The Mukden Incident [1931]: [Map: 2.1] Although the Marco Polo Bridge Incident on 7 July 1937 is usually regarded as the starting point of the *Second Sino-Japanese War*, arguably the war began six years earlier with the Mukden Incident, which precipitated the Japanese Army's occupation of Manchuria in 1931. In Japan the era of conflict including the *Second Sino-Japanese War* and the *Pacific War* is sometimes conflated and called the *Fifteen-Year War* [1931–1945] even though it fell short of that number of years.

By the end of the 1920s it was well understood within the Japanese military hierarchy in Tokyo that the annexation of Manchuria was a desirable goal of foreign policy. China's weakness, and the very real threat of the Soviet Union made the acquisition of Manchuria for the security of Japan's colonial occupation of Korea, now ruled as a vassal state, a compelling proposition. As diplomat and historian Takeo Iguchi has explained, "Japan felt threatened by the build-up of Soviet Military power as well as by the penetration of its ideology among the Japanese people."[4] For Japan the threat from the north was a linear development of a foreign policy that had seen Imperial Russia as the major threat to Japanese security from 1890 onwards, culminating in the

Russo-Japanese War of 1905. As early as 1928 Lieutenant-Colonel Kanji Ishiwara had been charged with producing a broad study of the operations needed for such a venture. His report was filed away. Numerous incidents began to raise tensions in the region. A Japanese spy was arrested by Chinese troops and shot. In July 1931 troops from the *Kwantung* Army were sent across the border to protect the rights of Korean immigrant workers, who were after all citizens of the Japanese Empire. At the Japanese Army compound in Mukden, two 9.5-inch cannon were put into place. Emplacement works had been carried out in the guise of building a swimming pool. The guns were trained on the Manchurian main barracks and Mukden's airfield.

Responsibility for the Korean border's security and the Manchurian Railway lay with Lieutenant-General Shigeru Honjo, the newly appointed commander of the *Kwantung* Army. In addition to Honjo, Colonel Kenji Doihara was appointed as Chief of the Special Service in Mukden. The significant upgrade of this position indicated the increased interest that the Imperial Army HQ was taking in Korea's border with Manchuria. If there were stirrings within the Imperial Japanese Army, it was not apparent to Chiang Kai-shek, who was busy chasing down the renegade communist leader Mao Zedong and the rival warlords. The Manchurian Army of warlord Chang Hsueh-liang, the Young Marshal, marched with Chiang, leaving Manchuria lightly defended. At the time, Chang Hsueh-liang was in Peking at the American Rockefeller Hospital, where he was being treated for opium addiction.

The Japanese Army's secret planning for war was finally hinted at when War Minister General Jiro Minami's public address to his commanders on 4 August was reported in the press. The liberal, anti-war newspaper, *Asahi Shimbu*, noted in its editorial that "The military seems to be openly disregarding public opinion and defying the government."[5] With rumors circulating in Tokyo, the liberal pro-peace government desperately fought to stave off military action. Kinmochi Saionji, the last remaining *genro* (elder statesman), intervened with Prime Minister Reijiro Wakatsuki and other civilian members of the cabinet to get them to deny funds for the military transfers. It was a losing battle. Saionji's influence led war minister, General Minami, to send an emissary, Major-General Yoshiji Tatekawa, to Mukden, to warn off the *Kwantung* Army. But ultranationalist hotheads Colonel Seishiro Itagaki and Lieutenant Kanji Ishiwara, both based in Mukden, were alerted to his arrival. Various telegrams were sent warning of Tatekawa's coming, including one from Lieutenant-Colonel Hashimoto that read "PLOT EXPOSED. ACT BEFORE TATEKAWA'S ARRIVAL."[6] Tatekawa, who was no shrinking liberal violet, having been a party to the assassination of former Manchurian warlord Chang Tso-lin in 1928, may well have been in on the plot. Both aggressive middle-ranking extreme nationalists Itagaki and Ishiwara, who was nicknamed 'Wild Shot,'[7] were well advanced in their planning for an incident that would give an excuse for the *Kwantung* Army to be drawn into Manchuria. Launch date was planned for the early hours of 18 September.

With knowledge of Tatekawa's journey-plan, Itagaki intercepted Minami's emissary on the train as he approached Mukden. When they reached Mukden at 7.05 p.m., Itagaki organized for them to be met and chauffeured to the best teahouse, Literary

Chrysanthemum, in Mukden's Japanese quarter. Tatekawa was happily plied with tea, sake, a bed and a *geisha*. At 10.20 p.m. that evening a small bomb was exploded next to the railway tracks near Mukden. A few minutes after the explosion a passenger train passed over the damaged track with barely a wobble—many of the passengers were unaware of even feeling a jolt. Chinese troops were accused of the crime and Japanese forces immediately went into action. By noon on 19 September most of the junction towns on the southern part of the Manchurian Railway had been taken over. Honjo, being informed of developments, made noises to suggest that Itagaki had acted without authorization. It was a charade that fooled nobody. At 11.50 p.m. Honjo approved the occupation of Mukden itself and ordered the transfer of the headquarters of the *Kwantung* Army. Meanwhile one of the secretly hidden cannon bombarded the airfield. China's modest air force was destroyed. In the fighting for Mukden that ensued, 500 Chinese troops were reported killed at the expense of 200 Japanese.

News spread worldwide. For foreign diplomats in Tokyo and Peking, the aggressive actions of the *Kwantung* Army came 'out of the blue.' At the League of Nations, Japan's ambassador assured his fellow diplomats that the Japanese troops would be recalled to barracks. The Japanese Army's carefully crafted plan fooled nobody. On 22 September, Stimson cabled to the chief US observer at the League of Nations that "It is apparent that the Japanese military have initiated a widely extended movement of aggression only after careful preparation . . ."[8] In a pusillanimous response the League of Nations voted to request the "Chinese and Japanese governments to refrain from action that might aggravate."[9] In Mukden the local commanders worried at actions that had been authorized on a 'nod and a wink' rather than with official orders. Tatekawa reassured them, "Just restrict operations to south Manchuria for the time being and everything will be all right,"[10] In Tokyo, Hirohito, his close advisers and the cabinet, divided between pro-war militarists and anti-war civilians, dithered.

On the Korea-Manchurian border, the Japanese Army in Korea massed its forces and waited for orders to deploy northwards to help General Honjo. Public pressure on the government grew and, fearful of being seen not to support Honjo's 10th Division, the cabinet, on 23 September, voted to fund troop movements for their advance into Manchuria. Hirohito rubber-stamped the northern advance of the Imperial Japanese Army from North Korea—a move that had technically breached Japan's constitution. Manchuria was annexed with minimal resistance. In Japan people rejoiced; business waited anxiously to see if League of Nations sanctions would follow. In October 1932, Lord Lytton finally reported to the League of Nations. He called for the "construction of a special regime for the administration of the Three Eastern Provinces [Manchuria]" consistent "with the sovereignty and administrative integrity of China" and "withdrawal of all armed forces, including any special bodies of police or railway guards, whether Chinese or Japanese."[11] Meanwhile, a furious Chiang sat impotently in southern China, aware that his armed forces were no match for those of the Japanese.

In spite of Article-35 of the Army code that stated "a commander who opens hostilities with a foreign country without provocation shall be punished by death"[12] there was little but token punishment for the instigators. In 1932, Lieutenant-General Honjo was relieved of command on the grounds of insubordination but returned to Japan as a hero. Even Emperor Hirohito honored him as such. It is interesting to note that at the beginning of the Manchurian venture, Hirohito had expressed serious doubts; it is reported that he plaintively told a court official, "I am striving to preserve world peace . . . But the forces overseas do not heed my commands and are recklessly expanding the incident."[13] He subsequently ordered restraint in Manchuria but was ignored. The Emperor may have been concerned at the risks of military action but once handed a successful *fait accompli* he seemed only too happy to go along with the projected Imperial expansion implicit in the Mukden Incident and the annexation of Manchuria. Honjo was elevated to the rank of baron (*danshaku*) and became a member of the Supreme War Council before being appointed as *aide-de-camp* to Hirohito with whom he developed a close relationship. After the acquisition of Manchuria, and the world's relative indifference to the event, the Emperor's liking for Japan's imperial quest seems to have increased.

In accepting the results of the Manchurian invasion it is open to question whether Hirohito was merely acting as a constitutional monarch or was simply expressing reservations that were characteristic of a man known for his caution. Given the later honoring of Lieutenant-General Honjo with his appointment as Chief *Aide-de-Camp* to Hirohito and the Emperor's subsequent good relations with him, one has to question whether Hirohito's protestations against the Army's annexation of Manchuria were in the nature of 'crocodile tears.'

Depression, Autarky and the Economic Imperatives for Japanese Aggression: Cordell Hull in his *Memoirs* wrote:

> If we could get a freer flow of trade—freer in the sense of fewer discriminations and obstructions—so that one country would not be deadly jealous of another and the living standards of all countries might rise, thereby eliminating the economic dissatisfaction that breeds war, we might have a reasonable chance for lasting peace.[14]

The problem for America was that Japan, over the course of the interwar years, moved in diametrically the opposite direction to the global model envisioned by the United States' leaders. At the critical conference with the Emperor on 6 September 1941, Tojo's government put forward an *Outline for the Execution of National Polity* that put autarky at its heart: point one noted that "In order to preserve the empire's self-sufficiency and self-defense, Japan was determined not to back away from war with the United States, Britain, and the Netherlands; consequently, war preparations were to be completed by the end of October."[15] Autarky was a philosophical difference that was one of the root causes of the looming conflict between the two countries.

In discussions with Ambassador Grew in Tokyo 1940, Foreign Minister Hachiro Arita explained,

> Japan has always advocated free movement of both men
> and commodities ... [but this principle] ... has been
> frequently violated and Japan has been obliged to undergo
> bitter experiences. Immigration [to America] is restricted,
> and markets are open or closed to suit the convenience of
> the importing nations while the importation of necessities
> into Japan is prohibited or limited at will by the exporting
> countries.[16]

On 1 August, Arita called for a Japanese controlled *Great East Asia Co-Prosperity Sphere*; it was the first time that this soon-to-be-famous expression was used. The fall of France and the Netherlands to *Nazi* Germany expanded the ambitions of Prime Minister Fumimaro Konoe, whose call for a New Order had largely envisaged a Japanese-dominated Asia comprising, Korea, Manchukuo, China, and Taiwan. By the summer of 1940 Dutch and French possessions were there for the taking and promised the possibility of control of raw materials vital to the prosperity of Japan, particularly oil and rubber. With the existence of Britain teetering on the edge as it engaged in the *Battle of Britain*, which would decide Hitler on whether to invade, there appeared to Japan the possibility of expanding its quasi-Empire even further.

By 1940 there was no expectation that Japan would view this sphere as one that would trade freely with the world. In the twenty years leading up to 1940 the concept of autarky, autonomous and indigenous economic development, had completely won the intellectual argument within Japan.

In the immediate aftermath of *World War I* there were two main arguments that made autarky attractive. First an analysis of *World War I* by serving Japanese officers came to the conclusion that Germany had lost the war primarily for economic reasons. Its economy, starved of vital commodities, had collapsed. It was thus concluded that in 'total' modern wars of a longer duration, combatant natons would no longer be able to depend just on their own resources. For the manufacture and operation of military equipment, nations would need secure supply of commodities such as coal, oil and iron ore. Colonel Kuniaki Koiso, a high-flyer on the General Staff, who was later to become Prime Minister in July 1944, was asked to study Japan's security problems. He concluded that Japan, Korea, and Taiwan alone could not provide the resources that Japan would require for a protracted war. It was a line of argument that other staff officers, including Major-General Tetsuzan Nagata, head of the Economic Mobilization Bureau, and Colonel Kanji Ishiwara and every other intelligence officer would have understood. For many in the Army the conquest of commodity-rich territories such as China was an imperative.

Secondly Article-16 of the Covenant of the League of Nations enshrined the principle that aggression by any country could be punished by a ban on trade and loans. It was a principle that seemed to favor those countries that were the 'haves' (such as the United States and Great Britain) in terms of resources rather than the 'have-nots'—in which camp the Japanese undoubtedly placed themselves. After all, how could Japan join the elite of countries to which it believed its destiny to be called, without being aggressive? Support for autarky was already coming from one of the most influential intellectuals of the interwar period. As early as 1918 Professor Kanogi argued that Japan's survival depended not only on becoming a totalitarian state but being "autonomous, independent, and self sufficient."[17] Similarly, figures as influential as Prince Konoe were arguing against the terms of a western peace that appeared to discriminate against the 'have-not' countries such as Japan.

On a more practical level, even as early as the 1920s the issue of oil became an imperative for the Navy. In *World War I*, oil had replaced coal as the source of energy for warships. It was a commodity of which Japan was bereft. Nor was it available in any significant amount in Manchuria. Given that the battleship had become the weapon that most clearly expressed international power, the need for oil was paramount. By the end of 1926 the Japanese Navy had already stored 1.5 million tons of the commodity but still it did not feel secure. For the Imperial Japanese Army too, the importance of oil was increasing with mechanization both in the form of tanks and trucks. However, it was the increasing importance of aviation that significantly boosted the demand for oil. The value of military aggression for the acquisition of oil seemed to have paid dividends when the Army's occupation of northern *Sakhalin* in 1925 ended with Japan gaining rights to half the area's oil production, an amount no less than 100,000 tons per annum. Such was the inexorable increase in the demand for oil that following the discovery of oil shale in Manchuria in 1926, the South Manchurian Railway and the Navy jointly ventured to look at the possibility of producing oil from coal.

The annexation of Manchuria and the economic development of Manchukuo was a component part of the military's quest for self-sufficiency. The drive to secure the northern provinces of China adjacent to Manchuria was also predicated on the need for their natural resources. The Military Affairs Bureau concluded that the area held more coal and iron ore than Manchuria. At a conference in 1934, attended by the Foreign Ministry, the Army and Navy, it was decided that the *Kuomintang* had to be denied occupation of northern China and that a Japanese corporation should be established to exploit the area's resources. Within the Army the primacy of economic self-sufficiency became a central plank of the Control Faction (*Toseiha*) committed to the development of Japan's civil economy so that it could engage in the 'total war' that it envisaged in the future.

Japan's vulnerability to embargo was as apparent to some international observers as it was to the Japanese military. Stanley Hornbeck, who had argued for an embargo of Japan in response to the Mukden Incident and Japan's annexation of Manchuria, noted that a sustained embargo "would impose on Japan the necessity of attempting to reorganize her economic life on a self-supporting basis. The immediate cost and the ultimate futility of such an effort would be evident to Japan's statesman from the beginning."[18]

The onset of the financial crash and the Great Depression starting in 1930 gave a further boost to Japan's autarkic tendencies. Capitalism appeared to have failed and increased the advocacy for protection and the acquisition of captive markets. In America, the passing of the *Tariff Act* [1930] (Smoot-Hawley), which increased import duties on 20,000 products showed that free trade was not sacrosanct even in those countries that most pleaded its cause. The collapse of the *Minseito* government in December 1931 brought to power right-wing politicians who believed in a more interventionist approach to solving Japan's economic problems. The maintenance of the Yen's gold parity caused capital outflows that were only solved by the Japanese Diet's passing of the *Capital Flight Prevention Act* [1932]. This was followed by the *Gold Purchase Act* [1934], which gave the Ministry of Finance complete power over specie holdings.

The social consequences of the economic recession were wide ranging. Interest in foreign culture that had marked the 1920s quickly dissipated. Japan turned back in on itself. Between 1929 and 1930 almost half of small businesses—more vulnerable than larger operations—were forced to close down. A wave of emigrants went to Brazil or Manchuria. Children from poor agricultural villages were sold as slaves. In the six prefectures of northeastern Japan the number of women sold rose from 12,180 in 1932 to 58,173 in 1934. In the pre-war years an estimated 200,000 women a year were sold as maids and nursemaids. In effect it was indentured service. It tailed off after 1937 as more and more women were employed as munitions workers, etc. Militarists took advantage of the economic and spiritual exhaustion of the Japanese people for whom the prospect of empire offered hope. Apart from falling commodity prices the misery in the countryside was compounded by the return of 211,990 factory workers, out of a total of 569,432, to the agricultural sector.

In 1936 the Resources Bureau that controlled the nation's mobilization plans submitted a proposal to the cabinet entitled *Measures Particularly Needed in Order to Establish a Basis for Mobilization*. It proposed "a powerful central organ to form and execute a policy of promoting natural and synthetic fuel production . . . there is a need for a Science Research Bureau to devise means to correct deficiencies of natural resources . . . we must plan for a stronger unity of administration in all trade matters."[19] Moving in this direction, the following year saw the creation of a Cabinet Planning Office that drafted a five-year economic plan aimed at the rapid expansion of production. By the start of the *Second Sino-Japanese War*, the Japanese military, who were the main promoters of autarkic policies that they believed were essential for Japan's survival, had wrought a substantial change in the nature of the Japanese economy from a free market system to one that was centrally directed by the state. The irony was that the increased militarization of Japan increased rather than decreased its reliance on products imported from America, whether it was oil, particularly high-octane aviation fuel, scrap iron or machine tools.

Fascism, Pan-Asianism and the Japanese Intelligentsia: It would be easy to assume that the collapse of Japan's parliamentary system and its replacement by an expansionist military was simply a reflection of the growing power of the Army in a country whose economy was subsumed by the Great Depression. In reality underlying Japanese expansionism of the 1930s was an intellectual movement that promoted both the ideas of fascism and Pan-Asianism. In broad terms it was an assumption of Asian and Japanese weakness and an affirmation that "something must be done to make it [Japan and Asia) stronger so that it may achieve recognition by the west."[20] A host of intellectuals who led the pan-Asian movement included Mitsuru Toyama (an old-generation rightist), Kametaro Mitsukawa, Shumei Okawa and Ikki Kita (three young right-wing activists and writers) Unosuke Wakamiya, Kojiro Sugimori, Yanunobu Kuchita, Kanoki Kazunobu, and politicians Kaku Mori, Ichiro Hatoyama,

It would be a mistake to think that ultra-nationalism was only a product of the 1930s. Born the son of a poor samurai in 1855, Mitsuru Toyama was the godfather of ultra-nationalist groups. In 1881 he had been a founding member of *Genyosha* (Black Ocean Society) a secret society initially campaigned for domestic reform before changing tack and agitating for the conquest of Asia. His career spanned the *Meiji Restoration*, the *First Sino-Japanese War* (before which he organized the *Tenyukyo*, a secret paramilitary force that operated in Korea), the *Russo-Japanese War, World War I*, the *Second Sino-Japanese War* and the *Pacific War*. As late as 1939 when he was in his eighties, Toyama established a national federation to suppress Christianity, which he described as "a device of Jewish ideas which threatens to encroach upon the spirit of the Japanese race."[21] Throughout his career he remained politically connected and was on friendly terms with future Prime Minister Tsuyoshi Inukai (in whose assassination his son was implicated) as well, ironically, as Chiang Kai-shek. His connections and support also ran to the Japanese underworld, a bastion of nationalist enthusiasm, which provided information and muscle when it was needed.

The gangster underworld comprised a seedy network of corrupt bureaucrats, terrorist groups, strike-breakers, extortionists and blackmailers who often worked hand-in-hand with ultra-nationalist groups. Ultra-nationalists worked within this soup of intrigue and illicit cash. At the Mitsui group, Japan's most illustrious *zaibatsu*, Mitsui Gomei, the holding company of the Mitsui family, was delegated to handle all issues of a political nature and set aside millions of yen for 'gifts' and 'contributions' to various causes. Thus, from 1932, Ikki Kita, one of the hardest hitting of the ultra-nationalist rabble-rousers was seen riding in a chauffeured limousine and living in a large house. Thanks to the generosity of Mitsui Gomei's 'research department' he was able to provide for disciples and henchmen.

Kametaro Mitsukawa, born to an impoverished merchant family in 1888, was somewhat typical of members of a dispossessed but educated middle-class who had found themselves losers in the capitalist transformation of Japan that had followed the *Meiji Restoration*. His personal humiliations were reflected on the international stage by the hurt he felt as a result of the Triple Intervention in 1895—a humiliation, perhaps retrospectively acquired, which would carry through to his biography entitled *After the Triple Intervention* [1935]. Japan's humiliation by the 'white man' led him to become an early exponent of Pan-Asianism which expounded the view that Asians should collectively stand up to the western imperialists: "Asia constitutes culturally, politically, economically, geographically and racially a single community that shares the same fate."[22] Although Mitsukawa proclaimed a pan-Asian brotherhood, he perversely insisted on Japan superiority and its rightful place as Asia's natural leader.

Having dropped out of Waseda University where he was studying politics and economics, he became a journalist with *Kaiyo Nippo* (the Maritime National Daily). It was a position that brought him into contact with senior figures in the Navy as well as civilian life. He became close to leading right-wing intellectuals including Nakano Seigo at the *Asahi Shimbun* and Professor Nagai Ryutaro. In 1918 he founded *Rosokai* (the Society of Old and Young Men) that attracted both generals and admirals and a mixed bag of right- and left-wing political adherents. More importantly, in 1919 Mitsukawa and Shumei Okawa founded *Yuzonsha Kokkyo Semmei-dan* (National Principle Society), which was an overtly radical pan-Asian group. In 1924 Mitsukawa, along with Shumei Okawa, took over the Social Education Institute which occupied rooms provided by Nobuaki Makino, an Imperial Household Ministry bureaucrat, within the grounds of the Imperial Palace.

Mitsukawa's contemporary right-wing figure Ikki Kita (born Terujiro Kita) was the son of a *sake* (rice wine) brewer on the island of *Sado,* in the *Sea of Japan* off Niigata Prefecture. Kita family's fortunes, like those of Mitsukawa, were in decline. His career followed a similar path to Mitsukawa. Kita dropped out of school and took up the career of a polemicist journalist and writer in Tokyo. He espoused a form of nationalistic statist socialism—in other words tending toward fascism. After spending almost a decade flirting with the Chinese revolution, Kita returned to Japan in 1920 and joined *Yuzonsha*, the pan-Asian club founded by Mitsukawa and Okawa. He also became a Nichiren Buddhist, which practiced a nationalistic form of the religion. Like Mitsukawa, Kita would also become influential in Army circles, where radicalised officers took up elements of his fascist philosophy. His best known work *Kokka Kaizo Hoan Daiko* [1919] (Outline of Plans for the Reconstruction of Japan), was sometimes misleadingly dubbed the Japanese *Mein Kampf* (My Struggle). It became a bible for the *Ketsumeidan* (Blood Pledge Band) and the Sakurakai (Cherry Blossom Society), a few of whose members participated in the coups and assassinations of the 1930s.

Perceived humiliations, such as the *London Naval Treaty* [1930] added grist to the grievances of right-wing intellectuals such as Ikki Kita and Mitsukawa. In 1930 Mitsukawa joined the *Aikoku Kinroto* (Patriotic Workers Party) that closely resembled the views and structure of the *Nazi* Party in Germany. However, in 1929 he wrote an article *Delusions about the Jewish Peril* in which he debunked the anti-Semitic conspiracy theories that had gained traction in Japan. He also joined the *Shin Kokumin Domei* (New Japan National Alliance). The development of an anti-capitalist Japanese statism was a philosophy that was in essence socialist, like that of the *Nazis*, but fiercely opposed to communism and the Soviet Union in particular. Unlike their European counterparts however, they revered tradition and the imperial system and were either unable or unwillingly to form a mass movement. In advocating a *Showa Isshin* (Showa

Restoration), Mitsukawa and others sought a political framework that did away with corrupt politicians and a dysfunctional parliamentary system. Professor Kazunobu Kanokogi, a philosopher at Kyushu University, was also a statist who rejected what he saw as the exploitative side of capitalism. He warned against the evils of party politics and the usurpation of power by big business. Capitalism was excoriated. In China, Kanokogi warned that unalloyed capitalism had turned the *Kuomintang* into 'running dogs' of international Jewish interests that spanned America, Britain, and the Soviet Union. He, like all his fellow intellectuals, viewed with dismay the war profiteers for whom *World War I* had produced a bonanza set against the poverty that was evident from the Rice Riots that swept Japan in 1918, forcing the resignation of Prime Minister Terauchi and his cabinet.

Kanokogi also drew the lesson from *World War I* that total mobilization of the economy was now a prerequisite of war. Rather than drawing the lesson that the winners, the liberal democratic powers, had outfought the Germans, Kanokogi, like many in the Japanese military, perversely concluded that a totalitarian system was preferable. Statism in Japan was a movement that meant different things to different groups. Some wanted simply a state-controlled economy, others a military junta, while some wanted a suspension of the constitution and promise of direct Imperial Rule. This was the solution favored by the Emperor's younger brother Prince Chichibu. For many the embrace of fascism simply represented a rejection of modern liberal values.

By contrast with Mitsukawa and Kita, their contemporary Kazunobu Kanokogi was a genuine academic and philosopher. He too had a significant impact on ultra-nationalist intellectual thought. Kanokogi became a cheerleader for Hitler when he came to power in 1933, in part because the Japanese philosopher's writing had advocated totalitarian and fascistic ideals in lectures as early as 1917. Kanokogi, originally a naval officer and a Christian pacifist, turned against liberalism after studying philosophy at Columbia in New York. In a symbolic rejection of Anglo-Saxon culture, he chose the philosophy of Nietzsche as the subject of his thesis for his Master's degree, *Freidrich Nietzsche, The Philosopher of Free Spirit and the Prophet of Übermensch* [1910]. A poem written in 1909 reveals the extent of his intellectual journey:

> Oh, Japan, at last your time has come. Your hour of destiny has at last arrived. You must awaken. Oh, Japan! You will achieve greatness. Difficulties make jewels out of people. Long ago tiny Prussia rose like a brave young lion. Now the tiny Japanese State . . . Ah, arise, Japan, the land of beauty and the nation of heroes, The stars will guide you higher and higher, With justice and with your strength.[23]

After his studies in New York, Kanokogi went to Germany where he studied philosophy at the University of Jena, Thuringia. Here, under Rudolph Eucken, who won the Nobel Prize for literature in 1908, Kanokogi recalled that he gained "a spiritual stimulus that at last guided me away from scepticism in a more positive direction."[24] Distaste for liberal democracy was now replaced by an admiration for the organic development of Japan's unique polity through the divinity of the Emperor. His rejection of parliamentary democracy inevitably led him to favor totalitarianism, which he managed to fuse into a doctrine that also incorporated Emperor worship. Thus, unlike some of his contemporaries, Kanokogi remained profoundly conservative in his view of the imperial family. It was therefore a right-wing philosophy that remained completely acceptable to Japan's social elite. His views, combined with a natural easy charm, enabled him to make influential contacts with Control Faction generals such as Jinzaburo Masaki and Shigeru Honjo as well as Rear-Admiral Hiroharo Kato. Friendly relationships were established with aristocrats such as Count Yoshinori Futara and Marquis Moritatsu Hosokawa. Imperial Princes such as Chichibu were part of the social and intellectual circle in which he swam.

Kanokogi's influence was not limited to the Japanese elite. He was similarly influential amongst a younger generation. After his return from India, where he was arrested and deported for his espousal of world revolution, he continued to further right-wing causes. These included the setting up of *Doshikai Kokoku* (Association of Patriotic Comrades) at Tokyo Imperial University. *Doshikai Kokoku,* for which he wrote the manifesto, became an important focus of dissemination of right-wing views to an educated elite who would find themselves well positioned as senior bureaucrats in 1930s Japan.

His influence spread beyond the salons of Tokyo. After his appointment to the post of Professor of Philosophy at Kyushu Imperial University, Kanokogi established two new study groups, *Man-Mo Kenkyukai* (Manchuria-Mongolia Study Group) and the *Kodokai* (the Imperial Way Society), which looked at uniqueness in Japanese thought through the lens of ancient Japanese texts such as *Kojiki*. Japan's uniqueness was to be protected and it is noticeable that the academic and bureaucratic compilers of the standard nationalist text *Kokutai no Hongi* [1937] (Basic Principles of the National Polity) warned that ". . . since the days of Meiji so many aspects of European and American culture, systems and learning have been imported, and that, too rapidly."[25]

Kanokogi joined the *Rosokai* and *Yuzonsha*, and participated in lecture programs with Indian Independence activists. It was one of the idiosyncrasies of Japanese Pan-Asianism that it was denouncing the British Empire at the same time that it was advocating the conquest of China. The rationale was that the Japanese, as 'superior Asians,' had right of conquest in order to create an Asian bloc against the west.

Matsukawa preached survival in the face of western aggression. In response to the limitation of Japanese naval building agreed in the *Washington Naval Treaty* [1922], Matsukawa claimed that the western powers were "plotting to subjugate Asia completely by the end of the twentieth century."[26] America was particularly to blame as he perspicaciously noted that, as a result of *World War I*, "Britain's wealth . . . migrated to New York."[27] To defeat the West, Mitsukawa promoted the ideal of an autarkic state that would be able to "destroy the evils of American capitalist aggression."[28] Kanokogi also suggested that Japan become "autonomous, independent and self-sufficent"[29] as a precondition for a totalitarian state's preparation for total war. Colonel Ishiwara, a Nichiren Buddhist, who was one of the key instigators of the Mukden Incident, was obsessed with the concept of Asian unity and believed that it would lead to a 'final war' between East and West.

Strongly influenced by Social Darwinism, some Japanese intellectuals went as far as to promote eugenics to sustain Japan's racial purity. Shigenori Ikeda, a leading journalist with two doctoral degrees from Germany wrote that "To sustain one's nation-state's superiority over other nation-states one must first ensure the superiority of its racial character."[30] He became a cheerleader for the *Race Eugenic Protection Act* [1940] that was promulgated by Konoe's government. The bill ordered compulsory sterilization of the mentally ill. Family centers were ordered to discourage marriage between Japanese and Koreans. These attitudes survived the war. In 1945 the Japanese government authorized a government-funded prostitution service for occupying American soldiers, declaring that "Through the sacrifice of thousands of [maidens, such as war widows] . . . we shall construct a dike to hold back the mad frenzy of the occupying troops and cultivate and preserve the purity of our race long into the future . . ."[31]

The Japanese notions of racial purity extended to anti-Semitism in spite of minimal contact with Jews. For the *Nazis*, the racial bogeymen were the Jews—for the Japanese ruling elite the racial bogeymen were members of any race that was not Japanese. For the anti-Semites in Japan, the Jews were considered a super-distasteful race protected by the Anglo-Saxon nations. Japan's nationalist intellectual elite was anti-Jewish even before they had heard of Hitler. His arrival on the international stage simply speeded up the dissemination of anti-Semitism in Japan. Baron Hiranuma later noted that "Hitler saw [the Jewish danger] and tried to eliminate it and that is why the Anglo-Americans hate him."[32] There were some Japanese who were 'Jew' obsessed. Lieutenant-General Nobutaka Shioden became a prolific writer of anti-Jewish texts. Shioden picked his anti-Semitic views after spending four years in France as military *attaché* and picked up on French anti-Semite conspiracists who blamed the Jews for the *Great War*.

Shioden was not alone in the military. Colonel Yasue Norihiro translated *The Protocols of the Elders of Zion* [1901], an anti-Jewish forgery initially propagated by the Russian secret service, which went to seventeen editions; the Nation Study Group, a military-civilian organization devoted itself to the study of the 'Jewish question'; Japanese Army interpreter, Tsuyanosuke Higuchi, published a book called *The Jewish Peril* [1923] and senior home office official Daizburo Tsugita warned that the *Bolsheviks* might use American Jews as agents and was concerned that the Japanese might be "unable to tell them from [genuine] Americans."[33] Anti-Semitism also penetrated the ranks of Japanese industrialists. Baron Mitsui Hachiroemon, scion of the great house of Mitsui & Co., and supposedly Japan's richest man, was strongly influenced by his closest adviser Shiro Sasaki who was an anti-Semite and fervent admirer of Hitler.

However, anti-Semitism was a minor racial concern compared to racial issues in Asia. Mitsukawa was dismissive of the Chinese, treating them as an inferior race. He gave Darwinian justifications for his view that ". . . in accordance with the laws of nature, the Japanese nation was entitled to colonize the neighboring areas of Manchuria and Mongolia."[34] The right-wing intellectual and rabble-rouser, Ikki Kita, who used the expression '*jakuniku kyoshoku*' (the weak are meek; the strong eat),[35] also embraced Social Darwinism while Kanokogi believed that war was a means of purifying humanity of its detritus, expunging "all elements that are weak, corrupt or negative, consigning them to hell."[36] By 1936 the overwhelming intellectual sentiment in Japan was that by invading China, Japan would liberate it. For Mitsukawa, Chiang's refusal to *kowtow* to Japan was a renunciation or betrayal of Sun Yat-sen's belief that the two countries should join forces against the west. Kanokogi meanwhile believed that China had been infected by western liberalism, which had caused them to resist Japan, against their true Asian nature. Ikki Kita averred that Japanese influence in China was acceptable because it was authentically Asian. China could be improved. Thus he recommended, "Everything about Japan's political system, law, literature, and military thought must be translated into Chinese."[37]

Even cultured intellectuals such as the poet Yonejiro Noguchi believed that China could be improved by Japan's governance. Noguchi called for the liberation of Asia in a heroic way and fell out with close friend, Rabindranath Tagore, when the great Bengali poet condemned Japan's invasion of China in 1937. Noguchi would no doubt have approved of Friedrich Ratzel, the German geopolitician who exerted a powerful influence on the *Nazis*, with his work *Das Meer als Quell der Völkergrösse* [1900] (The Sea as the Source of National Greatness). Ratzel, who was the first to use the word *lebensraum* (living space), which was to become the *leitmotif* for *Nazi* expansionism, observed that Japan had the potential to be a great empire. Kanokogi became a cheerleader for Ratzel's work along with that of Karl Haushofer, another leading *Nazi* intellectual.

Mitsukawa gave the familiar criticism of western hypocrisy regarding Japanese expansionism. In 1928 Herbert Hoover's inaugural address had proclaimed, "We have no desire for territorial expansion, for economic or other domination of other peoples."[38] Yet it was apparent to Japanese observers that America retained a string of imperial possessions stretching across the *Pacific* and that its soldiers still occupied Nicaragua, *Haiti* and the Philippines. Hypocrisy was a justification that General Kanji Ishiwara gave at his trial at the International Military Tribunal [1946] in Tokyo,

> Haven't you ever heard of Perry? Don't you know anything about your country's history ... Tokugawa Japan believed in isolation ... so for its own defense it took your country as its teacher and set about learning how to be aggressive. You might say we became your disciples. Why don't you subpoena Perry from the other world and try him as a war criminal.[39]

In 1936 the eminent Japanese legal scholar Sakutaro Tachi had also claimed inspiration from America when he accused the US of hypocrisy for its criticisms of Japan for

"following the very spirit of the Monroe Doctrine pronounced by the United States itself
. . . It is against its own principle to blame Japan for acting on behalf of the principles of
'Asia for Asiatics' especially since Asia is all within Japan's rightful sphere of
influence."[40] Kiyoshi Miki, a philosopher who had studied under Martin Heidegger (the
great German philosopher who specialized in existential phenomenology) and became
head of the Showa Cultural Research Group, wrote that

> The only way for this [China] incident to achieve world
> historical significance is for Japan to stand up to the task
> of [creating the cooperative body] with the ideal of the
> progress of world history along those unifying principles
> . . . unifying the ideal of the East goes with the task of
> breaking out of the so-called Europeanist perspective of
> world history, which equates the history of white people
> to the history of the world . . . the modernization of China
> is the prerequisite to the formation of the East Asian
> Cooperative Body.[41]

The Monroe Doctrine was not the only American ideal concept drawn upon by
Japanese intellectuals. Economic and military success in the post-*Meiji Era* convinced
many that Japan too was blessed by 'exceptionalism.' The concept combined both power
and philosophy. Kanokogi looked back to the ancients in suggesting, "Plato advocated
the noble ideal of rule by philosophy, saying that 'unless political power and philosophy
are combined to form one monolithic whole, the ideal of the state will not be realized'."[42]
Plato's ideal state was, according to Shumei Okawa, embodied in Japan. Another
Platonist, Shinkichi Uesugi argued that "the Japanese Empire possesses qualities that
make it possible to realize [Plato's] ideal state more easily than in any other country."[43]

Indeed there was a messianic quality to some of the pleadings of the intellectuals.
Japan had a duty to Asia to bring the ideals embodied in the Japanese state to the rest of
Asia. Mitsukawa hailed the annexation of Manchuria as a step along the path of regional
unification and was an "end to tyranny of the old Mukden military clique over thirty
million people."[44] As Japanese success increased so did the grandiosity of Mitsukawa's
vision as when he asserted that "The Japanese, the Sun race, must now engage in the
great task of world unification."[45] In 1936, Mitsukawa died at the prematurely young
age of forty-eight when he took a cold bath as part of a *Shinto* ritual. Ikki Kita, at fifty-
four years of age, also died young. With little or no evidence, Kita was charged with
masterminding the 26th February Incident and was duly arrested and executed as leader
of the Imperial Way Faction (*Kodoha*).

Pan-Asianism was not confined to the intellectual classes. In the late nineteenth
century, Prince Atsumaro Konoe, Fumimaro Konoe's father, had written an article
entitled *Let Nations of the Same Race Unite and Discuss Chinese Questions.*[46] In 1898
he urged, "Chinese and Japanese would need to stand together against the arch-enemy
of the white race."[47] He told a Chinese friend that Japan needed to operate an "Asiatic

Monroe Doctrine in the East" because "Asia is for the Asians."[48] As with Konoe, Pan-Asianism was not necessarily laced with aggressive racism. In imitation of a more moderate British paternalism, the internationalist, Inazo Nitobe, author of *Way of the Samurai* [1899], who worked for the League of Nations in the department that was a forerunner of UNESCO, argued with regard to the Koreans, "I like them. I think they are a capable people, who can be trained to a large measure of self-government, for which the present is a period of tutelage."[49]

No sooner had Manchuria been annexed than leaders were encouraged to expand their political and economic influence to the south. In March 1933, Kanokogi was one of the principal movers behind the setting up of *Dai Ajia Kyokai* (Greater Asian Association). Notable recruits included Koki Hirota and Prince Fumimaro Konoe, both future prime ministers, as well as senior military figures including General Araki Sadeo. The stated aim of *Dai Ajia Kyokai* was "to promote the harmony and fusion of the [Japanese] Empire and Asian countries, and the introduction and propagation of [Japan's] imperial culture in those countries."[50]

The apparent success of Japan's colonization of Korea and Taiwan had made the Japanese people quite open to the concept of territorial expansion. Their rapid acceptance of the concept of Manchukuo revealed a deep-seated belief in Pan-Asianism. Japanese people soon came to regard Manchukuo as an inalienable part of the Japanese Empire in a similar way that the British had come to see India as a part of the British Empire in the nineteenth century. As with the British in India, Japan believed that its empire brought a benefit to the world—not just to Japan. General Nobuyoshi Muto, Commander of *Kwantung* Army, affirmed that the building of Manchukuo "is a great work destined to contribute spiritually to world culture . . . I believe that not only could the co-prosperity of Japan and Manchukuo be realized, but also the pure development of world culture to be possible."[51] The broad acceptance of Manchukuo was soon shown in the rapid growth of the Japanese population of its cities. In the ten years to 1941 the Japanese population of Fengtian grew from 45,567 to 163,591, in Harbin from 4,151 to 53,295 and in Xinjing from 17,464 to 128,582.

Japan's intellectual leaders further fueled the fires of conspiracy theory that became apparent in their leaders' views of the west. Japan's perception of 'existential threat,' was fanned by Kanokogi who accused the Comintern of "mobilizing all liberal and capitalist forces, as well as those in between, into an antifascist camp . . . has formed an alliance with capitalist states such as Britain, the United States and France."[52] As early as 1917 Kanokogi was raising the alarm that "it is as clear as day that if Japan fails to build an empire on the Asian continent, [as a nation] we are all doomed to destruction."[53] The perceived threats were not just external. Kanokogi accused Japanese enemies of co-opting "senior advisers to the throne, bureaucrats, party politicians, entrepreneurs and financiers, journalists and academics."[54] Academics in Kanokogi's sights included Tatsukichi Minobe, Professor Emeritus at Tokyo Imperial University, whose conventional view of the Emperor as an organ of a democratic, constitution structure, was viewed as heresy by ultra-nationalist intellectuals. Attacking Minobe was a means of attacking the Emperor's moderate advisers such as Prince Saionji Kinmochi. According to Grand Chamberlain Suzuki, Hirohito had spoken to him about his constitutional role, and supported the sovereignty of the state over that of the ruler. Suzuki reported Hirohito's observation that "Many people are criticizing Minobe these days, but there is nothing disloyal about him . . . it is sad, indeed, that such a fine scholar should be treated in this manner."[55]

As Professor Christopher Szpilman has observed, Pan-Asianism "was an abstraction derived from poring over the political map of the world in salons and libraries, not from direct experience."[56] It nevertheless underlay the foreign-policy thinking of a generation of Japanese civil and military leaders. Thus Prime Minister Konoe's 3 November 1938 radio broadcast on the need for a New East Asia Order decried that "What the Empire craves is the construction of a new order to secure the perpetual stability of East Asia . . ."[57] Japan's leaders, whether politicians, generals, businessmen or intellectuals, may have harbored high-minded justifications for their support of Pan-Asianism but at a lower level these ideas carried little weight. Japanese racism predominated. *Kwantung* Army officer, Colonel (later General) Tanaka Ryukichi, interviewed by Shigeharu Matsumoto, a journalist and liberal internationalist, admitted, "To be perfectly frank, the ways you and I look at the Chinese are fundamentally different. You seem to think of them as human, but I see them as pigs."[58] In practice, intellectuals may have seen the conquest of China as the bringing of a cultural and ideological nirvana, but to the soldiers on the ground it was merely conquest and subjugation of an inferior enemy and a people that they viewed as sub-human.

Thought Control and Censorship: From various influences, Japan, like *Nazi* Germany, developed its own 'master race' philosophy. In part it was an organic development based on the development of *Shinto* that promoted the fusion of god and country into a racially exclusive creed not dissimilar to Hitler's Aryan teachings. However, in actively promoting the Emperor as a 'Godhead' in the aftermath of the *Meiji Restoration* as a means of justifying the overthrow of the Shogunate, the authors of the revolution inadvertently promoted Japan's racial superiority and laid the groundwork for ultra-nationalism to take root. As a result of the scares provided by the collapse of the world's monarchies in Europe and Asia at the beginning of the twentieth century as well as the rise of communism, the Japanese government in the 1930s expertly promoted Japan's unique *Shinto* faith, thus pouring oil on a groundswell of ultra-nationalism. The defeats of China and Russia as well as the conquest of Manchuria, which raised Japan to global prominence, brought with it a hubristic belief in Japan's 'manifest destiny'—a belief that it shared in common with the United States. However, there was one important difference. America may have baulked at Asian immigration at the beginning of the twentieth century but its belief in its national 'exceptionalism' was nevertheless based on the absorption of peoples of every nation, while Japan's 'exceptionalism,' more unconsciously than explicitly was entirely based on their own race.

Inazu Nitobe, Professor of Law at Kyoto Imperial University, author of the classic samurai book, *Bushido: The Soul of Japan* [1900], wrote that he expected that, compared to *Formosa*, the Japanization process "will be found easier in Korea, for the reason that the Korean race is very much allied to our own."[59] Nitobe, like most intellectuals of his generation, believed in Japanese superiority and distinctiveness. Nitobe, married to an American and particularly sensitive to western racism with regard to Japan, was fixed in his view of Japan's superiority to the rest of Asia. In the 1930s the debate about Japan's *kokutai* (national polity), embodying ideas of racial and religious identity, language, national identity and the sovereign Imperial system, grew in importance with the chorus of intellectual support expressed in the press as well as universities.

Prince Konoe, in his first prime ministership, called together a group of Japan's leading professors from the fields of history and philosophy to discuss the matter and formulate a construct of *kokutai* that could be adopted by the state. It was in part a reaction to the aforementioned persecution of Professor Tatsukichi Minobe, a constitutional expert who described the Emperor as an 'organ' (i.e. component) of the constitutional government. The outcome of the committee's deliberations was a 156-page pamphlet published by the Japanese Ministry of Education known as the *Kokutai no Hongi* (Cardinal Principles of the National Body Politic) that stressed the Emperor's position as being the embodiment of the nation but above the constitution.

In March 1937, Konoe's government issued the *Kokutai no Hongi*. Millions of copies were circulated to schools and institutions throughout the Japanese Empire, which required them to teach Japan's new religious-ideological text. One of the core teachings, not exactly new to Japan, was that the Japanese nation came before the individual whose importance was subsumed by the state and was not a separate entity. The bedrock of the document was support for Imperial Rule and its centrality to Japanese identity. *Kotukai no Hongi* covered almost every aspect of Japan's civic and public life including domestic policy, international affairs, culture and civilization.

Japanese expansionism was also supported in the catchphrase *hakko ichiu* (the world under one roof), that Prince Konoe popularized after he used it in a speech on 8 January 1940. *Hakko ichiu* (the eight corners of the world under one roof) was a phrase aimed at capturing the spirit of racial harmony and equality within a Japanese Empire—it was an ironic concept given the level of barbarity meted out to conquered Asian nations, whose peoples became little more than production ciphers for raw materials needed by the Japanese war economy. The development of the idea of *kokutai* turned the conflict with the west into a form of holy war. Thus the Imperial Rescript regarding the *Tripartite Pact* [September 1940] with Hitler and Mussolini averred,

> The teaching of the eight corners of the world under the roof [*hakko ichiu*] is the teaching of our imperial ancestors ... We sincerely hope to bring about a cessation of hostilities and a restoration of peace, and have therefore ordered the government to ally with Germany and Italy, nations that share the same intention as ourselves.[60]

Historian Daikichi Irokawa, who grew up in this environment offered the following reflections:

> The ideology of national polity enveloped the entire Japanese nation. It had an incredible presence. It is difficult to imagine the oppressive atmosphere that the people suffered under the canopy of national polity and the immutable emperor system. There was complete social consensus that those who violated these ideologies should be eliminated or that they inevitably would be eliminated.[61]

The Japanese government's determination to squash ideologies hostile to traditional Japanese values was evident long before the militarists' capture of the constitution. On 15 March 1928, there was a mass round up of 1,568 communist suspects; a second wave of arrests a month later secured the Communist Party's General Secretary, which effectively destroyed the party. According to post-war Communist Party mythology, cells moved underground from where they distributed propaganda vehemently attacking Japanese aggression in the *Second Sino-Japanese War*; in reality most of the pre-war communists simply joined the rising wave of Japanese nationalism.

Communist suspects, perhaps as few as 1,000, were arrested and interrogated. Women tended to be particularly badly affected by the government's crackdown on leftists. Setsu Tanno, the head of the Japanese Communist's women's section was arrested and imprisoned for several years. On release, Tanno found that her sister's husband, because of the societal shame, had divorced her. Many women committed suicide. Tanno recalled, "There was a man called Akira Asano, a communist and a writer. When he recanted in prison his wife, Chiyoko Ito, was unable to endure the pain. She lost her mind and was sent to Matsuzawa Hospital. She died there."[62] However, it should be noted that not a single Japanese communist was executed for his or her beliefs and no more than one or two died during interrogation. Japan's internal policing should not be compared with that of the *Nazis*; albeit extensively deployed, Japan's security forces in the 1930s were far less brutal.

With the onset of the *Second Sino-Japanese War*, the Japanese government, now completely dominated by the military, increasingly used the draconian powers of the *Public Security Preservation Law* [1925]. The Home Ministry created a 'special police,' known as *Tokko* (*Tokubetsu Koto Keisatsu*: abbreviated to *Tokko*). It had similarities to Britain's Special Branch, whose units were responsible for national security, or the Federal Bureau of Investigation in the United States. The *Tokko* expanded rapidly after the start of the *Second Sino-Japanese War* and undoubtedly became brutal in its operations as national security became more threatened. Branches of *Tokko* were set up throughout Japan to monitor undesirables such as socialists, communists, anarchists, trade unionists, and foreign nationals, particularly Koreans and Chinese. Interrogation and sometimes torture was standard. Informants were encouraged. A similar section was set up by the Ministry of Education to monitor students, high school teachers and university lecturers and professors. To bring prosecutions the Ministry of Justice trained up *shiso kenji* (thought prosecutors). Punishment usually meant confinement in re-education centers. The Japanese government's hostility to communism among the military elite was ironic given the deep-seated hostility to financiers, industrialists and capitalism itself. In 1941 the *Tokko* discovered that the Cabinet Planning Board (*Kikakuin*), set up to coordinate civilian and military policy in 1937, was not only antipathetic to Anglo-American style capitalism, but its members used texts such as Lenin's *The Development of Capitalism in Russia* [1899] and Rosa Luxemburg's *The Accumulation of Capital* [1913]. The *Tokko* concluded that *Kikakuin* had adopted 'left-wing progressiveness' which 'meshed' with the Japanese Communist Party. In spite of the development of *Tokko* and the *Shiso Kenji*, their methods, in terms of brutality, were by no means comparable with the *Gestapo* in *Nazi* Germany.

However, within the military, a secret police force, the *Kempeitai*, was developed not only to maintain political indoctrination within the Army but also within the broader population. As such it was less an internal organization and more closely resembled the *Gestapo* in *Nazi* Germany. The Navy also operated a similar, though much smaller, *Tokkeitai*. Between 1933 and 1936, the *Japan Times* reported that Japan's various internal security forces arrested 59,013 people charged with 'dangerous thoughts.' Only 5,000 went to trial and fewer than half were imprisoned. It was a reflection of the fact that Japan was a far more homogenous society than western nations and never did breed much political or social dissent. Nevertheless, the deterrence of what was increasingly a police state, was effective in limiting whatever dissent did exist with regard to Japan's domestic and political international direction.

The government controlled radio station, *Nihon Hoso Kyokai* (NHK), modeled on the BBC, which broadcast to five million radio sets, reinforced ideological indoctrination. People would gather round to listen. During what Irokawa described as a "brief period of sunlight—when people were enthralled with jazz, musical reviews, baseball, sumo, bars, dancehall and so on . . . [before] the pivotal 'February 26th' coup attempt took place."[63] People knew little about the incident other than that some soldiers had attacked some politicians . . . again. Japanese were more interested in the *sumo* champion, Sadaji Futabayama, who was set on his record-breaking run of sixty-nine victories—still a record. From mid-May, Sada Abe's murder of her lover by sexual asphyxiation, with its lurid details of her keeping his severed penis in her handbag, kept the Japanese media fully occupied.

Censorship played a significant role in keeping the media 'on message.' Fumio Kamei's documentary *Tatakau Heitai* [1939] (Fighting Soldiers), showing the tedium, as well as the physical and emotional drain of the war in China, was banned. Moviemakers were encouraged to portray the Japanese soldier as ideologically pure, dutiful heroes—a sharp contrast to Hollywood's macho types or the stereotypical samurai swordsman. The Japanese movies produced were not without skill. A group of Hollywood directors reviewed twenty Japanese movies made between 1937 and 1941 and unanimously agreed that they were much superior to American and European movies. Frank Capra, after viewing *Chocolate and Soldiers* [1938] acknowledged, "We can't beat this kind of thing. We make a film like that maybe once in a decade. We haven't got the actors."[64] Japanese films not only portrayed the enemies' ships and planes as an existential threat to the nation but also played on the psychological and cultural threats to Japan's *kokutai*. Anglo-American values were shown as corrupting and polluting. A popular slogan screamed, "*To Hell with Babe Ruth*."[65] Baseball, that had become a favorite Japanese sport, was suddenly decried as decadent. Audiences cheered when they were shown a newsreel of a judo master defeating an American boxer. Hollywood movies ceased to be shown. The playing of jazz in public was discouraged. Dance halls were visited by officials who censored the music. In October 1940 all dance halls were ordered shut. A women's National Spiritual Mobilization campaign, somewhat akin to Mao's later Cultural Revolution, shunned jewelry and cosmetics as well as western clothing. Government inspired slogans included "*100 million people, one mind*", "*Beware of spies*" and "*We'll never cease fire till our enemies cease to be.*"[66]

Japan's fascist ideology of the 1930s has often been considered a copycat of European ideas. In reality Japan's move toward fascism had its roots in ultra-nationalism based on Japanese cultural 'exceptionalism' and the Imperial system. For those few European right-wing nationalists who looked east, Japan's unique philosophies were much admired. Political journalist, Enrico Corradino, a follower of Gabriele D'Annunzio, who was a founding member of the Italian Nationalist Association and the weekly *L'Idea Nazionale*, wrote that by worshiping nature, heroes and the Emperor, the Japanese had developed an ideology of self-adulation: "Japan is the God of Japan," he wrote, "The strength of this people draws from religion is a strength drawn from its own bowels; its heroes are great men from the past, nature and the fatherland. It becomes self-adoration."[67] The success of Japan's ideological constructions was much lauded by *Nazi* propagandist Prince Albrecht Furst Von Urach who thought that Emperor worship was "the most unique fusion in the world of state form, state consciousness, and religious fanaticism."[68]

It is interesting to note that when in 1984 Prime Minister Yasuhiro Nakasone and German Chancellor Helmut Kohl agreed to restore the old Japanese Embassy in Berlin as a Japanese-German scholarly center, Japanese academics, not in the least bit ashamed of Japan's part in *World War II*, "proposed a seminar examining the parallels between *Shintoist* emperor worship and the myths of the German *Volk*."[69] It was an offer that Helmut Kohl's bureaucrats "politely declined."[70]

15 May Incident [1932]: The gunning down of former Finance Minister and head of the *Rikken Minseito*, Junnosuke Inoue, by a student member of *Ketsumeidan* (the League of Blood) on 7 February set off a wave of political assassinations. Next, Baron Takuma Dan, a graduate of MIT (Massachusetts Institute of Technology) and a leading lobbyist for closer relations with the western powers, was shot dead outside the offices of Mitsui Bank. The murder caused a severe loss of face for the Emperor coinciding as it did with the arrival of the Earl of Lytton, Chairman of the League of Nations committee that was investigating the Mukden Incident. Baron Dan had just held a dinner for the eminent international visitors. Members of the Blood Brotherhood were rounded up in a *Tokko* crackdown.

However, on 15 May 1932, eleven naval officers, all in their early twenties and four of them belonging to another nationalist anti-capitalist group, The Love of Native Village Academy, organized themselves into four 'hit' squads. One of them went to the *Shinto* shrine at Yasakuni and, after taking their vows, jumped into a taxi to the residence of Prime Minister Tsuyoshi Inukai. They walked into his house whereupon he calmly asked them to observe custom by removing their shoes. It did not save him. A young naval officer lost his temper and shot him in the face. The residence of the Lord Keeper of the Privy Seal was also attacked and hand grenades were thrown at the Mitsubishi Bank building. The most notable survivor was Charlie Chaplin, the Hollywood comic star. It had been planned to kill the famous visitor in the hope that his murder would precipitate war with America, whose *Washington Naval Treaty* had begun the 'humiliation' of Japan. Chaplin, a guest of the Prime Minister, was fortunate to be out with Inukai's son watching *sumo* wrestling at the Tokyo *Natsu Basho* (summer wrestling tournament).

Prime Minister Tsuyoshi Inukai was an unlikely target for an ultra-nationalist assassination. As head of the *Rikken Seiyukai* he had been vigorous in his condemnation of the *London Naval Treaty*, which limited Japan's shipbuilding program. When the *Kwantung* Army invaded Manchuria in 1931, he supported the annexation and criticized the League of Nations for their condemnation. When Inukai was appointed to form a minority government to replace the *Rikken Minseito* on 13 December 1931, he immediately reversed Prime Minister Hamaguchi's disastrous economic policies by taking the Yen off the Gold Standard and allowing the currency to depreciate. In foreign affairs Inukai acceded to the request from his ultra-nationalist Army Minister, Sadeo Araki, for further troops to be sent to Manchuria. Inukai policies were popularly received and in February 1932, his *Seiyukai* won a landslide election winning 301 seats to *Minseito's* 146 seats. Just over a week later the state of Manchukuo was formally announced.

It was a measure of the extent of ultra-nationalist sentiment that Prime Minister Inukai was too moderate. To a large extent Inukai's policies were irrelevant. He was an elected leader. That was enough to make him a target. The ultra-nationalists in the military demanded an end to parliamentary government to be replaced by a Showa Restoration—in other words that power should be returned to Emperor Hirohito. The wave of assassinations may well have been prompted by an attempt on the life of Emperor Hirohito by a Korean independence activist, Lee Bong-chang, who threw a grenade at the Emperor's carriage as it was leaving the Sakuradamon Gate on 9 January 1932. In the aftermath of the 15 May Incident, the perpetrators were popularly celebrated. Conspiracy theorists would later suggest that the gunmen had been put up to the murder by shadowy senior Army officers and even officials within Hirohito's court.

At their court martial, during which judges and prosecutors allowed the accused to have virtually unlimited time for incendiary nationalistic speeches, 350,000 people signed a petition in blood, which was presented to the court requesting lenient sentences. Short jail sentences followed. All but six of the fifty-four guilty men were released within three years and the remainder by 1940. The light sentences served to undermine both the rule of law and parliamentary democracy.

Japanese Political Parties: Minseito and Seiyukai Undermined [1932–1936]: In the 1930s pressure from the ultra-militarists, public anger at the economic depression and the rise of powerful elites in business and banking were putting considerable pressure on the pluralistic structure of the Meiji Constitution. It should be noted that Japan's electoral franchise was little more than window dressing in a constitution that was only nominally democratic. Japan's political structures were dominated by elite power groups. By 1932, Japan's parliamentary parties already had a 'thin' license to govern. The Emperor had the right to nominate a Prime Minister, whose name the Emperor, by tradition, took on advisement from the *genro* (elder statesman), whatever the result of parliamentary elections. More importantly the Army and Navy, in essence, had veto rights over the formation of any government. It was required that the cabinet posts of Army Minister and Navy Minister had to be held by a serving or former general officer. In theory by withholding their appointees the Army and Navy could hold the Prime Minister and the formation of a cabinet to ransom.

Over and above these constitutional niceties, the Emperor was, by definition of the *Meiji Constitution* [1889], an absolute monarch and Commander in Chief—a point often made by Emperor Hirohito in his wearing of military uniform. In one important respect, however, one powerful group that made up the 'royal' component of the constitution was in sharp decline. Although the institution of *genro*, a group of retired elder statesmen who acted as advisers to the Emperor, was extra-constitutional, it nevertheless played a central constitutional role in the Meiji and Taisho periods. The *genro* not only acted as wise counsellors to the Emperor; by dint of their seniority, reputation, and military background as well as Japan's cultural tradition of deference to elders, they could control the 'active military'. They could restrain ultranationalism behind the scenes. However, by the time that Hirohito assumed the Chrysanthemum Throne in 1926 only one *genro*, Kinmochi Saionji, remained. Prince Ito Hirobumi was assassinated in 1909. General Taro Katsura died in 1913; Marquis Kaoru Inoue in 1915; Field Marshal Prince Iwao Oyama in 1916; Field Marshal Prince Aritomo Yamagata in 1922; and Prince Masayoshi Matsukata in 1924.

Saionji, born to a noble Kyoto family, had been a playmate of the young Emperor Meiji, and despite his tender age of just seventeen, played a role in persuading the nobility to join in the fight to overthrow the Tokugawa Shogunate. After the *Meiji Restoration*, Saionji travelled to San Francisco and crossed America to Washington where he met President Ulysses Grant. Arriving in Paris in 1871 he stumbled into a street battle during the Commune and, after his tutor was shot, retired to Marseilles to learn French. He later studied law at the Sorbonne before returning to Japan with a considerably more liberal outlook on politics than when he had left. Saionji, who served several terms as prime minister before the war, was an internationalist who supported the new world order prescribed by the Washington Conference [1919–1922]. However, Saionji, who, by the standards of the period, was a liberal adherent of the Meiji Constitution, was alone not powerful enough to prevent the ebb of political power moving toward the military. By 1932, Saionji was eighty-three years of age and was in physical decline and mentally fragile. In effect the *genro* system, which provided a political glue to bind the pluralistic components of the Meiji Constitution, was all but gone.

About the same time that Saionji was left as the sole remaining *genro*, the power of the Privy Council also diminished. Up until 1924, the Privy Council ranked only behind the *genro* and the current prime minister. Thereafter Saionji lent his weight to the reform of the Privy Council proposed by the Kato cabinet in 1925 and told them "to get to work on the Privy Council."[71] On Saionji's advice, over the next two years academics were appointed to the Privy Council: four former or current law professors from *Todai*, the law faculty of Tokyo Imperial University. This was not entirely new. The Privy Council, in the 1920s, had been dominated by two reactionary legal experts Baron Kiichiro Hiranuma, a former Minister of Justice and staunch opponent of the *London Naval Treaty*, and Count Miyoji Ito (who had helped draft the constitution). Saionji's motives may have been to remove the power of political factions within the Privy Council, in contrast to Yamagata who had tried to pack it with his own faction members, or more likely to introduce a more liberal bias to their pronouncements. In the short term the reduction of the power of the Privy Council may have increased the power of the Diet but in the long term it also reduced a body that could have had a moderating effect on the increasing militarization of the government after 1932.

Another new feature of the politics of the post-war period was the decline in importance of the domain rivalries, which had been an important part of politics in the fifty years after the *Meiji Restoration*. The *Choshu* and *Satsuma* domains that had been largely responsible for the overthrow of the Tokugawa Shogunate, retained an oligarchic power as *genro*. The *Choshu* largely claimed control of the Army while the *Satsuma* traditionally controlled the Navy. As Taichiro Mitani, a *Todai* historian, has observed, "The Oligarchic clique could make the constitution work because its factional ties cut across the bureaucracy, the House of Peers, the Privy Council, the Army, and the Court."[72] By the 1920s the domain oligarchs, effectively the *genro*, had largely died out. It was another feature of the informal constitution, as opposed to the formal Meiji Constitution, that had simply vanished.

Following Inukai's assassination on 15 May 1932, it might have been expected that the prime ministerial post would have fallen to *Seiyukai*'s leadership successor, Kisaburo Suzuki. However, under the guise of a national emergency, Saionji counseled Hirohito to appoint Admiral Viscount Makoto Saito as head of a unity government. (Saito had had a long political career, though somewhat tarnished when he was forced to resign as

Navy Minister in 1914 as a result of the 'kickback' scandal involving Siemens AG and naval procurement.) It seems evident that Saionji's personal dislike of Kisaburo Suzuki and his reactionary militaristic politics played a decisive role in the appointment of Saito. Over the next few years the precedent set by Saionji would have a catastrophic effect on the political parties, which were not given the opportunity to form governments until after the war. In their weakened states, both main parties, *Seiyukai* and *Minseito*, for the time being, agreed to back the Saito administration. It was a time when support for the annexation of Manchuria was at its peak. Popular anger over the League of Nations' criticism of Japan for its aggression was also rampant. For the main parties, particularly Minseito, which had acquiesced in the Washington System, it was not a good moment for them to raise indignant protest.

Effectively sidelined, the political parties lost out to the bureaucracy, which became more and more important in the implementation of Prime Minister Saito's interventionist and stimulatory economic program—notably through the implementation of finance minister, Viscount Korekiyo Takahashi's *Plan for the Economic Resuscitation of Agrarian and Fishing Villages*. Increasingly the Home Ministry's disbursement of monies completely bypassed the political parties' control of local funds. The power of the bureaucracy was further enhanced by the Commission on the Guarantee of Officials' Status [1932], which gave the bureaucracy rights independent of political interference. A similar imperial ordnance in 1933, relating to the police force, introduced reforms that sharply reduced the power of political parties within the Home Ministry and police force.

The increased power of the bureaucracy helped the military, particularly the Army's Control Faction (*Toseiha*), which wanted to mobilize the economy to prepare for total war. It was, the lesson they had taken from their analysis of *World War I*. As Colonel Tetsuzan Nagata (later a general and leading member of *Toseiha*) remarked in 1927, "National mobilization (*kokka Sodoin*) is the task of marshalling the entire society of the state in times of need, then organize, unify and utilize all available resources, material and human, producing a maximum national strength as military power."[73]

In July 1934 the Saito government fell as a result of an alleged bribery scandal implicating the Ministry of Finance in a price support scheme for investors in Teikoku Rayon Co. (the Teijin Incident). It was another event deleterious to the cause of democracy. The Teijin Incident was followed by an 'electoral purification' movement led by home office minister, Fumio Goto, from 1934 to 1936. Again the political parties, *Seiyukai* and *Minseito*, were frozen out of the succession for prime minister. Admiral Keisuke Okada was chosen to form the next cabinet. Inadvertently Okada, a moderate, who voiced concerns about the increasing strength of the ultra-nationalists, created the Cabinet Research Institute [1935], which furthered the power of the military and the bureaucracy. As historian Gordon Berger has argued, this new agency, "brought together skilled bureaucrats, furnishing another new channel for military participation in civilian administration . . .".[74]

The Control Faction was rivaled for influence within the armed forces by the Imperial Way Faction (*Kodoha*), which, while it agreed with the need for increasing military strength, wanted a faster mobilization to confront the threat of the Soviet Union to Manchuria's northern borders. Ultimately however, it should be noted that the ideological differences between the Imperial Way Faction and the Control Faction were trifling and though they were played up, the conflict between the two factions was more about power than ideas. In hindsight it is difficult to discern significant ideological differences between the ultra-nationalistic rants of either side.

Nevertheless, the passion with which ultra-nationalist views were held by Army officers in this period is indicated by the murder of Major-General Tetsuzan Nagata, a leading Control Faction member, and Chief of the Mobilization Section of the Economic Mobilization Bureau of the Ministry of War. Lieutenant-Colonel Saburo Aizawa, who, like many of the Imperial Way Faction members, believed that the Control Faction was in the hands of the *Zaibatsu* (large business conglomerates) walked into Nagata's office and ran him through with a samurai sword.

Aizawa gave himself up, and, after a long drawn much fêted public trial, was found guilty and was executed by firing squad. In part the attack can also be explained by the frustration of the Imperial Way Faction, whose leaders were increasingly excluded from positions of power. Anger at the removal of *Kodoha* leader, General Sadao Araki, from his position as Minister of War in January 1934 was compounded by the removal of Jinzaburo Masaki as Inspector General of Military Education in 1935. His sacking probably triggered Aizawa's murderous attack. Masaki was removed by General Senjuro Hayashi and Field Marshal Prince Kotohito Kanin without reference to the convention that Masaki, as one of the 'big three' Generals had to agree. "Masaki was not even allowed an imperial audience to appeal against his removal."[75] The vehemence of his treatment is probably explained by disclosure of his intrigues and those of his confederate Araki. Masaki was considered a potentially dangerous figure who was bitterly disliked for surrounding himself with yes-men and for ousting those with talent who refused to be a member of his sycophantic clique.

Prince Kanin in 1919, had become the youngest Field Marshal in Japanese history by dint of his royal blood, not because of any military brilliance. As a military leader he was largely a figurehead but was important in the political intrigue within the Army because of his role as Chief of Staff of the Army from 1931 to 1940 and his position as great-uncle to both Emperor Hirohito and his wife. As a member of one of the four branches of the Imperial family eligible to succeed to the throne if the main line became extinct, Hirohito's great-grandfather Emperor Komei had adopted Prince Kanin as a potential heir. Originally intended by his family to be a Buddhist monk, Prince Kanin spent four years being trained as a *monzeki* (a Buddhist priest of aristocratic lineage) at Sanbo-in Temple, a sub-temple of the famed ninth-century Heian period Diago-ji Temple in Kyoto. Having been switched by his family to a military career, he graduated from the Imperial Japanese Military Academy in 1881, the Staff College in 1904 and served in both the *First Sino-Japanese War* [1894–5] and the *Russo-Japanese War* [1905]. His death was in sharp contrast to the grandeur of his elevated position in life. He died from infected haemorrhoids on 21 May 1945. The Chinese and Mongolian victims of Prince Kanin's authorization of the use of poison gas in the *Second Sino-Japanese War* would no doubt have rejoiced.

While vendettas were being played out between the factions, liberal voices were being silenced. The most renowned of these was Professor Taksukichi Minobe who was best known for his legal judgment that the Emperor was an 'organ' of the constitution—in other words presenting the Emperor as a constitutional monarch. Hirohito apparently supported Minobe's interpretation and commented to his military aide: "Is it not a great contradiction that the military should proceed to attack the organ theory in opposition to my views."[76] Interpretations of the Japanese constitution had differed since its inception but by the 1930s there had been a major shift in the national consensus.

The Minobe affair, which dominated headlines in 1935, indicates the degree to which opinion of the governing elite and the general public had shifted. In 1912 Professor Taksukichi Minobe posited the theory that the Japanese Emperor was an 'organ' of the constitution, not separate and above the constitution. The 'organ' theory may have been at the liberal end of the legal interpretation of the Meiji Constitution but was not considered heretical until the 1930s. Minobe had by then become a recognized member of Japan's intellectual, academic and political elite. Having served as a Professor of Law at Tokyo Imperial University, he went on to become the Dean of their Law Faculty from 1923 to 1927. In this period, historian Peter Duus concludes, "Minobe's constitutional theory thus had become authoritative doctrine."[77] Thereafter he became a counsellor in the Bureau of Legislation before, like many prominent academics, being appointed to the upper house of the *Kokkai* (Diet), *Kizoku-in* (the House of Peers) in 1932.

The period from 1918 to 1932 came to be seen as a brief 'golden age' of rule by the elected political parties. It was a measure of how far toward the ultra-nationalist camp that Japan's ruling elite had swung that in 1935, after a public campaign supported within the Diet, Prime Minister Okada was forced to ask Minobe to resign and proceeded to ban some of his works. Okada went on to finance a campaign to discredit Minobe and promote the position of the Emperor as being above the constitution—in other words, a publicly funded campaign to support the ultra-nationalist position.

The 26 February Incident [1936] and the Purge of the Imperial Way Faction: [Map: 2.2] On 26 February an attempted *coup d'état* by a group of young officers, which was loosely affiliated with and supported by the *Kodoha* (Imperial Way) faction, decisively changed the complexion of Japanese politics.

The rebels comprised about 100 young officers who had graduated from the Army Academy, but not the elite Army War College, from which all Imperial Japanese Army staff officers and ultimately the most senior commanders were drawn. Most of them were from the Imperial Guards Division and the 1st Division, supposedly hotbeds of political activism. The timing of their coup may have been linked to the fact that both units were about to be transferred to active service in Manchuria. In spite of this they had substantial support within the senior ranks of the Army and in particular the *Kwantung* Army stationed in Manchuria. Seven of their leaders, loosely linked to Ikki

Kita, persuaded eighteen officers to join them. The rebel forces would consist of the 1st Division, 1st and 3rd Regiments, with 1,393 troops, and 138 troops from the 3rd Imperial Guard Regiment.

Leaving their barracks at 4.00 a.m. on a cold, snowy night, they carried a flag of the rising sun inscribed with the legend, "*Revere the Emperor, Destroy the traitors.*" An hour later the rebels, comprising nine groups and 1,200 soldiers in total, launched simultaneous attacks on the four of the Emperor's senior advisers whom they intended to assassinate, as well as takeovers of the War Ministry, Tokyo Police Headquarters and the supposedly liberal *Asahi Shimbun* newspaper. An attempt was also made to take control of the Imperial Palace but their attack was beaten back. Their aim was to kill the men closest to the Emperor whom they believed were leading him away from the true *kokutai* of the nation. Their main target, Prime Minister General Keisuke Okada, upon hearing a gun battle outside his residence, was saved by his brother-in-law, Colonel Denzo Matsuo, who pushed him into a closet. The rebels mistook the unfortunate Colonel Matsuo for Okada and gunned him down.

Prince Saionji Kinmochi, the last remaining *genro*, who got a 'tip-off' and Nobuaki Makino, the former Lord Keeper of the Privy Seal, survived. The latter was on vacation in Yugawara near Atami and was saved by his twenty-year-old grand-daughter Kazuko who led him up the hill adjacent to his house. Admiral Kantaro Suzuki, the Grand Chamberlain, was even luckier. He had previously supported the *London Naval Treaty* and was much despised by the *Kodoha* rebels. Suzuki took several bullets and was left for dead. Another target was Admiral Viscount Makoto Saito, who, in the twilight of his career, had formed the 'unity government' that followed the assassination of Prime Minister Inukai in 1932. He was less fortunate than his colleagues.

The former prime minister and then Lord Keeper of the Privy Seal was shot, riddled with forty-seven bullets, at his home in Yotsuya after returning home from watching a movie (*Naughty Marietta* [1935] starring Jeannette MacDonald and Nelson Eddy) at the home of the American Ambassador, Joseph Grew: it was the first and last time Admiral Saito watched a 'talking movie.' Finance Minister Viscount Korekyio Takahashi, whose expansionary fiscal policy and abandonment of the Gold Standard had brought Japan out of the Great Depression, was shot and thrust through with a samurai sword while in his bed. Meanwhile General Jottaro Watanabe was cut down by a machine gun in front of his wife and daughter.

The attacks on the Keepers of the Privy Seal reflected a subtle recent shift in power and were a more significant blow to the 'liberal' cause than is often understood. With the dying out of the *genro*, the position of Lord Keeper of the Privy Seal had begun to take its place in the closest counsels of the Emperor. As the British Ambassador, Sir Robert Clive, noted in a report to London when Saito was appointed Lord Keeper of the Privy Seal in November 1935, "With the gradual depletion in the ranks of the *genro*, or elder statesmen, the political significance of the office of Lord Keeper of the Privy Seal has been greatly enhanced during recent times . . ."[78] Admiral Saito, a man who had been at the center of the process of building Japan into a great naval power, had spent years in

America and England and was very much an anglophile. During the *Russo-Japanese War*, as Chief of the Naval Affairs Bureau and the Navy Technical Department, Saito had overseen the logistics of the war. A ten-year career followed as Governor-General of Korea. Saito's assassination denuded the court of an ardent pacifist who, while he believed in the growth of Japan as a world power, believed that "we should not opportunistically attempt a sudden expansion of our navy . . . in one conference or two . . . we should gradually enhance our national strength—our economic and industrial power—while winning greater respect and understanding from the rest of the world."[79]

By contrast the rebel group believed in a return to traditional Japanese values, a rejection of modern capitalism and an emphasis on the need to defeat the Soviet Union whom they regarded as the greatest threat to Japan's existence. After seizing the War Ministry, which became their base for the next three days, the rebels parleyed with General Yoshiyuki Kawashima, the War Minister, who was secretly on their side. The *Kodoha* leaders, Generals Sadao Araki and Jinzaburo Mazaki, either fearing the repercussions of the rebellion or more likely hoping to benefit from it, went to the War Ministry to negotiate with the rebels. Kawashima left the rebels and went to the Imperial Palace to request an audience with Hirohito. Kawashima, whose career was finished by the failure of the coup, read out the rebels' manifesto. It was a diatribe full of romanticized gibberish aimed at the perceived enemies of the Emperor and Japan's *kokutai*:

> After humble reflection as children of the land of the gods we submit these grievances to the one eternal god, the Emperor, under whose high command we serve. The essence of our country consists first in accomplishing the evolutionary formation of a single nation that is one body and then in comprehending the entire earth under our roof . . . now once again we are reaching the autumn of an epoch in which we confront many outside lands and must make visible progress toward a new enlightenment. Despite the critical period ahead of us, gangs of effeminate sadists spring up in our midst like toadstools . . . The elder statesmen, the leaders of Army factions, the bureaucrats, the political parties, and so on have all contributed as leaders to this destruction of the national essence . . . the false counsels of false vessels sap the national essence, shade the divine radiance of the Throne, and retard the Restoration . . . We . . . take this opportunity to rise as one man. To make the traitor perish, to make the supreme righteousness righteous, to protect the national essence and make it manifest, we dedicate our own true hearts as children of the sacred land, thereby giving our livers and brains to be consumed in the fire. We humbly

> pray the sun goddess and the ancestors, riding on spirit
> wings, to lend us their dark assistance and second sight in
> our undertaking . . .[80]

Hirohito was less than sympathetic. He furiously told Kawashima that "whatever their excuses, I am displeased. They have put a blot on the nation. I call on you, War Minister, to suppress them quickly."[81] This was not what many of the senior officers wanted to hear. In general the *Kodoha* faction admired and even supported the sentiments of the rebel troops and sought to dissuade the Emperor from a brutal suppression of the rebels. In this most noted example of completely independent action by the Emperor, and the only one before the surrender of Japan in August 1945, Hirohito, who wore an Army uniform throughout the rebellion, overruled his advisers and demanded that the rebellion be put down without compromise.

In spite of the attempted intervention of General Kawashima, Major-General Tokoyuki Yamashita and Chief *Aide-de-Camp*, General Shigeru Honjo, as well as the Supreme War Council, which included *Kodoha* leaders such as General Mazaki and General Araki, the Privy Council and the Cabinet, the Emperor remained adamant not to yield an inch to the rebels. Hirohito, who declared to Honjo that "Those crazy violent officers may not be excused in any way—not even in terms of their 'psychological motivation,'"[82] rejected Yamashita's suggested compromise, which called on the rebels to commit *seppuku* (ritual suicide) with honor. This, the rebels were prepared to do, if it was officially sanctioned by the Palace. In response Honjo noted in his diary, "His majesty is extremely angry. He said that if they wanted to commit suicide, they should go ahead and do it, but that sending an imperial representative is out of the question . . . I have never heard His Majesty issue so stern a censure."[83] Senior Army commanders were stunned by the Emperor's intransigence. When his senior commanders hemmed and hawed, Hirohito raged against their "excessive caution and unnecessary procrastination" and threatened, that if the Army was not prepared to subdue the rebels, "I will personally lead the Imperial Guard and subdue them."[84]

Hirohito not only faced down his advisers but also his own family. His younger brother Prince Chichibu was associated with one of the leading rebels, Mitsugi Nishida. It has recently come to light that the rebels were open to the idea of replacing Hirohito with Prince Chichibu. An Imperial Family Council was called at which the Emperor whipped Chichibu and his siblings into line in spite of their concerns at his hard-line stance that was so at odds with his senior advisers. Subsequently Prince Chichibu wrote a note to Captain Nonaka asking him to surrender. In the background, Ikki Kita, who was in regular radio contact with the rebels, supposedly urged them to continue though it seems in hindsight that he was 'fitted-up' by the Army. In reality he opposed the coup and tried to dissuade the young officers. Only when it became clear on the third day that the Army was preparing to strike against the rebels, did they surrender. With war planes circling overhead, rebel troops began to defect on the morning of 29 February. At noon, Captain Nonaka put a pistol in his mouth and pulled the trigger. The remaining leaders were taken into police custody and looked forward to public trials at which they could air their grievances. At 3 p.m. a radio announcement declared that the rebellion was over.

Unlike the 15 May Incident in 1932, the rebels, who had this time attempted a *coup d'état*, were harshly dealt with. Secret trials were ordered held *in camera*. This time the young officers were unable to use their defense speeches as a pulpit for the public audience. The trials of the nineteen key defendants lasted less than one hour in front of a panel of Army officers. The defendants were found guilty and then executed by firing squad. They all gave a final *banzai* expressing loyalty to the Emperor. In August, the civilian rebels, including Ikki Kita, were shot. For Hirohito the attempted coup left an "indelible black mark on the history of the Showa reign"[85] and he determined that it would never be repeated. The results for the Army were far reaching. Hirohito demanded a purge of all *Kodoha* faction sympathizers and the new War Minister, General Hisaichi Terauchi, was charged with the role of orchestrating the cleansing of 2,000 of the Army's 8,000 officers. They were either sacked, retired or sent to outposts far away from political influence. The *Kodoha* faction was all but wiped out. Weighted toward the senior command, the purge opened up opportunities for many younger officers.

For the senior officers implicated in the uprising, the end of the affair brought humiliating expulsion from the Emperor's inner circle. General Honjo, Hirohito's Chief *Aide-de-Camp*, and formerly one of Hirohito's closest advisers, was unfortunate enough to have a son-in-law, Captain Yamaguchi, who was a rebel from the 1st Regiment. Honjo, a national hero for his command of the *Kwantung* Army during the invasion of Manchuria after the Mukden Incident, resigned on 28 March though the Emperor tried to mitigate the hurt by giving him gifts of money, art, a pair of paperweights from his desk, fresh fish and *omachi* (rice cakes) prepared by the Empress.

General Masaki, the *Kodoha* leader, who had been removed from his office as Inspector General of Military Education, was arrested and held by the secret police for a year and a half. He was eventually released without charge but his career was over. General Yoshiyuki Kawashima, who had attempted to negotiate with the rebels and represent their viewpoint to the Emperor, was forced into retirement. Major-General Yamashita was removed to Korea. In addition, control over the Army was further centralized by the revision of the 1913 law that required that the Ministries of the War and the Navy should be filled by generals and admirals from the active or reserve list. In May 1936 the Privy Council suggested to the new cabinet led by Prime Minister Koki Hirota that the law be changed to only allow active generals and admirals to fill these posts—a measure designed to ensure that the disgraced *Kodoha* on the retired list could never wheedle themselves back into office.

The Control Faction in the Ascendant [1936–1941]: The importance of the February 1936 *coup d'état* was that it resolved the long running factional rivalry within the Army between the *Kodoha* (Imperial Way Faction) and the *Toseiha* (Control Faction). The strike-north faction was in effect dead while *Toseiha,* the key advocates of 'strike south', were left completely in the ascendant. Although *Toseiha* influence had been increasing in the 1930s, after February 1936 there was in effect no opposition. For Hirohito, the faction, *Toseiha*, with which he felt more comfortable, was now in complete control. Factional rivalry, one of the major impediments to an expansionist war in China and later the United States and Great Britain had been removed.

After the humiliation of the 26 February Incident, Okada, having narrowly avoided assassination, resigned his cabinet. Even though national elections had only taken place in the previous week with *Minseito* regaining a narrow majority as the Diet's major party with 205 seats against *Seiyukai*'s 174 seats (down from 301 seats). However, there was no consideration of appointing a party leader to form a government. Saionji nominated Prince Fumimaro Konoe, a member of the Fujiwara family, who was personally close to the Emperor. Konoe vacillated and declined the post on health grounds. In his place, Koki Hirota, a former diplomat and ambassador to the Soviet Union, who had been Admiral Saito's foreign minister in 1933, was nominated to succeed Okada. Rather than diminish the role of the Army in the governing of Japan, the attempted *coup d'état* enhanced the role of the ultra-nationalist military.

Army Minister, General Count Hisaichi Terauchi gave an indication of the Army's new powers by refusing to accept Shigeru Yoshida as Minister of Foreign Affairs. (Yoshida, an experienced diplomat and noted liberal who opposed the war with America is credited with a major role in leading Japan in its post-war recovery as the first Prime Minister of the Liberal Democrat Party.) Henceforth the Japanese Diet would be completely hostage to the ambitions of Japan's military commanders. It was a decisive moment in Japan's progression toward a military dominated fascist dictatorship.

Under plans drawn up by Colonel Kanji Ishiwara, the powers of the Cabinet Research Bureau were to be expanded in order to enable the more rapid coordination of civilian and military mobilization. It was a plan supported by Finance Minister Eiichi Baba, who prepared an inflation-busting Y3.13bn budget. Hirota tried to block the reform program by consigning them to subcommittees for consideration. When it became clear to the Army that opposition within the bureaucracy and the Diet was intent on blocking their program, Army Minister General Count Hisaichi Terauchi resigned and brought down the Hirota cabinet on 27 January 1937. General Kazushige Ugaki was appointed to form a new government but his enemies in the Army refused to nominate a War Minister, which, because of the effective veto given to the Army and Navy over their respective ministries, meant that he was unable to form a government.

In his place General Senjuro Hayashi, a supporter of the slain Lieutenant-General Tetsuzan Nagata, presented a more modest version of the Ishiwara Plan. Nariakira Ikeda, former Managing Director of Mitsui Bank, who replaced Eiichi Baba as finance minister, refused to sanction the latter's budget. He declared that "the present plans are simply the fruits of the program of the middle-echelon Army officers and the *Kwantung* Army. We should be aware that they will have an extremely bad influence in financial circles."[86] Ikeda proposed Toyotaro Yuki, former Bank of Japan governor, as finance minister. Ikeda himself took up the post of governor of the Bank of Japan in February.

Together they worked in step to produce a watered down budget of Y2.77bn (down from Y3.13bn). Ishiwara was transferred back to Manchuria. Negotiations with the Army Ministry, relating particularly to the needs of Manchuria, came to a head with agreement on 15 May. Two weeks later, the Army Ministry drew up a revised program called *The Essentials of a Five-Year Plan for Key Industries*.

Although some could reflect that the Army had been forced to back down, the net result of Hayashi's cabinet was hardly supportive of the Diet and the main parties, whose members he completely excluded from government posts. In a miscalculation Hayashi called for new elections, just fifteen months after the previous ones. The two main parties, *Minseito* and *Seiyukai*, campaigned successfully against the government, returning to the Diet in force, but by now their voice was unimportant. Hayashi resigned and was replaced by the more Army friendly Prince Fumimaro Konoe, who at last accepted the post that many had long believed to be his destiny.

It should be noted that the new budgetary allocations agreed with Hayashi, albeit reduced, were hardly parsimonious. The military budget increased by 300 percent over the twelve months after the *coup d'état* against Okada's government. The Army's troop numbers were to be expanded by 41 percent. The fiscal conservatism of Finance Minister Takahashi, who had fallen to the '26 February' plotters, was overthrown by a binge of bond issuance to finance the aggressive new military strategy. However, it was not a strategy aimed at the Soviet Union. Russian spy, the German Richard Sorge, correctly interpreted the events of the 26 February Incident as proof that the 'strike south' factions had won. In his appraisement entitled *Views on the Housecleaning of the Army* [1936] he concluded that the target of Japanese military expansion would be China, not the Soviet Union.

Agnes Smedley, Ozaki and the Sorge Spy Ring: American writer Agnes Smedley was an unlikely instigator of arguably the most successful spy ring of *World War II*. Born in Osgood, Missouri in 1892, Smedley moved with her parents (her father was a coalminer), to Trinidad, Colorado where she witnessed first-hand a miners' strike in 1904. She became a teacher before going to business school and finding work as a travelling saleswoman. After a nervous breakdown and recovery in Arizona, she studied at Tempe Normal School (later, Arizona State University) where she started to edit the newspaper and met and later married a socialist, Ernest Brundin. Six years later she dumped the husband but not the socialism. She moved to New York where she fell in with radical Bengali socialists for whom she set up a communications center. After striking up a relationship with Virendranath Chattopadhyaya, a communist activist, she moved with him to Berlin.

In Berlin, she finished her autobiographical novel *Daughter of Earth* [1929], in which the main protagonist protests her psychological and physical problems with men and promotes her views on socialism and Indian independence. Having picked up German she left her Indian lover and decamped to Shanghai where she wrote for the liberal German press. Covering the Chinese civil war she was a cheerleader for Mao

Zedong and the communists and wrote for the *Frankfurter Zeitung* and the *Guardian* (then called the *Manchester Guardian*). In her years as a war correspondent, she travelled with the Chinese New Fourth Army and was disappointed to have her application to join the Chinese Communist Party rejected on the grounds of her excessive independence of mind. However, she is thought to have become a Soviet spy during her years in Shanghai and it was here that she introduced two of her lovers, Richard Sorge and Hotsumi Ozaki.

Richard Sorge was born in Baku, Azerbaijan, in 1895 to a German father, a mining engineer, who worked for the Caucasian Oil Company. Sorge's mother was Russian. Sorge served in the German Army on the Western Front where he was hit by shrapnel, losing three fingers. During his recuperation he read Marx's *Das Capital* and was converted. After the war he became a teacher but was sacked for his political views and fled to Moscow where he became a Comintern agent. He was sent back to Germany to infiltrate the *Nazi* Party but was moved to Shanghai in 1930 where he edited the German news service and wrote for the *Frankfurter Zeitung*, here he met Agnes Smedley. After a brief return to Berlin, where he refreshed his connections to the *Nazis*, Sorge returned to Asia in the autumn of 1933, this time to Tokyo with instructions to set up a spy ring. He summed up his mission as having a single main purpose to "observe Japan's Soviet policy closely . . . and to find out if Japan was planning to attack the Soviet Union. This was the most important assignment given to me and to my group . . . It would not be an overstatement to say that it was the entire purpose of my stay in Japan."[87]

With his relationship established with the *Nazi* Party in Berlin, Sorge was welcomed into the German Embassy and not just into the bed of the Ambassador's wife. Uniquely he would have access to secret information from Germany and Japan. His core network included radio operator Max Clausen, a Red Army officer, and his wife Anna, a courier, Branko Vukelic, a French journalist, and Yotoku Miyagi, who worked for an English language newspaper, the *Japan Advertiser*. Unquestionably his star agent, however, was Ozaki. Sorge, Ozaki and Smedley were true believers and shared the utmost respect. Ozaki would later describe his two confederates as being "loyal to their ideologies and profound in their principles, as well as being devoted to and talented in their work. If they were in any small way motivated by self-interest, or acted as if they were trying to use us, I at least would have refused and parted company."[88]

Ozaki, born of a samurai family in Shirakawa, Gifu prefecture, grew up in Taipei, *Formosa*, in a compound that had been organized by Emperor Taisho's Prime Minister, Prince Taro Katsura and by Marquis Kido's father-in-law, General Viscount Gentaro Kodama, Governor General of Taiwan. After Taipei, Ozaki returned to Japan to take up a place in the prestigious law department of Tokyo University. He made well-connected friends: Nobuhiko Ushiba, later a private secretary to Prince Konoe, and Matsumoto Shigeharu, who became another member of the Prince's inner circle. After being kicked out of university because of his association with the Japanese Communist Party, Ozaki went to work for the *Asahi Shimbun* who sent him to Shanghai in 1928. Here he met bevies of international Marxists and, most importantly, became connected to Richard Sorge through the good offices of Agnes Smedley.

In February 1934, four years after their first meeting, Sorge sent an intermediary to tell Ozaki to meet him in the deer park adjacent to the ancient Buddhist temples in the eighth-century Japanese capital of Nara, twenty-five miles south of Kyoto. At the meeting, Ozaki agreed to hand over whatever information came his way. The report that he and Sorge authored for the Soviets in response to the 26 February Incident was highly regarded in Moscow and significantly boosted Ozaki's value.

Thereafter Ozaki's importance increased exponentially. First he was recruited into the Breakfast Club by a group of young men closely associated with Prince Konoe, which gave him access to the rising star of Japanese politics. The Breakfast Club met twice a month. Members included such influential people as Konoe's secretary, Nobuhiko Ushiba, Kinzaku Saionji, and chief cabinet secretary, Akira Kazami. Secondly *Asahi Shimbun* made him a member of a China-study group with Kinzaku Saionji, grandson of the *genro*, and Lieutenant-General Rihachiro Banzai, later executive director of Japan's spy service, and then the country's foremost authority on China. Together with Ozaki they went to *Yosemite National Park* in Northern California to give a presentation to Americans on the Japanese position *vis-à-vis* China. Ozaki's well delivered and cogently argued address burnished his reputation within right-wing circles. Over the next three years, whenever Sino-Soviet issues came to the fore, Konoe would contact Kinkazu Saionji, who would in turn refer to Ozaki. Konoe, learning of Ozaki's skills through the young Saionji, appointed Ozaki to the *Showa Research Institute*, a cover name for a body employed to write cover papers and slogans for war.

The single most important result of Ozaki's activities as a Soviet spy is that he learned with certainty that Japan had no intention of invading the Soviet Union. It confirmed what Stalin probably already knew. He was thus able to lightly defend his eastern borders and concentrate his forces in the west against Germany. Eighteen divisions, 1,700 tanks and 1,500 aircraft were moved from Siberia. However, at no point during the *Pacific War* did Japan outnumber the Soviets on its Siberian frontier. Nevertheless, the withdrawal of Soviet forces from its eastern borders gave Japan's Army the confidence to deploy troops for its 'strike south' strategy.

The Long March and the Xian Incident [December 1936]: **[Map: 2.3] [Map: 2.4]** Mao's long march that started in October 1933 took two years to wind its way from southern China via the remote far western provinces of Yunnan, Xikang, and Quinghai before moving northeast and finally resting up at Yanan in northern Shaanxi Province on the southern part of the *Loess Plateau*. Along the way, Mao, not the acknowledged leader of the Communist Party at the beginning of the Long March, established his leadership, albeit tenuously in competition with more senior colleagues such as Wang Ming, Zhou Enlai and Zhang Guotao. The Long Marchers were chased all the way by *Kuomintang* armies, from which they barely escaped on numbers of occasions. Leaving aside survival, their aim was to connect with Soviet-controlled Outer Mongolia, from where they expected to receive supplies to continue the revolutionary fight against Chiang Kai-shek. Zhang Guotao had led the larger parallel Long March to the one led by Mao. After his CCP forces, 80,000 strong, were smashed at *Gansu* as they attempted to force a passage through to Soviet Mongolia, his now halved army made their bedraggled way to Yanan. Although he still commanded an army nominally twice the size of that of Mao, Zhang was a spent force and quickly lost out in the political power struggle. He was humiliated with minor appointments until Mao purged him in 1937. Eventually he went over to the *Kuomintang* after their retreat to Taiwan, before retiring to spend his later years in Toronto.

For Chiang Kai-shek, the communists were just one of three major problems. Leaving aside the issues of trying to modernize his still-feudal country, Chiang Kai-shek faced the problem of controlling unreliable warlords and, after the annexation of Manchuria, which he refused to recognize, he had to confront a Japanese Empire that was creeping southwards toward the ancient capital of Peking. Chiang wisely decided not to confront Japan in the knowledge that his huge but ill-equipped armies could not match them. Instead, he focused on the elimination of his domestic enemies, both warlords and communists, while gradually trying to modernize his armies. Adding to the confusion of the complex web of political alliance and betrayal, Chiang's armies, Mao and the Chinese Communist Party (CCP) notwithstanding, were being equipped and financed by the Soviets. Stalin saw Chiang as the best counterweight to Japan's ambitions for Russia's Far Eastern territories. For Chiang it was a delicate balancing act.

Having penned the communists into Shanxi Province by the end of 1935, Chiang planned to deliver the *coup de grâce* to Mao and his renegade forces in 1936. He had reckoned without Chang Hsueh-liang, usually referred to as the Young Marshal. Chang was the ousted warlord of Manchuria. He had succeeded his father, Chang Tso-lin, the Old Marshal, who the Japanese had assassinated in 1928. The Old Marshal had spent the 1920s battling with competing warlords for control of northern China with his Fengtian Army supported by harsh taxes levied from Chang's ancestral base of Manchuria. By the capture of the ancient capital of Peking and Anhui Province to the south, the Old Marshal showed that he had ambitions to be recognized as the ruler of the whole of China. Pushed back toward Peking by the *Kuomintang*, on 3 June 1928 Chang Tso-lin took a train back to Manchuria where he was coming under the increasing threat posed by Japan's Armies in North Korea.

As the Old Marshal's train reached the outskirts of Shenyang, a bomb planted by Colonel Daisaku Komoto, a *Kwantung* Army officer, collapsed a viaduct. After a two-week interlude, Chang Tso-lin was pronounced dead. At the Tokyo War Crimes Trial in 1946, Admiral Keisuke Okada, at the time Navy Minister in the cabinet of Prime Minister Giichi Tanaka, offered the not very plausible reason that Chang Tso-lin was murdered because he had failed to halt the advance of the communist-backed Chiang Kai-shek. The Old Marshal's place was taken by his 27-year-old son, Chang Hsueh-liang, a man at ease with westerners, who was best known for his reputation as a playboy and opium addict. In spite of this, an early interest in aircraft led him to being put in command of his father's airforce. His Texan pilot, Royal Leonard, recalled, "My first impression . . . was that here was the president of the Rotary Club: rotund, prosperous, with an easy, affable manner . . . we were friends in five minutes."[89] The *Kwantung* Army had probably hoped that the Old Marshal's son would prove to be more pliant than his father. If that was part of the Japanese plan in the murder of the Old Marshal, it backfired spectacularly when Chang Hsueh-liang switched allegiances from Japan to Chiang Kai-shek in December 1928. [The Young Marshal was cured of his opium addiction with the help of his friend, the journalist William Donald, an Australian and former editor of the *Far Eastern Review*, which he had left when the Managing Editor had insisted on a pro-Japanese line. An English novelist described Donald as a "red faced, serious man with a large, sensible nose."[90]]

After the annexation of Manchuria in 1931, Chang brought his 200,000-strong army south and joined forces with Chiang Kai-shek, formerly his father's bitter enemy. Chiang brought the Young Marshal into his inner circle and appointed him to senior government positions. He was thirteen years younger than Chiang, who he would describe as "like a daddy to me."[91] For Chiang the relationship may well have been more of the type described by Sun Tzu in *The Art of War* [sixth century BC], "keep your friends close and your enemies closer."[92] Nevertheless he had developed enough trust in his young protégé to give him the task of preventing Mao linking up with the Soviet Union and of destroying his stronghold near Yanan in Shaanxi Province.

Chiang was deceived. The Young Marshal, who was an admirer of European fascism and a friend of Mussolini and his family, had personal ambitions of his own to be China's leader. Chang Hsueh-liang had flirted with the Soviets before but they had not taken him seriously. That changed after he was given the job of bottling up Mao in Shaanxi Province. Now it was the Soviets who courted the Young Marshal. At the end of 1935 the Young Marshal flew to Shanghai to meet Russian agents. He threw off Chiang Kai-shek's agents by using one of his many girlfriends as cover. In 1993 he recalled in a meeting with Yung Chang and Jon Halliday, *Mao, The Unknown Story* [2005] "Tai Li [Chiang's intelligence chief] tried everything he could to find out my whereabouts, and he thought I went to have a good time with my girlfriends. But in fact, I was doing deals . . ."[93]

Chang Hsueh-liang was not just driven by personal ambition. Like many of his Manchurian troops he wanted to return to his homeland and to revenge himself on Manchuria's Japanese occupiers. Many Chinese, possibly a majority, thought it was absurd that Chinese were fighting Chinese while Japan was encroaching on their country to the north. In close combat, Chinese troops would call out to the *Kuomintang* troops asking them "Why do Chinese fight us, who are Chinese, to help a lot of worthless officers make money to ride about in motors cars, to get concubines, to gamble and to live a life of luxury?"[94] The Young Marshal complained to William Donald that CCP propaganda was "more damaging than their bullets."[95] His complaints to Chiang Kai-shek fell on deaf ears and they brought a froideur to the relationship. Chiang had noted in his diary on 24 November that the Young Marshal, "does not have the strength of will to endure the last five minutes of the [civil] war."[96]

Stalin strung the Young Marshal along. Unlike Chiang's 'softly, softly' approach, the Young Marshal wanted to join with Mao to fight the Japanese. In return he wanted Stalin's support for him to become China's new ruler. Stalin doubted his ability to lead and feared that a Chinese descent into civil war would merely open the door for Japan to conquer China and pose an even bigger threat to Soviet interests in the Far East. For the time being, Stalin played along and encouraged Chang Hsueh-liang to meet with a CCP agent in January 1936. Mao was more enthusiastic than Stalin for the alliance with the Young Marshal. The various negotiations placed Stalin firmly in the driving seat now that he was funding both Chiang Kai-shek and Mao and had the Young Marshal on the hook.

However, by the end of 1936, Mao and his CCP forces were clinging on for survival. Twenty thousand of their troops had managed to cross the Yellow River but Mao and the main force were forced to return to their freezing base on the edge of North Shanxi's high desert. Sandstorms blasted the CCP troops as they dug into the hills or the ground to find shelter. Mao was holed up in a dismal cave on the edge of the town of Baoan—his accommodation plagued by rats and scorpions. In *Red Star Over China* [1937] Edgar Snow glammed up his description of the tiny desert town where peasants eked out a living on feudal strips "once a frontier stronghold . . . Remains of its fortifications, flame-struck in that afternoon sun, could be seen flanking the narrow pass through which once emptied into this valley the conquering legions of the Mongols."[97] Mao pleaded with the Comintern for US$550,000 so that he could feed his half-starved troops. The very existence of Mao and his forces was on the line.

At the end of November events turned Mao's way. A regiment of the *Kuomintang* Army not only defected to the communists, but also caused the annihilation of a cavalry brigade and two infantry brigades. On 7 December, Chiang Kai-shek flew to Xian to take charge of the *Kuomintang* forces for the *Sixth Extermination Campaign* designed to finish off Mao once and for all. Chiang also threatened to dismiss the Young Marshal and disband his forces.

The Young Marshal was now in a bind. His personal plans for control of China would be jeopardized by Mao's demise. In a desperate bid for power, the Young Marshal plotted the capture of Chiang Kai-shek: "My philosophy is a gamble," he confided to his colleagues, "I might lose once or twice, but as long as the game goes on, the time will come when I get all my stakes back."[98] Chang Hsueh-liang did not inform Stalin of his plans. Mao meanwhile disingenuously led the Young Marshal to believe that he had Moscow's backing for the coup. By now the Soviet dictator was urging Mao to abandon his fight and join with Chiang to fight the Japanese. For Stalin, a unified Chinese Army under Chiang Kai-shek was the best stratagem for the defeat of Hirohito's armies. Stalin hoped to draw Japan into a long drawn out and costly war in the heart of China.

At 5.30 a.m. on 12 December, the Young Marshal, urged on by Mao, launched his *coup d'état*. Mao, informed of the plot a few hours in advance, was ecstatic. He told his secretary to "Go back to bed. There will be good news in the morning!"[99] A brief firefight with Chiang's guards gave Chiang the chance to escape through a window in his nightshirt, from where he scrambled barefoot up a hill and hid in a cave. He hurt his back in a fall and lost his dentures in the process. At dawn he was found barefoot and bleeding. Chiang asked whether he was going to be killed, to which his captor replied, "No, we just want you to fight the Japanese."[100] Chiang Kai-shek was taken prisoner and driven to a meeting with Chang Hsueh-liang where he rebuffed all attempts to discuss his policy toward Japan. Chiang refused to eat or talk. He prepared himself for martyrdom. William Donald would later reflect, ". . . I think he [Chiang Kai-shek] was very disappointed when he did not succeed in this respect."[101] Chiang would later compare his ordeal and suffering to that of Jesus Christ.

Mao, who was "laughing like mad"[102] when he heard of Chiang's capture, dispatched Zhou Enlai with orders to persuade the Young Marshal to kill his prisoner and then go to war against the *Kuomintang* government in Nanking while it was in disarray. Even at this stage Mao preferred a destabilized China to fighting Japan. For good reason Stalin was furious when he learned of Chiang's overthrow. When news of Chiang's capture reached Nanking, acting Prime Minister, H. H. Kung, the Generalissimo's brother-in-law, warned the Soviet *chargé d'affaires* that it risked a break in *Kuomintang*'s alliance with Russia and might lead to a realignment with, rather than against, Japan.

Stalin was incandescent—not with the *Kuomintang* but with those who were conspiring to topple Chiang Kai-shek. In Moscow, a telegram sent for Stalin to approve the execution of Chiang led to the arrest and execution of its author, Artur Artuzov, head of KGB foreign operations. Lead articles in *Pravda* and *Izvestia*, which condemned the Young Marshal's attempted coup, alerted Mao to Stalin's displeasure. In China, Dimitrov, Comintern's agent, hastily denied any involvement in the coup and blamed Mao to whom he sent a stern message. A peaceful resolution was demanded. Mao reportedly "flew into a rage . . . swore and stamped his feet."[103]

As for Chang Hsueh-liang, he soon realized that Mao had duped him. On 15 May, William Donald, a friend of Chiang, and Chang arrived from Nanking with sections of Chiang's diary which revealed Chiang Kai-shek's determination to destroy the Japanese invaders. The Young Marshal pleaded with the Generalissimo, "If he had known one-tenth of what is recorded in your diary, I would not have done this rash act."[104] Nevertheless the Young Marshal sent his private twin-engine Boeing, 'the Flying Palace' and his personal pilot, Leonard, to pick up Mao's emissary Zhou Enlai, who had travelled by donkey to the airfield at Yanan. Zhou Enlai brought the CCP's demand that Chiang Kai-shek should cease his bid to exterminate them and that together they should join forces to fight Japan.

In confinement Chiang Kai-shek stood on his honor and initially refused to speak to Zhou Enlai. It was only on Christmas Day 1936 that Chiang relented after word was brought from Moscow that Stalin would release his son, Ching-kuo, who was, in effect, being kept hostage in the Soviet Union. Unlike Mao, who was profoundly indifferent to his sons, Chiang Kai-shek was a devoted father. It was this medieval bargaining piece that helped bring an end for now to the civil war between the *Kuomintang* and the CCP. The arrival of Chiang's wife, Soong Meiling, and his secret police chief was also critical, with the latter playing a crucial role in persuading the Young Marshal that Chiang Kai-shek would guarantee his safety. In Xian, when Chiang Kai-shek finally met Zhou Enlai, his former *protégé* at Whampoa Military Academy in the 1920s, he greeted him warmly and suggested an end to the civil war: "All the time we have been fighting, I have often thought of you. I hope we can work together."[105] For both Mao and Chiang Kai-shek, the truce was a short-term expedient. Their joint paymaster, Stalin, had demanded an anti-Japanese alliance and ultimately, they both jumped to attention.

The Young Marshal, duped by Mao, despised by Stalin, fell back on the remnants of his relationship with Chiang Kai-shek. He calculated that if he did not place himself back in the Generalissimo's hands that he would be assassinated on the orders of the Nanking government. In doing so he bet that Chiang would not execute him for treachery. He was correct but his career was over. For the next fifty years he lived under Chiang's protective custody—effectively house arrest. He played *mahjong*, studied history and collected Chinese art. He died at his house in *Hawaii* in 2002 aged 101.

On his return to Nanking, Chiang purged his *Kuomintang* forces of any suspected communist sympathizers. However, he did not choose to renew his attack on the CCP stronghold in Shaanxi. Chiang had given his word to Zhou Enlai and kept it. Mao was furious but was persuaded by Zhou that Chiang would "probably not go back on his word," explaining that the Generalissimo had "the vainglory of a self-appointed hero."[106] In Nanking, Chiang Kai-shek pressed ahead with normalization of relations with the CCP, opening a bus and mail service to their stronghold at Yanan.

When the *Kuomintang* Central Committee refused to endorse the 'United Front' the Generalissimo ignored them and set about planning the resistance to Japan. Historian Jay Taylor, in his biography, *The Generalissimo, The Struggle for Modern China* [2011], speculates, with little evidence, that Chiang would have been forced by Stalin to abandon his attempt to exterminate Mao and the CCP. However, Stalin made little attempt to pull Chiang off his *Sixth Extermination Campaign* and it must remain debatable whether he would have done so. Stalin's main aim, far more important than the survival of Mao and the CCP, was to have a united China facing off with Japan. In any case Stalin saw Chiang as a socialist of sorts, whose type of rule was not a million miles away from his own. For Stalin, the urgency of priority drawing Japan into a conflict with a united China, had been brought into focus by the *Anti-Comintern Pact* [26 November 1936] between Germany, Italy and Japan, with its potential for a simultaneous Germany-Japan attack on its western and eastern borders respectively.

The Xian Incident, a story laced with intrigue, court politics, treachery and deception by the Young Marshal and three of the twentieth century's most infamous leaders, was to have profound consequences for China and the world. In the long term the survival of Mao and his ragtag CCP army enabled a communist takeover of China that otherwise would probably never have happened. In the medium term, the consequence of the Xian Incident was that it drew Japan into a war with a Chinese 'United Front,' which albeit heavily fractured, was, at least for the next four years, committed to fight Japan. The

CCP's secret defection from the 'United Front' to the Japanese was in the future. To Stalin's delight Japan would thus be occupied by a war of attrition that had 1.5 million of its troops bogged down in Central China for the next eight years. Daikichi Irokawa has gone as far as to suggest that Japan's political and military leadership's failure to understand the changing "situation in China after the Xian Incident was ultimately the most important reason for Japan's defeat in the *World War II*, even more important than the war with the United States."[107] Irokawa fails to mention that without the war with China, ultimately the *casus belli* of the *Pacific War*, there would have been no war with America—at least in the short term.

Kanji Ishiwara, one of the architects of the Mukden Incident, was one of the few to realize the dangers of a war of attrition in China. In sympathy with the soon to be purged *Kodoha* (Imperial Way Faction), he believed that Japan's immediate priority was a war with the Soviet Union. Conflict with the United States could wait. Ishiwara, a somewhat deranged religious fanatic, believed that a final war with America in the mid-*Pacific* was inevitable and crazily looked forward to this ultimate finale.

The Anti-Comintern Pact [November 1936]: The *Anti-Comintern Pact*, signed on 25 November between Germany and Japan (and later by Italy) was more grandly titled than it was substantive. Its signatories, Germany and Japan agreed to little more than to consult with each other on what measures to take if any of them were attacked by the Soviet Union. Originally the Pact was a plan conceived by Hitler's special ambassador, Joachim von Ribbentrop and the Japanese military *attaché* in Berlin, Lieutenant-General Hiroshi Oshima. Ribbentrop wanted to unite China, its historic ally, with Japan, with whom it was exploring a closer relationship, while Oshima hoped that such an alliance would assist in the subordination of China to Japan.

In the event, Chiang Kai-shek refused to participate, as did England and Poland who were also invited. Hitler's authorization of the project rested principally on his wish for an Anglo-German alliance against the recently formed Franco-Soviet alliance. Instead, a year later on 6 November 1937, a few months after the *Second Sino-Japanese War* had started, he bagged Italy, a poor substitute. The three nations formed what later became known as the Axis Powers. In the meantime, more importantly, Hitler had ditched the alliance with China and was now supporting Japan in its bid to defeat Chiang Kai-shek's National Revolutionary Army.

Preconditions for War: In China, following the Xian Incident, the pre-conditions for war were set. In the short term, with a CCP-*Kuomintang* alliance in place, Chiang Kai-shek, for the time being acknowledged as China's leader of a country unified in purpose and supported by the Soviet Union, was in a position to respond to any further Japanese incursions with a vigorous response and a willingness to risk full-scale war. It was a stance that would not have been possible without the CCP alliance and the backing of Stalin. Since the Mukden Incident, Chiang had taken Japan's incursions and insults and turned the other cheek. Now he didn't have to.

Japan too, was stoked for war. Since the Mukden Incident in 1931, Japan's parliamentary democracy had fallen into irreversible decline. Pluralistic centers of power that might have resisted the ultra-nationalist militarist advance, such as the *genro* and the Privy Council, had been muted. Ultra-nationalism gripped large important organs of the state, not only in the Army but also in the bureaucracy and academia. The general population, battered by the global depression of the early 1930s was equally dismissive of the political caste and easily stirred to patriotism by a government media that glorified cheap victories in Manchuria. Moderate voices, on which US Ambassador Grew in Tokyo continued to pin hopes, were quieted by waves of ultra-nationalist propaganda and the fear of the *Tokko*, the *Kempeitai*, right-wing assassins and the courts. Liberals such as Professor Minobe had been silenced.

Following the 26 February Incident in 1936, the Imperial Japanese Army, having purged the Imperial Way Faction, was now in the hands of the Control Faction. Their direction of foreign affairs was clear and unopposed; when the Army disagreed with cabinet direction, they brought it down. The Control Faction, less enthusiastic than the Imperial Way Faction for war with the Soviet Union, was determined to expand south from the *Kwantung* Army's bases in Manchuria. As they saw it, the move south and the annexation of northern China offered valuable assets, needed for the establishment of a powerful self-sufficient economic empire capable of standing up to the west. Unlike Soviet spy Richard Sorge, the government in Tokyo had not worked out that, as a result of the Xian Incident, Chiang Kai-shek and China, financed and equipped by the Soviet Union, were now united and ready for war.

Perversely the Control Faction, which had adamantly refused to fight a war with the Soviet Union on the Manchurian border, were now set up to be drawn into a proxy war with them in China. This was exactly Stalin's stratagem. Japan's southern expansionary course was set to clash with China's new determination to resist and it was therefore only a matter of time before a spark lit the well-kindled hearth of war. The Marco Polo Bridge Incident [July 1937] would provide that spark.

3 Japan versus China: From Phoney War to Total War

[1937–1941]

[Maps: 3.1, 3.2, 3.3, 3.4, 3.5, 3.6]

Manchukuo, the Marco Polo Bridge Incident and the Start of the Second Sino-Japanese War [July 1937]: [Map: 3.1] [Map: 3.2] On 4 June 1937, Prince Konoe, the newly appointed prime minister, and his cabinet were sworn into office. Just over a month later, on 7 July, the *Second Sino-Japanese War*, a conflict that was to bring the deaths of an estimated 30 million people, started with an innocuous-seeming incident that took place at the Marco Polo Bridge.

Foreign powers with trade rights in Peking were entitled to station troops along the railway that linked the city with its port of Tianjin forty miles away. By the established local protocols foreign troops were required to give notice to their Chinese military counterparts if they intended to engage in training maneuvers. The local Japanese commander failed to give the due warning and, when one of his soldiers went missing, shots were fired at the nearby Chinese garrison at Wanping, a town to the southwest of Peking accessed by the Marco Polo Bridge. The start of the *Second Sino-Japanese War* was, unlike the Mukden Incident, an unplanned episode, but one that, nevertheless, characterized Japan's gradual absorption of northern China.

It was a pattern of encroachment on China by Japanese forces, which had been in progress since the Mukden Incident of September 1931. The *agent provocateur* act of blowing up the railway from Port Arthur to Mukden had given the excuse for the occupation of Mukden by General Shigeru Honjo's 10th Division followed by the invasion of southern Manchuria. The annexation of all Manchuria and Inner Mongolia had followed. The 'independent' state of Manchukuo was subsequently established on 18 February 1932 with the last Qing Dynasty Emperor, Aisin-Gioro Pu-yi, put in place as its puppet ruler in the new capital of Hsinking. Two years later Pu-yi was proclaimed Emperor of Manchukuo. The head of the Japanese *Kwantung* Army who, in addition to his military role, held the role of ambassador, effectively controlled the Emperor. Japanese Vice-Ministers were placed in Emperor Pu-yi's Privy Council and over time they removed almost all his 'Manchu' advisers. The Chinese Legislative Council was merely window dressing with its sole function to rubber stamp Privy Council orders.

From Manchukuo, Japan expanded its regional authority southwards—much to the horror of Major-General Kanji Ishiwara, a convert to Nichiren Buddhism and one of the plotters instrumental in the Mukden Incident, who had dreamed of a Manchukuo under Japanese rule allied to a restored China. Manchukuo with Japan should, he believed, face down the Soviets on their northern border. Instead he found that Japan's new province was going to be used as a staging point for the invasion of China. He was a member of the 'strike north' or Imperial Way Faction (*Kodoha*). Ishiwara, who had graduated second at the Army Staff College in 1918, was rewarded for the Mukden Incident by an appointment to lead the 4th Regiment in Sendai followed by a return to the Army General Staff as Chief of Operations. Notwithstanding his disapproval of the southward military operations of the *Kwantung* Army, Ishiwara came out strongly against the rebels engaged in the 26 February Incident and not only escaped the succeeding purge of the *Kodoha* faction from the Army ranks but was promoted to the rank of Major-General in 1937 and sent back to Manchukuo as Deputy Chief of Staff of the *Kwantung* Army.

Having consolidated its hold on Manchuria, the *Kwantung* Army looked to expand their authority southwards. Chiang Kai-shek, fully aware of his country's economic weakness and his need to consolidate his own power, was forced to swallow his pride and bide his time. In 1935 the government of Manchukuo, in other words Japan, purchased the Chinese Eastern Railway from the Soviets. To the south of Manchuria, the provinces of Heibei and Chahar were occupied. On 9 June 1935, the *He-Umez Agreement* forced Chiang Kai-shek to agree to the 'neutrality' of these provinces. The 'East Heibei Autonomous Council' became another Japanese controlled puppet government. Peking was in effect surrounded. On the Peking–Tianjin railway, Japan deployed an estimated 10,000 soldiers, double the number of any other foreign contingent and far more than was authorized by the *Boxer Protocol* of 1901. In 1937, the *Kwantung* Army sought to further consolidate its position by buying land to build its own airport adjacent to Wanping, where the Marco Polo Bridge controlled the last route out of Peking into territory controlled by the *Kuomintang*.

Whether the flare-up of tension at Wanping was unintentional on the part of China, the intentions of the *Kwantung* Army were clear. In Tokyo, Prime Minister Konoe talked up the possibilities of negotiations while at the same time sending reinforcements from Japan. On 15 August 1937, Konoe's cabinet declared that "now we must take determined measures to punish the violent and unreasonable actions of the Chinese army and encourage the Nanking Government to reconsider."[1] Konoe would no doubt have agreed with former Japan Self Defense Force Chief of Staff, Toshio Tamogami when he wrote in 2008, "Our country was a victim, drawn into the *Sino-Japanese War* by Chiang Kai-shek."[2]

An Imperial Rescript issued in October explained that Japan was using its military "to urge grave reflection upon China and to establish peace in the East without delay."[3] The truce agreed provided a brief respite. Japanese reinforcements were poured into the area, and at the end of July the local commanders were instructed by Tokyo to "chastise the Chinese Army in the Peking-Tianjin area."[4] Chiang too was preparing to challenge Japan's advance. A message was sent to the Nineteenth Army in which he informed them "I am now determined to declare war on Japan."[5] On 29 July, any chance of a pullback from conflict was shattered by the massacre of Japanese citizens in the ancient town of Tongzhou, capital of the East Heibei Autonomous Region. Japanese soldiers rushed back to find that their women, old and young, had been raped and decapitated. Major Katura was shocked to find "a mother and child who had been slaughtered. The child's fingers had been hacked off."[6] A Japanese survivor told the *Asahi Shimbun* that he had seen "a man being dragged along by a wire . . . it was pierced through his nose."[7] Some 223 out of 385 Japanese and Korean residents of Tongzhou were slain. The Japanese Army responded with even greater brutality. A jingoistic press in Japan urged on the bloodlust of revenge.

However much the Imperial Army General Staff might have liked to pull back, as it was clear that they were cautious about a full-scale engagement in China, the rapid unfolding of events, including Chiang Kai-shek's determination to fight, and the push of public reaction back in Japan, meant that it became increasingly difficult to extricate themselves from this quagmire. After years of unopposed encroachment, China's sudden decision to push back had taken the *Kwantung* Army by surprise. Ultimately however, Japan's leaders found that moving forward was easier than moving back.

The Battles of Taiyuan and Shanghai [1937]: **[Map: 3.3] [Map: 3.4]** Chiang, at last, buoyed by increasing nationalist hatred of the Japanese invaders, and militarily enabled by the 'United Front' with Mao's communists, was no longer prepared to yield ground. For Chiang the time had come for China to stand tall and resist. However, his armies were not up to the challenge.

By the end of November 1937 Japan had secured control of northern China after the *Battle of Taiyuan*. The *Taiyuan Offensive* was fought over several months starting with General Hideki Tojo's invasion of Shanxi Province of which Taiyuan was the capital city. Five Japanese divisions, about 140,000 troops, engaged a joint *Kuomintang–* Communist Army comprising six army groups of 580,000 soldiers. After the capture of the coal-rich city of Datong, the Chinese Army retreated to the Great Wall of China where it was defeated at the *Battles of Pingxingguan and Niangziguan*. After the *Battle of Xinkou* in October, the Chinese divisions were largely wiped out and the remnants retreated either west toward the communist-controlled areas around Yanan or south to re-join the remaining *Kuomintang* forces. It was a heavy defeat for Chiang Kai-shek, which effectively lost northern China for the remainder of the war. Chinese casualties were estimated at 100,000 versus 30,000 for Japan. Having already occupied the former German naval base at Tientsin, which Japan had formerly held from 1914 to 1922, Japan extended its military power over the whole basin of the *Yellow River*.

In the south, the wealthy industrial and economic heartlands around the *Yangtze River*, including Shanghai, had been under attack since 13 August when a fracas between Chinese guards and Japanese guards on the edge of 'Little Tokyo' led to an extended firefight. Instead of the expected minor engagement and rapid conquest of Shanghai, Japan's senior Army commanders were surprised at the scale of resistance mounted by the *Kuomintang*. The 'Little Tokyo Incident' drew Japan into a full-scale war in southern China that it had not envisioned. Expansion in the north, moving south from Manchuria, was the *Kwantung* Army's intention, not the absorption of most of Japan's military resources in Shanghai. In a post-war interview General Zhang Fakui admitted, "Japan had no wish to fight at Shanghai . . ."[8] It is a statement that underestimates the extent to which Japan's commanders were champing for action. "The mood in the army today is that we're going to smash China," Prince Takamatsu, Hirohito's brother, wrote in his diary, "so that it will be ten years before they can stand up straight again."[9] Chiang Kai-shek threw 650,000 troops into the battle for the city and its environs as well as his modest air force of 200 aircraft. Chiang, whose forces were being advised by German officers led by General Alexander von Falkenhausen, was finally confident that his forces could take on the Japanese. A German officer told a British diplomat, "If the Chinese Army follows the advice of the German advisers, it is capable of driving the Japanese over the Great Wall."[10]

Chiang's advisers were overconfident. The modernization program was due for completion in eighteen months' time. Chiang's army had numbers on its side but in every type of modern equipment, from rifles, machine guns, field artillery, and tanks, it was deficient in both quantity and quality. Japan was also able to deploy some 3,000 aircraft, bombers and fighters, which quickly overwhelmed China's air force. In the defining battle of the *Second Sino-Japanese War*, Japan eventually committed over a quarter of a millions troops.

As in the north Japan's strength in tanks, an item of equipment virtually unknown to the Chinese Army, proved the decisive weapon in the *Battle of Shanghai*. In the city that had to be fought for street by street, these technological advantages were partially nullified. In one of the final confrontations at Nanshi on 11 November Japanese forces advanced against Chinese Army units pinned to *Siccawei Creek* on the edge of the French Concession. The French used thousands of small tricolors left over from the Bastille Day celebrations on 14 July, to cordon off their concession from Japanese incursion. Bombed and pressed by tanks, the Chinese troops fled into the French Concession where they surrendered their arms to the French authorities and were duly interned. At 3.34 p.m. Edgar Snow and other foreign journalists witnessed the hoisting of the Rising Sun Flag over *Nanshi* (old town) accompanied by the ritual calls of *banzai*.

The next day German correspondent Wolf Schenk observed, "What life, what crowds had been on the Broadway before! Now the rain poured incessantly from low hanging clouds on the fully deserted streets."[11] After three months of intensive fighting over one of the world's great cities, which had held the world's press in thrall, Shanghai had fallen. Europe and America, if not fully awakened to the Japanese threat, were, apart from *Nazi* Germany, swayed to the Chinese side. Overall 600,000 Chinese troops were pushed back after five months of fighting that ended in November—two months more than the 'three months' that Japanese commanders had promised the Emperor it would take them to conquer the whole of China. Both sides had reason to be dissatisfied with the short-term outcome of the conflict.

An estimated 250,000 Chinese casualties included 150,000 dead while the Japanese Army suffered an estimated 93,000 casualties. Although the battle was a major defeat for China, it gave time for the relocation of industrial assets to central China. It was the beginning of Chiang's strategy of drawing Japan into a long drawn out war of attrition in central China—Japan's worst nightmare and Stalin's perfect outcome.

A few weeks after the start of the war Leon Trotsky made the prophetic analysis that:

> Japan at present represents the weakest link in the capitalist chain. Its military-financial superstructure rests on a foundation of semi-feudal agrarian barbarism. The periodic explosions of the Japanese army simply reflect the unbearable tension of social relations in that country . . . The probable military success of Japan against China will be of significance only as historic episodes. China's resistance, closely linked with the rebirth of that nation, will grow stronger from year to year. Japan's growing difficulties will end in military catastrophe and social revolution.[12]

For Japanese industrialists the prospect of war in China was not altogether unattractive. Ginjiro Fujiwara, President of Oji Paper, and a member of the House of Peers, who later became Minister of Munitions, spoke for many when he argued that the conquest of China would bring benefits:

> A long war does not strike terror into the hearts of the Japanese people . . . Her [China's] military occupation may last from two to three years, even ten years if necessary, until China repents of her past stand . . . During this military occupation an army of robust and hustling Japanese go-getters may invade these territories . . . to double and treble Japanese exports.[13]

The Rape of Nanking [November 1937–January 1938]: In November Lieutenant-General Kasego Nakajima, given operational command of the Imperial Japanese Army's 16th Division, was ordered by ageing General Iwane Matsui, head of Japan's invasion force, to capture the Chinese capital at Nanking. From his sickbed Matsui commanded, "the entry of the Imperial Army into a foreign capital is a great event in our history . . . attracting the attention of the world. Therefore let no unit enter the city in a disorderly fashion."[14]

Matsui's wishes could not have been more brazenly ignored. Cities, towns and villages en route along the *Yangtze River* were destroyed. Suchow (now Suzhou), an ancient city criss-crossed by canals and sometimes described as the 'Venice of the East' was the first city to fall. Lieutenant-General Nakajima had a reputation as a brute and a sadist that was soon to be embellished. A Japanese officer commented, "Nakajima drank too much French civilization. He fancied himself a Robespierre or Danton. He came to

Nanking bringing in special Peking oil for burning bodies."[15] Nakajima did not hold back Japanese troops who were probably incensed by the heavy losses suffered at the *Battle of Shanghai*. Citizens who remained in the city were slaughtered. Younger women were rounded up and sold into sexual slavery, though many were simply raped and murdered. The city's gardens, temples, houses and buildings were ransacked. A British correspondent described a city in which "There is hardly a building standing which has not been gutted by fire. Smouldering ruins and deserted streets present an eerie spectacle, the only living creatures being dogs unnaturally fattened by feasting on corpses."[16]

An officer of the 11th Division that advanced along the *Yangtze River* parallel with Nakajima recalled that "Every night from my sleeping floor I could see the glare of the villages they were firing . . . Burned houses made bad billets. Only cowards are involved in such incidents."[17] Chiang Kai-shek would later claim that the 16th and 6th Japanese Divisions killed 390,000 people in the course of their advance to Nanking. Even allowing for Chiang's propaganda-driven exaggeration of numbers, it is clear that a terrific civilian massacre had taken place.

As the 16th Division approached Nanking, Prince Yasuhiko Asaka (Hirohito's uncle) was appointed to overall command of the Army in place of Matsui, who was sick with tuberculosis, and Nakajima who was wounded. Asaka was a slim taciturn aristocrat who walked with a limp after an accident from a car crash outside Paris in 1923 during his posting as a military intelligence officer. On 8 December an order was issued to senior commanders to "KILL ALL CAPTIVES." Asaka's intelligence officer claimed to have given the order on his own initiative; the truth of his claim could never be substantiated after the war because the intelligence officer died in the caves at Okinawa in 1945. A more detailed command was issued at battalion level: "All prisoners of war are to be executed . . . prisoners . . . are to be brought out from their imprisonment in groups of 50 to be executed . . . our intentions are absolutely not to be detected by the prisoners."[18] The brutal orders may in part have resulted from the Japanese Army's inability to feed its captives. From 9 to 11 December, the 6th and 11th Divisions moved around the walled city in a pincer movement before finally capturing the city on 12 December.

It is estimated that some 50,000 Japanese troops took the surrender of 90,000 Chinese troops within Nanking in addition to the city's 500,000 citizens. The diary of a Japanese soldier, Shiro Azuma, revealed their fears: "Although, we had two companies, and those seven thousand prisoners had already been disarmed, our troops could have been annihilated had they decided to rise up and revolt."[19].

Some were taken to grain fields and killed in small batches. However, in one instance thousands were marched to the river where their hands were tied. Another diarist, Riichi Kurihara, recorded that the Japanese troops then "encircled them in a crescent formation along the river and they were in the sights of many machine guns . . . suddenly all kinds of guns fired at once . . . the sounds of these firearms mingled with desperate yelling and screams."[20] After an hour of shooting, apart from the moans of a few there was silence. For the remainder of the night, Japanese soldiers bayoneted the bodies one by one. Some of the bodies were burnt but when they ran out of oil, many were simply turfed into the river. Later groups were herded into the river to drown. In Nanking itself, troops forced their way into shops and houses, butchered the inhabitants and then looted and set fire to the buildings. Sociologist Lewis Smythe saw that "Scores of refugees in camps and shelters had money and valuables removed from their slight possessions during mass searches."[21] Warehouses were filled with hundreds of pianos, carpets, antique screens and chests. Porcelain, silver and jade were more securely stored. Sales were made to defray Japan's military expenses.

Women suffered particular attention. Kozo Takokoro, a soldier of the 114th Division recalled that "we sent out coal trucks from Hsiakwan to the city streets and villages to seize a lot of women. And then each of them was allocated to 15 to 20 soldiers for sexual intercourse and abuse."[22] Soldiers roared around the city drunk, raping and butchering like a medieval army. In the documentary film *In the Name of the Emperor* [1991], Shiro Azuma admitted that after raping them "we always stabbed and killed them."[23]

Matsui, taken to inspect the city from the heights of the observatory on Chinlin Hill viewed the smouldering city through field glasses. He reflected, "If General Chiang had been patient for a few years longer and avoided hostilities, Japan would have understood the disadvantages of trying to solve the issue between the two countries by the use of arms."[24] In the city itself Matsui was appalled by what he found. To the press he said, "I offer my sympathy, with deep emotion, to a million innocent people."[25] Three hundred regimental commanders were harangued for the orgy of violence. Matsui later confessed that many of the soldiers had laughed at him. At the regimental level raw recruits were trained to be desensitized to torture and murder. Hakudo Nagatomi, who later became a respected doctor in Japan, recalled, "I beheaded people, starved them to death, burned them, and buried them alive, over two hundred in all. It is terrible that I could turn into an animal and do these things. There are really no words to explain what I was doing. I was truly a devil."[26]

Back in Japan the slaughter was welcomed. On 7 December the *Japanese Advertiser* showed no glimmer of shame in the headline '*Sub-Lieutenants in Race to Fell 100 Chinese Running Close Contest.*' It was happily reported that Mukai and Noda "are running neck-to-neck. On Sunday [5 December] . . . the 'score' was: Sub-Lieutenant Mukai 89, and Sub-Lieutenant Noda, 78."[27] Mukai declared that "The contest was fun."[28] Tang Shunsang, who miraculously survived by feigning death in a body pit full of his slaughtered compatriots, recalled the competition as officers shouted out "Kill and count! Kill and count."[29] Supposedly on-looking Japanese troops laughed and took pictures. Historian, Professor Bob Tadashi Wakabayashi and others have shown that while Japanese newspapers published the articles, the stories were apocryphal though as a parable for what actually happened the reported contest contained a large kernel of truth.

In Nanking itself the slaughter of troops turned into an orgy of blood lust. Women were not only raped but also sadistically mutilated. Men were sodomized. One Chinese man was murdered because he refused to commit necrophilia with a dead woman lying in the snow. Buddhist monks were castrated. Parents were humiliated, being forced to watch the rape of their children. Glutted with sex, soldiers amused themselves by ramming objects into the vaginas of captured women.

Foreign nationals intervened with mixed success. However, John Rabe, a committed *Nazi*, who was the head of Siemens China Co., was partially successful in setting up a neutral zone. He took to driving around Nanking sporting a *Nazi swastika* armband and ordering Japanese troops to cease their depredations. To try to raise international awareness Rabe organized photographs of the massacred victims. Surgeon, Dr. Robert Wilson, noted of Rabe, "what a splendid man he is and what a tremendous heart he has, it is hard to reconcile his personality with his adulation of '*Der Fuhrer.*' "[30] Other heroes included Willhelmina Vautrin, Dean of Studies at Ginling Women's Arts and Science College, Professor Lewis Smythe and Presbyterian minister, Plumer Mills.

At great personal risk, on 19 January 1938 George Fitch smuggled out film about the massacre on eight reels of 16 mm film. Stills were later printed in *Life* magazine and legendary photographer, Frank Capra, used them for the documentary movie *The Battle of China* [1944], which formed part of his *Why we Fight*—a US War Department propaganda series. As stories leached into the global media, John Magee in Nanking recalled that the Japanese military hated the Caucasian residents of Nanking more than the enemy for showing them up to the world. The scale of the killing has been widely disputed with just 1,000 deaths admitted to in Japanese histories. Rape of Nanking denial is still implicit in the silence on the subject by leading political figures. By contrast the estimated number of deaths at Nanking goes up from hundreds of thousands, to half a million in Chinese sources. Whatever the real number it should be noted that the Rape of Nanking was merely one incident in a wide-ranging brutal suppression in China, which is estimated to have cost 20 million lives during the course of the *Second Sino-Japanese War*. Broad dissemination of the news of the slaughter became a major factor in the hardening of American public feeling towards Japan. The Rape of Nanking considerably furthered the sentiment that America should help China fight the Japanese invaders.

After the capture of Nanking, Prime Minister Konoe's government offered Chiang Kai-shek harsh terms for peace. China would have to recognize Manchukuo, co-operate with Japan in fighting communism, permit the indefinite stationing of Japanese troops anywhere in China and agree to pay reparations. It was a blueprint for the absorption of China similar to the one that had taken place in Korea twenty-seven years earlier. Chiang refused. He determined to fight a war of liberation and moved his capital first to Wuhan and later to Chongqing. In a counter response to Chiang's refusal to negotiate, the Konoe government broke off any further negotiations and withdrew its recognition of Chiang Kai-shek's government. Over the next year war with China escalated. Large parts of northern, central and southern China were brought under Japanese control. In autumn offenses in 1938 Wuchang, Hankou and Hanyang (the three cities collectively known as Wuhan) were captured along the *Yangtze River* in central China, while in the south Canton (just sixty miles from *Hong Kong*) was also taken. The focus of military effort was the defeat of Chiang and the *Kuomintang* armies rather than the communists, who they largely regarded as bandits who could for the time being be ignored.

On 26 February 1938 Hirohito received Generals Matsui and Asaka at the Imperial court. As a reward for brilliant success achieved at Nanking, they were each gifted a pair of silver vases embossed with the imperial chrysanthemum. Prince Asaka, who had been in disgrace with the Emperor for his support of the *Kodoha*, the Imperial Way Faction, was rehabilitated within the court and could resume his passion for golf, with the odd game played with Hirohito. Matsui retired to Atami where he built a shrine of remorse for the dead at Nanking. In 1939 Nakajima retired in comfort on the spoils he took from Nanking. In the Tokyo War Crimes Trial after the *Pacific War*, Matsui, who had tried and failed to restrain his troops, was charged with responsibility for the Rape of Nanking, was found guilty and executed. Prince Asaka, benefitting from the protection given by General Douglas MacArthur to all the royal family, in spite of being in command throughout the Nanking massacre, was never even summoned to court as a witness.

In November 1937, the Nine-Power Treaty Conference meeting in Brussels, boycotted by Japan, which had assembled to agree what action to take regarding the outbreak of war, ended with no agreement on sanctions. Although in America and Europe, subsequent news of the massacres at Nanking shocked politicians and public alike, there were no further international attempts to coordinate sanctions. In large part the lack of reaction reflected American and British reluctance to antagonize Japan. In particular it was America, already perceived as the global superpower, which, under the guidance of Secretary of State, Cordell Hull, decided the course of passivity that guided international reaction to Japan's foreign policy aggression between 1937 and 1941.

Cordell Hull and the US State Department's Internecine Battles on Japan Policy:
Senator Cordell Hull, a lawyer from Tennessee, was appointed Secretary of State by Roosevelt in March 1933. Hull's political importance to Roosevelt lay in his influence with the southern Democrats. It was an importance that Hull would parley with great skill in protecting his fiefdom in the years ahead. With regard to China, Hull continued the policies of his predecessors in protesting Japan's annexation of Manchuria in 1931–1932, including a refusal to acknowledge the puppet state of Manchukuo. However, he refused to go any further than public condemnation. Although Cordell Hull was an impassioned believer in the virtues of democracy and free trade and pursued the traditional policies of 'open door' with regard to China, as well as the increasingly important doctrine of self-determination, he was set on avoiding any action that might precipitate conflict. Although Japan's launch of a full-scale war fundamentally altered America's perception of Japan and its intentions, Hull refused to budge from his non-interventionist stance.

Others within Roosevelt's administration were less sanguine. Admiral Harry Yarnell, commander of the Asiatic Fleet, spoke for many in the internationalist-minded US Navy when he declared that withdrawal of American engagement in Asia was not an option. "The time has passed when a great nation can increase her safety by such a method."[31] Admiral Leahy, Chief of Naval Operations, supported Yarnell's stance. Even within the

State Department there were murmurings of discontent at Hull's passivity. Asian expert, Stanley Hornbeck, thought, "Yarnell was doing a better job than their own department."[32] Yarnell's request for additional warships to be sent to Shanghai fell on deaf ears. Whatever Roosevelt's positive inclination toward the Navy, warmth from his time as Assistant Navy Secretary, he refused all pleas to undermine his Secretary of State. Even the sinking of USS *Panay* by Japanese bombers as it fled along the *Yangtze River* to escape the *Battle of Nanking*, was greeted with nothing more than strong words. American anger was quickly assuaged when Japan offered to pay full compensation.

In spite of Hull's caution, the *Panay* incident nevertheless hardened America's public attitude toward Japan. Within Roosevelt's administration it was Treasury Secretary, Henry Morgenthau, who took the lead in calling for the President to implement economic sanctions. However, although Roosevelt, in a speech in Chicago in October 1937, called for an international "quarantine of aggressor nations," his actions failed to match his rhetoric. Although America's economic interests in China were now being badly damaged Hull refused to sanction any action that could be construed as aggressive. By the summer of 1938 it became clear to observers in Washington that although Nanking had fallen, China would not easily be conquered. Chiang had removed his capital to Chongqing in the distant southwest of the country and his armies had drawn the Imperial Japanese Army into a costly stalemate in central China. Hull had good reason to do nothing.

However, public outrage was increasing. The bombing of Guangzhou (Canton) in May brought further public outrage. President Hoover's Secretary of State Henry Stimson wrote to Hull complaining of the Japanese barbarities and "future dangers" which were "soon going to explode again. I cannot believe that the opinion of this country would not back up still further expressions and non-military action against Japan's conduct."[33] Under pressure Hull approached Roosevelt to approve a modest plan to prevent American aircraft manufacturers from exporting to Japan by requiring them to seek licenses. It was another modest act that mollified public opinion without doing anything that might lead to open confrontation with Japan.

In Britain too, the public was beginning to pay attention to what was happening in Japan. On 21 January 1938 Winston Churchill drew attention to Japan and their war in China in an article entitled *What Japan Thinks of Us*. He noted that "British policemen in the International Settlement of Shanghai have been punched and manhandled by Japanese soldiers in a manner which shows a deep seated hatred of white people."[34] Churchill took note of Admiral Nobumasa Suetsugu (retired) who declared himself "in favor of driving the white race out of the Far East."[35] Neither did it escape Churchill's notice that soon afterwards, Suetsugu was appointed Home Minister in the First Konoe cabinet. Suetsugu was a strong supporter of German and Italian fascism.

Opinions within the Roosevelt administration covered a broad spectrum of opinion. Although the US Navy remained implacably opposed to Hull's pacifism, the US Army, by contrast, wanted to pull back the Army from Asia. It believed that, not only were the

Philippines indefensible but that Asia was not worth fighting for. The State Department was similarly split. Stanley Hornbeck wanted a tough response while Maxwell Hamilton, head of the Far Eastern Affairs Division, urged caution so as not to provoke Japan into even more aggressive action. In the junior ranks of the State Department, the China specialists favored stronger action to help China, while the Japan specialists warned of actions that might provoke Japan to more bellicose action. European specialists such as Hugh Wilson, who was briefly Ambassador to Germany, returning to the State Department after *Kristallnacht* (Anti-Jewish pogrom 9–10 November 1938), believed that America should leave Japan and China to fight it out and recommended that US foreign policy should focus on Europe alone. Others, like Ambassador Joseph Grew in Tokyo, believed that Japanese moderates would revive and return to power when Japan grew tired of the military excesses of the Army.

Roosevelt continued to talk tough and act weak. At a press conference in April 1939, he warned of the economic dangers faced by America from the 'autarkic' tendencies of the totalitarian states: "The nations of the world that pay better wages and work shorter hours are immediately faced, because of the barter system of the aggressor nations, with a loss of world trade. That is obvious."[36] However, although Roosevelt made it clear that America would not tolerate a loss of world trade to the totalitarian nations, he made no concrete proposals to combat their quest for autarky.

In looking at the economic cost of Japan's domination of Asia, the government in Washington produced figures showing the degree of America's reliance on the region. Asia produced 37 percent of the world's rubber, 17 percent of its tin, 90 percent of its quinine and 28 percent of its palm oil products. Yet in the final analysis none of these products posed an existential threat to the US economy. Tin could be sourced from Bolivia and rubber could be made synthetically. Of more concern to America was the loss of more global markets, Japan and China, to the autarkic ideology of its enemies, which already included the Soviet Union and Germany. In the short term there was no immediate crisis to trigger Roosevelt's interest in more aggressive policies toward Japan. However, with the looming aggression of both Germany and Japan, the threat to America's long-term aims of economic progress based on free trade remained very real. In this sense Japan's New Order and its promotion of a Japan-dominated Co-Prosperity Sphere did represent an existential threat to the United States. As Will Clayton, a cotton millionaire close to Roosevelt explained, "Standing alone in a hostile world, with our foreign trade destroyed, with the colossal readjustments this would entail, and with the enormous sacrifice imposed by total defense, the strain on our traditional way of life would probably be too great."[37] **[Chart: C.1]**

At the Treasury, Morgenthau was scheming to provide loans to China and seeking Roosevelt's support. Hull's under-secretary of state, Sumner Welles, who was a personal friend of the President, was, like Morgenthau, a 'hawk.' When Hull left Washington on 25 November 1939 for a conference of Latin American states in Lima, Bolivia, Welles took his opportunity to devise a broad ranging economic strategy against Japan including the end of gold sales, the blocking of credit, the embargoing of goods to Japan, the blacklisting of Japanese companies and the abrogation of the 1911 commercial treaty. However, after failing to enlist enough support within the administration for his measures, the only action left on the table for Roosevelt to consider on 9 December was the proposal for a China credit, which he duly approved. Even the US$25m, little more than a morale booster, was delayed by Hull when he returned.

A further indication of the extent of Hull's policy of appeasement was America's lack of protest when a pusillanimous British government, led by Prime Minister Neville Chamberlain, signed the *Craigie-Arita Agreement* in July 1939, which, in regard to British interests in its international settlements in Shanghai, curtailed their rights and allowed Japan 'special requirements.' The agreement came a few weeks after an isolationist Congress rejected a revised neutrality bill. To Japan's hawks, it appeared that the western powers were weak and not prepared to defend their Asian interests. Appeasement did not temper the appetite of Japan's militarists, but merely increased their hunger. At this moment of seeming spineless passivity, Congress forced Roosevelt into an aggressive response. In spite of Hull's prevarication, when Senator Arthur Vandenberg introduced a resolution calling for the abrogation of the 1911 *Treaty of Commerce and Navigation* with Japan, Hull, faced by a damaging public debate on the subject, decided to be proactive. The result was that on 26 July 1939 Roosevelt gave the required six months' notice to terminate the *Treaty of Commerce and Navigation*. Yet six months later, when the treaty expired, nothing changed. There were no embargoes. Without any assurances as to the future, however, Japan's rulers knew that they operated at America's sufferance. Far from allaying Japan's fear, American passivity merely highlighted its economic dependence on the major western power.

American policy toward Asia began to turn less conciliatory in 1940, not so much because of what the Japanese were doing but as a result of sweeping German victories in Europe. With France conquered and Britain isolated and facing invasion, Roosevelt's whole geopolitical stance was moved from his former position of rhetorical posturing. In May 1940 Roosevelt requested US$1.3bn in military appropriations; an American Congress fast losing its isolationist veneer readily granted this massive increase in defense expenditure. In June Roosevelt ordered immediate supply of US$41m of surplus military stocks to Great Britain. In the same month Roosevelt established what was in effect a war cabinet with the inclusion of two Republicans, Henry Stimson as Secretary of War and Frank Knox, Secretary of the Navy. While the ramp up in US defense expenditure was not exactly a mobilization for war, it was a mobilization to be prepared for war.

At the same time that America was gearing up its military capabilities, Japan began to give indications of its appetite for a region of control, which extended far beyond China. On 29 June 1940, Foreign Minister Hachiro Arita, during his third spell in the office since 1936, gave a radio address entitled *The International Situation and Japan's Position* in which he announced Japan's intention to establish a "bloc of Asian nations led by the Japanese and free of western powers."[38] Arita insisted that the world was destined to fall into four spheres of interest—a Europe controlled by Germany, the Soviet Union, America and an Asian sphere dominated by Japan:

> The countries of East Asia and the regions of the south seas are geographically, historically, racially and economically very closely related to each other. They are destined to co-operate and minister to one another's needs for their common wellbeing and prosperity and to promote peace and prosperity in their regions. The uniting of all these regions under a single sphere on the basis of common existence and ensuring thereby the stability of that sphere is, I think, a natural conclusion.[39]

While Japan's Asian ambitions were of concern to the White House, it was America's material needs for its military build-up that forced it toward a policy of embargo. In January 1940, the Army-Navy Munitions board had identified twenty-nine strategically essential products. In some cases supplies were limited yet America had no mechanism other than an agreed gentleman's 'moral embargo' to prevent foreign nations' purchase of those essential materials increasingly necessary for America's own military mobilization. A new agency was required. At first Hull attempted to thwart new legislation by bottling up proposals in committee but by April 1940 even he became persuaded of the need to build stockpiles of essential commodities. The *National Defense Act*, signed into law by Roosevelt on 2 July 1940 gave the President the power to declare certain goods vital to national defense and enabled him to put them on 'license,' without which they could not be exported.

Within a year 259 items were given 'license' status. In practice, exports continued to be allowed to friendly nations. It soon became evident to the petroleum section of the National Defense Advisory Commission (NDAC) charged with overseeing America's needs pertaining to the *National Defense Act* that there was a particular problem with regard to aviation gasoline. While America was currently self-sufficient in aviation gasoline, Robert Wilson, director of the NDAC's petroleum group pointed out that, bearing in mind the massive increase in intended military aircraft production, there were insufficient stocks of aviation gasoline to power the projected new air force. The Washington hawks, hitherto stymied by Hull, were now reinforced by the additions of Stimson and Knox. They pounced on this new information regarding a potential aviation gasoline shortage as a means of curtailing Japanese aggression. Morgenthau tried to use the opportunity to create an embargo for all oil products to Japan. He circulated information that not only was Japan buying up all available supplies from the west coast of America but that even exports to Spain were being redirected to Japan.

However, Hull remained determined not to give Japan any cause for provocation. In the end, a fudge was agreed. Roosevelt agreed to an embargo on all oil over 87-octane. It was a crucial number. American aircraft operated on 100-octane fuel while Japanese aero engines needed 86-octane fuel. At the same time as this announcement, the export of iron scrap to Japan was also embargoed. Perversely, the July 1940 ban on 87-octane fuel led to a 550 percent increase in the purchase of 86-octane fuel over the next five months compared to the preceding five months. Imports of oil into Japan increased from 1.2 million barrels in 1939 to 3.4 million barrels in the first six months after the so-called embargo. Most of this oil was at the 87-octane limit. Meanwhile in Japan, the mere threat of an embargo caused them to increase their demands on the Dutch East Indies to supply them with 3 million tons per annum versus 1 million tons previously. Japan also demanded that 20 percent of the crude that they received should be treated with tetraethyl lead to enable aviation gasoline to be produced after it was refined. What became clear from this episode was the critical touch-point of oil supply. **[Charts: I.1, I.3, I.5]**

Franklin D. Roosevelt: From Isolation to Intervention [1933–September 1941]: At the best of times Franklin Delano Roosevelt (FDR) was a difficult man to read. Henry Wallace, his former Vice-President said of him, "He doesn't know any man and no man knows him. Even his own family doesn't know anything about him."[40] "I am like a cat," he said about himself, "I make a stroke, and then I relax."[41] Loved and respected as a leader, seemingly happiest in the company of women, he was an enigma—detached, enigmatic and ruthless. While flying over Cairo, Roosevelt glanced out of the window and said "Ah my friend the Sphinx."[42] It was a testament to his ability to attract and deceive that in the 1940s, Roosevelt, a wheelchair cripple, seems to have been able to conduct concurrent affairs with Lucy Mercer, his wife's one time private secretary, Marguarite 'Missy' LeHand, his own private secretary and Princess Martha of Sweden who resided in the White House for part of the war. All the while he continued a marriage of political convenience with his wife Eleanor. Similarly in his public life, he seemed to prefer "unresolved jurisdictions."[43] His approach to foreign policy was no different, and having died in office and without an autobiography to guide the way, there is little evidence to go on with regard to a grand plan—if one ever existed.

In foreign affairs, as in his private life, Roosevelt never seems to have had a grand plan. For obvious reasons, when he came to office on 3 March 1933, his presidency would be largely occupied with the domestic US economy, which had contracted by 25 percent in the Great Depression that followed the Wall Street Crash. His main concerns would revolve around issues of the New Deal and the federal programs that helped sustain a partial recovery of the US economy in the 1930s from the depths of the deflation of the early 1930s. Foreign policy, for which the greater part of his fame lies today, took a distant back seat. In 1937, as China was being invaded, Roosevelt and the American press were far more interested in the *Judicial Procedures Reform Bill* (later known as the court packing plan), which was an ultimately failed attempt by the President to overcome a Republican majority on the Supreme Court.

In his first presidential election campaign against incumbent President Herbert Hoover, FDR said "I think Hoover's [foreign] policy is about right."[44] On 9 January 1933, Roosevelt asked Hoover's Secretary of State, Henry Stimson, to see him. They got along famously. So much so that Roosevelt appointed Stimson, a Republican, Secretary for War in July 1940. Roosevelt's preference for Republicans in foreign affairs probably reflected his suspicion of state department officials from his earlier days of public office. He would probably have agreed with his closest political friend and confidante, Harry Hopkins, that Foreign Service officers were "cookie pushers, pansies—and usually isolationists to boot."[45] Roosevelt, not only endorsed Stimson's embargo of arms to belligerents but also, more controversially, agreed with the 'Stimson Doctrine,' not to recognize territories that had been gained through aggression. The *leitmotif* of this doctrine was Japan's annexation of Manchuria. Much to Japan's chagrin, the 'autonomous' state of Manchukuo was never recognized. It was a policy of which many of his advisers disapproved. Roosevelt was not dissuadable: "I have always had the deepest sympathy for the Chinese. How could you expect me not to go along with Stimson on Japan."[46] In another controversial move, Roosevelt also recognized the Soviet Union, believing that not doing so had outlived its usefulness. He also noted that the Soviets' rivalry with Japan might put a brake on the latter's expansion in the Far East. It was a pragmatic, non-ideological approach that characterized his presidency.

If Roosevelt was pro-Chinese, he did very little to help them in his first seven years of office. Although America was alive to the economic possibilities of China, he did not view Chinese trade and the American concession in Shanghai as something worth fighting the Japanese over. The claim by the linguistic philosopher turned radical left-wing polemicist, Noam Chomsky, that America went to war over China in pursuit of economic interests misses the most important of nuances. While Roosevelt and Hull concluded that the China trade alone was not worth a war with Japan, Roosevelt did believe that war was worth fighting if it was to defend the world's free market trading system, which the rise of totalitarian states threatened in Europe and Asia. Free trade, after all, underlay the prosperity enjoyed by the United States. A more pertinent criticism of Roosevelt was made by George Kennan who argued in 1951 that the mistake of the Anglo-Saxon powers "had been to allow the totalitarian dictatorships to accumulate so much power that the aid of one would be necessary to defeat the other."[47]

While, like his Secretary of State, Cordell Hull, Roosevelt espoused 'open door' trade policies and the 'self-determination' of nations, in the calculation of America's self-interest, the Japanese occupation of Manchuria and later northern China were not issues over which America would either fight a war or provoke Japan to fight a war. This was not to say that Roosevelt had no interest in the region—far from it. As historian Christopher Thorne has written, "America's interest in the Far East was based on the undeniable fact that it had become a Great Power, and thus it had to be interested in the region."[48]

The United States had indisputably emerged from *World War I* as, in economic terms, the great world power. Its industrial, economic and political lead was clearly established: the Washington Conference in 1922, which fixed the ratios of capital ships that the United States, Britain, Japan, France and Italy could build, demonstrated the extent to which America had become the world's superpower. The British Navy was furious at the terms that they felt America had forced upon them. The Japanese were incandescent. Thereafter however, America had pulled back from international involvement. Congress refused to sanction participation in the League of Nations. The

American public, appalled by the carnage on the Western Front in *World War I*, turned its back on what they viewed to be the corrupt ways of monarchical old Europe. After the Wall Street Crash, foreign concerns moved even further away from the public consciousness. The annexation of Manchuria and Japan's creeping advance in north China was not enough to arouse American opinion. The legendary American columnist, Walter Lippmann, was expressing the majority view when he wrote in 1936, "The policy of the United States is to remain free and untangled. Let us follow that policy. Let us make no alliances. Let us make no commitments."[49]

Without American public opinion at his back, Roosevelt, whatever his views on trade or self-determination, was not going to go out on a limb for China. Furthermore Roosevelt was strict in his insistence that the conduct of policy did not leak from the control of his Secretary of State, Cordell Hull. On occasions when Roosevelt appeared to bend to the pleading of hawks such as Morgenthau, Ickes or individuals in the state department, he allowed Hull to whip him back into line. In part this reflected Hull's political importance and in part it reflected his understanding of Hull's line which was that, however abhorrent Japan's expansion, it was not in America's interest to provoke a war—a policy that remained consistent until the oil embargo of July 1941.

This policy did not prevent FDR from testing the water of public opinion as he did with his famous Chicago speech on 5 October 1937, in which he said,

> When an epidemic of physical disease starts to spread,
> the community approves and joins in a quarantine of the
> patients in order to protect the health of the community
> against the spread of the disease. War is a contagion . . .
> The peace of the world is today being threatened . . . We
> are determined to keep out of the war, yet we cannot
> insure ourselves against the disastrous effects of war and
> the dangers of involvement.[50]

The response was mixed. The American Federation of Labor resolved, "American labor does not wish to be involved in European or Asian wars."[51] The *Wall Street Journal* proclaimed: "Stop Foreign Meddling; America wants peace"[52] The *Chicago Tribune* and the Hearst press were caustic while the *New York Times* and *Washington Post* were supportive. International reaction was positive apart from Berlin and Tokyo. White House mail was four to one in favor. Nobody knew what quarantine meant—not even Roosevelt, who had no specific policies in mind. As the *Times* reported, "Mr. Roosevelt was defining an attitude not a program."[53] Roosevelt, still isolationist, was nevertheless against 'peace at any price.'

American policy did, by degrees, become more assertive in terms of trade. Public sentiment toward Japan began to change significantly after news of the Rape of Nanking and then the sinking of the USS *Panay*, a gunboat, twenty miles north of Nanking on the *Yangtze River*. The incident brought focus and outrage toward Japanese expansionism. On the *Panay* three people were killed and fifty wounded, including Lieutenant-

Commander James Hughes who was hit by shrapnel. Norman Alley, a *Universal News* photographer who happened to be aboard, remembered that Hughes, ". . . staggered; clutched suddenly at his neck. Blood spurted from his throat like water from a spigot."[54] Commander Hughes heroically returned to his post before being forced to abandon his sinking ship. Two Standard Oil tankers were also sunk. The US warship was clearly marked with American insignia. Norman Alley filmed the attack, the first ever of an aerial bombardment. At the cost of US$25,000, the film was flown in relays back to Washington. It took ten days to reach America where Roosevelt and his advisers viewed it first in the White House. It is a telling fact about Roosevelt's determination not to provoke the Japanese that he insisted that twenty seconds were taken out of the film because they were too incendiary. On New Year's Eve, the newsreel movie *The Sinking of the Gunboat Panay* [1937] premiered at Pantages Theater in Hollywood, before the main event, which was the comedy musical movie *Damsel in Distress* [1937], with a screenplay by P.G. Wodehouse and music by George Gershwin, starring Fred Astaire, George Burns and Gracie Allen. Putting Hollywood's finest into the shade, it was *The Sinking of the Gunboat Panay* that caused a sensation.

Before *The Sinking of the Gunboat Panay* [1937] was aired, both sides hushed up the whole episode. Admiral Yonai claimed that the bombardment of the *Panay* had been done above cloud cover, whereas Alley's newsreel showed that it had been a sunny blue-sky day making the US ship easily visible. In spite of these disclaimers, Foreign Minister, Koki Hirota, rushed to apologize for the 'mistake' and made a full compensation payment of US$2.2m. The Japanese bomber commander was relieved of his post.

It was not just the general public that had to be calmed down. Hawks in Roosevelt's administration urged him to take strong retaliatory action. At a cabinet meeting, Interior Secretary, Harold Ickes, spoke for many when he asked, "If we have to fight her, isn't this the best possible time?"[55] Congress, albeit riled, remained isolationist. Senator Henrik Shipstead from Minnesota asked for withdrawal of all forces from America's China concessions. In spite of his pacifist intent, Roosevelt was nevertheless determined to keep a free hand. In January 1938 Roosevelt fought vigorously to vote down a constitutional amendment introduced by Indianapolis democrat representative Lewis Ludlow, which called for a referendum before the US could go to war.

In spite of the Panay Incident, the widely reported atrocities of the *Second Sino-Japanese War* and Hitler's invasion of France, American public opinion remained firmly isolationist. In October 1939 a Gallup Poll revealed that 84 percent wanted Britain and France to win the war versus 2 percent who favored Germany. Yet 95 percent wanted America to stay out of the war. Roosevelt was with his electorate. He had an election to fight. Many would have agreed with Charles Lindbergh, the legendary aviator and a leading light of the isolationist America First Committee, who told a rally in New York, "We cannot win this war for England regardless of how much assistance we send."[56] Roosevelt's Republican opponent, Wendell Wilkie, had pacifist speechwriters such as Vicar-General Father James Drought who provided him with 'pulpit' lines such as "Must we dance to every rumbling of foreign drums?"[57] As late as July 1940, Roosevelt told the state department, "We are not going to get into a war by forcing Japan into a position where she is going to fight for some reason or another."[58] But that is exactly what he did a year later.

It is hard to disagree with Robert Dallek's conclusion in that he was abreast and possibly even a little ahead of public feeling. As one observer noted, he "listened to every rustle in the leaves and built up his own position with unending care and subtlety."[59]

It is clear that Roosevelt was prepared to deceive Congress and the US public when required. Critics such as the conspiracy theorist-historian Charles Beard claimed that Roosevelt misled the public and Congress and thus dragged them into war. The reality was quite the reverse. As the Panay Incident reveals, Roosevelt's deceptions were aimed at defusing the potential bellicosity of the American public—at least until it became clear that there was no recourse other than war. Roosevelt, through his speeches and famed 'fire-side' chats was a master of the media manipulation of the general public, but even he knew the limits and uses of these dark arts. He was determined that diplomacy and the maneuvering of international relations should be controlled without the interference of public hysteria. In diplomacy, he considered lying to the general public a necessary precondition for success, recognizing that international negotiation is made all but impossible if details of diplomatic maneuvering are publicly aired in the process. In this respect Roosevelt's deceits were perfectly acceptable by the standards of his or any other time.

There were domestic political considerations to his foreign policy. Although there had been some shift in public sentiment toward a more active foreign policy, the country was still in essence isolationist. Roosevelt, who had won a landslide victory in the 1936 presidential contest, was not confident that he could win a third term in 1940 against a Republican candidate with a peace platform. In part, political considerations may have contributed to his seemingly anaemic reaction to the Japanese occupation of North Vietnam in September 1940, two months before the presidential elections. Roosevelt embargoed all types of iron and steel for Japan and agreed a US$100m loan for China. It was a minimal response to partially assuage the hawks in the press, in Congress, and within his administration. But in October 1940 he refused to send to *Singapore* a naval squadron that Churchill had requested.

Even after his third and sweeping election victory against Republican Wendell Wilkie, Roosevelt continued to pursue a largely conciliatory line with Japan. Roosevelt said to the new, supposedly dovish, Ambassador Admiral Kichisaburo Nomura in early 1941, "There is plenty of room in the *Pacific* area for everybody. It would not do this country any good nor Japan any good, but both of them harm to get into war."[60] As late as 14 July 1941 when Morgenthau at cabinet pressed FDR for a response with regard to sanctions, Roosevelt was adamant in his desire to pursue peace with Japan: "Well to my surprise [wrote Morgenthau] the President gave us quite a lecture why we should not make any move because if we did, if we stopped all oil, it would simply drive the Japanese down to the Dutch East Indies, and it would mean war."[61] Stark and Marshall concurred. Admiral Stark voiced the opinion that "Every day that we are able to maintain peace and still support the British is valuable time gained."[62] As Roosevelt had told

Ickes, who had threatened to resign on the issue of supplying oil to Japan, " . . . it is terribly important for the control of the *Atlantic* for us to keep peace in the *Pacific*. I simply do not have enough navy to go around."[63]

From 1933 to the end of July 1941, it is clear that Roosevelt trod a carefully choreographed path in dealing with Japan. His purposes were various. Until the outbreak of war in Europe his political strategy was to stay in touch with American voters who were avowedly isolationist in sentiment and to warn Japan off by the possibility of economic consequences. After 1939 and until July 1941, Roosevelt's main focus was on the need to control the *Atlantic* in order to support Great Britain's war with *Nazi* Germany. As General Marshall advised the President, "If we lose in the Atlantic we lose everywhere."[64] The possibility of war with Japan was a distraction from Roosevelt's main purpose, which was to preserve a Europe free from tyranny and open to trade with America. While Roosevelt fully sympathized with China, compared to Europe it was never the main deal in terms of America's geopolitical priorities.

Mongolia and Northern China: Fulcrum of Dispute between Russia, China, America, Great Britain and Japan: The border disputes along the Russian-Manchurian borders that characterize the fraught geopolitical relationship between Russia, China and Japan in the early twentieth century were more obscurely played out further west in Mongolia.

Mongolia, with its miniscule population of less than a million citizens in 1911, was important because of its vast land mass—more than Great Britain, France and Germany combined—and its geographic location between Russia to the north, China to the south and Manchuria to the east. The state, which traced its modern origins to 1206 with the establishment of the Mongol Empire by Genghis Khan, had long been in decline. His grandson, Kublai Khan had conquered China and initiated the Mongol Yuan Dynasty in 1271. It was a short-lived dynasty. Just shy of 100 years later, in 1368, the Muslim Yuan dynasty, riven by corruption was overthrown by Muslim as well as Han nobles, thus laying the foundation for the Ming dynasty.

The Mongols retreated to their homelands where they fell back into a pattern of tribal rivalry. After the rise of Manchuria's Qing dynasty in the mid-nineteenth century, Mongolia was absorbed into the Chinese empire. Albeit allowed a significant degree of autonomy, Mongolia remained in this vassal relationship until the overthrow of the Qing dynasty in 1911.

In the power vacuum and chaos created by Sun Yat Sen's revolution, Mongolia launched its bid for independence—a bid that was characterized by a unique societal development derived from the sixteenth-century arrival of Tibetan Buddhism. By 1911 Buddhist monks comprised approximately one third of Mongolia's male population. Until then, social if not ultimate political power rested with the *Jebtsundamba Khutuktu* (Mongolian Holy Precious Master) who was the country's spiritual head, tracing his lineage back to the *Gelug* school of Tibetan Buddhism. Perhaps not surprisingly the revolutionary government that emerged created a theocratic state, which was led by the eighth *Jebtsundamba Khutuku* called Bogd Khan. Although his renouncement of any continuing contractual obligation that Mongolia had to the Qing dynasty was disputed by General Yuan Shikai, the new President of the Republic of China, the theocratic party remained in power until October 1919. Three years after Yuan Shikai's death, which brought to an end the 83-day Hongxian dynasty, Xu Shuzheng, cabinet secretary, confederate and deputy commander of Duan Qirui, who was China's new premier, invaded Mongolia with his grandly named Northwest Frontier Defense Army and forced Bogd Khan to renounce his declaration of autonomy.

It was a short-lived rule. When it became known that Premier Duan Qirui was being secretly financed by Japan, the so called Nishihara Loans, and that the Western powers had secretly concluded a treaty to transfer the former German coastal colonies of Shandong to Japan at the *Treaty of Versailles*, dissent erupted throughout China in what became known as the May Fourth Movement on 4 May 1919. It was an important moment in galvanizing the *Kuomintang*'s campaign to regain control of China from foreign imperialists and particularly Japan.

In the meantime, Duan mobilized his National Pacification Army to defeat his government rivals Cao Kun and Wu Peifu, the leading members of the Zhili clique. In the following *Zhili-Anhui War*, Duan's Japanese-financed army was smashed by the alliance of the Zhili's Traitor Suppression Army and the Fengtian (Manchurian) warlord army led by Zhang Zuolin. But the Zhili and Fengtian allies would fall out two years later, starting the First *Zhili-Fengtian War* in 1922, which ended with the temporary defeat and fall of the Fengtian leader, Zhang Zuolin. The Second *Zhili-Fengtian War*, starting in September 1924, was fought by the Japanese-backed Fengtian clique of warlords based in Manchuria and the Zhili clique in Peking backed by Anglo-American business interests. The Anglo-American Zhili interests were defeated at the *Battle of Tianjin* in October, leading to the re-emergence of the pro-Japanese Duan Qirui as China's figurehead premier. In the south meanwhile a *Kuomintang* Army, which was being trained up at the Whampoa Military Academy financed by the Soviet Union, and was unencumbered by the warlord civil war further north, prepared itself for the Great Northern Expedition. Led by Chiang Kai-shek, the *Kuomintang Army* eventually unified China in 1928.

In addition, in this new power vacuum created by the *Zhili-Fengtian Wars*, Mongolia became independent again under Bogd Khan in 1921 when the forces of Chen Yi, who had replaced Xu Shuzheng, were defeated by a Russian-Mogul army led by General Baron Roman von Ungern-Sternberg, an eccentric and famously violent White Russian commander with a partiality to Vajrayana Buddhism, who was known by his own troops as the "Mad Baron." Ungern-Sterberg's influence was short lived. When he invaded Siberia in support of anti-Bolshevik rebels, he was defeated by a Red Army-Mongolian force in June 1921, captured, tried and executed. Thereafter Bogd Khan theocratic government continued under Bolshevik protection until 1924 when the 8th *Jebtsundamba Khutuktu* died of cancer—though it was broadly assumed that he had been murdered by the NKVD (the forerunner of the KGB). Bogd Khan was not replaced.

Furthermore, Japan's ability to influence the outcome of the Mongolian civil war was cut short by the decision to withdraw its 70,000 strong army from Siberia in 1922, though Japan continued to finance the Fengtian cliques' attempts to control northern China. Japan's Siberian Expeditionary Army was the last remains of a pro-White Russian expedition force comprising American, British, Italian and French forces that had been sent to Siberia after the Russian Revolution. Thereafter a communist Mongolian People's Republic, backed by the Soviet Union, purged the state of independence sympathizers; it remained a Soviet vassal state until 1991.

As the story of Mongolia's brief post-war experience of independence and the extraordinarily chaotic smorgasbord of northern Chinese politics shows, the implosion of Chinese power and stability in the aftermath of the 1911 revolution was an open invitation to inference from foreign powers. Ultimately the importance of Mongolia's effective annexation by the Soviet Union and the interference of the US and Great Britain in Northern Chinese politics, was that it fitted into the Japanese ultranationalists' narrative that Japan was under threat of being surrounded and overwhelmed by the Soviet Union, Europe's greatest land power. If the Imperial Japanese Navy considered the American Navy from the east its greatest threat, the Imperial Japanese Army considered the Soviet Union in the north in the same light.

The geopolitical significance of the Soviet Union's effective annexation of Mongolia was most keenly felt by Japan's *Kwantung* Army in Korea. It was a key element in the background to the *Kwantung* Army's annexation of Manchuria in 1931 and their subsequent expansion into northern China. With some degree of logic, Japan's leaders began to fear that unless it took control of a weak Chinese state, the Soviet Union would fill the power vacuum. By 1939 therefore, it was not Chinese but Japanese and Soviet forces that glowered aggressively at each other across the borders of Siberia, Mongolia and Manchuria. **[See Chapter 39: Japanese–Soviet Conflict in Siberia, Mongolia and Manchuria]**

The Battles of Nomonhan (Khalkhin Gol) [May–September 1939] and the Soviet Threat to Japan: **[Map: 3.5]** The Soviet Union posed little threat to Japan in its early years. From 1918 the Soviets' main concerns were with security on its western and southern borders. However, after the Army reforms effected by General Mikail Frunze and then General Kliment Voroshilov, the situation changed. By 1935 the Red Army comprised 1.5 million soldiers, 16 cavalry divisions, 90 infantry divisions, 7,000 tanks, and 150,000 lorries.

Soviet interest in the Far East revived first with an agreement in 1924 signed with Manchurian warlord Chang Tso-lin for joint administration of the Chinese Eastern Railway by Russia and China. In 1929 Russia reasserted its military strength in the region when Marshal Vasily Blyukher led Soviet forces against raids by the new Manchurian ruler Chang Hsueh-liang at Fukdin on the Soviet side of the *Amur River*. As the Soviet Army revived so did Japanese fears about its intentions in the Far East. By the same measure the Mukden Incident and Japan's annexation of Manchuria led to an even greater Soviet interest in their eastern borders—their concerns only heightened when the Soviet offer of a non-aggression pact in 1932 was rejected by Japan. In the next two years there were 150 border incidents between the Soviet Union and Manchukuo, a rate that doubled again by 1936.

Japanese expansionism was evident from their developing interest in Inner Mongolia. Demchugdongrub, who was later given the title Prince De Wang by Emperor Pu-yi, was backed to create a puppet state comprising Inner Mongolia and the Northern Chinese province of Suiyan in 1936. De Wang's control of the region was finally established after the start of the *Second Sino-Japanese War* in 1937 following the defeat of the *Kuomintang* at the *Battle of Taiyuan*. In 1941 De Wang became Chairman of the Autonomous Mongolian Federation.

In May 1937, the Soviets inserted themselves more meaningfully into Chinese affairs when they agreed a non-aggression pact with Chiang Kai-shek in a deal which included a US$100m loan to buy military equipment from the Soviets. Meanwhile border clashes between Soviet and Japanese forces had increased in intensity. March 1936 saw Japanese scouting tanks attacked and destroyed by Soviet artillery. In June 1937, when three Soviet gunboats crossed the center-line of the *Amur River* to occupy *Kanchazu Island*, the 1st Division of the Imperial Japanese Army responded by launching an artillery barrage that sank Soviet gunboats, forcing the Soviets to retreat. The next year saw an even larger engagement of Soviet forces at the *Battle of Changkufeng*. The Soviets lost ninety-six tanks and suffered 5,000 casualties including 1,500 deaths. Conversely the Japanese government believed that the Soviets were not abiding by the border demarcations agreed at the *Treaty of Peking* [1860]. The Soviet irritant was such that the 'strike north' supporting Foreign Minister Sadao Araki suggested that "if the Soviets do not cease to annoy us, I shall have to purge Siberia as one cleans a room of flies."[65] Japanese attitudes to the Soviets veered from fear to contempt.

However, the ease with which these Soviet incursions were dealt with, led to complacency on the part of the *Kwantung* Army. It was a complacency that was heightened by the Case of Trotskyist Anti-Soviet Military Organization, a secret trial in the Soviet Union orchestrated by Stalin as part of the Great Purge, which weeded out perceived enemies in the armed forces. In his quest for absolute power, Stalin saw the 42-year-old Mikhail Tukhachevsky, who had just been promoted to Marshal, as his greatest threat. Tukhachevsky had transformed the Soviet Army and introduced sophisticated equipment in the form of modern tanks and aircraft and developed systems for their interlocking deployment. An educated and sophisticated man, Tukhachevsky, a violinist, whose friends included the composer Dimitri Shostakovich, was arrested and tortured. His signed confession was later found spattered with blood. Tukhachevsky and senior generals Iona Yakir, Ieronim Uborevich, Robert Eideman, August Kork, Vitovt Putna, Boris Feldman and Vitaly Primakov were accused of a conspiracy against the state, denied defense lawyers and were duly found guilty and executed on the night of 11–12 June 1937. Over the course of the next year 37,761 officers were purged from the Red Army of which 10,868 were arrested and 7,211 found guilty of anti-Soviet crimes.

It was assumed in Japan that the effectiveness of the Red Army had been badly compromised. General Masaharu Homma, Director of Military Intelligence in Tokyo, who would later lead Japanese forces in the defeat of General MacArthur in the Philippines, concluded that "The Soviet Army is down and out and can do nothing for some time."[66].

Nevertheless by 1938 the Soviets had built up their Far Eastern forces under Marshal Blyukher to twenty Infantry Divisions and three cavalry divisions, 330,000 troops in all. They had enough supplies for two years of war and outnumbered Japanese forces in Northern Manchukuo by two to one. Blyukher was tried and executed on Stalin's orders on 9 November 1938. Nevertheless Russian units began to reinforce Mongolian ones as far east as Tamsag Bulag, south of *Lake Buir* and the *Halha River*. Red Army movements seemed to pose a threat, spuriously as it turned out, to Manchukuo's security. Meanwhile total Japanese forces in Manchukuo had increased under the command of General Hideki Tojo from 95,000 to 400,000 by 1938 as he prepared the province for a war on two fronts.

With both the Soviet Union and Japan building up their forces in the region, given the disputes over borders, a conflagration was always a possibility. It finally occurred over an innocuous incursion by Mongol horsemen when they crossed east over the *Khalkhin Gol River* on 10 May 1939. For Japan, Manchuria's borders stood at the *Khalkhin Gol River* while the Soviets accepted a line that was 16 miles further east at Nomonhan. The Mongol horsemen were driven off but Lieutenant-General Michitaro Komatsubara, commander of the 23rd Division, a dandy poet, diarist and lover of whisky and sake, sent Lieutenant-Colonel Yaozo Azuma on a scouting mission. On 28 May Azuma's forces were surrounded by Mongolian units and destroyed. After suffering 97 men killed and 33 wounded, on 29 May, Azuma, with just 25 men remaining, perished in a final *banzai* charge. On 31 May Soviet Foreign Minister, Vyacheslav Molotov warned Tokyo that the *Soviet-Mongolian Treaty* [1936] included the Soviet undertaking to defend the borders of the Mongolian People's Republic.

In retaliation Lieutenant-General Komatsubara crossed the *Khalkhin Gol River* at the end of June. It was a disorderly, poorly prepared crossing in which Japanese forces lacked sufficient artillery or tanks. General Georgi Zhukov, a brilliant tank specialist much trusted by Stalin, who had recently arrived to take command of the Soviet Forces, launched a characteristically aggressive attack with 500 tanks. Zhukov later noted that "Our trump cards were the armored detachments . . . and we decided to use them immediately in order to destroy the Japanese troops that had just crossed the river, not letting them entrench themselves and organize anti-tank defense."[67] Heavy fighting continued for over a month along a 1.5 mile stretch of river but finally petered out into a stalemate.

Komatsubara planned another offensive for 20 August but was pre-empted by Zhukov's attack four days earlier. Japanese positions were bombarded by 557 aircraft. While 50,000 Soviet and Mongolian soldiers defended the east bank of the river, Zhukov launched three divisions across the river in a double envelopment that had completely surrounded the Japanese 23rd Division when the Soviet forces linked up at Nomonhan on 25 August. Komatsubara's breakout failed and within a week his forces were all but destroyed. Just 400 of his troops survived. His forces, short of food and water, plagued by mosquitoes, had suffered an ignominious and crushing defeat. Japanese forces suffered 45,000 casualties, mostly killed, four times the number of Soviets. Komatsubara reflected, "I thought I ought to have died, but I was ordered to return. I broke through the tight encirclement and came back. Now I'll do my bit to rebuild the Division and restore its reputation."[68] Six years later Zhukov boasted to Eisenhower's Chief of Staff, Bedell Smith, that "The Japanese are not good against armor. It took about ten days to beat them."[69]

The *Battles of Nomonhan* had shown that on the wide-open Siberian Steppes, the Japanese light tanks, mainly Type-89 I-Go medium tanks and Type-95 Ha-Go light tanks with their short barrels were no match for their much heavier, faster, long-barrelled Russian counterparts—mainly the Bystrokhodny 'Betushka' BT-5s and BT-7s which had been designed by the brilliant American Grand Prix driver and engineer, J. Walter Christie, who spent his life having his designs rejected by the US war department.

Nomonhan was also notable for its intensive use of aircraft—over 800 (250 lost) for the Soviets and 250 (160 lost) for the Japanese. The Soviets, who were still developing, supposedly more maneuverable, biplane fighters, found that the Polikarpov I-153 *Chayka* (Seagull), introduced in 1938, was no match for the standard Japanese Army monoplane fighter, the Nakajima Ki-27 (later called the 'Nate' by the Allies). However, by the end of the conflict, the Polikarpov I-16 *Ishak* (Donkey) monoplane, which was first introduced in 1934, was competitive when it was uprated in Type-18 format with a larger 830hp engine with a two-speed supercharger and a variable pitch propeller. More heavily built than the Ki-27, the *Ishak* could power dive out of a dogfight and could better withstand hits. The *Battles of Nomonhan* showed that the philosophy of producing planes that were more maneuverable was misguided and that in aerial combat "high speed, a strong structure and powerful armament turned out to be decisive for victory."[70]

Hitherto it was the most heavily fought aerial battle in history. Perversely the Japanese military and its manufacturers did not appear to learn any lessons from the *Battles of Nomonhan*, and continued to produce light, more maneuverable aircraft that were under-powered, under-armed and defensively highly susceptible to combat damage. However, the Japanese Army did learn one important lesson from the *Battles of Nomonhan*. Albeit a minor engagement in terms of what was to follow, the *Battles of Nomonhan* quashed whatever appetite Japan may have had for 'striking north.'

Hitler was dismissive of Japanese efforts and on 22 August in a remark that belied his pact with Japan and denoted his truly racist feelings about the Japanese, commented that "The Japanese Emperor is a companion piece for the late czars of Russia. He is weak, cowardly and irresolute and may be easily toppled by revolution . . . let us think of these people [the Japanese] as lacquered half-monkeys who need to feel the whip."[71]

Two days later on 24 August 1939, Hitler, to the astonishment of his Japanese allies, signed the *Nazi-Soviet Non-Aggression Pact*. A week later he invaded Poland, which led to a declaration of war against Germany by Britain and France on 3 September. Hitler was not the only foreigner contemptuous of Japan's performance. *Nomonhan* lured the western powers, notably Britain and America, into thinking that Japanese forces would be a 'push-over' in any conflict. The border war with the Soviets thus helped propagate an Allied air of complacency in the year ahead. Neither were the *Battles of Nomonhan* without consequences in Japan. Prime Minister Kiichiro Hiranuma, who had succeeded Prince Konoe in January 1939, was so embarrassed by military defeat in Manchukuo and by the *Nazi-Soviet Pact* that he announced, "The cabinet herewith resigns because of complicated and inscrutable situations recently arising in Europe."[72]

Prince Konoe and Japanese Domestic and International Politics [1937–July 1941]:
The fall of Hiranuma's cabinet brought to the fore Prince Fumimaro Konoe, one of the more mysterious figures of the pre-war period. Born into the Fujiwara family, whose dynasty had ruled Japan for more than a 100 years in the tenth and eleventh centuries, he was a nobleman born to privilege if not to a great fortune. By dint of his title, he was a member of the Upper Chamber of the Diet, the House of Peers. His access to power enabled him, at the age of twenty-eight, to lobby to be included in the delegation that went to the Paris Peace Conference in 1919. He came to public attention when he wrote an article denouncing the peace. The political spotlight fixed on Prince Konoe for life. While he was firmly in the nationalist camp, Konoe was so chameleon-like in his views that both major parties, *Minseito* and *Seiyukai* courted his support and sometimes his leadership. His refusal of the premiership after the 26 February Incident, did not damage his career and a year and half later, after the short premierships of Hirota and Hayashi, both of whose tenures of office were ended by irreconcilable differences between the Army, the bureaucracy and the lower house, in June 1937, Konoe was seen as a man able to bridge all sides and capable of managing a unity government.

The extremists of the Control Faction were mollified by the appointment of former finance minister, Eiichi Baba, as home minister. General Hayashi's Army and Navy ministers were kept in post. Two party members were given ministerial appointments and were allowed to keep their party affiliations. Former Prime Minister, Hirota, was brought back as Foreign Minister, and to pacify the powerful bankers Ikeda and Yuki, Okinori Kaya was appointed Minister of Finance. Shinji Yoshino, a *todai* (Tokyo University Law Department) educated bureaucrat, was made commerce minister.

Konoe sought to sustain Hayashi's policy of economic and military mobilization without ever reconciling it with the opposition of the lower house. Like his predecessors, Konoe had no mechanism for the mobilizing of popular support for a policy that would necessitate domestic sacrifices. The possibility of launching a new pro-government party was considered but rejected as impractical but in a bid to garner broad electoral support Konoe launched The Movement for Mobilizing Popular Morale, a popular campaign aimed at encouraging savings and limiting consumption.

At this juncture Konoe's government was carried away by events largely outside his control. The *Kwantung* Army, lavishly funded from Tokyo, had been chipping away at the *Kuomintang*'s writ in northern China when the Marco Polo Bridge Incident turned a minor episode into a full-scale war. Konoe's foreign policy, whose somewhat indeterminate aims seemed to be to steer Japan away from conflict either with China or the Soviet Union, was instantly derailed. In the initial stages, overwhelming patriotic sentiment stirred by the barbed reporting of a jingoistic Japanese press reporting on the war with China, enabled the cabinet to push through a five-year economic plan aimed at civil and military mobilization with virtually no opposition. On 9 September, a special session of the Diet authorized an exceptional Y2.2bn supplementary budget. The cost of Japan's mobilization for war is exemplified by the fact that during the course of 1937, Konoe's government sold 55 percent of its gold reserves for US$250m.

Bizarrely some government ministers believed that the war was economically beneficial. Commerce Minister Yoshino wrote, "The government takes the view that we should utilize the China incident [Marco Polo Bridge] as an opportunity to make another decisive stride in Japan's industry and economy . . . out of measures . . . adopted in connection with the Incident [26 February Incident]."[73] In addition, Konoe cajoled the Diet into passing the *National Mobilization Act* [March 1938] which gave the government far-reaching controls over all aspects of the economy including trade unions, strategic industries, education, corporate dividend policy, prices, rationing, and national media. When trade unions were abolished, the Minister of Welfare declared, "Our primary aim is to drive Communist ideas and dangerous social thoughts from the minds of the people by ordering the dissolution of the established labor unions, which have a tendency to sharpen class consciousness among workers . . ."[74] The National Service Draft Ordnance enabled the government to draft civilian labor to strategic industries during the *Pacific War*. More legislation enabled government control over power generation and transmission.

Konoe had not planned to implement the most draconian elements of the *National Mobilization Law*. Like most of the military elite, Ishiwara and a few others excepted, Konoe had expected that military victory would be rapid and it damaged his standing with some elements when he had to go back on his word and implement controls earlier than expected. Peace negotiations with the *Kuomintang* failed to produce results and in January 1939 Konoe lost interest, resigned and became President of the Privy Council. Albeit an intelligent politician Konoe had proved to be a weak leader with no clear agenda, who tended to be reticent in cabinet meetings and disinclined to confrontation. His passivity simply left the field to the ultra-nationalist military. As Ikeda complained in December 1938, "It is very difficult when the Prime Minister silently looks on while the right wing and part of the army interfere with what I am trying to do."[75]

The succeeding governments of Baron Kiichiro Hiranuma and General Nobuyuki Abe, which lasted for barely a year, failed to bring an end to the war with China while suffering the opprobrium of an economy that was beginning to suffer from severe food and power shortages. When a motion of no-confidence gained support in the lower house without the support of the party leaders who supported the government, Abe resigned. For the political parties, their exclusion from the office of Prime Minister meant that they were unable to reward their followers and maintain discipline. Abe was replaced by Admiral Mitsumasa Yonai, who was favored by the Emperor for his swift action in preventing naval officers from joining in with the 1936 insurrection. Yonai immediately resigned from active service and became Prime Minister on 16 January 1940.

A few months after Yonai came into office, Hitler's victories in Europe were opening up interesting possibilities with regard to the Asian empires of Holland, France and even Great Britain—a rerun beckoned of the opportunistic roll up of Germany's Asian Empire in *World War I*. However, Japan was not in a position to take advantage. In taking steps to set up a puppet Nanking government led by *Kuomintang* renegade Wang Jingwei, Japanese leaders were beginning to come to the conclusion that their army was in China for the long haul. Meanwhile in temporary political exile, Konoe reached the decision that the Japanese constitution had become dysfunctional to the point that the Prime Minister was no longer in control. His recipe for reform was the creation of a monolithic new political party that he could lead as party leader and prime minister. His ideas won broad acceptance from an Army that was less than enamored with a bi-party system and they engineered Prime Minister Yonai's fall by the expedient resignation of Army Minister Shunroku Hata on 16 June 1940.

By now Saionji, the last *genro*, was too weak to prevent his former protégé regaining the post of Prime Minister. Marquis Kido, Keeper of the Royal Seal, now took on the mantle of senior statesman (*jushin*). Before accepting the post of Prime Minister, Konoe, recommended to Hirohito by Kido, had taken the precaution of consulting with General Tojo, Army Minister, and Foreign Minister Yosuke Matsuoka to ensure a unity of purpose. In addition to these two men from the *Ni-ki-San-Suke* clique from Manchuria, two others included Naoki Hoshino, state minister in charge of the national planning board, and Nobusuke Kishi as vice-minister of commerce. To give some balance to these four from the Manchukuo clique, the *zaibatsu* (financial conglomerates) were represented by Ichizo Kobayashi, a former Mitsui Bank director who was made minister of commerce. Konoe appointed a Mitsubishi-related bureaucrat, Toyotaro Yuki, to the post of minister of finance. Within six weeks the main political parties dissolved themselves and committed to the new order.

On 12 October Konoe created the Imperial Rule Assistance Association (IRAA) as the embodiment of the new order, but this attempt at creating a *Nazi*-like state party failed to overcome entrenched political interests. In March 1941 the IRAA's management was transferred to the Home Ministry. Here it was allowed to wither. As for management of the economy, the cabinet adopted a new interventionist agenda, put forward by the Cabinet Planning Board on 7 December 1940. Major-General Tsukizo Akinaga proclaimed that Japan would "build while fighting."[76]

In effect Konoe tried to put all the tools in place for a one-party state designed to manage a planned economy with the aim of fighting war. It was a largely failed attempt to create a fascist structure not dissimilar to the one imposed by Hitler in Germany. Without the organ of a politicized party base, and with the abolition of the historic political parties, the ultra-nationalist Army and Navy factions increasingly captured the power vacuum at the heart of government. As the war in China expanded so did the demands on the Japanese economy. Already, because of the demands of the war economy and the shortage of capital, *zaibatsu*-controlled heavy industries were supported by special 'temporary military loans,' usually from the Industrial Bank of Japan, which provided for the specific needs of the military economy. After 1937 some 60 percent of special loans were focussed on heavy industry while 14 percent was directed toward trading companies for procurement of natural resources.

The Japanese Occupation of Vietnam and the Tripartite Alliance [September 1940]:
[Map: 3.6] Hull's string of victories against his hawkish subordinates and colleagues in his pursuit of a policy that would not provoke Japan to war did not end the internecine battles within Roosevelt's White House. Hawks including Hornbeck, Morgenthau, Knox, Stimson and Harold Ickes, Secretary of the Interior, continued to line up against the Secretary of State who seemed determined to avoid war at all costs. Pressure mounted on Hull when North Vietnam was invaded and occupied by Japan in September 1940. Washington had barely absorbed this news before Germany, Japan and Italy signed the *Tripartite Pact* on 27 September 1940 stating the following terms:

> ARTICLE 1. Japan recognizes and respects the leadership of Germany and Italy in the establishment of a new order in Europe.
> ARTICLE 2. Germany and Italy recognize and respect the leadership of Japan in the establishment of a new order in Greater East Asia.
> ARTICLE 3. Japan, Germany, and Italy agree to cooperate in their efforts on aforesaid lines. They further undertake to assist one another with all political, economic and military means if one of the Contracting Powers is attacked by a power at present not involved in the European War or in the Japanese-Chinese conflict.

Even though it had long been established that Germany and Japan were working together to establish new orders in Europe and Asia, the *Tripartite Pact* ratcheted up the pressure on the doves in Washington. The Axis was the most cynical of alliances. Hitler stated "It goes without saying that we have affinities with the Japanese."[77] In Japan the Axis alliance was greeted with more enthusiasm. The *Asahi Shimbun* predicted: "It seems inevitable that a collision should occur between Japan, determined to establish a sphere of influence in East Asia, including the *Southwest Pacific*, and the United States, which is determined to meddle in the affairs on the other side of a vast ocean by every means short of war."[78] Spurred on by a jingoistic press, the public in Tokyo rejoiced as did most generals and Army officers. Only in the Navy, among Admiral Yamamoto and some of his colleagues, was there a degree of apprehension about the German alliance. However, their post-war image as being pro-peace is very wide of the mark; Yamamoto and his ilk may not have liked the German link and may have feared confrontation with America, but were, in almost all other respects, in the mainstream of Japanese ultra-nationalism.

For the American public the Axis Pact was a bigger shock. It gave the cue for the hawks in Roosevelt's administration to launch another attack on the passivity of US foreign policy. Far from forcing the "United States to act more prudently"[79] as Matsuoka had hoped, the creation of the Axis alliance further increased Roosevelt's inclination to contain Japan's ambitions. Knox suggested that the 87-Octane Petroleum embargo should be reduced to 67-Octane. Roosevelt was at first supportive but Hull again blocked the move. The only real response to the *Tripartite Pact* was the call up of reserves to *Pearl Harbor* and the increase in supply ships to the *Pacific* naval base. At a cabinet meeting in November, Roosevelt confirmed that the policies of non-confrontation would continue "until the Japanese, by some overt act, cause us to change."[80]

In Japan the increasing fear, not entirely unfounded, was that America was biding its time until its military mobilization was completed. When this was finished, it was widely expected by Japan's leaders that the United States would begin to exert its power through embargoes of essential commodities, particularly oil. In America attention began to turn to how Japan could be blocked in case of war. The Army and sections of the Navy led by Admiral Stark, the new Chief of Naval Operations, wanted a defense that abandoned the Philippines and conserved its forces to the east. Stark's memo (later called Plan DOG) viewed Europe as the more important battleground and believed that the United States should concentrate on the *Atlantic* while Great Britain focused on the Far East. By contrast, Secretary of War, Stimson, wanted to reinforce the Philippines, whose defenses the Army had allowed to lapse. His argument was that the United States needed to support "that vital point of defense, *Singapore*."[81] Meanwhile Hornbeck argued that the best way to defeat Germany was to secure control of South East Asia. It was also argued that if America yielded South East Asia, China would be surrounded, cut off from supply and weakened to the point of collapse.

Roosevelt, not for the first time, sent out confusing signals. While accepting Stark's Plan DOG, with its emphasis on Europe, Roosevelt sent a letter to Ambassador Grew in which he gave a strong endorsement of America's commitment to *Singapore*. Thus Eugene Doorman, counsellor of the American Embassy in Tokyo, confidently told Japan's Vice Foreign Minister that "it would be absurd to suppose that the American people, while pouring munitions into Britain, would look with complacency upon the cutting of communications between Britain and the British dominions and colonies overseas."[82] In short, America's coordination of diplomacy, foreign policy and defense policy was hopelessly confused and could only have added to Japan's belief that America was not capable of defending its Empire.

Great Britain was also turning its attention to the Japanese threat. The British, fearful that the growth in Japanese stockpiles would make economic sanctions meaningless, put forward a proposal to block Japanese access to tankers. Given that Japan was buying far more oil than its own tanker fleet could carry, making it heavily dependent on

American tankers flying Liberian or Panamanian flags, the proposal represented a significant threat to Japan. In a repetition of past conflicts, lower-level executives in the State Department and the National Defense Advisory Commission (NDAC) supported the British proposal while Hull was intent on blocking it. Finally the Roosevelt administration did pull tankers out of the *Pacific,* not specifically to block Japan's access to oil but because in the *Atlantic*, in the spring of 1941, German submarines were sinking British ships faster than they could be built. By threatening legislation, Roosevelt achieved a 'voluntary' transfer of 200 ships from the *Pacific* to the *Atlantic*.

As for China, Roosevelt, in spite of public support, offered them only crumbs to sustain their resistance to Japan. Although the administration allowed the formation of the American Volunteer Group (AVG, the 'Flying Tigers'), giving officers leave to go to fight, and helping to finance the purchase of fighter planes, US support was trivial compared to the benefits brought by China's fight for survival in which they held down 1 million Japanese troops. As Jonathan Uttley succinctly expressed it in *Going to War with Japan* [2005], ". . . the Roosevelt administration treated China as a pawn whose inexhaustible manpower would be sacrificed to keep Japan from moving into the important region of Southeast Asia."[83]

Although the enactment of the *Lend-Lease Act* in March 1941, under the innocuous title of *An Act to Further Promote the Defense of the United States*, would be helpful to China in the future, its immediate aim was to finance Britain's continued effort to thwart Hitler's ambition to control all of Europe. Up until the passing of this act, Britain had been forced to buy war material from America on a 'cash and carry' basis. In the short term, the problem of supplying China related more to the shortage of war material in America than the giving of financial support. The US Army refused to supply the 0.30 caliber bullets that China needed for the Curtis P-40 Warhawk fighters that it had purchased. Harry Hopkins, Roosevelt's close advisor, complained that, with regard to the supply of bullets to China, ". . . I have come to the conclusion that the only hope is a directive from the President."[84] Eventually, under pressure, the Army yielded the barest minimum amount of 1 million 0.30 caliber and 500,000 0.50 caliber bullets.

In July 1941 Washington authorized the supply of 821,000 tons of supplies to Britain and just 16,000 tons to China, just 2 percent of the total. It was a balance that fully reflected the priority given by the Roosevelt administration to Europe over Asia. In effect Roosevelt and Hull's strategy was to focus virtually all their efforts on keeping Britain in the war with Hitler while hoping that China, largely unsupported, would keep Japan bogged down and incapable of extending its reach to the rest of Asia.

Operation BARBAROSSA, 'Strike South' and the Countdown to War in the Pacific [September 1940–December 1941]: On 22 June 1941, Operation BARBAROSSA, Germany's surprise invasion of its former confederate, the Soviet Union, proved to be a transformative moment in Japanese foreign policy.

Konoe's Foreign Minister, Yosuke Matsuoka, was famed for his speech at the League of Nations in 1933, where he defended his country's annexation of Manchuria and announced Japan's withdrawal from a collective security organization of which it had been a founding member. Matsuoka, a mercurial, acerbic character, was a fluent English speaker who had spent his formative years living in Portland, Oregon where he converted to Presbyterianism. It was not a religious belief that precluded regular visits to the Imperial Shrine at Ise. After returning to Japan, he became a career diplomat in the Foreign Office and rose through the ranks, participating at the Paris Peace Conference and, among other things, serving as secretary to Prime Minister Terauchi.

Later he went into politics, joining the *Rikken Seiyukai*, and becoming a representative in the Diet. After his noted performance at the League of Nations, he returned to Japan, resigned from *Rikken Seiyukai*, and set about planning the creation of a national socialist party based on the *Nazi* Party. It did not fly. Having overreached himself, Matsuoka took up a post as President of the South Manchuria Railway where he ingratiated himself with the increasingly powerful *Kwantung* Army.

After BARBAROSSA, Matsuoka's foreign policy plan, consisting of a *German-Soviet-Japanese Neutrality Pact* appeared to have gone up in smoke. In these changed circumstances, Matsuoka's instincts were to back his alliance with the *Nazis* and to push for an invasion of the Soviet Union's eastern empire. Matsuoka was alone. The Imperial Way Faction that had favored an attack on the Soviet Union had all but been annihilated after the 26 February Incident. Furthermore the Army was poorly equipped with the large tanks that they would have needed to compete with the Soviet Army in the wide expanses of Russia. Japan's defeat at the *Battles of Nomonhan*, in its brief border war with the Soviet Union in 1938–1939, convinced the Army's generals that this was no time for a major military campaign in Siberia. Although communism and the Soviet Union were perceived to be the greater long-term threat to Japan, neither the Navy nor the Army favored a northern military expedition. The Army, heavily embroiled in China, did not have the manpower for another major land war. They were happy to prepare for a war against the Soviets if they lost to Hitler, whose forces were now swarming through western Russia, but otherwise they were not prepared to move.

With Matsuoka noisily advocating an attack on the Soviet Union while upping his aggressive stance toward the United States, his continuing role as foreign minister became increasingly tenuous. Matsuoka refused to resign, leaving Konoe, who did not have the constitutional authority to sack a minister, with no option other than the resignation of his entire cabinet as a means of ridding himself of his recalcitrant foreign minister. Konoe was immediately reinstated and reformed his cabinet intact apart from Matsuoka, who was replaced by Admiral Teijiro Toyoda.

It occurred to almost nobody in the Japanese government that there should be no reaction to BARBAROSSA. In large part the idea of passivity had been eviscerated by the atmosphere of bellicosity that now permeated all echelons of the armed forces. Moreover, thanks to Konoe, the Japanese civilian economy was now prepared for total war. Within the Army much of the power with regard to the development of policy rested with the *bakuryo*, a generation of fifty-something senior officers at the Imperial General HQ and the service staffs; they included Shinichi Tanaka, head of Army General

Staff's Operations Division, Akira Muto, chief of the Army's Military Affairs Bureau and Rear-Admiral Takazumi Oka, chief of the Naval Ministry's Naval Affairs Bureau.

Oka had promoted Shingo Ishikawa, the well-known extremist and author, under a pseudonym, of *Nihon no Kiki* [1931] (Japan's Crisis) in which he had written about America's aim to control Asia since the mid-nineteenth century. He had concluded that Japan needed to embark on a "great national march to ensure its rights and survival."[85] Known as 'Wildshot,' Shingo Ishikawa was promoted by Oka to the position of head of the Navy's Arms Division. The Army had similar mid-level firebrands including Kanji Ishiwara who had inspired the annexation of Manchuria. In the absence of a clear overriding policy coming from above, these *bakuryo* officers pushed forward plans for expansion in the context of an intellectual background that accepted the rightfulness of the creation of a pan-Asian Empire. In this middle cadre, there was a forcefulness of purpose sometimes missing from their vacillating senior commanders.

In the absence of support for a northern strike against the Soviets, the *bakuryo* pushed for a 'strike south' strategy that was seen as low cost and low risk. Shinichi Tanaka argued that the southern advance was "nothing more than a means to secure naval replenishment and acquire funds and materials."[86] After the war the swagger of the middle ranks was recalled with embarrassment by one of their ilk, Colonel Akiho Ishii, an Army Ministry officer who co-drafted many of the pre-war attack plans: "Fools that we were, we could make an important policy decision as long as we took the initiative."[87]

For the *bakuryo*, the power vacuum in Asia created by the war in Europe was simply an opportunity of which Japan had to take advantage. The plan to occupy southern Indochina would give access to raw materials, would have little military cost, would block another supply route to Chiang Kai-shek, would expand Japan's Great East Asia Co-Prosperity Sphere and put pressure on the Dutch to supply them with more oil. Although Matsuoka the outcast warned of the risks of antagonizing America and announced "I predict that going south would bring a great disaster,"[88] the policy statement presented to the Emperor at the Imperial Conference on 2–3 July trumpeted the *bakuryo*'s lack of fear in this regard: "The Empire shall not flinch from war with Britain and the United States."[89] It was a statement that did not reflect the nervousness of senior officers, mainly within the Navy but also within the Army, from further antagonizing the United States.

Although the Navy's senior admirals, such as Yamamoto, were leery of risking a war with America, which they noted had started on a major shipbuilding program, they were never consulted. Admiral Mineichi Koga, commander of the Second Fleet reacted furiously: "How could you have endorsed such a critical policy without consulting us?"[90] Thus Japan sleepwalked into a military adventure because its senior commanders thought that they ought to do something and accepted a plan dreamt up by their underlings. Determined that their actions were low risk, Imperial General HQ seriously underestimated the American reaction. For the *bakuryo* the occupation of South Vietnam was no less than the first push for the conquest of all of South East Asia.

Hirohito's Role as Icon and Godhead in the Rise of Ultra-nationalism: When Hirohito
returned to Japan after his European sojourn he was probably infused with some, by
Japanese standards, liberal ideas. In England he received a crash course in Liberal
Democracy and on a trip to Scotland to stay with the Duke of Athol he joined in Scottish
reel dancing with the local villagers. Crossing to France, he visited Verdun and the
Somme where he walked through the bloody fields with blackened trees. "War is a truly
cruel thing," he remarked, "anyone who admires war should come and see this place."[91]

Back in Japan he played golf, skied, went to bars in Ginza to drink beer with his
friends from the Peer's school (*Gakushuin*). All of this changed after the 'leftist' son of
a conservative Diet member tried to assassinate Hirohito just a month before his
marriage to Princess Kuninomiya Nagako. The assassination attempt was revenge for
the wholesale slaughter of anarchists, leftists, Koreans and Chinese following the *Great
Tokyo Earthquake* on 21 September 1923. Thereafter, Hirohito, not surprisingly, given
the strictures of the court protocols, became introverted, and increasingly captive to
court officials and his Privy Council advisers. He was in any case usually timid and
cautious by nature. By the 1930s there is no evidence to suggest that his political views
were outside the right-wing consensus of Japan's elite, though he appears to have been
more liberal in his constitutional views than the ultra-nationalists.

Hirohito's gradual rightward shift can perhaps be traced to a steering of court policy
in the early 1920s. Following the death of Mutsuhito (Meiji) in 1912, Yoshihito (Taisho)
ascended the Chrysanthemum Throne. The succession of the physically and mentally
fragile Emperor coincided with increasing calls for 'democratization,' from liberal
intellectuals and from within the junior officer class. Articles began to appear in the
Kaikosha Kiji (the Army journal), which implied a need to re-evaluate the role of the
Emperor in binding the military with civil society. War in Europe, and the collapse of
the German, Austro-Hungarian, Russian and Ottoman Empires increased fears within
Japanese court circles as to the sustainability of the 'imperial system.' The emergence of
the Soviet Union also stoked fears of a spread of communist ideology that might
undermine the nationalist *Shinto* underpinnings of the Meiji Constitution.

At this critical junction Yoshihito's declining mental faculties made him wholly
dependent on his Privy Council and the *genro*. By 1918 the Emperor was no longer able
to carry out even the ceremonial, civil, military and religious duties required of him. The
future of the Imperial family was at crisis point. Social upheaval threatened. In 1918 rice
riots, caused by rocketing prices, erupted throughout Japan. The economy, which had
prospered at the expense of the European powers during *World War 1*, suffered a
post-war downturn. The country was rocked by violent strikes at the Tokyo Artillery
Arsenal (1919 and 1921), Kamaishi Iron Works (1919), Yawata Steel (1920), and
Kawasaki-Mitsubishi Shipyards (1921).

As a result of the threats to the Imperial system, the focus of the court elite now
turned to re-energizing a Japanese nationalism to counter the threat of foreign ideologies.
This drive to define a uniquely Japanese system, free from foreign contamination,
centered on the concept of *Kodo* (the Imperial way). Fortune favored the reformers.

The incapacity of Emperor Yoshihito allowed Prince Hirohito to become the new face of the Empire when he was appointed regent on 25 November 1921. This transfer of power, followed years later by the enthronement of Hirohito after Yoshihito's death in the early hours of Christmas Day 1926, provided an important centerpiece for the revival of Imperial legitimacy. As Emperor material, Hirohito was somewhat of an improvement on his degenerate father, but not a natural born leader. The 25-year old Emperor, socially ill at ease, with a stooping gait and nervous mannerisms, was neither charismatic nor very articulate. In spite of his interest in science, he was not regarded as academically gifted. After the war Russell Brines, an Associated Press Journalist, noted Hirohito's physical attributes: "He was short sighted, round shouldered . . . was weak chinned. His conversation consisted of inanities in a high-pitched voice."[92]

For the court bureaucrats, Hirohito was all they had; they would have to make do. Fortunately, in developing and promoting the myth of the Emperor's lineage from the God of the Earth and Sun Goddess, *Ameratsu Omikami*, the mystery was best sustained by keeping Hirohito out of sight and hearing. Until Japan's surrender in 1945, Hirohito's voice was never heard on Japanese radio, a medium whose influence expanded rapidly after the Ministry of Communications merger of the Tokyo, Osaka and Nagoya Radio Stations into the NHK (*Nippon Hoso Kyokai*: Japanese Broadcasting Corporation), modeled on the BBC, in August 1926.

The only photographs that the press was allowed to publish of the Emperor were carefully staged, showing him from the waist upward and never with another person. In schools, the *Imperial Rescript on Education* [1890] was used to install a mass program of Emperor worship. The Rescript was distributed to all schools with a photograph of the emperor for public display. Photographs were used as objects for esoteric veneration. Students were required to learn by rote a document that instructed the Japanese to "advance public good and promote common interests; always respect the Constitution and observe the laws; should emergency arise, offer yourselves courageously to the state; and thus guard and maintain the prosperity of Our Imperial Throne coeval with heaven and earth."[93] At source the state education system's promotion of *kokutai* from 1890 onwards grew a generation of indoctrinated young men who were reaching their majority in the 1920s. As Kaori Okano and Motonori Tsuchiya conclude in *Education in Contemporary Japan* [1999], "By this time [1918] the *Rescript on Education*'s influence on the practice of schooling was profound. State schooling focused on the legitimization of the state ideology and the socialization of youth for service to the imperial state . . ."[94]

At the same time as the introduction of the *Imperial Rescript on Education*, the government introduced the *Imperial Rescript for Seamen and Soldiers* [1890] that promoted their mission as the guardians of Japan as a 'sacred nation.' Traditional samurai values of *bushido* (the way of the warrior) were thus merged with modern weaponry and training. At the pinnacle of the Japanese government's propaganda campaign stood the iconic figure of the Emperor, the God creature who not only symbolized but also embodied the Japanese state. Hirohito was not only Japan's head of state—he and his family were the earthly representation of Japan's spiritual existence.

Hirohito's War Guilt Examined: In the post-war period there has been an intense focus and debate on Hirohito's role in the *Pacific War*, and specifically on his war guilt. The two main areas of debate concern his role in the initiation of Japan's imperial expansion and the decision for war with the West and secondly his knowledge and license of atrocities committed during the war by Japan's armed forces. The catalogue of atrocities was vast, including the dozens described in the following chapters. Shootings, torture, rape, and beheading were the common currency of Japan's occupation of Asia.

Less well understood was the issue of enslavement. Forced labor was common. With their menfolk fighting throughout Asia, foreign labor was needed in Japanese factories. More dangerously Koreans and Taiwanese were most often employed as construction workers attached to forces in the field where they often suffered the fate of the soldiers that they were supporting. Tens of thousands must have died in servitude in the *South Pacific*. Similarly the issue of rape or the use of forced 'comfort women' was a barely considered issue in the immediate aftermath of war.

The need for 'comfort women' was not insignificant. The War Ministry directed that "The psychological influence received from sexual comfort stations is most direct and profound . . . [they] greatly . . . affect the raising of morale."[95] In mid-1941 Zenshiro Hara, who commanded the Logistics Division of the *Kwantung* Army was sent to Seoul to demand that the government provide him with 20,000 'comfort women' within twenty days. They were provided by a combination of deception and coercion. It was estimated that one woman was required to service fifty to 100 men per day. During the course of the war hundreds of thousands of women of every nationality, including Caucasian, are thought to have been forced into prostitution for the army, though the main nationalities were Korean, Chinese and Filipino. However, the abuse of women and the use of slave labor by Japan during the war would only later become a *cause célèbre*. [See Appendix D: The Japanese Empire: From Co-Prosperity to Tyranny]

To a large extent the nature of the debate in the aftermath of the war was defined by the role played by General MacArthur's administration in the immediate post-war period. MacArthur was persuaded by his intelligence officers to retain Hirohito as a guarantor of Japan's social and political stability—a course action supported by President Truman. Leaving aside the logic of this conclusion, which has been challenged by historians such as John Dower, the result was that MacArthur set out to obfuscate the truth of Hirohito's involvement in the war. Hirohito and the Imperial family were given immunity from prosecution for war crimes. Defense attorneys were barred from calling the Imperial family as witnesses in the cases of those leading military and civilian figures who were prosecuted. According to translator Shuichi Mizota, Brigadier-General Fellers told Admiral Mitsumasa Yonai, ". . . it is extremely disadvantageous to MacArthur's standing in the United States to put on trial the very Emperor who is co-operating with and facilitating the smooth administration of the occupation."[96] Robert Dohini would later recall, "As we boarded the plane we learnt, from a letter delivered to Keenan [Chief Prosecutor] by President Truman practically at the airport, that we should lay off Hirohito and . . . the whole Imperial Household . . . I was told personally: do not attempt to interrogate any of them."[97]

In terms of deciding who was eligible to stand trial, MacArthur was not only arbitrary in his judgments, but also played fast and loose with common decency. General Ishii, who was responsible for the Unit-731, which used prisoners as guinea pigs for biological experimentation, bartered the scientific information that he had gathered in return for immunity from prosecution. Investigator Colonel Sanders recalled, "MacArthur agreed to immunity in return for all the information. I had MacArthur's word we would not prosecute."[98] Members of the Imperial family were also saved. Hirohito's uncle Prince Asaka, who commanded the Japanese forces at the Rape of Nanking was not prosecuted while General Matsui, who had been forced to step down from command because of ill health was tried and found guilty for the war crimes committed at Nanking even though he had attempted to restrain his officers from their brutal rampage.

It is interesting to note that a top-secret memo unearthed by Yoshiaki Yoshimi of Chuo University, dated 16 August 1938 authorizes the use of poison gas in China. The memo drafted by Prince Higashikuni, another of Hirohito's uncles, who later became Chairman of the International Martial Arts Federation, urged Japanese commanders to cover up the use of gas by claiming that it was being used by the Chinese. On 17 June 1925 a Geneva Protocol was added to the Hague Conventions permanently banning the use of all forms of chemical and biological warfare. Historian Nobumasa Tanaka argues that the use of chemical weapons in China could not have been done without Hirohito's authorization in the form of orders called *rinsan-mei* and *tairiku-mei* issued through the Army General Staff. Memos also show that the Emperor's cousin, Prince Takeo Tsuneyoshi, also condoned the use of chemical weapons.

Hirohito's court officials worked with MacArthur's officers to obfuscate the truth of Hirohito's involvement in the pre-war preparations for conflict. Even today the minutes of the meetings between Hirohito and MacArthur are restricted. The result is that most of the information about Hirohito's role comes from diaries of courtiers and senior military commanders. The *Sugiyama Memoranda*, a collection of papers belonging to Field Marshal Hajime Sugiyama, Chief of Staff and Minister of War from 1937 to 1944, revealed that Hirohito had known of the *Pearl Harbor* plan in August 1941 while Tojo was only told in November. Other important diaries came from Marquis Koichi Kido, Keeper of the Royal Seal, his secretary Baron Kumao Harada and General Baron Shigeru Honjo, Chief *Aide-de-Camp* to Hirohito from 1933 to 1936.

From a constitutional point of view, Hirohito's position was far from clear-cut. In theory the Meiji Constitution gave the Emperor absolute power. The Meiji Constitution, promulgated in 1889 asserted,

> . . . the emperor was the successor in an unbroken, sacred blood lineage, based on male descendants, and that government was subordinated to monarchy on that basis. It defined him as "sacred and inviolable," "head of empire" [*genshu*], supreme commander [*daigensu*] of the armed forces, and superintendent of all powers of

> sovereignty. He could convoke and dissolve the Imperial
> Diet; issue imperial ordinances in place of law; and
> appoint and dismiss ministers of state, civil officials, and
> military officers and determine their salaries.[99]

As the historian Tadashi Wakabayashi has concluded, Hirohito "wielded absolute moral authority in Japan by granting Imperial honors that conveyed incontestable prestige and by issuing imperial rescripts that had coercive power greater than law."[100] But to what extent did Hirohito simply sign the Imperial rescripts that were put in front of him by the government bureaucracy? The answer is unclear. An unwritten tradition of non-intervention by the emperor had developed. Hirohito saw himself as a 'constitutional' monarch. Supposedly he developed an admiration for constitutional monarchy after his long visit to Britain in 1921 just before he was appointed as regent in place of his terminally ill father. At Cambridge University Professor R. J. Tanner, who gave the lecture when Hirohito was given an honorary degree, warned that a constitutional monarch was obliged to approve the policies of his government. From reported conversations he supported Professor Tatsukichi Minobe, a lawyer specializing in constitutional law at Tokyo Imperial University, who argued that the emperor was an organ of the sovereign state rather than a sacred power standing above the state—an opinion that made Minobe a hate figure for right-wing political groups. *Sotto voce*, Hirohito told one of his advisers, "To hold that sovereignty resides not in the state but in the monarch is to court charges of [Imperial] despotism."[101] Hirohito was alive to the paradox of the position held by the ultra-nationalists: "Is it not a great contradiction that the military should proceed to attack the organ theory in opposition to my views?"[102]

Nevertheless, Hirohito clearly did not follow the constitutional role of monarch in the strict manner of British monarchs. The first of his three famous interventions was he refused to accept the advice of his ministers not to court-martial Colonel Daisaku Komoto, the officer who had organized the assassination of Manchurian warlord Chang Tso-lin in 1929. According to the Emperor his asking Prime Minister Giichi Tanaka to resign was merely a youthful indiscretion.

His second intervention during the 26 February Incident [1936] was to defend the constitution, though Hirohito argued that, given the disappearance of the Prime Minister, actually in hiding, but presumed dead, he had to take charge. The young officer rebels of the 26 February Incident, whose insurrection aimed to 'liberate' Hirohito from his moderate advisers, were humiliated. Hirohito refused to accept the rebels' suicide as an honourable solution to the crisis and ordered that they should be tried in a secret court to prevent them having a pulpit for their views. Members of his family, such as Prince Chichibu and Prince Asaka, who supported *Kodoha* (the Imperial Way Faction) and their wish for the crown to assume direct power, were whipped into line. This episode can be used to illustrate two contradictory views; first that the Emperor was a constitutional monarch but secondly that the Emperor *de facto* had absolute power. Moreover did his strong intervention demonstrate a distaste for ultra-nationalism or was he simply standing up for the powers of the Emperor in the face of an attempted coup?

His third intervention was to force surrender on a chaotic and dysfunctional government at the end of the war. Again it could be argued here that he only used power when authority around him collapsed. Were Hirohito's three interventions all exceptional circumstances or did he simply wield absolute power when it suited him?

Hirohito's defenders suggest that he was a shy, unworldly, peace-loving marine biologist, who had no interest in international politics. "The official portrait . . . represented Hirohito as a cultured, secluded biologist who left the management of his realm to generals and admirals and devoted all his energy to puttering about with fungi and small wormlike marine organisms."[103] Hirohito claimed that the military constantly undermined his will and that they alone determined on the course of war. After the Mukden Incident, one of his courtiers relayed Hirohito's opinion: "I believe that international justice and good faith are important and I am striving to preserve world peace, but the forces overseas do not heed my commands and are recklessly expanding the Incident. This causes me no end of anguish . . . When I think of all these problems, I cannot sleep at night."[104]

Toshiaki Kawahara in *Hirohito and his Times* [1990] gives the classic post-war view that "Hirohito had signed the declarations of war on 8 December, 1941, in spite of his reservations, under pressure from the military. After hostilities began, he felt duty bound to support the war effort."[105] The pro-Hirohito camp makes great play of Hirohito's actions at the crucial Imperial Conference of 6 September at which it was decided that Japan would go to war with America unless they could negotiate a lifting of the oil embargo. At his conference Hirohito took a piece of paper out of his pocket and read a poem that had been written by his grandfather, the Emperor Meiji:

> I believed this was a world
> In which all men were brothers.
> Across the four seas
> Why then do the waves and winds
> Arise now in such turmoil?[106]

The reading of the poem failed to produce a reaction from the assembled generals and assorted advisers. Hirohito broke the silence and added, "this poem by the Meiji Emperor is one which I have always loved. That great emperor's love for peace is a feeling I have also held as my own."[107]

Some commentators however, have taken Hirohito's words out of context. Kazutoshi Hando, a member of the Pacific War Research Society, who wrote the commentaries to the *Showa Tenno no Dokuhaku Roku* [1946] (Emperor's Soliloquy; his post-war testament), cited Marquis Kido's diary entry of 12 February to prove Hirohito's pacifist nature: "For the sake of peace and humanity, we shouldn't let the war drag on . . ."[108] Hando omits the end of the passage that says: "On the other hand, we can't give up our [newly won] resources in the south half-way through exploiting them."[109]

What never seems to be answered in this picture of the Emperor is why, given the importance of the decision to go to war, Hirohito did not use his 'absolute' powers to stop Japan going to war. After all Hirohito, in his third intervention to overrule his advisers, did insist on almost unconditional surrender on 9 August—a decision which was not only his alone but one that he decided to make by an unprecedented radio address to his own people. If he was as peace loving as his supporters suggest why did he not prevent the war with America? As his former *aide-de-camp* Vice-Admiral Noboru Hirata conjectured, "What [his Majesty] did at the end of the war, we might have had him do at the start."[110] Even behaving as a constitutional monarch, Hirohito had significant power to influence his ministers. There were constant behind the scenes meetings with individual ministers and advisers at which Hirohito could guide or direct policy. At the Imperial Conferences, Hirohito, by constitutional tradition, did not interfere; these formal meeting were used to 'rubber stamp' decisions that had already been made.

Hirohito's own words on the subject of his part in war responsibility are less than convincing. On Sunday 5 March 1946, five of Hirohito's Household Ministry officials, Yoshitami Matsudaira, Michio Kinoshita, Shichi Inada, Yasumasa Matsudaira and Hidenari Terasaki, came to the Palace and in front of them he recorded his version of the war, the *Dokuhaku Roku*. In a bizarre scene, the Emperor had a single bed set up on which he lay in pure white pyjamas on the finest soft cotton pillows. Inada later explained the reason for the strange post-war testament: "People might ask why at such a moment we were hastily requested to listen to the Emperor's account. Around that time, however, people were questioning his responsibility in connection with the war crimes trials, and there was a need to record the Emperor's candid feeling quickly."[111]

The 5 March meeting was the first such held over three weeks. Hirohito claimed that he had always stood aloof from politics. Not true. Furthermore he declared: "As a constitutional monarch in a constitutional political system, I had no choice but to sanction the decision by the Tojo cabinet to begin the war."[112] In an English summary of Hirohito's testimony, which along with the full Japanese text was deposited with MacArthur's secretary, the Emperor humbly concluded that "actually I was a virtual prisoner and powerless."[113] Even if Hirohito did behave most of the time as a constitutional monarch, choosing not to exercise his absolute powers, this is not a statement that is easy to reconcile with the three occasions when he formally intervened to overrule his advisers. Hirohito, on the rare occasions in later life when he was pinned down, became a master of obfuscation. When in October 1975 a reporter asked him how he interpreted the term 'responsibility for war,' Hirohito replied, "I can't comment on that figure of speech because I've never done research in literature."[114]

Inevitably, given the destruction of court documents, MacArthur's refusal to countenance Hirohito's prosecution, the obfuscation of courtiers and Hirohito himself, and the refusal of the Tokyo War Crime Trial defendants to implicate the Emperor, it was perhaps inevitable that some historians would seek to prove a conspiracy to hide a darker truth of Hirohito's involvement in the war. Hirohito's accusers argue that he only gave a façade of peaceful intent. Thus David Bergamini in *Japan's Imperial Conspiracy* [1971] argues that: "... I became convinced that the modern history of Japan, as presented since *World War II*, was a skilfully contrived illusion fabricated late in the war, partly by counter intelligence specialists in the general staff and partly by high-ranking palace courtiers."[115] Similarly Herbert Bix, author of *Hirohito, The Making of Modern Japan* [2001] argues that:

> From the very outset Hirohito was a dynamic emperor, but paradoxically also one who projected the defensive image of a passive monarch. While the rest of the world dissociated him from any meaningful personal role in the decision-making process and insisted on seeing him as an impotent figurehead lacking notable intellectual endowments, he was actually smarter and shrewder than most people gave him credit for, and more energetic too.[116]

In the absence of court papers, the advocates of Hirohito as war maker rely heavily on accounts of his interest in military affairs and other snippets of information. For example, Bergamini relates the story of one unnamed aristocrat who tells him, "I knew Hirohito as a boy. He was a romantic warlike idiot then and I suppose he still is . . . If you quote me by name I shall deny that I ever met you."[117] Similarly on 7 December 1938 Konoe complained to Marquis Kido: "I just met with the Emperor and he is talking of strategy all the way up to next March. He mentioned sending a division to Canton, which surprised me because I had heard nothing of such a strike before."[118]

Hirohito's primary interest may have been marine biology but he had a very real interest in military affairs. He frequently wore military uniform and during the *Second Sino-Japanese War* had a war room built underneath the imperial palace from where he could monitor movements of Japan's forces. On 11 July 1938, when a border clash with the Soviet Union was provoked by the commander of 19th Division, Baron Kamao Harada records in his diary that Hirohito gave Army Minister Itagaki a dressing down, and ordered that "Hereafter not a single soldier is to be moved without my permission."[119]

In 1932 Hirohito also gave direct orders to General Yoshinori Shirakawa to limit hostilities in Shanghai behind the back of Army Chief of Staff Prince Kanin Kotohito. Shirakawa was rewarded by being made a baron by Hirohito whose rescript published in *Fujin Gaho* declared that: "Your Lordship [Baron Shirakawa] commanded the Shanghai Expeditionary Forces, assiduously accomplished your mission on foreign shores, enhanced our military prestige, and so furthered international trust. We deeply appreciate your labors."[120] Foreign Minister, Yosuke Matsuoka, asked Hirohito to give a similar order to Kumataro Honda without cabinet approval. On Kido's advice, Hirohito refused because Honda "was such a blabber mouth."[121] In *Dokuhaku Roku*, Hirohito also revealed that, with regard to his attempt to solve the fighting arising from the Marco Polo Bridge Incident, he described his strategy thus, "I always advocated combining intimidation with peace offers."[122] This is not exactly the mild, retiring personality described by Hirohito's defenders. In addition, Hirohito has been charged with actively intervening in military strategy after the defeat at the *Battle of Guadalcanal* and to have insisted that Japan's main infantry divisions earmarked for the defense of *Luzon*, the Philippines main island, be committed to *Leyte Island* after MacArthur's invasion in autumn 1944.

With the absence of Imperial papers, the relationship of the Emperor to the Army can usually be glimpsed only in second-hand records. Thus after Prime Minister Konoe resigned on 16 October 1941, he explained to his chief cabinet secretary, Kenji Tomita, who recorded his words in his diary:

> Of course His Majesty is a pacifist, and there is no doubt he wished to avoid war. When I told him that to initiate war was a mistake, he agreed. But the next day, he would tell me: "You were worried about it yesterday, but you do not have to worry so much." Thus, gradually, he began to lean toward war. And the next time I met him, he leaned even more toward. In short, I felt the Emperor was telling me: my prime minister does not understand military matters, I know much more. In short, the Emperor had absorbed the view of the army and navy high commands.[123]

In spite of the sketchy anecdotal evidence put forward by Bix and Bergamini, there appears to be no hard evidence of the Emperor's taking a lead role in the decision to go to war. But neither is there reason to believe that Hirohito's opinions differed markedly from the *zeitgeist* of the Japan in which he lived. One imagines that if Hirohito had been strongly opposed to the ideas of Pan-Asianism, the New Order, or the Great East Asia Co-Prosperity Sphere then he would not have allowed the pseudo-intellectuals and right-wing propagandists, Mitsukawa and Shumei Okawa, to take over rooms inside the Imperial Palace for a Social Education Institute whose purpose seems to have been the indoctrination of leading members of Japan's elite. The existence of the Institute within the Palace grounds would seem to be clear *prima facie* evidence of how acceptable to the Imperial household were the pan-Asian ideals expounded by Mitsukawa. However, by other accounts, when their extreme views were understood, they were moved out. Kido seemingly undermines evidence of Hirohito's bellicosity, when he suggests in his diaries that Hirohito vacillated over the subjugation of South East Asia. Hirohito supposedly comments that brutal conquests were "actions such as those taken by Frederick and Napoleon . . . [but] our country does not want to act in such Machiavellian ways. Shouldn't we always try to bear in mind the true spirit of *hakkoichiu* [moral leadership] which has been our policy since the age of the Gods."[124] Like many people, Hirohito's views may simply have veered from one position to another. As Japan's nominal ruler, fear for his own position may have contributed to his vacillation.

A distinction should perhaps be made too regarding Hirohito's views of war in China versus war against the United States. The latter risked annihilation and the possible end of more than 2,000 years of unbroken family rule. The war with China carried no such risks and it seems likely that his desire for conquest was within the broad consensus of the military. By contrast Hirohito would have faced personal risks if he had opposed war against the West. There was some, not unreasonable, fear that he might be deposed by Prince Chichibu, who was much closer to the Army. Hirohito later reflected on this subject saying that if he had opposed the war, ". . . there would have been a great rebellion within the country, the people whom I trusted would have been killed and my own life would not have been guaranteed."[125] But as Wakabayashi has concluded, "Hirohito would no more have granted Korea independence or returned Manchuria to China than Roosevelt would have granted Hawaii independence or returned Texas to Mexico."[126]

After his death in 1989, Prime Minister Noboro Takeshita issued a government declaration stating that: "His majesty resolutely brought an end to the war that had broken out against his wishes."[127] Without court papers, Hirohito's personal papers and much other evidence that was deliberately destroyed by the Japanese, the truth of Takeshita's statement may never be clarified.

However, in a court of law, the wilful destruction of evidence would not have looked good. Even if the case for the conspiracy theorists has never been convincingly proven, it does not mean that Hirohito, Japan's Commander in Chief, was not guilty of responsibility for the *Pacific War*. As Stephen Large, Professor of History at Cambridge, concludes, "the fact that he formally sanctioned nearly every decision for war, notwithstanding his personal preferences for peace, means that he should have been held accountable for his share of war-responsibility."[128]

Underlying the problems of unraveling Hirohito's role in the prosecution of the wars in China and against the West is the problem of understanding 'decision making' in the context of Japanese culture. Unlike the West, the decision-making process in Japan is usually opaque. Decisions are not usually made by one man and often evolve after a long drawn out process of discussion or *nemawashi* (root binding). Opinions in Japan, not articulated in the blunt Anglo-Saxon empiric style, are often allowed to develop from inference. Furthermore the drive for discussion and policy direction, unlike in the West, comes from below—what was called in the Japan Imperial Army, the *bakuryo* (staff officers) were often the main drivers of policy. The upper-middle ranks of an organization in Japan are much more influential in decision making than their counterparts in western culture. Thus men such as Colonel Kanji Ishiwara, involved in both the Mukden Incident and the military expansion promoted after the 26 February Incident, were often prime movers. In the Japanese Army, senior officers would frequently act as gatekeepers who vetted decisions. In a further muddying of the waters of decision-making, Ministries would usually have *shingikai* (deliberative councils). In the 1930s there were upwards of 200 *shingikai* operating within the government system, peopled by relevant constituents such as businessmen. This is as true for Japanese corporations or political parties today as it was for the Japanese Army and Navy in the *Pacific War*. That is the reason why it is much more difficult and indeed sometimes pointless to identify Japanese leaders, including Hirohito, with specific decisions.

For reasons of Japanese culture, decisions tend to be far more collective than individual and in looking at the decisions made by Japan in the lead up to the *Pacific War*, it would be as well to look at Hirohito, the *genro*, Saionji, his courtiers such as Marquis Kido, Lord Keeper of the Privy Seal, his Privy Council, informal advisers, such as his extensive family and influential aristocrats such as Prince Konoe, as a collective. As the evidence shows it was only very rarely that Hirohito acted outside the parameters of the collective.

However, the Tokyo War Crimes Trials were conducted largely on the basis of Anglo-Saxon empirical logic and law. Guilt and blame would be individual not collective. As the Tokyo War Crimes Trials demonstrated, ignorance of war atrocities committed in contravention of the Hague Protocols of the Geneva Convention was no defense. Thus Yasuaki Onuma in *Beyond Victor's Justice* [1984] argues that the war crimes tribunal "regarded as criminal not only positive acts but also 'disregard' of the 'legal duty' to prevent breaches of the laws of war . . ."[129] Without MacArthur's intervention, Hirohito would almost certainly have been a Class A criminal charged with conspiracy to start and wage war. It seems likely that, had Hirohito been charged along with his military confederates, based on the criteria that were used at the Tokyo War Crimes Trials, he would almost certainly have been found guilty of war crimes and executed.

The judges presiding over the Tokyo tribunals were divided. B. V. A. Röling, the Dutch judge, who tried to put on 'Japanese clothing' in making his judgments, was adamant that the Emperor "had no power at all. He was a constitutional Emperor" and added that if he had not co-operated "he would have been murdered . . .."[130] Röling agreed with the decision not to prosecute the Emperor. However, President of the Tokyo Tribunal, Sir William Webb, observed, "No ruler can commit the crime of launching aggressive war and then validly claim to be excused for so doing because his life would otherwise have been in danger."[131] The French judge, Henri Bernard wrote one of the most discerning opinions when he wrote that the declaration of war by Japan, "had a principal author who escaped all prosecution and of whom in any case the present defendants could only be considered accomplices."[132]

Japanese historians have been equally divided and not always on the side of the Emperor. Professor Kiyoshi Inoue, a constitutional and legal historian at Kyoto University, in an article *Ho no Ronri Rekishi no Ronri* [1948] (The Logic of Law and the Logic of History) concluded:

> This was a man who, with all power in his hands, made the decision [to go to war] after taking into consideration all opinions and ascertaining all information with great care. It was not at all a decision made by a person whose freedom of action was deprived mentally or physically, or who had lost the ability to think.[133]

In 1975 Inoue, a doctrinaire communist, published '*Tenno no Senso Sekinin*' (The Emperor's Responsibility for War). Similarly Yasuaki Onuma, a professor of law at

Tokyo University in Tokyo '*Saiban Kara Sengo Sekinin no Shiso E*' [1987] (From the Tokyo Trial to the Concept of Post-war Responsibility) concluded that the victor nations knowingly overlooked Emperor Hirohito's guilt.

Richard Minear's *Victor's Justice: The Tokyo War Crimes Trial* [1971] argued that the failure to prosecute key war criminals—particularly the Emperor—showed that the trial was merely a political construct of the victor nations. The historian John Dower has also concluded, in his account of post-war Japan, *Embracing Defeat* [1999], that America, by choosing to ignore Hirohito's guilt and by participating in the cover-up of this fact, "came close to turning the whole issue of 'war responsibility' into a joke."[134] By refusing to countenance Hirohito's participation as either a defendant or witness, Supreme Commander Allied Powers, General MacArthur turned the Tokyo War Crimes Trials into a 'show trial' that besmirched the justice on offer and effectively relieved Japan of the guilt of their activities in the *Pacific War*, thus laying the grounds for the post-war hostility between Japan and the rest of Asia.

In summary, while there is not enough evidence to suggest as Bix and Bergamini do that Hirohito orchestrated the war behind the façade of a constitutional monarchy, neither does the available evidence suggest that Hirohito was entirely an innocent hostage to the ultra-nationalist militarists who had taken control of the Japanese government in the 1930s. On three occasions he did act as an absolute monarch, outside the normal conventions of collective decision-making. It is clear that, in a formal sense, in spite of the absolute powers implied by the Meiji Constitution, Hirohito largely operated within the conventions of a constitutional monarchy and within the Japanese cultural conventions of collective decision-making. Outside of these conventions, he would certainly have had the power of influence, though it is very unclear how far he used these powers. Allowing for the large quantity of 'unknowns,' because Hirohito and his courtiers destroyed most documentation relating to the war immediately after the surrender, it would be fair to conclude that Hirohito's opinions and actions probably fitted into the broad spectrum of nationalist views that represented the *zeitgeist* of Japan in the 1930s.

While broadly sympathetic to the expansionist ideals of Pan-Asianism, Hirohito was supportive of the Empire *post facto*, but was much more cautious with regard to fighting wars, particularly with America where he risked not only his Chrysanthemum Throne but also his head. Finally, in a strictly western legal sense, Hirohito was individually responsible for the war and the atrocities committed during the war and would almost certainly have been found guilty and executed if he had been prosecuted at the Tokyo War Crimes Trials.

Japan's Empire [1941]: [**Map: 3.6**] By summer 1941, Japan had opportunistically acquired an extensive empire—not just because the nationalists wanted to build a Japanese Empire but because geopolitical frailties in Asia presented 'golden opportunities.' As historian Professor Peter Duus has pointed out, without these "international" preconditions, "the Japanese Empire might not have expanded as dramatically as it did in the 1930s and 1940s—or perhaps not expanded at all."[135] The *Ryukyu Islands*, nominally vassal states to both China and the Satsuma Domain in southern *Kyushu*, ceased paying tribute to the Qing Dynasty in 1874 and were annexed by Japan in 1879. After defeat in the *Second Sino-Japanese War*, China ceded *Formosa* (later Taiwan) to Japan at the *Treaty of Shimonoseki* on 17 April 1895. China was forced to give up its claims to vassal suzerainty over Korea and in the same year, under the guise of 'protecting' Korea, Japanese plotters, probably with official connivance, murdered its Empress, Myeongseong. In 1910 the Korean government of Emperor Gojong was forced to sign a *Treaty of Annexation*. Further opportunity was provided by *World War I*, which gave Japan temporary command of the German colony of Tsingtau and by League of Nations mandate more or less permanent control of many of Germany's former *South Pacific* territories including Palau, the Northern Marianas Islands of Saipan, Tinion, and Rota as well as the Truk Lagoon and Kwajelein in the Marshall Islands. The global depression starting in the autumn of 1929 gave Japan the perfect cover to occupy China's province of Manchuria. Apart from the condemnations of the League of Nations' Lytton Commission, barely a whimper was raised from global leaders. Between 1932 and 1937, there followed the creeping occupation of northern China to the point that Peking was all but surrounded. In 1937 the Marco Polo Bridge Incident led to further conquests, which led to approximately half the country being brought under the effective control of Japan's puppet government in Nanking under the leadership of Wang Jingwei.

By the summer of 1941, Japan, taking advantage of the overthrow of the French government by the *Nazis* and its replacement by the puppet Vichy government, expanded further with the *de facto* take-over of French *Indochine* (Vietnam, Cambodia and Laos). In the summer of 1941 Japan controlled an empire of over 300 million people (including 200 million Chinese) and territories covering 3 million square miles. By comparison, in 1939 the British Empire had 449 million people and covered 22 million square miles; France, 56 million people over 7.5 million square miles; Holland 61 million over 1.3 million square miles; and America 17 million people over 1.3 million square miles (including the territories of the Philippines, Alaska and *Hawaii*). Japan had not only joined the ranks of Asia's great imperial powers, but perhaps more importantly had begun to threaten the geopolitical interests of its powerful neighbour to the south, the United States and its colonial possession of the Philippines. The occupation of French *Indochine* not only put the Japanese Army just across the water from *Luzon*, but also threatened to cut all supply to Chiang Kai-shek's *Kuomintang* government based in Chongqing.

Japan's imperialists had been fortunate to be able to take advantage of successive power vacuums in East Asia. Thus far the Japanese Empire had grown with little resistance from the West. By the summer of 1941 however, the United States was no longer prepared to stand by and see its regional power, and what it perceived as its right to 'open door' trade, particularly with China, further compromised by Japanese expansion. Though the United States' rulers largely eschewed such *realpolitik* terms, preferring instead to hark on about Japanese transgression of Chinese sovereignty, America's global geopolitical power was under threat. A response was required.

The Power of MAGIC: The value of code breaking had shown itself to great effect in 1921 when the intelligence gleaned from Japanese diplomatic traffic helped President Harding close out the Washington Naval Conference to America's advantage. Although there was a brief hiatus in America's code breaking, when Henry Stimson closed down the Army's intelligence unit in 1929 on the 'old school' grounds of ungentlemanly conduct, it was recreated by the Army in 1935 under the charge of Colonel William Friedman.

The Jewish son of a Rumanian wine merchant, Friedman was a geneticist who graduated from Cornell University. While working for the Riverbank Laboratories in Chicago, Friedman met and married Elizabeth Smith, a cryptographer assistant to the then famous cryptographer Elizabeth Wells Gallup, who specialized in the analysis of Shakespeare's work. Friedman began to work for the Army when in *World War I* Riverbank Laboratories offered his services to them. In 1921 Friedman became chief cryptanalyst at the war department, becoming the head of Signals and Intelligence Service (SIS). Thereafter Army officers were sent to Friedman for training. In the 1920s he studied the use of electronic rotor machines being developed for cryptography, which enabled him to crack the new cypher machine introduced for Japan's most important diplomatic traffic in 1937. It was Friedman's crucial insight that Japanese cryptologists had abandoned the rotor for a new mechanical system. This machine, called Alphabetic Typewriter 97 by the Japanese but codenamed PURPLE by SIS, had abandoned the use of a rotor in favour of stepper switches similar to those used in automated telephone exchanges. Friedman managed to reconstruct a duplicate machine.

By the spring of 1941, Friedman's unit, working in tandem with Lieutenant-Commander Alwyn's OP20GZ section of Naval Intelligence, were able to decrypt 97 percent of PURPLE's traffic. It was an ability that enabled them to decrypt the infamous Fourteen Part Message received by the Japanese Embassy on 7 December 1941, hours before the Japanese attack on *Pearl Harbor*.

Operation MAGIC was the name given to information gleaned from PURPLE and other codes broken by the intelligence services. Essentially MAGIC was a selected collation of the most important elements of the intelligence, which was circulated by courier to the President, the Secretaries of the Navy and War, the Directors of Naval and Military Intelligence, the Chief of the War Plans Directorate and the Secretary of State. This MAGIC source was almost jeopardized by British sloppiness in 1941; Germany, which had decrypted British diplomatic traffic from Washington that indicated that Japanese diplomatic traffic was being read, warned their associates in Tokyo. In spite of this Japan remained completely convinced of the security of their encryption machine and used it throughout the war. The combination of MAGIC intercepts and the insights provided by the Combat Intelligence Unit set up in *Hawaii* under Lieutenant Joseph Rochefort, who focused on the decryption of Japan's naval code, JN-25, would provide US commanders a decisive advantage throughout the war.

Friedman's unit worked closely with the British Government Code and Cypher School at Bletchley Park, exchanging a PURPLE machine for details of the German-designed Enigma machine and its decryption secrets. Intelligence from all these sources became known as ULTRA and provided US commanders with a compendium of intelligence information. **[See Appendix F: Intelligence in the Pacific War]**

Financial Freeze and Oil Embargo: America's Precipitation of the War with Japan [July 1941]: On 4 July 1941, the US government discovered from its MAGIC intercepts that the Japanese leaders had decided to 'strike south' toward South East Asia. The Russians confirmed this through their spy, Richard Sorge, a German journalist, who had access to secret information at the German Embassy. For Roosevelt, Hull and the cabinet, it was a Japanese plan that clearly demonstrated a Japanese intention to risk war with Great Britain, Holland and possibly America too. Thus the Japanese plan to occupy Vietnam, barely a military action at all given the quiescence of the Vichy government, was the straw that broke America's hitherto accommodative stance on Japanese expansion. On 22 July, Vichy Prime Minister, Admiral François Darlan, told US Ambassador Admiral William Leahy (later Chairman of the US Joint Chiefs of Staff), that at "the extremely strong insistence of the Japanese, he had been forced to grant permission for the Japanese to occupy all of Indochina."[136]

Japan's plan called for an American reaction. Cordell Hull, still intent on avoiding war at all costs, suggested China should be provided with a US$100m to US$200m loan combined with economic measures that would fall short of a provocation that would lead to war. The Navy also argued for measures that would not provoke Japan into an attack on the United States. All parties were agreed that any form of trade embargo, particularly involving oil, would lead to war with Japan. Roosevelt, for the first time in the on-going drama of Japanese expansionism, decided on firm actions that would make clear America's intent but fall short of provoking Japan to war. A military build-up was authorized for the Philippine Army, which was to be incorporated into the US Army with its head, Field Marshal Douglas MacArthur, appointed as commander. A major portion of the proposed deterrent was the transfer of B-17 Flying Fortress to America's Far Eastern colony. From Manila American bombers could threaten Japanese airbases on *Formosa*, and perhaps even strike as far as Japan.

Secondly Roosevelt planned a selective embargo on what could be exported to Japan. This would be achieved by the freezing of all of Japan's accounts in America. Funds would be released by license for approved goods. Exports could include oil and gasoline but only at octane levels below 80. To prevent stockpiling, Japan would be limited to oil imports at the average level of 1935–1936. The aim was to increase pressure on Japan while giving assurance to the voters on the East Coast who were about to face gasoline rationing.

On the evening of 25 July 1941, Roosevelt signed Executive Order No.8832, which subjected all of Japanese monetary assets held in the United States to control by license. The White House press release stated that: "this measure in effect brings all financial and import and export trade transactions in which Japanese interests are involved under the control of the government and imposes criminal penalties for violation of the order."[137]

The order extended to Japanese colonies including Manchukuo and China to protect them from looting by Japan's puppet government installed in Nanking. All assets owned 25 percent or more by Japanese interests were frozen. When Wall Street opened for business on Monday 28 July, the foreign exchange market for Yen simply disappeared. Japanese dollar bonds crashed to 20–30 percent of their par value. The Yokohama Silk Exchange closed. The New York Commodity Exchange suspended silk futures. In effect the entire Japanese international payments system seized up. Japan's gold held in America became immoveable and unusable. In South America modest amounts of gold and foreign exchange were similarly immobilized by governments that followed Roosevelt's lead. Cargoes destined for America remained stuck on Japanese wharves. When Great Britain and Holland followed America's lead, the Yen could only be used and traded within Japan's own empire. After the end of July only one dollar-license was granted—on 1 October to a Japanese company to pay a Cincinnati company for machinery shipped a year earlier.

The task of deleting and implementing the new system was assigned to Under Secretary of State, Sumner Welles, who in turn delegated the task to Assistant Secretary of State, Dean Acheson in his role as Chairman of the Foreign Funds Control Committee (FFCC). Along with hawks in the Treasury, Acheson determined to turn the license system into a full freeze. While Roosevelt and Welles were in Newfoundland meeting Churchill aboard USS *Augusta*, where they were being encouraged to employ ultimatums against Japan, Acheson and his co-conspirators, back in Washington, determined that Japan would get no oil at all. Roosevelt and Hull were completely unaware that their intended flexible economic policy had turned into an absolute financial freeze.

At the FFCC, which represented members from the State Department, the Justice Department and the Treasury, Acheson, the committee's chairman, explained that, after discussion with Welles, it was concluded that it was best "to take no action on Japanese applications."[138] Japanese officials were given an administrative 'run-around.' It was apparent that Japan was not the only country with *Bakuryo* (middle-ranking staffers) who tried to direct government policy beyond their pay-grade. A treasury official later admitted, "the Japanese tried every conceivable way of getting the precious crude oil, but to each proposal the Division of Foreign Funds Control had an evasive answer ready to camouflage its flat refusal."[139]

By the time that Hull found out what was going on after a remark made by the Japanese ambassador, Nomura, over five weeks had passed. Acheson's excuse was that in fear of an asset freeze, Japan had moved a great deal of its funds to South America. Acheson argued that Japan could buy its American oil with cash from these accounts. Hull and Roosevelt lunched on 5 September but no reversal of the effective oil embargo was forthcoming. By coincidence on the same day, Prime Minister Togo and his military cabinet were deciding on war with the United States. Previous attempts by Treasury Secretary Morgenthau and other hawks to harden the measure had been slapped down. With no record of what Roosevelt and Hull discussed at their lunch various historians have speculated that the failure to reverse the *de facto* oil embargo was the result of the

President's unwillingness to appear weak. They may also have surmised that, with intelligence information seeming to indicate that Japan was preparing for war, it made little sense to provide them with the resources that they needed.

However, given the importance of the decision and knowing that oil was a life or death issue for the Japanese and that its embargo was a quasi-hostile act, it is evident that over the summer Roosevelt's position on Japan had moved on. In Newfoundland, Churchill and Roosevelt had deepened the US-British alliance with the signing of the *Atlantic Charter*. Its eight declarations included the "desire to see no territorial changes that do not accord with the freely expressed wishes of the people concerned."[140] Perhaps most importantly, American public opinion polls had shifted. In early August 51 percent of Americans believed that Roosevelt should risk war rather than allow Japan to become more powerful. By September 67 percent of Americans agreed that they would "take steps to keep Japan from becoming more powerful even if this means risking war."[141] Ickes was also raising complaints, largely contrived, about domestic shortages of gasoline. Roosevelt disingenuously told reporters after returning to Rockland, Maine, that it had been "an interchange of views, that's all" and that the country was "no closer to war."[142] This was not true. Indeed Churchill had told his colleagues that Roosevelt had confided to him that "he would wage war, but not declare it" and "would become more and more provocative."[143]

An easy opportunity soon came for Hull to reverse Acheson's *de facto* financial and trade embargo. In early September a Japanese intermediary proposed to Hull that a barter trade should be made for US$15m of silk in exchange for a range of twenty commodities. Far from sidelining Acheson, Hull sent the matter to him for his opinion, which predictably was negative. Whatever the initial intentions of Roosevelt and Hull, by September they were clearly fully behind the policy of financial and trade exclusion of Japan. Remarkably no US agency carried out an analysis of how the financial freeze would affect the Japanese economy.

The effects of America's oil embargo in Japan were almost instantaneous. Without new oil supply, their stocks would run down every month. Japan's Cabinet Planning Board reported, "the Empire will shortly be impoverished and unable to hold its own."[144] The Board's president, Teiichi Suzuki concluded that essential inventories were below requirements and, in a review completed in November, he predicted that, on current levels of consumption, the stocks of eight out of eleven vital commodities would be 50 percent or more depleted in 1942. Stockpiles of copper, zinc and carbon black would be almost entirely used. As Prince Konoe reflected, "Confronted with military strangulation by oil embargoes and the choice of admitting defeat in China, thereby abandoning a large part of his continental empire and probably destabilizing the monarchy he had inherited, Hirohito opted for his third alternative: war against the United States and Britain."[145]

By its oil embargo, Japan had in effect been given the ultimatum demanded by the hawks in Roosevelt's administration. As Ambassador Grew in Tokyo wrote in his diary after the freeze order in August: "the vicious circle of reprisals and counter reprisals is on. *Facilis descensus averni est* . . . The obvious conclusion is eventual war."[146] Both sides were prepared to continue talks but in early September, another Japanese Imperial Conference decided that plans for a military assault on the US, Great Britain and the Netherlands must be developed. As Takeo Iguchi has argued, "The US economic sanctions against Japan became the decisive trigger for war."[147] America's *de facto* oil embargo, an act of war in all but name, had precipitated the countdown to military engagement. It was a decision effectively forced on Roosevelt by knowledge of Japan's intention to 'strike south' and his realization that America would have to fight to defend its geopolitical interests.

As the American financial freeze and oil embargo episode shows, the blame for starting the *Pacific War* was not one sided. As historian Professor Mark Peattie has commented, "the historical approach to the causes of the war has largely been shaped by 'praise and blame': a perspective from which evil forces of militarism, ultra-nationalism, and fascism were seen as crushing beleaguered elements of progress and democracy . . ."[148] While it is evident that Japan did follow an ultra-nationalist path in its attempt to co-opt China into its pan-Asian empire, America too had Asian geopolitical interests that it wanted to protect, and not only its possession of the Philippines. America predicated its existence on its right to trade globally. By the 1930 this perceived right was not only ideological, but also existential. America's economy had grown so large, its international commercial interests so extensive that it simply could not afford to allow a world in which Germany and Japan carved out autarkic spheres. America's oil embargo showed that it was fully prepared to risk war, not only with Japan but also, because of the *Tripartite Pact* [September 1940], with Germany, which Roosevelt perceived as a much greater threat to his nation's geopolitical and imperial interests.

Indeed Roosevelt's decision to apply pressure to Japan through the oil embargo was inextricably linked to his desire to support Great Britain in its war with Germany and Italy. He did not want to see Britain, the nation that he was straining to sustain, further weakened. While Roosevelt was aware that the oil embargo risked war, he and his administration must fervently have hoped, and indeed some certainly expected, that the Japanese governement would fold under the pressure. Roosevelt's administration not only underestimated the internal pressures on Japan's ruling elite not to back down but also misjudged Japan's ability to fight war. Misled by Japan's defeat at the *Battles of Nomonhan* [1939] and by Japan's military difficulties in fighting Chiang Kai-shek's *Kuomintang* forces in central China, Japan's fighting capability was significantly underrated in Washington and London. Moreover Roosevelt's administration, albeit aware of the need to mobilize and re-arm, nevertheless overestimated its preparedness for war in the *Pacific*.

4 Mobilization for War in Asia: America and Japan

[1931–December 1941]

[Chart: 4.1] [Maps: 4.1A, 4.1B, 4.2, 4.3]

Lack of US Preparedness for War: With the imposition of a financial freeze and effective oil embargo against Japan, Roosevelt had begun the countdown to war. By September 1941, after his lunch with Secretary of State Cordell Hull, where Roosevelt decided not to reverse the *de facto* oil embargo of Japan, the President knew that war, with both Japan and Germany, was not only likely but also probable. Furthermore he knew that the United States was not prepared for war. While Roosevelt had pushed through a huge program of military rearmament from the beginning of 1940, after July 1941 a frantic US mobilization was required to meet an enemy that had fully mobilized for the *Second Sino-Japanese War* four years earlier. Roosevelt not only had to prepare for war in the *Pacific* but more importantly from the American point of view, prepare for war in Europe.

The problem for America before 1941 was not simply that it was not prepared for war in the *Pacific*; it was not prepared for war anywhere. Bernard Baruch, who had run the War Industries Board at the end of *World War I*, spent the interwar years as a lone prophet of doom—warning of America's military weakness. It might have been thought that America would have wanted "to prevent a repetition of its utter unpreparedness of 1917,"[1] but, on the eve of *World War II*, it found itself in an even worse position. In 1938 Baruch told the President, "the condition of American defense is unknown only to Americans. Every foreign power knows what we are doing and exactly what we lack."[2] Unlike the politicians, who appeared to have their heads firmly stuck in the sand, America's Army and Navy were not unaware of Japan's strengths. During the visit of the USS *Augusta* to Japan in June 1934, US Naval officers had ample time and opportunity to view the equipment of the Japanese Navy. "One thing was that it was big," observed Lloyd Mustin, "and the other was that it was good . . . this was indeed a tough, professional navy . . ."[3] Mustin, from a famous twentieth century naval family, noted that, in spite of their cordial reception, "There was a clear sense of world rivalry, well recognized. When your instinctive reaction is that you two are on an inevitable collision course, social relationships are inclined to be a little stiff, and they were."[4]

When war in Europe was declared on 3 September 1939, two days after the *blitzkrieg* invasion of Poland, Germany had been rearming for seven years and was the only major power other than Japan that was wholly geared to the immediate conduct of war. Worse was to follow. The German invasion of France on 10 May 1940 and its rapid defeat and capitulation gave Roosevelt and America a severe jolt. As the economist, author and journalist, Eliot Janeway, noted, "the fall of France had found the American economy unprepared even to become prepared."[5]

It is salutary to look at American economic capacity for war at the end of the 1930s. Although America produced 26.4 million tons of steel in 1938 this was not far ahead of that of Germany, with half the population, on 20.7 million tons. However, whereas German steel plants were working at full output, US plants were operating at little more than a third of capacity utilization. In the post-war period, America's ability to wage war had shrivelled. Both the American military machine and its arms industries were skeletal. Because American tax law did not allow companies to write off obsolete plant, it was sometimes more economic to demolish facilities rather than mothball them. Thus Remington, the biggest rifle manufacturer in the world, destroyed its factory at Eddystone, Pennsylvania. In the summer of 1940, America had an army of just 280,000 men. Its widely dispersed forces, stationed in small units, did not possess a single combat division. The War Department history would note that when Germany invaded Poland, "the state of equipment was such that not even a single division could have been put in the field on short notice."[6] Even more concerning, Henry Stimson, who became Secretary of Defense in 1940, noted, "We did not have enough [gun] powder in the whole United States to last the men we now have fighting overseas for anything like a day's fighting, and what is worse we did not have the [gun] powder plants or facilities to make it; they had all been destroyed after the last war."[7] America even failed to meet its own limited legal defense requirements. In 1939 the number of staff officers available to the Assistant Secretary of Defense was just seventeen compared to the seventy-eight mandated in the *Defense Act* of 1920.

In spite of being the world's most powerful economy, militarily America, with fewer than 100,000 combat soldiers, was a pigmy. Her armed forces ranked eighteenth in the world, trailing countries such as Spain, Portugal, Switzerland, Holland and Belgium. The US Navy was also short 20,000 men. While America, given time, could have scraped together five or six divisions to put in the field, Hitler had 136 divisions in action with a further seventy in reserve. Germany's armies were over five million strong with a further 500,000 men in the Luftwaffe. With regard to equipment, even the modest aim to increase the US Army to 375,000 in the summer of 1940 meant that new recruits had to practice their drill with sticks. Needless to add, but the existing US forces were equipped with hopelessly out-dated rifles, machines guns, artillery and tanks. The Navy's shipbuilding program had fallen to a fraction of that of Japan. Investment in military technology post *World War I* had been negligible. Hitler was not ignorant of the facts when he boasted, ". . . Germany today, is together with her allies strong enough to oppose any combination of powers in the world."[8]

As well as being unprepared for war in Europe, there was little idea about how to go about gearing up the economy for conflict. US economic mobilization had been so bungled in 1918 that at the beginning of their mobilization, General Pershing, the

American leader of the American Expeditionary Force, had had to buy his grenades from the British, as well as rifles and machine guns.

Logically, Roosevelt would have turned to Bernard Baruch to reproduce his *World War I* War Industries Board and it is a measure of his distrust for this Democrat businessman that, in spite of taking his advice, he declined to appoint him to reconstruct his former efforts. Roosevelt was determined not to be in the clutch of businessmen and vaguely asserted that: "If war does come we will make it a New Deal war."[9] Thus when Roosevelt passed the appropriations bill on 1 July 1938, on the same day he passed an *Excess Profits Tax Act*, which was impossible to define but was thrown as a sop to his liberal supporters. There must on no account be any 'war millionaires.' As Henry Stimson observed, ". . . there are a great many people in Congress who think that they can tax business out of all proportion and still have businessmen work diligently and quickly. That is not human nature."[10] Ultimately Roosevelt erred on the side of pragmatism and his liberal leanings did not hold back the process of economic mobilization.

If Roosevelt was cautious, his Congress was hostile. Although Marshall forcefully persuaded the President that massive increases in funding were required even to defend America from the possibilities of a German invasion, the Congress would not be easily overcome. A strong anti-war bloc in the Midwest tried to divert funds for the Army toward farm benefits, with their leader, Alva Adams from Colorado, arguing, "We can make savings by reducing appropriations for war which is not coming."[11] Not even the American industrialists were unanimous in their support of developing a war economy. William Knudsen, a General Motors auto executive who was later made a Lieutenant-General and Chairman of the Office of Production Management, pleaded with Henry Ford to produce Rolls Royce engines for British's Spitfires. Ford refused on the grounds of his isolationist convictions. Ultimately it was the threat of war with Japan in 1941 and then its actuality that proved to be the main recruiting master and economic mobilizer of America's war effort. It was only with the approval of the *Lend-Lease Act* by Congress in the second week of March 1941 that America began to commit itself to being "the great arsenal of democracy."[12]

*America's **Global Task of Production and Supply:*** For the United States to equip itself to fight wars on two fronts, Europe and the *Pacific*, would have been a formidable task in itself. However, from early on it became clear that this was not the only task required of the US economy. In November 1940 the British Ambassador to Washington, Lord Lothian, announced with brutal honesty, "boys we're broke, all we need now is your money."[13]

This statement must have come as a shock if not disbelief to the many people who saw Great Britain as the world's largest and richest empire. In reality Britain, whose economic strength had been much dissipated by *World War I* and by the Great Depression was a great power in decline. In 1939 its industrial production was just 17 percent of that of the United States. Moreover Britain's strength in engineering and manufacturing was undermined by its need for imported raw materials that were denied it by the German U-boat blockade.

Although the US Lend-Lease program, which provided Britain with the destroyers it needed to beat the U-boat threat in the so-called *Battle of the Atlantic*, was a much needed palliative for Britain's economic weakness, there was a constant fear on the part of the Roosevelt administration that Britain might be forced out of the war by its enfeebled economy. Ultimately US manufacturing was required to provide a large portion of the war *matériel* used by the British, including items such as Sherman tanks, transport ships, aircraft for use on fleet carriers, etc. Soviet requirements were also substantial. After Hitler's invasion of the Soviet Union, American interest lay in keeping Stalin in the war where his forces, on Hitler's Eastern Front, could wear down Germany's military strength. Roosevelt needed to sustain his unexpected new Allies with the fear gnawing at the back of his mind that Stalin might do a U-turn and settle with the *Nazis*, making the task of the US ground forces in re-conquering Europe even more onerous. Thus substantial feeding of the Soviet war machine was required in term of tanks and aircraft. Finally China, under Chiang Kai-shek was virtually bereft of manufacturing capability. What capacity it had in this area had been severely depleted by Japan in their occupation of China's commercial heartlands on its eastern sea border. The efforts to supply China with everything from manufactured goods such as arms, trucks, and aircraft were more than equalled by the need to transport all of its aviation fuel and oil by air. This phenomenal logistic task achieved via the Hump (the airlift over the Himalayas between Assam and Kunming) kept China in the war and tied down some 1.5 million Japanese troops and their arms in the process.

America's wartime economic effort therefore, not only needed manufacturing and logistics capacity to keep its own armies in the field, eventually 8.3 million men in aggregate, but also needed to provide critical supply of *matériel* to sustain all of its Allied partners including Britain, China, Canada, Australia, and the Soviet Union. It was a global economic and logistic challenge that the US economy, ravaged by almost a decade of depression, seemed ill equipped to deal with when war broke out in 1939.

The New Deal and Technological Advance in Pre-War America: [Chart: I.4] H. E.

Forman, Managing Director of the Associated General Contractors of America, observed, "A sense of urgency prevailed throughout the war construction program. Work drove ahead through all kinds of weather and obstacles. Projects of unprecedented size and complexity were completed at speeds which surprised even the industry."[14]

The attack on *Pearl Harbor* may have been a catalyst for energizing a nation, but in spite of the economic stagnation of the 1930s, the Roosevelt administration's 'Keynesian' intervention in the economy had seen the completion of some of the largest infrastructure projects ever attempted. The Tennessee Valley Authority (TVA), established in May 1933 to regenerate impoverished agrarian areas of Alabama, Mississippi and Kentucky, initiated dam building and electricity generating projects which were the largest infrastructure projects that the world had ever seen. The Grand Coulee Dam on the *Columbia River* remains the world's largest concrete structure. The TVA became a worldwide model for agrarian modernization often taken up by totalitarian economies. The Public Works Administration (PWA), set up by Roosevelt as part of the 'New Deal' under the *National Recovery Industrial Act* [1933], left an important legacy for America's wartime requirements. By 1939 the PWA had built 166,000 buildings and constructed over 700,000 miles of new roads. The US route system, nearly all with two lane highways, was completed by 1941. The expansion of America's road system would prove vital in relieving congestion of the rail system that had so bedevilled Pershing's logistical planning in *World War I*.

From 1930 America also greatly expanded electricity capacity, particularly hydro. Between 1930 and 1941 America's electricity output rose by 87 percent. When the Bonneville Dam started to be constructed in 1933 it was not foreseen that the power generated would supply the huge amount required by the shipyards of Portland, Oregon a decade later. Aluminum Company of America (ALCOA), attracted by the availability of cheap power opened the region's first aluminum plant in 1940. To a large extent public works projects in the 1930s powered America's military mobilization in the 1940s. Perhaps the most significant contribution of 1930s pump priming however, was the impact on manpower. Established in 1933, the Civil Conservation Corp (CCC) paid unemployed young men aged between eighteen and twenty-five to work on public projects in return for board and lodging (often in vast tented villages) and US$30 per week; US$25 had to be sent home to their families. The CCC, which at its peak employed 50,000 young adults, created a cadre of disciplined young workers with construction skills. By 1940 there were 2.6 million construction workers in the United States, of whom 58,000 were engineers and 266,000 were electricians.

To a large degree the public works programs of the 1930s provided America with people with the skill sets and know-how to scale up the industrial infrastructure required by the onset of war in Europe and Asia. By the end of 1941 infrastructure projects completed by the Corps of Engineers included 371 troop cantonments (with 220 under way), 20 ordnance plants (with 40 under way) and 9 storage depots (with 23 under way). In 1942, expenditure on military construction tripled and expenditure on the expansion of industrial facilities doubled. In the civilian sector the number of workers employed by construction contractors increased from 1.15 million in 1939 to 2.17 million in 1942.

While the public sector provided much-needed investment in infrastructure and created skilled employment in the stagnant 1930s, one sector of the private economy continued to see relative prosperity over the decade. The automobile industry enjoyed robust growth in the 1920s with aggregate production reaching 5.3 million vehicles in 1928. By 1930 America had produced 50 million vehicles since the advent of the automobile; there was a vehicle for every five people—a level of consumer penetration far in advance of any other country. In that year some 85 percent of the world's automobiles were in the United States. In Japan only 500 vehicles were produced in 1930. Although production collapsed at the beginning of the depression to just 2.4 million vehicles per annum, a healthy recovery to 4.6 million aggregate production had been achieved by 1940. The scale of the industry was important in terms of the number of trained mechanics needed to service the huge accumulated stock of private vehicles that grew from 23.1 million registrations in 1930 to 29.6 million by 1940; truck registrations grew even faster from 3.5 million in 1929 to 5.2 million in 1941. It was also the decade in which car radios, heaters and hydraulic brakes became standard. New options for car purchasers included automatic transmission, power steering and larger, more powerful engines.

By 1941 the US automobile industry was the largest employer in America with 6.7 million people dependent on its jobs. Remarkably within a year, starting on 1 February 1942, the entire industry would be shut down and retooled for the production of war *matériel*. The energies of US enterprise that had created the world's first 'auto economy' would now be directed at winning the wars against Germany and Japan. It was a happy chance that the auto sector had the tools for the job. As Bruce Catton noted, the auto industry discovered that "all but a fraction of its tools could be used to make munitions."[15] In addition the mass motorization of American society produced a workforce whose skills as mechanics and drivers would be ideally suited to the mechanized needs of *World War II*.

Furthermore the depression rationalized the production of motor vehicles. Before 1930 there had been as many as 1,800 automobile manufacturers; the depression winnowed out hundreds of inefficient vehicle companies and by the end of the decade there were just three main manufacturers, Ford, General Motors and Chrysler producing over 90 percent of all vehicle output. These companies had the technology, logistical and management ability to gear up many of the emerging wartime industries to mass production. Factory scale, layout, and quality control changed fundamentally over the decade and significantly aided the creation of a highly efficient war economy. New assembly line technologies transformed the productive potential of manufacturing. The development of small electric motors enabled assembly lines to be modernized, reducing the need for thermal energy that was more difficult to apply to the flexible needs of assembly and the production line. Between 1929 and 1939 the Bureau of the Census (*Statistical Abstract of the United States*: [1948]) calculated that electric horsepower within the manufacturing industry increased from 33.8 million to 45.3 million. All of the major auto companies were heavily involved in the mass manufacture of equipment needed by America's armies after war broke out in 1941.

In addition, General Electric (GE), another American industrial behemoth, had pioneered the development of the diesel-electric motor in 1920, which powered the assembly line transformation of the 1930s. Their diesel-electric motors became a mainstay of the new power generation technologies for ships and particularly submarines. After 1935 GE was involved in the construction of every submarine built.

In the home, electrification had as great an impact as in the factory. The 1930s saw rapid take up of electric refrigeration that took over from the 'icebox,' which was what was typically understood as refrigeration before the depression. By 1940 some 56 percent of urban households had refrigerators run by electricity. It was a technology that would have a significant impact on America's ability to keep its troops well fed across the vast reaches of the *Pacific*.

In spite of the depression the aeronautical industry also made significant technological advances. In 1936 Donald Douglas introduced the then revolutionary Douglas DC-3; the plane not only starred in the final scenes of *Casablanca* [1942] with Humphrey Bogart, Ingmar Bergman and Claude Rains, but more importantly, the DC-3 demonstrated that the aeronautical industry sustained a high level of technological inventiveness in the face of difficult business conditions of the 1930s. With the onset of war, Douglas would be one of the main industrial innovators in the race to produce more technologically advanced planes for the US Army and Navy.

Productivity gains were also seen in other areas of new technology. Advances in instrumentation improved process control and raised quality as well as productivity. Hydraulics and analogue computer systems hastened the advances in automated control. The 1930s saw the development of technologies that would change the industrial world from one which relied on mechanical technology to one that increasingly switched to electro-mechanical technology in the 1940s. The era saw similarly spectacular advances in the development of special steels using complex alloys. A carbon steel blade used to cut plastics might need to be sharpened every sixty feet while a tungsten carbon alloy blade would last for 10,000 feet. US output/capital unit input that had grown by just 1.09 percent per annum from 1919 to 1929 grew by 3.56 percent per annum from 1929 to 1939.

The US Economy in the 1930s: **[Map: 4.1A, 4.1B, 4.3A] [Charts: C.4, C.11]** By 1941 the US population had grown to 132 million people, having more than quadrupled in the previous eighty years. During this period of explosive population growth the United States had also become the world's dominant industrial economy. By 1929 America accounted for over half of the planet's industrial output.

However, economic activity declined precipitously after the Wall Street Crash in 1929. While the period leading up to the crash saw significant overinvestment in the economy, between 1929 and 1933 private fixed capital formation (investment) fell from US$20.1bn to barely US$3.0bn. In the 1930s unemployment rose to 20m, while more than half the population was in effect under-employed. Personal incomes fell by 40 percent. Although the job creating policies of the 'New Deal' such as the Tennessee Valley project helped bring about a modest recovery in demand and economic activity by 1941, there is no doubt that the US economy was operating significantly below its productive capacity when Roosevelt took the momentous decision to freeze Japanese financial assets.

The start of *World War II* initiated a huge increase in military expenditures. In 1940 US spending on defense was US$1.7bn; 16.6% of a US$10.1bn budget. Thereafter defense spending rose to US$6.4bn (+276%) in 1941, US$25.6bn (+300%) in 1942, US$66.6bn (+160%) in 1943, US$79.2bn (+18.1%) in 1944 and US$81.9bn (+3.4%) in 1945. In that year defense spending accounted for over 80% of the government's

US$106.8bn budget. The surge in President Roosevelt's military spending was initially accounted for by the increase in investment for new processing plants, factories and shipyards. The voting of funds by Congress greatly exceeded its ability to issue contracts. In June 1941, of the US$46.9bn thus far authorized by Congress, only US$21bn worth of work or products had been contracted for. After 1943 investment in capacity was barely 6 percent of the total and suggests that between July 1941 and December 1942, the United States had largely built the new capacity to produce the war *matériel* that enabled them to win the war. Thereafter military expenditures were largely concentrated on buying the produce of this new capacity—military equipment and munitions. Within a remarkably short time frame therefore, the United States produced a vast military manufacturing engine to take on the productive might of both *Nazi* controlled Europe and Japan. What is very clear from the figures is that many months before Japan initiated armed conflict with America with its attack on *Pearl Harbor*, the United States was gearing up for war on a scale that made it clear that armed conflict was considered by Washington to be a 'racing certainty.'

Wall Street certainly indicated as much. In 1941 trading plummeted to its lowest level since 1921. Office vacancies on Wall Street in 1939 stood at 4.4 million square feet—20 percent more than in 1932. Employment in New York's financial sector fell 200,000 from its pre-crash peak. Daily trading volume fell as low as 216 shares for each of the Exchange's 1,375 members. Although industrial output reached an all-time high in October 1940, with economic recovery fueled only by American and British defense orders, sentiment was nervous; the prospect of war, and increased taxes to pay for it focused attention on the negatives. The market traded within the narrowest of ranges. As in the auto industry, financial sector assets could be retooled for military tasks. Thus it was found that young investment bankers were ideally suited to be trained as command and control operators of America's new war fleet, particularly its aircraft carriers whose complex operations needed copious amounts of intellectual dexterity.

In spite of booming profits reported by oil companies, auto manufacturers and toolmakers in the first three quarters of 1941, *Business Week* magazine reflected the overall mood: "Signs multiply that the economic system is in for heavy weather. Has the defense program produced a real depression or is it merely going through an unpleasant phase as a prelude to prosperity."[16] The *Washington Post* was similarly gloomy. Fearing the harmful effects of the move toward a war economy it predicted that the "swiftly mounting impact of priorities will assume perfectly appalling proportions before many weeks."[17] Doom lay around every corner. *Fortune* magazine's quarterly management poll revealed that 75.6 percent of managers in 1941 thought that Roosevelt's appeal to the national emergency was a pretext to advance the cause of radical New Deal economics.

America's Pre-War Mobilization Plans: In 1918 the inept War Industries Board (WIB) had been put under the charge of financier Bernard Baruch who centralized it and made it into an efficient war machine. According to one source "The great principle followed throughout the board's dealings with industry was that of voluntary co-operation with the big stick in the closet."[18] However, in the backlash to war, the WIB was dismantled in 1920.

An Industrial Mobilization Plan (IMP) was put forward in 1931 with Bernard Baruch again being the main architect. However, it was largely ignored in a period of isolationism. The Great Depression, not global war, became the focus of Franklin D. Roosevelt's new administration in 1933. Baruch, like Churchill, feared the aggressions of Hitler and remained the 'Cassandra' in Washington's corridors of power. "In the modern world neutrality is a delusion. Carried to its ultimate end of refusing commercial intercourse with belligerents, it can amount to economic sanctions—which are in effect an act of war."[19]

After a trip to Europe in 1937 Baruch reported that the German Army was sleek and powerful while English defenses were sketchy. He reported that the French Army, and particularly its air force, was a joke. He told Roosevelt that the democracies were in no shape to face Hitler. In reaction to this news Roosevelt appointed a War Resources Board (WRB) in 1937. Edward Stettinius Jr., a partner at J. P. Morgan, was appointed as its chairman. The Board was charged with updating the Industrial Mobilization Plan (IMP). However, the WRB was abolished just six weeks later following complaints from New Dealers that Wall Street bankers dominated the WRB. For some liberals and New Dealers, politics took precedence over national security. Nevertheless the writing of the revised IMP by the WRB continued surreptitiously under the guiding hand of Bernard Baruch who gained the coveted role of leading a mobilization organization. The new IMP was written with a considerable amount of help from Baruch's deputy, John Hancock, and the proposals also took on board all of Roosevelt's views.

Nevertheless there remained a basic problem. How to mobilize while preserving the essential machinery of democratic government? New Dealers were suspicious that big business would attempt to roll back the social and economic reforms of the 1930s, while big business was concerned that the New Dealers would extend what they deemed to be a quasi-socialist revolution. The still dominant isolationist sentiment and it supporters in the press were also alert to anything that could be conceived of as a strategy likely to lead to foreign entanglements. Roosevelt may have wanted to rearm and mobilize more aggressively but he was only prepared to remain slightly ahead of the curve of popular opinion that was only gradually raising its concerns about the situation in Europe.

As early as December 1940 Roosevelt stated that America's role in the emerging war in Europe was to become the "Arsenal of Democracy."[20] Looking at the situation from Washington, the democracies needed all the help they could get. On 13 March 1940, after battling heroically against the Soviets in the *Winter War*, Finland reluctantly came to an accommodation with Stalin. A few weeks later Germany invaded a practically defenseless Denmark and Norway. On 10 May the so-called 'Phoney War' ended when Hitler's *panzer* divisions overran Holland and Belgium and stormed into France. The march of the dictatorships was seemingly strengthened with the addition of Mussolini to the totalitarian coalition—coming to fruition with the *Tripartite Pact* of Germany,

Japan and Italy signed on 27 September 1940. It may have come as little surprise to the Roosevelt administration in Washington but after the formation of the Axis alliance, even the isolationists in the US called for a massive increase in defense spending.

In this respect Roosevelt was ahead of the curve in his calling for industrial military mobilization. Speaking on 16 May 1941, Roosevelt observed: "These are ominous days . . . the clear fact is that the American people must recast their thinking about national protection."[21] Roosevelt shocked everyone in calling for annual production of 50,000 planes per annum. Including light planes, existing capacity was only 15,000 per annum. To pay for this expansion Roosevelt called on Congress for a $1.2bn budget to add to the $1.7bn already appropriated for military purposes. Through the newly established Office of Emergency Management (OEM), Roosevelt also formed the National Defense Advisory Commission (NDAC).

Roosevelt clearly learned from the backlash against the War Resources Board (WRB). While the National Defense Advisory Commission (NDAC) included three businessmen including Stettinius and William Knudsen, farmers, unions, consumer protectionists and a New-Dealer economist, Leon Henderson, were also appointed. Changes came thick and fast. In a fighting speech on 10 June 1940, Roosevelt announced that 365 warplanes would be delivered to Britain and France along with $50m of surplus *World War I* arms. Knudsen, a fierce patriot who had left his US$300,000 (US$5m in today's money) per annum job to go to work for the NDAC for US$1 per year, typified much of the spirit of the American businessmen who threw themselves into the role of mobilizing America for war. Knudsen was the archetype no-nonsense businessman. When a public relations man managed to procure a meeting, Knudsen asked, without looking up from his papers, "Can you build a tank?" When the man replied in the negative, Knudsen followed up with "Then I won't be seeing much of you,"[22] thereby ending the meeting.

Knudsen would be given valuable support by Stacy May, a plump, balding bespectacled statistician who had left the Rockefeller Foundation to become head of the NDAC's Bureau of Research and Statistics. He persuaded the British to reveal their war plans and put the statistics together with those of the United States to produce a comprehensive moving statistical compendium of plans and resources that proved vital to the coordination of the United States' industrial mobilization for war. By the end of the month Roosevelt's cabinet had been reshuffled. The experienced 73-year-old Henry Stimson, a former secretary of war under President Hoover, was brought in to run the War Department while Frank Knox, a 'Rough Rider' friend of former President Theodore 'Teddy' Roosevelt, was appointed Navy Secretary. To the astonishment of the Democrats, both of these appointees were Republicans. Roosevelt was clearly moving toward a war cabinet of all parties. Two days after the announcements of cabinet changes, France surrendered to Germany on 22 June 1940.

In Europe, Britain stood alone. From a purely pragmatic viewpoint, as British Ambassador Lord Lothian reminded his audience of Yale alumni on 19 June, the United

States had long relied on the British Navy for the protection of its own commerce. As for Britain, the last bastion of democracy on the continent, Lothian emphasized that "if Britain goes it will be difficult to preserve it [democracy] for long . . . anywhere else."[23] If Britain came to an accommodation with Hitler, the entire Mediterranean as well as the *Suez Canal* would fall into Axis hands while the British Colonies in Asia would be open to the threat of the Japanese. A month later the new direction set by Roosevelt and the Congress was best signposted by the passing of the *Two Ocean Naval Expansion Act* [July 1940]—a US$4bn building program that would provide 18 new aircraft carriers and seven battleships as well as dozens of cruisers and destroyers.

America's VICTORY Plan: With the United States preparing for but not yet committed to war, full mobilization of the economy for war remained theoretical. In spite of increased budget appropriations there was still something missing. Roosevelt filled the gap in July 1941 when he formally called for studies for an integrated national industrial war plan that would enable the US economy to provide munitions for the fighting of war on two fronts if necessary. From the mobilization plans, which got under way in the summer of 1940, it is clear that Roosevelt and his administration considered the likelihood of war with Germany or Japan, or both of them, to be high. The Japanese invasion of North Vietnam had only served to ratchet up the odds. The 'how' or 'when' of the impending war was still unclear.

The so-called VICTORY Plan that was published in October 1941 as a result of Roosevelt's request for an integrated study was largely worked on by a team led by Major Albert Wedemeyer, a staff officer in the War Plans Division of the Army General Staff. (Wedemeyer would later be promoted to general and become Lord Mountbatten's number two at South East Asia Command.) Wedemeyer had recently returned from two years spent on secondment at the German officer staff college. He set about estimating the amount of US working hours, male and female, that would be required to fulfil the requirements of wartime industrial production with the balance left over for service in the armed forces.

Wedemeyer's estimates proved relatively close to the final outcome. Although he grossly overestimated the need for armored, airborne and motorized divisions, his call for 88 Infantry Divisions compared to the actual deployment of 66 divisions in 1944. In terms of military manpower his estimate of 10.5 million was reasonably close to the eventual outcome of 8.3 million. Wedemeyer's forecasts would have been closer still if America, not the Soviet Union, had had to face the full might of the German Army. Because of Germany's necessary commitment to the Eastern Front, the British and American armies never faced more than 25 percent of the Germany Army at any given time.

The Navy did little to alter their estimates of naval requirements from the 'two ocean' plan put forward in July 1940. However, the Air Force under the guidance of 'Hap' Arnold saw the opportunity to significantly increase its role with the long-term aim of establishing an independent service. The lugubriously titled 'Air War Plans Division

Plan No. 1' put forward a framework of 64,000 aircraft in 239 groups. The manpower requirement was put at 2 million. Reflecting the strategic ascendancy of the 'bomber' faction in the interwar years, the centerpiece of the plan was the development of a long-range bomber with a 4,000 miles round-trip range while carrying a bomb load of twenty tons. This plan would come to fruition with the Boeing B-29 Superfortress in 1943.

As war drew nearer, Wall Street financier and industrialist, Ferdinand Eberstadt, was brought in to the War and Navy Departments to look closely at the steps needed to improve the procurement process and speed industrial mobilization. With some knowledge of the auto industry and a realization of the imperative need for machinery capable of bending, stamping, boring, milling, drilling, and punching metal, Eberstadt realized that at a first stage there would need to be a huge increase in machine tool capacity and proposed appropriate organizations to deal with this. The American *attaché* in Berlin warned that "the production of German machine tools in 1938 was eight times the volume in 1933."[24] Over the same period American machine tool production had stagnated. Eighty-five percent of US equipment was over ten years old with some dating back to the American Civil War. Perversely, in the following year, 1939, America was swamped with orders for new machine tools from Britain, France and Russia. Half of US output went overseas while manufacturers projected that the export total would be 75 percent in 1940. By comparison, US companies, military equipment industries apart, facing flat demand for their products, were disinclined to invest in new equipment.

Eberstadt counseled closely with Bernard Baruch who had performed the key role in industrial mobilization in *World War I*. When in November 1941 he proposed that the Joint Army-Navy Munitions Board be strengthened into an executive body with responsibility for facilities and procurement planning, production and administration, Eberstadt was promptly rewarded with the offer of the Chairmanship of the Joint Army-Navy Munitions Board. Until the spring of 1943 he was the driving force behind US industrial mobilization. Although the job was far from complete when the Japanese Navy attacked *Pearl Harbor*, "the fundamental process of defining the size and equipment needs of the American armed forces was now understood."[25]

However, the United States was still a long way from having fully mobilized its economy to enable its armed forces to be put on a war footing. But neither was America starting from zero. From mid-summer 1940 Roosevelt had increasingly put his foot on the gas pedal with regard to the rebuilding of America's industrial-military capacity. War was fully expected. It was largely a question of how ready America would be when it started. Perhaps the greatest good fortune for Roosevelt and his administration was that the US economy and its labor force were operating at such a low level of capacity that in gearing up for war the President did not have to weigh up the choice between guns and butter. As events showed they could have both. **[See Appendix C: Economics of the Pacific War: The 'New Deal' Mobilized] [Charts: C.1, C.2, C.4, C.5]**

The Development of Japan's Economy in the 1930s: Japan entered the *Pacific War* in a very different condition to the United States. While the US economy had been stagnant during the 1930s ending the decade with a high level of spare capacity, Japan was growing strongly. Japan's industrial production index rose from 100 in 1929 to 182.5 in 1939. Vehicle production had risen from 500 per annum to 48,000 by 1941 while aircraft production had risen from 400 per annum to 5,000 over the same period. In 1937 Japan had double the shipbuilding capacity of the United States. Economic growth over the decade was 3.9 percent per annum compared to 1.1 percent in the United States and 0.7 percent in Great Britain.

While the traditional *zaibatsu* (particularly the big four, Mitsubishi, Mitsui, Sumitomo and Yasuda) continued to dominate the economy, new industries spawned aggressive start-up companies. Toyoda Automatic Loom Works spawned the first Toyota automobile in 1935 under the direction of the company's eldest son Kiichiro Toyoda who established the Toyota Motor Company in 1937. Many well-known companies of the post-war period were created in this decade of technological change. Reflecting the increasing mechanization of the textile industry, machine tool manufacture began to grow rapidly. Okamoto Machine Tool Works, which produced its first gear grinder in 1930, was incorporated in 1935. New companies were also spawned in the developing chemical sector. In 1939 Showa Denko KK, a fast-growing chemical and engineering company was established out of the merger of Nihon Electric Industries and Showa Fertilizers. Two years earlier Canon, the renowned global camera manufacturer, was founded as the Precision Optical Instruments Company. Hoya Corporation, another optical products company, was founded in 1941.

Electrification and mechanization not only helped the advance of major companies but also enabled the myriad of small family businesses to survive as components suppliers to larger assembly companies. As American bombers would discover, it was only with the mass firebombing of Tokyo and the major urban centers that industrial output began to be seriously affected when the residentially based 'mom-and-pop' lathes were incinerated. Production was also growing in the most important outpost of Empire, Manchuria. Coal production here had risen from 8.9 million tons to 13.8 million tons in 1936 while iron ore rose from 673,000 to 1.325 million. Mineable reserves of magnesite, molybdenum, tungsten, and vanadium had also been discovered. On the *Yalu River* in northern China, Japan constructed a hydroelectric dam larger than the famous Boulder Dam in Colorado. In spite of this seemingly rosy picture, there were significant problems in Japan's economy. Extraordinarily high levels of fixed capital formation by both government and the private sector had driven the growth in the Japanese economy. Investment in heavy industry, which already accounted for a high level of 38.3 percent of Japan's aggregate investment in 1930, rose to 72.6 percent in 1942. Inevitably Japanese consumption and with it living standards were compromised.

In general the Japanese government in the 1930s sustained a policy of free market economics that saw its role as one of coordination and the provision of infrastructure. To this effect the development of nationwide electrification in the 1930s enabled the take up of electrical machinery that transformed the all-important textile industry. New technologies brought about a sharp increase in productivity and with it a consolidation in the number of companies. Increasingly their product output turned to the manufacture of western clothing that could be sold at home as well as being exported. The 1930s saw a significant increase in the national provision of paved roads and highways that helped industrial integration. The development of universities and technical colleges kept pace with industry's demand for engineers.

Nevertheless, after 1931 the relationship of industry with the Japanese government began to change. In Manchukuo, the Army, operating a style of government completely different from that in Japan, implemented a more Soviet-style command economy. Investment in emigration of farming families to build colonies in Manchuria aped the Soviet colonization of its Empire. Industrial plans were also implemented though with mixed results. Companies were subsidized in order to speed up their relocation and investment. New breeds of companies with strong links to the Army were encouraged. These so-called *shinzaibatsu* (new *zaibatsu*) were new companies outside the traditional *zaibatsu* framework. Often they were associated with the new industries of chemicals, aerospace, vehicle manufacture, and munitions—areas that were of particular interest to the Army. In addition their business activity was particularly skewed towards the new colonies of Taiwan, Korea and Manchuria.

Aikawa Yoshisuke, the most high profile of these new entrepreneurs, used his holding company Nihon Sangyo (Japan Industries) established in 1928 to buy out Dat Motors (DAT Jidosha Seizo Co. Ltd.) in a stock market operation in 1933; two years earlier Dat had produced the first 'Datsun' (literally son of Dat) motor car and Aikawa saw the potential of this new industrial sector that had hitherto relied largely on American imports. In 1935 Datsun diversified into the production of trucks. Aikawa, who issued stock in Nihon Sangyo under the ticker name Nissan, grew his conglomerate rapidly by expanding into metals, machinery, chemicals, autos and trucks.

By the end of the war there were seventy-four companies listed under Nihon Sangyo's umbrella. By some measures in 1941, Aikawa's *shinzaibatsu* had even outpaced Mitsui and Mitsubishi. However, the growing influence of the Army and Empire revealed itself in the transfer of the Nissan holding company to Manchuria. The relationship with the Army was not always beneficial. In 1936 the Diet passed the *Automobile Manufacturing Business Act*, designed to establish a domestic motor manufacturing sector, which scotched Datsun's plans to form a joint venture with America's General Motors. More damaging for Datsun was the Army's insistence that the company should abandon cars and focus entirely on trucks. It was symptomatic of the increasing militarization of the economy and the Army's power to bully the private sector into submission. In effect, as the 1930s progressed, the command-and-control model developed by the Army in the colonies, particularly Manchukuo, was brought back to Japan as the Army's political clout increased.

In 1938 the government further introduced command economy modes with the introduction of the Materials Mobilization Plan. At first applied to cotton, the aim was to restrict imports and to increase production aimed at export. Domestic consumption was downgraded. Similar restrictions were soon applied to leather and rubber products manufactured for domestic consumption. As the decade ended military cabinets increasingly relied on a Central Price Committee to set rice prices and control supply. The military governments also shifted taxation based on land sales, luxuries and imports to taxation of household incomes and corporate profits. Intervention in the capital markets resulted in limits put on dividend payments.

Japan's Economic Preparations for War: In July 1929 new finance minister Junnosuke Inoue, with the support of Minseito, was determined to return Japan to the pre-*World War I* parity of 100 Yen to US$49.85. This sound money policy required an upward revaluation of the Yen by between 7 and 10 percent. The policy was announced just one month after the Wall Street Crash of 1929; Japan was thus committed to a policy of fiscal rectitude and contraction of its money supply just as the world was about to descend into a destructive deflationary cycle. Sanji Muto, President of *Kanebo*, Japan's largest cotton spinning company, likened it to "opening a window in the middle of a typhoon."[26] Fueled by a collapse in American demand for silk, the agricultural sector, which continued to employ over half of Japan's labor, collapsed. Farmers suddenly found themselves unable to repay loans. Bankruptcies swept the country while speculators accumulated gold and depleted Japanese reserves.

For a country still highly dependent on exports the sudden deterioration in their terms of trade impacted dramatically on economic output. It was not helped by Britain's currency devaluation following their exit from the Gold Standard on 21 September 1930. In addition Japan's major trading partners started to turn protectionist. The US Congress passed the infamous *Tariff Act* [June 1930] (Smoot-Hawley), which imposed record high tariffs on over 20,000 products imported into America. Great Britain followed suit, passing the *Import Duties Act* [1931]. For Japan's Generals the benefits of an autarkic empire were clearly signposted by the Anglo-Saxon powers.

Faced with a run on specie, in December 1931, finance minister, Korekiyo Takahashi, abandoned the gold standard. Takahashi, the illegitimate son of a court painter in Tokyo, had been adopted by a poor samurai household. He led a peripatetic life; learning English as a manservant in London before travelling to Oakland, California where he worked as a manual laborer. On returning to Japan he worked first as an English teacher, then as a bureaucrat in the Ministry of Education. Later at the Ministry of Agriculture, Takahashi founded the Japan Patent Bureau. After emigrating to Peru where he failed in a business venture, he returned to join the Bank of Japan and after becoming a Vice-President and helping to organize the finances that made the *Russo-Japanese War* possible, was elevated to the House of Peers.

In successive governments until his assassination in 1936, Takahashi increased money supply and embarked on a fiscal expansion that led him to be referred to as "the Keynes of Japan."[27] By some accounts Takahashi had already read and understood Keynes's economic papers before they were brought together in his famed *General Theory of Employment, Interest and Money* [1936]. In addition to land reclamation, irrigation, drainage and river repairs, state spending also went to the military; subsidies were given for the manufacture of military vehicles in 1932 and for shipbuilding in 1933. Tax breaks and protection were afforded for the steel and oil refining industries. Takahashi's intervention inevitably began the inexorable rise in the defense sector of the economy.

After the death of Takahashi and the beginnings of full-scale military operations against China following the Marco Polo Bridge Incident, the scope of government control of the economy increased markedly. In September 1937 the *Temporary Capital Adjustment Act* put in place controls on the allocation of capital to make sure that industries essential to the war effort could be funded. Civilian industries such as textiles were barred access to bank or outside funding. Similar restrictions were applied to raw materials by the *Temporary Export and Import Commodities Act* [1937]. The *Emergency Shipping Management Act* [1937] gave the Japanese government the power to requisition private vessels. To oversee what was clearly a command economy model, in October 1937 the government established the Cabinet Planning Board to control the sourcing of materials and the direction of foreign trade.

The intent to move toward central planning took an important step further when Prince Fumimaro Konoe ensured the passage of the *National Mobilization Law* [1938]. In his second administration Konoe went further down the route of imperial fascism when he proclaimed the Political New Order in July 1940 and created the Imperial Rule Assistance Association. In doing so Konoe moved toward the radical wing of the Army that wanted a "powerful organ of mass mobilization necessary to channel the economic and spiritual energies of the citizenry toward the implementation of a new system of state."[28] After 1936, a combination of the aristocracy, the military, the bureaucracy, the Army and the Emperor himself acquiesced in the overthrow of the party political system that they had supported with decreasing enthusiasm since 1930. In effect a 'New Political Order' was required to enable Japan to transit toward its aggressive new role in the 'World Order.'

The New Order aimed to redefine the role of big business. Individual industries were placed on a list for government guidance: *Automobile Industry Act* [1936]; *Synthetic Oil Industry Act* [1937]; *Machine Tool Industry Act* and the *Aircraft Industry Act* [1938]; the *Shipbuilding Law and the Light Metal Industry Act* [1939]; and the *Machines Manufacturing Act* [1941]. The Economic New Order, advocated by Prince Fumimaro Konoe when he returned as Prime Minister for his second administration in July 1940, sought to "restructure the economy to ensure that industry fulfilled 'public goals' of the state, not private goals of capital."[29] It was a concept that followed in lock-step with *Nazi* Germany; in 1927 Hitler had averred in a speech, "we are socialists, we are enemies of today's capitalistic economic system."[30] Like Hitler, Konoe's 'New Order' did not want to disband private enterprise but merely to guide it towards the service of the state.

At his famed 'book burning' in Berlin in front of the Berlin *Staatsoper* in May 1933, Goebbels had pronounced the end of "the age of extreme Jewish intellectualism." The *Nazi* distaste for intellectuals was not imitated in Japan where support for the Fascist Third Way ordering of the economy came from bureaucrats such as Shinji Yoshino, author of *Japan's Industrial Policy* [1935]. Other advocates of the Third Way included economist Professor Hiromi Arisawa, whose teachings outlined in *Nihon kogyo Tosei-Ron* (The Industrial Control in Japan) [1937] combined the "Marxist perspective of planning with the German theory of total war."[31] Arisawa thus advocated, "step by step we must progress toward state capitalism."[32]

Labor Mobilization in Japan: With the embarkation of Japan on a much more aggressive international policy after the invasion of mainland China in 1936, the Army became increasingly conscious of the risks posed by a disaffected proletariat. General Ugaki, a moderate in the Army's political spectrum, noted that Japan's imperial expansion "did not have truly healthy roots [social and economic]."[33]

The liberal tolerance of trade unions, that had been a hallmark of Japan's economic governance changed dramatically after 1936. The Army took the lead. In 1936 they forced 8,000 munitions workers to withdraw from *Sodemei*, the government employees union. The Japanese trade unions had already moved their rhetoric away from the confrontational approach of earlier decades. In December 1931 *Sodemei*'s journal called for "comprehensive national economic planning . . . Unions are less organizations to demand fair distribution of profits than important organs for control of industry."[34] In effect they were anticipating the move by the Japanese government toward state capitalism. Taking the Army's lead the Home Ministry announced, "it would be appropriate to legally sanction unionism as the leading spirit of a social movement."[35] To remodel government-union relations, bureaucrats such as Iwao Minami, a bureaucrat and former labor manager, proposed the creation of 'discussion councils' based on *the Organisation of National Labor Act* [1934] whereby the Nazis established Councils of Trust in all German factories with more than twenty employees. Minami would later recap his *Nazi* lessons for Japan in a book entitled *Germany on the Rise* [1938].

The transformation reached its apogee in 1938 with the first Konoe government's creation of Patriotic Industrial Society (*Sangyo Hokoku Renmei*); the *Sanpo* as it became known was modeled on the *Nazi*'s *Deutsche Arbeitsfront* (The German Labor Front). Under the direction of the Minister of Labor, Marquis Koichi Kido, worker organizations were structured on a company-by-company basis. Enterprises became a functional community whereby labor and capital were fused into a 'single body' (*ittai*). The number of *Sanpo* grew rapidly from 19,000 enterprises registered in 1939 to 85,000 units in 1941. Inevitably the ability to run or organize universal trade unions became compromised. By 1940 virtually all trade unions had been abolished with barely a whimper. In July 1940 Prime Minister Konoe's Labor New Order forced a voluntary dissolution of the remaining 500 unions with some 360,000 members.

The Structure of Japan's Pre-War Economy: **[Chart: 4.1]** The country's over-reliance on imports troubled the political and military elite. Japanese industry needed to import 24 percent of its bauxite, 59 percent of copper, 71 percent of iron ore, 78 percent of industrial salts and 80 percent of lead, tin and rubber. Japan was highly dependent on trade by sea. It is ironic that as a country that depended on foreign ships to carry 33 percent of its imports, Japan went to war with the world's two largest merchant fleets. In 1941 Great Britain had 425 tankers (aggregate 3 million tons), the United States had 389 tankers (aggregate 2.8 million tons), while Japan had just 49 tankers with an aggregate tonnage of 0.6 million tons. At the start of 1941, Japan needed to import 85 percent of its crude oil with the remainder accounted for by lower quality synthetic production. Most of Japan's imported oil was carried in foreign ships, mainly American, as the greater part of its crude oil came from Standard Oil of California (SOCAL, later renamed Chevron). It was less expensive to transport oil from California to Japan than from California to the east coast of America.

Most alarmingly the rate of growth in government investment in military equipment was crowding out investment in the private sector. In 1936 Japanese shipbuilding yards produced 442,000 tons of merchant shipping and 55,000 tons of warships. By 1941 annual tonnage of merchant ships launched had fallen to 237,000 tons while the tonnage of warships produced had risen to 225,000 tons. The squeeze on merchant shipping was not only in new production. By the end of 1941, 21.6 percent of Japan's cargo fleet was idle while waiting for berths for maintenance or refit. As the historian H. P. Wilmot has noted in *Empires in the Balance* [2008], "the amount of shipping available declined . . . at the moment when [Japan's] commitments and needs increased."[36]

It is clear that even before the outbreak of the *Pacific War* between Japan on the one side and the United States, Great Britain, Australia, and Holland on the other, the Japanese economy was already running at full capacity. With 1.5 million troops stationed and active in China, the Japanese economy was already in a total war mode. The need to invest in armaments and heavy industry had severely impacted Japanese living standards by 1941. In the four years from 1937 to 1941, the food production index had fallen by 21.9 percent. Over the same period textile purchases fell by 39.6 percent. As shipping needs for the *Second Sino-Japanese War* expanded so pressure had increased on domestic consumption that required the import of 20 percent of rice and wheat, 66 percent of soy and almost 100 percent sugar. By the time that Japanese aircraft carriers were bearing down on *Pearl Harbor*, Japanese citizens were already feeling the pinch in their diet. To expand their war effort further, much deeper cuts to Japanese living standards would be required. The entirety of Japan's economic and social function would have to be molded to the exigencies of war. Japan was a 'Sparta' in the making.

In anticipation of the possibility of war with America, in October 1940 the Japanese government set up a think tank called *Soryokusen Kenkyujo* (Institute of Total War Studies) to evaluate the economic impact of war with the United States. Thirty individuals were drawn from institutions ranging from the Army, Navy, civil service, major corporations, and the press. The report completed in the summer of 1941 concluded that Japan could not even sustain its war with China much beyond five years. As for war with America, the *Soryokusen Kenkyujo*'s analysis showed that the shortage in cargo ships would become critical in 1943 and that war would be unsustainable after 1944; in other words a long war with America was unwinnable.

Soryukusen Kenkyujo's report was buried and afterwards both ministries and the GHQ staffs of both the Army and Navy were purged of men who spoke negatively of the alliance with Germany and the possibility of war with the US and Great Britain. Instead of taking note of the *Soryukusen Kenkyujo*'s warnings, the Navy went to war using a report prepared by a single officer in the summer of 1941. This report assumed that losses from submarines could amount to 75,000 tons or 900,000 tons per annum. While the report assumed that Japanese shipbuilders could produce this quantity of commercial shipping annually, actual production never exceeded half of this figure. What is clear from these calculations is that Japan's logistical basis for engaging in a conflict with the United States was flawed. With Japan already fully mobilized in its war with China, the projected conflict with the United States allowed it a window of little more than a year to achieve a victory that might force America to the negotiating table. **[See Appendix B: Oil, Raw Materials and Logistics: 'Just Start Swinging']**

Plan DOG [November 1940]: **[Map: 4.2]** As the Roosevelt administration came to the conclusion that war was very likely, if not inevitable, it became clear to some in the US military that America was not only unprepared in terms of *matériel* but also in terms of strategy. Former plans for war with Japan, notably Plan ORANGE, which had been the overwhelming focus of naval war planning in the interwar years did not reflect the fact that America was now likely to face war on two fronts, *Atlantic* as well as *Pacific*. Plan DOG was the response to this developing situation. The name derived from option *(d)* (d for dog) listed in a memo written by Admiral Harold Stark, Chief of Naval Operations, on 12 November 1940. Plan DOG suggested that the focus of war planning should be to defeat Hitler and therefore, strong offensive action was recommended for the *Atlantic* and a concurrent more passive defensive strategy for the *Pacific*. The alternatives, (a) hemispheric defense, (b) offensive in the *Pacific* and defensive in the *Atlantic*, and (c) a balanced two-ocean strategy, were rejected.

Perhaps most importantly Stark's Plan DOG memo advised that secret talks be undertaken with their British counterparts so that an agreed and coordinated plan was on the table if hostilities broke out. Thus covert discussions between US and British staff, begun in the late 1930s, intensified in 1940 and again in the early months of 1941. US negotiators were instructed not to agree to anything that might put American assets under British command or commit themselves to any strategy aimed at preserving the British Empire: the US Joint Board warned: "The proposals of the British representatives will have been drawn up with the chief regard to the support of the British commonwealth. Never absent from their minds are their post-war interests, commercial and military."[37] Perhaps this viewpoint was not surprising given Churchill's nineteenth-century character, which was somewhat out of step with his time; as British historian John Costello has pointed out, "Churchill's view of China was quintessentially Victorian, British, and imperialistic."[38] However, the British Prime Minister was not the only person with an Imperial obsession. Though few Americans would have admitted it, Plan ORANGE (the cornerstone strategy for war with Japan) was aimed at the preservation of the American Empire in the *Pacific*.

Reaching agreement that Europe and the defeat of Germany and Italy should be the priority was rapidly agreed. Asia was more contentious. Britain, with more to lose in the region, favored *Singapore* as the hub of regional defense. Although vast sums had been invested in the interwar years in 'state of the art' naval facilities and defenses to match, America's naval experts doubted whether it could sustain a defense if Japan mounted an air campaign from airfields in Indochina. British admirals suggested that portions of the American *Pacific* fleet should be posted to *Singapore*—in hindsight a decision that would have been disastrous. The US Navy preferred a strategy of limited naval offensive in the *Marshall Islands* to draw Japanese naval strength away from South East Asia. Ultimately it was agreed that the US would send more ships to the *Atlantic* to allow Britain to send naval forces to *Singapore*. The agreements allowed for Plan DOG to be inserted almost seamlessly into Plan ORANGE—the basic plan designed in the interwar years for dealing with any attempt by Japan to conquer the Philippines, which was their expected prime target if Japan and America came to blows. What neither DOG nor ORANGE envisioned was that America forces in Asia would be so feeble or that Japanese military capability would be so good. **[See Chapter 6: Plan ORANGE and MacArthur's Philippines Debacle]**

'Flying Tigers': America's Plans for a Backdoor War against Japan in China: While military and naval officers in Washington were planning for a possible war with Japan, some Americans, supported by Roosevelt's government, were already going to China to fight the Japanese. In effect Roosevelt sanctioned the fighting of Japan by the backdoor. In large part, it was a development brought about by one of the more colourful characters of the *Pacific War*, Claire Lee Chennault.

Chennault was born in Commerce, Texas, to John Stonewall Jackson Chennault. It was a frontiersman life. At the outset of *World War I*, Chennault joined the officer training school at Fort Benjamin Harrison before joining the Air Division of the Signal Corps when the *National Defense Act* of 1920 made the Army Air Service a specialty like the infantry or artillery. He became a specialist pursuit (fighter) pilot with a flair for aerobatics. Within four years he had become the commander of the 19th Pursuit Squadron in *Hawaii*. In the 1930s he was promoted to Chief of the Pursuit Section of the Air Corps Tactical School located at Maxwell Field, Alabama.

But four years later, Chennault left the US Air Force largely as a result of long-running disputes with the bomber-oriented senior commanders of the Air Corps Tactical School. The 'bomber mafia' believed that technological developments in high-level bombing would make fighters redundant whereas Chennault countered that the same technological developments would allow fighters to attack at higher altitudes. He was right. As a result of bomber-centric thinking the US Air Force's investment priorities meant that in *World War II*, US long-range fighter escort capability lagged the development of strategic long-range bombing—a problem that would haunt them until the last year of the war. After leaving the Air Force, Chennault, spurning offers from the Soviet Union, travelled to China where he became adviser to Chiang Kai-shek who was attempting to establish a credible air arm. Help was urgently needed as China sought to hold back the Japanese Army that had increased its control of western China after the Marco Polo Bridge Incident that had propelled Japan into full-scale conflict with China in 1937.

At the time of Chennault's arrival in 1937, the Chinese Air Force possessed 500 aircraft of which only ninety-one were serviceable. They mainly comprised obsolete warplanes manufactured by *Fabricca Italiana Automobili Torino* (FIAT). In addition, it was an appallingly badly organized force riven with corruption. An exasperated Chiang had handed over control of the air force to his wife, Soong Meiling—Madame Chiang Kai-shek. In effect Chennault reported to Meiling, who took a keen interest in the establishment of a Chinese Air Force. At first Chennault was hired at US$1,000 per month for three months to advise the Generalissimo on why his planes seemed incapable of flying. This soon turned into a long-term appointment. On 1 September 1937 Chiang put Chennault in charge of the Chinese Air Force's operations and training. He quickly established a warm working rapport with his employers. Of Madame Chiang, Chennault would later say, "She will always be a Princess to me."[39] From the beginning he exaggerated what he would be able to achieve with the Chinese Air Force, writing to Major-General Haywood 'Possum' Hansell to tell him, "Boy, if the Chinese only had 100 good pursuit planes and 100 fair pilots, they'd exterminate the Jap air force."[40]

However, Chennault's first effort to establish a credible Chinese Air Force was not successful. With the backing of Meiling and with Chiang's imprimatur, Chennault managed to procure twenty-four Vultee V–11 light bombers. They were nearly all destroyed in a single Japanese bombing attack. The problem simply was that the *Kuomintang* did not possess the foreign exchange resources to fund the creation of a credible air arm. But the fortunes of a virtually bankrupt *Kuomintang* government would change as the Japanese threat to South East Asia began to impinge on American and British interests.

In June 1940 T. V. Soong, Chiang's financier brother-in-law, approached Washington to ask for arms and credit. T. V. Soong, or just T. V. as he became known, who had been smuggled out of Shanghai by the Green Gang, the city's main crime organization, had set himself up at the Yellowbrick Shoreham Hotel where he assiduously lobbied on Chiang's behalf. T. V.'s 'walrus' figure, usually sporting a snorkel, became a familiar sight in the hotel's swimming pool. He was positively received though there were questions as to whether the supply of arms to China was an action that might push Japan into an alliance with Germany. T. V. proved an effective negotiator. William Donovan, head of the Office for Strategic Studies (OSS), the forerunner of the CIA, commented, "T. V. reminds me of . . . the star Wisconsin halfback, very quick on the ball and inclined to plough through between guard and tackle rather than waste time going around the end."[41]

Delicate questions of protocol *vis-à-vis* Japan became redundant on 27 September 1940 when Japan signed the *Tripartite Pact* with Germany and Italy. Three days earlier

Japan had occupied northern Indochina, which put them on China's southwestern border. Ambassador Johnson in Chongqing advised the US State Department, "failure of the United States . . . to afford timely aid . . . may in the end result in communist ascendancy in China."[42] Fighter planes were urgently needed for the defense of Chongqing, which was taking a daily pounding. The American Ambassador reported a scale of Japanese bombing that "is beyond all description in its brutality . . . daily visits of a hundred or more bombers swinging back and forth over a city of helpless people who cower for hours in dugouts where many are overcome just by the bad air . . ."[43]

In November 1940, Chennault flew to New York and Washington with a Chinese delegation and, with the help of Chiang's financier, T. V. Soong, and the Chinese Ambassador, arranged a complex financial scheme involving two US$50m loans. They were arranged to help stabilize the Chinese currency and to buy 100 Curtis P-40 Kittyhawk fighters. Roosevelt sealed the deal with Congress on 2 December, barely a month after his election to a third term as President. *Life* magazine told its readers that they (the Chinese) were getting a great deal, ". . . China promised to keep 1,250,000 Japanese troops pinned in the field; to keep Japan's formidable fleet blockading the Japanese shore; to retard the aggressors' march in the direction of immediate US interests. The merchandise was fantastically cheap at the price."[44]

In addition Bob Pawley, who had earlier set up the Central Aircraft Manufacturing Company (CAMCO) to supply the Vultee Bombers to the *Kuomintang,* was employed to recruit pilots to man the Kittyhawk fighters. The Americans who first arrived in Asia posing as tourists were mainly adventurers out for excitement and to make a quick 'buck.' David Lee recalled,

> Tex Hill, "had a map and it showed Burma and the Burma Road. He said they were looking for pilots to patrol the area. That sounded real good to us, adventurous. He explained it real fast. 'You'll get $600 a month . . .' " A US$500 bonus was also paid for every plane shot down. Everything was real vague.[45]

Bored flight instructors, Robert Smith and Paul Greene, were turned down by one recruiting agent, C. B. 'Skip' Adair, because they had only ever flown trainers rather than fighters, but they plied him with drink until he changed his mind. Apart from squadron leaders there were no ranks—just pilots. Some of them, such as Frank Tinker from Arkansas and John Allison from Florida, who eventually became a US Air Force major-general, were veterans of the *Spanish Civil War* that had ended in the spring of 1939 with victory for Franco's fascists. Chennault's pilots were a highly paid, unstable, fast-living cast of characters. Tinker would eventually commit suicide, putting a gun to his head in a hotel in Little Rock, Arkansas. Even Chennault acknowledged that the pilots "subsisted almost entirely on high-octane beverages."[46] Suitably the recruits' first billet in Burma was at a base called Johnny Walker Airfield. Later many of the crews came from the US Air Force, enabled by a special dispensation from Roosevelt for pilots and crew who were to pledge allegiance to the force of another nation—an act that would normally have been deemed both treacherous and illegal. The US government also gave the pilots dispensation to return to the US Air Force with the same rank with which they had left. Pawley's recruits were formalized as the American Volunteer Group (AVG). In effect, the sending of Kittyhawks and pilots to Asia was a covert act of war against Japan.

From now on Japan would have competition in the air over Burma and China. However, in northeastern China the bombing of the *Kuomintang* strongholds of Chongqing and Kunming was relentless. AVG pilot, David 'Tex' Hill, born in Korea to Texan missionaries, recalled that "The Japanese had been bombing Kunming for years, with no military objective—just bombing right into the people, that was my first indication of war, seeing all those dead and wounded people, with arms and legs blown off. It was terrible."[47] Chennault himself proved a talented and inspirational leader. 'Tex' Hill described Chennault as,

> a very dynamic person . . . The first time you met him, you got the message loud and clear that he was a no-nonsense guy who really knew what he was talking about. You immediately had a lot of confidence in him. He never used a lot of verbiage; he was straight to the point, mission-wise. He was a wonderful person, very loyal to the people who worked for him . . .[48]

War or Peace? The Final Negotiations [1940–December 1941]: A former foreign minister, who claimed to be a great admirer of America after the war, Admiral Kichisaburo Nomura was sent to Washington on 27 November 1940 to take up the position of Ambassador with a view to securing a lasting peace. He was an outgoing popular character in Washington. Over the next year Nomura would become a familiar figure at the service entrance of the Carlton Hotel where he would slip in for peace negotiation meetings with Cordell Hull in the Secretary of State's suite of rooms. Arriving in Washington just a few months after the *Tripartite Alliance* and the occupation of northern Indochina, Nomura arrived at another low point in American regard for Japan.

With war in the air, others tried to get aboard the peace train. Bishop James Walsh (Superior General of the Catholic Foreign Mission Society of America) and Vicar General Father James Drought went to Japan to inspect missions but their real purpose was diplomatic. The plan was supported by Postmaster General Frank Walker, a Catholic, and Taro Terasaki, the spymaster based in Japan's Washington embassy. Discussions with bankers and a senior member of the Army Ministry's Military Affairs Bureau led to meetings with Foreign Minister Matsuoka. The Japanese wanted to use Walsh and Drought as secret intermediaries to negotiate a deal, which would allow them control of China without interrupting the flow of oil. Ultimately the prospects of a deal foundered when Matsuoka rowed back on the proposals set out in the draft

The priests submitted their *Draft Understanding* at the beginning of April 1941. It had been drawn up after consultation with enemy agents and laid out a minimal negotiating stance. Hull rejected it as "much more accommodating than we had been led to believe it would be and all that the most ardent Japanese imperialist could want."[49] Ambassador Kichisaburo Nomura was over optimistic. The US demanded 'open door' trade, no change in Asia except by peaceful means, a 'geopolitical' status quo, and no interference in internal affairs of nations—all difficult demands for Japan to accept. Moreover, Nomura did not understand the importance of the *Tripartite Alliance* when the US began to insist on a break with Hitler. In the negotiations it did not help that Nomura suffered from advanced deafness, which exasperated Hull.

A further impediment to successful peace negotiations was the breaking of Japan's Code PURPLE. Japan's highest level code, used by high level diplomats and Japanese ministers, allowed the elite circle in Washington access to what became known as the MAGIC intercepts. It was clear that Japan was preparing for war—making it all but impossible for Washington to take Nomura's peace overtures seriously. Japan's leaders believed that they could make war preparations at the same time that they were negotiating and no doubt hoping for peace on reasonable terms; the MAGIC intercepts may well have given Roosevelt and Cordell Hull the mistaken impression that Japan's aggressive stance was harder than it actually was.

Over the course of the year Nomura's attempts to achieve peace had become ever more forlorn. Japan and France's Vichy government in Indochina signed the *Protocol Concerning Joint Defense and Joint Military Cooperation* on 29 July 1941. The agreement gave Japan use of eight airfields, vital stepping off points for an attack on South East Asia as well as the right to station more troops in Vietnam. In Tokyo, Matsuoka was convinced that diplomatic steps would deter America whereas in reality they had the opposite effect. One of the major problems was that neither side believed that a deal was likely. The Japanese believed that after its financial and oil embargo of Japan, the United States was stalling and playing for time—not an entirely unfair assessment. Washington knew it would be summer of 1942 at the earliest for their defensive preparations in the Philippines to be complete. Japan by contrast was forced to prepare for war because the armed forces were under time pressure because of the depletion of their oil stocks.

In reaction to America's financial freeze and *de facto* oil embargo, on 3 September 1941 Konoe's cabinet convened to discuss the '*Outline Plan for the Execution of the Empire's National Policy*' that had been produced by the Imperial General Headquarters. After much haggling it was duly approved the following day. Unless the western powers backed off from interference in the 'China Incident' and agreed to the closing of the Burma Road through which they were supplying Chiang Kai-shek's armies, the cabinet resolved that: "Our Empire, for the purpose of self-defense and self-preservation, will complete preparations for war, with the last ten days of October as a tentative deadline, resolved to go to war with the United States, Great Britain and the Netherlands if necessary."[50] In addition, it was required that the western powers "cooperate in the acquisition of goods needed by our Empire."[51] In other words America would have to rescind its trade embargoes and allow Japan to gather the material wherewithal to sustain its empire. The Army had few doubts as to the outcome and General Uchida noted in his diary on 3 September, "Mobilization of the Army is expected to begin about mid-September."[52]

At 4.40 p.m. on 5 September 1941, Konoe met the Emperor to discuss the 'Outline Plan.' Hirohito pointed out that the cabinet's plans placed war preparations first and diplomatic negotiations second. He was clearly unhappy that Konoe's government was giving precedence to war over diplomatic activities and demanded that the Chiefs of the Army and Navy General Staffs be called immediately to explain themselves. By ignoring the Ministers of War and the Navy, Hirohito, by implication, was blaming the senior staff commanders for the aggressive stance of the Outline Plan.

Army Chief General Sugiyama and Navy Chief Admiral Nagao hurried to the Palace and at 6.00 p.m. they and Konoe were ushered into an audience with the Emperor who questioned his military chiefs on the specifics of the planned operations. When Sugiyama estimated that the *South Pacific* could be rolled up in three months, Hirohito raised his voice and said, "As War Minister at the outbreak of the China Incident, you asked me to approve sending Army troops there, saying that the Incident would be settled in a short time. But has it [the *Second Sino-Japanese War*] yet been ended after more than four years? Are you trying to tell me the same thing again?"[53] When Sugiyama mumbled excuses about the extent of the Chinese hinterland, Hirohito responded by pointing out, "if the Chinese hinterland was extensive, the *Pacific* was boundless."[54] The Emperor's visitors were forced to give assurances that diplomacy would be given precedence over war. A chastened Nagano reflected later that evening that "I have never seen the Emperor reprimand us in such a manner, his face turning red and raising his voice."[55]

At the formal Imperial Conference on the following day, the Outline Plan, an operational directive that started a mobilization for war against America, Britain and Holland, against a background of a faltering war in China, was approved. Before giving his assent Hirohito read a poem written by his grandfather, explaining that he was "striving to introduce into the present the Emperor Meiji's ideal of international peace."[56]

After the meeting Konoe secretly met US Ambassador Grew and not only agreed to accept Hull's four principles but also assured him that he had the support of the Navy and War Ministries. The more conciliatory tone of Konoe at this point may have been explained in part by the failure of their *Nazi* allies to achieve the comprehensive victory in Europe in the summer of 1941 that had been hoped for. Britain and the Soviet Union may have suffered a battering, but they were still alive. However, Konoe, whose cabinets had been so closely associated with Japanese expansionism, was in a difficult position with regard to discarding the Axis alliance or rowing back on an aggressive international policy. In trying to reach agreement with the United States Japan risked having to accept a stunning loss of face. Konoe might accept this but would the Japanese people, whipped up into a frenzy of nationalist fervor, be so accommodating? Most importantly would the Army and Navy Staff Officers, who, as a result of their constitutional right to have serving officers as ministers of the Army and Navy, had an effective veto on Cabinet decisions, be so accommodating as to accept a pullback? When presented with Konoe's proposal that he should meet Roosevelt, even Ambassador Grew, perhaps the leading dove in the negotiations with Japan, acknowledged that "Nobody in the world can prove that even if Konoe had met the President and even if he had been able to give satisfactory commitments that he would have implemented them after he came back. That was definitely in the control of the military."[57]

The Rise of General Hideki Tojo [October 1941]: By October 1941, Konoe was coming to the end of his tether. Albeit a nationalist who was a steadfast believer in the development of the Japanese Empire, he vacillated between the logic of Imperial expansion and fear as to the consequences. Behind him the normally timid and cautious Hirohito was probably even more uncertain as to the way forward. War with America carried enormous risk but so did meeting America's demands for Japan's withdrawal from China. To his right stood the Army's ultra-nationalists for whom the yielding of ground in China at America's behest was beyond acceptability. When the offer to meet Roosevelt in person was turned down by the White House on the advice of Hull, Konoe felt that he had little left to offer. At the 14 October cabinet meeting, War Minister, General Hideki Tojo, dominated the proceedings, banging on with bullying eloquence about the dangers of giving in to the Americans. "Manchukuo will be endangered," Tojo asserted, "and our control of Korea undermined."[58] Konoe, always reticent to express his views in large meetings, resigned.

Who could the Emperor turn to? After considering various Army figures, the Emperor, advised by the *Jushin* (council of advisers, which included Admiral Yonai and Konoe) decided for Tojo who was known to be a fanatical devotee of the Emperor and would thus be expected to follow Hirohito's lead. Tojo also commanded respect and often fear within the Army itself. Perhaps, some argued, Tojo could keep the Army hotheads under control. Not everyone agreed. When word was brought to Colonel Akiyama that the Emperor had asked Tojo to form a cabinet, the Army information officer smiled and predicted, "Now we will have war."[59]

Hideki Tojo was the son of a samurai convert to the new military system after the Meiji Restoration in 1868. Although his father was promoted to general, he never got the posting that he felt he deserved because he came from the northeast of Japan, an area that carried little clout in military circles. Tojo resented his father's treatment. In 1899 he graduated tenth from the Japanese Military Academy. Tojo's rise began at the Military Affairs Bureau in 1931 when he was based in Manchuria. He became an intimate with Naoki Hoshino, head of economic affairs in Manchukuo, and was close to Lieutenant-General Tetsuzan Nagata, one of the leading members of the *Toseiha* Faction before his murder by Lieutenant-Colonel Saburo Aizawa in 1935. He proved his loyalty to the Emperor by participating with other *Toseiha* members in ruthlessly suppressing the *Kodoha* (Imperial Way Faction) after the 26 February Incident. Appointed to the Army General Affairs office, he ran censorship and press control. He was eloquent, important in an age when most information was disseminated by radio, bull headed, and believed in Japanese racial superiority. Nicknamed *kamsiori* (the razor), he was perceived to have a sharp cutting mind but was known for his use of the *kempeitai* (Army police) in Manchuria to install an ideological purity within the *Kwantung* Army. If he had an expertise it was supposedly his knowledge of the Soviet Union and he believed, as did many of his colleagues, that they were Japan's ultimate enemy. Failure at the *Battles of Nomonhan* convinced him of the need to back off this project for the time being.

Ian Mutsu (later President of the International Motion Picture Company of Japan), a correspondent for United Press Associations noted, "during the war crimes trial he [Tojo] in effect testified that the Emperor ultimately had been responsible for the war, because he could have stopped it if he wished."[60] At the war crimes trials he also denied any knowledge of the "torture and mistreatment . . . carried out by the *kempeitai*."[61]

Tojo was not held in particular awe when he came to power. That would change. When Tojo was appointed Prime Minister he immediately defied convention by adopting the War Minister portfolio in addition to his position as Prime Minister. By 1943 Tojo had become a virtual dictator having added to his roles by assuming the positions of Chief of Imperial Army General Staff, Minister of Armaments, and Minister of Education. If Hirohito and his courtiers had hoped that the appointment of Tojo would hold back the bellicosity of the Army, the choice backfired spectacularly. For Tojo, his promotion would enable him to fulfull the ambitions he expressed in *Hijoji Kokumin Zenshi* (Essays on the time of emergency confronting the Nation) [1934], a seven volume collection of essays presented by fifteen senior Army officers: Japan he asserted must "spread [its own] moral principles to the world [for] the cultural and ideological warfare of the 'Imperial Way' is about to begin."[62]

Japan's Decision for War and the Hull Note [5 November–1 December 1941]: At the Imperial Conference of 5 November 1941 Hirohito approved the plan of attack for *Pearl Harbor*, a scheme that had been broached to him at the end of August. Nevertheless it was decided that a last bid for peace should be made. On 6 November Nomura presented a proposal, 'Proposal-A,' for a partial withdrawal of troops from China. However, the US, through its MAGIC intercepts, was aware that this was 'Proposal-A,' which, if rejected, would be followed by 'Proposal-B.' The US stalled, rejected 'Proposal-A' and duly waited for the submission of 'Proposal-B,' which arrived on 20 November. Now the Japanese government proposed a withdrawal of troops from southern Indochina and the cancellation of any deployments in South East Asia— northern Indochina excluded. In return the US would have to agree to end financial or material assistance to Chiang Kai-shek and the *Kuomintang*, and allow Japan to buy oil. A US counter-offer was scotched by Roosevelt when he learnt through MAGIC intercepts that Japanese troop ships had set sail for Indochina. Doubting the sincerity of Japan's offers, Roosevelt ordered Hull to drop the counter-proposals.

Aware by 26 November that Japan had put a deadline of three days later for any agreement to be reached and assuming that Japan would launch an attack somewhere shortly afterwards, the Roosevelt administration was by now convinced that war was all but inevitable. A surprise attack was expected—though given the known troop movements, South East Asia was the expected target. Secretary of State, Cordell Hull, probably aware that there was now nothing to negotiate, on 26 November, presented the Japanese Ambassador with a ten-point ultimatum, the Hull Note, demanding complete Japanese withdrawal from Indochina and China. The Japanese assumed that by China, America included Manchuria in its demands, as it had not formally accepted Japan's occupation of the area that they now ruled as Manchukuo. The Hull Note, clearly stating a more trenchant US position than had previously been laid out, came as a body blow to any remaining hopes that Japan had of extricating itself from the dilemma of either accepting utter humiliation and defeat in China or going to war with America, the world's most powerful country. Unable to back down, on 1 December at a conference with Hirohito attended by Tojo, the Emperor gave the final sanction for war against the United States, Britain and Holland.

Some commentators would later describe the Hull Note as a *casus belli*. In 1948, historian Charles Beard argued that the Hull Note was an ultimatum that led to the *Pacific War*—part of a conspiracy theory that had Roosevelt deliberately causing the war to enable him to engage in Britain's war against Germany. More recently Benn Steil, Director of International Economics at the Council on Foreign Relations has added to the conspiracy agenda by claiming that assistant secretary of the treasury and Soviet spy, Harry Dexter White, wrote the Hull Note as part of a Soviet plot to draw Japan into the *Pacific War*. In similar vein Toshio Tamogami, Chief of Staff of the Japan Self Defence Force (JASDF), wrote in an article '*Was Japan an Aggressor?*' [2008]: "If Japan had accepted the conditions laid out by the United States in the Hull Note, perhaps the war could have been temporarily avoided . . . As a result, those of us living today could very well have been living in a Japan that was a white nation's colony."[63] Thus Tojo argued, as Tamogami has suggested, that the Hull Note left no alternative to war.

Pacific War historians have comprehensively discredited the arguments of Beard, Steil, Tamogami, and other conspiracy theorists. Leaving aside the fact that the Emperor had authorized war against the United States at the Liaison Conference on 6 September 1941, the Hull Note is a barely credible causal explanation of the *Pacific War*, given that Japan was already deploying to attack the Philippines, Malaya and *Pearl Harbor* if its 20 November 'Proposal-B' was not accepted. As for Steil's theory that the Hull Note was a Soviet plot, it is hotly disputed whether Harry Dexter White wrote it. Furthermore, Hull, obviously not a communist, authorized the sending of the note. Harry Dexter White, a Soviet spy, albeit an American patriot who never joined the communist party, did not provide the *casus belli* of the *Pacific War*. Single factor interpretations of the causes of the *Pacific War* are in any case an absurd over-simplification of the path of the conflict.

Summary of Causes of the Pacific War: The causes of the *Pacific War* are a complex fabric woven over decades, as Chapters 1–4 of this book have argued. The *Pacific War* resulted from the long drawn out imperial rivalry starting in the mid-nineteenth century between the established western powers and a rapidly emerging Japan for supremacy in an Asia, particularly China, which had failed to sustain an economy that was able to provide for its self-defense. The implosion of Chinese power set in train the events that led to *World War II*. The rise to power in Germany and Japan of ultra-nationalists bent on territorial aggrandisement, combined with the Anglo-Saxon nations' failure to enforce the Washington System and the League of Nations, in combination a barely veiled post-*World War I* 'Pax Anglo-Saxon,' allowed a global geopolitical framework to develop that, by the 1930s, was unstable and untenable. In the later 1930s the Anglo-Saxon powers were in a state of naked disarmament. The US Army had been whittled down to a force smaller than that of Belgium. The perceived weakness of China, combined with a lack of response from the Anglo-Saxon powers, whetted the appetite of an assertive and increasingly nationalistic Japanese political and military elite.

The annexation of Manchuria was an appetizer that only increased Japan's hunger for empire. The main driver for imperial expansion was the Japanese Army and particularly its recalcitrant ultra-nationalist *Kwantung* Army in Manchuria. In the aftermath of the 26th February Incident, an attempted *coup d'etat* by the Imperial Way Faction, the Control Faction emerged triumphant and purged the Japanese Army of its enemies—a process which unified and strengthened the Army even further.

Added to this mix, the role of the Soviet Union and Germany in the origins of the *Pacific War* is often overlooked. Stalin, concerned about the alliance of Germany and Japan after their signing of the *Anti-Comintern Pact* in November 1936, feared a concurrent attack on both its East and West fronts. In response Stalin used the Xian Incident to unite Mao and Chiang Kai-shek, at least temporarily, against the Japanese invaders with the aim of drawing Japanese forces away from the Soviet Union's eastern border and into a conflict in central China. The combination of Stalin's machinations, Chiang Kai-shek's patient rebuilding of *Kuomintang*'s military strength in the 1930s under Germany's guidance (provided by General Alexander von Falkenhausen until the *Anti-Comintern Pact*), and the increasingly imperialistic Japanese Army, pushed Japan and China toward all-out war with each other. The resulting *Second Sino-Japanese War* in July 1937 was arguably, in hindsight, the real starting date of *World War II*.

The trigger for the war was a seemingly innocuous little skirmish between Japanese and Chinese troops at the Marco Polo Bridge on the outskirts of Peking. It began a war that initially involved Japan and China and behind the scenes, the Soviet Union, which, after the *Anti-Comintern Pact*, had taken over the former German role of financing and equipping the *Kuomintang*'s National Revolutionary Army. However, within months, because of the special status of the Chinese treaty concessions in Shanghai and elsewhere, the interests of virtually all the western powers were drawn into the conflict—none more so than the United States, which, as the *Pacific Ocean*'s most powerful nation, had long cast covetous eyes on the potential of China trade. The heavy fighting between Chiang Kai-shek's National Revolutionary Army and Hirohito's *Kwantung* Army in northern China and in the *Yangtze River Delta* around Shanghai and Nanking set the course for a global conflict. In essence, the *Second Sino-Japanese War* morphed into *World War II* when Japan's ally Germany invaded Poland some two years later, on 1 September 1939. At this point Roosevelt, standing behind Great Britain and France, just as he was standing behind China, began to realize that America's isolationist stance was beginning to unravel as its existential interests were increasingly drawn into the vortex of conflict in both Europe and Asia.

It is only by dint of the western-centric view of global history that the Marco Polo Bridge Incident is not remembered as the start of *World War II* in the same way that the assassination of Archduke Ferdinand in June 1914 is recalled as the starting point of *World War I.*

Ultimately the United States would fully merge the conflicts in Europe and Asia when Roosevelt decided to cut off Japanese access to international finance, creating a *de facto* oil embargo of Japan at the end of July 1941. At the same time Roosevelt turned what had been a significant rearmament of the US Army starting in 1940, into a full-blooded mobilization for an anticipated war against Japan and Germany. The triggers for this aggressive shift in Roosevelt's foreign policy came after Japan's occupation of Vichy French-controlled northern Indochina in September 1940, Germany's invasion of the Soviet Union (Operation BARBAROSSA) in June 1941 and Japan's invasion of southern Indochina on 28 July 1941—each event ratcheting up the pressure on Roosevelt to take action.

With regard to Germany, the Roosevelt administration, albeit hostile to Japan's expansion in China, would have been much more sanguine about Japanese domination or even perhaps the conquest of China, if Hitler had not been in the process of constructing an even more threatening autarkic empire in Europe. Ultimately the Roosevelt administration precipitated the war with Japan by an oil embargo because it was not prepared to allow the world to be Balkanized into autarkic spheres, in both Europe and Asia, which would be inimical to America's economic and geopolitical interests. Roosevelt's bid to support Chiang Kai-shek's efforts to maintain Chinese independence was not determined by moral values concerning the rights of nations, which underlay the League of Nations; it was determined by Roosevelt's hard-nosed *realpolitik.* The fates of China and Europe were thus umbilically linked and made doubly so by the *Tripartite Pact* signed by Germany, Japan and Italy in September 1940, which determined in effect that if America went to war with Japan, it would also go to war with Germany. Faced by economic strangulation after the July 1941 oil embargo imposed by Roosevelt, Japanese leaders felt unable to back down and refused to meet America's terms that required them to withdraw from China after four and a half years of the *Second Sino-Japanese War* in which Japan had suffered over one million casualties. The oil embargo was a key turning point for both sides.

Six weeks after the oil embargo, on 6 September 1941, Emperor Hirohito authorized his Army's plans for war with the United States, Britain and Holland—providing very little margin for peaceful negotiation. Meanwhile Roosevelt, fully aware that the oil embargo was likely to lead to war, had authorized a massive military and naval mobilization. This included a build-up of US forces in the Philippines and a recall to active duty of General Douglas MacArthur, the US Army's former Chief of Staff who was already working for the Philippine government as Field Marshal of its Army. In addition forces and armaments were being assembled in the United States to combat the increasingly likely eventuality of war with *Nazi* Germany. The adoption of Plan DOG, based on Admiral Stark's memorandum of November 1940, showed that Europe remained America's geopolitical priority, not only because its economic importance to America was paramount but also because it perceived Germany as the greater military threat—it was a plan that implicitly underrated Japanese military capability as well as overrating Allied strength in the Asia-Pacific region.

Thus as early as the summer of 1940, some eighteen months before *Pearl Harbor*, America was already gearing up for war. Japan, already fully mobilized to fight in China, and by now operating a total war economy, had a head start. By November 1941 Japan, with its battle-hardened Army, was ready for war against the West while America, from a standing start, with an Army enfeebled by twenty years of neglect, was less than half done in its preparations for war with both Japan and Germany. At this point the American and Japanese governments may still have hoped for peace but neither had much leeway for negotiation; their overriding geopolitical objectives were, in effect, mutually incompatible. For both countries, the path to war was established. By its oil embargo America may have initiated the *Pacific War* but ultimately Japan, the aggressor nation that had sought to overthrow the established balance of power in Asia, had to commence armed hostilities because the clock was running down on its oil stockpiles. By contrast America, desperately trying to get its industrial war machine up to speed, had every advantage in waiting and delaying the start of a conflict that they nevertheless believed was all but inevitable. In terms of the causes of the *Pacific War*, the last diplomatic act, Cordell Hull's Note, was no more than the stationmaster's whistle for a train, fully booked and loaded, that was already pulling out of the station.

Part III
Hirohito's Whirlwind Conquests: December 1941–June 1942

5 Pearl Harbor: Yamamoto's Great Mistake

[7 December 1941 in Hawaii and Washington: 8 December 1941 in Tokyo]

[Drawing: 5.1] [Maps: 5.2, 5.3, 5.4]

The Conquest of Hawaii and Captain Mahan: While surveying the *Pacific Ocean* in 1845, US Navy Commodore, Charles Wilkes, opined that on the *Hawaiian Island* of *Oahu, Pearl Harbor* "would afford the best and most capacious harbor in the *Pacific*."[1] The natural harbor was seemingly carved into the center of *Oahu* for this very purpose.

However, it was opportunity for missionaries, trade and sugar cultivation that first attracted American settlers to *Hawaii*. In 1875 President Ulysses S. Grant beat off competition from France and Great Britain to conclude an exclusive trade agreement with Queen Liliuokalani. Twelve years later, the port of *Pearl Harbor* was ceded to the United States. The creep of Empire continued. After a coup by American missionaries and sugar planters on 17 January 1893, which deposed Queen Liliuokalani and replaced her with a Committee of Safety, *Hawaii* was formally annexed by the United States on 7 July 1898. In 1908 Congress authorized the dredging of the harbor's entrance to enable it to take the Navy's largest ships; this was followed by the construction of harbor facilities and dry docks and in 1919 by the acquisition of *Ford Island* in the center of the harbor. By then, not only had *Hawaii*'s native population been decimated by disease, but also *Pearl Harbor*'s strategic importance had been fully recognized.

In part this was due to the strategic thinking of Captain Alfred Thayer Mahan, a flag officer who became a geopolitical strategist and lecturer at the US Naval College in Annapolis, Maryland in 1885 and subsequently its President where, among other important contacts, he befriended Theodore Roosevelt. Mahan's major work on *The Influence of Sea Power upon History 1660–1783* [1890], with its emphasis on naval power as the route to world power, became a must-read for navy officers around the world, including Japan, where it was translated. In addition, Mahan authored over 100 articles. He was without question the most influential naval strategist of his age. The development of *Pearl Harbor* as a major naval base was central to his creed of growing US naval power in the *Pacific*. Inevitably Japanese politicians, naval planners and ultra-nationalists took note of the implicit aim of expansion of American power in the *Pacific*. Confirmation of America's expansionary intent came with the conquest of the Philippines after their sinking of the Spanish fleet in 1898.

'Range Extension' and Armament Technology Developments in the Interwar Years: [Drawing: 5.1] Historically 'Davids' have shown that 'Goliaths' can be defeated.

Although Japan's economy was just one-seventh the size of the United States, the *Washington Naval Treaty* [1922] allowed Japan 60 percent of the tonnage of the United States, its increasingly feared regional competitor. In the *Naval Treaty of London* [1930] Japan's ratio was upped to 70 percent. Although the United States had to split its naval forces between the Atlantic and the Pacific, Japan was still paranoid about its naval disadvantage. In 1928 Vice-Admiral Kichisaburo Nomura produced a review of Japan's naval needs in view of the restrictions required by the *Washington Naval Treaty*. It concluded that the Imperial Japanese Navy needed to develop superior, higher quality weaponry and better training and tactics to compensate for its inferior tonnage allocation. One of the key advantages to be developed was 'range-extending' technology. If Japan could attack the American Navy before it could return fire, a decisive advantage could be gained in a major naval engagement that Japan believed, like the *Battle of Tsushima*, could win them the war.

The development of 'super-battleships,' after the lapse of the naval limitation treaties, was designed to win a range-advantage for the Imperial Japanese Navy. The massive 18-inch guns of the super-battleship *Yamato* that came into service a week after *Pearl Harbor*, to be followed months later by her sister ship *Musashi*, were designed to demolish the American battle fleet as soon as it came within their 26-mile range. Their shells weighed 1.5 tons and could fire every forty seconds. (In 1942 the keel of a third *Yamato* Class battleship, the *Shinano* was converted to being an aircraft carrier.) By comparison America's biggest battleship guns, the 16-inch Mark-6 guns could hurl a 1.35 ton armor piercing shell twenty miles—a six-mile deficit compared to the Yamato Class though the rate of fire at two rounds per minute was slightly faster than the Japanese 18-inch gun.

A second range-extender development came in the form of torpedoes. As a result of the *Washington Naval Treaty*, which limited Japan's capital ships' total displacement compared to the Anglo-Saxon nations, the Japanese Navy invested heavily in new technologies such as submarines, aircraft carriers and torpedoes, weapons that were not limited. In 1928 Rear-Admiral Kaneji Kishimoto and Captain Toshide Asakuma began development of a new long-range torpedo. A year earlier an eight-man Japanese team of naval engineers had visited the Whitehead Torpedo Works at Weymouth with a view to buying their torpedoes. Believing, erroneously, that the British were working on an oxygen-powered torpedo, engineers from the Kure Naval Yard began work on one of their own. The British gave up, the Japanese succeeded. The Type-93 was introduced into service in 1933.

The secret of the Type-93's speed was the mastering of compressed oxygen technology for driving propulsion, which was much harder to handle safely than the traditional compressed air technology, but which was five times more efficient per given volume. Ingeniously, to reduce the risk of explosion on release, Kishimoto's team developed a means of starting ignition with natural air and gradually replacing it with compressed pure oxygen during its run. The risk of on-board explosion was thus significantly reduced. Mechanisms were designed with careful precision to prevent any contact between hot lubricants and the oxygen. Fuel lines were designed to flow without sharp angles and their linings were finely ground to prevent residual oxygen, oil and grease from collecting in microscopic pits. A special potassium-cleaning compound was also developed. Tests were successfully carried out in 1933 when it was designated as Type-93. The formidable new weapon weighed 2.8 tons, was nine yards long and had a 24-inch width. It could carry a 1,100 lb payload at forty-eight knots with a phenomenal range of 40,000 yards. It proved technologically far superior to any torpedo produced by the British or Americans during the course of the war. Apart from range, speed and warhead size, the Type-93 left almost no observable wake. Every precaution was taken to keep the weapon a secret. To take advantage of the Type-93, special light cruisers, *jurai sokan* (torpedo cruisers), were fitted out with torpedo tubes. Tactics of long distance concealed firing were developed for fleet engagements. As naval historians Peattie and Evans have pointed out, "The cruisers could deal the enemy a severe blow at the outset before he even knew he was in danger and before he even thought of evasive maneuver."[2] By comparison the American Navy assumed that a torpedo's lack of distance, judged from their own torpedoes' capabilities, would prevent them from being of any offensive use in a long-range gun duel between capital ships (defined as battleships until the advent of the aircraft carrier). During the war, unlike the Allies, it became normal for the Japanese Navy to arm its cruisers and destroyers with torpedoes as their main strike weapon.

Along with torpedo design, the Imperial Japanese Navy became world leaders in the development of large long-range submarines. These were designed to extend the offensive range of the Japanese Navy, including the remarkable I-400 series, which were vast submersible aircraft carriers that in their strategic capabilities presaged the post-war development of submarines armed with nuclear ballistic missiles. **[See Appendix A: Submarines: America Draws Tight the Noose]**

The fourth—and arguably the most important—major 'range-extender' was the development of new aircraft for use on aircraft carriers—the new weapon of mass destruction. Aircraft carriers themselves were by definition 'range-extenders' in terms of their ability to project power. Yet at the beginning of the interwar period carriers were little more than an emerging technology. HMS *Argus* (a converted ocean liner 1918), and USS *Langley* (a converted collier 1920) were the world's first aircraft carriers. Both were soon obsolete. Two years later the Imperial Japanese Navy's *Hosho* became the world's first purpose-built aircraft carrier. But for the next decade they would be little more than auxiliary ships—carriers of airplanes, mainly for reconnaissance. The limited scope of ambitions for the aircraft carrier was perhaps not surprising given the general scepticism that still remained about the role of the air force. Famously, the American maverick Brigadier-General 'Billy' Mitchell had returned from Europe in 1918 convinced of two things: first that the air force needed to become a third branch of the armed forces on a par with the Army and the Navy; secondly that the *Great War* was not the war to end all wars. "If a nation ambitious for universal conquest gets off to a flying start in a war of the future," he said, "it may be able to control the whole world more easily than a nation has controlled a continent in the past."[3] What Mitchell understood was that the aircraft would become a 'range-extender' that could rapidly transpose the power of arms from one region to another. It was a crucial insight that few of his contemporaries shared. Mitchell also understood that aircraft would bring an end to the 'Dreadnought Era,' which had made the battleship the weapon of mass destruction from the 1890s to the 1930s. In *Winged Defense* [1925], Mitchell observed, "the day has passed when armies on the ground or navies on the sea can be the arbiter of a nation's destiny in war. The main power of defense and the power of initiative against an enemy has passed to the air," and he concluded that ". . . air power has not only come to stay but is, and will be, a dominating factor in the world's development."[4]

From 1921 Mitchell, Assistant Chief of the Air Corps, carried out tests on stationary redundant battleships to show that bombers could sink battleships. The tests caused such a controversy between the US Navy's battleship brigade and the nascent air force that it even became the subject of cartoons in the *Chicago Tribune*. Mitchell, increasingly exasperated with the military and naval hierarchy, slammed their competence before the US House of Representatives' Lampert Committee. He paid the price of his outspokenness in October 1925 when, after another withering attack on senior military commanders, President Calvin Coolidge ordered that he be prosecuted for the violation of the Ninety-sixth Article of War (a catch-all article used to punish Mitchell's perceived insubordination). To General Douglas MacArthur's great distaste, he was appointed the youngest judge on the court. Although MacArthur supposedly voted for acquittal, Mitchell was found guilty on all counts in spite of the support of such luminaries as Fiorello La Guardia, airman, Congressman and a future highly popular Republican Mayor of New York, and 'Hap' Arnold, who was to serve as US Army Air Force Chief of Staff during *World War II*. Mitchell resigned from the Army but continued to preach his cause behind the scenes—even helping to convince President Roosevelt of the importance of air power in 1932. Largely spurned in his own time, Mitchell became a colossus of legend in the history of the US Air Force.

By 1932 in Japan a similar, albeit quieter, if no less acrimonious revolution was also under way. After a decade of first assembling and then manufacturing American and European aircraft, the Naval Air Arsenal took the important step to move toward self-sufficiency in design and manufacture. The prime mover for this step change was the Naval Aviation Department, whose Chief of the Technical Division from 1930 to 1933 was Rear-Admiral Isoroku Yamamoto. In 1934 Yamamoto, now promoted to Vice-Admiral, went to the London Naval Conference before returning the following year to take up the post of head of the Naval Aviation Department. Yamamoto, contrary to the widely held view that he was a pro-western moderate, was an ardent nationalist who believed that Japan should build an empire to rival that of the United States but should avoid war at least until Japan had developed military and naval parity. Writing to a young officer in 1934, Yamamoto expressed the view that: "the time has come for this mighty empire rising in the east to devote itself, with all due circumspection, to advancing its fortunes."[5] He went on to warn that: "The example afforded by the Great

War by Germany—which if only it had exercised forbearance for another five or ten years would by now be unrivalled in Europe—suggest that the task facing us now is to build up our strength calmly and with circumspection."[6] His views were broadly in sync with other leading naval officers including Admiral Mitsumasa Yonai and Admiral Shigeyoshi Inoue.

Yamamoto turned Japan's conventional strategic thinking on its head. Rapid development in aircraft technology and aircraft carrier design had begun to challenge every textbook strategic calculation. Working closely with Mitsubishi, the strongest of the *zaibatsu* in manufacturing terms, Yamamoto helped to develop more powerful aircraft to be used on aircraft carriers. Paradoxically, Yamamoto, adamant in his opposition to the invasion of Manchuria in 1931 and the aggression of the *Kwantung Army* that precipitated the formal start of the *Second Sino-Japanese War* in 1937, created the conditions for the development of weapons without which the conquest of South East Asia and the *South* and *Central Pacific* would not have been possible. Not satisfied with the production of the radical Mitsubishi A5M 'Claude' in 1935, the Navy department called for a fighter aircraft with even higher specifications. What followed was Mitsubishi's winning design for the A6M Zero, which, when it went into production for the Imperial Japanese Navy in 1940 was arguably the finest fighter of its generation. With the simultaneous development of an excellent dive-bomber and carrier attack bomber, the Aichi D3A 'Val' and Nakajima B5N 'Kate' respectively, as well as a land-based bomber, the Mitsubishi G3M 'Nell,' the Japanese Imperial Navy had the tools to go to war with the United States. All of these planes possessed world leading 'range' statistics in their class. Japanese airplanes were the ultimate expression of the Japanese interwar mantra of 'range-extension.'

Yamamoto's Great Gamble: **[Map: 5.2]** In 1939, then Prime Minister Yonai sent his friend and fellow admiral, Yamamoto, to be Commander in Chief of the Combined Fleet. Yonai would claim that the decision was "the only way to save his life"[7] because of Yamamoto's continual criticism of Army policy and his belief that America had too much industrial might to be defeated in a precipitate war. "Anyone who has seen the auto factories in Detroit and the oil fields of Texas," he noted, "knows that Japan lacks the power for a naval race with America."[8] Yamamoto insisted, "a war between Japan and the United States would be a major calamity."[9]

Nevertheless, increasingly faced by the certainty of war because America's economic blockade of Japan left it with no acceptable alternative, Yamamoto prepared plans that he believed could enable Japan to win. Given his background, it is perhaps not surprising that Yamamoto was one of the earliest proponents of a navy and a strategy led by carriers rather than by battleships. In 1923 Yamamoto had become second in command of the Kasumigaura Aviation Corps where he started to develop his legendary popularity. Later as Naval *attaché* to Washington in 1925 and again in 1928, Yamamoto was not unaware of the achievements of Charles Lindbergh in flying across the *Atlantic* in the previous year and he was also *au fait* with the technical importance of this achievement.

A naval colleague Miwa Yoshitake, in *Recollections of Fleet Admiral Yamamoto* noted, "he had a far clearer perception than myself both of the nature of instrumental flight as such and of the need for the Japanese Navy to adopt it."[10] Not surprisingly, in 1936, Yamamoto fiercely opposed the building of the battleships *Yamato* and *Musashi* which were to be the world's largest but which he viewed as little more than 'white elephants.'

The Imperial Japanese Navy's pre-prepared plans for war with the United States centered on the strategic principles of *Yogeki Sakusen* (Interceptive Operations). Its intellectual origins lay in the strategic naval thinking of Mahan, who was much studied by the Japanese and Tetsutaro Sato, 'the Japanese Mahan.' The plan was predicated on the assumption that Japan would invade and defeat American forces in the Philippines. It was then assumed that the US Navy would steam across the *Pacific* to relieve or retake the Philippines from Japan. Interwar naval investment had focused intensively on the development of submarines and torpedoes that it believed could reduce an American *Pacific Fleet* by 30 percent before it arrived at the *Marshall Islands*, which it was assumed they would pass on their way to the Philippines. The remainder of the US fleet would then be engaged in a decisive battle in the manner of *Tsushima*, the epic battle that annihilated the Russian Fleet as it cruised through the *Sea of Japan* toward Russia's eastern port of Vladivostok. The 'super-battleships' *Yamato* and *Musashi* with the 'range extension' provided by their big guns would win them another great victory that would end the war in their favor—allowing them to keep their Asian empire. The epic *Battle of Tsushima*, that had allowed a geopolitical minnow, Japan, to defeat the Russian Empire, one of the great powers, created a precedent for Japan's dealing with the United States. *Tsushima* was the dominant influence on the Japanese Navy's strategic planning. Thus in 1941 the Imperial Japanese Navy's operations manual (*Kaisen Yoh-murei*) declared that: "Battle is the sole means of victory. So everything should satisfy what the battle demands."[11]

For Yamamoto the problem with existing naval strategy was that America might simply delay its *Pacific* Fleet advance until Japan was weakened by its lack of resources and/or the US had built up overwhelming naval resources. On 7 January 1941, Yamamoto issued a memorandum '*Gumbi ni kansuru shiken*' (Views on Military Preparations), which pointed out that in fleet training exercises, Japan had never won a war game on the basis of their grand strategic 'wait and react' plan. How could Japan be sure that US Navy would be drawn into battle at an early stage of the war? If America simply pursued a war of attrition, given their massive industrial superiority, how could Japan win? "If in the face of such odds we decide to go to war," Yamamoto speculated, ". . . I can see little hope of success in any ordinary strategy."[12] Attacking first might even the odds. As the widely published air strategist Brigadier-General 'Billy' Mitchell wrote, "No nation can afford to decline the role of aggressor and sacrifice the opportunity of attacking an enemy that may be unprepared."[13] Yamamoto increasingly came to the view that, with no certainty of bringing the US Navy to them, the Imperial Japanese Navy would have to seek out the enemy. Aircraft carriers had arrived at the point of technological development that they gave Yamamoto a range-extension option that was not available to a battleship fleet. Following the success of mock battles with carriers, Yamamoto had been led to reflect to his Chief of Staff, Rear-Admiral Shigeru Fukudome, "It makes me wonder if they [the Japanese carriers] couldn't get to Pearl Harbor."[14] From these various considerations emerged the nine-page plan *Views on the Preparation of War*.

In the plan that he outlined, Yamamoto argued that if he could wipe out the US *Pacific* Navy in one fell swoop, the US might accept a truce that would give Japan time to develop oilfields and other sources of supply of raw materials. He was emphatic that "the outcome must be decided on the first day."[15] It was a plan for a *Pearl Harbor* attack, which the noted aviation tactical expert, Commander Minoru Genda, who had closely studied modern naval battles, believed was feasible. Torpedoes could sink battleships.

Two examples were closely studied. On 10 June 1918, the Austro-Hungarian Navy's SMS *Tegetthoff* and its sister dreadnought SMS *Szent Istvan* (Saint Stephen), which had been built at the Ganz & Company's Danubius Yard in the Hungarian-controlled port of Fiume (now Rijeka in Croatia), were returning from a patrol along the *Dalmatian Coast* when they were attacked by two Italian motor torpedo boats, MAS-*15* and MAS-*21*. MAS-*15*, commanded by Captain Armando Gori, scored two torpedo hits in *Szent Istvan*'s boiler rooms and shut down electrical power for the battleship's pumps. *Szent Istvan* continued to flood and eventually capsized before it could be towed back to port.

More importantly Genda had studied the British aerial torpedo attack on the Italian Navy at the *Battle of Taranto* on 11 November 1940. A single British aircraft carrier, HMS *Illustrious*, with its complement of just twenty-one out-dated biplane torpedo bombers had sunk one Italian battleship, the *Conte di Cavour*, and seriously damaged two others, *Caio Duilio* and *Littorio*, which were saved by being run aground. British carriers had a total complement of just 36–57 planes. What damage might the Japanese Navy inflict with six fleet carriers carrying some 70–85 planes each, an aggregate of 423 modern monoplane dive-bombers and torpedo bombers?

Strategically Yamamoto believed that a surprise attack that crippled America's *Pacific* Fleet would give Japan breathing space to overrun South East Asia and capture the vital oil resources of the Dutch East Indies, without which Japan would be unable to fight a protracted war. To provoke an attack in the Philippines and allow the American fleet a free run in the *Pacific* might invite attack and set back operations in South East Asia. Thus an attack on the US fleet at *Pearl Harbor* would, for six months at least, secure Japan from attack. From a technical point of view there were considerable attractions to catching an enemy fleet at anchor. At sea a major capital ship could twist and turn at a speed of up to thirty knots, almost as fast as the latest torpedoes. Coming in low at the slow speeds needed to aim and release torpedoes, aircraft were also easy targets for anti-aircraft gunners. Scoring a hit on a speeding warship was difficult. Diving 15,000ft at a speed of 300mph with anti-aircraft all around, in a cramped cockpit where the windscreen often fogged up, was not conducive to accuracy. As one pilot described it, hitting an enemy warship was "similar to dropping a marble from eye height on a scampering cockroach."[16] Fortunately for Yamamoto, at least at the beginning of the war, he had a stock of superbly trained pilots—probably the best, man for man, in the world.

For modern examples of sneak attacks, Yamamoto could draw on the successful surprise attack by Admiral Togo on Port Arthur in 1904 at the start of the *Russo-Japanese War*. To a great extent the concept of stealth and surprise attacks fell very much into the samurai tradition. In battle, groups of samurai would sometimes charge to the center of the enemy line in the hope of 'decapitating' the commanding general.

The sneak assassination of enemy commanders in the dead of night was also the stuff of samurai legend. In the Satsuma rebellion of 1877 led by Takamori Saigo, a sneak attack by sword-wielding samurai at 4 a.m. caught Imperial forces off-guard at the *Battle of Kumamoto*. When outnumbered or faced by a more powerful enemy the tactics of 'assassination' were acceptable. The *47 Ronin* was an early-eighteenth-century story about an incident at Edo Castle (Tokyo) involving forty-seven *ronin* (masterless samurai), who set out to assassinate a corrupt court official, Yoshinaka Kira, to whom their master, Naganori Asano, had refused to pay a bribe. Asano, after a violent altercation with Kira, was ordered to commit *seppuku* (literally 'stomach-cutting': ritual suicide by self-disembowelment with a *tanto*, short blade sword, followed by slashing of the neck to cut the main carotid artery). In revenge, the forty-seven *ronin* plotted to kill Kira, which they did a year later. In turn they then committed *seppuku* as a codified and honorable means of avoiding having to work for a new master. In this archetype of the samurai code of *bushido*, the sneak attack and murder of the corrupt official was perfectly morally acceptable—as was suicide. To western culture, a surprise attack on *Pearl Harbor* might be morally damnable, but interpreted by *bushido* it was not. Hence too the lack of moral outrage when ultra-nationalists murdered political opponents in the 1930s.

In April, Yamamoto was given the go-ahead to develop detailed plans for Operation Z, named after the famous pennant from Admiral Togo's flagship at the *Battle of Tsushima* [1905]. To his staff gunnery officer, Captain Yasuji Watanabe, Yamamoto confided, "If we fail we'd better give up the war."[17] Yamamoto's plans were not without opponents. As soon as he started to work on the details of the attack on *Pearl Harbor*, opposition started to fester within the Navy's General Staff and built up in the summer and early autumn. In particular the First Air Fleet Commander, Vice-Admiral Chuichi Nagumo, a cautious officer with little aviation background, who had been appointed in April 1941, and his Chief of Staff, Rear-Admiral Ryunosuke Kusaka strongly opposed Yamamoto's intended gambit. Apart from the undoubted risks, which even Yamamoto went out of his way to highlight, there was also concern that the absorption of resources by Yamamoto's strike force might fatally undermine the South East Asia campaigns. For the Philippines campaign in particular, the Army needed carriers to provide air cover for their landings. Entrenched opposition from the 'battleship brigade' within the Japanese Navy officer cadre, as in the US Navy, attempted to pull back the trend toward an aircraft-dominated Navy.

The internal battle regarding war strategy raged throughout the late summer and early autumn. On 3 October Yamamoto argued against a policy of only going for the oil in the Dutch East Indies: "What would you do," he asked his colleagues, "if the US fleet launched air raids on Japan from the east? Are you suggesting that it's all right for Tokyo and Osaka to be burned to the ground so long as we get hold of oil."[18] It was a pertinent question. Yamamoto cleverly hit at the Navy's pride in being able to prevent any attack on Japan's capital and the Imperial Palace. Furthermore, by October, several critical factors swung the arguments towards Yamamoto's *Pearl Harbor* operation. First the commissioning of the new fleet carriers, *Shokaku* and *Zuikaku*, probably the best in the world in 1941, relieved pressure on available carrier resources. Secondly engine modifications to the Zero fighter's engines allowed them to fly and return to the Philippines from *Formosa*, which would enable the Japanese Army's Air Force to provide additional support for their amphibious landings. Finally Yamamoto nudged the decision his way by threatening to resign.

In the weeks that followed, meticulous preparation continued for the attack on *Pearl Harbor*. *Hawaii* would need to be approached by Japan's carrier fleet without being observed. A route via the *Kuril Islands* off Siberia was selected from where Yamamoto planned to swoop down from the north. In October a passenger liner, *Taiyho Maru*, was sent along this route to see if any other ships were in the area. They were not. On 1 November the *Taiyho Maru* arrived in *Oahu, Hawaii* with Lieutenant Matsuo on board, charged with the task of reconnoitring the harbor entrance to the US Naval Base. Two weeks later the *Taiyho Maru* returned to Japan with three Navy spies who had been based in *Hawaii*. They were in time to brief the midget submarine crews who would lead the underwater attack on *Pearl Harbor*.

For detailed planning of flight operations, particularly the complex synchronization required for mass attacks involving the aircrews of six fleet carriers, Yamamoto brought in Commander Mitsuo Fuchida. It would have taken years for American carriers to be able to manage the same feat of communication and coordination of attack that Japanese officers such as Fuchida were able to achieve in a matter of weeks with little of the technology available later to US flight direction officers. Commander Kosei Maeda, a torpedo operations expert, was recruited to fine-tune the requirements of attack in a harbor that was known to be very shallow. Special fins were designed to prevent torpedoes running too deep when they first hit the water. Training was done in *Kagoshima Bay* (*Kyushu Island*), which had a passing resemblance to *Pearl Harbor*. Commander Minoru Genda, who had made a careful study of the British attack on the Italian fleet at Taranto, was put in charge of designing a tactical plan of attack on *Pearl Harbor*. Overall command of the carrier fleet had been given to Vice-Admiral Chuichi Nagumo, an officer with an uncanny resemblance to Yamamoto. Unlike the commander of the Combined Fleet, Nagumo was grouchy and uncommunicative.

On 8 November, flag officers of the combined fleet were assembled and told that:

> The success of our attack on Pearl Harbor will prove to be
> the Waterloo of the war to follow . . . It is clear that even
> if America's enormous heavy industry is immediately
> converted to manufacture of ships, aircraft and other raw

> materials, it will take several months for her manpower to
> be mobilized against us. If we assure our strategic
> supremacy from the outset ... by attacking and seizing
> all key points at one blow while America is still
> unprepared, we can swing the scale of operations in our
> favor.[19]

Operating under conditions of strict radio silence, Yamamoto ordered his forces to leave Japan's home waters from the great ports of Japan's *Inland Sea* to head north. False radio traffic was generated to mislead American listeners into believing that the Combined Fleet was still in home waters. Although US intelligence deduced that the Japanese fleet was on the move, *Hawaii* was never seriously considered as a destination. On 23 November, the great carrier force was finally assembled at *Hitokappu Bay* on *Iturup*, the largest of the *Kuril Islands* that stretch out in a line northeast from *Hokkaido*, the northernmost of Japan's four main islands, to the Kamchatka Peninsula in eastern Siberia. In this remote location bordering the *Sea of Okhotsk* and the *North Pacific*, preparation could be made far from curious eyes.

The Strike Force, led by Admiral Chuichi Nagumo, consisted of six fleet carriers including the *Akagi* (flagship), *Kaga, Soryu, Hiryu, Shokaku* and *Zuikaku*. On 26 November, Nagumo left the *Kurile Islands* and headed into the *North Pacific* at a leisurely thirteen knots while desperate last peace negotiations were taking place in Washington. All the while intelligence from Japanese spies in Honolulu was keeping the Naval General HQ updated on activity at *Pearl Harbor*. Winter storms and fog hid their advance. A vanguard of twenty-seven, mainly C-Class submarines had already been dispatched to *Oahu* to surround the island and report on ship movements and were charged to sink anything that managed to escape the attack on *Pearl Harbor*. Five further C-Class submarines, *I-16, I-18, I-20, I-22,* and *I-24* left port on 18 November carrying five midget submarines, which were scheduled to sneak into *Pearl Harbor* on the morning of 7 December.

Two days after leaving *Iturup*, on 28 November, the fleet had a *rendezvous* for refueling. On 1 December the final decision to attack was authorized by Emperor Hirohito and the following day, at 8 p.m. Admiral Nagumo received the coded message '*Niitaka Yama Nobore*' (Climb Mount Niitaka) ordering him to execute the attack on *Pearl Harbor*. At 9 p.m. on 6 December Nagumo sent an emotional message to all hands, recalling Admiral Heihachiro Togo's 'Nelsonesque' message before the *Battle of Tsushima*, "The Rise and Fall of the Empire depends upon this battle. Everyone will do his duty to his utmost."[20]

Pearl Harbor Prepares for War: **[Map: 5.3]** The logic of *Pearl Harbor*'s strategic location was finally recognized when President Franklin D. Roosevelt moved the *Pacific Fleet*'s main operating base to *Hawaii* from San Diego in early 1941. It was a move that put *Pearl Harbor* center stage and closer to its destiny in history. For Japan, it was a move that confirmed the existential threat that they feared from America's advance into Asia and the *Pacific*. After America's financial freeze and oil embargo in July 1941, followed by the peace negotiations, which were in effect a countdown to war, *Hawaii* was alive with activity in preparation for hostilities. The last peacetime edition of *Time* magazine concluded, "everything was ready. From Rangoon to *Honolulu*, every man was at battle stations ... A vast array of armies, of navies, of air fleets were stretched now in the position of track runners, in the tension of the moment before the starter's gun."[21]

Vice-Admiral 'Bull' Halsey set out from *Pearl Harbor* with Task Force 2 on 28 November 1941 aboard the USS *Enterprise* (CV-6), accompanied by a second fleet carrier, USS *Lexington* (CV-2). Halsey's task force was escorted by nine destroyers and was followed by Rear-Admiral Milo Draemel in a squadron of slower ships. They were ordered to ferry twelve fighter planes to *Wake Island* to prepare it for the possibility of Japanese attack. Regarding any encounter with the Japanese, Admiral Husband E. Kimmel, Commander in Chief, US Fleet and *Pacific* Fleet told Halsey "Goddam it, use your common sense."[22] Halsey told his crew that they were now operating under wartime conditions and, "Anything we saw in the sky was to be shot down, anything on the sea was to be bombed."[23] According to Lieutenant Clarence Dickinson, a member of Scouting Squadron-6, Halsey was not worried about firing the opening shots of the war. Dickinson recalled, "Admiral Halsey had made it quite clear to us repeatedly that under any circumstances he stands behind us. Right or wrong, if we act he takes responsibility."[24] Operations officer Commander William Buracker was stunned and asked "Do you realize that this means war?"[25] Halsey nodded. "Goddammit Admiral, you can't start a private war of your own! Who's going to take the responsibility?"[26] "I'll take it. Shoot first and we'll argue afterwards. I am going to fire if anything gets in my way"[27]

Commander of the Hawaiian Air Force was Major-General Frederick Martin under General Short while his counterpart in the Navy was Rear-Admiral Patrick Bellamy who reported to Admiral Husband Kimmel. Remarkably Martin and Bellamy had collaborated on a report on 1 March 1941 that outlined a scenario and warning that a surprise early morning attack might destroy the US *Pacific* fleet. The defensive recommendations springing from this report were largely ignored even though war games had been played in exercises that had featured carriers approaching and attacking from the north.

Tora! Tora! Tora!: **[Map: 5.4]** In the blue skies above *Oahu* on 7 December 1942, *Pearl Harbor*'s history would be marked forever. At 7.47 a.m., "*Tora! Tora! Tora!* (Tiger! Tiger! Tiger!)"[28] were the code words shouted by Commander Mitsuo Fuchida to his radio operator above the noise of his cockpit to alert Admiral Nagumo, aboard his flagship *Akagi*, that the US forces at *Pearl Harbor* in *Hawaii* had been taken completely by surprise. It was to be the most infamous surprise attack in history. As soon as he had relayed his message, Fuchida fired a flare and started the first strike of 183 aircraft led by Lieutenant Commander Shigeharu Murata's torpedo bombers.

Fuchida's first wave had set off from the Japanese Strike Force, lying 230 miles north of *Oahu*, at 6.15 a.m.

At 7.00 a.m., at Opana Radar Station on *Hawaii*, Privates George Elliot and Joseph Lockard should have already shut down their spanking new radar set. However, to get in extra practice, they stayed focused on their screens. At 7.02 a.m. they plotted a major incoming formation from the north about 127 miles away. When they called the information center at temporary operation rooms at Fort Shafter, they were greeted by Lieutenant Kermit Tyler, whose only experience of radar was a similar four hour shift a few days earlier. Tyler told the young radio operators that they must have seen a flight of Boeing B-17 Flying Fortress that was due in from California and that there was nothing to worry about. It was not the first strange sighting of the morning.

At 3.57 a.m. Captain William Outerbridge of the USS *Ward*, an ageing destroyer, was informed that the minesweeper USS *Condor* had spotted a periscope a few miles from the entrance of *Pearl Harbor*. At 6.37 a.m. Captain Outerbridge was again awoken and told that a small submarine had been spotted trailing the repair ship USS *Antares* into *Pearl Harbor*. USS *Ward* gave chase and scored a hit on the fast submerging conning tower of the Japanese submarine. Depth charges were dropped and when explosions brought oil and debris to the surface, a kill, first blood to the United States in the *Pacific War*, was confirmed. Captain Outerbridge immediately sent a message back to *Pearl Harbor*, "We have attacked, fired upon, and dropped depth charges upon submarine operating in defensive sea area."[29] The report was dismissed as a false alarm.

It was a peaceful scene that greeted the lead Japanese aircraft as they approached *Hawaii*. Fuchida would recall, "We could see that the sky over *Pearl Harbor* was clear . . . a film of morning mist hanging over it. I peered intently through my binoculars at the ships riding peacefully at anchor."[30] The layout of the island, its naval facilities, even the disposition of its fleet was already familiar to Fuchida. For months a 28-year-old spy, Takeo Yoshikawa, masquerading as a convivial consul official under the name Morimura Tadashi had been joy riding with the many young Japanese American women to be found on *Oahu*; he built up a detailed knowledge of *Pearl Harbor*. Based on this information Yamamoto, aboard the flagship *Nagato*, would keep a continually updated copy in his desk of: '*The Habits, Strengths and Defenses of the American Fleet in the Hawaiian Area.*'[31]

Fuchida's first-wave strike comprised 183 planes; a 1st Group consisted of fifty Nakajima 'Kate' B5N bombers armed with 800 kg armor piercing bombs and another forty 'Kates' armed with Type-91 torpedoes. The tactics of the attack were simple; a group of dive-bombers would neutralize the US airfields and the remainder along with the torpedo bombers would aim for the ships berthed in *Pearl Harbor*. Their primary targets were capital ships—aircraft carriers and battleships. A 2nd Group of 54 Aichi D3A 'Val' dive-bombers were targeted at *Ford Island*, Hickam Field (the largest airfield) and Wheeler Field (second airfield), while a 3rd Group of forty-five Mitsubishi A6M Zero fighters would provide cover and also strafe targets at Hickam and Wheeler. A second wave of 171 planes, led by Commander Shigekazu Shimazaki attacked Hickam Field as well as the aircraft and hangars at *Kaneohe, Ford Island* and *Barbers Point*.

As the first wave approached *Hawaii* a number of airborne US aircraft were taken unawares and shot down although one did manage to fire off a radioed warning, albeit somewhat incoherent. On the ground at 7.55 a.m. the surprise was total. "I was in the bunk room and everyone thought it was a joke to have an air raid drill on Sunday," recalled Ensign Guy Flannigan, "Then I heard an explosion."[32] Anti-aircraft guns were completely unmanned. None of the Navy's 5-inch thirty-eight caliber anti-aircraft guns fired a shot; just four of the Army's anti-aircraft batteries gave any action while only one in four machine guns were used. On the *Nevada,* sailors rushed to hack off the locks on their ammunition stores. At Hickam Field, when Lieutenant Overstreet went to the Ordnance store to get guns and ammunition, he was told by the desk sergeant, "I doubt if I'm authorized to give you any without a hand receipt."[33]

Fuchida found no aircraft carriers in place. Fortuitously for the US Navy, Admiral Husband Kimmel had sent Vice-Admiral Halsey and his carriers to *Wake Island*. The third carrier, USS *Saratoga* (CV-3) was finishing a refit in San Diego. By default the US Navy's battleships became the main targets for Fuchida's attack. The seven battleships lying in 'battleship row' were completely exposed. Admiral Kimmel had failed to protect his battleships with torpedo nets.

On the dockside sailors were preparing to raise the Stars and Stripes; the brass band of the USS *Nevada* started to play *The Star Spangled Banner*. A nurse at the Naval Hospital merely noticed ". . . planes roaring overhead . . ."; she turned to a colleague and said, "The flyboys are really busy at *Ford Island* this morning."[34] At Fort Shafter, Major-General Walter Short, while getting ready for a Sunday morning round of golf with Admiral Husband Kimmel, Commander in Chief Pacific Fleet, heard explosions from his quarters and rang to ask what was going on; his intelligence officer replied "I'm not sure, General but I just saw two battleships sunk." Short exploded, "That's ridiculous!"[35] His shocked reaction came just as the battleship, USS *West Virginia*, hit by bombs and seven torpedoes, was settling on the shallow bottom of *Pearl Harbor*. A torpedo hit on her rudder made maneuver impossible. Rapid counter-flooding measures carried out by Lieutenant Claude Ricketts prevented the 'Wee Vee' from capsizing, limiting the loss of life to 105 men. From chalk marks scratched on the walls, sixty-six of the dead were later found to have survived for sixteen days in an airtight storeroom. Captain Mervyn Bennion, while inspecting damage to the *West Virginia* was hit in the stomach by shrapnel from a bomb hitting the neighboring battleship, USS *Tennessee*, and later died.

Rear-Admiral William Furlong, who commanded the fleet service vessels, was on the quarter-deck of the minelayer USS *Oglala* when he saw a bomb drop on the Naval Air Station at *Ford Island*; at first he thought it must have been a faulty release from a US plane but as the aircraft flew past he could not help but notice its Rising Sun roundel. Furlong raised the alarm, though within minutes this was hardly necessary. However, it was Commander Logan Ramsey, who, having dashed into the radio room at *Ford Island* Operations Center sent the now immortal radio message relayed across the island as well as to Washington and Manila, "Air raid *Pearl Harbor*. This is not a drill."[36] Perhaps the sailor aboard the *Oklahoma*, who grabbed the public address system and yelled, "Man your battle stations. This is no shit,"[37] more graphically expressed the sentiments of the serving men.

The battleship, USS *Nevada*, in spite of taking a torpedo hit, got under way and headed for the channel out to sea until it was hit by further bombs; at this point it was decided to beach *Nevada* and allow the battleship to sink in shallow waters. An 800 kg bomb penetrated the battleship USS *Arizona*'s teak decks and landed on 450 tons of munitions in the forward magazine; at 8.10 a.m. a massive explosion sent a plume of smoke 1,000 feet in the air. Flames leapt from the forward turrets. On the signal bridge, Rear-Admiral Isaac Kidd and Captain Franklin Van Valkenburgh were atomized by the blast; their only residual trace being a Naval Academy ring found embedded and soldered into the superstructure. Survivors of the blast who jumped overboard were heard to sizzle as they hit the water. Most of the crew was killed instantly and the battleship sank taking some 1,177 men with her. Admiral Kimmel saw the *Arizona* "lift out of the water, then sink down—way down."[38]

USS *California* was hit by two bombs and two torpedoes; with her bow ruptured and water rushing in, the crew was ordered to abandon ship. *California* settled into the mud with just her superstructure jutting above water. *Oklahoma*, whose anti-aircraft guns even lacked firing pins, was hit by four torpedoes, immediately listed to port and soon capsized. Four hundred men were trapped below decks. Miraculously the battleship USS *Maryland* escaped with minor damage. Smaller ships were ignored by Fuchida attackers. Light cruisers USS *Helena* and USS *Honolulu* were torpedoed. The explosion on USS *Helena* capsized the minelayer USS *Ogala* lying alongside. Arriving at 9.15 a.m. the second wave of 167 aircraft faced more resistance, particularly from onshore and ship anti-aircraft fire. Although further chaos ensued on the ground the major portion of the damage had already been done by the first wave.

Meanwhile in Washington: In Washington news of the attack would be received with equal incredulity. Secretary of the Navy, Frank Knox, was conferring with Cordell Hull and Henry Stimson when he was handed a dispatch. *Pearl Harbor* had been attacked. Knox, shocked out of his wits exclaimed, "This cannot be true. This must mean the Philippines." "No Sir; this is *Pearl*"[39] came the reply. Shortly afterwards, at the State Department, Cordell Hull received Ambassador Nomura who arrived with his government's Fourteen Part Message with its declaration of intent to terminate negotiations—in effect a declaration of war. It was late. In spite of Yamamoto's strict condition that the note had to be delivered by 1.00 p.m. Washington time, translation and typing up of the note delayed Nomura. Thus Japan's surprise attack on *Hawaii* failed to stay within the notional bounds of honorable behavior. The delay caused by the slowness in typing up the declaration has been the center of much historical attention. In recent years Professor Takeo Iguchi at the International Christian University in Tokyo has uncovered documents, which suggest that there was never any intention to give the

United States notice that war was about to start. Yet it seems unlikely that, even if the message of war had arrived before the attack on *Pearl Harbor*, Roosevelt and the American public would have regarded the Japanese raid as anything other than a sneak attack.

Nomura's failure to get the translation of the Fourteen Part Message completed in time added to the Ambassador's noticeable discomfort. Although Hull already knew its contents from the MAGIC intercepts, he feigned shock although his fury and indignation was real enough: "In all my 50 years of public service, I have never seen a document that was more crowded with infamous falsehoods and distortions—infamous falsehoods and distortions on a scale so huge that I have never imagined until today that any government on this planet was capable of uttering them."[40]

Meanwhile the attacks at *Pearl Harbor* were still continuing. A dive-bomber attack on USS *Pennsylvania* lying in its dry dock blew up guns and ammunition, killing sixteen men. Flooding the dry dock to put out the fires on the *Pennsylvania* proved to be a bad idea; oily water caught fire and both destroyers lying in dry dock, the USS *Cassin* and USS *Downes,* were burned out. The destroyer USS *Shaw* was also damaged, as was the seaplane tender USS *Curtis* and the repair vessel USS *Vestal*. At Navy headquarters, a despairing Kimmel tore off his four-star insignia. He must have known that he would take the blame for the disaster. When a spent bullet smashed through a window and struck him lightly on the chest, leaving a smudge on his spotless white uniform, Kimmel turned to his aide and said, "Too bad it didn't kill me."[41]

As for *Hawaii*'s aircraft defenses, they were largely destroyed. Out of 402 planes on the islands 347 were either destroyed or heavily damaged. Most of them were hit while on the ground. The US Air Force was almost completely lacking in preparation for defense of any kind. Just eight Army Air Corps fighter pilots managed to take off. Lieutenant Gordon Sterling, who had planned a Sunday date with his fiancée, Ada Olsson, was shot down and killed. His body has never been recovered. Five planes flying back to *Hawaii* from the carrier USS *Enterprise* were shot down by 'friendly' fire. However, two Curtiss P-40 Warhawk fighter pilots, George Walch and Kenneth Taylor, barely in their beds after an all-night game of poker, rushed to their planes at Wheeler Field and managed not only to take off but also to engage in a dogfight with withdrawing Japanese aircraft. They were credited with seven 'kills' between them though only three were later confirmed.

In all US forces suffered 2,402 dead and 1,247 wounded plus about 100 civilian casualties. Material losses were four battleships sunk, three damaged and one beached. Two other ships were sunk and nine damaged. By comparison the Japanese lost twenty-nine aircraft and had sixty-four men killed; losses included five midget submarines of which four were sunk. In spite of the element of surprise, the midget submarines performed with little reward. One midget submarine's navigation system and engines failed. After it was abandoned one crewman drowned but the other Japanese submariner, Kazuo Sakamaki, swam to shore and was captured by US Sergeant David Akui. Sakamaki was the first prisoner of the *Pacific War*.

Reaction in America and the World: In America, football fans listening to the New York Giants-Brooklyn Dodgers game were the first people to learn of the Japanese attack on *Pearl Harbor* when the transmission was interrupted at 2.26 p.m. WQXR (New York's classical music radio station) tactfully changed its radio transmission of Gilbert and Sullivan's *The Mikado* and played *HMS Pinafore* instead. A group representing Manhattan *Nisei* (Americans of Japanese descent) sent a telegram to Roosevelt telling him, "We the American citizens of Japanese descent of New York City and vicinity join all Americans in condemning Japan's aggressions against our country, and support all measures taken for the defense of the nation."[42]

In Washington, the shock to President Roosevelt, a Navy man at heart, was profound. Secretary of Labor, Frances Perkins, noted his extreme pallor at a meeting with his senior advisers and cabinet officers in the Oval Office. She noted, "his pride in the navy was so terrific that he was having physical difficulty in getting out the words that put him on record as knowing that the navy was caught unawares, that bombs dropped on ships that were not in fighting shape and not prepared to move, but were just tied up . . . ."[43] The mood in the Navy Department was equally stunned and despairing. To the Bureau of Navigation's director of recruiting, Nimitz said "Red . . . we have suffered a terrible defeat. I don't know whether we can ever recover from it."[44] For American soldiers and sailors of all ranks, the bubble of complacency had burst. America knew that it was in for a fight. Seaman William Fomby, a mess cook on USS *Oklahoma*, noted that "When you see all these people in bed sheets laying out stacked up like corkwood, it takes all the glamor out of war."[45] It was a far cry from the Marine, Lieutenant-Colonel Cornelius Smith's boast a few weeks earlier: "Hell, we could blow them out of the water in three weeks."[46] Panic swept the nation. The structure of American life changed instantly. Citing the war in the *Pacific*, union leaders called off a nationwide strike by 125,000 welders.

In London Churchill heard about *Pearl Harbor* on BBC's nine o'clock news while he was listening to a US$15 portable radio given to him by President Roosevelt's close friend and adviser, Harry Hopkins. Churchill, barely able to contain his delight that America was now in the war, immediately rang Roosevelt who confirmed, "It's quite true. They have attacked us at *Pearl Harbor*. We're all in the same boat now."[47] At the end of this extraordinary day, Churchill recalled that he went to bed and "slept the sleep of the saved and thankful."[48]

Back in Japan, Tokyo Radio announced a crushing victory against the American Fleet at *Pearl Harbor*. Crowds burst into spontaneous applause. Robert Guillain, a French reporter, noted the reaction of Japanese civilians in the *chic* Ginza quarter of downtown Tokyo, "Joyous relief and intense satisfaction shone in every face . . . across every face was spread a look of smug pride mixed with naiveté."[49] At the Navy Department in Tokyo, Lieutenant Yoshida recalled that Naval staff "were swaggering up and down the halls, swinging their shoulders. Full of pride."[50] Many were stunned at the Japanese success. "To be perfectly honest," recorded Masatake Okumiya, an airman, "I personally was astounded at the enemy's inexplicably weak resistance . . . prior to the attack no one would have dared to anticipate the actual results of our initial assaults."[51]

Prime Minister, General Tojo, explained the war to the Japanese public; in the face of western aggression Japan planned "to annihilate this enemy and to establish a stable new order in East Asia, the nation must anticipate a long war."[52] Meanwhile at the Imperial Palace, Eiichiro Jo, Emperor Hirohito's naval aide noted in his diary that at 8.30 p.m. "The chief of the Navy General Staff reported on the achievements of the *Hawaii* air attack . . . Throughout the day the Emperor wore his naval uniform and seemed to be in a splendid mood."[53] A formal declaration of war with an Imperial Rescript was issued. The west was accused of "economic and political pressure to compel thereby our Empire to submission . . ." which, "has no other recourse but to appeal to arms and crush every obstacle in its path."[54]

Hirohito's main ally, Hitler, received the news at the Wolf's Lair, the Führer's headquarters in the Masurian Woods east of Berlin. It was "The turning point!" he exuberantly told his assembled staff, "We now have an ally who has never been vanquished in 3,000 years."[55] Hitler did not wait for an American declaration of war. "The American President and his plutocrat clique have mocked us as the *Have-nots*— that is true," Hitler announced to his followers, "but the *Have-nots* will see to it that they are not robbed of the little they have."[56] He urged his allies to destroy "the Anglo-Saxon-Jewish-Capitalist World."[57]

The day after the attack on *Pearl Harbor*, Admiral 'Bull' Halsey, aboard the USS *Enterprise* as it returned from *Wake Island*, exploded with anger as he witnessed the scene of devastation on entering *Pearl Harbor*. Regarding Japan's infamous 'sneak' attack on *Pearl Harbor*, Halsey's response was "The dirty little bastards!"[58] "Before we're through with them," he raged, "the Japanese language will be spoken only in hell!"[59] The immediate reactions to the surprise attack at *Pearl Harbor* bore little resemblance to the subsequent debates that were to dog both sides in the aftermath of the attack. These debates still rage today. The first relates to the question of blame allocation in the United States for *Hawaii*'s lack of preparedness for attack while the second revolves around the role of Admiral Yamamoto and the wisdom or otherwise of Japan's war plan.

The US Navy: Recriminations and Blame: If the raid on *Pearl Harbor* posed questions for the Japanese leadership, it was no less problematic for America. Within the week Secretary of State for the Navy, Frank Knox, had visited *Hawaii* and decided that Admiral Kimmel would have to be replaced. Similarly Lieutenant-General Walter Short, who was technically responsible for the defense of *Hawaii*, was also relieved of his command. However, it was Kimmel, because of the battleships that were lost, who became the most notable scapegoat for the debacle at *Pearl Harbor*. How could he have been so unprepared? From the outset the 'blame game' became of paramount importance to the senior officers involved. In Washington Admiral Rainsford Stark, Chief of Naval Operation warned Rear-Admiral Claude Bloch, commander of the 14th Naval District in *Hawaii*, "Tell Kimmel I will be asking him how far out (the patrol craft) were and in what sectors."[60]

The Navy's 14th Naval District Combat Intelligence Unit on *Oahu*, known as Station Hypo, under the command of Lieutenant-Commander Edwin Layton, had warned Kimmel on 2 December, "As there had been no radio traffic from four Japanese carriers for fully fifteen and possibly twenty-five days, their location was unknown."[61] On 27 November Secretary of State for War Henry Stimson had sent a message to Kimmel and Short to the effect that a war with Japan could start at any moment. Should this not have warranted a high level of alert, particularly as they were fully aware that negotiations with Japan in Washington were reaching a critical point? Major-General Martin, who had asked for control of recently arrived radar sets, was denied by General Short who insisted that they remain under the operation of the Signal Corps.

Admiral Stark had himself sent a warning to British Admiral Hart in *Singapore* and Admiral Kimmel in *Hawaii*, ". . . an aggressive move by Japan is expected within the next few days."[62] On 3 December Stark also informed them that the Japanese embassies had destroyed their codebooks in *Hong Kong, Singapore*, Manila, Washington, and London. In spite of these warnings Kimmel was bizarrely complacent. The day before the attack on *Pearl Harbor*, when Joseph Harsch of the *Christian Science Monitor* had asked Kimmel whether Japan would attack America, he answered categorically, "No, young man, I don't think they'd be such damned fools."[63]

However, the blame cannot be apportioned to Kimmel and Short alone. In Washington Admiral Rainsford Stark, Chief of Naval Operations and Rear-Admiral Richmond Kelly 'Terrible' Turner, head of War Plans Division of the Navy Department failed to give Kimmel all the information that was available from PURPLE, a diplomatic crypto-graphical machine used by the Japanese Foreign Office, and JN-25, the name given by code-breakers to the chief, and most secure, command and control communications scheme used by the Imperial Japanese Navy. Access to this information would have given Kimmel a much more direct warning that a Japanese attack was imminent. Political machinations within the Naval hierarchy were at the heart of the problem. Naval Intelligence under Captain Theodore Wilkinson was allowed to collect information but, after an internal political battle with Rear-Admiral Turner, he was forced to give up the role of intelligence dissemination.

Thus whereas the Army passed the full MAGIC intercept information package to MacArthur, Rear-Admiral Turner, protecting key pieces of information, failed to pass on the same critical information to Kimmel in *Hawaii*. At a later government inquiry into *Pearl Harbor*, Admiral Bellinger, Kimmel's Air Defense Officer testified that "The information available to me—limited and unofficial as it was—did not indicate that I should recommend to the Commander in Chief Pacific Fleet [Kimmel] that distant patrol plane search for the security of *Pearl Harbor* be undertaken at this time."[64] It was a self-serving explanation also given by Kimmel, albeit with some justification. Whether Short and Kimmel would have acted on this information will never be known. MacArthur, who was privy to all the information known in Washington, as well as having eight hours' notice of what happened at *Pearl Harbor*, failed to react at all.

Within the Navy sympathy was clearly with Stark and Kimmel. After the first *Pearl Harbor* inquiry conducted by Supreme Court Justice Owen Roberts, Admiral Ernest King, who had replaced Stark as head of the Navy, scathingly reflected that the Roberts's committee had "merely selected a 'scapegoat' to satisfy the popular demand . . ."[65] King was also incandescent that the demotion of Stark from CNO to Commander of the US Naval Forces in Europe was a punishment not meted out to General Marshall. King's more than reasonable contention was that the US Army was just as much at fault as the US Navy for the *Pearl Harbor* debacle, perhaps more so because General Short had primary responsibility for the protection of *Hawaii*. Admiral Ernest King endorsed the blame allocated to Admirals Stark and Kimmel by Supreme Justice Owen Roberts for the disaster; however, by the time that Admiral Kent Hewitt began to conduct the second inquiry, the *Pearl Harbor* Court of Inquiry, King was having doubts about his earlier harsh judgment. In August 1945, under pressure from Secretary of the Navy, James Forrestal, (the replacement for Frank Knox when he died of a heart attack in 1944), had to push King to endorse the Hewitt report with an endorsement that read:

> Admiral Stark and Admiral Kimmel though not culpable to a degree warranting formal disciplinary action, were nevertheless inadequate in emergency, due to the lack of the superior judgment necessary for exercising command commensurate with their duties. Appropriate action appears to me to be the relegation of both of these officers to positions in which their lack of superior strategic judgment may not result in future errors.[66]

King later recanted his endorsement of Admiral Hewitt's judgment. In April 1948 he went as far as to write to the Navy Department to say that he had been in error in endorsing Hewitt's report and requested that his endorsement be withdrawn. It was one of the few times in his life that he admitted an error of judgment. As for Nimitz, when he met Kimmel he said, "You have my sympathy. The same thing could have happened to anybody."[67] These were not just kind words to a good friend; it was a stance that Nimitz would maintain throughout this life.

In 1985 Edwin T. Layton co-authored an autobiography with John Costello, entitled *And I Was There: Pearl Harbor and Midway—Breaking the Secrets* in which he placed the blame for the lack of intelligence available to Kimmel squarely on the shoulders of Rear-Admiral Turner. Many *Pacific War* historians now endorse this view. Remarkably Turner went on to have an extremely successful war in his role as commander of the amphibious forces in the *Central Pacific* campaign, eventually becoming a full admiral. After the war he became the US Naval Representative on the United Nations Military Staff Committee. Even now the issue of blame for *Pearl Harbor* divides opinions. On 25 May 1999, the US Senate passed a non-binding resolution exonerating Kimmel and Short; however, the resolution only passed by fifty-two to forty-seven votes and was not endorsed by President Bill Clinton.

Debunking the Conspiracy Theories: As for the assertion by a raft of conspiracy theorists that President Roosevelt knew details in advance of the impending attack on *Pearl Harbor*, they have no basis in fact. The conclusions of the Roberts and Hewitt inquiries should be evidence enough that the United States did not willingly open its navy to be sunk on purpose. Grounds for the conspiracy theory came from the many warnings of the risk of attack at *Pearl Harbor*. Brigadier-General 'Billy' Mitchell posited the possibility as early as 1924. Army-Navy war games at the end of January 1931 were based on an enemy carrier attack on *Pearl Harbor*. In 1935, Major-General Hugh Drum, commander of the *Hawaiian* Department, pleaded for the building of airfields on *Hawaii*'s outlying islands arguing that ". . . to prevent the destruction of or serious damage to our airfields on *Oahu* and *Pearl Harbor* by hostile aircraft, carriers must be sunk or driven off before they can launch their aircraft . . . ."[68] FDR's administration had been warned of the possibility of an attack on *Pearl Harbor* by Ambassador Grew's sources in Peru. On 28 January 1941 Grew warned that "in the event of trouble breaking out between the US and Japan, the Japanese intend to make a surprise attack against *Pearl Harbor* with all their strength and employing all their equipment."[69] The Martin-Bellinger report in March 1941 had similarly warned of an existential carrier threat to *Pearl Harbor*. This warning was made months before the attack was even a thought in Admiral Yamamoto's mind.

In August 1941 the Farthing Report, postulating a six-carrier attack on *Pearl Harbor*, was circulated in Washington. It concluded, "With the United States living and working under a condition of unlimited National Emergency, Japan making its southward movement, and the world in general in a complete state of turmoil, we must be prepared for D day at any time."[70] Intelligence and analysis concerning the risks to *Pearl Harbor* abounded. Why was it not acted on? In situations of impending war—theories, conspiracies, rumors, fact and misinformation whirl around decision makers in bewildering streams. Only in hindsight does the correct 'intelligence' become apparent.

Seemingly at the time the US Navy was much more obsessed by the possibility of sabotage by the 160,000 Japanese in *Hawaii* than they were by existential threats. In Washington General Marshall treated these threats as equals: "The risk of sabotage and the risk involved in a surprise raid by air and by submarine constitutes the real perils of the situation."[71] In spite of these many warnings, complacency was even more prevalent than intelligence. Journalist Clarke Beach assured his readers that "A Japanese attack on *Hawaii* is regarded as the most unlikely thing in the world, with one chance in a million of being successful. Besides having more powerful defenses than any other post under the American flag, it is protected by distance."[72] As Gordon Prange had concluded in his exhaustive account, *At Dawn We Slept* [1981], "[*Pearl Harbor*] was less a failure of intelligence than a failure to evaluate properly the excellent intelligence available."[73] In other words the failures at *Pearl Harbor* were a screw-up not a conspiracy.

That Roosevelt was determined that Japan should be seen to strike the first blow in the war is undisputed. Understandably he did not want to appear in the role of aggressor. In public, not wanting to provoke widespread panic, he also played down the risks of attack or even war. However, from the point of view of sheer political calculation it is inconceivable that he would have allowed the death of thousands of US sailors to achieve this end let alone the possible destruction of the country's fleet and the possible loss of the war before it started. It should be remembered that as far as Roosevelt was aware, all America's forces were alert to the possibility of attack. After *Pearl Harbor*, Roosevelt was as shaken as any man in Washington and when he turned to Knox and demanded, "Find out, for God's sake, why the ships were tied up in rows,"[74] his exasperation was not faked.

Apart from hubris, perhaps the main culprit of the American failure at *Pearl Harbor* was the US Navy's institutional ossification. Leaving aside the issues of intelligence dissemination and divided command structure, (changed on 17 December when command of *Hawaii* was handed to the Navy), at the start of the war the US Navy's leadership retained the mind-set of a battleship fleet. Before the start of the *Pacific War*, consensus in the US Navy was that the battleship was still the main strike weapon. At *Pearl Harbor*, the US Navy had stationed seven battleships and just three carriers. The US warship program in 1941 shows that carriers were still not a priority; although the keel of the first Essex Class carrier had been laid down, it was not planned for the USS *Essex* to be commissioned until 1944. In the eighteen months before *Pearl Harbor* the US Navy built two new battleships, bringing its full complement to seventeen while adding just one new fleet carrier, bringing the total to seven. There was an evident disconnection between the known risks to *Pearl Harbor* and the US Navy's build program. That changed rapidly after *Pearl Harbor* with a speeded up program that produced the *Essex* by December 1942 and twenty-two more Essex Class carriers by the time of Japan's defeat in 1945. In addition, after *Pearl Harbor*, at Roosevelt's insistence cruiser keels were converted to Independence Class light carriers.

In December 1941, while the US Navy's senior admirals may have recognized the theoretical possibility of a carrier attack on *Pearl Harbor*, it is doubtful that they considered it a *real* possibility. It took *Pearl Harbor* to wake up the US Navy to the new realities of naval warfare, notably the central role of carriers. Although it may not have appeared so at the time, *Pearl Harbor* gave the US a lucky break. At what in hindsight was minimal material cost in terms of the loss of battleships, the US Navy learnt lessons that would enable them to win the war in the *Pacific*.

Reflections on Yamamoto's Failure at Pearl Harbor: In spite of the shockwaves created in *Hawaii*, Washington and throughout America, Yamamoto's attack on *Pearl Harbor* was at best a superficial success and at worst a colossal mistake. For a man who had lived in the United States, Yamamoto's understanding of his enemy was strangely flawed. After *World War I* he had studied at Harvard and spent two spells as Japanese Naval *attaché* in Washington. As a rear-admiral, he also participated at the London Naval Conference in 1930 and again in 1934. He was intelligent, English-speaking, knowledgeable about the west and much adored within the Japanese Navy. His views on

US industrial strength and his famed dislike of the Japanese Army in general and Tojo in particular have sometimes led him to being portrayed as a neglected sage.

Nothing could be further from the truth. Yamamoto once wrote,

> To die for Emperor and Nation is the highest hope of a military man. After a brave hard fight the blossoms are scattered on the fighting field. But if a person wants to take a life instead, still the fighting man will go to eternity for Emperor and country. One man's life or death is a matter of no importance. All that matters is the Empire.[75]

He was a Confucian traditionalist who shared the *bushido* disdain for death. His extraordinary popularity within the Navy reflected the fact that he epitomized the *zeitgeist* of 1930s Japan, not because he opposed it. Just before *Pearl Harbor* Yamamoto composed a *waka* (a thirty-one syllable poem) in which he wrote, "It is my sole wish to serve the Emperor as His Shield, I will not spare my honor or my life."[76] The post-war legend that the Japanese Navy was enlightened and anti-war, while only the Japanese Army was 'culturally Neanderthal' and war-mongering is simply incorrect. While Yamamoto himself, fully aware of America's industrial strength, tried to persuade Prince Konoe to "make every effort to avoid war with America,"[77] this did not mean that Yamamoto was anti-war or against the expansion of the Japanese Empire.

Like his compatriots he believed that Americans were essentially weak—dispirited by a major defeat they could be persuaded to agree to a truce and to allow Japan to keep its Empire. He naively insisted that the Fourteen Part Message should be delivered half an hour before his surprise attack on *Pearl Harbor* on the grounds that this would not antagonize America to the point of seeking revenge; it shows a remarkable lack of knowledge—indeed common sense—to think that President Roosevelt and the American people would have considered Japan any less dastardly had Ambassador Nomura been able to type up the Fourteen Part Message in time for his 1.00 p.m. meeting with Secretary of State, Cordell Hull.

Rear-Admiral Takijiro Onishi pointed out one of the key misjudgements made by Konoe, Yamamoto and other supporters of the *Pearl Harbor* Plan. If Japan's war objectives were to draw the United States into negotiations, then an invasion of the Philippines might work, but to attack *Pearl Harbor*, part of US sovereign territory, risked driving the Americans "so insanely mad"[78] that they would seek a revenge without temporization. "You are an amateur naval strategist, and your ideas are not good for Japan," Onishi told Yamamoto, "This operation is a gamble." Yamamoto angrily replied, "I like games of chance."[79] The *Pearl Harbor* project was fraught with risk. Yet that was an important element in Yamamoto's character. His friend, Admiral Takagi Sokichi, noted, ". . . Admiral Yamamoto was no saint. Few men could have been as fond of gambling and games of chance as he . . . shogi, go, mahjong, billiards, cards, roulette—anything would do."[80] Even Yamamoto understood that his plan was a gamble and the risk of discovery very high; he warned his officers on the decks of the *Akagi* before the flagship departed on its mission, that "you must take into careful consideration the possibility that the attack may not be a surprise after all. You may have to fight your way into the target."[81] Indeed Admiral Osami Nagano, Chief of the Navy General Staff initially rejected the *Pearl Harbor* project and it was only given the 'green light' on 19 October after Yamamoto threatened resignation.

If the risk of discovery was high, there was also the risk that the prime targets, the US carrier fleet, would not be at *Pearl Harbor* when the Japanese surprise attack took place. Indeed, this is actually what happened. So what did Yamamoto achieve by his gambit? The port was shallow and none of the eight battleships actually sank to the bottom of the ocean. The shallowness of the water and the proximity of the battleships to shore facilities saved six out of the eight battleships from total destruction—proof of the flawed logic of Yamamoto's plan. Only USS *Arizona*, which blew up, and USS *Oklahoma*, which capsized, were permanently lost to the *Pacific* Fleet; the remainder were salvaged and rebuilt and served later in the *Pacific Campaign*. *West Virginia*, *Tennessee*, *California*, *Maryland*, and *Pennsylvania* all fought at the *Battle of Leyte Gulf* where the Japanese fleet was effectively dealt a *coup de grâce*. Had the US fleet suffered a beating of the scale of *Pearl Harbor* at sea, all of these US battleships would likely have been lost. As the historian E. B. Potter has observed, ". . . had Kimmel put to sea and met the enemy, his whole fleet would almost certainly have been sunk—in deep water beyond salvage, with a loss of 20,000 men."[82] For Japan, the 'partial' sinking of US battleships at *Pearl Harbor* was a paltry return for such a major effort. The fact that the US carriers were not at *Pearl Harbor* further compounded the failure of a poorly conceived plan.

The absence of the US carriers had a tangential effect on another important aspect of the attack, namely the supposed failure to launch a second strike at *Pearl Harbor* by Admiral Nagumo. It is a subject on which there was much controversy both at the time and subsequently. Mitsuo Fuchida's *I Led the Attack on Pearl Harbor* [1954] suggests that Fuchida confronted Nagumo about his decision to call off a second strike. In general Nagumo is portrayed as a plodder in the epic Hollywood film *Tora! Tora! Tora!* [1970]. However, Fuchida's claims regarding the second strike do not seem to tally with other contemporaneous accounts.

Nagumo had very good reasons for not pursing a second strike. With the absence of the US carriers from *Pearl Harbor* and their whereabouts unknown, Nagumo must have been aware of the possibility that his position was now known and that he might be the object of an American counter-attack. Furthermore the second wave strike planes did not get back to their carriers until after midday. By the time they had been rearmed, refueled and 'spotted' (the word for the arrangement of aircraft on deck ready for take-off), it would have been well into the afternoon before they could have taken off again. A nighttime carrier landing would almost certainly have been required. This was an exercise for which the Japanese carriers were not equipped nor its flyers trained. In 1941 only the British Royal Navy had thus far developed the expertise for landing aircraft on carriers at night. For this reason alone Nagumo would have been reluctant to authorize another attack. As for waiting till the next morning, this was not possible because of a lack of enough fuel for the carriers to wait on station for another day. Logistical support was limited and he risked losing ships if he delayed his return. It was going to be a long war and conservation of resources after such an apparently successful attack was not an inappropriate response by Nagumo.

At first Yamamoto was supportive of Nagumo, though later he declared that not launching a second strike was a mistake. Indeed he must soon have realized that the destruction of the dockyards, particularly the dry docks, maintenance facilities, not to mention the huge oil depots amounting to 4.5 million barrels (which were all targets for a third strike) might have brought greater rewards in terms of delaying America's *Pacific War* efforts than the crippling of her battleship fleet. A curious omission on Genda's target list was the US submarines and their pens; it was a strange oversight given the emphasis given to the development of this arm by the Japanese themselves. In the course of the war, US submarines would have a far greater influence on the outcome than battleships, whose main activity turned out to be the provision of offshore battery cover for the Marine's amphibious landings across the *Pacific*.

In looking at the causes of the failure of *Pearl Harbor* from a tactical or strategic viewpoint therefore it would be invidious to point the finger of blame at Admiral Nagumo. The poor returns from the attack on *Pearl Harbor* were a result of the weakness of Yamamoto's strategic concept. Having identified the need to bring America to battle rather than risk a war of attrition that they could only lose, Yamamoto's plan of attack lacked ambition. The conquest of *Hawaii*, a project that was later considered at the time of the *Midway* venture, might have been a more ambitious but much more effective way of holding back America's industrial might than the mere raid on *Pearl Harbor* that was undertaken. Indeed Rear-Admiral Richmond Turner, Director of War Plans in Washington had warned that *Hawaii* would be invaded. Given the ease with which Japanese forces defeated much larger American forces in the Philippines, it is not inconceivable that Japan could have taken *Hawaii* even more speedily. A Japanese occupation of *Hawaii* could have retarded the American reoccupation of the *Pacific* for years and would have left Australia effectively defenceless.

In the west the Japanese attack on *Pearl Harbor* has usually been characterized in the post-war period as being audacious and daring as well as dastardly—a brilliant, albeit evil *coup de théâtre* by Admiral Yamamoto. It is clear in hindsight however, that Yamamoto did not go all the way in his radical upending of Japan's conventional battle plan. Yamamoto never planned more than the buying of time. "Six months" was his often quoted mantra: "In the first six months to a year of war against the US and England I will run wild, and I will show you an uninterrupted succession of victories; I must also tell you that, should the war be prolonged for two or three years, I have no confidence in our ultimate victory."[83] Yamamoto, like his colleagues at the Imperial Navy's general staff in Tokyo, was not able to throw off the yoke of historic strategic conventions. At the Imperial Liaison Conference on 15 November 1941, just three weeks before *Pearl Harbor*, Admiral Osami Nagano, Chief of the General Staff, informed Hirohito that: "at the appropriate time, we will endeavour by various means to lure the main fleet of the

United States [toward Japan] and destroy it."[84] For the Japanese Navy's general staff, the attack on *Pearl Harbor* was never designed to provide them with ultimate victory but simply as a means of delaying the epic engagement with battleships until South East Asia, particularly the oil-bearing Dutch East Indies, could be conquered. As the historian Rotem Kowner in his *The Impact of the War* [Russo-Japanese] *on Naval Warfare* [2007] has concluded: "The attack on *Pearl Harbor* was not a refutation of this view [of the large determining engagement], but a gamble intended to realize it."[85] Even Yamamoto never refuted the logic of this master plan.

Within the ranks of the Imperial Japanese Navy there was a different voice that went unheeded. Vice-Admiral Shigeyoshi Inoue, another Navy moderate, was the most scathing of the General Staff's critics regarding their adherence to a battleship policy. At a meeting in January 1941, at which the General Staff discussed the building of yet more *Yamato* Class battleships, Inoue became apoplectic with rage. He subsequently produced a memo on *Shin Gumbi Keikaku Ron* (On Modern Weapons Procurement Planning) in which he proposed the radical idea that an intelligent enemy would avoid the battle strategy proposed by the General Staff and fight a protracted war of attrition aimed at the long-term strangulation of Japan's economic vitality. He believed that submarines and aircraft would sink Japan's battleships long before they could participate in a decisive naval engagement. Inoue even made the radical conjecture that aircraft carriers would become redundant when the newly developed long-range bombers and fighters could control the air from land bases. In his view aircraft technology was becoming the paramount driver of strategy. Alone, he saw the war as an economic battle where boring ideas of conservation of the commercial fleet were of paramount importance and accordingly emphasized the need to build escort destroyers.

While his colleagues saw the coming war as a matter of creating the conditions for tactical advantage in a great 'winner-takes-all' naval battle, Inoue saw the coming *Pacific* war in strategic terms. Above all he recognized the attritional nature of the war and understood that the Japanese Navy, geared up to winning a single great victory, was not prepared for a war of long duration. It was an understanding that made nonsense of the strategic aim of the attack on *Pearl Harbor*, whose purpose was only to buy time. Inoue was the 'Cassandra' within the Imperial Japanese Navy's staff, whom they chose to ignore.

The attack on *Pearl Harbor* was designed to give Japan six months breathing space and nothing more. The tragedy for Yamamoto's reputation is that having been the first Admiral to realize the strategic importance of aircraft carriers and their primacy over battleships, he produced a plan for their utilization that was a strategic and tactical dud as regards winning the war or even putting Japan into a position from which it could negotiate from strength.

In December 1941, the Japanese Navy had the opportunity to seek out and destroy the US Navy in its lair, *Pearl Harbor*, and fluffed it. With overwhelming superiority in terms of numbers of carriers, quality of aircraft and above all, superb fliers, brilliantly led and trained, Japan needed to bring the US *Pacific* Navy to battle as soon as possible. A *Hawaii* conquered would have given Japan a naval base, *Pearl Harbor*, from which the Imperial Japanese Navy could have put the west coast of America and the *Panama Canal* under economic siege—in a prolonged war of attrition that Admiral Inoue alone seems to have advocated. To protect *Hawaii*, the US carrier fleet may also have been forced to engage with the then superior Japanese carrier fleet. The Japanese military and naval leadership should have understood that the only force that had the potential to defeat them in 1941 was the United States Navy. There was no other force in Asia or the *Pacific*, which offered that same existential threat to Japan.

In hindsight, whatever the risks, it would have been better to have secured an early overwhelming victory in the *Pacific* by invading and securing *Hawaii*. The necessary conquest of South East Asia, with the Dutch East Indies and its supply of oil the main prize, could have been put on hold for a few months. The problem for Japan was that, by their raid on *Pearl Harbor*, instead of slaying the dragon, they had merely tweaked its tail and woken it. In a monumental misunderstanding of the psyche of the American people, Yamamoto's half-hearted strategy only succeeded in stirring America to its full economic and military potential. After *Shinjuwan Kogeki* (the *Attack on Pearl Harbor*), even Yamamoto was unable to raise much enthusiasm for the victory. Shortly afterwards he wrote to a friend, "This war will give us much trouble in the future. The fact that we have had a small success at *Pearl Harbor* is nothing."[86]

6 Plan ORANGE and MacArthur's Philippines Debacle

[December 1941–April 1942]

[Maps: 6.1, 6.2, 6.3, 6.4, 6.5]

Plans ORANGE and RAINBOW-5: In 1939, War Plan RED was a United States military plan dealing with the outbreak of a war with Great Britain; War Plan BLACK was for a war versus Germany and War Plan ORANGE was for a war versus Japan, which was considered the most likely to be put into use. Developed by the US Joint Army and Navy Board in the 1920s and 1930s, the color-coded plans were designed for every eventuality; a War Plan BROWN was even developed for the US to deal with a colonial uprising in the Philippines.

However, after the Austrian *Anschluss*, the occupation of Czechoslovakia, the *Molotov-Ribbentrop Pact* and other aggressive actions by Hitler, the US Army considered it a strong possibility that it could be called upon to fight on several fronts against multiple enemies. In response, the Joint Planning Board developed RAINBOW Plans 1–5 that combined the color-coded plans such as ORANGE with multi-enemy combinations. By the autumn of 1941, with war with Japan considered by Washington to be all but inevitable, War Plan RAINBOW-5 (incorporating ORANGE) had become the operational default plan for American Forces. It assumed that America would be fighting a war against a combined German-Japanese alliance. War Plan RAINBOW-5, taking account of Plan DOG that Admiral Stark had proposed a year earlier, putting an overall emphasis of effort on the war in Europe and the *Atlantic*, called for America to defend the Philippines (or at least the Bataan Peninsula and the island of *Corregidor*) until such time that the US Navy could fight its away across the *Pacific* to relieve US forces.

At 3.30 a.m. on 8 December 1941, Major-General Lewis Brereton, who, after a career that had survived a nervous breakdown and accusations of alcoholism, had become head of the Far East Air Force (FEAF) of the US Army Air Forces based in the Philippines, learned there was a Japanese attack in progress at *Pearl Harbor*. General Douglas MacArthur, Commander in Chief of the US Army of the Far East was also awoken in his penthouse atop the Manila Hotel by a call from his Chief of Staff, Lieutenant-General Richard Sutherland. A stunned MacArthur exclaimed, "It [*Pearl Harbor*] should be our strongest point."[1] While he dressed hurriedly, Brigadier-General Leonard Gerow, head of the Army's War Plans Division, called MacArthur to tell him the news and suggested that he "wouldn't be surprised if you get an attack there [the Philippines] in the near future."[2] MacArthur sat down to read his bible. Meanwhile

Philippine President Quezon refused to believe the news. He asked his secretary Jorge Vargas, "Where did you get that nonsense?"[3] The future of the Philippines rested in the hands of General MacArthur who, if not the elected ruler of a Philippines moving towards independence, was undoubtedly its most powerful man.

General MacArthur, Soldier and Propagandist: General Douglas MacArthur was born an army brat in Little Rock, Arkansas. Though his grandfather was a lawyer and politician, his father, Arthur MacArthur, became a career soldier and went on to win the Medal of Honor fighting for the Unionist Army at the *Battle of Missionary Ridge* during the *American Civil War*, eventually becoming a lieutenant-general. By contrast Douglas MacArthur's mother, Pinky, was a southern belle from a Norfolk, Virginia, Confederate family. Two of Pinky's brothers, steadfast in their allegiance to the Southern Confederacy, refused to attend her wedding. Pinky would always remind her son of his southern roots and taught him its fastidious if slightly pedantic form of politeness.

MacArthur would remain a dutiful son in awe of his mother until her death in 1935. It may well have been this relationship, and the inner insecurity that this fostered, which was the key to understanding his remarkable psychological make-up. Dressed up in girl's clothes until the age of eight, the young MacArthur sported long curling locks of blond hair while at the same time he was admonished for crying—only tears of patriotic fervor were allowed in his father's household. MacArthur's peripatetic childhood was lonely and emotionally circumscribed. The death of his younger brother and the long absences of his soldiering father no doubt exacerbated his isolation and forced him ever closer to his mother. Perhaps it was an Oedipus complex that was the root cause of his monstrous egomania; as President Dwight Eisenhower, for ten years MacArthur's aide and Chief of Staff, commented, "[He] could never see another sun . . . in the heavens."[4]

When his father was posted to San Antonio, MacArthur attended the West Texas Military Academy and then went on to the US Military Academy at West Point. His mother followed him and took rooms overlooking the grounds. MacArthur was athletic and played football and baseball for the Academy. However, it was for his intellectual ability that MacArthur became legendary; his recall of names and dates in military history was often dazzling. He graduated top of his class and was valedictorian at West Point. His early military career was no less successful. Tours of duty, sometimes as aide to his father, took him to the Philippines, to Japan, China and India. He also served as an assistant to Theodore Roosevelt at the President's request. Later he served in Panama and then in the office of the Army Chief of Staff in 1912.

In 1914 he was recommended for, but was refused, a Medal of Honor after an escapade at the port of Veracruz on the *Mexican Gulf*, where he supposedly fought off three separate attacks by Mexican forces, including cavalry, as he tried to commandeer locomotives needed for carrying US troops. Although his commanding officer strongly supported the award for bravery in this escapade, from which he survived with no fewer than three bullet holes in his clothing, he was turned down for the Medal of Honor on the grounds that he initiated an action without it having been authorized. There was also some scepticism about MacArthur's fantastical account of the engagement—a familiar pattern later in his life.

MacArthur's participation in *World War I* turbo-charged his career. In 1915 he was promoted to the rank of major when he moved to the War Department and the following year he became head of the Information Bureau at the office of the Secretary of War. It was here that MacArthur learnt the skills of press management that, it could be argued, became his greatest professional accomplishment. In 1917, he was promoted to Colonel when he moved to become Chief of Staff to Major-General William Mann, head of the National Guard, renamed the 42nd Division, when it was posted to fight on the Western Front. MacArthur enjoyed a short but heroic war. After participating in a French raiding attack, he was awarded the *Croix de Guerre* and for continued acts of bravery went on to win a remarkable seven Silver Stars and a second *Croix de Guerre* as well as being made a commander of the *Légion d'honneur*. Throughout his life he would display exceptional personal bravery. Meticulous and often flamboyant in dress, he became known as the Beau Brummell of the trenches. General Brereton would later record in his diary, "He is one of the best dressed soldiers in the world . . . I have never seen him looking otherwise than if he had just put on a new uniform."[5]

Although he was recommended for a Medal of Honor after being wounded by machine guns during a reconnaissance mission, for the second time in his life the recommendation for the award was ignored though he did receive a second Distinguished Service Cross. Later promoted to Brigadier-General as commander of the 42nd Division, MacArthur was also awarded the Distinguished Service Medal.

After *World War I*, MacArthur became Superintendent of the US Military Academy at West Point, at thirty-nine the youngest for two hundred years. Based on his experience of war he transformed and modernized training and introduced a rigorous program of athletic pursuits. During this period he fell in love with a hugely rich Washington socialite, Louise Cromwell Brook. Louise, a licentious divorcee, was also the *inamorata* of General John Pershing, Commander of the US Expeditionary Force in *World War II*; supposedly Pershing threatened to end MacArthur's career when he decided to marry Brook. Pinky was equally furious. "Of course the attraction is purely physical,"[6] Pinky complained to a friend. Predictably, bored by the constraints of military life and with enough money to go her own way, Louise effectively left MacArthur after five years. She went on to have several more husbands and several more divorces.

In 1927, MacArthur became President of the American Olympics Committee and led a US team that won 22 gold medals, 18 silver and 16 bronze medals as well as garnering 17 Olympic records and 7 world records at Amsterdam's 1928 Olympic Games. A posting to command the US Army in the Philippines in 1928 was followed by his appointment as Chief of Staff of the US Army in Washington in November 1930. Here he would sit at his desk cooling himself with a Japanese fan while wearing a *Kimono* and smoking cigarettes in a bejewelled holder. Thus, in Washington, he became a 'figure.' However, few would ever claim to know him; such was the theatrical, play-acting façade presented by MacArthur that he would remain an enigma even to those who worked with him for years. In a characteristic sign of megalomania, MacArthur now started to refer to himself in the third person: "MacArthur will be leaving for Fort Myer now. . . ."[7]

At this time, MacArthur, a phenomenal polymath, became famous for his 'discussions.' Eisenhower recalled, " 'Discuss' is hardly the correct word; discussion suggests dialogue and the General's conversations were usually monologues."[8] However, Eisenhower, who worked for MacArthur for ten years would always acknowledge the benefits of this tutelage, and was quick to praise his positive qualities while recognizing his worst: ". . . he did have a hell of an intellect! My God, but he was smart. He had a brain."[9] However, during his apprenticeship, Eisenhower may have learnt more about 'what-not-to-do' than what to do.

In Washington, MacArthur would ride his horse back home to have lunch with his by now 80-year-old mother. The 50-year-old General had brought back from Manila a 16-year-old Filipino mistress, Isabel Rosario 'Dimples' Cooper, for whom he found an apartment—and a poodle. A sexually precocious girl, already a film star famous for the first onscreen kiss in a Filipino movie, *An Tatlong Hambog* [1926] (The Arrogant Three), Dimples was a great beauty who soon attracted many alternative lovers while MacArthur was on his travels. Fearful that his mother would find out about Dimples, he dropped a lawsuit against Drew Pearson of *The Washington Post* when the journalist, having acquired MacArthur's love letters to her, threatened to call Dimples as a witness. Eventually, bored by his courtesan, he paid off the increasingly embarrassing Dimples with US$15,000 delivered in cash by an aide to the lobby of the Warren Hotel. She went to the Midwest and bought a beauty salon before moving to Los Angeles. She died there in 1960 after taking an overdose of barbiturates.

More controversially MacArthur would command the troops that fired on the Bonus Army protestors, unemployed *World War I* veterans who demanded immediate redemption of their service bonds, when they marched on Washington in 1932 during the Great Depression. He could have sent another officer and did not have to make a public spectacle of his command but did so against the advice of a junior aide, Dwight Eisenhower, who in early signs of political wisdom, "told that dumb son-of-a-bitch [MacArthur] not to go down there." He added, "I told him it was no place for the Chief of Staff . . ."[10]

As his career went from strength to strength, in spite of the hiccups described above, confrontation with authority, never far away in his youth, was an increasingly likely possibility. Having reached the pinnacle of military power as Chief of Staff, all restraints on his ego fell away. "His visits to the White House often took on the aura of a State visit."[11] As early as 1932 he clashed with President Roosevelt. In his pompously titled autobiography *Reminiscences of General of the Army Douglas MacArthur* [1964] published a few months before his death, MacArthur claimed to have responded to Roosevelt's demands for a 50 percent cut in military expenditure by telling him that ". . . when we lose the next war, and an American boy, lying in the mud with an enemy bayonet through his belly and an enemy foot on his dying throat, spits out his last curse, I wanted the name not to be MacArthur, but Roosevelt."[12] In response, Roosevelt supposedly yelled, "You must not talk that way to the President!"[13] MacArthur claimed that he offered his resignation and that when Roosevelt refused to accept it, he left the Oval office only to vomit on the front steps of the White House.

In spite of his clashes with the President, Roosevelt extended MacArthur's term as Chief of Staff. On leaving office in October 1935, MacArthur was awarded a second Distinguished Service Medal and retroactively engineered for himself two Purple Heart awards for his *World War I* service; the first of which he inscribed with the number '1' as he insisted on being the first to receive the award of which he had also been the inventor. The love of military paraphernalia was a lifetime obsession.

After Manuel Quezon became President of the Philippines following the country's gaining of semi-independent status in 1935, MacArthur, whose father was an old friend of Quezon's father, was invited to establish the Philippine Army. On his way out to Manila on board SS *Herbert Hoover*, he met the petite 37-year-old Jean Faircloth. She was, like his mother and MacArthur's first wife, a wealthy southern socialite. They married two years later. However, unlike his first wife, she loved the attention of being married to a famous General and was genuinely in awe of her husband. Thus adored, she and their son Arthur would become the bedrock of his life. Arthur, perhaps overawed by the fame or possibly infamy of his father, did not take up a place at West Point but changed his name and dropped out of the public eye, adopting, given his upbringing, a strangely alternative lifestyle in which he supposedly became a musician-artist in Greenwich Village, New York.

In Manila, Quezon was inveigled into granting General MacArthur the title Field Marshal for which MacArthur, the inveterate popinjay, designed his own resplendent white uniform with lots of gold braid and a silly Ruritanian hat. Eisenhower, who thought the whole thing was very "banana republic," added, "It was pompous and rather ridiculous to be the Field Marshal of a virtually non-existing army."[14] MacArthur's 'Napoleon Complex' could only have been further enhanced by a grandiose ceremony in which Quezon presented him with a baton made of solid gold. Roosevelt's funding of MacArthur's new army was less generous. Even with hand-me-down equipment provided by the US Army, annual funding of US$6m was grossly inadequate.

Everything changed after President Roosevelt's administration was shocked to its core by Japan's sudden move to expand its empire southwards by invading Indochina and occupying Saigon on 26 July 1940. Roosevelt's reaction to this very real threat to its nearby Philippine colonial possession was almost immediate: within five days Roosevelt federalized the Philippine Army and massively increased funding for MacArthur's 22,000 man Army (10,000 US soldiers and 12,000 Philippine Scouts). At the same time MacArthur was formally brought out of retirement to be appointed Commander of the US Armed Forces in the Philippines. 8,500 US soldiers were immediately dispatched to Manila. In addition MacArthur set about recruiting and equipping some 120,000 new recruits for a hugely expanded Philippine Army. MacArthur talked about having a 200,000 strong army by the end of 1942. He would not have the time to achieve this expansion. Some four months after his appointment as Commander in Chief in July 1941, the building of a sizeable Philippine Army was a project that was still very much work-in-progress.

MacArthur in 'Cloud Cuckoo Land': Imminent air attack and probably an invasion was the situation General MacArthur faced at 5.00 a.m. on 8 December 1941 when General Brereton came to the headquarters of US Army Forces in Manila. Brereton wanted to see his Commander in Chief to seek permission to attack the enemy. Why he was not allowed to see MacArthur in person later became a cause of much dispute. Whatever the reason, MacArthur's Chief of Staff, Brigadier-General Richard Sutherland, refused Brereton's request to implement immediately the provisions of RAINBOW-5 (ORANGE) that called for an air attack on Japan's nearest airbases on *Formosa* some 800 miles away.

Thirty minutes later, in response to a direct order to implement War Plan RAINBOW-5 (ORANGE) from General George Marshall in Washington, Sutherland ordered Brereton to prepare an air strike against Japanese airbases though not to implement it. According to Brereton, he asked for permission to strike three times from Sutherland and was thrice denied. Finally, some eight hours after news of *Pearl Harbor* had reached the Philippines, Brereton claims finally to have spoken to MacArthur directly (though MacArthur later denied this), and at last received permission to attack Japan's Formosan bases, but only after a reconnaissance mission had been undertaken. By this time, Brereton, who had wisely put all his planes in the air to avoid them being caught on the ground as had happened at *Pearl Harbor*, needed to bring his fighters and bombers down for refueling. By sheer bad luck for Brereton, the Japanese attack, expected in the early morning, had not materialized because of fog that had delayed departure of their aircraft.

At midday on Clark Field, the main Far East Air Force (FEAF) airfield some thirty miles north of Manila, the aircrews spotted two perfect 'V' formations. Sergeant King, of the 20th Pursuit Group, called Major Grover to sound the air raid alarm; Grover asked, "How does he know they are Japanese planes?"; King yelled back "We don't have so Goddamn many!"[15] A similarly shocked Sergeant Tim Gage exclaimed, "My God, look at the enemy planes—there are thousands of them."[16] The same surprise greeted the crews at Iba Field. "Look at the pretty formation of B-17s" observed a young crewman; Second Lieutenant Glenn Cave reacted differently, "You're crazy—there aren't that many B-17s in the Philippines."[17]

A Japanese attack by Mitsubishi M4B 'Betty' bombers after midday, delayed by six hours of fog over *Formosa*, caught two squadrons of Boeing B-17 Flying Fortress on the ground and most of the P-40 Kittyhawk fighters that were preparing for action. Miscommunication, lack of radar, and failure to implement land-based spotters meant that Clark Field was virtually undefended. Only four fighters managed to take off; the remainder were destroyed along with 12 out of 17 American bombers. Returning P-40 fighter pilot Don Steel remembered the sight from 8,000 feet: "There was beautiful

Clark Field, all in flames ... every building on the airdrome was on fire ... large columns of smoke rising to 18,000 foot ... sleek and shining B-17s that we were so proud of and had just received from the States were all sitting on the ground, blazing."[18]

In a dogfight over Clark Field, six P-40Es of 3rd Squadron managed to intercept the incoming Japanese bandits and claimed three kills. Two of the US pilots were killed including Lieutenant Herbert Ellis who had laid claim to two of the kills. Having been hit and set on fire, Ellis baled out of his plane but was gunned down as he drifted down by parachute. The air war with Japan was not going to be a 'gentleman's' affair.

For the pursuit pilots, the inferiority of their P-40s was a problem, but of greater concern was the complete failure of aircraft warning systems. As Grant Mahony complained, "The first warning any of us on the ground would get that Japs were in the vicinity would come when we saw them diving over the hills shooting at us."[19] Nicholas Hobrecht, who told his friend 'Dub' Balfanz that "I'll be killed in the first dogfight I get in,"[20] hardly made it off the ground from Nichols Field before a Zero latched on his tail and hit him with 20 mm cannon shells. Hobrecht bailed out but hit his P-40's stabilizer and crashed to the ground dead with his parachute unopened. In a post-war analysis of the battle it was clear the Japanese had only used two *kokutai* (air group) of 89 Zeros in the first *Battle of Luzon* compared with the 114 operational P-40s and P-35s of the 24th Pursuit Group. Although some 30 Japanese aircraft were shot down, almost all the American fighters were destroyed. 20 percent of their pilots were killed. Of the 165 pilots, half were captured and entered the Japanese POW camps while 30 percent managed to hobble their way south with whatever aircraft they could find that were still airworthy. Their performance compared miserably with the American Volunteer Group (AVG) that operated in Thailand and China.

What became clear is that the P-40s and P-35s were reasonably competitive but only if they had the chance to climb to altitude and build air speed. It quickly became apparent that attempting to out-dogfight the more maneuverable Zero would result in almost certain death. Unlike the AVG in Burma and China, where Lieutenant-General Claire Chennault had placed significant emphasis on the build-up of an air warning system, in the Philippines, this service had been woefully inadequately prepared. It was a mistake that cost the American force dearly both in the air and on the ground. In addition, American pilots suffered constant problems with their guns. A lack of belt ammunition meant that there had been inadequate testing of their weapons systems. Also American pilots only learnt from trial and error how to fight a Zero—not by engaging in a dogfight, but only by using hit and run tactics. By swooping from altitude, selecting a target, firing a burst of their machine guns and out-diving the pursuing Zero, P-40s could hope to escape a dogfight. These were lessons from the AVG that the US Air Force had simply failed to glean or pass on.

In aggregate it seems that American losses on the ground were forty-nine planes destroyed. In the air the Japanese made fifteen confirmed kills with seven probables and one aircraft forced to crash. The US had lost half of its bombers and a quarter of its fighters. At Clark Field, only three B-17 Flying Fortress remained intact. Ground casualties amounted to 100 dead and 250 wounded. As for the Japanese losses, they totaled six Zero A6Ms. A simultaneous attack by fifty-four Mitsubishi G4M 'Betty' bombers destroyed most of the US aircraft on the ground at the auxiliary field at Iba. By 1.30 p.m., forty-five minutes after the Japanese attack began at Clark Field, the US had lost half of its aircraft in the Philippines. Meanwhile on *Formosa*, Japanese soldiers put on gas masks as they waited for an American air strike that never came. After the war, a Japanese officer recalled, "We were worried because we were sure after learning of *Pearl Harbor* you would disperse your planes or make an attack on our base at *Formosa*."[21]

Altogether, the destruction of the US Air Force on the ground in the Philippines was a much less forgivable catastrophe than *Pearl Harbor*. On 27 November, MacArthur, along with other US field commanders in the Army and Navy including Kimmel, was alerted by radio message that "negotiations with Japan appear terminated . . . Japanese future action unpredictable but hostile action possible at any moment. If hostilities cannot repeat cannot be avoided the United States desires Japan commit the first act."[22] In spite of these messages, MacArthur remained upbeat and dismissive of the reports from Washington. At the end of November, at a meeting with Francis Sayre, the US High Commissioner in Manila, MacArthur said, "the existing alignment and movement of Japanese troops convinced him that there would be no Japanese attack before the spring."[23] In spite of this assertion, on 28 November MacArthur radioed an optimistic message to General Marshall in Washington that "Everything is in readiness for the conduct of a successful defense."[24]

MacArthur had not only been informed that war was imminent but *Luzon*, rather than *Pearl Harbor*, was the expected first point of attack for any Japanese opening of hostilities against the United States. Furthermore MacArthur, unlike Admiral Kimmel in the Philippines, was fully aware of all available intelligence regarding Japanese negotiations and troop movements from the cracking of Code PURPLE produced by a Japanese diplomatic crypto-graphical machine, and JN-25, the Imperial Japanese Navy's internal message code. General MacArthur, given the warnings of imminent Japanese attack, and his access to all the highest-level intelligence, and knowledge that Japan's most likely prime target was Manila and the US Army on *Luzon*, had no excuse for his Air Force to be 'surprised' and wiped out. History has not found other scapegoats for the disaster. The head of the Far East Air Force, (FEAF), General Brereton, had been fully up to speed and ready to launch operations at 5.00 a.m. (Philippines time), within several hours of the Japanese attack on *Pearl Harbor*. However, the failure to adequately prepare attack-warning systems can largely be laid at Brereton's door.

Remarkably, unlike *Pearl Harbor*, there was no inquiry into the Air Force debacle on 8 December or indeed the reasons for the loss of the Philippines against numerically inferior forces. So what happened in the nine hours between MacArthur learning of the attack on *Pearl Harbor* and the destruction of the Far East Air Force (FEAF) on the ground at Clark Field? In the absence of an inquiry there were never any official answers to this question. Apart from MacArthur's call from Washington and receipt of a message from the war department directing him to implement War Plan RAINBOW-5, little else is known. There is no record of MacArthur's telephone conversation with President Quezon. Presumably MacArthur was in contact with his Chief of Staff, Major-General Richard Sutherland. It was subsequently reported that those who saw him described him as looking nervous, ill and exhausted.

The most commonly accepted explanation is that MacArthur simply 'froze' in shock at the unfolding events. It seems beyond comprehension that MacArthur did not talk to Brereton, the head of his air force, until eight hours after he had learnt of the attack on *Pearl Harbor*. However, the truth may never be known. In his memoir, *Reminiscences* [1964], MacArthur made no mention of the missing hours, merely explaining, "at 11.45 a.m. a report came in of an overpowering enemy formation closing in on Clark Field. Our fighters went up to meet them, but our bombers were slow in taking off and our losses were heavy. Our force was simply too small to smash the odds against them."[25] In keeping with much of what MacArthur would write during the *Pacific War* and afterwards, it was an explanation that was entirely disingenuous. MacArthur's assertion in his autobiography, that he "was under the impression that Japan had suffered a setback at *Pearl Harbor*"[26] lacks any credence. Psychologically unable to deal with his own failure in the Philippines in the *Pacific War*, with regard to the disasters on *Luzon* and later at Bataan and *Corregidor*, Macarthur would forever live in 'cloud cuckoo land.'

However, MacArthur may not have been the only senior officer 'out of sorts' on 8 December. General Brereton, a known alcoholic, had spent the evening carousing, only returning to his quarters an hour before being woken with the news of *Pearl Harbor*. In the aftermath of the Philippines debacle, Marshall, puzzled by MacArthur's failure, would offer the excuse that his 'airmen' were "not up to standard."[27] It has even been suggested that Sutherland's refusal to allow Brereton to see MacArthur was because the US air force commander was too 'wrecked' to be presentable. Sutherland had been at the same party.

By 10 December, most of the remaining antiquated American Seversky P-35s had also been wiped out while eleven Curtiss P-40 Warhawks were shot down. Just twenty-two serviceable P-40s were left. Clark Field was abandoned the following day and on 17 December, fourteen surviving B-17s were ordered to transfer to Australia. With Manila's airfields put out of action and the remnants of the Far East Air Force departed, the Japanese bombers could focus on the US Navy's port infrastructure at Cavite Navy Yard—it proved a far more destructive attack than that at *Pearl Harbor*. "They'd flattened it [Cavite Navy Yard]," Lieutenant John Buckley grimly noted. "There isn't any other word. Here was the only American naval base in the Orient beyond *Pearl Harbor* pounded into bloody rubbish."[28] Experienced war correspondent Carl Mydans of *Life* magazine remarked to his colleague about the exceptional accuracy of the Japanese bombing. Port buildings and infrastructure were devastated. The loss of 230 torpedoes in the attack was only mitigated by the fact that they were mainly shipboard destroyer torpedoes rather than submarine torpedoes, which had already been moved to *Corregidor Island*. However, thanks to Admiral Thomas Hart's disbursement of his assets, vessel losses were minimal; only the submarine USS *Sealion* was lost along with the minesweeper USS *Bittern*.

Perhaps the greatest tragedy of the early days of the war was the sinking of the inter-island ferry, USS *Corregidor*, which was carrying some 1,200, mainly Filipino, passengers to the south, because the crew had failed to register their departure, and the Army's Seaward Defense Commander refused to switch off the electrically controlled mines that guarded the exit to *Manila Bay*. In the early hours of 17 December, a huge explosion on the starboard side near the stern caused the ship to sink in minutes. Only 296 passengers and crew were rescued. The dead included the captain as well as several Filipino legislators.

The historian and Washington defense analyst, John Gordon, has described MacArthur's reaction to the developing military catastrophe in the Philippines, as "delusional."[29] On 10 December, MacArthur radioed General Marshall in Washington to recommend an "immediate attack on Japan from north . . . a golden opportunity exists for a master stroke while enemy is engaged in overextended air effort."[30] By comparison the US Navy, more realistically, was already guiding Washington to expect the Philippines to be lost.

When Admiral Hart directed that a merchant ship convoy bound for Manila with their cargo of fifty-two Douglas A-24 Banshee dive-bombers and eighteen Curtiss P-40 Warhawk fighters should be escorted by the USS *Pensacola* to Brisbane, MacArthur exploded and sent Marshall a message on 13 December demanding that: "Every resource of the Democratic Allies in sea, air and land should be converged here immediately and overwhelmingly . . ."[31] Redeployment of the *Pensacola* convoy to the Philippines was an absurd suggestion given Japan's establishment of air control and could only have ended in disaster. MacArthur also briefed against the Navy and Admiral Hart in particular and may even have been going behind Marshall's back to get to Secretary of the Army, Henry Stimson. Unlike Hart, MacArthur's behavior was "desperate [which is understandable] but also out of touch with reality."[32] Formerly Hart had considered himself to be a friend of MacArthur but in the lead up to the outbreak of war their relationship had deteriorated dramatically. Indeed Hart confided to his wife before the outbreak of hostilities that "Douglas is, I think, no longer altogether sane—he may not have been for a long time."[33]

Homma, the 'Poet General,' Invades Luzon: **[Map: 6.1]** Commanding Japan's Fourteenth Army invasion force was Lieutenant-General Masaharu Homma. Known as the 'Poet General,' Homma was a cultured man known as an amateur playwright and painter. Born on *Sado Island* in Niigata Prefecture in northeastern Japan, Homma graduated from the Army Staff College in 1915 and was soon sent to the UK as a military *attaché*. He even served in combat with the British Army in Northern France in 1915. In all, he spent eight years in England and was a fluent English speaker. A prominent moderate in the army, he protested openly against the continuance of the war in China after the Rape of Nanking and insisted that peace should be negotiated. His liberal stance and humanitarian concerns for conquered people would lead him into conflict with General Count Hisaichi Terauchi, a hard-line former War Minister, who commanded the Southern Army's push throughout South East Asia.

On 8 December, General Homma's 48th Division began its invasion of *Northern Luzon*. Aware of the broad dispersal of American forces, Homma planned to encircle the American forces and cut off their line of retreat to Manila. In the only action of any worth by the US Far East Air Force (FEAF), a Japanese minesweeper was sunk and several other ships slightly damaged. Two days later, triple landings were made on the main Philippines island of *Luzon*, with 4,000 Japanese troops landing at Aparri and Vigan in the north. On 12 December a further 2,500 men were landed at Legazpi in the south. These diversions failed to draw MacArthur's forces away from the main landing point, which most military analysts had expected, correctly, to be *Lingayen Gulf*.

Indeed on 21 December, the main Fourteenth Army units, consisting of 43,000 men of the 48th Division landed at *Lingayen Gulf* some 150 miles north of Manila. Against them MacArthur had 32,000 American troops (of which 12,000 were Philippine Scouts), and an estimated 120,000 strong conscript Philippine Army. The defenders massively outnumbered their Japanese attackers. Japanese forces pressed rapidly south from *Lingayen Bay* and cut off some 60,000 troops of the Army that MacArthur had built up in the previous five months. The mistake of MacArthur's forward beach defense strategy was now exposed. Belatedly MacArthur, previously dismissive of War Plan RAINBOW-5 (ORANGE) reverted to its plans, which had prescribed a defense of the Bataan Peninsula and the island of *Corregidor* until forces from the United States could come to their relief. Too late MacArthur ordered the construction of a defensive corral on the Bataan Peninsula with the addition of *Corregidor Island* at its southern tip. In the meantime Major-General Wainwright planned to defend Homma's advance at the *Agno River*, sixteen miles south of *Lingayen Bay*, with the aim of holding the Japanese advance long enough to enable the Bataan Peninsula to be supplied and manned.

The best strategic and tactical minds in the US had been working on Plan ORANGE since before *World War I*; no matter how many times successive Army analysts had looked at the problem of how to defend the Philippines, the 'siege' option, albeit in many iterations, remained steadfastly the strategy of choice, with the Bataan Peninsula the preferred location. MacArthur, knowing better, had earlier written in a memo to Washington regarding Operations Plan RAINBOW, "The strategic mission as formerly envisualized, of defending merely the entrance to *Manila Bay* by a citadel type defense with a small token force, should be broadened to include the defense of the Philippine Islands."[34] Essentially, MacArthur viewed War Plan RAINBOW-5 (ORANGE) as defeatist. In the event MacArthur withdrew his troops from the beaches without contest.

Unfortunately for the US and the Philippines, MacArthur's alternative plans to RAINBOW-5 were an unmitigated disaster for the US and the Philippines. The main Japanese landing on *Luzon Island* started on 22 December with the US Air Force only capable of putting up a token resistance. The early morning saw an attack by two light bombers with no results. Later two Warhawk P-40Es strafed the destroyer *Nagatsuki*, a minesweeper, killing one Japanese man and wounding eight. One of the US fighters was shot down while the other piloted by Lieutenant Boyd 'Buzz' Wagner was flown back to base even though his windscreen was shattered and he was half blinded by glass.

Wagner, leader of 17th Pursuit Squadron, was the first US flying hero of the *Pacific War* after he had claimed four Nakajima Ki 27 'Nates' in a single sortie on 12 December. Andy Krieger of 3rd Pursuit recalled, "When Wagner went out, he knew he'd be all right, because there was not another man on earth who could fly like him."[35] Although four Philippine-based B-17 Flying Fortress did manage to drop bombs on the advancing Japanese armada and they all returned safely, there were no reported hits. Landing day had brought a desultory performance by the now virtually annihilated US Air Force.

After the ignominious flight from *Lingayan Bay*, the last US troops to enter the Bataan Peninsula were the 26th Cavalry, the 11th and 12th Divisions of the Philippine Army, and a force of American Stuart M3 tanks. In addition to these forces, the 31st Infantry fought fierce rear-guard actions at Zigzag Pass and Layac Junction to hold back the advancing Japanese 48th Division. Harold K. Johnson of the 57th Infantry on *Luzon*, who would later become Chairman of the Joint Chiefs of Staff, later described MacArthur's decision to fight the Japanese at the beaches of *Lingayen Bay* as "a tragic error."[36] It was only the brilliant defensive campaign fought by Lieutenant-General Jonathan 'Skinny' Wainwright that enabled Major-General George Parker to extricate 15,000 troops from south *Luzon*. Even then MacArthur was not helpful. When Wainwright called for tank reinforcements to help him hold off the Japanese advance toward Manila, General Sutherland said, "No," though on further reflection he agreed to, "ask the general [MacArthur]."[37] Instead of sending the tank battalion that Wainwright demanded, MacArthur sent five tanks. When Wainwright withdrew to the line of the *Agno River*, Wainwright called on MacArthur to give him his well-trained former command, the Philippine Division, to enable him to launch a surprise counter-attack. MacArthur refused, preferring to hold the division in reserve.

Nevertheless, Wainwright managed to hold up the Japanese advance by leading his troops in spirited defense and the blowing up of 184 bridges. In the course of one of these bridge engagements, Major Thomas 'Trap' Trapnell's 26th Cavalry conducted the last cavalry charge in US history. Trapnell was awarded a Distinguished Service Cross for his leadership. On 23 December, MacArthur authorized the planned withdrawal to the Bataan Peninsula, too late for it to be successfully defended.

Ultimately Wainwright's fighting retreat was helped by General Homma's not realizing that US forces would make their last stand at the Bataan Peninsula rather than Manila. Indeed the Japanese Army General Staff had only ever envisioned that the US Army's last stand would be made in Manila; "they never planned for or expected a withdrawal to Bataan."[38]

MacArthur's Lies and Obfuscation: In spite of giving up the beaches without a contest, Major LeGrande 'Pick' Diller, MacArthur's press officer, put out a statement that the Japanese landings at *Lingayen Bay* had been repelled. However, *Life* magazine's photographer was unable to find evidence of a battle. Based on LeGrande Diller's press release the *New York Times* trumpeted a headline, "JAPANESE FORCES WIPED OUT IN WESTERN *LUZON*."[39] Meanwhile the *United Press* reported that there had been a three-day battle with 154 enemy boats sunk; supposedly not a single Japanese soldier had reached the shores. It was a seemingly remarkable testament to MacArthur's wisdom in fighting the Japanese on the beaches. However, all of MacArthur's press releases, which formed the basis of US newspaper reports, were entire fabrications— stories about battles that never took place. While trumpeting his 'successes' to the press, MacArthur moved very quickly to establish a narrative with Washington that covered up his own incompetence. As early as 10 December, MacArthur wrote to General 'Hap' Arnold in Washington to explain the annihilation of his Air Force. "Their losses were due entirely to the overwhelming superiority of enemy force," he wrote, "No Unit could have done better . . . No item of loss can properly be attributed to neglect or lack of care. . . ."[40] Not surprisingly, given the circumstances of the debacle on 8 December, MacArthur was paranoid about losing his reputation. It is interesting to note that when General Brereton took the last transport ship out of Manila on Christmas Eve, the last words said to him by MacArthur were, "I hope that you will tell the people outside what we have done and protect my reputation as a fighter."[41]

As well as duping the press and muffling internal criticism, MacArthur would also look to blame others for the loss of the Philippines; Admiral Thomas Hart, Commander in Chief, Asiatic Fleet, became an early target of MacArthur's sniping with his claim that Hart's forces should have halted the Japanese landing. In reality Hart, equipped with a single outmoded heavy cruiser, USS *Houston* and a *World War I* light cruiser, USS *Marblehead* along with thirteen destroyers of similar vintage was ill equipped to deal with a modern Japanese Navy. Slow-moving coastal gunboats supported them. As for the twenty-nine American submarines and their new Mark IV magnetic torpedoes, far from being the potent weapon that had been hoped for, they would soon prove to be the weakest of all American weapon systems.

Hart's suggestion before the start of the war that the US Navy should coordinate and control air attacks on Japanese shipping was rudely rejected by MacArthur, at this point Hart's ranking junior, "It would be manifestly illogical to assign control of tactical command of such a powerful Army air striking force to an element of such combat inferiority as your Command or that of the 16th Naval District."[42] Unlike MacArthur who failed to move his aircraft, Hart took Admiral Stark's 24 November warning of imminent war very seriously and moved his ships from Manila southwards and out of harm's way. MacArthur would write that the US admirals made "no effort to keep open our lines of supply."[43] Ironically Admiral Hart conducted the investigation into the *Pearl Harbor* catastrophe on behalf of the US Navy; a similar exercise was never carried out to investigate the more costly catastrophe in the Philippines.

MacArthur went to his grave insisting that larger forces overwhelmed his army on the Philippines. On 22 December 1941 MacArthur had reported to Marshall that a Japanese Army of between 80,000–100,000 troops had landed at *Lingayen Bay*, more than double the actual force. MacArthur also lied about the size of his own forces, stating that he had just 40,000 partly equipped troops. That his forces were inadequately trained and equipped had some truth but as for being outnumbered the reverse was true; leaving aside the issue of training and equipment, on a simple numerical calculation, MacArthur's forces outnumbered the Japanese on *Luzon* by 2:1. Trying to cover up his failings in the Philippines by obfuscating the facts and by making spurious criticisms of the Navy would become a lifetime occupation.

In addition to providing misinformation about numbers, MacArthur made great play of the 'sinking' of the *Haruna*, a Japanese battleship supposedly participating in the Japanese armada attacking the Philippines. A legend was manufactured that on 10 December, Captain Collin Kelly had crashed his plane into the *Haruna* after he had given time to his crew members to escape from the damaged aircraft. In fact the *Haruna* was 1,500 miles away; Kelly's B-17 Flying Fortress actually scored a hit which damaged the cruiser *Natori* on 10 December and the pilot and crew had to bale out after being shot down by Japanese 'ace' pilot Saburo Sakai flying a Mitsubishi Zero. Kelly's parachute failed to open before he hit the ground. Kelly's killer, Saburo Sakai, was from a samurai family in Saga Prefecture in Japan's southern *Kyushu Island*, an area famous for its *Arita-yaki* (Imari porcelain) much beloved of European and American collectors. Sakai graduated as a flier from the Japanese Navy Fliers School at Tsuchiura in 1937, earning him a silver watch presented to him by Emperor Hirohito. He scored his first 'kill' in October 1939 on the borders of Manchuria, shooting down a Soviet Ilyushin DB-3 bomber. Then he flew combat missions against the Chinese during the Japanese advance into South and Central China. Already a seasoned pilot by the time he joined the Tainan Air group whose Mitsubishi A6M Zero fighters supported General Homma's invasion of the Philippines, Sakai went on to record an estimated 64 kills, becoming possibly the most famous Japanese pilot of the *Pacific War*.

At sea, a US victory of sorts was recorded by the antiquated 18-year-old US submarine *S-38*, an S-Class submarine built by the Union Iron Works in San Francisco in 1919. While patrolling in *Lingayen Gulf*, it managed to plant two torpedoes into the flank of the 5,445-ton *Hayo Maru*, a cargo and troop transport. It was only the second US submarine success since *Pearl Harbor*. Lieutenant Wreford 'Moon' Chapple, captain of *S-38*, had gone some way toward making up for the mistaken sinking of a Norwegian freighter ten days earlier.

On land, only the 26th Cavalry put up any fight and after taking heavy casualties, they too were forced to withdraw. By nightfall on 23 December Japanese forces had moved ten miles inland. On 24 December 7,000 more Japanese troops landed at three locations in *Lamon Bay* on the southeast coast of *Luzon*, some thirty miles from Manila. Again the beach defense was almost non-existent; General MacArthur's dispersed and over-stretched forces were now caught in a pincer movement as the Japanese forces consolidated their hold on eastern *Luzon* and then began their march on Manila.

On 26 December Hart and fifteen of his staff boarded the submarine, USS *Shark*, and headed for Surabaya in *Eastern Java* to take command of the naval forces that he had dispatched to the Dutch East Indies. On arrival it became clear that MacArthur's poison against Hart was continuing to drip into the ears of Washington-based military and naval staffs. By 2 January Hart felt compelled to send a stiff message:

> Having sensed since about 10 December that this fleet might be charged with the loss of the Philippines I have kept records straight to prove otherwise. I really think that my preceding dispatches with your general knowledge of the situation should be sufficient to combat erroneous impressions. A defeat in the Philippines will be primarily incident to total loss of the air that followed close upon the first Japanese attack made nine hours after that on Pearl Harbor. It is axiomatic that fleets must have basing facilities for their operations and our base had had no fighter protection whatsoever . . .[44]

The Battle of the Bataan Peninsula: [Map: 6.2] [Map: 6.3] Belatedly MacArthur had adopted 'War Plan ORANGE,' which he had hitherto spurned. Major-General Parker was removed from command of the southern forces and transferred to Bataan where he was ordered to prepare for defense of the peninsula and to organize American army forces when they arrived. Bataan, a peninsula some thirty miles long and fifteen miles wide, with mountainous jungle and Mount Bataan at its southern point, separated *Manila Bay* from the *South China Sea*. A mile and a half off its southern tip lay the island of *Corregidor*, a lozenge-shaped island roughly two miles by 1.2 miles with a four mile long tail giving it the appearance of a tadpole.

Some 75,000 troops (15,000 American troops supported by 60,000 Filipinos) and 26,000 refugees fled to Bataan. The logistical chaos that ensued need not have arisen if War Plan ORANGE had been implemented in the months after the federalization of the Philippine Army. At least MacArthur was now ensconced in a superb defensive position. However, their first line of defense was overrun almost immediately when, making the same mistake as the British in Malaya, MacArthur failed to extend his lines into the jungle and the mountains. The result was that the US-Filipino forces were quickly outflanked through the jungle by Japanese troops and were forced back to a new defensive line halfway down the Bataan Peninsula. It was now a case of how long could MacArthur sustain his defense against the forces arranged against him. Although the Japanese had about 40,000 troops, about half the number of MacArthur's Philippine Army, they were better equipped and fed and their morale was high. The Japanese also possessed complete control of air and sea. Bottled up on the Bataan Peninsula, American and Filipino troops now asked—when would help arrive?

With the devastation of naval resources at *Pearl Harbor*, combined with the weakness of the US aircraft carrier fleet, the power of Japan's carrier fleet and Japan's defensive string of 'fortified' islands between *Hawaii* and the Philippines, it was soon clear to all high level commanders that the US Navy would not have the capability to steam across the *Pacific Ocean* to relieve the Philippines in the foreseeable future. In spite of some desultory plans to relieve MacArthur's stranded army and various failed attempts to buy or hire cargo ships to take supplies to Bataan, it is inconceivable that MacArthur, no matter how limited his accomplishments as a strategist, could not have known that there was going to be no rescue. Indeed War Plan RAINBOW-5 (ORANGE), with its outline of a 'siege' strategy for the Philippines in case of war with Japan, implicitly accepted the possibility of the loss of the Philippines, *Wake* and *Guam*. MacArthur's acceptance of defeat was clearly evident in the message he sent to Washington as his troops occupied the defensive lines on Bataan: "With its [Bataan] occupation all maneuvering possibilities will cease. I intend to fight it out to complete destruction."[45]

Nevertheless MacArthur merely obfuscated with the press and with his own troops. "Help is on the way from the United States," he promised, "Thousands of troops and hundreds of planes are being dispatched . . . . no further retreat is possible."[46] "We have more troops than the Japanese have thrown against us; our supplies are ample; a determined defense will defeat the enemy's attack."[47] Roosevelt may have been guilty of giving the truth of the impossibility of rescuing the Philippines in "mean little doses"[48] as *Time* magazine's, later Pulitzer Prize winning journalist, John Hersey, described Washington's pronouncements, but in this respect MacArthur was no less guilty of raising hopes that he must have known were unrealistic. Not content with lying to the US press, MacArthur also lied to his own troops and officers.

For the rest of his life MacArthur made a great play of President Roosevelt's 'supposed' promises to relieve the Philippines; when Roosevelt died in 1945, MacArthur turned to staff officer Bonner Feller and said, "So Roosevelt is dead; a man who would never tell the truth when a lie would serve him just as well."[49] Leaving aside the lack of gratitude for a man who had promoted him to his elevated post, and his distasteful disrespect for a deceased president, MacArthur must have been fully aware, if not beforehand at the very least with hindsight, that the Philippines could not have been rescued in 1941. MacArthur's blaming of Roosevelt was another self-serving attempt to deflect blame.

Eisenhower, now seated in Washington and soon to be General Marshall's right hand, showing that he could never quite shake off the awe he had for a man for whom he worked for ten years, and revealing a far more generous nature than his erstwhile boss, confided in his diary that he felt that MacArthur, "might have made a better showing at the beaches and passes, and certainly he should have saved his planes on December 8th . . . but he's still my hero."[50] It was an observation that clearly highlighted the paradox of their relationship.

Reluctantly General Marshall only decided on New Year's Day that the Philippines would perforce have to be abandoned, though he did not tell MacArthur immediately. In spite of MacArthur's upbeat pronouncements, morale on Bataan was not good. Aside from the overall lack of supplies and preparation to withstand a prolonged siege, the giving of larger rations to American troops did not improve the mood of the largely

Filipino troops on Bataan. Antonio Aquino (son of sugar baron Benigno Aquino) risked shark-infested waters to swim the mile and a half from Bataan to *Corregidor* to warn Quezon of the increasing rift between US and Filipino troops. "We feel we should have the same rations as the Americans,"[51] he complained. It was not just the Filipino troops that were shabbily treated. In a sign of the inter-force rivalries to come, MacArthur ordered his Chief of Staff, General Sutherland, to remove the 4th Marines from the general recommendations for Presidential unit citation awards: "The marines had enough glory in *World War I*,"[52] he said by way of explanation.

The lies were not just about the possibility of relief. Contrary to MacArthur's assertions, supplies in Bataan were not plentiful; his failure to plan a defensive campaign around War Plan RAINBOW-5 (ORANGE) would prove fatal to the peninsula's defense. Fifty million bushels (1,700 million litres) of rice stored in central *Luzon* could not be moved in time to Bataan; it would have been enough to sustain MacArthur's entire army and 20,000 civilians for four years. In addition large stockpiles of food and munitions were simply left at the Manila docks. Colonel Ernest Miller of the 194th Tank Regiment wrote, "food and materiel of war [was] sabotaged by that same mismanagement and indecision which had destroyed our airpower."[53]

Available supplies were much larger than Plan ORANGE had called for, which was for sufficient supplies to be held at Bataan to sustain 43,000 men for six months. Brigadier-General Charles Drake, the US Army's quartermaster in the Philippines had calculated it would take fourteen days to transport sufficient supplies to Bataan; in practice he only had eight days. In the chaos of roads crowded with troops and refugees the management of this exercise became impossible in spite of Drake's desperate efforts. Before the retreat to Bataan, Drake had pleaded with MacArthur to take supplies to Bataan as a precaution. MacArthur had refused to allow it.

As a result, the supply situation on Bataan quickly descended into chaos. From 5 January, MacArthur put his troops on half rations. In practice many received much less. MacArthur's logistical failures left his men to subsist on just 1,000–1,500 calories per day—far below a survival diet. By the end of January meat and fish supplies had dwindled to 11 days, flour to 6 days and vegetables to 4 days. Sugar was gone. Wainwright confided to Major 'Trap' Trapnell of the 26th Cavalry, "I don't worry about the Japs. I worry about the chow."[54] Through lack of nutrition, the US troops' resistance to disease collapsed and over 80 percent of them succumbed to malaria and other tropical diseases. The failure of supply was also reflected in inadequate oil and munitions dumps.

By comparison MacArthur and his men ensconced on *Corregidor* had more than adequate food supplies for 7,000 men for six months in the Malinta Tunnels on the island. One day of barge supply across *Manila Bay* brought that supply up to 180 days of food for 10,000 men. Life in the tunnels may have been safe but it was not pleasant. On 9 January 'Pick' Diller noted that ". . . suddenly the lights went out. The tunnel wall began to shake. Japs were dropping 1,000 pounders. Air inside the tunnel was pressing against the lungs. More bombs dropped. Detonation reverberates louder in tunnel than outside. Nurses started mumbling prayers."[55] Afterward Diller and the officers started to talk about when the convoy would arrive. Romulo quietly told the soldiers around that he had inside information that "the convoy is very near and may be here in a week's time but keep that under your hat."[56] As if.

If MacArthur's promises were little more than wishful thinking, because he of all people, as a former US Army chief of staff, would have known that War Plan RAINBOW-5 gave priority to Europe over the Far East, at least Quezon was more realistic in his aggrieved outpourings at the fickleness of American pledges: "I cannot stand this constant reference to England, to Europe. Where are the planes this *sinverguanze* [scoundrel] is boasting of? How American to writhe in anguish at the fate of a distant cousin while a daughter is being raped in the back of the room!"[57] From this it can reasonably be assumed that MacArthur had not fully informed Quezon about RAINBOW-5 (ORANGE) and its strategic implications.

When the realization finally dawned on Quezon that the Philippines was to be abandoned, the furious President and his cabinet demanded instant independence from US suzerainty and declared their intention to announce their country's neutrality. A memo from MacArthur seemed to give some support to Quezon's position. Indeed MacArthur's equivocation on this subject was more astonishing to Washington than Quezon's impassioned demands. Roosevelt rejected Quezon's proposal and Quezon himself had second thoughts about the neutrality idea after meeting his Vice President, Sergio Osmeña, in the bathroom of their shared bunker on *Corregidor*. When Osmeña pointed out that in going back to Manila, Quezon's daughters might be raped by Japanese soldiers, the President, squatting on his primitive wooden latrine, replied thoughtfully, "Compadre, perhaps you are right. I shall think it over."[58] He never raised the matter of neutrality again.

Meanwhile MacArthur fished out an old double-barreled Remington 'Derringer' pistol from his belongings and scrounged two cartridges from his personal aide and naval adviser, Colonel Sydney Huff; displaying his 'drama-queen' personality, MacArthur proclaimed, "Sid, they will never take me alive."[59] He undoubtedly meant it; for all his bravura, MacArthur was a genuinely brave man and displayed a fearlessness that astonished colleagues throughout his life.

Homma, having penned MacArthur's forces into the bottom half of the Bataan Peninsula, consolidated his positions and prepared for the next phase of the engagement. At this critical junction the Japanese commanders relieved the crack 48th Division and prepared them instead for an attack on the Dutch East Indies. While this decision has sometimes been characterized as a mistake that showed Japanese commanders' underestimation of the strengths of the defenses at Bataan and *Corregidor*, it may have been tactically astute. Japan's senior commanders may have decided that they could afford to ignore MacArthur's forces; holed up on the Bataan Peninsula, US forces could be left to 'wither on the vine.' The Dutch East Indies, with its wealth of oil, was, after all, the strategic prize for which Japan's southern campaigns were being fought. In the place of Homma's 48th Division, the job of clearing out the American defenders from

Bataan was given to the much less capable 65th Brigade that had originally been designated to be a garrison unit.

On 13 January Emperor Hirohito, eagerly following campaign developments while ensconced in the war room built underneath his Imperial Palace in Tokyo, made his first direct intervention in the running of a war whose advances thus far, had run like clockwork. He pressed General Sugiyama, Army Chief of Staff, to reinforce the troops on the Philippines so as to speed up the taking of Bataan. A week later Hirohito pressed Sugiyama again on reinforcement. Although Sugiyama pointed out that with the US army bottled up in Bataan, it posed no danger, he nevertheless assured the Emperor that fresh troops would be sought. Hirohito would raise the problem of Bataan for a third time on 9 February and again on 26 February.

Contrary to MacArthur's post-war assertion that Hirohito was a constitutional monarch who had no day-to-day role in the running of the war, thereby excusing him from standing as a criminal suspect in the Tokyo War Crimes Trial, the Emperor was actively involved in the discussion and approval of all strategic war plans. Later, when the war started to turn against Japan, weakening the Army's power, Hirohito's interventions became more insistent. In spite of the unsatisfactory conclusion of the campaign in the Philippines, on 18 February the Emperor conducted a public celebration of the victories in the war to date; the conquering Emperor rode on his pure white horse to the Nijubashi Bridge in front of the Imperial Palace where he waved to the adoring crowds. Hirohito was clearly not overly worried by the delay in wrapping up the Philippines; a month later, on 9 March, he commented to Marquis Kido, his Lord Privy Seal, "The fruits of victory are tumbling into our mouths too quickly."[60]

Meanwhile, after a failed counter-attack on Japanese forces on 16 January, the weakened US Philippine Division withdrew to the reserve battle line in the center of the Bataan Peninsula. The withdrawal was made just in time, as Major-General Naoki Kimura outflanked General Wainwright's lines on the western slopes of Mount Natib. Trapped to the north, Wainwright tried but failed to break the Japanese road blockade with a tank attack that he led in person. Afterwards he and his men were forced to abandon their vehicles and artillery and withdraw to the south via the beach. The Philippine 51st Division was similarly enveloped on the other side of the mountain.

On the night of 22–23 January Wainwright began a hazardous withdrawal from the Abucay Line to a new defensive line ten miles to the south. Meanwhile MacArthur kept up a stream of inanities to Washington; the defeat and retreat was described as a planned maneuver; "Under cover of darkness I broke contact with the enemy and without loss of a man or an ounce of material I am now firmly established on my main battle position. The execution of the movement would have done credit to the best troops in the world."[61] By comparison the 16th Naval District intelligence officer, Lieutenant Commander Cheek, sent a message reporting the same event; "The panic spread to all this regiment [53rd] . . . and even to the reserve [52nd] Regiment a mile in rear of the front. Machine guns, rifles, ammunition and equipment were abandoned—the former were turned on the disorganized 51st Division by the enemy."[62] Far from not losing a man, as MacArthur claimed, Commander Cheek's meeting with a US Army colonel confirmed that 40 percent of the Philippine Army divisions had been lost through desertion. I-Philippine Corp alone had abandoned tens of artillery pieces, scores of machine guns and thousands of rifles along with copious amounts of munitions and supply. Cheek's reports, which revealed the dissembling nature of MacArthur, must have been seen by Admiral Ernest King in Washington, and provided another reason for King's detestation of America's most senior military commander.

With no reserves available, untrained sailors, their white uniforms blacked-up, were thrown into the battle. Marine NCOs, who were salted into the sailors' ranks, commanded them. Marines provided leadership. In some cases the most basic knowledge was imparted to the sailors. As they were preparing to deploy, one sailor called out, "Hey Sarge, how do you get the bullets into this thing?"[63] In spite of their rawness, the sailors would prove their worth in defensive actions as General Kimura attempted to outflank the new American line by amphibious landings. Japanese troops who landed at Longoskawauan Point and Quinauan Point were annihilated in the so-called *Battle of the Points*.

The strength of the new defensive positions was similarly displayed with US victory in the *Battle of the Pockets* when a Japanese salient was cut off. Homma managed to extricate just 378 men. Indeed the Japanese front line had to withdraw for several miles on 22 February 1942. In total three battalions of the Japanese 20th Infantry had in effect been destroyed. It was a humiliating retreat and the first serious setback that the Japanese Army suffered in the *Pacific War*; much to General Terauchi's annoyance it now seemed likely that Homma would miss the fifty-day campaign target that had originally been set. The two minor victories in January and February hinted at how strongly constructed defences could combat Japanese rapid flanking movements. MacArthur completely failed to learn the important lessons of the *Battle of the Points* and the *Battle of the Pockets* that a flanking movement could quickly be turned into an enemy surrounded if defense remained resolute. America's hold on the Bataan Peninsula would ultimately be denied not by a poor defensive line but by logistical failings.

MacArthur's Escape to Australia: At this point President Roosevelt ordered General MacArthur to relocate from *Corregidor* to Australia. It was Army Chief of Staff, General Marshall's call. Noticeably it was not Marshall's idea but that of John Curtin, the Australian Prime Minister. Eisenhower had argued that MacArthur was expendable but Marshall had second thoughts and decided that the capture or death of MacArthur would hand a propaganda coup to Japan. Marshall was not unaware of the furious rows that MacArthur would unleash—particularly in respect of the US Navy. The new military and geopolitical importance of Australia was another fact to be considered. What if Curtin came to an arrangement with Japan—not entirely far-fetched given his fury at Churchill for his perceived abandonment of Australia. America had not yet fully committed itself to Australia and Britain was considered at best incompetent. As an Australian officer had vented, the British Army had been "forced back by a small

Japanese army of only two divisions, riding stolen bicycles and without artillery support."[64] Taking MacArthur to Australia would help shore up their willingness for the cause. Other voices were calling for MacArthur's rescue. Republicans as well as the *New York Times* led the call for him to be brought back from *Corregidor*. Roosevelt, probably more for political reasons than military, concurred with Marshall and ordered MacArthur to leave *Corregidor*.

At first MacArthur resisted the call to relocate; he declared that rather than obey the President, he would resign his commission and cross over to Bataan to offer himself as a volunteer. It was a theatrical gesture, as fantastical as the reports he was sending from the Philippines. On 12 March he left *Corregidor* in a convoy of four PT boats with his wife and son; without informing or getting permission from General Marshall, and much to Washington's later astonishment, he also took his Chief of Staff, General Sutherland and his key staff members: Colonel Sydney Huff (personal aide), Brigadier Spencer Akin (Intelligence), Captain Hugh Casey, Lieutenant-Colonel Richard Marshall, Colonel Charles Willoughby (Intelligence), Lieutenant-Colonel LeGrande 'Pick' Diller (press officer), and Colonel Harold George. The lucky few, who became known as the 'Bataan gang,' were to be his loyal assistants throughout the war. It could never be said that MacArthur was not loyal to his staff; in return he demanded absolute loyalty too with the implicit understanding that all the plaudits of any campaign would be his and his alone.

Setting out under cover of darkness, PT boats took them at high speed through tempestuous seas to the southern Philippine island of *Mindanao*, narrowly avoiding detection by Japanese destroyers and coastal batteries. MacArthur, who suffered chronic seasickness on the journey, later described it as like "a trip in a concrete mixer."[65] A B-17 Flying Fortress took them onwards to Australia. After getting to Alice Springs, Australia, MacArthur carefully crafted a statement for the benefit of the press; on arrival in Adelaide by train, he pompously declared, "I came through and *I shall return*."[66] MacArthur ignored a request by Washington to replace 'I' with 'We.' The phrase, "*I shall return*,"[67] much burnished by the press, became MacArthur's most famous quotation—at least until his equally famous, "*I have returned*."[68]

However, a less famous quotation from the same interview perhaps gives an even greater insight into some of the inter-force conflicts that lay ahead. "The President of the United States," proclaimed MacArthur, "ordered me to break through the Japanese lines ... for the purpose, as I understand it, of organizing the American offensive against Japan, a primary object of which is the relief of the Philippines."[69] MacArthur's understanding that he would be in charge, and secondly, 'relief of the Philippines,' would be a 'primary object' were assumptions of decisions that would be made above his 'pay-grade.'

As ever this would not deter MacArthur. Indeed it was a feature of his entire life that he assumed command even when it was not authorized. If baulked, as he would be for a while over these two assumptions, MacArthur would invariably invoke conspiracy by an enemy that he referred to knowingly as an indeterminate 'They.' Paranoia had been a constant companion throughout his career; conspiracy was always imagined when he was thwarted. Now in Australia, the 'Navy Cabal' would become the enemy that he tried to defeat almost as ruthlessly as the Japanese themselves. However, the first target was Lieutenant-General George Brett, Head of the Allied Air Force, who he immediately tried and failed to replace with one of his 'Bataan gang.'

MacArthur's departure from *Corregidor* coincided with a lull in the fighting as General Homma reorganized his forces and waited for reinforcements. Meanwhile the effects of MacArthur's neglectful attitude toward fulfilling the logistical requirements of War Plan RAINBOW-5 (ORANGE) meant that a sharp decline was now visible in General Wainwright's troops. It had not helped that Bataan's food reserves had been transferred by MacArthur to the better-provisioned *Corregidor*. By the end, the US and Filipino troops were driven to eat their horses and mules.

Curiously in spite of his well-known personal bravery, and his oft-repeated declaration of love for his troops, MacArthur had only made one visit to the Bataan front from his HQ in the hidden tunnels of Malinta Hill on *Corregidor*. Throughout MacArthur's career, the proclamations of love for his troops were much more frequent than actions that gave evidence to these declarations. In spite of this, MacArthur remained a hero, particularly to his Filipino troops; in this deeply Catholic country, his return was waited for as if he was the 'Messiah'—an image that MacArthur's propaganda machine would carefully exploit.

The Destruction of the US Army on Bataan: MacArthur's disappearance to Australia could not have helped morale on Bataan and *Corregidor*, though the arrival of Wainwright to take MacArthur's place immediately improved relationships between Army and Navy personnel. When Japan re-launched its attacks on 28 March with a heavy artillery barrage, US forces were in desperate straits. Although Imperial HQ was furious that MacArthur had been allowed to escape, there was optimism that the recently arrived 4th Division from the Imperial General Headquarters reserve in Shanghai, under Colonel Takushiro Hattori, Army Chief of Operations, would be able to finish the job. The Imperial Japanese Navy Air Force supplied a fresh squadron of Zero fighters and 24 'Betty' bombers. The Japanese Army air was also strengthened with the arrival of 60 Ki-21 'Sally' Bombers.

By the end of March some 67,100 Japanese troops (out of a total strength of 85,200 troops on *Luzon*), 80 bombers and 140 artillery pieces were ready for the final assault. Their plan was to launch their main attack on the *Manila Bay* side of Bataan where the II-Philippine Corps held the American line. Homma, fearing disgrace, wrote in a rather defensive tone on 2 April, "There is no reason why this attack should not succeed."[70] Wainwright, aware that his troops were starving and dispirited was in no doubt as to the outcome. Homma need not have worried. On 3 April the American lines crumbled along Mount Samat. Now safely out of harm's way, MacArthur issued orders from Australia: "When the supply situation becomes impossible, there must be no thought to surrender. You must attack."[71] However, his abandoned troops were now demoralized. On 8 April the 57th Infantry Regiment and the 31st Division were overrun at the *Alangan River*.

The 45th Infantry, ordered to get to *Corregidor*, failed to reach their embarkation point before they were cut off and eventually only 300 men of the 31st Infantry managed to get across to the island. In total about 2,100 men had managed to find their way to *Corregidor*; about half of them were sailors and Marines. As for the Filipino Army, Major-General Edward King, Wainwright's field commander on Bataan reported, "in two days an army vanished into thin air."[72]

When news of the defeat on Bataan arrived, MacArthur turned immediately from ordering his troops to fight to the last man, to covering up the reasons for the American Army's greatest military defeat in its history. On 9 April, MacArthur told a press conference, "No army has done so much with so little, and nothing became it more than its last hours of trial and agony."[73] The truth was somewhat different. In no small part the army had 'so little' because of MacArthur's irresponsible neglect of War Plan RAINBOW-5 (ORANGE). As for the 'last hours' mentioned at his press conference, they were characterized by an undignified flight in complete chaos. This was not the heroic last stand that he had demanded.

The Fall of Corregidor: **[Map: 6.4]** On *Corregidor* or 'the Rock' as it was commonly known, 13,000 troops defended a heavily fortified garrison. Laced with anti-aircraft guns, artillery and cannon, it was considered by some to be impregnable. However, with shortages of water allowing for two small rations per day, the defenders were on their last legs. Heavy bombing had also sapped their morale. Although submarines had brought in food, mail and munitions in March, the garrison was doomed by lack of supplies. It was a question of when, not whether, it would fall.

From 12 April *Corregidor*'s famed gun emplacements fought a protracted duel with Japanese artillery units on Bataan. The 12-inch guns from batteries on *Corregidor* and Fort Drum, the fortified island with its 36 foot reinforced concrete encasements, placed in the southern channel into *Manila Bay*, battered the Japanese positions. However, over the next two weeks Japanese artillery gradually wore down the American guns and more particularly their crews. Gunner Sergeant Waldron described the experience of being under fire: "Sometimes the shells would come so fast and explode so close together that we stayed inside our tunnels. Nothing could survive that shelling. The enemy would pick out an area and start walking shells across it and when they were through, it would look like No-Man's-Land."[74]

For the troops the tension of being under fire for long periods of time was unbearable. The noise of guns drove some men crazy. Waldron recalled a Sergeant Rollings whose "nerves just went to pieces and whenever he gave the command to commence firing, he would take off through the jungle, not knowing or caring where he ran."[75] Already undermanned before the engagement started, by the end of April the American troops' ability to return fire had fallen off sharply in spite of the continued availability of thousands of shells. By contrast the Japanese bombardment increased in intensity, pouring thousands of shells into the 'Rock.' By 5 May most of *Corregidor*'s guns had been silenced and the defenders anticipated that an invasion would soon follow.

On the night of 5–6 May, the Japanese 61st Regiment landed on the northeast corner of *Corregidor* and in spite of some fierce resistance established a beachhead to which they brought tanks and artillery. In hindsight it was a mistake that MacArthur did not bring tanks to assist in the defense of *Corregidor*. From the beachhead the defenders were quickly pushed back toward the stronghold of Malinta Hill at the neck of the island, where tunnels sheltered senior officers and their families. Having lost some 800 soldiers, General Wainwright decided that further resistance was pointless. Little did Wainwright know that the Japanese, who had taken 70 percent casualty rates in their landing of 2,000 troops on 4 May, were also on their last legs. General Homma had used up the last of his reserves. Unbeknownst to the Americans it had been a close run battle.

On the evening of 6 May, General Wainwright, fearful of the slaughter of civilians pressed into Malinta Hill's tunnels, asked for 'terms' and Homma responded by insisting on the surrender of all US forces in the Philippines. Wainwright would later write, ". . . it was the terror that is vested in a tank that was the deciding factor. I thought of the havoc that even one of these could wreak if it nosed into the tunnel, where lay our helpless wounded and their brave nurses."[76] For the fighting soldiers it was a traumatic moment. 4th Marine Colonel Howard broke down and sobbed, "My God, and I had to be the first Marine officer ever to surrender a regiment."[77]

In his last message addressed directly to President Roosevelt, Wainwright wrote:

> There is a limit to human endurance and that limit has long since passed. Without prospect of relief I feel it is my duty to my country and to my gallant troops to end this useless effusion of blood and human sacrifice. If you agree, Mr. President, please say to the nation that my troops and I have accomplished all that is humanly possible and that we have upheld the best tradition of the United States and its Army. May God bless and preserve you and guide you and the nation in the effort to ultimate victory.[78]

On *Mindanao Island* in the southern Philippine Archipelago, General Sharpe acquiesced to Homma's demand for his surrender though many individuals went into the jungle and continued the struggle as guerrillas. *Corregidor*, according to MacArthur, "the strongest single fortified point in the world"[79] had fallen in less than two days. The *Pacific War*'s first *Battle of Luzon* was over.

As had been the case throughout Japan's South East Asia onslaught, an army with its main resources bogged down on the Chinese mainland had managed a remarkable victory on a shoe-string; not only in terms of the number of troops it could muster, but also in the already very thin logistical support it could provide its armies in the field. The quality of Japanese military leadership during this period, as well as the remarkable endurance, skill and spirit of its infantry, has rarely been adequately acknowledged. General Homma, hugely outnumbered, had fought a brilliant campaign in which he had also gone out of his way to instruct his troops to treat conquered subjects with dignity and respect. However, in Tokyo, Army Chief of Staff Hajime Sugiyama did not appreciate Homma's efforts. Sugiyama reckoned that the Fourteenth Army's commander was not aggressive enough and shortly after *Corregidor*, Homma was removed from active command.

Eisenhower noted in his diary, "*Corregidor* surrendered last night. Poor Wainwright! He did the fighting in the Philippine Islands, another [MacArthur] got such glory as the public could find in the operation."[80] In fact, the dividends reaped by MacArthur from this disaster would be far greater than Eisenhower could ever have imagined.

The Bataan Death March: [**Map: 6.5**] The Bataan Death March began on 9 April almost a month before General Wainwright's surrender to General Homma on *Corregidor*. Prisoners numbered 76,000 including 12,000 Americans captured on the Bataan Peninsula. They were marched for sixty miles from its tip to Capas, which lay almost due north. Homma and his staff had no plans prepared for the transport of the huge volumes of captured troops and civilians and had to make *ad hoc* arrangements that contributed to the horrors of the march in which Allied soldiers, Americans and Filipino, many of the latter civilians, were murdered and brutalized. An estimated 500 Americans and ten times that number of Filipinos were estimated to have died en route during the ten-day journey to Camp O'Donnell in Capas, Tarlac Province. It should be noted that some estimates put the number of deaths much higher. In the fog of war counting was all but impossible and it cannot be gauged how many Filipino civilians and soldiers managed to slip away during the march.

Denied fresh water and food, the marchers had to drink whatever foul water they could find. Dysentery quickly became rampant. Those who could not keep up were beaten and if they fell behind were shot or bayonetted. Japanese officers on horseback beheaded some of the prisoners with samurai swords.

At the end of the war General Masaharu Homma, in spite of his attempts to mitigate the harsh treatment of prisoners and Filipino civilians, took the blame for the designated war crime though it was clear that he had not ordered the atrocities and far from clear whether he was even aware of what had taken place. Homma accepted his capital sentence with remarkable grace, thanking the five man military commission for his treatment during his confinement. He was executed by firing squad on 3 April 1946.

In line with all the tribunals after *World War II*, responsibility for war crimes was not dependent on knowledge of atrocities let alone orders for atrocities. Luckily for Hirohito, the Commander in Chief of the Japanese Army, he was excused on MacArthur's instructions from responsibility for all Japanese war crimes—so too were Generals MacArthur and Kenney after the massacre of 1,000 defenseless Japanese troops at the *Battle of the Bismarck Sea* in March 1943. [**See Chapter 21: Battle of the Bismarck Sea: Tipping Point of US Air Supremacy**] However constructed, the Tokyo War Crimes Trials and their regional counterparts in Manila and Shanghai were at least partly based on arbitrary victor's justice. Ironically MacArthur's father,

Lieutenant-General Arthur MacArthur had been the commander of the US Army's 2nd Division, 8th Corp at the *Battle of Manila* against Philippine forces in 1899 and afterward in the brutal suppression of Filipino forces in *Luzon*—campaigns in which an estimated 250,000 Filipinos lost their lives.

Dissenting opinions in the Homma case included the former High Commissioner for the Philippines and later Supreme Court Associate Judge 'Frank' Murphy who concluded, "the lives of Yamashita and Homma, leaders of enemy forces vanquished in the field of battle, are being taken without regard to due process of law."[81] Appalling though it was, the Bataan Death March was trivial in terms of numbers compared to the many millions of Chinese who were slaughtered by the Japanese Army in the course of the *Pacific War* and the *Second Sino-Japanese War* that preceded.

MacArthur: Culpability, Honors and Money: It has to be asked what was MacArthur's culpability for the military denouement of the Philippines campaign. Some leeway has to be given for the constrained time schedule of little more than four months that he had to get 120,000 new recruits armed and into shape. In August 1941, Major-General Wainwright wrote to his daughter-in-law and mentioned that the Philippine Army troops "are not well trained so I will have a job getting them ready to fight."[82] There were also genuine issues of supply and armament; when Japan invaded the Philippines there was an estimated 1.1 million tons of Manila-bound *matériel* waiting at America's west coast docks. Yet it is also clear that MacArthur had very little interest in the detail of training or logistical management.

As a general he was more of a 'bar stool' strategist, a constant lecturer on the history of warfare from Olympian heights, rather than a master and implementer of tactics and logistics; these tasks were thoroughly delegated to his staff. The beach defense strategy and tactics that he adopted in preference to War Plan ORANGE were pure folly. Even his subordinates considered MacArthur's belief, that his Air Force would drive the Japanese from the beaches, to be utterly risible. While to his credit MacArthur was not averse to the introduction of the new weaponry employed by a modern air force, he remained wholly unrealistic about the usages and limitations of the new breed of aircraft. The same applied to the development of the PT boat that he championed. A fast boat that could travel at forty knots and fire torpedoes was a useful tool but not a weapon that could defend the Philippines from a determined invader such as Japan with its powerful carrier fleet.

Given the ability of the Japanese to concentrate their forces at the point of attack, a strategy based on the defense of *Luzon's* hundreds of miles of beaches was a wholly inadequate concept and would have failed even if all of his 152,000 soldiers had been well armed and trained. Even elementary precautions against a Japanese attack were not taken. Bizarrely MacArthur forbade Lieutenant-General Brereton, Commander in Chief of his Air Force, to take reconnaissance photographs of the Japanese airfields on *Formosa*. With the benefit of hindsight and the knowledge that Japan's resources were already severely stretched, a well-managed defense of the Philippines could have held out indefinitely, or at least absorbed a vastly greater Japanese military effort, thereby draining resources from other theaters.

With regard to MacArthur's abilities, Brigadier-General Bradford Chynoweth, who commanded the 61st Infantry Division of the Philippine Army, wrote of the appalling conditions for troops that he found when he arrived; his division was equipped with obsolescent Lee Enfield rifles, had no artillery, and had only an average of nine weeks training. More saliently, Chynoweth placed a large measure of the blame for this on General MacArthur who he described as "lazy, almost shiftless, frivolous, uncommunicative, uncooperative. He never visits his troops. His tactical judgment was nil. He was the poorest judge of subordinates that I ever knew. Yet he achieved GREATNESS!"[83] In part the problem was simply that by the end of 1941 the 65-year-old MacArthur, as an operational commander, was past his sell-by-date. He had last seen action in 1918 although in 1924 he had commanded forces against a mutiny by the Philippines Scouts. Since then he had occupied desk jobs including Chief of Staff of the US Army.

The nature of MacArthur's relationship with Quezon has also been called into question. When the Japanese occupied Manila on 2 January 1942, Quezon agreed to work with the invaders, a strategy supposedly agreed with MacArthur on the condition that there was no formal alliance with Tokyo. MacArthur later denied any knowledge of this agreement. However, it has to be asked why MacArthur and his staff secretly pocketed the US$500,000 that Quezon's government awarded them 'supposedly' for pre-war services on 3 January 1942. But for a technicality that Roosevelt had been persuaded by MacArthur to adopt in regard to service in the Philippines, acceptance of funds was a violation of army rules that would normally have required his instant dismissal. At the very least it was morally dubious behavior. US$500,000 was transferred to MacArthur's personal account on 15 February, the day before Quezon was taken from *Corregidor* to safety by submarine. Noticeably, when Eisenhower was similarly offered money, he declined. In his memoirs Eisenhower disclosed, "I explained that while I understood this to be unquestionably legal, and that the President's motives were of the highest, the danger of misapprehension or misunderstanding on the part of some individuals might operate to destroy whatever usefulness I might have to the allied cause in the present War."[84]

Remarkably the payments to MacArthur and his staff were covered up until public disclosure by the historian Carol Petillo in 1979, after she found a copy of the order in General Sutherland's papers (Sutherland's cut of Quezon's 'loot' was US$75,000). MacArthur, who copiously recorded every award he ever received in his memoirs, failed to mention this one; in effect MacArthur knew that his financial dealings with the Quezon government stank. Perhaps most tellingly, MacArthur's main activity as a commander during his time in the Philippines after the Japanese attack was the issue of press releases. In the course of his ten weeks as ground commander of the Philippine Army, MacArthur oversaw the release of a remarkable 142 press releases; he personally oversaw each one. Astonishingly 109 of the releases only mentioned one soldier—General Douglas

MacArthur. Not everyone in Washington was fooled. Eisenhower, who was to become the greatest of the US wartime generals, had worked with MacArthur for ten years and saw through his combination of public bombast and private whingeing. He described MacArthur as being "as big a baby as ever."[85]

Nevertheless, General Marshall recommended MacArthur for the Medal of Honor for his defense of the Philippines and it was duly bestowed. However, when General Marshall sought MacArthur's approval for a Medal of Honor to be awarded to the imprisoned General Wainwright, MacArthur baulked. It would be a 'grave injustice' he declared to the other generals who had fought at Bataan. Furthermore MacArthur sent Marshall a vitriolic message that blamed Wainwright's tactics and accused him of being responsible for the high level of casualties on Bataan. It was an appalling betrayal of a much-admired 'fighting general,' whom history has shown to have displayed a bravery and competence on *Luzon* that MacArthur had lacked.

MacArthur's own citation, written by Marshall, reads, "For conspicuous leadership in preparing the Philippine Islands to resist conquest, for gallantry and intrepidity above and beyond the call of duty in action against invading Japanese forces . . . etc."[86] In spite of a broad level of concern in Washington about MacArthur's competence given the fiasco that was the defense of the Philippines, US leaders now felt that, after the catastrophe of *Pearl Harbor*, an American hero was required. MacArthur fitted the bill; brave and inspirational leader though he undoubtedly was to some—the monomaniacal, paranoid and delusional Douglas MacArthur, whose incompetence and neglect had brought disaster to the US Army in the Philippines, was to become the Army's pin-up in *World War II*. It was a decision which many would have cause to regret as the *Pacific War* unfolded.

7 Invasion of Malaya: Yamashita's 'Bicycle Blitzkrieg'

[December 1941–February 1942]

[Maps: 7.1A, 7.1B, 7.2, 7.3, 7.4, 7.5]

General Yamashita and the Plan of Attack: **[Maps: 7.1A, 7.1B]** The invasion of Malaya was planned as one of the three 'surprise' attacks which comprised the opening moves of Japan's aggressive plan to 'strike south'; their ultimate aim to capture the rich oil fields of *Borneo* and the Dutch East Indies (now Indonesia). The invasion of the Philippines was intended to cut off America's ability to disrupt the supply lines between Japan and their intended supply of oil, while the attack on *Pearl Harbor* was designed to put the American fleet out of action for long enough to prevent it from either saving the Philippines or preventing Japan from acquiring oil assets. The third leg of Japan's opening gambit was equally important. A simultaneous attack on Malaya was designed to eviscerate the only other credible military threat in South East Asia, the British and their naval stronghold in *Singapore*.

In planning for the Malayan Campaign, Japanese high command had benefited from information that had fallen into its hands from the German capture of the passenger and cargo steamer SS *Automedon* by the surface raider *Atlantis* on 11 November 1940. The documents, discovered in a chest meant for British Far East Command, were taken to Rear-Admiral Paul Wenneker, the naval *attaché*, at the German embassy in Tokyo and then handed over to Japan.

The captured documents disclosed that there was no British fleet to help *Singapore*, and that Britain would not declare war if Thailand was invaded. The virtually helpless state of Britain's Asian Empire was fully displayed. The same document had also disclosed that *Hong Kong* was expendable. As Wenneker noted in his diary, "As anticipated, the contents were read with extraordinary interest."[1] Vice-Admiral Nobutake Kondo was delighted, "Such a significant weakening of the British Empire could not have been identified from outward appearances."[2]

Lieutenant-General Tomoyuki Yamashita was the commander designated to lead the Japanese attack on British Malaya. Born on 8 November 1885, Yamashita was the son of a village doctor near the city of Kochi on the island of *Shikoku* (the smallest of Japan's four main islands). Joining the Army was his father's idea, "because I was big and healthy"[3] as he later recalled. The strongly built Yamashita joined the Army at the age of twenty-one after graduating with some distinction in the eighteenth place in his class at the Imperial Japanese Army Academy. Eight years later he served in the action that secured Shantung from the Germans in one of the actions that dismembered the German Empire in Japan's favor during *World War I*.

In 1916, he entered the elite Army War College at Minato in Tokyo that had been founded in 1882 as an elite school for Japan's most capable officers. Modeled on the *Preussische Kriegsakademie* (Prussian War Academy) that had produced such legendary officers as famous theoretician Major-General von Clausewitz as well as Field Marshal von Moltke, the General who won the *Franco-Prussian War*, Japan's Army War College taught military tactics with a strongly German influence. Attending the college was an essential prerequisite to reaching the highest levels of Japanese military command. Again Yamashita excelled and not just in his academic studies. In addition to graduating sixth in his class, which won him one of the six Army Swords presented by the Emperor, Yamashita married the daughter of retired General Nagayama. Yamashita was a powerful heavy-set figure, whose physical presence, as well as intellect, commanded attention.

Later he became something of an authority on Germany, serving as a military *attaché* first in Berne in Switzerland and then in Berlin, returning to Japan in 1922 where he joined the Imperial Army General Staff. Whether it was a love of German beer and sausage that, over time, was to give him his unusually large girth is unclear. Back in Tokyo Yamashita garnered considerable opprobrium by making a plan and recommendations for the reduction of the military in line with post-war budgetary requirements. After joining the Imperial Army General Staff, Yamashita became sympathetic to the Imperial Way Faction (*Kodoha*) within the Army and clashed with General Hideki Tojo, future wartime prime minister, who was a leading member of the Control Faction (*Toseiha*). Although Yamashita was not an overtly political soldier he nevertheless developed a rivalry with Tojo that was to last the remainder of their lives.

After another posting to Europe as military *attaché* in Vienna, Yamashita, now a colonel, was given command of the 3rd Imperial Infantry Regiment in 1930. However, the attempted *coup d'état* in the 26 February Incident in 1936 by disaffected junior officers of the 3rd Regiment belonging to the Imperial Way Faction was an embarrassment to its former commanding officer. Hirohito rejected Yamashita's appeals for leniency for the conspirators. Yamashita had advised the conspirators to commit *seppuku* (ritual suicide by disembowelment) as a dignified way out of the impasse, but the Emperor refused to permit them this dignified exit. Hirohito, in an action that showed that he was not the constitutional puppet of post-war mythology, ordered the rebels to return to their barracks and insisted on their execution. Yamashita, suspected of having promoted the uprising in the Emperor's name, was effectively banished by the *Toseiha* leaders to Seoul where he served as brigade commander. Other *Kodoha* leaders were similarly purged from influential positions and banished to the provinces. From this point onward, *Kodoha* effectively ceased to exist. Believing his career was over, Yamashita took up calligraphy and signed himself *Daisen* (Giant Cedar). Later as commander of the Imperial Japanese Army's Fourth Division, he was involved in desultory actions against Chinese insurgents.

Then because of his knowledge of Germany, Yamashita's fortunes changed and he was sent on a secret mission to Berlin in December 1940. Here he met Hitler, whom he considered "an unimpressive little man"[4] and Foreign Minister Joachim von Ribbentrop, with a view to acquiring German military technology. Hitler told Yamashita, "All our secrets are open to you."[5]

Most of all Japan needed radar, the lack of which was to be a significant disadvantage in the forthcoming *Pacific War*. Yamashita left empty handed. "His [Hitler's] promise to show all his equipment was meaningless,"[6] complained Yamashita, who thought that Hitler behaved like a clerk. Hitler was also disappointed. He wanted Japan to declare war on Britain and America. Although his role was not diplomatic, Yamashita, never one to shy away from expressing his view, told the Germans that with the on-going *Second Sino-Japanese War*, Japan had its hands full with China and was also concerned about the Soviet threat on its northern Manchurian border. Yamashita, like many *Kodoha* (Imperial Way) officers, believed that the real threat to Japan's existence came from the Soviet Union rather than the United States. Only after Roosevelt threatened Japan with economic starvation and the loss of all it had won in China, did Yamashita and other *Kodoha* officers come to believe completely in the necessity for war against the United States.

Yamashita also managed a final visit to Vienna where a decade previously he had taken a German war widow, Kitty, the daughter of a general, as his mistress. He noted in his diary, ". . . in the afternoon Kitty came to see me. It was memorable."[7] It was a very rare personal moment in a life devoted to military duty. He came back from Germany convinced that the Japanese Army needed to modernize by increased mechanization, particularly with regard to the development of tank corps.

He also reported back to Imperial Army HQ that the use of airpower would be much more critical in future warfare than they had yet considered. Already on the Chinese Front, Yamashita had come to the conclusion that while the classic *banzai* charge might work against a low-grade Chinese Army, it would not work against more sophisticated infantry and modern weaponry. Much to Japan's future cost, General Tojo dismissed Yamashita's findings and recommendations. Yamashita's unusual interest in technological development did not prevent his adherence to traditional values. He was a fierce devotee of the Emperor. Indeed whenever he moved office, he reoriented his desk so that it would be facing the Imperial Palace. In spite of Tojo's disfavor, Yamashita's brilliance was not completely unrecognized. To win the war, Japan had need of its best commanders. On 6 November Yamashita was transferred again from northern China to take command of the Twenty-fifth Army and its planned defeat of the British Empire. He had just over a month to prepare.

Fortunately in Lieutenant-Colonel Masanobu Tsuji, Chief of Staff, Operations and Planning, Yamashita possessed a brilliant if frequently insubordinate and politically scheming officer. Tsuji, who was to develop a reputation for his unsavoury savagery toward conquered peoples, was nevertheless a supremely hard working and astute tactician. A Control Faction fanatic, Tsuji even took a vow not to indulge in sex, alcohol or tobacco until *Singapore* was captured. As a Control Faction member and ally of Tojo, Tsuji was not a reliable supporter of Yamashita. Yamashita, commentating on Tsuji in his diary, wrote that he "is egotistical and wily. He is a sly dog and unworthy to serve the country. He is a manipulator to be carefully watched."[8] Tsuji who had trained in jungle warfare on *Formosa* had come to the conclusion that *Singapore* was most vulnerable from the *Johor Straits* from the north. The Taiwan Army Research Unit (*Doro Nawa*) under the direction of Tsuji undertook a detailed terrain analysis of the Malay Peninsula and carried out covert reconnaissance flights. It was noted that roads on the Malay Peninsula were mainly concentrated down through Kuala Lumpur on the west coast and Tsuji assumed correctly that the British forces would rely heavily on moving their forces along these axis points. The Japanese therefore planned to outflank the British Army either by amphibious assault or by flanking movements, moving infantry through the jungle on bicycles.

Having learnt from Germany, Yamashita supported this strategy with overwhelming air support. The 3rd Air Division provided 459 aircraft and a further 159 carrier-based airplanes also supported the invasion force. The invasion fleet set out from the southern Chinese island of *Hainan* picking up further forces at Saigon in Vietnam, where, over eighteen months previously, the Japanese had strong-armed France's *Nazi*-supporting Vichy government into giving them use of military and naval bases as well as the right to station up to 25,000 troops in the country.

Complacency and Weakness of British Air Defenses: Civilians in *Singapore* remained steeped in the complacency that seemed to characterize British Malaya's attitude to impending war. Maisie Prout remembered, "We were so sure that the British forces would mop up the Japanese in no time. We thought they wouldn't get much further. According to British propaganda, the Japanese were all bow-legged and squinty-eyed and they all had very bad teeth . . . they would be annihilated before they reached Kuala Lumpur."[9] A sense of racial superiority underlay British war planning throughout the Far East. As late as January 1938, Winston Churchill declared: "It is quite certain that Japan cannot possibly compete with the productive energies of either branch of the English speaking peoples."[10]

Complacency abounded at all levels of the British Army. Senior British officers in Malaya had never made a serious attempt to understand the nature of the terrain in which they were stationed. There was no guidance from Malaya Command on how to fight in the jungle. Most British officers simply assumed that the jungle was not a terrain in which fighting could take place. British tactics amounted to no more than to hold the open ground around major routes and at bridges. Troops were to be trucked from one static position to another.

There were just a few British officers who disagreed with this approach. Lieutenant-Colonel Ian Stewart, commanding officer of the 2nd Battalion of the Argyll and Sutherland Highlanders stationed on *Singapore Island*, took his troops up country to the jungles, plantations and mangrove swamps. Stewart's young subaltern, David Wilson, noted, "There was talk of 'impenetrable' jungle, 'unfordable rivers' and the like, but in fact the countryside in which we were to operate was almost entirely cultivated plantations of rubber and palm with well-developed roads and estate tracks."[11] After the debacles in Malaya and Burma both Stewart and Wilson would go to lecture at Indian training colleges about jungle warfare and they played a significant role in rebuilding the fighting expertise of the Indian Army.

Explanations for British military complacency are various. Aside from the innate sense of racial superiority, peacetime ossification of military command was clearly a factor. There were more understandable explanations too; a captured British captain explained to Colonel Tsuji that they were confident of holding up the Japanese for months in northern Malaya, because ". . . the Japanese Army had not beaten the weak Chinese Army after four years fighting in China we did not consider it [Japan] a very formidable enemy."[12] The confidence of British military aviators was equally misplaced. Although there were twenty-one airfields in *Singapore* and Malaya, few of them boasted modern facilities and only fifteen of them had concrete runways. In heavy rain, grass airstrips became unusable. All the airfields were each allocated eight heavy and eight light anti-aircraft guns. However, by the end of 1941 only 17 percent of the promised guns had been supplied. The number and quality of operational radar units was also inadequate. Even more importantly the Chief of Staff informed Air Chief Marshal Sir Robert Brooke-Popham, Commander in Chief for the Far East, in mid-September 1941 that the plan to have 336 aircraft by the end of 1941 could not be met. Far East Command was also short of experienced pilots. Indeed in the nine months to September 1941, Far East Command suffered sixty-seven accidents, twenty-two of which ended in planes being written off while thirty-one others were described as resulting in serious damage.

Malaya's defenses were reliant on many out-dated hand-me-down aircraft. Air-Chief Marshal Brooke-Popham made light of any deficiencies in the available equipment, "Let England have the 'Super' Spitfire and the 'Hyper' Hurricane, 'Buffaloes' are quite good enough for Malaya."[13] Even the Brewster Buffaloes were in short supply, however. The Brewster 339 Buffalo was a development of the first American monoplane fighter, which replaced the Grumman F3F bi-plane fighter. Although it was introduced in 1939, the Brewster, as a result of its weight, immediately disappointed. Of the 144 fighter aircraft available to the British in Malaya there were only 44 Buffaloes with the remaining aircraft being even more antique.

The version of the Buffalo used by the Royal Air Force (RAF) had been given a more powerful engine that was regarded as being beyond the limits of its airframe with the result that speed, climb, manoeuvrability and ceiling were all deleteriously affected. Fitted with two 0.30 mm guns and 2x 0.50 mm cannons that fired through the synchronized propellers, the Brewster Buffalo was also considered to be under-gunned. About 20 mph slower than the Mitsubishi A6M Zero, the Buffalo's rate of climb of 2,400 feet per second was poor compared to the Zeros' 3,100 feet per second. The Buffalo's range of 960 miles was also half that of the Zero. Moreover as a night fighter it was, according to one pilot, "hopeless because the flames from the exhaust stubs of the engine of the Buffalo could not be dampened, and the enemy could see me coming miles off, whilst I could not see them!"[14]

Nevertheless it had some defenders. Dutch pilot, Captain Pieter Tideman thought, "the Brewster was a good, sturdy, fast fighter with two half inch armor plates behind the seat. She would take a hell of a lot of beating."[15] In the event the Zero (introduced in 1940) and the Army Nakajima-43 (1941) did give them a 'hell of a beating.' One year was a long time in the rapidly developing technology of aircraft manufacture and there was no question that the Japanese planes were at least two years ahead of the hand-me-down equipment provided to Allied forces in Asia at the start of the *Pacific War*.

The less famous Nakajima *Hayabusa* (Peregrine Falcon) was the standard Army fighter known as the 'Oscar' and used the same Ki-43 radial engine as the Zero. Like the Zero, it was light, easy to fly and highly manoeuvrable. Because of it similar profile, it was sometimes called the Army Zero. The 'Oscar' also suffered the same deficiencies in being relatively under-armed and lacking defensive armor. But the 'Oscar' scored more kills during the *Pacific War* than any other aircraft including its more famous sibling, the Mitsubishi Zero. In total 5,919 Nakajima 'Oscars' were produced by the end of the war.

The ease with which the Nakajima Ki-43 overcame Allied opposition probably helped to take Japan down the wrong design track in terms of the development of their fighter aircraft. The *Battles of Nomonhan* against the Soviets had shown that power, armament, dive speed and armor for pilots and fuel tanks were more important than maneuverability. The Japanese military failed to learn these lessons and instead of developing the heavier and bigger engined Nakajima 'Tojo' Ki-44 *Shoki* (Zhong Kui: Demon Killer, top speed 376 mph versus 329 mph for the Ki-43) they chose maneuverability over power—probably because for the pilots, the lighter Ki-43 'Oscar' was more enjoyable to fly and was more effective in the early days of the war when traditional one-on-one dogfights were the tactical norm in air duels. As Dimitar Nedialkov concludes in his study of the air battles *In the Skies of Nomonhan* [2011], ". . . as often happens in military establishments, the Japanese war machine did not respond properly [to the Ki-44 'Tojo' attributes] and this powerful and rapid fighter was displaced by the Nakajima Ki-43 *Hayabusa* [Peregrine Falcon] which shared its earlier and smaller brother's [Nakajima Ki-27 'Nate'] shortcomings."[16]

During the war Nakajima produced just one Ki-44 'Tojo' for every five Ki-43 'Oscars'. In terms of aircraft design, Japan's armed forces took a wrong turn in persisting with lightweight maneuverable fighter aircraft—though arguably Japan's lack of resources in terms of metals and production capacity made their choice inevitable. By contrast the United States decision to make more robust, heavily armed fighter aircraft such as the Hellcat and Corsair was the better longer-term call.

Similarly Squadron Leader G. B. M. Bell fondly recalled: "We were equipped with Brewster Buffaloes, an American aircraft designed for use on carriers and at that time discarded by the US Navy as obsolete. However, we were proud to be flying the Buffalo which was, despite it obsolescence, modern when compared to the other aircraft with which the Command was equipped."[17] Moreover, not only was the supply of modern planes non-existent but there was an inadequate supply of munitions. Fighter pilots had to practice air gunnery with no bullets. Beer bottles were dropped to simulate bombs. As Sergeant Peter Ballard recalled, "What silly games we played!"[18]

The Royal Air Force (RAF)'s Bristol Blenheim Bombers (introduced 1937) and the Lockheed Hudson (introduced in 1939 but based on the Canadian Lockheed-14) were also inferior in quality to the Japanese Navy's twin-engine Mitsubishi G3M 'Nell' (1936), Mitsubishi G4M 'Betty' (1941) and its Army's heavier bomber, the Mitsubishi Ki-21 'Sally' (1938). Although the British bombers had the advantage of protective armor and self-sealing fuel tanks, with just two or three machine guns, they were poorly armed for defense. The Japanese bombers with their lighter more modern construction could fly 3,000 miles compared to less than half that for a Blenheim. Most importantly with a speed of between 255mph and 265mph the British bombers could not outrun the Japanese fighters that were to prove their nemesis.

Many Allied pilots would have read an American magazine article entitled *Japan's Bush League Air Force* that rubbished Japanese pilots as only fit to fly light aircraft, while their aircraft manufacturers were written off simply as producers of cheap 'knock-offs' of western models. Remarkably, articles such as this were given credence at a time when information was available that the new Mitsubishi A6M Zero had effectively destroyed Chiang Kai-shek's Chinese Air Force a year earlier. The appearance of Zero should not therefore have been such a shock. In 1940 western observers had sent back reports from Japan, China and Indochina regarding the appearance of a remarkable new fighter aircraft. There was clearly more than a touch of racial superiority in the widely held belief that the 'Nip' could neither build a better aircraft nor fly better than his western counterpart. Indeed, as the war started, stories circulated suggesting that Germans were flying Japanese planes.

Not only were the British aircraft in Malaya antique in a field of rapidly developing technology, but also supplies of newer fighters, such as the Hurricane and Spitfire that had just seen off General Herman Göring's attempt to defeat Great Britain by air in the *Battle of Britain*, were not forthcoming. Although production was being rapidly ramped up under Lord Beaverbrook's direction (aircraft production increased by 153 percent in the two years to 1941), the Middle East was given absolute priority. Commitments to supply the Soviet Union with fighters also took precedence to the Far East. The Allies were terrifyingly aware that keeping the Soviet Union in the war was an essential prerequisite to an invasion of France and an early defeat of Hitler. Thus, although British aircraft production exceeded that of Germany by 39 percent in 1940 (15,049:10,826) and by 62 percent in 1941 (20,094:12,401), precious little was to be made available to the British forces in *Singapore* and Malaya. **[Charts: C.14, C.15]**

In contrast to his days at the Admiralty, by mid-1941 Churchill had become one of the few realists with regard to British prospects in the Far East. *Hong Kong* he expected to lose and *Singapore* was always a doubt. He had prophesied that he "expected terrible forfeits in the East; but all this would be merely a passing phase."[19] Even he did not anticipate the scale of the military catastrophe to come.

Japanese air superiority was quickly established on 8 December. Japanese bombers stationed in Vietnam bombed *Singapore*. More importantly the Royal Air Force (RAF) defense capability in northern Malaya was quickly reduced. The supremacy of the Japanese fighters, the Mitsubishi Zero and the Nakajima Ki-43 'Oscar,' delivered arguably the biggest psychological shock to the western defenders of Malaya at the start of the *Pacific War*. The aerial dominance of the Zero and the 'Oscar' in the air served to undermine the morale of the British infantryman on the ground. As historian H. P. Wilmot has observed, "in the opening phase of the war the Zero-sen was just what the Japanese needed, and the Allies were devastated by the appearance of a 'super fighter.' "[20]

Although lightly armed with single or double 12.7 mm (0.5-inch) machine guns and poorly protected by armor, the highly maneuverable Japanese fighters overwhelmed the RAF's Buffaloes. After dispatching the British fighter cover the Bristol Blenheim and Lockheed Hudson bombers as well as the obsolete Vickers Vildebeest torpedo bomber were easily destroyed by Japan's 'Oscars,' Zeros and 'Nates.' Within three days the RAF in Northern Malaysia had effectively been wiped out. With the airfields secured, the Japanese Army Air Force could cover Yamashita's southern advance down the Malay Peninsula. The captured British airfields also provided bases from which to bomb *Singapore*.

Invasion of Thailand and Malaya: Two days earlier on 6 December Japanese armed convoys had been spotted in Thailand's coastal waters. Still there was no alarm in *Singapore*. In part the British may have succumbed to the delusion that the Japanese would never attack during the November to February monsoon season. Commander in Chief, Sir Robert Brooke-Popham publicly continued to play down the likelihood of war that was much speculated about in the press. In Fleet Street, the *Sunday Times* had demanded, "Why, if Japan's intentions are honorable and peaceful, does she send twenty-seven transports, heavily laden with troops, even to Siam?"[21] Even in private Brooke-Popham was confident. Two days before the Japanese invasion, he told his cipher clerk, Mrs. Muriel Reilly, "You can take it from me there will never be a Japanese bomb dropped in *Singapore*—there will never be a Japanese set foot in Malaya."[22] Similarly, Churchill, when asked by a young sub-lieutenant whether Japan would attack, while he was coming back across the *Atlantic* from a meeting with Roosevelt, was equally confident, at least in public, that Japan would not dare attack Britain or America: "No I don't think so. If they do, they'll find they've bitten off more than they can chew."[23]

Just after midnight on 8 December, almost an hour and a half before Yamamoto's planes arrived to bomb *Pearl Harbor*, Indian soldiers observed the shadowy forms of troop transports dropping anchor off Kota Bharu. In *Singapore* General Percival gave the news to the Governor, Sir Shenton Thomas; seemingly unconcerned Thomas said to Percival, "Well, I suppose you'll shove the little men off."[24] Bombardment began half an hour later; the 'strike south' phase of the *Pacific War* had begun. Contrary to common perception the first bombs of the *Pacific War* were dropped on Malaya not *Pearl Harbor*.

At 1.00 a.m., 5,300 infantry headed for the beaches of Kota Bharu. Troops also landed on the east coast of the southern provinces of Thailand at Pattani and Songkhla. From here they advanced toward Jitri on the west coast of Malaya.

The *Battle of Kota Bharu* was fought on the beaches of Malaya by elements of the 9th Infantry Division under Major-General Barstow. The two beaches, split by the *Pengkalan Chapa River*, led inland to the strategically important Kota Bharu Airfield and the roads that led inland and across to the west coast. The 8th Infantry Brigade under Brigadier 'Billy' Key had fortified the narrow beaches with pillboxes, barbed wire and land mines. After fierce fighting in which the Japanese landing forces took heavy losses, a breach was made in the beach defenses. By the afternoon of 8 December, Japanese Twenty Fifth Army troops had exploited these gaps to the extent that Brigadier Key asked permission to withdraw.

The Royal Air Force (RAF) Hudson bombers flew seventeen sorties from Kota Bharu Airfield sinking the *Awazisan Maru* transport ship and leaving others damaged. Two Hudsons were shot down. One Japanese account recorded a British suicide attack:

> One British aircraft which attacked the landing parties was heavily damaged by AA fire from the shore. So badly damaged, in fact, that the pilot must have known his chances of getting back to base were slender. He turned his limping aircraft round in the face of the Japanese fire, flew back to the beach, positioned himself over one of the largest of the landing barges, and then deliberately turned the nose of his aircraft down in a power dive. The aircraft struck the landing barge with a terrific impact. As a result, all 60 of the Japanese soldiers aboard were either killed outright or drowned as their craft sank.[25]

The first *kamikaze* pilot of the war was British.

It was a disastrous first day of aerial encounters. Far from being a joke as perceived by the British, the Japanese Army and Navy Air Forces had provided the cutting edge to Japan's invasion of Thailand and Malaya. As General Percival grimly commented, "The rapidity with which the Japanese got their air attacks going against our aerodromes was quite remarkable. Practically all the aerodromes in Kelantan, Kedah, Province Wellesley, and Penang, were attacked, and in most cases fighters escorted the bombers. The performance of Japanese aircraft of all types, and the accuracy of their bombing, came as an unpleasant surprise. By the evening our own air force had already been seriously weakened."[26] During the night Lieutenant-Colonel Arthur Cumming's 2nd Battalion of 12th Frontier Force Regiment fought a rear-guard action to hold the airfield for which he was later awarded the Victoria Cross. However, after causing the Japanese some 800 casualties (320 killed) versus 465 allied casualties (105 killed or missing) Brigadier Key was forced to withdraw. By Japanese accounts it was the heaviest fighting of the Malay campaign and showed what traditional well-prepared fortifications could achieve. At the same time as Kota Bharu was being fought over, Lieutenant-General Arthur Percival authorized Operation KROHCOL whereby British forces crossed into Thailand to intercept the Japanese forces that had landed at Pattani Beach. However, the Japanese 5th Division easily pushed back the British force.

By 22 December 1941, just two weeks after the start of the war, the denouement of the British Air Force (RAF) in northern Malaya was complete. In the biggest dogfight yet over Malaya, fifteen Buffaloes from 453 Squadron based at Kuala Lumpur were set upon by eighteen Nakajima 'Oscars' of the 64th *Sentai* (combat group) and later by the 59th *Sentai* (squadron). In the fighting that followed only three Buffaloes survived and the remnants of 453 Squadron were merged with Royal Australian Air Force (RAAF) 21-Squadron Flight.

Three days later news filtered through to the Allied forces in Malaya that *Hong Kong* had fallen. The defensive Gin Drinkers Line on the mainland had been quickly overrun and Major-General Christopher Maltby was forced to retreat to *Hong Kong*. After eighteen days of fighting, the Governor of *Hong Kong*, Sir Mark Aitchison Young, surrendered to Lieutenant-General Takashi Sakai on Christmas Day. The 14,000 strong British forces suffered 2,113 dead and over 2,000 wounded. As a result of the extreme brutality meted out to the British colony, after the war, General Sakai faced charges at the Chinese War Crimes Military Tribunal and was found guilty and executed by firing squad in August 1946. **[See Chapter 8: Battle of Hong Kong]**

Admiral Phillips and the Naval Reinforcement of the Far East Fleet: A far greater catastrophe was now visited on the British Empire. On 2 December Admiral Sir Thomas 'Tom Thumb' Phillips (so small that he had to stand on a box on the bridge of his ship) arrived in *Singapore* with the battleship HMS *Prince of Wales* accompanied by HMS *Repulse*, a reliable and well-armed if somewhat out-dated battle-cruiser, that had been launched shortly after the *Battle of Jutland* in 1916. Equipped with six 15-inch guns in three turrets, the *Repulse* had a nine-inch armor belt.

Launched in 1939, the *Prince of Wales* was the pride of the fleet. Capable of cruising at twenty-eight knots, the new battleship was armed with ten 14-inch guns, sixteen 5.25-inch guns, forty-two 40 mm 'pom-pom' anti-aircraft guns and seven 20 mm Oerlikon guns, and a single 40 mm Bofors, perhaps the most effective anti-aircraft gun of the period. In spite of this armament it was considered that the number of anti-aircraft guns was insufficient. A 14.7-inch upper belt of armor protected her. However, as on the *Repulse*, the armor belts were designed to protect ships from shells not torpedoes. In 1941 in the eastern *Atlantic*, the *Prince of Wales* had engaged with the great German battleship *Bismarck* and scored three hits on her, before torpedoes launched from antiquated Fairey Swordfish, biplanes from a foregone era, disabled the pride of the German fleet. It should have been a portent. Even the greatest of capital ships was vulnerable to torpedoes.

Although in hindsight Phillips has come to be considered a controversial choice for the role of Commander in Chief of the Eastern Fleet, at the time the selection of a man renowned for his intelligence, and holding the post of Vice-Chief of the Naval Staff, was perfectly sensible. Field Marshal Smuts thought he was an "admirable choice,"[27] and continued to praise him after his death. American Commander in Chief of the Asiatic Fleet, Admiral Thomas Hart described him "as good an Englishman to work with as I have had for some time."[28] He was evidently a good 'office' admiral. According to Captain Bell, Phillips "had a knack of getting along well with others outside the Navy: the services, civil servants, diplomats, and particularly foreign naval officers."[29] Whether he was as good a fighting officer was another matter. He was certainly not liked by 'fighting admirals' in the Navy such as Vice-Admiral Sir Geoffrey Layton. Nevertheless on certain strategic issues, Phillips has been proved correct even if his opinions were ignored at the time. He had strongly asserted the need for tanks in Malaya and had doubted the virtues of the Brewster Buffalo, suggesting instead that the Hurricane be sent to the Far East. But, in spite of this interest in the air war, he seems to have been slower than some in the British Navy to accept the airborne threat to capital ships. Thus the proposal by Flight-Lieutenant Tom Vigors, to provide Z Force with the cover of six fighters, albeit still an inadequate number, was turned down.

This was not the naval force originally planned for *Singapore*. Unfortunately for Admiral Phillips, the brand new carrier HMS *Indomitable* had not been able to join the Navy force sent to *Singapore* because she had run aground in the middle of trials in the *Caribbean*. Regardless of this misfortune, *Indomitable*, unlike the *Prince of Wales*, was never considered an essential component of Britain's Far Eastern Fleet. There were other problems faced by Z Force. Extreme humidity had caused the failure of the *Prince of Wales*' analogue, electro-mechanical computer that guided the battleship's anti-aircraft batteries. There was not enough time to fix it before the *Prince of Wales* set off to engage the invading Japanese amphibious forces; the result was that Britain's technologically world-leading anti-aircraft High Angle Control System (HACS) could not be used.

Whether the *Prince of Wales* and the *Repulse* should have been sent to *Singapore* at all is open to question. The Admiralty was dead set against it. With some accuracy Captain William Davis and his colleagues had outlined the risks involved:

> We in Plans and Operations Foreign [in the Admiralty] were solidly against sending out *Prince of Wales* to the Far East, as it were almost by herself, as also was the First Sea Lord who argued strongly against the wisdom of dispatching a wholly unbalanced force into an area where we did not know the strengths or capabilities of the potential enemy. We suggested that such action would make *Prince of Wales* a hostage to fortune.[30]

However, Winston Churchill insisted on a show of defiance with more than a hint of deterrence attached. The British Prime Minister felt it was necessary to keep in with the Americans. In a speech at the Mansion House on 10 November, Churchill affirmed,

". . . this movement of our naval forces, in conjunction with the United States main fleet, may give a practical proof to all who have eyes that the forces of freedom and democracy have not by any means reached the limits of their power."[31] It was a gesture that was a pale shadow of the interwar plan to send the main fleet to *Singapore* in case of a conflict with Japan. It was a gesture that was too little too late. As such, the sending of the *Prince of Wales* to *Singapore* can be marked down as a blunder on Churchill's part.

Nevertheless Z Force, led by the *Prince of Wales*, which had arrived in *Singapore* in high optimism and not a little complacency, left port confident of success. As Richard Smith, a 19-year-old rating on the *Repulse* remembered:

> Everybody was told that the Japanese fleet was absolutely useless and that it was just a lot of rice paper and string. We would go up there and knock them about and cause havoc—it would be a walkover and we would enjoy ourselves. This was the whole mentality when we were lying in the harbor with all lights on. Everybody was ashore wining and dining and all the colonials we saw were making merry and having a wonderful time. The fleet had arrived and Japan would not now enter the war.[32]

If the sending of the *Prince of Wales* had been intended as a deterrent, it did not work. British press hyperbole regarding the arrival of the great new ship simply alerted the Japanese to the threat. In response Admiral Yamamoto diverted two heavy cruisers to his Southern Force. Having expected that there would only be one capital ship to face the British Z Force, Phillips now faced a Japanese fleet that was more powerful. More importantly in terms of the outcome of the battle, the Kanoya Air Group, that performed a major role in the battle, was transferred from *Formosa* to Saigon. Without a carrier or cruisers and with too few destroyers, Phillips's Z Force was considered by many senior officers to be unbalanced and vulnerable; that opinion was formed before the attack on *Pearl Harbor* precipitated a quantum shift in the perception of the threat of aircraft to battleships.

The Naval Battle of Malaya: The Sinking of HMS Prince of Wales: [Map: 7.2] On 7

December 1941 the Admiralty, now fully aware that a Japanese strike somewhere in South East Asia was imminent, sent what has been considered a "prodding message" asking "What action it would be possible to take with naval or air forces."[33] Phillips replied that he would 'endeavor' to engage the enemy.

Z Force, under Admiral Phillips, headed toward northern Malaya to intercept the Japanese invasion fleet in an operation opposed by his deputy Vice-Admiral Sir Geoffrey Layton. The latter advised Phillips not to move "unless the Air Force could guarantee . . . reconnaissance and fighter protection."[34] Nevertheless, Phillips set sail to intercept the Japanese expeditionary forces in the full knowledge that the Japanese had bombers in the vicinity (based in Indochina) and that he could not rely on fighter support.

Vice-Air Marshal Pullford had not been able to give Philips any assurances that there would be any available air cover off Kota Bharu on 10 December. Indeed a few hours after leaving harbor, Phillips received a message from Pullford that read: "REGRET FIGHTER PROTECTION IMPOSSIBLE."[35]

In response Phillips is reported to have said, "Well, we must get on without it."[36] Thereafter Z Force, HMS *Prince of Wales* and the battle-cruiser HMS *Repulse*, with four accompanying destroyers, proceeded without land-based air cover and without communication in order to sustain radio silence. In hindsight it was an extraordinary decision that was both brave and foolhardy, though it could be argued that if he had not set sail to intercept Japan's amphibious forces, he would also have faced harsh criticism from some quarters and possibly even court martial. That night, in the officers' wardroom, a journalist noted the complacency of the British officers who ". . . don't think the enemy is much good. They could not beat China for five years . . ."[37]

London certainly expected action as the prodding message, undoubtedly supported by Churchill, clearly indicated. First Sea Lord, Admiral Sir Dudley Pound would subsequently continue to support Phillips's actions; to Lady Phillips he wrote that the Board of the Admiralty were unanimous in their support for his embarkation and he concluded, "It might well have been a brilliant success."[38] Quite possibly however, Pound was soft-soaping Admiral Phillips's widow in her hour of bereavement. By contrast Churchill would later claim that after *Pearl Harbor*, it was his intention that "they [*Prince of Wales* and *Repulse*] should go across the *Pacific* to join what was left of the American Fleet."[39] It was not an account that tallies with his speech to the House of Commons on 8 December at 3.00 p.m., some two hours after Phillips had set sail, in which he said, "some of the finest ships of the Royal Navy have reached their stations in the Far East . . . and I do not doubt that we shall give a good account of ourselves."[40] It seems likely that both Churchill and the Admiralty knew about Phillips's course of action though they may not have been aware of the limitations of Z Force's fighter support.

Having failed to find the Japanese invasion force, Phillips turned back toward *Singapore*. He must have realized the mistake he had made because on the evening of 9 December he told Engineering Officer, Commander L. J. Goudy that he would "never again put capital ships in the position we are now in."[41] It was too late. At 2.40 a.m. on 10 December, a Japanese submarine signaled: "A battleship is in flight to *Singapore* at a speed of twenty knots. We hope to intercept it fifty miles south of the Anambas Islands."[42] All the while Japanese submarines and seaplanes had tracked Admiral Phillips's force. Without the British knowing it, in the early hours of 10 December, Japanese submarine *I-58* had fired five torpedoes at the Z Force but they had all missed. By good planning, *I-58*, which had been placed on picket to watch out for the emergence of Z Force from *Singapore*, radioed ahead the fact of the British fleet's departure. Although the *Prince of Wales* had survived *I-58*s torpedo attack, Japan's naval and air commanders were nevertheless alerted to her presence.

At 10.00 a.m. the S-Class destroyer HMS *Tenedos*, which had been dispatched from Z Force and was some 140 miles to the southeast, survived an attack by Japanese

Mitsubishi G3M 'Nell' medium bombers from Saigon. The 'Nell' could carry either 1,700 lbs of bombs or one Type-93 aerial torpedo. At 11.13 a.m. eight 'Nell' bombers scored a hit on the *Repulse* with a 250 lb bomb that exploded in the Marine quarters but the damage and casualties were not severe. Heavy anti-aircraft fire damaged five of the attackers. Half an hour later, seventeen more 'Nell' bombers from *Genzen* Air Group attacked both of the British capital ships scoring at least two torpedo hits on the *Prince of Wales* at 11.44 a.m. as it turned to try to avoid them. One torpedo hit the port side forward of the aft 14-inch gun turret. The second torpedo exploded on the hull at the point of exit of the port-side propeller screw and immediately the *Prince of Wales* took on water through a twelve-foot gash. ". . . I have a vivid memory of her just keeling over as she was hit," recalled Richard Poole watching the *Prince of Wales* from on board the *Repulse*, "and an enormous column of dirty, grey water shot up close to her stern."[43] Worse still for the *Prince of Wales*, the torpedo had destroyed the bracket that held the 17.5-inch diameter propeller shaft in place. The wildly churning propeller shaft tore apart the shaft alley and thousands of tons of water poured in. She was soon listing at eleven degrees.

The stern hit, where the screws, shafts and boilers are located, is one of the 'Achilles heels' of naval ships. Germany's greatest battleship, *Bismarck*, was similarly disabled as a result of a stern shot and at the end of the war, the behemoth Japanese battleship *Yamato* would also succumb in this manner. The *Prince of Wales'* subsequent reputation as a 'Jonah' ship was never fair. She was a great ship that took a hit at her weakest point. However, even if she had been able to make it back to *Singapore*, it seems likely that the damage might still have put her at the mercy of Japanese bombing attacks. The *Prince of Wales* would probably not have survived the fall of *Singapore* and might even have fallen into enemy hands to be used against the Allies.

The *Prince of Wales'* list started to degrade its defense capabilities. Anti-aircraft guns on her port side could not now achieve enough elevation to defend the battleship. In addition speed dropped to just sixteen knots. At 12.20 p.m. a further attack by the Kanoya Air Group's Mitsubishi G4M 'Betty' bombers (the Imperial Royal Navy's main land-based anti-shipping strike aircraft) scored four more torpedo hits on the *Prince of Wales*, holing her from stem to stern. Sub-Lieutenant Geoffrey Brooke, along with other crewmembers watched helpless; Brooke remembered thinking, "There goes my cabin."[44] The remaining 'Bettys' scored a torpedo hit on the *Repulse* amidships.

Lieutenant Sadao Takai, leading Genzan Combat Group's 2nd *Chutai* (combat group), expressed the surprise of all of his colleagues that:

> All the crewmembers searched the sky vigilantly for the enemy fighters, which we expected would be diving in to attack us at any moment. Much to our surprise, not a single enemy plane was in sight. This was all the more amazing since the scene of the battle was well within the fighting range of the British fighters.[45]

Shortly after the holing of the *Prince of Wales*, the *Repulse*, which had thus far taken one torpedo hit and avoided nineteen, was cornered by a pincer attack by nine 'Bettys' from the *Kanoya* Group on port and starboard sides and took four torpedoes in her flanks. One of Group Leader Lieutenant Iki Haruki's pilots told him afterwards, "As we dived for the attack, I didn't want to launch my torpedo. It was such a beautiful ship, such a beautiful ship."[46] Lieutenant Herb Plenty, who watched the action from above in his Hudson bomber, noted that "The efficacy of splitting into elements to attack simultaneously from different directions was not lost on subsequent Japanese leaders. Five minutes later three more squadrons were in position; individual pilots flew in from different directions. *Repulse* was confronted with a criss-cross of torpedoes. We counted three explosions. A list quickly developed."[47] An older ship, without watertight compartments, the *Repulse* soon took on water. Captain Tennant immediately ordered his crew to abandon ship, saying, "Save yourselves and good luck."[48] Within ten minutes of being hit, the *Repulse* rolled over and sank at 12.33 p.m. Midshipman R. I. Davies staying at his 20 mm Oerlikon fired on the Japanese 'Bettys' to the last and went down with his gun. As she sank there was a chorus of three cheers from the crew in the water.

Eight minutes later the Japanese made their last attack of the day. A squadron of eight 'Nells' from the *Mihiro* Group each carrying a 1,100 lb bomb attacked the *Prince of Wales*. Five of the attackers were damaged but a single bomb hit aft exploding under the catapult deck. More importantly, it put out of action the last remaining boiler. Now dead in the water, the battleship soon started to list even more to port and the destroyer HMS *Express* came alongside to take off her crew. At 13.13 p.m. the *Prince of Wales* capsized almost taking the *Express* with it. For the loss of just three aircraft, Japan had effectively destroyed British naval power in Asia. Both of Britain's capital ships had succumbed to aerial torpedoes launched at long range. Indeed their defense against torpedo bombers which was to put up a fixed barrage of fire where shells would explode at a pre-determined range failed because the Japanese bombers were able to drop their torpedoes at a much farther range than had previously been considered possible.

The sinking of the *Prince of Wales* was another devastating demonstration of Japan's prowess in torpedo technology. Japan's marine engineers had developed world-leading technology for its aerial Type-91 torpedoes with sophisticated anti-roll fins and a PID (Proportional-integral-derivative) controller which dramatically increased range and accuracy and enabled attacks in open sea conditions. Historically, the British, with their strong naval tradition had been thought to be the world leaders in torpedo technology. Japan's aerial Type-91 literally blew this reputation out of the water. British ship-launched torpedoes were even more outclassed by Japan's Type-93 pure oxygen fueled Long Lance torpedoes. By comparison, at the start of the war, the British twenty-one inch Mark VIII, which ran on oxygen-enriched air, was 6.5m long, with a 750lb warhead (30 percent less than the Type-93) and a range of just 4,500m (one-sixth the range of the Type-93). The Mark VIII could travel at forty knots (20 percent slower than the Type-93) and produced a noticeable wake compared to the Long Lance.

Richard Poole, a young officer on the *Repulse*, recalled his first sighting of a Type-91, "It's quite frightening to see this enormous thing with 1,000 lb of TNT in the head coming straight at you . . ."[49] American torpedoes were similarly outclassed even when they worked, which, at the beginning of the war was a rare occurrence. **[See Appendix A: Submarines: America Draws Tight the Noose]**

Admiral Philips, Captain John Leach and a number of other senior officers decided to go down with the *Prince of Wales*. Before the end Phillips was heard to say, "I cannot survive this."[50] In addition to Phillips the *Prince of Wales* lost nineteen officers and 307 crew while 24 officers and 486 crew were lost on the *Repulse*. HMS *Vampire* rescued Captain William Tennant of the *Repulse*.

In the aftermath of the battle it was widely questioned why Phillips had not called for air cover. Disputes on this subject are still alive today. There are numbers of explanations including the lack of time to get off a message, damage to the *Prince of Wales* communications, fear of breaking radio silence, complacency over the flying skills of the Japanese who he may have assumed to be 'Italian' rather than 'German,' or simply a mistake as a result of exhaustion. Whatever the truth, the *Prince of Wales* went down with the British Admiral. His assistant private secretary later speculated, "I can only surmise that T. P. thought it was pointless to call for something [aircraft cover] which was not available."[51] Had the Buffaloes arrived in time, despite their deficiencies when faced with the Zero, there is reason to believe that they could have seen off unescorted Japanese 'Nells' and 'Bettys.'

The next morning First Sea Lord, Sir Dudley Pound, called Winston Churchill to give him the news. He recalled:

> In all the war, I never received a more direct shock . . . As
> I turned over and twisted in bed, the full horror of the news
> sank in upon me. There were no British or American ships
> in the Indian Ocean or the Pacific except the American
> survivors of Pearl Harbor, who were hastening back to
> California. Over all this vast expanse of waters Japan was
> supreme, and we everywhere were weak and naked.[52]

In *Singapore*, Duff Cooper, Resident Cabinet Minister, tried to strike a balance between realism and stoicism, by saying that not much had changed over a month, "We were not safe then; we are not safe now. But in these great days, safety seems hardly honorable and danger is glorious."[53] By contrast Hitler was ecstatic at the news of Japan's naval victory and promptly declared war on the United States. On hearing of the sinking of the *Prince of Wales*, the normally taciturn, expressionless Admiral Yamamoto broke into a large smile though he later confided over a game of *shogi* (Japanese chess), "In spite of this new victory today, our success cannot possibly continue for more than a year . . . I feel great sympathy for the British commander who apparently went down with the *Prince of Wales*. The same thing may happen to me someday in the not-too-distant future."[54]

The *Battle of Malaya* as the Japanese called this naval engagement showed that even the most modern high-speed battleships were completely exposed to aerial attack. The vulnerability of battleships at anchor had been demonstrated two days earlier at *Pearl Harbor*, but this was the first time that capital ships, while at sea, had been sunk by aircraft alone. Admiral Phillips had not believed that Japanese aircraft could operate so far from land, and like many of his colleagues in the British Royal Navy, he hugely underestimated Japan's new aircraft as well as their pilots' fighting capabilities. However, he could not reasonably have been blamed for lack of knowledge of Japan's secret weapon, the Type-91 torpedo, and its destructive power.

A bitter Tom Vigors, whose squadron of Buffaloes arrived on the scene just as the *Prince of Wales* sank, later reflected,

> I reckon this must have been the last battle in which the Navy reckoned they could get along without the RAF. A pretty damned costly way of learning. Phillips had known that he was being shadowed the night before, and also at dawn that day. He did not call for air support. He was attacked and still did not call for help.[55]

For the British Army, fighting the Japanese advance, the loss of the totemic *Prince of Wales* was a shattering blow to morale. From now on the Allied infantrymen would have to fight in the knowledge that they were cut off by sea from reinforcement or escape.

Preparations for the Defense of Malaya: Having destroyed the British Navy and Air Force within days, and after establishing an airbase at Kota Bharu, Japan's Twenty-fifth Army was now ready for its advance down the Malay Peninsula. The blimpish Major-General Bond, Percival's predecessor in *Singapore*, had thought that the short sightedness of Japanese troops was one of the reasons for their poor fighting ability and declared, "You can take it from me, we have little to fear."[56]

Lieutenant-General Arthur Percival, who had replaced Bond in May 1941, had a different opinion. Tall and spindly, Percival was also bucktoothed; strangely his appearance was like an English caricature of what a typical Japanese looked like. Born of a staunch middle-class family from Hertfordshire where his father was a successful land agent, Percival was solid and dependable. Academically average at Rugby School, he became a clerk for iron-ore merchants Naylor, Benzon & Company before joining the Army on the day that *World War I* broke out. As often happens in wartime his career progress was meteoric; he won a Military Cross, the *Croix de Guerre* and several mentions in dispatches. By the end of *World War I* he commanded a brigade and attained the rank of lieutenant-colonel. However, there were many, like Major John Wyett, who doubted his abilities as a commander or leader: "He was a mild-mannered, relatively useless fellow. I quite like him as an individual but he was utterly unable to cope with the situation he'd been placed in."[57]

On arriving in *Singapore* Percival was immediately alarmed by the lack of tanks and heavier equipment in Malaya. He demanded a minimum reinforcement of forty-eight infantry battalions as well as two tank battalions. Unlike some others he did not underestimate the Japanese. Colonel G. T. Wards, an assistant military *attaché*, who had witnessed, at first hand, Japanese military capability in China, wrote one of the briefing papers in Percival's Mission files. Wards described the Japanese Army "as a formidable force, well able to cope with any opposition likely to be met with at the present time in the Far East."[58] Wards was also convinced that Japan intended to expunge all western nations from Asia. As for Percival he soon came to the conclusion that *Singapore* would not be able to hold out for six months against such an enemy.

Percival was aware of the weaknesses of defense across the *Straits of Johor* and correctly predicted that the Japanese would attack through the southern provinces of Thailand. He made another prediction that was not far off the mark; in terms of the opportunities and dangers of his new job in *Singapore* he wrote,

> I realized that there was a double danger ... either of being left in an active command for some years if the war did not break out in the East or, if it did, of finding myself involved in a pretty sticky business with inadequate forces which are usually to be found in the distant parts of our Empire in the early stages of war.[59]

It was indeed going to be a sticky business. Even the usually optimistic Churchill was not altogether confident. "The idea of trying to defend the whole of the Malay Peninsula cannot be entertained,"[60] he told General Hasting Lionel 'Pug' Ismay, the Army Chief of Staff. South Africa's General Jan Smuts was also alarmed: "If the Japanese are really nippy there is an opening here for a first class disaster."[61] Nevertheless, Churchill had not been alone in thinking that the Japanese would not be foolish enough to attack the US and UK at the same time.

Arriving in Malaya on 16 May, little did Percival know that he had just 205 days to get *Singapore* into shape for an attack that by now was fully expected in private, if not in public. He set about the completion of *Singapore*'s defenses but immediately found obstacles put in the way by the War Office. They would only pay *Singapore* laborers forty-five cents per day, which was less than half the going rate. Inevitably work sputtered along. Chief Engineer Brigadier Ivan Simson, arriving in *Singapore* just before Percival, complained that senior commanders in *Singapore* were largely indifferent to the modernization of defenses; they had forgotten "the tremendous stopping power of barbed wire covered by fire from trenches and pillboxes."[62] Percival himself dismissed the importance of building defensive fortifications that he suggested might create a spirit of defeatism.

Perhaps most importantly Percival failed to get the *matériel* he needed from the UK. By midsummer 1941, the Far East's needs had fallen down the pecking order behind the Middle East and the Soviet Union, who Churchill was now bending over backwards to supply with the latest tanks and Hurricane fighters. From August 1941, Churchill had promised Stalin 250 tanks and 200 planes per month until June 1942. What would Percival have given for even one month's worth of this precious hoard?

Instead of *matériel*, in September 1941, Churchill had sent his Minister of Information to *Singapore* to oversee the defense of the island. The playboy politician Duff Cooper arrived to much fanfare with his wife, the great bohemian society beauty, Lady Diana Cooper, the illegitimate daughter of the Duchess of Rutland and the writer Henry Cust, who had been a stage actress, movie star and then pig farmer before her marriage. Duff Cooper's arrival did little to improve the defenses of *Singapore*. Indeed his presence was deeply resented by the Governor, Sir Shenton Thomas, and Sir Robert Brooke-Popham who had been appointed in November 1940 as Commander in Chief, British Far East Command. In spite of Brooke-Popham's position, the island's bureaucrats reported directly to London, as did the Royal Navy. The scheming and defeatist Colonial Secretary, Stanley Jones, further added to the dysfunctional management of Malaya. In a letter Lady Diana Cooper wrote, "There seems to me no defense at all . . . Today a little fleet arrived to help."[63]

From the outset Cooper was seen as Churchill's spy in *Singapore*, which of course he was. A stream of poisonous missives from Cooper about his colleagues soon followed. The *Singapore* establishment responded in kind. Shenton Thomas wrote to his boss Lord Moyne, the Secretary of State for the Colonies, "We felt we were being landed with a failure [Duff Cooper]. We remembered Sir Stafford Cripps's description of him as 'a petulant little pipsqueak.' "[64] The result was a highly confused, political and divided leadership in *Singapore*.

Churchill would eventually try to resolve the leadership dilemma by appointing General Wavell as head of American-British-Dutch-Australian Command (ABDA) in the *Southwest Pacific*. Duff Cooper refused to stay and serve under Wavell, being only too happy to leave a *Singapore* that he detested. In a parting shot, Duff Cooper advised Churchill and Lord Moyne, "There exists a widespread and profound lack of confidence in the administration. I believe that the simplest solution would be to declare a state of siege and appoint a military governor for the duration of the emergency."[65] However, the appointment of Wavell did little to solve the military problems facing Malaya. Churchill found the taciturn and inarticulate Wavell uninspiring and personally unappealing, while Wavell soon came to the conclusion that Percival was not up to the fight.

With the British forces now in retreat from Kota Bharu, Yamashita's Twenty-fifth Army moved westward unopposed towards the stronghold of *Penang Island*. With the other Japanese forces advancing from the northeast, the British residents were soon in danger of being cut off. On 17 December, *Penang*'s British residents abandoned the island and its inhabitants in undignified flight.

Asians were abandoned on the piers as only whites were allowed on the ferries to the mainland. Mrs. Muriel Reilly recalled, "It still hurts to think how the white race 'let down' hundreds of similarly faithful servants who trusted in us, and looked to us for protection from the hated Japanese."[66] Arms and supplies were left to the invaders to help themselves. Yamashita's lightly provisioned forces made good use of them. As for the local Malays and Chinese, many turned against their former colonial masters. It was a bitterness that lingered even after the hated Japanese had been removed from their shores. As the young *Singapore*an student Lee Kuan Yew, later the founding father of his country, observed, before the Japanese invasion of Malaya:

> The superior status of the British government and society was simply a fact of life. After all, they were the greatest people in the world. They had the biggest empire that history had ever known, stretching over all time zones, across all four oceans and five continents. We learnt that in history lessons at school . . . I was brought up by my parents and grandparents to accept that this was the natural order of things.[67]

Japan's 'Bicycle Blitzkrieg': [Map: 7.3] Percival made his first major stand at Jitra on 11 December. The strategic logic for the defense of Jitra was the safeguarding of the northern airfields. Given that Malaya was not provided with aircraft of either sufficient quality or quantity to defend Malaya, Percival's decision to protect airfields can only be described as perverse. At the *Battle of Jitra* the folly of not sending tanks to Malaya was also cruelly exposed. Colonel Tsuji, Chief of Staff of Combat Operations, who witnessed the fighting, reported that first contact: "Our tanks were ready on the road, and the twenty or so enemy armored cars ahead were literally trampled underfoot . . . The enemy armored cars could not escape by running away, and were sandwiched between our medium tanks . . . It was speed and weight of armor that decided the issue."[68]

The British forces had been too thinly spread across a fourteen mile front with jungle on the right flank, monsoon-drenched rice fields and rubber plantations in the middle bisected by two roads and the railway and mangrove swamps on the left. Hampered by poorly prepared defenses and bad communication, when Allied lines were punctured by Yamashita's concentrated attacks, Percival was forced to issue the order for a costly retreat in terms of men and equipment. As Percival later explained in his post-war memoir, *War in Malaya* [1949]:

> This withdrawal would have been difficult under the most favorable conditions. With the troops tired, units mixed as the result of the fighting, communications broken and the night dark, it was inevitable that orders should be delayed and that in some cases they should never reach the addressees. This is what in fact occurred . . . the withdrawal, necessary as it may have been, was too fast and too complicated for disorganized and exhausted troops, whose disorganization and exhaustion it only increased.[69]

The defeat at the *Battle of Jitra* revealed the folly of using an undermanned army to try to defend Malaya in its entirety. A lower line, possibly as far south as northern Johore, would have shortened British lines of supply and extended those of the Japanese; holding up the Japanese would have exposed Japan's weak logistical capabilities. By the end of December Japanese forces controlled most of northern Malaya and they now began their move southwards. Successive lines of defense failed to hold. The Japanese, armed with tanks, were able to overwhelm the British and Indian forces; when frontal force failed, Japanese troops requisitioned bicycles and outflanked the British by moving rapidly along jungle tracks. Also when held by the Indian 11th Division at Kampar, halfway between *Penang* and Kuala Lumpur, where the Japanese came across terrain unsuitable for their tanks, Yamashita turned their flanks by an amphibious landing further south on Malaya's west coast.

After three weeks of perpetual fighting and retreat, the morale of British troops had all but collapsed. As Colonel Alfred Harrison of the 11th Indian Division observed on Christmas Day, "Fatigue had stretched the men's mind to the limit and the moral ascendancy which the Japanese had achieved in these few weeks included a 'psychic' side. The troops were beginning to attribute almost supernatural powers to the Japanese."[70] By contrast, the well-trained, battle-hardened Japanese troops were used to victory and went into battle believing that they would win. Battle tactics showed that the Japanese had learnt from the Germans. Bomber aircraft were used as a form of mobile artillery where the jungle terrain made the siting and use of ground artillery difficult. An engagement would start with a bombing attack on an Allied roadblock and would be quickly followed up with a frontal attack until a front line had been established; Japanese troops would then search for the opportunity for enveloping movements through the jungle. It was a piecemeal approach—roadblock by roadblock.

Coordination of the air and ground forces was impressive. Yamashita had signals officers placed in Air-to-Ground Communication Squads in operational headquarters. The advance along the Malay Peninsula had been rehearsed. In June 1941 amphibious landings, the destruction and repair of bridges, and jungle craft were practiced in a ten-day exercise in China's *Hainan Island*, under the supervision of the Army Research Section. The 600-mile circumference of *Hainan* closely matched the distance between Thailand and the tip of *Singapore* as simulated amphibious operations circumnavigated the island. As early as March 1941, the 5th Division and combined service elements had even practiced an invasion of *Singapore*. In the event, the combination of air, land and sea operations was brilliantly executed. The speed and energy of these attacks was dazzling Malaya's defenders and drained the resolve of the British and Allied troops.

It was not just the troops who were demoralized. Sir Henry Pownall, who had arrived on 23 December to replace Brooke-Popham as Commander in Chief Far East, found Brooke-Popham close to breakdown and noted in his diary, "It is of course time B-Popham left; he is pretty tired and is quite out of business [drunk] from dinnertime onwards."[71]

The Battle of Slim River and the Fall of Kuala Lumpur: [Map: 7.4] The crushing setbacks in Malaya wrought other changes. In a monumental shift in the perception of where power lay in the region, Australian Prime Minister Curtin, increasingly unhappy with Churchill's unfulfilled promises, let it be known in the *Melbourne Herald* that his hopes now rested with the United States:

> The Australian government, therefore, regards the Pacific struggle as primarily one in which the United States and Australia must have the fullest say in the direction of the democracies' fighting plan. Without inhibitions of any kind, I make it quite clear that Australia looks to America, free of any pangs as to our traditional links or kinship with the United Kingdom.[72]

Open dissension at the political level fed rebellious sentiment lower down. The famously egomaniacal Major-General Gordon Bennett demanded operational control of the III-Indian Corps if a retreat to Johor on the southern tip of Malaya was required.

Meanwhile further south but still north of Kuala Lumpur, a new line of defense was established at the *Slim River*. The defenses were poorly constructed with virtually no mines or anti-tank guns to cover the Allied lines in spite of the availability of both. In addition artillery had been placed in reserve in the mistaken belief that their line of sight was compromised. At the *Battle of Slim River*, the ever-inventive Yamashita used a surprise night attack supported by tanks to overwhelm the Indian 11th Division. In a direct assault the defenders' roadblocks were quickly taken and dismantled. An astonishing seventeen-mile advance was accomplished in two hours. Two British brigades perished almost in their entirety and Percival was forced to try to relieve them by pushing forward the Australian 8th Division. The rapid defeat of British forces at the *Battle of Slim River* on the west coast opened up the whole of central Malaya.

Kuala Lumpur was next to fall as the city, considered indefensible, was abandoned without a fight on 11 January. In the north, Japan consolidated their control without having to leave large garrisons by signing a loose alliance with the Thai military dictator, Field Marshal Plaek Phibunsongkhram (usually known as Phibun), who was allowed to take control of Malaya's northern provinces. The folly of the British high command in rejecting the concept of 'leave behind' forces, to coordinate guerrilla operations that could have significantly affected the Japanese speed of advance, was now fully exposed.

Another line of defense was established further south where the rambunctious Major-General Gordon Bennett achieved one of the few successes of the Malayan campaign. His 8th Division briefly held back the Japanese at Gemas, where a particularly bloody battle took place at the Gemencheh Bridge on 18 January. Sergeant Gunner Thornton described the scene:

> A couple [of Japanese tanks] attempted to turn and make
> a get-away but still those boys with the anti-tank guns

were sending a stream of shells into them. At last they could not move forward any further and became as pill-boxes surrounded, sending fire in all directions; until one by one they were smashed, set on fire, and rendered useless and uninhabitable. There came then from the tanks sounds which resembled an Empire Day celebration as the ammunition within them burnt, and cracked with sharp bursts, and hissed, with every now and again a louder explosion as larger ammunition ignited.[73]

After crossing the bridge, Colonel Mukaide's infantry, riding on bicycles ahead of the First Tank Regiment, were ambushed by devastating machine gun fire. As ever when the Japanese came to an impasse, the extraordinary courage of their troops and commanders came to the rescue, sustaining the momentum of Yamashita's advance that was calibrated on a strict timetable in keeping with traditional Japanese military practice. Although the Japanese incurred over 600 casualties in the ambush at Gemencheh Bridge, the Twenty-fifth Army quickly reinforced its front and recovered its drive south within hours.

The Battle of Muar: **[Map: 7.5]** Gordon Bennett fell back to positions south of the *Muar River*. In *Singapore* it was widely believed that here finally the Japanese advance would be halted. However, Bennett's 45th Indian Brigade, set to defend the river's south bank, was outflanked by an amphibious landing of the Imperial Guards Division led by Colonel Masakazu Ogaki. Hemmed in by another brilliant tactical pincer movement, Brigadier Duncan and his entire 45th Indian Brigade were forced to retreat to the town of Muar. Duncan was concussed and most of his HQ staff was killed in a Japanese air attack. By nightfall of the 16 January Muar town was completely in Japanese hands.

While the Imperial Guards were moving down the coastal route, the Japanese 5th Infantry Division followed the parallel route through central Malaya. At this point Percival's ability to hold the west was further undermined by the threat posed by Yamashita's 18th Division that had landed near Endau on Malaya's *South China Sea* coast. Falling back to Bakri, the 45th Indian Brigade took up new defensive positions but were again outflanked and surrounded. They took heavy casualties from the Imperial Japanese Guards Division and its tanks. On 20 January Brigadier Herbert Duncan was killed in a bayonet charge in an attempt to recover lost vehicles. The *Battle of Muar* was lost. Command of the defeated 45th Indian Brigade was taken over by Lieutenant-Colonel Charles 'Andy' Anderson who had arrived three days earlier with a supporting battalion of the Australian Imperial Force. Anderson, a South African-born game hunter, who had married an Australian girl and moved to New South Wales, Australia in 1934, now had to carry out a fighting retreat to break through the Japanese encirclement. He fought his way through fifteen miles of Japanese lines. The lightly built, bespectacled Anderson was an unlikely hero. In the withdrawal to Parit Sulong, Anderson, with

Australian troops singing *Waltzing Matilda*, led from the front, at one point leading a bayonet charge and personally destroying two machine gun posts with well-thrown grenades and shooting two enemy soldiers with his revolver.

In a doggerel verse entitled the *Battle of Muar*, 'Tich' Jelley of the 4th Anti-Tank Regiment wrote:

> The Colonel gave the order
> "We must fight to get out
> The 19th boys can do it!"
> And the 19th gave a shout!
>
> . . . .
>
> And good it is to recollect
> Our heroes—particularly one.
> Our Andy—that's him over there
> With the calculating face,
> A man, a soldier and a mate
> And none can take his place.[74]

Even after a night march Anderson still found himself surrounded. The bridge at Parit Sulong had been heavily reinforced and Anderson's calls for airstrikes and airdrops failed to bring any relief. Gordon Bennett wished him good luck and Anderson, having destroyed his heavy equipment, was left to his own devices to bring home some 900 survivors, 500 Australians and 400 Indians, including many of the wounded, through swamps and thick jungle. For his exploits in the fighting retreat Anderson was subsequently awarded the Victoria Cross. On 13 February 1942, the *London Gazette* recorded Anderson's achievements; his Victoria Cross citation concluded, "He not only showed fighting qualities of very high order but throughout exposed himself to danger without any regard for his own safety."[75] General Yamashita would record that "In a week long, bloody battle, without heavy tank or air support, they [Anderson's force] had held up the whole of my army."[76]

Later captured in *Singapore*, Anderson survived years of hardship on the infamous construction of the Burma Railway and after the war became a member of Australia's House of Representatives. Over 3,000 men had been lost as well as virtually all of their equipment and supplies. The 45th Brigade was disbanded. It was a devastating blow to the morale of the defenders now waiting for the advancing Japanese Army. As for Gordon Bennett's generalship, he would later be much criticized for fighting the *Battle of Muar* with four companies of the 45th Brigade left north of the river rather than concentrating his defenders on the south bank. After the *Battle of Muar*, British forces fell back pell-mell toward the *Straits of Johor* that separated the Malay mainland from *Singapore*. As M. C. Hay, lance bombardier in the FMS Volunteer Force, incredulously observed, "It was one of the features of this incredible campaign that if a handful of Japanese were reported in our rear the whole British army must perforce retire—infantry, guns, and armored cars—often without firing a shot."[77] The nature of the retreat was similarly described by Australian Charles Edwards of 2/19th Battalion. "The Japs who with superiority in the air, and with tanks, we had neither, gradually pushed us about 16 miles to a kampong Parit Sulong on the banks of the Sungei Simpang Kiri where on the 21 January 1942 we found ourselves surrounded, again the Japs had encircled around and held the bridge."[78]

The *Battle of Muar* was a stunning victory for Yamashita's Twenty-fifth Army, which significantly undermined what remained of British confidence. The tactical brilliance of Yamashita's flanking operation had now destroyed the British Army's belief that the Japanese could be held. The Japanese soldier gained a mythical status as a jungle fighter *nonpareil*. Thus an awestruck Punjabi officer described them as "being absolutely first-class. The speed with which they tumbled out of their lorries, and commenced an enveloping operation against us was incredible."[79] Similarly another British officer noted that "They were bold, fearless, fanatical and highly skilled in jungle craft, made use of the tree tops for observation and field of fire and even perfected a system for climbing."[80] It was a reputation burnished by the fact that the Japanese infantryman was backed by firepower, in the form of tanks and air superiority, denied to the British, Indian and Australian soldiers.

By contrast many of the British forces were inexperienced and poorly led. Major-General Elliot, who served in India in 1942–1943, would later explain that the rapid build-up of the Indian Armies after the start of the war with Germany, led to the 'milking' of experienced units to provide seed experience to new forces being raised and trained. The result was that many of the older and supposedly experienced units contained officers and non-commissioned officers "recently promoted; and more than half the men would be recruits with less than a year's service."[81]

General Percival's strategy to fight delaying actions until the arrival of reinforcements in *Singapore* was fatally undermined by the inability of his troops to construct and hold defensive lines. In part this was due to poor training and morale as well as the disappearance of civilian workers as soon as Japanese aircraft appeared; however, it was the speed of Japanese engagement that most severely undermined his plans. Neither was he helped by the intervention of recently appointed General Wavell who, unimpressed by Percival's campaigning in the first month of the war, overrode his deployments and backed Major-General Gordon Bennett's flawed plans to hold Muar.

By now the tactical and strategic failure of the British Army in Malaya was clear for all to see. Even the British Governor of the Straits Settlement, Sir Shenton Thomas, could recognize the problems. As early as 6 January he had noted in his diary, "We . . . have gone in for mechanized transport to the nth degree. It is a fearsomely cumbersome method. We have pinned our faith to the few roads but the enemy used tracks and paths, and gets round to our rear very much as he likes."[82] With the loss of a thousand fifteen-hundred-weight trucks by the end of January, the efficiency of Allied troop withdrawals and redeployment was further impaired as troops could no longer carry all the heavy equipment allocated to them.

Japanese Infantry: 'Supermen' and Brutes: It was imagined incorrectly that Japanese troops were 'to the jungle born' whereas in fact Japan, a northerly country, was devoid of tropical jungle except on its colonized southern islands. Moreover in 1941 Japan was far more industrialized and urbanized than all the Asian countries that they invaded. A high percentage of Japanese soldiers were actually 'townies.' Their superior performance in the jungles of Malaya was not the result of some predisposition to comfort in jungle conditions, but can be attributed to their much higher levels of motivation and *esprit de corps*, combined with better training and tactical leadership. It is often overlooked that Yamashita's troops had mainly been deployed in northern China, their experience hitherto had been in cold climates. On the journey south, however, they were briefed in detail about tropical conditions based on the work done by Colonel Tsuji on jungle warfare.

After the war General Percival correctly concluded, "Japanese successes were due primarily to training, previous war experience, discipline and morale. The Japanese has strong offensive spirit . . . they were tough."[83] Japanese infantry units, throughout the war, maintained a fighting effectiveness with a higher rate of casualties, sometimes over 70 percent, which was way beyond the capabilities of British and American troops. It was normally estimated by Allied commanders that combat effectiveness collapsed after units sustained casualty rates of more than 30 percent. Indeed it was only the German crack *Waffen-SS* units on the Eastern Front, toward the end of the war, that were able to achieve similar levels of casualty/combat effectiveness as the Japanese.

In addition to their fighting qualities, Japanese soldiers developed a reputation for committing appalling atrocities. At Parit Sulong Bridge to the south of Muar, Captain Rewi Snelling was left behind in command of 150 severely wounded Australian and Indian soldiers who were not capable of undergoing the tough jungle retreat led by Lieutenant-Colonel Anderson. After Snelling offered his surrender, the Japanese herded the wounded prisoners into buildings where they were denied medical attention. The Indians were beheaded and others randomly shot in what became known as the Parit Sulong Massacre. Later, on 22 January, Lieutenant-General Takuma Nishimura gave the orders for the prisoners to be forced outside, doused with petrol, set alight and raked by machine gun. Lieutenant Ben Hackney, one of the three survivors recalled, "Rifles and machine guns belched forth a storm of death, a few fell, a group fell . . . The prisoners were then set alight and amid screams and yells of pain, fright, nervousness and delirium, burnt . . ."[84]

At the end of the war, Nishimura was convicted and sentenced to life imprisonment by a *Singapore* court for another massacre at *Sook Ching* in the eastern part of *Singapore* where he had been the commander in charge. However, on his way back to Japan to serve the remainder of his sentence, Nishimura was hijacked by Australian military police in *Hong Kong*. He was taken to *Manus Island*, New Guinea, today a detention center for boat people trying to gain entry to Australia. Here Nishimura was tried for the Parit Sulong Massacre, found guilty and hanged on 11 June 1951. Doubts remain about the evidence presented at the trial, particularly as a confession to the massacre by a Lieutenant Seizaburo Fujita was ignored.

Japanese atrocities were not confined to the land war. Parachuting British pilots would soon realize that they were targets to be shot at. On Saturday 13 December Tom Vigors was hit in a dogfight, baled out of his Brewster Buffalo but made the mistake of pulling the ripcord on his parachute too early "with the result that within seconds I had what seemed like the whole Japanese air force shooting at me, from 10,000 feet down to where I eventually hit the deck, on the top of the Penang Mountains."[85] Even when he landed on the ground he was pursued by enemy pilots; he recalled that "The Japs continued to shoot at me until I made cover of some convenient jungle."[86] Sergeant Ross Leys had a similar experience. Finding himself outnumbered in a dogfight, a Zero managed to turn inside his Buffalo and pumped machine gun fire into his engine. He bailed out at 4,000 feet; "There seemed to be Zeros coming at me from every direction . . . as the Japanese fighter came close to me, I could see puffs of smoke coming out of his machine-guns. I thought to myself that this was it. He made three or four attacks at me. Others were less fortunate."[87] For Japanese pilots, many of whom spurned the use of a parachute as a cowardly way to escape death in battle, an escaping pilot was a justifiable target.

The Race to the Straits of Johor and the Dwindling Hopes of Saving Singapore: After the retreat from the *Battle of Muar*, the remaining British forces were forced back to their last lines of defense in the southernmost state of Johor between Batu Pahat on the west coast and Mersing on the east coast. This could be little more than a holding position. The British Forces, now shorn of much of their supporting artillery and heavy equipment, which had been lost or abandoned at engagements further up the Malay Peninsula, were demoralized and barely battle-worthy. The defeat at the *Battle of Muar* had put in jeopardy the possibility of defending *Singapore* that was anyway woefully underprepared and later called into question Wavell's decision to continue to divert fresh troops to the colony if *Singapore* could only be held for a short period.

For the Japanese army, their arrival in Johor Bahru on 31 January 1942, facing across the channel to *Singapore* was a stunning finale to their rampaging campaign down the Malay Peninsula. Colonel Tsuji noted, "Since landing in southern Thailand barely fifty five days ago, we had made an overland dash of eleven hundred kilometers . . . half the length of *Honshu*, the principal island of Japan. We had fought ninety five engagements, and repaired more than two hundred and fifty bridges."[88] It is difficult to disagree with a report by the US Joint Forces Staff College, *The Japanese Campaign in Malaya: December 1941–February 1942 A Study in Joint Warfighting* [2002], that concluded "the Japanese succeeded in Malaya because they applied the tenets of joint war-fighting doctrine; they were able to conduct an effective multidimensional joint war-fighting campaign against a one-dimensional enemy who was not."[89]

As on the north shores of *Singapore* itself, the defense positions during the long retreat through Malaya were wholly inadequate. This could not be blamed on any shortage of materials. The latest anti-tank Dannert Wire (concertinas of high-grade steel razor wire) barbed wire and sandbags had been made available in Malaya in considerable quantity. The British administrators in *Singapore* had simply failed to engage enough civilian labor to construct the necessary defensive positions. Again and again in the retreat south through Malaya, retreating Allied forces would have to march and then dig in their own defensive positions. On 27 January, General Wavell, recently appointed commander of American, British, Dutch and American forces (ABDA) ordered Percival to retreat across the causeway from Johor to *Singapore*.

Explanations for British Defeat in Malaya: In London, British commanders were deeply shocked by the military catastrophe in Malaya. In trying to explain the problem, Wavell wrote to General Alanbrooke, Chief of the Imperial General Staff,

> The trouble goes a long way back, climate, the atmosphere of the country . . . lack of vigor in our peacetime training, the cumbrousness of our tactics and equipment, and the very real difficulty of finding an answer to the very skilful tactics of the Japanese in this jungle fighting. But the real problem is that for the time being we have lost a good deal of our hardness and fighting spirit.[90]

As usual, Wavell, like most senior British commanders, neglected to give much credit to General Yamashita, who, in Japan, garnered the epithet 'Tiger of Malaya,' for the sheer brilliance of his campaign. By the standards of any military operation in *World War II*, Yamashita's handling of troops, tanks, amphibious operations and air support was masterful. In spite of inter-force rivalries, the Twenty-fifth Army, 3rd Air Group, the Southern Squadron, 22nd Air Flotilla and the 4th and 5th Submarine Squadrons worked together to move rapidly and concentrate force where it was required. British strategy was to delay the enemy long enough to bring up reinforcements; Yamashita's speed of advance never allowed them that luxury. In its skilful mix of services, Japan perhaps had the advantage of culture, geography and history. As the military historian, John Keegan has noted, ". . . the Japanese who, as an island people, had long been accustomed to using land and sea forces in concert to preserve the security of the archipelago they inhabit and extend national power into adjoining regions."[91]

With barely enough supplies or logistical support available for his campaign, Yamashita's rapid advance down the Malay Peninsula walked the tightrope of what was possible. His force of just 70,000 troops, of which just 30,000 were frontline soldiers, had overcome a British force double that number. It seems likely that had Yamashita ended the war on the winning side, rather than being condemned to death to take responsibility for war crimes committed under his charge, he would have been lauded for his Malay Campaign and as one of the great generals of the twentieth century.

8 Battle of Hong Kong: A Murderous Siege

[7–25 December 1941]

[Maps: 8.1, 8.2, 8.3]

A Hopeless Cause: **[Map 8.1]** The *Battle of Hong Kong* does not sit easily into the campaign narratives around which *Hirohito's War* has been structured. Although the battle started on the same day as *Pearl Harbor* and the invasions of Malaya and the Philippines, it was an outlying battle on the Chinese mainland whose eastern seaboard and its hinterland had already been largely subsumed by Japanese forces in the first four years of the *Second Sino-Japanese War*. To a large extent therefore, with regards to the ongoing war in China, Japan's occupation of Hong Kong was a tying up of loose ends—a minor military exercise. For the British, Hong Kong had already been given up as of negligible strategic value—it must have come as a surprise to both sides therefore that this British colony was yielded at much greater cost than Singapore, around which British defense of its empire in the Far East had been based.

There was no realistic prospect of Hong Kong surviving an attack by the Japanese Army. As Japan became increasingly engaged in fighting Chiang Kai-shek's *Kuomintang* Armies after the Marco Polo Bridge incident in July 1937, which signaled the start of the *Second Sino-Japanese War*, the government in London was fully awakened to the Japanese threat in Asia. In a review of the international situation in the same year, the British Chiefs of Staff had concluded that after Germany, Britain's most likely enemy was Japan. As for Hong Kong, the British Chiefs of Staff decided that it should be regarded as an important though not vital outpost; its defense was more a matter of honor than a strategic imperative.

The issue of Hong Kong's defense gathered more urgency after 21 October 1938 when the Japanese occupied the province of Canton (*Guangzhou*) that surrounds Hong Kong. It was decided that Singapore and Malaya could be defended but studies showed that Hong Kong was indefensible to a Japanese attack. Not only was the Japanese Army fully embedded in Eastern China, but Hong Kong was vulnerable to a Japanese fleet that controlled the *South China Sea*. The British Fleet in Singapore was both weak and, at 1,600 miles, was too far distant to be able to render assistance. Moreover Japan's colony of *Formosa*, with its numerous Japanese airfields, was just 400 miles across the water. Combined with the absence of a sufficient American naval presence in the Philippines, it meant that Hong Kong was pincered between Japan's armies and their Navy's control of the seas between Vietnam and *Formosa*.

In reviewing their Asian assets therefore, Hong Kong's ability to sustain a meaningful or protracted defense was largely discounted. In April 1938 Hong Kong's General

Commanding Officer (GOC) wrote to the war office to warn that, "In the event of a wanton attack on Hong Kong, the garrison would have no option but to fight"; but he concluded gloomily, " The chances of effecting prolonged resistance even in the best circumstances seem slight."[1] Britain even considered making Hong Kong an open city as they later did with the concessions at Tianjin (Tientsin) when Japanese troops were allowed uncontested access. By August 1940 little had changed and, determined not to waste resources on indefensible assets in China, the British Joint Chiefs of Staff withdrew two battalions from the Shanghai International Settlement. About Hong Kong they concluded, "We should resist the strong pressure to reinforce Hong Kong and we should certainly be unable to relieve it."[2] Their conclusions were in part based on the recommendations of Air Chief Marshal Sir Robert Brooke-Popham, Commander-in-Chief of the British Far East Command, though the logic of not committing to the defense of Hong Kong must have been obvious to any observer.

A dispatch sent to Hong Kong on 15 August for the eyes of the GOC only made it clear that "Hong Kong is not a vital interest and the garrison could not withstand a Japanese attack."[3] The message, sent on the cargo-liner SS *Automedon*, was intercepted on 11 November en route from Liverpool to Hong Kong by a German attack cargo ship, *Atlantis,* which boarded the captured British ship before sinking it; eventually the stash of secret documents found on board *Automedon* ended up in the hands of the German Ambassador in Tokyo, who passed it on to the Japanese government.

A Change of Heart: The Defense of Hong Kong Upgraded: Churchill too was realistic about the defense of Hong Kong. "We must avoid frittering away our resources on untenable positions"[4] he declared. In January 1941, he opined that Hong Kong garrison should be "reduced to a symbolic scale."[5] However, if the British and American governments were counting on China to resist a Japanese advance in Asia, how could they encourage Chiang Kai-shek if they simply abandoned Hong Kong to its fate? In 1941 therefore, there was a change of heart in London. Hong Kong would be reinforced by Canadian troops. It was a politically driven compromise. Churchill reversed the decision not to reinforce Hong Kong in September 1941 as a sop to appease Chiang Kai-shek, whose armies were holding down 1.5m Japanese troops in China. On 19 September the Dominion Office cabled Ottawa stating, "a small reinforcement of the garrison of Hong Kong . . . would be very fully justified . . . have a very great moral effect in the whole of the Far East and would reassure Chiang Kai-shek as to the reality of our intent to hold the island."[6] In spite of the indisputable logic of Churchill's geopolitical calculation, the hopeless military situation of Hong Kong had not changed. Inevitably, the decision to reinforce a doomed Hong Kong generated considerable heat in post-war debate.

As a result of the Chief of Staffs' reappraisement, the defense of *Hong Kong* was upgraded. This included not only *Hong Kong Island*, which was transferred to Britain on a perpetual rent free lease in the *First Convention of Peking* [1860] after the *Second Opium War*, but also the New Territories, comprising some 200 islands and the mainland up to the *Sham Chun River*, which was transferred to Britain on a 99-year lease by the

Second Convention of Peking [1898]. A defensive line was constructed to protect the New Territories from attack; it was a series of bunkers, machine gun posts, entrenchments and artillery positions that stretched for 18 miles across the New Territories from *Shenzen Bay* to the *Starling Inlet*. The New Territories defensive barrier, sometimes referred to as the Maginot Line of the East, became better known as the Gin Drinker's Line. On Hong Kong as well as New Kowloon, defenses were beefed up at the Wong Nai Chung Gap, Lye Moon Passage, Shing Mun Redoubt, Devil's Peak and Stanley Fort. However the efforts made to beef up Hong Kong's defenses were patchy at best. There were not even enough troops to fully man the Gin Drinkers Line.

Furthermore Wing Commander H. G. Sullivan arrived at Kai Tak Airfield to find three Vildebeeste torpedo bombers and two Walrus amphibians—all over ten years old. He reported, "It had been suggested that dispersal bays be carved out of the hills, but like everything else in Hong Kong these did not materialize."[7] The Royal Air Force based at Kai Tak Airfield was an embarrassing token. A request for a fighter squadron had been rejected. The nearest RAF station was at Kota Bharu some 1,400 miles away. Naval resources were even more derisory. Just a single destroyer, HMS *Thracian*, remained in Hong Kong with several gunboats and a number of torpedo boats.

An offer by the Canadian government to send two infantry battalions to Hong Kong comprising 1,975 troops was accepted. It seems unlikely that they were fully aware of the pessimistic military assessment. Thus the Royal Rifles from Quebec and the Winnipeg Grenadiers, minus a considerable portion of their motorized equipment, arrived on 16 November aboard the troop ship *Awatea* and the merchant cruiser HMCS *Prince Robert*. This merchant vessel had been dragooned into service by the Canadian Navy, which boasted just six modern destroyers. Bizarrely, the colonial authorities refused to organize a mass armament of the native Hong Kong Chinese—a cause of not a little resentment toward the British. As Hong Kong's Chief Information Officer admitted, "there cannot have been less than 75,000 Chinese who would willingly have borne arms and fought."[8] Although it was still a token defense, it nevertheless doomed thousands more soldiers to either death or the hardships of imprisonment. As the military historian B. H. Liddell Hart concluded, "Even the Japanese never committed such folly for face, as did the British in this case."[9] As a military exercise it was folly—but perhaps not so pointless in a geopolitical context. Keeping Chiang Kai-shek in the war, given his tying down of 1.5m Japanese troops, was considered essential in both London and in Washington.

Canada's Prime Minister and leader of the Liberal Party, Mackenzie King, had brought a motion to the House of Commons on 10 September 1939 to declare war on Germany. This had been done a week after George VI's declaration of war so as to make clear that it was Canada's independent decision. Clearly Mackenzie King had overcome his previous conviction, developed on a tour to Europe in 1937 that "the world will yet come to see a very great man-mystic in Hitler."[10] The motion was supported by the opposition Conservative Party led by Robert Manion.

Canada's reinforcements had brought the Allied troops up to 12,500. After their arrival in Hong Kong, Jan Henrik Marsman, a construction engineer wrote, "After the arrival of a few thousand Canadians, everybody felt that the Crown Colony could and would be defended successfully. It was a psychological miracle."[11] Other infantry forces included the Royal Scots Regiment, the Queens Own Royal West Kent Regiment, 1st Battalion Middlesex Regiment, 5th Battalion 7th Rajput Regiment, and the Winnipeg Grenadiers. Infantry contingents had also been provided by the Hong Kong Volunteer Defence Corps; Indian and Chinese troops comprised 35 percent of the Allied defense forces.

British forces in Hong Kong were not in prime condition. Brigadier Cedric Watts noted, "with many young and inexperienced officers and newly arrived recruits in Indian units, all units were badly in need of training."[12] This apart, his Indian units had been 'milked' of its best soldiers to seed newly raised battalions.

In spite of this assessment, Britain's Commander-in-Chief in the Far East, Air Vice Marshal Sir Robert Brooke-Popham, was adamant that Hong Kong's troops were far superior to the Japanese. Addressing officers at the main theatre in the disreputable Wanchai district of Hong Kong, Brooke-Popham told them that the Japanese had "dirty uniforms" and were a "sub-human species" and he could not "believe that they would form an intelligent fighting force."[13] Not everybody present agreed. Brigadier Cedric Wallis said about Brooke-Popham, "the Air Marshal must be very badly informed and making a great mistake in belittling the Japs."[14] Throughout Asia British officers with knowledge of the Japanese Army were ignored. When Colonel G.T. Ward, a military *attaché* in Tokyo, lectured a group of officers in Tokyo on the excellent morale and superb training of Japanese troops, the senior British officer present became distinctly agitated and gave his opinion that Ward's views were "far from the truth."[15] Another staff officer in Hong Kong, when asked whether Hong Kong could be overrun, pompously dismissed the possibility: "Preposterous notion old boy. The Japs haven't the manpower or the skill. Why, one of our soldiers is worth three of theirs."[16]

Major-General Maltby Leads Hong Kong's Defense: The British General Officer in Command (GOC) was Major-General Christopher Maltby, a slim fair-haired fifty-year-old thirty-year veteran of the Indian Army. His battle experience was against rebellious Pathans on the Northwest Frontier. He had a reputation for coolness, which was won in the *Persian Gulf* in *World War I*. He reacted calmly when his forces were attacked at 8.00 a.m. on 8 December 1941. Set against them were 52,000 Japanese troops of the 38th Division commanded by Lieutenant-General Takashi Sakai. As an opener, Kai Tak Airfield was bombarded by Japan's 45th Air Regiment and Hong Kong's aircraft destroyed. Imperial GHQ gave Sakai ten days to capture Hong Kong. In London, Douglas Amaron optimistically reported that Hong Kong "may develop into a Tobruk of the Pacific."[17]

Many Hong Kong residents must have wondered why the Japanese Army would bother with a Hong Kong that represented no military threat to its interests in China. As with other Imperial acquisitions Japan's leaders believed that they could use this famously rich financial center and *entrepôt* to its economic advantage. Hong Kong also had an important naval base with concomitant docking and repair facilities. In the event, as in the rest of the Empire, Japan was able to destroy but not rebuild. Hong Kong became an Imperial burden while the naval facilities did not prove to be usefully located.

At the beginning of December reports that Japanese troops were massing on the border began to filter through to Hong Kong. The threats were ignored by a complacent Hong Kong social elite. With war fast approaching the British expatriates in Hong Kong sustained the niceties of colonial life to the last. Beach parties and picnics, bridge afternoons, regattas at the Yacht Club, cocktails at the Jockey Club and sundowners at the Repulse Bay Hotel were the fabric of colonial life in Hong Kong. Dances at the Peak Club or dinners at the Peninsula Hotel were much more important than worrying about the Japanese, who were not considered militarily capable in the face of western trained forces. As one British officer noted about the colonial laziness and complacency for which Singapore has become more famous, there was "a determined unwillingness to have the pleasant routine of their lives disturbed by those 'short-arsed yellow bastards' who were overrunning China."[18] Indeed in 1934 a Colonial Office bureaucrat in London reported that Hong Kong was "the most self-satisfied of all the colonies except Malaya."[19]

Up until the last minute many Englishmen believed that Japan would never have the nerve to attack the British Empire. When reports arrived from the Punjabi units on the mainland front that a force of 38,000 Japanese was maneuvering for an attack, many were incredulous. When Captain Iain McGregor, Maltby's ADC, met with the Chairman of Hong Kong Shanghai Bank to propose a mobilization of the Hong Kong Volunteers—a move that would seriously inconvenience operations at the bank, he received a less than friendly welcome: "Good God, Iain. You know how these army fellows flap. You know our intelligence is far better than theirs [Army Intelligence]."[20] The Chairman had been told that one their managers in Manchuria had dined with the Commander-in-Chief of Japan's *Kwantung* Army the night before and had been assured that Japan would never attack its old ally, Great Britain. Another banker was reported as scoffing at the suggestion of an attack: "There is no war, sir, and there never will be. The Japanese have more sense than to attack a British colony."[21]

Although the senior intelligence officer in Hong Kong, Major Charles Boxer had long warned of the Japanese threat, it seems that he misread the imminence of their attack. Boxer, a graduate of Sandhurst in 1923, had learnt Dutch and Portuguese before going to the School of Oriental and African Studies (SOAS) to learn Japanese. After the war he would become the professor of Portuguese at King's College, London. Boxer took up with Emily 'Mickey' Hahn, a dazzlingly beautiful bohemian feminist adventuress. Hahn, albeit qualified as a mining engineer, became a writer, opium addict and figure in Shanghai's cultural *beau monde* where she met and married Sinmay Zau, a leading Chinese poet. (Her Chinese marriage papers would later save her from internment.) After the start of the *Sino-Japanese War*, she left Shanghai and moved to Hong Kong to write a book about the Soong sisters—including Meiling, Chiang Kai-Shek's wife. Hahn tarried in Hong Kong to live quite scandalously with the otherwise married Boxer with whom she bore an illegitimate child—though ultimately after the vicissitudes of war and his imprisonment, they did eventually marry.

Japanese Forces Cross the Gin Drinkers Line: [**Map: 8.2**] On the morning of 7 December 1941 a Punjabi patrol spotted the movement of Japanese forces and the information was speedily relayed to Maltby, who was attending Anglican Sunday morning service. "The Punjabis say there are at least 20,000 soldiers in the area, perhaps even more," he was told; "they must be exaggerating," he replied, "Our intelligence people are certain there are only 5,000 at most."[22]

The same evening Boxer went to the frontier and could see no evidence of Japanese movement. Rumors of troop movements were thought to have been spread by the Japanese themselves. That night an intelligence missive to the War Office in London, which was either written or approved by Boxer, suggested, "the reports (of Japanese movements) are certainly exaggerated."[23] Two days earlier the Japanese-speaking Boxer had dined with a senior Japanese officer across the border. Japanese intentions had been well camouflaged.

Even on the day of the Japanese attack, the famous Palace Floating Restaurant was full; the *South China Morning Post* reported the next day that life went on "as if we were taking part in yet another exercise."[24] John Harris of the Royal Engineers recalled, "The city carried on as usual. The shops and offices were all open . . . the story still prevailed that the Japanese could neither move nor see at night!"[25] British officer, Lieutenant Colonel Holmes complained, "We seem to be on some peacetime festival rather than on the brink of war."[26]

Maltby had already decided to make no attempt to hold the Japanese at the *Sham Chung River*, but deployed three battalions along the Gin Drinkers Line. Having crossed the river, on 8 December, General Sakai launched attacks at the Shing Mun Redoubt and Golden Hill, which after being retaken by the Royal Scots, had to be evacuated later in the day. The end of the Royal Scots' resistance seemingly came when 'friendly fire' scored a direct hit on a concrete pillbox on the Shing Mun Redoubt. The position was rapidly yielded. Three infantrymen were later dug out alive from the collapsed pillbox by Japanese troops. With battle-lines set Maltby had given his order of the day with a rousing Nelsonesque flourish: "I expect each and every man of my force to stick it out unflinchingly, and that my force will become a great example of high-hearted courage to all the rest of the Empire who are fighting to preserve the truth, justice and liberty for the world."[27]

On Hong Kong's peaks the start of the war was plainly visible. Seeing black smoke billowing from Kai Tak Airfield, Emily Hahn, from the comfort of her terrace, assumed that the RAF's pathetic force had been destroyed. Others were more sanguine. From the terrace of an adjoining property she heard a pipe-smoking Englishmen complain, "That's it. The Japanese have committed suicide."[28] He was right, but not perhaps in the timeframe that he imagined.

Having been forced to give up the relatively short-lived defense of the Gin Drinker's Line, which meant that the New Territories and Kowloon were now considered indefensible, Maltby began the withdrawal of his troops to *Hong Kong Island* on 11 December. The Rajput battalions were the last to be withdrawn in a fighting retreat two days later. Lieutenant-General Takashi Sakai demanded a surrender, which was refused. Almost all heavy equipment was successfully withdrawn.

In Hong Kong mixed messages were coming back from the mainland front. James Bertram at the Ministry of Information was writing a press release saying the Japanese were being wiped out in the New Territories when Hilda Selwyn-Clarke, on her way to the Red Cross office next door told him: "Better scrap that one. Rumor has it Gin Drinkers is in trouble and the Japanese will soon be entering Kowloon."[29]

Sakai had expected that Britain's main effort to defend the city would be on the mainland. Colonel Doi explained their surprisingly "inactive" defense as a result of "their estimate that it would take at least several days for the Japanese troops to approach their position."[30] Similarly a surprised Colonel Tosaka recalled, "In actuality the British Army did not show great resistance on the expected Gin Drinkers Line."[31] The result was that "little thought had been given to an attack on Hong Kong Island."[32] The decision to fight on *Hong Kong Island* and Sakai's frustration at the delay to the "10-day" operational deadline given by his commanders at Imperial General Headquarters may partially explain the later brutality of the Japanese Army.

Now in a panic, Major Boxer contacted Colonel "Fatty" Liao, an officer of Chiang Kai-shek's 8th Route Army, to see if he could conduct guerilla action but it soon became clear that the Chinese were short of arms and that the British forces had none to spare. A senior British officer told Boxer, "I am sorry, old fellow, but we simply don't have the guns to spare. Like everything else, the guerilla plan has been left too late."[33]

The retreat from the mainland was swiftly followed by a demand by General Sakai for the colony to surrender. Governor Sir Mark Young, a diplomat who had formerly worked in Ceylon, the Carribean and the Middle East, declined the invitation. When Boxer gave the reply, the Japanese interpreter remarked, "It will be a pity if we have to level this beautiful city."[34]

In the lull that followed the retreat from the mainland, the Governor remained upbeat. "There is every reason for confidence," he declaimed in the *South China Morning Post*, "Reserves of food, guns and ammunition are ample for a protracted defense on a siege scale. The garrison is in good spirits and the staunchness of the civilian population is marked."[35] Rumors that Chang Kai-shek's *Kuomintang* Armies were preparing to attack Japanese forces from the rear gave some grounds for optimism. But in reality *Kuomintang* efforts were limited to a few desultory acts of sabotage on the Canton–Kowloon railway. In London, Winston Churchill also attempted to keep up spirits in his inimical way,

> We are all watching day by day and hour by hour your stubborn defense of the port of Hong Kong. You guard a link between the Far East and Europe long famous in world civilization. We are sure that the defense of Hong Kong against barbarous and unprovoked attack will add a glorious page to the British annals. All our hearts are with you and your ordeal. Every day of your existence brings nearer our certain final victory.[36]

The Battle for Hong Kong Island: **[Map: 8.3]** A heavy bombardment of *Hong Kong Island* began on 15 December and two days later a further demand for the British to surrender was made. Somewhat bizarrely in view of the Japanese Army's stance on fighting to the last man and treating surrender as the worst form of personal dishonor, Sakai was flabbergasted by the second British refusal to surrender. Maltby wrote on 1 January 1942,

> The (Japanese) envoys seemed genuinely surprised and disconcerted when the proposals were summarily rejected. The second delegation, coming within four days of the first, suggested that either a) they disliked the prospect of attacking across the water, b) that the Chinese threat in their rear was taking effect, or c) that it was an attempt to undermine our morale by fostering thoughts of peace and quiet.[37]

In contrast to the upbeat public pronouncements, Lord Alanbrooke, Chief of Staff of the British Army in London, noted in his diary on that day, "I doubt whether Hong Kong will hold out for a fortnight."[38] British newspapers were equally gloomy. A *Daily Express* editorial concluded that Hong Kong "has neither the strategic value nor the fighting chance of Tobruk. We must be prepared for its fall."[39] The *Daily Mirror* meanwhile summed up Governor Mark Young's reply in a suitably feisty headline: "GO TO HELL."[40]

Japanese landings began on the north side of the island on the evening of 18 December at North Point and Braemar Point. Specially trained swimmers cleared mines guarding the approaches to the shore to enable light landing skiffs to bring across troops. When they arrived, soldiers entered Chinese homes and confiscated clothing, particularly male apparel; this they used "to infiltrate unobserved through the streets."[41]

A parallel landing was made at *Aldrich Bay* to the northeast. Expertise at night fighting helped the Japanese to sweep inland with little resistance, in spite of the much-hyped reports of an island bristling with defenses including a honeycomb of shelters and tunnels and a 'gun encrusted backbone.' Twenty gunners who surrendered were executed; when they bayonetted the "unsuspecting men from the rear amidst cheers from enemy (Japanese) onlookers ... All the while, the Japanese were talking and laughing."[42] Meanwhile at the Silesian mission at Shau Kei Wan, medics were surrounded. Two wounded Indian soldiers who arrived in a Red Cross ambulance were summarily killed. Male staff were rounded up and murdered. When a Canadian doctor protested, "We are medical personnel. Noncombattants", he was told, "I'm sorry. We have instructions from our commander-in-chief. You must all die."[43] Dr. Martin Banfill, a witness to the slaughter, survived because a Japanese officer took him off for questioning. He was lucky to be put into a POW camp. Just as there were random victims of Japanese sadism and brutality, so there were random survivors.

The defenders would be disappointed by false reports that Chang Kai-shek's armies under General Tsai Tingkai were attacking just twenty-eight miles north of the New

Territories. Meanwhile on 18 December, Churchill relayed a message to Hong Kong: "We expect you to resist to the end. The honor of the Empire is in your hands."[44]

Only ten hours after landing, Japanese troops were so close to West Brigade headquarters at Wong Nei Chong Gap that Canadian Brigadier John Lawson was forced to destroy his cyphers. Lawson sent a message: "SITUATION GRAVE. DEEP PENETRATION MADE BY ENEMY."[44] Fighting continued on 19 December with the headquarters of West Brigade (comprising the Royal Scots, the Winnipeg Grenadiers, the Punjab unit and the Canadian signalers) being overrun. Their commanders, Canadians Brigadier John Lawson and his Chief-of-Staff, Colonel Patrick Hennessy, were killed. Lawson, with his bunker under attack, had decided to go out to fight and did so with a pistol in either hand.

The rapid acquisition of strategic points by advanced Japanese troops was a tactic originally developed by a French officer, Captain Lafarge, during *World War I*. The tactic, later adopted in the German Army training manual, was to use crack troops to launch rapid and aggressive attacks on key points. As each key target was taken, standard troops occupied their positions. The fast paced infiltration was enabled by fifth columnists who supplied maps and information.

At the Repulse Bay Hotel guests were dining on the terrace when Japanese snipers opened fire. A seventy-two-hour battle followed. Filled with Swiss, French, German and Russian patrons, the them-and-us nature of the colony continued in the hotel's refined surroundings, gunfire notwithstanding. When a grey-haired matron complained at the hotel reception that a group of Indians were lurking in her corridor, she protested to the manager, Marjorie Matheson, "What is the matter with you. Can't you keep those creatures in the basement."[45] After three days of fighting, British troops fell back to Port Stanley. Miraculously the non-combatant guests at the hotel were left unharmed. When Japanese troops approached the forty or so wounded officers housed in the bar, the elderly nurse Elizabeth Mosey intervened: "These are sick men. If you want to kill them, you'll have to kill me first."[46]

An Allied counterattack failed to dislodge the Japanese from the Wong Nai Chung Gap that passaged from the north to south across the mountainous island. Over the next two days Sakai focused on seizing the central reservoirs, which fed the island. On Mount Butler a defensive action by the Winnipeg Grenadiers ended with the award of the only Victoria Cross in the *Battle for Hong Kong* when Company Sergeant Major John Osborn, who had retrieved and thrown back numbers of Japanese grenades, threw himself on top of another, an action that killed him but saved up to ten others. Sugar Loaf Hill was taken by the Japanese at noon on 22 December and later that day the Royal Scots were driven off Stanley Mound. That night Maltby ordered a retreat to Stanley Fort. With the defenders split into two, fighting continued around strongholds in the west and around Stanley Fort to the southeast.

Murder at St. Stephen's College: On 25 December, Sakai's forces seized St. Stephen's College, which was being used as a makeshift hospital. Dr. George Black had seen no point in evacuating the ninety-five British and Canadian wounded. Where was there to go? "Frankly I'd rather be here than with the soldiers at Fort Stanley."[47] It turned out to be a poor bet. In spite of putting a Red Cross flag on the roof, when the elderly doctor, Captain Whitney opened the door to the Japanese troops, telling them "this is a hospital. You musn't come in. Leave us in peace,"[49] he was shot and killed at point blank range. Fifty-six wounded soldiers lying in the hallway were bayonetted.

A further forty male prisoners were locked into an upstairs storeroom, 10 feet by 20 feet. From here they were taken from the storeroom two or three at a time every twenty or thirty minutes and were mutilated and then killed. Those waiting must have heard the piercing screams of their colleagues. Three young British and two young Chinese nurses were later dragged off screaming and writhing from their room, thrown on to a pile of bodies, gang raped and then murdered. Canadian officer Captain Overton Hickey, was murdered when he tried to stop the Japanese troops from raping nurses. Just two older nurses were spared. Injured soldiers and medics were tortured and killed. One surviving doctor asked to see his wife, a nurse, and was shown her butchered corpse. He lost his mind. Four other men were spared and released but not before two of them had their ears and tongues cut off. They were told: "Go to Fort Stanley and tell your officers what you have seen."[50] As many as 150 people may have been massacred here, including British, Indian, Canadian and Chinese.

Other murders and massacres were recorded at Jardine's Lookout, *Causeway Bay*, *Deepwater Bay*, Maryknoll Mission, Brick Hill and Blue Pool Road. Thirty civilians of mixed nationality were murdered in this last event but the worst massacre of prisoners took place after the *Battle of The Ridge*; in aggregate about 100 soldiers were massacred in a number of locations, including British and Canadians.

Hong Kong Surrenders: In the west action centered on a defensive line around *Victoria Harbor* with the Royal Scots dug into the slopes of Mount Cameron and the Grenadiers covering Bennet's Hill. In spite of fierce fighting on Christmas Eve, their positions were eventually overrun and the defenders were forced to surrender. With water running short, at 3.15 p.m. on Christmas Day, Maltby advised the Governor of Hong Kong, Sir Mark Aitchison Young, that further resistance was pointless. When Young appeared in person in front of Lieutenant-Colonel Tokuchi Tada at the Peninsula Hotel, Japan's Headquarters, Hong Kong became the first British Crown Colony to surrender to an invasion.

In aggregate 1,528 defenders were killed. The remaining 11,000 soldiers were sent to prison camps. Exactly how many survived the war is unknown but of the 1,689 captured Canadians 267 died in captivity (17.5 percent); a further 600 Canadian troops were wounded. Hong Kong itself was looted. In January 1942 a semblance of order was restored with the setting up of a Hong Kong police force manned with Indian and Chinese recruits but commanded by Japanese officers. Similar forces were organized for the New Territories. Europeans were paraded through the streets to humiliate them in front of the Chinese populace. Years of forced labor, brutality and malnutrition would follow. But the civilian prisoners kept in Stanley Internment Camp were the lucky ones. On 1 October, USS *Grouper*, a Gato Class submarine, torpedoed the *Lisbon Maru*, on its way to Japan with 1,834 POWs. The sinking of the *Lisbon Maru* cost the lives of 824 men, either drowned, shot or bayonetted as they tried to escape the sinking ship. A further 200 died in Japan's bitter winter of 1942–1943. As the US reporter George Baxter concluded, "it was plain that humiliation was part of the Jap scheme to convince the natives that the white man had been conquered."[51]

During the Japanese occupation a reign of terror continued in Hong Kong; summary executions were frequent. These were carried out by the new police force at King's Park in Kowloon, either by beheading, shooting or during the course of bayonet practice. Furthermore, in spite of the establishment of a police force, it was estimated that over 10,000 Hong Kong Chinese women were raped during the Japanese years. The Hong Kong dollar was outlawed and citizens were forced to exchange their currency for Japanese military yen. The functions of the Hong Kong Shanghai Bank were sequestered and transferred to the Yokohama Specie Bank. As the Japanese economy disintegrated toward the end of the war, rampant inflation effectively wiped out the wealth of Hong Kong's inhabitants. The new yen scrip had become worthless.

The speaking of English was banned and the education system was Japanized. Street names and places were given Japanese names; Queen's Road Central became the *Meiji Dori* and the Peninsula Hotel became the *Matsumoto*. Radio and press were censored and only Japanese movies were allowed; these included *The Battle of Hong Kong* [1942], which was made on location in Hong Kong by the Dai Nippon Film Company and was shown on the anniversary of Hong Kong's capture. Food had to be rationed and civilian allocations were not enough to keep many people from dying of starvation. The result of death and deportations to the mainland meant that the population of the city fell from 1.6m to just 600,000 by the end of the war. The surrender came just in time; by August 1945 there were just 4,000 tons of rice left in the city, just enough to keep the population alive for a month.

In London the fall of Hong Kong was mentioned in a brief sentence in Alanbrooke's diary entrance on 25 December 1941; he was far more concerned with plans for deployment in Africa and the Middle East. Britain's interest in Hong Kong thereafter remained mute, at least until after the dropping of the atom bomb on Hiroshima. An immediate end to the war loomed large. Although the British Foreign Office had earlier warned, "we have lost a dreadful amount of face and prestige over the fall of Hong Kong and we shall never regain what was lost,"[52] Britain immediately set about the recovery of its former colonial asset.

Hong Kong, neglected for so long before and during the war, now became the febrile center of attention in London. Alanbrooke noted in his diary on 21 August, "Hong Kong and its relief by British forces before the arrival of either Chinese or American forces filled most of our COS [Chief of Staff Committee] discussion and plans."[53] Further COS discussions centered around Hong Kong on 24 and 27 August, with much disagreement as to whether Lord Louis Mountbatten, nominally the head of Allied Forces in the Far

East, should be in charge. A British task force had been quickly formed in Ceylon and sailed for Hong Kong. Rear-Admiral Cecil Harcourt duly arrived and set up a military administration with himself at its head. Japan's surrender was formally accepted on 16 September 1945.

Harcourt realized that Hong Kong could not go back to the 1941 *status quo*; Hong Kong Chinese were given positions of authority and allowed to live on the peak. Alexander Graham, returning as Governor in 1947, remarked on a "decline in social snobbishness . . . I observed, too, a greater mixing of the races."[54] For a while, the Hong Kong Cricket Club remained stubbornly resistant to Chinese membership, though that too eventually changed. That the resident Hong Kong Chinese accepted the return of Great Britain was not surprising. No matter how racist and patronizing the pre-war British colonists, no better advertisement for the British Empire could have been given than the brutal depravities of Japan's Co-Prosperity Sphere; both British and Chinese learnt something from this mutually ghastly experience, which helped them to rub along with surprising ease in the post-war period. However the granting of any political power to the Chinese in Hong Kong had to wait until just before the handing back of the city to China in 1997.

After the battle, Lieutenant-General Sakai became the governor of Hong Kong before being replaced in February 1942. He retired from active service in 1943. This did not save him after the war. Arrested and brought before the war crimes tribunal in Nanking, Sakai was found guilty of murder and was sentenced to death and executed by firing squad in September 1946. Perhaps surprisingly in Hong Kong "the number of killings and trials with executions and jail terms was stunningly small"[55] though the East River Column, a group of about 6,000 guerilla fighters did expend most of its energy on killing collaborators as the war drew to an end. If nothing else the *Battle of Hong Kong* showed that the murder of civilians and the mass rape of women in Nanking in 1937 was not an isolated aberration.

The story of Hong Kong's heroic defense may have been irrelevant to the strategic determination of the war but it was meaningful to the thousands of soldiers and civilians who lost their lives in a battle whose only justification was the preservation of British face *vis-à-vis* Chiang Kai-shek and the *Kuomintang*.

9 Fall of Singapore: Churchill's Sacrificial Pawn

[January 1942–February 1942]

[Map: 9.1]

The Strategic Logic of Singapore: Before *World War I*, Britain had seen Japan as one of its closest allies; the country had watched its back in the Far East against the rising threat of Germany imperialism. This attitude began to change in 1915 when Japan gobbled up Germany's Shantung Concession and made clear in the process its future intentions toward China. A further shift in British sentiment came following the *Washington Naval Agreement* [1921] when America not only forced a 5:5:3 capital ship ratio on Britain and Japan but also forced them to give up their long established alliance.

The *Washington Naval Agreement* caused change in Japan as well. A slighted Japanese military and naval elite, believing that the Anglo-Saxons had 'ganged up' against them, now became increasingly anglophobe. Similarly British geopolitical analysts at the Foreign Office began to view Japan as the biggest threat to its Empire. In the past, threats to its Asian Empire came mainly from other European powers. They could be dealt with in Europe. Japan presented a non-European threat that would have to be dealt with in Asia. Thus on 16 June 1921 the British cabinet formally agreed that a naval base should be built in *Singapore*. The Australians had pressed for Sydney but the case for *Singapore*, which was several thousand miles closer to Britain, was hard to rebuff. Thereafter *Singapore* became more than an important naval base; in effect *Singapore* became the symbol of British power in Asia and the fulcrum of its vast Empire. Although *Singapore* was built into a first class fleet naval base, Britain was no longer economically capable of supporting two fleets. Furthermore the *Washington Naval Treaty* [1921] effectively prevented Britain from having two full fleets. America had a similar problem with having to support both the *Atlantic* and *Pacific* Fleets. By contrast Japan's naval interests were focused in the *Pacific* alone. Thus Britain and her Far Eastern colonies were left with vague assurances that in case of an outbreak of war in Asia, the 'Main Fleet' would be dispatched to *Singapore*. With the outbreak of war in Europe in 1939 Britain's commitment to send the main fleet to Asia was inevitably watered down. By 1941, the over-stretch of Britain's fleet in the *Atlantic, North Sea*, and the *Mediterranean* meant that the ability to send any force to Asia had all but evaporated.

Even more importantly advances in aircraft technology in the interwar years had completely undermined *Singapore*'s original *raison d'être*. By 1937, an assessment by Major-General William Dobbie and his chief of staff, Brigadier Arthur Percival (later Lieutenant-General Percival) correctly concluded that any Japanese attack would advance from Thailand and Northern Malaya. It was a premise based on the rapidly developing capabilities of modern aircraft and the recognition that the British defense of *Singapore* would rely heavily on air power and airfields placed judiciously along the east coast of Malaya. This requirement drove military tactics. The British Army would have to defend a high line in northern Malaya in order to protect the strategically important airfields located there. Ultimately British high command, having reneged on the concept that the navy would provide *Singapore*'s defense, failed even to provide adequate aircraft either in number or quality for their Asian bastion's defense. Ground defenses were required to make up for the shortfall. Even here they were short-changed. Leaving aside the issue of training, the decision not to send tanks to Malaya left the Allied troops badly under-gunned.

The troops consisted of 20,000 British, 15,000 Australian, 37,000 Indian and 17,000 sundry Malay and Asian troops, 89,000 in aggregate. Even London considered that the troops were of relatively low quality. Malay Command itself believed that its 31 battalions were 17 short of what was required. Starting on 3 January, reinforcements arrived to make up this shortfall. The 45th Indian Brigade was followed by the British 53rd Brigade; the 44th Indian Brigade arrived on 22 January. Two days later an Australian machine gun battalion arrived along with 1,900 reinforcements to supplement the Australian 8th Division. On 29 January the British 54th and 55th Brigades arrived to complete the transfer of the 18th British Division. Various smaller elements continued to arrive until 5 February. The dribbling-in of troops, in terms of acclimatization, training and deployment was less than ideal in military terms; arguably after the loss of the *Battle of Jitra* on 11–12 December it was already too late for reinforcements to have any impact on the outcome.

In the post-war analysis official British Historian, Major-General S. Woodburn Kirby concluded that ". . . a physically unfit British Division, two almost untrained Indian Brigades, a number of partially trained Indian and Australian reinforcements and aircraft which could only be a wasting asset."[1] Churchill and the Chiefs of Staff in London, knowing that *Singapore* was lost nevertheless continued to pour in fresh soldiers and therefore increased the magnitude of the disaster. In spite of Britain's equivocation as to how to defend *Singapore*, the city and its naval bastion had come to occupy a totemic position in Britain's Asian Empire. As historian H. P. Wilmott has commented, "By December 1941 *Singapore* had become nothing less than a British virility symbol."[2]

America too, increasingly committed to helping Britain to fight the *Atlantic War* with Germany, was too stretched to be able to provide a *Pacific* fleet capable of matching Japan. America was confident in its ability to win any naval war in the *Pacific* but not yet. With rising concern about Japan's threat to its Asian Empire, comprising the Philippines and *Hawaii*, America's Congress, in spite of its isolationist mode, was sufficiently alarmed to pass the *Two Ocean Naval Expansion Act* [June 1940]—a US$4bn building program that would provide 18 aircraft carriers, seven battleships, 27 cruisers, 115 destroyers and 43 submarines. The program would give America massive superiority in firepower in the *Pacific* but was planned for completion only in 1946.

Plans for the Defense of Singapore: In spite of Britain's Asian strategic conundrum, in December 1939, Winston Churchill, while he was still First Lord of the Admiralty, produced a cabinet paper that assured his colleagues that *Singapore* was safe:

> *Singapore* is a fortress armed with five 15-inch guns and garrisoned by nearly 20,000 men. It could only be taken after a siege by an enemy of at least 50,000 men. As *Singapore* is as far away from Japan as Southampton is from New York, the operation of moving a Japanese Army with all its troop ships and maintaining it during the siege, which should take at least four or five months, would be liable to be intercepted, if at any time Britain chose to send a superior fleet to the scene.[3]

Although the causeway was blown up on 31 January 1942, Japanese infiltrators would later take small boats or wade across the low water that separated the island of *Singapore* from Johor. The destruction of the causeway badly affected morale. Gordon Bennett observed "There was a feeling that all was lost and from now on we were achieving nothing. To say that one was depressed was to put it very mildly."[4] As for the naval port at Sembawang on the northernmost part of *Singapore*, on which such vast sums had been expended in the pre-war decades, Japanese control of the straits after the destruction of Z Force made it worthless, and it was not only abandoned but also destroyed by demolition experts. As Tom Kitching, *Singapore*'s chief surveyor, noted with some bitterness: "The Naval Base is evacuated . . . so much for all the millions spent on it . . ."[5]

Much to Churchill's astonishment, the British Prime minister had only recently learnt from Wavell that the north side of *Singapore* was not fortified; *Singapore* was not the fortress that he had imagined. Furious, he raced off a memorandum to the Chiefs of Staff Committee, "I must confess to being staggered by Wavell's telegram. It never occurred to me for a moment that . . . *Singapore* . . . was not entirely fortified against an attack from the Northwards . . ."[6] Churchill also warned his colleagues "this will be one of the greatest scandals that could possibly be exposed."[7] Whether an island with a civilian population of 500,000 could be described as a fortress is open to question. In siege situations the presence of civilians, especially women and children, has, throughout history, tended to sap the morale not to mention the logistics of defenders. Even the best of besieged fortresses need the possibility of relief; given the need to deploy the British fleet in Europe, this was never a possibility.

But while Churchill had every right to be apoplectic that basic fortifications had not been put in place, and while his prophecy of scandal proved all too accurate, it was too late to do anything. He believed that *Singapore* was lost but refused to countenance an evacuation and insisted that the defenders put up a face-saving spirited fight. He wrote to Wavell telling him:

> I was greatly distressed by your telegrams, and I want to
> make it absolutely clear that I expect every inch of ground
> to be defended, every scrap of material or defenses to be
> blown to pieces to prevent capture by the enemy, and no
> question of surrender to be entertained until after
> protracted fighting among the ruins of Singapore City.[8]

In reply Wavell was far from optimistic about how long *Singapore* could hold out if General Percival was driven out of Malaya's southernmost province of Johor; "The fortress guns are sited for use against ships, and have mostly ammunition for that purpose only; many can only fire seawards . . . many troops remaining are of doubtful value."[9]

Having arrived at the shores of Johor, Yamashita planned his invasion with meticulous care based on the intelligence that had been gleaned. In addition to spies and aerial reconnaissance, Yamashita could also view *Singapore* from the high ground of Istana Bukit Serene, the Sultan of Johor's magnificent palace. As Colonel Tsuji would later recall in his war memoir of the Malayan Campaign, "the heights of the Imperial Palace had been selected for Army Combat Command Post because of the view the position afforded over the whole battlefield."[10] Reading British psychology perfectly, as he had done for the past two months, Yamashita decided it was completely safe to make it his HQ as he believed that the reverential British would never bomb it.

Percival had a total of 70,000 infantry of mixed experience plus 15,000 others, clerks and support staff, who could be pulled into the line if necessary. The thirty-eight battalions comprised 17 Indian, 13 British, 6 Australian, and 2 Malayan. In addition there were three machine gun battalions. The defenders were not helped by Lieutenant-General Arthur Percival's bitter dislike of the Australian Major-General Gordon Bennett. Neither was the constant interference of Australia's Prime Minister particularly helpful. Bennett's two brigades from the Australian 8th Division in addition to the 44th Indian Brigade were given the western and northwestern sectors of the island where *Singapore*'s main airfield, Royal Air Force (RAF) Tengah was located. Percival had placed what he considered to be his weakest troops west of the causeway where he did not expect Yamashita's main attack. East of the causeway, near the now abandoned naval base, rather than the nearby airfield, was considered the likely target of Yamashita's main thrust. Here Percival placed his strongest forces. Percival guessed wrong. Yamashita's main attack would arrive west of the causeway.

The west and northwest of the island was an area full of mangrove swamp, dense jungle interspersed by rivers and creeks. That it was not an area suitable for defense had not been previously identified; there were no open fields of fire in which to restrict enemy movement. Even the barbed wire that was available in large quantities at Nee Soon Ordnance Base was not made available to the Australians, who were told it was reserved for elsewhere. Frank Baker, a mortar platoon lance corporal, recalled, "It was an absolute shambles—we had no defenses."[11] In the north and west, Indian troops were stationed under Lieutenant-General Sir Lewis Heath and Major-General B. W. Key. This area included the Sembawang Naval Base. The mainly urban southern area was allotted to Major-General Frank Simmons who had a mixed bag of Malayan, Indian and Straits Settlements Volunteer Force troops. Reserves were thin, comprising five shattered battalions from the Malay Peninsula retreat, and were more nominal than real.

Against them Yamashita could muster just 30,000 troops. He was outnumbered by more than 2:1 by Percival's troops. For an amphibious assault military textbooks would normally recommend that the attacker needs a 2:1 advantage to be successful. A Japanese victory, often seen as inevitable in post-war writing, was far from assured. Yamashita's troops included the Imperial Guards Division with an accompanying light tank brigade, the 5th Division under Lieutenant-General Takuro Matsui and the 18th Division under Lieutenant-General Renya Mutaguchi. The 'eastern sector' was awarded to Major-General Takuma Nishimura's Imperial Guards Division, whose erratic performance in the Malaya Campaign had relegated them to Yamashita's secondary front to the east of the causeway. The main attack operation was awarded to the 5th and 18th Divisions to the west of causeway.

Leaving aside Yamashita's significant troop disadvantage, it was still a far from straightforward operation. His lines of communication were stretched and supply was problematic. Indeed, had it not been for the capture of the west coast seaport of Endau (Johor) by the Japanese 55th Division on 21 January, which allowed a supply convoy to land *matériel* on 26 January, Yamashita would have run out of bullets. Such was the fine margin on which Japan's Malayan Campaign had been predicated. Furthermore Yamashita's troops were exhausted. They had bicycled and fought their way down the Malay Peninsula and inevitably suffered from the usual bevy of tropical diseases. Nevertheless, in spite of having suffered 4,565 casualties (including 1,793 dead) in their 55-day advance south, it was an army, unlike their enemy, that was victorious. High spirits put the fatigue of Japanese troops on hold.

Air Battles over Singapore: Earlier by the end of December 1941, with the airfields of Malaya now under Yamashita's control, Japan had moved forward its air units to begin more sustained operations against *Singapore*. Japan's 22nd Air Flotilla moved nineteen Zeros and five C5Ms from Soc Trang Airfield in Indochina to Kota Bharu while the rest of the flotilla went to airfields on Mir and Kuching on the northwest coast of *Borneo*. From here Japanese aircraft were able to intercept any Allied shipping heading for *Singapore*. On the night of 29 December oil tanks in *Singapore* were bombed causing fires while thirty-one G3Ms from Genzan Combat Group raided Seletar, *Singapore* City and Keppel Harbor. During the day Japanese raiding sorties strafed and bombed retreating British army positions in Malaya.

As ever, the British underrated the Japanese. Kuala Lumpur Airfield and Port Swettenham Airfield had been booby-trapped and it was estimated that it would take three months for the Japanese to make them operational. In retaliation for the death of a few Japanese troops who were killed in the airfield battles, the invaders forced

Australian prisoners to walk through minefields to detonate land mines. Kuala Lumpur Airfield became operational within three days. The Japanese were now set for a full-scale air assault on *Singapore*.

The shortcomings of the British Brewster Buffalo fighters continued to be exposed as they sought to defend against the incessant Japanese bombing raids. On 12 January 1942 eight Buffaloes scrambled from Sembawang Airfield and gave chase to a departing formation of twenty-seven Japanese bombers. The Japanese opened their throttles and went into a shallow dive leaving the Buffaloes in their wake. One British pilot remarked, "Bombers outpacing fighters—you've got to f . . . well laugh!"[12] The Buffaloes were equally hard done by in their attempts to outfly Japanese fighters.

The problem was well illustrated by Flight-Lieutenant Garden's description of a dogfight involving Nakajima Ki-27 'Nates' that he attacked head-on on 12 January, the first disastrous day of the bombing blitz on *Singapore*. He saw the face of one Japanese pilot as he passed so close that the 'Nate's' aerial dented the starboard wing of his Buffalo. He wrote,

> There were three of them in formation on my tail and I could not out-turn them. Meanwhile they were hammering my main-planes and fuselage with their machine guns. I was dying for an excuse to bale out, until I remembered the advice of Flight-Lieutenant Tim Vigors, which was to the effect that when you think all is lost and death and destruction are imminent, just shut your eyes, work the rudder left and right, open the throttle to maximum and "pudding basin" the control column—and I did just that and when I opened my eyes there was not an aircraft in the sky to be seen, but my aircraft had suffered considerable damage and was flying extremely badly and vibrating severely. I turned for home. As the aircraft came to a halt at the end of the runway, it slowly collapsed around me.[13]

As for dealing with the Zero, the Buffalo pilots learned early on that to try to out-fight a Zero was virtually suicidal. If a British pilot was lucky enough to get off a few rounds, he soon learnt to push the joystick forward, dive and head for the 'decks'; the Zero could outpace, out-climb and outmaneuver but it could not out-dive. By the end of 12 January, the first day of Japan's first major air attack on *Singapore*, fifty-four British sorties had been made at a cost of six Buffaloes shot down, three lost in accidents and a further four damaged. Sergeant Webster reflected, "the Japs have been sending fighter pilots over here all day and our lads have been doing their best, but as I have known well all the time—thanks to the inability of lots of people to organize, train and run a fighter force—it was just a great shambles."[14]

Not all the Allied pilot losses were down to Japan's air superiority. Not helped by inexperience and fatigue, there were frequent accidents. Sergeant Arthur noted in his diary on 5 January that "Shortie Elliott [from Wellington and, at nineteen years of age, the youngest pilot on the squadron] went west."[15] Elliott was just taking off while Ron Shields, also from Wellington, had aborted a sortie when his engine started to misfire. Shields took a short cut across the aerodrome and hit Elliot head on in a massive explosion. In spite of the chaotic scenes at British airfields, reinforcement convoys managed to arrive from India intact. In the second convoy (DM-1) arriving on 13 January, crates of fifty-one Hurricane fighter planes were hurriedly prepared for battle by the men of 151-Maintenance Unit. Within four days twenty-one Hurricanes were prepared for action. However, many of the pilots had little or no flying time with Hurricanes. Furthermore, while the addition of four guns increased the aircraft's firepower, their weight significantly reduced speed and maneuverability. For some Japanese pilots the Hurricane, or the 'Hullicane' as they called it, was more difficult to pronounce than to fight against.

Great faith was put in the new aircraft and Sergeant Weber of 243-Squadron noted in his diary that "we had the great thrill when we saw our Hurricanes overhead. And today to see the squadron in the air was a sight for sore eyes. They are indeed sleek looking creatures—streamlined and speed personified."[16] In reality the performance of the planes, in large part due to the inexperience of their pilots, was lacklustre. It was not the game-changing weapon that had been hoped for.

Meanwhile the Japanese raids were taking a toll on the effective running of British airfields. After the first big raid on Sembawang Airfield (*Singapore*), the local Chinese labor force evaporated. It meant that British Service staff had to take on work done by service personnel such as cooking and cleaning as well as, more importantly, filling in bomb craters. With a lack of earth-moving equipment and rollers, this task had to be done mainly by hand. On most days at least half the new Hurricanes were not in a serviceable condition to fly. By 27 January 243-Squadron was so reduced and Kallang Airfield riven with craters that they were unable to land and were ordered to fly on to Sembawang Airfield instead. Here their four remaining pilots were merged with 453-Squadron. The demoralized squad was then investigated by the Service Police for suspected deserters—a result of problems with certain Hudson bomber units in Malaya. The station commander and Air Vice-Marshal Sir Paul Maltby (later Black Rod in the House of Lords) gave a pep talk that backfired when they spoke about the Australians being "Yellow"; the squadron diary reported the pilots as being "very, very upset and angry."[17] The pilots' time in *Singapore* was by now nearly up. By 28 January of the fifty-one Hurricanes delivered, only twenty-one were in flying condition. Three days later, with *Singapore*'s airfields increasing unusable, the orders were given to move to *Java*.

In eleven days of intense fighting 232-Squadron had claimed thirty-eight confirmed kills with ten probables for the loss of eighteen Hurricanes in operational sorties. Seven more were very badly damaged and two had been lost on the ground. 232-Squadron and stragglers from elsewhere were ordered to *Sumatra*. Only a handful of aircraft remained on *Singapore*. On Wednesday 4 February a handful of Hurricane pilots arrived at their field to find that their ground crews had disappeared and that their aircraft were unprepared. As for the runways these could only be repaired using Chinese labor under armed guard—some of whom were shot as they attempted to flee. When the Hurricane mission had to be cancelled, Group-Captain Watts received a message of inquiry as to why the fighters had not been ready. Watts finished his drink in the mess and went to his room and shot himself. Writing about this tragedy later, Sergeant Peter Ballard recalled that Watts had become increasingly demoralized and had had a "death wish on him for some time."[18] It seems that "during daylight high level bombing attacks on Tengah, he would be seen walking about the airfield, out in the open, refusing to take cover at all while everybody else jumped into the nearest slit trenches available. If his behavior was meant to be an inspiration it had the opposite effect, and we thought him out of his mind."[19]

With just twelve aircraft left to defend the city, the pilots were in a desperate situation. Enemy patrols over the aerodrome were constant. To try to un-camouflage, prepare for flight and try to take-off was not practicable. As Sergeant Jack Burton concluded "it is suicide to take off."[20] Inevitably planes were at their most vulnerable as they were climbing because fighters above them had the advantage of speed. In *Singapore* the increasingly desperate government notices in newspapers and on the radio were urging workers to carry on regardless of the air raids. From the Japanese a different message was being broadcast. "Hello *Singapore*!" trilled the Japanese broadcaster from a radio station set up on *Penang*, "How do you like our bombing? You saw what happened yesterday? That is a trifle to what is in store for you."[21] By Thursday 15 February, Sembawang Airfield had become the front line and Sergeant Weber of 453-Squadron noted in his diary that "Ridiculous as it may seem to we lesser individuals, our squadron is now situated in no-man's-land, between two opposing armies . . ."[22]

The Attack on Singapore: Yamashita's Bluff: **[Map: 9.1]** On 3 February Yamashita started the artillery and aerial bombardment of the island. Five days of intense fire poured down on *Singapore*. On the evening of 7 February the 400 troops of the Konoe Imperial Guards crossed to *Ibin Island* to the east of the causeway; it was here that Percival had placed his main forces, the Third Army comprising the 9th, 11th and 18th Divisions.

The *Ibin Island* maneuver was a feint. Yamashita's main attack was planned for the western side of the causeway. There, on the evening of 8 February Japanese 5th and 18th Divisions assembled on the carefully camouflaged roads that would take them to the water's edge for embarkation. At 8.30 p.m., a first wave of 4,000 Japanese infantry landed from 150 small boats on the beaches of Sarimbun on the northwestern coast. The noise of the boats was drowned out by the artillery barrage; "Silently the men jumped out of the boats, sinking up to their loins in the mud of the shore; but they forced their way through the mud, mangrove roots and broken wire entanglements protecting the enemy position, and rushed their [Australian] trenches and pillboxes."[23]

In one notable act of bravery Lance-Corporal Yamamoto, one of the boat commanders, guided a raft of three launches lashed together to the shores of *Singapore*. On arrival

Yamamoto collapsed to the ground whereupon the squad commander could see that his lungs were protruding through his ribs. He had said nothing about his wounds from an exploding artillery shell. "Long live the Emperor!" Yamamoto whispered to the squad commander, "I am indebted to you for your kind assistance. Excuse me for going a step ahead of you."[24] He then expired. Yamamoto was posthumously awarded an individual letter of commendation and was promoted two grades in rank.

The thinly spread Australian lines had been badly deployed by Major-General Gordon Bennett and comprising just 3,000 soldiers, the lines were soon breached, leading to pockets of Australian troops being surrounded and destroyed. This was not surprising given the lackadaisical, unfocused defense plans. Lewis gunner Cliff Olsen remembered, "We were horribly spread out and it was pitch black and they [Japanese troops] were very hard to see. They walked through us half the time."[25] It was also noted by Frank Baker that, whereas he had a 0.303 Lee Enfield rifle, ". . . the Japs all seemed to be armed with automatic weapons. The shocking thing was that in our briefings we had been told their armaments were inferior to ours and their grenades were just toys."[26] Having achieved a beachhead Yamashita was able to land some 14,000 troops by dawn.

Communications to the Australian front broke down. Not believing that the Japanese attack from the west was the main Japanese thrust Percival declined to send reinforcements. Percival believed that the Japanese main invasion would be to the east of the causeway because he believed that the naval base, albeit already abandoned by the British would be Yamashita's primary target. Bizarrely, in a dispatch, he affirmed that "the object of the defense was not to hold *Singapore Island*, but to protect the Naval Base"[27] though how he could protect one and not the other was not explained. Surprisingly, on realizing that the main attack was being made in the west, Percival failed to withdraw troops from the quiet sectors to form a strong reserve. Once the Japanese had broken through in the west, the holding of positions in the east and south was largely redundant.

Although fierce fighting continued through the night and following morning, Japanese superiority in air cover and artillery told. A general uncoordinated retreat ensued. Although in some instances they had fought bravely it was overall a shambolic performance by the defenders. Australian soldiers had been disastrously let down by their commanders; their morale was shattered. Defeatism became rampant and not just among the troops. At Wavell's HQ at Lembang in the hills of *Java*, Sir Henry Pownall, Brooke-Popham's replacement, noted in his diary, "*Singapore* is on its last legs . . . I fear that we were frankly out-generalled, outwitted and out-fought."[28] Private Paul Gemmell described the action as ". . . a foul up from start to finish. General Percival had been advised that the Japanese would land on the west coast, so he sent all his troops to the east . . . We felt we could have held them with reinforcements . . . We felt betrayed."[29] Yamashita's concentration of forces against an outnumbered and weakly organized defense was always going to overwhelm the defenders no matter how valiantly they fought. As Churchill noted in *Hinge of Fate* [1950], "There were no permanent defenses on the front about to be attacked."[30]

Although fifty-one Mark II Hurricane fighters had arrived in *Singapore* in December followed by a further forty-eight stationed in *Sumatra*, Mitsubishi 'Betty' and 'Nell' bombers destroyed many of them on the ground. Although there were dogfights over Sarimbun Beach and half a dozen Japanese bombers were shot down, by the end of the first day of fighting, Percival had just eight serviceable Hurricanes at his disposal at Kallang Airfield on *Singapore*. These were now moved to *Sumatra*.

From the air *Singapore* was not a pretty picture. On 5 February Hudson bomber pilot Sergeant Ian Newlands who was designated to fly one of the planes to pick up Air Vice-Marshal Pullford and his staff and fly them to *Sumatra* noted "Approaching *Singapore* the future did not look bright. Thick palls of smoke hung in the air fed by burning oil tanks and various ships. It looked like pictures we had seen of Dunkirk."[31] By 9 February Japanese bombing attacks were raining bombs down on Allied positions and there was little that the remaining Hurricanes could do. As for the 15-inch coastal guns that had been installed at vast expense to defend *Singapore*, they could not be used, not, as is often believed because they were in fixed positions facing out to sea. Most of them could be swiveled to face inland but in another cruel tale of chronic mismanagement these behemoth guns were supplied only with armor piecing shells to bombard ships, not the dispersion shells that could have wrought havoc on invading infantry forces. The following day when Japanese landings moved to go to the southwest, the 44th Infantry Brigade was forced to retreat and General Bennett decided to fall back to a new line of defense, from the east of Tengah Airfield to north Jurong.

Meanwhile poor communications hampered the 22nd Australian Brigade in the northern sector under Brigadier Duncan Maxwell whose troops had battered the Imperial Guards when they landed at 10.00 p.m. on the evening of 9 February. Although Japanese troops had managed to gain a foothold on the beach, Maxwell, fearing that he was being surrounded unnecessarily ordered a retreat against Bennett's orders. The retreat opened up the 11th Indian Division's flank and also allowed Japanese troops to advance directly to *Singapore* from Woodlands, thereby undermining the Jurong Line. Maxwell, a doctor in civilian life, had earlier called on Percival to tell him that the loss of *Singapore* was not worth a single life. The *Battle of Kranji* as it came to be called was therefore lost after a propitious beginning.

All of the beaches west of the causeway were now open. Yamashita used this opportunity to float over his light tanks and they speedily turned the flank of the Jurong Line set up by Bennett. They could have stormed into the city center itself but decided to hold back. Churchill, clearly mystified as to how a small Japanese army was pushing back a much larger British army, cabled Wavell with exhortations: "I rely on you to show no mercy to weakness in any form. With the Russians fighting as they are and the Americans so stubborn at *Luzon*, the whole reputation of our country and our race is involved. It is expected that every unit will be brought into close contact with the enemy and fight it out."[32] Indeed at this point, and embarrassingly for Churchill, MacArthur's troops, trapped on the Bataan Peninsula seemed to be performing much better than their British counterparts. In a cable to Wavell on 9 February, Churchill vexed his extreme frustration:

> I think you ought to realize the way we view the situation in Singapore. It was reported to the Cabinet by the Chiefs of Staff of the Imperial General Staff that Percival has over 100,000 men. It is doubtful whether the Japanese have as many in the whole Malay Peninsula. In the circumstances, the defenders must greatly outnumber Japanese forces who have crossed the Straits, and in a well-contested battle they should destroy them. There must at this stage be no thought of saving the troops or sparing the civilian population. The battle must be fought to the bitter end at all costs. Commanders and senior officers should die with their troops. The honor of the British Empire and of the British Army is at stake. With the Russians fighting as they are and the Americans so stubborn at *Luzon*, the whole reputation of our country and our race is involved.[33]

The Australian 22nd Brigade that had borne the brunt of the fighting was 'all-in' and could only muster 200 troops. By now Yamashita was also running out of reserves of troops and his attack was stretched to the limits; he needed to end the battle quickly. The anxiety of Japan's leading military commanders was also growing; Admiral Matome Ugaki wrote in his diary, "I hope it won't turn out to be another Bataan."[34] Yamashita therefore called on Percival to end his pointless resistance. ". . . the war situation is already determined and in the meantime the surrender of *Singapore* is imminent," Yamashita warned Percival in a message dropped behind British lines. "From now on," he continued, "resistance is futile and merely increases the danger to the million civilian inhabitants without good reason exposing them to infliction of pain by fire and sword."[35] A dispirited Percival, surrounded by feuding senior commanders, decided to fight on.

The following day battles were fought at Pasir Panjang and Bukit Timah. After fierce resistance from the Malay soldiers these areas were overwhelmed and the major allied munitions store at Bukit Timah was captured. The Japanese soldiers were so enraged by the resistance put up by the 1st Malay Infantry Brigade that they tied Second Lieutenant Adnan bin Saidi to a cherry tree and bayonetted him to death. His platoon had held up the Japanese for two days at Pasir Panjang.

Surrender and Humiliation: On 13 February senior British officers advised Percival to surrender to save civilian lives. A repetition of the already infamous Rape of Nanking was feared. Percival claimed to have his "honour to consider"[36]; General Sir Lewis Heath, another fractious colleague, who commanded the 3rd Indian Division shot back, "You need not bother about your honor. You lost that a long time ago up north."[37] Percival remained adamant that he would not surrender though he nevertheless agreed to seek discretionary permission to do so. The prospects of holding out worsened the following day when Percival was informed that with the water pipes shattered by bombing, supply would run out within a day or two.

On 14 February the Imperial Konoe Division completed the repairs of the causeway allowing Yamashita to bring all his forces to bear on *Singapore*. With the causeway open, heavy guns were brought up to heights east of the reservoir. Bombardment of the center of *Singapore* could now begin in earnest.

At 1.00 p.m. on 14 February Japanese soldiers were seen approaching Alexandra Barracks Hospital. At 1.40 p.m. a British lieutenant greeted them waving a white flag. He was immediately butchered with a bayonet thrust. Japanese troops then entered the hospital and proceeded to murder staff and patients. The following day 200 male staff and patients, many badly wounded, who had been bound up overnight, were marched to an industrial estate half a mile away. When anyone collapsed they were bayonetted. Pushed into dingy rooms without water many died of their ailments. The following day the remainder were taken off in small groups to be bayonetted or hacked to death with machete. In all about 320 men and women were massacred over several days. There were just five known lucky survivors. It was later suspected that Colonel Tsuji was the architect of the massacre; a tactic designed to persuade Percival of the consequences of not surrendering.

By the morning of 15 February both sides were desperate. The last lines of British defense had been breached, food and water for the besieged were running low, ammunition was in short supply and many Allied troops had deserted their posts and were now looting the city. Captain A. G. Menz of the Australian Provost Company reported, "Arms and equipment being discarded all over *Singapore*. Wharves crowded with soldiers viewing chances of getting off in boats . . . morale shocking. A lot of men hid themselves . . ."[38] At 9.30 a.m. Percival called a conference of his commanders and after discussing but rejecting the possibility of a counter-attack, decided to surrender. In hindsight, given the exhaustion of Japanese resources, a bold attack by Percival might have succeeded. As Yamashita later admitted, "They . . . had more bullets and other munitions than I had."[39]

Percival was ordered to proceed to the Ford Motor Factory where Yamashita gave the terms of surrender. Unconditional surrender was asked for and given; the British were ordered to provide 1,000 troops to serve as police. Percival asked for a guarantee of safety for his troops. It was required that a flag of the rising sun be hoisted immediately on the Cathay Building, *Singapore*'s tallest construction. Some were not convinced that surrender was necessary; one resident thought it was "a most extraordinary situation. British troops all over the place. Fully armed . . . and yet we have surrendered. And the number of Jap troops to be seen is negligible."[40] However, the Malayan civil service put out a circular to all troops that surrender was because of shortage of stores and ammunition. There was considerable Japanese surprise that the British had not destroyed the airfields and harbor. A junior British officer was interrogated and asked why this had not been done. He replied, "Because we will return again."[41]

In the campaign-ending *Battle of Singapore*, the Japanese had lost 1,714 men killed in action in addition to 3,378 wounded. They had captured "roughly 100,000 prisoners of war, of whom about 50,000 were white soldiers."[42] Also taken were 740 artillery pieces, 2,500 machine guns, 65,000 rifles, 1,000 locomotives and wagons, 200 armored cars, 10 light airplanes, and several thousand motorcars and trucks. Nevertheless for Tsuji the British surrender was a bittersweet moment. He later recalled that

> Since my appointment to the 25th Army as Staff Officer in Charge of Operations, I had vowed to the Gods to abstain from wine and tobacco until my cherished wish was accomplished. We had expected that on this day we would drink until our glasses were "bottoms up". But what actually happened was that we could not enjoy our wine or eat our delicacies. They tasted bitter and seemed to choke one's throat because of the three thousand several hundred seniors, colleagues, and soldiers with whom we could not share this day's joy.[43]

Hirohito duly sent a congratulatory Imperial Rescript: "Officers and men, risking malaria, and enduring intense heat, have struck violently at the enemy, engaged in unremitting pursuit at lightning speed, destroyed his powerful army, and captured *Singapore*. As a consequence Britain's base of operations in the Far East is overthrown and annihilated. I deeply approve of this."[44] For Yamashita the surrender came just in time. He could not have fought on for much longer. He recalled,

> My attack on Singapore was a bluff—a bluff that worked. I had 30,000 men and was outnumbered more than three to one. I knew that if I had to fight for long for Singapore, I would be beaten. That is why the surrender had to be at once. I was very frightened all the time that the British would discover our numerical weakness and lack of supplies and force me into disastrous street fighting.[45]

Over the course of three months of fighting, Yamashita, at cost of 3,506 dead and 6,150 wounded had inflicted casualties of 17,500 on Percival of which 7,500 were killed. In addition, the Japanese had taken 120,000 prisoners over the duration of the Malaya campaign. For the last week of the campaign the Japanese had had complete control of the air over *Singapore*. Total Allied fighter aircraft shot down in *Singapore* and Malaya had been 122 Buffaloes and forty-five Hurricanes. However, the 3rd Composite Air Division reported the loss of 331 aircraft of all types from all causes. In addition 500 personnel were killed. Although the Allies claimed to have shot down 183 Japanese planes, this was a considerable overstatement. The more likely figure is estimated at closer to 100.

Consequences of the Fall of Singapore: For Britain the defeat of the British Army in Malaya and *Singapore* was, according to Churchill, the single biggest disaster in their entire history. Given that the British forces had 90,000 troops at the beginning of the war compared to a Japanese combat force of three divisions comprising just 50,197, it is easy to comprehend Churchill's amazement and incomprehension. The scale of the victory is even more impressive in terms of its speed and number of casualties on the Japanese side given that, in textbook terms, the attacking force needed a two to one superiority in numbers to have a chance of victory.

The defeat at the *Battle of Singapore* also did lasting damage to Britain's reputation as a great power. Writing after the war, Colonel Tsuji, the brilliant strategist and brutal instigator of atrocities, who miraculously escaped prosecution as a war criminal, wrote in the preface to *Singapore 1941–1942, The Japanese Version of the Malayan Campaign of World War II* [1988] that with regard to *Singapore*, "England was weighed in the balance and found wanting, and she forfeited the dignity of one hundred and twenty years."[46] It was a dignity never to be recovered. In Tokyo the victory against the 'arrogant' British and their empire was sweet indeed. Tokyo Radio announced, "There will be no Dunkirk at Singapore. The British are not going to be allowed to get away with it this time. All ships leaving will be destroyed."[47] The Japanese government distributed cakes and caramel drops to children; families were also given beer, sake and red beans.

The *Asahi Shimbun* captured the mood of the press and public when it declared a headline that stated, "GENERAL SITUATION OF THE WAR DECIDED."[48] Similarly Colonel Hideo Ohira, Chief of the Army Press Division, stated "with the fall of Singapore the general situation of the war has been determined. The ultimate victory will be ours."[49]

Tojo told the Diet (Japan's bicameral national assembly) that while Burma and the Philippines would be granted independence, *Hong Kong* and Malaya would be retained as vital bases; he went on to add that,

> The objective in the Great East Asia War [Japanese name for *Second Sino-Japanese War* and the *Pacific War*] is founded on the exalted ideals of the founding of the Empire and it will enable all the nations and peoples of Greater East Asia to enjoy life and to establish a new order of co-existence and co-prosperity on the basis of justice with Japan as the nucleus.[50]

Tojo also took the opportunity to call on Australia and New Zealand to abandon Britain and America and join Japan in building a "New Order in the World."[51] General Ugaki gloated in his diary that "I am sure that the Australians were scared stiff."[52] They were. Arguably the British relationship with Australia was permanently damaged. Their troops had been used in the Middle East and Malaya. They felt aggrieved that so little had seemingly been done to protect *Singapore*. In their eyes promises of protection had been reneged upon. The loss of *Singapore* was a blow to Britain but not one that threatened its national security. For Australia the fall of *Singapore* represented an existential threat. Australian Prime Minister Curtin described it as "Australia's Dunkirk."[53] For many Australians the British were a 'busted flush' who had failed to honor their commitments to defend them. Curtin prepared his countrymen for the worst as he predicted the "battle for Australia"[54] would soon follow. The Australian Chiefs of Staff concluded that Japan would likely attack Port Moresby and "thence the mainland of Australia."[55] After the fall of *Singapore*, Curtin understandably turned to America for salvation. Much to Churchill's chagrin, Curtin declared, "Without any inhibitions of any kind, I make it quite clear that Australia looks to America, free of any pangs as to our traditional links or kinship with the United Kingdom."[56]

It can only be imagined how the war might have developed differently if Churchill had taken the realistic course of abandoning Malaya, Burma and *Singapore* and concentrating instead on a defense centered on *Ceylon* and India. The sacrifice of an army in Malaya alone of 120,000 trained troops was a devastating blow to Britain's ability to have a decisive impact on the outcome of the war. By the time that General Slim had rebuilt the British-Indian Army in India, America and Australia had already won the decisive 'turning point' battles of the *Pacific War*. However, it would have taken a political leader even braver and stronger than Churchill to abandon *Singapore* without a fight, whatever the strategic logic might have suggested.

The Fall of Singapore and Malaya in Retrospect: After the war Percival would attempt to salvage his reputation and put the blame for the humiliating loss of Malaya squarely on Churchill and the government in London for their lack of support in terms of tanks and aircraft. He had a point. However, it is quite clear that on the ground British strategy and tactics were wholly inadequate. Had General Percival accepted the loss of Malaya that he had previously acknowledged to be 'not-defendable,' strong defensive positions could have been constructed both in the southern tip of Malaya and northern *Singapore Island*. It was a strategy that he rejected as being too defeatist. The failure to construct adequate defenses for *Singapore* was the glaring oversight for which Percival, Shenton Thomas, Brooke-Popham, the Malay civil service, and ministers in London were all responsible. With hindsight it is clear that Yamashita, with his small army and fragile logistics, had the slimmest margin of victory in Malaya and *Singapore* and one can only surmise that even a modest amount of governmental effort or better general-ship by British generals and bureaucrats, might have seen Britain victorious. For Britain the defeat was abject and shaming. Tom Kitching summed it up perfectly: ". . . the manner of the fall of *Singapore* provides the blackest page in the History of the British Empire."[57] It is a catastrophe that still haunts Britain's reputation today in Asia.

Native support could have been much better coordinated by the organization of jungle-based guerrilla groups dispersed throughout central and Northern Malaya, which could have constantly harried Yamashita's lines of supply. The Malay Chinese in particular, were especially 'up for the fight' given the long war waged by the Japanese against their compatriots on the Chinese mainland since 1931. Percival's complacency was reflected throughout the Malay civil service that had become lazy, racist in their view of the Japanese and wholly complacent. As Duff Cooper complained regarding the Malayan civil service, they "failed lamentably in making adequate preparations for war."[58]

Critiques of the catastrophic Malayan campaign have tended to focus on the inadequacies of the colonial armies and leadership in Malaya. Typically, British historians such as Corelli Barnett, have written excoriatingly about the intellectual and moral corruption and incompetence of

> a handful of Imperial rulers in white duck or khaki drill whose minds . . . were ossified by the arrogance of race and empire and hierarchical snobberies of colonial society, and whose energies had been un-sprung by long service in damp heat, by a social round lubricated by an excess of gin-slings and *stengahs* [Malayan word for *half*; an abbreviated name for a drink consisting of *half* whisky, *half* water, over ice].[59]

While this is an undoubtedly accurate description of the structural failings of the British Empire at the end of the 1930s, there has often been a lack of due respect given to the military brilliance of the Japanese during the Malayan Campaign. *Singapore's* capitulation was not simply a story of 'guns pointing the wrong way' and other post-war mythologies. Yamashita's tactics, the ability to concentrate force, the speed of attack, the adroitness of flanking movements, the superb discipline and morale of the Japanese troops, the coordination of air and ground forces were all components of a remarkably skilled military operation. In part the historic downplaying or neglect of Yamashita's generalship may be due to the atrocities committed by the Japanese in the aftermath of their victories. 'Military brilliance' and 'civilian massacre' were not, and are not now concepts that sit comfortably together.

Moreover, plaudits for generalship rarely go to generals who end up on the losing side. There may also be a racial undertone to the lack of respect for the abilities of an Asian soldier. There has been a general tendency to blame Britain's defeats in the *Pacific War* as almost entirely the result of incompetence while praising the later victories as almost entirely the result of military brilliance. However, General Wavell recognized that the enemy had performed exceptionally well and admitted to his confidante Joan Bright, who ran the Commander in Chief's information room in London, that Japan had used its "forces boldly and has been too quick for us."[60]

General Yamashita, possibly set up to fail by both Tojo, as well as his immediate commander General Terauchi, who he also loathed, won a stunning victory with a small force of infantry that was significantly outnumbered in Malaya. Such was Yamashita's mastery that Percival remained convinced throughout that he was facing five Japanese divisions rather than the three that Yamashita actually had at his disposal. Though he had been offered a further two divisions, Yamashita had declined them because the Japanese Army did not possess adequate logistical support for a larger force; an extraordinary testament to how Japan achieved its early *Pacific War* victories operating on a logistical 'shoe-string.' Indeed Yamashita's advance down the Malay Peninsula became highly dependent on captured British supplies—what became known to the Japanese as 'Churchill Stores.'

Yamashita's belief that he could conquer Malaya with an outnumbered force also reflected the deeply racist view of the Japanese Army that Asian troops, India and Indian Malaya, were virtually worthless. In Yamashita's mind he was confronting 45,000 Caucasian troops. That was all that counted. In the event it was a correct assessment though one that would be turned on its head once Lieutenant-General 'Bill' Slim set about building a professional Indian Army in 1943.

Even allowing for their expert destruction of Britain's naval and aerial capabilities, and the relative paucity of the troops facing them, the Japanese foot soldier nevertheless had to win the battle on the ground, often over terrain where aerial power was of little assistance. Yamashita was assisted by the meticulous research and planning carried out by Lieutenant-Colonel Tsuji. It is usually overlooked that Japanese troops had to operate in hostile and unfamiliar environments; this was after all home turf for the British and colonial defenders. Yet Japanese forces acquitted themselves far better than the home team, Great Britain. Japan's armies were largely trained and experienced in operations in the cold climate and terrain of northern China. Here, horses were the principal means of transport. For the move south, Tsuji needed to switch Japanese troops to the use of trucks and bicycles for deployment. It is also often overlooked that Japan had relatively little time to prepare its southern campaigns given that until mid-1941 her main concerns were the defeat of China and the defense of Manchuria's northern borders. For ten years, the Japanese GHQ staff had planned a mobilization and invasion strategy against its number one enemy, the Soviet Union.

By contrast in mid-1941, after the American oil embargo of July, Tsuji, with just thirty colleagues of the *Doro Nawa* (the Taiwan Army Research unit), was given the responsibility for the planning of the new Southern Advance strategy that was implemented in December 1941:

> . . . in a period not exceeding six months, [they] planned
> the military operations of the whole army which was to
> move south, and also the administration of the territories
> to be occupied, and I declare with humility that it provided
> the greatest and in fact the only instruction book on
> tropical warfare available to the Japanese armies.[61]

In terms of timing Tsuji asserts "not until September 1941 did we begin active preparations for military operations to the south."[62] In a remarkably short period Tsuji and his colleagues assembled intelligence on British troop deployments, terrain, equipment, defenses, and beachheads. The gathering of information was achieved through the use of agents and reconnaissance flights. Information was collected from the Southward Association and from bankers, sea captains, university professors and mine engineers. Maps were a particular problem. By comparison with Russia, for which Imperial General HQ had extremely accurate maps to 1:100,000 scale, for Malaya there were only inaccurate local offerings.

Inevitably the shortness of time available considerably diminished the quality and accuracy of the work done. Tsuji complained bitterly about the under-planning of the Southern Advance. The conquest of Malaya by Japan should not therefore be considered to be the result of superb, long-prepared plans; rather it should be concluded that Japan won the first stages of the war in spite of hastily thrown together plans. Yamashita had to overcome these handicaps. Fortunately for Yamashita, the superb discipline and morale of the Japanese troops was a weighty asset in his account. His use of rapid movement, night attacks, jungle flanking operations and amphibious assaults behind allied lines were carried out with supreme confidence and precision and enabled the Japanese to defeat a significantly superior force. These were tactics that required superb troop discipline and technical proficiency on the part of junior officers. For all of Britain's glaring mistakes, General Yamashita's Malayan Campaign deserves to go down in history as one of the greatest feats of arms by any military commander of any country during *World War II*.

10 Burma Corps: Humiliation Then a Fighting Retreat

[January 1941–May 1942]

[Maps: 10.1, 10.2, 10.3, 10.4, 10.5]

Why Burma? In the opening gambits of Japan's war against the West, the three primary targets were *Pearl Harbor*, Malaya (including *Singapore*) and the Philippines. The destruction of Anglo-American military and naval resources in these three locations would allow Japan to occupy the oil rich areas of the Dutch East Indies. Tin, rare metals (such as tungsten), and rubber were secondary economic allures that came with the conquest of Malaya. However, oil, denied to Japan by Roosevelt's embargo, was the Holy Grail of Japan's 'strike south' strategy. So why was Burma an important secondary target of Japanese expansion?

Although the invasion of Burma was never central to Japan's East Asian strategy, and it could be argued that throughout the war, the India-Burma theatre was a sideshow to the main events elsewhere, it nevertheless served a number of subsidiary purposes. First the occupation of Burma would protect the *Singapore*-Malay flank of its Asian Empire. Secondly as the idea of the Japanese Empire became the dominant credo of Japan's southeastern military expansion, the idea of 'liberating' another Asian colony became a motivation, and a justification in its own right.

It was assumed, in part correctly, that the Burmese, who were agitating for independence, would be particularly receptive to helping them overthrow their colonial masters. Although Burma's prime minister, U Pu, expressed the opinion of a large swathe of Burmans that they should stand by the British, ultra-nationalists such as U Maw and Bogyoke Aung San (father of current Burmese leader Aung San Suu Kyi) saw the war with Japan as the opportunity for immediate independence. It was a movement that mixed nationalism with socialism. II. G. Wells on a world lecture tour noted "the Burmese mix-up of resentful nationalism, a sort of crude communism. . . ."[1] As in India the presumption of the British regarding the loyalties of their colonial subjects was not well received by nationalists. Without consultation with his subjects, the Governor General of India informed them that "I Victor Alexander John, Marquis of Linlithgow . . . do hereby proclaim that war has broken out between His Majesty and Germany."[2] In India Nehru was appalled, "One man and he a foreigner, plunged four hundred million of human beings into war without the slightest reference to them."[3] The Burmese nationalists were equally dismayed. The pro-Japanese Burmese leader Ba Maw resigned from the House of Representatives and attacked U Pu's policy of supporting the war.

While some Burman people went along with the British out of respect or awe for their historic power, others deeply resented the overtly racist superiority of their colonial rulers. Even the mixed blood, *café au lait* soldiers were frequently treated with contempt. Officer George Robertson, son of a Scottish forester and a Shan woman, enlisted in the Burma Royal Navy Reserve and noted that when he traveled in a car with a fellow expat officer, "I tried to strike up conversation, but he would have none of it. He neither spoke nor took any notice of me . . ."[4]

In early May 1940, Colonel Keiji Suzuki, using the alias Masuyo Minami, arrived in Rangoon as a secret agent acting for Imperial General HQ in Tokyo. He worked undercover as the correspondent for *Yomiuri Shimbun* (a national Japanese newspaper) and as General Secretary of the Japan-Burma Association. His instructions were to sound out Burmese political opinion about the possibility of cutting supply from Rangoon into China along the Burma Road.

Indeed, beyond any considerations of liberation, the most important reason for Japan's move into Burma was to win control of the Rangoon-Kunming supply route, and thus prevent American Lend-Lease *matériel* from reaching Chiang Kai-shek. With the Japanese occupation of *Hong Kong*, and their naval control of the South China Sea, the Burma Road that wound from Lashio in northern Burma to Kunming in China's Yunnan Province and thence to Chongqing, Chiang's capital, had become the only supply route to the *Kuomintang* (Chinese nationalists). It can be too easily forgotten that at the start of the West's involvement in the Asian component of *World War II*, Japan had already been fighting in China for ten years (though intensively for four years). Emperor Hirohito's armies there, including the thirteen divisions stationed on the Mongolian border, comprised some forty divisions in total: 1.35 million troops out of its entire army of 1.7 million. The importance attached by the Japanese to knocking China 'out of the game' to enable the release of more resources to fight the United States and Britain and her colonies was mirrored by Britain and America's determination to keep China 'in the game.' At the outset of the conflict, the British Chiefs of Staff sent a message to Wavell instructing him that it was "of the highest importance Chiang Kai-shek should be given every possible support and encouragement. We must in conjunction with him ensure that the Burma Road is kept open and that a flow of warlike stores reaches him. Continuation of Chinese resistance is indispensable and will pay a good dividend. Americans feel very strongly on this."[5]

Japan's war with the West was largely justified on the basis of it being unreasonable for the country to be forced to give up the gains that it had made in China over ten years; that was America's price for lifting its oil embargo and unfreezing Japanese assets in the United States. The complete defeat and encirclement of China was therefore a key strategic aim of the push into Burma. Additionally Burma itself was not without natural resources. As well as rice from the central plains, and the rubber plantations, Burma was a prime source of cobalt and produced 30 percent of the world's supply of wolfram (tungsten). There were also oil fields at Yenangyaung to the southwest of Mandalay in Central Burma. Here some 5,000 oil wells produced 250 million gallons of oil per year.

The importance of Burma to the Japanese was matched by the determination of Britain to hold it. The difference in attitude to Malaya and *Singapore* was marked. Efforts made on their behalf were little more than face saving. Burma they intended to hold. On 17 December 1941 Lord Alanbrooke, British Army Chief of Staff, noted, "Personally I do feel there is not much hope of saving *Singapore*, but feel that we ought to try to make certain of Burma."[6]

General Shojiro Iida: The Burma campaign was put under the command of General Shojiro Iida, like General Yamashita in Malaya, a graduate of the Army Staff College. After graduating twenty-seventh in the Class of 1916, a year before Yamashita, Iida, a composed and unflamboyant officer, pursued a much quieter and more conventional military career than some his fellow commanders of the first stage of the *Pacific War*. As with many of Japan's other leading officers, Iida, except in his devotion to the Emperor, was not the typical military type caricatured in the West.

In Burma, Ba-Maw, who was later asked by Iida to form the Burmese Executive Administration in August 1942, wrote that he

> had found him to be a unique type of Japanese soldier, human, fatherly, and very understanding, a militarist on the surface but not altogether so deeper down; at least he always tried to see things your way too, which was what made him different from the other militarists ... The general was a samurai in his almost mystical devotion to his emperor, his warrior caste and code, and his country, but this very devotion, which consumed him made him understand the devotion of others to their own gods.[7]

Promoted to the rank of captain in 1918, Iida took part in the Japanese Expeditionary Force that fought the Bolsheviks in Siberia. After various positions on the Army General Staff, Iida became commander of the Imperial Guards 4th Regiment in 1934. Subsequently he became Chief of Staff of the Japanese First Army in China in 1938 and the following year he was promoted to the rank of Lieutenant-General. Later in 1939 he was appointed commander of the Japanese Army in Taiwan. Iida returned to command the Imperial Guard in 1941 before being sent to Saigon to head the Twenty-fifth Army, a position that he relinquished to General Yamashita in November 1941. Iida was moved to command the Fifteenth Army, newly formed for the invasion of Burma, comprising the 33rd and 55th Divisions of the Imperial Japanese Army.

Iida's Advance from Malaya and Thailand: [Map: 10.1] From December 1941, the Japanese 5th Air Division, commanded by Lieutenant-General Obata, with a total complement of 200 aircraft including the Mitsubishi Ki-21 'Sally' heavy bomber, started to bomb Rangoon and British airfields in Burma after they arrived in Thailand from *Formosa* in early January. By 14 February, Vice-Marshal D. F. Stevenson, who had only been in his post as Allied Air Force commander in Burma for five weeks, was forced to report that all that remained were about thirty serviceable fighters, mainly Hurricanes and P-40 Tomahawks of the American Volunteer Group (AVG).

However, Iida had not waited for complete air superiority. Contrary to General Wavell's belief that if the Japanese did invade it would be in the middle of the country through the Shan States, Iida invaded the long southern strip of Burma that faces India across the *Bay of Bengal*. On 15 January 1942 Iida swept aside the 3rd and 6th Battalions of the Burma Rifles that had been sent by Lieutenant-General Hutton to defend the airfields of Tavoy and Mergui. On the insistence of Wavell, who grossly overestimated the competence of his troops, Hutton had been forced to organize a forward defense that was easily outflanked. Tavoy Airfield and Mergui Airfield were considered to be important by Iida for use in the battles for both Burma and Malaya. Iida then proceeded to advance northwards toward Rangoon. Meanwhile the small Royal Air Force (RAF) detachment of out-dated Buffalo fighters plus an American Volunteer Group (AVG) of 'Flying Tigers' flying Tomahawk P-40s were soon overwhelmed when the Japanese established bases at Tavoy Airfield and Mergui Airfield. Squadron leader Monty 'Bush' Cotton recalled, "The whole of the RAF ground organization was a complete mess."[8]

Nevertheless the bombing attacks launched on Rangoon in December were not without cost to the invaders. On Christmas Day 1941 Chennault's 'Flying Tigers' AVG shot down ten aircraft and their squadron leader reported, "It was like shooting ducks!"[9] The Japanese commander, Major Kato, was mortified. In his diary he wrote, "I felt terribly chagrined while at the same time I felt a strong sense of responsibility for not having trained my men more thoroughly. I offered my apologies to Colonel Kitajima ... Spent the whole day in mortification tortured by the sense of responsibility."[10] Nevertheless seven AVG planes were shot down and four of their pilots killed. Logistics support for sustained air defense was not forthcoming. By the end of February, of 267 Group's three squadrons of Hurricanes, they were barely capable of keeping ten in the air at any one time. Former US Navy and AVG ace veteran 'Scarsdale' Jack Newkirk reported, "The planes that we have here now are beginning to look like patchwork quilts for the holes in them. The engines are also getting tired . . ."[11] Jack Newkirk had little more than three weeks to live. Returning from a strafing mission to Japan's Lamphan Airfield in Thailand, Newkirk was shot down and killed as he sought to strafe two Japanese vehicles that turned out to be bullock carts. He was supposedly struck by fire from a Japanese armored car nearby.

At least the Allied air force had dispelled the Japanese belief that westerners were too effete to fight. Major Hiroshi Yoshioka, commander of the 77th *Sentai*, who had previously seen distinguished service in the war with China but was now based in the forward airstrip at Raheng, 200 miles east of Rangoon, reported, "the enemy had a great will to fight" though he added that "their technique in the air was not superior."[12]

The main Japanese invasion force, having transited to northwest Thailand now launched the main invasion of Burma. Japan's 55th Division attacked westward coming through the Kawkareik Pass forcing Hutton's 16th Brigade of the 17th Division to retreat northwestwards. Wavell signaled Hutton, "Cannot understand why with troops at your disposal you should be unable to hold Moulmein and trust you will do so."[13] However, the Japanese advance was so rapid that it came close to trapping the 2nd Burma Brigade on the southeast side of the *Salween River* near Moulmein. James Lunt noted in his diary, "They say they are going to turn Moulmein into a second Tobruk . . . They must be crazy."[14] Indeed Lunt and his brigade were only able to escape by ferry but at the cost of large amounts of equipment. The *Battle of Moulmein* also brought the Japanese a captured store of 5,000 drums of aviation fuel that enabled their air force to get quickly into action.

The military setbacks immediately revealed the poor training and preparation of British and Indian troops. James Lunt serving with the 4th Burma Rifles in 1940, noted that training consisted of

> no tactical instruction of any kind . . . [on exercise] we attacked in line up the gentle slope, the commanding officer galloping to and fro as he adjured us to "keep our dressing." Afterwards during the critique, he told us that British officers should always lead the line, waving their walking sticks. I wonder what the Japanese were being told around about the same time? Perhaps they did not carry walking sticks?[15]

The 17th Indian Division now fell back northwards toward the apex of the *Bay of Bengal* where the *Sittang River* fed south. Wavell's new plan of action was to hold this point while fresh troops were shipped into Rangoon from India. Somewhat ludicrously, on 6 February, completely unaware of the extent to which his forces were outclassed, Wavell shouted orders to the officers of the 2nd Burma Brigade telling them to "Take back all you have lost!"[16] At least some of Wavell's troops knew how to die bravely. When Captain Suzuki Tadashi entered the tent of Lieutenant-Colonel Jerry Dyer, he found the British officer with his jaw shattered by a bullet. Tadashi recalled him "sitting upright with several of his men. He signed us to shoot him and died in a serene frame of mind. His attitude really was in keeping with the honour of a military man. I sincerely respected him and wished I might do the same."[17]

By 12 February London was already becoming pessimistic about the fate of Burma. Army Chief of Staff, General Alanbrooke noted in his diary that news from Burma was "rapidly deteriorating . . . I am getting very nervous . . . We are paying very heavily now for failing to face the insurance premium essential for security of an Empire! This has usually been the main cause for the loss of Empires in the past."[18] Within days of this diary entry, British forces had suffered yet another defeat at the *Battle of Bilin River* just thirty miles east of the *Sittang River*.

The Royal Air Force (RAF) and the 'Flying Tigers' (American Volunteer Group: AVG): The AVG, or the 'Flying Tigers' as they became known, started operations out of

Rangoon and Kunming in the summer of 1941 and brought much-needed expertise to Chiang's air operations. Having arrived in Burma with the expectation of fighting as mercenaries for the Chinese, after the attack on *Pearl Harbor*, the American pilots found that, money apart, they had another reason to fight. As one flier noted in his diary, "We are stunned . . . we realized that we are in the middle of one hell of a big war! . . . I wonder when we'll get a chance at them."[19] After pilot Eric Shilling painted his engine cowlings as an open-mouthed shark, Chennault adopted this for all his fighter planes, which soon became a familiar and much-loved sight in northeastern China. Within weeks of the Japanese attack on *Pearl Harbor*, the exploits of the 'Flying Tigers' became headline news in America. In Chongqing, Graham Peck, working for the US Office of War Information, noted the arrival of the P-40s with their "thick powerful roar, smooth as the tearing of heavy silk."[20] For Americans, the exploits of the 'Flying Tigers' were a welcome propaganda fillip in the depressing weeks after *Pearl Harbor*.

The Kittyhawks (a variant of the Curtiss P-40 Warhawk) arrived via Burma in the spring of 1940 but the whole operation took more than six months to set up. In their first sortie over Rangoon on 20 December 1941 (some two weeks after *Pearl Harbor*), Chennault's P-40s surprised a Japanese raid by Mitsubishi Ki-21 'Sally' bombers. Six Japanese bombers and four fighters were shot down, though they lost pilots Neil Martin and Henry Gilbert—the first 'Flying Tigers' to lose their lives.

By Christmas 1941 'Duke' Hedman had become the AVG's first ace with five kills. Remarkably he achieved the rare feat of becoming an ace in a single day—in fact within 15 minutes. Hedman was an "unassuming farm boy from South Dakota" reported the *Chicago Daily News*.[21] A delighted Chennault wrote to his banker father in rural South Dakota saying, "He is a first rate combat pilot and the reckless bravery of his attacks, both on strafing and bombing missions, and in aerial combat with the Japanese, are something you can well be proud of."[22] Indeed the 'Flying Tigers' became renowned for their exceptionally aggressive tactics, often flying, as Hedman had done, straight into the middle of formations of Japanese bombers, where Japanese fighters were afraid to shoot at them for fear of hitting their own aircraft. Many more aces followed. Charles 'Chuck' Older, leader of the 'Flying Tigers' 3rd Squadron, the Hell's Angels, scored eighteen kills. After the war, the squadron gave its name to a San Bernadino motorcycle club, which later became the well-known global Hell's Angels Motorcycle Club, on the suggestion of another 'Flying Tiger' pilot, Arvid Olsen. As for 'Chuck' Older, he became a Superior Court Judge in California and achieved greater fame as the presiding judge in the Charles Manson murder case involving the drug and sex-crazed cult killing of Sharon Tate, the actress wife of movie director Roman Polanski.

The success and aura that surrounded Chennault and his 'Flying Tigers' created a groundswell of support for his recall to service in the US Army Air Force. Subsequently, this able leader won the promotions denied to him in the 1930s and was rapidly promoted to brigadier-general. Strangely he would now report to General 'Hap' Arnold with whom he had formerly been in conflict over fighter-bomber tactics in the 1930s. From the end of December 1941 the 'Flying Tigers' were absorbed back into the regular US Army Air Force and they became the nucleus of the China-based US Fourteenth Air Force in March 1942. Chennault loomed into American public consciousness as a great American hero when his picture was displayed on the front cover of *Life* magazine on 10 August 1942. *Time* magazine would also carry his portrait on the front cover of their 6 December 1943 issue. Hollywood was quickly into the act, releasing *Flying Tigers* [1942] starring John Wayne; the movie even used real footage from the war in China. It was on the set of this movie that Wayne picked up the nickname 'Duke.'

As in Malaya a key aspect of this early British failure was heavy defeat in the air. Just as in Malaya, as well as by the Americans in the Philippines, the potential threat of Japanese air power had been treated prior to the war with stereotypical arrogance. Sub-Lieutenant Russell Spurr's father wrote to tell him that: "Their eyesight is so bad they can't fly fighter planes. That's assuming the little bastards could even build them."[23]

In reality the Royal Air Force (RAF) was quickly overwhelmed. On Christmas Day 1941 twenty-seven Ki-21 'Sally' heavy bombers from the 12th *Sentai* and a further thirty-six from the 60th *Sentai* raided Rangoon Airfield. They were escorted by twenty-five Ki-43 'Oscar' fighters from the 64th *Sentai*. A follow-up attack involved 8 Ki-21 'Sally' heavy bombers, 27 Ki-30 'Anne' light bombers and 32 Ki-27s. In a pattern similar to the invasion of Malaya, British radar was found wanting. Sergeant Beable complained, "Once again because of the inadequate warning system we found ourselves in the unenviable and vulnerable position of having to climb at very low airspeed into the Japanese formation some 5,000 feet or more above us."[24] Highly optimistic claims were made of Japanese bombers shot down. British fighters took heavy losses, airfield buildings were badly damaged and anti-aircraft batteries destroyed with the bodies of gunners "scattered in a bloody broken mess for hundreds of yards around."[25] Civilian casualties in Rangoon were also severe with an estimated 5,000 killed. Flight-Lieutenant Brandt reported that "Chaos reigned in Rangoon. The jails were opened, the lepers were let out and a lot of fifth column activity carried out."[26]

Even the arrival of the first Hurricanes did little to dent Japan's overwhelming air superiority. Three Hurricane IIB Trops (Tropicalized) were flown in by Squadron Leader 'Jimmy' Elsdon. Within minutes of arriving at Mingaladon Airfield warning of a Japanese raid sounded off. Squadron Leader 'Bunny' Stone wrote that the Hurricanes were attacked before they reached altitude: "We were promptly jumped by about ten of them [Japanese Army fighters]. Couldn't do a damned thing with the tanks on, never got a shot while the little buggers queued up on my tail and filled me full of holes . . . Decided I had had enough and dived down to the estuary, among the shipping."[27] Given the importance of attacking from altitude, the failure to give timely warnings of approaching enemy aircraft was a very significant factor in the failure of the Allies to stem the tide of Japanese air supremacy. Navigator Sergeant Don Purdon gave a graphic account of the peculiarities of the warning system on which they had to rely:

> For warning we had to rely on an outpost in the hills manned by Burma Frontier Force soldiers who spoke little English—communications was by heliograph. I don't think any of us could read it so we had to rely on a Burma Frontier counterpart first to read and then translate from Burmese! One never knew if the flashes in the hills meant an air raid under way or whether it was a call for rations or other mundane needs.[28]

On 3 February the Allied air forces were struck by an unforeseen disaster. Eighteen fighters that left Calcutta's Dum Dum Airfield bound for Lashio in eastern Burma, lost their way over the Shan Highlands and crashed one by one. It was a reminder that the hazards of flying in the *Pacific War* were not all about combat. Interwoven with fierce dogfights were quiet days without bombing raids; pilots on the eastern front played golf at the Rangoon Country Club and swam at the Kokine Swimming Club and generally "acted like rich kids."[29] For men facing death every other day carousing was almost obligatory. Brawls were frequent. When the owner of the Silver Grills whorehouse in Rangoon tried to eject the American pilots they pulled out their pistols and shot out his chandelier causing panic among the prostitutes. As more of Rangoon's white population departed taking with them their daughters, the American pilots who had hitherto almost exclusively chased girls in this social strata, began to turn their eyes toward the Anglo-Burman girls who had previously been the preserve of the flight technicians. A disapproving British officer told them, "We don't mind you sleeping with them but don't for God's sake drag them around in our hotels and restaurants."[30]

The bar at the famous Strand Hotel was the scene of much heavy drinking. After one heavy night, seven pilots missed morning roll call and one of them, Robert Smith, was still too drunk to fly. It was not just the pilots who misbehaved. Rangoon crew chief, George Reynolds, crashed an American Volunteer Group (AVG) car and, fearing attack by two approaching Burman, shot one and wounded the other. Reynolds was jailed but released the next morning with the whole affair quietly hushed up. Houses, abandoned by owners who were fleeing Rangoon, were occupied by pilots and crew who proceeded to loot the properties. Pilot George Burgard purloined a truck and with crew chief Ed McClure filled it with stolen goods. Burgard wrote in his diary that he had acquired "so much stuff it would not be believed if I listed it."[31] He was clearly an optimist about his chances of survival. On 21 February the AVG met a mission by the whole 77th *Sentai* (squadron): "There were . . . Jap planes all over the sky. I tried to shoot them all down myself, but got only two in a full hour of fighting. It was a wild scramble . . . I got one [bullet] thru my wing that shot out my right tire. Some fun."[32] Thieving was not just personal. At the ports, the AVG commandeered crates and stole whatever was useful at the base: spare parts, tools, guns and ammunition. Normal logistics had simply broken down. The entrepreneurial Burgard survived the war and eventually became a supplier of parts for NASA (National Aeronautics and Space Agency).

Blowing the Sittang Bridge: [**Map: 10.2**] Constant air attacks hastened an already disorderly retreat toward the *Sittang River* and its major bridge, the crossing of which would open the invader's route to Rangoon. With typical speed, fast-moving Japanese forces had cut round the flank and were less than an hour from the bridge. With most of the division stranded on the eastern side of the river, on 23 February Major-General John 'Jackie' Smyth VC ordered the bridge to be destroyed. "Hard though it is," he later recalled, "there is very little doubt as to what is the correct course; I give the order that the bridge shall be blown immediately."[33]

It proved to be the most controversial decision of the retreat from Burma. Indeed it has been questioned whether Smyth was in any fit state to command. Suffering from an anal fissure, he was in such excruciating pain that his doctors were injecting him with arsenic and strychnine in order to give him some relief. In any circumstance it would have been a difficult decision. "If we blew it," Smyth wrote, "it was in the knowledge that two-thirds of my division would be cut off on the far bank. But if we didn't, a complete Japanese division might march straight on to Rangoon . . . it was not really a very difficult [decision] . . . from a purely military point of view."[34]

By chance Smyth was not the only senior commander in severe physical pain. A few weeks earlier Wavell himself had fallen off a jetty in the dark and had broken bones in his back. Brigadier 'Taffy' Davies, on General Hutton's staff wrote, "A terrible decision had to be made. If he blew the bridge he sacrificed the bulk of his division. If he failed to blow the bridge and it was secured by the enemy, the way to Rangoon lay open . . . General Smyth blew the bridge. In my opinion a heroic and inevitable decision."[35]

Even General Slim, writing later about the Sittang Bridge debacle was unable to criticize Smyth's call. "It is easy to criticize the decision; it is not easy to make such a decision. Only those who have been faced with the immediate choice of grim alternatives can understand the weight of decision that presses on a commander."[36] But if the decision to destroy the bridge could easily be justified, much criticism has later been showered on Smyth for not organizing a garrison to defend the bridge. For the soldiers stranded on the east bank of the *Sittang River*, the deafening sound of the explosion was followed by disbelief and fury. Captain Bruce Kinloch of the 1st Battalion 3rd Gurkha Regiment recalled, "as the echoes died away there was complete silence. All firing ceased, and every living thing seemed to be holding its breath. Then the Japanese, like a troop of chattering monkeys, broke into shrill chattering. Believing that everyone else had crossed over and abandoned us to our fate, we were filled with anger."[37]

With the bridge blown about 3,500 troops had subsequently made their way across the *Sittang River* either by swimming or by constructing amateurish rafts such as empty petrol cans tied to bamboo poles. Four hundred men managed to cross a makeshift lifeline suspended between the spans of the destroyed bridge. Sergeant Bill Crowther and bandsman Les Williams manned a machine gun to the last bullet and made ready to dive into the *Sittang River*. Williams told him, "I've to take my chances with the Japs. I can't swim."[38] Having spent his youth swimming in the Tyne near Newcastle, Crowther was an adept swimmer and helped other colleagues; he recalled, ". . . so the *Sittang* held no terror for me. Mind you, there were still some snipers and aircraft. How long I spent in that river I don't know—helping other chaps to anything that floated."[39] However, many British troops were drowned or picked off by Japanese soldiers as they tried to swim across. One British officer sank into the mud and drowned. Some 5,000 men were killed or captured. Between them the survivors had 550 rifles, 10 Bren guns and 12 Tommy guns. The delay may have cost the Japanese ten days in getting to Rangoon, but at the cost of almost 20 percent of the British Army's fighting strength and all the 17th Indian Division's weapons and supplies. The result was that the British forces were now too weak to hold even the west side of the river.

As in Malaya, the British troops were imbued with extreme complacency about the fighting capabilities of their Japanese opponents. Peter Young, a British Commando who had fought in Europe, expressed the racial stereotypes that characterized the views of officers and foot soldiers alike, describing the Japanese as "dwarf-like figures under their medieval helmets, their Mongol faces, many with glasses and gold teeth which made them look like creatures from another world."[40] Similarly a British officer harrumphed, "The little yellow bastards shouldn't give you chaps too much trouble, they're only little runts."[41] It was an attitude that imbued Wavell's own thinking. He had largely discounted the possibility of Japan's being able to attack Burma through the mountainous jungle terrain of eastern Burma. Indeed Major-General John Smyth recalled that when he was first transferred to Rangoon, "Wavell did not give the impression that he thought there was any threat to Burma at all."[42] In the game of blame that followed the loss of Rangoon, Hutton noted that a major contributing factor to the city's loss was "the failure of the command in Burma to appreciate that the holding of Rangoon was fundamental to the effective protection of Upper Burma and the Burma Road to China."[43] Wavell himself would later acknowledge his mistakes to Hutton telling him that he "never expected the Japanese to get along as fast as he did, or in such strength."[44]

Foolishly, and much to Chiang Kai-shek's chagrin, Wavell also refused the offer of Chinese troops to help repel a Japanese invasion. Faced with the reality of the Japanese Army's performance, attitudes changed with remarkable speed. Within days, in the eyes of British soldiers, the 'Japs' went from being dwarfs to 'superhuman' fighters. Apart from complacency the British Army in Burma was also hampered by the quality of some of its units; the Burmese Division comprised largely of raw recruits while General Smyth found that the Indian Division had been trained and equipped for desert warfare. The British troops were little better prepared. Lieutenant Anthony Dillon, 1st Battalion Gloucestershire Regiment, noted that: "We were badly equipped signalling by heliograph or line. We had few vehicles our mortars and machine guns were carried on mules. We were unfit for modern war."[45]

As a result of the thus far inept defense of Burma, on 28 February, Field Marshal Wavell, Commander in Chief of ABDA (American-British-Dutch-Australian Command), although partly responsible for the shambles himself, replaced Lieutenant-General Sir Thomas Hutton with General Sir Harold Alexander. By now British high command was clutching at straws; a bewildered Wavell had written to Churchill and Alanbrooke admitting,

> I am very disturbed altogether at lack of real fighting spirit in our troops shown in Malaya and so far in Burma ... causes go deep, softness of last twenty years, lack of vigour in peace training, effects of climate and atmosphere of Far East ... I have no reason to think otherwise but agree that Alexander's forceful personality might act as a surplus to troops.[46]

As we have seen, the Royal Air Force (RAF) was as lacking in preparedness as the British Army. In spite of information available from Japan's war with China from 1937 onwards, British commanders were chronically lacking in intelligence about the latest Japanese aircraft. Crashed Japanese aircraft in Burma soon enlightened them. Too late, in a post-campaign dispatch the quality of Japan's aircraft was acknowledged: "Technical examination of these—although many were burnt or otherwise destroyed beyond recognition—established the quality of equipment about which little was previously known."[47]

Alexander, the Irish Guardsman who had been the hero of the rear-guard action at Dunkirk, and was regarded by Churchill as Britain's finest general, was pushed forward as Burma's savior. It was not a universal view. Lieutenant-General Sir Francis Tuker wrote, "I think he is quite the least intelligent commander I have ever met in a high position."[48] As punishment for the debacle at Sittang Bridge, Wavell summarily dismissed General Smyth, demoted him and forced his immediate retirement from the Army. A guilt-ridden staff officer involved in the Sittang Bridge decision, Brigadier Hugh-Jones, would later walk into the sea and drown himself. In hindsight it is clear that Wavell's 'forward' strategy in confronting the Japanese invasion was in large measure to blame for the *Sittang River* catastrophe. It later transpired that Wavell, when pressed by Lieutenant-General Hutton ten days earlier, had refused his subordinate's request to withdraw all forces east of the *Sittang* to create a strong defense on the western side of the river. Smyth would later record that Hutton, who had been considered a capable Chief of Staff in India, was a bureaucrat unsuited to command in the field; he was "not the dynamic fighting commander which the coming events in Burma really demanded."[49]

Alexander arrived to take over from Hutton with instructions "to hold Rangoon if possible and failing that to withdraw northward to defend upper Burma, while keeping contact with the Chinese."[50] It was a forlorn task. Although Alexander ordered a counter-attack against the Japanese invaders to the northwest of Rangoon, he nevertheless determined that the city was not defendable and prepared to evacuate. The British forces in Rangoon faced encirclement and annihilation if they stayed; there were not enough ships to take them back to India even if there had been adequate air cover to protect an evacuation fleet. Striking north to protect the Burma Road supply route to China may have been strategically desirable but it was also the only escape route for British forces. In Rangoon itself the city fell into an unseemly panic. An eyewitness quoted in the official report said, "I do not think there was one sober man anywhere. The crews of the ships alongside, and the troops, had looted cases of liquor and were rolling about the place in the last stages of drunkenness."[51]

'Vinegar Joe' Stilwell and the Chinese Army in Burma: By moving north, Alexander could attempt to make a stand before Mandalay and defend the Burma Road by linking up with the Chinese Expeditionary Force under General Luo Zhuoying. The presence of Chinese troops in Burma was not wholly welcome to the British. Wavell had rejected them before being overruled by Churchill. As Stilwell noted acidly, Wavell "didn't want the dirty Chinese in Burma."[52] In theory it was a force that was under the command of General 'Vinegar Joe' Stilwell whom Roosevelt and General Marshall had ordered to Chongqing to be Chiang Kai-shek's Chief of Staff and to oversee the American Lend-Lease operation. On March 11 1941, Roosevelt signed a Lend-Lease Act that eventually provided US$43.6bn of materiel of which China received US$1.6bn, 3.6 per cent of the total and accounting for just 0.6 per cent of aggregate US war spending – a small price to pay for the holding down of 1.5m Japanese troops.

It was a command that even Marshall admitted presented unique difficulties. It led to one of the more bizarre relationships of the war between two notoriously difficult men, General Joseph Stilwell and Chiang Kai-shek. 'Vinegar Joe' Stillwell, born in Palatka, Florida, had colonial family roots dating back to the seventeenth century. In spite of the patrician blood of an early colonist, Stilwell developed the rebellious spirit of an outsider. With the help of family connections to President William McKinley, and under the guidance of his father, he secured a place at West Point Military Academy. Here he excelled at sports including basketball (which he supposedly introduced to the academy), cross-country running, which he captained, and American football. He also proved himself to be a capable linguist topping the lists in French. He would go on to learn Spanish and more importantly, Chinese. In 1904, he graduated 32nd of 124 from West Point.

Stilwell's famous sobriquet 'Vinegar' came from his time as commander at Fort Benning in Georgia. Here a subordinate drew a cartoon of Stilwell emerging from a vinegar bottle. The name 'Vinegar Joe' stuck. In recognition of his linguistic skills, after *World War I* Stilwell was sent to China where he quickly mastered the Mandarin language. Two more tours to China followed in the interwar years. Meanwhile, during his years of service in America he came to be regarded as the best corps commander in the US Army. However, Stilwell was an acquired taste. His acerbic tongue was lacerating and he only rarely strayed into the realms of dry humor. Predictably Mountbatten loathed the hard-talking American who spared nothing to look as ornery as possible. The loathing was mutual. Stilwell described Mountbatten sneeringly as a "glamour boy" suited only to win Britain's "last chukka in India."[53] The American would also delight in imitating the 'toff' accents of English officers. In general Stilwell loathed and distrusted British officers though he did rate General Slim—the only "good limey."[54] Conventional British officers were unimpressed. British Army Chief of Staff, General Alanbrooke thought Stilwell was "a hopeless crank with no vision."[55]

As for Roosevelt, Stilwell regarded him as weak—Churchill's patsy: "The Limeys have his ear, while we have his hind tit. . . ."[56] Of greater importance for his career, General Marshall respected Stilwell's abilities and uniquely, was able to tease him. A smart uniform, an insignia of office or a medal, never adorned this shabbiest of officers. Visually his appearance was not helped by a prominent nose and scrawny neck that made him seem prematurely old. Added to this, the squint that he developed after being injured by the explosion of an ammunition dump, gave him a look that was the complete opposite of a parade ground officer. Stilwell defined the phrase 'down to earth'—a quality which appealed to some. For some officers this was perfect. For Slim, "He was not a great leader in the highest sense, but he was a leader in the field; no one else I know could have made his Chinese do what they did. He was undoubtedly the most colorful character in South East Asia—and I like him."[57]

Having prepared his top field commander for the invasion of North Africa, General Marshall had suddenly dispatched Stilwell to the court of Chiang Kai-shek. Keeping China in the war against Japan was seen as critically important. Just as Marshall believed that everything should be done to keep Stalin in the war with Hitler on the Eastern Front, so he believed that the Chinese Army could occupy and absorb Japanese resources in China. Chiang Kai-shek was as keen to have American help as they were to give it. In offering Stilwell the role as his Chief of Staff, Chiang demonstrated the importance of the American alliance to his cause. However, if Stilwell possessed the linguistic skills to talk to the non-English speaking Chiang, he nevertheless failed to understand the nuances of Chinese culture. Misunderstandings about the nature of his role were inherent from the beginning. Stilwell essentially saw himself as a *de facto* commander in chief; Chiang's commanders saw Stilwell as a superior form of adviser. Chiang probably saw Stilwell as little more than the quartermaster for American supplies. The commander of the Chinese Fifth Army, General Du Yuming pointed out to the Governor of Burma, Reginald Dorman-Smith that Stilwell "thinks he is commanding. In fact he is doing no such thing . . ."[58]

Not surprisingly Chiang never wanted to relinquish ultimate control of an army that was the source of his power. As a general who had conquered most of China with his Nationalist Armies, Chiang also rated himself as a better than shabby military performer. That he was prepared to relinquish as much power as he did to an American chief of staff was, in itself, remarkable. Even Stilwell, in a rare moment of empathy, confided in his diary, ". . . in justice to all of them, it is expecting a great deal to have them turn over a couple of armies in a vital area to a goddamn foreigner that they don't know and in whom they can't have much confidence."[59] Unfortunately, Stilwell, with his black and white view of the world, found it difficult to understand that his role needed to be nuanced to the peculiarities and subtleties of Chinese politics.

On arriving in China, however, the Mandarin-speaking Stilwell was probably better disposed to Chiang and the Chinese than his British allies whom he loathed. On meeting

General Alexander for the first time, he noted in his diary on 13 March 1942, "Very cautious. Long sharp nose. Rather brusque and *yang chi* [stand-offish] . . . Astonished to find me—mere me, a goddam American—in command of Chinese troops. '*Extrawdinrey*!' Looked me over as if I had just crawled out from under a rock."[60] Although by character Stilwell was a deeply flawed choice as far as dealing with superiors and his allies, he was a brilliant motivator of foot soldiers. Chinese troops in particular seem to have worshipped him.

Escape from Rangoon: **[Map: 10.3]** On 7 March Alexander and Slim struck north with the intention of joining up with the Chinese Expeditionary Forces. Before leaving Rangoon, he oversaw the demolition of the oil terminal and key port installations. But the move north was already too late. General Iida's 33rd Division was already circling round to the west of Rangoon. To the north, at Satthwadaw, Colonel Takanobu Sakuma blocked the main road toward Prome. The town was an important inland commercial center on the *Irrawaddy River* 175 miles from Rangoon.

The first attempt to break out by retreating English and Indian troops was thrown back by the roadblock set up by Colonel Sakuma. Alexander's second attempt at a break out met no resistance at all and the British Army was able to make good its escape. By a slice of luck, the local Japanese commander, General Sakurai, failed to maintain Colonel Sakuma's roadblock that cut off Slim's only line of retreat to the north. It later transpired that Sakurai had expected the British to mount a vigorous defense of Rangoon and then to retreat westward; a retreat of all Allied forces to the north was never anticipated.

Having prepared for a desperate battle to break through on 8 March, Major J. Bonham-Carter (great-uncle to British actress Helena Bonham-Carter) became suspicious of the silence as morning broke and crept forward to find that the Japanese forces had departed. As Slim later observed, "All the Japanese commander had to do then was to keep his road-block in position and with the rest of his troops attack the forty-mile column strung out along the road. Nothing could have saved the British, tied as they were by their mechanical transport to the ribbon of road."[61] It was Slim's luckiest moment; he would make full use of his reprieve. It is quite conceivable that without this slice of good fortune, Alexander's army would have been surrounded and annihilated or forced to surrender.

The Battle of Magwe: **[Map: 10.4]** On the retreat northwards to Prome (Pyay) General Alexander's troops were strung out over forty miles. They were fortunate not to be attacked from the air. As was usual in Japanese campaigns of the first six months of the war, infantry and tanks advanced so fast that they ran ahead of the Army's supply chain. For a few precious weeks Japan's rolling advance came to a grinding halt. The same applied in the air. Lieutenant-General Hideyoshi Obata's fighter *sentai* (squadron) ran out of range extension drop-tanks (fuel tanks that could be jettisoned after fuel was used). It would also take some weeks to repair Mingaladon Airport and its satellite strips before the *sentai* could be moved forward. As a Japan Army Air Force (JAAF) officer reported after the war they were "busily occupied with maintenance and repair work."[62]

Major Ishikawa's 50th *Sentai* occupied Mingaladon while fifteen miles to the northwest Hiroshi Yoshioka, promoted to Lieutenant-Colonel, settled his 77th *Sentai* into Highland Queen Airfield at Hmawabi. The heavy bomber groups, 98th *Sentai* and 12th *Sentai* were dispatched to northwest Thailand at Nakon Sawan and Lampang respectively. Thailand's national socialist dictator Field Marshal Phibu (Plaek Phibunsongkhram), who maintained an ostensibly neutral stance during the *Pacific War*, nevertheless allowed the Imperial Japan Army access to facilities on demand. He was powerless to do otherwise.

On 9 March the Allies new main airfield was discovered at Magwe, near the oilfields of Yenangyaung to the southwest of Mandalay. They did not attack immediately. The Japan Army Air Force (JAAF) reported that "in order to deceive the enemy, we supported operations in other areas, awaiting a greater assemblage of the enemy's strength."[63] On 20 March Obata set out his Central Burma Attack Mission. With a force of 80 fighters, 70 bombers and 40 fighter-bombers he intended to destroy the Royal Air Force (RAF) and the American Volunteer Group (AVG). On the same day an RAF Blenheim spotter noted a massive build-up of Japanese aircraft around Rangoon. At Magwe, Dan Hoyle reported that "We are prepared to be attacked tomorrow morning or at dawn."[64] On 21 March the 12th *Sentai*'s Mitsubishi Ki-21 'Sally' bombers struck Magwe in spite of cloud cover obscuring the target. The 98th *Sentai* followed. Allied pilots who went up to intercept noted the superb formation flying of the Japanese; as a 'Sally' was damaged it would move inside the formation while another plane took its place on the flank. They found the cloud cover cleared and the target marked out by the fires lit by the 12th *Sentai*. Thirty-one Nakajima 'Nates' from the 1st and 11th *Sentai*, which had recently arrived in Rangoon, joined the 98th *Sentai*. Hurricane pilot Kenneth Hemmingway of the 17th Squadron was awe struck by the sight of the approaching Japanese armada. "Wherever I looked," he marveled, "I could pick out bunches of weaving Jap fighters protecting formation after formation of bombers."[65]

Obata's final waves of attackers, the 8th Sentai, comprised seventeen, twin-engine Kawasaki Ki-48 'Lily' bombers and ten single engine Mitsubishi Ki-30 'Ann' light bombers. Altogether Obata had put 151 bombers and fighters in the air. American Volunteer Group (AVG) pilot Cliff Groh, who had recently arrived in Burma, achieved a rare success in a beaten up old Tomahawk fighter. After brawling with Obata's 'Sallys,' Groh was on his way back to base when he happened across a 'Nate.' Forgetting that he had locked his guns, he had to dive beneath the Japanese fighter:

> I charged my guns and made an approach from his port side. I gave a deflection shot and fired several bursts before he turned toward me . . . I kept firing burst after burst until just before I passed him. I saw the plane lurch but dived down in case . . . As I pulled out of my dive I turned and saw the Jap plane crash . . .[66]

Groh had killed Major Tadashi Okabe, commander of the 11th *Sentai*, a veteran of the *Battles of Nomonhan* (alternatively *Khalkhin Gol*) in the border war with the Soviet Union in 1939. Cliff Groh from Wilmette, Chicago survived the war—but only just. A few weeks after killing Major Okabe, Groh recalled

> I was assigned last April 2 to fly a P-40 [Warhawk] back to a reconditioning base for repair. The plane's guns were disconnected. I ran into a terrific storm and had to follow an unknown river [*Mekong*] and landed on a sand bar near the Siam border only fifteen miles from a Jap airbase. Luckily, in a nearby town I found a Presbyterian mission and was given invaluable aid. They tended to my injuries and later I rushed out and destroyed the P-40 before they could capture it. Then, with the help of the missionaries I dispatched a wire to General Claire Chennault. I then started to walk the 350 miles through the mountains and jungles. I was on that little jaunt from April 22 to June 6. I never would have made it but for help from Chinese army guides and an occasional horseback hitch-hike.[67]

On Sunday 22 March, Lieutenant-General Hideyoshi Obata launched further heavy attacks. Oley Olson complained to Chennault by radio that they had received "Absolutely no warning . . ." and as a result at Magwe Airfield, "The runways were rendered unserviceable, communications were broken down and a number of aircraft, both bombers and fighters, were destroyed on the ground."[68] Olen reported "One shark badly burned up four hit badly. Three planes left now. Repairing and possibly have two others to fly away."[69] For the American Volunteer Group (AVG), the game was up. Chennault ordered them to get out of Burma. Technicians working through the night got four Tomahawks in condition to fly the 300 miles to Loiwing on the China-Burma border. The Royal Air Force (RAF) also took flight and managed to get eight Hurricanes to *Akyab* in the west of Burma close to the Indian border. Obata's officers made exaggerated claims to 120 Allied planes destroyed in the two-day attack. Nevertheless Obata had achieved his objective of wiping out all Allied air capability in Burma.

Allied Deployment in Central Burma: Having escaped north, it was now planned for the Chinese 6th and 66th Armies (the equivalent of two British Divisions) to hold the Japanese on a front south of Mandalay while the Burma Army would attempt to hold the *Irrawaddy River Valley* further to the west. However, the speed of the Japanese Army's advance gave the Allies little chance to establish strong positions. Using captured British trucks, Japanese forces moved rapidly up the south-to-north road networks.

With the retreat of Chennault's American Volunteer Group (AVG) and the Royal Air Force (RAF), Burma Corps had to make the remainder of the 900-mile retreat without air cover. Its new commander was Lieutenant-General William Slim, fresh from fighting the

Vichy French in Syria. Slim, appointed to his command on 8 March, noted that his troop casualties to Japanese air attack were not great. He also observed, "The effect on morale, while not as great as might have been expected, at first was serious, but later the troops seemed in some ways to become accustomed to constant air attack and to adjust themselves to it."[70] The retreating British force were hampered by a flood of refugees, estimated at about 900,000 people, many of them Indians, fleeing from the carnage. Adding to the disruption many Burmese deserted the Burma Rifles and joined the Burma Independence Army, which began to harry the retreating British forces. As many as 100,000 refugees pressed into Mandalay where British civilian administration collapsed. It did not help that Japanese bombing, virtually uninterrupted by any British air cover, had quickly degraded Burmese respect for the British. When Stilwell and Chiang Kai-shek met in Mandalay on 6 April, the Generalissimo was utterly shocked by the chaos that he found. He wrote to Churchill, chiding him that "In all my life of long military experience I have seen nothing to compare with the deplorable unprepared state, confusion and degradation of the war area in Burma."[71] Chiang was swept with a rapid sense of disillusionment with his new ally; he must have wondered how Britain had managed to sustain its illusion of strength for so long in its hold of the major Treaty Concessions in China.

During April Mandalay was practically razed to the ground by Japanese bombing. Much to the merriment of hostile Burmans, the first bombs landed in the middle of a British lunch party at the 'high society' colonial Upper Burma Club, blowing some of the guests into Fort Dufferin's moat. Indian official N. S. Tayabi described the destruction of Mandalay as a blow that "doomed any lingering sense of loyalty or sympathy for the British cause among the Burmese and Chinese elements of the local population."[72] Inevitably General Alexander's 'burnt earth' policy also brought increasing misery to the Burmans.

Fears for the whole region were heightened by a 9 April attack on *Ceylon* by Japanese aircraft carriers. In Washington, General Marshall agreed to station the Tenth Air Force in Northern India to help in its defense. It was a move that shored up the gathering concern that America would abandon its support for the India-Burma theater. In return Marshall extracted a promise of Britain's agreement for a cross-*Channel* invasion of Europe. In truth however, America was committed to India by dint of the importance of keeping China in the war; it was not lost on Marshall that Chinese troops were tying down a 1.5 million strong Japanese Army. On 28 April Roosevelt announced, "Ways and means would be found to deliver airplanes and munitions of war to the armies of General Chiang Kai-shek."[73] In May the operations of the Tenth Air Force began in northern India with twenty-five transport planes assembled in Assam. The airlift of supplies to China, which became known as 'the Hump' would become one of the largest logistical operations of the war. **[See Chapter 12: Limits of Empire: Doolittle and New Military Strategies]**

Aung San and the Burmans: The tactical switching of loyalties by Burmese civilians that ensued after Japan's invasion, rendered the entire population increasingly untrustworthy. General Slim recalled that one patrol was lured into a seemingly friendly Burmese village only to be massacred by hidden Japanese troops. Those captured were used by the Japanese troops as bayonet practice the following day. The appalling practices that had been seen so often in Malaya were repeated in Burma. Slim noted in his biographical account *Defeat into Victory* [1956] that "The fate of a prisoner in the field depended largely on the caprice of the officer into whose hands he fell. He might be tortured and brutally murdered, shot or killed by the sword, or merely maltreated, starved, bound, and beaten."[74]

The Burmese, always less favoured by the British by comparison with the tribal peoples such as the Karen or Shan, had never been loved and neither were their saffron robed priests. Novelist George Orwell, a policeman in Burma, admitted that he would happily have bayoneted the canting Buddhist monks, while fellow writer H. G. Wells complained that the Burmese were "unpleasant, negative and peevish."[75] President Roosevelt was even less complimentary about them. To Churchill, he opined, "I have never liked Burma or the Burmese . . . Thank the Lord you have He-Saw, We-Saw, You-Saw under lock and key. I wish you could put the whole bunch of them into a frying pan and let them stew in their own juices."[76]

Neither should it be forgotten that the Burmese, the racial group that occupied the flat lands between Burma's great rivers, the *Irrawaddy, Chindwin* and *Salween*, were a conquered people that had fought three wars against the British in the nineteenth century. Resentments lingered under the surface. Within their own country, the British, who favored the hill tribes living along Burma's long jungle borders, discriminated against the Burmese. Karens, Chins and Kachins dominated government positions, the police, and above all the army. Noticeably in 1939 the Burmese Army consisted of just 472 Burmans compared to 3,197 tribal soldiers, comprising Karens, Chins and Kachins. Furthermore many of the tribes converted to Christianity and unlike the Burmans were largely left to rule their fiefdoms without interference. With the rise of Asian nationalism in the 1930s, spurred by the examples of Chiang Kai-shek in China and Mahatma Gandhi in India, it was perhaps not surprising, given the historic background, that an independence movement, laced with increasingly fashionable Marxist-Leninist dogmas and National Socialist methods, should have reared its head in Burma's fertile ground. Such were the opportunities for an aspiring dictator, that young student, Bogyoke Aung San, gave up his law degree to join a fascist-style paramilitary group, *Dobama Ye Tat* (our brave Burma Army). Aung San also became a member of the 'Freedom Bloc'; "Colonialism's difficulty," he argued, "is Freedom's opportunity."[77] Next, Aung San, an enthusiastic linguist, volunteered to go overseas to seek weapons.

Ba Maw's arrest and jailing on 6 August 1940 caused considerable stir and U Maw's confederate Bogyoke Aung San departed Burma some months later to seek financing for the fight against the British. Initially aiming for help from Mao Zedong in China when he set out on 8 August 1940, Aung San was hijacked by the Japanese *Kempeitai* (Secret Police) who persuaded him to go with them to Tokyo. Here he was persuaded of the merits of the Japanese cause, for whom he wrote a pamphlet outlining a *Blueprint for a*

Free Burma. He later explained, "I went to Japan to save my people who were struggling like bullocks under the British."[78]

Aung and his 'Thirty Heroes' as they were later called by the Burmese press, cut their fingers and pooled their blood in a silver bowl with strong liquor in a ceremony with Colonel Suzuki that tied their respective causes. Ba Maw recalled that in unison they swore an oath "to be indissolubly bound together by this bond of blood when fighting the British."[79] Bogyoke Aung San recruited soldiers to bring back to Japan for training and in 1942 they marched into Burma behind the troops of Lieutenant-General Iida's Fifteenth Army. The 300 strong Burma Independence Army (BIA) led by Colonel Suzuki and Aung San soon multiplied rapidly as they picked up disaffected Burman. Although the BIA did none of the fighting against the British, the Japanese found them useful as a means of keeping the less pliable hill tribes under control. However, as their looting spree grew in scale, Lieutenant-General Iida decided on 4 June to ban the BIA from participating in government. Iida also put an end to their daily execution of Karen hostages. The following month Iida abolished the BIA and carefully recruited a new Burman force renamed the Burma Defense Army.

The Battle of Toungoo: After a brief consolidation of their capture of Rangoon, General Iida rapidly pushed his forces northwards. Four Japanese divisions broadly followed the tracks of the three great rivers, the *Irrawaddy* (west), the *Sittang* (center), and the *Salween* (east) that quadrisected Burma.

Iida's 55th Division pressed northwards along the main Rangoon–Mandalay Road and engaged Chiang Kai-shek's Chinese Expeditionary Force, under the command of General Luo Zhuoying. The Chinese forces comprised three armies, 5th, 6th and 66th; each was the equivalent to a British Division. The campaign began well for the Chinese as they ambushed the Japanese advance at the *River Kan*. From here Stilwell's forces made a tactical retreat to Oktwin. The Japanese were now more circumspect; however, after a failed Chinese attack and flanking movement at the *Battle of Oktwin*, on 23 March, Major-General Dai Anlan's Chinese 200th Division retired to Toungoo, an ancient walled city about 130 miles south of Mandalay and 180 miles north of Rangoon on the west bank of the *Sittang River*. Toungoo was the former capital of the sixteenth century independent kingdom of the same name. The same day Major-General Chennault withdrew the remnants of the American Volunteer Group (AVG), the 'Flying Tigers,' to India. Stilwell noted in his diary, "No air support left now."[80]

On 25 March the 55th Division, commanded by Lieutenant-General Tadashi Hanaya, and the 56th Division, commanded by Lieutenant-General Yuzo Matsuyama, attacked from the north, west and south. General Dai Anlan's only line of retreat was an upcountry bridge across the *Sittang River* with a road toward Lashio and the relative safety of China's Yunnan Province some 250 miles away. Dai Anlan had approximately 8,000 troops to the Japanese commanders 15,000 strong army. Although heavily outnumbered not just in troops but also in equipment, Dai Anlan's forces put up a strong defense that continued even after heavy artillery shelling of Toungoo's *Sittang Bridge* made it impassable for vehicles. The advance of Major-General Liao Yao-shiang's Chinese New 22nd Division from the north reduced some of the pressure as Japanese troops were diverted to fend them off. In spite of heavy bombing and strafing attacks, Chinese soldiers fought on from the rubble repelling fierce Japanese infantry attacks on 26, 27 and 28 March. Casualties were high on both sides with an estimated 2,000 Chinese dead and wounded to 5,000 for the Japanese.

On 29 March, Chiang, to Stilwell's fury, ordered his Chinese forces to withdraw. The Fifth Army's withdrawal of its field artillery exasperated British and American officers. When asked to justify his actions, Lieutenant-General Du Yuming, Chiang's *protégé*, explained that "The 5th Army is our best army because it is the only one which has field guns, and I cannot afford to risk those guns. If I lose them the 5th Army will no longer be our best."[81] General Tai An-lan organized an orderly withdrawal across the *Sittang River* and then tracked northwards along its eastern bank. The Japanese 56th Division followed in its wake. In his diary, Stilwell noted bitterly, "Liao [Major-General Liao Yao-shiang, New 22nd Division] and Tu [Lieutenant-General Du Yuming, commander of the 5th Army and second in command to China's Expedition Leader, Luo Zhuoying] have dogged it again. The pusillanimous bastards . . ."[82] On 1 April Stilwell asked himself despairingly in his diary "Am I an April fool? . . ."[83]

Chiang wanted to save one of his best armies. Stilwell saw it otherwise. "Through stupidity, fear, and that defensive attitude we have lost a grand chance to slap the Japanese back at Toungoo. The basic reason is Chiang Kai-shek's meddling."[84] With a few notable exceptions, Stilwell's first experience of dealing with Chinese arms was completely exasperating. He found Chinese generals reluctant to move forward without express orders from Chiang in Chongqing. In his characteristic vinegary tones, Stilwell complained of the Chinese generals under his nominal command, "I can't shoot them; I can't relieve them, and just talking to them does no good."[85] Stilwell returned to Chongqing to have the first of many rows with Chiang. On one occasion Stilwell lost a whole Chinese division. Having ordered an advance by the Sixth Army's 55th Division commanded by Lieutenant-General Chen Mien-wu, Stilwell found that by the next morning it had disappeared without trace into the hills. Stilwell was almost in awe of this 'supernatural' event: "There's not a trace of it. It's the god-dammest thing I ever saw. Last night I had a division, and today there isn't any."[86] Stilwell demanded that Chen be court-martialed. Chiang Kai-shek refused. Even Slim, who was usually complimentary about the Chinese suggested that to get a Chinese unit to hold its position was "like enticing a shy sparrow to perch on your windowsill."[87]

Chiang's priority was to preserve the Fifth and Sixth Armies. It was easy for Stilwell to recommend attack; China was not his country. If his armies were lost, Chiang faced the possibility that Japanese forces would invade China by the backdoor leaving him pincered between Japan's occupying Armies in East China and Iida's advancing forces from the southwest. Advancing, fighting, retreating had been the pattern of Chiang's long war with Japan. It had served him well. Against a vastly better equipped army he had kept his forces intact and exhausted Japan's logistical capacity. It was a way of fighting completely alien to the Stilwell-MacArthur school of command that was based on constant attack.

At this point in the *Pacific War* however, Chiang's contempt was mainly reserved for the efforts of the British rather than his new Chief of Staff Stilwell. Like the Americans, Chiang believed that the British were not prepared to fight and were merely using the Chinese with American money, to save their colonies for them. Chiang expressed himself "fed up with British retreat and lethargy."[88] It was a view that many Americans agreed with. Major Frank Merrill (later the commander of the famous US jungle unit, Merrill's Marauders), who was acting as liaison with the British campaign in Burma, described the British effort to Stilwell as "no plan, no reconnaissance, no security, no intelligence, no prisoners."[89] Not surprisingly Chiang was resistant to sacrificing his best troops when the British seemed so little interested in fighting.

The Battle of Yenangyaung: On Burma's western front Lieutenant-General Slim, commanding the 1st Burma Division, counter-attacked Iida's 33rd Division with his Gurkha troops, winning an engagement at the *Battle of Kokkogawa*, the only British victory in the whole of their retreat from Burma. However, southwest of Mandalay at Yenangyaung, the center of Burma's oil industry, Slim found that his forces were quickly encircled by fast-moving Japanese forces in one of their usual flanking operations. Slim's 7,000 troops needed rescuing. Lieutenant-General Alexander pleaded with General Luo Zhuoying for the help of the Chinese 38th Division led by Lieutenant-General Sun. Luo refused to budge but General Sun Li-jen on his own initiative counter-attacked with just 1,100 men of his 113th Regiment. Slim's 7th Armoured Brigade supported Sun with M-3 Stuart tanks.

At the *Battle of Yenangyaung*, Lieutenant Gerald Fitzpatrick viewed the scene as Chinese troops swept forward; he was amazed by a "spectacular show of a superbly trained and drilled Chinese Army moving like clockwork, to the bugling and signalling of the boys and the calls of commanders."[90] They had appeared seemingly out of nowhere carrying a strange assortment of weapons and with a large bandwagon of porters and animals. One British liaison officer referred to them as "Genghis Khan's horde."[91] General Alexander, grateful for the extrication of his troops, would reward Sun by pinning the ribbon of the CBE (Companion of the British Empire) on his chest to the delight of the Chinese general "who left us beaming all over his face."[92] Alexander would later receive a severe reprimand from King George VI for his action in decorating a Chinese soldier without the authority of the Palace.

In spite of Sun's intervention, which enabled most of 1st Burma Division to escape their encirclement, the end result of the four-day engagement that ended on 20 April was a victory for the Japanese and another forced retreat by the British. Major-General Scott's 1st Burma Division lost 1,000 troops either killed, wounded or missing. Scott himself collapsed from exhaustion and had to be taken back in a bullock cart. Scott recovered but Yenangyaung's area commander, Brigadier Roughton died from heat exhaustion. It was noted by Japan's official history, "The enemy's fighting spirit suddenly collapsed. He abandoned his vehicles and retreated northwards. Soon he went to pieces. It was a rout."[93] However, it was not such a rout that Slim forgot to blow up 1 million gallons of oil to deny it to the Japanese. After the war the oil company unsuccessfully tried to sue Slim for the damage.

General Sun, who won the confidence of General Slim, was born in Anhui province, Shanghai's hinterland. After participating with the Scouts at Tiananmen Square as a member of the May 4th Movement (criticizing the Chinese government's weak response to the *Treaty of Versailles*), Sun studied engineering at the prestigious Tsinghua University in Peking where, apart from his studies in civil engineering, he became a baseball star. After the award of a Boxer Indemnity Scholarship to study in America, Sun graduated from Purdue University, Indiana. A few years later he gave up civil engineering and decided to become a career soldier when he won admission to Virginia Military Academy from where he graduated in 1927. As a Colonel in the Chinese Army fighting the Japanese, as they invaded China at the start of the *Second Sino-Japanese War*, Sun was wounded at the *Second Battle of Shanghai*, known in Chinese as the *Battle of Songhu*. Some fragments of a rifle grenade would remain lodged in his body for the rest of his life. For his gallantry he was awarded the *Blue-Sky-White-Sun Medal of the Republic of China*. Sun would later become one of Stilwell's principal commanders. As such Sun earned the sobriquet of the 'Rommel of the East' for his aggression. American missionary surgeon, Gordon Seagrave described General Sun as a "tall, handsome figure, looking much younger than his years"[94] who treated his troops with unusual courtesy and consideration. After fleeing with Chiang Kai-shek to *Taiwan*, Sun's stellar career shuddered to a halt when Chiang and his son, Chiang Ching-kuo, fearing that the Americans would try to replace the Generalissimo with Sun, trumped up charges of an attempted coup and locked him up for thirty-three years. Released in 1988, he died two years later; his obituary in the *New York Times* on 21 November 1991 referred to him by his other sobriquet "the ever victorious general."[95]

The performance of General Sun and Chiang's Armies in general should have put paid to the lie that the Chinese could not fight—a canard that was frequently made both during and after the war. Compared to the British, they had the advantage of experience in fighting the Japanese. As Lieutenant-General Chen Mien-wu, commander of the Chinese Sixth Army, said to the deflated Governor Doorman-Smith, "We are sorry for you. You have been defeated so often. But don't lose heart. Look at us. We now know all about war, as we've been fighting the Japanese for the last ten years. You too will learn if you stick to it."[96] What Chiang's generals understood better than Stilwell, was that a fighting retreat when faced by a superior enemy preserved a fighting capability. By contrast Stilwell's constant call for aggression risked annihilation.

1st Burma Division fought its way out of the Japanese encirclement with Sun's intervention rescuing some 200 British prisoners but transportation for the British troops was lost. It would be a long walk to safety. The actions in front of Mandalay proved to be the nadir of Britain's Burma campaign with fifty-nine suicides and desertions in a single British unit after it was ordered to move forward. In spite of Sun's efforts however, almost all the 1st Burma Division's heavy weaponry was lost during the battle and subsequent rapid retreat. Burma Corps managed to cross to the west bank of the *Irrawaddy River* by 30 April and thereupon blew up the Ava Bridge in front of the advancing Japanese.

Headlong Retreat by the Allied Armies in Burma: Meanwhile the Chinese Expeditionary Force had withdrawn to Hopong to the southeast of Mandalay. General Dai Anlan's Chinese 200th Division scored a minor victory in driving the Japanese out of the town at the *Battle of Hopong-Taunggyion* from 20 April to 24 April. Stilwell was largely instrumental in this success by his taking personal command of the attack. As Slim generously admitted, "it was a magnificent achievement—only made possible by Stilwell's personal leadership with the very front units."[97] However, Chiang had become increasingly unhappy with what he considered to be Stilwell's recklessly aggressive offensive tactics. It had not helped that Stilwell had grossly underestimated the size of Japan's advancing forces, being unaware that the 18th Division was in Burma at all. "I know that I've sacrificed a great deal for nothing, for the sake of this plan of the Americans and British," wrote a despairing Chiang, "But now I do have to stick it out to the end."[98] The intervention of Chinese troops provided the briefest of respites. Chiang, bitterly disappointed at the performance of the British Army in Burma and concerned at what he considered to be Stilwell's recklessly aggressive tactics, decided to cut his losses and get what troops he could back to western China.

Having failed to hold central Burma, and cut off from China, the only route left for Burma Corps was a retreat westwards across country to Manipur Province in India. It was an epic fighting retreat that almost ended in disaster at Shwegyin on the east bank of the *Chindwin River*. Alexander was amazed at the speed at which Sakurai could advance. "Anyone seeing this track for the first time would find it difficult to imagine how a fully mechanized force could possibly move over it."[99] Sakurai's speed was not altogether unrelated to the 'boot' that he had received from the Japanese Army Chief of Staff who, according to Sakurai's diary, had ordered, "Not one Allied soldier is to get back to India."[100]

At Shwegyin the Japanese penned the British forces into a basin while troops were ferried across the river. Numbers of Japanese soldiers were able to flank the retreat and had to be fought off around the perimeter of the basin in which the retreating troops were herded while they waited for boats to cross the *Chindwin River*. "The Gurkhas," recorded Slim, ". . . put in a very spirited counter-attack."[101] Swimming in the *Chindwin*, Brigadier Mike Calvert came face to face with a Japanese officer and the two of them engaged in a hand-to-hand fight. Having killed his opponent Calvert vomited; he later confessed that he "had never felt so wretched before . . . In fact this had been a fair fight. The Jap had asked for no quarter and would certainly have given none. I told myself all this but it did not help much . . . I felt like a murderer that afternoon."[102]

Having escaped across the *Chindwin River*, many British soldiers asked how they would get back to India. "You walk mate or you die."[103] It was 130 miles of dusty paths ahead—or at least until the rains came and turned the tracks to mud. For Burma Corps' fighting units, it was a predictably appalling trek lasting two to three weeks with little or no provision or shelter. Captain John Randle recalled, "We were often short of food and water . . ."[104] Lieutenant Fitzpatrick lost 46 lbs, almost a third of his body weight. After almost four months of constant retreat Burma Corps reached Imphal in Manipur in May 1942.

Arrival was little better than the journey. Fitzpatrick complained that conditions were "uncomfortable, not only because it was raining hard . . . but because we had no shelter or unsoiled ground on which to lie, thousands of people having previously occupied it, with surprisingly primitive ideas for soldiers, on the most rudimentary rules of sanitation."[105] Similarly, reaching Kanglatongbi on 18 May 1942, Major Lyall Grant wrote that although his men had mosquito nets, they were without ground sheets or blankets; "It was indeed a cold and miserable reception to India."[106] The only consolation for Lieutenant-General Slim was that his soldiers to the end of the retreat kept rank and carried their weapons. As he later wrote, "They might look like scarecrows, but they looked like soldiers too."[107] In spite of the British escape across the *Chindwin*, General Iida noted with some pleasure in his diary that on occupying Kalewa on 12 May, they counted 1,200 bodies, 2,000 vehicles, 110 tanks and 40 guns.

Meanwhile the Chinese Sixth Army was destroyed along the Karen tribal states in the east and the Japanese then advanced north through the Shan states to capture Lashio, cutting off General Sun's 38th Division from a retreat back to China. Japanese forces entered Lashio on 29 April; some 10,000 tons of Lend-Lease supplies that could not be shipped to China in time had to be destroyed but an estimated 44,000 tons of supplies are thought to have fallen into Japanese hands. Sun, by now 100 miles north of Mandalay, decided to cut west to make for the safety of India. His forces would later be rearmed and trained, becoming Stilwell's X-Force. The remaining Chinese forces to the north and east retired toward Yunnan Province. With the destruction of one of his best armies and the severe mauling of another, Chiang had paid a high price for his alliance with the West.

The Chinese 200th Division that had performed creditably at the *Battle of Toungoo* and then at the *Battle of Hopong-Taunggyi* ran out of luck as they retreated toward Yunan. In the last battle of their Burma campaign on 23 May, they suffered a shattering defeat at the *Battle of Hsipaw-Mogok Highway* where Dai Anlan and his troops found themselves surrounded by Japanese armored forces. Major-General Dai Anlan was wounded and died of his wounds as the 200th Division continued its retreat. The remnants managed to break through the Japanese lines on 2 June and made their way to the border reaching Tenchong on 27 June.

The retreat eastward by the elements of the Chinese 96th division was equally desperate. Against the advice, indeed pleading, of Brigadier John Bowman, the British liaison officer with the Chinese Fifth Army, the Chinese 96th Division, having reached Hukawng from where the logical route would have been into India, was led by its commander cross country eastwards toward China's border. Bowerman reported, ". . . doubtless imagining he could loot sufficient food, refuse to take advice and continued on his way . . . began to run out of food along the refugee trail . . . robbed and looted everything it could obtain from the refugees and completely cleaned out Sumprabum and other villages. . . ."[108] When complaints were made by British officers to Major-General Yu Shao, commander of the 96th Division, part of Lieutenant-General Du Yuming's Fifth Army, he coolly replied, "Soldiers in every army rob and rape in time of war. It is not surprising that some of my men conform to pattern."[109] Depredations cut both ways; the Kachins killed many Chinese soldiers. Combined with disease and starvation the 96th Division lost approximately 75 percent of its strength.

The retreat gave some British officers, caught up in the escape from Burma, the opportunity to see the Chinese Army close up. Captain Jack Barnard recalled hearing shots one night; a colleague calmed his alarm:

> . . . it's not the Japs. It happens to be the Chinese. They're shooting any soldiers who are too badly wounded to continue the march. It's no use looking horrified about it. You'll just have to get used to the idea, because you'll be coming up against it regularly between here and Yunnan. The sanctity of life means very little in this part of the world.[110]

Discipline in the Chinese Army was often brutal. Chinese guards caught smoking opium were shot on the spot. A Chinese lieutenant explained his actions after one such summary execution: "Did not take life. Opium addict is already dead. Moral fibre gone. Intellectual vigor gone. Physical strength gone. Army on march cannot carry passengers. Centipede does not stop for gammy leg."[111]

Life as a Chinese soldier was hard beyond description. New recruits, usually conscripts, were often tied together with rope until they arrived at base camp, where they were given three weeks training. The average Chinese soldier wore straw sandals and usually had to share a blanket with five others. Daily rations of 25 ounces of rice with the addition of pickled vegetables and salt kept troops at barely subsistence levels. Even officers went hungry. Pay, when it was received would have to be spent on food to keep a soldier alive. Diseases such as dysentery, smallpox and typhus wracked the infantry. Hygiene and medical care were rudimentary in spite of the efforts of Dr. Robert 'Bobby' K. S. Lim, head of the Chinese Red Cross, the energetic physician who helped transform China's hospital services before and after the *Pacific War*. At Stilwell's insistence 'Bobby Lim' was later awarded the American Order of Merit. Losses from desertion or death from disease and malnutrition could cause depletion of 40 percent of an entire division every year; thus requiring 3,000 recruits for a single Chinese division.

The retreat to Yunnan of Major Yu Shao's 96th Division also revealed the corruption and brutality that Stilwell would have to deal with as Chiang Kai-shek's Chief of Staff. Captain Oscar Milton, on finding a dead Chinaman by the trail, noted that the dead soldier's body was naked: "I wonder if he was still alive when they stripped him . . . The

Brutes have left him nothing, not even his dignity as a soldier . . . These Chinese are inhuman, especially the officers. I've still to hear an officer address a friendly word to one of his men."[112] Barnard responded, "I imagine Yu Show will be drawing this poor chap's pay and rations until the end of the war."[113] It had already become apparent to Bernard that corruption in the *Kuomintang* was endemic. Barnard would later write, " . . . no reputable General would dream of putting in an accurate strength return. He automatically adds on 25 percent, lines his own pocket and gives his officers a cash bonus, if they're lucky. If he's in a benevolent mood, he sometimes dishes out an extra bowl of rice to his grateful warriors."[114]

If the retreat from Burma was tough for soldiers, it was worse for civilians fleeing the advancing Japanese army. Many thousands of civilians died by the roadsides whether they fled to the east or west. Apart from illness and starvation, the refugees also suffered from the brutality of hostile tribals, bandits and retreating soldiers. Eleven-year-old Colin McPhedran, an Anglo-Burmese cousin of Ba Maw, set out with his mother, brother and sister to Hukawng in China, was forced to abandon his mother to die by the roadside while she urged him on: "The world is full of good people . . . I know you will find them and be well cared for, for the rest of your life. Son, you must walk on . . . don't look back."[115] Taking his brother and sister in hand, he staggered onwards. Robert, his brother, died in the night and he later collapsed. Colin woke up in a refugee camp in Ledo that had been set up by a Scottish tea planter. Weighing just 50 lbs he had lost more than half his body weight. His sister had also been rescued but it was too late to save her. Out of 600,000 refugees, as many as 100,000 may have died en route to safety.

Many refugees were robbed and killed by the Burmese who took advantage of the discomfort of their former colonial masters. Lieutenant Pat Carmichael of the Indian Mountain Artillery recalled: "we loathed the Burmans almost as much as we did the Japanese, for their persistent treachery and murderous attacks on refugees."[116] Atrocities were not all on the Burmese side. During the retreat Lieutenant Gerald Fitzpatrick ordered twenty-seven Burmans to be shot, supposedly for banditry and giving intelligence to the Japanese. However, bad it was for those who retreated, it was preferable to the treatment meted out to those captured and imprisoned by the rampaging Japanese Army. Indian soldiers who fell into Japanese hands were tied up and put in bamboo houses that were doused with gasoline and set alight. Even British officers were stripped, tied to trees and used for bayonet practice. There was a litany of barbaric encounters that repeated the sorry record of brutality seen in the Japanese conquest of Malaya.

In London the fall of Burma was noted but in the general hubbub of world war far greater attention was being paid to new crisis points in the Middle East and North Africa, areas that were at least adjacent and critical to the future of Europe. By mid-summer Alanbrooke seemed much more concerned by the progress of his portrait by the society painter Sir Oswald Birley, than by the fate of British troops on the Burma-Assam border. It truly was the forgotten army.

Effect of Defeat on India: The retreat from Burma was inconsequential in its effect on Indian politics. The speed and chaos of Britain's defeat undermined India's National Congress Party's belief in the ability of the British to withstand the Japanese onslaught. Taking advantage of the situation, Gandhi called for Britain to depart India immediately. Such was the seriousness of the crisis that even Chiang, himself a fierce opponent of western influence in China, bestirred himself to fly to India to tell Gandhi that this was not the time to stir trouble.

However, Gandhi was adamant that the war gave India the opportunity to push for independence. Indeed, he argued that the British presence in India had given "an invitation to Japan" to invade and he insisted, "Britain must abandon her hold on India."[117] Although a British government mission by Sir Stafford Cripps promised consideration of self-government for India after the war, a track toward independence down which Britain had already led India before the war, Gandhi's intransigence led both him and Nehru to being interned for the duration of the war. Fortunately for the British war effort, neither Indian leader went as far as their former Indian National Congress colleague, Subhas Chandra Bose, who escaped Indian authorities early in 1941 and organized a 30,000 strong Indian National Army to help Japan 'liberate' India.

But if its impact on domestic politics was injurious, the war turned out to be a boon for the development of the Indian economy as the British Army turned to the continent to support the war effort against the Japanese occupation of Burma. "New industries included motor manufacture, chemicals and pharmaceuticals and light engineering. With an annual output of 1.5 million tons, the Tata family, *Parsi* [Zoroastrian] from Bombay, became the largest producer of iron and steel in the British Empire. Electric power production grew by 45 percent during the course of the war."[118] Even with hindsight it is debatable whether the war hastened or delayed the coming of independence to the Indian sub-continent.

Stilwell's Long Walk and Chiang's Lost Armies: **[Map: 10.5]** Meanwhile in Burma, the fleeing civil service under Governor Reginald Dorman-Smith fled further north to Myitkyina where the remains of the Burmese civil government were re-established. Civilian flight followed, and while a fortunate few were airlifted to India, many tens of thousands perished in the long march through the Hukawng Valley and across the dense jungles of the Patkai mountain range. Some 8,616 personnel and 2,600 wounded were airlifted out of Shwebo and Myitkyina.

As for General Sun's 38th Division, they too retreated along this route to India. Arriving finally at Ramgarh in Bihar they were put under the command of General Stilwell who would now attempt the building of a 'New Model' Chinese Army on western principles. As Stilwell proclaimed during the retreat, "God, if we can only get those 100,000 Chinese to India, we'll have something."[119]

Stilwell, who had originally intended to make a last stand with his troops in northern Burma with Myitkyina as his new headquarters, found that the Japanese were already ahead of him at Bhamo. On 5 May therefore Stilwell decided that there was no other alternative than striking out for India. Stilwell refused to be airlifted out of harm's way and on 7 May led out on foot with a 114 strong party, including 18 American officers, 6 enlisted men, some stray British officers, 16 Chinese guards, an American missionary, 19 Burmese nurses, Mr. Case (President of the Agricultural College at Pyinmana who spoke various dialects of the hill tribes), correspondent Jack Belden and Indian mechanics. Together they began a trek across Burma's northern jungles for 140 miles to reach India. The day after their departure, the Japanese entered Myitkyina. Stilwell did not rate the chances of his out-of-condition charges; leaving at 5.00 a.m., by midday his officers were "pooped" or suffering from heat exhaustion: "Christ we are a poor lot."[120] Later he complained to another "older" member of the party, "Dammit, Williams, you and I can stand it. We're older than any of them. Why can't they take it?"[121] Forcing them to march at his pace, they used elephant trails, even journeys downstream on rafts, to reach safety. It was an epic journey. The discomforts of the trail were varied. Malaria and dysentery were rampant. Food was hard to come by. The hardships failed to stop the constant refrain of Christian singing by the Burmese nurses. Stilwell noted in his diary that he woke one morning to find a leech that he had to remove, "Big, bright green sucker, about eight inches long."[122] The monsoons broke making the 3,000 foot vertical descent into the Naga Valley particularly treacherous. "By the time we get out of here," he told his ragged charges, "many of you will hate my guts but I'll tell you one thing; you'll all get out."[123] They all finally arrived at Homalin in India on 15 May.

It was a remarkable escapade for a 63-year-old three-star American general. As one of his staff boasted on Stilwell's behalf, "Hell, that was a picnic excursion for him. He's just made of steel wire, rubber and concrete for guts."[124] It did not endear him to Chiang. He thought it was completely hare-brained for the commander of his Chinese troops to abandon them for a jungle 'frolic' no matter how daring and courageous. Chiang fumed, "Stilwell deserted our troops and left for India without my permission."[125] He even wondered whether, "because of the battle, his [Stilwell's] nerves have given way."[126]

The Chinese Fifth Army that he had abandoned made their way northwestwards to India under the leadership of General Sun. Soldiers, no longer strong enough to carry their weapons, destroyed them. Chinese soldier Luo Gu noted: "the soldiers are all in rags and look very gaunt. Everyone is carrying a bag of rice, a water-can, a diesel tin, and in the other hand, a walking-stick."[127] Nevertheless Sun's 38th Division made their way westward through the Chin Hills reaching India on 25 May. The rear-guard 113th Regiment had to fight their way through encircling Japanese forces before crossing the *Chindwin River* and reaching safety on 30 May. Colonel Wyman, a member of Stilwell's staff noted, "The story of the 113th is really an epic."[128] Meanwhile the 22nd, plus fragments of the 28th, 96th, and 200th, took the longer northerly route to India; 23,000 out of 30,000 Chinese troops that had set off reached Ledo between July and August.

If the Burma campaign was bad for British forces, it was worse for Chiang Kai-shek. As the price to pay for his alliance with the United States, he had agreed against his instincts to send three of his best armies to Burma to help the British defend their colony against the Japanese. For his pains, he had seen the Fifth Army escape to be stranded in

India while the Sixty-sixth Army was all but annihilated as it tried to escape back to Kunming along the Burma Road. Out of an estimated 100,000 troops sent to Burma, an estimated 50 percent of them had been killed and most of their equipment had been lost. Chiang had paid a heavy price for America's offer of military and financial assistance to defeat Japan.

Stilwell's loss of his precious armies naturally alarmed Chiang Kai-shek. This, combined with the woeful performance of the British in their defense of Burma, not surprisingly undermined Chiang's confidence in western military ability. As for Stilwell, he told reporters at New Delhi, "All retreats are ignominious as hell. I claim we got a hell of a beating. We got run out of Burma and it was humiliating as hell. I think we ought to find out what caused it and go back and retake it."[129] Stilwell's blunt honesty came as a shock to American journalists more used to the honeyed words of Roosevelt and Churchill.

There were downsides to Stilwell's 'tell it as it is' style. Stilwell's ensuing report on the reasons for the defeat in Burma was so vicious about the Chinese and British that Marshall ordered that all copies should be destroyed. In essence Stilwell fantastically accused Britain of deliberately losing the Burma campaign in order to weaken China; it was a sign of mental instability that did not augur well for his future relations with the Allied partners with whom he would have to work. For Stilwell, the unintended consequence of his retreat to India was that he was able to divert the 45,000 tons of accumulated supplies intended for China to re-equip the Chinese Army in India.

To his wife, Stilwell wrote that after his epic walk he hoped to catch a few days rest "at a place called Carmel, where there are a few people I know who will welcome a vulgar man, even though he has proven a flop and has been kicked around by the Japs."[130] Stilwell was just as vinegary about himself as he was about others. If there was a glimmer of hope for Stilwell it lay in the performance of the Chinese soldier. Their commanding officers may have lacked the qualities he wanted but the soldiers themselves had been a revelation, showing grit that the British had lacked. For the Japanese the resistance they faced from General Tai An-lan's 200th Division at the *Battle of Toungoo* was the fiercest that they faced throughout the entire Burma campaign. Meanwhile Sun Li-jen's intervention at the *Battle of Yangyaung* was a model of aggressive action as was the fighting retreat of his 38th Division to India.

Stilwell strongly believed that if Chinese soldiers were better fed, better paid, better trained and better equipped they would be more than a match for the Japanese and would provide him with a force with which he could reconquer Burma, an ambition that became as much an abiding preoccupation as MacArthur's focus on the Philippines. To a foreign correspondent he confided that "If I can prove the Chinese soldier is as good as any Allied soldier, I'll die a happy man."[131]

General Alexander Loses an Army: About 13,000 of Britain's 25,000 troops emerged from the jungles of Burma after their 900-mile journey on foot over four months of fighting. The British suffered 10,036 casualties of which 3,670 were killed. In addition the Burmese Army suffered a further 3,400 casualties. Only 2,000 soldiers were fit for further active duty while 122 out of 150 pieces of artillery had had to be abandoned. In essence Britain had lost an Army. It would take two years to replace it.

Apart from appalling weather conditions, and the crossing of rivers and gorges, the British Army had had to face the usual bevy of tropical diseases as well as poisonous spiders, insects and snakes including Giant Pythons, King Cobras that could grow up to 18 foot, the deadly Banded Krait (just one foot long) and the Russell's viper. Even Stilwell complained about the snakes. To his wife he wrote, "The damn snakes are starting to appear. One got into my office and one tried to get into my tent."[132]

In spite of the hardships endured, Slim observed with some pride that although, "All of them, British, Indian, and Gurkha, were gaunt and ragged as scarecrows. Yet, as they trudged behind their surviving officers in groups pitifully small, they still carried their arms and kept their ranks, they were still recognizable as fighting units."[133] Mixed with pride there was also a certain grievance that the survivors of the Burma Corps were not treated with the same respect that greeted the returnees from Dunkirk. Slim knew that it would be a huge task to turn around the morale of his troops. As he pointed out, "Defeated soldiers in their own defence have to protest that their adversary was something out of the ordinary . . . that he had all the advantages of preparation, equipment and terrain, and that they themselves suffered from every corresponding handicap. The harder they have to run away, the more they must exaggerate the unfair superiority of the enemy."[134]

For the British there was now the job of rebuilding an army both to defend India and to take on the task of recapturing Burma. But first, why had Burma been lost? In his official dispatches, Wavell admitted that:

> More might have been done, in spite of all deficiencies, to place the country on a war footing. Political considerations, the climate, under-estimation of the enemy, over-estimation of the natural strength of the frontiers, the complacency of many years of freedom from external threat, all combined to prevent the defense problem being taken sufficiently seriously.[135]

General Iida's Burma Triumph: For Lieutenant-General Shojiro Iida and the Japanese Army, the conquest of Burma, though against lesser forces and with better odds than in Malaya, nevertheless represented another startling feat of arms. For sheer brilliance it compares with General Yamashita's achievement in Malaya. With an invasion force comprising four divisions, approximately 35,000 men, Iida had defeated a combined British-Chinese army more than three times that number. In exceptionally difficult terrain, over a five-month campaign from January to May, Iida managed to conquer a country 20 percent larger than Great Britain.

Again it was the rapidity with which the Japanese were able to move their army that astonished the British commanders. They were well supported by Obata's 5th Air

Division, which proved yet again the essential role of air dominance in *Pacific War* land battles. Never allowed to rest, regroup or consolidate, Iida's forces constantly kept the Burma Corps on the move and when counter-attacks were made they moved rapidly to encircle and trap their opponents. Speed was considered of the essence because of the Japanese belief that in getting to close quarters they could make their superior *seishin* (spiritual energy and pure heart) count. *Seishin* worked in the early months of the war partly because Japanese troops were well led, were given intelligent jungle tactics and were trained and prepared to fight in conditions that were no more familiar to the Japanese that they were to the British and Indians. When the Commander in Chief ordered the 1st Infantry Brigade to move from the North West Frontier to Manipur, Brigadier F. V. Wodehouse complained that "It must be remembered that both the battalions going with this Brigade have been concentrating on Mountain Warfare on the NWFP [North West Frontier Province]."[136] He also noted that these battalions were not trained in the use of modern weapons or "the technique of modern warfare against a first-class enemy."[137]

Typically two or three Japanese columns would advance in parallel until contact was made with the enemy. The column in contact would fight a holding engagement while the other columns would envelop the enemy flank several miles to one side, sometimes on both sides, and having completed an encirclement would then establish roadblocks on the enemy's route of retreat. Japanese commanders gave a relatively low importance to 'intelligence,' believing that speed of closing would make up for deficiencies in this area. On the offensive against a disorganized enemy in 1941, Japanese commanders got away with weak intelligence capability though it would come to hurt them later when their war in Burma became defensive. As the military historian Gordon Rottman has observed in *The Japanese Army in World War II* [2005], the Japanese "completed most initial operations well within schedule. In fact this 'victory disease' led many officers to believe that staff intelligence sections no longer had a purpose."[138]

In addition to weak intelligence, Japanese forces were also hampered by poor communications equipment. While the 1932, Type-92 telephone using single wire connection carried by a soldier with a 600-yard spool, was fine for static engagement, fast moving action required radio. Even the newer radio sets were obsolescent by western standards. Although some Japanese Army units were issued with AM sets, they had no FM capability. Japanese field sets were complex, poorly built and badly waterproofed. The most common sets were Type-94s that had been introduced in 1934. The forty-eight-symbol *kana* alphabet was used for Morse code; messenger dogs and carrier pigeons were also used as well as red, white and green flares fired from grenade dischargers.

The personal bravery of the troops played no small part in enabling the rapid advance. As Lieutenant-Colonel John Masters would later testify, Japanese troops "pressed home their attacks when no other troops in the world would have done so . . . The Japanese simply came on, using all their skill and rage, until they were stopped by death."[139] For the Japanese, Lieutenant-General Iida's Burma campaign must rate as one of the great feats of arms of the twentieth century. Lieutenant-General Shozo Sakurai's division marched and fought for 127 days; his campaign took in thirty-four battles over a span of 1,500 miles. Much of their advance was made on foot. Casualties, including soldiers killed, were just 4,597. Iida had conquered a large Asian country and in the process defeated the British Empire, one of the world's acknowledged superpowers. The strategic goal of isolating and blockading China had been achieved. For Britain the defeat in Burma was a devastating setback. Their Chinese allies were now completely cut off from western supply. As Wavell observed in a message to London in July, "The loss of Burma has been from a strategic point of view our most serious reverse of the war. It has deprived our Chinese Allies of a flow of munitions to continue their long resistance."[140] New threats now faced Britain. Defeat "has exposed India to a serious threat of invasion," Wavell continued, "and it has had a disastrous effect on British prestige in the East."[141]

In Tokyo, the fall of Rangoon was greeted with pleasure, even though by now the scent of victory was becoming commonplace. Nevertheless, Privy Seal Kido noted on 9 March, "The Emperor was obviously delighted. I could only express congratulations."[142]

Strategic Hindsight: Great Britain's defense of its empire in Malaya and Burma was shambolic. In hindsight it is clear that British commanders hugely underestimated japan's military capability. Complacency, political expediency and racial arrogance underlay the disaster. The result was humiliating defeat. In the space of two months Japanese Armies comprising some 140,000 troops defeated 160,000 British, Indian and Australian soldiers supported by 90,000 Chinese. Britain's Far Eastern Armies, as well two of China's elite divisions, were in effect wiped out. It took two years to rebuild.

In hindsight there were clear failures in almost all aspects of military craft. Logistics, equipment, training, construction of defenses and tactical deployment were all deficient. However, perhaps the greatest mistakes were made in the strategic overlay. The naval base at Singapore, built at vast expense in the interwar period, was designed as the fulcrum of defense. However, the £60m (£3.0bn today) spent was a waste without a British Far Eastern Navy and a concomitant provision of air cover.

Although a more determined and tactically more astute defense of Singapore and Malaya could have set back the Japanese advance, without provision by sea or air, Britain was doomed to eventual defeat. A withdrawn defense in Central Burma, shortening the lines of supply to India and drawing on the support of Chiang Kai-shek's forces, would have significantly nullified Japan's naval and air strengths. In addition it would have stretched Japan's logistical capabilities. It was a strategy that Chiang Kai-shek and Stalin adopted with great success in China and the Soviet Union respectively. British arrogance, lack of strategic imagination and political posturing were to blame – Churchill, Alanbrooke, Wavell, and Brooke-Popham all stand accused.

11 Dutch East Indies and Japan's Quest for Oil

[December 1941–June 1942]

[Maps: 11.1, 11.3, 11.4] [Diagram: 11.2]

Rajah Brooke's Defense of Sarawak: Rajah Charles Vyner Brooke, the third and last 'White Rajah' of *Sarawak* in *North Borneo*, was 67 years old when the Japanese invasion force arrived off the town of Miri in *Sarawak* on 16 December 1941; fortunately for him he was on vacation in Australia when his kingdom was invaded.

Brooke's great-uncle, the famous Rajah James Brooke, had been a young army officer in Bengal when he inherited £30,000 and invested it in the purchase of a schooner, *The Royalist*. Setting off for *North Borneo* in 1838, he had helped put down a local rebellion, won the confidence of the Sultan of Brunei and had been rewarded with the Governorship of *Sarawak* in 1841. In the following year the Sultan transferred sovereignty to Brooke and he took the title of Rajah. In effect he and his heirs became the only 'white' kings of Asia in a country about the same size as Denmark. Britain, given the island of *Labuan* off the coast of Brunei in 1846, only became formally responsible for *Sarawak*'s international protection in 1888 when it sought to deny the area to any other interested foreign power. In the same year the neighboring Sultanate of Brunei also became a British protectorate.

Although Brooke had overseen the building of airfields at three of the major settlements of *Sarawak* including Miri, the major oil producing area of the region, Air Chief Marshal Sir Brooke-Popham had pre-determined that the Kingdom could not be defended in the event of a Japanese attack. As soon as the Japanese invasions of 8 December 1941 were underway, British-trained teams began the work of demolishing the oil fields of Miri and Seria (in Brunei) and their joint refinery at Lutong. It was well understood by all, that the end goal of any Japanese 'strike south' policy would be a grab for the oil fields of *North Borneo* and the Dutch East Indies. The region was the fourth largest exporter of oil after the US, Iran and Romania. With a gross output of 65 million barrels of oil per annum, the Dutch East Indies could theoretically more than make up any shortfall from imports denied to them by President Roosevelt.

Brooke's Sarawak Force comprised a mixed group of local tribal volunteers, Sarawak Rangers, coast guards and police under the command of Lieutenant-Colonel C. M. Lane. As General Percival, commander of the British forces in *Singapore* and Malaysia had concluded with a vast reserve of understatement, "Nobody could pretend that this was a satisfactory situation, but at least it would make the enemy deploy a larger force to capture *Sarawak* than would have been necessary if it had not been defended at all . . ."[1] Even this overstated the usefulness of *Sarawak*'s defensive capability. With no British aircraft available to make use of the airfields that had been constructed, a total of 2,565 troops presented little threat to Major-General Kiyotake Kawaguchi's forces that left *Cam Ranh Bay* in Vietnam on 13 December.

General Kawaguchi: Major-General Kiyotake Kawaguchi was of the same generation of officers who commanded the invasions of the Philippines (Lieutenant-General Masaharu), Malaya (Lieutenant-General Tomoyuki) and Burma (Lieutenant-General Shojiro). Similarly, Kawaguchi graduated from the Army Staff College at Minato during the years of *World War I*. Like Lieutenant-General Yamashita, he came from an ordinary family from the provincial backwater of Kochi on Japan's fourth island of *Shikoku*.

It was a generation of young provincial officers who had grown up on the stories of the glorious *Meiji era* triumphs of the *First Sino-Japanese War* and the *Sino-Russian War*. They were deeply patriotic men, utterly devoted to the cause of the Emperor. It is also striking that they were chosen for command not for their birth or connections, but simply because they had proved themselves the most capable of their generation. The Japanese Army was nothing if not meritocratic. Like his colleagues, Kawaguchi was neither the ruthless nor colorless figure that fits the caricature image usually portrayed by Hollywood. A photograph of Kawaguchi shows a balding, round faced, dome headed figure with a huge and incongruous looking 'handlebar' moustache. He was a sad-eyed reflective man who cared deeply for his troops but who, throughout his career, showed an unusual sensitivity toward the fate of the occupied. These were not sentiments shared by all of his colleagues, many of whom were responsible for acts of merciless barbarity throughout the Dutch East Indies Campaign.

Most of his career was spent in staff jobs in northern China. He was promoted to the rank of major-general in 1940. After being given the task of organizing the invasions of *Borneo* and the Dutch East Indies, Kawaguchi went to Sanya on *Hainan Island* off southern China to discuss and plan operations with his staff. Detailed knowledge of the region was limited and maps were largely deficient. However, Kawaguchi prepared his troops as best he could with training on the health and sanitation requirements of jungle warfare. New equipment and clothing were provided for the tropical climate. Most importantly perhaps, with no roads available in many parts of the region, considerable effort was made to train troops for amphibious landings. Meanwhile detailed plans were made for the conquest of this vast, maritime Empire consisting of some 12,000 islands. Kawaguchi's plan would involve a complex series of rolling advances southwards towards the populous and fertile island of *Java* that was the heart of Holland's East Indies Empire. Three semi-autonomous forces would cover the breadth of a region that spanned almost 2,000 miles from east to west and 1,000 miles from north to south.

The Eastern Force would advance from the city of Davao on the southern Philippine island of *Mindanao* to take control of the island of *Celebes* (now *Sulawesi*), *Ambon*, the famed spice islands of the *Moluccas* and *Timor*. The Western Force would attack

Palembang on the north *Sumatra* coast and would take control of this 'second' island of the Dutch Empire that lies adjacent to Malaya. The Center Force, having taken Sarawak, the British protectorate on the north coast of *Borneo*, would then advance down its east coast, taking the important oil installations at Tarakan and Balikpapan, before clearing out remaining Dutch forces occupying *Borneo* itself.

The final piece of the intricate mosaic of actions in the Dutch East Indies would be a joint assault on *Java*. It was an organizational and logistical task involving the use of Army, Navy and their respective air forces that was exceptionally complex. Even for a man of Kawaguchi's proven administrative capabilities, it must have been a mind-boggling task.

Borneo Invaded: [**Map: 11.1**] The *Battle of Borneo* began with Japanese landings at dawn on 16 December 1941. Having taken possession of Miri and nearby Seria (in Brunei), Major-General Kawaguchi, made aware that there were no roads linking the major settlements of *Sarawak*, organized further landings at the key points along the west coast including Jesselton, Sandakan and Kuching. Only the latter was seriously defended. As Brooke-Popham explained, "The only place which it was decided to hold was Kuching, the reason for this being not only that there was a modern airfield at this location, but that its occupation by the enemy might give access to the Dutch airfields in *Borneo*, furthermore, it would also give the enemy access to Singapore."[2] However, after stiff resistance from the 2nd Battalion, 15th Punjab Regiment, the only significant British military force on *Borneo*, the Allied troops were forced to give up their defense of the airfield on Christmas Day.

Subsequent to the *Battle of Kuching*, the British island of *Labuan* was invaded on 1 January and the British resident Hugh Humphrey was taken prisoner. Humphrey later complained that his punishment for destroying all the fuel oil on the island was that "I was repeatedly hit by a Japanese officer with his sword [in its scabbard] and exhibited for 24 hours to the public in an improvised cage."[3] With *North Borneo* secured, the Japanese now planned an advance that placed *Java* and its capital Batavia (current day Jakarta), the richest center of the Dutch Empire, as the prime target of its southward advance. Along the way the Central Thrust would advance southwards down the east coast of *Borneo* via the *Makassar Strait* toward *Bali* and *East Java*.

The Dutch East Indies Attacked: Having completed their primary objectives in *North Borneo* by the middle of January, Kawaguchi planned the next stages of the advance against the Dutch East Indies. The Dutch, who had ruled the *Indonesian Archipelago* for 300 years, had, like Britain, thought little about the likelihood of invasion by an aggressive regional power until a year before Japan's attack. This small European nation controlled the third largest global empire after the British and French. However, Holland by January 1942 was a country defeated and occupied by the Germans.

A few weeks prior to the German invasion of Holland on 10 May 1940, which had been widely expected, Japan's Foreign Minister, Hachiro Arita, expressed the sort of 'sympathetic' concern that indicated that Japan might offer the Dutch East Indies the kind of 'protection' that they had formerly offered to *Formosa* and Korea. Alerted to this, the American Secretary of State announced on the following day that "intervention in the domestic affairs of the Netherlands Indies or any alteration of their *status quo* by other than peaceful processes would be prejudicial to the cause of stability, peace, and security not only in the region of the Netherlands Indies but in the entire Pacific area."[4] It was already clear to all, especially the Dutch, that the Japanese had its Asian territories in their sights. In 1939 the Dutch government, suddenly aware of the vulnerability of its Empire, had already authorized the construction of three new 28,000-ton cruisers carrying nine modern 12-inch guns each. It would be too little, too late. In spite of its constrained circumstances, the Dutch government-in-exile in London, as soon as the attack on *Pearl Harbor* was confirmed, pre-empted the inevitable by declaring war on Japan. Queen Wilhemina's government proclaimed, "The Kingdom of the Netherlands considers itself in a state of war with Japan."[5]

Many Dutch colonials believed that the Japanese would never reach the East Indies let alone *Java*. Elizabeth Van Kampen, the daughter of a Dutch businessman in Sumber Sewu near Malang recalled the usual jokes that went around regarding Japanese military prowess, "the Japanese while shooting would always miss, because they were slit-eyed. Or the Japanese planes were made out of meat tins. Or the Japanese couldn't run fast enough because of their crooked legs. And so on."[6]

The main oil rich target of *Tarakan Island* off the *East Borneo* coast was assaulted by Kawaguchi's Center Force on 11 January. Within twenty-four hours the Dutch garrison had been overcome. During the first engagement a group of thirty soldiers from the Royal Netherland East Indies Army were bayoneted for refusing to give directions to the main town. At the *Battle of Tarakan* some 870 Dutch were taken as prisoners of war. On the same day a force of 2,500 Japanese naval marines supported by 500 paratroopers landed at *Manado* on the northern part of *Celebes Island* with the aim of exercising control over the mineral-rich eastern part of the Dutch East Indies. The cutting thrust of the attacks came from the 21st Air Flotilla that were deployed from Davao on the southern Philippines island of *Mindanao*. After fierce fighting for the airport, the Dutch commander ordered his troops to retreat into the jungle to carry on a guerrilla campaign that continued to the end of February. As was to become commonplace in the Dutch East Indies campaign after the *Battle of Menado* a large number of prisoners of war were executed.

Although the Japanese thrust southwards was carried out piecemeal with small-scale military operations, in aggregate the commitment of resources to the invasion of the East Indies was significant and fully reflected the importance of Dutch oil wealth to their future conduct of the war.

The American, British, Dutch, and Australian (ABDA) Command: By now a unified command had been set up combining the American, British, Dutch and Australian forces (ABDA). The ABDA Command was created on 15 January 1942. It was, given its multi-national composition, an inevitably rushed and confused *ad hoc* structure. The unification of command had been forced on Britain by General Marshall and Roosevelt at the ARCADIA Conference on Christmas Day 1941. The appointment of General Wavell as ABDA's commander was reluctantly agreed by Churchill who feared that "the theater in which he would act would soon be overrun and the forces which would be placed at his disposal would be destroyed by the Japanese onslaught."[7]

Wavell was an unusual soldier. A fluent Russian speaker, he read Greek and Latin and was also an avid reader of history. He was also a hugely experienced commander with a strong record of performance; German generals as capable as Rommel and Reichenau were counted among his admirers. Perhaps inevitably, from the outset, there was considerable resentment from the Australians, Dutch and New Zealanders as to what was seen as an Anglo-American stitch-up. The relationship was made even more difficult when the fall of *Singapore* killed any lingering deference in Australia's relationship with Great Britain.

At the start of the *Pacific War* Allied forces never had the combined naval resources to match Japan. Although on 8 December 1941 they matched each other with 10 battleships apiece, by the end of that momentous day at *Pearl Harbor*, Japan outnumbered the Allies by 3:1 in capital ships. The Allies were similarly outnumbered in other categories; aircraft carriers 10 to 3; heavy cruisers 18 to 17; destroyers 112 to 93. Only in light cruisers (27 to 20) and submarines (71 to 65) did the Allies have a slight advantage. However, by the time that ABDA was established, the overwhelmingly important US component of the Allied naval forces in the *Pacific* was committed to the defense of the American West Coast. What remained to ABDA was a weak force of surface ships comprising a mishmash of Dutch and Australian cruisers supported by a small American destroyer squadron and a smattering of small British ships. With three light cruisers, *de Ruyter, Java* and *Tromp*, supported by seven destroyers and fifteen submarines, the Dutch had a naval force roughly equal to that of the British/Australians in the Far East. However, the Dutch ships were far from modern. The *Java* was of Jutland period design with single turret 5.9-inch guns; *de Ruyter* was also under-gunned. Wavell was rightly not optimistic. He noted, "over such a wide area our resources by land, sea and air are extremely limited."[8]

The Army comprising 38,000 *Koninklijk Nederlandsch-Indisch Leger* (KNIL) troops plus 8,000 sundry others was under the command of Lieutenant-General Hein Ter Poorten. About a quarter of the KNIL were Europeans or Eurasians. The forces were stretched over a vast area. Piecemeal deployment meant that just a single Dutch battalion was available to defend the crucially important oil fields at Palembang, Sungeigerong and Pladju in *South Sumatra*. Moreover it was a force that was largely trained and organized for dealing with internal insurrection rather than foreign invaders. Furthermore although Ter Poorten was responsible for deployment, the sending of reinforcements was the prerogative of each country.

The ABDA Command Air Force was under the command of Major-General Lewis Brereton with British Air-Marshal Sir Richard Pierse as his deputy. However, the respective heads of the national air forces continued to preside over day-to-day management of their contingents. For the Dutch this was Lieutenant-General Ludolph van Oyen. Dutch aircraft were largely 'hand-me-downs' from the US including the obsolete Martin B-10 bomber designed in 1931. It was not a force capable of withstanding the Japanese aerial onslaught that provided the cutting edge of their advances in the first six months of the war. At no point did the Japanese ever consider the use of naval and land forces without first securing total control of the air.

Most importantly Wavell's strategy to defend the Dutch East Indies was fatally compromised by the priority that he gave first to Malaya and *Singapore* and secondly to Burma. When *Singapore* was about to fall, Wavell floated the idea that if *Sumatra* and *Java* fell, the 6th and 7th Australian Divisions should be sent to Burma; apart from the deeply pessimistic stance implied, Wavell's concerns were clearly self-serving and naturally angered the Australian government in Canberra. Saving the British Empire was Wavell's main concern, while for the Americans, the security of Australia took precedence over the Dutch East Indies. The Dutch government in *Java* was in effect on its own.

For the Japanese, the piecemeal deployment of the ABDA Command forces meant that they could concentrate overwhelming force against the Allied garrisons in *Borneo* and the Dutch East Indies. It was a low risk strategy that virtually guaranteed success. For the ABDA forces meanwhile, having set out their stall in terms of piecemeal defense, it was soon impossible for them for logistical reasons, to change course and mount a determined and concentrated defense around a single strategic point. Thus, using a skilful combination of forces on air, sea and land, Japan's Imperial forces pursued the familiar pattern of determined and rapid advance that characterized their military initiatives elsewhere in the first months of the war.

Japan's 'Central Thrust' and the Battle of Balikpapan: Notwithstanding the disadvantages of their forces and the structural deficiencies of the Allied command, their naval war in the Dutch East Indies started well. At the *Naval Battle of Balikpapan* on 23/24 January 1942, Hart gave the American-British-Dutch-Australian Command (ABDA) Allies their only major success of the Dutch East Indies campaign. USS *Paul Jones*, USS *Parrot*, USS *Pope* and USS *John D. Ford* of the 59th US Navy Destroyer Division led by Commander Paul H. Talbot, under cover of darkness, advanced unnoticed into the middle of the Japanese landing convoys and sank four of them with torpedoes. The attack would have been more devastating if the defective American Mark XV torpedoes had not run too deep. Earlier an air attack on the convoy by Dutch Martin bombers supported by British Brewster Buffaloes sank a transport and damaged another.

Unfortunately for the Allies, the Japanese troops had already disembarked by landing craft and Japanese casualties were light. Again the first thrust of the attack on 22 January came from Japanese airpower provided by the 23rd Air Flotilla based in Davao. They cleared the skies of Dutch fighters within a few days. By the evening of 25 January Balikpapan City had been taken and mopping up operations continued the following day. Only minor damage was done to the valuable oilfields as Lieutenant-Colonel Van den Hoogenband failed to complete their destruction. Again the Japanese operations under Major-General Shizuo Sakaguchi were marked by atrocities. After seeing the destruction of the Tarakan oilfields by Dutch troops, Sakaguchi had been determined that the same thing would not be done to the oil installations at Balikpapan. Two captured Dutch officers were sent as emissaries to warn Lieutenant-Colonel Van den Hoogenband that all Dutch soldiers and civilians would be rounded up and shot if the oil fields were damaged. The warning was ignored. In spite of the minimal damage done to the oilfields, seventy-eight soldiers and civilians, including eight patients dragged out of the hospital, were taken to the beach near the old Klandasan Fortress. Two victims were beheaded while the rest, including doctors, priests and clerks were driven into the sea and shot. The native population was forced to watch.

The *Naval Battle of Balikpapan*, while it did not cause the Japanese advance on *Java* to lose momentum, nevertheless pointed the way to the type of engagement that would characterize the eighteen month period from the summer of 1942 to the end of 1943 when a series of small scale naval battles starting with the *Battle of Savo Island* on *Guadalcanal* would gradually degrade Japan's Navy as it sought to sustain amphibious troop movements. After consolidating their positions at Balikpapan and preparing the airfield for the next 'jump' in the 'central thrust,' Japanese forces moved down the *Makassar Strait* toward *East Java*. On 4 February, a four strong cruiser force led by Rear-Admiral Karel Doorman, while entering the *Makassar Strait* near *Bali*, was attacked by a sixty strong force of 'Nell' and 'Betty' bombers. Doorman's force, which had been looking to intercept Japanese transports, suffered damage to two cruisers. USS *Houston* suffered a direct hit on its rear turret, killing forty-eight men and rendering its two 8-inch guns useless. The *Battle of Makassar Strait* represented a major first failure by the ABDA Command to interdict the flow of Japanese troops towards *Java*. "As a result of this battle," a Japanese Navy officer recalled, "the Japanese Navy gained great confidence in its ability to fight night engagements."[9]

Ambon (the Moluccas) and the 'Eastern Thrust': The next move was along the axis of the 'Eastern Thrust' toward *Timor* where Japan's ultimate strategic aim was to block supplies from Darwin in northwest Australia to *Java*. Kendari on the east coast of the *Celebes* was quickly overrun on 24 January and its airfield made available to the 21st Air Flotilla. Next, on 4 February, the Japanese led by Major-General Takeo Ito invaded *Ambon*, the major port of the *Molucca* 'spice' islands, located half way between Manado in the northern *Celebes* (*Sulawesi*) and *Timor*. *Ambon*'s somewhat pathetic air defenses, consisting of two Buffalo fighters, had been destroyed a fortnight earlier. On 24 and 25 January aircraft from the Japanese carriers *Hiryu* and *Soryu* attacked the airfield at *Ambon* that Japanese intelligence had mistakenly identified as a major Allied airfield base. In fact the Australian squadron of Hudson bombers, that had been located on *Ambon*, were moved after the fall of *Menado*.

The handful of remaining fighter aircraft that had been flown to defend *Ambon* were massively outnumbered. Flight-Lieutenant Cornfoot of Royal Australian Air Force (RAAF) 13th Squadron recalled, "The valiant pilots had taken off against the Japanese after sitting for hours beside the strip . . . the loss of the Dutch pilots saddened us indeed. We had profoundly admired their heroism even though it was futile."[10] Lieutenant F. E. Broers was shot down immediately and in spite of being wounded survived the war in captivity. On the ground 2,600 troops from the Molukken Brigade and 1,200 Australian troops put up fierce resistance over a four-day period.

Following the *Battle of Ambon* 300 prisoners were taken. In a wood near the village of Tawiri, adjacent to Laha Airfield, Japanese troops dug two graves, both six yards in diameter and three wide. On the late afternoon of 9 February, on the orders of Rear-Admiral Koichiro Hatakeyama Dutch and Australian prisoners were brought to the site and made to kneel one by one next to the open pits. The first beheading, using a samurai sword, was carried out by Warrant Officer Kakutaro Sasaki. Four crewmembers of Mine-sweeper No. 9 that had been sunk by a mine eagerly stepped forward to wreak revenge on the next four victims. As light faded torches were shone on the necks of the victims to guide the swordsmen's aims. Eighty-five prisoners perished. Two weeks later a further 227 prisoners were similarly slaughtered through the night. After the war Rear-Admiral Hatakeyama died shortly before his war-crimes trial in Melbourne.

As *Ambon* was falling America started to feed P-40 pursuit group squadrons into *Java*. The fighter reinforcements included 17th Pursuit Group led by Buzz Wagner who had gained fame as a pilot in the early days of fighting on *Luzon* in the Philippines. Pilots were a mixture of Philippine veterans and raw recruits who had arrived a month earlier from the United States. Flying from Darwin, they stopped over in Kupang on the western tip of *Timor* and then to Waingapu on *Samba Island* before making the last part of their 530-mile trip over *Lombok* and *Bali* to the major port city of Surabaya on the eastern tip of *Java*. The Dutch made them more than welcome; 17th Pursuit pilot, George Kiser recalled, "The Dutch assisted us in every way possible, furnishing guards on the field, food and medicine. Living conditions were not too bad. We had nice quarters, the food was not good but sufficient and altogether everything was as good as could be expected considering the supply situation at this stage of the war."[11] The small number of American fighters were welcome but they were too few to make a difference.

> By the first of February 1942 there were about 30 airplanes [P-40s] and about 45 pilots in Java. Three-fourths of the pilots were just graduated from flying school and had never flown a pursuit ship until they landed in Australia. About three hours of transition were given them and they started up toward Java. The first time they ever fired a machine gun was at a Japanese aircraft.

> In 30 or 40 hours of combat flying, however, they grew
> very proficient in flying ability. A few of them were killed.
> Almost every time it was a case of not looking around.[12]

In Washington, Brigadier-General Dwight Eisenhower who was keeping a watching brief for Marshall on events in the Dutch East Indies, noted in his diary on 30 January, "The news from Wavell is all bad."[13]

Palembang (Sumatra) and the 'Western Thrust': On 13 February the focus of attack moved to Palembang on the *North Sumatra* coast where Royal Dutch Shell had major refineries. Here 2,000 Dutch troops with a force of 118 Royal Air Force aircraft including 40 Blenheim bombers, 30 American-built Hudson light bombers and 48 Hurricane fighters, sought to hold back an invasion led by Vice-Admiral Jisaburo Ozawa. Prior to the Japanese landing intense air battles were fought with Japanese aircraft based at Kahang Airfield in southern Malaya. By 13 February only fifteen Hurricanes remained serviceable though they had achieved a 1:1 kill ratio against the Japanese.

On the same day, in one of the more celebrated incidents of the East Indies Campaign, a former 1,000 ton *Yangtze River* gunboat, HMS *Li Wo*, was one the many ships fleeing from *Singapore*, which fell two days later. The *Li Wo*, which had already been battered by four aircraft attacks, chanced upon the Japanese amphibious fleet and bravely attacked the troop transport armed with just a single 4-inch gun and two machine guns. For over an hour and a half, Lieutenant Thomas Wilkinson, commander of *Li Wo*, battled with Japanese fleet transports, setting one on fire and ramming another with his doomed ship. Only ten of the eighty mixed crew and personnel survived. Wilkinson went down with his ship; he was awarded a posthumous Victoria Cross, the only one awarded for the Dutch East Indies campaign.

The *Li Wo* incident made a small dent in the Japanese amphibious advance led by Vice-Admiral Jisaburo Ozawa. On 12 February, 3,000 Japanese troops of 229th Infantry Regiment supported by a battalion from the 230th Regiment had embarked on twenty-two transports from *Cam Ranh Bay* in Vietnam. One heavy cruiser, *Chokai*, one light cruiser, *Sendai*, and eight destroyers supported the invasion transports. A covering force consisted of the light carrier *Ryujo* and five more cruisers and three destroyers plus additional land-based air support. Ahead of them, 350 paratroops were landed to try to take the main airfield in advance but were driven back with heavy casualties. However, thanks to the timely arrival of more Japanese paratroopers, they managed to deactivate most of the demolition charges at the Royal Dutch Shell refineries at Palembang.

On 14 February 1942 Japanese bombers sank the SS *Vyner Brook* in the *Bangka Strait* near *Sumatra*. It was a merchant ship belonging to Sir Charles Vyner Brook, Rajah of *Sarawak*, which was carrying sixty-five Australian Army nurses and 265 other passengers, mainly women and children. Survivors managed to wade ashore where they gave themselves up to the Japanese, along with thirty to forty British servicemen who had arrived in another lifeboat from a ship sunk earlier. The men were marched into the jungle and murdered, while the women were forced to wade into the sea at *Radji Beach* where they were machine-gunned. Sister Vivian Bullwinkel, who was shot in the side, feigned death in shallow waters, survived and lived to tell the story.

On 15 February, Rear-Admiral Karel Doorman led a force of 5 cruisers and 10 destroyers to intercept the invasion force. However, Doorman was forced to turn back to *South Sumatra* by aggressive air attacks. Although Hurricanes made strafing sorties against the Japanese landing craft, the remaining American-British-Dutch-Australian Command (ABDA) aircraft were withdrawn to Java where another major Japanese attack was expected. By 16 February all remaining ABDA personnel were withdrawn to *Java* or to India. For the loss of a single transport, the *Otawa Maru*, to British bombers, Ozawa's force arrived intact and occupied all the Dutch facilities. Apart from the area's oil fields, which reputedly produced the world's 'sweetest' crude oil, nearby Pangkalanbenteng Airfield (called P1 by the British) was a major target of the operation. The Japanese planned that P1 would serve as their main airbase for operations against other Dutch garrisons on *Sumatra* as well as neighboring *Java*. After the *Battle of Palembang*, Japanese ground forces moved south and completed the takeover of *Sumatra*.

Furthermore the capture of Palembang Airfield enabled the first Japan Army Air Force (JAAF) units to advance to a base from where they could launch attacks on the heart of the Dutch Empire at Batavia (modern day Jakarta) in *West Java*. On 19 February the first such raids were carried out on Buitenzorg by five Ki-48 'Lily' light bombers of the 90th *Sentai* escorted by 19 Nakajima 'Oscars' of the 59th and 64th *Sentai*. It was a calling card to be followed up the same day by a much heavier attack by 12 bombers and 36 Zeros. It produced a pattern of engagement similar to that experienced in Malaya. Dutch Captain Tideman leading a squadron of a dozen Brewster Buffaloes complained, "We could not reach the bombers properly—we did not shoot down any but got tangled up in huge dogfights with the Zero."[14] Tideman's airfield at Bandung was badly hit with six aircraft under repair destroyed. Two of Tideman's squadron colleagues were shot down although one parachuted to safety. Tideman himself survived but only just; he recalled, "During the action I was hit badly several times . . . I remember the first hit I received came from a cannon shell hitting my right wing, where I could see a huge hole. I was shocked to death at first—later I got used to the sound of hitting bullets."[15] On another occasion Lieutenant Simons told Tideman after they landed that "all of a sudden he had seen the Jap climbing up from below behind my tail . . . opening up on me at close quarters. Certainly I was lucky that time and my armour plate behind my seat took the beating as we later discovered."[16]

By the beginning of March the Dutch were down to their last remaining Brewster Buffaloes. They fought against better equipment and hopeless odds. Although many of the Dutch fighter pilots had headed off to Australia, on 7 March Captain Jacob van Helsdingen, on his thirty-fifth birthday, led a flight of four Buffaloes to attack Kalidjati. They were set upon by six Zeros. Helsdingen was killed.

Bali Invaded and the Raid on Darwin: **[Diagram: 11.2]** Further humiliation for American-British-Dutch-Australian Command's (ABDA) naval forces soon followed a week after the *Battle of Palembang*. After the Japanese had landed a battalion of troops from the 48th Infantry Division on the island of *Bali*, an ABDA force of three cruisers, seven destroyers and two submarines was sent to attack Japan's invasion force. The two departing Japanese transports were accompanied by four destroyers. On the night of 18–19 February, in spite of the huge discrepancy in forces, the Japanese destroyers crossed the 'T' of the Allied line; *Asashio* proved the worth of Japan's development of the Long Lance torpedo by sinking the HNLMS *Piet Hein*. An Allied cruiser and destroyer were also damaged. Although three of the Japanese destroyers were damaged, the *Battle of Badung Strait* proved the significant advantage enjoyed by the Imperial Japanese Navy in both torpedo and gun technology and training. Crossing the 'T' in naval terminology is when the forces of a naval force in a warship gun duel manage to sail across the line of an advancing enemy column thereby allowing all the guns of the 'crossing' force, fore and aft, to swivel and target the enemy. The advancing column is necessarily disadvantaged because only its forward guns, usually half to two-thirds of its guns depending on configuration, can fire. To cross the 'T' is therefore the optimum maneuver for a naval force commander in a duel between surface ships. This technique was used to devastating effect by Admiral Togo to destroy the Russian fleet at the *Battle of Tsushima* [1905].

With the fall of *Bali*, the end objective of the 'central thrust' and the capture of its airfield, the Japanese invasion forces could now interdict ABDA operations based in Surabaya on *Java*'s eastern tip. In addition *Java* was now cut off from any possible source of help from Australia. In his diary Admiral Matome Ugaki, Yamamoto's chief of staff, noted that "the enemy must know well that Java is doomed by our capture of Bali, the paradise of the world, only 22 kilometres away."[17]

Further to the east the island of *Timor*, the end objective of the 'eastern thrust' was invaded on 20 February, the day after *Bali*'s fall. Dili, the defenceless Dutch capital of *Timor* was bombed. Fierce fighting ensued with Dutch, Australian and British defenders over the next two days. *Timor* proved the hardest nut for Kawaguchi's forces to crack as guerrilla forces led by a contingent of Australians continued to harass them for the rest of the year until August when the Japanese 48th Division, commanded by Lieutenant-General Yuitsu Tsuchihashi launched a counter-offensive. After November, in a classic 'burnt earth' strategy, Japanese forces carried out a brutal and systematic destruction of food stocks and villages in the Allied controlled areas. The tightening of the net forced most of the remaining Allied forces to escape by nightly US submarine pick-ups from December to February 1943. The *Timor* campaign cost the lives of 450 Allied troops versus an estimated 2,000 Japanese. As usual in war it was the civilian population that suffered worst—it is thought that as many as 70,000 Timorese and Portuguese civilians died during the Japanese campaign.

After the fall of *Bali* in February 1942, ABDA Command gloom became rampant. Although Japanese troop numbers set to invade *Java* would not be significantly different from the defenders, Wavell's attitude showed an increasing pessimism about the ability to compete with the Japanese on equal terms. After the surrender of *Singapore* a week earlier this was not surprising; nevertheless his attitude showed the extraordinary psychological upper hand that the Japanese Army had achieved over the first two months of the war. Resignedly Wavell wrote to Churchill, "I hate the idea of leaving these stout hearted Dutchmen and will remain here and fight it out with them as long as possible."[18] Churchill cabled a farewell message to his troops, "I know that you will do everything humanly possible to prolong the battle."[19] His hopes proved illusory. With the occupation of *Bali*, a now alarmed and pessimistic Wavell perceived an increasing threat to Australia that was 1,650 miles away. Meanwhile Japanese-occupied *Timor* was only 450 miles from Darwin. Would the seemingly unstoppable Japanese military machine stop at the Dutch East Indies? Wavell concluded, "Loss of Java, though a severe blow from every point of view, would not be fatal. Efforts should not therefore be made to reinforce Java, which might compromise defense of Burma and Australia."[20] Fears for Australia were significantly heightened when, on 19 February, four Japanese carriers launched 36 fighters, 71 dive-bombers and 81 altitude bombers for an attack on Darwin. In addition 50 bombers of the 21st Flotilla flew from the captured airfields at Kendari and *Ambon*.

The attack achieved complete surprise. With minimal air defense and virtually no anti-aircraft guns Darwin was defenseless. At the airfield about twenty aircraft were destroyed on the ground. Darwin's mainly wooden buildings were set ablaze. Unlike *Pearl Harbor*, the Japanese attack focused on dockyard installations and the oil depot as much as ships in harbor. The destroyer, USS *Peary*, was sunk along with nine merchantmen and auxiliaries that were either sunk or beached. In all 243 Australians were killed with over 300 wounded. Half the civilian population of Darwin fled. Prime Minister Curtin, fearing that the Darwin attack might presage an invasion, immediately blocked any possibility of sending the Australia Corps to reinforce Burma.

The Battle of the Java Sea: **[Map: 11.3]** By the end of February Japan had virtually closed the noose on *Java*, the beating heart of the Netherlands' East Indies Empire. The three southward thrusts of the Japanese army were ready to converge on *Java*. To the north key airfields and oil installations had been captured on the east coast of *Borneo*. Meanwhile on the eastern side of the *Makassar Strait*, which fed the most direct route from the Philippines southwards to *Java*, Japanese airbases had been established on *Celebes* (*Sulawesi*). Due east of *Java*, Japan controlled *Bali* while key locations in *Timor* had also been taken. To the west of *Java*, the island of *Sumatra* and its main airbases and oil installations were under Japanese control. *Java* was pinned from the east, west and north. Perth, Australia, 3,500 miles to the south, was too far away to help. The stage was set for the assault on *Java* itself.

The American-British-Dutch-Australian Command (ABDA) in effect had already given up psychologically if not in the field. With about eighty aircraft remaining, Wavell was advised on 19 February that Allied air power was virtually spent. Air Chief Marshal

Peirse spoke for ABDA when he forecast that the life expectancy for its air force was just two weeks. He was too optimistic. On 20 February Churchill advised Wavell that General MacArthur would be evacuated from *Corregidor* to set up a command in Australia. The Combined Chiefs in Washington urged Wavell to buy time: "Java should be defended with the utmost resolution ... every day gained is of importance."[21] However, there would be no attempt to reinforce *Java*. Everyone except the Dutch thought that the diversion of the veteran USS *Langley* with a planeload of P-40 Warhawks would be a case of throwing the good after the bad. The lessons of *Singapore* had been learned. The *Langley* and its aircraft were held back. Unlike *Singapore*, politicians and commanders in London and Washington as well as Wavell himself anticipated the loss of *Java* with almost unseemly haste.

On 20 February, Wavell and his deputy, Lieutenant-General George Brett, who led the air defenses, concluded that ABDA Command should be wound up "When the fighter defense of *Java* would no longer be possible."[22] At the front, the aircrews were becoming increasingly dispirited; Hubert Eugenes of 17th Pursuit B Flight complained that "It's no fun when the Jap Zero come at you ... the Japs are super pilots, they must have thousands of airplanes, and their planes are the best."[23] In later briefings Shepherd and Gilmore would report that "First, it is very foolish to attack Jap fighters without superior altitude unless it is necessary. Second, when Jap fighters are operating in pairs, if you attack the leader, always be on the watch for his wingman. The wingman will try and get on your tail after he has broken from formation."[24]

George Kiser, clearly with some exaggeration reported, "At all times we were out-numbered at the least 10 to 1, but still we managed to get official credit for in excess of sixty-five victories with only a loss of about nine pilots."[25] The 17th Pursuits P-40 Warhawks, in spite of being out-dated, performed creditably and as with the 'Flying Tigers' in China should have provided the Japanese with ominous warning about the future course of aerial combat if America could supply its aviators with more modern equipment. In spite of these encouraging victories the outlook was far from healthy; ultimately all the American Warhawks were shot down and there were no replacements. On 21 February Jim McAffe, a US Army Air Force administrative officer noted in his diary that he had "an awful feeling about Java. The Japs will certainly take a crack at it, and I know it'll fall flatter than a cake and twice as quick."[26] The Japanese were as confident as the Allies were gloomy. Izawa summarized the situation on *Java* at the end of February; "Japanese preparations could not have been more complete, thorough or effective. Virtually defenseless, Java now hung like a ripe plum, ready to fall into the invader's outstretched hand."[27] With the permission of Wavell and Marshall in Washington, on 22 February, Brett withdrew his aircraft from *Java*. On the same day the Combined Chiefs of Staff (CCS) in Washington informed Wavell that while "all fighting units for which there are arms must continue to fight ..." they ordered the withdrawal of "air forces which can more usefully operate from bases outside of Java. ..."[28]

On 25 February, Wavell formally abandoned the Dutch when he handed over command of ABDA Command. That evening he left *Java* with his staff for Colombo in *Ceylon*. In his last telegram from Java, he wrote, "I deeply regret the failure to hold the ABDA area . . . It was a race against time, and the enemy was too quick for us."[29] In spite of the resignation of their commander, ABDA's naval forces looked for battle. On 27 February 1942, a combined force of ships from each of the four nations of ABDA left Surabaya to intercept the Japanese eastern invasion fleet coming down the *Makassar Strait*, a little in advance of the western invasion fleet that was heading south toward west *Java* from the *South China Sea*. The Allied fleet, which was not large enough to block both invasion forces had chosen to stand and fight against the earlier arriving 'eastern' invasion force. Both fleets were intent on a full-blooded naval shoot-out. For the Dutch a naval victory was the only means of denying *Java* to the Japanese; for the Japanese Navy an engagement was their only means of protecting their troop transports.

Under the leadership of Rear-Admiral Doorman, the ABDA Command force comprised heavy cruisers, USS *Houston* and HMS *Exeter*, three light cruisers, HNLMS *De Ruyter* (Doorman's flagship), HMAS *Perth* and HNLMS *Java*. In addition there were nine supporting destroyers. Ranged against them Rear-Admiral Takeo Takagi commanded two heavy cruisers, *Nachi* and *Haguro*, supported by light cruisers *Naka* and *Jintsu*. Fourteen destroyers, as well as the light carrier *Ryujo*, accompanied the heavier ships. Seemingly the two forces were well matched. However, Japan's heavy cruisers, with an aggregate of twenty 8-inch guns, outgunned the ABDA heavy cruisers twelve 8-inch guns on the *Exeter* and *Houston*. The Japanese force's command and control capability was also superior to the mixed force confronting them.

Having failed to locate the Japanese fleet, Doorman's forces were returning to the port of Surabaya when a scout plane located Takagi's fleet fifty miles to the north. Doorman immediately reversed course to intercept. The naval forces opened fire shortly after 4 p.m. on 27 February. In the early exchanges HMS *Exeter*'s boiler room took a hit and the ship had to retire toward Surabaya. A single Japanese Type-93 Long Lance torpedo sank the Dutch destroyer HNLMS *Kortenaer*. Meanwhile the Japanese light cruiser *Jintsu* and destroyer *Asagumo* engaged the destroyer HMS *Electra* in a gun duel that ended with such severe damage to the British ship that she had to be abandoned.

Some two hours after the action began Doorman broke off southwards seeking to evade the Japanese covering fleet in the dark so as to fall on their troop transports. The US destroyer force meanwhile returned to port to refuel and rearm. The remaining ABDA Command fleet, now comprising just four cruisers found Takagi's force again at 11 p.m. and exchanged fire. A Long Lance torpedo fired by the heavy cruiser *Haguro* sank Doorman's flagship, *De Ruyter*. "It was like the ship was lifted from the water;" recalled Dutch Marine Corps command bridge operator, Corporal Rozier, "all lights went out, we were listing and fire broke out on the AA [anti-aircraft] deck . . ."[30] Heavy cruiser *Nachi* delivered a similar fate to *Java*, another ABDA light cruiser, though it took an hour and a half to sink. Survivors from both ships numbered just 111 sailors. In all, the day's engagement cost some 2,300 ABDA lives. In character, the brave but unlucky Doorman, who, in the naval battles for the Dutch East Indies, had fought a series of engagements, always on the losing side, chose to go down with his ship.

After this catastrophic follow-up engagement of the *Battle of Java Sea* the remaining Allied cruisers retired from the battle to the Tandjong Priok Naval Base in *West Java*. To complete the rout, the destroyer HMS *Jupiter* had earlier been sunk by a mine. Takagi's invasion fleet had suffered minimal disruption with the loss of just twenty-four hours to its invasion schedule, four transports sunk and a single destroyer damaged. Takagi's cruisers dispatched most of the remainder of Doorman's fleet on the following two days. At the *Battle of Sunda Strait*, the cruisers *Perth* and *Houston* were sunk in the early hours of 1 March, as they stumbled into the Japanese naval forces in *Banten Bay*, which were guarding the western bound invasion convoy headed for Batavia (Jakarta). Surrounded on all sides, the ABDA Command ships suffered a withering gun barrage and a series of torpedo attacks from Japanese destroyers and the heavy cruisers *Mogami* and *Mikuma*. In total over ninety Long Lance torpedoes were fired at the Allied cruisers. The *Perth* sank first, losing 353 of its 681 crew. Of the 328 survivors, 106 died in captivity. On the *Houston*, Captain Albert Rooks was killed by gunfire, but it was four torpedo hits that finally holed the cruiser causing it to roll over and sink. Just 368 of 1,061 crew survived. A Japanese transport and a minesweeper were sunk and several Japanese destroyers took hits. On the *Houston* Lieutenant-Commander Arthur Mayer gave the flavor of the chaotic engagement when he reported,

> The disposition of the enemy vessels was such as to completely encircle the *Houston* . . . Enemy planes were overhead . . . Enemy ships believed to be cruisers or carriers were firing at the *Houston* from about 12,000 yards to seaward. Having established hitting range, they were pouring fire into the ship and causing considerable damage. Destroyers operating in formations of three to four ships were making repeated attacks upon the bows and quarters of the *Houston*, using both guns and torpedoes . . . All communication systems which were still operative were hopelessly overloaded with reports of damage received, or approaching torpedoes, or new enemy attacks begun, or changes in targets engaged.[31]

Nevertheless one Japanese transport was sunk immediately and three others were damaged and then beached. The invasion commander, Lieutenant-General Imamura, along with tanks, trucks and cargo, was unceremoniously dunked in the sea.

At noon later the same day the badly limping *Exeter* was caught up by Takagi's heavy cruisers and sunk along with the destroyer HMS *Encounter* at the *Second Battle of Java Sea*. Meanwhile the US Navy's four destroyers made their escape via *Bali* where there was a brief encounter with a Japanese destroyer. They arrived in Freemantle, Australia four days later. Two other US destroyers were not so lucky and another Dutch destroyer was sunk while trying to head for Australia. A similar retreat to Australia was also carried out by what remained of the ABDA Command Air Force.

The *Battle of the Java Sea*, the first major fleet engagement since the *Battle of Jutland*, had ended with a decisive victory for Japan. Nevertheless the ease with which the Japanese Navy had triumphed troubled some. Captain Mitsugo Ihara, a staff officer of the Japanese Third Fleet would later lament, "[Allied] opposition [in the Java area] was so light that the Japanese forces were not put to a severe test and consequently they concluded that equipment available and the tactics used were satisfactory for future operations. It would have been better for the Japanese if they had encountered more opposition."[32]

The Collapse of Dutch Resistance on Java: [Map: 11.4] The *Battle of Java* took place over a two-week period starting on 28 February. Lieutenant-General Hitoshi Imamura led the invasion forces from the Sixteenth Army with the 2nd Division and 230th Regiment totalling 35,000 troops under his command. Against him were ranged a Dutch force of 25,000 troops, mainly poorly trained Javanese recruits supported by 3,500 British troops, 2,500 Australians and 1,000 Americans. Imamura concentrated his actions against the main American-British-Dutch-Australian Command (ABDA) forces located in Batavia (Jakarta) in western *Java* while the 48th Division, which had served so effectively in the opening campaign against MacArthur on the Philippines, landed in *East Java* at Kragan forty miles west of Surabaya after Admiral Takagi's defeat of the ABDA navy at the *Battle of the Java Sea*.

In the east Japanese forces, having enveloped the major port city of Surabaya, advanced southwest with their customary rapidity taking Blora, Soerakarta, Bojolali, Jogjakarta (the great Javanese cultural centre nearby the ninth-century Buddhist temple complex of Borobudur), Magelang, Salatiga, Ambarawa and Poerwordejo.

Their eventual target was the port town of Tjilatjap (Cilacap) situated on the southern coast of central Java, the port city from which it was suspected that the Dutch forces might attempt an evacuation to Australia. Major-General Yuitsu Tsuchihashi led his triumphant 48th Division into Tjilatjap on 8 March and the following day Major-General Pierre Cox surrendered his forces at the nearby town of Wangon. By then the fight had gone out of the Dutch. Lieutenant-Colonel Humphries noted: "The determination and morale of all ranks was of the highest order, the Dutch Commander could not however be persuaded . . . I took this to be a definite indication of the Dutch lack of intention to fight at this juncture, and was in no way surprised when subsequent events took the form they did . . ."[33]

Meanwhile from their two-pronged landings on the western tip of *Java* at Merak-Bantam and on the north coast at Eratan Wetan to the east of Batavia (Jakarta), Lieutenant-General Masao Maruyama's 2nd Division forces took the key airfields. Batavia was enveloped. Maruyama's 2nd Division then moved on toward the major central Javanese city of Bandung. Although there were some notable rear-guard actions, in general the Dutch retreat descended in chaotic flight. C. W. de Iongh recalled: "The retreat of the KNIL [*Koninklijk Nederlandsch-Indisch Leger*] troops from Porong and Pandakan was a complete 'stampede.' Panic without any organization. Officers and troops of the division yelled at us: 'Flee, flee, the Japanese tanks are coming!' "[34] At 9 a.m. on 8 March Lieutenant-General Hein ter Poorten broadcast that Dutch forces should lay down their arms and a few hours later British and Australian forces followed suit. A formal instrument of surrender was signed four days later. The *Java* campaign was ended. The ABDA Command forces had suffered 2,383 dead compared to 671 killed on the Japanese side. The conquest of the Dutch East Indies had finished three months ahead of schedule. In Malang Elizabeth Van Kampen soon saw the Japanese arrive: "They came on bicycles or were just walking. They looked terrible, all with some cloths attached at the back of their caps, they looked very strange to us. This was a type of Japanese we had never seen before."[35]

Many Dutchmen, who felt that they should have continued a guerrilla campaign, greeted the surrender of Ter Poorten's army with bitter recrimination. In truth, after 300 years of often harsh Dutch rule, the equivocal sentiment of native Indonesians toward their Dutch rulers ruled out that possibility

The Japanese *Borneo*-Dutch East Indies Campaign has rarely been accorded its due place in the history of the *Pacific War*. Lacking the great set piece battles and dramas of the Philippines, Malaya, *Singapore* or Burma, the myriad petty military and naval actions which comprised this most complex of advances by Japanese forces are difficult to follow or describe. Relative lack of interest by British and American historians in what was a largely Dutch conflict in spite of the ABDA Command structure has also diminished the perceived historical importance of the campaign.

In many ways however the *Borneo*-East Indies Campaign shows Japanese military capability at its best. Intricately planned and coordinated multi-service actions delivered at blinding speed wove a web of confusion around the ponderous efforts of the defenders. With 58,000 troops, the defenders were not heavily outnumbered. However, the Japanese, who were able to bring some 350 bombers and 450 fighters, heavily outnumbered ABDA Command with just 234 aircraft. Japan, with over fifty warships, also outgunned ABDA's thirty-three ships. Yet, even allowing for the discrepancy in available *matériel*, the entire campaign always appeared far more one sided than their respective resources would suggest. The ABDA commanders appeared resigned to defeat almost from the start. At the start of Japan's offensive against the West on 8 December, the Dutch had believed that Japan would never invade *Java* and Lieutenant-Colonel Saunders noted the ". . . baseless confidence engendered into the Dutch people by their own public men . . ."[36] This veneer of calm soon collapsed. Over the two-week period of the campaign, the Japanese armed services, Army, Navy and Air Forces, outperformed their counterparts through better equipment, better training, better morale and better leadership.

The Brutal Rule of the Conquerors: [Charts: D.1, D.2, D.3] For the defeated soldiers of the *Koninklijk Nederlandsch-Indisch Leger* (KNIL), the surrender to Japan was just the beginning of the horrors of their war. Frans J. Nicolaas Ponder was in the town of Muntilan in *Central Java* when he was taken into captivity. On 18 March the Japanese Army marched into town. "They were greeted with cheers from the natives . . . the very next day, the camp guard was doubled and visiting hours were drastically curtailed."[37] A week later he and the other prisoners were transported in galvanized zinc freight cars; it was boiling hot and they were forced to stand.

There were thousands of personal tragedies. In Batavia, after the surrender of the KNIL, Ralf Ockerse remembered that his mother, wife of a Dutch officer rushed to see her army officer husband as he was herded into the prison camp at Koningsplein. By good fortune she was able to wave at him in the distance and catch his attention; "She was able to signal that she was pregnant . . . and Father seemed to have understood this."[38] It was the last time she would see him. In some cases, captured Australian soldiers were transported in the bamboo cages used to transport pigs. Smaller men were folded up two to a cage. In one case a witness noticed that the prisoners were "tied up with their hands on their backs. Also the legs were tied up . . ."[39] A child witness recalled, "My sister and I saw how the Japanese pushed Australian military, saw those typical Australian hats, into those baskets. When the men were not quick enough then the Japanese stung them with a bayonet."[40] If they were lucky their Japanese drivers drove them to the camps; many died from heat and asphyxiation but in some cases the bamboo cases were reported to have been dropped into harbors, rivers or the *Java Sea*. Elizabeth Van Kampen, who saw these bamboo-caged prisoners, described her haunting memories: "Up till today I can still hear the harsh voices of these poor men crying and screaming for help and for water."[41]

In villages outside Malang, for many months, life continued without much Japanese intervention. The main inconvenience was that expatriate workers were no longer able to receive salaries and had to eat as the local Indonesians did. However, life began to change when Japanese troops entered Dutch family homes for the first time on Christmas Day 1942. Two months later Elizabeth Van Kampen's father was taken away to a camp in Malang. On her sixteenth birthday, she was taken to Malang to see him. It was the last time they would speak. In a notable incident an accompanying woman "Mrs. Hoebregts made the mistake to talk in Dutch to my mother while a Japanese soldier stood not far away from us. He walked up to her and slapped her in the face: 'You have to speak Malay or Japanese' he told her."[42] The following year Elizabeth Van Kampen and her mother and sister were also taken to Banyu Biru prison.

For the Dutch troops arriving in an assembly camp outside Surabaya in *Eastern Java*, the brutality started more immediately. Frans Ponder recalled,

> During a roll call, a Jap commanded us in Japanese. Nobody understood what he said. Attention! Right face! Count off! Etc. All in Japanese. The first blows soon fell. It was advisable not to attempt to ward them off because they would soon be followed by numerous kicks and thrusts with the butt of a rifle. Blood of the first victim flowed freely and we learned the first Japanese cuss words, *bagero* and *kanero*.[43]

Jan Voss, a 15-year-old Dutch-Indonesian boy at the time of the surrender remembered being taken to a prison outside Bandung. "The very first time I came to hate the Jap was the morning after our arrival in camp. They confiscated our precious personal documents and family pictures and just burned them."[44] Worse was to come. The camp commander Matsuoka was considered a 'good Jap' but his assistant, a former Tokyo taxi driver, Matsumura, was a bully who became nicknamed 'the slapper.' He administered punishment with a bamboo stick.

On 29 May Frans Ponder was given a medical examination whereby "a Japanese doctor stuck a glass rod in the behind to determine if the person had dysentery . . ."[45] Five days later he was kicked and rifle butted into the steamy cargo hold of a Japanese cargo ship and taken to *Singapore* where he was put into the infamous Chiangi Prison. Numbers of his colleagues died of dysentery en route and were buried at sea. At least Ponder survived his journey to *Singapore*. In 1944, as MacArthur began to threaten the Philippines, shipments of prisoners on *Java* were sent to *Sumatra* to help build a railroad being constructed to transport coal from the west of the island to the east coast and thence to *Singapore*. Willem Wanrooy recalled a hellish journey on a rusty old freighter from Jakarta to *Sumatra*; he suffered from "blazing sun during the day, and bone chilling rains at night."[46] There was little food or water for the 2,200 prisoners and 4,000 natives on board. Three days out torpedoes slammed into the *Junyo Maru*. "I saw human bodies and pieces of wood, metal and other debris blown high in the sky from somewhere mid-ship . . . howls, screams and cries filled the air."[47] Wanrooy had been fortunate to find a place on deck and managed to swim to safety and the good fortune of a passing ship the next day. He had watched more than 5,620 men die. In terms of lives lost it was the biggest maritime disaster of the Pacific war.

This was no accident however. The Japanese deliberately failed to mark their prisoner transports as POW ships with the result that seventeen ships, carrying mainly Dutch soldiers as well as native Indonesians to *Sumatra* or Burma, were sunk; 17,909 people died in this way. On other prison ships, inmates died from disease. Arthur Stock, a Royal Air Force (RAF) engineer, became a British prisoner of war on *Java*, and recalled that a ship that left the island of *Ambon* for *Java* with prisoners aboard had to anchor off

Makassar Bay for four weeks while an epidemic of blackwater fever took its toll of the prisoners of war. Half of those who embarked died.

Certain POWs such as guerrilla fighters, escapees, captured demolition units or special forces were put in *Jahat* Camps (for dangerous prisoners). After interrogation by the *Kempeitai* they would be killed, usually by decapitation. Andrew Van Dyke, the 12-year-old son of a sugar plantation manager was a boy prisoner at the start of the war and observed life in numbers of different camps during the course of the war. His aunt was kept in jail in Surabaya on charges of aiding resistance fighters; "She endured the nightly attention of the Kempeitai and was ultimately decapitated many days after the war had ended."[48]

In Malang, 16-year-old Elizabeth Van Kampen recalled venturing out of her camp with other girlfriends in the middle of the night and making their way to the known *Kempeitai* house in

> Welirang Street. The three houses behind the Kempeitai were empty, and the doors were locked, so the six of us crawled to the back garden. Luckily there were trees and shrubs so we could hide ourselves behind them. We couldn't see much, but what we heard was more than enough. I was really scared when I heard people, men and women, screaming in death agony.[49]

Elizabeth Van Kampen's liberty to roam came to an end in January 1944 when she was notified by her camp leader that now she too was considered a POW. She noted that their treatment became noticeably worse as it became clear to their Japanese prison guards that the war was being lost. When Allied planes dropped leaflets to this effect, camp guards "became even more strict than before, and several women were really beaten up very nasty with rough bamboo sticks."[50] Naturally the Japanese prison guards used split bamboo that left painful splints in the skin.

Dutch conscript soldier Denis Dutrieux remembered being made to watch the execution of three POWs who had tried to escape. One of the Dutch prisoners refused the blindfold and spat in the eye of the Japanese prison commander, yelling "Long live the Queen! . . . the prisoners were then barbarically bayoneted to death . . . accompanied by the most revolting, blood chilling, beastly screams I have ever heard . . ."[51] Their bodies were tied to poles as a grim warning. "Bastards. They can't be human beings,"[52] the POWs muttered. Brutality was not reserved only for westerners. The Indonesians whom Hirohito's government claimed that they were liberating were treated with the arbitrary cruelty of conquerors. Property, life and liberty were claimed at will. Punishment was liberally meted out. Ralph Ockerse recalled in his memoir *Our Childhood in the Former Colonial East Indies* [2011] that he saw an Indonesian caught stealing, whereupon "As a Japanese soldier happened to be nearby, he took his samurai sword and cut off the Indonesian's hand as punishment for his actions . . . such incidents were periodic occurrences."[53]

Torture was *de rigueur*. Willem Maaskamp remembered being beaten "with whips, military belts, fists and every other item at their disposal. . ."[54] The *Kempeitai* interrogators also "extinguished burning cigarettes on our bodies."[55] Even when they were not killed, prisoners were frequently taunted with the possibility of execution. "After a cruel beating," Maaskamp recalled, "the *Kempeitai* officer in the interrogation room tied my wrists, made me kneel in front of him, pulled out his revolver and held it against my forehead."[56] Jan Vos meanwhile recalled the regular visits of a Mr. Matsuda from the *Kempeitai*. "He dressed in a grey suit and an Indonesian hat. He always greeted us with exaggerated politeness but he could probably be considered the worst executioner around. Matsuda had no qualms at torturing a Jewish dentist . . . he drove needles underneath the man's fingernails and toenails in order to extract a confession."[57]

Women and boys under twelve were herded into concentration camps of various sizes ranging from just 100 to an 18,000-person camp at Cihapit outside Bandung in *West Java*. At Cihapit in 1944 numbers of Dutch women would be coerced into prostitution to service Japanese army personnel after it became logistically impossible to transport more Korea 'comfort' women to replace those that had died in captivity. Other large camps included Cideng near Jakarta, the capital city; here a particularly brutal commandant Captain Kenichi Sonei terrorized the inmates, killing hundreds. Particularly at full moon, the psychopathic Sonei became a demented murderer. After the war he would be executed as a war criminal.

Rita La Fontaine De Clercq Zubli, the 13-year-old daughter of the postmaster of the town of Jambi on *Sumatra*, escaped rape by masquerading as a boy. However, she was shocked to spy local women at a party given by the invaders being "too submissive to the amorous advances of the Japanese officers accompanying them. I knew that some of these women were married . . ."[58] As with all occupying armies fraternization became a normal accompaniment to conquest. Rita's parents were alarmed to discover that their masquerade would not necessarily protect their daughter as her father was told, "young boys were hired to work in Japanese households as houseboys. It was a known fact that these boys were often abused and exposed to drugs."[59] However, Rita survived the war and married a Dutchman and relocated to the US in 1960 where she worked as a technical typist at the Smithsonian Astrophysical Observatory in Cambridge, Massachusetts.

Bedding in the camps consisted of little more than matting. Up to forty people were crowded into huts and inmates would have to lay head to toe. In some camps basic bunks were stacked against walls. Huts were frequently made from bamboo and constructed in jungle clearings. The baked earth floors turned to mud when it rained. In the jungle clothes quickly rotted or wore out. Replacement clothing was virtually non-existent. Women would often be seen working in native shorts, clogs and brassieres. Men were given the shreds of Japanese army uniforms. When boots perished, they were replaced by wooden clogs. The lack of clothing was particularly harsh for inmates settled in the many mountain camps where the nights were cold.

Food was organized by communal food kitchens operated by designated inmates. Hunger could never be satisfied and food that was "either found or stolen, was most often prepared on bricks, using modified tin cans with twigs underneath to fuel the fire."[60] In prisons however food was often provided just once a day and pushed through windows or under doors. Only the strongest prisoners ate as POWs pressed to the front of the queue. The old and feeble perished from starvation. Food in the camps was often little better than a slow-starvation diet even for the healthy. Elizabeth Van Kampen described a diet of

> Tea early in the morning before the roll call. Breakfast: a bowl of starch. Lunch: a cup of boiled rice, a tablespoon heaped up of boiled green cabbage and a teaspoon also heaped up *sambal*, a sort of Spanish pepper. Tea in the afternoon. Dinner: starch soup with a few leaves of cabbage, one could count the small pieces. As my mother said it so well: It was just enough not to die . . . too soon.[61]

In a country of abundance, there was no fruit. In camps such as Banyu Biru nearly all the inmates suffered *pallagra* in various degrees of seriousness; symptoms included skin lesions, *dermatitis, alopecia* (hair loss), *edema* (swelling of limbs), *glossitis* (inflammation of the tongue), *ataxia* (lack of physical coordination), *neuritis* (nerve damage), *dilated cardyomyopathy* (enlarged heart) and *diarrhea*. Eventually the condition could lead to incurable dementia. Within a few years of captivity, from a population of previously sturdy young women and children, thousands died from starvation at Banyu Biru Prison. Old people considered 'useless' by the Japanese were often killed rather than being taken into camps. In Bogor, one young woman attested that "The Japanese locked my grandmother's stepmother together with other fellow sufferers up in a big bamboo cage and plunged this cage many times under water in the river, until all the patients were dead."[62]

In some camps urine was collected and turned into a rich vitamin drink. "I personally had a chance to sample this drink, "Jan Vos wrote, "and I must say it tasted like palm wine."[63] Medical care was virtually non-existent. Although there were doctors and nurses there were no medicines or equipment. Tropical ulcers ate away flesh until the bones were exposed. Open wounds would attract maggots. Washed out wounds would be bound with filthy rags. As a last resort limbs would be amputated. Cholera, dysentery, dengue fever and typhoid were commonplace. Beriberi was particularly nasty. "The 'wet' version of the disease, caused by poor nutrition, would release body fluid from the cells. Fluid would collect primarily in the legs, rising up the torso and towards the lungs. This would ultimately result in death by drowning."[64] The dry version of beriberi was hardly better. A patient lost fluid from the bodily orifices. When they fell and hit their heads, "it could split open like a dropped watermelon."[65]

After the Dutch surrender, their language was banned in schools and institutions throughout the East Indies. Even in camps only Japanese and Indonesian was permitted. Violations were punished by severe beatings. Forgetting to bow was a cardinal sin. The

12-year-old Van Dyke recalled that one time when he was sitting on the garbage wagon to prevent the garbage from falling off while other boys and girls were pushing it, they arrived at the main gate of the camp only to be bellowed at by an angry sentry. Van Dyke had failed to "come down from the cart to bow for him. As a penalty I had to remain still in a bowing position for a minute or so. Suddenly I felt a severe whack on my back. The Japanese had hit me with the butt of his rifle to vent his wrath. I was in great pain for days and could barely straighten up."[66]

After the Japanese surrender, officers were ordered to paint POW on the roofs of the prisoner huts so that food could be sent to prisoners as quickly as possible. At first this was done by dropping supplies from B-24 Liberators flying in from West Australia. "Big drums, attached to parachutes, came tumbling down. Some fell right through the roofs of our barracks . . . oh boy did we have a treat! . . . they did a good job doling out the 'manna from heaven.' "[67] Elizabeth Van Kampen only learned that the Japanese had surrendered on 24 August. Her happiness was short lived. News arrived that her uncle Pierre had died in a *Kempeitai* prison in December 1944. Neither did her captivity end. The Dutch had to be kept locked up for their safety after future President Sukarno's nationalists started killing Dutch people. Eventually on 28 December 1945 Elizabeth Van Kampen and her mother and two sisters were evacuated by boat to Sri Lanka. In February 1946 they were notified that their father Theo had died of dehydration in Malang Prison shortly before the end of the war.

Some prisoners' survival appeared miraculous both to themselves and others. Willem Maaskamp, a 17-year-old Dutch prisoner wrote that his brother disappeared after a Japanese submarine sank his destroyer. He suddenly appeared after the end of the war having survived the sinking of his ship, Chiangi Prison, work on the 'railways of death' in Burma and Thailand, shipment to Japan and work in the Japanese coalmines. After liberation in August 1945 he was shipped out by a US aircraft carrier to Manila and then to hospital in Australia before being sent home to *Java*. Maaskamp's elder brother, a pilot in the Netherlands East Indies Air Force was less fortunate. After being ordered to fly out to Australia, Maaskamp's mother received a telegram declaring him to be 'missing in action'; "We never heard from him since, and after the war he was declared killed in action. Fred was 24 years old when he died for Queen and country."[68]

Japan's Bitter Fruits of Victory in the Dutch East Indies: Apart from mopping up exercises, Japan's conquest of the oil rich territories of the Dutch East Indies was complete by 8 March 1942. American-British-Dutch-Australian Command's (ABDA) forces, that on paper should have had the wherewithal at least to put a brake on the Japanese advance, failed even in that mission. Japanese forces, in a complex coordinated web of inter-service action, had won another astonishing victory with minimal losses. It remains one of the least heralded campaigns of *World War II*.

What had the Japanese Empire gained? The ABDA Command demolition of oil wells, storage facilities and refineries proved to be a relatively temporary brake on oil production in the region. The longer term outcome proved less satisfactory to Japan.

While output was quickly restarted under Japanese management, the post-1942 output of the Dutch East Indies and *Borneo* never regained the annual production of 65 million barrels achieved in 1940. Japan lacked technicians and more importantly oil industry technology and equipment.

Nevertheless even 4 million barrels per month (48 million barrels per annum) should 'on paper' have provided Japan with enough oil to cover its needs without dipping into strategic inventories. In theory South East Asian production combined with synthetic domestic production, easily met Japan's required annual consumption that was 36.9 million tons in 1941 (of which the Army and Navy accounted for approximately 24 million barrels), rising to a peak of 43.9 million tons in 1943. However, imports of all oil products to Japan never exceeded 1.4 million tons per month and the highest annual figure for imports was achieved with 13.5 million tons in 1943.

The problem was simply that there were not enough tankers. Although a boosted building program increased aggregate tanker tonnage from 575,000 tons in January 1942 to a peak of 809,000 in July 1943, it was never enough to bring the oil treasures from its newly acquired East Indies Empire. **[See Appendix B: Oil, Raw Materials and Logistics: 'Just Start Swinging']** Thereafter as the US submarine campaign found its stride, tanker tonnage began to fall alarmingly. The net result of this failure to bring enough oil from the Dutch East Indies was that after 1943, the largest portions of the Imperial Navy's oil-guzzling fleet (18 million barrels per annum) had to be kept in southern waters, close to the source of supply. What should have been a huge advantage in terms of short lines of communication to the Japanese home islands versus a US fleet that had to haul its logistical support across the *Pacific*, was therefore largely negated. Even with the Japanese fleet thus parked several thousands of miles from the home islands, Japan was still burning through its stockpiles of crude oil and refined products. Inventories fell from 48.9 million tons in 1941 to just 13.8 million barrels by the end of 1944. Thereafter falls in domestic production and the cessation of all imports caused a precipitate erosion of remaining oil supplies. In the first six months of 1945, Japan's inventory was reduced by a further 9 million leaving it with an inventory of only 4.9 million barrels by the end of June.

The last oil tanker with Dutch crude arrived in March 1945. By then the need for oil was so great that the Japanese government initiated a program to make low grade oil from pine roots that civilians as well as school children were assigned to dig up. For all this effort, 70,000 barrels of pine oil produced 3,000 barrels of aviation fuel. It was the economics of pure desperation. By the time the US dropped an atom bomb on Hiroshima, Japan was literally scraping the barrel. Japan's entire 'strike south' gamble, predicated on the thesis that the Dutch East Indies could replace oil imports from America, not only failed to bring enough oil to Japan to enable it to sustain its oil inventories but even failed to bring enough oil to cover the annual consumption of the Navy on whose security Japan depended. In effect Japan was 'eating its own tail.'

Part IV
'Victory Disease': Japan's Reversal of Fortune: June 1942–December 1942

12 Limits of Empire: Doolittle and New Military Strategies

[February 1942–May 1942]

[Maps: 12.1A, 12.1B, 12.2, 12.3, 12.4, 12.5, 12.6A, 12.6B, 12.7]

The ARCADIA Conference: **[Maps: 12.1A, 12.1B]** With America drawn into the war with Germany by the Japanese attack on *Pearl Harbor*, Churchill and Roosevelt quickly needed to determine how the war with Germany, Italy and Japan should be fought and what were to be its objectives. The First Washington Conference (ARCADIA) took place at a series of meetings in Washington between 22 December 1941 and 14 January 1942. The first declaration from the conference appeared on 1 January 1942 and was clearly intended as a New Year declaration of intention. Twenty-six Allied nations (not including France whose Vichy Government had allied itself with *Nazi* Germany) declared that they would adhere to the principles of the *Atlantic Charter* signed by Britain and America on 12 August 1941. In hindsight it can be seen that this declaration foreshadowed the creation of the United Nations. The *Atlantic Charter* gave warning that total war would be waged until total victory had been achieved. There was also an undertaking that each nation would not conclude a separate peace with their enemies. At a stroke Japan's notion that it could fight a limited war and force America to the negotiating table was demolished.

In the course of the conference, British and American military committees worked out details of co-operation. The outcome was a formal standing organization known as the Combined Chiefs of Staff (CCS) that was permanently established in Washington for the coordination and management of British and American war efforts. Although there were frequent disagreements within this organization, it worked in a largely productive manner for the duration of the war. Noticeably it was not something replicated by the Axis powers, though for reasons of geography and logistics it is arguable that Germany and Japan were never in a position to support each other.

Perhaps the most important decision of the conference, and one from which the Allies never wavered, was that, notwithstanding *Pearl Harbor*, the war in Europe would take precedence over the war in Asia. For Churchill this decision was a huge relief. For Asia, it meant that the Allied response to the rapid expansion of the Japanese Empire would necessarily be compromised.

Size Matters: The Limits of Empire: The whole premise of Japan's aggressive military action in attacking the United States was to retain its gains in China and to expand on them so as to create a Great East Asia Co-Prosperity Sphere. An Asian bloc with Japan at its head would be able to compete with the western powers, notably the United States, Russia and Great Britain. Empire was not only necessary economically but had, by 1940, become a spiritual quest. As Foreign Minister, Matsuoka proclaimed somewhat grandiosely before the war, "The Co-prosperity Sphere in the Far East is based on the spirit of Hakko Ichiu, or the Eight Corners of the Universe under One Roof. . . We must control the western Pacific . . ."[1]

Before the occupation of Manchuria in 1931, Japan's 'Empire' consisted of Korea (85,000 square miles) and Taiwan (13,500 square miles); the effective annexation of Manchuria added a further 425,000 square miles, which was an area three times bigger than the Japanese home islands (145,000 square miles). By the time of the Marco Polo Bridge Incident in July 1937, Japan ruled an area comprising 655,000 square miles. What started out as a skirmish with China soon turned into a further justification for the creation of an enlarged Empire or Great East Asia Co-Prosperity Sphere. The aim was the complete subjugation of China. Some five years later, in 1941, Japan controlled almost half of China including its most productive maritime and industrial provinces; if Indochina (285,000 square miles), effectively added to the Japanese Great East Asia Co-Prosperity Sphere after the defeat of France and its replacement by a 'collaborator' Vichy government, is included, Japan's ruled area had increased from 655,000 square miles to approximately 1.6 million square miles.

Faced with the choice of yielding to America's demands to reduce its empire back to the level of 655,000 square miles, or 243,500 square miles if Manchuria had to be yielded, wiping out the costly gains of almost ten years of war with China, Japan opted to launch a daring assault on both the European Empires in South East Asia as well as the United States Empire in Asia and the *Pacific*. In the four months of military and naval victories, which shocked the world, Japan conquered America's prize imperial possession, the Philippines and its Archipelago (115,000 square miles), as well as inflicting a serious defeat of its navy in its home base of *Hawaii*.

In addition by March 1942, Japan had seized *Singapore* and Malaysia (127,000 square miles), humiliating the British Empire in the process. Furthermore the remnants of Britain's army were fighting their way to the Indian border to escape Japan's occupation of Burma (260,000 square miles). The Netherlands' Indonesian colonies (735,000 square miles) were subsumed by Japan after the surrender of Dutch forces on 9 March. Added to these new territories, Japan also took *Guam* (US territory), *Wake Island* (US territory), *Hong Kong* (British territory) and the mandated Australian territories of the *Bismarck Archipelago*. In addition the islands of *Attu* and *Kiska* in the *Aleutian* chain linked with Alaska were captured as a prelude to Yamamoto's *Midway* campaign. In just over ten years, Japan had achieved a remarkable expansion of its empire from 243,500 square miles to 2.9 million square miles—a growth factor of twelve times. In the space of a few months Hirohito's government had brought 500 million Asians under its direct rule. Did this strengthen Japan? Economically it would be hard to argue that even Manchuria, absorbed into the Japanese economic empire after 1931, could be considered to have contributed to Japan's economic strength.

Five years of war with China had drained Japan and required a standing army of 120 divisions (1.5 million troops) just to maintain its hold over half of the country. Now with its sweeping victories over America, Great Britain, Holland and Australia, Japan had an additional 1.25 million square miles to administer and garrison.

Japan's expansion therefore added significant burdens to an already stretched economy; even without having to fight a war with China, the United States, Great Britain and Australia, the mere management of this suddenly acquired empire would have been difficult. However, simple addition of the new 'real estate' requiring Japan's attention underestimates the task facing Japan in March 1942. While the increase in Japan's Empire in terms of territory was daunting, the scale of the Empire in terms of distances was even greater.

Japan's Empire at its peak in June 1942 stretched from the Russian borders in the north, the barren wastes of Kamchatka and the islands of Alaska in the northeast, to Jakarta in the southwest and *Timor* in the south, and from the borders of Burma/India in the west to the *Marshall Islands* in the east, and *Guadalcanal* in the southeast. The area covered by Japan's Empire including oceans was now 20 million square miles, an area almost 140 times larger than Japan's home islands. The diameter of Japan's Imperial borders had expanded to 5,000 miles. The logistics of managing this newly acquired empire were breathtaking in their scale and complexity; this task had to be accomplished at the same time that Japan was fighting an all-out war with the United States, the world's most powerful economy, Great Britain, the world's largest empire and China, the world's most populous country.

Victory Disease: Japanese forces achieved victories so stunning and in such rapid succession that some including the Emperor were concerned about hubris and complacency. Japan now faced the problem of 'what next?' Curiously Japan's planning had not gone beyond March. In April 1942, Admiral Yamamoto wrote to his geisha, Plum Dragon, "The first stage of operations has been a kind of children's hour, and will soon be over; now comes the adults' hour, so perhaps I'd better stop dozing and bestir myself."[2] Yamamoto did bestir himself but the consequence of victory was not certainty but confusion.

In his post-war *Showa-Tenno Dokuhaku Roku* (The Emperor's Soliloquy), Hirohito recalled, "[In 1941] we thought we could achieve a draw with the US, or at best win by a six to four margin; but total victory was nearly impossible . . . When the war actually began, however, we gained a miraculous victory at Pearl Harbor and our invasions of Malaya and Burma succeeded far quicker than expected."[3] Great victories were won but what had they actually gained? Japan, by its own estimation, could not invade and conquer America, so how could they force the United States to come to terms that would allow them to keep their Great East Asia Co-Prosperity Sphere? Apart from how to force America to the negotiating table, Japan faced another problem, which was that the Tripartite Alliance with Germany and Italy forbade Japan from seeking a separate agreement with the United States. In the *Dokuhaku Roku*, Hirohito surmised, "if not for this [agreement], we might have achieved peace when we were in an advantageous position."[4] This was surely wishful thinking however because there was no indication that Roosevelt and his government ever considered a negotiated peace with Japan at any stage.

For the Japanese Navy the strategy was clear; a task force should conquer *Hawaii*. As Rear-Admiral Matame Ugaki pointed out: "Time would work against Japan because of the vastly superior national resources of the United States . . . Unless Japan quickly resumed the offensive—sooner, the better—she would eventually become incapable of doing anything more than sitting down and waiting for the American forces to counter-attack."[5] For Ugaki the American fleet, this time with its carriers, had to be drawn into *the* decisive battle; a Japanese victory in this decisive engagement might force America to negotiate. It was a plan soon scotched by the Imperial High Command, which came to the conclusion that there were insufficient resources to conquer *Hawaii*. Not surprisingly the Army was reluctant to commit manpower to an extension of the *Pacific* perimeter that would increase demand from an already stretched garrison service in China. Thus the Army categorically refused to accede to the *Hawaii* invasion plan.

Japan's logistical overstretch was already evident after a mere three months of fighting. From a defensive point of view the Navy was concerned that its naval perimeter in the *Pacific* was made vulnerable at its southern flank by the ability of America to supply Australia by convoy. The danger of allowing a counter-invasion force to be built in northern Australia, capable of rolling up Japan's southern perimeter, was immediately perceived as a major threat. Indeed at this stage Japan was largely oblivious to the idea of a thrust through the *Central Pacific* that was envisaged by Admiral Ernest King, Commander in Chief, United States Fleet. For the time being Japanese strategists correctly understood that the US fleet at *Hawaii* was too weak to launch an attack on Japan through the *Central Pacific*—though eventually it was believed that the war with America would be won by a great naval battle in this corridor in the mode of the *Battle of Tsushima*. In the short term therefore Japanese planners were much more concerned with an American attempt to attack the Japanese home islands from a base in Australia. The potential threat, ultimately realized, would come through New Guinea and then the Philippines. To counter the American military threat, Japan's Naval General Staff suggested an invasion of north Australia. As early as 11 March Prime Minister, General Hideki Tojo, had warned that "Australia must learn that defense against our invincible forces is impossible in view of her sparse population, the vastness of her territories and her geographical position which makes her so distant from the United States and Britain."[6]

It was a warning that an alarmed Australian Prime Minister took seriously. Speaking on 13 March, Curtin said, "This is a warning. Australia is the last Allied bastion between the west coast of America and Japan. If she succumbs, the entire American continent will be wide open to invasion . . . I tell you that saving Australia will be the same as saving the western side of the United States."[7] It was a bizarre, self-serving speech that contained little logic. Australia, some 7,000 miles from the west coast of America, was never going to be the launch pad for an invasion of the United States. Eisenhower, in an early strategic study for General Marshall, had even concluded that while an attempt should be made to defend Australia, it was, in the final analysis, expendable.

In spite of Prime Minister, General Tojo's aggressive words, the plan to invade Australia was also squashed. With some 70 percent of its troops tied up in China the Japanese Army had neither the manpower nor the transport capacity to launch or provision such a large-scale campaign. China, a country where the Japanese Army had been fighting a war for ten years, continued to be a priority. Military men, many with a background in Manchukuo's *Kwantung* Army, also remained fearful of the Soviet Union. Many in the Navy suspected that the *Kwantung* Army was hoarding troops for the expected eventual conflict with the Soviet Union. For the Army the campaign in Burma would also absorb more troops than had originally been expected. After the war, Tojo, with regard to the mooted invasion of Australia, reported, "We never had enough troops to do so . . . We did not have the armed strength of supply facilities to mount such a terrific extension of our already overstrained and too thinly spread forces."[8]

Vice-Admiral Shigeyoshi Inou, commander of Japan's southern fleet, pushed for a more limited campaign. It was a compromise deal. By occupying Port Moresby in New Guinea and *Tulagi* in the southeastern *Solomon Islands*, it was believed that supply to Australia from America could be disrupted. Captain Sadatoshi Tomioka, Head of the Project Section at Naval HQ, had first enunciated the 'Australia Doctrine.' He proposed that Australia's potential as a base for counter-attack could be neutered without the logistical cost of conquest and occupation. Furthermore by securing these *South Pacific* bases, Japan's 'outer perimeter' could also be strengthened by a second phase *South Pacific* Campaign: the seizure of *New Caledonia, Fiji* and *American Samoa*. Thus Japan's perimeter would be extended and supply to Australia disrupted. Australia might even be cajoled into signing a peace agreement with Japan.

It was a plan that both the Army and Navy could live with. However, it was not a plan that was unanimously supported in the Navy. While Ugaki and the Imperial Naval HQ advocated the southward drive, it was not the preferred strategy of the Navy's new hero Admiral Yamamoto. With the invasion of *Hawaii* ruled out on the grounds of a lack of resources, Yamamoto planned an attack on *Midway*, an island whose airfield would supposedly enable Japan to put constant pressure on *Hawaii* and American convoys. (As US cargo ships traveling to Australia could easily have circumvented the effective range of bomber patrols from *Midway*, the efficacy of this strategy has been questioned.) While Yamamoto was not wholly averse to the aims of the southward strategy, his primary focus was on the destruction of the carrier fleet. His staff gunnery officer and close confidante, Commander Watanabe, averred that "by launching the proposed operation against Midway, we can succeed in drawing out the enemy's carrier strength and destroying it in decisive battle."[9] The memories of the war-winning *Battle of Tsushima* lived on. As Watanabe, representing Yamamoto at the strategy conference with Imperial Naval General Staff, argued, "In the last analysis, the success or failure of our entire strategy in the Pacific will be determined by whether or not we succeed in destroying the United States Fleet, more particularly its carrier task forces."[10]

Even if the US carrier fleet did not take the bait, Japan could add *Midway* and the *Aleutians* to its defensive perimeter. It was also argued that the taking of the *Midway*, like the 'Australia Doctrine,' would similarly cut American supply to Australia. Perhaps most importantly the Imperial Japanese Navy Staff in Tokyo was reluctant to refuse the plans of Yamamoto who was being lionized by Japan's national media. Vice-Admiral Chuichi Nagumo, Commander in Chief of the First Air Fleet, could not risk Yamamoto's resignation.

Japan's Naval HQ was doubtful. Naval Staff Commander Miyo noted, "The combined fleet's view that the seizure of Midway threatening Hawaii would effectively undermine America's will to fight and thus pave the way to a negotiated peace was far too optimistic."[11] In addition the *Midway* strategy was not the only alternative on the drawing board. Studies were being made to invade *Ceylon* with a view to using this as a launch pad for the conquest of India. Even a link-up with the Germans in the Middle East was mooted, though Hitler quickly squashed the idea. Meanwhile the Japanese Army briefly considered an attack on the Soviet Union.

What is evident from the disputes that appeared after the remarkable series of victories won in the aftermath of *Pearl Harbor*, is that there was no clear vision as to how the war was going to be fought or won. Just as Japan had stumbled into a war with China without a pre-conceived 'war plan,' just as they had stumbled into a war with the United States and Great Britain without a clear vision of an 'end game,' so Japan arrived at the second phase of the *Pacific War* without any idea how to progress. It was a muddle. Furthermore there was no single guiding mind behind Japanese strategy. As winners up to this point, initiative for the direction of the war was still in Japanese hands. Japan could make the choices; America would have to react. At this critical juncture Japan's high command did not follow a stratagem, it stumbled forward with a smorgasbord of military and naval plans.

Japan's Indian Ocean Raid and Divided Strategies: **[Map: 12.2]** Before implementing the 'southern strategy' and *Midway* campaign, Admiral Chuichi Nagumo's fleet carrier force comprising *Akagi, Ryujo, Hiryu, Soryu, Shokaku* and *Zuikaku* was sent on a raid of the British naval base on *Ceylon*. Having supported the conquest of the Dutch East Indies, Nagumo's fleet departed the *Celebes Islands* on 26 March. First the light carrier *Ryujo*, with a diversionary force of six cruisers under Admiral Jisaburo Ozawa, was sent to attack shipping in the *Bay of Bengal*. Twenty-three Allied ships were sunk in addition to five bagged by Japanese submarines. But, warned by decrypted intercepts of Nagumo's advance, Vice-Admiral Sir James Somerville had retreated to the *Maldive Islands*.

Nagumo's main force was spotted 400 miles south of *Ceylon* on 4 April and the following day a strike force of 125 bombers with thirty-six Zero escorts led by Commander Mitsuo Fuchida flew over the Royal Air Force (RAF) base at Ratmalana Airfield. Faulty warning procedures meant that RAF fighters did not scramble to meet them. Perhaps fortunately for the lives of the RAF pilots, Fuchida's target was the naval base at Colombo where they sank HMS *Hector* (armed merchant cruiser) and HMS *Tenedos* (destroyer), as well as merchantmen *Cornwall* and *Dorsetshire*. Fuchida's forces lost eighteen aircraft but downed twenty-seven RAF aircraft in the course of the attack. Five more Allied merchantmen were sunk on 6 April as well as HMIS *Indus* (sloop) off *Akyab* in Southwest Burma.

The most damaging engagement took place three days later at Trincomalee Harbor. At 10.55 a.m. on 9 April, the returning British Carrier, HMS *Hermes*, a small *World War I* era carrier that had been ordered in 1917 and was commissioned in 1924, was caught by eighty-five Aichi D3A 'Val' dive-bombers. Marooned without escorts or aircraft, the *Hermes* was an isolated target. Taking over forty hits, the *Hermes* sank off Batticaloa with the loss of 307 men including Captain Onslow. Nagumo's carriers lost four 'Vals.' Other attacks sank HMAS *Vampire* (destroyer) and HMS *Hollyhock* (corvette). In spite of giving British forces a mauling, the widely expected invasion did not take place. Although the *Andaman Islands* were occupied, Japan did not have the resources to mount an occupation of *Ceylon*, which would have given Britain significant problems in terms of logistical supply to Calcutta, the lynchpin port for the supply of the British–Indian Army ensconced on the border with Burma. Overall, the *Indian Ocean Raid* appears a slightly random even aimless operation. It achievements did little to match Japan's imperative strategic requirement, which was to bring the United States to the negotiating table. Indeed during the *Indian Ocean Raid*, arguments over Japan's strategic direction festered.

Finally, unable to agree a single strategy, the Japanese Navy planned two. In support of the invasion force for Port Moresby, the first stage of the 'Southern Plan,' Yamamoto dispatched Admiral Shigeyoshi Inoue with two brand-new fleet carriers, the *Shokaku* and the *Zuikaku*, as well as the light carrier *Shoho*, and a force of cruisers and destroyers. The Fourth Fleet thus set out from *Truk*, the huge lagoon in the *Caroline Islands* that served as its forward base. Yamamoto meanwhile planned his attack on *Midway* and the diversionary raid on the *Aleutian Islands*.

Indeed the only plan that was comprehensively abandoned was the 'consolidation strategy' advocated by yet another naval faction led by Nagumo's Chief of Staff Rear-Admiral Kusaka; he wanted time to train more pilots, consolidate logistics and refurbish the fleet before the next round of warfare. Kusaka's advice was wholly ignored. While each part of the three-legged strategy had its own internal logic, none of them delivered a credible means of delivering a knockout blow to the United States. More importantly with regard to the dispersal of naval forces, Yamamoto disregarded the importance of 'concentration of forces' that is a cardinal rule of offensive military strategy.

The plans eventually chosen for the second stage of the *Pacific War* displayed muddled thinking, hubris and political compromise. However, what is most evident is that the Japanese Imperial forces had not started the war with a clear plan as to how America was to be defeated. It is a startling realization. Moreover if Japan's commanders could be so muddled in victory, how would they fare when faced by setbacks?

The American Strategic Dilemma: For American strategists, there were also dilemmas and choices to be made. It should be noted that even after their resounding defeats at *Pearl Harbor* and in the Philippines, America enjoyed certain advantages. First they had time. With its massive industrial capacity, the United States could prepare a build-up of forces to launch a counter-attack; furthermore it could be secure in the knowledge that it would eventually be able to obtain the *matériel* to attack Japan while doubting that Japan had the *matériel* to attack America. Apart from the occasional febrile moment in the panicky days after *Pearl Harbor*, it was never genuinely considered likely that Japan would invade America. Whatever the fears and exigencies that followed the setbacks of the early months of the war, America could follow a strategic path with the comforting knowledge that every day that passed without a heavy defeat moved the outcome of the war in its favor.

In the short term however America had to decide an appropriate strategy balanced between the needs of the *Atlantic* and *Pacific* campaigns. The key strategic decisions would come to a head at the ARCADIA Conference in Washington in the first weeks of 1942. Churchill, who had arrived at the end of December 1941, stayed in the White House with Roosevelt until 15 January. It alarmed both the US and British military that they were cocooned together. Alexander Cadogan reflected the British view when he opined in his diary that Churchill worshipped Roosevelt. Before *Pearl Harbor* Churchill had tried to woo Roosevelt into war; after Churchill told King George VI at lunch, "Britain and America were now married after many months of walking out."[12]

America's fears related to what Roosevelt might promise Churchill in terms of supplies. The US had potential for the production of war *matériel* on a massive scale but in the short term resources were highly stretched. Something had to give; priorities would have to be considered. Admiral Ernest King, the anglophobe Naval Chief of Staff, wanted a speeded up *Pacific* campaign that would guarantee the security of Australia as an impregnable Asian base; he had an obsessive fear that Churchill dripped poisonous advice in the ears of the sickly President Roosevelt. On 3 March King sent a memorandum to Roosevelt in which he outlined his plans for operations in the *Pacific*; they were summarized as "Hold Hawaii, Support Australasia, Drive north-westward from New Hebrides."[13]

However, Marshall and his Chief of Staff, Eisenhower, had logical concerns about a '*Pacific* First' strategy. Taking a global strategic view, it was above all essential to keep both Britain and Russia in the war. Britain, America's cultural and geopolitical soul mate, still had survival at stake in the spring of 1942. Just as importantly sustaining Soviet resistance was essential as a means of occupying a high percentage of Germany's war *matériel* on the Eastern Front. Indeed the Soviet role was at this stage not dissimilar to the role being played by China in the *Pacific War*. Faced by these priorities Eisenhower's conclusion that keeping Australia supplied was "desirable not essential"[14] was not unreasonable; neither was his assertion that preventing an invasion of Australia was "not immediately vital to the outcome of the war."[15] "Germany is the predominant member of the Axis Powers," Marshall asserted and in spite of the entry of Japan into the conflict, "our view remains that Germany is still the prime enemy and her defeat is the key to victory."[16]

However, Marshall did not intend to bat for his 'Europe First' strategy without haggling some advantage with the British. He insisted to British Army Chief of Staff, General Alanbrooke (and through him to Churchill) that his support for a 'Europe First' strategy at the ARCADIA Conference was very dependent on British support for a 'Second Front' to relieve pressure on the Soviets. Brooke was won over; to Churchill, who preferred a Middle East strategy rather than a European front to relieve the Soviets, Alanbrooke said, "To counter these moves [by King] Marshall has started a European plan and is going one hundred percent all out on it."[17] Marshall had also won over Air Force Chief of Staff, 'Hap' Arnold, and secured the Joint Chief's unanimity by agreeing a compromise deal with King, which guaranteed some support for *Hawaii* and Australia while pushing ahead with a 'Europe First' strategy underwritten by an agreement with Britain for the opening up of a 'Second Front.' It was agreed to divide resources 70:30 in favor of the European theater.

With the Army largely winning its battle for a 'Europe First' strategy, it was hardly likely that King would submit the US *Pacific* Fleet to operate under a unified military command even though this is what MacArthur now expected. He later commented, "of all the faulty decisions of the war, perhaps the most inexplicable was not to unify command in the *Pacific*."[18] However, King was able to argue convincingly that the war in the *Pacific* was a maritime rather than a land-based war; this was particularly true given that because of the 'Europe First' strategy for the conduct of the war, King was told that he would largely have to rely on his Marines for ground support. It was a logic that MacArthur, already unreasonably furious with the Navy for not rescuing him in the Philippines, declined to see. For the remainder of the war MacArthur would allude to dark Navy conspiracies against him in the corridors of power in Washington.

But MacArthur could not be denied altogether. His brilliant campaign to win over the press, his relaying of self-burnishing information about completely fictional battles, and his overall brilliance in the field of propaganda had completely obliterated the reality of his failed command. If Admiral Husband Kimmel was held accountable for the failures at *Pearl Harbor*, judged by the same standards, MacArthur was doubly responsible for the debacle on the Philippines. Remarkably in early 1942, Congress was already calling for MacArthur, this most preposterous egomaniac and liar to be awarded with the Medal Honor. *Time* magazine considered him to be a true American hero. Insiders like Eisenhower, who served for ten years as his chief of staff, knew the truth but the MacArthur bandwagon was unstoppable. The result was a divided *Pacific* Command with MacArthur made Supreme Commander, South West Pacific Area and Admiral Nimitz, in ranking terms MacArthur's junior, made Commander-in-chief, Pacific Ocean Areas. Nimitz's sphere would include the *Pacific* west to the 160th meridian longitude including New Zealand, *Samoa* and *Fiji*. MacArthur was given Australia, New Guinea, the *Solomons* and the Philippines. Meanwhile the British sphere was India, the *Indian Ocean* and Burma.

However, while American inter-service rivalry was intense, it was not, unlike Japan, dysfunctional. As for his support for the British-led America, Britain, Dutch, and Australian (ABDA) force in the *Southwest Pacific*, even Admiral King supported unified command. On the Joint Chiefs of Staff, Leahy (who replaced Stark when he was appointed to command the US Navy in Europe), Marshall, Arnold and King may have argued their corners, but ultimately they worked as partners. As one of King's staff officers noted, "King knew he had to get along [with other co-commanders]. That was the compelling influence on all of them. They knew they had to get along."[19] Even MacArthur would strike up friendships, as he did with Admiral 'Bull' Halsey, and with the clear line of operation as set out, and in spite of the occasional spat and niggle, operational and strategic command worked. In MacArthur's area of command Nimitz ceded him all naval authority, while in the *Central Pacific* area Nimitz may have been challenged for his strategy and tactics but never for his authority to execute command. Ultimately too, the US Joint Chiefs of Staff had the opportunity to sanction all major strategic decisions. Where agreements needed to be made with Allies, the regular meetings of the Combined Chiefs of Staff, with their permanent staff in Washington, were supported by successive conferences, first in Washington and then in more far reaching locations such as Casablanca, Cairo, Tehran and Yalta, as both Stalin and Chiang Kai-shek were drawn into the broad Allied coalition. At these high level meetings with political leaders and generals, broad strategies were discussed and agreed.

In regard to strategic management, Japan's task should have been easier; there were no allies to deal with, as neither of its two Axis partners were geographically able to offer much in the way of co-operation or assistance. Apart from a briefly considered plan for the armies of Germany and Japan to meet up in Persia, the Japanese via northern India, there were only sparse contacts between the Axis powers.

By comparison with the Allies' collective command structure in the form of the Joint Chiefs of Staff, in Japan its leaders failed to develop a coercive mechanism by which the Army could commit the Navy to a task and vice versa. A central command group may have existed in theory at the Imperial General Headquarters, but in practice it was a meeting point at which each service presented to the other what they were not prepared to do. It did not help that in meetings with the Army, Admiral Nagumo developed the habit of falling asleep. Even within the rival services, command was dysfunctional; Yamamoto was even prepared to threaten resignation with his entire staff if he did not get his way in the development and execution of war strategy. Far from the stereotype of Japanese reverence for discipline and authority, leadership was confused and their strategic direction was sclerotic; it was the Allied Forces that were ultimately better organized and operationally more effective.

The Logistics of Supply to China: With the military and naval defeat of the Allied powers in the Philippines, Malaya, Burma and the Dutch East Indies, the only Allied power still fighting the Japanese was China. As early as January 1942 it had become apparent to General George Marshall, Chief of Staff of the US Army, that keeping China in the war was essential. Chinese forces alone were holding down 1.5 million Japanese soldiers and a large proportion of their war *matériel*.

At the beginning of 1942, General George Marshall, US Army Chief of Staff, recommended to President Franklin D. Roosevelt that General 'Vinegar Joe' Stilwell, America's top Corps Commander, should be appointed to command the China-Burma-India (CBI) Theater and the North Combat Area Command (NCAC). He would be stationed at Chongqing, where, in addition to his region US commands, he would serve as Chief of Staff to Chiang Kai-shek, the President of the Republic of China, who the Allies had appointed Supreme Commander of the region. Stilwell was one of Marshall's closest friends and a highly respected, Chinese-speaking officer. T. V. Soong, Chiang Kai-shek's man in Washington, who had checked out Stilwell's record, let Marshall know that he thought, "the best man in the Army for the job had been chosen."[20]

Chiang too sent a message confirming his pleasure at the selection: "General Stilwell's coming to China and assuming duty here is most welcome."[21] On 23 January Marshall duly asked Stilwell whether he was happy to go to China. "I'll go where I'm sent,"[22] Stilwell stoically replied. Stilwell immediately prepared for his task by meeting Lauchlin Currie, who was responsible for administrating Lend-Lease for China.

Stilwell's task, in its most basic form was clear: China had to be kept in the war. Sustaining China was therefore considered to be an essential component of the long-term strategy to defeat Japan. Stilwell was charged with the organization and control of America's Lend-Lease supplies to China and with the coordination of the military response to Japan as Commander of the NCAC. Although America's leaders could see the value of keeping China in the war, it did not mean that the China-Burma-India Theater was at the center of their strategic thoughts. The *Sino-Japanese War* had been regarded as a sideshow according to *Time* magazine: "yellow man killing yellow man."[23] Stilwell would find that in terms of importance, his region of command would continue to be treated as a sideshow—albeit an important one. He arrived in India on 25 February 1942 to find that Malaya and *Singapore* had fallen and that the British Army was in retreat in Burma. Allied supply routes to Burma were under threat. Indeed on the day of Stilwell's arrival, President Roosevelt wrote to Marshall to tell him, "it is of the utmost urgency that the pathway to China be kept open."[24]

Japan's aim to squeeze-shut China's supply routes was not new. In the summer of 1940, the Conservative British government, led by Prime Minister Winston Churchill, appeased Japan's military threats by closing the Burma Road for three months. Minutes of the War Cabinet meeting at noon on Friday 5 July 1940 noted that the "General view of the War cabinet was that the military situation did not justify us in taking action which might involve us in war with Japan."[25] Surprisingly it was Viscount Halifax, Secretary of State for Foreign Affairs, not Churchill, who was the staunchest in the view that Britain should not give in to Japanese bullying on the issue. By contrast Churchill felt that the US should take responsibility for the decision and doubted the wisdom of Britain standing alone when she was fully committed militarily elsewhere; "In the present state of affairs," he stated at the same War Cabinet meeting, "he did not think that we [Britain] ought to incur Japanese hostility for reasons mainly of prestige."[26] It was a pragmatic, even cynical response from Churchill. Britain duly acquiesced to Japan's demands to close the Burma Road. However, Tojo's government did not respond to weakness with restraint. Shortly thereafter, in September 1940, Japan occupied North Indochina.

Previously goods arriving at the Vietnamese port of Haiphong were transited to the railhead thirty miles away at Hanoi in North Vietnam from where the railway ran to Kunming in Yunnan Province. From here Chiang Kai-shek could provision his armies in China's remote eastern province of Sechuan where he had located his capital, Chongqing. After the Japanese occupation of Indochina in September 1940 this route was closed. Japan's noose around China tightened further in April 1941 when the *Soviet-Japanese Neutrality Pact* closed the possibility of supply to China via Turkestan. At this point the Burma Road, from Lashio in northern Burma and then across to Kunming was the only supply route to the *Kuomintang* (Nationalist) government that remained open—even this route was only viable as long as Rangoon and its railway to Myitkyina remained in British hands. The encirclement of China was further signaled on 29 July 1941 when Japan and the Vichy government in Indochina signed a Protocol Concerning Joint Defence and Joint Military Cooperation. In effect, in return for a fig leaf of autonomy, France had ceded control of all Indochina to Japan.

Roosevelt Agrees an Airlift: [Map: 12.3] On 15 January 1942 Japanese troops began to infiltrate mountain passes into Burma from Thailand. Rangoon was clearly threatened. Anticipating the possible fall of Burma to the Japanese, the British Joint Chiefs of Staff had already discussed the likely consequences. Churchill, recently returned from his ARCADIA Conference with Roosevelt, shocked his colleagues when he told them that he regarded "keeping the Burma Road open [to China] as more important than the retention of *Singapore*."[27] Looking at the issue as dispassionately as Churchill did, keeping China in the war was indeed of greater strategic importance than saving *Singapore*. However, colonial politics intervened. The last available British reinforcements were sent only to *Singapore* rather than Burma because Australian Prime Minister Curtin, who had sent troops to fight in the Middle East, declared that the abandonment of *Singapore* would be 'inexcusable.' British Chief of Staff, Lord Alanbrooke later reflected: "Looking back on our decision to send 18th Division to *Singapore*, in the light of after events, I think we were wrong to send it to *Singapore*, and that it would have served a more useful purpose had it been sent to Rangoon."[28]

With the British and Chinese Armies in retreat in Burma, the prospect of losing the last remaining supply route to China began to ring alarm bells in the United States. The administration in Washington was already discussing the issue of supply to China. T. V. Soong and Averill Harriman, the senior partner of the investment bank, Brown Brothers Harriman, and a *confidante* of Roosevelt, pored over maps looking at exotic land routes via Persia, the *Caspian Sea* and Turkestan before concluding that an airlift from Assam to China would be a more efficacious method of supplying China. The flight from Ledo in northern Assam to Myitkyina (in northern Burma) was 167 miles; from there goods could be trucked to Kunming in China's southwest Yunnan Province. At first sight the choice of new supply route was a cinch. However, it was soon complicated when it became clear that Myitkyina would fall to the Japanese onslaught as Iida's armies surged into northern Burma. Supply flights to China would now have to be routed direct to Kunming by the roundabout Himalayan route—a distance of 614 miles.

Soong had proposed air supply to Roosevelt on 31 January. Harriman concurred. He concluded in a report for Roosevelt that one hundred DC-3 transports could supply Chiang Kai-shek with up to 12,000 tons of supplies per month. The port of Calcutta would be the starting supply point. Roosevelt signed off on 5,000 tons. Harriman's jaunty back-of-the-envelope calculations were wide of the mark. To deliver just 5,000 tons a month of supply would require 304 aircraft and 275 crewmen as well as 3,400 engineers and support staff on the ground. Around Ledo and Kunming there would need to be five airfields at each end, not to mention warehousing and transport infrastructure. The supply of China would end up becoming a mammoth task, perhaps the biggest and most complex logistical exercise of *World War II*.

The primary importance of supply was made clear to Stilwell before his departure for the east. In addition to an airlift, he determined that a road should be built skirting the Himalayas in northern India and Burma and feeding into northwest China. The strategic imperatives were clear and Stilwell affirmed, "Events are forcing all concerned to see the vital importance of Burma. We must get the airline going at once and build the back-country road."[29] Within weeks of his arrival in China, the supply route to Lashio, where the Burma Road began, was effectively closed when the port city and capital of Burma, Rangoon, fell to General Iida's Japanese Army's 33rd Division on 8 March 1942. To keep China in the war, Stilwell would have to sustain the flow of supply to Chiang's army's without the now compromised rail transit from Rangoon to Myitkyina. Stilwell needed to create his new supply lines and quickly.

The Hump: [Map: 12.4] Stilwell immediately set about planning to airlift supplies from India. Losing little time, the US Tenth Army Air Force led by Brigadier-General Earl Naiden opened its office in New Delhi in March 1942 to build up the logistics needed to create an 'Air Ferry.' The 'Air Ferry' operation, which became known as the Hump, came under the joint command of Stilwell and American Air Force commander General 'Hap' Arnold. Supplies would arrive by ship in Calcutta, Bengal, on the northeast coast of India. Alternatively shipments arrived in Bombay and were transited by rail to Calcutta. From there *matériel* would be moved by rail 800 miles north to Ledo in Assam.

The last 400 miles to the British Army's main depot at Dimapur was by a rackety narrow gauge railway. The railway itself, originally built to take tea from Assam to Calcutta, was a hotchpotch of different track gauges necessitating the loading and unloading of *matériel* three times. Along the way supplies had to be debarked and ferried across the *Brahmaputra River*, the largest of the 700 riverines that filigreed northern Bengal (now Bangladesh). Supplies destined for China over the Hump had to be transported the last 200 miles to Ledo. Bridges required strengthening to cope with the increased loads. The railway would remain a constant bottleneck until it was agreed to militarize the entire route under American command in February 1944.

From hastily built airfields constructed around Ledo it was planned that an airlift would transport 3,000 tons of supplies per month over the Hump to a major supply dump in Myitkyina and thence by barge to Bhamo to connect with the Burma Road running to Kunming. Eventually the Hump would use thirteen airfields in India and fly to six in China. At one time more than a million Indians were employed in the building of airfields for the United States' logistical operations. A similar number would be employed in China.

In spite of being given Chiang's best trained army of 70,000 soldiers, Stilwell, along with Slim's Burma Corp failed to hold General Iida's fast-moving army in central Burma. By May 1942 central and northern Burma, including Lashio and Myitkyina, had been lost. Japan was now in occupation of a fertile, rice producing country with 16 million people, and important resources including oil, manganese, and tungsten. Even more importantly all external supply was denied to 'free China.' Piled up in Calcutta's docks and warehouses, 45,000 tons of Lend-Lease material was, for the time being, unusable.

Stilwell's 'Air Ferry' that had been planned to make the 167-mile 'hop' from Ledo in Assam to Myitkyina in northern Burma would now have to make the much longer 614-mile 'hop' from Assam direct to Kunming in China. From here much of the supply would have to be taken 450 miles by road to Chiang Kai-shek's new capital at Chongqing. Furthermore, with Japanese fighter aircraft stationed in northern Burma, the transport planes would have to fly around the East Himalayan Uplift. With a cruising speed of just 230 mph the Douglas DC-3, one of the early transport aircraft on the route, was a 'sitting duck' for Japanese fighters. The avoiding route over the Himalayas was almost as hazardous. As pilot Cedric Mah recalled, "We lost more aircraft due to navigation and weather conditions than to enemy action."[30] If crews were forced down by technical failure or bad weather and were lucky enough to survive a crash-landing, getting home was still far from guaranteed; hostile natives would often kill them. As an incentive to persuade the natives to bring them to safety, pilots carried colored silk or leather patches, known as 'blood chits' that would provide rewards for bringing them back alive; natives often taking their pay in the form of salt.

The route from Ledo took pilots over the Patkai Range and the *Chindwin River* Valley bounded by the 14,000 foot Kumon Mountains. Pilots then needed to traverse ridges as high as 16,000 foot through which ran the source valleys of the *Irrawaddy, Salween* and *Mekong Rivers*. Finally transport planes would have to negotiate the Satsung Range, the largest mountain range of the route before landing at Kunming Airfield, which itself stood at over 6,000 foot above sea level. "Imagine, in the black of the night blasting off with a heavily loaded transport and staggering into a void" wrote Cedric Mah, "No sooner airborne you begin a climb and circle to 6,000 feet. There are mountains to all sides of you rearing to 18,000 feet . . . You see nothing, not a single light, just a myriad of stars."[31] At these altitudes pilots needed oxygen.

Flying conditions changed dramatically from season to season.

> From June to October, pilots would encounter the clouds and the rain of the tropical monsoon season. They would switch from VFR [visual flight rules] flying to straight instrument flying. En route, the sky and track would be hidden. Cumulus nimbus clouds could soar up to 50,000ft. (15,000m) . . . Severe updrafts and downdrafts would bar their progress while heavy downpours with icing would nullify their passage.[32]

In the best of times it was a dangerous route. Cargo planes, difficult to maintain in tropical conditions, were unreliable. They had to operate in extremes of heat and cold. Emergency landing and rescue were less than certain. Moreover the weather was rarely good and even less predictable. Turbulence could flip a plane on its back. Downdrafts sometimes dropped planes thousands of feet in seconds and, over 12,000 foot, icing up of wings could sometimes prove fatal.

Maintenance was a further problem. Lack of spare parts meant that teams would be sent into the jungle to cannibalize planes that had crashed. There were no hangars and on sunny days maintenance was impossible. As Colonel Edward H. Alexander, Commander of the India-China Wing, reported: "Except on rainy days, maintenance work cannot be accomplished because shade temperatures of from 100 degrees to 130 degrees Fahrenheit render all metal exposed to the sun so hot that it cannot be touched by the human hand without causing second-degree burns."[33]

Not the least of the Hump's drawbacks was that it was an expensive way of supplying China. 'Hap' Arnold who flew the Hump noted that a C-87 Liberator transport plane used 3.5 tons of 100-Octane gasoline to take four tons of fuel to Kunming. It took four such flights to give the Fourteenth Air Force enough fuel to manage a single bombardment mission. At the airfields in Assam elephants were trained to pick up and load fuel drums onto cargo planes. Arnold's ground visit was not unproductive. At the end of 1942 he transferred Hump operations to Air Transport Command (ATC) and reorganized their command structure. The operations began to improve rapidly both in efficiency and uplift in tonnage.

At first ATC had to operate with an assortment of twenty-five planes, not the 100 promised by Roosevelt. It would take time to build up the operation further in the face of the demands of the European theater where resources were being built up for Operation BOLERO (the Second Front in Europe). War *matériel* was also urgently needed by the Soviet Union. Planes, crew and munitions were in short supply. At first the Hump could only meet a fraction of the supply needed by Chiang.

As transports operated by Air Transport Command (ATC) fell from the promised 100 to fifty-seven, Chiang Kai-shek became increasingly vexed. In June 1942, as Rommel punctured British defenses in North Africa, including the capture of Tobruk, transport planes destined for Kunming were purloined from India. On 25 June, Stilwell noted in his diary, "Bang! Brereton [Air Force General] to go to Egypt with all the heavy bombers and all the transports he needs. Bang! The A-29s [Lockheed Hudson light bomber] are to be held up in Khartoum and diverted to the British. Now what can I say to the G-mo [Chiang Kai-shek]?"[34] The excuses provided by Stilwell were of little interest to a Chinese leadership only remotely interested in the war in Europe. Unfairly Stilwell took the brunt of Chiang's fury.

Stilwell, not averse to mischief of his own, used Lend-Lease supplies as a lever to greater control over Chiang's army's. It was one of the many grievances that would ultimately bring about a complete breakdown in their relationship. For Washington the real fear was that Chiang might conclude a separate peace with Japan. In diverting supplies from China, America was walking a tightrope. Thus in October 1942, Roosevelt, under pressure to get Chiang Kai-shek to agree to the British planned Operation ANNAKIM to retake Rangoon in an amphibious attack, agreed that from the beginning of 1943, ATC would be provided with enough planes to bring 5,000 tons a month to China. In addition, Brigadier-General Claire Chennault, founder of the 'Flying Tigers' who, like MacArthur, had re-joined the US Army, was appointed commander of the Fourteenth Air Force which would be assigned 265 combat aircraft.

The Hump's operation began using any type of plane available from the US or China including Douglas DC-3s, Douglas C-47 Skytrains (Dakota was the British name), Douglas C-53s (a troop version of the C-47) and Douglas C-39s (DC-2). When fully loaded Douglas DC-3s could not climb high enough to clear all the peaks and were forced to weave a perilous path through the mountains; a task that was virtually impossible when the treacherous Himalayan weather closed in. In April 1943 the Air Transport Command's (ATC) aircraft began to be supplemented and eventually replaced with new Curtis-Wright C-46 Commandos that could fly at a higher ceiling and with a larger capacity—at 8 tons it could carry double the load of a Douglas DC-3.

Introduction of the new planes was not pain free however. Stilwell complained that the Commandos' "Carburettor ices up," and lamented that "We have lost six over the Hump and the boys' morale is lower and lower."[35] At the sharp end, Pilot Bill Gilmore recalled at the last Hump pilots' reunion that "The C-46 was rushed into production and the bugs hadn't been worked out. The bugs were worked out over the Hump."[36] Later additions to the air fleet included the Consolidated C-87 Liberator. By the end of 1943, the Hump had 142 aircraft in operation: 93 C-46 Commandos, 24 C-87 Liberators and 25 C-47 Skytrains. They frequently operated around the clock with five crews for each aircraft.

At the TRIDENT Conference in Washington in May 1943, following demands from Chiang Kai-shek, Roosevelt ordered an increase in this force to 500 planes and a further uplift in tonnage over the Hump to 10,000 tons per month by September. It was the price demanded by Chiang for his support of the planned invasion into Burma in November. In the end the Operation ANAKIM campaign, intended to be an amphibious operation to take Rangoon and the Burma Railway, never got off the ground. Such was Chiang's disappointment at the British cancellation of an operation that would have lifted the *matériel* siege of China, that T. V. Soong, Chiang's Foreign Minister (formerly Finance Minister) and representative at TRIDENT, hinted, quite untruthfully, that Chiang might make a separate peace with Japan unless there was a whole-hearted commitment "to undertake its [China's] relief and discharge the post-Casablanca commitments began."[37]

As tonnage shipped increased however, so did casualties. As flights increased to supply Chiang's armies for operations in northern Burma US aircraft losses mounted; forty-seven planes lost in January–February 1943, one out of every 218 flights. However, as time went on casualty rates fell dramatically. At its peak the Hump was using over 700 aircraft with a plane crossing the Hump every two minutes. Numbers employed in the airlift rose to a veritable army of 84,000 pilots, crews, technicians and logistics support staff.

In addition to the extreme danger of the missions, the boredom of the remote jungle airfields of northern Burma took their toll. An idea of the living conditions was illustrated by an extract of a piece of doggerel verse written by Private Robert L. Looney published in the 'CBI Roundup' (CBI: China-Burma-India) on 22 October 1942.

> I am weary of curry and rice
> All mingled with highly spiced dope
> I am weary of bathing with lysol
> And washing with carbolic soap.
> I am tired of itch and spin diseases
> Mosquitoes and vermin and flies
> I am fed up with the tropical breezes
> And sunshine that dazzles your eyes
> To eat without fear of infection
> To sleep without using a net
> And throw away all my collection
> Of iodine, quinine, et cet.[38]

Given that a tour of duty for pilot and crew was 'officially' meant to be eighty flights, there was an approximately one in three chance of being killed—a far higher 'kill rate' than for Australians fighting in the early jungle battles of New Guinea, the Kokoda Trail and the *Battles of Buna, Gona* and *Sanananda*. Lieutenant-Colonel George Laben of the 2nd Troop Carrier Squadron, reckoned that during his period of service, because of his squadron's losses, it had "turned over about four times."[39] Some pilots recorded many more than eighty flights; Laben did 245 missions in his C-47 while Canadian Albert Mah (Cedric's elder brother) flew more than 420 times over the Hump. It was a stressful and often brief life for the pilots, "They were killed, or they quit, wore out or just broke down . . . Release from one's tour of duty in Burma was almost impossible, unless you were shot down, wounded or could get someone to relieve you."[40] As one observer noted, the Hump crews were "living like dogs and flying like fiends."[41]

Some cargoes were worse for the crews than others. Conditions for the 'body bag' pilots, who flew home the dead, were so bad that they were awarded special commendations. They had to fly with windows open and their planes stank so appallingly that they were unusable for anything else after just a few such missions. 'Lucky escape' stories were the grist of the pilots' existence. Cedric Mah recalled that after ice had caused his hydraulics to fail, dropping his plane "like a stone,"[42] he survived by junking US$4.3m worth of new Chinese currency over the jungle to lighten his aircraft.

Miraculous escapes became the stuff of legend. Joe Rosbert, a 'Flying Tiger' veteran who threw in his lot with the China National Aviation Corporation (CNAC) to fly the Hump, lost altitude as ice began to build up on his wings. After scraping away ice from his windscreen, "suddenly, there was a swirl in the clouds, and directly ahead, a mountain."[43] Desperately trying a right turn, he heard "almost instantly a scraping sound under the fuselage. The nose tipped down and we crashed into the mountain of snow."[44] With a broken ankle, Rosbert and his co-pilot stayed with the plane for two days before striking out. After a two week descent during which they feasted on a dead bird, they came across Himalayan natives, "like creatures out of the stone age,"[45] who fed them. Forty-six days later, much to the astonishment of their colleagues, they suddenly appeared back at base.

General Albert C. Wedemeyer opined, "Flying the Hump was the foremost and by far the most dangerous, difficult and historic achievement of the entire war."[46] Chick Marrs Quin's *The Aluminum Trail* [1989] lists more than 700 planes lost in the course of the Hump operation at a cost of some 1,200 lives. It is a measure of the remoteness of the region and its inhospitable landscape that more than 500 of these cargo planes and their crews remain missing. Even take-off was hazardous. The phrase 'CBI (China-Burma-India) take-off' came to be defined as "If you can see the end of the runway through the rain and mist, then a take-off is expected."[47] Every 340 tons delivered cost the life of a pilot. For the most part, the perilous lives of the Hump pilots have been barely acknowledged let alone recorded. Slim, notably, gave them due, if typically modest, applause, "The young American pilots of the Hump should be remembered with admiration and gratitude by their countrymen and their allies."[48]

The Ledo–Burma Road: The Strategic Need for a Land Supply Route to China:
[Map: 12.5] Stilwell believed, incorrectly as it transpired, that the Hump could never supply enough material to sustain the ground and air forces in China. Stilwell thus wrote to Secretary of War, Henry Stimson, asserting that the Air Transport Command (ATC) "will never be able to do more than supply very small quantities of important materials."[49] As early as December 1941 the Chinese government had been considering the problems of supply. Watching the situation in Malaya with alarm, Chiang Kai-shek was aware earlier than his allies that Burma could be at risk; the loss of Rangoon would leave him cut off. On 1 January 1942 the *Kuomintang* government, prompted by Stilwell, formally requested material for the construction of a road from Ledo in Assam across the eastern Himalayas in northeast India and Burma to Lashio where it could pick up the Burma

Road to Kunming in China's southeast. The War Department did not agree; however they admitted that air supply would be greatly helped by the re-occupation of northern Burma, which, by eliminating Japan's fighter airfields, would relieve the ATC from its perilous mountain routes.

If the building of the 'Air Ferry' from northern Assam to Kunming was an astonishing logistical task, the building of the Ledo Road, planned to wind through the same mountains as the Hump was traversing by air, was even more ambitious. Bernard Hoffman, an Army Photographer, who followed the road's progress, described it as the "toughest road-building job Army engineers have ever known, any time or anywhere."[50] Stilwell's proposal to General Wavell, to whom he reported before the setting up of the South East Asia Command, was for a road to be carved through the 14,000 foot Patkai Range.

The road would pass southeastwards from Ledo in Assam where the railway from Calcutta terminated, to Shingbwiyan in northern Burma as it exited the Patkai Range. From there the road would be built almost due south to Myitkyina. Stilwell assumed that by the time the Ledo Road was built to Myitkyina, he would have recaptured this important northern border town. Having later won the *Battle of Myitkyina*, Pick continued to build the Ledo Road southwards to Lashio where it hooked up with the Burma Road that turned back up to the northeast to the Chinese border and then eastwards to Kunming after it crossed the *Mekong River* in Yunnan Province. By linking the Ledo Road with the Burma Road, Stilwell planned to supply the Chinese armies directly by vehicle convoys running 1,079 miles from Ledo in north India to Kunming in eastern China.

Stilwell's demands for a Ledo Road were not universally supported. Slim recalled, "Stilwell was almost alone in his faith that, not only could the road be built, but that it would be the most potent winning factor in the war against Japan."[51] Building roads across the natural mountain barriers, which divided the country north to south, seemed to many observers to be a perverse strategy. Although Slim believed that the road could be built, he "doubted the overwhelming war-winning value of this road."[52] If China needed to be supplied, Slim believed, along with most strategists, that an amphibious landing to take Rangoon and an advance to Lashio along Burma's main access routes provided the best way to supply China. It was the strategic logic of Operation ANNAKIM. The problem was that the powers in Washington and London always found reasons not to prioritize the supplies necessary to conduct this operation; in particular, landing craft, being hoarded for Operation OVERLORD's Normandy landings, denied transport needed for an amphibious flanking attack in Burma. General Slim also doubted Stilwell's premise, sold to Roosevelt and Churchill, that the war could be won from China: "The American amphibious strategy in the *Pacific*, of hopping from island to island would, I was sure bring much quicker results than an overland advance across Asia with a Chinese Army yet to be formed."[53]

Churchill, like Slim, was among a number of people who believed that the Ledo Road would become a 'white elephant' that would be surplus to requirements by the time it was built. Although Churchill backed Wavell and Stilwell and approved the Ledo Road's construction at the Allied meeting in Casablanca (SYMBOL Conference) in January 1943, he always suspected that by the time it was built it would be redundant: "an immense, laborious task, unlikely to be finished until the need for it has passed."[54] It was prophetic. The Ledo Road highlighted a fundamental difference between the strategic goals of the Americans and the British. For Churchill the retaking of Burma was a worthy end in itself; for the Americans "the re-conquest of Burma was merely incidental to the reopening of land communications with China . . ."[55] The Joint Chiefs of Staff bluntly made clear to the British that "US forces and resources are committed to the China-Burma-India area for the purpose of assisting China."[56]

The Restructuring of US Naval Command: In the immediate aftermath of *Pearl Harbor*, Secretary of the Navy, Frank Knox had flown out to *Hawaii* to assess the situation. He came back resolved on two issues; first Admiral Kimmel should be recalled to face investigation and Admiral Chester Nimitz should replace him as Commander in Chief of the *Pacific* Fleet; secondly Admiral Ernest King, then Chief of the Bureau of Navigation, should become Commander in Chief, US Fleet (CINCUS), the resurrection of a position that Roosevelt had abolished in January 1941.

At first King showed some reluctance as Admiral Stark, Commander of the Naval Office (CNO) was the Navy's senior officer. King eventually agreed but on certain conditions. He wanted to substitute the acronym CINCUS, 'Sink-us,' with the less pun-strewn name COMINCH (Commander in Chief, US Navy). The fleet would have to be commanded from Washington. As King explained, "Where the power is that is where the headquarters have to be."[57] More dramatically he insisted that he wanted direct command over the bureaus in the Navy Department. This would require an act of Congress but Roosevelt made it clear that he would replace any bureau chief who did not co-operate with King. On Knox's recommendation King's position was defined by an executive order drawn up by two members of the General Board, Walter Sexton and J. O. Richardson. On 17 December, Roosevelt signed Executive Order 8984 that gave King unprecedented powers.

King would have "supreme command of the operating forces comprising the several fleets of the United States Navy and the operating forces of the Naval Coastal Frontier Command . . ."[58] Even more dramatically, King would be answerable only to the President not to the Secretary of the Navy to whom he would vaguely report only for 'general direction.'

King went to his tawdry office at the Navy Department and began to build his organization. He later noted, "Nothing was ready. I had to start with nothing."[59] Rear-Admiral Wilson, Superintendent of the Naval Academy, was chosen as his Chief of Staff. Getting staff was not easy. When Captain Charles Cooke on the USS *Pennsylvania* was told to report to Washington to become King's chief planning officer, he resisted and had to be told, "we all must serve where we can do the most for the Navy and that has to be judged by other people than ourselves."[60] Eventually Cooke would live aboard the USS *Dauntless*, a 257-foot family yacht, the *Delphine*, formerly belonging to the automotive Dodge family, that King commandeered as his flagship. Moored up at the Washington Navy Yard, at great expense, King made the *Delphine* his home for the duration of the war.

King had bullied and cajoled his way to a position of unprecedented power. One of the least known major figures of *World War II*, King avoided a public profile and disdained the press. Taciturn, a man of few words, King was both highly intelligent and fierce. King's daughter would say that her father was the most even-tempered man she knew because he was "always in a rage."[61] In public he would berate his wife, a fact that was even noted in his Navy personnel records. Tall, immaculately dressed, King was an energetic womanizer and enjoyed his drink; he distrusted men who did not share these vices. Academic brilliance took him from an upbringing as the son of a railroad repair foreman to the US Naval Academy in 1897. He graduated fourth in his class in 1901.

In complete contrast to General MacArthur, who he detested, King garnered power by stealth not bombast. During the course of the war he met Roosevelt almost every day, becoming one of his key advisers. King managed through fear. "I don't care how good they are," he said, "unless they get a kick in the ass every six weeks, they slack off."[62] King's authoritarian ways were soon noticed; Eisenhower wrote in his diary, "Admiral King is an arbitrary, stubborn type with too much brain and a tendency to bullying his juniors but I think he wants to fight which is encouraging."[63] The role of Admiral Stark, Chief of Naval Operations, was made redundant and he was moved to London to take command of US Naval forces in Europe.

Admiral Nimitz: The Cool Commander: If the fates had been harsh on Admirals Stark and Kimmel, they were kind to Chester W. Nimitz who had originally been tapped up for the job in *Hawaii* that Kimmel eventually took. Nimitz had turned down the commander-in-chief, US Fleet (CINCUS) role in *Honolulu* that President Roosevelt offered him and Admiral Husband Kimmel was the alternate choice. Nimitz refused on the grounds of his being too junior. Having fortuitously dodged this bullet, not surprisingly Admiral Nimitz said about Kimmel, "It could have happened to anyone."[64] Even Admiral King was prepared to admit, "No one thought the Japs would strike—or even that they were ready to strike."[65]

On agreeing to the appointment of Admiral Nimitz as Kimmel's successor, President Roosevelt said to Naval Secretary Knox, "Tell Nimitz to get the hell out to *Pearl* and stay there till the war is won."[66] The fact that King disliked Nimitz with whom he had clashed throughout their careers did not bother either King or Roosevelt. King disliked almost everyone while Roosevelt liked personal antagonism that allowed vigorous policy debate. Neither was Roosevelt averse to the idea of divide and rule. Ultimately both King and Nimitz were professionals and overall Roosevelt's restructuring of the system of naval command worked with a relatively high degree of harmony and efficiency throughout the *Pacific War*, which was in marked contrast to the operation of the Imperial Japanese Navy.

While Admiral Chester Nimitz may have been a lucky man, he was more than a reasonable choice. His experience was rounded. His time in Washington as Chief of the Bureau of Navigation proved useful in giving Nimitz a broad perspective of the Navy and knowledge of senior personnel. The Navigation Bureau, in essence the US Navy's personnel office, was charged with the manning of the build-up of the fleet after the 1934 *Congressional Act* authorized funding to build up its fleet to 'Treaty Strength'— meaning the size of navy allowed under the *London Naval Treaty* [1930]. Perhaps more importantly he had relevant operational experience for the task ahead. He had spent time as a submarine commander and had even supervised the construction of a submarine base on *Honolulu*. He had also campaigned to have submarine gasoline engines replaced with diesel, which were considerably safer as well as producing less noxious fumes. In 1909 Nimitz had described submarines as "a cross between a Jules Verne fantasy and a humpbacked whale."[67] His later support for this unglamorous branch of the Navy would bring spectacular if largely unheralded success in the later stages of the *Pacific War*.

Nimitz was instrumental in bringing the concept of the 'Circle Formation' into the US Fleet. This tactic developed by Nimitz's close friend and contemporary, Commander Roscoe MacFall, at the Naval War College, as a result of observations of the lack of control inherent at the *Battle of Jutland* in *World War I*, enabled a more fluid and mobile deployment than the traditional box or 'Multiple Line Formation.' By ordering cruisers and destroyers to deploy in concentric circles around the principal ships (battleships and later aircraft carriers), a single order, rather than a complex series of orders, could change the direction of the entire fleet. Though slow to be implemented even by the US, the new system would be copied by all navies by the end of the war.

Even more important was Nimitz's experience with aircraft carriers. The importance of air power was recognized by a limited few at the start of the 1920s. Fortunately, Rear-Admiral William Sims, President of the Naval War College was one of the tactical pioneers of this emerging arm during Nimitz's student years. For Sims, aircraft carriers were the Navy's new capital ships. He predicted quite correctly, that carrier-based planes would be able to outgun battleships in range and destructive power. It was a forecast made before Brigadier-General 'Billy' Mitchell's flyers had proved the concept of bombing ships by the sinking of a former German battleship, *Ostfriesland*, in a field test carried out in 1921. This was a revolutionary concept. Previously it was thought that the use of carriers and their aircraft was to act as intelligence gatherers (in effect binoculars) for large modern battle fleets that had to operate over huge distances. In spite of Sims' predictions, the role of aircraft carriers remained operationally limited. The US Navy's first aircraft carrier was USS *Langley*, a converted collier, which was used (like a collier) as a support vessel rather than as an integral part of the battle convoy formation. In fact it was Nimitz who was the first officer not only to advocate but also to implement the integration of the *Langley* into the 'Circle Formation' in 1924. It was a brilliant conjunction of two of Nimitz's great tactical achievements. The carrier was perfectly in sync with the philosophy of the new battle formation because the ease of turning enabled by 'Circle Formation' was essential for an aircraft carrier that needed to turn into the wind in order to launch its aircraft.

In addition to the technical and command skills that Nimitz had learned during his career, he was also by nature intelligent, disciplined and organized. A well-known raconteur, Nimitz was a convivial but thoughtful man, a good spotter of talent, and proved capable of delegating to his fleet commanders and restrained himself from trying to micro-manage them from afar. His meetings were famous for being open to discussion and opinions from all ranks in attendance. Nimitz listened carefully and then decided. His impact on arrival at *Pearl Harbor* was immediate. He did not sweep out his inherited staff but supported and invigorated them for the fight ahead; winnowing out poor performers was something that he would accomplish gradually. Rear-Admiral Raymond Spruance noted that Nimitz's arrival was "like being in a stuffy room and having someone open a window and let in a breath of fresh air."[68] US Navy morale quickly recovered. Indeed one of Nimitz's early concerns was to raise the morale and ethos of a Navy that had been badly mauled. Instead of plotting a purely defensive strategy, Nimitz decided to use the attacking potential of his inferior carrier fleet. Indeed it was limited in both quantity and quality. As Nimitz reported to King on 7 February 1942, "Pacific Fleet markedly inferior in all types to enemy. Cannot conduct aggressive action Pacific except raids of hit-and-run character."[69] This is exactly what he did.

Admiral 'Bull' Halsey: The Fighting Admiral: Halsey's father was a Navy man and by his teens he had lived in six cities. The family eventually settled in Coronado, California near the Mexican border. Big chested, stocky, short-legged, Halsey was a boisterous man who came to be nicknamed 'Billy big head.' Short and aggressive, he loved football in spite of his diminutive size. His mother Anne cajoled US President William McKinley into giving her son a chance to apply to Annapolis Naval Academy. In a rare display of academic discipline Halsey crammed for exams and got in. At Annapolis he played football as full back for two years. Coaches liked his grit. Not academically bright or particularly gifted, he graduated forty-third out of sixty-two in 1904.

In the early eighteenth century, a Captain Halsey was a brigand privateer during Queen Anne's war with the French. Halsey loved this association with his forbear; he later wrote, "I enjoy reading how his little brigantine once took on four ships together and captured two of them, with $250,000 in booty."[70] His life was noted in the 1926 book *The History of the Lives and Bloody Exploits of the Most Noted Pirates.*[71] Halsey became known for bravery, and rapid decision making. He showed his fearlessness when he stared down a huge and crazed US sailor wielding a club. His first command was a rust bucket, torpedo boat USS *Du Pont*. After two years Halsey was given the destroyer USS *Flusser*. *World War I* offered Halsey the hope of active service and he arrived in Europe in January 1918 hoping to fight. He was given USS *Benham*, a destroyer. It was a dirty ship and poorly disciplined. He made it shipshape in six weeks without alienating his crew who quickly warmed to their young captain. His popularity with seaman would be a feature of his career. He transferred to USS *Shaw*, another destroyer. *World War I* ended without him seeing action. However, even his minor participation in the war left him "as a dog with two tails."[72] Halsey loved war. His time would come again.

Robert Carney, later his chief of staff, recalled that "In destroyers he found an outlet for his command talent, his inherent boldness, and his gift for dealing with people."[73] During his destroyer years Halsey formed a close attachment to Captain Raymond Spruance who was a fellow destroyer commander and subordinate. It was an attraction of opposites. Halsey respected Spruance's soft-spoken professionalism. Spruance admired Halsey's fighting spirit. Halsey wrote a report describing Spruance as "one of the best all around officers I have ever served with. He's quiet, efficient, always on the job, and with a clear thinking brain always working."[74] By contrast Halsey famously loathed paperwork and avoided it at all costs.

In February 1927 Halsey was given command of his first aviation detail aboard his command, USS *Reina Mercedes*. He cadged flights at every opportunity. "Soon I was eating, drinking, and breathing aviation, and I continued to do so during the remainder of my duty on Reina."[75] Though he failed the eye exam for the aviation course at Pensacola Airfield, he remained addicted to the air arm. After a long and glittering destroyer career, he was tabbed for higher things and sent to the Naval War College in Newport, Rhode Island in June 1932.

At Newport Halsey wrote an essay on *The Relationship in War of Naval Strategy, Tactics and Command* [1933], which goes some way to explaining his actions at the *San Bernadino Straits* move during the *Battle of Leyte Gulf*. Of the requirements of a good admiral Halsey believed that "the greatest of these was command."[76] He did not believe that pre-designed plans should dictate the course of battle: "Decisions need to be made by commanders on the spot, though sound plans were a foundation . . . only."[77] Halsey believed that "Ideas can never be so clearly conveyed in writing, as they can by personal and intimate discussion."[78] Plans without understanding were useless. "It is of paramount importance that unit groups be not broken up, except by urgent necessity."[79] Halsey also quoted *Civil War* cavalry General Nathan Bedford Forrest, "Get there fastest with the mostest men."[80] "The man on the spot may have information not available to the commander that gives an entirely different picture. The subordinate must be trusted, or if not trusted removed."[81] Accordingly he advised that the Navy should adopt the slogan, "Tell him what to do, but not how to do it."[82] For Halsey a good officer was one whose "courage both moral and physical must be unquestionable."[83]

Halsey was sent to Pensacola Air Force Base to do an aviation observer course prior to taking command of the USS *Saratoga*, a former battle-cruiser that had been turned into an aircraft carrier in 1922. His navigation class, for which he gave up Scotch, gathered on 1 July 1934. In spite of his poor eyesight he was not to be denied his switch to a student pilot course. His wife, Frances, exploded with anger when she found that he was flying. Halsey, already a 51-year-old grandfather, soon flew solo. On one landing he flipped the aircraft on its back—an episode that added to his popularity with his young colleagues. After graduating he reported to USS *Saratoga* in July 1935. He returned to

Pensacola as base commander in 1937 and was promoted to rear-admiral while in Florida. A fine showing in destroyer exercises in January 1939 would bring him to the attention of President Roosevelt.

Throughout his career the sailors lionized him. Lieutenant Thomas Moorer noted, "Everybody was crazy about Admiral Halsey, I think, because he could kind of get with it, let us say ... so there wasn't such a separation between junior officers and the Admiral."[84] His popularity was enhanced by his penchant for partying. Halsey was an early riser whose hyperactive nature was fed by ten cups of coffee and forty cigarettes a day. In the evening he liberally indulged his love of Scotch whisky. Halsey once noted, "A bottle of Scotch on the table always bore fruit in our dealings with other commands."[85] Halsey's popularity extended beyond the Navy. A note from Owen Cedarburg of Bonne Terre, Missouri, typified the thousands of letters of fan mail received by Admiral Halsey: "Ever since I heard of your exploits I have liked you," wrote Cedarburg, "I like your seagoing looks and the manner in which you fight and just about everything else ... when you went in the Japs went out."[86]

However, those who worked with him closely also noted the relative chaos of his commanding style. Halsey fired directives in a scattergun approach that could be disconcerting for staff, as one officer noted, "My feeling was one of confidence when Spruance was there and one of concern when Halsey was there."[87] Halsey was obsessed with sinking carriers. Perhaps he wanted to live up to the press image that he clearly enjoyed. On other military subjects he could tend to caution and advised Nimitz against the taking of the island of *Peleliu*, "because I envisioned another Guadalcanal."[88] He advocated bypassing this island and making a landing in the central Philippines.

During the action on *Peleliu*, Halsey advocated the use of poison gas to dispose of the cave-hiding defenders. "It is a question of slow progress in digging out the rats. Poison gas is indicated as an economical weapon."[89] Even by the mores of the age Halsey's description of Japanese soldiers as "monkey meat"[90] was considered crude and distasteful, though it endeared him to the more nationalistic American audiences.

America's Fight Back Begins: [Maps: 12.6A, 12.6B] King and Nimitz determined that in spite of the devastating setback at *Pearl Harbor* and the risk of further losses, their carrier forces would be used aggressively. Admiral Halsey was chosen to lead out the first attacks. The USS *Yorktown* and USS *Enterprise* were dispatched to raid the *Gilbert* and *Marshall Islands*; it was a brave move as it left just the USS *Saratoga* and USS *Lexington* to guard *Hawaii*.

The raiding force left early on 11 January 1942 and in spite of the fact that USS *Saratoga* was hit by a torpedo and had to limp back to *Honolulu*, and then the West Coast for repairs, Nimitz did not recall Halsey. His raid claimed the sinking of two submarines, a small carrier, a light cruiser and various supply ships and auxiliaries. The bombing attack on *Kwajalein* on 1 February 1942 was launched from USS *Enterprise* with thirty-seven dive-bombers. Meanwhile Halsey's cruisers under Admiral Spruance blasted *Wotje* and *Maloelap* while Admiral Fletcher commanding the carrier USS

Yorktown attacked *Jaluit, Makin* and *Mili*. Spruance sank one Japanese transport and two smaller vessels. At 1.38 p.m. *Enterprise* had to swerve to avoid five twin-engine bombers led by Lieutenant Kazuo Nakai. Nakai's plane was damaged and he swung back in a suicide dive that clipped the port edge and sent its wing skidding into the port catwalk. The rest of the bomber skimmed over the deck, spraying gasoline and dumped itself into the sea on the other side. Nakai's was one of the first *kamikaze* though his was an *ad hoc* rather than a pre-planned attack.

Although Halsey massively overestimated the damage done to the Japanese, the psychological impact of the raid was important. At last America had a victory to shout about. Even more importantly it had a naval hero for journalists to lionize and the general public to adore. Nimitz may have been a good choice as head of *Central Pacific* command but he was not exciting; a foreign observer described Nimitz in 1942 as "an old man, slow and perhaps slightly deaf."[91] By contrast Halsey, though occasionally abrasive, was a genial man who was built up as a hyper-aggressive old seadog, a role for which his bulldog face was clearly designed. Armed with an ability to provide a pithy remark, he was perfect for an American press gluttonous for good news and a hero to boot. It was a role that Nimitz was happy to yield. The legend of 'Bull Halsey' was born.

Nimitz gave Halsey the Distinguished Service Medal. The *New York Times* heralded Halsey "for planning and conducting these brilliant and audacious attacks on Japanese strongholds and for driving them home with great skill and determination."[92] Nimitz had little time to rest on the laurels of this minor victory. Learning from intelligence that Japanese troops were being assembled at Rabaul on *New Britain*, it was assumed, partially correctly, that their new targets could be the *South Pacific Islands* of *New Caledonia* and *New Hebrides* to the east of New Zealand; islands that, in Japanese possession, would enable Australia to be blockaded.

In mid-February, to interdict the build-up of forces in Rabaul, a Task Group comprising the USS *Lexington*, under the command of Vice-Admiral Wilson Brown mounted a raid on the growing Japanese logistical base. However, before an attack could be launched they were spotted and attacked by two waves of Japanese 'Betty' twin-engine bombers. The Japanese attack was disrupted by one of the most audacious aerial exploits of the war when Lieutenant O'Hare, flying an F4F Grumman Wildcat, attacked the enemy squadron and shot down three bombers in as many minutes of action. Vice-Admiral Brown reckoned that O'Hare's lone attack on a squadron of bombers had saved the *Lexington*.

O'Hare, whose father had the unlikely distinction of having been murdered by Al Capone, became the US Navy's first air ace, winning the Medal of Honor. He was taken back to the United States to raise war bonds. After becoming a successful squadron commander, on 26 November 1943 he was killed by a lucky shot from a 'Betty's' front machine gunner during a rare nighttime mission. O'Hare International Airport in Chicago was named in his honor.

Deciding that he had had a lucky escape, Brown withdrew the precious *Lexington*. A second raid against Rabaul led by the *Lexington* set out on 8 March—this time with the addition of USS *Yorktown*. Japanese landings at Lae and Salamaua on the north coast of southern New Guinea changed Vice-Admiral Wilson Brown's plans. Brown entered the *Gulf of Papua* and launched a carrier attack force of 103 aircraft across the Owen Stanley Mountains and against the Japanese beachheads. The raid was seemingly successful although the US Air Force exaggerated the effects of the damage done to the Japanese, who were not long disrupted.

Although Nimitz's raiding strategy produced relatively minor results, the aggravation to Japan reinforced Yamamoto's belief that the destruction of the US carrier fleet was vital to the management of their newly acquired Empire as well as the conduct of the war.

Public Relations and Roosevelt's Plan to Bomb Japan: A number of daring raids notwithstanding, in early 1942 the United States had suffered and was continuing to suffer a series of reverses on land and sea. It was not meant to be like this. Although President Roosevelt was fully aware that the banning of US oil exports to Japan would very likely cause war with Japan, he had hoped to defer their initiation of military action until the spring of 1942 at the earliest so as to allow more time for cranking up America's war machine and sending of troops, equipment, munitions and supplies to MacArthur's incipient Philippine Army. When the war did indeed start, the last thing that Roosevelt expected was to find his *Pacific* Fleet's battleships at the bottom of *Pearl Harbor*. Added to the profound shock of this attack, the failure of MacArthur's Philippines deployments compounded the gloom.

Both for mobilizing the energy of the American people and for uplifting the morale of the soldiers and sailors of his Army and Navy, the President needed some good news stories. Allowing the media to write up General MacArthur as a great national leader and a heroic defender of the Bataan Peninsula, in spite of the full knowledge that MacArthur's troop deployments and battle plan on *Luzon* had been catastrophic, was a clear sign of the President's desperation. Defensive heroism, albeit largely faked, was all very well but Roosevelt wanted news of a successful 'attack mission' as soon as possible. Thus the President declared his intention "to find ways and means of carrying home to Japan proper, in the form of a bombing raid, the real meaning of war."[93] The Doolittle Raid on Japan on 18 April was proposed originally by President Roosevelt to his Joint Chiefs of Staff a few weeks after *Pearl Harbor*.

Given that there was no Allied territory close enough to Japan from which to launch an air attack, it was quickly realized that only a raid made by the United States' precious carriers could achieve the mainland strike that Roosevelt required. It was a high-risk strategy for what was in essence a public relations exercise, "to bolster morale of America and her allies."[94]

The concept for the plan had originated with Admiral King at the ARCADIA Conference. He envisioned one carrier with bombers that had a longer range than normal carrier bombers and a second carrier with fighters. The advantage of range was that the carriers would be less exposed to the risk of detection. It seemed a plausible plan but medium bombers had never taken off from a carrier; it was an unproven concept. Captain Francis Low and other members of King's staff further developed the plan. First they had to find a suitable aircraft. The Douglas B-18 Bolo was discounted as obsolete; its upgrade, the Douglas B-23 Dragon had wings that were too large. The Martin B-26 Marauder needed a longer runway. It was a possibility but only if it could be lightened and given a larger fuel capacity.

The planners finally decided on North American Aviation's B-25 Mitchell, a medium bomber, named after the maverick Navy officer Brigadier-General 'Billy' Mitchell, which fulfilled both the runway and payload requirements of take-off from the deck of a carrier. The main problem was how the B-25s could bring their crews to safety. Whatever the risks a suicide mission was not envisaged. With a tricycle landing gear and a high approach speed, landing a B-25 on a carrier would not be possible. A friendly country would be needed. America's new ally, Russia, refused to take part for fear of provoking a Japanese attack on its eastern borders. Chiang Kai-shek, in thrall to the United States, was agreeable, though he feared reprisals.

Lieutenant-Colonel 'Jimmy' Doolittle: To pull off the plan in detail, King agreed to bring in Lieutenant-Colonel Doolittle. If ever a man was misnamed it was James 'Jimmy' Doolittle. A well-known Army aviator, aerobatics performer and test pilot after *World War I*, Doolittle was already a minor celebrity. In 1921 he had taken part in Brigadier-General 'Billy' Mitchell's famous test that showed that airplanes could sink battleships. His aerial 'firsts' included the 'outside loop,' the setting of a world speed record and the crossing of America for the first time in less than twenty-four hours. In 1925 he was watched by 200,000 people on *Chesapeake Bay*'s shoreline as he won the Schneider Marine Trophy (the *Coupe d'Aviation Maritime Jacques Schneider*) in a Curtiss RC3-2 at a record 232 mph. In the same year Doolittle was awarded a doctorate in aeronautical engineering from the Massachusetts Institute of Technology. His most important technical contribution to aviation was his development of instruments that would allow pilots to fly blind; the artificial horizon and directional gyroscope instrument that he developed is still standard equipment. Doolittle would test himself by landing a plane in a blacked-out cockpit.

Constrained within the peacetime military Doolittle resigned from the Army and joined Shell Oil Company after they agreed to triple his salary. At Shell he worked on the project to develop 100-octane aviation fuel. However, he remained on the reserve list and after *Pearl Harbor* immediately requested a recall to active duty. 'Hap' Arnold refused to allow him to become a combat pilot but, recognizing his immense technical skills, assigned him to work on special projects reporting directly to the US Air Force Chief. He was a natural choice to lead the quest to solve the difficult technical challenges presented by a carrier bomber raid on Tokyo.

Doolittle oversaw the reconfiguration of the B-25 for the purposes of the Tokyo Raid. Mid-Continental Airlines in Minneapolis added extra fuel tanks and removed the ventral gun turret and the weighty radio; given the need for radio silence it was not needed.

Having shaved 12 percent off its maximum take-off weight, the B-25 was ready for testing. With modifications done, Doolittle marked out the length of carrier decks on land-based airfields, and proved the workability of the concept on 1 and 2 February. Doolittle planned to use fifteen B-25 bombers. Each aircraft was armed with a 500 lb M-43 high explosive bomb and an M-54 that contained 128 4 lb cluster bombs.

Doolittle then set about recruiting volunteers from the 17th Bomber Group. Twenty-four crews and aircraft were assembled (allowing for nine spares), and were sent to Elgin Field, Florida. Night flying and low altitude bombing was practiced as was fuel-saving flying technique. The B-25 crews flew their aircraft to March Field in southern California. The Sacramento Air Depot replaced parts and did a final service. Unbeknownst to the crews the carburettors were mistakenly readjusted to standard settings, which meant that the aircraft would not have met their peak performance; fortunately an eagle-eyed member of the aircrew noticed a different serial number on his aircraft carburettor and the mistake was rectified. It was a measure of the fine tolerances on which the *Doolittle Raid* was planned.

The Tokyo strike group arrived at Almeda in *San Francisco Bay* on 1 April and their aircraft were loaded onto the Navy's newest carrier, USS *Hornet*. The following day, Task Force 18 set sail and slipped out to sea under cover of fog. From now on communication was done by semaphore. The USS *Hornet* that was to carry the B-25s was commissioned on 20 October 1940. The *Hornet* was the last of the Yorktown Class carriers and was sorely needed to supplement the United States' outnumbered *Pacific Ocean* carriers. The *Hornet* had to survive; the next US carrier, the USS *Essex* (the first of twenty-four Essex Class carriers) would not be commissioned for another fourteen months. Captain Marc 'Pete' Mitscher was given command of the *Hornet*, the centerpiece of Task Force 18, which included the cruiser USS *Vincennes* and the light cruiser USS *Nashville*. The 22nd Destroyer Division, comprising USS *Gwin*, USS *Meredith*, USS *Grayson* and USS *Monssen*, was sent to accompany the special mission along with the oiler USS *Cimarron*.

Nimitz also ordered Admiral Halsey's Task Force 16 with its flagship, USS *Enterprise*, to join the *Hornet* Task Force; Halsey the ranking officer would take overall command. Unlike the *Hornet* that was loaded with the specially prepared B-25s, the *Enterprise* was conventionally equipped with 42 dive-bombers, 22 F4F Wildcat fighters, and 5 F4F-3s as well as 18 TBD-1 Devastator torpedo bombers. Two elderly cruisers, USS *Salt Lake City* and USS *Northampton*, accompanied the *Enterprise*. The accompanying destroyers included USS *Balch*, USS *Benham*, USS *Ellet* and USS *Fanning* plus the fleet oiler USS *Sabine*. The combined force (Task Force 16 and Task Force 18) was further supported by submarines USS *Thresher* and USS *Trout*.

The Doolittle Raid: **[Map: 12.7]** The crews of Halsey's Task Force 16 were shocked when Task Force 18 hove into view on 13 April to the northwest of *Hawaii*. AOM1 James Barnhill recalled, "We could not believe what we were seeing as the *Hornet* slipped into close range. She was carrying sixteen North American B-25s . . . we knew for certain if they got off the deck, they would never be able to return."[95] It was only now that an exuberant Halsey announced details of their mission: "This force is bound for Tokyo. In all my experience in the Navy I have never heard such a resounding cheer as came up from the ship's company."[96] According to *Hornet*'s commander, Mitscher, "morale reached a new high . . ."[97]

While the merged Task Force 16 steamed toward Tokyo, the *Thresher* and *Trout* acted as pickets looking out for signs of any Japanese surface vessels. They also attacked Japanese cargo ships and *Thresher* sank a 5,000-ton freighter off Yokohama, the major port city forty miles to the south of Tokyo.

On board the *Hornet* final preparations were made for the take-off and flight. Medals given to US sailors by the Japanese government during the US Navy's port call in 1908 had been forwarded to Nimitz and then to Mitscher with the expectation that they would be returned with interest. Mitscher duly obliged and attached them to the ordnance. Meanwhile in China, Stilwell and Chiang Kai-shek were preparing a reception committee; English-speaking ground crews and aviation fuel had to be brought in to the target airfields in southern China—no easy task at the beginning of 1942. Kweilin, the preferred landing site, was provided with 10,000 gallons of 100-octane fuel as well as 500 gallons of 120-weight oil. In total 30,000 gallons of fuel were delivered to the five sites. 'Hap' Arnold notified Stillwell to expect that on "APRIL 20, SPECIAL PROJECT WILL ARRIVE DESTINATION."[98] Once they had landed, it was planned that the planes would be sent to Chengdu and the crews to Chongqing from where they could be repatriated back to America.

At 3.20 a.m. on 18 April, the radar officer aboard *Enterprise* picked up two vessels at about 20,000 yards; the crew was called to general quarters. A change of course evaded detection. However, one of the three Dauntless dive-bombers launched from *Enterprise* at dawn was spotted by a ship forty-two miles ahead of Task Force 16. Halsey changed course but at 7.44 a.m. a Japanese picket ship, the *Nitto Maru*, was spotted at 10,000 yards. The armed *sampan* reported to Imperial Japanese Navy General Staff, "Three carriers sighted Position 650 nautical miles east of *Inubo Saki*."[99] Intercept ships were immediately dispatched from Yokosuka and Hiroshima. In the *Indian Ocean*, Vice-Admiral Chuichi Nagumo, who was leading a carrier force, was notified and he too changed course towards Japan. Meanwhile after strikes by the *Enterprise*'s aircraft had failed to sink the *Nitto Maru*, Halsey sent USS *Nashville* to finish the job. It took half an hour and 928 rounds of 6-inch shells to finish her off. It did not augur well for future surface naval battles.

However, if it was a raid, the Japanese staff commanders believed that it would have close to 200 miles to be able to launch and return Wildcat fighters; this was the benchmark distance set by Halsey's carrier raids on the *Marshall* and *Marcus Islands*. The expectation was that the US force would arrive at its launch point no earlier than 19 April. Now that they had been spotted Halsey had to make a decision whether to launch sooner than planned or retreat. It was 650 miles to Tokyo; the B-25 crews were 100 miles away from their planned strike point. At this range only a landing at Yushan

Airfield would be possible; however with expected headwinds now anticipated by *Enterprise*'s aerologists to be as strong as twenty-seven knots, fuel consumption was going to be borderline. At 8 a.m. *Hornet* received Halsey's message: "Launch planes. To Colonel Doolittle and Gallant Crew: Good luck and God Bless You."[100]

Doolittle was first off at 8.20 a.m. The remaining fifteen followed. They proudly displayed their idiosyncratic names: '*Whisky Pete*,' '*Whirling Dervish*,' '*Ruptured Duck*,' and '*Hari Kari-er*.'[101] It was an alarming sight. Wind was gusting at forty knots and with heavy seas, some of the aircraft disappeared from view as they came to the end of the carrier deck, only to re-emerge as if from out of the sea. At heights of little more than 100 feet above the water, Halsey described the take-offs as "most spectacular . . . The wind and the sea were so strong that morning that green water was breaking over the carrier's ramps. Jimmy led his squadron off. When his plane buzzed down the *Hornet*'s deck at 8.25 a.m. there wasn't a man topside in the task force who didn't sweat him into the air."[102] The last plane to take off, First-Lieutenant William Farrow's '*Bat out of Hell*,' slid backwards as the swell took the *Hornet* and sliced off the arm of a deck crewman.

Doolittle had organized the sixteen planes into five flights. Three flights would cover northern, central and southern Tokyo, Doolittle's flight would hit Yokohama and the naval base at Yokosuka while the last flight would hit Nagoya and Osaka. Targets selected included utility companies such as Tokyo Gas and Electric Company, Nippon as well as major arsenals. Other targets were Mitsubishi Aircraft Works, where the Zero was produced, and Kawasaki Aircraft Company. Ogura Oil Company and other storage facilities were also targeted. To hamper any defenders that they might come across, Doolittle spread out his flights over a wide area.

It was a four-hour trip to Tokyo. Although the B-25s flew over warships, cargo boats, tankers, patrol vessels and assorted smaller craft no warning message was relayed to Tokyo. Lulled into a false sense of security by the distance of Halsey's carriers from Tokyo, no warnings had been given and no preparations made. At 11.55 p.m. in Tokyo an announcer for a musical program announced that only Japan had been free from enemy attack. "We ask ourselves. What has become of the advertised American air power? What has become of the British and American Fleets, if any?"[103] Just over an hour later the announcer had his answer. At 12.00 p.m. seventy miles away an observation post north of Tokyo reported the sighting of enemy bombers. By then it was too late to intercept the oncoming Mitchells. Ki-27 'Nates' were too slow to scramble and failed to catch the B-25s. As for anti-aircraft fire, the US planes were flying too low for them to lock on to their targets.

The last B-25 from first flight was unfortunate to develop a gasoline leak that pushed them off target. Commanded by Lieutenant Everett Holstrom, his B-25 was set upon by two Kawasaki Ki-61 '*Hien*'—called 'Tonies' by the Allies—which were prototypes still in development. To add to Holstrom's problems his top gun turret malfunctioned; he dropped his bombs in *Tokyo Bay* and scarpered as best he could. Similarly Captain Edward 'Ski' York, who subsequently found out that the Sacramento Air Depot had replaced his specially tuned carburettors, was also running short of fuel. He found some 'opportunist' industrial targets. Realizing that he would land 300 miles short of China, York, against instructions, headed for the Soviet Union.

Lieutenant Ted Lawson in '*Ruptured Duck*' was more fortunate. Incendiaries were dropped on Tokyo that a crewmember had inscribed with "I don't want to set the world on fire—just Tokyo!"[104] Large fires were seen as they left the area. Remarkably in view of the fact that many of the B-25s were pursued and engaged by Japanese fighter aircraft, all sixteen emerged from their attacks unscathed. But could they reach China and safety?

Intended and Unintended Consequences of the Doolittle Raid: At 2.45 p.m. a Japanese news flash issued a report that had been dressed up by the government's propaganda team, "Enemy bombers appeared over Tokyo today shortly after noon for the first time in the current East Asia War. Heavy and telling damage was inflicted on schools and hospitals."[105] A death toll of three to four thousand was also reported though this was almost certainly an exaggeration. Japan would later claim, falsely, that nine planes had been shot down.

Of the sixteen US Mitchel B-25s only two made it to a Chinese airfield as planned. Ten crews had to bale out over China when their planes ran out of gas. Four others had to ditch at sea. As with the trip to Japan, the flight to China was gas-guzzlingly bad in spite of the benefits of a tailwind on this leg of the journey. Poor visibility had also led to navigation problems. The surviving crews went to Chongqing as planned and were decorated by Chiang Kai-shek. Most of the crews were lost. Doolittle, the propaganda 'mascot' of the raid was fortunate to land just seventy miles north of Chuchow. A downcast Doolittle believed that he had failed and fully expected to be court-martialed.

As planned it was indeed a spectacular propaganda coup for the American war effort. But the costs were significant. The Japanese Army began a hunt for the downed crews that extended over 20,000 square miles for three months. By ditching in China, seventy-one of the eighty crewmembers survived their trip with help from the Chinese; two were drowned, eight were captured by the Japanese, of whom three crewmembers were tried and beheaded for the supposed strafing of civilians. Of the remaining five, one died from the appalling mistreatment meted out to them while four members survived the war. The most adventurous trip was that of Captain Edward 'Ski' York and his crew. Judging that he would not reach China, 'Ski' landed his Mitchell at an airfield near Vladivostok where they were interned according to the rules of the Geneva Convention. They were sent first to Okuna, south of Moscow, and then to Okhansk (Perm) on the western fringe of Siberia. When they were moved to Ashkabad near the Iranian border, York succeeded in bribing his Soviet guards and made his way across the bordering Mashhad Mountains to the British consulate in Tehran in Iran. Many of the crewmen went on to serve in the China-Burma theater. Chiang would later notify Roosevelt that, in southern China, the Japanese Army slaughtered 250,000 Chinese civilians in a campaign of vengeance. Even allowing for some exaggeration on Chiang's part, the Doolittle Raid thus caused the death of more than twice the number of Chinese than the United States military suffered during the entire *Pacific War*.

A frightened Japanese commentator speculated that the US must have developed a super-carrier with a quarter mile flight deck; others speculated China or the Philippines as the origin of the attack. Destruction of one of the Japanese picket ships soon disabused the Navy of this notion; tortured pilots also gave up exact details of how the raid was carried out. An embarrassed Yamamoto diverted a submarine squadron from *Bonin Islands* to hunt down the intruders. Carrier forces returning from operations in the *Indian Ocean* were ordered to give chase. The raid itself did minimal damage to Japan's war fighting capability. However, the psychological and propaganda effects within America were more than Roosevelt could have hoped for. Far from being court-martialed, Doolittle came back a hero. The Doolittle Raid may have been a propaganda coup for America, but 'Hap' Arnold's realistic appraisal was that "From the viewpoint of an Air Force operation the raid was not a success, for no raid is a success in which losses exceed ten percent and it now appears that probably all of the airplanes were lost."[106]

Clark Lee of the *Los Angeles Times* stated, "It was electrifying. Almost too good to be true after we had been waiting so many long, bitter weeks for the United States to get started."[107] Hollywood immediately started to produce *Thirty Seconds over Tokyo* [1944] starring Robert Mitchum and Spencer Tracey who played Lieutenant-Colonel James Doolittle. In Japan the attack was a stunning blow to the pride of the Japanese Navy. Yamamoto made a grovelling apology to the Emperor. Admiral Ugaki recorded in his diary, ". . . this [raid] shattered my firm determination never to let the enemy attack Tokyo or the mainland."[108] From a practical point of view the raid's most significant and lasting effect was to draw more war resources to home defense than had previously been the case.

Roosevelt told reporters that planes came from the mythical 'Shangri-La.' A year later the true story was released and further burnished Halsey's reputation. The *New York Times* concluded that nobody could have dreamed "of sending big land bombers careening off naval carriers, built to accommodate smaller aircraft."[109] Roosevelt's administration reported that the raid was led by Halsey, "the hard-boiled fighter from Elizabeth, New Jersey."[110] It was the first of many instances in which Halsey, whether responsible or not responsible, whether successful or not successful, always emerged with the cloak of success. Like MacArthur it was a 'cloak' that fed his vanity, ultimately with near disastrous consequences.

In Japan, in response to the Doolittle Raid, Yamamoto's aggressive *Midway Island* strategy sold itself to a hierarchy bent on revenge. Accordingly the Imperial Navy staff urgently set about organizing their next move—the destruction of America's pesky carrier fleet. The aim would be to take *Midway Island* and the *Aleutian Islands* while drawing out the US carrier force from *Pearl Harbor* and destroying it. Before implementing this primary strategy, Yamamoto would dispatch two carriers to the *Coral Sea* to take care of the seemingly little matter of taking *Tulagi Island* in the southern *Solomons* and Port Moresby in southern New Guinea with the aim of tightening the noose around Australia. The intentions of Japan's Operation MO, as the southern operations were called, were summarized by a General Staff spokesman at Imperial Naval HQ;

> We shall first occupy Port Moresby, together with important positions at Tulagi and in southeast New Guinea, by close collaboration between the Navy and a detachment of South-Sea forces. We shall set up airbases and intensify our air operations on the Australia sector. Later, one of our groups will occupy the islands of Nauru and Ocean so as to ensure a supply of the phosphates so much needed by our agriculture.[111]

In hindsight it can be seen that Japan's military and naval leaders were guilty of a complacent, strategic overstretch—a clear belief that they only had to show up to defeat an enemy whom they had defeated with supreme ease in the early months of the war.

13 Battle of the Coral Sea: The First Carrier 'Shoot-Out'

[April 1942–May 1942]

[Maps: 13.1A, 13.1B, 13.2]

The US Naval Intelligence Network: [Map: F.1] Unbeknownst to the Japanese, one of the main ingredients in their early war successes disappeared in the early months. 'Surprise,' their major weapon in the first few weeks of the *Pacific War*, was completely negated by the development of an American intelligence and decryption capability that the Japanese were never able to match. The tables were turned. The Americans, with remarkable speed, had developed an intelligence network and capability that meant that they now possessed the advantage of 'surprise.' It proved to be one of the key turning points of the war and perhaps the main reason why the US Navy was able to turn around its disastrous start to the *Pacific War* within little more than six months of *Pearl Harbor*.

Commander Edwin Layton was appointed Chief Intelligence officer to Admiral Husband Kimmel on 8 December 1940. His position was such, given the debacle of *Pearl Harbor* exactly a year later, that it would have been no surprise if Nimitz had dispensed with his services. In fact Kimmel and his intelligence team were never given access to the decryption transcripts PURPLE, the high level Japanese diplomatic code, which might have enabled them to raise a higher level of preparedness before the attack on *Pearl Harbor*. Nevertheless it speaks well of Nimitz's man management skills that he retained existing staff and assessed them on the basis of the work they did for him. The retention of Layton was inspired. He proved to be adept at piecing together and analysing multiple pieces of intelligence information. Weeding out the 'noise' of intelligence that was often conflicting, Layton was able to predict Japanese movement with uncanny accuracy from listening posts set up around the *Pacific*. It was a far from easy task as the Japanese, as a precaution, would often transfer call signs between warships of different size in order to better hide their capital ships. It was a critical skill in the early stages of the *Pacific War* when the Japanese and American resources were so evenly matched. Superior intelligence would tip the balance in the US Navy's favor.

Layton was half of a double act. Joseph Rochefort had become close friends with Layton when they had studied Japanese together in Tokyo from 1929 to 1932. While Layton specialized in intelligence analysis, Rochefort went on to specialize in cryptology. In 1941 he was sent to *Hawaii* by Commander Laurence Safford, head of the code and signal section of the Navy HQ in Washington known as OP–20-G. Rochefort set up the so-called HYPO Station (H for *Hawaii*) in a disused basement in *Pearl Harbor*'s new administration building; it was to become known as the 'Dungeon.'

There he recruited a team of cryptologists and linguists to monitor and decode Japanese Navy transmissions.

It was an unlikely operation. Rochefort's team worked day and night by rotation under florescent lighting. They lived on coffee and sandwiches and rarely saw daylight. Often they slept on cots laid down between IBM tabulating machines. Rochefort himself, usually unshaven, always dishevelled, famously worked in his carpet slippers and wore a stained red velvet smoking jacket or a bathrobe over his khaki uniform. Rochefort and his team of twenty worked largely on the FLAG OFFICERS Code while other code breaking teams in Washington and the Philippines worked on the Navy's main code known as JN-25 (JAPAN NAVY). Remarkably, the Japanese would never discover the breaking of the Imperial Japanese Navy's code.

British code breakers in Asia also contributed as did 'spotters,' often plantation managers, dotted around the *South Pacific*. Thus a broad spectrum of intelligence information was brought to Layton's attention. In addition the Doolittle Raid brought an unexpected intelligence benefit. The Japanese Navy's pursuit of Halsey brought a wealth of information by the revelation of five digit code groups on which the Japanese JN-25 Code was based.

Japanese Carriers to the South Pacific: [Maps: 13.1A, 13.1B] The result of Nimitz's development of a strong intelligence capability was that the US Navy was given two weeks warning of the Japanese Navy's southward push. Layton predicted landings in the New Guinea area around 3 May. It was also known that two Japanese fleet carriers would leave *Truk* for the *Coral Sea*. It was correctly guessed that the target was Port Moresby.

A few days after the Doolittle Raid, Japanese Imperial General HQ put into action the first phase of its 'Australia Doctrine' strategy, Operation MO, to occupy Port Moresby on the south coast of New Guinea and *Tulagi* in the *Solomon Islands*. Rear-Admiral Kose Abe led the invasion force with eleven transports carrying 5,500 troops. Rear-Admiral Sadamichi Kajioka escorted the convoy with one light cruiser and six destroyers. Meanwhile 500 troops were sent to *Tulagi* with two destroyers and an assortment of minelayers and auxiliary ships with a view to establishing a seaplane and communications base. The light carrier *Shoho* and four heavy cruisers under the command of Rear-Admiral Aritomo Goto also covered the *Tulagi* force.

Japan's main strike force in the form of carriers *Zuikaku* and *Shokaku*, protected by two heavy cruisers and six destroyers left *Truk* on 1 May and proceeded via the east coast of the *Solomons* to the *Coral Sea*. Positioning itself off the south coast of New Guinea, the fleet would provide air cover for Vice-Admiral Abe's troop transports bound for Port Moresby. In addition the area was screened by seven submarines (five I-Class and two RO-Class).

In the pattern of Japan's expansionary march across Asia in the early months of the *Pacific War*, its plans were complex and detailed, using numbers of separate task forces with multiple objectives. Also typical was the relatively small number of Japanese troops used in offensive operations relative to defenders, just 1:1 in the case of Port

Moresby—a further sign of Japanese hubris with regard to their estimation of their military capability *vis-à-vis* the Allies. Added pressure came from Yamamoto to complete Operation MO and by 1 May so that the carriers could *rendezvous* with Yamamoto in preparation for the attack on *Midway* planned for early June. However, the odds had changed since the early days of the war. Even the Japanese, in spite of their overarching self-belief, were aware, from the series of raids by the US Navy in the *South Pacific* as well as the Doolittle Raid that the American fight-back had begun.

Preparations for Battle: Although the *Coral Sea* was in MacArthur's area of operations, it was logically concluded that Nimitz should remain in command of directing the battle that was now anticipated. Nimitz responded to the Japanese initiative by sending Admiral Fletcher's carrier USS *Yorktown* (CV-5) and Task Force 17 USS *Lexington* (CV-2) under Rear-Admiral Aubrey Fitch.

Fitch's Task Force 11 was ordered to re-join Fletcher's Task Group on 1 May at *Batchelor's Button* about 250 miles southwest of *Espiritu Santo* in the *New Hebrides*. (It was not a leadership that pleased King who, somewhat irrationally, believed that Fletcher was a defeatist.)

Sending two of his precious carriers some 2,175 miles was a risky strategy and Nimitz flew to Washington to explain his actions; although Nimitz had the advantage of intelligence, he was well aware that Japan's carrier crews were better prepared for battle. Nimitz's orders, which relied on the localized execution of tactics, was a model of simplicity: "Rear-Admiral Fletcher will operate in the *Coral Sea* from 1 May onwards and will be in command of all the forces assigned to him. He will have discretion to take action to intercept the enemy and keep open vital lines of communication between the United States and Australia."[1] Admiral Fletcher was an old-school 'black shoe' fleet Admiral. ('black shoe' admirals were sailors first, while the new breed of 'brown shoe' admirals were airmen first.) Tall, lean, youthful, a noted womanizer, Fletcher believed that an American Navy officer needed to be a sailor before becoming a fighter. Cool and decisive, Fletcher had distinguished himself in *World War I* and subsequently spent a large part of his career in Asia and the *Pacific*.

The whole Japanese operation was directed by Admiral Shigeyoshi Inoue from the cruiser *Kashima* at Rabaul. Inoue, Fletcher's opposite number, was short and overweight, his physical opposite. Born in Sendai on the northeast coast of *Honshu Island*, the largest of the big four Japanese islands, Inoue proved to be a brilliant officer and graduated second out of 179 graduates from the class of 1909 at the Imperial Japanese Naval Academy. He was an accomplished linguist learning both English and French and became a good enough guitarist to become a music teacher after the war. A *protégé* of Admiral Yamamoto, Inoue shared his enthusiasm for naval aviation, believing as early as 1937, "The days of the battleship are gone. It has been replaced by the aircraft."[2] He also shared Yamamoto's political inclinations and was even more vehement than Yamamoto in believing that it was "impossible . . . for Japan to defeat America."[3] He was seen as part of the 'liberal' faction within the Navy and opposed the alliance with the *Nazis* and the aggressive international expansionism. American naval intelligence described Inoue as "an exceptionally brilliant and capable officer."[4]

Like many of his colleagues, Inoue was also a meticulous planner. For months he had been sending detailed reports and plans proposing an extension of the Great East Asia Co-Prosperity Sphere into the *Southwest Pacific*. Put in charge of Operation MO, now was his chance for glory. Like most of the Japanese Navy, recent successes made him certain that victory was simply there for the taking; it was assumed they would be too good for anything that the American Navy could throw at them. Even with the limited forces available to him, given that the bulk of the fleet was in the north preparing for the attack on *Midway Island*, Inoue commanded a force that comprised 282 aircraft, half of them carrier-based on two modern fleet carriers and one modern light carrier. Sixty-two further ships supported Operation MO, including six heavy cruisers, three light cruisers, fourteen destroyers and six submarines. Their task was to protect the 28-ship convoy of troops and supplies as it traversed the *Louisiade Archipelago* (a group of islands off the eastern tip of New Guinea) as it headed toward a landing site adjacent to Port Moresby. With New Guinea's capital city under Japanese control, an airbase would be able to interdict supplies to northern Australia and the major *entrepôt* city of Brisbane in Queensland. In addition Inoue planned to disrupt the bomber attacks from Australia's northern airfields in Townsville and Cooktown, which had proved so troublesome to the Japanese forces at Lae and Salamaua on the southeastern coast of New Guinea.

To achieve his task Inoue divided his operations into three. Rear-Admiral Kuninori's support force, based on two old light cruisers would begin to establish airbases on a southeast axis from Rabaul through the *Solomon* chains starting with the small island of *Tulagi* in the southern *Solomons* on 3 May. The second force and main force under Rear-Admiral Aritomo Goto with four heavy cruisers and the light carrier *Shoho* carrying twenty planes would provide air cover for this assault that was expected to take only one day. *Shoho* was a brand-new carrier having just been converted from the sub tender *Tsurugisaki* a few months previously.

The third force for Operation MO would be a strike group comprising the two fleet carriers, *Shokaku* and *Zuikaku*, carrying 124 planes, under the command of Rear-Admiral Chuichi 'King Kong' Hara. He in turn would be under the command of Rear-Admiral Takeo Takagi whose 5th Cruiser force, comprising the *Myoko* and *Haguro* along with six destroyers, would provide defensive support. The dependable Takagi, not an aviator himself, would delegate air operations to Hara, a tall, bulky, 53-year-old officer with an aggressive reputation who had led the Fifth Carrier Fleet against *Pearl Harbor* and later Rabaul.

Takagi was charged with disrupting the Australian airbases at Townsville and Cooktown and to prevent them attacking the troop convoys advancing on Port Moresby. To avoid early discovery Takagi's force would take a circuitous easterly course steering them around the east coast of the *Solomons* and allowing them to approach the *Coral Sea* from due east from where air attacks would be launched on the Allied airbases in northern Australia on 7 May. While Takagi's forces rounded the southern tip of the

Solomons', flying boats, by now stationed at *Tulagi*, would provide reconnaissance as they moved toward the *Coral Sea*. In addition four submarines were stationed as pickets southwest of *Guadalcanal Island* in the southwest *Solomons* to alert Takagi of any Allied forces scurrying out from Brisbane to meet them. Meanwhile Goto's main force would double back to meet and accompany the invasion force of troop transports that left Rabaul on 4 May en route to Port Moresby.

Hara, alone of the senior commanders, doubted the wisdom of approaching the northern shores of Australia and putting Japan's precious large carriers at risk of discovery and attack from land-based bombers. The falsely reported sighting of an Allied carrier fleet southeast of Rabaul reopened the debate about the wisdom of the attack on Australia's northern airfields. On 29 April, Admiral Yamamoto, from his flagship *Yamato*, ordered the raid on Townsville and Cooktown Airfield to be cancelled. With the emphasis now put on the land-based aircraft at Rabaul, Hara was ordered to transfer nine of his pilots to additional planes from *Truk Atoll*. The delay caused by this minor maneuver would have a significant impact on the forthcoming engagement at *Tulagi Island*.

Japanese Invasion of Tulagi Island: By 1 May both Japanese and Allied navies were headed toward a conflict that both sides anticipated. Admiral Inoue was under the illusion that his plans were unknown; however, US code breaking meant that the US Navy already had their carriers placed at *Butternut Point*, 400 miles southwest of *Guadalcanal* and 200 miles to the south of the *Louisiade Archipelago* at the easterly entrance of the *Coral Sea*. Indeed intelligence had even identified *Deboyne Atoll* in the central *Louisiades* as the *rendezvous* location for Japanese naval forces and the troop transports sailing from Rabaul.

Meanwhile Nimitz and his admirals, who may have had the jump on Inoue in terms of his advance warning of their intentions to take Port Moresby, were unaware that *Tulagi* in the southern *Solomon Islands* was a target and did not know that the Japanese fleet led by Takagi would make a left hook by taking the long way around the *Solomons* and approaching the *Coral Sea* from the east rather than from the north as expected. For Fletcher refueling was problematic. Fitch's Task Force 11 with carrier USS *Lexington* had started refueling on 2 May. As night fell on 3 May he was still not finished and completion was not expected until noon on the following day. Refueling at sea was still an 'art' in its infancy; it was one of the US Navy's previously overlooked areas of technical and logistical expertise that was to become increasingly important as America's long-range war across the *Pacific* gathered momentum.

Fletcher was concerned on two counts. First he believed "reports of enemy forces precluded remaining so far to the southward"[5] and secondly he was nervous about their being targeted by Japanese submarines if they hung around and waited in a small refuelling area. The previous day dive-bombers from USS *Yorktown* had attacked a Japanese I-Class submarine just twenty-three miles to the north. Fletcher wanted to get further north and west where he expected to find the advancing Japanese forces. He therefore split his carrier forces, headed north with Task Force 17 and ordered Rear-Admiral Fitch to join him thirty-six hours later. The reunion was delayed by news of Japanese landings on *Tulagi* that sent Fletcher scurrying to the northeast. The USS *Neosho* and USS *Russell* were left behind to meet up with Fitch and the USS *Lexington*, and direct them to a new *rendezvous* at Point Corn, 325 miles south of *Guadalcanal*.

Battle action began on 4 May. Admiral Fletcher launched forty sorties at dawn from Task Force 17 to disrupt the Japanese landings at *Tulagi*. USS *Yorktown*'s aircraft sank the *Kikuzuki*, a destroyer, as well as three minesweepers and four seaplanes. When Flight Commander William Burch, leader of fifteen Douglas Dauntless SDBs, returned at 9.45 a.m., he raced to the bridge to tell Fletcher that they "had hit the Japs but didn't do any good."[6] Although Fletcher launched a second-wave attack, Japanese losses did not prevent the Japanese force from building its communication outpost. Fletcher's strike on *Tulagi*, too far to have been made from north Australia, alerted Inoue's carrier strike force that there was an American carrier in the area.

Takagi reacted to this information by sending out reconnaissance planes. Takagi's carrier force, delayed by having to transfer fighters to Rabaul, was 350 miles north of *Tulagi* rather than the 120 miles that had been planned. Takagi was also refueling. His search planes scoured the sea to the east of *Tulagi* and the *Solomons*. However, Fletcher was in the south, out of range of Takagi's search. Admirals Fletcher and Fitch, as well as Nimitz back at *Pearl Harbor*, still believed that the main threat of Japan's carrier fleet would come via the *Louisiades*. Nobody anticipated Inoue's left hook from the east. At dawn on 5 May, Task Force 11 and Task Force 17 met up as planned at *Point Corn*. As they met, a Japanese seaplane was shot down; although it failed to fire off a warning signal, its failure to appear back at base nevertheless eventually gave a clue to Admiral Inoue that there was an American carrier force close by. After his oil-consuming high-speed run to attack *Tulagi*, Fletcher took the opportunity to refuel Task Force 17 again.

In reporting back to *Pearl Harbor*, Admiral Fletcher was scrupulously honest about the mixed fortunes of the attack on Japanese positions and ships at *Tulagi Island*. "This operation is indisputably disappointing in the quality of results achieved, particularly in view of the cost in ammunition and equipment. It shows the need for training in dropping of bombs and torpedoes whenever possible."[7] Nimitz, well aware of the shortcomings of the US Navy, was always anxious to support his commanders in the field and answered, "Congratulations and well done to you and your force. Hope you can exploit your success with your augmented force."[8]

Maneuverings for a First Carrier to Carrier Battle: During 5 May, as Admiral Takagi's carrier force rounded *San Cristobel Island*, the southern tip of the *Solomons*, and then turned north to enter the passage between *San Cristobel* and *Rennell Island*, his carrier force was much closer to Fletcher's forces than either side realized. Meanwhile Fletcher was heading northwest from Point Corn with Fitch's Task Force 11 kept at a ten-mile distance in keeping with US practice of carrier separation. Reconnaissance flights by both fleets just failed to locate each other.

On 6 May it was confirmed from *Pearl Harbor* that the Japanese now intended to land their troops at Port Moresby on 10 May and that their carrier fleet would be nearby. Fletcher aimed to find them on the following day, 7 May, after refueling was complete. In fact on the morning of 6 May, Takagi's carrier fleet was not to the north of *Bougainville* as Fletcher believed but had already entered the *Coral Sea* west of *Tulagi* where it too stopped to refuel though just out of range of his spotter planes. Fueling completed, Takagi headed south. He believed that enemy forces were likely to be further west and wanted to block off their escape route back to *Hawaii*. Japanese strategy was no less than the complete destruction of any US fleet lurking in the *Coral Sea* trying to protect Port Moresby.

Preparing for battle Fletcher sent the oiler USS *Neosho* and the destroyer USS *Sims* south to keep them out of any action. That evening it was announced that the besieged American-Philippine garrison at *Corregidor*, the island to the south of the Bataan Peninsula, had been surrendered by Lieutenant-General Wainwright. No doubt Imperial command in Tokyo, fully aware of the developing action in the *Coral Sea*, was expecting a great naval victory to follow the next day. However, in mid-morning a Japanese flying-boat reconnaissance plane from *Tulagi* reported a sighting of Fletcher's fleet and Takagi hurried his carriers south so as to get in range in preparation for an early morning strike on 7 May. At Rabaul, Admiral Inoue who had earlier predicted, "It is not likely that powerful enemy forces are in the area"[9] was completely shocked to hear that there was a strong enemy carrier force in the *Coral Sea*.

Meanwhile Fletcher, unaware that Japanese carriers were just 100 miles to the north, sent Vice-Admiral Jack Crace's surface force Task Force 44, including the cruisers HMAS *Australia* and HMAS *Hobart*, to head off the southern exit from the *Louisiades*, the order blinkered to Crace read, "Proceed at daylight with your group to destroy enemy ships reported passing through Jomard Passage and threatening Moresby. Conserve fuel. Fuel destroyers from cruisers. Retire to Townsville [northern Australia] when necessary to fuel."[10] Crace headed north toward the *Jomard Passage*. In separating his fleet, Fletcher wanted to make sure that even if his carrier fleet was incapacitated, Crace would be able to intercept the Japanese troop convoy bound for Port Moresby. Submarines under Captain Christie were also sent to guard the coast of New Guinea as well as the *Louisiade* and *Bismarck Archipelagos*. Much criticized after the war by naval historians Bates and Morison, Crace fully endorsed a decision that necessarily weakened the anti-aircraft defenses around Task Force 17; "Under the circumstances prevailing at the time I am certain Fletcher was right and the advantage to be gained by possibly catching the Moresby invasion Group in the *Jomard Passage* far outweighed that gained by increasing the anti-aircraft screen by the ships of my force."[11] Moreover it was well known that anti-aircraft fire in the early days of the *Pacific War* was largely ineffective. A Task Force 17 gunnery officer concluded that Crace's potential defensive contribution was "a very minor consideration as far as AA (anti-aircraft) was concerned."[12]

The Battle of the Coral Sea: First Blood to Admiral Fletcher [7 May 1942]: **[Map: 13.2]** At 7.22 a.m. a Japanese spotter plane mistakenly relayed a sighting of the US carrier fleet. *Shokaku* and *Zuikaku* immediately launched a full air strike only to find the oiler USS *Neosho* and the destroyer, USS *Sims*, which was duly sunk. Sixty-eight American survivors spent ten days on life rafts before they were rescued.

Similar miscommunications were afflicting Fletcher. At dawn on 7 May Fletcher turned into the wind to enable ten Douglas SBD Dauntless reconnaissance planes to take off. He had come to rest at a point 115 miles south of *Rossel Island*, the most easterly point of the *Louisiade Archipelago*. Hours later a Dauntless dive-bomber piloted by Lieutenant John Nielsen spotted an Aichi E–13A 'Jake' seaplane. Not wanting the 'Jake' to report the presence of an enemy plane, Nielsen went after it. In the ensuing dogfight Nielsen eventually shot down his prey: "He couldn't have been twenty feet off the water when I hit him," Nielsen recalled, "and he went down and under like a rock."[13] A quarter of an hour later, Walter Straub, Nielsen's rear gunner, spotted a group of warships near *Misima Island* in the *Louisiade Archipelago*. Nielsen reported back to *Yorktown* that he had seen "TWO **CRUISERS** AND FOUR DESTROYERS."[14] Straub transcribed the message but couldn't send it because he found that the rear antenna, probably shot away by the 'Jake,' was gone. Needing to use his short wave band, Nielsen sped back toward the *Yorktown* until he was near enough to get back a 'Roger' call sign at 8.15 a.m. Using his code tables Straub sent back a message that was reconfigured on board the *Yorktown* as "TWO **CARRIERS** AND FOUR CRUISERS."[15] A printing misalignment in his codebook had caused Straub to make a near catastrophic error, an example of the slender margins on which major battles can turn. Fletcher would never have sent his strike carrier force against a surface force led by two cruisers.

Fletcher, determined to get in the first shot at the Japanese carriers headed his Task Force 17 north towards the *Louisiade Archipelago*, which was 225 miles away and prepared his carrier for launch. By 9.26 a.m. *Yorktown*'s entire strike force of ninety-three planes had been spotted (fueled and armed on deck) on deck and Fletcher came onto the bridge wing with a bullhorn and ordered them to "Get that Goddamn carrier."[16] Forty-five minutes later the strike force was on its way. Nielson and Straub now returned to the *Yorktown* dropping a beanbag with an attached note that confirmed the location of the Japanese force. Fletcher was horrified to see that the note mentioned "TWO **CRUISERS** AND FOUR DESTROYERS"; not a word about carriers. As a result of the miscommunication, Fletcher had launched his entire strike force against a small cruiser force—leaving his own carriers bare to attack from Japan's carriers. When Nielsen landed Fletcher asked him "What about the carriers?" The shocked Admiral, according to one witness, told Nielsen, "Young man, do you know what you have done? You have just cost the United States two carriers."[17]

Fletcher's full attack force was now headed toward an insignificant target. His own defenses were wide open. At this point the bridge received an Australian bomber report of a Japanese carrier and twenty or more ships just thirty miles from Nielsen's sighting off the *Louisiade Archipelago*. Deciding to give credence to this report, Fletcher redirected his strike force in this new direction. Fortune favored Fletcher after all. At 10.40 a.m. Fletcher's aircraft spotted Admiral Goto's force with the light carrier *Shoho* to the northeast of *Misima Island*. Fifteen Douglas Dauntless dive-bombers and twelve Douglas Devastator torpedo bombers moved down to attack. Just as Captain Izawa turned *Shoho* into the wind and prepared its aircraft for a strike against Fletcher's carriers, *Shoho* was hit by two 1,000 lb bombs and four torpedoes from the USS *Lexington*'s strike force. Twenty minutes later the *Lexington*'s attack was followed up by an even more devastating attack by twenty-five Dauntless dive-bombers from the USS *Yorktown*. Its strike planes hit the now stationary Japanese carrier with eleven more bombs and two more torpedoes. Lieutenant Commander William Burch recalled that "It was the best attack I ever made in my life" and that "She [*Shoho*] . . . was under the waves seven minutes after our first bomb hit her."[18]

Dive-bomber commander Lieutenant Commander Weldon Hamilton reported,

> We began from 16,500 feet and pushed over in our dive at 12,000. The Jap was exactly downwind as I nosed down, simplifying my problem tremendously. My bomb, which was the first 1,000-pounder to hit, struck in the middle of the flight deck's width, just abaft midships. As I looked back the entire after-portion of the flight deck was ablaze and pouring forth heavy smoke.[19]

During the battle Wildcat pilot Lieutenant Junior Grade Walter Haas swooped down on a squadron of Zeros and scored the first confirmed kill of a Zero by a Wildcat.

The *Shoho* sank at 11.35 a.m., taking with it 631 crewmen. It was America's first sinking of a Japanese carrier, albeit a light carrier. With great excitement, Commander Dixon, USS *Yorktown*'s VS-2 commander, radioed the message, "Scratch one flattop! Dixon to carrier: I repeat: scratch one flattop!"[20] Fletcher danced a jig of delight and hugged his flight commanders. By contrast Admiral Inoue, with the air cover for his troop ships now sunk, ordered the Port Moresby invasion force to turn back. *Yorktown*'s pilots may have been cock-a-hoop but in reality they had missed the Japanese fleet carriers and pounded a sprat. "It was a successful attack,"[21] noted Lieutenant-Commander Paul Stroop, "except that we had an overkill on the carrier [*Shoho*] . . . this being the first battle of that kind, everybody went after the big prize, and they sank this rather soft carrier very quickly."[22]

Fletcher recovered his planes and, deciding that at 2 p.m. it was too late for a second strike, moved his carrier forces southwest reflecting his belief that the battle would turn in this direction. He was still uncertain as to the whereabouts of Inoue's main strike carriers. Bad weather and the lateness of the hour by now precluded further searches for the Japanese strike carriers. At 2.29 p.m. Fletcher sent a message to Fitch informing him, "Will hold off. Awaiting information from Army. Hoping to repeat in the morning this day's excellent work."[23] Fitch concurred though some senior officers, such as Captain Frederick Sherman thought that further reconnaissance missions should be undertaken.

Meanwhile minutes later Admiral Crace fended off a Japanese bomb and torpedo attack. After that three friendly B-26 Martin Marauders mistook Crace's force for the fleeing Japanese troop convoy and bombed their own ships; fortunately they missed. The only damage done was to the Australian Navy's relationship with General MacArthur who received a stinging telegram at his headquarters.

Later that afternoon Fletcher received confirmation for the first time that USS *Slim* was sunk and that USS *Neosho* was sinking. The captain of the tanker had radioed that his ship was "as full of holes as a colander."[24] The *Slim* sank in minutes; ". . . a terrific explosion occurred. What remained of the ship was lifted 10 to 15 feet out of the water, and the surface of the water around the ship was covered with oil . . . One man who couldn't swim was seen hanging onto the anchor until the stern disappeared into the water."[25] Fletcher, ever concerned about fuel supply, reduced the speed of the fleet to eight knots; he reported that the loss of the *Neosho* "upsets our logistics."[26] Fletcher headed west assuming that the Japanese strike carriers were nearer to Crace. Similarly the Japanese assumed that Crace's force was the US carrier force and also headed in a westerly direction. Waiting for his returning aircraft and the stormy weather also persuaded Hara and Takagi to call off their planned second wave attack in the early afternoon.

Admiral Hara, unlike Fletcher, had some capability for nighttime carrier flying. However, it was still a largely undeveloped skill and the Japanese admiral was loath to put pilots to the test. But when new reconnaissance information indicated that the two fleets were closing, Hara changed his mind about a second attack and decided to risk his more experienced crews on a night attack. Admiral Takagi approved the mission and at 4.15 p.m. Commander Takashi took off with twelve Aichi D3A 'Val' dive-bombers and fifteen Nakajima B5N 'Kate' torpedo bombers. By the time that they were expected to find the American carriers some 280 miles away it was anticipated that the storms would have passed and that the night sky would be clear. On the part of Hara and Takagi it was an immense gamble with their most experienced crews.

At 5.45 p.m., near sundown, just as Fletcher believed that he had got away with a whole day without an air attack on his strike carriers, USS *Lexington*'s radar picked up groups of enemy bogeys some 22–28 miles away. Fletcher's dozen or so air patrol fighters were now too low on fuel to mount a long-distance raid so fresh Wildcats were scrambled from *Lexington* and *Yorktown* to provide a thirty-strong plane defense. At 6.03 p.m. Lieutenant Commander Paul Ramsey ambushed the Japanese bogeys and claimed five shot down while other Wildcats claimed several kills of Japanese torpedo planes. Takahashi's attack was now in disarray. One radio transmission by a Japanese pilot that was picked up by the *Lexington* reported, "Attack squadron has been annihilated by enemy fighters."[27] Takahashi aborted the mission.

However, as they returned toward their own carriers, three of the disoriented Japanese pilots, whose radio homing signals were jammed by US fighter director transmissions, attempted to land on *Yorktown* and *Lexington* at the same time that their own Wildcats were circling to land. Greeted by a hail of tracer bullets the Japanese 'cuckoos' opened their throttles and sped away though one them was felled by anti-aircraft fire. In the confusion, at 19.09 p.m. anti-aircraft fire broke out from the surface cruisers and destroyers as well as the *Yorktown*'s entire starboard anti-aircraft battery. A despairing Wildcat fighter pilot complained, "What are you shooting at me for? What have I done now?"[28]

Ensign John D. Baker was driven off by the anti-aircraft fire and disappeared off the radar. In spite of the evident presence of enemy aircraft, Fletcher went up to the air plot room himself, insisted that the radio be kept open to try to reach Baker. Flight Director Officer, Lieutenant Commander Oscar Pederson gave up on getting Baker back onto radar at 8.28 p.m. and gave him the course to the nearest landfall: "I remember the talker with me was practically in tears when I had to tell the pilot [Baker] good-bye and good luck."[29] John Baker was never seen again. Fletcher may have lost Ensign Baker but Admiral Hara had lost nine of the precious twenty-seven experienced crews that he had sent out on a night mission and with nothing to show for it. In addition during the day American pilots had shot down nineteen Japanese planes at a cost of just three fighters and three bombers. It had been Fletcher's day.

At 8.00 p.m. the opposing carrier fleets had converged to little more than 100 miles distant. It was a gap that increased thereafter as Fletcher steamed southeast while Takagi headed east. Admiral Fitch mistakenly believed that the Japanese carriers were closer and at 9.51 p.m. advised Fletcher, "Presence of enemy planes during recovery of our fighters and analysis of later radar plots indicate enemy carrier or carriers about thirty miles bearing 090 at 1930."[30] Fletcher rejected the idea of night surface attack, a technique for which the US fleet was poorly trained, as was soon to be fully demonstrated a few months later at *Guadalcanal*, and decided to retain his surface forces for the expected carrier engagement the following day. "All in all," Fletcher later wrote, "it seemed best to keep our forces concentrated and to prepare to confront the enemy's aircraft carriers on the following morning."[31] Nimitz would later strongly endorse Fletcher's decision: ". . . not to attempt such an attack [surface] was sound . . . [Fletcher] was correct in not dispersing his forces at that particular time when he did not know the composition of the enemy."[32] Even if Fitch's information had been correct, a surface attack would have been a grave risk given that the direction of movement of Japan's carrier fleet was completely unknown. Furthermore high-speed steaming, using up precious reserves of oil, would have been risky given the sinking of the fleet's oiler, the USS *Neosho*.

Neither was a night air attack considered. Flight executive officer, Turner Caldwell, later an admiral himself recalled that the young carrier fliers, "did not have much respect for Fletcher, as he was indecisive and knew little about aviation," but on mature reflection in later life Caldwell admitted that although all the pilots were qualified in night landings "at that time we had no doctrine nor training for night combat."[33] Takagi and Hara also discussed the possibility of a night surface attack with Inoue and their staffs. Although the Imperial Japanese Navy was famously very well trained and skilful at night fighting, their forces included just two heavy cruisers and they were uncertain as to American strength. After the war Admiral Hara admitted, "We gave up the idea because our main mission, as defined in Operation MO, was to provide distant cover to the invasion force. This was for us all the more essential because we guessed that the following day would be the decisive one."[34] Although the successful return of eighteen of his twenty-seven attack aircraft was testament to the night flying skills of his pilots the loss of nine experienced crews was necessarily a blow to the offensive capability of Admiral Inoue's force. For the following day Takagi would have just ninety-six serviceable planes versus Fletcher's 117. Thus ended a crushingly disappointing day for the Japanese offensive. Inoue bore the shame of being the first commander to lose a major warship, a carrier to boot. The invasion force had also been turned back.

During the night the opposing fleets prepared for dawn searches and the expected carrier engagement the next day. Though the two carrier fleets moved away from each other during the night, both Admirals knew that the following day, 8 May, would bring on the major battle. Inoue and Fletcher were anxious for action; Inoue to avenge the day's failures and to clear the way for the Port Moresby invasion, while Fletcher needed to interdict the Japanese troop convoy knowing that, with the loss of his oiler, *Neosho*, he could only stay on station for a further two days. Aboard the *Lexington*, Captain Frederick Sherman was so well prepared that he had calculated within minutes the time that Japanese aircraft would launch their attack on the US fleet.

In hindsight 7 May had been a 'comedy of errors' for both fleets, mainly in terms of reconnaissance, identification and communication. H. S. Duckworth, *Lexington*'s flight officer, would later reflect, "Without doubt, May 7 1942, vicinity of *Coral Sea*, was the most confused battle area in world history."[35] Fletcher had enjoyed the lion's share of the luck; the detachment of Crace's support force had fortuitously drawn away the bomber attacks of Takagi's planes that would otherwise have been available to attack the *Lexington* and *Yorktown*. Perhaps more importantly bad weather had shrouded Fletcher's carrier force.

The Battle of the Coral Sea Continued: Shokaku Wounded, USS Lexington Sunk [8 May 1942]: Just after midnight, Admiral Fitch, in command of the tactical operations of the battle, suggested to Fletcher that at dawn he wanted his reconnaissance pilots to search 200 miles north and 125 miles south where the chance of finding the Japanese fleet was highly likely. Fletcher answered, "As usual I agree with you thoroughly. I will change course to the west."[36]

The two fleets found each other at almost the same time. At 8.02 a.m. Fletcher's radar had picked up a bogey eighteen miles to the northwest and it was clear that Task Force 17 had been spotted. In return, twenty minutes later, Lieutenant Joseph Smith spotted Takagi's strike force. They were placed some 120 miles to the north of Fletcher's carriers whereas Inoue's search operators were much closer to the mark in their estimate that the fleets were 225 miles apart. By 9.25 a.m. both *Lexington* and *Yorktown* had launched their strike forces. Fletcher dispatched 22 Dauntless dive-bombers, 12 Devastator torpedo planes and 9 Wildcat fighters from the *Lexington* and 24 Dauntless, 9 Devastators, and

6 Wildcats from the *Yorktown*; a US strike force of 82 aircraft in total. Takagi's strike forces, comprising sixty-nine planes were launched shortly before; the Japanese admiral steamed south after them. At 9.08 a.m. Fletcher transferred tactical command to Fitch, leaving himself free for the complexities of strategic command, most importantly the logistical problems posed by the lack of available fuel.

At 10.43 a.m. Fitch turned his fleet northward and formed his fleet into the classic 'Victor' formation that had originally been devised by Vice-Admiral Frederick Sherman, who now commanded the *Lexington*; a circle with the two carriers placed at the center some 3,000 yards apart. By contrast Japanese defense required supporting cruisers and destroyers to back away to give their aircraft carriers maximum capability to maneuver away from torpedoes.

Fletcher placed little reliance on anti-aircraft defense and knew that the fleet's main defense would come from the seventeen Wildcat air patrol planes and the twenty-three dive-bombers on anti-torpedo plane patrol. At 10.57 a.m. Lieutenant-Commander Joe Taylor, commander of VT-5, broke the tension aboard *Yorktown* when he told his flight commander, "OK Bill, I'm starting in."[37] Two minutes earlier *Lexington*'s radar operator had announced, "Large numbers of echoes 70 miles north-east."[38] Six minutes later both US aircraft carriers scrambled their nine reserve Wildcat fighters to meet the incoming Japanese bogeys. Battle was imminent. Given the accuracy of Sherman's predictions as to the timing of the arrival of the Japanese attack, it was a gross oversight by the defense operations commander that there were only eight Wildcats in the air guarding the fleet; furthermore these aircraft were running short of fuel and needed to land. Meanwhile the scrambled Wildcats were disadvantaged by having to climb into the fight with Zeros, which were already advantaged by their maneuverability. Outnumbered, Admiral Fitch suggested that the spare twenty-three Dauntless dive-bombers, albeit hopelessly outclassed by the Zero, could nevertheless be used to disrupt the Japanese bombers. However, given the number of bombers and torpedo planes that got through to the US carrier fleet, the competence of Fitch's defensive plans has to be questioned.

At 11.13 a.m. the 5-inch port side anti-aircraft guns on the *Lexington* opened fire. Pilot Ralph Wilhelm reported that the "sky was just a solid blanket of anti-aircraft burst all between 1,000 and 3,000 feet altitude." Thirteen torpedo planes surrounded the *Lexington* and at 11.18 a.m. Sherman turned sharp to starboard to avoid the 'fish' dropped by the leading attacker. Later as the Japanese 'Kate' bombers attacked, Sherman gave orders to turn his stern to the attacker to minimize the target; as the aircraft carrier started to move Commander H. S. Duckworth screamed "Don't change course, Captain! There's a torpedo on each side of us running parallel!"[39] Japanese torpedoes were fired from all angles. Captain Sherman reported,

> I turned to port with full rudder to bring the first torpedoes ahead. From then on the torpedoes were coming from both starboard and port, and I maneuvered with full rudder both ways as I considered best to avoid torpedoes.

> Some from starboard crossed ahead; two others ran
> parallel to the ship, one on each side; some from port ran
> ahead; two ran under the ship without hitting. At 11.20
> a.m., first torpedo hit ship and exploded just forward of
> the port forward gun gallery . . .[40]

The 40,000 ton fully laden carrier had avoided eleven torpedoes but took two hits. In sick bay Chaplain Markle remembered "several heavy shocks which seemed to raise the ship up as if going over a hump."[41] Markle was quickly introduced to the horror of battle at sea. Amidships he found

> four men nearly naked and crying for help, having been
> horribly burned. A Filipino cook who was there in the
> passageway helped me get the men on cots, take off the
> remainder of their clothes and give them a drink of water.
> One of these injured men was given a morphine injection
> to relieve his suffering . . . men kept coming in from the
> 5-inch gun galleries on the port bow, some alone, others
> with help of a shipmate, many with clothes blown off and
> skin literally dripping from their bodies.[42]

US Navy commanders may have had doubts about the accuracy and effectiveness of their anti-aircraft batteries, but that is not how it appeared from the point of view of Japanese pilots. After the battle Flight Captain Shigekazu Shimazaki reported, "We encountered a veritable wall of anti-aircraft fire. The aircraft carriers and their escorts darkened the sky with their tracer bullets, shells and shrapnel. It seemed impossible that we could survive such a stream of anti-aircraft gunfire."[43] Several of the attacking torpedo planes were shot down by anti-aircraft fire. Similarly the USS *Yorktown*, urged on by frequent course changes ordered by Captain Elliot Buckmaster as he saw each dive-bomber commit to his dive, weaved from side to side to avoid *Zuikaku*'s bomber squadron. Observing Buckmaster yank the *Yorktown* in desperate defensive maneuvers, Commander Elliot Shanklin, gunnery officer of the USS *Astoria* noted the "violent maneuvers, the most radical I saw during the war."[44]

Apart from two torpedo hits on the port side and two glancing bomb strikes that killed a 5-inch gun crew and caused sixty-six casualties in all, *Lexington* appeared to have escaped the first Japanese attack relatively intact and was still able to steam at twenty-five knots. At 12.40 p.m. Commander 'Pop' Healy, in charge of *Lexington*'s damage control teams, reported to Captain Sherman, ". . . we have stopped up the holes made by the torpedoes, the fires are now out and the vessel will be almost back on an even keel in a few moments, but, may I suggest, Captain, that if you intend to be hit by any other torpedoes it would be as well to take them on the starboard side."[45] However, one torpedo hit had forced the shutdown of some of USS *Lexington*'s boilers. More seriously the other torpedo had fractured the aviation fuel gasoline pipelines causing vapors to seep into an adjoining electrical generator compartment. *Yorktown*, apart from a few opened plate seams from near misses, was unscathed. Fletcher radioed to Nimitz, "First enemy attack completed, no vital damage our force."[46] Fletcher's carriers suffered the loss of thirty-three planes that appeared to be a reasonable exchange for the reported sinking of the *Shokaku*. Jay Taylor had reported after his torpedo attack on the fleet carrier *Shokaku*,

> The area on the port side from the bow aft for about 50 to 100 feet was one mass of flames from the waterline to the flight deck. The flame was exceptionally intense. It looked like an acetylene torch, and appeared to be coming from inside the ship. Another small fire was burning at the starboard quarter . . . the fires were burning so fiercely. It is believed probable that this carrier was so badly damaged that it finally sank.[47]

However, this turned out to be a false report. In fact poor American attack techniques allowed both the Japanese fleet carriers to survive, although the *Shokaku* did take two hits from 1,000 lb bombs from *Yorktown*'s twenty-four Dauntless dive-bombers; the second killed 223 crewmembers and rendered its flight decks inoperable. The pilot, Lieutenant John Powers, who dropped the telling second bomb from his VB-5 Dauntless dive-bomber, had been hit by Japanese fighter cannon but continued to descend to 1,000 foot before releasing. He failed to pull out of his dive when the blast from his bomb blew the wings off his Dauntless dive-bomber. Subsequently he was posthumously awarded the Congressional Medal of Honor. Nevertheless the failure of the US to land torpedo hits was significant; the Japanese reported that the Americans had "slow torpedoes and long range. We could turn away from them."[48] Both of Japan's fleet carriers survived. It was the first indication of the US Navy's chronic deficiency in torpedo technology.

All eleven torpedoes dropped by Commander Brett's VT-2 Douglas Devastators missed their target. The *Zuikaku* was not touched. At 11.45 a.m. a third bomb was landed on the *Shokaku* by Dauntless dive-bombers from the *Lexington*; 108 Japanese sailors were killed and a further forty wounded. Captain Jojima requested permission to retire. Without aircraft lifting capability the *Shokaku* had effectively been put out of action and needed to return to Japan for repair. Returning aircraft were directed to the *Zuikaku*. At midday the two carrier forces' returning aircraft crossed and engaged in a dogfight before getting back to their carriers. The returning Japanese pilots claimed that one of the US carriers had been sunk and the other badly hit by three bombs. The torpedoing of an American battleship (even though none were present) was also claimed as well as damage to a light cruiser. Massive exaggeration of bombing results would become a feature of Japanese carrier pilots reporting during the course of the war.

Licking their Wounds: While the attacks on the *Lexington* and *Yorktown* had officially cost thirty Japanese aircraft, thirteen more planes were lost in landing and other accidents; others needed servicing or repair while many were stuck below decks on the damaged *Shokaku*. Rear-Admiral Ugaki, with *Shokaku* inoperable and with just nine remaining serviceable planes on board *Zuikaku*, informed Admiral Inoue that a second strike was not possible. Ugaki was ordered to retire. It should be noted that even at this stage of the war, strains were already evident in the logistics for the Japanese Navy. Japan's fleet carriers entered the engagement at the *Coral Sea* with a 25 percent shortfall in strike aircraft. As for *Shoho*, she started the battle with eighteen aircraft, nine fewer than her full complement (i.e. 30 percent under capacity). Takagi reported to Inoue that there were "no prospects for a second attack today."[49] Apart from the lack of planes, Takagi was also concerned that a number of his ships were short of fuel. At 3.45 p.m. Takagi's forces were formally instructed to "suspend attack and head north."[50]

Further reports of US ships prowling in the *Louisiades* by a Rabaul-based reconnaissance plane, clearly referring to Admiral Crace's support group, helped persuade Inoue that the slow moving troop convoy was still at risk. Given that their information was that at least one of the US carriers was sunk and the other one severely damaged, withdrawal was a curious decision. After all Japan still had one operational carrier. However, Japanese intelligence had completely failed to work out the US force dispositions and there lurked the suspicion that there might still be an American carrier unaccounted for. Admirals Fletcher and Fitch had come to believe erroneously that there was a third Japanese fleet carrier in the vicinity. Japan's troop ships retreated back to Rabaul—their commanders believing that a further opportunity to take Port Moresby would soon present itself.

It appeared that both US carriers had survived and would be able to launch further strikes, but at 12.47 p.m. a huge explosion, caused by the ignition of gasoline vapors by an electrical spark, killed twenty-five men and started a fire on the *Lexington*. The wounded included 'Pop' Healy who was seriously injured and later died; although the officers and crew did not know it, the *Lexington* was doomed. With one carrier wounded, concerns about fuel, the number of available serviceable aircraft, enemy fighter superiority, as well as uncertainty about the ability to find the Japanese fleet in the worsening weather, Fletcher, after conferring with Fitch, decided that he should remove his carrier fleet to safety. As his friend and cruiser commander Rear-Admiral 'Poco' Smith recalled, "Fletcher was forced to clear the area, get well south, fuel his units, ascertain damage and lick wounds."[51] At 13.52 p.m. Fletcher radioed Nimitz, "*Yorktown* can now make 30 knots. I propose retire tonight to fill *Yorktown* complement planes as far as possible from *Lexington* and send that ship to Pearl."[52]

Fletcher was considering a night surface attack when a second explosion on the *Lexington* produced billows of black smoke. At 14.50 p.m. Sherman signaled, "Fire amidships is not under control."[53] By now temperatures below decks were approaching the critical level of sixty degrees at which level torpedoes could spontaneously combust. Some twenty minutes later another huge explosion blew out hull plating. All plans for a surface attack were forgotten. The fires were deemed to be uncontrollable at 15.38 p.m. and the USS *Lexington* was abandoned at 17.05 p.m. From his flag room Admiral Fitch called down to Sherman and said, "Well Ted, let's get the men off."[54] The only good news Fletcher received that afternoon was that the Japanese troop convoy was spotted steaming north 180 miles north of the *Jomard Passage*.

It would take time to move the nearly 2,735 men off the *Lexington*; in the meantime a massive explosion ripped open the *Lexington*'s flight deck hurling planes and debris in the air. In places the carrier's hull glowed red with the heat. Two hours later Rear-Admiral Fitch ordered his flagship to be torpedoed by the USS *Phelps*; at 7.52 p.m. the *Lexington* rolled over and sank with its last breath a mighty underwater explosion. The scuttling of USS *Lexington* proved a controversial decision and Admiral King would take the view that she could have been saved. Nimitz was more supportive of Fletcher.

In this first ever carrier battle, the first sea battle in history in which the capital ships of the combatants never sighted each other, respective losses would suggest that Japan had had the better of the contest. Japan had lost the light carrier *Shoho* (11,000 tons), 1,074 men and seventy-seven aircraft; meanwhile the US Navy lost a full fleet carrier, USS *Lexington* (42,000 tons), sixty-six aircraft and 543 men, plus a tanker and destroyer. In addition the USS *Yorktown* was damaged and would require repair back at *Pearl Harbor*. Just thirty-six planes were operational with a further twelve able to be repaired. On the *Yorktown* bodies and body parts were collected and put under canvas to take home. However, when Captain Buckmaster realized that many of his crew were turning back from the canteen when faced by this ghastly sight, he ordered the bodies to be quietly buried at sea during the night.

Twenty-year-old Howard Stein, normally a drummer and violinist with the ship's band (Navy musicians train on two instruments: one for entertainment and one for ceremonies), volunteered for the burial detail. The teetotal Stein recalled that they were ordered to take a large shot of liquor before facing this gruesome task—but it had little effect. "The corpsman came by with this bottle of Ten-High whisky and poured a shot for each of us before we went up to the parachute locker. It went down like water."[55]

On the evening of 8 May, Fletcher was composing a report for Commander in Chief, Pacific Area Command (CINCPAC) when he received a message from Nimitz starting, "Congratulations on your glorious accomplishments of the last two days. Your aggressive actions have the admiration of the entire fleet. Well done to you and your officers and men."[56] Nimitz would later report that Fletcher had "utilized with consummate skill the information supplied to him, and by these engagements . . . won a victory with decisive and far-reaching consequences for the Allied cause."[57] It was scant comfort for the loss of the USS *Lexington* and Fletcher would have been much more content had he known that happiness in the Japanese camp was in even shorter supply.

Back in Washington, Admiral Ernest King had been kept out of the loop in terms of what was happening during the two days of battle. Radio silence was a necessary precaution of battle. Also King's 'rule' as he referred to it was to 'let them go on' rather than to signal "How are you doing?"[58] King believed that an operating fleet needed "all the communications they can use in order to coordinate their work effectively."[59] King may have been kept in the dark during the battle but afterwards he closely inspected the performance of his sea commanders. Over Rear-Admiral Fletcher's performance at the *Battle of the Coral Sea*, Nimitz and King were in profound disagreement. While Nimitz proposed Fletcher's promotion to vice-admiral and the award of a Distinguished Service Medal, an admiral who had lost his beloved *Lexington* did not impress King, who had previously averred that he would not give medals to commanders who lost ships. King refused to reward Fletcher. In a pattern that would become familiar, King was slow to release information about losses. The loss of a fleet carrier could only be bad news. As Nimitz noted in a private letter to King, "At the present stage of our carrier building program, we cannot afford to swap losses . . ."[60] For three weeks, his British counterpart First Sea Lord, Sir Dudley Pound, was kept under the impression that the *Lexington* had merely been damaged. Even his own naval secretary, Frank Knox, was kept in the dark.

In Japan, the ramifications of *Coral Sea* were equally stark. Inoue had the humiliation of having to report Japan's first major setback since the start of the *Pacific War*. At 10.00 p.m. Yamamoto sent a message to his former protégé ordering him to "destroy the enemy to the fullest extent of your power."[61] This was no longer a realistic prospect with *Zuikaku*, Japan's only functioning strike carrier in the *South Pacific*, having only a few planes still operational.

Bombers and Bombs: There were lessons to be learnt from the battle. The American 1,000 lb bombs proved to be significantly more destructive than the Japanese relatively small 250 lb bombs. The Douglas SBD Dauntless dive-bomber had proved to be the American carriers' most potent aircraft. It was a tough heavily built plane affectionately referred to as 'the barge' by its crew of two, a pilot plus an enlisted radioman-gunner. It was about 25 percent heavier than its Japanese equivalent, the 'Val' and, unusually for an American plane, had a longer range than its counterpart. The Dauntless' more powerful engines gave it a top speed of 250 mph and a cruising speed of 152 mph. It had two 0.50 caliber machine guns in its cowling and could be used for reconnaissance or patrol. In operation, the Dauntless pilot would aim to approach from 20,000 feet and then dive out of the sun to avoid detection. The target would be lined up using a small glass window in the floor under the pilot's seat. Diving at seventy degrees the pilot would deploy dive-breaks on the trailing edge of his wing. At speed the pilot would experience weightlessness. At about 2,000 feet, the pilot would pull a bomb release lever and then have to pull hard on his joystick to climb out of the dive. The snap pull-out would often result in a momentary black out.

By comparison the US Devastator torpedo plane, introduced in 1937, was slow and only had a range of 150 miles. Furthermore the American Mark XIII torpedo was notoriously unreliable if dropped above 120 foot or at more than 100mph; at this height and speed the Devastator was exposed to greater and longer defensive fire than its Japanese counterpart. For the Japanese, the Nakajima B5N Type-97 'Kate' carrier attack plane and its air-launched torpedo proved itself to be a reliable ship killer with a range double that of the Devastator. There were drawbacks however. Like the Mitsubishi A6M

Type-O Zero fighter, the Type-97's range and maneuverability came at the expense of armor protection for pilot and 'self-sealing' fuel systems.

However, though the Aichi D3A1 Type-99 dive-bomber 'Val' proved a reliable performer, its inability to carry large bombs made it inferior to the Dauntless. As for the legendary Zero fighter, in the early phases of the war, because of its speed, ability to climb and maneuverability, it generally had the upper hand against the US Navy's Grumman F4F-4 Wildcat, though, like the Nakajima 'Kate,' it too suffered from poor armor and a lack of a self-sealing fuel tank. As a fighter the Wildcat was sturdy and reliable and was never completely overwhelmed by the more maneuverable Zero. Some pilots rated it highly. British test pilots viewed the Wildcat as the outstanding naval fighter of the early years. Japanese pilots often rated the Wildcats higher than American flyers. Kaname Harada recalled, "the only American fighter that I fought against was the Grumman F4F Wildcat, and the performance was probably the same as the Zero fighter."[62]

As for tactics, by comparison with the Japanese, US Navy pilots were relatively poorly trained and tactically inept. A further handicap was that US aircraft carrier communications and their coordination of bomb and torpedo attacks remained woefully deficient. The policy of single air strikes by single air groups (i.e. each carrier independently) was less effective than coordinated fleet strikes. Some lessons from the *Coral Sea* were mutual. Both fleets learnt that air defenses for their carriers were insufficient both in terms of available fighters and anti-aircraft weaponry. Radar, which would give a major boost to coordination of carrier defense, was not sufficiently developed to be of use to the commanders at the *Coral Sea*. Overall it was a confusing, muddled battle, perhaps displaying more than anything the novelty of the first action in naval history where the combatant's capital ships never came into view of each other. For both sides it was also a first live workout of their aircraft carriers, a new capital ship weapons system that had finally come of age.

Halsey, commanding USS *Enterprise* and Task Force 16, raced to get to the *Coral Sea* to join Fletcher's *Yorktown* and *Lexington*. He was itching to get into battle— literally. Exhaustion, lack of sleep and anxiety brought a skin rash that became progressively more irritable. Halsey later described his ailment as "a general eruption of the skin and a tremendous itching. It took more will power than I had to prevent an occasional scratch, although I knew it was the worst possible thing to do."[63] Halsey missed out on the *Battle of the Coral Sea* by one day as he scurried down from *Pearl Harbor* with carriers USS *Enterprise* and USS *Hornet*. However, because the US Navy would not release the battle commander's name, on 18 May 1942 *Time* magazine assumed it was Halsey, their favorite mariner, who had led the line at the *Battle of the Coral Sea*. *Time* reported that Nimitz "could thank his task-force commanders, sea dogs like bushy-browed Vice-Admiral William Frederick Halsey Jr., a naval aviator who knows the potency of the swift attack, sighted and powered from the air . . ."[64]

The Battle of Words: Both the US Navy press liaison department and the US press grasped eagerly at the first major piece of good news for American force of arms. With at best massive exaggeration, the *New York Times* reported, "The Japanese have been beaten back after a long battle in the Pacific, in which between seventeen and twenty-two of their ships were either sunk or damaged. The enemy is in flight, pursued by the Allied forces."[65] Meanwhile Japan also declared a famous victory. Two US carriers were announced as sunk. On 12 May *Radio Tokyo* had jubilantly announced that:

> In the great Battle of the Coral Sea on 7 and 8 May the Japanese fleet succeeded in sinking the American Saratoga and the Yorktown Class and a capital ship of the California Class, a British warship of the Warspite Class; a cruiser of the Canberra Class was severely damaged; another cruiser sunk, a 20,000 ton oil tanker sunk, and a destroyer sunk. Planes destroyed were 98. Japanese losses were negligible—one small aircraft carrier converted from a tanker and 31 planes.[66]

Japanese hubris was rampant. Admiral Sankichi Takahashi, retired former Commander in Chief of the combined fleet, told a correspondent from the *Asashi Shimbun* that the smashing of the American fleet at the *Battle of the Coral Sea*, unlike the static attack at *Pearl Harbor*, proved that the British and American navies could not live with the matchless Japanese Navy. Hitler sent a warm congratulatory telegram to Hirohito, "After this fresh defeat, the warships of the American navy will hardly dare to oppose the Imperial Navy, since any vessels with presumption enough to join battle with the Japanese fleet may be regarded as already lost."[67] The US Navy publicly and vigorously denied these reports.

In truth the *Battle of the Coral Sea* was a confused encounter in which luck played a greater hand in the outcome than well-engineered plans and skill. Not surprisingly given the newness of carriers as a weapons system there were many operational errors. In particular, air-to-air and air-to-ground radio communications, the use of cyphers and encryption, cutting edge technologies in their infancy, proved highly unreliable. Planes too, performing at the edge of their technological envelope were shown to be fragile pieces of equipment. Just two days' worth of fighting saw both fleets lose their air arms' effective offensive capability. No wonder that the United States set about building streams of escort carrier, effectively airplane transport ships, to enable rapid resupply of new aircraft. The precariousness of oil supply was also noted and helped the United States reassess the long-term needs of fighting a war thousands of miles from a home base. The confusion of the battle was matched by the lack of clarity as to outcome.

As the pre-eminent post-war American naval historian, Samuel Eliot Morison concluded, the *Battle of the Coral Sea* was "a tactical victory for the Japanese but a strategic victory for the United States."[68] The overwhelming importance of the battle to the Allied cause was not the insignificant matter of the sinking of the light carrier *Shoho* or the putting out of action of the *Shokako*, but the saving of Port Moresby that was then weakly defended by inexperienced Australian troops.

In hindsight the importance of the *Battle of the Coral Sea* was even greater than had first been imagined. The fleet carrier *Shokaku* was badly damaged and was lucky to survive sinking when damaged plates sprang loose on the journey home. Moreover the *Shokaku* was fortunate to avoid American submarines and get back to Japan for major repairs. Although the *Zuikaku* escaped any hits, it was also forced to return to Japan to pick up replacement aircraft and pilots. Japanese commanders' belief that both US carriers had been sunk was in hindsight a double boon to the Americans. First Yamamoto and his colleagues were unaware that the *Yorktown* would be available to fight at *Midway* and secondly they believed that there was no necessity to get *Zuikaku* back on station for the *Midway* campaign. Thus neither of Japan's newest fleet carriers would be available for Yamato's *Midway* expedition while *Yorktown* was repaired and played a decisive role—conceivably a major factor in tipping the balance of advantage toward the United States in what would arguably prove to be the deciding battle of the *Pacific War*.

Psychologically it was a turning point. Even if the Japanese public was misled, the Japanese Navy now understood that they were facing a capable fighting force. Furthermore the US Navy knew that, while its performance in the battle was far from perfect, it could at least compete. Lastly, in the final analysis, the invasion force for Port Moresby had been turned back. The limits of Japan's Empire had been reached.

14 Battle of Midway: Nimitz's Lucky Day

[4–7 June 1942]

[Maps: 14.1, 14.2, 14.3]

Yamamoto's Advance to Midway and the Aleutians: **[Map: 14.1]** Imperial Navy Order No.18, "The Commander in Chief of the Combined Fleet is to cooperate with the army in the occupation of the Midway and strategic points west of the Aleutians."[1] Thus Yamamoto's plan to win a decisive naval encounter and thus the *Pacific War* was set in motion. By 5 May 1942 Yamamoto had won his battle with the army to further expand Japan's defensive perimeter while at the same time trying to tease out the American carrier fleet with the aim, as always with Japanese strategy, of trying to win the '*Tsushima*-style' mega-victory. But how would the US carrier fleet be cajoled into putting to sea? **[See Appendix L: The Battles of Attu and Kiska]**

The plan was to occupy America's *Aleutian Islands*, which curl out into the northwest *Pacific* like a dog's tail from the south of Alaska. In addition Yamamoto's new naval expedition intended to extend Japan's reach by the occupation of the *Midway Islands* that Vice-Admiral Chuichi Nagumo described as the "sentry for *Hawaii*,"[2] albeit one that lay a not inconsiderable 1,300 miles west of *Honolulu*. These were US territories and surely Admiral Nimitz would have to send his fleet, including his carriers, to their rescue? If so, for Yamamoto and Japan, the hoped for 'knock-out' victory could be at hand. As the Americans had done with MacArthur, the Imperial Japanese HQ had plumped up Yamamoto's reputation for propaganda purposes and in doing so had handed him power, which they would later regret. Opposition to Yamamoto's plans within Naval HQ in Tokyo was swept aside when he threatened to resign unless he got his way. In terms of his popularity in Japan, Yamamoto was in his pomp.

Yamamoto's strategy would unfold with an invasion of the *Aleutians* to be followed immediately with the capture of *Midway Island* with transports carrying 2,000 troops sent from *Saipan*. Air support would come from Vice-Admiral Nagumo's carrier force lying off *Midway*. Meanwhile Yamamoto, with Japan's main force, would wait north of *Midway* blocking the path of the US carrier fleet's fastest route from *Pearl Harbor* to the *Aleutians*. It was a battle plan with split objectives for the Japanese navy; providing support for the occupation of the *Aleutians*, providing air cover for the amphibious invasion of the heavily defended *Midway* some 1,670 miles to the south, and lying in wait to destroy the US carrier fleet. Above all Yamamoto assumed that he would dictate the course of events. As Mitsuo Fuchida, a fleet aircrew captain, and Yamamoto's strike coordinator, who had led the first strike at the *Battle of Pearl Harbor*, would later point out, there was a "blithe assumption that [the enemy] would be taken by surprise."[3]

As was typical of Japanese war planning, a complex disposition of its forces was planned for Operation MI (Midway). The cream of Japan's naval forces would be utilised, including 4 modern fleet carriers, 4 inferior assorted light carriers, 3 seaplane tenders, 11 battleships, 22 cruisers, 65 destroyers and 21 submarines. Yamamoto's battle fleet would be divided in two; the four fleet carriers of the First Carrier Strike Force would advance to the north of *Midway* to support the planned amphibious landing while the main battle fleet would lie 300 miles further north, ready to support either the *Midway* strike force or the *Aleutian* campaign (Operation AL). For Nagumo there were concerns that the main fleet was so far away. Meanwhile Vice-Admiral Nobutake Kondo, the Second Fleet commander, had pointed out the risks of attacking *Midway* with its two airfields capable of sending heavy bombers against the Japanese carrier force.

At the heart of the plan there was a degree of complacency and hubris. Yamamoto believed that Admiral Chester Nimitz, after the heavy losses taken by the American fleet at *Pearl Harbor*, would necessarily adopt a defensive posture. Indeed it was assumed that, after *Pearl Harbor*, US naval strategy would be based only on attrition and that Nimitz would seek to save his fleet until America's industrial might and its productive capacity could come to his rescue with streams of new war *matériel*. At the beginning of May 1941, in a naval war table game conducted to simulate the attack on *Midway*, Vice-Admiral Matome Ugaki, the selected umpire, decreed that the early deployment of Red Force (US) commander's carriers on the flank of Blue Force's (Japan) approach was not allowed. Ugaki justified his intervention by arguing that Americans did not have the fighting spirit necessary to carry out such an aggressive maneuver. Officially it was decreed, "Although the enemy lacks the will to fight, it is likely that he will counter-attack if our occupation operations progress successfully."[4]

Why it was likely that a frightened enemy would be more likely to engage in counter-attack rather than a surprise flanking attack was never explained. Even the raid on *Tulagi* in the *Solomon Islands* on 4 May by a US carrier (Rear-Admiral Jack Fletcher's USS *Yorktown*) did not alert the fixed mind-set of the Japanese hierarchy that Americans were capable of springing surprises. Yet two years earlier Yamamoto had told a group of Japanese schoolchildren, "It is a mistake to regard the Americans as luxury loving and weak. I can tell you Americans are full of spirit of justice, fight, and adventure."[5] Perhaps hubris fostered by the lavish plaudits he received after *Pearl Harbor* had subsequently dimmed his objectivity. The sending of two fleet carriers to the *Coral Sea*, some 2,200 miles from *Hawaii*, should have alerted Japan's naval high command to the US Navy's aggressive mind-set. Likewise the daring Doolittle Raid. In their estimation of the enemy, Yamamoto and the Imperial Japanese General Staff had mistakenly concluded that the Americans would only risk a carrier engagement if goaded. While Admirals Ernest King and Chester Nimitz certainly wanted to preserve their fleet carriers, both men were 'aggressively minded' and were well prepared to take justified offensive risks.

Either Yamamoto chose to ignore the warnings or indeed hoped that the Americans would fall for the bait and let their aggression lead their fleet carriers to be drawn into a decisive engagement. If Nimitz responded to the invasion of *Midway*, US sovereign territory, by sending his carriers out from *Pearl Harbor*, Yamamoto intended to destroy them and win the conclusive battle on which Japan's whole war strategy depended. Alternatively *Midway* and the *Aleutians* would be taken at minimal cost. The value of these assets was debatable. American command would never understand the logic of the Japanese invasion of the *Aleutians* where its soldiers, difficult to resupply, were left to huddle cold and starved in primitive huts. Even the value of the *Midway* was questioned. A Japanese airbase on *Midway* would have a maximum radius of 600 to 700 miles that could easily be avoided in the vast expanses of the *Pacific*. As with the *Aleutians*, supply was another problem. "Had he [Yamamoto] really taken into thorough account the enormous drain on resources and difficulty in maintaining supplies on such an isolated island," observed Commander Tatsukichi Miyo, First Section Air Officer of the Navy General Staff, "or the reduction in air strength necessary in other areas in order to keep it [Midway] up . . ."[6]

Commander Layton, Captain Rochefort, and Naval Intelligence: What never seemed to have occurred to Yamamoto was that Nimitz and his Chief of Intelligence, Commander Edwin Layton, would develop the capability of tracking his every move. In their intelligence network the Americans developed a weapon, which, if it could not win a sea battle, could at least make sure that their fleet carriers, which had immediately been elevated to the status of capital ships (previously battleships) after *Pearl Harbor*, were perfectly positioned to gain tactical advantage through surprise. Intelligence enabled Nimitz to be strategically more aggressive than would otherwise have been warranted.

In the months since the start of the war, the intelligence unit in *Pearl Harbor*, the *Pacific* Fleet Combat Intelligence Unit (HYPO) under Captain Joseph Rochefort, working with similar units in Washington and Brisbane, had developed sophisticated decrypting techniques. Using *katakana* (the phonetic Japanese script), the JAPAN NAVY Code No. 25 (JN-25) had ascribed 45,000 randomly selected five-digit numbers to different phrases and words that were then mixed with five digit numbers from a second book. Using coding clues picked up from the papers of a downed Japanese aircraft at *Pearl Harbor*, Rochefort and his team broke the JN-25 Code, turning the intelligence failures at the start of the war on their head. As Rochefort's most able cryptographer noted, "if you observe something long enough, you'll see something peculiar . . . and then you try to explain the peculiarity."[7]

By the time of the *Battle of Midway*, they were able to decrypt about 5 percent of all Japanese messages, opening an Aladdin's cave of information. Using banks of IBM tabulating machines producing their piles of punch cards, HYPO built up a vast information repository. Thus they were gradually able to build a comprehensive understanding of Japanese naval units and their movements. Just as important as his technical skills, Rochefort, a strong-minded individualist, refused to toe the line fed by intelligence HQ in Washington. He was convinced, 'AF' stood for *Midway* while Washington was equally convinced otherwise. Rochefort, by his force of character and his friendship with Layton, insisted that AF meant Midway and convinced Nimitz. In combination with Commander Layton's uncanny ability to intuit the psychology of the Japanese commanders, he and Rochefort made a formidable team.

Before *Midway*, Rochefort was helped by Japan's delay in the introduction of new JN-25 Codebooks from the planned 1 April start date to 1 June; too late. Throughout the *Pacific War*, the US was helped by Japanese complacency with regard to intelligence. "Unbelievably, the Japanese never tumbled throughout the entire war to the fact that their codes had been broken, and the US Navy, equally blind, continued to believe that its ability to read one after another of the Japanese codes remained a deep, dark secret from its own sailors."[8]

"EXPEDITE DELIVERY OF FUELLING HOSE"[9] may not seem to be the most revelatory of messages but it was enough for Layton and Rochefort to deduce that the Japanese fleet needed to be able to refuel in a mid-Ocean operation. The 'fuelling hose' request suggested to them that an operation in the *South Pacific*, where they could refuel at Truk or Rabaul, was not being considered. Snippets of information from message intercepts were assembled and matched with other intelligence. The result was evidence of a build-up of forces in *Guam* and *Saipan*, a natural launch base for any eastward campaign. Furthermore repetitive mention of 'AF' and 'AO' enabled them to work out that they represented *Midway* and the *Aleutians* respectively. It was a three-dimensional puzzle and Layton and Rochefort, the former engineer and skilled crossword player, were its master. Yamamoto's invasion targets and his force dispositions were discovered.

It settled the Allied quandary as to where the main Japanese fleet would strike next after *Pearl Harbor*. In the intervening months there was a distinct lack of consensus within Allied high command about Japan's likely targets. In the political battle for resources it was opportune for regional commanders to pitch their own areas as the likeliest source of danger. After *Pearl Harbor*, MacArthur feared an invasion of Australia; the British feared an attack in the *Indian Ocean*; 'Hap' Arnold feared an attack on the West Coast of America. Meanwhile Nimitz, supported by Admiral Ernest King, Commander in Chief of the Navy in Washington, called for more resources in the *Pacific*. Meanwhile Army Chief of Staff, General George Marshall had largely won from Roosevelt his demand for prioritisation of support for Great Britain and the Soviet Union in the war with Germany.

In fact Admiral King was largely disposed to support MacArthur's view that the Japanese would strike in the *South Pacific* and he ordered Nimitz to keep Admiral 'Bull' Halsey's Task Force 16 in the area. It was only on 17 May, nine days after the conclusion of the *Battle of the Coral Sea*, when Layton and Rochefort were able to provide overwhelming evidence of Japanese plans for a further *Central Pacific* campaign, that Nimitz was able to recall Halsey to *Hawaii* to prepare for a possible engagement with Yamamoto's fleet.

"Will Admiralty entertain request for carrier from Eastern Fleet,"[10] Admiral King demanded of Churchill on 18 May in an attempt to beef up the carrier force of what he considered to be the more vulnerable *Central Pacific* Region. He had clearly been alarmed by the intelligence insights of Layton and Rochefort. King's concerns were such that, overcoming his antipathy to the British, he wanted Churchill to provide one of the three British carriers, based off Africa, to come to the *Pacific*. Churchill politely declined and thereby missed the chance to have a British 'flat-top' at the *Battle of Midway*. Instead, on 4 May Churchill sent a force of two carriers from Durban to attack *Madagascar* but still failed to persuade its Vichy government to capitulate to the Allies. In exchange for this somewhat unrewarding raid, Churchill earned the undying enmity of Admiral King, who was to be a source of constant friction for the remainder of the war.

Meanwhile Rochefort's team floated a ruse to ensnare the Japanese into giving away more information. *Midway Island*'s garrison commander was instructed to radio that he had a water problem because of the breakdown of a filtration plant on the atoll. By means of this misinformation, which elicited a rush of communication from the Japanese listening post on *Wake Island* regarding the plight of 'AF' (*Midway*), Rochefort managed to glean enough information to suggest that the main attack would be on *Midway* while 'AO' (the *Aleutians*), it was now correctly asserted, was a secondary target. The *Aleutians* were never simply a diversionary target as has been frequently suggested by many historians in the post-war period, because there were very real fears within Japanese high command that America might launch an invasion of northeast Asia from this northerly direction.

Further intelligence refinements were to come. Called for an early morning meeting with Nimitz, a dishevelled, unshaven, bloodshot Rochefort arrived late. He had emerged from his windowless subterranean lair where he led a team of similarly pasty-faced, crypto-analyst troglodytes in their '24 hours a day, seven days a week' quest for information. One of the team of eight recalled that they were "sealed off from the rest of the world like a submarine."[11] Nimitz, a stickler for punctuality, was angry at Rochefort's late appearance, though perhaps less so when his unconventional intelligence officer told him with uncanny precision that the *Aleutians* would be attacked on 3 June and *Midway*, the following day, 4 June. Layton was also prepared to stick his neck out by telling Nimitz, "They'll come in from the northwest on a bearing 325 degrees and they will be sighted at about 175 miles from *Midway*, and the time will be about 6.00 a.m."[12] It was an intelligence *tour de force* that would prove to be the decisive factor in the coming battle.

Such was the familiarity of Rochefort and his team with the Japanese fleet's Morse code operators that he could say of the *Akagi*'s chief warrant officer that he "hits the key like he's kicking it with his foot."[13] More importantly Rochefort's team was able to work out the almost exact disposition of Japanese forces. Indeed it was this intelligence, knowing that Yamamoto's divided force gave him strike force parity, which gave Nimitz confidence to send his carriers to *Midway Island*. Parity; tactical surprise made giving battle a justifiable gamble.

In a less well-known example of the importance of Layton's team, they managed to foil Yamamoto's attempt to get intelligence regarding the location of the US carriers before the *Midway* campaign. In March 1941 Yamamoto had authorized Operation K, a seaplane attack on *Pearl Harbor*. Japanese submarine fuel tenders, a unique Japanese development, had refueled two Kawanashi N8K seaplanes, armed with four 500 lb bombs, at *French Frigate Shoals*. Layton had correctly worked out that the Japanese had used the *French Frigate Shoals* to make this possible and Nimitz duly sent the USS *Ballard* to patrol the area. It meant that when Yamamoto sent submarines there to refuel float planes, they were forced to abandon their reconnaissance mission; another reason why Yamamoto's forces went into the *Battle of Midway*, blind.

Nimitz's Plans and Preparations: Aware of the disposition of Japanese forces, Nimitz came to the conclusion that there was an opportunity for a surprise attack on the Japanese carrier force; he was of course aware from intelligence that the *Battle of the Coral Sea*, which had inflicted modest levels of damage on the Japanese fleet's most modern carriers *Zuikaku* and *Shokaku*, had forced their return to Japan. As a result Nimitz knew that his carrier forces would be evenly matched.

Rear-Admiral Fletcher, aboard the damaged USS *Yorktown* [CV-5], was recalled at haste from the *Coral Sea*, to be ready to lead a force of three carriers to go up against Nagumo's task force that was now heading for *Midway Island*. Denuded of their *Coral Sea* carriers, the Japanese would have four fleet carriers instead of the six that Yamamoto had originally planned for: *Akagi* (Nagumo's flagship), *Hiryu, Kaga* and *Soryu*. Up against them were the US Navy's three carriers, USS *Enterprise* [CV-6], USS *Hornet* [CV-8] and USS *Yorktown* [CV-5].

Although outnumbered in carriers there was almost parity in terms of aircraft. The four Japanese carriers could muster 248 aircraft against 233 on the three American carriers. However, with the *Midway Islands* and their two runways counted, the US also possessed an 'unsinkable' fourth carrier, with an additional 141 aircraft (31 Catalina seaplanes, six Grumman TBF Avengers, four B-26 Marauder medium bombers, 17 B-17 Flying Fortress heavy bombers, 27 Douglas Dauntless torpedo planes, 17 Chance Vought Vindicator dive-bombers, 21 Brewster Buffalo fighters, 7 Grumman F4F-3A fighters, and 1 light utility aircraft). In effect, at the *Battle of Midway*, the US had 353 aircraft versus 248 for Japan as well as five runways to Japan's four. Contrary to much of the *Battle of Midway* mythology of the post-war period, the aerial firepower of the US Navy 'on paper' significantly outweighed that of the Imperial Japanese Navy at the *Battle of Midway*. The legend of America as the plucky little underdog facing overwhelming odds is not supported by the facts.

Japanese and US Aircraft Compared: However, in terms of training, combat experience, and equipment, the balance was in favor of the Imperial Japanese Navy. As Alvin Kernan, an aviator at *Midway* and author of the remarkable account *The Unknown Battle of Midway* [2005], noted, "The Battle of the Coral Sea, just before Midway, had shocked the

American navy with what it revealed about both our planes and those of our enemy. Our fighter planes were inferior to the Japanese Zero, and our torpedo plane was obsolete."[14]

The Grumman Wildcat F4F could be out-turned and out-climbed by the Mitsubishi Zero and there were rumours after *Midway* that the failure of the Wildcats to protect the torpedo bombers was because their pilots had sought to avoid combat. There may be an element of truth in this accusation; the US Navy 'grapevine' had turned the Zero into an all but mythical aircraft. After successive defeats an aura of invincibility attached to the Zero in the same way that in the US military, the Japanese soldier had become a jungle fighter of mythical powers. To be fair to the US fighter flight commanders however, it was clear that fighters were needed to protect the US carriers from attack. Furthermore the best chance of a Grumman Wildcat defeating a Zero was to make a shoot and dive attack from altitude, which meant keeping them at 20,000 feet, a long way from the attack zone of the US torpedo bombers, which was at deck level.

The Nakajima 'Kate' torpedo bomber was also vastly superior to the out-dated Douglas Devastator, "a real turkey,"[15] which was replaced immediately after the *Battle of Midway* by the Grumman TBF Avenger. By comparison in the first year of the war the Nakajima 'Kate,' using torpedoes, put out of action three US fleet carriers, the *Lexington, Yorktown* and *Hornet*.

Even more important was the match-up of the two sides' respective torpedoes. Japan's Type-91 aerial torpedoes, (although not a version of the famous Long Lance torpedo used by submarines and destroyers), were nevertheless longer and thinner than the American Mark XIII torpedo (Length: 17.8 foot versus 13.4 foot and Diameter: 17.75 inches versus 23.4 inches). Their weight (1,847 lbs versus 1,949 lbs) and explosive payload (between 400 and 500 lbs depending on the model) were similar. The important advantages of the Type-91 lay in a speed of forty-two knots versus just 33.5 knots for the Mark XIII. This was a critical difference given that the speed of the carriers on both sides exceeded thirty knots. Ultimately the main defense that a carrier had against a torpedo was the ability to turn away from them as soon as their tracks had been picked up. Speed far outweighed the importance of range with regard to air launch torpedoes. Thus although the Type-91 could only manage 2,100 yards, compared to the 6,000 yards range of the American Mark XIII, this was not as important as it looks on paper. A torpedo plane needed to plant its 'fish' reasonably close to a fast moving target such as an aircraft carrier in order to have a realistic chance of scoring a hit.

Above all, the Japanese, thwarted by the *Washington Naval Treaty*, which limited their tonnage of capital ships, had used the interwar years to develop 'non-controlled' weapons systems, in particular submarines and aircraft carriers. Thus they had focused heavily on aerial torpedo technology and training, had developed mass production for torpedoes and had thoroughly tested them. In the *Pacific War* Japan's Type-91, unlike the Mark XIII, worked from the get-go. Moreover Japanese pilots, unlike their American counterparts, were thoroughly trained in their use.

In the early years of the war US torpedoes were invariably 'duds.' Little attention had been paid to the development of aerial torpedoes in the interwar years. The Newport

Torpedo Station manufacturing facility at *Goat Island*, an important employer in the US state of Rhode Island, providing 4,800 jobs, controlled a monopoly position and was complacent in both manufacture and testing. At a trial of the Mark XIII on 1 July 1942, a month after the *Battle of Midway*, out of ten torpedoes dropped, four sank, five ran wild and only one ran straight and true to the target. Even if their gyroscopes worked, the faulty design of the Mark XIII magnetic triggers as well as the pin contact mechanisms meant that they rarely exploded when they did hit the target. Remarkably, major corrections to the design and manufacture of the Mark XIII were not made until the end of 1943.

A further significant advantage enjoyed by the Japanese carriers was that because of the longer flying range of their more lightly armored planes, Japan's fleet carriers could launch their attack aircraft further out from their target. A US carrier had a safe launch range of just 150 miles though their commanders would have preferred 100 miles. By comparison Japanese carriers had a safe launch range of at least 250 miles. The outstanding Nakajima 'Kate' torpedo bomber had a range of 1,200 miles compared to the Douglas Devastators' 716 miles. Without the element of surprise therefore, the US aircraft carriers were always going to be at a disadvantage against their Japanese counterparts in terms of first launch capability. It should be noted that aircraft never performed at the envelope of their 'book' performance, particularly in combat conditions where gasoline usage in a dogfight could be two to three times greater than at normal cruising speed. Also, as Alvin Kernan noted,

> A carrier plane spent some time on deck warming up and taxiing, burning gas all the time, before taking off at full power, gulping fuel. And once in the air it might circle for up to an hour . . . waiting for other squadrons to get airborne . . . before departing for the concerted group attack that was doctrine in both navies.[16]

The advantages at *Midway* were not all with the Japanese, however. The Douglas Dauntless was possibly the best dive-bomber on either side. The US superiority in aircraft numbers was not only because the US Navy's carriers could carry more planes but also because the Japanese carriers were not fully resourced. Production of key carrier aircraft such as the Nakajima 'Kate' B5N had been stopped or, like the Aichi 'Val' D3A, reduced. In addition, many of the Japanese carriers' aircraft, which had been in continual operation in regions as far apart as Africa, the *Indian Ocean*, the *South and Central Pacific* since before *Pearl Harbor*, were clapped out. Throughout the war the Japanese Air Force was weak on service and repair capability. In wartime conditions and operation, the performance, of what for the *époque* were technically highly advanced aircraft, fell precipitately from optimum levels.

The Missing Carriers: In terms of being 'clapped out,' the same could be said for the crews. Rotation was never built into Japan's armed services' operations. The Imperial

Japanese Navy's training program already seemed to have failed before the *Battle of the Midway*. Navy flying cadets were in such short supply that instructors from the Yokosuka Air Corps were by necessity being drafted into the new aircrews for the returning *Shokaku* and *Zuikaku*. In Japan in the 1930s, overly rigorous screening of naval pilot candidates often reduced the number of graduated pilots to less than one hundred per annum; an absurdly low figure for a Navy that was beginning to reorganize its tactics around its growing fleet of aircraft carriers. When the *Pacific War* started the Japanese Navy unquestionably had around 600 superb pilots with over 800 hours of fly-time. However, what they needed was a whole lot more fliers who were simply 'good.' By contrast the United States Navy took a decision to radically overhaul and expand its training of pilots three years before the start of the *Pacific War*; a decision that the Imperial Japanese Navy only took in 1941; too late. Japan never caught up with its need for Navy pilots as attrition began to take its toll from the first carrier engagement at the *Coral Sea*.

Noticeably, Yamamoto, perhaps aware of the shortage of trained crews, made no serious efforts to get the largely undamaged *Zuikaku* re-equipped in time to join Nagumo's First Carrier Strike Force as it headed for *Midway*. The contrast in urgency shown by Nimitz could not have been starker. His hopes of parity depended on getting the damaged *Yorktown* back into operation. With the carrier, USS *Saratoga*, returned to the West Coast for repair and formation of a new task force, it was imperative that the *Yorktown* was available for the impending action. This was no easy task. A destroyed hanger and lift as well as damaged hull plates would normally take three months to repair; Nimitz told them categorically, "We must have this ship back in three days."[17] Getting *Yorktown* back into action was important not only for giving the US Navy numerical aircraft superiority, but also in terms of confusing Yamamoto and the Japanese navy's senior officers to whom it never occurred that there could be more than two US carriers at *Pearl Harbor* in June 1942. They knew that the *Saratoga* had returned to the American west coast while they believed that the *Yorktown* had been heavily damaged and probably sunk in the *Coral Sea*.

In *Honolulu* 1,400 US workers downed tools on all other projects and worked around the clock to get the repairs done on the *Yorktown*. 'Sprung' plates were covered by new plates and welded into place, then braced with timber. Loaded on board were new upgraded Grumman Wildcat fighters, the F4F-4, for which the unprepared crew had to consult manuals to learn how to operate them. Nimitz also authorised Fletcher to filch several new squadrons earmarked for the *Saratoga*. So short was the turnaround that engineers from the repair ship USS *Vestal* stayed on board to carry on working as *Yorktown* sailed from *Pearl Harbor* on 30 May. Albeit a necessarily 'bodged' repair job, the patched up carrier was ready to leave port and capable of engaging the enemy.

Admiral Spruance to the Fore: This was more than could be said for its commander. Vice-Admiral 'Bull' Halsey was sick. The commander of Task Force 16, comprising the carriers *Enterprise* and *Hornet* had returned to *Pearl Harbor* suffering from

Dermatitis-psoriasis, a severe skin allergy probably brought on by exhaustion after months of hit and run missions in the *Pacific* including the Doolittle Raid. Halsey reported that the itching "was becoming increasingly violent and I was getting little or no sleep."[18] The now frail Admiral had to be stretchered off the *Enterprise*. He was ordered to sick bay from where he recommended Rear-Admiral Raymond Spruance, his cruiser commander, as his replacement.

News of Spruance's appointment was a huge shock to Halsey's task force commanders. There was much mumbling about Spruance being a surface ship sailor—a 'black shoe' officer. Nothing becomes Halsey better than his choice of Spruance for the *Midway* task. In a letter to Fletcher, Halsey praised Spruance's "excellent judgment and quiet courage."[19] Spruance would prove himself to be a brilliant naval commander throughout the course of the *Pacific War* in which he even outperformed his friend and mentor, 'Bull' Halsey. CINCPAC's (Commander in Chief, Pacific Area Command) official Grey Book, a daily synopsis of events, stated on 3 June "The whole course of the war in the *Pacific* may hinge on the developments of the next two or three days."[20] Spruance, a quietly thoughtful and able officer, a lover of gardening and symphonic music, was concerned at his lack of carrier experience. However, in Task Force 16, he had Chief of Staff Commander Browning, who was by reputation the outstanding US Navy air operations tactician. Spruance took command of the *Enterprise* while Captain Marc Mitscher commanded the *Hornet*. For the *Midway* operation, Spruance, while responsible for Task Force 16, would be under the nominal command of the more senior ranked Rear-Admiral Jack Fletcher with Task Force 17, which, after the loss of USS *Lexington* at the *Coral Sea*, consisted just of his own *Yorktown*.

Fletcher's appointment was one that Admiral King, back in Washington, fiercely questioned; he believed that Fletcher had been too timid at the *Battle of the Coral Sea*. Nimitz however had no doubts; he replied to King, "I hope, and believe that after reading the enclosed letter, you will agree with me that Fletcher did a fine job and exercised superior judgment."[21] In reality Fletcher's command was fairly nominal; because of the proximity to *Midway Island* Nimitz decided for once to retain overall operational command. He briefed his commanders individually before the battle and remarkably Nimitz, Fletcher and Spruance never actually met to coordinate tactics or battle plans.

Where were the Pickets? Where were the Spotter Planes? Planning and Operation Failures of the Japanese Navy: For the Japanese, the *Midway* operation was the biggest of the entire war. Operation MI involved some 145 ships and would burn more oil than the Imperial fleet had consumed in the whole of the previous year. It was a great deal of energy to expend for a few square miles of coral and sand. Presumptuously, they renamed *Midway*, the 'Island of the Setting Sun.' Aware of the importance of the *Midway* operation to the entire war, Yamamoto wrote to Plum Dragon, his favourite geisha, "Now comes the crucial time."[22]

The divided Japanese fleet, heading for their respective stations, maintained strict radio silence. Thus when Yamamoto's communications officer picked up a surprisingly large volume of radio traffic coming from the *Hawaii* area, which could well have indicated the presence of the US carrier fleet, Vice-Admiral Nagumo, commander of the main Fleet's Strike Force, was not informed. For Yamamoto surprise trumped everything. In effect the Japanese naval commanders trumped themselves. Until he was attacked, Nagumo believed that there was only the possibility of the *Enterprise* and the *Hornet* being in the area. He knew that the *Saratoga* had returned to the US mainland for repair, while, as he understood it, the *Yorktown* had been sunk at the *Battle of the Coral Sea*. Unlike Nimitz and his commanders, on the eve of battle, Nagumo was completely unaware of the location of the enemy let alone the composition or disposition of its forces.

As a result of failures by Yamamoto to make timely placement of his submarine pickets, the arrival of the three American carriers at *Point Luck* to the northeast of *Midway* went undetected. Poor operational planning meant that submarines, which should have been in place on 1 June, did not arrive until 3 June. The man responsible for this serious failure, Vice-Admiral Marquis Teruhisa Komatsu, was a cousin of the Empress and one of Emperor Hirohito's closest friends. As commander of the Sixth Fleet's submarine forces he was responsible for the placement of pickets but he failed even to attend planning sessions held aboard the battleship *Yamato*, sending juniors in his place. Apparently the hubristic Marquis Komatsu, perhaps typical of many senior officers in the Japanese Navy, was so confident of victory at *Midway* that he was preoccupied with follow-up plans for the seizure of the *Panama Canal* and parts of California. The failure of the Japanese pickets, another of those slices of luck that were to assist the US fleet at *Midway*, enabled Nimitz to sustain that essential element of surprise that Layton and his intelligence group had handed him.

On 3 June, as the American carriers steamed toward *Midway* to intercept Nagumo's carrier force, Lieutenant Dick Crowell aboard *Yorktown* reflected, "The fate of the United States now rests in the hands of two hundred and forty pilots."[23] At 9.35 a.m. on the same day a PBY Catalina reconnaissance mission by Ensign Jewell Reid spotted Vice-Admiral Nobutake Kondo's main fleet and sent back a message. Nimitz grinned and handed Layton the report, which suggested that Rochefort's intercepts and predictions were spot on: "This ought to make you happy."[24] A nine plane B-17 strike was sent from *Hawaii* and found Tanaka's transport force and accompanying warships. In spite of dropping 11,000 tons of bombs, they fell harmlessly among his warships and did no damage, though the US pilots erroneously claimed five hits and one probable. A follow-up night raid by Rear-Admiral Patrick Bellinger's PBY Patrol Wing Two was more successful. He improvised and armed his four modified Catalina flying boats with Mark XIII torpedoes. They found Rear-Admiral Raizo Tanaka's troop transports and accompanying destroyers silhouetted by moonlight. They dropped their torpedoes and skedaddled. The *Akebono Maru*, a small oiler was hit, but managed to stay with the convoy. Even though Yamamoto knew from these attacks that his force's approach had been discovered, he did not warn Nagumo that the *Midway* invasion plan had been rumbled.

At noon on 3 June, Nagumo's *Kido Butai* (carrier strike force), still shrouded by poor weather, altered course from east to southeast and increased its speed to twenty-six knots to reach its launch point. On the Japanese carriers, in the early hours of 4 June, the airmen aboard *Akagi, Kaga, Soryu* and *Hiryu*, having been woken by a bugle call at 4 a.m., were eating rice, miso soup, pickles, chestnuts and warm sake before preparing for their strike on the airfields of *Midway*. The maintenance crews had been working since 2.45 a.m., arming and fueling their planes and manhandling them into elevators. The planes were then pushed into take-off order on deck and fired up to warm their engines, usually a twenty minute process. Nagumo met with his officers at dawn and was able to conclude, "There is no evidence of an enemy task force in our vicinity."[25] It was a false sense of security that came from a number of basic failures in his task force's intelligence gathering. At 4.30 a.m. Nagumo ordered the first strike against *Midway Island*. Thus, completely unaware of the presence of an enemy carrier force, Nagumo prepared a force of 76 bombers and 36 fighters to strike at *Midway*; 126 planes were held in reserve.

Apart from the submarine picket failure, Nagumo did not send out the floatplanes from his surface ships to search for enemy ships in the vicinity of *Midway*. Flight operations had been delegated to a precociously talented young officer, Commodore Minoru Genda, usually credited with the development of massed air attack; some of his tactics had been developed while acting as the Japanese air *attaché* to the Japanese Embassy in London during the *Battle of Britain*. Genda, the young genius of the Navy flying corps, was picked out by Yamamoto to mastermind flight operations at *Pearl Harbor*. Either because of complacency or poor planning, Genda only sent out a single-phase reconnaissance of the area around Nagumo's battle fleet. Only two 'Kates' were used for the most important southerly quadrant, while five Aichi E13A 'Jakes,' floatplanes launched by his escort ships, covered the remaining quadrants. In failing to take this seemingly elementary precaution it should perhaps be remembered that *Midway* was only the second carrier-to-carrier battle in history and that no naval commander on either side, with the exception of Rear-Admiral Fletcher, who had been at the *Battle of the Coral Sea*, was experienced in this form of combat. At the outbreak of the *Pacific War*, aircraft carriers were an immature weapons system. Their complexity is such that, almost seventy-five years later, only six nations have ever built and operated fleet carriers.

Cautious practice would have been to send out a two-phase reconnaissance, whereby a second wave of spotter planes was sent out along the same axis at a half hour gap. As Air Group Commander Mitsuo Fuchida of the *Akagi* commented rather self-servingly after the war,

> A two-phase search would have been wiser ... if we recognized the possibility that this assumption might be wrong and that an enemy force might be present, our searches should have been such as to assure that we could locate and attack it before it could strike at us. For this purpose a two-phase dawn search was the logical answer.[26]

Of the six planes sent out to scout the area around the carrier fleet, the one designated to fly in an eastern sweep failed to leave because of a jammed catapult on the cruiser *Tone*. Nevertheless from the known evidence of the flight paths taken by the reconnaissance airplanes, the heavy cruiser *Chikume*'s No.1 plane flying a 77-degree course should have spotted Task Forces 17 and 18 at approximately 6.30 a.m. Either the plane was way off course or the pilot was flying above cloud cover and peeking through the gaps rather than flying below the clouds. Had Spruance's task force been spotted at this juncture, the outcome of the battle would almost certainly have been different. Nagumo could have ordered a strike by his reserve aircraft against the US carriers and would have prepared his fighter defenses in anticipation of an incoming US attack.

Unlike the US Navy, which believed in a split carrier force as the best means of defense, the Japanese command held their four carriers in tight formation to concentrate the escorting surface ship's anti-aircraft fire as well as maximise the effectiveness of air cover provide by their Zero fighters.

On *Midway* too the crews had been up early: "The atmosphere was quiet and somber, more or less foreboding, you might say."[27] At 5.34 a.m. they received the news that they had been anxiously waiting for from Lieutenant Howard Ady, piloting a Catalina northwest of *Midway*: "ENEMY CARRIER BEARING 320 [degrees], DISTANCE 180 [miles]."[28] US pilots scrambled to their planes. Aboard the USS *Yorktown* at *Point Luck*, Admiral Fletcher received the news at 6.03 a.m. and using short wave radio, TBS, ordered Spruance's group, USS *Enterprise* and USS *Hornet*, "Proceed south-westerly and attack enemy carriers when definitely located. I will follow as soon as the planes are recovered."[29]

First Contact over Midway: **[Map: 14.2]** With Commander Fuchida, who had led the attack on *Pearl Harbor*, not able to fly because of an appendix operation performed en route on the *Akagi*, the attack on *Midway* was led by the strikingly handsome Lieutenant Joichi Tomonaga. 'Val' bombers formed the main part of the strike force that arrived at 14,000 feet over *Midway* at 6.20 a.m. Tomonaga's bombers found themselves barely inconvenienced by fighters that Nagumo's Zero had quickly dealt with. One of *Akagi*'s aviators dismissively reported to Commodore Fuchida, "Enemy fighters are lousy indeed. I think they were almost wiped out."[30]

Seventeen of the American Wildcats and Buffaloes sent out to meet them were shot down. One of the surviving US pilots at the *Battle of Midway* later filed an angry report saying that the Brewster Buffalo "is not a combat aeroplane. The Japanese Zero can run rings around it . . . It is my belief that any commander that orders a pilot out for combat in it should consider them lost before leaving the ground."[31] Tomonaga, whose strike force had lost just four bombers and two fighters, radioed the *Akagi* at 6.50 a.m. and called for a second strike. *Midway*'s airfield was still operable and would need to be shut down to ensure that the Japanese amphibious landing planned for the 7 June was not attacked by US aircraft.

Meanwhile the US fleet's reconnaissance planes had been active. Lieutenant William Chase had spotted Tomonaga's strike force heading for *Midway*; also Lieutenant Howard Ady caught sight of the Japanese fleet and radioed back its location to Rear-Admiral Spruance. Nimitz was informed. Remarkably, the Japanese fleet was just five miles away from the spot predicted by Commander Layton. Nimitz made a suitably laconic remark to his Chief of Intelligence, "Well you were only five miles, five degrees and five minutes off."[32] Aboard the *Enterprise, Hornet* and *Yorktown*, commanders made final plans for strikes against the Japanese carriers. Aircrews had been woken at 1.30 a.m. and were served steak and eggs so as to be fed and well prepared for dawn. When news of the sightings of the Japanese fleet arrived, Rear-Admiral Fletcher, initially holding his flagship *Yorktown* in reserve, ordered Rear-Admiral Spruance and Captain Mitscher to attack as soon as possible. However, the first US attack on the Japanese carrier fleet came from *Midway Island*. At 7.00 a.m. Lieutenant L. K. Fieberling led the initial attack on the *Akagi*. Even with their spanking new Grumman TBF Avenger torpedo bombers, the US pilots' attack approach at deck height, without fighter cover, was suicidal.

Fuchida sitting up on deck, propped up against a parachute pack, wrote in his post-war biography, *Midway: The Battle That Doomed Japan, The Japanese Navy's Story* [1955], "Still they kept coming in, flying low over the water. Black bursts of anti-aircraft fire blossomed all around them, but none of the raiders went down. As *Akagi*'s guns commenced firing, three Zero braved our own fire and dove on the Americans. In a moment's time, three of the enemy were aflame and splashed into the water, raising tall columns of smoke. The three remaining planes kept bravely on and finally released their torpedoes."[33] One of the Avengers struck the flight deck, bounced off and exploded. A single Avenger survived the attack. Meanwhile the *Akagi*, capable of cruising at 31.5 knots, was easily able to turn away from the Americans' slow-moving Mark XIII torpedoes.

At 7.15 a.m., twenty-five minutes after Tomonaga's request for a second strike at *Midway*, Nagumo ordered his reserve aircraft to be fitted with contact fuse bombs. For Nagumo's primary strike force it would be another hour and quarter, about 8.30 a.m., before they would start to land on their carriers.

Spruance Launches Carrier Attack: At 200 miles away from the Japanese carrier fleet but closing, Rear-Admiral Spruance advised by his Chief of Staff, Captain Miles Browning, an aviator, knew that Nagumo's Task Force, distracted by their attack on *Midway*, was at its most vulnerable. Spruance decided to launch all of his bombers from *Enterprise* and *Hornet*. In a meeting convened with his senior flight commanders, Browning took charge and organized the flight plans with a detailed knowledge of enemy positions, which surprised colleagues who were unaware of US access to JAPAN NAVY code-25 and the FLAG OFFICERS code. About forty-five minutes later, when Spruance got to within an estimated 'safe' launch range of 155 miles, planes started to launch from the *Enterprise* and *Hornet*. *Yorktown*, under Fletcher, started its own launches an hour later. Naval historian Rear-Admiral Samuel Eliot Morison observed,

> This fourth of June was a beautiful day, perfect for carrier war if the wind had only been stronger from the enemy's direction. At 19,000 feet the pilots could see all around a circle of 50 miles radius. Only a few fluffy cumulus clouds were between them and an ocean that looked like a dish of wrinkled blue Persian porcelain.[34]

The carriers had turned south away from the Japanese fleet to turn into the wind for take-off. It took Spruance an hour to launch his sixty-seven Dauntless dive-bombers and twenty-nine Devastator torpedo planes. Additionally twenty Wildcat fighters were put up. Because the American strike force was at the edge of its estimated 'safe' range, Captain Browning, not wanting to use up his aircrafts' fuel in time-consuming circling, sent Lieutenant Clarence McClusky's squadron of dive-bombers ahead for a first strike. An hour later, Rear-Admiral Fletcher, lying twenty-five miles astern, launched 17 Dauntless dive-bombers, 16 Devastator torpedo bombers and 6 Wildcats from *Yorktown*. Unlike Spruance, Fletcher kept back half of his strike force. Nevertheless by 8.30 a.m. the US Navy had a numerically impressive 155 strike planes in the air. The fate of the Japanese fleet carriers was now cast.

Thus far superior intelligence and good luck had favoured Spruance and Fletcher. Luck now turned. *Tone*'s floatplane that had been delayed for half an hour by a faulty catapult did an abbreviated dogleg reconnaissance as a result of which it happened on the US fleet. Irritatingly for Nagumo however, the radio message from *Tone*'s spotter plane, received at 8.00 a.m., did not mention whether the US force included carriers. However, twenty minutes later, at 8.20 a.m., Nagumo received the stunning news, "Enemy is accompanied by what appears to be a carrier."[35] Nagumo immediately reversed his earlier decision to fit contact bombs for the planned second raid on *Midway*. Torpedoes were brought out from the stores to ready his Nakajima torpedo planes for an immediate attack against US carriers.

Nagumo now faced a dilemma. With his strike force returning from *Midway* in the next fifteen minutes, should he launch an immediate strike against the US carriers with his reserve force? In which case many of his precious aircraft from the *Midway* strike would have to ditch in the sea. If he waited however, he might be caught by a first strike from the US carriers' torpedo planes and dive-bombers. It was a classic 'horns of a dilemma'; the sacrifice of up to 106 returning aircraft or get off a strike at the US carriers? An immediate launch was not an option. 'Val' dive-bombers on Yamaguchi's *Soryu* and *Hiryu* may have been ready to go but the 'Kates' with their torpedoes were not even armed let alone taken up from the hangar deck and 'spotted' for launch. Before launch of a strike attack, all the participating planes would be 'spotted'/arranged on the fight deck. Nagumo could have sent his dive-bombers, in contravention of the standard practice of combined mass attack, but they would have had to go without a fighter escort because his Zeros needed to be refueled and rearmed. As Vice-Admiral Ryunosuke Kusaka, Nagumo's Chief of Staff, later testified, "I witnessed [how] enemy planes without cover were almost annihilated . . . I wanted most earnestly to provide them [our bombers] with fighters by all means."[36]

Action came thick and fast. While Nagumo was deliberating, another wave of US aircraft arrived from *Midway*. Half of the Marine's sixteen Douglas SDB Dauntless dive-bombers were shot down and the remainder were badly mauled. Again *Midway*'s torpedo bombers went scoreless. Additionally fifteen B-17 Flying Fortress bombers dropped their bombs from 20,000 feet and scored no hits. The wave of Dauntless dive-bombers was followed by eleven Vought SB2U Vindicator dive-bombers led by Major Ben Norris; miraculously nine of them managed to get back to base in spite of the fact that their slow speed made them the butt of Japanese fighter pilot jokes. The Vought Vindicator had been the first monoplane dive-bomber when it was introduced in the early 1930s but was now thoroughly obsolete.

Meanwhile the failure of the more modern *Midway Island*'s Dauntless dive-bombers to land hits on the Japanese carriers was later ascribed to the fact that their Marine pilots had not been trained to 'dive-bomb' but only to 'glide bomb' which was significantly less accurate.

Nagumo's apparent dithering did not please some of his colleagues. Fuchida would later reflect,

> Looking back on this critical moment, ultimately was to decide the battle, I can easily realize what a difficult choice faced the Force Commander [Nagumo]. Yet, even now, I find it hard to justify the decision he took. Should he not have sacrificed every other consideration in favor of sending the dive-bombers immediately against the enemy ships?[37]

An incredulous Vice-Admiral Tamon Yamaguchi, a former Princeton student and then a naval *attaché* in Washington, who commanded the *Hiryu*, wanted an immediate strike against the US carriers even if 'Vals' had to use fragmentation bombs with which they had been armed. He sent an urgent message, "Consider it advisable to launch attack force immediately."[38] Yamaguchi was no fool; in 1912 he had graduated second out of 144 cadets at the Imperial Japanese Naval Academy. Yamaguchi wanted to attack the American carriers with the bombs that were already attached rather than lose time by switching to torpedoes. However, Nagumo decided to land the returning *Midway* strike force and to get them rearmed before going on the offensive against the US carrier forces. Nagumo also radioed Yamamoto to alert him to the presence of a US carrier force and tell him of his plans to launch an attack. Believing there was just one enemy carrier, Nagumo instructed his colleagues: "After completing recovery operations, proceed northward. We plan to contact and destroy the enemy task force."[39]

With the last plane landed at 9.00 a.m. on the *Akagi*, the race was now on to refuel and rearm its aircraft as quickly as possible. On board the *Akagi*, flight officer Masuda observed, "Here we go again. This is getting to be like a quick-change contest."[40] The under-deck hangers were frantic with activity. Bombs, torpedoes, tracer ammunition, fuel lines and loading equipment were littered everywhere. Almost as soon as the *Midway* strike force was landed, Nagumo received a spotter plane report of approaching torpedo planes. At 9.18 a.m. the Japanese destroyer screen signaled the near approach of the enemy aircraft. Zero fighters took off to intercept. On the *Akagi*, Fuchida recalled, "An electric thrill ran throughout the fleet as our interceptors took off amid the cheers of all who had time and opportunity to see them."[41]

US Torpedo Bombers into the 'Meatgrinder': Lieutenant John 'Redskin' Waldron, the hard drinking, "shaggy . . . somewhat uncouth"[42] one-eighth *Sioux*, squadron commander of Torpedo-8 from USS *Hornet*, must have realized that the pilots of his fifteen lumbering Devastator torpedo planes faced almost certain death. Even if they survived the attack an uncertain fate awaited as they had already covered 175 miles to get to the Japanese fleet and only had enough fuel for a 300 mile round trip. The straight talking Waldron, aware that their odds on survival were slim, had earlier told his colleagues, "If there is only one plane left to make a final run in I want that man to go in and get a hit."[43]

At 9.20 a.m. Waldron spotted the Japanese fleet, waggled his wings to signal his squadron to attack and dived towards the Japanese carriers. All the Devastators, bar one piloted by Lieutenant Ensign George Gay, were shot down by the fighter escort cover of forty Zeros before they could make their torpedo drops. "Their distant wings flashed in the sun. . ." wrote the poetic Fuchida after the war, "Occasionally one of the specks burst into flame and trailed black smoke as it fell into the water."[44] Gay managed to release his torpedo but was then shot down. He made a landing in the sea. His machine gunner was killed but Gay escaped capture and almost certain death by hiding under his seat cushion and only inflated his life raft after the Japanese fleet had sailed off. He was the only survivor from Waldron's squadron.

At least Waldron reached his target. The attacks from the US carriers had been launched at such extreme limits of their range that ten Wildcat pilots from USS *Hornet* had to ditch their planes. For reasons never fully explained, Commander Stanhope Ring, a smooth talking naval '*beau ideal*'[45] not known for his piloting or navigational skills but destined to become an Admiral, who had been given the plum command of the whole of the *Hornet*'s air group, chose a course setting at 265 degrees, which was some thirty degrees further north than the actual position of the Japanese fleet. Waldron, who had violently argued with his air group commander before take-off, subsequently broke-off from the others to go south with his squadron to find the Japanese. After an airborne altercation, Waldron told Ring, "Well, the hell with you. I know where they are and I'm going to them."[46] Ring's entire command, the so-called 'flight-to-nowhere' managed to lose half its planes through aircraft being forced to ditch without any engagement with the enemy at *Midway*. The reason why the 'flight-to-nowhere' was so off target remains a mystery with some blaming Ring and others Captain Marc Mitscher, the 'brown shoe' commander of the *Hornet*. To Mitscher's horror only twenty of the fifty-nine planes launched in the morning returned to his ship.

Next into the 'meatgrinder' of Nagumo's carrier defense were Commander Eugene Lindsey and his fourteen Devastators from *Enterprise*'s Torpedo Squadron-6. He had to dive straight into the attack without his covering Wildcat fighters because like Waldron before him he was short of fuel and could not afford to wait. Ten Devastators were shot down. No torpedo hits were scored on the *Kaga*.

From *Yorktown* Commander Lance E. Massey was next to attack with his twelve Devastator torpedo planes from Torpedo-3 Squadron, covered by six Wildcat escorts. They made toward the *Hiryu*. Massey was killed early in an attack described by surviving gunner Lloyd Childers as a "melee with about thirty Zero going crazy in the most undisciplined, uncoordinated attack that could be imagined."[47] Just five planes managed to reach the *Hiryu*; the fast-turning carriers maneuvered to avoid the slow running *Mark XIII* torpedoes. Just two Devastators returned to the *Enterprise*. The survivors of Torpedo-3 Squadron did not include pilot Ensign Wesley Osmus, a stocky, dark haired 23-year-old from Chicago who ditched into the sea and survived until the destroyer *Arashi* picked him up. On board he was interrogated before being taken to the back of the ship where a fire axe was smashed into the back of his neck. Remarkably, when the sailors tried to throw his body overboard, he still managed to cling to the rails until his fingers were crushed; forced to let go, he fell into the *Pacific Ocean* where he drowned. The perpetrators of this war crime were never identified. Quite possibly, Osmus's murderers died when the *Arashi* was later sunk at the *Battle of Vella Lavella* (6 October 1943).

Thus far the slaughter of US torpedo planes, in five waves of attack (the first two from *Midway*), amounted to forty-one planes and eighty crewmen. On board the *Akagi*, Fuchida noted that

> Most of the credit for this success belongs to the brilliant interception of our fighters . . . No less impressive was the dauntless courage shown by the American fliers, who carried out the attack despite heavy losses. Shipboard spectators of the thrilling drama watched spellbound, blissfully unaware that the worst was yet to come . . . As our fighters ran out of ammunition, during the fierce fight battle, they returned to the carriers for replenishment, but a few ran low on fuel.[48]

Lieutenant McClusky's Lucky Strike and Thirty Minutes that Changed the War:
[Map: 14.3] America's fortunes now turned on what proved to be a decisive stroke of good luck. Lieutenant Clarence McClusky with thirty-seven Dauntless dive-bombers was frantically searching for the Japanese fleet. Fuel was getting low. McClusky later recalled, "Call it fate, luck or what you may . . . I spied a lone Jap cruiser scurrying under full power to the North East. Concluding that she possibly was a liaison ship between the occupation forces and the striking forces, I altered my course to that of the

cruiser . . . that decision paid dividends."[49] He guessed correctly, but for the wrong reasons. The Japanese destroyer, *Arashi* (not a cruiser as McClusky had thought) had been left behind to seek out the US submarine, *Nautilus*, after its earlier failed torpedo attack. Nimitz would later attribute the successful outcome of the battle to McClusky's instincts in following the Japanese destroyer.

Finding the Japanese fleet, McClusky now enjoyed a second piece of luck. The last Devastator torpedo attack may have been slaughtered but it had brought the remaining Zero escort fighters down to 'deck' level. It has also been argued that there was a Japanese command failure to hold some Zeros back at a higher level and that they had been poorly coordinated—a somewhat 'armchair' criticism in view of the primitive nature of ship-to-plane communication as well as the confusing 'mists' of battle. Furthermore the evasive action taken by the Japanese carriers had split up the tight carrier defensive box formation that normally held them at 1,300-yard intervals; *Kaga* and *Soryu* were 6,000 yards from *Akagi* while *Hiryu* was out of sight. Before the Zero escorts could climb back to an attack altitude, McClusky's Dauntless dive-bombers, aiming at the 'rising sun' roundels on the decks of the *Akagi* and *Kaga*, bore down from 10,000 feet at a seventy-degree angle.

Enterprise's dive-bomber squadron split in two. McClusky headed for *Kaga* while the other section went after the *Akagi*. McClusky had time to note, "As we neared the bomb-dropping point, another stroke of luck met our eyes. Both enemy carriers had their decks full of planes, which had just returned from the attack on *Midway*."[50]

At 10.22 a.m. a bomb took out the *Kaga*'s rear elevator, while a second bomb hit the forward elevator and went through the upper hangar deck. The aircraft being refueled and rearmed were ripped apart by fire and explosions. Meanwhile a 1,000 lb bomb scored a direct hit on the bridge killing Captain Okada and most of his officers outright. Even worse than the damage to bridge, decks, elevators and hangars, was the rupturing of the aviation fuel lines and the failure of the carrier's fire prevention systems, including the emergency generators and the carbon dioxide fire suppression equipment. Fires soon caused a vast explosion of some 36,000 kg of bombs and torpedoes that blew out the *Kaga*'s sides.

However, it was a day of mixed fortunes for McClusky's squadron. The Dauntless of Frank O'Flaherty and his rear gunner/radio operator, Bruno Gaido, suffered punctures to its fuel tank and they were forced to ditch. Picked up and interrogated by the crew of the destroyer *Makigumo*, O'Flaherty and Gaido were tied up with ropes, attached to weighted fuel cans and thrown overboard. Their murderers were never identified. A mine off *Guadalcanal* would later sink the *Makigumo*. Four other crews from McClusky's squadron flew back but took the wrong bearings and were never seen again. McClusky himself was more fortunate; attacked by several Zeros, one of which his rear gunner, Walter Chochalousek, shot down, his cockpit was shot out and he was fortunate to get back to the *Enterprise* where he found that his plane was riddled by fifty-five bullet holes.

At 10.26 a.m. *Enterprise*'s Dauntless bombers hit Nagumo's flagship, *Akagi*. "The terrifying scream of the dive-bombers reached me first," recalled Fuchida on the *Akagi*, "followed by the crashing of a direct hit. There was a blinding flash and then a second explosion much louder than the first. I was shaken by a weird blast of warm air."[51] The second bomb had exploded on the upper hangar deck and destroyed the middle elevator. A gaping hole in the deck revealed a hangar full of battered aircraft; through the smoke and fire a mangled elevator could be seen. Fuchida recalled, "Deck plates reeled upwards in grotesque configurations. Planes stood tail up, belching livid flame and jet-black smoke."[52]

Secondary combustion occurred as aircraft bombs, heated up by burning aviation fuel, exploded. *Akagi*'s rudder jammed but even more importantly the fire control systems appeared to fail. Fire rampaged uncontrollably throughout the stricken carrier. Nagumo's chief of staff, Ryunosuke Kusaka reported, "When I got down the deck was on fire and anti-aircraft and machine guns were firing automatically having been set off by the fire aboard ship. I had my hands and feet burned . . . Bodies were all over the place . . . that is the way we eventually abandoned *Akagi*—helter-skelter, no order of any sort."[53]

At 10.25 a.m., just three minutes after bombs had wrecked the *Kaga*, thirteen Dauntless dive-bombers from *Yorktown*, led by Lieutenant Richard Best's VB-3 scored three devastating hits on the *Soryu* with 1,000 lb bombs. Two exploded on the upper hangar deck while a third penetrated to the lower hangar deck. Best later recorded, "*Soryu* threw everything at us. I never tried to look where my bomb hit: she was shooting, the battleships were shooting, and the Zeros were swarming around. I dropped all the way to the deck to get out of there."[54] The carrier, which had launched a first strike against the US carriers, was preparing a second strike when the bombs hit home. Within minutes the *Soryu* was an uncontrollable fireball. Seven hundred and eleven crewmen were killed including her captain, Yanagimoto. The remainder of the crew started to be taken off at 10.40 a.m., just fifteen minutes after the first bomb had struck. The *Soryu* was scuttled with a torpedo from the destroyer *Isokaze* at 7.00 p.m.

While the returning McClusky was landing on *Enterprise* with just two gallons left in his tanks, Nagumo set about informing Yamamoto of the early morning disaster. In the space of four minutes, Dauntless dive-bombing squadrons from *Enterprise* and *Yorktown* had destroyed three Japanese aircraft carriers, half of its fleet carriers. "Fires raging aboard *Kaga, Soryu, Akagi* resulting from attacks carried out by enemy land-based and carrier based planes. We plan to have *Hiryu* engage the enemy carriers, in the meantime we are retiring to the North."[55] (Nagumo's assertion that the successful attacks on his carriers were carried out by land-based US dive-bombers was incorrect.) Yamamoto ordered Admiral Kondo with his light carrier *Zuiho* from the *Aleutians* to *Midway* at full speed. Twenty-five minutes after the *Soryu* was scuttled, the destroyer *Hagikaze* put the *Kaga* out of its misery with two torpedoes fired into her side. The *Kaga* sank stern first. Injured Ensign Takeshi Meada noted ruefully that a "comrade carried me up to the deck so I could see the last moments of our beloved carrier, which was nearby. Even though I was in pain tears started to run down my cheeks, and everyone around me was crying; it was a very sad sight."[56] *Kaga* suffered 811 killed including most mechanics, boiler-men, hangar crews and twenty-one pilots. Most were trapped below burning decks from which there was no escape.

As the *Kaga* was sinking, the *Akagi* too was nearing its end. The carrier's increasingly heated fuel tanks exploded. The *Akagi* stayed afloat a little longer. In the early afternoon a shell-shocked Admiral Nagumo was levered out of the window of the bridge and was forced to shimmy down a rope. By the time Fuchida's turn to escape arrived, both the iron ladder and the smouldering rope were too hot to hold; he fell and broke both his ankles. Although a last evacuation had been ordered, Captain Aoki, determined to go down with his ship, lashed himself to the bulkhead. With the carrier still afloat at midnight, *Akagi*'s officers boarded the ship and forcibly rescued him.

The Hiryu versus USS Yorktown: Meanwhile the *Hiryu* alone escaped unscathed as torpedo planes from *Yorktown* failed to score any hits from their attack. *Hiryu* was thus able to launch eighteen 'Val' dive-bombers and six Zeros led by veteran Lieutenant Michio Kobayashi to search out the US carriers. Just before midday, Wildcat fighters above the *Yorktown* intercepted dive-bombers from the *Hiryu*. Although three Zero and six 'Val' bombers were shot down, and a further two 'Vals' were hit by the *Yorktown*'s anti-aircraft gunners, the crew prepared themselves for hits. The carriers' fuel lines were flooded with carbon dioxide. Admiral Fletcher observed, "Well, I've got my tin hat. I can't do any more."[57]

Six Aichi D3A 'Val' dive-bombers weaved through the defensive screen. A bomb rolled along *Yorktown*'s deck and exploded. Another went straight down the smokestack and knocked out five of the carrier's six boilers. A third bomb penetrated the main deck and both hangar decks before exploding in Deck Four. Within an hour the fire fighting crews had managed to put out fires and re-plank the landing deck. Because *Yorktown*'s radar had been knocked out, Fletcher removed his flag to the cruiser USS *Astoria*. Kobayashi failed to return to the *Hiryu* and perished.

Until now Nagumo had believed that there were a maximum of two enemy carriers operating against him with one of them now incapacitated. He must have been astonished to learn that there were still two more carriers 200 miles to the southwest of *Yorktown*. Meanwhile aboard the *Hiryu*, Yamaguchi sent his last ten torpedo planes against the *Yorktown*. The attack was led by the *Hiryu*'s senior pilot, Lieutenant Tomonaga. Knowing that he had ruptured fuel tanks, he realized that he was on a one-way mission.

In spite of the cover provided by twelve Wildcats, four Japanese pilots got through and dropped their torpedoes. On board *Yorktown*, crew could see Japanese pilots shaking their fists. Torpedoes hit the port side; the rudder also jammed. *Yorktown* began to list to the right and Captain Buckmeister gave the order to 'abandon ship' shortly before 3.00 p.m. Hopes of salvaging the long-suffering *Yorktown* evaporated when, as it was being towed back to *Pearl Harbor*, Japanese submarine *I-168* put torpedoes into its side. *Yorktown* rolled over and sank. The destruction of the *Yorktown* demonstrated what might have happened to the rest of the US carrier fleet if McClusky and his dive-bombers from *Enterprise* had not fortuitously found the Japanese carriers first. It has also been pointed out that, had Commander Ring, in charge of the *Hornet*'s air group, not chosen a wrong course "the fourth Japanese carrier *Hiryu*, would likely have not survived to launch the counter-attack that led to the sinking of the *Yorktown*."[58] However, the *Yorktown* would have its revenge. Lieutenant Earl Gallagher, leading his squadron of twenty-four Dauntless dive-bombers from the *Enterprise* including ten Dauntless from the *Yorktown*, which had sought refuge on the *Enterprise*, attacked the *Hiryu*. On board the last Japanese carrier, Admiral Yamaguchi, believing that he had only one more US carrier to sink, was feeding his pilots and rearming and spotting his aircraft for take-off.

With their guard down, Zeros intercepted just three of the US Dauntless dive-bombers. Seeing that Gallagher's group had failed to hit *Hiryu*, *Yorktown*'s Lieutenant DeWitt Shumway, leading his VB-3 group, switched targets from the battleship, which he had been designated to attack and crashed four bombs through *Hiryu*'s decks. Some of the hits may also have come from Richard Best's VB-6. In a now familiar pattern, bombs and fuel in the hangar decks exploded. Below decks those who survived, unable to move upwards, were forced into the bowels of the ship to escape the inferno. At 1.00 a.m. the next morning the order was given for *Hiryu* to be abandoned. At 4.30 a.m. Captain Kaku and Vice-Admiral Yamaguchi waved farewell to their colleagues and stayed on board with the intention of going down with their ship; legend has it that Yamaguchi drowned while calmly watching the moon.

At 4.50 a.m. on 5 June, Yamamoto ordered *Akagi* scuttled, saying to his staff, "I was once the captain of *Akagi*, and it is with heartfelt regret that I must now order that she be sunk."[59] *Akagi*'s accompanying four destroyers fired a torpedo each and put an end to the Japanese strike force's flagship's tortured final hours; 267 men had died. Shortly afterwards the smouldering hulk of the *Hiryu* was also dispatched.

Aftermath and Reactions to Midway: Yamamoto was not yet fully aware of the enormity of the disaster. Three Japanese forces were converging on *Midway*; Vice-Admiral Takeo Kurita from the north with a force of cruisers, destroyers and a seaplane tender; Vice-Admiral Nobutake Kondo from the northeast with two battleships, four cruisers and the light carrier *Zuiho*; and Yamamoto with three battleships, the antiquated *Hosho* (Japan's first carrier commissioned in 1922), and two seaplane carriers. His converging forces were told, "The enemy has been practically destroyed and is retiring to the eastward."[60]

As they raced through the afternoon and early evening, operational command was transferred to Vice-Admiral Kondo. Yamamoto hoped to catch the remaining US carriers by dawn on 5 June and salvage a victory. Spruance would not give him the opportunity; he explained, "I did not feel justified in risking a night encounter with possibly superior enemy forces."[61] Spruance withdrew eastwards though he reversed course the next day to cover *Midway Island*. He later wrote that he had a "feeling, an intuition perhaps, that we had pushed our luck as far to the westward as was good for us."[62] History has never seriously questioned Spruance's decision not to pursue. Having failed to catch up with the US fleet, Yamamoto retired from the battle and headed home.

At *Pearl Harbor*, Nimitz was ecstatic. To Spruance he signaled, "You who have participated in the *Battle of Midway* today have written a glorious page in our history. I am proud to be associated with you."[63] On the island of *Oahu* there was joy and relief. *Hawaii* had lived under the threat of invasion for months. Washington was equally joyous, with Admiral King reflecting that the battle had "put an end to the long period of Japanese offensive action, and restored the balance of naval power in the *Pacific*."[64] This was an understatement. Given the vast advantages that America's pipeline of *matériel* could provide, the balance of naval power in the *Pacific* had swung wholly to their advantage. In exchange for the *Yorktown*, Nagumo had lost four fleet carriers and 2,200 of their crew including precious pilots, along with 234 planes. Some 800 more sailors were lost from the heavy cruisers *Mikuma* (sunk) and *Mogami*.

If King was understated in his conclusion, Vice-Admiral Ugaki, Chief of Staff to Yamamoto, overstated the Japanese position after *Midway*; ". . . [though] we must accept defeat in this operation, we will not have lost the war. There will still be eight carriers in the fleet, counting those, which are to be completed soon. In battle as in chess, it is the fool who let himself be led into a reckless move through desperation."[65] When Lord Privy Seal, Kido Koichi, informed Hirohito of the defeat at the *Battle of Midway*, his facial expression remained impassive; he simply commented that the Navy should "not lose its fighting spirit."[66]

In Japan news of the battle was not made public. The Imperial Japanese Navy orchestrated a cover up. It was claimed that two US carriers had been lost for just one Japanese carrier. The *Japan Times and Advertiser*'s headline proclaimed, "Navy Scores another Epochal Victory!"[67] Hirohito even floated the idea of issuing an Imperial Rescript to *Midway*'s commanders to commemorate their victory. Hirohito was dissuaded but the Naval Ministry sent a message to field commanders with instructions "to quote our damage in the Midway Sea Battle as one carrier lost, one carrier badly damaged, once cruiser heavily damaged, and thirty-five planes failing to return."[68] Any survivors of the disaster were quietly shipped off to the remoter parts of the Japanese Empire. Emperor Hirohito issued a directive to Japanese Naval Staff on 11 June that the wounded should be surrounded by security and prevented from making contact with friends and family "until they could be healed, heartened, hushed and reassigned."[69]

For Vice-Admiral Halsey, recovering in hospital in *Honolulu*, the US victory at *Midway* was bittersweet. It should have been his command, his glory. "Missing the *Battle of the Midway* has been the greatest disappointment of my career, but I am going back to the Pacific where I intend personally to have a crack at those yellow bellied sons of bitches and their carriers"[70] he told a wildly applauding audience of young midshipmen at the US Naval Academy at Annapolis. It would later be said by some that it was disappointment at missing *Midway* that led to the numerous episodes of reckless aggressiveness that marked his later actions in the *Pacific War*.

If the *Midway* was a disappointment for Halsey, it was a disaster for Nagumo's hitherto spotless record. In some quarters, in the post-war period, he had received some criticism for not following up at the *Battle of Pearl Harbor* with a second strike. In spite of considered study of the issue that shows that Nagumo's decision was correct and that Fuchida's critical account is somewhat suspect, his reputation as overly cautious tended to stick. Noticeably, *Tora! Tora! Tora!* [1970], a highly successful Oscar winning Hollywood film about *Pearl Harbor*, fully endorsed the Fuchida line.

Nevertheless in the months leading up to *Pearl Harbor* Nagumo had not put a foot wrong. The *Battle of Midway* has tended to build on Nagumo's somewhat unfair reputation for caution. However, after such a massive defeat, it would have been surprising if some fingers of blame had not pointed to the strike fleet's commander. By June 1942, Vice-Admiral Nagumo was a prematurely aged 54-year-old suffering from bad arthritis, which many ascribed to his over indulgence as a *Kendo* swordsman in his youth. Albeit a 'surface' specialist, inevitable given his graduation from the Imperial Naval Academy in 1908, where he graduated eighth out of 191 cadets, Nagumo was an undoubtedly intelligent officer who had been a fierce advocate of aircraft carrier development and operation. However, the stark fact remains that even if Nagumo had decided not to change his bombers' weapons from bombs to torpedoes, the fate of *Kaga, Akagi* and *Soryu* was decided as soon as the dive-bomber squadrons had taken off from *Enterprise* and *Yorktown*—a maneuver that was completed by 8.30 a.m. After this point there was no way that Nagumo could have forestalled the eventual outcome of the battle.

As for the bomb versus torpedo debate, famously raised by Yamaguchi aboard *Hiryu*, it was a fine judgment particularly given that the Nakajima 'Kate' torpedo plane was the carrier fleet's most potent weapon. Launching an attack with his reserve at 8.30 a.m., when his spotters confirmed the presence of a US carrier in the vicinity, might also have meant forcing large numbers of his first wave to ditch in the ocean. It is more credible to criticize Nagumo for not sending out more scout planes at dawn covering a wider area. A degree of complacency, later described by the Japanese as 'Victory Disease,' may have accounted for this mistake. However, it was not Nagumo's fault that the Japanese picket submarines were not in place in time. To forestall the sinking of his carrier force Nagumo would have needed to have had a fix on the US Fleet and launched his attack aircraft by about 6.00–6.30 a.m. on 4 June; a tall order. There is no getting around the fact that US intelligence, which virtually put the location of the Japanese fleet on a pinhead in the early morning of 4 June, all but guaranteed the Americans' first strike advantage.

Nevertheless in the post-war period it came to be seen as miraculous that America won such an overwhelming victory. This idea gained traction among some historians. Walter Lord, author of *Incredible Victory* [1998] wrote, "By any ordinary standard, they were hopelessly outclassed . . . They had no right to win . . . Like Marathon, the Armada . . . Even against the greatest of odds, there is something in the human spirit—a magic blend of skill, faith and valor—that can lift men from certain defeat to incredible victory."[71] A similar sentiment is imparted by Gordon Prange's book, *Miracle of Midway* [1983]. However, the odds were not stacked against a US victory. As has been explained, US aircraft significantly outnumbered the Japanese at *Midway* while intelligence had given Nimitz invaluable first strike advantage.

Yamamoto had divided his force in part because he wanted to draw out the US carriers from *Pearl Harbor*. He did not have Nimitz's advantage of intelligence and felt that his carrier forces would be able to deal quite comfortably with any American carrier threat. Given the intelligence available, it was not foolish of him to believe that there were only two 'serviceable' US carriers capable of being at *Midway*. That *Yorktown* had survived the *Coral Sea* was completely unknown to him. Yamamoto was also correct in thinking that his aircrews, albeit wearied by months of constant action, were superior in experience and battle-craft and that on past evidence they had the better equipment in terms of aircraft capability particularly with the Zero fighter and the Nakajima 'Kate' torpedo plane. However, due to their superior intelligence and the advantages conferred by 'first strike,' the odds clearly favored the United States. Even then Spruance's victory was highly dependent on McClusky's good fortune and judgment in spotting them following the destroyer *Arashi*, as it was scurrying back to the main fleet after its fruitless attempt to sink the US submarine, *Nautilus*.

US and Japanese Aircraft Carriers: Performance and Design: What neither side fully understood was how their aircraft carriers would perform in battle conditions. The aircraft carrier was still a relatively new type of capital ship. The first American carrier, USS *Langley*, a converted collier (USS *Jupiter*) was launched in 1920 while the first purpose built aircraft carrier of the Japanese Navy, *Hosho*, was completed in 1922. Curiously Japan took an early lead in carrier development in part because of the very *Washington Treaty* [1922] designed to limit Japanese naval power. In order to meet compliance with the *Washington Treaty*, in 1920 Japan built two carriers by converting the *Kaga* (from the hull of a battleship) and the *Akagi* from the hull of a battle-cruiser. Both ships were very extensively rebuilt in the 1930s; it was in this form that they appeared at *Midway*.

Japanese carriers reached their apogee with the construction of the *Shokaku* and its sister ship *Zuikaku*. The two *Shokaku* Class carriers were commissioned in the autumn of 1941 and, had they not suffered damage at the *Battle of the Coral Sea*, should have been available for the attack on *Midway*. Their design benefitted from the lifting of restrictions after the expiry of the *Naval Treaty of London* [1930]. At 32,000 tons displacement they were 10,000 tons heavier than the *Soryu* Class they replaced, which reflected their heavier armament (particularly overhead protection for aviation fuel tanks and munitions stores) and larger engines, producing 160,000 horsepower, which was even more than the super *Yamato* Class battleships. They carried a standard complement of 84 aircraft including 27 dive-bombers, 27 torpedo bombers, 18 fighters and a further 12 in reserve. The *Shokaku* Class carriers were probably the best of their kind until the Americans started to churn out the Essex Class in 1943. Like their American counterparts, armor was used sparingly, mainly for the hull and as extra protection for fuel tanks and magazines. Speed, essential for both offensive and defensive action, was considered paramount.

The main difference between American and Japanese carriers was that, like the British, the Japanese carriers stored their craft on the hangar decks. In general the

America carriers stored their planes on deck and used their hangars for repair and maintenance. The American practice and configuration meant that their carriers could carry about 20 percent more planes than the Japanese and double the number of British carriers. Given the premium on hangar space, it was perhaps surprising that the Japanese did not develop planes with hinged wings to the same extent as US aircraft manufacturers.

Apart from storage capacity, the US deck system was also operationally more efficient. Because US planes were stored, refueled and rearmed on deck the process of turnaround was quicker. Planes could be kept on deck at the same time as being operated for landing and take-off. Planes on deck were protected by safety nets from the not infrequent possibility of planes veering off. Japanese decks were only operational when aircraft were stored below. Japanese aircraft carriers needed to refuel on the hangar decks, which meant that their timetable for landing, refueling-rearming and launching planes was largely governed by the speed and logistics of elevators. Even though the *Shokaku* Class's three elevators could move up or down in twenty seconds, maneuvering planes on, off, and around elevators took time. Loading planes on deck for take-off, 'spotting,' took forty minutes with a further twenty minutes needed to warm up engines. American carriers were advantaged because the bulk of their planes had foldable wings, giving more 'spotting' space on deck.

Operationally, US carriers were far better designed. By 1943 the Americans were able to speed up their deck operations even further by the use of jeeps and specially designed deck tractors. Deck management was a highly skilled task and needed well-trained and motivated teams of deck crew working in perfect unison in an environment that was extremely hazardous. As came to be seen in the five carrier-to-carrier battles of the *Pacific War*, the only such in history, the difference of a few minutes could be critical. The slower process of refueling and rearming of Japanese carrier aircraft, compared to the deck-based refueling and rearming of the American carriers, almost certainly cost the Japanese the *Akagi* and the *Kaga*.

In spite of the offensive capability of Japanese carriers, the *Battle of Midway* (and to some extent the *Battle of Coral Sea* shortly beforehand), showed up some serious design faults. Like the American carriers, Japanese carriers had wooden main decks rather than steel because of weight; seaworthiness and deck stability for landing and take-off required a low center of gravity. Problematically, bombs easily penetrated wooden decks; this made the design of the two hangar decks critical. Japanese hangars had closed sides while US carriers' hangars had rolling doors. The percussive impact of bombs exploding in the enclosed Japanese hangars was vastly more devastating than in the US carriers' 'open' hangars. American crew could quickly and easily throw damaged aircraft or munitions out of the hangar sides. Neither were Japanese carriers helped by their operating practices. Whereas American crews fueled and loaded munitions after aircraft had been 'spotted' on deck, Japanese planes were fueled and equipped with bombs in the enclosed hangers making them a potentially much more deadly environment than on American carriers. There were other weaknesses. Fuel tanks in the Japanese carriers were integral to the hull and designers almost certainly underestimated the degree to which aviation gas fuel (some 150,000 tons on the *Shokako* Class) would leach under battle conditions, where even a near miss could wrench steel plates and cause fumes to escape and build up within the ship. With enclosed hangars on Japanese carriers, these noxious and highly explosive fumes had nowhere to escape.

Furthermore Japanese carriers had not developed self-sealing fuel lines. In another operational weakness, Japanese carriers assigned less than half the number of their crew to fire fighter duties than their American counterparts. At the best of times, aircraft carriers, with their combination of fuel and munitions and aircraft preparation within enclosed hangers, could be described as 'floating bombs' but Japan's 'closed' design exacerbated these characteristics. At the *Battle of Midway*, the US Navy's dive-bombers turned all four of Nagumo's fleet carriers, *Akagi, Kaga, Soryu* and *Hiryu* into burning infernos within minutes. In effect the Japanese carriers, because of their design flaws, became inoperable and unsalvageable as soon as the first bomb strikes from US dive-bombers hit home. By comparison what is very noticeable is that *Yorktown*, which was very heavily damaged by dive-bombers at the *Coral Sea*, was able to be brought back to *Pearl Harbor* and repaired in time to play a critical role at *Midway*. Even after *Midway* the damaged *Yorktown* would have been salvageable if it had not been torpedoed as it was being towed back to *Hawaii*.

The US Navy learnt rapidly. At the *Battle of the Coral Sea*, a lesson learned from the sinking of the *Lexington*, which was destroyed by an explosion of aviation gases that had leached from the ship's oil tanks, was that tanks and fuel lines could be made safer by the use of inert gases. These changes were immediately implemented on the *Yorktown*. By contrast the rigidities of the Imperial Japanese Navy's command structure never allowed such rapid response to problems. Post-war analysis has shown that if the *Soryu* and *Horyu* had had self-sealing fuel lines, they would probably not have been lost at the *Battle of Midway*.

Explanations, Recriminations and Plaudits: The technical defensive deficiencies of the Japanese carrier fleet made the importance of 'first strike' in the *Battle of the Midway* even more critical. Japanese carriers, with their better trained and more experienced aviators, superior battle-craft and capable planes made them a brilliant offensive weapon; but it was a fragile weapon given that the carriers themselves were so brittle in defense. It is this factor that made the US Navy's intelligence so critical to the outcome of the battle. Thanks to Layton and Rochefort, Nimitz was able to place his carriers with detailed advance knowledge of the disposition of Yamamoto's forces as well as their battle plans. Ultimately the *Battle of Midway* was won because Spruance and Fletcher were able to launch their aircraft to give themselves 'first strike' advantage.

Nevertheless Fletcher's carrier fleet enjoyed immense slices of luck, notably McClusky's sighting of the destroyer returning to the main fleet after hounding the American submarine, *Nautilus*; and the *Enterprise*'s dive-bombers' good fortune in finding an almost complete absence of fighter cover at the exact moment that McClusky and Best attacked the *Kaga* and *Akagi* respectively. Battles can turn on good fortune and at *Midway* the division of this precious commodity was far from even. Spruance modestly wrote, "We were shot with luck on the morning of 4 June, when the fate of the operation was decided."[72]

If the American victory at *Midway* was fortunate it was not because they were outnumbered—as already discussed they were not—but because they were not made to pay for the gross inadequacies of their battle plans, tactics, training and equipment. Each Task Force (TF) Admiral—Fletcher (TF 17) on *Yorktown* and Spruance (TF 16) with *Enterprise* and *Hornet* (commanded by Captain Mitscher)—operated in isolation. Not only did the carrier commanders not meet, they barely communicated with each other. Ship-to-ship and ship-to-air communications technology, which would change beyond recognition by the time of the great *Pacific War* fleet battles of 1944, was still in its infancy, as was command experience of groups of carriers. Even within ships coordination was lacking; flight squadron commanders appear to have made their own decisions about the course to set to intercept the Japanese fleet. Waldron was only able to make his doomed torpedo attack because he unilaterally abandoned the course set by his superior officer, Commander Stanhope Ring.

In theory US aircraft carrier tactics demanded that dive-bombers, covered by fighters, attacked first, leaving the slow moving torpedo bombers to sneak into the attack to deliver the *coup de grâce* in the confusion of the *mêlée* above. In the event Marine torpedo bombers from *Midway* and then three aircraft carrier squadrons of Devastator torpedo bombers went in first. Travelling at as little as 100 miles an hour just fifty feet above water, the torpedo bombers were sent to their doom without any fighter cover from the Wildcats which were stationed at an altitude of 20,000 feet. The only action seen by US fighters other than over *Midway* itself was by Lieutenant-Commander Jimmy Thach from the *Yorktown* whose Grumman Wildcats rode shotgun for Massey's doomed Torpedo-3 Squadron. In the event Thach's group was so preoccupied with fighting off Zeros, three of which he shot down using his new 'weave' tactics, that they gave little effective support apart from drawing off some of the enemy aircraft.

Compounding the catastrophe, because of the lack of torpedoes, many of the Devastator pilots had never actually dropped one in practice let alone in anger. Those torpedoes that were dropped did not work. Scandalously, because of political corruption in the American government's 1930s weapons procurement system, the Mark XIII torpedo did not work until corrections were finally made to its manufacture in 1943 after months of political shenanigans. **[See Appendix A: Submarines: America Draws Tight the Noose]** Given the shattering losses suffered by the torpedo squadrons, had the battle been lost, their sacrifice might easily have lived in legend alongside the 'Charge of the Light Brigade' at the *Battle of Balaclava* [1854], as an exercise in futility.

That the US dive-bombers arrived *en masse* at an opportune moment with regard to the disarray of the defending Japanese Zeros as well as the chaotic changeover in weaponry in the under-hangars aboard the Japanese carriers was entirely luck. The complete lack of US air attack coordination at *Midway* is in stark contrast to the precision of the coordinated Japanese attack by the air groups of six carriers at *Pearl Harbor*.

Essentially there was no US battle plan for the fighting of the *Battle of Midway*; each squadron took its chances and, collectively, they were rewarded with stunning good fortune for extraordinary acts of individual heroism bordering on foolhardiness, which compensated for their lack of training and poor equipment.

As for the performance of the *Hornet*, it can only be concluded that Captain Mitscher and Commander Ring were lucky not to have had their careers truncated, which is what they themselves expected in the aftermath. Theirs was effectively a no-show because of the gross miscalculation of the course settings chosen by Commander Ring. Even Vice-Admiral Spruance treated Mitscher's 'after action report,' a report that mysteriously and in contravention of regulations did not include a contribution from Commander Ring, as an unreliable concoction. In a high level report, Spruance noted, "Where discrepancies exist between *Enterprise* and *Hornet* reports, the *Enterprise* report should be taken as the more accurate."[73] Because a great victory had been won, the cover-up of the US Navy's operational and technical fiascos at *Midway* suited everyone involved. Strangely it was a battle in which both sides, victors and losers, tried to cover up the truth.

After the *Battle of Midway*, Commander Ring was awarded the Navy Cross, as was his *Hornet* colleague Waldron . . . albeit posthumously. Remarkably both Mitscher and Ring, in spite of what became known as "the flight to nowhere,"[74] went on to have glittering careers while Captain Rochefort, who historian Alvin Kernan described as "MVP (Most Valuable Player) of the battle"[75] was later sent to run a dry dock in San Francisco after falling foul of internal US Navy politics. However, the smell of failure haunted Ring for the remainder of his life. Reportedly he let it be known in an officer's club in *Pearl Harbor*, "The pilots on the *Hornet* think I'm a real shit."[76] Because of the *Hornet*'s virtual non-participation in the battle, it is worth noting that the Japanese fleet carrier force was in effect destroyed by just two US carriers, the *Enterprise* and the *Yorktown*.

Layton and Rochefort apart, whose intelligence work gave the US Navy its all-important first strike advantage, it is difficult to identify a great 'hero of *Midway*.' All the US commanders made mistakes with Spruance probably making fewer than the others. Spruance had timed his strike force launch to perfection, catching the Japanese carriers between operations, and had also taken the risk of sending everything in a single mass attack that gave the possibility of overwhelming the Japanese defenses. Spruance also made the correct decision to withdraw during the night rather than risk a night fight. Given that the US carriers' Admirals appear to have exerted no control over aerial coordination, tactics or approach, their only significant contribution to the battle was the decision as to when to launch their bomber attacks.

It is debatable whether it was wise for Admiral Nimitz to take personal command of the operation leaving Fletcher as little more than a nominal figurehead. Had the US lost the battle, Nimitz must surely have taken the blame for not fully handing over command and for the appalling failures of flight coordination at *Midway*. Fletcher certainly did not receive the plaudits that a commanding Admiral would normally have received after such a historic and devastating victory. Unlike the *Battle of Trafalgar* there is no 'Horatio Nelson' figure at the *Battle of Midway*, though Spruance would gain most in reputation by his handling of Task Force 16 comprising USS *Enterprise* and USS *Hornet*. Indeed because of the mistaken attribution of the sinking of Japanese aircraft carriers to the Army's land-based aircraft on *Midway*, the cover up with regard to the Mark XIII torpedo, the failure to train and then to protect the doomed torpedo airmen, the cover up of the *Hornet*'s 'flight to nowhere,' and the treatment of Rochefort, the *Battle of Midway*, on paper the greatest naval victory that the US will ever achieve, left a curiously sour taste in the mouths of many of those who participated. In the end the heroes of the day, apart from Nimitz's intelligence officers, were the extraordinarily brave US Navy and Marine pilots of the torpedo and dive-bomber squadrons. Their success was aided by the superb performance of the Douglas Dauntless dive-bomber and the chink in the armor of the Japanese Navy's vast technical and combat superiority, namely the design faults, the operation deficiencies, the weak defensive capabilities and the lack of structural robustness of their aircraft carriers.

In hindsight we know that Yamamoto's division of his carrier forces, the split objectives at *Midway* (destruction of the island's defenses as well as defeat of the US carrier fleet) and his failure to get at least *Zuikaku* back to the central *Pacific* after the battle of the *Coral Sea*, were mistakes. But was Yamamoto not correct to try to score a stunning naval victory and reduce the US front line capital ships before America's industrial largesse came on-stream? Ultimately Yamamoto knew that in the long term he had a weak hand when faced with the potential of US military production; this fact alone was responsible for him forcing his strategy at *Midway* in order to bring out the American carriers. It probably never occurred to Yamamoto that the US would *not* be on the defensive. In fact the opposite was true. Both King in Washington and Nimitz at *Pearl Harbor* were inclined to attack and looked for the opportunity to do so on reasonable terms of advantage.

Nimitz's strategic imperatives were the inverse of Yamamoto's. For the latter it was essential to seek out overwhelming victory; by contrast Nimitz could bide his time until favorable circumstances and relatively even force disposition gave him the opportunity to give battle. He also had the luxury of withdrawal if necessary. With the advantage of intelligence he could choose when to ride his luck; his calculated gamble paid off.

Within the Japanese Navy, many felt that hubris was the main cause of defeat. Commander Mitsuo Fuchida accused the Navy of "arrogant underestimation of the enemy" as well as its "blithe assumption that [the enemy] would be taken by surprise."[77] "Victory Disease" he would assert was the "root cause of Japan's defeat . . . in the entire war."[78] Similarly Commander Chihaya Masatake caustically opined, "We as good as planned for it [defeat]. If we had escaped that terrible disaster on that occasion, we should have met the same fate somewhere else in the Pacific theater . . . [defeat] was visited on the Japanese navy to penalize its absurd self-conceit."[79] Vice-Admiral Ugaki was similarly convinced that the main cause of defeat was over-confidence, "We had become conceited with past successes and did not make studies of steps to be taken when an enemy air force appeared on the flank while we were engaged in launching an attack on another target."[80]

In reality the reason for Yamamoto's failure was more complex. He failed to learn an important lesson from the *Battle of the Coral Sea* that fast fleet carriers could travel vast distances rapidly and could appear where they were not expected. Yamamoto should have assumed the possibility of US carriers being in the area. Had he done so it is possible that Admiral Nagumo would have instituted a two-phase search pattern rather than the single-phase search that failed to spot the US fleet. As soon as Spruance and Fletcher's planes took off unobserved, the fate of Nagumo's task force was out of his hands.

Perhaps even more importantly Yamamoto failed to concentrate his fleet and provide them with overwhelming firepower. Contrary to most western accounts, the US Fleet was quite evenly matched with the Japanese force at *Midway*. Instead of ensuring the application of overwhelming force, it was simply assumed that the better quality of his forces would prevail.

The Rewards of Victory: By the time of the *Battle of Midway*, Nimitz knew that thirteen Essex Class carriers with a 27,000-ton displacement were on order, with the first of these to be completed by the end of the year. This did not make Nimitz complacent but, unlike Yamamoto, the broader strategic picture did not make him desperate and prone to take excessive risks. US Naval command could take risks that were better calibrated to reward than their Japanese opponents. This approach was made clear in Nimitz's instructions to Fletcher and Spruance, "In carrying out the task assigned . . . you will be governed by the principle of calculated risk, which you shall interpret to mean the avoidance of exposure to your force, to attack by superior enemy forces without good prospect of inflicting, as a result of such exposure, greater damage to the enemy."[81]

Japan's human losses from the battle at *Midway* were significant. Out of 2,000 naval airman available to Japan in total, 110 airmen were lost from the four carriers at *Midway*; *Kaga* (21), *Soryu* (10), *Akagi* (7) and *Hiryu* (72). Moreover 721 aircraft technicians were killed, which represented 40 percent of those who embarked. More significant in terms of the balance of naval power was the loss of four of Japan's six fleet carriers; the weapon that above all, after *Pearl Harbor* and until the development of the atom bomb just four years later, defined the ability of the maritime nations to design their war strategies and project their power.

At the start of the battle Japan had six fleet carriers (*Kaga, Akagi, Horyu, Soryu, Shokaku* and *Zuikaku*) and one modern light carrier, *Zuiho* as well as the small carriers *Hosho* and *Ryujo* that were almost obsolescent, and the converted cruise liner *Junyo*. (The newly built light aircraft carrier *Shoho* was commissioned after *Pearl Harbor* and its short life brought to an end at the *Coral Sea*.) In addition Japan also possessed three seaplane tenders. Unlike the Americans, whose reconnaissance was integrated into the operations of the fleet carriers, Japan organized scouting with specialist seaplane tenders or seaplanes carried by destroyers. Japan's small and light carriers were only ever capable of playing bit parts in the war in the *Pacific*. Ranged against the Japanese carrier fleet at the start of the *Pacific War* the US Navy had five fleet carriers (*Lexington, Saratoga, Yorktown, Enterprise* and *Hornet*). With *Lexington* lost at the *Coral Sea* before the *Battle of Midway*, America had a deficit of four fleet carriers to Japan's six. After the battle the balance of power in fleet carriers swung to three for the United States versus two for Japan. The US Navy may have lost *Lexington* at the *Coral Sea* and then USS *Yorktown* at *Midway* but Japan lost four fleet carriers. The scale of the disaster can be seen when put into the context that Japan's fleet carrier force, which had taken fourteen years to build up, was reduced by two-thirds in a single morning at *Midway*.

For Japan, the dominance of their fleet carrier force in the first six months of the *Pacific War* gave them the ability to take the initiative. As historian H. P. Willmot has noted, "The ability to concentrate mobile forces to dictate the direction and tempo of future operations was the all important factor in the conduct of the *Pacific War*."[82] Losing the *Battle of Midway* ended Japan's hitherto strategic dominance of the conflict. As the US Naval War College concluded after the battle, *Midway* "put an end to Japanese offensive action . . . and. . . [restored] the balance of naval power in the *Pacific*."[83]

Without their fleet carrier advantage, for the rest of the war, Japan's military and naval operations in the *Pacific* would have to march to the beat and direction of an American drum. Admiral King in Washington was quick to see the dramatic change in the balance of power. He wrote to Army Chief of Staff George Marshall, insisting, "It is urgent in my opinion, that we lose no time in taking the initiative."[84] Possession of the dominant carrier force would allow America's commanders to move the focus of the *Pacific War* at will. From now on America would increasingly dominate the pattern of engagement. Meanwhile Japan's losses were irredeemable. After the *Battle of Midway*, Japan was never capable of replacing its carrier fleet. Japan's industrial capacity was such that it was only ever able to produce two new-built fleet carriers in time to take part in an active operation in the *Pacific War*; the *Taiho* (a modified *Shokaku* design) was launched in April 1943 while the Shinano was produced from the half-built hull of a Yamato Class super-battleship. Meanwhile the new Unryu Class carrier spawned just 3 of the 16 new carriers ordered by the Japanese Navy two months after the *Midway* catastrophe; but, commissioned late in the war, none of these carriers—*Unryu, Amagi* and *Katsuragi*—would see action other than being targets for US air attacks. Other new Japanese carriers were conversions from seaplane tenders into light carriers, *Chitose* and *Chiyoda*. By contrast America produced fifteen new Essex Class fleet carriers and nine Independence Class light carriers by the end of 1945. Arguably the *Battle of Midway*, in many respects a fortuitous victory for the United States, was for Japan the most devastating single strategic defeat suffered by any country in *World War II*—only General von Manstein's defeats to General Zhukov at the *Battle of Stalingrad* [1942] and the *Battle of Kursk* [1943] beg comparison. In hindsight, if not at the time, it is clear that almost any chance that Japan had of winning the war, or at least of negotiating its way to a favorable peace deal, had died.

15 Battles of the Kokoda Trail: Aussies Triumphant

[June 1942–September 1942]

[Maps: 15.1, 15.2, 15.3]

Admiral Inoue and Strategies of the South Pacific: **[Map: 15.1]** "We've got to go to Europe and fight," wrote Eisenhower, "We've got to quit wasting resources all over the world—and still worse—wasting time."[1] General Marshall, soon to be Chief of Staff, was clear, from a strategic point of view, that Europe should be the absolute priority for the United States. England and the Soviet Union had to be kept in the war. In essence his thinking ran along the lines of RAINBOW-5—a plan that had been developed after the realization, following the Anschluss and Munich Agreements, and the *Ribbentrop-Molotov Pact* in the late 1930s, that America might have to face multilateral enemies on different continents.

War Plan RAINBOW-5 in effect superseded Plan ORANGE, conceived before *World War I* but formally adopted by the Army Navy Board in 1924 to deal with commencement of war with Japan alone. While Plan ORANGE range remained alive as a means of rescuing the Philippines by a thrust through the *Marshall* and *Caroline Islands* in mid-*Pacific* by the US Navy, it would now have to be subservient in timescale to the global requirements of RAINBOW-5.

At the First Washington Conference meeting between Churchill and Roosevelt and their military and naval chiefs, code-named ARCADIA, held from 22 December 1941 to 14 January 1942, RAINBOW-5, with its emphasis on European prioritization, was confirmed, much to Churchill's relief, as the principal strategic platform from which the war would be fought. The Army in particular, as evinced by Marshall and Eisenhower, was adamant that, for the time being the *Pacific* should be little more than a holding operation. It was based on the correct assumption that Japan did not have the resources to attack America. If necessary, Army logic ran, even Australia was expendable. While they met in Washington however, circumstances were leading to a nuanced change to the balance envisaged by the Army.

In large part the nuanced changes reflected a response to Japan's own strategic thrusts. At the start of the war Japan's main targets had been the neutralization of the US Navy in *Hawaii*, wresting US control of the Philippines, as well as British control of Malaya and *Singapore*, and South Burma, all leading to Japan's ultimate strategic objective, the acquisition of the oil fields of British controlled *Borneo* and the Dutch East Indies. These goals encompassed the strategic aims set out for the First Operational Stage of the war devised by Imperial General Headquarters. The Second Operational

Stage envisioned the conquest of eastern New Guinea, *New Britain, Fiji, Samoa*, the *Aleutians, Midway* and "strategic points in the Australian area."[2]

Within the framework of the First Operational Stage, Vice-Admiral Shigeyoshi Inoue, commander of the Imperial Japanese Navy's *South Pacific* Fourth Fleet, who had been heavily involved in operational planning before the start of the war, was responsible for the gathering in of *Pacific* assets not already under Japanese League of Nations mandated control, including *Guam* (US), *Wake Island* (US), and the *Gilbert Islands* (UK). Added to this list was Rabaul, a perfectly positioned deep water port and garrison lying 700 miles to the south of Japan's *Pacific* Fleet Headquarters at *Truk Lagoon*. Rabaul was located at the eastern tip of *New Britain* (formerly *Neu Pommern*) and adjacent to the second largest island of the *Bismarck Archipelago, New Ireland* (formerly *Neu Mecklenberg*). Renamed, after the *Treaty of Versailles*, German imperial possessions in New Guinea had been transferred to an Australian Mandate in 1921.

Vice-Admiral Inoue, born in the city of Sendai, in Miyage Prefecture on the northeast coast of Japan's main *Honshu Island*, has often been seen as the *protégé* of Admiral Yamamoto but arguably, in his own right, he was the greater naval tactician and theorist. Graduating second in his year (1909) from the Imperial Japanese Navy Academy at Etajima near Hiroshima, he was marked early on for his intellectual prowess. Sent to learn German as a naval *attaché* in Switzerland, he served as a staff member of the Japanese delegation at Versailles and was then asked to learn French and work as the naval *attaché* in Paris. His sojourn in France did not stop him mastering English. To round off his linguistic accomplishments he also served as naval *attaché* in Italy from 1929 to 1931. A keen musician, Inoue added to his accomplishments by becoming a skilled guitar player.

Inoue was politically well connected albeit to an increasingly minority faction within the Army: he was married to the sister of General Nobuyuke Abe who served as Japan's prime minister for five months and concurrently as Foreign Minister until January 1940 when his position of neutrality in the European War and his opposition to closer links with *Nazi* Germany brought him down.

Like Yamamoto, Inoue became an outspoken critic of the Tripartite Alliance with Germany and Italy and believed that it would be foolish to challenge America's industrial might. He thought that the Japanese Army ". . . underestimated America's natural strength and the spiritual strength of its people, particularly its women. They had a childish notion that since women had such a powerful say there, it wouldn't be long before they started objecting to the war."[3] As a strategist he was equally outspoken. He probably realized more clearly than anyone in the Japanese Navy that the development of submarine and torpedo technologies as well as aircraft power had fundamentally changed the nature of naval war. Thus he predicted that the next naval war would be 'three-dimensional.' He bitterly opposed the building of the super-battleships, *Musashi* and *Yamato*, authorized by the Imperial Japanese Navy in the late 1930s arguing that the aircraft carrier should be prioritized as the Navy's primary strike weapon.

Inoue even made the revolutionary suggestion that the development of new bomber aircraft meant that it would be possible to defend the *Pacific* perimeter just using land-based bombers; Inoue could be considered a Japanese equivalent to the farsighted US aviator Brigadier-General 'Billy' Mitchell. Perhaps alone amongst the senior ranking naval staff and contrary to Admiral Yamamoto, he questioned the wisdom of depending on the single 'knock-out' victory strategy adopted by the Imperial US navy.

Realizing that the crucial Navy stronghold at *Truk Lagoon* could be compromised at its southern flank by any Allied airbases located in the islands of the *Bismarck Archipelago*, Inoue had pushed for the annexation of Rabaul. Carrier-based air attacks on 21 January easily dispatched Australia's antiquated air defenses, and troops led by Major-General Tomitoro Horii landed outside Rabaul on 23 January and quickly took the garrison—the same day that General Wainwright began a hazardous withdrawal from the Abucay Line on the Bataan Peninsula. Over a thousand Australian troops retreated into the jungle to continue a guerrilla fight but were completely unprepared for this type of campaign. All but a few surrendered within a few weeks.

One hundred and thirty of these Australian troops were taken in small groups to Tol Plantation where they were bayonetted to death. As a concession, Australian officers were shot. One of the two survivors noted, "Most of the Australians died very bravely, promising the Japanese, 'You'll pay for this when our chaps catch you!' "[4] A further thirty-five Australian prisoners were also executed at the nearby Waitavalo Plantation. As was often the case with Japanese atrocities during their *Pacific* campaigns, it was a fanatical middle-ranking officer, Colonel Masao Kusunose who ordered the killings. He later committed suicide. Remarkably in the New Guinea Campaign not a single Australian soldier survived capture by the Japanese. After interrogation, all were put to death.

Having established himself at Rabaul and organized its incorporation into the 'First Operation Stage' of Japan's war plan, Inoue set about securing the key garrisons that could undermine this new stronghold. In early 1942 'Navy Instruction-47' and Army 'Instruction-596' ordered the taking of "all key locations in British New Guinea."[5] On 29 January the Imperial Naval Staff approved the further extension of Japan's outer perimeter along the lines envisaged in the Second Operational Stage. Thus the islands of *Manus* and *Negros* to the north of *New Britain* were secured as well as *Buna* on the New Guinea mainland. To the south of Buna, Gona, Lae and Salamaua were easily overcome on 8 March.

Reverend James Benson, an Anglican missionary at *Gona*, heard the deafening barrage that started the Japanese invasion of the north coast of New Guinea. It seemed as "though hundreds of guns were spitting fire" wrote Benson, and, "the deep woof! Crump! Crump! of bursting bombs a mile away, gave me a queer feeling in the pit of my stomach. But we still continued to sit on as though it were all a play."[6] The next targets on Admiral Inoue's list were Port Moresby on the southern coast of eastern New Guinea and *Tulagi*, a small island in the *Solomon Straits* with a secure port and amphibious aircraft base. Opposite *Tulagi* it was planned to build an airbase on the sparsely inhabited island of

Guadalcanal. For two weeks the Army and Navy argued over the possibility of invading Australia. At Japanese Navy General Staff HQ, an invasion plan was drawn up by Captain Sadatoshi Tomioka. It was ridiculed by Colonel Takushiro Hattori who pointed out that the Army alone would need 1.5 million tons of shipping to transport and feed the twelve infantry divisions needed to conquer a country bigger than China. An exasperated Hattori picked up a cup of tea and spilled it on the floor, "The tea in this cup represents out total strength. You see it goes so far. If your plan is approved I will resign."[7]

Although the Japanese Army put the kibosh on the Navy's suggestion that Australia could be invaded, Inoue nevertheless knew that from bases in southern New Guinea, including Buna, Gona, and Port Moresby, he could control northern Australia and be prepared for any counter-offensive in the region. In addition, with the establishment of a naval base at *Tulagi* and a planned airfield on the island of *Guadalcanal* in the southern *Solomons*, Inoue could use them as bases for the onward advance to *New Caledonia, Samoa* and *Fiji.* The Army agreed to this more modest mooted expansion as a *quid pro quo* with the Navy for giving up its own 'pet' project to carve through India to join up with the Germans in the Middle East. (In fact Hitler quickly rejected this plan. His main interest was the defeat of the Soviet Union on his Eastern Front.) By capturing the *Pacific Islands* to the east of Australia, Japan's naval leaders believed that they could cut supply to Australia from the west coast of America. Although the Japanese plans appeared aggressive in intent, the aims were strategically defensive with the aim of cutting off America's ability to launch a counter-offensive from Australia. The occupation of Port Moresby, Lae, Wau, Buna, *Milne Bay*, and *Guadalcanal* would also deny airfields to the Allies, which could potentially threaten Japan's major regional garrison at Rabaul.

Admiral King and the Defense of Australia: Thus far Japan's rapid advance of relatively modest forces under Inoue's command had barely been impeded. Australian garrisons, massively outgunned by Inoue's fleet and its aircraft superiority, were left flat-footed by the speed and deftness of Japanese landings and had succumbed with little resistance offered.

It seems certain that, without the critical intervention of Admiral Ernest King in Washington, who subtly altered the strategic priorities implicit in War Plan RAINBOW-5, Inoue would almost certainly have completed his Second Operational Stage. Like Inoue, Ernest King was a top performer at the US Naval Academy at Annapolis, graduating fourth in his class in 1901. His background on both sides of the family was recent immigrant stock. His paternal grandfather was a builder from Scotland while his maternal grandfather was a master woodworker with the Royal Navy in Plymouth. Ernest King's father James became an itinerant bridge builder before settling down to work at a locomotive repair yard in Lorain, Ohio. Ernest King grew up with the attributes of a no-nonsense, pragmatic, skilled, workingman.

As a teenager, King developed a fascination with military and naval history, and determined on a career in the Navy. When his father asked his local Congressman for help in getting his son put forward for the US Naval Academy, Ernest was allowed to stand in competitive examination for a place at Annapolis. Out of thirty candidates, King ranked first. Confident to the point of arrogance in his ability, King was not averse to insubordination for which he was frequently reprimanded and disciplined. He was far from being an intellectual however, being well known for his enjoyment of liquor and women: "You ought to be very suspicious of anyone who won't take a drink or doesn't like women,"[8] he once averred. At the US Naval Academy, he chased, won and married 'Mattie' Egerton, supposedly "the most beautiful, the most sought after young woman at Annapolis,"[9] with whom he would eventually have seven children.

After a distinguished career that took him to the command of the carrier *Lexington* in 1930 and subsequently Vice-Admiral in command of the *Pacific* Air Fleet, King was then disappointed to be overlooked as Chief of Naval Operations, the highest-ranking uniformed job in the Navy. With his career now seemingly over, Hitler's invasion of France rescued King. Having impressed Secretary of State for the Navy, Charles Edison, and then Roosevelt by his intellectual ability and aggressive intent, in 1941 King was appointed to command the *Atlantic* Fleet. Nine days after *Pearl Harbor*, King was appointed Commander in Chief of the US Fleet above Chief of Naval Operations, Admiral Harold Stark. In effect, King leapfrogged the man who had beaten him to the post of Chief of Naval Operations.

King inherited a strategy that would cede all the central *Pacific* to Japan while calling for him to hold line at the *Samoa Islands* and points south including the *New Hebrides, New Caledonia, Fiji* and *Tonga*. Thus Marines were dispatched to *Samoa* while the Army sent 1,500 troops to *Canton Island* and 2,000 to *Christmas Island*. A refueling base was also established at *Bora-Bora* while 17,000 troops were sent to *New Caledonia* to safeguard its important deposits of nickel and chrome. The unit became known as the Americal Division (**Ameri**cans in New **Cal**edonia).

While he grudgingly accepted War Plan RAINBOW-5's 'Europe First' bias as necessary for a global war strategy in spite of his visceral loathing of 'upper-crust' Englishmen, the First Washington Conference, ARCADIA, with its vague summary paper, which required "maintaining only such positions in the [*Pacific*] theater as will safeguard vital interests,"[10] gave King 'wiggle room.' King interpreted ARCADIA as giving the Navy scope for the acquiring of island assets from where future offensives against Japan could be developed. The Army and quasi-independent Army Air Force however, were more clearly focused on their European priorities. They drew the line at putting more soldiers at Funafuti on the *Ellice Islands* that were stepping-stones to *Guadalcanal* at the foot of the *Solomon Islands*. However, political and geopolitical concerns were moving Roosevelt toward adopting a more flexible approach to Australia and the *Pacific* than ARCADIA had originally envisioned. On 21 January 1942, Australian Prime Minister John Curtin, alarmed at the possibility that his country would be invaded, insisted to Churchill that two of its four best divisions that were in the Middle East (3) and Malaya (1) should be returned home. As Curtin's predecessor

Australian Prime Minister, Robert Menzies, told the Canberra parliament in May 1939, "What Britain calls the Far East is to us the Near North."[11]

It was a suggestion, which, if crystallized, would jeopardize the Allied hold on the Middle East. Given that one of the priorities of ARCADIA was not to allow Germany and Japan to join forces through India and the Middle East, Roosevelt stepped in to guarantee the security of both Australia and New Zealand. On 15 February Roosevelt ordered that the 41st Infantry Division be sent to Australia. In early March further pressure from Prime Minister Curtin leveraged Roosevelt to send the 32nd Infantry Division to Australia as well as the 37th Infantry Division to New Zealand. It was a 'tipping point' moment. From now on America, not Britain, would be the guarantor of Australian security.

Australia's security became further assured when Roosevelt, on Army Chief of Staff Marshall's advice, ordered General MacArthur to escape from *Corregidor*, the fortified island at the tip of Bataan where he and his family were ensconced with his surrounded American troops. He landed in Australia firm in the belief that, from his Antipodean base, he would take command of all American forces in the *Pacific*, with the task of leading a combined military and naval force to liberate the Philippines and thence move on to defeat Japan. MacArthur was to be grievously disappointed in an assumption of a command that was never promised to him; it increased the intense bitterness that henceforth characterized his relationship with the Navy.

Perversely MacArthur's very presence in Australia, because of his power with the press, further increased the importance of more aggressive action in the *South Pacific* and thus the power of Admiral King and the Navy to increase the scope of their mandate. For Australian morale, MacArthur's presence proved a welcome tonic. As war correspondent George Johnson noted, "The arrival of MacArthur—as much by his own colorful personality and career as by the spectacular story of his escape from the Philippines—has done more to lift morale on the mainland than anything else that has happened in the war."[12] Lastly Roosevelt, with his acute political antenna, was not unaware that the American public, because of the trauma caused by *Pearl Harbor*, was more focused on Emperor Hirohito rather than Hitler as its number one 'boogeyman.' Admiral King tacked with these subtle shifts in the political winds, to pilot a more aggressive 'defense' of the *South Pacific* than might otherwise have been the case. Most importantly at the end of January, Admiral King authorized the sending of aircraft carrier USS *Lexington* to lead a task force to the *South Pacific*.

The benefits of this positive approach were soon apparent. The Japanese Navy, used to having their aggressive advances virtually unimpeded from the air, were surprised by *Lexington*'s raid on Rabaul in east *New Britain*. On 20 February, after twenty-three Japanese bombers were shot down for the loss of just two fighters, Inoue was forced to postpone his invasion of Lae and Salamaua on the east coast of New Guinea for several weeks. When Inoue did invade New Guinea on 3 March, another carrier attack by the *Lexington* and *Yorktown*, launched across the Owen Stanley Range from the *Gulf of Papua* on 10 March, sank or damaged thirteen of Inoue's warships and transports in the

Huon Gulf. Crucially it led to a two-month postponement of Inoue's planned attack on Port Moresby.

On 15 February, the day that *Singapore* fell, King maintained his aggressive intent by sending the carrier USS *Yorktown* to *Canton Island* (part of the *Phoenix Islands* halfway between *Hawaii* and *Fiji*). This aggressive move, taking away carriers that could otherwise be protecting *Hawaii*, was not one that the Japanese expected. To protect the supply route to Australia, King also authorized the setting up of naval bases at Tongatabu in the *Tonga Islands* and Efate in the *New Hebrides*. King's expansionism was not without dissent. At a Joint Chiefs of Staff meeting on 16 March, the Army put its foot down over more soldiers being sent to the *Pacific*, limiting numbers to 41,000 Army personnel and 15,000 Marines. Europe remained the priority for the US Army just as China and the Asian continent remained the priority for the Japanese Army. For the time being King's determination to make inroads into the *Solomons* was stymied. More troops would be needed for an aggressive action in this direction. As Rear-Admiral Richmond 'Terrible' Turner pointed out, "It is a far different matter attempting to establish advanced bases in the *Solomons* than in the islands heretofore occupied."[13]

A week earlier, the Joint Chiefs of Staff had come to the momentous and controversial decision to split command in the *Pacific*. Much to MacArthur's chagrin, he was only appointed to command the South West Pacific Area that would include Australia, New Guinea and the Philippines. Meanwhile Nimitz would command the whole of the *Pacific* as Commander in Chief of the Pacific Area Command. The concept of a split command to achieve a single strategic goal, the defeat of Japan, must have seemed illogical to all; why did the Joint Chiefs of Staff arrive at this peculiar structure?

In part, all parties, including Marshall and 'Hap' Arnold must have questioned MacArthur's poor performance in the Philippines. They may also have feared handing MacArthur too much power given his well-known 'megalomaniac' tendencies. King in particular, whose leadership role was much more central to the *Pacific War* than the war in Europe, was completely resistant to being reduced to the role of MacArthur's 'whipping boy.' In addition, he was not prepared to hand over the spanking new navy now on order at shipyards all over America to a man who so bitterly loathed the naval service—a dislike so intense that MacArthur, on his escape from *Corregidor*, had even refused to fly in a Navy B-17 from *Mindanao* to Australia. On the other hand, Marshall and 'Hap' Arnold were not prepared to allow their forces to be put under the control of Admiral Nimitz, thus far an untested leader. An Army-Navy stand-off at the highest echelons meant that a divided *Pacific* command structure was the sensible compromise solution. Perversely it turned out to be a more than workable one.

Although King and Nimitz were held back in their broad strategic plans by a lack of war *matériel* to start the fight back in the *South Pacific*, their aggressive actions in Halsey's hit-and-run raids had nevertheless begun to put pressure on Japan's naval command. In hindsight the most important development resulting from these attacks was the dispatch of two fleet carriers, the *Zuikaku* and *Shokaku* as well as the light carrier *Shoho* to the *South Pacific* region to support the invasion of Port Moresby, which was seen as a crucial stepping stone on the route toward 'Operation FS' (*Fiji* and *Samoa*).

Operation MO (Port Moresby) and the First Battle of Kokoda: **[Map: 15.2] [Map: 15.3]** Operation MO was planned as part of the Japanese Imperial General Staff Second Operational Stage which aimed to establish airfields at Buna, Kokoda, and *Milne Bay* and a naval and airbase at Port Moresby, as well as to capture the island groups flanking the Australian east coast. For reasons of supply, major airfield bases were needed at coastal locations. The first part of Operation MO developed with the sending of 400 *Rikusentai* (Marine paratroops) from the 3rd Kure Special Landing Force to *Tulagi*, just off the coast of *Florida Island* in the *Solomon Sea.* The invasion force landed on 3 May with the aim of taking over the naval base there, in addition to which work was begun on building an airfield on the larger island of *Guadalcanal* facing *Tulagi*. The accompanying force consisted of two destroyers, six minesweepers, two minelayers, a transport ship and two submarine chasers. More distant cover was provided by Rear-Admiral Goto and a force consisting of the light carrier *Shoho* plus four heavy cruisers and one destroyer. A further support group consisted of two light cruisers, a seaplane tender and three gunboats.

After depositing the *Tulagi* invasion force the Cover Group and Support Group were required to join the eleven troop transport ships headed toward Port Moresby and scheduled to arrive on 10 May 1942. The invasion force for New Guinea consisted of 5,000 troops of the Imperial Japanese Army accompanied by another 500 *Rikusentai* (Marine paratroops) from the 3rd Kure Special Landing Force. The landing force under Admiral Koso Abe was protected by a detachment of six destroyers and a cruiser led by Admiral Kajioka Sadamichi. Longer-range cover was provided by two of Japan's latest fleet carriers, the *Zuikaku* and the *Shokaku* in addition to the light carrier *Shoho*. At Port Moresby 5,300 poorly trained Australian soldiers awaited them. Based on performances in the war to date they were probably not over optimistic about their chances of holding out.

Fortunately for them Abe's invasion force never arrived. Having anticipated their invasion force by a combination of guesswork and MAGIC intercept, Vice-Admiral Ghormley, *Southern Pacific* commander, had sent carriers *Lexington* and *Yorktown* to intercept. **[See Chapter 13: Battle of the Coral Sea: The First Carrier-on-Carrier Action]** Over the course of a two-day aircraft carrier engagement, the first in history, the *Lexington* was sunk and so was the *Shoho*. A badly damaged *Yorktown* limped back to *Hawaii* in time to get to the *Battle of Midway*. By contrast both *Zuikaku* and *Shokaku* were forced to return to Japan for repairs and resupply. The *Battle of the Coral Sea* was to have far reaching repercussions on the *Battle of Midway*, but its immediate impact on Japan's New Guinea Campaign was that the Navy gave up on the idea of an amphibious landing to take Port Moresby. Although on a pure *matériel* count, the *Battle of the Coral Sea* was a Japanese victory, it was an indication that the engagement came to be seen by the Japanese as a major strategic defeat that Admiral Inoue was recalled to Japan in

October 1942. His active fleet career was over. Inoue became commander of the Imperial Japanese Naval Academy and was recalled to a central role as Vice-Minister of the Navy at the end of the war when he was promoted to full Admiral.

While the Japanese forces were retiring from the *Gulf of Papua* and began preparing for an overland attack on Port Moresby from the northern coast of east New Guinea, the Australian Army began a massive expansion of its resources to face the threat of invasion. General MacArthur planned to use Port Moresby as the fulcrum of the Allied strategy to eject the Japanese from New Guinea. After MacArthur's arrival from the Philippines, Curtin immediately deferred to him and put General Thomas Blamey and all of Australia's forces under his command. By the summer of 1942 Australian forces amounted to a not insubstantial ten infantry Divisions and three armored Divisions. By the appointment of MacArthur, at a stroke America, not its colonial masters, Great Britain, became the guarantor of Australia's survival.

Instead of amphibious assault Japan's military leaders decided to take Port Moresby by land. Intelligence had already reached Australia that Port Moresby was still a target and on 22 June, General Blamey sent a message to the commander of New Guinea Force that he should send 'white troops' to defend the strategically important airfield at Kokoda. An assault on Port Moresby was planned for July—after the *Midway* Campaign.

On 21 July, Japanese beachheads were established at Buna, Gona and Sanananda on the north coast of eastern New Guinea, beating off light resistance from Australian forces. Sadaharu Imanishi, a diminutive Japanese foot soldier, recalled that he landed at Gona carrying a bag of rice weighing 50 lbs, 180 bullets, 2 grenades, a steel helmet and tooth brush: "There was little resistance. Soon after we landed, Australian aircraft attacked, but we escaped into the jungle. We headed straight for Kokoda."[14] Reinforcement troop transports came over the following week. Although one was sunk by Allied bombing on 29 July most Japanese troops managed to struggle ashore. As had become the norm, atrocities soon followed. Two young missionaries, May Hayman and Mavis Parkinson went into hiding in the jungle but were given away by Embogi, a village councillor. Hayman and Parkinson were held in a coffee mill by the *Kempeitai* and when they refused to give up any information, they were taken to a plantation near Buna, bayoneted and turfed into shallow graves.

Australian Anglican priest, Father James Benson was more fortunate. He was taken prisoner and transported to Rabaul and miraculously survived the war. In another incident at the Anglican mission in Sangara, the Reverend Henry Holland and Reverend Vivian Hedlich were beheaded along with co-workers. Showing a peculiar mercy a captured six-year-old boy who became distraught was shot in the head. Sasebo 5th SNLF (Special Naval Landing Force) troops, according to the captured Japanese diary of Toshio Sato, beheaded seven Australian men and women including a 16-year-old girl: "They held her down screaming and crying while they cut off her head."[15] Even Toshio Sato, an interpreter working in Buna, was horrified. Records of murders and massacres by Japanese troops were perfunctorily recorded. First-Class Seaman Shunji Shin noted in his diary, "14 August: About 8.00 a.m. decapitated or shot the nine prisoners."[16]

War correspondents noted that New Guinea natives had also indulged in atrocities against the foreigners. After the capture of Lae and Salamaua in February, drums from the Sepik villages beat out "Japan'e' come. White man 'e go bush."[17] Most of the planters fled but farm laborers often turned on those who remained, in some cases eating them. "The well fleshed" one native told Father Benson, "used to be tied by their hands to a tree; then as meat was needed, slices would be cut from their legs and buttocks' in a practice called 'living meat.' "[18] Anarchy reigned for a while, but when large Japanese armies arrived many of the natives fled into the bush. Some returned to work for the Japanese as porters but found that their new masters were far crueler than the white men they had replaced. As the war in New Guinea progressed, the native population increasingly shifted their allegiance to the Allies.

With superhuman effort the Japanese troops of Sakigawa Transport Unit cut down six miles of rough track between Buna and Soputa. Nevertheless with motorized transport remaining scarce and difficult to operate, troops carried their own provisions up toward the village of Kokoda. Private Toshio Watanabe of the Tsukamoto Battalion wrote, "I am completely exhausted because I walked 40 *ri* [five miles] with one *To* 9 *Sho* [9.54 gallons] of rice and *miso* on my back."[19] A large force of 3,000 Korean and Taiwanese construction troops were landed on 14 August, followed three days later by *Rikusentai* (Special Landing Forces) from the 5th Sasebo Force. Troops from the 144th Regiment, 55th Mountain Artillery, 55th Cavalry and 47th Anti-Aircraft Artillery were also landed. On 21 August they were joined by two battalions of the 41st Regiment. Reconnaissance of New Guinea had been done with typical Japanese thoroughness. In March 1942, an intelligence report noted that in eastern New Guinea, "on an average two pigs are raised by each family in a village . . . they are small and thin, average weight 30 kg . . . wild pigs are found all over the mountains but it is difficult to catch them."[20]

Before the war, maps of the area had been sourced by Japanese spies in Australia. As late as 1941, many of Australia's 3,000 Japanese residents were buying maps of New Guinea in Sydney's bookshops. German spies based around the former German colonies of the *Bismarck Archipelago* had also supplied maps and intelligence. Josef Hoffstetter, a Swiss itinerant worker for twenty-two years, who, as a citizen of a neutral state, had escaped a round-up of German nationals, provided Japan with valuable information. Hoffstetter later worked for the Japanese as a guide and adviser and was given officer status. In June 1942, Prince Tsuneyoshi Takeda provided Imperial HQ with a map of the region that had been made by a British explorer in the 1920s. Historian Peter Williams has concluded that with regards to southeastern New Guinea, even as late as "August 1942, Japanese maps of the area of operations were superior, although not greatly so."[21]

It was perhaps a symptom of 'victory disease' that the Japanese never expected MacArthur and the Australians to defend New Guinea. After the war, Navy Captain Toshikazu Ohmai, a senior staff officer stationed at Rabaul admitted, "The Japanese did not think that General MacArthur would establish himself in New Guinea and defend Australia from that position."[22] By contrast Curtin and his ministers suffered from what could be described as 'defeat syndrome,' fully expecting that Port Moresby would be overrun and that an invasion of Australia would force them to adopt the 'Brisbane' line, a defensive scorched earth policy that would relinquish the northern territories to the Japanese. On discovering the arrival of Japanese troops at Buna, General Morris, who had previously believed that an amphibious landing adjacent to Port Moresby was the most likely threat, immediately ordered the 39th Battalion to march overland to Kokoda. Major-General Morris who yielded command of the New Guinea Force to Lieutenant-General Sydney Rowell in August remained optimistic about the Australian ability to hold back the Japanese and told his successor, "The mountains will beat the Nips and we must be careful they don't beat us."[23]

A force of 13,500 Japanese troops from Gona would weave its way along trails over the spine of the Owen Stanley Mountains that ran through New Guinea's eastern peninsula and approach Port Moresby from its northern flank. The so-called Kokoda Trail was not a single trail but a complex web of intertwining paths. Japan's first target was the village of Kokoda, halfway inland from Gona toward the spine of the 7,000-foot high Owen Stanley Mountains. Its airfield was a key target.

For MacArthur the Japanese invasion of Buna was a major setback. He too had planned to occupy the Buna-Gona area with a view to building an airbase from where Rabaul could be attacked as early as 10 August. Lieutenant-General Harukichi Hyakutake, the younger brother of the Emperor's Grand Chamberlain, had beaten him to it by two weeks. Australian forces of the Papuan Infantry Battalion fought a rear-guard action on the trail leading up to Kokoda for six days from 23 July. During this action Corporal Senopa of the Royal Papuan Constabulary became the first Papuan to win a Military Medal. (The main service provided by the Papuan population was to act as porters for the Australian Army; some 18,000 Papuans would serve in this capacity.) The Japanese infantry commanders, veterans of Malaya, used the same tactics that served them so well on the advance to *Singapore*. Probing patrols would seek out the enemy, "feel for the weakness in his position, break through and cut up his supply lines."[24] Where possible Japanese officers would work around the flanks.

The 39th Battalion's commanding officer, Lieutenant-Colonel William Owen flew into Kokoda Airfield to take command of his troops and he led its defense. As Owen patrolled around to show leadership he took a sniper's bullet in the forehead. Just seventy-seven soldiers had held up an army of more than 10,000 troops under the command of Major-General Tomitaro Horii although the advance guard that they fought numbered just 230 men led by Captain Ogawa. The *First Battle of Kokoda* with its close combat and hand-to-hand fighting was a foretaste of the hard slog ahead for both sides. Ogawa, like his counterpart, was killed in the battle for the airfield.

The Second Battle of Kokoda: With the loss of the airfield the Australians reinforced their troops with units forced to slog their way over the Owen Stanleys toward Kokoda. Australian forces had regrouped at Deniki, some three hours journey from Kokoda. To add to their difficulties supplies would have to be airdropped while wounded soldiers were laboriously manhandled by Papuan native porters whom the Australian troops affectionately called 'fuzzy wuzzy angels.' Logistics along the narrow mountainous tracks that wound around the Owen Stanley Mountains would become the critical factor in the long battle ahead.

The Kokoda Trail, with the exception of an hour's walk along the *Brown River* about two-thirds of the way along the 96 mile route, consisted almost entirely of ridges. The ridges, although somewhat lower in the south than the north, were precipitous, and were difficult even to climb let alone fight over. Supply was arduous in the extreme. Sometimes log steps were cut into the dank jungles flanking the ridges. However, the step itself was frequently little more than a pool of mud and water. A fully laden soldier might take an hour to walk one or two miles in the most vertiginous stretches. Warrant Officer Wilkinson wrote, "A long day . . . last downhill to camp very hard to take. Many falls as knees gave way."[25] From Kokoda Village to the north the trail rose gradually to 2,190m at Bellamy's Peak before descending southwards toward ever more precipitous ridges as Port Moresby was approached. Cloud and mist often descended to 1,000 foot in the Owen Stanleys making the march for soldiers sunless, humid and dank. Temperatures as low as five degrees at night replaced tropical conditions during the day.

Sir Kingsley Norris, senior medical officer of the 7th Division gave a graphic account of life on the trail for a marching soldier, describing

> series of ridges, each rising higher and higher until seven thousand feet is reached, then declining in ridges to three thousand feet . . . short trees and tall trees, tangled with great, entwining savage vines. Through an oppression of this density, cut a little native track, two or three feet wide, up the ridges, over the spurs, round gorges and down across swiftly-flowing, happy mountain streams. Where the track clambers up the mountain sides, cut steps—big steps, little steps, steep steps . . . Every few miles, bring the track through a small patch of sunlit kunai grass, or an old deserted native garden, and every seven or ten miles, build a group of dilapidated grass huts—as staging shelters—generally set in a foul, offensive clearing. Every now and then, left beside the track dumps of discarded, putrefying food, occasional dead bodies and human foulings. In the morning, flicker the sunlight through the tall trees, flutter green and blue and purple and white butterflies lazily through the air, and hide birds of deep-throated song, or harsh cockatoos, in the foliage . . . About midday, and through the night, pour water over the forest, so that the steps become broken, and a continual yellow stream flows downwards, and the

> few level areas become pools and puddles of putrid black
> mud. In the high ridges above Myola, drip this water day
> and night over the track through a fetid forest grotesque
> with moss and glowing phosphorescent fungi. Such is the
> . . . route for ten days.[26]

It would be difficult to imagine a more difficult terrain in which to fight or to keep troops supplied. Critically the senior Allied commanders, neither MacArthur nor his deputy, Sutherland, nor Australia's General Blamey made the effort to see the conditions on the ground.

With confirmation from MAGIC intercepts that Australia would not be invaded, thus discounting the possibility that the landings at Gona were a diversion, MacArthur and Blamey could now countenance a more full-blooded reinforcement of East New Guinea. The backbone of New Guinea's defense would rely on Australia's 21st Brigade, led by Brigadier Arnold Potts. In addition Major-General Arthur 'Tubby' Allen's battle hardened 7th Division, back from the Middle East, was sent to Port Moresby where they were held in reserve. While both sides were preparing their forces for the next engagement, a battle for air supremacy raged above them. On 17 August, Port Moresby was hit by its seventy-eighth air raid, often a twice-daily occurrence. Better radar equipment did not arrive from America until mid-September, which meant that Allied fighter pilots in their Bell P-39 Airacobras and Curtiss P-40 Warhawks depended heavily on coastal spotters. Fighter pilot casualties were high while the Allied bombers had to make their attacks from bases situated in north Australia, with their main targets the key Japanese bottleneck along the Kokoda Trail, as well as Kokoda Airfield where they tried to prevent Japanese resupply.

The pell-mell nature of the fighting is indicated in Warrant Officer Wilkinson's account of a skirmish at Pirivi village near Kokoda on 5 August:

> Shot two Japs in village and one in garden. Snipers held
> us up for One? Hours. Lost two killed five wounded. Hell
> of a mess in village during scrimmage. Believe I pinned
> one Jap to the ground with bayonet and screamed with
> laughter. Remember putting field dressing on one of our
> chaps and firing at the roof at the same time.[27]

Three days later, Major Allen Cameron launched an attack on Kokoda with the 39th Battalion. At the same time Lieutenant-Colonel Hatsuo Tsukamoto, feared as a strict disciplinarian, was preparing to launch his own offensive. It was a rare engagement of the *Pacific War* where two offensive actions met head on. Cameron's aim was to recapture the village and its airbase. Splitting his force into three companies, D-Company met heavy Japanese opposition and spent the next two days in a fighting withdrawal. C-Company was ambushed, its commander was killed and it had to withdraw; A-Company took the virtually undefended village of Kokoda but was surrounded and had to fight its way back toward Deniki village which, after a brief fight, was abandoned by the Australians on 13 August. A-Company finally joined up with the remainder of 39th Battalion at Isurava.

Cameron's attempted counter-attack taught him and his officers a new lesson, that the Japanese were as able in defense as attack. Australian troops were shocked by the brilliance of Horii's troops. One soldier reported that on one attack, "We got to within 15 feet, but we still couldn't see them." He complained with grudging admiration, "You don't even see the Jap who gets you! It's like fighting the invisible man. Those Japs are tough, hard fighters and their camouflage is perfect."[28] In hindsight it seems likely that Cameron's reckless counter-attack on Kokoda severely depleted the strength of the 39th Battalion, which was now required to block the Japanese advance. Cameron would later claim that he was heavily outnumbered though how he could have gauged this is hard to fathom. Post-war evidence suggests that both sides were evenly matched with between 400 and 500 men each, though Tsukamoto's forces probably had the advantage in terms of field guns. After marching the ninety-six miles of the Kokoda Trail and having been rebuffed at the *Battle of Kokoda Airfield*, the soldiers of the 39th Battalion were a spent force. Years later, Lieutenant-Colonel Ralph Honner described his first impression of his new battalion:

> Physically, the pathetically young warriors of the 39th were in poor shape. Worn out by strenuous fighting and exhausting movement, and weakened by lack of food and sleep and shelter, many of them had literally come to a standstill. Practically every day torrential rains fell all through the afternoon and night, cascading into their cheerless weapon pits and soaking the clothes they wore—the only ones they had. In these they shivered through the long chill vigil of the lonely nights when they were required to stand awake and alert, but still silent.[29]

Potts' Fighting Withdrawal: The Battles of Isurava, Brigade Hill, Ioribaiwa and Imita Ridge: After a two-week period of consolidation after the *Second Battle of Kokoda*, General Horii moved forward toward Isurava on 26 August. Having won the first and second *Battles of Kokoda Airfield*, his troops now faced the hard slog upwards to the highest point of the Kokoda Trail's passage through the Owen Stanley Mountains. A Japanese soldier noted in his diary, "The road gradually gets steeper. The sun is fierce here. We make our way through a jungle where there are no roads. The jungle is beyond description. Thirst for water. Stomach empty."[30] Many of the Japanese soldiers were forced to make the trek to Isurava direct from the beaches with little or no respite. Sergeant Kawate Ryozo noted in his diary that on beaching, he was surprised that "it was only jungle there" and went on to record, "We all carried 30 kg packs and started walking at night . . . It was rainy and the path was very muddy and we could hardly move forward. Some of the newly recruited soldiers, started saying, 'I cannot walk anymore. Kill me right here, please.' We had to beat them and force them to walk."[31]

At its steepest 2,000 steps were cut out of mud on the side of the mountain and reinforced by cut saplings. Each step was two-foot high and there were no resting places. To the Australian troops the track became known as 'The Bloody Track'; sections acquired nicknames such as 'The Golden Staircase' and 'The Wall.' On Saturday 29 August, Private Stuart Clarke described his life thus: "bullets everywhere—hell on earth amongst the clouds in the mountains."[32]

Horii's first wave of 2,500 troops supported by an equal reserve, faced 2,300 Australian soldiers from the 39th and 53rd Battalions as well as some units of the 49th. Under fierce mortar and artillery fire, the 39th held firm as Japanese troops made fierce frontal attacks, while another Japanese force sought to encircle them and cut off their line of retreat. Lieutenant-Colonel Horner later gave a graphic account of an engagement that was the heaviest of the campaign to date:

> Heavy machine-guns—the dread "wood-peckers"—chopped through the trees . . . the enveloping forest erupted into violent action as Nippon's screaming warriors streamed out of its shadows to the assault . . . The enemy came on in waves over a short stretch of open ground, regardless of casualties . . . They were met with Bren-gun and Tommy-gun, with bayonet and grenade; but still they came, to close with the buffet of fist and boot and rifle-butt, the steel of crashing helmets and of straining, strangling fingers. [It was] vicious fighting, man to man and hand to hand.[33]

As thousands of men would find after them, jungle battles were peculiar in terms of the closeness of combat. A study by US medical officers later in the war showed that in jungle engagements such as the *Battle of Isurava*, 50 percent of casualties received their wounds at distances of less than 25 yards, and 85 percent at distances less than 50 yards. One private recalled that "When the Japs were about ten feet away . . . I shrivelled up into almost nothing."[34]

The 53rd Battalion defending the alternative trail beyond Isurava, was bombarded with mortar fire from the ridges overlooking their perimeter. Some platoons were overrun. A survivor from one of these engagements, Private Bruce Kingsbury, joined up with another platoon in a counter-attack. Picking up a Bren gun, he charged forward and cleared a swathe through the advancing Japanese forces. Although he was shot dead by a sniper, Kingsbury's charge, for which he was awarded a posthumous Victoria Cross, temporarily halted the Japanese advance. However, the imminent threat of encirclement of the 39th Battalion forced Brigadier Arnold Potts to order a withdrawal. Although the *Battle of Isurava* was another victory for Horii, it did not achieve the annihilation of the Australian forces that he had hoped for. Furthermore, over the six days of fighting to

31 August the Japanese had lost 140 men killed and 231 wounded compared to 99 Australian dead and 111 further casualties. A battle of attrition did not suit General Horii whose lines of supply were becoming ever more tenuous. A fighting retreat took Potts backwards to Eora Creek on 30 August, Templeton's Crossing on 2 September and Efogi on 5 September. The fighting retreat to Efogi was helped by the decidedly slow pace of Colonel Kyomi Yazawa's advance. Major Koiwai who had led the pursuit wrote about the advance after the war:

> Since yesterday's failed attack he had not liked my cautious approach. He seemed to be anxious for a quick victory but it was not easy to attack the enemy without knowing where they were. Being too eager for a victory could result in delaying the pursuit and increasing our losses. This is the last thing a commander should do.[35]

In spite of Yazawa's cautious approach, forty-three Japanese dead still outnumbered Australians killed by a two to one margin. The week-long advance that covered less than two miles a day gave time for the Australians to prepare their defenses to make another stand at Efogi. An irritated Horii decided that Colonel Kunusone's 144th Regiment, which had fought at Isurava, should replace Yazawa's regiment as leaders of the pursuit.

At Efogi, General MacArthur again called for Potts to resume the offensive. In spite of his demands for aggressive action, MacArthur denied Potts the 2/27th Battalion reinforcements requested because they needed to be held back while the outcome of the concurrent *Battle of Milne Bay* on the southern tip of east New Guinea remained uncertain. MacArthur's demands for offense paid scant regard to the conditions of the Australian troops after a week of fighting retreat. One soldier noted,

> During this time most of them had been unable even to brew themselves a mug of tea and certainly had not had a hot meal. Now shelter-less, their feet pulpy and shrivelled from the constant wet, they were soaked by continuous rain. They were worn out by fighting in country where movement alone for even unencumbered men was a hardship.[36]

Although Potts was ordered to hold the forward supply base on the open, dry lakebed at Myola that was being supplied, inadequately, by air, further Japanese outflanking attacks made the Australian position indefensible.

Importantly Potts was able to destroy what remained of his supplies and withdraw. When Horii's HQ was later captured at Isurava, the Allies found an order from Horii to his officers to "exercise the most painstaking control and supervision, so that every bullet accounts for an enemy, and every grain of rice furthers the task of the Shitai. Full use must be made of captured ammunition and provisions."[37] In hindsight it was clear that the Japanese advance to Port Moresby was conducted on the tightest of margins regarding logistical support. Horii's task was not made easier by the fact that because of a lack of maps, a problem shared equally with the Australians, he had only a loose idea of where he was going or what was the nature of the landscape; his direction was largely guided by the pursuit of an enemy that he guessed knew its way.

Neither had it helped Horii that he had not been able to capture all the Allied supply dumps that he had anticipated would fall into his hands. There were some exceptions. After the *Battle of Isurava*, Japanese troops came across a food dump at Alola where a Japanese soldier noted that "We had as much food as we could carry . . . our regiment could not carry it all and the rest was handed to the main force . . . Everyone was as excited as a child with their gorgeous breakfast of hardtack and butter."[38] Seizo Okada, an *Asahi Shimbun* war correspondent embedded with the troops, reported, "It seemed as though we had suddenly landed in fairyland."[39] As he gorged on captured Allied food he reflected on "the appalling power of Anglo-American civilization that Japan had so recklessly challenged."[40] Further supply was sought by Japanese troops who scoured the jungle for wayward food drops by the Royal Australian Air Force (RAAF). In spite of these sporadic windfalls, by September, the issue of rice was down to a small handful per day. Perversely, the more advanced the troops the less food they received. Seizo Okada noted, "All the troops showed unmistakable signs of weakness and exhaustion."[41] For the Japanese troops, the slog over the Owen Stanley Range seemed to be never ending. When they finally saw the sea, still miles from their ultimate objective, the Japanese troops hugged each other with joy and wept.

The next stop on the retreat was Mission Ridge. Here Potts finally placed his newly arrived 2/27th Battalion (21st Brigade/7th Division) reinforcements from Port Moresby and on 6 September he was further resupplied with troops of the 2/14th and 2/16th Battalions. On 7 September Horii, also reinforced, led a total force of 3,000 troops in a frontal attack on Mission Ridge. There soon followed a typical Japanese jungle flanking movement from the right. The Japanese flankers came out of the jungle behind the 2/27th and engaged Potts' reserve that had been placed on Brigade Hill.

Horii's right hook cut Potts off from three of his battalions and threatened to overrun his headquarters. Yet again an Australian retreat had to be ordered along the trail toward the village of Menari. Eighty-eight troops of the 2/14th and 2/16th were killed as they tried to break through Japanese encirclement. As for the 2/27th at the head of the trail, they found themselves completely cut off. For a while, they were thought to have been completely annihilated. However, the 2/27th negotiated an arduous two-week trek along a different path through the mountains to Jawarere where they re-joined the main Australian forces. These 500 troops, about half the troops at Mission Ridge, were effectively lost to the defenders that now assembled at Ioribaiwa.

Unbeknownst to the Allies, their task had been made considerably easier by the decision of Japan's Imperial HQ to downgrade the importance of the assault on Port Moresby. US Marines had landed on the island of *Guadalcanal* in the southern *Solomons* on 7 August and by 28 August it had become clear that this was more than the raiding party initially suspected and it was envisioned that new assets both in terms of troops and logistics would have to be switched to this hitherto unforeseen area of operations. **[See Chapter 16: Guadalcanal I: Battles of Tulagi, Savo Island, Tenaru and East Solomons]** Thus even as the *Battle of Isurava* was being fought Horii's new order was to "advance to the southern slopes of the Owen Stanley Range and destroy the enemy troop positions there."[42] However, Horii's further instructions clearly limited the scope of his further operations on the 'downhill' route toward Port Moresby: "Use a portion of your strength to secure the front but amass your main strength on the north side of the range in preparation for future operations."[43] Thus instead of the 5,000 troops originally intended for the final attack on Port Moresby, Horii sent only 3,500 troops over the high point of the Owen Stanley Range while the plan for a combined land and amphibious attack, with an additional 5,000 troops, on the main Australia garrison at Port Moresby was put on hold. With just 3,500 troops there was no intention to take on the 22,000 strong Australian Army at Port Moresby. On 31 August Imperial HQ issued Directive-127 confirming that *Guadalcanal* was now Seventeenth Army's principal area of operation and that the attack on Port Moresby was postponed until "after the development of *Guadalcanal* operations."[44]

The change in strategy forced by the situation on *Guadalcanal* was too late to save Potts. After his series of defeats Potts was relieved of command and replaced by Ivan Dougherty on 10 September. For MacArthur the successive defeats were a humiliation after his theatrical promise to the world's press: "We must attack, attack, attack!"[45] After relieving Potts, General Blamey addressed the assembled 21st Brigade and lashed them for failing to halt an inferior enemy, though he never made it clear on what grounds he considered the Japanese inferior. Reportedly Blamey told his troops that "no soldier should be afraid to die . . . Remember it's the rabbit who runs who get shot, not the man who holds the gun."[46] By all accounts the troops turned mutinous and sang *Run, Rabbit, Run* [1939], a favorite wartime ditty, whenever Blamey appeared within hearing of the enlisted men. Potts, who was blamed by the appropriately named Blamey for not launching a counter-attack at Kokoda, wrote to his wife swearing to "fry [Blamey's] soul in the afterlife."[47]

It is ironic that Potts, who, contrary to his own estimate of being heavily outnumbered, enjoyed rough troop parity with Horii's advancing forces, was sacked for failing to hold the Japanese. By contrast MacArthur, whose defeated army in the Philippines outnumbered Japanese forces by 2:1, was lauded as a hero, awarded the Medal of Honor and promoted to South West Area Command. For Australian soldiers to be told in effect that they were cowards was demoralizing. In the jungle meanwhile crude Japanese propaganda leaflets were telling them that their womenfolk were being seduced by the much better paid American troops in Australia. One Japanese leaflet depicted a GI having sex with an Australian girl with the caption, "Take your sweet time at the front Aussie. I got my hands full right now with your sweet tootsie at home."[48]

The irony of his own humiliation in the Philippines was lost on MacArthur who blamed his Australian soldiers for this latest reverse, telling Marshall, "the Australians have proven themselves unable to match the enemy in jungle fighting. Aggressive leadership is lacking."[49] MacArthur was preparing the ground to pass the buck on to General Blamey if Port Moresby was lost. Although MacArthur had formerly considered Blamey to be an effective officer, he now suggested that he was failing to 'energize' his troops. Blamey was a divisive figure: a whisky-drinking womanizer, he was described by one of MacArthur's officers as a "non-professional Australian drunk."[50] Disliked by many, Blamey was a skilled staff officer and administrator and in spite of his poor man-management skills would nevertheless emerge from the *Pacific War* with his reputation largely intact—though this may reflect more on his political skills.

In hindsight, in terms of performance, the Australian forces, untrained in jungle warfare, had proved themselves no different in performance against a Japanese flanking advance than MacArthur's US troops in the Philippines or General Percival's British troops in Malaya. In Australia, constant retreats were increasingly becoming a public scandal, largely because of misinformation being fed to them by MacArthur and his associates. In the international press, on 22 September, editorials in the *New York Times* and *The Herald Times* savaged the Australian leadership. They viewed the Japanese campaign toward Port Moresby as another '*Singapore.*' Complaints were reaching their crescendo just as the strategic and logistical balance of the battle was about to turn in the Allies' favor.

In Australia, a totalitarian censorship was imposed by MacArthur and the Australian government—journalists were proscribed from writing anything that was not in one of 'Doug's' *communiqués*. Remarkably Japanese reporter Seizo Okada, who marched with Horii's troops over the Owen Stanleys, was able to write with far more freedom than his peers from the 'liberal' west. In effect MacArthur stifled the possibility of press freedom and cleared the field for his own personal propaganda to dominate all accounts of the campaigns for which he was responsible.

Prime Minister Curtin, reacting to the public mood, ordered General Blamey to go to Port Moresby and take personal command. MacArthur raised no objections to a suggestion that provided him with the perfect scapegoat if Port Moresby were to fall. In Port Moresby, Blamey replaced Lieutenant-General Sydney Rowell, commander of I Corps, with Lieutenant-General Edmund 'Ned' Herring. Rowell, who loathed Blamey after his experience as his Chief of Staff in the Middle East, complained to General Cyril Clowes at *Milne Bay* that "He comes here when the tide is on the turn and all is likely to be well."[51] In this respect, Rowell was prescient. Subsequent to sacking Rowell, Blamey pursued him with a vicious ferocity, refusing to allow him overseas appointments and demanding his demotion and early retirement.

Reinforcements were again sent to the new front line that was now formed at Ioribaiwa Ridge, including the 3rd Battalion Militia, 2nd Battalion, 1st Pioneer Battalion, 2nd/6th Independent Company and a unit comprising elements of the 39th Battalion and 2nd/6th Independent Company. Freshly trained forces from the 25th Brigade also arrived on 13 September under the command of Brigadier Ken Eather. Eather's soldiers fought Colonel Kunusone's pursuers to a standstill at Ioribaiwa where the defenders outnumbered the attackers by two to one. Kunusone's forces were stuck with no reserves available to break the deadlock. However, Eather appears to have convinced himself that he had been defeated and it was recorded in the brigade diary that "Owing to enemy penetration on both flanks of our position on 'Ioribaiwa Ridge' Brigadier Eather considered that enemy could not be held in present position and ordered Brigade to withdraw to vicinity of Imita Ridge."[52]

Later analysis showed that Australian forces were significantly hampered by lack of field artillery. They had no artillery light enough to carry for use in mountain warfare unlike Horii's forces, which were provided with sixteen 75 mm and 70 mm field guns. These guns were carried by packhorses or by the troops themselves. Field guns could be devastating in jungle conditions. At the *Battle of Iroibaiwa* half the Australian casualties were from artillery fire. Private Eric Williams noted that even shells exploding high in the jungle trees could be deadly: he recalled one such explosion "killed the blokes with their head on the tree, because the percussion went straight down, split their skulls open . . . I could see they were dead."[53]

At Imita Ridge, it was decided to make a stand on one of the most precipitous ridges on the whole Kokoda Trail. It was also the last major barrier before the Kokoda Trail led down to the gentler slopes toward Port Moresby that was twenty-five miles away. Strong defensive positions were constructed along Imita Ridge, strong defensive positions were built, significantly aided by the now very short lines of communication and supply.

Asaku Koryu versus 'K' Rations versus Starvation: The Japanese advance from Buna had covered the first forty miles in five days, while the next thirty miles took fifty days. How long would the last twenty-five miles take? A war correspondent noted that "the speed of their advance slackens every day" and surmised that the Japanese were "now facing the difficulties, which caused our retreat from Kokoda, when we could not maintain almost impossible supply lines across a scarcely negotiable goat-track."[54]

Horii's Japanese forces, having come within sight of Port Moresby were indeed stretched to breaking point. Forced by Imperial HQ's changing priorities to keep back significant forces on the north side of the Owen Stanley Range, Horii did not have sufficient troop resources to complete his mission. It had been a remarkable advance in which his forces had suffered just 900 casualties. In the absence of any amphibious support, now shelved, Horii could only hold a defensive line. It has often been reported that the Japanese were denied supplies by the Australians' destruction of stores along their route of retreat and by Royal Australian Air Force (RAAF) sorties. In reality the weather was a greater danger than the RAAF. Although the RAAF dominated the skies throughout the campaign, they did little damage to the Japanese supply chain. According to one officer, "enemy bombing did not so seriously interfere because the land movement of supply was carried out during the night or [during] intervals of the bombing."[55] Cover provided by jungle foliage severely limited the effectiveness of bombing.

Horii only lacked the wherewithal to supply his troops when long periods of torrential rain swelled streams into raging torrents and swamped or swept away pathways and bridges. Poor weather also disrupted air supply to Kokoda Airfield. Unseasonably heavy rain fell from 9 September to 13 September when it seems that Horii's supply lines broke down completely. For the next four weeks it is estimated that the Japanese 'Stanley Detachment' were reduced to a ration providing just 4,000 kilojoules per day compared to the 12,000 kilojoules required for light work and 16,000 required for heavy duty. Lieutenant Sakamoto was able to provide his troops with some captured, albeit spoiled American rations but he noted that there was "Not a grain of rice left."[56] Korean and native porters, usually fed less than the troops, often stole from the thin line of provisions that managed to get to the front. Japanese transport troops would also help themselves. As one Japanese transport officer confessed, "Though we focused on the fact that we must not let the front line starve, in our hearts, we couldn't but be aware that we ourselves would die [on two cups of rice per day]."[57] To try to stave off hunger troops ate native taro plants and sucked on sugar cane sticks. By eking out sustenance from foraging it took several weeks of inadequate calorie intake from rations for unit effectiveness to tail off.

Advanced Japanese forces were the most badly affected. At times daily rations were reduced to a cup of rice and many failed to get even that. Soldiers were forced to exert themselves to forage for bananas or search out native gardens for yams and pumpkins. Rather than attack, Horii ordered his weak, bedraggled and starving troops to dig in defensive lines. "The detachment will stay here and firmly hold its position in order to perfect its organization and replenish its fighting spirit," ordered General Horii, "We will strike a hammer blow at the stronghold of Port Moresby."[58] However, while Japan's 'thin' logistics could just about sustain rapid offensive action, it was poorly designed for long drawn out defensive battles of attrition. In spite of the Japanese supply problems however, the forces operating over the Kokoda Trail never suffered the mass starvation that would later be experienced at the siege of Buna.

Reinforcements never came. They were being diverted to *Guadalcanal*. It would have been little comfort to MacArthur that it was the US Navy's Marines' heroic stand at Henderson Field on *Guadalcanal* that was saving his South Pacific Area Command from the humiliation of losing Port Moresby. After a setback to Lieutenant-General Harukichi Hyakutake's attempt to retake Henderson Field on 14 September, Imperial General Headquarters decided that it could no long support two fronts in the *South Pacific*. On New Guinea, Horii was ordered to withdraw. The *Battle of Milne Bay* apart, it was Japan's first significant retreat since the start of the war, and Horii's demoralized and starving troops had to make the arduous journey back over the Owen Stanley Range toward Gona where they were ordered to arrange the defense of the Gona-Buna coastal garrisons. "The order came like a bolt from the blue," said Captain Nakhashi, "causing an overflow of emotion ... feelings of anger, sorrow and frustration."[59] It was a demoralizing moment for the Japanese troops. Second Lieutenant Hirano recorded, "It left us momentarily dazed to have to retreat from our present position, after advancing so close to our goal at the cost of enormous sacrifices and casualties."[60] Japanese troops who had advanced on half rations or less found it more difficult to retreat on the same amount. The journalist Okada wrote that the order to retreat "had crushed the spirit of the troops."[61] The hiatus in the supply of food made the retreat even more strenuous. Major Koiwai's memoir recalled that "Our bodies were completely fatigued, so climbing even the smallest hill required a great effort . . . gasping for each breath . . . many were stooped over, their eyes filled with tears and without even the strength to urge themselves on."[62] Men on stretchers pleaded to be left and allowed to die.

In theory Japanese soldiers on campaign were entitled to *Assaku Koryo* (compressed ration) consisting of dried rice, pickled plums, dried fish, salt and vinegar. The individual components were delivered in tins or cellophane bags. Most of the foods were wrapped in waterproof paper and during the war was often prepared by Japanese schoolchildren who were thus drafted into the patriotic effort. In addition there were emergency rations. *'A' Rations* consisted of 825 grams of rice in a paper sack, 170 grams of meat or fish, 15 grams of *miso* powder and 15 grams of sugar. *'B' Rations* consisted just of high carbohydrate *kanpan* (hardtack crackers). In practice Japanese logistics of food supply to front line areas broke down within a year of the start of the *Pacific War*. Thereafter food supply was often *ad hoc* and highly dependent on local supply or foraging.

American rations were somewhat different, both in type of foods and quantity. When Marines went ashore they were provided with two canteens of water and 'K' Rations, which consisted of a breakfast, lunch and dinner. The 'K' Ration designed by University of Minnesota physiologist, Dr. Ancel Keys in 1941, included high-energy foods such as hard biscuits, candy, dry sausage and chocolate. Weighing 28 ounces and providing 3,200 calories, a 'K' Ration could be eaten by Marines every meal for a maximum of fifteen meals before being supplemented by an 'A' or 'B' Field Ration. It was tested in tropical conditions in Panama and seemed to induce no significant weight loss though in combat it proved to be not enough—1,200 calories short of what was needed for highly active men. Merrill's Marauders on operation in Burma found that living on 'K' Rations for prolonged periods of time reduced average body weight by 20 percent. 'K' Rations were packed in generic tan-colored rectangular boxes with black lettering US Army field Ration K. The units were marked B, D, S for breakfast, dinner (lunch) and supper respectively.

The breakfast unit consisted of veal loaf or canned ham and eggs, biscuits, dried fruit or cereal bar, Halazone water purification tablets, a 4-pack of cigarettes, chewing gum, instant coffee and sugar cubes. Dinner (lunch) offered the troops ham and cheese, biscuits, caramel candies, chewing gum, powdered lemon, cube sugar, salt packet, four cigarettes, matches. Supper was canned meat, chicken, beef or pork, biscuits, a 2 ounce chocolate bar, a fruit bar, more chewing gum, soup packet, toilet tissue and four more cigarettes.

In garrison conditions US soldiers were provided with 'A' Rations, while field kitchens served up 'B' Rations. While the quality of Army food could never compare with the Navy, it was nevertheless significantly better than most of their allies or enemies. 'C' Rations, a complete high protein, high carbohydrate meal in a single can, were the most disliked. Although the American GI had significantly better thought out and varied rations than the Japanese equivalent, it was much more important that the US Army was logistically capable of delivering the rations, even in the most trying of circumstances. US soldiers in the *Pacific*, unlike their Japanese counterparts, rarely had to resort to foraging and never had to turn to cannibalism.

Horii's Retreat: Cannibalism and Destruction: In the mountainous jungles along the Kokoda Trail the pursued now turned pursuer. As the Japanese Army retreated, the Australians harassed them. The advance along the Kokoda Trail brought back unhappy memories; at the juncture where 2nd Battalion 27th Regiment had been outflanked at the *Battle of Isurava*, "Dead men [Australians] were found in treetops. Others were sitting in their trenches, with the bones of their fingers clutched around the triggers of their weapons."[63] The area still smelt of death.

Horii's fighting retreat back to Gona was a nightmare of endurance. If the advance was hard, the retreat was harder across "a terrible terrain of thick mountain timber, great rocks drenched in rain, terrifying precipices and chasms . . . the track itself is knee deep in thick, black mud . . . every hour"[64] There was a bond of hatred for the Kokoda Trail shared by friend and foe alike. Troops overcome by disease and malnutrition simply expired by the wayside. The 2,000-foot climb to the highest of the Owen Stanley ridges was gut wrenching even for a fit man and the descent almost as bad. "Near Efogi," reported George Johnson, "on a slimy section of the track that reeks with the stench of death, the remains of an enemy soldier lies on a crude stretcher, abandoned by the Japanese retreat. The flesh had gone from his bones, and a white, bony claw sticks out of a ragged uniform sleeve. . ."[65]

In appealing for supplies of food to be brought to his army, the chief of staff of the Japanese Seventeenth Army pleaded that his troops were "only keeping themselves alive by eating tree buds, coconuts, and seaweed."[66] In fact the supply situation was much worse. As well as eating grass and roots, the evidence of mutilated bodies also revealed that retreating Japanese soldiers were reduced to cannibalism. The documentary, *Yuki te Shingun* [1987] (The Emperor's Naked Army Marches), which won the Calgary Film Award for director Kuzuo at the Berlin International Film Festival, showed former Japanese soldiers admitting to cannibalism in New Guinea. Sometimes they ate their own fallen colleagues but on occasion 'White pigs' (Australian soldiers) as well as 'Black pigs' (native Papuans) were also killed and eaten. The film was seen through the eyes of New Guinea veteran, Kenzo Okuzaki, who is filmed seeking out other former soldiers from the campaign. Okuzaki was in no doubt as who was to blame: ". . . the most cowardly man in Japan, is the Emperor Hirohito."[67]

As became normal during the New Guinea Campaign, soldiers on both sides were ten times more likely to become casualties of the jungle than from fighting. As MacArthur would repeatedly tell his commanders, from the comfort of his mansion—the jungle, if used correctly to drain Japanese resources, was their greatest ally. Although Horii set up strong defensive points at Templeton's Crossing and Eora Creek, exacting a heavy toll on the advancing Australian troops, it was the disease and the terrain that was most destructive to the retreating Japanese forces. By 19 October, Lieutenant Sakamoto was recording that "Because of the food shortage, some companies have been eating the flesh of Australian soldiers . . ."[68] Cannibalism was usually random but on occasions it seems that Japanese commanders planned and organized the eating and distribution of human flesh.

The Australians suffered almost as badly as the Japanese. Untrained in jungle survival, Australian troops wore shorts and short-sleeved shirts in the evenings when malaria-carrying mosquitoes were at their most predatory. Junior commanders failed to supervise the regular daily intake of quinine to prevent malaria. However, the mosquito was not the only flying predator in a jungle in which leeches, jungle mites and sand flies also vied for the real estate of a soldier's exposed flesh. At New Guinea's airfields the joke was that mosquitoes were so big that ground crews tried to refuel them mistaking them for airplanes. For the soldiers forced to live in the open during the campaign, the 'New Guinea Salute' referred to the waving away of swarms of black flies. As MacArthur was to discover at great cost to his troops, the jungle was a more deadly enemy than the Japanese.

Blithely unaware of the conditions, MacArthur complained about the slow progress in pushing Horii's forces back over the Owen Stanley Range, suggesting, "extremely light casualties indicate no serious effort yet made to displace the enemy."[69] With greater troop numbers than the Japanese, MacArthur and Blamey wanted to push harder even if that meant that Australian troops would have to fight on short rations and take higher casualties. If MacArthur had been informed by his liaison officers about the difficulties of terrain, weather, disease and supply faced by the Australian soldiers, his decisions gave little indication of any understanding. The Allies' front line commander, Major-General 'Tubby' Allen, a short overweight 48-year-old, who had trekked up the Kokoda Trail with a pack on his back wrote a message for Blamey telling him, "If you can do any better come up here and try."[70] Just in time, he cancelled the message before it was sent. His troops were not short of supplies after 70,000 pounds of food, ammunition and medical supplies were air dropped. Recovery was another matter. 'Tubby' Allen had to send virtually his entire force on a 'treasure hunt.' MacArthur remained oblivious to problems of command and forced Blamey to relieve the popular 'Tubby' Allen of his command on 28 October just before the vital breakthrough was made to re-take Isurava.

When a 1,250 man force of US 32nd Division led by Lieutenant-Colonel Henry Geeds, was sent on an extended flanking maneuver over the Owen Stanley Mountains by the Kapa Trail, a much harder trail even than the Kokoda Trail, it took them forty-two days fighting their way through dense jungle and near vertical ridges to arrive at Gona. By the time they reached Gona, the GIs, ravaged by malaria, dysentery and dengue fever, were left barely capable of fighting. On the journey Sergeant Paul Lutjens noted in his diary, "Our strength is gone. Most of us have dysentery. Boys are falling out and dropping back with fever."[71] MacArthur's disastrous flanking operation was yet another indication of how out of touch he and his command were with regard to the terrain and fighting conditions on New Guinea. As for Geeds, he suffered a heart attack and had to be carried out of the jungle. By the end of the *Battle of Buna-Gona* on 9 January only 165 of Geeds' men were left standing, though most of them were barely able to walk.

The Kokoda Trail finally yielded to the Australian advance in heavy fighting at the villages of Oivi and Gorari that lie a little beyond Kokoda itself. On 5 November the 2nd Battalion 2nd Regiment and 2nd Battalion 3rd Regiment were stopped by a strong defensive position set up at Oivi Village, which the 25th Brigade proceeded to envelope by a flanking operation. By the night of 9 November the Japanese retreat had been blocked at Gorari. Fierce fighting took place on 10 and 11 November as the surrounded Japanese troops tried to force their way through to safety. It was a bloodbath that took the lives of 440 Japanese soldiers for the loss of 121 Australians. All fifteen assembled Japanese field guns were captured. The *Battle of Oivi and Gorari* was the first real disaster suffered by Japanese forces on the Kokoda Trail.

By 13 November, engineers from the 2nd Battalion 31st Regiment had swum across the *Kumusi River* at Wairopi. Material was ferried across and a footbridge constructed. Within a few days all seven Australian battalions that had chased the retreating Japanese up and down the Owen Stanley Range had successfully traversed. The *Battle of Kokoda* was finally ended. It had cost over 2,200 Australian casualties: just under a third were killed. However, if casualties included sickness from tropical diseases the number could be multiplied by ten. It is a reflection of the bitterness of the fighting and the conditions of combat that the casualty rate in the *Battle of the Kokoda Trail* was double that of the *Battle of Guadalcanal*, an engagement that is often seen as a benchmark for the ghastliness of combat in the *South Pacific*. Many of the Japanese taken prisoner were murdered by embittered Australian troops. "To men with no respect for the humanity of their enemy," wrote Mark Johnson, "the practical difficulties of the situation probably made killing them on the spot seem reasonable"[72]: it was a situation that must have been familiar to many Japanese soldiers during their rapid conquest of Asia. Without logistical and administrative support, keeping prisoners was often all but impossible. Neither were the conditions of terrain and geography conducive to generosity toward a captured soldier.

Japanese soldiers were not the only troops consumed by visceral racial loathing. Australian hatred of the Japanese was tinged with racism. One soldier who had fought Italians and Germans in Libya and Greece reflected, "My regard for Tony [the Italian] was always impersonal and Fritz . . . tinged with admiration, but none of us know anything but vindictive hatred for the Jap."[73]

The Battle of Milne Bay: *Milne Bay* on the southeastern tip of New Guinea was developed as an airbase for Royal Australian Air Force (RAAF) bombers to intercept Japanese naval attempts to take Port Moresby and also as a relay station for bombers transiting from attacking the Japanese stronghold at Rabaul. Troops and equipment had started to arrive on 25 June and a rapid build-up continued thereafter. A first runway was built on marshy but useable ground with matting cover. A further two runways were started.

When Japanese planes discovered the building of an RAAF airbase, Lieutenant-General Harukichi Hyakutake requested Vice-Admiral Gunichi Mikawa to capture *Milne Bay* with his 8th Fleet. For Japan the importance of *Milne Bay* was to deny the Americans an airfield base from which they could attack Rabaul and also a base from which an amphibious assault on Port Moresby could be made. After making an intelligence misjudgement about the number of Allied troops (mainly Australian) at *Milne Bay*, a small assault force was assembled including 612 *Rikusentai* Troops from the 5th Sasebo SNLF (Special Naval Landing Forces), commanded by Commander Masajiro Hayashi. A second force of 350 troops from the 10th Naval Landing Force and 100 men from the 2nd Air Advance Party were landed at another site. Two light Type-95 Ha-Go tanks were also brought ashore to support the attack. The main Japanese force of 1,000 troops landed at Waga at the northern edge of the bay.

The attack had been anticipated. When decrypted intelligence revealed the operation of a submarine picket around *Milne Bay*, MacArthur's intelligence chief, Brigadier-General Charles Willoughby, warned of an impending attack. MacArthur had rushed in the 18th Infantry Brigade as reinforcement. When the first Japanese attacks came on 26 and 27 August they were met with unexpectedly heavy resistance particularly around Airfield No.3 where reportedly "the Japanese went down like corn . . . they were forced to withdraw when the line of Japanese dead at the edge of the airfield was almost six feet high."[74] It did not help that in the heavy mud flats around the airfield the Japanese tanks became stuck and had to be abandoned; realizing that they had underestimated the size of the Australian units at *Milne Bay*, a further 567 *Rikusentai* from the 3rd Kure SNLF as well as 200 more from 5th Yokosuka SNLF were sent by convoy. On 29 August Commander Masajiro Hayashi's reinforcements and more supplies of food, munitions and equipment arrived off Waga and were unloaded. Although the SNLF enjoyed a reputation as crack troops, within the Imperial Japanese Navy their quality was less esteemed and even the US War Department handbook noted that they had "a surprising lack of ability in infantry combat."[75]

With new Japanese forces, Hayashi prepared another attack for the early hours of 31 August. *Banzai* charges across the airfield, which the Australians lit by flares, were cut down by heavy machine gun fire. Heavy Japanese casualties included Hayashi himself. The commander of the fresh *Rikusentai* forces, Minoru Yano, then attempted to outflank the Australian positions but they too found themselves hosed down by Bren machine gun fire and were forced to retreat. In the coconut groves there was hand to hand fighting: "One Australian was walking through a coconut grove when a Jap dropped on him from the trees, He was impaled on the Australian's bayonet . . . finished him off, as he thought . . . the Jap, with a dying effort . . . emptied his Tommy gun into the Australian"; another Australian, severely wounded after being, "stabbed in the back by a stalking Jap wrestled with his assailant and strangled him to death with his bare hands."[76]

On 31 August 2nd Battalion 12th Infantry Regiment commanded by Lieutenant-General Cyril Clowes led the Australian counter-offensive and recaptured the third airstrip and the 'KB Mission.' That night 300 retreating Japanese who had found themselves cut off were ambushed and lost some ninety soldiers killed. In the night Japanese troops infiltrated Australian lines:

> Some of the Japs were without firearms . . . Completely naked and armed only with long knives, they raided inside the Australian lines at night, or swam along the foreshore to get behind our positions. The awful bubbling scream of a man whose throat had been cut was often the only evidence that these night-prowling killers were in the Australian positions.[77]

After a night of fighting off Japanese infiltration, the Australians again went on the offensive on the morning of 1 September, this time led by the 2nd Battalion 9th Regiment. Corporal John French typified the fighting spirit of the Australian troops when he attacked and destroyed two machine gun posts single-handedly with grenades before being killed as he attacked a third with his Thompson sub-machine gun. He was later awarded a posthumous Victoria Cross.

By now, Yano had given up all hope of taking the airfield and determined simply to hang on until they could be rescued. By the time that the light cruiser *Tatsuta* and the rescue convoy arrived on 5 September there were only fifty fully fit Japanese troops left fighting with all their company commanders killed and a handful of platoon leaders still alive. Overall the Japanese forces suffered 936 casualties of whom 625 were killed. On the other side, 167 Australians were killed as well as 373 wounded. The Australian dead included thirty-six Australians who were captured by the Japanese and subsequently executed. In some cases it was found that their bodies had been mutilated. In addition some fifty-nine civilians were also murdered.

If the *Battle of the Kokoda Trail*, which ended two weeks earlier, was the first campaign in which Japan suffered defeat, the *Battle of Milne Bay*, leaving aside a few temporary repulses in the course of their *Pacific* advance, was their first military defeat, predating the *Battle of Edson's Ridge* on *Guadalcanal* by a week. Albeit a minor engagement in the context of the *Pacific War*, the *Battle of Milne Bay* dispelled the myth that Japanese troops were unbeatable supermen. The importance of air cover was also underlined. Whereas the Royal Australian Air Force (RAAF) could give air cover to their troops within minutes of a break in the clouds that hung over *Milne Bay*, it was later estimated by the Japanese 4th Fleet that only one in every four missions from airfields at Buna or Lae provided any meaningful assistance.

In spite of the Australian victory there was sniping from MacArthur's HQ in Brisbane: in response, Major-General Clowes complained that the Americans should "visit the jungle to see what conditions are, instead of sitting back and criticizing."[78] In spite of this, the uplift on morale was to have a hugely beneficial effect on Australian troops for the long New Guinea Campaign that lay ahead. As an elated war correspondent, George Johnson reported, "This is our first big success against the much publicized Japanese *tadori*, and it deserves to be set down in some detail . . ."[79] On hearing of the Japanese withdrawal from *Milne Bay*, staff at the American HQ at the Lenon Hotel in Brisbane cracked open the champagne and sycophantically hailed their victorious Commander in Chief, MacArthur. While MacArthur congratulated the Australians in public, in private he wrote to General Marshall and suggested, "[Australian] Aggressive leadership is lacking . . . The decisive factor was the complete surprise obtained over him by our preliminary concentration of superior forces."[80] It was a curmudgeonly, wholly disingenuous note that tried to deflect the glory of the hour onto MacArthur's own actions.

Reflections on the Importance of the Battles of the Kokoda Trail: Throughout their advance in South East Asia from December 1941 onwards, Japanese forces had always trodden a fine line in terms of margin for error or setback. Their rapid and aggressive frontal attacks combined with peerless jungle flanking movements enabled them to sustain rapid forward momentum. As a result they planned logistics for short campaigns; it was all that Japan's 'thin' logistical capabilities could stretch to. An advancing Japanese Army could operate on just four tons per thousand men per day (PTMD) while American and Allied armies needed a minimum of twelve tons PTMD. In 1944 the US Army in Europe was being supplied for operations at an astonishing rate of seventy tons PTMD. As early as the *Russo-Japanese War* [1904–1905], it was noted by observer Captain Frederick Sedgwick, "the Japanese soldier can live for days on rice and fish . . . no European troops could march and fight on such a diet."[81] Even in terms of troop transportation, Japanese requirements were a fraction of those of the United States. In ships, space for a Japanese infantryman was calculated at 2 square meters compared to 6 square meters for an American. Where it would take three Japanese ships to move 5,000 troops, it would take nine American ships to move the same number. Nevertheless Japan's 'thin' logistics made them extremely vulnerable in the event of failure in meeting the 'timed' schedule of advance.

In the field the Japanese soldier could also operate at tolerances beyond those of the Allied soldier. Second Lieutenant Kanemoto, a supply officer, noted that they carried out research on how many days their troops could carry food and fight offensively. A special frame was designed for their backs, which enabled them to fight while carrying eight *sho* (11.2 kg) of rice. If daily consumption was temporarily reduced to just four *go* (560 grams) it was reckoned that at the extreme limit, Japanese troops could carry their own food and advance for twenty days without resupply from the rear. Kanemoto concluded, "this experiment was the key to the overland advance on Port Moresby."[82] As was common with Japanese armies, food supply was supplemented by well-organized foraging. Taro, a starchy root vegetable was common along with sweet potatoes while pigs, domesticated and wild, were plentiful. Troops were trained in foraging techniques and references to pig chasing are common in Japanese war diaries. Contrary to much post-war speculation the Japanese advance was not halted by their troops' lack of supply but rather by the shift in Japan's strategic priorities.

It can be speculated that had it not been for Vandegrift's Marines' spirited defense of *Henderson Field* on *Guadalcanal*, Horii might quite possibly have received the resources that could have pushed him 'over the line' in his bid to take Port Moresby. Certainly Japanese high command did not blame Horii for the failure. Horii was drowned when he took a raft down to the Buna coast. After the raft became stuck, Horii commandeered a canoe, which overturned when he got to the open sea: Colonel Tanaka drowned first and then the exhausted Horii told Private Shigeji Fukuoka, formerly a fisherman, that "I haven't the strength to swim further. Tell the troops I died here."[83] Lifting his arms above his head he shouted, "*Tenno Heika Banzai*" (long live the Emperor) before sinking under the water. Horii was awarded a posthumous promotion to lieutenant-general.

As for the Australian troops and their officers, much abused at the time, they kept their forces intact, which thus enabled them to conduct an orderly retreat. Although Potts' tactical decisions were sometimes suspect and his claims of being massively outnumbered shown to be incorrect, his retreat had advantages. By fighting and giving ground, not dissimilar to the tactics used by Chiang Kai-shek in China, Australian commanders used up the Japanese 'timeline' and ate into their logistical capabilities. By ignoring MacArthur's orders to counter-attack, which would surely have wiped them out, Brigadier Potts' fighting withdrawals created the conditions for the ultimate victory of Australian forces on the Kokoda Trail. It was an epic battle in the context of the whole *Pacific War*, important for being the first major ground setback suffered by Japan in *World War II*; a tag that is usually allocated by historians to the US Marines at *Guadalcanal*, should rightfully belong to the Australian Army for its heroic fight along the length of the Kokoda Trail.

MacArthur, in complete disregard of the facts told General Marshall, "The Australians have proven themselves unable to match the enemy in jungle fighting."[84] If the Australian troops never won MacArthur's respect, they did at least win over the appreciation of the Japanese. In a memorandum on *Enemy Fighting Methods*, the Australian soldier was characterized as "A slow firer, but skilful in covering roads and precipices: fires and throws grenades at close range; fond of using grenades; fighting spirit is unexpectedly intense. He does not retreat in single firing combat."[85] Infantryman Susumu Kawano, who had arrived in New Guinea on 18 August, noted in his diary on 27 November, "The strength of the Australian soldier is superior to that of the Nippon soldier."[86] That is not to say that the Japanese forces lacked skill: "Japanese doctrine laid stress on winning by cunning and with as few casualties as possible."[87]

While reasonable criticisms were made of junior commanders and other unit failings at the start of the *Battle of the Kokoda Trail*, these were trivial compared to the colossal mistakes made by Generals MacArthur and Blamey. Having failed to acquire appropriate intelligence, they appeared to be entirely without knowledge of the monstrosity of the terrain and fighting conditions or the sophisticated nature of either the Japanese offensive capabilities or later, their defense systems. The Australian soldiers were sent into battle underprepared and ill-trained, as well as lacking in adequate equipment and support. Given MacArthur's previous experience in the Philippines, it seems remarkable in hindsight that he appeared to have learnt nothing from this humiliating defeat. Ultimately

Australia won the *Battle of the Kokoda Trail* because the Japanese were incapable of providing reinforcements of new fresh troops to the front lines and the logistical resources to support them. In this respect the Australians were significantly helped by the diversion of Japanese troops and resources to *Guadalcanal*. By the end of the *Battle of Kokoda Trail*, General Blamey was able to deploy more than double the number of troops of his opposite number, Major-General Horii.

Since *World War II*, the role of the militiamen of the 39th Battalion in defending Australia at the *Battle of Kokoda Trail*, the first and only time the country was ever seemingly on the point of being invaded, has become a legendary encounter comparable to the *Battle of the Alamo* in American history or the Spartan defense at the *Battle of Thermopylae* in European history. Although a slightly exaggerated mythology, fanned by the exuberant reporting of George Johnson and others, has sometimes been created around the story of the *Battle of the Kokoda Trail*, the extended battle was nevertheless one of the turning points of the *Pacific War*. After initial fragility, the performance of Australian troops was exceptional in some of the most difficult battle conditions of the war. Much overlooked relative to the engagements at *Guadalcanal*, the Australian victory at the *Battle of the Kokoda Trail* was a major event in the *Pacific War* that has frequently been overlooked in American histories. John Toland's Pulitzer Prize-winning account *The Rising Sun: The Decline and Fall of the Japanese Empire 1936–1945* [1970] manages to omit the *Battle of the Kokoda Trail* by name. More annoyingly from an Australian viewpoint, Toland credited American troops and General Eichelberger with fighting their way over the Owen Stanley Mountains—an engagement in which neither American troops nor Eichelberger were present. Unlike the Australians, almost all the Americans who fought at the *Battle of Buna-Gona* were flown over the Owen Stanley Mountains.

For Japan's high command the *Battle of the Kokoda Trail* was regarded as a major turning point even at the time. In his post-war *Showa Tenno no Dokuhaku Roku Hachi-Jikan* (the Emperor's Eight Hour Soliloquy) Hirohito observed, "I knew we had lost any hope for victory when we failed to hold the Stanley Mountain Range on New Guinea . . ."[88] Thereafter Hirohito's hopes of getting something out of the *Pacific War* diminished rapidly and he reflected that after the *Battle of the Kokoda Trail*, "I hoped to give the enemy one good bashing somewhere, and then seize a chance for peace."[89]

16 Guadalcanal I: Battles of Tulagi, Savo Island, Tenaru and East Solomons

[May 1942–August 1942]

[Maps: 16.1, 16.2A, 16.2B, 16.3, 16.4, 16.5, 16.6, 16.7]

Strategies, Plans and Dissensions: [Map: 16.1] While Japan was pushing Australian forces back over the Owen Stanley Mountains in their advance on Port Moresby, the US Navy was initiating its own offensive in the southern *Solomon Islands*—the ultimate aim being to interdict Japan's expansion into the southern *Pacific Ocean*, which could have threatened supply routes to MacArthur's Allied Forces in Australia. Furthermore Admiral Ernest King wanted to put pressure on Japan's key *South Pacific* garrison at Rabaul.

Rabaul is a township on the easternmost tip of *New Britain*, an island 320 miles long and up to twenty-nine miles wide off the east coast of New Guinea. An unlikely place perhaps for a full-scale Japanese invasion faced by its garrison of just 1,400 Australian troops on 23 January 1942. Three days earlier, Japanese planes had appeared overhead. The Royal Australian Air Force's eight multi-purpose Wirraway fighter-bombers, based on a 1934 design bought from North American Aviation, were no match for over a hundred Japanese planes from Vice-Admiral Nagumo's four carriers, *Akagi, Kaga, Zuikaku* and *Shokaku*, fresh from their victory at *Pearl Harbor*. The Wirraways were quickly dispatched. As Gunner David Bloomfield recalled, "It was like hawks attacking sparrows."[1] On the ground, in spite of fierce initial resistance, the defenders were quickly overcome by Major-General Tomitaro Horii's invasion forces and the Australian troops fled into the jungle from where, piecemeal, they proceeded to surrender over the following weeks. Those who stayed and fought were less fortunate. Natives recalled that "some retreating Australians were killed in a fight and their heads were cut with axes, bellies sliced open, and limbs removed with bayonets."[2]

Rabaul, formerly the capital of Imperial Germany's New Guinea colony, was built partly on the mangrove swamps from which it took its name. Tavurvur, a volcano, which had largely destroyed Rabaul in 1937, overlooks it. The town's importance rested only on the scale and perfection of its almost totally enclosed natural harbor. Taken over from Germany by Australia as spoils of war after the *Treaty of Versailles* [1919], it was awarded to Australia as part of a League of Nations 'New Guinea Mandate' and remained a quiet backwater of the Australian Empire until Japan's Imperial HQ decided that its harbor would make it a perfect military and naval garrison for the outer perimeter of its *Pacific* Empire.

Lieutenant Saiji Matsuda, a junior *Kempeitai* officer, described the base in romantic terms:

> the first time I saw Rabaul, it was truly beautiful. It was like an oil painting in primary colors. I couldn't help but be struck by the master hand of God of creation. In the sky, our navy planes bravely flew back and forth, and in the bay, several hundred ships vied for space and gallantry of form . . . morale was high. Natives were cheerful. The Southern Cross I saw in the sky that first night gleamed its silvery rays, giving one a feeling of mystery and romance.[3]

Soldiers enjoyed the hot springs and the singing and dancing under moonlight. Matsuda recalled, "the sight was truly a paradise on earth."[4] For the lower ranks conditions were not so favorable. Petty Officer Yasato Ichikawa described the barracks for enlisted men at Yunakanau Airfield:

> The barracks were made of panels which were crudely put together . . . 80 men of a division lived together. However, if a plane did not return, seven or eight men of a section ended up missing. Therefore there was always enough space in the barracks . . . oil drums were placed at the corner of the yard as bathtubs, as if they were there in a construction site.[5]

Ichikawa and his colleagues would soon learn the horrors of war. 'Betty' bombers, whose fuel tanks caught fire so easily that they were nicknamed 'Type-I *Raita*' [cigarette lighter] often returned full of dead crewmen. A *Shinto* funeral would be arranged at the foot of South Daughter, an extinct volcano that formed the tip of Crater Peninsula. Flimsy coffins would be lit with waste oil. Ishikawa recorded that "The coffins and pilot suits were burned down soon. It was hell on earth to see the naked corpses burning. Only organs didn't burn easily. They smouldered forever . . . I was learning the fragility of life and the cruelty of the human world."[6]

Eight hundred miles to the north, the lagoon of *Truk*, sometimes described as Japan's *Pearl Harbor*, had been sequestered by Japan from the German Empire during *World War I*, after which Japan was awarded the administrative mandate by the League of Nations. The Imperial Japanese Navy saw Rabaul as a southern defensive garrison for *Truk* and a jumping off point for the extension of their defensive perimeter to New Guinea in the southwest, the southern *Solomon Islands* in the south and the *New Hebrides* (*Vanuatu*), the *New Caledonian Islands, Fiji, Tonga* and *American Samoa* in the southeast. From these strongpoints it was hoped that the logistical supply to Australia could be blocked. Japanese military hubris was at its peak. The Navy even considered the possibility of invading Australia. On Emperor Hirohito's forty-second birthday, 9 March, he remarked to his Lord Privy Seal, Marquis Kido, "The fruits of victory are tumbling into our mouths too quickly."[7]

When the Imperial Japanese Army, tied down as it was in China, refused to provide the additional troops and transports required for an invasion of Australia, the Navy decided to pursue the less ambitious strategy of interdicting the supply of American arms and troops. In the first week of May 1942 an invasion force was sent to Port Moresby supported by the fleet carriers *Zuikaku* and *Shokaku*. At the same time Rear-Admiral Kiyohide Shima and the 3rd Kure Special Landing Force stormed the lightly defended port of *Tulagi* in the southern *Solomon Islands*.

Although the sea invasion of Port Moresby was temporarily abandoned after the *Battle of the Coral Sea* in May 1942, the development of a naval and seaplane station at *Tulagi,* an island with a natural port opposite *Guadalcanal*, continued. Seventeen miles across the water, on the remote and sparsely inhabited island of *Guadalcanal*, the Japanese established control of plains inland from Lunga Point where they began construction of an airfield. The Japanese advance was barely interrupted but for an air attack launched by the USS *Yorktown* on 4 May, the day of its occupation of *Tulagi*. A destroyer, *Kikutsuki* was sunk along with a number of smaller boats. A week later another US raid sank the cruiser-minelayer *Okinoshima*.

The Japanese planned to build up an air capability on Lunga Point with a force of bombers and support fighters with which it could interdict any shipping from the United States to Australia. In spite of the disaster at the *Battle of Midway* in June, the Japanese Navy's plans continued to be aggressive and expansionist; using Lunga Point and *Tulagi* as advance posts, they looked to capture *New Caledonia* and *Fiji* to effect a blockade of Australia. As a Japanese strategic paper had argued in late January 1942, "acquisition of airbases in the Solomons and Papua Areas would vitally strengthen Japan's strategic position, giving the Navy the advantage of expanded aerial reconnaissance over waters in which enemy naval forces must maneuver for a counter-offensive from the southeast."[8] It was further reckoned that "Japanese control over these areas would intensify pressure on north-eastern Australia and hinder its use as a base of Allied [particularly air] operations."[9]

If Japan's plans at the beginning of the year had been riven by dissension between the Army and Navy, this was no less true of the US armed forces. On 18 February 1942 Admiral King, Commander in Chief of the Navy in Washington, wrote to General George Marshall, Chief of Staff of the Army, calling for army garrisons to occupy islands in the *Pacific* southwest. These were needed to block the Japanese advance. Marshall, who was above all committed to the European theater and the defeat of Nazi Germany, questioned the need for the island occupations and whether, if they needed to be garrisoned, the Marines could not be used for this task. "In general," Marshall concluded in his letter to King on 24 February, "it would seem to appear that our effort in the southwest Pacific must for several reasons be limited to the strategic defensive for air and ground troops."[10] In a more detailed response King stated that at the very least he needed bases at *Tonga* (a member of the *Friendly Islands* adjacent to *Fiji*) and

Espiritu Santo (in the *New Hebrides* group of islands south of the *Solomons*) to prevent Japan's threat to the supply of Allied forces in Australia. The Marines, he argued, would be better used to launch amphibious assaults rather than man garrisons. King's superior strategic logic won the debate. Neither Roosevelt nor Marshall wanted MacArthur and American Army forces in Australia marooned without logistic support from the United States. After Bataan, the idea of a second American army lost was too appalling to contemplate.

As a first stage of the US Navy's island advance, *Noumea*, in *French New Caledonia*, the group of islands to the southwest of the *New Hebrides*, was occupied on 12 March. There Tontouta Airfield was constructed. *Noumea* was in the 'middle of nowhere,' some 900 miles east of Australia and 800 miles north of New Zealand. There was no infrastructure but it possessed a large natural harbor. The occupation was quietly done. The Allies feared that if a Japanese reconnaissance plane spotted the Marines building an airstrip, they would quickly move down and take it. Marine Engineer Captain John Little recalled, "We were right up there under Tojo's chin. If he only opened his mouth we'd fall right in. A couple of Jap destroyers could have cleaned us out at any time."[11] The anchorage at *Noumea* rapidly became congested as the US Navy struggled to build the requisite port facilities to cope with the sudden influx. Many ships were used simply as 'floating storage.' Heavy equipment had to be manhandled ashore—a task that needed huge resources of manpower that itself required organizational support. It was a logistic task of gargantuan proportions that the Navy at this stage of the war was barely equipped to deal with. Admiral King remarked that "I don't know what the hell this logistics is but I want some of it."[12] Indeed logistics were to be the core problem that faced both the United States and Japan at the *Battle of Guadalcanal*.

Next, on 29 March, a mixed group of Australian forces, Marines and soldiers, took Port Vila, on the island of *Efate* in the *Vanuatu* chain. Construction of an airfield began in early May. Ultimately this island base proved a disappointment as *Efate* became renowned as the worst malarial island in the *South Pacific*. Being posted to *Efate* became a punishment assignment. A week after the 3rd Construction Detachment arrived in *Efate*, the 2nd Construction Detachment arrived to develop the airfield on *Tonga* as a refueling depot for long haul flights on their way to or from the US to Australia. As in the opening gambits of a game of chess, in the first half of 1942 both Japan and the US maneuvered their pieces into place; by August 1942, like a 'pawn advance' on a chessboard, both sides in the *South Pacific* had matched each other's moves. Who would now make the first aggressive play?

After the *Battle of Midway* on 4 June, the United States' strategic options were re-examined. To forestall an expected Japanese advance on the *New Hebrides* (Vanuatu), the US Joint Chiefs directed that the *Santa Cruz Islands*, 200 miles to the north, should be occupied and denied to the Japanese. Two hundred miles to the south of the *Santa Cruz Islands, Espirito Santo*, the largest island in the *New Hebrides* (Vanuatu), also possessed an excellent natural anchorage. At the beginning of June 1942 American Seabees rushed to complete an airfield on *Espirito Santo* before the Japanese could build theirs on *Guadalcanal*. Within a month B-17 Flying Fortress were able to take off from *Espirito Santo* and bomb *Guadalcanal*, which lay 500 miles to the northwest. From *Espirito Santo*, it was planned that the Marines would seize *Tulagi* and the Japanese airbase under construction at Lunga Point on *Guadalcanal*. It was a 'pawn snatch' by Admiral King that developed into the longest land battle of the war.

The longest and arguably the most critical land battles of the *Pacific War* were about to take place on *Guadalcanal*, this most obscure of islands in the *Solomon* chain. Major-General Alexander Vandegrift, who would lead the Marines, confessed, "he didn't even know the location of *Guadalcanal*."[13] Apart from dozens of engagements on land, the island of *Guadalcanal* was the focal location of the least well known but, collectively, some of the most important naval battles of the *Pacific* campaign, with at least seven major engagements and innumerable minor sorties. Admiral King's directive of 25 June ordered that the operation would be under the command of Admiral Nimitz and Vice-Admiral Robert L. Ghormley his Commander, *South Pacific* Force. Their invasion target date was 1 August.

In Australia MacArthur was not happy. Predictably he made conspiratorial accusations that there was a master plan for "the complete absorption of the national defense function by the Navy ..."[14] In Washington General Marshall tried to engineer General MacArthur's overall command of the operation. While Admiral King was prepared to allow MacArthur and the Army to garrison *Guadalcanal* after it was taken, he insisted that Admiral Nimitz was responsible for actions within the *Southwest Pacific* area— particularly as it was a Marine operation that expected little aerial support from the US Army Air Force, whose closest base was some 975 miles from *Tulagi*; this compared with the Boeing B-17 Flying Fortress's maximum operating range of 925 miles. Although MacArthur continued to rail against the "Navy cabal"[15] in Washington, and orchestrated a *Time* magazine piece, *Hero on Ice* [3 August 1942], in order to advertise his complaints, much to MacArthur's chagrin, Admiral King stood firm. His carriers would not be put in MacArthur's charge. Not surprisingly MacArthur became an outspoken prophet of doom regarding the *Guadalcanal* Campaign. While he generally proffered support to the embattled Marines, this did not mean that MacArthur would not snipe from the sideline.

The fight for command presaged what would be a continual battle between the Army and Navy for power over *Pacific* Theater operations. Refusing to accept the *prima facie* logic of what was in essence a 'Navy' dominated war, MacArthur sniped, wheedled and bullied. His obsessive protection and promotion of his own position and power was equaled only by his paranoid delusion about plots against him. Even General Marshall, who invariably backed his Army commander, MacArthur, throughout the war, thought that the notoriously 'prickly' Admiral King was far easier to deal with than his own Army commander in Australia. Marshall recalled that MacArthur was "supersensitive about everything ..."; Marshall made the additional observation that with regard to Washington's military politics, "everybody had ulterior motives about everything."[16]

Guadalcanal's Topography and Japanese Overreach: **[Maps: 16.2A, 16.2B, 16.3]**
Foot-soldiers often die for the vanity of their commanders. Had MacArthur won the
leading role for his army troops for the invasion of *Guadalcanal* it is unlikely that
they would have thanked him. This *South Pacific* island, some ninety miles long
and twenty-five miles wide, was not a tropical paradise. Although there was lush,
tall-grassed meadows in the northeast around the *Lunga River*, for the most
part *Guadalcanal* was divided by a mountainous ridge, 8,000 foot high, along its
spine. The mountains fall precipitously down to the unapproachable western coast.
The island is largely covered by tropical jungle; swarms of mosquitos, vicious white
ants, crocodiles, giant lizards, poisonous spiders and plants, scorpions and leeches
guarded this brutally unwelcoming place. However, a few plantation settlers had
been able to land at the island's northeastern shores and had eked out a plantation
life with the island's sparse native population. Jack London, the peripatetic early-
twentieth-century journalist and author, said of the *Solomon Islands* as a whole, "If I
was a king the worst punishment I could inflict on my enemies would be to banish
them to the Solomons. On second thought, king or no king, I don't think I'd have the
heart to do it."[17]

A few Catholic missionaries served a small native population of 15,000 people, while
a few hardy Anglo-Saxon managers ran coconut plantations. There was also a Burns
Philp & Co. trading station. The most famous and distinguished inhabitant was the
British colonial District Officer, Martin Clemens, a young Scotsman in his late twenties.
Born in Aberdeen to a musician father, Clemens won scholarships to Bedford School
and then to Christ's College, Cambridge. He was an undergraduate rower and intrepid
'night climber' who once managed to place chamber pots on all the pinnacles of Kings
College Chapel. It was a fearlessness that soon became evident after the Japanese
invasion of the *Solomons*. He had stationed men around *Guadalcanal* as watch-outs for
the Australian Navy and had alerted the Allies to the fact that the Japanese were building
an airfield. Clemens and his natives were to prove an invaluable source of intelligence
for the US Marines during the campaign.

By comparison to *Guadalcanal, Tulagi* is a tiny 2.2-mile by 0.6-mile island set into
the coastline of *Florida*, the largest of the *Nggela Group of Islands* facing *Guadalcanal*.
Hilly and heavily wooded, *Tulagi* had no other purpose than to guard the small but
useful harbor that was the center of colonial government in the *British Solomon Islands*.
In the *Solomons* natural harbors and airfields were what counted. Like all the locations
of the New Guinea-*Solomons* arena, islands were not territories that needed to be
dominated in their entirety. There was nothing worth fighting for in terrain that was
some of the most inhospitable in the world. Beyond the value of the military installations
that the combatants put in place, these islands had almost no intrinsic value, arguably
negative value, as virtually all manpower, construction equipment, weapons, munitions,
gasoline, food and medical supplies had to be shipped at vast expense in terms of time,
ships and logistic complexity. With rampant malaria and other tropical diseases, simply
stationing troops in these locations was to guarantee their rapid degradation.

Land-based linkages between military bases even in New Guinea were of limited use because of the hostile terrain that needed to be traversed. There were no roads. Traversing a few miles of jungle was the equivalent to hundreds of miles of normal country. Thus bases were entirely dependent on the naval and air power that supported them. While supply by sea was essential, it was nevertheless the case that, because of the rapid advances made in aircraft technology in the interwar years, air power, whether by carrier or land based, trumped sea power in all daylight hours. The key to military success in the *South Pacific* therefore was the ability to defend and supply airfields. The military dynamic of the airfield at the *Battle of Guadalcanal*, was, in essence, fundamentally the same throughout the entire conflict in the *Pacific*.

The importance of airpower also gave island airfields a defined combat radius; in other words the distance from which a military base could be supported by the next nearest airfield. For the Japanese the combat radius of fighter planes was 250–350 miles; for the Allies, with fighters that had much shorter overall operating ranges, the combat radius from airbases was 150–250 miles. Japanese bombers and American bombers had longer ranges but were restricted at these distances by their need for fighter protection. At 650 miles from Rabaul, the airfield built by the Japanese at Lunga Point on *Guadalcanal* was, as they were to discover, a significant overreach. At the very least, Japan's commanders should, in hindsight, have developed an intermediate staging airfield at *Shortland Island* (just to the south of *Bougainville*); something that was eventually done but far too late. Japan was not the only side to overreach, however, as the American invasion of *Guadalcanal* soon demonstrated.

The US Invasion of Tulagi and Guadalcanal: **[Map: 16.4]** When the plans for the invasion of *Guadalcanal* and the capture of *Tulagi* were handed down from the US Joint Chiefs of Staff to Admiral Nimitz, his *South Pacific* commander, Vice-Admiral Ghormley, and General MacArthur protested that Allied forces were not yet ready to carry out the exercise. With just thirty-five additional bombers made available from *Hawaii,* they were unconvinced that the landing could be adequately protected. Ghormley warned, "I desire to emphasize that the basic problem of this operation is the protection of surface ships against land-based aircraft attack during the approach, the landing, and the unloading."[18]

Operation WATCHTOWER, as the invasion was called, under the operational command that Ghormley had given to Vice-Admiral Jack Fletcher, was supported by a total aircraft force of 291 planes under the command of Rear-Admiral John S. McCain. A fast new battleship, USS *North Carolina*, five cruisers and sixteen destroyers escorted the carriers, USS *Enterprise* (CV–6), USS *Wasp* (CV–7) and USS *Saratoga* (CV–3). The carrier force was to be led by Rear-Admiral Leigh Noyes. In total there were eighty-nine ships involved in the planned amphibious invasion. The Amphibious Force was led by Rear-Admiral Richmond Kelly Turner while the Marines were led by veteran Major-General Vandegrift, a courteous Virginian of 'confederate' stock. His troops were a mixture of "leathernecks, the old breed of American regular"[19] and angry new recruits who had poured into the recruiting offices after *Pearl Harbor*. Above all of this complex soup of command stood Vice-Admiral Ghormley with Nimitz and the Joint Chiefs also involved. It was an overly complex structure that perhaps reflected the competing political interest and inexperience. The invasion of *Guadalcanal* was the first US attempt at a combined forces operation.

The assemblage of intelligence about *Guadalcanal* and Japanese force dispositions was put in the hands of Lieutenant-Colonel Frank Goettge of the 1st Marine Division. In spite of the economic development of the island by Anglo-Saxon business interests, there were no complete maps of *Guadalcanal* or *Tulagi*. In the main, the Marines had to rely on information provided by former residents and by flights over the area. As to enemy dispositions, the invading forces relied largely on the local lookouts organized by Martin Clemens, the British district officer. Along with numbers of planters, gold-miners and other intrepid loners, he had been trained in the use of the tele-radio sent by Lieutenant-Commander Eric Feldt to report on Japanese naval movements. In the event estimates of 1,850 defenders at *Tulagi* and 5,250 at *Guadalcanal* proved to be too high by over 3,000.

The logistic operations did not start well. Marines, having just completed the arduous 18-day crossing of the *Pacific* had to unload, rearrange and 'combat-load' supplies onto transports at Wellington in New Zealand. Remarkably the heavily unionized New Zealander dockside stevedores did not help them. Lieutenant William Twining, in command of the advance logistics force, reported, "They work differently from us. They stop for morning tea, lunch, and afternoon tea. If it's raining they don't work at all."[20] An industrial dispute followed and notwithstanding US forces being about to go into battle, the stevedores simply stood aside as the Marines had to undertake unloading unassisted. The plan envisaged taking sixty days of supplies.

On meeting Vice-Admiral Ghormley, Vandegrift received a dispatch from Washington requiring him to land on *Guadalcanal* and *Tulagi* on 1 August, five weeks hence. Given that the 1st Marine Division's troops were split between *Samoa*, Wellington and boats still at sea, it was a tall order. Not only were logistics in chaos but also the men were out of shape and untrained for jungle warfare. Alarmingly the Americans possessed no maps for the islands of the southern *Solomons*, some of the most remote places on the planet. Vandegrift complained "I do not see how we can land anywhere by 1 August."[21] In spite of the Army's 648th Engineer Topographical Battalion carrying out a 'red-rush' aerial photographic mapping of the island, the results, because of bureaucratic incompetence, were lost in a corner of an Auckland warehouse. Vandegrift never received the photographs. It was fortunate that Marine Corps officers Lieutenant-Colonel Merrill Twining and Major William Mckean had accompanied the photographers on their flight on 17 July and were verbally able to relay information. They observed Korean 'slave' workers building the airfield at *Guadalcanal*. Twining hoped "they build a good one. We are going to use it."[22] He could have had little idea that this small airfield, being constructed at the backend of nowhere, would become the fulcrum on which the balance of power in the *Pacific* would come to rest.

At the planning conference aboard USS *Saratoga* on 26 July, some 367 miles south of *Fiji*, misunderstandings came to light. In particular, Vandegrift was alarmed to find that while it would take three or four days to unload supplies, the Navy carrier force covering the landings would be withdrawn by Vice-Admiral Fletcher after just two days. Vandegrift would therefore be left at the mercy of Japanese aircraft that would be unchallenged until the runway at Lunga Point could be completed. Copies of Fletcher's orders and plans were so limited that there were not enough to go round and Ghormley did not receive a set until a month after Operation WATCHTOWER had begun. After the meeting there was little time for landing rehearsals and those that were done, Vandegrift considered to be a complete waste of time.

Nineteen thousand mainly 'green' Marines embarked on nineteen transports and four destroyer transports from the *Fijian* island of *Koro* on 31 July. They were aided by fine weather for their approach combined with bad weather around Rabaul that prevented the Japanese from launching their normal patrol and scouting operations. Nevertheless in Tokyo, Lieutenant-Commander Haruki Itoh at the Naval Intelligence Center deduced from a massive increase in US naval radio traffic that an Allied offensive in the *Solomons* was likely. His warnings were ignored. Remarkably, thanks to good fortune and the ineptitude of Japanese defenders and their commanders in Rabaul, the entire convoy arrived undetected and announced their arrival with a bombardment of the island at 6.14 a.m. on 7 August, a week later than originally planned. It was also the date that had originally been set by the Japanese for the completion of the airfield on *Guadalcanal* and the receipt of sixty aircraft. The American invasion was just in time. Vice-Admiral Gunichi Mikawa received a message from *Guadalcanal* informing him that his Japanese troops had "encountered American troops" and that his forces were "retreating into the jungle."[23] At 6.30 a.m. *Tulagi*'s commander radioed Rabaul to report the scale of the US attack and assured his superiors, "We will defend our posts to the death."[24] They were as good as their word.

In Tokyo, at Japanese Army Staff HQ, news of the American landings was received with surprise—not so much about the landings themselves but that the Japanese Navy was building an airfield on an insignificant island in the *South Pacific*. The Navy had omitted to tell the Army of their perimeter expansion in the South Pacific. The Army surmised that the American attack was merely a raiding party. By contrast Admiral Osami Nagano at Imperial Navy HQ was far from relaxed. He immediately ordered the combined fleet to retake *Guadalcanal*. Yamamoto, not sensing the importance of the impending conflict, did not take charge of operations himself and sent Vice-Admiral Nishizo Tsukahara from *Saipan* to oversee naval operations that had formerly been the sole preserve of Mikawa. In fact both Admirals maintained separate HQs leading to constant problems of confused and countermanded orders.

At 7.40 a.m. elements from the 1st Raider Battalion and the 5th Marine Division disembarked into Higgins boats, under the command of Brigadier-General William Rupertus, and then waded ashore after their landing craft stuck on the coral reefs thirty yards from shore. They found no opposition. Once ashore they assembled and prepared to advance along the island. At 8.10 a.m. Japanese radio transmission broke contact with Rabaul after reporting the enemy attack and concluded with the message, "Enemy troop strength is overwhelming. We will defend to the last man."[25] Fighting began almost as soon as the Marines pressed forward at midday. The night was spent repelling four Japanese frontal charges and innumerable stealth attacks. It was not until late afternoon of the following day that resistance was largely overcome, though fighting with isolated Japanese elements continued thereafter. By 9 August the Marines had also secured the even smaller islands of *Gavutu* and *Tanambogo* that were joined to *Tulagi* by a causeway.

Across the soon to be named *Ironbottom Sound*, on *Guadalcanal* Marine landings commenced unopposed at 9.10 a.m.; 11,000 Marines of the 1st and 5th Divisions were landed on 'Red Beach' to the east of the *Tenaru River* and the airfield at Lunga Point. Moving along the shore the Marines also secured the area to the east of *Alligator Creek*. Advancing inland the airfield was taken with little resistance at 4.00 p.m. on the following day.

On *Guadalcanal* Captain Kanae Monzen's 11th Construction Battalion had panicked in the face of the US Navy's sudden and unexpected bombardment and he was forced to retreat to a position three miles to the west. Most of their food, and considerable amounts of construction equipment and installations, were left behind including wharves, jetties, ice plants, and a radio station and assorted buildings. The Japanese and their construction laborers had departed rapidly as evidenced by the debris of half-eaten breakfasts, teacups and *hashi* (chopsticks). Helmets, clothing, mosquito netting, *tabis* (rubber-soled flip-flops), blankets and even rifles were left strewn around. Stocks included 900 drums of aviation fuel. This was less helpful than it seemed. Using the 90-octane fuel was tricky. American aero engines, which required at least 100-octane aviation fuel, could not use it, while for trucks 90-octane fuel burnt too hot and could only work if diluted.

The End of Zero Supremacy: On the morning of 7 August, Japan's 25th Air Flotilla was about to take off to attack Australian positions at *Milne Bay*. **[See Chapter 15: Battles of the Kokoda Trail: Aussies Triumphant]** News of the US attack on *Guadalcanal* suddenly changed priorities. Vice-Admiral Tsukahara sent a message to 11th Air Fleet HQ on *Tinian* requesting 25th Air Flotilla to "destroy the enemy invasion forces with all its might."[26] 'Betty' bombers and their escort Zero fighters were immediately dispatched from airfields at Kavieng on *New Ireland* and from Rabaul on *New Britain* to attack the US armada led by three fleet carriers that were assembled off *Guadalcanal*. The Japanese attacks precipitated what turned out to be one of the longest running air battles of *World War II*.

The 650-mile flight from Rabaul to *Guadalcanal* was no small effort. The distance was particularly problematic for the Japanese Navy's main fighter. The legendary Zero fighter, the Mitsubishi A6M, in the early phases of the war, because of its speed, ability to climb and maneuverability, was considered untouchable. Japanese fighter ace, Saburo Sakai, recalled that in his first flight in a Zero during the Philippine campaign, "She handled like a dream. Just a flick of the wrists and she was gone."[27] The Zero generally had the upper hand against the US Navy's Grumman F4F-4 Wildcat, though, like the Type-97, the Japanese fighter suffered from poor armor and a lack of a self-sealing fuel tank.

However, with regard to missions from Rabaul to *Guadalcanal*, the Zero had never flown on operations at this distance. Although the fourteen-cylinder Sakai-12 radial engine produced by Nakajima was thrifty, in order to make the distance, the Zeros needed to wear a 330-liter detachable belly tank. Even with the availability of this attachment, the new Model 32 Zero of the 2nd Air Group could not be used. The Model-32 (A6M3 Type-0) had a more powerful Sakai-21 engine with double superchargers. Wings were shorter and squared off for maneuverability. Speed increased from 316 mph to 336 mph while climb rate increased from 3,100 foot per minute to over 4,500 foot per minute. However, the increased weight of these engines destabilized the aircraft and forced the manufacturers to bring the engine 21cms closer to the cockpit. While these changes improved the handling of the new Zero, the gasoline tank had to be reduced in size. Inevitably the older Model-21 version of the Zero (A6M2 Type-0), which could make the distance, was subject to significant wear and tear caused by the long haul to *Guadalcanal*; the cruising techniques used to fly the long distances were particularly hard on the engines. Japanese maintenance crews, not logistically well supported at the best of times, were stretched to the limit.

The light frame of the Zero made the plane inherently difficult to upgrade with the armor and heavier weaponry that would have made it competitive with fighter aircraft being produced by America and Great Britain. Whereas North American Aviation's P-51 Mustang and Supermarine Aviation Works' Spitfire made significant strides in their upgrades during the war, the Zeros made in 1944–1945 were little better than the ones that had swept the Allies aside in the early months of the war. By the end of the war the Allies had not just updated their aircraft but replaced them with technically far more advanced weapons such as the Grumman Aircraft Engineering Corporation's F6F Hellcat (a replacement for the F4F Wildcat) and the Chance Vought Corporation's F4U Corsair.

The main problem faced by Japan was that the Zero, a brilliant plane when it was designed, quickly became obsolete. As Mitsubishi's chief designer, Jiro Horikoshi, noted, "Even the best fighters become obsolete within two years during times of war and four years during times of peace."[28] Reflecting the much smaller industrial base of Japan, Horikoshi never had a development team or budget that could have enabled the rapid production of new aircraft. The Zero's successor, the Mitsubishi J2M *Raiden* (Thunderbolt), only came into operation at the end of 1944 and only 628 were produced by Mitsubishi Jukogyo KK at its plants in Nagoya and Suzuka. A further 128 *Raiden* were built at *Koza Kaigun Kokusho* (the Koza Naval Air Arsenal).

The *Raiden* was designed to carry four 20 mm cannon capable of knocking out American bombers. They were also capable of reaching a high ceiling at a fast rate of climb. However, the *Raiden*'s development time was almost two years longer than for an equivalent American aircraft and was far too late to influence the air war in the

Pacific. A similar killer of high-flying US bombers such as the Boeing B-29 Superfortress killer, the Kyushi Hikoki KK's J7W *Shinden* (Magnificent Lightning), with its revolutionary rear propeller 'canard' design and its four frame-mounted 0.30 mm cannon, never made it beyond prototype phase. The only example was transferred to Washington's Smithsonian Institution in 1960.

A further disadvantage of the Zero versus its American counterparts was its weaponry. The Zero was equipped with two light 0.30 (7.7 mm) caliber machine guns and two 20 mm cannon. The rifle-caliber 0.30 machine gun came with a high rate of fire but with a weight of just 0.5 ounces, its bullets had limited penetrative power against heavily armored US planes. Even engine blocks were normally impervious to a 0.30 caliber round. As for the Japanese 20 mm cannons, although they fired a projectile 4.5 ounces in weight plus an explosive charge, they had a limited rate of fire, a low initial muzzle velocity and were inaccurate except at the closest range. The weight of cannon rounds also reduced the number that could be carried. Early Zeros carried just sixty cannon rounds for a mission. As Saburai Sakai observed, "Our 20 mm cannons were big, heavy and slow firing. It was extremely hard to hit a moving target. Shooting down an enemy aircraft was like hitting a dragonfly with a rifle!"[29]

By comparison the 0.50 (12.7 mm) caliber round of the heavy machine guns favored by the American Air Force weighed 1.7 ounces, which was more than three times heavier than a 0.30 caliber round. American machine guns also had a much a higher rate of fire. The weight and velocity of an American 0.50 caliber machine gun bullet could penetrate cockpit, gas tanks and engine blocks—the three most vulnerable targets of an enemy aircraft.

For Japanese fighters coming from Rabaul, the defects in their equipment were compounded by the effects of exhaustion on pilots who had to fly long distances in steamy and sometimes stormy weather and then had to fight for their lives. Japanese pilots knew that if they were shot down, their chances of being rescued were minimal. In the *Solomon Islands* even ditching a plane because of mechanical problems, a frequent occurrence, was likely to result in death. By contrast the US pilots defending their base at Henderson Field would be likely to parachute or ditch closer to home. US flight rescue officers would quickly put into operation sophisticated search and rescue missions, which saved a high percentage of the American pilots who were shot down or had to ditch because of mechanical failure.

Anxiety for Zero pilots could not have been lessened by instructions to fight with their belly tanks attached to give them the extra fuel needed to make it back to Rabaul. Not only did this disrupt the fighting aerodynamics of the plane, it also significantly increased the Zeros' defensive weakness. The Zero, without self-sealing fuel tanks, was prone to explode when hit. The attachment of the belly tank during combat, which was normally required to be released before combat, simply increased the Zeros' vulnerability. Veteran Zero pilot Takao Tanimazu noted, "you could always tell if it was a Zero or enemy plane that had crashed in the sea. The Zero left a fire on the surface, but the American plane just left an oil slick."[30] In the course of the war Mitsubishi never managed to develop a reliable self-sealing tank. When looking at the suddenly degraded performance of the Zero in the air over *Guadalcanal* by comparison with fighter encounters earlier in the war, the issue of distance was clearly a major factor.

Saburo Sakai's Dogfight: On 7 August 1942 Guadalcanal was the location of the most famous aerial dogfight of the *Pacific War*. It was highly unusual in that both fighter pilots, Saburo Sakai and James 'Pug' Southerland, both of them 'aces,' survived the war and lived to tell a story, which was also verified by the findings from their respective planes. The account was interesting for what it said about the respective qualities of the two main fighters of the first year of the *Pacific War*: the Mitsubishi A6M Zero versus the Gunman F4F Wildcat. Moreover the fight between the two men, who were able to distinguish each other physically during the engagement, also shows the extent to which pilots of this era clearly saw combat as a form of personal duel—a codified duel to the death.

Saburo Sakai's account is the more graphic description of this epic encounter:

> On the fifth spiral, the Wildcat skidded slightly, I had him, I thought. But the Grumman dropped his nose, gained speed, and the pilot again had his plane in full control. There was a terrific man [Southerland] behind that stick. He made his error, however, in the next moment. Instead of swinging back to go into a sixth spiral, he fed power to his engine, broke away at an angle, and looped. That was the decisive split second. I went right after him, cutting inside the Grumman's arc, and came out on his tail. I had him. He kept flying loops, trying to narrow the distance of each arc. Every time he went up and around I cut inside his arc and lessened the distance between our two planes. The Zero could out fly any fighter in the world in this kind of maneuver. When I was only fifty yards away, the Wildcat broke out of his loop and astonished me by flying straight and level. At this distance I would not need the cannon; I pumped 200 rounds into the Grumman's cockpit, watching the bullets chewing up the thin metal skin and shattering the glass. I could not believe what I saw; the Wildcat continued flying almost as if nothing had happened. A Zero, which had taken that many bullets into its vital cockpit would have been a ball of fire by now. I could not understand it. I slammed the throttle forward and closed in to the American plane, just as the enemy fighter lost speed. In a moment I was ten yards ahead of the Wildcat, trying to slow down. I hunched my shoulders, prepared for the onslaught of his guns, I was

trapped. No bullets came. [Southerland's guns jammed.] The Wildcat's guns remained silent. The entire situation was unbelievable. I dropped my speed until our planes were flying in wing-to-wing formation. I opened my cockpit window and stared out. The Wildcat's cockpit canopy was already back, and I could see the pilot clearly. He was a big man, with a round face. He wore a light khaki uniform. He appeared to be middle-aged, not as young as I had expected. For several seconds, we flew along in our bizarre formation, our eyes meeting across the narrow space between the two planes. The Wildcat was a shambles. Bullet holes had cut the fuselage and wings up from one end to the other.[31]

Southerland, his guns jammed, had to bail out of his damaged Wildcat. As he was trying to free himself from his cockpit to parachute to safety, his Colt M1911 0.45 caliber automatic pistol became entangled and he was forced to leave it behind. Landing behind enemy lines, suffering eleven wounds, Southerland managed to evade Japanese troops and struggled through the bush to the coast. Natives treated him and eventually managed to guide him back to Henderson Field some two weeks later. On 14 February 1998, Southerland's crashed Wildcat was found in the jungles of *Guadalcanal*; damage to the aircraft matched the accounts of the battle. Southerland's Colt 0.45 automatic pistol was recovered.

In a later dogfight over *Guadalcanal*, Sakai survived a bullet that passed through his brain and still managed to guide his damaged fighter back to the airbase at Rabaul. At Rabaul, Sakai was carried from his cockpit unconscious. He was fortunate to survive. His cockpit was riddled with bullets and covered in blood. Remarkably Sakai survived an eye operation done without anaesthetic and recovered, not only to train pilots, but also to persuade the Japanese Air Force to send him back into combat at the end of the war. He fought one of his most famous dogfights at *Iwo Jima* in 1944 where he shot down a much superior F6F Hellcat. It was his sixty-fourth kill, making him the highest scoring Japanese pilot to survive the *Pacific War*. Shoichi Sugita, one of the escort fighter pilots on the flight on which Admiral Yamamoto was assassinated, scored the Japanese *Pacific War* record of more than 120 kills; he was shot down and killed after taking off from Kanoya Airfield on *Kyushu* in April 1945.

Sakai was one of the few pre-war pilots who survived the war. He subsequently became a devout Buddhist. Unusually, he was a fierce post-war critic of Japan for its role in starting the *Pacific War*. When asked by the *Associated Press*, "Who gave the orders for that stupid war?" Sakai replied, "The closer you get to the emperor, the fuzzier everything gets." He encouraged his daughter to go to America, to "learn English and democracy."[32] She duly married an American. Sakai's autobiography *Samurai!* was published in 1957.

The Start of the Bomber War in the Solomons: While Sakai and Sutherland were dueling, Japanese aircraft attacks from Rabaul caused heavy damage to the destroyer USS *Jarvis* that was struck by a torpedo while the transport USS *George F Elliot* was set on fire and eventually sank. The Japanese bombers paid a heavy price for their attack on the US armada as anti-aircraft guns took their toll on low flying 'Betty' bombers. "Boy, they're shooting them down like flies, one, two, three," shouted an over-exuberant radio operator, "I can see them coming down in the sea right now!"[33] Thirty-six Japanese aircraft were shot down versus nineteen US planes lost including fourteen fighters.

In spite of MacArthur's general scepticism and gloom regarding the *Guadalcanal* operations, to his credit he did everything he could to support Vandegrift's operations with his own still sparsely supplied air force. MacArthur was not unaware that keeping American forces on *Guadalcanal* would prevent Japan from interdicting American supplies to his own forces in Australia. At 900 miles distance, *Guadalcanal* was too far from the airbase at Port Moresby to provide bombing support for Vandegrift's Marines. However, he could damage the airports around Rabaul that were launching bombing raids on *Guadalcanal*. Major-General George Kenney, the newly appointed commander of the Fifth Air Force in MacArthur's South West Pacific Area, would later write that when on 6 August he promised to bomb Vanakanau Airfield (Rabaul) with 16 B-17 Flying Fortresses, MacArthur "looked as though he was about to kiss me."[34]

In fact attacking Rabaul would serve a double purpose as the Japanese had also just landed a large force at Buna on the southeast coast of New Guinea with the objective of moving south to control the Papuan Peninsula. The degrading of Rabaul would become a major objective of American strategy for the next eighteen months. The first assault on Rabaul's Vanakanau Airfield on 7 August was ineffectual. Despite the extravagant claims of General Kenny, the raid by West Point graduate Major 'Dick' Carmichael's 28th Bomb Squadron did little more than superficial damage. One B-17 Flying Fortress crashed on take-off because of a faulty supercharger while two more soon had to turn back because of an engine problem on one and an electrical failure on another. Two of the remaining thirteen Flying Fortress were shot down with the loss of eleven men. The new Model-32 Zero might not be able to go the distance to *Guadalcanal* but it could make life miserable for American bombing missions to Rabaul.

It was an uncomfortable initiation for the B-17 survivors as Zeros buzzed around them firing tracers that zipped through the thin-skinned aluminum fuselages of their B-17s. Equally deadly shrapnel tore through the aircraft. Most alarming for the attackers was seeing Vanakanau Airfield's defenders swarm over the Flying Fortress of Captain Harl Pease. His bomber lost an engine and fell behind. Later it came to light that Pease's aircraft, named '*Why Don't We Do This More Often*,' had an auxiliary tank fitted without a self-sealing liner. Carmichael would later reflect that it was this that "did him in on the way back. He was hit and caught fire."[35] Nevertheless the claims made for the raid did raise morale. MacArthur ordered Kenney "to pass out as many decorations as you think fit."[36]

On the presumption that Captain Pease had been killed, he was awarded a Medal of Honor that was presented to his parents by Roosevelt on 4 November. In fact Pease survived. In spite of being machine gunned by Zeros as he parachuted to earth, taking a shot in the lower leg, Pease was patched up by a civilian prisoner; this after a Japanese prison guard laughingly told him, "We don't treat American airmen."[37]

On 8 October Pease and five other combatants plus two captured native coast-watchers were taken to Tavurvur Crater where Warrant Officer Minoru Yoshimura ordered several recruits to bayonet the eight prisoners and push them into a pit. Three of them fell in as intended but five captives continued to writhe on the floor in agony. According to Yoshimura's testimony a medical officer had been given permission to "carry out a dissection."[38] "This doctor," Yoshimura continued, "then cut the jugular vein of the suffering prisoner of war before opening his abdomen. He then took some dark-looking object out (presumably his liver) . . ."[39] A second prisoner was similarly eviscerated. Yoshimura ended with the matter-of-fact confession, "As soon as all the prisoners were placed in the hole I gave the *coup de grâce* by stabbing each one in the throat."[40] A month later, on 4 November, eleven more captured crewmen were taken to Tavurvur Crater. Blindfolded and tied with wire in a kneeling position, they were all decapitated with a *katana* (a long curving single edged samurai sword) by soldiers of Rabaul's 81st Naval Garrison Unit. During the course of the war, apart from a few prisoners transported to Tokyo for interrogation, none of the hundreds of the Allied aviation crewmembers taken to Rabaul survived captivity.

Many crews disappeared without trace. On 14 August 1942, a brand-new Boeing B-17E of the Kangaroo Squadron took off on a reconnaissance mission. The plane, piloted by Lieutenant Wilson Cook, was named '*Chief Seattle from the Pacific Northwest*' in honor of the citizens of Washington state who paid for it. Much of the US$280,500 cost of the plane came from a bond campaign by Seattle's newspapers with much of the money raised by schoolchildren. No distress call was made and neither plane nor crew were ever found. Cook's B-17 may have been shot down. Quite possibly however, the navigator had become disorientated and lost—a common occurrence for pilots flying over sea. On 17 September Lieutenant Claude Burcky's B-17 lost its way in bad weather and the crew were forced to bail out. Burcky and seven others were picked up and survived but the plane's navigator paid the ultimate price for his error. Given the paucity of Japanese radio communications, it seems likely that Japanese navigators and their crews fared even worse from disorientation. In terms of numbers, downed Japanese planes, flying at the limits of their ranges to *Guadalcanal*, vastly exceeded the number of B-17s lost over Rabaul. Thirty of the fifty-one Japanese aircraft that took off from Rabaul on 7 August 1942 to attack *Guadalcanal* did not return.

The severe losses of what Captain Yoshiyotsu Moritama of the 4th Air Group called the '*First Battle of the Solomons*' (7–8 August) were a profound shock to Japanese commanders. Even the grossly inflated damage reports relayed back to Tokyo did not assuage the guilt felt by the Japanese bomber commanders. In reporting to his superiors Moritama indulged in extravagant self-criticism when he concluded, "As the direct leader of the unit, I am strongly aware that I am to blame for it, and humbly accept the responsibility."[41] While captured Japanese bomber crews may not have been treated to medical vivisection or decapitation, they usually met an appalling end if they were forced to parachute or ditch their planes in the sea. Many refused to be taken prisoner and preferred death by drowning. Some encouraged American crews to shoot them. Often US pilots and seamen needed little or no encouragement. Other Japanese pilots and crew were picked off in the water by sharks or salt-water crocodiles.

Battles of the 'Slot' and Fletcher Does a Bunk: Japanese losses were not limited to the air. On the evening of 8 August, US Submarine, *S-38*, an antiquated S-1 type submarine launched in 1917, commanded by Lieutenant-Commander H. G. Munson, using updated underwater radar equipment, picked up telltale sonar echoes and tracked a convoy of six Japanese troop transports carrying 2,000 Japanese soldiers bound for *Guadalcanal*. Fifteen miles west of Cape St. George, Munson closed in to 1,000 yards and fired two torpedoes that sank the 5,600-ton *Meiyo Maru*. Fourteen Japanese officers and 328 men were killed or later drowned. The 'Slot' had claimed one of its first victims. The remaining five troop transports reversed course and scuttled back to Rabaul. The 'Slot' (*New Georgia Sound*) was the American name given to the direct route down which Japanese troops and their supplies were convoyed through the central sea passage of the *Solomon Islands* to 'Guadalcanal', where Japanese forces battled almost daily with the Marines for control of Henderson Field. The *Battles of the 'Slot'* refers to the bewildering series of naval engagements that developed from the Imperial Navy's attempt to supply Japanese troops on *Guadalcanal* between August and November 1942.

The *Battle of Guadalcanal* is central to the narrative of America's ultimate victory against Japan in the *Pacific War*. As a military engagement *Guadalcanal* holds a place similar to that of the *Battle of Midway* for naval operations. Sometimes overlooked in the process was the extent to which, over the course of four months of naval engagements, the US Navy significantly diminished Japanese naval strength to a degree that paved the way for the later one-sided annihilation of the Japanese fleet at the *Battle of the Philippine Sea* and finally at *The Battle of Leyte Gulf*.

Admiral Yamamoto ordered Vice-Admiral Mikawa from his naval bases at *New Britain* and *New Ireland* with seven cruisers (five heavy; two light) and one destroyer to disrupt the American amphibious landings on *Guadalcanal*. Rear-Admiral Turner's amphibious landing force was protected by a surface force of eight cruisers (six heavy; two light) and fifteen destroyers and given cover by three fleet carriers under the command of Vice-Admiral Fletcher. As a result of a failure to send out sufficient spotter planes on 8 August, Rear-Admiral Turner, commander of the transport fleet, was unaware that Mikawa's force of five heavy cruisers, two light cruisers and a destroyer were advancing down the 'Slot.'

However, as Mikawa's forces *rendezvoused*, they sighted a US submarine. Lieutenant-Commander Munson's *S-38* dived but later reported "two destroyers and three larger ships of unknown type, heading 140 degrees true, at high speed, eight miles west of

Cape St. George."[42] The warnings, which underestimated the size of Mikawa's force, were ignored by Turner. Meanwhile Vice-Admiral Fletcher had decided to retire two days early from the *Solomons* to refuel and more importantly to protect his carriers, USS *Saratoga* (CV-3), USS *Enterprise* (CV-6), and USS *Wasp* (CV-7), from the possibility of air attack. After losing USS *Lexington* (CV-2) at the *Battle of Coral Sea* and USS *Yorktown* (CV-5) at the *Battle of Midway* on 4 June, both under his command, Fletcher was acutely sensitive, arguably too much so, about the possibility of losing another carrier. His fears were heightened on hearing that the Japanese were deploying up to forty twin-engine torpedo planes.

At 6.07 p.m. on 8 August, Fletcher sent a message to Ghormley and Turner; "Fighter plane strength reduced from 99 to 78. In view of large numbers of enemy torpedo planes and bombers in this area, I recommend the immediate withdrawal of my carriers. Request tankers to be sent forward immediately as fuel running low."[43] As a result of logistic mistakes, Fletcher's screening destroyers were short of the fuel required to remain on-station to protect the fleet carriers. Ghormley supported Fletcher, leaving Rear-Admiral Turner, in charge of the amphibious landings, to curse "He's [Fletcher] left us bare ass!"[44] Brigadier-General Vandegrift felt let down by both Admirals. In hindsight Fetcher's excuse for withdrawal appeared flimsy.

Indeed the planning for the *Guadalcanal* mission had been beset by discord from the start. Rear-Admiral Turner would later report that Fletcher was "very much opposed in Pearl Harbor to undertaking the attempt against Guadalcanal, as he felt sure it would be a failure."[45] Just ten days before the landings at *Tulagi*, on 27 July 1942, Fletcher and Turner had engaged in a vigorous four hour argument about how long America's fleet carriers would stay in the vicinity to give cover to the unloading of supplies for the *Guadalcanal* Campaign.

The Naval Battle of Savo Island: [**Map: 16.5**] Hearing of Fletcher's intended departure, Turner was dismayed, as he had expected continued coverage of his disembarkation. In the face of this sudden crisis he called a conference to which he invited his commanders. They included Marine Brigadier-General Vandegrift and Western Defense heavy cruiser commander, British Rear-Admiral Sir Victor Crutchley, the last British admiral to serve in the Australian Navy. Crutchley withdrew his heavy cruiser HMAS *Australia* from the line of ships that was patroling west of *Savo Island* at the throat of the 'Slot' guarding the entrance to *Ironbottom Sound*. It was in *Ironbottom Sound*, between *Guadalcanal* and *Florida Island,* that Turner's transports were in the process of unloading supplies. Crutchley had placed his six heavy cruisers in two lines patroling either side of *Savo Island*.

While Crutchley had been leading the western line with HMAS *Australia*, HMAS *Canberra* and USS *Chicago*, he placed Captain Frederick Riefkohl aboard the USS *Vincennes* to lead the eastern line with two other heavy cruisers, USS *Quincy* and USS *Astoria*. Meanwhile Crutchley had placed the radar destroyers USS *Blue* and USS *Ralph Talbot* outside these two lines of destroyers; they were required to sail back and forth across the entrance to *Ironbottom Sound* as lookouts for any approaching enemy warships. US destroyers USS *Helm* and USS *Wilson* also formed a screen. With no Japanese force having been reported in the 'Slot' during the day, Crutchley had reduced his force's state of readiness from Condition-I to Condition-II, which meant reduced manning on guns and other critical stations. This was an appropriate order given that his force had been operating at full stretch for two days in helping to fend off bomber attacks on Turner's transports.

In Crutchley's absence, while he attended Turner's conference aboard his flagship USS *McCawley* (an APA-4 attack transport), Captain Howard Bode of USS *Chicago* was put in charge of the southern cruiser force. After being woken up to be told of the new command arrangements, Bode simply went back to sleep. Expecting that Crutchley would soon return to his post, Bode, understandably, did not move his ship to the head of the line. Neither did Bode or Crutchley inform their fellow captains of the new command structure. As for Rear-Admiral Turner's conference at 11 p.m. on 8 August, the objective was to inform his colleagues that Fletcher had retired, a day earlier than Turner had expected. Now that his own transports were left without air cover, he announced that he too would be 'off' early next morning, a day earlier than previously anticipated, without delivering the full complement of stores that the Marines required.

At 6.42 p.m. on 8 August, Vice-Admiral Mikawa, in a fine imitation of Nelson's famous message before the *Battle of Trafalgar*, sent a message to his ships, "In the finest tradition of the Imperial Navy we shall engage the enemy in night battle. Every man is expected to do his utmost."[46] He then dashed full speed toward *Savo Island*.

While Bode slept, Mikawa nervously approached *Savo Island*, convinced that US planes and submarines had alerted the US Navy of his approach. At 0.54 a.m. on 9 August the *Chōkai* spotted the USS *Blue* in the darkness on the starboard side and Mikawa's force trained their guns on the American destroyer. Luckily for USS *Blue*'s crew, if not for Admiral Crutchley's Allied surface force, their radar did not pick up the presence of Japanese forces. USS *Blue* sailed blithely on. Thus, by good fortune, Mikawa aboard *Chōkai*, with *Aoba, Kako, Kinugasa, Furutaka, Tenryū, Yubari*, and *Yunagi* following in line, sailed straight through the 75-mile hole in the radar screen of USS *Blue* and USS *Ralph Talbot* just as the two ships were approaching the outer limits of their search-legs.

However, Mikawa was far from sanguine. Above all he feared that he was entering a trap that included the air power of three US fleet carriers. Mikawa and his crew cheered up when they received the false news from Rabaul that the previous day's air attacks had sunk an American carrier. Half an hour later, at 1.25 a.m., Mikawa's cruiser force caught Admiral Crutchley's cruiser force completely unawares. Sighting the cruisers USS *Chicago* and HMAS *Canberra* with the destroyer USS *Patterson*, Mikawa gave the order "PREPARE TO FIRE TORPEDOES."[47] Long Lance torpedoes leapt from the deck tubes of Mikawa's cruisers. Meanwhile USS *Patterson* sighted a ship 5,000 yards ahead and broadcast a radio alarm, "WARNING, WARNING: STRANGE SHIPS ENTERING HARBOR!"[48] Within seconds of the warning, *Chokai, Aoba* and *Furutaka* opened fire. The Allied warships were lit up by Japanese spotlights and flares. On the USS *Wilson*, Lieutenant-Commander Walter Price later recalled, "Our cruisers appeared to be enveloped in a plunging fire as soon as they were illuminated."[49]

> The effect on the Allied commanders was almost stupefying. They confused the situation; mistook the enemy for friends; failed to make reports of the enemy's presence; made numerous incorrect decisions; and almost completely forgot their primary objective—the defense of their transports and cargo ships ... The net result of this, plus a reduced radius of visibility owing to smoke and fire, was that the *Quincy* was delayed in firing her first salvo for about twelve minutes. Both the *Quincy* and the *Vincennes* appeared un-able to open fire with the Condition of Readiness-Two.[50]

Within a few minutes HMAS *Canberra*, whose guns had not been loaded when the action commenced, was badly damaged and sinking. On USS *Chicago* an explosion threw Captain Bode out of bed. At 1.47 a.m. *Chicago*'s bow was blown off by a torpedo hit and he ordered his ship away from the battle area. In his panic Bode had failed to inform the northern force of US cruisers that the Japanese were attacking. On the *Canberra*, navigation officer, Sub-Lieutenant Mat Gregory recalled the complete surprise of the attack and complained, "It was unbelievable that we could be working with American ships and not have been equipped with radio-telephone. *Patterson* tried to warn us by blinker but it was too late—something exploded on the starboard side."[51]

Next Mikawa, dividing his forces into two columns, caught the cruisers USS *Astoria*, USS *Quincy* and USS *Vincennes* in crossfire. USS *Astoria* was first to be pounded by shells from the *Chokai*'s big guns; the blazing *Astoria* sank the following day. USS *Quincy* then came under attack from the *Aoba*. Crewmen were still dashing to their stations as shells began to rain down. The American cruiser's No. 2 turret took a direct hit and exploded; Captain Samuel Moore called his gunners, shouting, "We're going down between them—give them hell."[52] Soon after a shell blew away the *Quincy*'s plot-house (map and strategy room located behind the bridge), killing her captain. At 2.35 a.m. she rolled over, stern lifting in the air, and sank with men still clinging to her sides. Although the *Vincennes* managed to score hits on *Kinugasa*, the US cruiser was pounded by wave after wave of gunfire from the line of Japanese cruisers.

It was later confirmed that the *Vincennes* took seventy-four hits from 8-inch, 5.5-inch and 4.7-inch shells. The *Vincennes* also took two torpedo strikes. The Bureau of Ships concluded that the loss of the *Vincennes* was inevitable; the cruiser went down by the bow and rolled to port. Close to a thousand men were left in the water, many of them wounded. Hundreds drowned or were taken by swarms of sharks; during rescue efforts in the early morning, US ships had to deploy riflemen to ward them off. At 2.32 a.m. action ceased as heavy rain set in.

Unbeknownst to the Americans, the Japanese fleet had, unlike its US counterpart been practicing night combat. As Ozawa testified to his interrogator, Rear-Admiral R. A. Ofstie after the war, "Strategically speaking, I think the night battle is a very favorable method for the side which had the weaker force, and so we stressed training on that type of battle from before the war."[53] In the 'interwar years' the Japanese Navy developed the use of parachute-suspended star shells and parachute flares to enable them to fight effectively at night. By contrast most of the 5-inch star shells fired at Mikawa's forces malfunctioned. Powerful searchlights had also been developed by Japan. Although their radar development was backward, nighttime lookouts were selected and trained to be able to see objects at night up to two and a half miles away. In the 1920s and 1930s Nippon Kogaku KK [Japan Optical Company—now better known as camera-maker Nikon Corporation] produced increasingly high quality optical products such as range finders, binoculars, periscopes and aiming sights. The Type-88, Model-1, binoculars adopted in 1932 were particularly effective for night vision. By the start of the *Pacific War*, the Japanese Navy was probably the best equipped in terms of optical aids. Night tactics and maneuvers were also practiced.

The Japanese Navy Publication Battle Instructions [1934] placed heavy emphasis on the role of nighttime engagement. It was estimated that a successful destroyer flotilla attack could launch a cross-woven spread of up to 130 torpedoes at an enemy force. The nighttime strengths of the Japanese Navy were played out to the full at the *Battle of Savo Island*. The result of the US operational disarray, the surprise engagement and the technically more proficient Japanese commanders and crews, had dealt a harsh lesson. Alarmingly it was later discovered that the Allies had no prepared plans for night fighting.

Mikawa's force suffered moderate damage to three cruisers and fifty-eight Japanese sailors were killed. However, on the way back to its base at Kavieng, the heavy cruiser, *Kako*, was sunk by US submarine *S-44*, under the command of Lieutenant-Commander 'Dinty' Moore. *S-44* was an out-dated S-Class submarine built by Bethlehem Shipbuilding Corporation in Quincy, Massachusetts in 1923. 'Dinty' Moore followed the *Kako* and closed in to 700 yards before releasing four torpedoes at point blank range. The *Kako* broke up and sank in minutes.

Because of atmospheric interference of radio signals it took two days for Turner's report on the *Battle of Savo Island* to reach Nimitz at *Pearl Harbor*: "Heavy running actions continued about forty minutes. No knowledge of damage to enemy . . . We lost [heavy cruisers] Astoria, Vincennes, Quincy, Canberra; [heavy cruiser] Chicago torpedoed in bow; [destroyers] Ralph Talbot, Patterson damaged. Heavy casualties, majority saved."[54] For Nimitz it was news that shocked him deeply and gave him a sharp reality check in the heady weeks after the *Battle of Midway*. Only the last sentence of Turner's report "Attack did not reach [our] transports or shore forces," gave Nimitz a crumb of comfort. As a result Commodore Richard Bates, in his report for the US Naval College, would conclude that the *Battle of Savo Island* was "a limited tactical victory"[55] for the Japanese Navy.

Seen from the shore, the battle provided a spectacular if confusing picture to the Marines looking on. Corporal 'Rube' Garrett, ammo-chief for I-Battery, 3rd Battalion, noted in his diary on 9 August,

> I saw the Battle for Iron Bottom Bay [aka Savo Island] . . . I nearly had a beachside view. But I remember us in a coconut grove . . . It was raining like the dickens and I got under a truck . . . When you watch a naval gun battle eight miles away, you see tremendous flashes in the gloom. When you see continuous flashes like lightning, what that is 16-inch guns. We didn't realize it at the time but that was our ships getting blown to hell. But we thought we were winning the battle, and every time a ship would go down we'd start cheering "Rah, Rah, that's the good guys" . . . and they were kicking our butts every time. We finally found out by word of mouth I guess.[56]

It was a stunning victory for the Japanese Navy. Unlike the disaster at the *Battle of Midway* that had not been reported in the press, victory at the *Battle of Savo Island* was widely extolled in Japan. Exaggeration was rampant. It was claimed that |twenty-four American warships had been sunk as well as eleven transports. According to the Japanese media, Australia had become "absolutely an orphan of the southwest Pacific."[57] 'Tokyo Rose' (the name given to an English language Japanese propaganda radio station hosted by women) boasted that the US Marines on *Guadalcanal* were like "summer insects, which have been dropped into the fire."[58] In spite of Japanese exaggeration, with 1,979 casualties, including 1,270 dead, the engagement at *Savo Island* was a disaster for the US Navy. Four heavy cruisers had been sunk and one badly damaged.

Admiral Yamamoto was somewhat less pleased with the victory and his commander. Mikawa had lost the opportunity to fall on Turner's disembarking convoys with their 16,000 troops. Unaware of Fletcher's withdrawal of the US carrier force, Mikawa decided at 2.40 a.m. to retreat before dawn revealed his ships. Mikawa later explained, "To remain in the area by sunrise would mean that we would only meet the fate our carriers had suffered at Midway."[59] Judged in hindsight it was a catastrophic mistake. Mikawa's remarks are perhaps a good indication of the huge psychological blow that the defeat at the *Battle of Midway* dealt to the Japan's naval commanders. The fear of American dive-bombers, which had devastated their carrier force at *Midway*, was overwhelming. Mikawa's caution was good fortune for the Allied commanders who were let off lightly for their errors. "The fact must be faced," admitted Admiral Crutchley, "that we had an adequate force placed with the very purpose of repelling surface attack and when that surface attack was made, it destroyed our force." Nimitz was deeply suspicious of the causes of the defeat. Weeks later he was still in the dark. His Commander in Chief, Pacific Area Command (CINCPAC) Command Summary on 19 August noted,

"Our losses were heavy and there is still no explanation of why. The enemy seems to have suffered little or no damage."[60]

In December 1942, the Secretary of the Navy ordered a formal inquiry to determine the "primary and contributing causes of the losses and whether or not culpability attaches to any individual engaged in the operation."[61] The results of the inquiry brought a smattering of conclusions including, "Inadequate condition of readiness on all ships to meet sudden night attack"; "Failure to recognize the implications of the presence of enemy planes in the vicinity of the previous attack"; issues with the "capabilities of radar" and "failure in communications."[62] Commodore Bates, in his later strategic analysis for the Naval War College, noted:

> The Allies . . . relied on their radars and appear to have attached little importance to their visual means of detection. Nor were they familiar with the limitations of the radar . . . or with its failure in the presence of land masses . . . As a consequence, the Japanese almost invariably made visual contact on Allied ships long before the Allied ships made radar or visual contact on the Japanese ships.[63]

What was clear from the analysis was that the US Navy relied too much on technology and too little on basic old-fashioned seamanship. It was a theme that would recur throughout the *Pacific War*.

Australian views of the defeat at the *Battle of Savo Island* were less flattering about Vice-Admiral Fletcher. Sub-Lieutenant Mat Gregory of the HMAS *Canberra* noted that it was Fletcher's abandonment of the landing forces that led to the disaster. "He nicked off, even though it was later shown he wasn't short of fuel at all. I've never forgiven him. He just walked off and left us to the mercy of the Japanese."[64] The US Navy's Hepburn Investigation report (after Admiral A. J. Hepburn) was more polite though he made the same point about the causes of the disaster; "as a contributory cause . . . must be placed the withdrawal of the carrier groups on the evening before the battle . . . for the fact that there was no force available to inflict damage on the withdrawing enemy."[65]

However, the US Navy board, in spite of reservations, did not take disciplinary action against the fleet commanders. The failures were deemed so widely spread that it was concluded that it would be invidious to single out any of the senior commanders for blame. Thereafter Admirals Turner, McCain and Crutchley all had careers that prospered during the war. However, Fletcher, in spite of his leading role at the *Battle of the Coral Sea* and at the *Battle of Midway*, was never liked by Admiral King, and was placed in charge of the *Northern Pacific* in November 1942, an area that became a backwater for the remainder of the *Pacific War*. Only the more junior Captain Howard Bode was picked out for special criticism and, not able to face disgrace, committed suicide. Lessons were learned from the inquiry. Peacetime luxuries like flammable furniture and wall decorations were removed from ships. Internal steel structures were stripped of paint to prevent fire from spreading and the release of toxic fumes. The US Navy also looked to improve ship-to-ship communications.

Rear-Admiral Turner blamed the disaster on "a fatal lethargy of mind which induced a confidence without readiness, and a routine acceptance of outworn peacetime standards of conduct. I believe that this psychological factor, as a cause of our defeat, was even more important than the element of surprise."[66] Similarly the board's main investigator, Admiral Japy Hepburn, concluded, "The primary cause of this defeat must be ascribed generally to the complete surprise achieved by the enemy . . . [and] an inadequate state of readiness on all ships to meet a sudden night attack."[67] Surprise does appear to have been the key element. Even Admiral Mikawa admitted, "Had they [the US surface force] had even a few minutes warning of our approach, the results of the action would have been quite different."[68] As ever, in the naval battles of the *Pacific War*, luck was a factor—notably Mikawa's fortunate passage through the blind spot of Crutchley's picket destroyers. There was some consolation for the Allies. As Admiral Crutchley later, self-servingly, pointed out, "Our forces did achieve our object, which was to prevent the enemy from reaching the transports."[69]

Ultimately the *Battle of Savo Island*, a decisive tactical naval victory for the Japanese Navy, proved to be little more than a pyrrhic triumph. At the time however, commanders on the ground were less sanguine. Major-General Millard Harmon who led the Army forces in the southwest under Vice-Admiral Ghormley's command, wrote on 11 August, "The thing that impresses me more than anything else in connection with the *Solomons* action is that we are not prepared 'to follow up' . . . Can the Marines hold it? [*Guadalcanal*] There is considerable room for doubt."[70]

Even before the *Battle of Savo Island* had begun, the strategic objectives of Mikawa's mission were lost. American troops and some of their supplies had already landed on *Guadalcanal*, the US carriers had left the area and troops sent to reinforce the Japanese garrison there had been dispersed. However, the Marines "shot themselves in the foot"[71] by not helping the crews on Turner's transports to manhandle the supplies to higher ground. When the tide rose, large quantities of supplies were washed out to sea—a disaster in the weeks ahead, when the Marines ran out of food. It was a problem compounded by Turner's insistence on recalling his remaining transports from *Iron Bottom Bay* the next morning. The bay was now eerily abandoned and the US Marines were alone with their Japanese enemies on the jungle- and swamp-infested tropical island of *Guadalcanal*. Marine Ore Marion bitterly recalled,

> We were surrounded and abandoned all the way down the line . . . we little snuffies who fought the war, not those assholes in Washington, Pearl or Australia, let it be known, "the goddamn Navy brought us here and when those bastards are ready to take us off this island—that's when we'll go." That's how we, just kids, felt: and that's what we did.[72]

In Washington the crushing defeat suffered by the US Navy at the *Battle of Savo Island* was an embarrassment to be covered up. After the great victory at the *Battle of Midway*, senior Naval command in Washington were not prepared for the disaster at the *Battle of Savo Island*. By his own admission King was crushed by the news and demanded that the message be decoded again to make sure that it was not a mistake. "[*The Battle of Savo Island*] as far as I am concerned, was the blackest day of the war," he recalled later, "The whole future became unpredictable."[73]

When the respected journalist Hanson Baldwin, on his return from the *South Pacific*, was invited to appear before the Joint Staff Planners (JSP) Committee to comment on his impressions, he was astonished to find that the Army had been kept in the dark about the *Battle of Savo Island*. Baldwin was fully aware of what had happened at *Savo Island* but when he mentioned it an alarmed Captain Charles Brown, one of Admiral King's naval planners jumped up to protest. It became clear to Baldwin that the Army and the Air Corps officers on the JSP, "had no idea of what had happened at Guadalcanal or Savo, no idea at all."[74]

Henderson Field and the Seabees: After landing, the next four days were spent in the backbreaking task of transferring supplies to dumps placed within the perimeter, which had been established around Lunga Point and the airfield. Using equipment left by the Japanese, the 6th Naval Construction Battalion then began work on completing the landing strip.

The Seabees battalion (named from an abbreviation of the Seabees formal title of Construction Battalion; CB) comprised 32 officers and 1073 men. The brought 2 bulldozers, 6 dump trucks and 25 other vehicles. A tractor and roller left by the Japanese were also appropriated. The Seabees used 10,000 barrels of cement and 18,000 feet of soil pipe. The airfield was named Henderson Field in memory of Lofton R. Henderson who led the first air attack on the Japanese fleet at the *Battle of Midway*. Putting the sloth of the Japanese to shame the airfield was completed in just six days. Just 2,600ft in length and bumpy to boot, it worked. Its rapid construction was a reflection of the far better training, equipment and motivation of the American Seabees than the usual forced and unskilled Korean labor employed by the Japanese. By contrast, within their ranks, the Seabees had specialist teams of tractor drivers, carpenters, masons, dynamiters, electricians, shop-fitters and machinists. Even General MacArthur, rarely complementary about the Navy was moved to remark, "The only trouble with your Seabees is that you don't have enough of them."[75]

In spite of the rapid construction of the airport, the scale of Vandegrift's task was monumental. Before quitting his transport mission Rear-Admiral Turner landed enough rations for just one month. Vandegrift was without landmines, barbed wire, heavy weapons or even trenching tools. Neither did he have enough men to fully man his perimeter. Here sentries set passwords containing lots of 'L's (Lollipop, Lallapaloozer etc.) knowing that it was the roman letter that the Japanese found difficult to pronounce.

Seabees not only built stuff, they also filled in doing whatever jobs were needed—including manning the perimeter defences and fighting. At sunset Seabees also guided planes in by flashlight and lit up the perimeter of the airfield. It was a job not without danger. Seabees Commander, Joseph Blundon, recalled, "if they [landing planes] caught a little air pocket even the brush of a wingtip would sever the head of any man holding a light."[76] The Seabees, created just nine months earlier at the suggestion of Admiral Ben Morell, then Chief of the Navy's Bureau of Yards and Docks, became one of the greatest successes of the *Pacific War* . . . and the most unsung. Camp Endicott established at Davisville would train more than 100,000 Seabee engineers during the course of the war and in total some 325,000 troops served in the Navy's Construction Battalions. Many were construction veterans of Roosevelt's New Deal projects of the 1930s. Rarely has enough prominence been given to the remarkable feat of carrying and constructing America's naval and military power 5,000 miles across the *Pacific*; it was the Seabees that made this task possible.

Rear-Admiral Ben Morell coined the Seabees motto, "*Construimus Batuimus*—We build, we fight."[77] Arguably these US engineers were one of the main differences between the forces of Japan and the United States in the *Solomons* campaign. In the *Pacific* theater, the Seabees worked closely with the Corps of Engineers. Together they would go on to construct 111 airfields, many of them still used, as well as building housing for 1.5 million men. At the end of war, in *Okinawa*, 100,000 Seabees were engaged in construction projects as the US Army prepared to invade mainland Japan.

A less heralded but essential unofficial function of the Seabees was to provide the alcohol that kept up military spirits. Within days of arriving on any island, they set up distilleries. Many of the Seabees were older men recruited for their technical skills. A not inconsiderable number had been 'moonshiners' in the Prohibition period, which had only ended in 1933. Many of these volunteers came from the Appalachian Mountains in the south where illegal stills had been a way of life. So-called 'White Lighting' was distilled from anything that would ferment. The Seabees also took care of storage and distribution. Seabee Jim Rothermal declared, "You didn't want a nosy CO or master of arms [Navy MP] to find it. We'd hide it in foxholes. In about 20 days it was ready . . . one batch was outstanding. I filled a soup bowl full, drank it down, and in twenty minutes I could barely walk. Good stuff."[78]

Japanese planners, obsessed as they were by the production of glamorous weapons of attack for the winning of the decisive encounter, paid scant regard to the boring aspects of war. Japanese industry should have produced more bulldozers and other assorted construction equipment and better organized its transportation to the *South Pacific* where the ability to build high quality airfields rapidly was one of the key determinants of the *Solomons* and New Guinea campaigns. Of course, underlying Japan's logistics failure was the lack of capacity of an economy unable to produce enough *matériel* for a war being fought on so many fronts. It is interesting to note that the best airfields in Japan's *Pacific* empire were those at Clark Field (the Philippines), built by the Americans and at Rabaul, built by the Australians.

The Battle of Tenaru: [**Map: 16.6**] In his diary on 17 August 'Rube' Garrett noted the pleasure of swimming on *Guadalcanal*:

> We always went to the river to bathe—the Lunga River—
> it was only knee deep . . . fresh running water. We'd go in
> there and strip off. There was a big old tree, it was laying
> down in the river. We would wash our clothes in there and
> all, lay them on a limb while we swam . . . But every now
> and then we'd see a dead Jap floating in the river. That's
> the river we fished with hand grenades.[79]

The pleasures of swimming and fishing would be short lived. Along with the four weeks of food that they had managed to land, the Marines had nine days of food captured from the Japanese. To conserve supplies meals were immediately reduced to two a day. The Marines were soon afflicted by severe dysentery and within a few weeks over 20 percent had been taken ill. If conditions were bad for the Marines, they were far worse for the Japanese who had withdrawn west and established positions behind the *Matanikau River*. Here they had to subsist largely on coconuts and foraged food.

Vandegrift established an oval-shaped perimeter defense around the airfield and down to the coast. Lacking resources for this to be a continuous line of defense, strongpoints were heavily defended and lookout posts were supplemented by frequent patrols. In the short time available the Marines had to prepare against counter-attack as best they could. Lines of fire were cleared through the dense undergrowth. In his diary Garret noted,

> We had to burn off all the tall Johnson type grass on
> Henderson Field—Japanese snipers were using it to slip
> in amongst us at night. They would strap a light machine
> gun to one man's back. He would run and lay down—
> they would fire a few rounds then he would jump up and
> the gun would move to another position.[80]

While they waited for the Japanese onslaught, the Marines were pounded by day by Japanese bombers and by night by warships. Japanese warships would use the cover of darkness to slip down the 'Slot' to deliver fresh Japanese troops to *Guadalcanal* and to bombard Henderson Field.

On 20 August flight operations from Henderson Field went live after the delivery of nineteen Wildcat fighters and twelve of Douglas Aircraft's SBD Dauntless dive-bombers. They saw action almost immediately as bombers from Rabaul started their daily air strikes. A reinforcement of fourteen out-dated Bell Corporation P-400/P-39 Airacobra arrived between 22 and 27 August. The rear-engine Airacobra was agile but with its Allison 1200 HP engine lacking a supercharger, it was deficient in speed, climb rate or the ability to fight above a 5,000 foot ceiling, which made it unsuitable as an interceptor for Japanese bombers that could fly much higher. A supercharger compressed air into an aero engine to give it more oxygen to burn, enabling a plane to fly faster and at higher altitude where oxygen was thinner. Even though its introduction was as recent as 1939, the P-39 Airacobra was already technologically redundant. In spite of the Airacobra's frailties, in August 1941 any available aircraft were more than welcome on *Guadalcanal*.

Marine attitudes to the Japanese hardened as a US patrol was deceived by a white flag seemingly proffered by Japanese forces. Lieutenant-Colonel Frank Goettge, Vandegrift's intelligence officer, was mown down by machine gun and most of his force wiped out with many of the captured American wounded slashed to death by samurai swords. The story spread and from now on Marines would take no prisoners. The Marine encampment on *Guadalcanal* at this stage was small and sparsely equipped. David Galvan, a rear gunner on a Marine dive-bomber recalled,

> Henderson looked like a very small pasture with a whole lot of holes in it when I first arrived. I mean a narrow one too. When you come into Guadalcanal there was a grove of coconut trees . . . a little kind of meadow that extended from the Tenaru River running east by southeast. On the opposite side was jungle—thick jungle; a solid mass of trees and brush. There was no transition zone . . . For a while in late August we only had about 10 aircraft. We'd work in the open or in the jungle, which was a few feet away; it gave us a lot of shade. . .[81]

A minor first engagement took place on 19 August as three companies probed *Matanikau River* to the west of Henderson Field. In a daylight *banzai* charge, supposedly the first of the war, sixty-five Japanese soldiers were killed for the loss of just four Marines dead and eleven wounded. Second Lieutenant John Jackym recalled that they "came across the Japanese quite suddenly; they were all cleverly camouflaged and hard to see until they all seemed to pop up out of the bush only yards away. It was horribly frightening, uncertain and confused; they seemed to be all around. I just fired furiously whenever one of them came into view."[82]

On the same day Roosevelt radioed Stalin from Washington to convey the good news of *Guadalcanal*'s occupation, "we have gained, I believe, a toehold in the Southwest Pacific from which the Japanese will find it very difficult to dislodge us. We have had substantial naval losses there, but the advantage gained was worth the sacrifice and we are going to maintain hard pressure on the enemy."[83] It was an optimistic assessment. On the positive side for *Guadalcanal*'s Marines, it meant that Roosevelt had a shoe in the game, namely his pride and personal authority. Above and beyond strategy, Roosevelt had staked his name on the ability of the Marines to hold out.

Meanwhile at Rabaul the Seventeenth Army under Lieutenant-General Harukichi Hyakutake had been ordered to retake Henderson Field. Accordingly Yamamoto launched Operation KA to expel the Americans from *Guadalcanal*. However, Japanese intelligence was still operating in the belief that the American forces were a lightly armed raiding party. Available units were sent to clear out the US raiders. The 28th Infantry Regiment from the Imperial Japanese Army's 7th Division, commanded by Colonel Kiyonao Ichiki, arrived from *Guam* on a nighttime convoy on 20 August, landing at Taivu to the east of Henderson Field. Major-General Kiyotake Kawaguchi's 35th Infantry Brigade was coming from *Palau* while the 4th Infantry Regiment would arrive from the Philippines. Colonel Ichiki and his so-called Ichiki Detachment were authorized to attack without waiting for the other units to arrive. Lieutenant-General Hyakutake had ordered him to "... quickly recapture and maintain the airfields at Guadalcanal. If this is not possible, this detachment will occupy a part of Guadalcanal and await the arrival of troops in its rear."[84]

With this license, Colonel Ichiki, by reputation a superb officer, with his crack troops, chose the 'glory' option. His men were ordered to read the Army battle instructions, which started, "when you encounter the enemy after landing, regard yourself as an avenger come at last face to face with his father's murderer."[85] Ichiki, much criticized later for his recklessness, was undoubtedly imbued with the Japanese view that western troops were badly disciplined, poor-spirited fighters. One can hardly blame him. Up to this point Japanese military contact with the enemy throughout Asia had been one-way traffic. Rapid advances, combined with flanking movements had routed all before it. Vandegrift's Marines on *Guadalcanal* provided the Japanese with their first real test against first-class American troops with a proud fighting tradition.

Carrying just a week's rations, Ichiki advanced confidently on the Lunga Point perimeter boasting in a radioed report, "No enemy at all, like marching through no-man's-land."[86] Thus, after landing with 917 troops at Taivu Point, that was ten miles to the east of Henderson Field, at 2.00 a.m. Ichiki launched an overconfident frontal attack across the sandbar of the *Ilu River* in the darkness of the early hours of the morning of 21 August. Ichiki's troops were mown down by 'dug-in' machine guns and several M3 37 mm anti-tank guns loaded with buckshot canisters, which proved deadly against the advancing infantry. Private Leckie recalled, "Here was booming, sounding, shrieking, wailing, hissing, crashing, shaking, gibbering noise. Here was hell!"[87] Marine David Moss was amazed by the bravery of the Japanese troops, "They seemed so invincible. They just could not believe they could die. It was a crack unit . . . The fellow next to me was killed. I picked up his Tommy gun."[88]

At 5 a.m. a second attack attempted to flank the Marine's positions. Having waded into the sea and circled round from the east, Japanese troops charged through the surf. Again they were cut down by artillery and machine gun. "We were picking them off in the river," David Moss reported, "and later on in the morning some were trying to swim around us, in the ocean to the north, and we picked them off there. I know I did."[89] In places bodies lay three deep like wet sandbags in the lapping sea. Not only was the attack repelled, but a Marine flanking counter-attack by a reserve battalion in the morning forced the surviving twenty-eight Japanese soldiers, mostly wounded, to retire to their starting point where Ichiki had left a 100-strong garrison. In the aftermath of the battle a number of US Marines were shot by Japanese troops who feigned death. As a result it soon became standard practice for Marines to bayonet bodies they came across on the battlefield. Some fifteen Japanese soldiers were taken prisoner. Ichiki was dead; supposedly the scale of the defeat led him by some accounts to commit *seppuku* (ritual suicide by disembowelment). Fighting continued to 5 p.m. by which time US casualties amounted to thirty-four killed and seventy-five wounded.

Returning to view the scene of the battle some weeks later Private Leckie was horrified to find the ground still corpse-ridden with "swarms of flies; black, circling funnels that seemed to emerge from every orifice . . . the beating of their myriad wings made a dreadful low hum . . . All my elation at the victory, all of my fanciful cockiness fled before the horror of what my eyes beheld."[90] Nevertheless for the Marines in the Lunga Perimeter, the overwhelming defeat of Ichiki's infantry provided a huge morale boost. The first engagement of Operation KA was a disaster for the Japanese. One of their officers said it was "like a housefly attacking a tortoise. The odds were against it."[91] Ist Marine Private Jack Means described it as "an absolute massacre."[92] After the battle the condition of the surviving Japanese attackers declined dramatically. Rations were reduced to one-third of normal. A diet of mouldy rice and soybean was a staple that left them pathetically weak. A Japanese soldier recorded, "Our bodies are so weak they are like raw cotton."[93]

Though a small engagement in the context of the war, it was the first time that a jungle-trained Japanese force had been dealt such a setback; a defeat that was in effect a massacre and one of the most lopsided engagements in the *South* Pacific conflict to date. (The *Battle of Milne Bay* fought by the Australians on the tip of New Guinea a week later brought an even more crushing Allied victory.) Defeat was a new experience for a Japanese Army and its officers consumed by hubris. Apart from a few temporary setbacks on the Bataan Peninsula, Malaya and Burma, the advance of Japanese forces in the *Pacific* had hitherto been one-way traffic. For the US Marines and the American armed forces the *Battle of Tenaru* gave them confidence that they could compete in 'slugging it out' with Japan's jungle-trained troops.

In Rabaul, Lieutenant-General Hyakutake received the astonishing news from the remnants of the force left behind at Taivu that Ichiki's force had been annihilated. Hyakutake duly informed Imperial General HQ in Tokyo: "The attack of the Ichiki Detachment was not entirely successful."[94] It was a message that was not 'entirely truthful.'

With regard to truth, the canonization over subsequent decades of the Marine actions at *Guadalcanal* has tended to obscure the reality that in the next year and a half it was largely the Australian and then the US Army that fought the Japanese as they painstakingly advanced up the *Solomons* towards Rabaul and then along the north coast of New Guinea. Nevertheless it was the Marines, smaller in number, who tended to be saved for the most difficult of actions in which the need for aggression was paramount.

Machine Guns and Field Artillery: The *Battle of Tenaru* was one of the first demonstrations of the power of the machine gun as a defensive weapon against the high-speed Japanese infiltration and advance tactics. The Browning Automatic Rifle (BAR) was, in spite of its name, a machine gun made mainly for ground emplacement resting on a bipod, though at twenty pounds, more than double the weight of the Springfield Rifle that was the Marines' standard issue in the first stages of *Guadalcanal*, it was in theory capable of being carried and fired from the hip. The BAR was fully automatic and fired a 0.30 caliber round. The BAR M1918A2 was adopted by the US Army as its standard squad automatic weapon (one per squad of twelve) in 1938. For most effective operation however, the BAR needed three men to carry and load the machine gun. With a box magazine containing just twenty rounds, troops would have to carry numbers of spare magazines. One man was in effect a spare in case one of the others was killed. All squad members would be trained to use the BAR.

In addition to the BAR, Marines units were supported by specialist machine gun platoons, typically containing forty-eight men at full strength. They would operate eight heavy machine guns, four water-cooled M1917 Brownings, with the barrels enclosed in a water-filled casing, and four air-cooled M1919 Brownings. Bullets of 0.30 caliber were loaded in fabric belts strung from ammunition boxes carrying 250 rounds. Although the air-cooled version was lighter, many specialists preferred the water-cooled version that tended to be more reliable. Whichever type was used constant attention to maintenance was required. Sustained synchronized use of the Browning produced a wall of lead. Firing up to 600 rounds per minute with a muzzle velocity of 2,800 foot per second, triple the velocity of the BAR, the heavy Browning machine guns proved to be devastating defensive weapons against Japanese troops charging in open terrain. The *Battle of Tenaru* was the first of many actions across the *Pacific* in which the Browning would prove invaluable.

By comparison the Japanese mainly used the Nambu Model-11 Light Machine Gun that was a poorly manufactured copy of a Czech design that was itself modeled on the British Bren gun. The side mounted, open, hopper type magazine could carry just thirty rounds but had the advantage of taking the same bullets used by the standard infantry Type-38 Arisaka Rifle. However, its rate of fire of 400–425 rounds per minute was 20 percent less than the BAR while its muzzle velocity was similarly lower. Firing a 0.256 caliber bullet, the Nambu fired with less weight but like the Arisaka rifle, its poor manufacture led its bullets to wobble causing severe injuries. The Nambu Model-11 and the Arisaka rifle also had the advantage of showing little smoke during daytime or 'flash' at night.

In addition to Browning machine guns, the Marines also deployed 75 mm M1 Pack Howitzers, which were the standard field artillery unit employed by the United States in *World War II*. The Pack Howitzer, so named because it could be taken to pieces and assembled in the field, was devastating against troops in open terrain. Only 188 pieces were manufactured in 1941 and production only took off in the following year with an increase in output of 575 percent. On *Guadalcanal* the 37 mm M3 Cannon proved even more effective than the howitzer. Originally designed as an anti-tank gun by the Watervliet Arsenal on Long Island, NY, the 37 mm M3 Cannon could fire anti-personnel canister rounds that proved the most devastating weapon of all at the *Battle of Tenaru*.

At the *Battle of Tenaru*, as in many subsequent battles, the Japanese frontal charge tactics made the combination of Browning light and heavy machine guns, 75 mm Pack Howitzers and 37 mm cannon, winning weapons as they could lay a mass of lead ahead of charging and fully exposed Japanese troops. Rear-Admiral Tanaka later had this to say about the disaster:

> I knew Colonel Ichiki from the Midway operation and was well aware of his magnificent leadership and indomitable fighting spirit. But this episode made it abundantly clear that infantrymen armed with rifles and bayonets had no chance against an enemy equipped with modern heavy arms. This tragedy should have taught us the hopelessness of "bamboo-spear" tactics.[95]

Against *Banzai* charging troops, weight of lead was much more important than accuracy.

The Naval Battle of the East Solomons: **[Map: 16.7]** By the middle of August, the problems faced by Japan from the loss of Henderson Field on *Guadalcanal* were becoming ever more apparent. The US carrier fleet was not only giving air support for the Marines defending the airfield but was also interdicting supplies for the Japanese troops trying to take Henderson Field. In addition US carriers were starting to feed in fighters and bombers to Henderson Field. As infrastructure and capacity were gradually increased, US bombers from there were able to intercept attempted Japanese convoys to *Guadalcanal* making daytime re-supply of Japanese forces all but impossible. Furthermore, for Yamamoto there was the prospect that permanent occupation of Henderson Field would disrupt all Japanese movement throughout the *Solomons*. Ultimately the US development there threatened Rabaul.

Yamamoto seemed slow to react to the danger. On 21 August a supply convoy set off for *Guadalcanal* from *Truk* with provisions for the Japanese forces at *Guadalcanal* as well as the 1,500 troops from the 28th 'Ichiki' Infantry that Colonel Kiyonao Ichiki had refused to wait for. (Unbeknownst to Yamamoto, Ichiki had been killed just as the convoy was setting off.) The troop convoy led by Rear-Admiral Raizo Tanaka was escorted by his flagship, the light cruiser *Jintsu*, eight destroyers and patrol boats. Two fleet carriers, *Shokaku* and *Zuikaku*, as well as the light carrier *Ryujo* under the command of Vice-Admiral Chuichi Nagumo would support the convoy. The carrier force was screened by a heavy cruiser and eight destroyers. As ever Yamamoto's deployments were complex. Preceding Nagumo was a force of two battleships, three heavy cruisers, one light cruiser and six destroyers commanded by Rear-Admiral Hiroaki Abe.

Yet another force, commanded by Vice-Admiral Nobutake Kondo, even further in advance, consisted of five heavy cruisers, one light cruiser, six destroyers, as well as the *Chitose*, which carried seaplanes. Supporting the whole enterprise were 100 land-based fighters and bombers provided by the Imperial Japanese Navy at Rabaul. A spread of twelve submarines was also placed to the southeast of *Guadalcanal*. The concept of Operation KA was for the advance forces to locate the US carriers and to destroy them with the light carrier *Ryujo* used as bait to draw away the American carriers' aircraft. Destruction of the US carrier force would lead to the unfolding of stage two. The two Japanese surface forces would engage the remaining US fleet in a conventional surface action, leaving Henderson Field at the mercy of prolonged naval bombardment until Japanese troops could retake it.

Meanwhile on 21 August, the US carrier force consisting of three fleet carriers USS *Enterprise*, USS *Saratoga* and USS *Wasp* lay 400 miles south in their reserve positions. As the ground battle for Henderson Field on 19–20 August developed, Admiral Fletcher was ordered by Southern Fleet Commander Vice-Admiral Ghormley to move forward to give close support to the embattled Marines. By 22 August, the US and Japanese carriers began to close on each other in preparation for what would be the third carrier battle of the *Pacific War*. On 22 August one of USS *Enterprise*'s scouting planes, which was shot down before it could relay a message, gave the Japanese a clue as to the presence of US carriers in the area. At 9.50 a.m. on 23 August, Tanaka's troop convoy force was spotted by a Catalina flying boat and USS *Saratoga* immediately sent off a strike force to attack. However, Tanaka, aware that he had been observed turned away from *Guadalcanal* and thus evaded attack. On 24 August Tanaka reversed course again and steamed back toward *Guadalcanal*. Planned landings of fresh Japanese troops would now be pushed back to the 25 August.

With no further sightings of the Japanese fleet, Vice-Admiral Fletcher sent USS *Wasp* back south for refuelling on the evening of 23 August. Both fleets "groped for each other like tired wrestlers with smoke in their eyes."[96] However, in the early hours of 24 August, Nagumo sent the light carrier *Ryujo*, heavy cruiser *Tone* and two destroyers ahead of the main force to launch an attack on Henderson Field by both air and surface bombardment. *Ryujo* was thus offered as a decoy. At 9.30 a.m. the *Ryujo*'s task force was spotted. At 12.20 p.m., at a point in the 'Slot' some 230 miles from Lunga Point, the *Ryujo* launched six Nakajima B5N 'Kate' and fifteen Zeros. Meanwhile the Japanese fleet carriers were prepared for strikes against the US fleet carriers—if they could be found. Having sent off a force of bombers and fighters to attack Henderson Field, the light carrier *Ryujo* was left with just nine Zero fighters for defense. At midday *Ryujo*'s aircraft fought with Henderson Field's defenders and suffered a loss of three 'Kate' bombers and three Zeros in exchanges for three Wildcats. Commander Tameichi Hara aboard the destroyer *Amatsukaze* was incredulous that the *Ryujo* had not put up all its fighters, seven of which were only brought on deck after Hara sent a scolding message suggesting, "Your flight operations are far short of expectations. What is the matter?"[97]

The seven Zeros parked on the deck of the *Ryujo* had only just started up their propellers when USS *Saratoga*'s 30 Douglas Dauntless dive-bombers and 8 Grumman TBF Avenger torpedo planes, led by Commander Harry Felt, launched their attack. As at the *Battle of Midway* Vice-Admiral Fletcher had left half of his planes in reserve.

They were not needed. Lieutenant Syd Bottomley lined up the *Ryujo* and released a 1,000 lb bomb from 1,500 foot. It struck squarely amidships. It was followed by two more 1,000 lb bombs dropped by Lieutenant Gordon Sherwood and Lieutenant Roy Isaman, which crashed through *Ryujo*'s decks. Bob Hansen, in a scouting Dauntless recalled: "Heavy black smoke was curling from the sides and rolling over the deck in a streaming curtain. An occasional lick of flame appeared from amidships."

From his sea-level view Commodore Tameichi Hara on the *Amatsukaze* saw the same scene noting "Water pillars surrounded the carrier, and it was engulfed in thick, black smoke. This was no deliberate smokescreen. Her fuel tanks had been hit and set afire."[98] She was also hit by at least one torpedo after *Ryujo* was cornered by a pincer attack by three planes approaching from the starboard flank and two planes from the port. As a bonus, one of the torpedoes that missed their target went on to hit a Japanese destroyer. Turned almost instantly into a stationary fireball, *Ryujo* keeled over in mid-afternoon and sank later that evening. One hundred and twenty officers and crew were killed. *Ryujo*'s returning aircrews had to ditch their planes.

Some two and a half hours after the attack on Henderson Field, the US carrier force was finally sighted and *Shokaku* and *Zuikaku* launched a strike force comprising 36 dive-bombers, 12 torpedo planes and 27 fighters. Before these aircraft arrived to strike the USS *Enterprise* and USS *Saratoga*, the American carriers launched their own attack-aircraft. Fletcher's carriers were also able to muster a considerable defense force of fifty Wildcat fighters. In spite of this, *Enterprise* took the brunt of the Japanese strike attack. At 5.09 p.m. 'Radar Plot' (radar plot room at the back of the Captain's bridge) on *Enterprise* reported "the enemy planes are directly overhead now!"[99] At least half of the thirty-six Japanese 'Val' dive-bombers breached the US fighter defenses and reached their target. It was a testament to the quality of anti-aircraft defenses on the *Enterprise* and her escorting warships that at least ten Japanese dive-bombers crashed out around the carrier. USS *Grayson*, a Gleaves Class destroyer, reported that the battleship USS *North Carolina*'s "volume of fire was so great that the ship appeared to be in flames."[100] The *North Carolina*, a fast new battleship that had been commissioned only four months earlier at the New York Naval Shipyard, went on to become the most decorated American battleship of *World War II*.

Julian Burke, later a rear-admiral, aboard the *North Carolina* recalled:

> The engagement only lasted seven minutes. It seemed like hours at the time. I remember talking to the men in my division in the starboard battery. The seamen were manning these machine guns—50 mm calibers and 20 mm, and they were the most excited and proud people. They fought like they had knocked down every single plane in the ocean. We were all claiming having shot down 350 aircraft, and really there were only about 75. The Japanese did suffer a terrible loss that afternoon. But

> we became men. The maturity of our seamen and our officers after that ... and the way we approached problems, was entirely different. We had grown up in seven minutes.[101]

In spite of the efforts of the anti-aircraft gunners 'Val' dive-bombers led by Lieutenant Keiichi Arima, dived toward the *Enterprise*. A first hit was scored by Petty Officer Furuta with a 250 lb semi-armor piercing bomb. It passed through the teak decks and penetrated 42 foot through three steel lower decks before exploding in the petty officer's quarters. Thirty-five men died instantly and seventy were wounded. Fortunately Bill Fluitt, the ship's gasoline officer had drained and vented the aviation fuel lines and filled them with inert carbon dioxide a few minutes before the attack. A secondary blast threw metal and body parts out as far as the escorting USS *Monssen*. At 4.46 p.m. another 'Val' from Arima's *shotai* (squadron) was hit and fell apart as it swooped toward the *Enterprise*. Its bomb continued to fall, hit a part of the structure of the aft elevator and exploded. Boatswain's Mate 2nd Class Arthur Davis, who had been standing next to the elevator, was blown to bits and a large chunk of his body landed in the lap of an anti-aircraft gunner.

Remarkably war photographer Marion Riley caught the attack and explosions on film, though his colleague, Robert Read, Photographer's Mate 2nd Class was killed instantly by the third bomb that struck just in front of the *Enterprise*'s stack. A pilot looking at the scene below decks recalled, "most of the men died from concussion and were then roasted ... They looked like iron statues of men ... The faces were indistinguishable, but in almost every case the lips were drawn back in a wizened grin giving the men the expression of rodents."[102]

Remarkably, and in stark contrast to the result of bomb hits on the Japanese carriers at the *Battle of Midway*, the crew of the heavily damaged USS *Enterprise* managed to contain the fires and had the decks operational within the hour. Holes were trimmed with axes, steel boilerplates were hammered into place and deck planks were replaced to enable planes to land. A jammed rudder that had started to send the *Enterprise* in circles was quickly repaired. Fortunately for the US carriers, a second Japanese strike force failed to find them due navigational errors. Fletcher's dive-bombers and torpedo bombers returned without having found their Japanese fleet carrier targets. Fletcher, wishing to avoid the possibility of a night engagement with Japanese surface forces, withdrew his carriers southwards. The *Enterprise* retired to *Pearl Harbor* for repairs. Admiral Kondo's surface task force gave chase but was forced to give up.

Criticisms were later made of US flight direction, which had enabled so many of Japan's dive-bombers to evade the fifty-three fighter planes that had been deployed above Fletcher's carrier fleet. Admiral Nimitz concluded that direction was "not as effective as it should have been."[103] In part the problem was created by the indiscipline of American pilots and their unnecessary chatter that clogged the airwaves with such superfluous transmissions as "Look at that one go down" or "I'm in high blower, where are you, Bill?"[104] (A 'blower' referred to a plane being in supercharger mode.)

On the following day, 25 August, Admiral Tanaka's troop convoy continued toward *Guadalcanal*. Some 150 miles from their destination, Tanaka's flagship *Jintsu* was hit by an attack from eighteen planes from Henderson Field and Tanaka himself was laid unconscious. *Jintsu* was able to limp back to Rabaul but the troop carrier *Kinryu Maru* was sunk along with the destroyer *Mutsuki*. The latter's captain, after being lifted from the water, commented laconically, "even the B-17 could make a hit once in a while."[105] Faced by mounting losses Tanaka turned his convoy back up the 'Slot' toward the *Shortland Islands*; he concluded, "it would be folly to land the remainder of this battered force on *Guadalcanal*."[106] Japan's naval forces lingered in the northern *Solomons* out of range of Henderson Field but retired back to *Truk* on 5 September. On *Guadalcanal* itself General Vandegrift joshed, "Everyone is withdrawing but the Marines."[107]

The third carrier battle of the *Pacific War* was a clear though not overwhelming victory for the US Navy. As well as sinking a light carrier and three other ships, seventy-five Japanese aircraft had been destroyed and 290 of their aircrew killed. The seaplane carrier *Chitose* was also badly damaged. In return American forces had suffered heavy damage to the *Enterprise* and lost twenty aircraft with ninety killed. From an American viewpoint, albeit a victory, the *Battle of the Eastern Solomons* was something of a disappointment. As Lieutenant Henry Mustin recorded in his account of the battle for Naval Intelligence, there was a failure of communications with the scout planes regarding the whereabouts of the *Zuikaku* and the *Shokaku*. "The attack group which was sent out at 1435 on 24th [August] to strike the Ryujo," Mustin noted, "should have had the two large carriers for targets . . . they were closer to us."[108] Although wounded, the 'Big E,' as the battle-weary *Enterprise* had become known, would live to fight again. Most importantly, Hyakutake had failed to reinforce his Japanese forces on *Guadalcanal*. As a Japanese officer noted in his diary, "Our plan to capture *Guadalcanal* came unavoidably to a standstill, owing to the appearance of the enemy."[109]

Slow-moving convoy ships, because of their inability to get down the 'Slot' and back under cover of darkness, could no longer be used to supply Japanese forces on *Guadalcanal*. They were too vulnerable to Dauntless dive-bombers from Henderson Field. In future all Japanese troops and supplies would have to be carried by fast destroyers; a poor use of this resource in terms of ships and fuel. The value of Henderson Field was thus significantly enhanced. Japanese vulnerability in the 'Slot' was shown to good effect a week later when bombers from Henderson Field sank the Japanese destroyer *Asagiri* and damaged two other destroyers as they travelled down the 'Slot.'

Perhaps the most mystifying element of the battle is why, given the importance of Henderson Field, Yamamoto, having assembled a considerable fleet, failed to press his attack with greater determination. It can only be concluded that the scars of the *Battle of Midway* had cut deeply into his confidence. For Nimitz the result of the battle was more than satisfactory. After the slapping given to the Allied Navy by Vice-Admiral Gunichi Mikawa at the *Battle of Savo Island*, the US Navy's victory at the *Battle of Eastern*

Solomons was a quick restorative. Furthermore Japanese re-supply of its forces on *Guadalcanal* had been thwarted and a serious defeat avoided. More precious time had been bought before the flood of new US warships came on stream at the end of the year. Before the battle Nimitz had expressed concerns about the state of his carriers' aircrews; "pilots with experience are spread thin and those recently in battle are shaken."[110] Now the recent pilot graduates had been 'blooded' and would be better prepared for future action. An American toehold in the southern *Solomons* had been established. Round one in the battle for *Guadalcanal* had been won by the United States.

17 Guadalcanal II: Battle of Edson's (Bloody) Ridge

[August 1942–November 1942]

[Maps: 17.1, 17.2, 17.3]

Air War over Besieged Henderson Field: In the air battles over Henderson Field starting on 20 August, the Japanese had held the upper hand in the early encounters. Armed at first with eighteen Grumman F4F Wildcats and five Bell P-400s (an older export version of the P-39 Airacobra, which was lightly armed with a single Hispano-Suiza 20 mm cannon in the nose and four wing-fitted 0.30 caliber machine guns) Marine Brigadier-General Alexander Vandegrift's fighters had found themselves hopelessly outmatched. Saburo Sakai and his colleagues' Zeros had outfought the Wildcat in the early engagements over Henderson Field. The P-400 was even more mismatched. They lacked superchargers and could only fly at between 10,000 to 12,000 feet because there were no high-pressure oxygen tanks available on *Guadalcanal*; it was a ceiling below that at which Japanese bombers and Zero fighters could operate.

Within six days of their arrival in the *Solomons* only three out of the original eighteen Wildcats were operational. Airacobras, useless in aerial combat, were converted to ground attack aircraft. Fortunately at the end of the month Rear-Admiral John McCain supplied nineteen more Wildcats and twelve more Douglas Dauntless dive-bombers led by Major Robert Galer. They arrived on 30 August while a dogfight was raging over Henderson Field. Galer's Wildcats immediately pitched in, while the dive-bombers headed for the airfield. From now on there would be a constant battle to resupply Vandegrift's 'Cactus' Air Force (as it became known after the code word for *Guadalcanal*) before its stock of planes was diminished by combat loss and accidents—on Henderson Field's muddy, bomb crater pocked runways, landing and take-off were extremely hazardous.

By early September Vandegrift had eighty-six pilots and sixty-four planes: 3 Army, 10 Navy and 51 Marines. Nevertheless the Japanese were winning the arms race. On the same day that Galer arrived on *Guadalcanal*, Rabaul received fifty-eight replacement aircraft. Furthermore the short range of his aircraft prevented Vandegrift from interdicting Japanese destroyers that were speeding down the 'Slot' each night at dusk and speeding back before dawn. The range handicap of Vandegrift's aircraft enabled Japanese destroyers to feed fresh troops onto *Guadalcanal* while giving Henderson Field a pounding for good measure.

On 31 August Rear-Admiral John 'Slew' McCain, a naval aviator appointed COMAIRSOPAC (Commander of Air South Pacific), made his first visit to *Guadalcanal*. Vandegrift opened his only bottle of bourbon in his honor. As they drank, Japanese

Mitsubishi 'Bettys' bombed the Marine positions and that night a cruiser pounded Henderson Field. More Japanese bombers arrived to greet the morning of 1 September. A shocked and bleary-eyed McCain exclaimed, "By God, Vandegrift, this is your war and you sure are welcome to it. But when I get back tomorrow I am going to try to get you what you need for your air force here."[1] McCain urgently requested an additional two squadrons of Lockheed P-38 Lightnings or Wildcats to be sent to Vandegrift. His request was accompanied by a warning, "If the reinforcement requested is not made available *Guadalcanal* cannot be supplied and hence cannot be held."[2] McCain's description of the plight of 1st Marine Division stirred Vice-Admiral Robert Ghormley into seeking more immediate help. He even dared to ask General MacArthur for the loan of some Lockheed P-38 Lightnings. MacArthur refused; they were needed for the defense of Australia. MacArthur mischievously asked Ghormley whether he could spare a couple of his carriers. Vandegrift's needs were clearly greater, but there was no one 'in-theater' to overrule MacArthur.

If new planes were not forthcoming, new supplies of liquor arrived with Brigadier-General Roy Geiger who flew up to *Guadalcanal* from the *New Hebrides* on 3 September to take command of the 'Cactus' Air Force. Geiger brought a case of 'scotch,' a gift from Nimitz. Geiger, like Vandegrift, a southern gentleman, realizing, "scotch' was not the drink for a southerner, offered to swap it for the case of bourbon residing in his quarters. When a monumentally angry Geiger discovered that an intrepid Marine had snaffled his prize liquor, Vandegrift decided that as he was 'not in Virginia' he could keep Nimitz's proffered gift of 'scotch.'

Geiger, a single-minded and aggressive commander with a ferocious temper, proved to be a superb commander who drove on his outnumbered fliers. In the battles raging above Henderson Field, the US pilots, armed with better equipment and tactics, were starting to get the better of their Japanese counterparts but new Japanese aircraft were arriving faster than they could shoot them down. By mid-September reinforcements at Rabaul and Buka gave the Japanese an advantage of 180 planes to the 'Cactus' Air Force's seventy. Moreover many of these American aircraft were by now clapped out. Some were kept simply for their spare parts. On 10 September Geiger had just ten serviceable Wildcats. While exhausted pilots stuck doggedly to their daily air skirmishes with the Japanese, it was the Seabees who kept the runways operational. At regular intervals alongside the runway, the Seabees would deposit and hide the materials (matting, earth and sand), transport and tools needed to repair a crater made by the standard 500 lb Japanese bomb. All hands, cooks included, raced to their stations to make repairs as soon as the bombers had departed. Somehow craters would be filled in time to land returning aircraft. However, the Marines were hard pressed, living on half-rotten Japanese rice. They would soon be on half rations.

On 1 September, the morning of McCain's departure from *Guadalcanal*, USS *Saratoga* (CV-3), just a week after the *Battle of the East Solomons*, was hit by a torpedo launched by *I-26*, captained by Commander Yokota Minoru. Admiral Fletcher was blown off his feet, one of twelve men injured by the blast. The carrier was towed back to *Tongabatu* where it was found that the damage was more serious than first thought and had to retire first to *Hawaii* for repairs. She would be out of action for three months. With the *Enterprise* also under repair America's carrier presence in the *Pacific* was down to just USS *Wasp* and USS *Hornet*. Vandegrift had lost his floating backup aircraft force. Three days later the plucky old four stack destroyers, USS *Little* and USS *Gregory*, which had been converted into APDs (fast transport destroyers) used to bring Vandegrift supplies and new troops were both sunk in a night action in the early hours of 5 September when a US Navy pilot mistakenly dropped flares above them. Three modern Japanese destroyers, *Yudachi, Hatsuyuki* and *Murakumo*, which had been bombarding Henderson Field turned their guns on the hapless US destroyers. The situation for the Marines appeared ever more desperate.

In the White House, Roosevelt's spin-merchants, preparing the ground for defeat on *Guadalcanal* started to deprecate the importance of the struggle. It was now a "local operation."[3] In his annual Labor Day speech, the President seemingly wanted to downplay the importance of the conflict in the south *Pacific*; "We must not overrate the importance of our successes in the *Solomons*."[4] Evidently Roosevelt was readying the American public for bad news.

Skirmishes and Reconnaissance: Air battles continued daily over Henderson Field. Japanese bombers aimed to put the airfield out of commission and it proved to be a daily race between their work and that of the Seabees who attempted to repair bomb damage in time to get the landing strip serviceable again. (The importance of the Seabees was recognized by their reinforcement with 392 further engineers who had been brought by convoy on 1 September.)

For the Japanese bombers it was an unnerving four-hour trip of 560 miles just to get to Henderson Field with the knowledge that there was very little hope of being rescued if they were shot down. By contrast most US aircrews were recovered. In the nine days to 5 September, the US lost 15 aircraft to 19 Japanese. The Marine aircraft wing benefitted from the information relayed from Australian coast watchers on the islands of *Bougainville* and *New Georgia* who warned of Japanese attacks.

On *Guadalcanal*, Vandegrift, realizing that the main prize for the Japanese attackers would be Henderson Field rather than *Tulagi*, had increased his defense resources by transferring Colonel Edson's 1st Raider Battalion and the 1st Parachute Battalion to *Guadalcanal*, thus adding 1,500 men to the 11,000 who started the *Guadalcanal* Campaign. The Japanese too were building up their forces. Between 29 August and 4 September some 5,000 troops under Major-General Kiyotake Kawaguchi, including the Seventeenth Army's 35th Infantry Regiment and 4th Regiment were brought down the 'Slot' by destroyer and deposited at Taivu Point to the east of Henderson Field. A further 1,000 troops under the command of Colonel Akinosuke Oka went by barge to the west of Lunga Point.

Meanwhile Admiral Yamamoto retired his fifty-vessel fleet from its station in the *North Solomons* to refuel at *Truk*. At a conference called aboard his flagship, the super-battleship *Yamato*, the head of the Japanese fleet gave two orders: "to keep the location and movements of Japanese carriers unknown to the enemy" and secondly "to make initial air assaults against the enemy as strong as possible."[5] He prepared his forces for the support of Kawaguchi's land assault on Henderson Field. Kawaguchi planned a three-pronged assault. Colonel Oka would come from the west, the Kuma brigade from the east and the main attack with 3,000 men would flank round to attack from the jungles in the south. Kawaguchi's troops deployed to prepare their assault on 7 September.

On 8 September Colonel Edson mounted a surprise seaborne raid on the village of Tasimboko near Taivu Point and after forcing its Japanese defenders back into the jungle, happened across Kawaguchi's main store of supplies that were promptly destroyed. They were surprised to discover, and indeed fortunate, that 4,000 Japanese troops had recently left the area. Kawaguchi had embarked on his flanking movement through the jungle toward Henderson Field's vulnerable southern perimeter: "tunnelling through the jungle"[6] as he described it. Yard by yard Kawaguchi's troops hacked their way toward their launch point with their troops stretched out in a two-mile long single file. The match up with Edson would have to wait.

Edson's Raiders withdrew with captured documents that indicated that an attack was imminent. One infuriated Japanese diarist noted, "It is maddening to be the recipients of these daring and insulting raids."[7] Perhaps he should have been more concerned with the loss of food and other supplies which now precluded any possibility of retreat to the east of Henderson Field. For Edson's Raiders it was an attack with benefits. They returned to base with tins of crab and beef as well as twenty-one cases of beer and gallons of *sake* (rice wine). More importantly they came back with the certain knowledge that Kawaguchi was on a jungle march on what was clearly a flanking operation.

After the American evacuation of the Taivu region, Mr. Ishimoto, the surly carpenter who had worked for Lever Brothers Plantation on *Tulagi*, took revenge for the attack on Tasimboko. Father Oude-Engberink was tied up, thrown into a hut and butchered; two young Sisters, Sylvia and Odilia, were raped and murdered.

The Battle of Edson's (Bloody) Ridge: **[Map: 17.1]** Edson and Vandegrift's operations officer correctly forecast that the main attack would come at a grassy coral ridge that ran parallel to the *Lunga River* just to the south of Henderson Field. The mile long ridge was interspersed by spurs that caused the Japanese to dub it, 'The centipede.'[8] 'Lunga Ridge,' later to be known as 'Edson's Ridge,' was reinforced with 840 men of Edson's battalion on 11 September. They furiously dug themselves into foxholes for the battle ahead and to survive the Japanese bombing raids that would kill those foolish enough to disdain their use. Warning wires were quickly strung out and artillery and machine gun pits dug to provide enfilades of fire. Piles of grenades and machine gun belts were placed to hand.

On the airstrip, David Galvin recalled that the Dauntless SDB dive-bombers were lined up wing to wing with their rear machine guns facing the jungle treeline: "so afraid we were that the Japanese would break through. They also had F4Fs with the tails jacked up so someone could fire the six 0.50 caliber machine guns."[9]

Back at *South Pacific* HQ, on 12 September both Ghormley and MacArthur were gloomily pessimistic about Vandegrift's chances of avoiding defeat—a likelihood they rated as close to nil. Ghormley, short of cruisers, carriers, attack transports and cargo vessels felt that he could no longer support the Marines on *Guadalcanal*. In spite of his pessimism, Ghormley sent all the planes he had to support the besieged troops. Wildcats came in from carriers *Hornet* and *Wasp*. The Japanese threw even more planes into the increasingly desperate showdown at Henderson Field. On 12 September, 140 aircraft of the 26th Flotilla were added to the bases at Rabaul and *Bougainville*. Final plans for a fly-down of senior officers from Rabaul were drawn up. However, even Vandegrift was drawing up plans to take the remnants of his force into the mountainous jungle to fight as guerrillas. He told Major-General Roy Geiger, "If the time comes when we no longer can hold the perimeter I expect you to fly out your planes."[10]

MacArthur with usual dramatic grand-eloquence expounded, "The Japanese were better fighting men than the Germans. He [Vandegrift] didn't have enough men to hold them . . . The Japanese could take New Guinea and the Fijis any time they pleased, after which they would control the Pacific for a hundred years."[11] It seems quite likely that the defeats he suffered at the hands of the Japanese in spite of outnumbering them, had severely shaken MacArthur's confidence. General 'Hap' Arnold noted that MacArthur was ". . . much more nervous than when I formerly knew him. Hands twitch and tremble—shell shock."[12] Perhaps Vandegrift's predicament reminded MacArthur of Bataan. However, this was *Guadalcanal*, not Bataan, and Vandegrift believed in his Marines; indeed he resolutely kept his HQ behind Lunga Ridge, at the expected point of the Japanese attack.

Undetected by aircraft from Henderson Field because the thick jungle cover obscured any sight of his column, Kawaguchi arrived unobserved at his assembly and 'take-off' point in the jungle south of the Henderson Field perimeter. However, Martin Clemens' scouts were coming in with reports that three thousand Japanese soldiers were assembling at positions to the east of the *Lunga River*. On 11 September, senior officers gave their final exhortations to their officers. *My Guadalcanal* [1992] based on a diary kept by Lieutenant Genirou Inui of the 8th Independent Anti-tank Gun Company (8-TAS) recorded the address given by Major-General Kawaguchi before the all-out attack:

> It's the time to offer your life for His Majesty the Emperor. The flower of Japanese infantrymen is in the bayonet-charge. This is what the enemy soldiers are most afraid of. The strong point of the enemy is superiority of firepower. But it will be able to do nothing in the night and in the jungle. When all-out-attack begins, break through the enemy's defenses without delay. Recapture our bitterest airfield. Rout, stab, kill, and exterminate the

enemy before daybreak. We are sure of ultimate victory of the Imperial Army![13]

At 9 p.m. a cruiser and three destroyers shelled the Marine positions on Lunga Ridge. In the early hours of 12 September Kawaguchi launched his first probing attacks between *Lunga River* and the ridge and pressed until daylight. "The sky and jungle were blazing with fireworks and a hellish bedlam of howls."[14] Fortunately for the Marines, it was a poorly coordinated attack, reflecting the difficulties of field 'command and control' and many Japanese units either became separated or lost altogether. Kawaguchi's troops suffered an estimated 500 casualties. In the morning, while sitting on a log eating cold meat and potatoes, Edson warned his officers, "They were just testing, just testing. They'll be back . . . Today we dig, wire up tight, get some sleep. We'll all need it."[15]

Edson pulled back his front to form a tighter line of defense between the *Lunga River* and the ridge, which it crossed just 150 yards in front of 'Hill-123,' Edson's HQ. Around this strongpoint Edson deployed five companies. New positions had to be quickly dug and prepared. Heavy Browning machine guns were placed to give as many converging fields of fire as possible. "The Nip will be back," warned 'Red Mike' Edson, "I want to surprise him."[16] Having fought all night the Marines were exhausted; Edson standing on a grenade box in the late afternoon addressed his men, "You men have done a great job, and I have just one more thing to ask of you. Hold out just one more night. I know we've been without sleep a long time. But we expect another attack from them tonight and they may come through here. I have every reason to believe that we will have reliefs here for all of us in the morning."[17]

Waiting out the day, Kawaguchi resumed the attack on the night of 13 September with his remaining 2,500 troops—a four to one advantage against the American defenders. Kawaguchi's 1st Battalion led by Major Yukichi Kokusho breached the first line between the *Lunga River* and the ridge forcing the Marines back toward 'Hill 123.' Kokusho's battalion forced their way through the swamps in the open land aside the *Lunga River* and toward the airfield. Coming across a store of Marine rations, the ravenous Japanese troops stopped to scoff what they found. However, at 3.00 a.m., Kokusho, moving eastwards toward the northern section of the ridge, engaged the Marines in a fierce firefight. Major Kokusho was killed and his remaining troops were wiped out as a fierce counter-attack by Captain Torgeson, promoted in the field to take charge of B-Company and C-company of the Parachutists, saved this last line of defense in front of Henderson Field.

In another attack the Marines were pushed back along the east side of the ridge by Lieutenant-Colonel Kusukichi Watanabe's battalion and began to fall back toward the airfield. For a short time 'Hill 123' was exposed and cut off. Fortunately Major Kenneth Bailey, one of Edson's staff officers, managed to rally the retreating Marines and bring them back to positions on 'Hill 123's' flank. Desperate frontal assaults now tried to dislodge the positions around 'Hill 123,' the key fulcrum of the battlefield. Machine gun barrels glowed red with heat. However, in some instances, it was with fierce hand-to-hand fighting that the attackers were eventually repulsed.

At night, when not attacking, the Japanese troops would chant in rhythmic unison, "US Marines be dead tomorrow. US Marines be dead tomorrow";[18] it was as Captain William J. McKennon recalled, like "a mad religious rite."[19] The *banzai* charges were suicidal in their intensity. McKennon noted, "When one wave was mowed down—and I mean mowed down—another followed it into death."[20] During the heavy fighting for 'Hill 123,' three companies managed to reach the edge of Henderson Field before being repulsed by a counter-attack by Seabee engineers. This was the last important action. As dawn broke pockets of Kawaguchi's troops littered the field only to be strafed by fighters from Henderson Field. The battle was over. Lieutenant-Colonel Griffith recalled the sight of the Japanese dead, "With heads lolling and mouths agape, the inscrutable dead stared with glazed and sightless eyes at the morning sun."[21]

The undoubted hero of the action was Edson himself who exposed himself to danger all night in exhorting his troops in their efforts. "I can say that if there is such a thing as one man holding a battalion together Edson did it" reported Captain 'Tex' Smith, "He just stood behind the front lines—stood, when most of us hugged the ground."[22] When Marines tried to fall back Edson simply screamed at them "Listen, the only thing those people have got that you haven't is guts!"[23] Edson not only lived up to his 'Red Mike' nickname but, having already been awarded his second Navy Cross for the taking of *Tulagi*, would now be awarded promotion to command of the 5th Marine Regiment and a Medal of Honor. Attacks on the western and eastern perimeter flanks by Oka and the Kuma battalions respectively were more easily beaten back.

Pilots and mechanics waited anxiously for the Japanese to break through. Rear gunner, David Galvin, recalled,

> That night was savagery on both sides. That night everything was firing; nothing was held back. Shells went flying over our head. We were very close to the battle and could hear the artillery, the gunfire, the screaming . . . The next morning everybody was worn out and exhausted but elated. Nobody was saying anything, nobody talking because it was so horrible . . . we were quiet, we had our private thoughts. Everybody had a cigarette. I didn't smoke, but even I had one to calm down.[24]

Kawaguchi had failed but it was not for lack of effort. He had correctly identified the Marines' weakest point; the plan of attack was well conceived though hampered by the inability of the main attack force to take artillery on their jungle trek to exit the jungle south of Henderson Field. Significantly Kawaguchi was left to rue the failure of one of his battalions to enter the battlefield at all; at the critical junction when victory or defeat balanced on a knife-edge, the addition of this single battalion could have turned the course of battle. "This powerful battalion, the one I had counted on most, was completely mismanaged. When I heard of this I could not help shedding tears of disappointment, anger, and regret."[25] However, having spent a week trekking through the jungle to reach the jump-off point south of Henderson Field, the launch of a night attack, with an exhausted and half-starved force, was never going to be an easy task.

The courage of Kawaguchi's troops was remarkable throughout. On the morning of 14 September survivors continued to make suicidal charges. Snipers and hidden Japanese soldiers fought on, causing Marine casualties including Edson's head of operations, Major Robert Brown. But already at 2.30 a.m. Edson had called headquarters to tell them, "we can hold."[26] For the loss of fifty-nine Marines killed and 204 wounded, Edson had won the day. Other units were similarly depleted. By comparison Kawaguchi had lost 708 soldiers killed and a further 505 were wounded. His second day of fighting had cost him half of his force.

Even General Vandegrift, standing in front of his command post reading a message, was surprised by a sword-wielding Japanese officer and two *banzai*-screaming soldiers. A Marine was run through with a single sword thrust but the attackers were shot down at Vandegrift's feet. Vandegrift may not have realized it at the time, but his Marines' victory against Kawaguchi's forces was probably the tipping point of the whole prolonged battle for *Guadalcanal*. Before his attack Kawaguchi admitted to Nishino, a Japanese reporter, "No matter what the War College says, it's extremely difficult to take an enemy position by night assault. There were a few cases in the Russo-Japanese War but they were only small-scale actions. If we succeed here on Guadalcanal, it will be a wonder in the military history of the world."[27] Kawaguchi had a point. The key issue however was that daylight attack was out of the question. As the Japanese Navy was finding to its cost, US control of Henderson Field gave them control of the skies in daylight hours. Henderson Field remained the key to the battle.

In the final analysis, Kawaguchi's forces were simply overwhelmed by superior US firepower. Lieutenant Genjirou Inoue noted in his diary on 14 September, ". . . firepower had overwhelmed us, and we had put too much confidence in our charging-power. Only after our superior firepower can compete with their superior firepower, will the charging-power of the Imperial Army win a victory. I wish to say 'Root out the old concept of the battle!' "[28] Given how little space could be given over on the transports to heavier guns and ammunition, it is easy to imagine how Lieutenant Inoue felt when Kawaguchi ordered all guns to be destroyed or buried before the retreat.

Kawaguchi fell back west to Matanikau Valley where he joined Oka's unit. Having lost their supply store to Edson's earlier attack, Kawaguchi's starving remnants lost more than half their remaining force from wounds and illness on their week-long retreat. In his diary entry of 16 September, Lieutenant Inoue recorded with a bitter humor, "For the first time since 13 [September] we got thin rice gruel. The greatest dinner in this war!"[29] Food was not their only concern. As Kawaguchi's troops escaped piecemeal through the jungle, Martin Clemens' scouts were picking off groups of stragglers. On 5 October Constable Saku, a talented scout, ambushed a group of ten Japanese soldiers scavenging for wild nuts; his native forces slaughtered them with spears and axes.

Japanese troops survived mainly on grass, moss and the luxury of an occasional foraged betel nut; Inoue's diary recorded how grenades thrown into a river brought an unexpected haul of fish—a luxury indeed. But on 25 September when the news of rice supply was dashed, "a soldier flung himself down on the sands in tears, crying 'Rice is coming! Rice is coming!' "[30] When a little rice was found and shared, soldiers relished the experience grain by grain. Kawaguchi and his ragged survivors emerged from the jungle at Point Cruz, some seven miles west of the airfield. They were suffering from chronic dysentery and dehydration. Japanese troops soon renamed *Guadalcanal*, 'Starvation Island.'

Interlude: The War of Supply and Logistics: **[Map: 17.2]** For a Japanese Army that was used to easy victories over western armies this was a defeat that stunned the Imperial High Command. One of Yamamoto's staff officers was a little ruder, "The army had been used to fighting Chinese."[31] It now dawned on them that what had seemed to be a minor military operation in the southern *Solomons*, was turning into a major engagement with significant strategic consequences. In Rabaul, Lieutenant-General Harukichi Hyakutake prepared to send more troops to *Guadalcanal*. In addition he planned to provide them with 100 mm artillery pieces and 150 mm howitzers.

In spite of the US victory and the positive propaganda being spun in Washington, Ghormley's pessimism began to leak to the press. On 19 September Hanson Baldwin, military correspondent for the *New York Times*, met Vandegrift and let it be known that senior officials in Washington, no doubt influenced by General MacArthur, were gloomy about the outcome. When Baldwin asked sceptically, "Are you going to hold the beachhead?" Vandegrift replied, "Hell yes, why not?"[32] He could afford to be expansive. For the first time in the *Second World War*, American soldiers had thwarted a Japanese offensive. As promised, Rear-Admiral Kelly Turner arrived on the USS *McCawley* leading a group of transports carrying supplies, and the 7th Marines and a battalion of the 11th Marine Regiment. Turner had braved the hostile seas and the opposition of Vice-Admiral Ghormley to bring 4,000 fresh soldiers. They included a charismatic commanding officer, Lieutenant-Colonel Herman Hanneken, a veteran of the Caribbean *Banana Wars* [1915–1919] during which he had been awarded the Medal of Honor for personally killing 'King' Charlemagne Péralte, the leader of the *Haitian* guerrillas known as the *Cacos*. Another of 7th Marine's *Banana War* veterans was the legendary Major 'Chesty' Puller. Thus reinforced, Vandegrift could consider going on the offensive.

For the time being fighting had given way to supply as key to the battle for *Guadalcanal*. As Richard Frank, the eminent historian of the *Battle of Guadalcanal* observed, it "had become a competition to see who could reinforce the fastest . . ."[33] In addition to troop reinforcements Turner's convoy also managed to land 147 vehicles, 1,000 tons of rations, tents and 400 drums of aviation fuel. Vandegrift now possessed 19,000 troops plus fifty planes of the 1st Marine Air Wing. Further units were also deployed from *Tulagi* to *Guadalcanal*. The US Navy was beginning to win the logistical battle. Resupplied with fresh troops, Vandegrift was presented with opportunities for a more expansive strategy and in his *Final Action Report* he concluded, "This accretion of force required us to re-examine and readjust our plans in accordance with improved circumstances and in the light of lessons learned from the bitter fighting of mid-September."[34]

In the lull in fighting, the Marines turned their hands to domesticity. In the "great *Guadalcanal* housing boom"[35] Marines scavenged for building materials such as old crates, packing materials, Japanese rice bags, palm fronds and tree trunks. They built personalized ramshackle bivouacs. Some Marines burrowed into rocky outcrops while the Seabees busied themselves with building deeper and sturdier dugouts. For many it was a relief to escape the glutinous mud on which they had made their beds for weeks. However, there was little that could be done to clean up tattered uniforms. As for socks and underwear, for many Marines, they were now a distant memory.

More importantly Vandegrift, armed with new supplies and fresh troops, set about building deadly defenses around Henderson Field. Barbed wire was now plentiful. Jungle and kunai grass were cleared to provide artillery and machine gun entrenchments with wide fields of fire. Booby traps were designed using grenades, trip wires and hidden cans of petrol. Fortunately for Vandegrift, General Harmon managed to thwart the plans of the interfering Rear-Admiral Turner who had decided that the occupation of *Ndeni* in the *Santa Cruz Islands* was more important than reinforcing and consolidating the position on *Guadalcanal*. Harman argued successfully with Vice-Admiral Ghormley, "It is my personal conviction that the Jap is capable of retaking *Guadalcanal*, and that he will do so in the near future unless it is materially strengthened."[36] From now on Vandegrift began to enjoy a concentration of focus by his fellow commanders on the logistics and supply of his Marines.

In the aftermath of the *Battle of Edson's Ridge*, Japanese attention also turned to regrouping and resupply. Too late to join Kawaguchi's assault, the 4th Aoba Infantry Regiment landed at *Kamimbo Bay* on the western tip of *Guadalcanal* on 11 September. This in itself was an indication of Japan's supply problems. By landing at *Guadalcanal*'s western tip, the supply trips down the 'Slot' were foreshortened but it created an extended supply line to the front and ultimate strategic objective, the re-capture of Henderson Field. 'Tokyo Express' runs down the 'Slot' on the 14, 20, 21 and 24 September brought desperately needed food supplies to the troops on *Guadalcanal*. By 13 September, the Imperial Japanese Army had already started the transfer of troops from the 2nd and 38th Infantry Divisions to Rabaul. The plan was to land a new force of 17,500 troops on *Guadalcanal* for another major offensive planned for 20 October.

Finally Japanese high command had been woken from their slumber. Influential men were returning from *Guadalcanal* with alarming stories. Gen Nishino, a journalist who had been with Major-General Kawaguchi on *Guadalcanal* and fully witnessed the horrors of the campaign, returned to Rabaul where he encountered an old friend, Major-General Yumio Nasu, commander of the Infantry Group of the 2nd Division. In a revealing exchange, Nishino advised Nasu, "I would say that if we keep sending in forces piecemeal, they will be swallowed up one by one. It's the worst thing to do, don't you agree, sir? If I talked like this to anyone else, I'd probably be sent off to jail." Nasu replied, "I agree. It's a great pity we don't have enough planes and ships to do what you want."[37]

Others in Rabaul were less inclined to accept these tales from the battlefront. Taken to see Lieutenant-Colonel Fukunaga at Seventeenth Army HQ, a man that Nishino described as greasy and well fed, Nishino was told in no uncertain terms that he was defeatist and lacking in *seishin* (purity of heart), "Just remember we'll never let you return to Japan. It would be like sending a spy back home."[38] However, opinion at the higher level of army command in Rabaul was far from unanimous. Lieutenant-General Hyakutake's Chief of Staff, Major-General Futami Akisaburo was adamant that *Guadalcanal* was lost and would repeatedly make known his views. "We must not try to retake Guadalcanal" he declared, "we have no chance of winning there."[39] Lieutenant-Commander Fumio Iwatani must have expressed the fears of many officers when he expressed the opinion that it

> was impossible for us to continue this affluent operation as long as our logistical strength was weak ... It was taught to us that even when we were gasping under heavy damage, the enemy was also suffering. Therefore, we should press the enemy even harder, with all our might and grab the victory. However, facing an enemy seemingly immortal to damage, we felt utterly incapable of keeping up. In the face of this war of attrition, our replacement troops, which were sent to us several times, disappeared like bubbles. The food and arms supply for [soldiers on] Guadalcanal became increasingly difficult to provide, despite our best effort. . .[40]

The ubiquitous Army tactician and fanatic, Colonel Masanobu Tsuji, who had come to prominence in Manchuria, found his way to *Guadalcanal*. He returned to Rabaul and castigated the Navy for their failure to supply their beleaguered troops. At an Army-Navy meeting, Tsuji offered to fly to *Truk* to confront Yamamoto himself: "Our supply has been cut off for more than a month. Officers and men have to dig up grass roots, scrape moss and pick bugs from trees and drink sea water to survive."[41] Tsuji even reported that Kawaguchi, not his favorite officer, was "thinner than Gandhi." Hyakutake threatened, "If the Navy lacks the strength to escort the Second Division properly to *Guadalcanal*, we will go in transports without any escort. And 17th Army HQ will lead the way."[42] However, for once the shock of defeat temporarily buried inter-force rivalry as Yamamoto became convinced of the need to support to the hilt the Army's efforts to retake *Guadalcanal*.

Immediately after the *Battle of Edson's Ridge*, Vandegrift, aware that Kawaguchi's forces had been able to arrive at his southern flank undetected increased patrol activity around the Lunga Perimeter. Also, after taking ten days to rest his troops, Vandegrift, after rotating his commanders and taking stock of his new resources, began to organize raids on the Japanese forces billeted around the *Matanikau River*. However, an assault on Japanese forces west of the *Matanikau River* between 23 and 27 September showed that even a poorly fed Japanese force could remain full of fight.

After being surrounded near Point Cruz, the Marines took heavy losses and had to be rescued by the destroyer USS *Monssen*, which shipped them back to safety. In what was the worst military setback suffered by the US Marines in the *Guadalcanal* Campaign, Colonel Samuel B. Griffiths later explained the key problem thus,

> It can be said that we had most faulty intelligence of
> Japanese strength and dispositions. No orders would ever
> have been given for a battalion to go up to Kokumbona
> and patrol from there had there been any realization that
> there were several thousand Japanese between the
> Matanikau and Kokumbona. Faulty intelligence was the
> cause of the whole breakdown at that time.[43]

Apart from this unhappy excursion the main activity of the troops was perimeter patrols. In the early morning and evening, the US artillery would cease it interdictory artillery fire and reconnaissance patrols would be sent out. Frequently nothing was reported other than signs of Japanese presence. Because of the dense jungle or swamp terrain, patrols would usually advance in single file, occasionally in double file though it was sometimes difficult to stay in touch. Scouts at the front were the most vulnerable as they would come upon Japanese troops at very short notice and often lacked the possibility of quick support.

The odd patrol would end up with a brief firefight with a group of Japanese troops, who were probably also on patrol. These brief fights usually ended with one or both groups making a hasty withdrawal. Marine Clifford Fox, a frequent patroller, noted, "Sometimes you'd exchange fire with Japanese along a ridgeline. That might be a little way off. But in the jungle, it was always close, very close. It was face to face sometimes. Lord, sometimes men fought with bayonets."[44] On *Guadalcanal*, casualties from battle action and from malaria and other tropical illness usually meant that units had to fill their patrols with cooks, mechanics or bandsmen. Everyone became a rifleman. Between the well-known hard fought named engagements, it was a pattern of warfare in the *Solomons* and New Guinea that would become the standard daily fare of Marines and GIs over the next eighteen months.

The Sinking of USS Wasp: On 15 September, the loss of the fleet carrier USS *Wasp* (CV-7) had piled yet more suffering on the embattled Vice-Admiral Ghormley. Sitting southeast of *San Cristobal*, the southernmost major island of the *Solomons*, USS *Wasp* was providing air cover for Rear-Admiral Turner's landing of troops and supplies, when it was spotted by Commander Takaichi Kinashi, skipper of the submarine *I-19*. Unobserved by *Wasp*'s six escort destroyers, Kinashi fired off a spread of six Type 95 torpedoes. Hit by three torpedoes, the *Wasp* was lifted out of the water hurling men and planes in the air. All the carrier's forward water mains were broken. Fire fighting became impossible.

The carrier immediately burst into flames, listed and took on water. Although Sherman turned the ship to make the smoke and flames blow out to sea and managed to right his ship by rebalancing the fuel ballast, there was no way to put out the fires. USS *Wasp* became little more than an out of control fireball, and Captain Sherman ordered his crew to abandon ship. Already men at the bow of the ship were being forced to jump into a sea lit up by fiery oil and gasoline. 193 men of the ship's 2,247 complement were killed; a further 366 were wounded. Rear-Admiral Scott aboard the cruiser *San Francisco* ordered USS *Lansdowne* to fire torpedoes and scuttle the *Wasp*. That evening Radio Berlin proudly announced, "Enemy 22,000 ton carrier has been sunk."[45]

Another of *I-19*'s torpedo spread ploughed on straight under the USS *Mustin* and went on to hit USS *North Carolina*. Ordered in 1937, the North Carolina Class was launched with this ship in April 1941 and was considered the most modern Allied battleship of its time. In spite of an explosion that killed five men and put a 32-foot hole in its side, the *North Carolina* managed to counter-flood a compartment to right the list and continued to steam on at twenty-five knots. Yet another of *I-19*'s torpedoes holed the destroyer USS *O'Brien*, which would eventually sink under-tow as it returned to the west coast of America. Five of *I-19*'s six shot spread hit US warships, sinking two ships and badly damaging a third: it was the most productive torpedo shot in history.

Hornet was more fortunate. Warned by the destroyer USS *Mustin*, the *Hornet* managed to avoid the torpedoes aimed in its direction by *I-15*, another *B-1* type submarine (one of twenty built, it was perhaps the archetypal Japanese submarine capable of carrying a seaplane as well as carrying seventeen Long Lance torpedoes that could be fired from its six forward mounted torpedo tubes). They all missed the *Hornet*.

The loss of the *Wasp* was a heavy blow but without the 4,000 men of the 7th Marines put ashore by 18 September, the US would probably have lost *Guadalcanal*; to that end the sacrifice of a carrier was worthwhile. Nevertheless the *Wasp*'s demise had the effect of firing up Admiral King in Washington. His *Pacific* Navy had lost one carrier and had had two (*Enterprise* and *Saratoga*) severely damaged within the space of a month. He now realized that there was a need for more aircraft to be based on *Guadalcanal* itself rather than relying on aircraft carriers to provide air cover. Fewer than half the Wildcats delivered to *Guadalcanal* since August, were still operational. The Navy did not have the resources to man its aircraft carriers as well as supply land-based planes. The Army would have to make up the difference. In a stormy meeting on 16 September, General Arnold refused. The following day Admiral King, Chief of Naval Operations in Washington, wrote to General Marshall arguing that it was "imperative that the future continuous flow of Army fighters be planned, starting at once, irrespective of, and in higher priority than, the commitments to any other theater."[46] King's campaign was only partially won.

However, Vandegrift's raid on 6 October was more successful. Marines led by promoted Lieutenant-Colonel 'Chesty' Puller crossed the *Matanikau River* and launched an assault on the 4th Infantry Regiment of the 2nd Infantry Division that had recently arrived on *Guadalcanal*. Trapped in a ravine, the Japanese troops were bombarded by artillery and mown down by machine guns as they attempted to clamber the ridges guarding the ravine. Several hundred of Lieutenant-General Masao Maruyama's fresh troops were slaughtered. It was a sharp lesson for the Japanese regarding the huge improvements in US jungle fighting performance.

Renewed Bombing of Rabaul: **[Map: 17.3]** By now there was a new overall commander for the *South Pacific*. Nimitz, who had visited *Guadalcanal* on 29 September, shared the same humidity, mosquitoes and gruesome rations as the Marine defenders and, immediately alerted to their plight, determined on a plan of reinforcement of men and supply. Nimitz, having decorated Marines on *Guadalcanal* until he ran out of medals, flew back to *Noumea*, to confront Vice-Admiral Ghormley at his HQ aboard USS *Argonne*. Ghormley, in tremendous pain from an abscessed tooth, made a poor impression on Nimitz, seemingly depressed, pessimistic and overly anxious.

Nevertheless they attended a joint Allied commanders meeting to discuss the increasingly desperate situation of *Guadalcanal*. The gathering of a dozen generals included General 'Hap' Arnold, head of the Army Air Force, who was on a tour of inspection in Asia. As usual MacArthur refused to attend and instead grandly sent his deputy Major-General Dick Sutherland as well as Lieutenant-General George Kenney. The latter was again pressed to provide more help in bombing Rabaul in spite of the active engagement of all his forces against Japanese convoys reinforcing Buna as the Australian and American troops started the arduous task of retaking ground along the Kokoda Trail. Kenney agreed to "try to burn the place down."[47] Bombing missions were duly dispatched on 2 October and again on 5 October; the first was a token mission with just 6 B-17 Flying Fortress but the second comprised 14 B-17s, 6 from 30th Bomb Squadron and 8 from the 28th Squadron. 30th Bomb Squadron planes took a severe beating with the loss of Lieutenant Earl Hagman's plane after the loss of its right inboard motor soon followed by the left inboard. The last that was seen or heard of his flight was his heading into cloud with eleven Zeros in pursuit. On board another plane, Royal Australian Air Force (RAAF) navigator Pilot Officer Allen Davenport had his leg shot off by a 20 mm shell; he died of trauma soon after getting back to Port Moresby.

On 6 October MacArthur pushed for further action against Rabaul. Reconnaissance appeared to show the unloading of large amounts of supply indicating a renewed Japanese push in Buna and *Guadalcanal*. In response Kenney planned a larger thirty-six-plane mission from Port Moresby to Rabaul on 8 October. Six of the Flying Fortresses had to drop out because of technical problems but the remaining aircraft made their way to Rabaul. Four Catalina flying boats preceded them and firebombed the residential areas north of Simpson Harbor.

The now 'illuminated' Rabaul presented an easier target for the Flying Fortresses. Bombs damaged the coaling jetty as well as exploding a munitions and fuel dump in the Bayloo district. Parts of China Town were destroyed while, according to Radio Tokyo, a bomb landing on a hotel in the city killed fifty *geisha*; it seems that the Japanese had shipped out some 3,000 'comfort women,' mainly Koreans and Taiwanese, to Rabaul in early 1942. Unbeknownst to the pilots their 8 October raid saved the life of Father George Lepping. The day before, Captain Mitzusaki, commander of the 81st Naval Garrison, who had just murdered Harl Pease and seven other prisoner, pointed at Father Lepping and told him, "You go tomorrow."[48] Fortunately Mitzusaki was wounded by shrapnel in the raid and was replaced. The plan to murder Father Lepping was forgotten.

While a follow-up photo reconnaissance mission showed the extent of the damage on Rabaul, it also revealed that the important targets had been missed. The harbor was full: 26 transport ships, 2 submarines, 1 cruiser, 4 destroyers and 2 minelayers. Furthermore Lakunai Airfield was crammed with 72 fighters as well as other aircraft. In all, the photographs on 9 October revealed over 80 Zeros, 50 medium bombers, 28 dive-bombers and 8 flying boats. Some of the Zeros had not been transported by ship but had flown the 3,000 miles from Tokyo taking stops at *Iwo Jima, Saipan* and *Truk*; an extraordinary feat.

The increasing importance of the actions in New Guinea and *Guadalcanal* had already been revealed in Vice-Admiral Tsukahara's moving of the 11th Air Fleet HQ to Rabaul in August. In addition the Fifth and Sixth Attack Air Forces were established at Rabaul, while the First Attack Air Force was headquartered at Kavieng. Two further raids were made in October and Kenney complained that he wore out the skin of his finger and thumbs pinning 250 decorations to the chests of his men.

Recognizing the threat revealed by the new troop and equipment build-up at Rabaul, Kenney launched another attack on 10 October with seven Catalinas and twenty-one B-17s. Three American bombers hit Lakunai Airfield with newly modified 300lb bombs; wrapped with wire, on detonation they broke into 6–12 inch pieces making a noise that Kenney described as "like a whole tribe of disconsolate *banshees* [mythological Irish spirits]."[50] More importantly the wire pieces could cut through two-inch limbs of trees up to 200 yards from impact. Air force troops caught in the open on the airfield were torn to shreds. Admiral Ugaki aboard battleship *Yamato* in *Truk Lagoon* noted in his diary that the raid caused 110 dead and wounded.

Kenney's efforts nevertheless failed to stem the flow of new supplies to Rabaul. Photographs taken on 20 and 22 October showed that there were now over seventy ships at anchor. Four Flying Fortresses attacked the harbor on 23 October. It was claimed that four ships sustained direct hits while a near miss sank a cruiser. In fact post-war analysis showed that the raid only sank two small 150-foot submarine chasers. In spite of Kenney's efforts to degrade Rabaul the autumn attacks on Henderson Field showed little sign of let-up. Tony Betchik, a crew chief working on Marine Wildcats noted, "October was especially bad because we often had few planes in the air. I tried to keep a record of all the strafing, bombing, and shelling and counted close to 200."[49]

New Japanese Commanders: Lieutenant-General Hyakutake and Vice-Admiral Kusaka: Newly arrived Lieutenant-General Masao Maruyama and Major-General Yumio Nasu were forced to withdraw their forces from the eastern side of the *Matanikau River*. Further smaller raids by the 1st Battalion of the 2nd Marines followed on 9 and 11 October against Japanese outposts at *Aola Bay*, some thirty miles east of Lunga Point. For the first time in its history the recently arrived Sendai Division had been forced to retreat. It was an ominous start to Lieutenant-General Hyakutake's arrival on *Guadalcanal* as he took charge of the operation to recapture the island.

Japanese air leadership had already changed. At the end of September 1942 Vice-Admiral Tsukahara, Commander of 11th Air Fleet, overstressed after two months in which his aircraft had taken unprecedented losses, was suffering dengue fever, malaria and stomach complaints. He was sent home and replaced by Vice-Admiral Jinichi Kusaka, cousin of Admiral Ryunosuke Kusaka, who became Chief of Staff of the Combined Fleet in 1944. Kusaka, born in Ishikawa Prefecture, graduated twenty-first out of 179 cadets from the Imperial Naval Academy in 1917. In *World War I*, he served on a cruiser and battleship but did not see action. In 1921 Kusaka was promoted to Lieutenant-Commander and became a gunnery expert after graduating from the Naval College in that year. In 1930 he was sent to the United States and Europe for a year. At the end of 1936 he was appointed commandant of the Naval Gunnery School before promotion to head of the Imperial Japanese Naval College in 1940. Kusaka was a refined *bon viveur* who made full use of the 4,500 horses sent to *New Britain* with the invasion fleet at the beginning of 1942.

He rode every morning and took a siesta every afternoon. His arrival coincided with the massive build-up of Japanese forces in the *Solomons*. Coconut plantations were cleared and a new airfield was built near Rabaul, a slow process given that the Japanese engineers and their construction crews were not provided with bulldozers. Kavieng Airfield on *New Ireland* was similarly expanded though at 780 miles from *Guadalcanal* it was too far for operations in that theater. Development of the existing airstrip at *Buka Island*, north of *Bougainville* in the northern *Solomons* was more important. Another airfield was constructed near the village of Buin on the southern tip of *Bougainville*. American bomber attacks meant slow progress in development of an airfield that was plagued with operational and logistical problems. A poor workforce and lack of equipment delayed the project and the final airfield was barely usable. On 25 October, Rear-Admiral Ugaki noted in his diary, "every time it rained heavily, about ten planes were damaged due to skidding."[51] An even more advanced southerly airfield was planned for Munda Point on *New Georgia Island*. A single 350-yard landing strip suitable for fighters was put into service on 17 December 1942.

Nimitz Replaces Vice-Admiral Ghormley with Vice-Admiral Halsey: Hyakutake and Kusaka were not the only new commanders settling into new roles. Back on *Noumea*, Nimitz and Ghormley discussed relieving the exhausted 1st Marine Division and proper employment of carriers but Nimitz quickly came to the conclusion that first it was his regional commander who was in urgent need of relief. Rumors of problems had already filtered back to *Hawaii*. Hanson Baldwin of the *New York Times* had told Nimitz that Ghormley "was really completely defeatist. He was almost despairing."[52] 'Hap' Arnold during his September visit noted, "My estimate, upon leaving Admiral Ghormley's headquarters was this: so far, the Navy had taken one hell of a beating and at the same time was hanging on by a shoestring. They did not have a logistic set up efficient enough to guarantee success."[53] Commander in Chief, Pacific Area Command's (CINCPAC) Grey Book recorded on 15 October, "The situation is not hopeless but it is certainly critical."[54] 'Hap' Arnold opined, "the best shot is getting new leaders who know and understand modern warfare; men who are aggressive and not afraid to fight their ships. So far, I'm afraid it's been the other way around."[55]

For Nimitz the sacking of Ghormley, an old navel academy chum and football teammate, was a difficult decision. However, the gloom and negativity surrounding the *South Pacific* Command had to be lifted; Nimitz needed an Admiral who would "sail into hell itself if need be."[56] 'The Bull' as MacArthur called Admiral Halsey, was the obvious choice. Halsey, recovered from the chronic dermatitis and exhaustion that had prevented him from taking command at the *Battle of Midway*, told a captive audience of midshipmen at the Naval Academy on 31 August that "I am going back to the *Pacific* where I intend personally to have a crack at those yellow-bellied sons of bitches and their carriers."[57] Halsey, furious at missing *Midway* was desperate to get back into action.

On 18 October, Admiral 'Bull' Halsey was informed that he would take over from Ghormley, who was sent back to Washington to recuperate. In typical 'Bull' fashion, Halsey exclaimed, "Jesus Christ and General Jackson! This is the hottest potato they ever handed me."[58] Halsey immediately put his renowned energy and optimism into the task. Halsey's leadership qualities were needed. By October 1942, Vandegrift could see that his men were teetering on the edge, "They were a salty lot, bronzed and lean, their dungarees practically in shreds. They held the enemy in terrible contempt. They joked about nearly everything but their humour didn't fool me. They were tired men. I wanted desperately to get them off the island."[59] Even the news of Halsey's promotion had an immediate impact. An air combat intelligence officer on *Guadalcanal* recalled, "I'll never forget it. One minute we were too limp with malaria to crawl out of our foxholes; the next we were running around whooping like kids."[60] The qualities of bullying and cajoling, which he possessed in abundance, were immediately applied to those logistics officers who controlled the supply of war material. "Europe was Washington's darling, the *South Pacific* was only a stepchild,"[61] Halsey could not understand ". . . why we should not have some of the gravy that is being shipped in great quantities to Europe."[62]

He would bring a badly needed new focus and exuberance to the conduct of the *Guadalcanal* Campaign. With personal charisma and a snappy sound bite, Halsey quickly became an even greater favorite of the rapidly expanding ranks of the American press crowd in the *South Pacific*. The *New York Times* was infected with a revived spirit of optimism: "Shift to Offensive is Seen in Washington Selection of 'Fighting' Admiral Halsey as Commander in the Pacific."[63]

It was a view that was beginning to gain traction in Washington. War Plan RAINBOW-5 may have given priority to Europe in terms of supply but American troops based in Great Britain were making their long drawn out preparations for an invasion of France, while on *Guadalcanal* Marines were fighting. The eyes of the American public and the US President were on the *South Pacific*. Roosevelt asserted, "My anxiety about the Southwest Pacific is to make sure that every possible weapon gets into that area to hold Guadalcanal."[64]

Halsey dispensed paper work and authority to his staff. That was delegation that he was always happy to do. Unlike Ghormley he focused solely on the key issues. As for staff morale, he was a natural inspiration to men around him. He was quick to conduct rousing award ceremonies and, again unlike Ghormley, made it a priority to visit hospitals to personally thank the wounded for their service. His first decision was to cancel Turner's plan for an airfield to be constructed in the *Santa Cruz Islands* and instead diverted the fresh troops to Vandegrift. He also transferred 8th Marines from *Samoa* and brought in a specialist Marine Battalion, Carlson's Raiders. More artillery was found and sent in to *Guadalcanal* with a Seabee construction unit. Halsey wanted his ships at sea and fighting. At *Noumea* he exhorted maximum effort to get ships repaired and operational and back in the fight. On 16 November, Halsey put the entire logistic operation in the hands of Army Brigadier-General Raymond Williamson; logistical bottlenecks were relieved within a month and the flow of *matériel* to *Guadalcanal* increased by 40 percent.

Halsey's eminently quotable and usually racist lines delighted American war reporters. "Kill japs, kill japs and keep on killing japs,"[65] Halsey told a reporter who asked him what his objectives were. He was more than confident that his troops would beat the enemy. "When we started out, I held that one of our men was the equal of three Japs. I have since increased that to twenty. They are just monkeys, and I say 'Monkeys' because I cannot say what I should like to call them. Japan's next move will be to retreat; and they will keep on retreating."[66] Occasionally Halsey went too far, even for the 'Jap-hating' American media and its audiences.

> These yellow bastards are beasts alright and it's not me, but the greatest fighting men this country ever produced that are teaching them their manners . . . We are trying to keep our swords sharp on these yellow bellied sons of bitches and will continue to give them hell every time they want. The day is not in the too distant future when we will be able to go after them and kick them off the face of the earth. In order to save the world, I am going to advocate at the peace table for the few yellow bellies that are left—emasculation for the males and spaying for the females.[67]

Regarding losses he told reporters, "You can't make an omelet without breaking eggs. You can't fight a war safely without losing ships."[68] In spite of Halsey's racist bigotry, his qualities of leadership could not be gainsaid. He was undoubtedly the best leader of men in the *Pacific War*. Positive decisions and actions quickly defused negativity. Urgency always drove him. When the commanding officer of a division told Halsey, "Give me three weeks to . . . combat load my transports and then I'll be ready to go anywhere," Halsey laughed and told him that his division was "leaving for *Guadalcanal* tomorrow."[69] It was quickly noted that Halsey had transformed the atmosphere of command. Vandegrift noted on 8 November, "Admiral Halsey flew in like a wonderful breath of fresh air."[70] It was a much needed change. In spite of the *Battles of Tenaru, Savo Island* and *Edson's Ridge*, the hardest yards of the *Guadalcanal* Campaign lay in the future.

18 Guadalcanal III: Battles of Henderson Field and the Santa Cruz Islands

[September 1942–January 1943]

[Maps: 18.1, 18.2, 18.3, 18.4, 18.5]

The Battle of Cape Esperance: [**Map: 18.1**] With the failure of Captain Tanaka's convoy mission on 25 August at the *Battle of the Eastern Solomons* the Japanese had been forced to rely on the nightly runs by destroyer to supply them with food, munitions and reinforcements. Destroyers, submarines, or PT boats would aim to speed down the 'Slot' at more than thirty knots in the early evening and then return again by daybreak to avoid air attacks from the bombers at Henderson Field. Albeit costly in terms of resources, the 'Tokyo Express' as it became known by the Americans (or *Nezumi Yuso,* 'Rat Transportation,' by the Japanese forces) kept Japanese hopes alive that Henderson Field could be retaken.

In an order direct from the Emperor's chief of staff that stemmed from the Army and Navy agreements reached in mid-September, operations in New Guinea were downgraded in favor of a major push to recapture *Guadalcanal.* Horii's advance on Port Moresby was brought to a halt. [**See Chapter 15: Battle of the Kokoda Trail: Aussies Triumphant**] The opening lines of the new orders read, "After reinforcement of Army forces has been completed, Army and Navy forces will combine and in one action attack and retake Guadalcanal Island airfield. During this operation the Navy will take all necessary action to halt the efforts of the enemy to augment his forces in the Solomons area."[1]

For three weeks from mid-September nightly runs down the 250-mile long 'Slot' kept their forces supplied. In addition there was a gradual 'feed in' of 17,500 troops of the 2nd and 38th Infantry Division. However, Japanese troops were quickly degraded by the lack of food, malaria and the miserable conditions. Indeed when Lieutenant-General Masao Maruyama, commander of the 2nd Infantry Division, arrived on *Guadalcanal* on 3 October, it was soon revealed that of the original 9,000 Japanese soldiers that had come to the island, 2,000 were dead, and 5,000 were too crippled by illness, disease and exhaustion to be considered for offensive action. It was therefore realized that to sustain a bigger Japanese force on *Guadalcanal* a larger logistics effort would be required.

Reinforcements would include Emperor Hirohito's crack Sendai Division. Founded in 1870, the Sendai Division had distinguished itself in the *Sino-Japanese War* and the *Russo-Japanese War* of 1904–1905 by the capture of Crescent Hill at the *Siege of Port Arthur.* Somewhat less honorably, the Sendai Division had been partly responsible for the Rape of Nanking. Hirohito's devoted troops had taken a couplet from the Emperor Meiji's rescript to his armed forces as their motto;

Remember that death is lighter than a feather,
But that Duty is heavier than a mountain.[2]

However, in spite of being provided with crack troops, it was a far from rosy situation that Lieutenant-General Harukichi Hyakutake had found on arriving in *Guadalcanal* after his appointment as commander of all the island's forces. Hyakutake was genuinely shocked by the skeletal condition of the remnants of previous actions. Colonel Tsuji reported that Major-General Kiyotake Kawaguchi was "thinner than Ghandi." He radioed Rabaul to tell them that the situation was much worse than he had thought possible. Supplies unloaded on 9 October had been promptly stolen. Hyakutake didn't blame them; on being informed of the theft, he merely said, "it is my fault for having brought such loyal soldiers to such a miserable lot. May they fill their stomachs with our food and be remade into good soldiers."[3]

As for Major-General Kiyotake Kawaguchi, in spite of the now well-understood failure in supply, he was not just relieved of command but was sent home in disgrace. He was a compassionate man, who was firmly opposed to the fanatical brutality of men such as Colonel Tsuji with whom he had crossed swords first in the Philippines over Tsuji's butchering of the local population. Kawaguchi had argued with him, "shooting defeated opponents in cold blood was a violation of the true *Bushido* [The Way of the Warrior]."[4] Kawaguchi was retired to the reserve list in 1943. Later he was put in charge of the defenses of the island of *Tsushima*, located between Japan and Korea. Ironically, given his fight to treat conquered civilians with decency, Kawaguchi was arrested by General MacArthur in his role as SCAP (Supreme Commander for the Allied Powers) after the war and tried and imprisoned as a war criminal. In stark contrast his nemesis, Colonel Tsuji, a major war criminal, was never arrested.

Reflecting Hyakutake's concern for the condition of his troops and in preparation for the attempt to take Henderson Field in a major engagement in October, Vice-Admiral Mikawa at Rabaul again decided to risk sending a much-needed larger supply convoy. The 'reinforcement group,' as it was called by the Japanese under Rear-Admiral Takatsugu Jojima, left their *Shortland Islands* anchorage on 11 October 1942 with the cruiser seaplane tenders *Nisshin* and *Chitose* accompanied by six destroyers; his convoy would carry 728 soldiers, four 15 cm howitzers, two field guns and munitions. The importance placed on the convoy was indicated by the quantity of air coverage planned from airbases at Rabaul, Kavieng and Buin. Henderson Field was bombed with a force of forty-five 'Betty' bombers and thirty Zeros. Seven bombers and four Zeros were shot down and relatively little damage was done apart from the loss of two Wildcats and one of their pilots. Nevertheless the distraction of the attack did allow Rear-Admiral Aritomo Goto to lead, unobserved, a force of three cruisers, *Aoba, Kinugasa* and *Furutaka* and two destroyers, *Fubuki* and *Hatsuyuki* down the 'Slot.' The objective of Goto's mission was to stand off Henderson Field and bombard it. To prevent Henderson Field scouts from finding the convoy, six Zeros were ordered to remain over Henderson Field until darkness and then to ditch their aircraft and wait to be picked up—in effect a suicide mission. Only one pilot survived.

As Admiral Jojima's convoy was heading south, scout planes spotted Jojima's supply convoy some 200 miles from *Guadalcanal* in the early afternoon of 11 October and Rear-Admiral Norman Scott, who had been practicing night maneuvers with his force of two heavy cruisers USS *San Francisco* and USS *Salt Lake City*, two light cruisers USS *Boise* and USS *Helena* and five destroyers, moved to intercept at night. It was the first occasion that the US Navy had sought to challenge Japan's nighttime control of the 'Slot.' It was a typically aggressive move by Vice-Admiral Halsey, which reflected the analysis of failings in the August engagements at the *Battle of Savo Island* and the *Battle of the East Solomons*. An evaluation from Admiral King's staff in Washington suggested that "Surface ships should be employed as striking forces . . . we must use our ships more boldly as opportunity warrants."[5]

Although USS *San Francisco*'s aircraft spotted Jojima's force off *Guadalcanal* and reported it to Scott at 11 p.m., some forty-five minutes later the enemy ships picked up by the new SG radar systems of USS *Boise* and the destroyer USS *Duncan*, were those of Goto's surface force rather than Jojima's convoy. The enemy ships closed to a few thousand yards, enabling Rear-Admiral Scott to cross the 'T' as they did so. Scott's line could fire a complete broadside while Goto's ships could only use their forward guns— and even that was restricted because of the possibility of the advancing column hitting its own ships. At such a short range, effectively point blank range, the tension was immense; USS *Helena*'s radar operator asked, "What are we going to do, board them?"[6]

In a confused action, US shelling started at 11.36 p.m. when Scott had not even given his permission to 'open fire.' Although Scott was concerned his ships were firing at 'friendly' targets, his cruisers inflicted severe damage on Admiral Goto's flagship *Aoba*. Struck by forty shells, which knocked out two of its main guns, the bombardment mortally wounded Admiral Goto. Fortunately Scott's commanders had chosen to ignore their Admiral's order to cease fire. Scott was not the only confused admiral. Goto was still unaware that he had stumbled into the path of American ships and thought that he had been done for by friendly fire; lying on the remains of his bridge, the dying Admiral repeatedly said, "*Bakayaro! Bakayaro!* [Stupid Bastard! Stupid Bastard!]"[7]

Furutaka took a torpedo hit on her engine rooms and later sank. Meanwhile the destroyer *Fubuki* was pounded and started to sink. The entire action lasted barely thirty minutes before Goto's forces turned tail. Scott's attempted pursuit proved fruitless and he soon broke off the attack. For the loss of the destroyer USS *Duncan* in addition to heavy damage to the *Boise*, for which she returned to Philadelphia for repair, Scott's force had sunk a cruiser, *Furutaka*, and had badly damaged another, *Aoba*. As well as sinking a Japanese destroyer *Fubuki*, in the early morning two destroyers sent by Admiral Jojima to pick up survivors were sunk by Dauntless dive-bombers from *Henderson Field*. One hundred Japanese survivors, who spent twenty-four hours refusing to be picked up by the US Navy, were eventually rescued and taken as prisoners.

Four hundred Japanese sailors were killed in the action. Although it was a clear victory, a nighttime first for the US Navy, it was of little strategic consequence given the unopposed and unseen landing of the 4,600 strong 'Reinforcement Group' on the north coast of *Guadalcanal*. The retirement of Scott's forces also allowed the Japanese Navy to continue their nighttime control of the 'Slot.'

The *Battle of Cape Esperance* was thus a US tactical naval victory but a strategic failure, in that Rear-Admiral Tanaka's troop convoy reinforced Japan's beleaguered troops on *Guadalcanal*. On the morning of 12 October, Vice-Admiral Mikawa managed to deliver 728 fresh troops with ammunition, supplies and artillery. In this sense the *Battle of Cape Esperance* was the exact reverse of *Savo Island* where Japan won the naval battle but failed to land their troops. Nevertheless, Tanaka believed that the *Battle of Cape Esperance* was a crushing defeat for the Imperial Japanese Navy.

For the US Navy a negative consequence of the action was that it continued to believe in the superiority of the gun over the torpedo in naval engagement. Scott's deployment actually prevented his destroyers from using their torpedoes. Ease of targeting in two dimensions (torpedoes) rather than calculation in three dimensions (shells) should have made the preference obvious although the repeated failures of US torpedoes may partially have explained US Naval commanders' preference for shelling. Rear-Admiral Scott would claim credit for having practiced nighttime gunnery, but Charles Cook, a junior officer on the *Helena* was probably more correct when he later wrote, "Cape Esperance was a three-sided battle in which chance was the major winner."[8] However, on the positive side for the United States, it was another engagement that added to the gradual attrition that was to prove fatal to the Japanese Navy's war effort. The *Battle of Cape Esperance* further proved the value of the new microwave-frequency SG surface-search radar with its circular display, which gave an unprecedented view of the enemy at night.

Japanese defeat at the *Battle of Cape Esperance* must in part be ascribed to complacency about the US Navy's night fighting capability. Like the Americans at the *Battle of Savo Island* in August, Admiral Goto's cruisers were not prepared for an attack—hardly believing that a US Naval force would have the temerity to challenge the Japanese in a night attack. Reviewing the battle afterwards Vice-Admiral Matome Ugaki, Chief of Staff of the combined fleet, noted in his diary that Goto should have followed the Japanese proverb, "Treat a stranger as a thief."[9] After the *Battle of Cape Esperance* the Japanese confidence in their overwhelming superiority in night fighting was shattered. A Japanese officer would comment, "providence abandoned us . . . The future looked bleak for our surface forces, whose forte was night warfare."[10]

As well as the build-up of Japanese forces on *Guadalcanal*, Nimitz was also bringing new forces to support his beleaguered Marines. On the back of Nimitz's cajoling of Marshall, who had been reluctant to support the *Guadalcanal* Campaign, 8 October saw 2,837 men of the army's 164th Infantry Regiment embarked on convoys for reinforcement of *Guadalcanal*. They arrived on October 13. More routine air supply, evacuation of the wounded, improvement in quality and quantity of food also helped to some degree to sustain the morale of Marines who had now been on active combat duty for over two months. However, malaria was increasingly taking its toll in terms of the number reporting to sick bay, while those sick troops who remained in the field were weakened to the point where their operational usefulness was significantly degraded.

Before any such further help could reach them, the defenders on Henderson Field would have to deal with another major Japanese resupply convoy coming down the 'Slot.' Before midnight on 14 October, the Japanese convoy reached Tassafaronga on *Guadalcanal*; troops and supplies were unloaded. During the following day, the convoy, open to air attack, suffered the loss of three of its cargo ships. They had erroneously thought that Henderson Field and its aircraft had been completely destroyed by the battleship attack. The remainder of the convoy, with a third of their supplies unloaded, slipped away during the night of the 15 October. Nevertheless by 17 October, Rabaul had been able over a period of several weeks to feed 15,000 fresh troops into *Guadalcanal* giving Lieutenant-General Hyakutake a total force of 20,000 men.

With the aim of crushing the US ability to send up bombers from *Guadalcanal* to disrupt the convoy, Yamamoto sent two battleships *Kongo* and *Haruna* ahead to pound the runways of Henderson Field. At 1.30 a.m. on 14 October they opened fire with their sixteen 14-inch guns. Each shell that they fired was five-foot long and weighed 1,400 lbs. It was perhaps fortunate that the two Japanese battleships carried only 300 high-explosive shells compared to the 600 armor-piercing shells used for ship-to-ship combat. Nevertheless for an hour and a half US forces absorbed a fearful pounding. Using their high explosive fragmentation bombs the Japanese destroyed forty-eight of Henderson Field's aircraft and killed forty-one men including six pilots. Marine Fred Heit recalled, "When the battleship shells went over, it sounded like an express train; a whooshing noise."[11] Martin Clemens wrote, "the ground shook with the most awful convulsions."[12] Clemens' own cook, Michael, was buried alive and had to be dug out. One near miss flung Major-General Vandegrift to the floor of his dugout. "The next morning we saw cattle and pigs wandering around the jungle," observed Fred Heidt, "They were shell shocked because of the shelling and the bombs. A lot of us were too."[13]

Yamamoto, satisfied that his battleships had put the airfield out of action, ventured closer to *Guadalcanal* with his carriers. Vice-Admiral Chuichi Nagumo, in command of the carrier fleet, and Vice-Admiral Nobutake Kondo with a covering cruiser force, was ordered forward. Not only was Kondo ordered to cover Lieutenant-General Hyakutake's attack on Henderson Field but also he was to prepare to engage with the American carriers, which Yamamoto erroneously believed to be in the area. In his searches south of *Guadalcanal* Nagumo only found the destroyer USS *Meredith* that was ripped to shreds by dive-bombers and torpedo planes. *Meredith* sank almost instantly. Survivors clung to life rafts and their lines in the water. Sharks pulled them off. One shark leapt onto a life raft and gouged a chunk out of a dying man's thigh before it could be pushed back into the water. There were just eighty-eight survivors out of 324 men.

In spite of the intensity of the Japanese naval bombardment, within several hours of daylight the Seabees had managed to make the airfield operational. Replacement dive-bombers and Wildcats were sent from *Espirito Santo* in the *New Hebrides*, although Japanese heavy cruisers continued to shell Henderson Field on the night of 14 and 15 October. Shortage of high octane aviation gasoline made it unclear as to what further part the 'Cactus' Air Force would play in the upcoming battle. Vandegrift and his troops knew that the heavy bombardments presaged a new assault on Henderson Field. At this critical juncture, Nimitz displayed unusual jitteriness. On 15 October he reported that his forces were "unable to control the sea in the Guadalcanal area. Thus our supply of the positions will be done at great expense to us. The situation is not hopeless but it is certainly critical."[14] In desperation Rear-Admiral Turner on *Espirito Santo* loaded the destroyer USS *McFarland* with 40,000 gallons of gasoline to make the run to *Guadalcanal*. Arriving in *Ironbottom Sound* on 16 October, the *McFarland* delivered its precious cargo, in spite of coming under heavy attack from Japanese bombers.

Lieutenant-Colonel 'Indian Joe' Bauer, coming in to land with a squadron of nineteen Wildcats, saw the attack and immediately went to the rescue even though his tanks were nearly empty. In one of the most famous aerial feats of the *Guadalcanal* Campaign, Bauer singlehandedly shot down four Japanese planes. His wingman boasted, "The Chief stitched four of the bastards end to end."[15] Notwithstanding Bauer's heroics and the supply of gasoline for the 'Cactus Force's' aircraft the American situation on *Guadalcanal* remained critical.

The Battle of Henderson Field: [Map 18.2] By 24 October even President Roosevelt appears to have joined in with the spirit of panic and desperation concerning the situation on *Guadalcanal*. He ordered the Joint Chiefs to rush all available weapons to Vandegrift's Marines. If Vandegrift's situation on *Guadalcanal* was critical, at least the long interlude while Japan built up it forces and supply had not been without a strategic cost to the Japanese. The loss of their positions east of the *Matanikau River* reduced the feasibility of Hyakutake's making a coastal advance on the Marines' Lunga Perimeter. An attack from the south remained their best chance of success. Hyakutake therefore dispatched Lieutenant-General Masao Maruyama with 7,000 troops to trek through the jungle to put himself in a position to launch an offensive on 22 October.

Maruyama was not unaware of the importance of his offensive. Before setting out to *Guadalcanal*, he warned his officers, "This is the decisive battle between Japan and the United States, a battle in which the rise or fall of the Japanese Empire will be decided."[16] In addition to Maruyama's jungle assault, a diversionary attack would be made along the coast from the west with tanks, artillery and 2,900 soldiers, led by Major-General Tadashi Sumiyoshi.

Construction of the so-called 'Maruyama Road' was begun on 12 October. The trail wound through dense jungle and traversed rivers, ridges and ravines. Often little more than a footpath twenty inches wide, it sometimes resembled a green tunnel burrowing through the dense jungle undergrowth. Each soldier of the Sendai Division had to carry 60 lb of personal equipment, food and munitions as well as an artillery shell. Rations were halved. Artillery had to be manhandled by ropes over jungle-covered cliffs. It was a hard 35-mile slog that took two days longer than planned, forcing Hyakutake to postpone the attack to 7.00 p.m. on 24 October. As in the previous month's attack from the jungles to the south of the Lunga Perimeter, the advance of Japanese forces remained unobserved. That night, at a meeting at Vice-Admiral 'Bull' Halsey's *Noumea* HQ with Major-General Millard Harmon and Rear-Admiral Richmond Turner, Vandegrift was asked whether he could hold out. "Yes I can hold but I have to have more active support than I have been getting." Halsey promised "everything I have."[17]

However, because of a breakdown in communications, Sumiyoshi was unable to inform his troops that the attack from the south was delayed, their assault began at dusk on 23 October. Increased activity in the area had alerted the Marines to the likelihood of impending attack and it was no surprise when it finally arrived. The tank and infantry attacks by the 4th Regiment of the Sendai Division at the mouth of the *Matanikau River* were repulsed with relative ease by intense fire provided by twelve batteries of US artillery (75 mm and 105 mm guns); in addition there were concentrated fusillades from cannon, 37 mm anti-tank guns, Browning machine guns and Garand M1 semi-automatic rifles. All the Japanese light tanks were destroyed with only one managing to reach the east bank before being destroyed by a grenade put in its tracks by the occupants of a foxhole. As dawn broke, the sandbar on the *Mataniku River* revealed a clog of burnt out tanks and bodies. Crocodiles helped themselves to the leftovers. Japanese infantry suffered heavy losses with an estimated 650 men killed.

With no action on the southern perimeter, it was now assumed by Vandegrift and his staff that captured maps, indicating a three-pronged attack including the southern perimeter, were a ruse; Vandegrift therefore withdrew units from Lieutenant-Colonel 'Chesty' Pullar's forces dug into 'Edson's Ridge' to the south of Henderson Field. Martin Clemens described this outstanding 44-year-old, barrel-chested officer as having "A chin like a bulldozer blade."[18] Meshed with Pullar's Marines were the 164th Infantry under Lieutenant-Colonel Robert Hall. However, Vandegrift and his senior officers had managed to bluff themselves. Arriving late on 24 October, Maruyama's troops started their attack on the southern perimeter. It was piecemeal and uncoordinated as units lurched out of the jungle. As with Kawaguchi before him, a night attack without field communication was almost impossible to control. Vandegrift was better prepared than a month previously. The entire Marine perimeter had been wired, the cutting of which alerted the Marines to Japanese movements and enabled the defenders to concentrate their fields of artillery and mortar fire. Marine Sergeant Mitchell Paige, a 'China Marine,' who in the interwar years had been stationed to protect the Shanghai International Concession (a joint operation of British and American areas), developed new tactics for use of the machine guns in enfilade defense.

Paige had shown that the barrels of water-cooled guns did not stop working when water ran out and that the guns continued to fire even when they were red hot. He noted, "A lot of guys were changing barrels for no reason. I would have been dead."[19] Although heat would eventually wear down the grooves, the BAR would keep on firing, which was the most important issue when facing a Japanese infantry charge. Paige also knew how to use the BAR to best effect, advising, "When the Japanese get that close, just pull the trigger and used search and traverse [move the gun side to side and up and down] . . . Close your eyes if you want to. With eight guns firing, a mosquito couldn't get through."[20]

In spite of this the sheer numbers in the Japanese attack overwhelmed the ridge on which Paige's platoon was stationed. With a few survivors Paige turned the guns and fired into the rear of the advancing Japanese as they attacked the next ridge. Three of his colleagues were either killed or wounded: "Star . . . got his in the stomach. Then Reilly got hit in the groin. Joneck had been hit earlier, but when he reached my gun he got hit in the neck . . . A piece of flesh just disappeared from his neck."[21] With blood curdling cries of "Blood for the Emperor! Marine you die!"[22] Japanese infantry made suicidal advances. The diary of a dead Japanese officer was revealing as far as the difficulties that they faced:

> the terrain and enemy situation were completely obscure, and it was necessary to advance along a road, which had been made by the enemy. To make matters worse, the enemy had excellent detectors set up which discovered our movements and there was intense machine gun and mortar fire. Even though it was night, the enemy . . . were able to inflict extremely heavy losses in this way.[23]

One American machine gunner claimed to have fired 26,000 rounds during the night.

At 10.00 p.m. Major-General Yumio Nasu ordered a general assault on the eastern ridge. As at the *Battle of Tenaru*, M3 37 mm gun emplacements proved devastating against mass advancing infantry. The Browning heavy machine gun also enjoyed one of its finest hours. Sergeant John Basilone would win a Medal of Honor for manning two machine guns. Bodies of Japanese infantrymen piled so high that they obscured the field of fire. During lulls in the fighting, Basilone had to send out detachments to clear away the bodies. Private Nash W. Phillips recalled, "Basilone had a machine gun on the go for three days and nights without sleep, rest, or food. He was in a good emplacement, and causing the Japanese lots of trouble, not only firing his machine gun, but also using his pistol."[24]

On the ground, as dawn broke the Japanese retreated and the Marines counterattacked the rear ridge. Sergeant Paige ripped a Browning off its tripod and chased the Japanese down the hill. "The men followed me, shooting and yelling. At one time I almost ran into a Japanese field officer. He had emptied his revolver and was reaching for his two-handed sword. He was no more than four or five feet away when I cut him down."[25] The remaining Japanese disappeared into the jungle. Three hundred dead Japanese troops were found on the ridge behind them. An hour before Nasu's charge, Yamamoto had received a message: "The Kawaguchi Detachment captured the airfield and the western force is fighting to the west of the field."[26] Although Yamamoto learnt the truth the next morning, others were less well updated. At the Seventeenth Army HQ in Rabaul, Rear-Admiral Kusaka of the Eleventh Air Fleet, believing that Henderson

Field had been taken, sent fighters to land there. Instead the Japanese Zero fighters were intercepted by American Wildcats, which shot down seventeen of the incoming 'bandits.'

It can be debated whether Nasu's fate was better or worse than that of Maruyama's survivors. Over two days the lightly armed Japanese troops, who had had to ditch much of their heavier equipment in the slog through the jungle, were massacred. Although small groups of Japanese attackers were able to make incursions through the Marine lines, Pullar's Marines hunted them down over succeeding days. An estimated 1,500 Japanese troops of the renowned Sendai Division were killed versus just sixty Americans. As for Colonel Pullar, after being wounded by shrapnel, he refused to allow the medical corpsman to write out an order for transfer to the field hospital, bellowing, "I remain in command here."[27] 'Chesty' Pullar, from Saluda, Virginia, had risen from the rank of private in *World War I* and was already a legendary figure in the Marines; this larger than life figure was the only Marine ever to win five Navy Crosses in a career total of fourteen separate awards for bravery. He would later be sent on tours of US bases to dispel any lingering myths concerning the 'invincibility' of the Japanese soldier.

Over the two days of battle, Henderson Field was pounded by shells from Japanese cruisers and bomber sorties flew constantly from Rabaul. So confident was the high command that Maruyama would take Henderson Field that it was expected that their fighters would be able to land there on the afternoon of the 24 October. The following day some twenty-seven Japanese planes were shot down, five by anti-aircraft batteries. Although further attacks were launched near *Matanikau River* on 26 October, Lieutenant-General Hyakutake was forced to call off any further engagement at 8.00 a.m. Lieutenant-General Maruyama retreated with his shattered forces back to Seventeenth Army HQ at Kokumbona to the west of Matanikau. He arrived on 4 November. It was a miserable journey for his troops now suffering from extreme malnutrition.

Combat above Guadalcanal: By October 1942 it was increasingly noticeable that the US Navy's Grumman F4F Wildcat fighter, so brilliantly outfought by Japanese Zero fighters at the start of the war, had turned the tables. It was partly the result of the superior tactical training, with leader and 'wingman' using the 'Thach Weave' to 'double-tag' Japanese Zeros. As early as mid-1942 Commander John Thach developed a defensive maneuver to combat the more agile Mitsubishi Zero. Known as the 'Weave,' the principle was for two fliers to work in conjunction to shoot down an enemy plane. When an enemy bandit locked onto an American fighter, the target fighter would weave away from his fighter partner who would weave in the opposite direction before turning to attack the chasing aircraft from the enemy's flank. Thach worked out his tactics using matchsticks on his kitchen table. He trialled the maneuver successfully at *Midway* where he served aboard USS *Yorktown*.

Thach, born in Pine Bluff, Jefferson County, graduated from the US Naval Academy in 1927 and served on the USS *Mississippi* and then on the USS *California*. He transferred to aviation in 1929 and became a member of the crack group of aviators known as 'Top Hat.' As a consequence Hollywood chased them down to perform in the

Hollywood movie *Hell Divers* [1932], an aviation drama made with the co-operation of the US Navy. It was Clarke Gable's first starring role, albeit without the trademark moustache. The 'Thach Weave' proved to be one of the most significant tactical innovations of *World War II* and was a major contributory factor to the increased performance of US fighters. Thach went on to become a Rear-Admiral after serving in the Korean War where he commanded the escort carrier USS *Sicily*.

On 25 September Rabaul had received reinforcements amounting to 100 Zeros and eighty bombers. Stationed at Vunakanau and Lakunai Fields, the new aircraft went into action two days later. Six 'Bettys' and five Zeros were shot down. The following day saw an even larger attack by sixty aircraft. Twenty-three bombers and a Zero were destroyed. Vandegrift radioed *Noumea* to boast, "Our losses: no pilots, no planes, no damage. How's that for a record."[28] The aerial combats over *Guadalcanal* began to make legends of the American fliers. Captain John Smith, leader of Henderson Field's so-called 'Cactus' Air Force, would go on to score nineteen victories in his Wildcat. Along with Captain Smith, First-Lieutenant Jefferson Deblanc and Lieutenant James Swett, he would win a Medal of Honor at *Guadalcanal*. Major Robert Galer also won a Medal of Honor with thirteen 'kills' to his name.

Probably the most famous of the Medal of Honor winners however was Lieutenant-Colonel Harold 'Indian Joe' Bauer; of Volga German stock, raised in Woodruff, Kansas, he had become a renowned fighter pilot before the war. At the start of the war, his exceptional skills as a flier, trainer and inspirational leader brought rapid promotion. A month after his famous saving of USS *McFarland* 'Indian Joe' was forced to ditch at sea and, though he appeared in complete good health, rescuers failed to find him the following day; it was assumed that he had been taken by sharks. Of equal fame to 'Indian Joe' was Joe Foss. Starting his combat duty on *Guadalcanal* on 10 October, by 23 October he had nursed four shot-up Wildcats back to Henderson Field. In just fourteen days he had downed eleven enemy aircraft making him a 'double' ace. Foss would go on to achieve twenty-six kills and tie the record of Captain Eddie Rickenbacker in *World War I*.

The scale of the air war over *Guadalcanal*, sometimes neglected in comparison to the famous sea and land battles, is indicated by the fact that between 1 September and 18 November there were 140 raids on Henderson Field in which the airbase was hit at least once. On 14 October, after a particularly heavy raid, US aircraft were forced to circle the landing strip for an hour while thirteen bomb craters were hastily filled in. Seabees Commander Joseph Blunden recalled that in desperation to get the planes landed and "because there were not enough shovels to go around, some men used their helmets to scoop up earth and carry it to the bomb craters."[29] As for unexploded bombs, defusing teams would dive into the holes to begin their work. To cope with the problem, the Seabees therefore constructed an alternative grass runway.

The Battle of the Santa Cruz Islands: **[Map: 18.3]** It was a diminished American carrier force that would face the Imperial Japanese Navy in the last carrier battle of the

Guadalcanal Campaign. As previously noted, USS *Saratoga* had been torpedoed by *I-26* on 31 August and was being repaired. Worse still on 14 September, USS *Wasp* had been lost to a submarine torpedo attack. With almost half a year to wait before new US aircraft carriers came on stream, these were serious setbacks.

Halsey, who inherited a command with just one carrier, USS *Hornet*, was reinforced a week later by the returning USS *Enterprise*, which had been under repair and refit in *Honolulu*. He immediately sought a decisive encounter; it was a wish that was reciprocated by his Japanese counterparts who wanted to break the stalemate that threatened their control of the *Solomon Islands*. In early October two fleet carriers, *Hiyo* and *Junyo*, along with the light carrier, *Zuiho*, arrived at *Truk* where they joined fleet carriers *Shokaku* and *Zuikaku*; 5 battleships, 14 cruisers and 44 destroyers were assembled to accompany them. Finally it seems that Yamamoto was taking the issue of control in the *South Pacific* with the seriousness it deserved. A major showdown was in the offing. The assembly of five Japanese carriers in the *South Pacific* showed that this major strike weapon of the Imperial Japanese Navy had not been completely shattered at the *Battle of the Midway* as is sometimes assumed.

As usual Yamamoto organized a divided command as the fleet approached the southern *Solomons*. An 'Advance' force under Vice-Admiral Nobutake Kondo (also fleet commander) consisted of the carrier *Junyo*, 2 battleships, 4 heavy cruisers, 1 light cruiser and 10 destroyers; the 'Main' force, led by Vice-Admiral Chuichi Nagumo, contained the fleet carriers, *Shokaku* and *Zuikaku* as well as the light carrier *Zuiho*, 1 heavy cruiser and 8 destroyers; a 'Vanguard' force comprised 2 battleships including Rear-Admiral Hiroaki Abe's flagship *Hiei*, 3 heavy cruisers, 1 light cruiser and 7 destroyers. Even without the fleet carrier *Hiyo* that was forced to retire to *Truk* on 22 October because of an accidental on-board fire, the attacking Japanese fleet amounted to an impressive 40 ships and 199 aircraft; by far the largest force that Yamamoto had put into the *South Pacific*. As ever he sought a decisive naval encounter.

Facing them Halsey had put a force of 23 ships including 1 battleship and 2 carriers, *Hornet* and *Enterprise*. As was standard US practice, the carriers were split into two carrier groups some twelve miles apart. They carried a complement of 136 aircraft, though as at *Midway* they enjoyed the benefit of land-based aircraft at Henderson Field. In addition Task Force 61, as the carrier force was designated, could be supported by land-based aircraft at *Espirto Santo*. However, at the range at which land-based aircraft would have to operate, the effectiveness of this support was necessarily limited. It was an undoubtedly risky plan to allow his carriers to move north of the *Santa Cruz Islands*—250 miles to the east of the *Solomon Islands* chain—where the effectiveness of land-based support would begin to diminish sharply. Halsey gave Task Force 61 command to Rear-Admiral Thomas Kinkaid.

Arguably the more prudent course would have been for Halsey to station his carriers to the south or southeast of *Guadalcanal*. From here Catalina spotter planes would be able to give local intelligence as to the movement of the Japanese fleet against the US toehold on *Guadalcanal*. This was the more cautious approach previously taken by

Vice-Admiral Robert Ghormley and his carrier commander Vice-Admiral Jack Fletcher. By contrast the Rear-Admiral Kinkaid expedition's move north of the *Santa Cruz Islands*, with the intention of launching a bombing attack on the Japanese naval bases and shipping off southern *Bougainville*, risked America's diminished carriers being attacked by a superior force of Japanese carriers as well as Japan's long-range land-based bombers based at *Rabaul*.

Even though the 21 October ground attack on *Guadalcanal* by Japanese troops appeared to have failed by 25 October, Vice-Admiral Kondo's carrier force remained in the southern *Solomons* seeking to engage the American carrier fleet. Halsey, following events in the ground *Battle of Henderson Field* from his HQ at *Noumea*, recalled, "The crescendo of the fighting ashore made it plain that the climax was rushing towards us. I thought that the 25 October would precipitate it."[30] At mid-morning a Catalina flying boat spotted the main Japanese fleet and relayed a message to Kinkaid. Although out of range, Kinkaid sped further north to try to engage the Japanese carriers and sent off a strike force of twenty-three aircraft in the early afternoon. However, Kondo's fleet turned north and out of range of the American strike. At dawn the next day, 26 October, Halsey sent a typically uncompromising message to all his commanders, "Attack—repeat—Attack!"[31]

The Japanese fleet reversed course and turned south at 2.50 a.m. on 26 October and the two forces now closed to within 250 miles of each other by daybreak. At 5.10 a.m. Kinkaid began launching eight pairs of Douglas SDB Dauntless dive-bombers. The scale of the widespread searches would later reduce the number of planes available for a strike. At about the same time Kinkaid had received a 3.10 a.m. sighting report of vice-Admiral Nagumo's strike force. Similarly Nagumo launched thirteen 'Kates' to do a spotter sweep of the south where they expected to find the American carriers. In fact by now Nagumo's forces were due west of Task Force 61.

At 6.30 a.m. the US spotters picked up Rear-Admiral Hiroaki Abe's 'Vanguard Group' with its two battleships. At 6.45 a.m. Lieutenant-Commodore Bucky Lee and his wingman Ensign William Johnson spotted two carriers that quickly launched Zeros with the aim of shooting down the American spotters of Scouting-10. After a game of ducking and diving in the sporadic cloud, both spotters made their way back safely. Meanwhile *Hornet*'s Task Force 17 had also been discovered. At 6.58 a.m. a *Zuikaku*-based 'Kate' reported, "LARGE ENEMY UNIT SIGHTED. ONE CARRIER, FIVE OTHER VESSELS."[32] Sighting each other almost simultaneously just before 7.00 a.m., both fleets raced to launch their attacks; 64 airplanes including 21 Aichi D3A 'Val' dive-bombers, 20 Nakajima 'Kate' torpedo bombers, 21 Mitsubishi Zero fighters and 2 scouters, set off to attack the *Hornet*. Twenty minutes later *Shokaku* and *Zuikaku* launched a second wave of torpedo planes and bombers to strike the American carriers. Kondo also ordered Abe's 'Vanguard Force' surface ships to join his 'Advanced Force' in pressing forward to engage Kinkaid's fleet. A total of 110 aircraft were now headed toward the US fleet. They crossed with the seventy-five planes launched by Kinkaid to attack the Japanese carriers.

At 6.30 a.m. two Dauntless scout planes, led by an aggressive young flyer, Lieutenant Birney Strong, who had heard the call giving the sighting of Abe's Vanguard Group, immediately headed south to attack—even though they had reached the limit of their 200-mile patrol. At 7.40 a.m. Strong found the carrier group, and, using cloud cover, launched a surprise attack on the *Zuiho*. Both Dauntless landed 500 lb bombs on its flight deck, rendering the light carrier unable to land aircraft. During a 45-mile chase back toward his carrier, Strong's rear gunner, Clarence Garlow, managed to shoot down a pursuing Zero. Strong was awarded the Navy Cross for his action. The *Zuiho*, unable to land aircraft, would have to make its way back to Japan for repair.

Meanwhile a series of American attack squadrons, comprising Avenger torpedo bombers, Dauntless dive-bombers and accompanying Wildcat fighters, were bearing down on the Japanese carriers. The respective attacking aircraft crossed and tangled in a fighter dogfight which saw 4 Zeros, 3 Wildcats and 2 Avengers shot down. Eleven Dauntless dive-bombers that managed to get past *Shokaku*'s fighter defense planted 3–6 hits on her decks causing severe damage to lower decks. Lieutenant Moe Vose, who planted a 1,000 lb bomb on the *Shokaku*, provided a souvenir for the following Dauntless of Fred Bates, whose open cockpit gratefully received a large charred splinter of one of the carriers that had attacked *Pearl Harbor*. Another squadron from *Hornet* found Abe's force and two 1,000 lb bombs hit the heavy cruiser *Chikuma*. The *Chikuma* was then hit by another bomb dropped by three Dauntless bombers from the USS *Enterprise*.

Meanwhile the US carriers found themselves almost defenseless as Japanese strike forces hove into view. Mistakes made by Flight-Direction Officer, Commodore Jack Griffen, who had ordered fighter cover to patrol in the wrong direction, meant that there were only eight covering Wildcat fighters. Kept at just fifteen miles distance from the carriers, the US fighters were too close and flying at too low an altitude (12,000 foot) to intercept effectively. The Wildcat cover had to climb to a higher altitude just as the Japanese dive-bombers and torpedo planes began to dive toward their targets. Flight-Director Griffen screamed at his fighter pilots to "Climb, Climb!"[33] At the same time Lieutenant-Commodore Shigeharu Murata who had led the torpedo attack forces against 'battleship row' at *Pearl Harbor*, sent out the message "TO-TO-TO"[34] (All forces Attack). It was Murata's last communication; within a few minutes, having released his torpedo, he was shot out of the sky. Nevertheless the Japanese strike force, comprising fifteen 'Val' dive-bombers and twelve torpedo-carrying 'Kates,' managed to avoid most of the American fighter protection. Aboard the *Hornet*, bridge officers attempted to shoo Rear-Admiral George Murray into the protection of steel shutters, but he protested "Leave them open. I want to see the show."[35] The show, a horror show at that, was not long in coming.

At five miles distance the 'Kate' torpedo bombers split into two groups and began circling their prey looking for the best angles of attack. At 9.10 a.m. six 'Val' dive-bombers led by Lieutenant Toshio Tsuda made their attack. The 'Vals' planted three bombs on USS *Hornet*'s deck. In addition at 9.14 a.m. a damaged and flaming dive-bomber piloted by Warrant-Officer Sato crashed on the stricken carrier's smoke stack and glanced off into the base of the flight deck's island. The stricken 'Val' spewed gasoline onto the signalling bridge incinerating seven of *Hornet*'s crewmen. One uninjured signalman raced to rescue his twin brother who was on fire. Both died. It was not the end of *Hornet*'s suffering. At 9.17 a.m. the two torpedoes launched by the now deceased Murata and his wingman, crashed into her side and knocked out her engines and communications. All electrical power was lost. The forward engine room was immediately flooded and the *Hornet* came to a halt with a list ten degrees to the starboard. The carrier's rudder was jammed hard right.

A few seconds later, a damaged Japanese bomber deliberately rammed into the stricken carrier—penetrating the flight deck and causing fires in the hangar deck. Gunner's Mate Alvin Grahn recalled, "One of them dropped a torpedo and then swooped up and over the flight deck. Somebody hit him good and he caught fire. Just a mass of flames . . . The pilot laid his plane right over and made a tight circle and came back and smashed into the port side . . ."[36] It was a foretaste of the *kamikaze* to come. The attack cost twenty-seven Japanese aircraft but USS *Hornet* was dead in the water. Destroyers USS *Morris*, USS *Russell* and USS *Mustin* came alongside to offer firefighting assistance. The fires were brought under control within forty-five minutes. Attempts were then made to tow away the stricken carrier.

Japanese attacks on the USS *Enterprise* were less successful. Thanks to the work of the US carrier's Wildcat fighter support only five Japanese torpedo bombers got through the security net. *Enterprise* kept its stern to the incoming bombers and thus narrowed the target. By good fortune all the torpedoes missed and only one came close to scoring a hit. USS *Enterprise* had survived. Meanwhile, 170 miles to the north, the USS *Hornet* was being avenged. Her Dauntless dive-bombers swooped down on the *Shokaku* and planted at least three 1,000 lb bombs onto her decks. She survived but her flight decks were ruined and her hangars burnt out and useless. The USS *Hornet*'s Avenger torpedo planes failed to locate the *Shokaku*.

The *Enterprise* received returning craft from both US carriers until it ran out of space and forced others to ditch their craft. One of these, a damaged Avenger TBF, crashed near the destroyer USS *Porter*. The ditched Avengers' torpedo launched and, running in a wild circle, came back to strike *Porter*, which was in the process of rescuing the TBF's crew. The freak accident killed fifteen sailors and the heavily damaged *Porter* had to be scuttled.

At 10.15 a.m. the second Japanese strike wave of 'Val' dive-bombers, again largely unimpeded by the covering Wildcat fighters, dived towards the *Enterprise*. The carrier's gunnery officer, Lieutenant-Commodore Orlin Livdahl sitting in 'Sky Control' high up on the main mast above the bridge, watched in alarm as the damaged and smoking 'Val' piloted by Mamoru Seki, headed straight toward him. Seemingly facing certain death, at the last moment the *Enterprise* pitched to one side and Seki's plane crashed into the water. Still armed with its bomb the dive-bomber exploded sending debris and water over the flight deck—rising so high that even Livdahl was showered. The third, fifth and seventh plane of the leading seven-plane *shotai* were blown out of the air by anti-aircraft fire. The *Enterprise*'s avoiding turn meant that Lieutenant Keiichi Arima's *shotai* would make its attack from the stern. Emerging from the cloud a few minutes after Seki's doomed *shotai*, an anti-aircraft officer used his bullhorn to yell a warning: "Four o'clock! Four o'clock! Get him."[37] To no avail. At 10.17 a.m. the 250 kg bomb hit the forward part of the carrier and passed straight through and out in front of the bow where it exploded mid-air. A Dauntless rear-Gunner, Sam Davis Presley, was killed when the blast turfed his plane into the water. Another Dauntless that caught fire was pushed off the side before its 500 lb bomb exploded.

More fortunately, Gun director, Lieutenant Marshall Field Jr., a grandson of the famous Chicago department store's founder and son of the owner of the *Chicago Sun*, was blown upwards onto the flight deck, full of shrapnel but alive. Field staggered back to his gun position and later his quad of 1.1-inch guns shot down a 'Kate' torpedo bomber. The ditched 'Kate' crew got out of their aircraft alive and as the *Enterprise* passed close by, several American machine guns burst into life and ripped them to shreds. Concerning the murder of unarmed enemy pilots, anti-aircraft gunnery officer, Lieutenant-Commodore Benny Mott would later claim that his gun crews had misunderstood his commands.

A second bomb penetrated the flight deck just aft of the *Enterprise's* forward elevator. It hit a girder and split in two with one half blowing up the hangar deck and the second part penetrating to the third deck where it demolished officers' state rooms. On the hangar deck, eight Dauntless bombers were damaged or destroyed by fire. Many sailors were killed. The forward elevator was jammed in the up position. At 10.20 a.m. a third bomb delivered by Lieutenant Yamada's rear *shotai* exploded at the waterline, rupturing fuel tanks and putting a fifty-foot gash in the side. A Wildcat was bounced into the water and a Dauntless was left suspended from a gun galley by its landing gear. In the attack, Yamada, a *Pearl Harbor* veteran, was killed. As with the *Hornet*, air cover was thin. Wildcats shot down just two of the nineteen dive-bombers. However, the *Enterprise*, the *Pacific War*'s luckiest ship, was more fortunate than the *Hornet* because *Zuikaku*'s torpedo planes failed to land a strike. However, a damaged Japanese plane deliberately flew into the destroyer USS *Smith*, killing fifty-seven crewmembers. The blazing ship was kept afloat by the determined efforts of its remaining crew in putting out the fire. It was an action that won its crew nine Navy Crosses, thirteen Silver Stars and two Bronze medals. The saving of the *Smith* won them more than they had bargained for when the *Smith*'s crewmen found the latest Imperial Japanese Navy aircraft codes in the remains of the crashed 'Kate.'

An hour later, a strike force from the *Junyo* attacked the *Enterprise* carrier group and scored hits on the battleship *South Dakota* and the light cruiser *San Juan*. Eleven of the seventeen Japanese dive-bombers were shot down. At 11.35 a.m. Rear-Admiral Kinkaid, aware that there were two undamaged Japanese carriers in the area, decided to retire. With the *Hornet* disabled and not able to take returning aircraft, the *Enterprise* landed forty-seven aircraft. The flight barriers that prevented runaway planes crashing into parked aircraft had to be lowered to provide extra parking space that was at a premium because the Dauntless, unlike the Wildcat or Avenger did not have folding wings. Landing-Signal Officers, Lieutenant Jim Daniels and Lieutenant Robin Lindsey operating their direction paddles bravely determined to land aircraft even with only two remaining landing wires available as parked planes crowded towards the aft flight deck. All, except five planes, which were forced to ditch, landed safely without overshooting.

Believing that he had destroyed *Enterprise* and *Hornet*, Admiral Yamamoto ordered his fleet to "Chase and mop up fleeing enemy."[38] Although the Japanese carriers had scored many hits on Kinkaid's task force, the loss of their aircrews was significant. The Japanese strike forces had taken a mauling. A staff officer on board the *Junyo* described the scene as the Japanese pilots returned:

> We searched the sky with apprehension. There were only
> a few planes in the air in comparison with the numbers
> launched several hours before . . . The planes lurched and
> staggered onto the deck, every single fighter and bomber
> bullet holed . . . As the pilots climbed wearily from their
> cramped cockpits, they told of unbelievable opposition,
> of skies choked with anti-aircraft shell bursts and tracers.[39]

The surviving 'Vals' returned claiming six hits in all. Kondo, with the 'Advanced' and 'Vanguard Forces,' raced toward the last position of Kinkaid's carriers and launched final strike waves. Aboard the *Junyo*, Lieutenant Shunko Kato, having returned from the attack on the *Enterprise*, was so exhausted he could not deliver a coherent account of the engagement to his captain. When he was informed that he was required to buckle up for another mission, Kato exclaimed in disbelief, "Again? Am I to fly again today?"[40] Zero pilot, Flight-Commander Lieutenant Yoshio Shiga, shouted at Kato, telling him, "This is war! There can be no rest against the enemy . . . We have no choice . . . We go!"[41] Shiga proceeded to tell him, "We cannot afford to give them a chance when their ships are crippled."[42] Kato raised himself and agreed to fly even though previous losses had considerably reduced their numbers. Nevertheless the floundering US carrier was found. Leading his four 'Kates,' Kato's group, escorted by Shiga's six Zeros, scored the decisive bomb hit that sealed the fate of the *Hornet*. Listing heavily the USS *Hornet* was abandoned and finished off with torpedoes by the destroyers *Makigumo* and *Akigumo* whose captains decided that the stricken US carrier was too damaged to viably tow back to Japan. It was the last action of the *Battle of the Santa Cruz Island*. Kondo's forces, critically short of fuel, were ordered to return to *Truk*. It was a clear material victory for Kondo's forces. A precious US fleet carrier had been destroyed while America's last remaining carrier in the *South Pacific*, the USS *Enterprise*, was heavily damaged again though it was at least patched up to be operational within several weeks.

In Japan a great victory was proclaimed. Emperor Hirohito announced, "The Combined Fleet is at present striking heavy blows at the enemy fleet in the South Pacific Ocean. We are deeply gratified. I charge each of you to exert yourselves to the utmost in all things toward the critical turning point in the war."[43] But Japan too had paid a heavy price. The *Shokaku* had survived, in large part due to much-improved fire control systems introduced since the *Battle of Midway*. However, it took Japan almost nine months to get the *Shokaku* back into action. The *Zuiho* was out of action for the next three months. However, undoubtedly the most significant loss to the Japanese Navy was its aircrews. Ninety-nine aircraft were lost and with them sixty-eight pilots and seventy-seven observers. Twenty-three squadron, group, section or flight leaders were killed— the cream of the Imperial Japanese Navy's Aviation Corps. One of the few surviving bomber squadron leaders on returning to the *Junyo* was "so shaken that at times he could not speak coherently."[44]

Overall 49 percent of the Japanese torpedo bomber crews were killed as well as 39 percent of dive-bomber crews and 20 percent of fighter pilots. Indeed the vastly improved performance of US anti-aircraft fire from screening destroyers and the carriers demonstrated the significant improvement in equipment and training in this area. In particular Bofors 40 mm guns showed marked improvement on previous armament and together with proven 20 mm guns they accounted for a high percentage of downed planes. The new Twin-Bofors mounts fitted to the USS *Enterprise* automatically ejected spent magazines and were able to put up a wall of lead at the intermediate range that Japanese dive-bombers needed to make their run. Accuracy of fire was also helped by the development of an automated gun director. The *Enterprise*'s batteries were reinforced by a screen of fire put up by USS *Dakota* and the light anti-aircraft cruiser USS *San Juan*, which was equipped with sixteen 5-inch rapid fire guns as well as a multitude of 1.1-inch anti-aircraft guns. The defense weapons of the heavy cruiser USS *Portland* and five destroyers had made up the remainder of the *Enterprise*'s screen.

Rear-Admiral Kinkaid commented, "There cannot be too many 40 mm and 20 mm guns on any type of ship. They knock down planes."[45] There was also a noticeable decline in the performance of Japanese aircrews; Commander Arnold True, who had been witness to both the *Battles of Coral Sea* and *Midway*, noted a "marked decrease in [Japanese] skill."[46] Nevertheless Commander True also observed that there was "no diminution in the courage and daring of the individual [Japanese] pilot."[47] The net result of these different factors was that Japanese loss of 148 aircrew was extraordinarily high compared to the three previous carrier battles; 90 at *Coral Sea*, 110 at *Midway* and 61 at *East Solomons*. So severe was the manning crisis, that *Zuikaku* and *Hiyo* were forced to return home because of lack of trained aircrew. For the next phase of the *Guadalcanal* Campaign only the *Junyo* was left on station. In all, the Japanese carrier fleet lost ninety out of 203 combat aircraft.

By comparison Kinkaid's carriers lost eighty out of 175 aircraft. Just eighteen crewmen and eight pilots were lost, including two captured. Just as significantly only five section or group leaders were killed. Given that at the critical juncture of the battle, the US carriers' defense fighters, because of operational mistakes, had failed to turn up, the relative difference in performance reflected well on the rapidly improving performance of the US fleet's anti-aircraft gunnery crews and their new weapons.

However, the American action during the battle was far from faultless. US torpedo planes again proved completely ineffective, particularly when compared to their Japanese counterparts. Communications faults during the battle were common. The failure of the covering fighter squadrons to intercept the incoming bombers was a cause of much internal dissension. Coordination of air attacks remained poor. Squadron Commanders Flatley and Sanchez were scathing about Rear-Admiral Kinkaid's organization of fighter-direction.

Captain Hara, a Japanese destroyer captain concluded "Numerically or tactically, it was a Japanese victory."[48] Hara also surmised, "The enemy [the Americans] had entered the fray with a tactical and psychological advantage, but complacency had cost them a high price . . . contrary to *Midway* . . . they [the Japanese] struck back effectively with what force they had."[49] Indeed, the *Battle of Santa Cruz Islands* was a salutary reminder of what might have been at *Midway* if the Japanese carriers had had better luck and better intelligence of American force disposition. Nevertheless there was a more sanguine view of the *Santa Cruz Islands* action. Vice-Admiral Nagumo, who was transferred to shore duty after the battle, reported to the Combined Fleet with greater than usual insight and honesty, "This battle was a tactical win, but a shattering strategic loss for Japan. Considering the great superiority of our enemy's industrial capacity, we must win every battle overwhelmingly to win this war. This last one, although a victory, unfortunately, was not an overwhelming victory."[50] Naval victories are usually counted in ships lost but given the destruction of the cream of the Japanese Navy's aircrews, it could even be argued that, in the case of the *Battle of the Santa Cruz Islands*, the Japanese came off worst.

Reporting several weeks after the battle, Nimitz too correctly calibrated the result of the battle: "This battle cost us the lives of many gallant men, many planes and two ships that could ill be spared . . . We nevertheless turned back the Japanese again in their offensive to regain *Guadalcanal* and shattered their carrier air strength on the eve of the critical days of mid-November. It was indeed a pyrrhic victory."[51] Nimitz's observation now was that "the general situation at *Guadalcanal* is not unfavorable,"[52] a much more upbeat assessment than the one made a month previously.

Maruyama's Retreat: Writing in his diary on 27 October, Lieutenant Keijiro Minegishi wrote, "I must take a rest every two meters. It is quite disheartening to have only one tiny teaspoon of salt per day and a palm full of rice porridge."[53] By 30 October Minegishi was writing, ". . . I am surprised how food captures the mind to the degree that one is always thinking of it, I try to think of other things but can't."[54] Indeed, with its obsession on food, Minegishi's diary could almost be exchanged paragraph for paragraph with that written by Lieutenant Inoue who had done the same retreat six weeks earlier after the *Battle of Edson's Ridge*.

On 4 November, Colonel Toshinari's 230th Infantry, ordered to retreat eastwards by Maruyama, arrived in similarly wrecked condition at Koli Point. It is estimated that aggregate Japanese losses in the *Battle of Henderson Field* were as high as 3,000 compared to eighty for the defenders. While the defenders of Henderson Field has significantly upped their capabilities during the month since the *Battle of Edson's Ridge*, it nevertheless has to be questioned why the crack Sendai Division, able to concentrate its attack with 7,000 troops at the weak southern perimeter, failed so miserably? In part there was a failure of intelligence. Hyakutake and Maruyama were led to believe that there were just 10,000 defenders rather than the 19,000 who were present. In addition there was a complete breakdown of logistics, which meant that troops went into battle not only half-starved but also short of equipment, particularly artillery. For Maruyama, simply getting his troops through the jungle to the attack point at the southern perimeter was an achievement. Not surprisingly the appalling conditions led to fractious relationships between the senior commanders while Maruyama's chronic neuralgia was hardly helpful.

Though the inflexibility of Japanese tactics has been much criticized, what choices did Maruyama have in practice? In the conditions of a night attack, impenetrable jungle terrain and no communications, field control was virtually impossible while troops lacked the support of heavier equipment such as mortars, artillery and heavy machine guns. Without the ability to maneuver or reconnoiter effectively, and with no maps of the terrain, virtually the only choice for commanders was to cross open terrain as quickly as possible and close with the enemy. Massively outgunned, the Japanese officers were left with few options other than the *banzai* charge. As Colonel Furimiya concluded in his diary before committing suicide, "We must not overlook firepower."[55] Similarly Tsuji admitted the Japanese troops had "failed because I underestimated the enemy's fire power."[56]

At a more junior level, officers knew that they were going to be outgunned. Lieutenant Genirou Inoue, an anti-tank gun officer noted as early as August that there was not enough transport to take enough heavy guns to *Guadalcanal*. In his diary of 26 August, he railed, "four antitank guns can't defeat 30. Only the Regimental guns [heavy guns] gain control of the enemy. Only a drop in the bucket! A fool hunts for misfortune! A shortage of firepower will force us into inconsistent battles, double our losses, and must raise the morale of the enemy."[57] On 29 October Emperor Hirohito, increasingly concerned by reports from *Guadalcanal* sent a message to senior commanders: "As Guadalcanal is the place of bitter struggle and is also an important base for the Navy, I wish you would make efforts to recapture it swiftly without being satisfied with success at this time."[58]

On 1 November, following the crushing defeat of Japanese forces at Henderson Field, Vandegrift sent six Marine battalions to attack the remaining Japanese forces to the west of Matanikau. With the objective of capturing the Seventeenth Army HQ, the American force led by Colonel Edson destroyed the defensive positions at Point Cruz. The 4th Infantry Regiment under the command of Colonel Nomasu Nakaguma was forced to retreat west. At Point Cruz, Japanese troops were cornered with their backs to the wall; Edson ordered his men to make a rare US bayonet charge. Some 400 Japanese were killed for the loss of seventy Marines. However, when the Japanese were being driven back to Kokumbona, Vandegrift got wind of a new landing of Japanese troops near Koli Point to the east of the Lunga Perimeter.

There on 3 November Japanese destroyers landed 300 army soldiers with the objective of linking up with Shoji's forces still retreating from the jungles south of Henderson Field. The battalion of Marines, sent to counter the newly arrived forces, were driven back to the Lunga Perimeter. To counter this new threat Vandegrift ordered Edson to break off the Kokumbona offensive. Puller's Marine battalion, two battalions from the 164th Infantry and Hanneken's battalion were now dispatched to shore up the newly active front to the east of Henderson Field.

The arrival of these fresh American forces coincided with the return of Shoji's remnants to Koli Point. American forces encircled the exhausted Japanese troops at *Gavagi Creek*, an area adjacent to Koli Point. Lieutenant-General Hyakutake ordered Shoji to extricate his troops from the entrapment. Filtering troops through a swampy creek to the south of the American lines, Shoji managed to escape into the jungle with several thousand men. The remaining 450 soldiers, trapped in a pocket near Koli Point, were wiped out; stores and heavy weapons were also captured in an operation that cost forty Marine lives and 120 wounded.

In a further demonstration of Vandegrift expansive inclinations and capabilities, on 4 November a raiding force led by Lieutenant-Colonel Evans Carlson was landed by boat at *Aola Bay*, forty miles to the east of Lunga Point. Carlson's 2nd Raider Battalion along with infantry from the 147th Regiment were required to provide security cover for the building of another airfield. Five hundred Seabees were also shipped to this location although by the end of the month it became clear that the site was unsuitable and had to be abandoned. On 8 November, in the midst of these skirmishes, Vice-Admiral Halsey arrived for an inspection and won much admiration for touring the perimeter where he chatted with the Marines in their dugouts. With victory now in sight, it was a suitable moment for the 'harrumphing' for which he became famous. Asked for his strategy by a journalist, Halsey replied, "To kill Japs, kill Japs, and keep on killing Japs."[59] It was great stuff for morale. Three weeks later Halsey was awarded his fourth star to become a full admiral. On 30 November his stars shone even brighter when he was featured on the front cover of *Time* magazine. Nimitz was quoted as saying, "He possesses superb leadership qualities which have earned him a tremendous following of his men. His only enemies are Japs."[60]

Nevertheless there was more than verbal jousting still to be done. With troops available in the area east of Lunga Point, Vandegrift ordered Carlson's Raiders to march from Aola and cut off and pursue Shoji's troops who had escaped from Koli Point. On an epic 29-day march, Carlson's forces killed some 488 Japanese troops for the loss of just sixteen men. As for Shoji, just 750 survivors managed to get back to the new Japanese line at Mount Austen in the region of the upper *Matanikau River*. Here new troops from the Japanese 38th Infantry Division, which were landed by destroyers on the 5, 7 and 9 November, enabled the Seventeenth Army to hold back further American attacks in the week beginning 10 November. The Japanese now had a numerical advantage of 30,000 to 23,000. Escalation continued on 11–12 November with the arrival of 6,000 fresh Marines as well as the 182nd Regiment, which evened up the numbers. For the next six weeks Japanese and American forces faced each other in an uneasy stalemate.

By now it was not just Japanese troops who were in a sorry state. After four months on *Guadalcanal* the Marines were physically and psychologically shattered; young men were grown old. Many of the Marines were too exhausted to make their way back to the field kitchens to eat. 1st Marine was ravaged by malaria. Cases grew from 239 in September to 1,941 in October and 3,200 in November. Others had contracted dengue fever, jaundice or dysentery.

The First Naval Battle of Guadalcanal: **[Map: 18.4]** After the failure of the 24 October Japanese offensive to recapture Henderson Field, a new attack was planned for November. Again the issue was resupply. Yamamoto was asked for assistance in bringing 7,000 troops of the 38th Infantry in eleven convoy ships. In addition significant quantities of food, munitions and heavy equipment were urgently needed. Yamamoto, convinced for the time being that America's carrier fleet had been destroyed at the *Battle of Santa Cruz* ten days earlier, decided to send two battleships, the *Hiei* and the *Kirishima*, with the intention of bombarding Henderson Field with specially developed fragmentation shells. As ever the aim was to put the American's 'land aircraft carrier,' Henderson Field, out of commission. Vice-Admiral Hiroaki Abe led the Japanese force. In addition to his battleships, he would bring six heavy cruisers, four light cruisers, and sixteen destroyers.

After gathering intelligence of another attempt to take Henderson Field, Halsey prepared a reinforcement task force, Task Force 67, which prepared to leave on 11 November. Even *Enterprise* with one of its elevators stuck in the up position, was rushed back into service. The force, in two groups, was put under the overall command of Rear-Admiral Richmond Turner, with each group led by Rear-Admirals Daniel Callaghan and Norman Scott respectively. Turner put Admiral Callaghan, a few days senior to Rear-Admiral Scott, in local command even though the latter was more experienced particularly given his experience at the *Battle of Cape Esperance*. Turner's forces comprised two battleships, two heavy cruisers, three light cruisers and twelve destroyers. The supply ships and transports, in spite of air attacks from Buin, in the northern *Solomons*, were able to unload their cargoes of food and munitions as well as fresh troops. With news of Abe's approaching surface force, Turner ordered all supply ships to leave *Guadalcanal* by the early evening of 12 November.

Although Callaghan had five ships with the new SG radar he failed to put them in the lead of the column and failed to issue a battle plan to his commanders. In spite of this, radar detected Japanese ships at 1.24 a.m. though the information was slow to reach Callaghan who chose to manage the battle from the bridge rather than the command center. Both forces visually sighted each other at about the same time; it seems that Callaghan had the opportunity to cross the 'T' (the classic and best way to confront an enemy surface force) but failed to give orders in a timely and coherent manner. The result was a confused and pell-mell gun battle. An officer from the *Monssen* described the battle as "a bar room brawl after the lights had been shot out."[61] In the confusion, when Captain Jenkins of the light cruiser USS *Atlanta*, used by Rear-Admiral Scott as his flagship, swung hard left, he received a radio call from Callaghan asking "What are you doing?" Jenkins answered, "Avoiding our own destroyers."[62] From *Guadalcanal* itself, the battle provided a spectacular show for the troops ashore. Private Leckie poetically described the surreal scene before him, "The star shells rose, terrible and red. Giant tracers flashed across the night in orange arches . . . the sea seemed a sheet of polished obsidian on which the warships seemed to have been dropped and were immobilized, centered amid concentric circles like shock waves that form around a stone dropped in mud."[63]

The *Akatsuki*, a *Fubuki* Class destroyer, with its searchlight turned on, became a close quarters target for at least six US ships, was hit repeatedly and blew up. The battle was at such short range that USS *Laffey* came within twenty feet of colliding with the *Hiei*. At this range the battleship *Hiei* could not lower its larger guns while the smaller *Laffey* was able to rake the battleship's taller superstructure. Vice-Admiral Abe was wounded and his chief of staff was killed. Gun-Pointer Richard Hale, noted, "it was so close we could throw hand grenades and hit it."[64] The *Laffey*'s torpedoes struck the *Hiei* but at such short distance that they failed to arm. The unfortunate *Laffey* was then hit and left burning while the USS *O'Bannon* also passed close to the *Hiei* and scored numerous hits. Rear-Admiral Callaghan fared worse. The *Hiei*, along with *Kirishima, Inazuma* and *Ikazuchi* scored repeated hits on Callaghan's flagship USS *San Francisco* and killed him along with most of his senior staff and crew.

By this point Callaghan had already inadvertently killed his putative successor, Rear-Admiral Scott, whose flagship USS *Atlanta*, the inappropriately nicknamed 'Lucky A,' hit by a torpedo, drifted into the *San Francisco*'s line of fire and took nineteen hits from its 8-inch shells. *Atlanta* was scuttled the next morning. USS *Juneau* also took a torpedo hit and the listing light cruiser retired from the battle. The destroyer USS *Barton*, only commissioned on 29 May 1942, lasted for all of seven minutes. After opening fire and letting off four torpedoes, she took a torpedo in the forward fire room and another in the engine room; she broke in two and sank in seconds. Another destroyer, USS *Monssen* was deluged with thirty-seven shells that reduced her to a burning wreck. Meanwhile at 1.58 a.m. the heavy cruiser USS *Portland* took a torpedo in her stern and, with her steering destroyed, spent the night turning in circles. After frantic efforts by her engineers, the *Portland*, nicknamed 'Sweet Pea,' managed to hobble to an anchorage at *Tulagi*.

As dawn broke the destroyer USS *Cushing* was burning and abandoned along with the USS *Monssen*. In the afternoon they sank. The destroyer USS *Aaron Ward* survived albeit being put out of action after receiving a salvo of eight hits. While trying to get a tow in the early morning, the *Aaron Ward* was on the receiving end of second helpings from the crippled Japanese battleship *Hiei* but made her escape after the intervention of attack planes from Henderson Field. Having escaped the clutches of *Ironbottom Sound*, the *Aaron Ward* would get back to *Pearl Harbor*, be repaired and return to action at *Guadalcanal* at the beginning of 1943. However, while on an escort mission to *Savo Island* on 6 April 1943, the destroyer was sunk by Japanese dive-bombers, and after failing to beach itself on *Florida Island*, sank stern first in 200 foot of water, thus joining the thirty other naval skeletons lining the *Sound*.

As for the venerable *Hiei*, launched in 1911 as a battle-cruiser, but reconstructed into a fast battleship just prior to the *Pacific War*, her superstructure had been obliterated from fearsome close combat attacks, which had killed her chief of staff and wounded Rear-Admiral Hiroaki Abe. Like the USS *Portland, Hiei*'s steering had been disabled. At dawn *Hiei* was found turning in a circle to starboard at a speed of five knots leaving her as a sitting duck for Grumman Avengers from Henderson Field. After two torpedo hits from Grumman Avengers, the *Hiei* was scuttled.

Of the thirteen ships dispatched by Vice-Admiral Halsey, apart from Hoover's own ship, USS *Helena*, USS *Fletcher* was the only American ship not to receive a hit. It had been a bloody encounter, considered by many to be the most brutal surface engagement of *World War II*.

Tony Betchik, the Wildcat Crew Chief recalled,

> There were huge naval battles at night. We could see the flashes and see the ships hit . . . there were many prayers on my lips for those poor guys. I can see those flashes of red lighting the sky as they fired, as they hit, and as the ships blew up. It was an astounding sight. The time seemed to stand still you were so engulfed by the spectacle, a spectator. You knew what was happening and that it affected you. But it was spectacular.[65]

Thomas Furlow, a young Marine pilot, described the scene the next morning; USS *Atlanta*, hit by an estimated fifty large caliber shells,

> was sitting there dead in the water and it looked like someone had taken a knife and scraped the ship from one end to the other. The turrets were bent. The damage was terrible. I remember sailors hanging on to all sorts of things offshore. They brought in dozens to the canal: guys with legs missing and everything. . .[66]

Often forgotten in accounts of *Pacific War* sea battles was the appalling effect of shell and torpedo strikes on warships and their crews. On board USS *Sterett*, Perry Hall remembered "Bits of burning bedding smouldered on the bunks, burnt bodies were scattered above the decks, and water poured into a shell hole, just above the waterline, whenever the ship wheeled to port or starboard . . . The stench of burning flesh and powder made breathing difficult."[67]

Why Abe's force retired is unclear. His force had demonstrated yet again that Japanese night training in gunnery and use of torpedoes was vastly superior to their US opponents. However, it should be remembered that his forces were widely scattered and that he himself was wounded.

Next morning, 13 November, the passage between *Savo Island* and *Guadalcanal* was littered with crippled ships and swimming sailors, both American and Japanese. The abandoned *Yudachi* was sunk while the battered *Amatsukaze* made a miraculous escape to *Truk*. *Akatsuki* was also sinking. Meanwhile the tugboat USS *Bobolink* spent the day rescuing US sailors in *Ironbottom Sound* while shooting Japanese swimmers *en passant*.

Departing the *Solomon Islands*, the damaged USS *Juneau*, USS *San Francisco* and USS *Helena* were attacked by *I-26*, the submarine commanded by Minoru Yokata whose torpedo shots had almost sunk the carrier USS *Saratoga* at the end of August. Two torpedoes intended for the *San Francisco* missed their target but scored hits on the *Juneau*. The light cruiser blew up, broke in two and sank in twenty seconds. Fearing further torpedo attacks, the *San Francisco* and *Helena* did not wait to pick up survivors. Out of *Juneau*'s 697 crewmen, 100 survived the sinking, but, after eight days in the water, only ten remained alive with the rest taken by their injuries, heat, exhaustion and sharks. It was later revealed that a report of the missing ship and request for a search was mistakenly left in a file-pending tray for several days. The lucky survivors did not include five brothers. The Sullivans—George, Francis, Joseph, Madison, and Albert— were from Waterloo, Iowa, a town previously best known as the place where depression era bank robber and Dillinger gang member 'Tommy Carroll' was gunned down by FBI agents. After the sinking of the *Juneau*, Halsey relieved Captain Hoover of the *Helena* from command for not going back to rescue the survivors. On reflection Halsey admitted to acting too hastily against a man with a superb combat record. Hoover was reinstated and Halsey apologized and wrote accordingly to the Navy Department to withdraw his charges.

With two light cruisers and four destroyers sunk and two heavy cruisers badly mauled, the *First Naval Battle of Guadalcanal* was a crushing defeat for the US Navy only relieved by Abe's decision not to press the attack further. Some 1,439 American sailors had perished, more than double the fatalities suffered by the Japanese. The dead included two rear-admirals—Callaghan and Scott; curiously they died within minutes of each other and together accounted for two of the three US Admirals to die in combat in *World War II*. When Halsey was awarded his four stars, he removed his two three-star clusters and told an officer, "Send one of these to Mrs. Scott and the other to Mrs. Callaghan. Tell them it was their husband's bravery that got me my new ones."[68]

Abe's forces had also taken a heavy pounding. The *Hiei* became not only the first Japanese battleship sunk in the *Pacific War* but also the first battleship the Japanese Navy had ever lost. The battle cost Japan two destroyers with another two put out of action. Most significantly Abe's force failed in its primary mission to land the transports and to decimate Henderson Field with fragmentation shells.

In spite of the battle and retirement of Abe's forces, Rear-Admiral Raizo Tanaka decided to continue the transport convoy to *Guadalcanal* on the evening of 13 November. They were sanguine about their prospects because, as *Hayashio*'s Commander Tadashi Yamamoto recalled, they "thought that the bombardment groups succeeded in destroying [the American] planes the night before."[69] With the withdrawal of all US naval units, Vice-Admiral Gunichi Mikawa had a free hand to pass down *Ironbottom Sound* with heavy cruisers *Chokai, Kinugasa, Maya* and *Suzuya* as well as light cruisers *Isuzu* and *Tenryu* and six destroyers; Henderson Field was duly bombarded in the early hours of 14 November.

Nevertheless with the Seabees able to repair Henderson Field, the 'Cactus' Air Force was still able to launch attacks on Mikawa's retiring force. Neither had Mikawa and Tanaka counted on the nearby presence of USS *Enterprise*. *Kinugasa* was hit by bombs, which killed 511 of her crew and sank her. The damaged *Maya* needed to retire to Japan to be repaired. In perhaps the most important action of the battle, a force of 18 Dauntless dive-bombers and 7 TBF Avengers sank 7 out of 11 of Tanaka's transports. Survivors from these ships were picked up by the escort destroyers and taken to *Shortland*. Crucial Japanese troop reinforcement of *Guadalcanal* had been thwarted. If the *First Naval Battle of Guadalcanal* had been a great naval victory for Japan, its aftermath was another strategic failure. Once again a Japanese Naval victory had not led to any significant degradation of US aerial or military strength on *Guadalcanal*.

The Second Naval Battle of Guadalcanal: [Map: 18.5] In the aftermath of the battle, a furious Yamamoto sacked Abe for his failure to follow up his victory and forced him into retirement. Vice-Admiral Nobutake Kondo, commanding the Second Fleet at *Truk*, was ordered to form a new surface force to pursue the original mission to destroy Henderson Field. As well as the battleship *Kirishima*, the Kondo Force that headed toward *Guadalcanal* on 13 November included heavy cruisers *Atago* and *Takao*, light cruisers *Nagara* and *Sendai* plus nine destroyers. The *Kirishima* was a vintage *World War I* battle-cruiser designed by the British naval architect George Thurston. It was rebuilt as a fully-fledged battleship in 1927 and again as a fast battleship in 1934. Kondo took *Atago* as his flagship.

Meanwhile Vice-Admiral 'Bull' Halsey, now low on available ships, as usual took an aggressive approach by sending his brand new battleships USS *Washington* and USS *South Dakota*, which were part of the USS *Enterprise* carrier group, to confront the new Japanese threat. With their 16-inch guns (compared to the 14-inch guns of the *Kirishima*) they were more than a match for their Japanese counterparts, but suffered from the relative inexperience of their crews. Under the command of Rear-Admiral Willis Lee Jr., they arrived with four escort destroyers in *Ironbottom Sound* on the evening of 14 November. At 11.00 p.m. radar picked up the arriving Japanese force at some 20,000-yard distance.

However, the US screening destroyers took a fearsome beating from the much more accurate night fire of the Japanese and USS *Walk* and USS *Preston* were sunk within minutes. Meanwhile the destroyer USS *Benham* lost her bow to a torpedo and was forced to retire while USS *Gwin* was hit in her engine room. The *Benham* was later scuttled. In their flaming retreat, the advancing *South Dakota*, compromised by electrical problems caused by mistakes made by her chief engineer, was lit up by Japanese searchlights and attracted fire from Kondo's main force including the *Kirishima*. Taking hits from twenty-five medium and one large caliber shell, the *South Dakota*, with no radar and effectively blind in a night battle, turned away from the battle at 12.17 a.m. on 15 November. As Captain Thomas Gatch's post-battle report outlined, the loss of electrical power and radar was devastating, "The psychological effect on the officers and crew was most depressing . . . gave all hands a feeling of being blindfolded."[70]

Following behind *South Dakota, Washington*, largely unobserved, tracked the *Kirishima* with her SG radar, whose technical capabilities were better used by Rear-Admiral Lee than his late predecessor Rear-Admiral Callaghan. Lee used his superior 16-inch guns to telling effect on the *Kirishima*, scoring hits with 9 main battery shells and 40 5-inch shells. One of the hits jammed *Kirishima*'s rudder and she started to circle out of control.

On *Tulagi*, downed Wildcat fighter pilot, Jake Stub, who was waiting to be transported back to *Guadalcanal*, took up a grandstand view thanks to a pair of binoculars left at an elevated lookout post:

> I would estimate that I was twenty miles away . . . Flare shells went up and illuminated a portion of the area. You could see the shells clearly. They were red hot when they left the guns and looked liked glowing tennis balls almost floating across the sky. The Japanese battleship *Kurishima* [*Kirishima*] started burning, so I could see it very clearly.[71]

The heavy cruisers *Atago* (Admiral Kondo's flagship) and *Takao* also took hits. When Lee withdrew *Washington* to the northeast, Kondo ordered his ships to follow and tried to land torpedo hits without success; at 1.00 a.m. Admiral Kondo ordered his ships to reform and retire north from the battle. By 1.30 a.m. on 15 November, the action was over.

Besiegers Become the Besieged: *Kirishima* and the destroyer *Ayanami* were scuttled an hour and a half later. Meanwhile Tanaka's remaining transports beached themselves at Tassafaronga on *Guadalcanal* at 4.00 a.m. while their accompanying destroyers raced back up the 'Slot' to get out of range of Henderson Field. Only a few thousand of the 38th Army's reinforcement troops reached their destination. The failure of Abe and then Kondo's mission doomed Japanese attempts to retake Henderson Field.

From now on Japanese troops had to be sustained by fast destroyers' 'Tokyo Express' down the 'Slot'; it was never enough to sustain a Japanese ground force that was losing fifty men a day from malnutrition and disease. On 12 December the Japanese Navy, suffering badly from the attrition of the naval battles of the 'Slot,' requested the abandonment of *Guadalcanal*. Withdrawal of the Japanese Army was approved by Imperial General HQ and the Emperor on 31 December; it came with a decision to rebase the line of defense on *New Georgia* in the central *Solomon Islands*.

For the US Navy, the attempt to scuttle USS *Benham* highlighted the weakest aspect of their combat performance. Of the four torpedoes aimed at the stationary *Benham*, the first exploded prior to contact, the second missed to bow, the third ran wild and the fourth missed to stern. The Mark XIV torpedo was a disaster and its performance was shown in even starker contrast to the Japanese torpedoes, which the Japanese Navy, unlike the US Navy, considered their main strike weapon. Combined with their failure to improve night gunnery to Japanese standards, the US Navy was perhaps fortunate not to suffer worse in the battles of the 'Slot.' In general the US Navy was tactically outfought even though, with the development of SG radar, they should have won tactical advantage. Rear-Admiral Lee was at least realistic when he concluded, "We . . . realized then and it should not be forgotten now, that our entire superiority was due almost entirely to our possession of radar. Certainly we have no edge on the Japs in experience, skill, training or performance or personnel."[72]

The importance of propaganda was such that news of the death of the five Sullivan boys and the story of incompetence that shrouded the terrible human losses on the *Juneau*, was covered up. By contrast Rear-Admiral Dan Callaghan, the dead Admiral, in spite of his colossal mistakes on the first night of the battle that contributed to his own death and that of his colleague Rear-Admiral Scott, became a newspaper hero who was posthumously awarded a Congressional Medal of Honor.

In the three days of battle covering the *First and Second Naval Battles of Guadalcanal*, America had lost two cruisers and seven destroyers with numbers of other ships damaged; 1,732 US sailors were killed. Meanwhile the Imperial Japanese Navy had lost two battleships, one heavy cruiser and three destroyers. About 2,000 Japanese sailors were lost. In the air battles Japan lost sixty-four aircraft to thirty-six US aircraft. Most importantly however all eleven of its troop transports had been lost. Almost all the 3,000 troops of the Naval Landing Force had drowned and half of the 38th Division had been lost. On hearing of the fate of Tanaka's transports, a jubilant Vandegrift concluded, "We've got the bastards licked!"[73] After victory in the two *Naval Battles of Guadalcanal*, Halsey reflected, "The sun began to rise on me." The more prosaic official report concluded, "The sea and air power of the Japanese in the *Guadalcanal* area was decisively smashed."[74] But after disappointment with Rear-Admiral Kinkaid for being too conservative at *Santa Cruz* and *Guadalcanal*, Halsey replaced him with Rear-Admiral Ted Sherman. Halsey's treatment of Kinkaid rankled and may have contributed to their mutual misunderstanding and bad feeling at the later *Battle of Leyte Gulf*. Kinkaid after a year at sea was sent home for a rest. Meanwhile Halsey's popularity in the American media reached new heights. Halsey was profiled on the front cover of *Time* magazine on 30 November; the article was titled, *"Hit Hard, Hit Fast, Hit Often."*[75]

President Roosevelt mourned for his friend Rear-Admiral Callaghan but was upbeat about the results of the battle and tentatively announced, "It would seem that the turning point in this war has at last been reached."[76] It helped that November saw good news for the Allies with victories at the *Battle of El Alamein* in North Africa, at the *Battle of Stalingrad* and in New Guinea. The result of the *Naval Battles of Guadalcanal* was a tactical victory for Japan but a strategic victory for the US Navy. The strenuous Naval efforts to reinforce the Japanese troops surrounding Henderson Field had failed. In a development reminiscent of the great Athenian disaster in their military expedition to capture Syracuse in *Sicily* in 415 BC—on *Guadalcanal*, the Japanese besiegers would now become the besieged.

19 Battles of Buna-Gona-Sanananda: MacArthur's Lies and Neglect

[November 1942–February 1943]

[Maps: 19.1, 19.2]

MacArthur's Failures of Strategy, Planning and Supply: [**Map: 19.1**] By November 1942, having battled Japanese forces back across the Owen Stanley Range, Australian troops now came up against their strongholds, at Buna, Gona and Sanananda. It was from here that Major-General Horii had launched his campaign to wrest control of Port Moresby and eastern New Guinea. [**See Chapter 15: Battles of the Kokoda Trail: Aussies Triumphant**] The crushing defeat inflicted on Japan by Australian troops on the Kokoda Trail must have boosted Allied hopes of an easy victory against a demoralised enemy. MacArthur's chief of intelligence Lieutenant-Colonel Charles Willoughby predicted that Buna, Gona and Sanananda were lightly defended with fewer than 1,500 soldiers; in fact there were 6,500 Japanese defenders under the command of Horii's replacement, Major-General Oda. They had every intention of fighting for and holding their heavily fortified garrisons, which were regarded as essential assets in denying the Allies airfields that could threaten Rabaul. For the first time in the New Guinea Campaign, US troops would join the Australians who had fought their way over the Owen Stanley Mountains. The Americans were in for a shock that would force them to re-evaluate the fighting quality of their antipodean allies' troops, whom they had hitherto treated with barbed criticism if not derision.

The three semi-independent strongholds were able to remain connected by the work of the Japanese troops who manned barges and motorized landing craft that shifted troops, supplies and munitions between the garrisons, as they were needed. Complacency due to poor intelligence was not MacArthur's team's only mistake. A further intelligence mistake was the failure of Willoughby to supply available photographs of the area to the local commanders. Eichelberger, who was appointed as MacArthur's corps commander during the battle, was appalled to discover that not even his Corps HQ had been provided with photographs.

The area surrounding the three coastal strongholds was swampland full of shoulder-high jungle scrub and intersected by numerous creeks. On drier parts stood tall six-foot high razor-sharp kunai grass. In some areas there were overgrown coconut plantations. In these varied terrains the digging of foxholes served to protect the troops but little more. Not only did they immediately fill with water but they provided no outlook above the surrounding dense vegetation. George Johnson described a foot soldier's life at Buna-Gona thus: "They live almost perpetually in a dripping green twilight, hiding by day amid the dank palms and underbrush and twisting vines and creepers; moving by night through an eerie, moist blackness into which the light of tropical stars seldom penetrates."[1]

Furthermore the US troops and their officers lacked experience in jungle action. Little advance intelligence or planning had been done to ascertain knowledge of the conditions in which their soldiers would have to fight. MacArthur's chief of staff, Major-General Sutherland was certain that Japanese defenses consisted of light field entrenchments and noted that there was "little indication of an attempt to make a strong stand against the Allied advance."[2] When they launched their attack on 19 November, troops who had been in jovial spirits expecting an easy victory, were completely shocked by the ferocity of the Japanese defense. As the Marines were discovering on *Guadalcanal*, the Japanese soldiers were as brave in defense as in attack; their acceptance of hardship, their ability to fight through it, and their bravery individually and collectively was unmatched. A US soldier at Buna commented, "They are tough babies all right, but I guess part of the toughness comes from them not being able to go any place else; they just stay there and die."[3] In deference to the skilfully constructed Japanese defenses, Allied soldiers were soon on their bellies crawling through the dense undergrowth and glutinous mud.

US logistics were not helped by the lack of naval support available to the Allied forces. In Washington Admiral King, who had been a fervent opponent of MacArthur's appointment as commander in chief of the South West Pacific Forces, focused his resources on the build-up of a big blue-water navy at *Hawaii*. In March 1943, when 'MacArthur's navy' as it was derogatorily referred to in US Navy ranks, was given the title Seventh Fleet, it consisted of just two remaining Australian cruisers and one light US cruiser. By contrast Halsey's Third Fleet consisted of five carriers, six battleships, and thirteen cruisers. As well as a paucity of naval resources allocated to MacArthur, Admiral Nimitz insisted that the ships assigned to him remained under naval command. The divided command made relations extremely fractious, first with Vice-Admiral Herbert Leary and then with Vice-Admiral Arthur Carpender who replaced him in September 1942. The situation was further complicated by the need for the Navy's forces in the *Southwest Pacific* to support the Marines' operations on *Guadalcanal*—a greater priority in Washington than the remote southeast corner of New Guinea where the Australians were operating.

The result was that MacArthur's forces, simultaneously fighting at Buna, were starved of naval support. *Matériel* to the Buna-Gona region had to be supplied in small craft provided by a Dutch maritime company. In addition the US Navy, concerned about the reach of Japanese aircraft from Rabaul, was loath to risk its ships in providing naval bombardment against Japanese positions at Buna. MacArthur noted ruefully, "The attitude of the Navy in regard to destroyers appears to avoid risk at a time when all the services should give a maximum of cooperation to defeat the enemy."[4]

Japan's Bunker Defenses and Problems of Supply: **[Diagram: 19.2]** For the sick and injured Japanese troops at Kokoda Hospital, a stark choice faced them. Having run out of stretchers, patients somehow had to make their way back to the coast, otherwise orders were given for them to be shot if they were incapable or unwilling to commit suicide. The plan worked. At Giruwa—located on the coast between Sanananda and Gona—the 500-bed hospital soon overflowed with 2,000 soldiers, arriving in twos and threes, often with only the clothes they stood in. There was little to welcome them. Food was running short and a report by medical officer Lieutenant Fukunobu Okubo revealed that the hospital had run out of morphine. Surgical instruments had rusted in the humidity. Canvas tents had rotted.

The Japanese Army, albeit denied the luxury of adequate logistical supply had nevertheless constructed a series of bunkers using coconut logs and fifty-gallon drums full of sand topped with ammunition boxes full of earth. Above that were *kapok* (natural fibrous down) mattresses topped by soil and then rice-bags filled with earth. The Japanese defenders were thus well dug in to heavily constructed pillboxes with firing slits for machine guns. The entire ensemble was then camouflaged to the extent that attackers were virtually on top of the pillboxes before they could see them. It was later found that their roofs were usually three to four feet thick with a front wall six feet thick. Larger bunkers could be forty feet in length or as small as six feet in length and, although they were usually manned with a machine gun, were largely used for troop protection during artillery or air bombardment. They were interlocked with 'crawl-entrenchments' and firing pits that could be quickly filled with troops to give withering cross fusillades of fire on advancing troops. Bunkers and entrenchments were similarly expertly camouflaged. Furthermore the garrisons were set out in a large triangle with short lines of communication, which allowed troops to be shifted rapidly from one area to another. As they had demonstrated in attack, the Japanese commanders showed both invention and sophistication in their organization of defense. When the Americans probed forward to make their first attacks, US engineer Major Porter observed, "Our troops were pinned down everywhere by extremely effective fire. It was dangerous even to show a finger from behind one's cover . . ."[5]

Meanwhile Lieutenant-General George Kenney, US commander of the South West Pacific Area's Fifth Air Force, assured MacArthur, "Tanks and heavy artillery can be reserved for the battlefields of Europe and Africa. They have no place in jungle warfare."[6] Kenney convinced him that his air support would suffice to soften up Japanese defensive positions. The result was that field commander Major-General Edwin Harding left the US 32nd Division's thirty-six 4.1-inch howitzers and twelve 6.1-inch back at base in Australia. It proved a serious mistake.

Kenney's Air Force began to soften up the defenders at Buna in November. On 16 November along with the Allied Air Force (AAF) they dropped two 2,000 pounders and 319 other bombs. It was the heaviest air attack that the Japanese troops on New Guinea had yet faced. Noboru Wada of the 5th Yokosuka Special Landing Party noted that it was "The most terrific bombing ever experienced since our landing at Buna two months ago. On several occasions I thought my end had come."[7] But in spite of the heavy aerial bombardment, Kenney's attacks made little impression on the bunkered Japanese positions.

American troops, trained in the Australian outback, were completely unprepared for the conditions and type of warfare required of them. Even their uniforms, which their commanders had ordered dyed dark green, were hopelessly inadequate for the task; the dyes closed the uniform material's natural ventilation so that sweat was trapped inside, in conditions where temperatures rarely fell below ninety degrees and humidity was a constant 85 percent. Ten inches of rain could fall on a daily basis. There was a good reason why New Guinea was the world's second largest island but one of its most sparsely inhabited. Later MacArthur would write that the jungle was "as tough and tenacious an enemy as the Japanese"[8] as if it was an insightful revelation; sadly for the troops who fought in the three-pronged *Battles for Buna, Gona and Sanananda*, MacArthur's failure ever to visit the front meant that the conditions in which they had to fight were never recognized at the time. Unfortunately for the Australian and American troops the revelation of the dire fighting conditions came as a result of their bitter tribulations in the jungle around Buna, in part caused by the gross negligence of MacArthur and his senior commanders.

Unlike the Australians who had to march the Kokoda Trail, sometimes twice if they participated in the original retreat, the US 32nd Division, led by Major-General Edwin Harding, had the luxury of being flown over the Owen Stanley Mountains. Only the US 2nd Battalion 126th Infantry walked the Kokoda Trail. Sergeant Paul Lutjens wrote in his diary, "Most of us have dysentery. Boys are falling out and dropping back with fever. Continual downpour of rain . . . Bully beef makes us sick. We seem to climb straight up for hours, then down again. God, will it never end?"[9] For most of the US 32nd Division GIs, untrained in jungle warfare, the conditions of combat came as a rude shock. But at least they were acclimatized

Just as the Japanese had suffered from stretched supply lines as they approached Port Moresby along the Kokoda Trail in the other direction, so the American and Australian forces at Buna-Gona suffered from the Allies' inadequate logistical capabilities. Soldiers would frequently have to share their already inadequate C-Ration packs. Tents were in short supply and soldiers spent most days and nights drenched by constant downpours. As well as artillery, troops lacked flame-throwers and grenade launchers. Airdrops were weather-dependent and unreliable in their accuracy, as were bombing raids on Japanese positions. Poor communication and lack of reliable maps meant that Allied aircraft sometimes bombed their own troops. Then there was the enemy. Near the plantation a brief firefight ended with two Australian soldiers being captured and then executed by medical officer, Captain Kato. Concerning the problems of supply, Captain H. T. 'Bert' Kienzle, an officer of the Australian New Guinea Administrative Unit (ANGAU) gave acute reflections on the peculiarity of the problems,

> . . . with limited supply of carriers available, maintenance of supplies was going to be impossible along this route without the aid of droppings by plane. A carrier carrying only foodstuffs consumes his load in 13 days and if he

carries food supplies for a soldier it means six days supply for both soldier and carrier. This does not allow for the porterage of arms, ammunition, equipment, medical stores, ordnance, mail and dozens of other items needed to wage war, carried on the backs of men. The track to Kokoda takes eight days, so the maintenance of supplies is a physical impossibility without large-scale co-operation of plane droppings.[10]

Although well prepared in their defenses, Japanese troops also suffered. Like the Allied troops in their foxholes, Japanese troops would have to eat, sleep, urinate and defecate in waterlogged hideouts. Hunkered down in their bunkers, sometimes for days on end, Japanese troops had to live in foot-deep water. It was not unknown for Japanese troops to drown in their sleep. To guard against this many would sleep propped up in a sitting position. Inevitably jungle diseases were rampant on both sides. Food was problematic. Although supply by submarine continued until Christmas Day 1942, food was in short supply for Japanese troops from the beginning of the battle. The 2,500 fresh troops who arrived by destroyer from Rabaul on 17 November were soon hungry. On the same day that the reinforcements arrived, a Japanese machine gunner on the front line of the Allied attacks that had begun the day before, noted in his typically food-obsessed diary, "Our food is completely gone. We are eating tree bark and grass"; two days later he observed, "In other units there are men eating the flesh of dead Australians. There is nothing to eat."[11] Soldiers were forced to eat grass, bark, even caked earth, which destroyed their digestive systems and often made them unable to eat when food did become available: some Japanese soldiers would suddenly cough blood and die.

The Battles of Buna-Gona-Sanananda: The new troops brought by the destroyer *Makigumo* were soon in action. Private Seiichi Uchiyama, who had fought in *Hong Kong* and then spent eight months in *Sumatra* was in combat almost immediately. He recorded a "fierce hand grenade battle with enemy twenty meters away in the jungle. Horiguchi was wounded. I dragged him to the rear and became a machine gunner."[12] In the fighting that followed Uchiyama's section lost three killed and two wounded. His own section commander was killed as well as two others in the platoon.

On 19 November bad weather stopped virtually all flights out of Port Moresby. The US supply situation was soon critical. While the Americans had enough ammunition, reserves of food were almost depleted. In response to the crisis, Lieutenant-General Kenney's technicians came up with an aerial supply system that did not require his pilots to see the drop zone. A radio compass was designed that could lock on to a radio beacon below. From now on pilots were able to deliver 'sight unseen.' It was a development that significantly advanced the Allies' ability to conduct aggressive jungle operations in the months ahead. However, in the short term drops did not improve and, on 22 November, C-47 transports circled overhead and proceeded to drop supplies of which only 5 percent were recovered. Most of the food drop was picked up by Japanese troops—manna from heaven. The 25th Brigade diary described it as "one of the worst displays by the Air Force in the campaign."[13]

When Harding's first attack stalled, on 20 November, MacArthur had ordered him to attack saying, "All columns will be driven through to objectives regardless of losses."[14] Buna had to be taken that day. Failure left MacArthur apoplectic. On 21 November, he again ordered "Take Buna today at all costs."[15] Repeated orders for Major-General Harding to accomplish this task appeared to take no account of the mounting evidence of significantly greater Japanese troop numbers than MacArthur's intelligence officers had estimated. Harding admitted that he was facing "a catastrophe of the first magnitude."[16] For the GIs, the fighting terrain and conditions were a complete shock. "Tommy guns . . . were full of muck and dirt," complained one soldier, "even the M1s fired well only for the first clip, and then jammed because clips taken from belts were wet and full of muck from the swamp."[17] The horror of the action was recalled by Lieutenant Robert Odell, a 126th Infantry platoon leader: "Everywhere men cursed, shouted and screamed. Order followed order. Brave men led and others followed. Cowards crouched in the grass, frightened out of their skins."[18]

Japanese fire was intense. Captain Cattens, on 20–21 November, led a flanking operation to attack the Japanese artillery blocking the road to Sanananda. He ran into a wall of fire. Lieutenant Stewart Blakiston later described the pounding, which they had had to withstand;

> When we first occupied our little defense position, we were hemmed in by jungle. When we left, it looked like a sports field. Every blade of grass had been levelled and all the scrub and trees had been cut down by machine gun fire . . . Sometimes the Japanese would circle our defenses with their gunfire like Red Indians attacking a wagon train in the old wild Western films. How any of us survived that day defies imagination. Some of us almost cried with relief when we got out.[19]

Of Cattens' 90 soldiers, 31 were killed, 36 wounded and only 23 were physically unscathed. Five of his ten officers alone were killed in the first attack. The lack of progress was not for want of trying. On the same day Major-General Harding called for air strikes to support his attempted advance. As Major-General Herbert Blakeley recalled,

> The air attack, by A-20s [Douglas Havoc] and B-25s [North American Mitchell], came in around 1600; it was not a success. Most of the planes could not find the target area; one flight dropped its bombs in the sea, and one B-25 got a direct hit on Companies B and C of the 128th,

> killing six, wounding twelve, and seriously affecting the
> will to fight of the whole battalion. The Japanese positions
> were virtually untouched and the attacks against them
> were easily repulsed.[20]

By 23 November it had become increasingly apparent that tanks and artillery were essential to prise out the Japanese and to enable any movement against their positions. Barely any advance had been made by 25th Brigade, which over the previous four days had suffered sixty men killed, three missing and 141 wounded. A day of air attacks was ordered on 24 November along with constant mortar bombardment. Eighty bomber sorties were flown to Buna, Gona or Sanananda. The sound was impressive and a Japanese officer reported, "Today's bombing was so terrific I did not feel as if I was alive."[21] However, even Kenney's massed aerial bombardment failed to penetrate the prepared Japanese defenses. Realizing their earlier mistakes, airlifts over the Owen Stanleys brought the first disassembled artillery pieces. However, the 126th Regiment's artillery companies did not arrive until 27 November and even thereafter munitions supply problems continued. By the end of five days of fighting I Corp's troops had been reduced dramatically in condition. Major-General Harding reported,

> The troops were half-starved. Most of them had been
> living on short rations for weeks and their food intake
> since the fighting began had averaged about a third of a C
> ration per day—just enough to sustain life. They were
> shaggy and bearded and their clothes were ragged. Their
> feet were swollen and in bad shape. Their shoes, which
> had shrunk in the wet, often had to be cut away so that the
> troops could even get their feet into them.[22]

The Japanese Air Force flying out of Rabaul had managed to cut supply by sea and the airlift of supplies over the Owen Stanley Mountains was inadequate even when weather conditions allowed planes to fly. As Flying Officer Ken Dineen recalled, "Flying conditions were always adventurous because of the tremendous cloud formation over the Owen Stanleys . . . As the 'gap' through which we had to fly [from Port Moresby] to reach Buna and Gona was frequently closed by clouds. . . many operational flights had to be cancelled."[23] Dineen further recorded that he "was appalled to see the condition of our troops arriving from the Owen Stanleys. They all seemed to be riddled with malaria, and suffering from malnutrition."[24] Meanwhile the sending of supply ships was still considered too dangerous because of the strength of Japanese air cover from Rabaul. Kenney was reporting that his transport planes were "bringing back loads of shell shocked troops" while Australia's Lieutenant-General Sir Thomas Blamey suggested that, instead of US soldiers, it might be better to send battle-trained Australians who "would fight."[25] It was "a bitter pill for General MacArthur to swallow"[26] noted Lieutenant-General Kenney who was present for the lunch at MacArthur's government mansion in Port Moresby at which Blamey had criticized the performance of the US 32nd Infantry. The 'Red Arrows,' as they were known, traced their roots back to the famed Iron Brigade in the *American Civil War* [1861–1865]. Warrant Officer Paul Rogers who observed the scene noted that Blamey thoroughly enjoyed MacArthur's discomfort. It was 'pay-back' time for the Australians whose efforts at the *Battle of Kokoda Trail* had been derided by American officers and their troops. "Now it was our turn to rub salt into the wound,"[27] noted an Australian soldier.

While it was clear that MacArthur and the senior commanders were out of touch with what kind of equipment was required to tackle the Imperial Japanese Army's thoroughly thought out defense emplacements, it was also true that the nature of the fighting and terrain had come as a severe shock to US infantry battalions more used to the climate and countryside in Wisconsin and Michigan from where they had been recruited. The 32nd Division's GIs had quickly become demoralized to the extent that even simple survival disciplines such as gun maintenance were found wanting. Basic discipline disintegrated. Men were even digging their fox-holes using helmets and bare hands because they had misplaced their personal issue of entrenchment tools; this item was almost as important as a gun in terms of survival in the field. On the ground, officers were just as poor as their troops, failing to regulate their troops attention to care of equipment, clothing, disease prevention and most importantly supply of regular sustenance. By 1 December, ten days after the fighting began, 492 American GIs had been killed or wounded with little advance to show for it.

In spite of the appalling conditions and the gruesome fighting, GIs enjoyed moments of humor. At the end of November, Chaplain Father Dzienis left his dugout to find the recently constructed 'two-hole' outside—only to be sent scurrying inside when a salvo from Japanese destroyers landed nearby. Father Dzienis, his pants still round his ankles was "as mad as a hornet" and thundered, "To Hell with the Geneva Conventions. Give me a pistol."[28]

An intensely frustrated MacArthur decided on 29 November to relieve the 'under-performing' Major-General Harding. MacArthur appointed US I Corps' Major-General Robert Eichelberger, telling him,

> Bob, I'm putting you in command at Buna. Relieve Harding . . . I want you to remove all officers who won't fight. Relieve regimental and battalion commanders; if necessary, put sergeants in charge of battalions and corporals in charge of companies—anyone who will fight. Time is of the essence . . . Bob, I want you to take Buna, or not come back alive . . . And that goes for your chief of staff, too.[29]

On 30 November Blamey, wallowing in *schadenfreude*, reported that the Americans "outnumber the Japs by at least five to one on the Buna front but to date have made no progress . . ."[30]

Robert Eichelberger, born in Urbana, Ohio on 9 March 1886 was the son of a farmer turned lawyer. Through the influence of his father's former law partner, William Warnock, who had become a Congressman, Eichelberger entered the US Military Academy at West Point in June 1905. He was a modest student and graduated sixty-eighth out of 103 in the class of 1909; an unusually distinguished group that produced twenty-eight starred generals including General George Patton. Eichelberger's modest academic performance did not diminish a massive ego, albeit better concealed than MacArthur's, which drove his career.

Eichelberger achieved rapid promotion after winning a Distinguished Service Cross for bravery at the *Battle of Novitskaya* [1919] while serving with the American Expeditionary Force Siberia, which had been sent to Russia to support the 'White' Russians against the communists. Postings followed in Mexico, the Philippines and China where he set up an intelligence office in Peking and Tientsin. In 1924 he attended the General Staff College at Fort Leavenworth; seated alphabetically he sat next to Major Dwight Eisenhower. Also placed in his graduating class was Joseph Stilwell, later to become known by his nickname 'Vinegar Joe.' In 1940 he was about to be made Stilwell's deputy when he was suddenly picked out to be Superintendent of the United States Military Academy at West Point. Here he downgraded traditional occupations such as horse-riding and introduced up-to-date instruction in field combat. Eichelberger speeded up the pace of graduation to meet the increased demands of US military mobilization from mid-1940.

For his reputation and career, it did Eichelberger no harm that he recruited Earl 'Red' Blaik to coach the Academy's football team producing the most successful period of its history. MacArthur was a staunch football fan and Blaik had been one of his cadets. Marshall too took note. Eichelberger was promoted to Major-General in July 1941 and at the outbreak of war immediately applied for active command. Marshall plucked him out of an expected career in Europe where he had been designated to lead Operation TORCH (the Anglo-American invasion of French North Africa). It was thought that Eichelberger's training in amphibious warfare in *Chesapeake Bay* would stand him in good stead as MacArthur's head of Corps. Having worked previously with MacArthur, it was a role that Eichelberger approached with not a little trepidation. However, it was an opportunity for a man of formidable ambition, who even described himself as a "man possessed."

Meanwhile in Rabaul Major-General Yamagata's HQ staff had prepared a remarkably accurate account of the status of MacArthur's forces:

> The enemy's land forces, taking advantage of our army's reversals, is advancing ... now face Buna, Giruwa [Sanananda] and Basabua [Gona]. They are at close grips with our forces and persistently carry out small attacks. The enemy air force, having established air superiority, is daily bombing and strafing our army bases ... However,

it can be presumed that the enemy is having difficulty with rear supplies and is suffering exhaustion.[31]

Arrival of General Eichelberger and a Change in Fortunes: Major-General Eichelberger, on arriving at Buna to replace Harding, true to his immense ego, immediately engaged in furious argument with his commanders accusing them of poor tactics and of being cowards who had been 'licked.' Eichelberger's intelligence officer reported that the GIs' morale and discipline were shot. He found the troops "dazed by the hazards of swamp and jungle."[32] "The troops were deplorable," he wrote, "They wore dirty long beards. Their clothing was in rags. Their shoes were uncared for, or worn out."[33] Most senior officers and battalion commanders were sacked. Unfair perhaps, given the poor planning of MacArthur, Blamey and the senior command, but probably the only choice given that American morale had completely collapsed. Eichelberger noted, "There was no front line discipline of any kind. There was never any idea of the men going forward."[34] However, he did not underestimate the task at hand. "When the stink of the swamp hit our nostrils," recalled Eichelberger, "we knew that we . . . were prisoners of geography."[35]

Eichelberger was not the only soldier unhappy with his troops. The inexperience of raw troops was a problem that afflicted both sides. Company diarist Lieutenant Yamasaki wrote on 28 November, "In this trench filled with dead bodies, the following thoughts occurred to me. It is difficult to wage war with conscripts with two months' training . . . the men don't know the officers. I cannot trust the men, and wonder if I can carry out operations in this situation."[36] The next day an attack by seventy B-17s and P-40s scored a direct bomb hit on Yamasaki's HQ and killed him. His body was never found.

For new commanders good luck and timing is often essential. Eichelberger profited from the latter. By mid-November the efficacy of Allied air attacks on Japanese supply convoys to Buna had increased markedly. The number of available aircraft was more or less the same but Lieutenant-General Kenney, with his characteristic energy, had, by reorganizing supply and maintenance at airfields, been able to make his assets work harder. By the end of November, Kenney was sending twice as many aircraft against convoys compared to two months earlier. In a switch in tactics, aircraft were assigned away from attacking well-constructed bunkers to targeting rear areas where more effective damage could be done. With the likelihood of fresh troops and supplies rapidly diminishing, Japanese officers in desperation began to organize suicide squads and *banzai* charges. Some soldiers did not wait for the *banzai* charges and committed suicide. Death was often preferable to living with the ever-present smell of putrescent flesh that forced men to wear gas masks. Thus Corporal Tanaka wrote a final letter to his friends, "Today Battalion Commander Yamamoto and subordinates organized a suicide squad. Guard leader Fujita and four men are included. Death is the ultimate honor."[37] It was a pattern of self-destruction in the Japanese Army's rear-guard actions that would be played out again and again over the coming years.

As soon as Eichelberger recognized the deficiencies in supply to his troops, he replaced his logistics officer with one who would ignore all protocols to get the food and medicines that his men needed. Kenney proved a more than reliable partner in increasing air supply. Eichelberger generously remarked, "Both Australian and American ground forces would have perished without 'George Kenney's Air.' "[38] On his most productive day, 14 December 1942, Kenney managed to ship 178 tons of supply from Port Moresby to Popondetta, near Buna. Importantly Eichelberger quickly came to understand the importance of preventing malaria infection that had decimated and enervated his troops. The more effective Atrazine replaced Quinine, though it was too late to prevent malaria's already catastrophic impact on the health of Allied troops. Even the well-fed General Eichelberger lost one pound in weight for every day he spent in the jungle over the next month. GIs returning from the front line were unrecognizable: "thin, bearded men with hollow cheeks and the marks of strain and pain around their eyes."[39]

If life was difficult for Eichelberger's men it was certainly worse for the Japanese. Lieutenant Kiyoie who had landed with the fresh troops had assumed that further reinforcements would soon follow. Theft of food by starving troops was now rife. Discipline began to disintegrate. All the while new troops and supplies expected daily never arrived. A message sent to the Chief of Staff of the Eighth Army at Rabaul was indicative of the increasing despair. "When we advanced with the reinforcements, we lost the chance because of the small support of the air force, and are in a very difficult situation. Ammunition and food are almost gone and fighting power is very low."[40] On 30 November, Corporal Tanaka, a military policeman wrote his farewell letter:

> . . . it is now merely a case of waiting for death. Most of the officers have been killed, so there isn't much we can do. The garrison of 600 has been reduced to 200 . . . We have not eaten for over a week and have no energy. As soldiers, we are ready to die gallantly . . . Take care of yourself and do your best. Excuse my hasty writing.[41]

Eichelberger spent the beginning of December reorganizing his troops. However, it was the individual bravery of a 'Red Arrows' platoon sergeant, Herman Bottcher, ironically a German veteran of the Loyalist International Brigade in Spain, who made the first significant breakthrough on 5 December. Bottcher was not even a US citizen. He cut a path through virgin forest and outflanked the Japanese positions. Leading a frontal attack with grenade and machine gun, he and his squad overwhelmed the Japanese troop positions and broke through to the beach, thereafter named the 'Bottcher Salient,' thereby isolating the enemy positions. A machine gun was set up and he mowed down Japanese troops as they waded toward his position from east and west. Eichelberger's staff made strenuous efforts to supply his position and when they asked him what he needed he yelled, "Pants. For God's sake, General, pants!"[42] His clothes were rotting. On one occasion, Major-General Eichelberger, crawling there on his belly, visited Bottcher's platoon during the night and took turns with his GIs to take shots at Japanese snipers in the trees—not something that one could have imagined Major-General Sutherland doing. Bottcher's daring did wonders for the morale of the 32nd Division.

Bottcher, who was later killed in the Philippines, was credited with killing 120 Japanese soldiers and won two Distinguished Service Cross medals, a battlefield promotion to captain and most importantly for him, American citizenship. Nevertheless advances against enemy positions at Buna-Gona-Sanananda were painfully slow over the next few weeks. Fighting frequently ended with hand-to-hand combat. An Australian infantryman complained, "Those bastards fight to the last. They keep fighting until your bayonet sinks into them."[43]

It was the Australians who achieved the first major success in overrunning Gona in mid-December. On 9 December the last fortified Japanese position at Gona was taken. Lieutenant-Colonel Ralph Honner sent back a brief message, "GONA'S GONE!"[44] Buna however remained obstinately resistant. On 13 December, MacArthur wrote to Eichelberger noting, "Time is fleeting and our dangers increase with its passage . . . however splendid and electrifying your presence has proven; remember that your mission is to take Buna."[45]

By mid-December, the remaining Japanese troops knew that they were doomed and that there would be no relief from Rabaul and no rescue. Surrender though was not considered. A Japanese diary entry recorded,

> With the dawn the enemy starts shooting all over. All I can do is shed tears of resentment. Now we are waiting only for death. The news that reinforcement had come turned out to be a rumor. All day we stay in the bunkers. We are filled with vexation. Comrades, are you going to stand by and watch us die? Even the invincible Imperial Army is at a loss.[46]

The arrival of the first tanks on 18 December, hitherto regarded as surplus to requirements, provided an important addition to Eichelberger's armory.

Even at this relatively early stage of the battle the appalling conditions in which the Japanese were fighting beggared belief: a journalist observed,

> Rotting bodies, sometimes weeks old, formed part of the fortifications. The living fired over the bodies of the dead, slept side by side with them. In one trench was a Japanese who had not been able to stand the strain. His rifle was still pointed at his head, his big toe was on the trigger, and the top of his head was blown off . . . Everywhere, pervading everything, was the stench of putrescent flesh.[47]

Similarly infantryman Kiyoshi Wada noted, "Went to get water from the stream. On the way the jungle was full of dead, killed by shrapnel. There is something awful about the smell of the dead."[48] Private Yoriichi Yokoyama recalled, "We talked only about food every day, like how much we missed Japanese food and craved plain rice, pickles, miso soup, sushi and so on. Ironically, most of us starved to death."[49]

After the fall of Gona, Brigadier George Wootten's Australian 8th Brigade moved to come to the aid of the US 32nd Division at Buna. On 18 December, an attack on the Buna stronghold by the Australia Imperial Force's (AIF) Brigadier Wootten (soon afterwards promoted to Major-General) broke the deadlock. When General Blamey arrived in Port Moresby with the Australian 163rd Infantry, MacArthur ordered them to support the American attacks on Buna rather than to aid the stalling Australian attack on Sanananda. Tank attacks dramatically increased the potency of the Allied advance. They could roll up to within three or four yards of the bunker and blast away until it was destroyed. A new kind of phosphorous grenade, which induced horrendous burns, was also deployed by the troops to attack Japanese foxholes. The new weapons left the Japanese troops demoralized. The tanks, which helped Wootten's Australian infantry to clear the entire Duropa Plantation and Cape Endaiadere, enabled MacArthur, with great aplomb, to report a victory at Buna to the US media—his adoring American public little knowing that it was the Australians commanded by Wootten who had completed the task.

It was only when Buna was secured that the US sent its 126th Infantry to support and give fresh impetus to Major-General George Vasey's Australian 7th Division at Sanananda. By this time many of the Australian forces, which had fought their way down the Kokoda Trail were completely 'clapped-out.' However, for MacArthur only the "American" victory at Buna "mattered." For him the Australian efforts at Gona and Sanananda bordered on the inconsequential. Later, MacArthur described the *Battle of Sanananda* as merely a "mopping-up" operation.

His *Reminiscences* [1964] focused almost entirely on the American action at Buna. 'Mopping up' was not the experience of men on the ground. Brigadier Selwyn Porter, a highly reputed officer who led the 30th Brigade at Sanananda, after its relief of the 16th Brigade and US units, wrote to a friend to tell him, "Really, there is just no possibility of depicting the conditions of fighting here . . . it sometimes takes a day to move a mile or two; so, all the science of rapid counter-attack goes by the board . . ."[50] Porter, no friend of the rebellious trade unions back home, reserved some choice remarks for some of his countrymen; "The Jap uses coolies to carry loads. He should use our pacifists, politicians and wharf humpers. These boys have done more work for their dollars, in one day, than the wharfies and coalminers have done in a year."[51] The relieved 16th Brigade retained a strong spirit in spite of having been severely degraded; 605 soldiers had been killed or wounded while another 978 troops had been evacuated for sickness— usually defined as having a temperature over 103 degrees.

Buna had still not been won. In mid-December Eichelberger's construction of a bridge across *Boreo Creek* allowed him to bring up M3 Stuart tanks under cover of darkness. A frustrated MacArthur, still wholly dissatisfied with the progress being made, and feeling that this would count against him in Washington, sent Major-General Sutherland to the front with instructions to replace Eichelberger and take command himself if he thought it was appropriate. Sutherland was far too comfortable at MacArthur's HQ to have contemplated putting himself in the combat zone. By contrast Eichelberger, a fearless soldier, had led his troops from the front. For a middle-aged officer of major-general rank to lead an attack on enemy bunkers was more than exceptional—it was a unique event in *World War II*. Several of Eichelberger's personal staff were wounded along with three senior commanders, one of them hit just seventy-five yards from the Japanese front. At Buna they probably took more casualties than any Allied general staff group of the entire war. With Eichelberger's example of leadership, GI morale soared.

A combination of heavy artillery and tanks supported by aggressive infantry finally started to wipe out the hitherto impregnable Japanese positions at Sanananda. Over the next five days of heavy fighting the Japanese defenders were pushed back as Major-General Oda was rushed to the front with reinforcements. Kiyoshi noted in his diary, "According to Major-General Oda . . . the policy of the Empire of Japan is that it will absolutely not give up Giruwa [Buna]."[52] He showed himself to be either a gullible if not delusional soldier or alternatively a master of sarcasm when he confided to his diary, "It goes without saying that we will also attack Port Moresby. We will place New Guinea under our complete control."[53] A more junior Japanese soldier, Lance Corporal Uchiyama, was more realistic. He waxed poetic as his end neared; he had

> no thoughts of returning home alive. Want to die like a soldier and go to Yasakuni Shrine. Writing in this diary word by word, not knowing when a shell may strike and I will be killed . . . full moon shining through the trees in the jungle. Hearing the cries of the birds and insects, the breeze blowing gently and peacefully.[54]

Uchiyama was killed on Christmas Eve.

Some Japanese troops made miraculous escapes. On 18 January Wada's diary was found amidst bodies and debris and he was assumed to be dead. In fact Wada was one of the lucky few who escaped from the final encirclement at Sanananda by swimming to safety. In 1991 he was located in Japan and participated in an Australian Army documentary on the campaign. At Sanananda on 28 December 1942, Wada had noted in his diary, "I took out a picture of my parents and looked at it."[55] He must have been as surprised as anyone that he did eventually get back to Japan to see them.

While the Japanese were receiving their last supplies from Rabaul on Christmas Day, gifts of boiled lollies, tobacco and matches were being distributed to the Allied troops. Field kitchens served a special dinner of meatloaf and preserved peaches. The smell of American delicacies drove the Japanese to despair. Private Nishimura recorded a bizarre incident in which one of his colleagues, an English speaker, declared "I've had enough":[56] he stripped to his underpants and feigning drunkenness staggered toward the American lines. Silence followed, only occasionally interrupted by laughter. The

Japanese soldier returned several hours later bearing food—a gift from the American soldiers a few yards away. Few Japanese soldiers were as fortunate.

Meanwhile Eichelberger was receiving MacArthur's Chief of Staff, Major-General Sutherland, carrying 'gifts' of another kind from the commander in chief; the letter from MacArthur read, ". . . your attacks, instead of being made up of two or three hundred rifles, should be made up by two or three thousand . . . Your battle casualties to date compared with your total strength are slight so that you have a big margin to work with."[57] As the campaign continued so did Eichelberger's contempt and detestation of Sutherland. While Sutherland scampered back to Port Moresby for the lavish headquarters festivities to be enjoyed with the mistress he had smuggled into MacArthur's HQ, Eichelberger's celebratory meal consisted of a cup of soup and a cup of coffee at a field medical post; he spilt them both when an artillery shell exploded nearby. After the end of the war, Eichelberger would refuse to speak a single word to Sutherland when the two of them met. Almost universally disliked, Sutherland's character was so repellent that when General Walter Krueger learnt of his death years after the war, he commented, "It is a good thing for humanity."[58]

By Christmas Day, Lieutenant Yamamoto recorded that there were no more reserves left. Every man available was in the line. On 26 December fierce fighting ensued at Buna as the Australians tried to take the airfield. Private Tim Hughes distinguished himself by making three individual sorties to lob grenades at Japanese positions, following them up with fire from his Thompson sub-machine gun. He was awarded a Military Medal for his "remarkable bravery" and "exceptional coolness."[59] Sergeant Frank Duffy was similarly rewarded for gallantry.

Japanese ingenuity continued to surprise the advancing Allied troops. Using a rope and pulley, dummy snipers would suddenly be released from trees making soldiers think that the way forward was clear. Thus lulled, when they advanced a concealed sniper would open fire. In desperation the Japanese also set fire to the kunai grass to delay the Allied advance. As their hold on the battlefield contracted, Japanese soldiers continued to chop down trees to construct new bunkers. There was still fight in the depleted Japanese ranks. A counter-attack was launched at Major Trevivian's force at 9 p.m. on 27 December. It was beaten back by a reserve of B Company, twenty-five men led by Captain M. J. Brown, whose assault completely annihilated the Japanese raiders. Brown had charged into the attack holding a bayonet in his hand. There were no reserves left on either side.

US and Australian troops pressed forward their attacks as New Year arrived. According to one Japanese diarist the occasion was celebrated in style; "Welcomed the New Year in a trench. We had one cigarette . . . a can of sardines for seven men."[60] As the US forces closed in on the last redoubts, as dusk came some Japanese soldiers were seen swimming out to sea. It was the first sign that the defenders were cracking.

However, some bunkers thought to have been taken, were re-infiltrated and came alive again, killing unaware US troops. To destroy the remaining Japanese bunkers tanks were deployed followed closely by Bren-gunners to protect them from lurking Japanese infantry. As they approached a bunker it was fired on to distract the occupants while a GI was handed an Ammonal charge through the side hatch of the tank's turret. The GI would then scramble atop the bunker and pull the pin on the grenade attached to the charge and drop it down the ventilation shaft. By nightfall on New Year's Day 1943 all that remained to the Japanese defenders was a pocket 100 yards by 200 yards; its lines were manned by any remaining troops to hand including surviving medics. Of the eight prisoners taken, six were laborers and only two were soldiers. The day cost members of the 2nd Battalion 12th Regiment, forty-five killed and 127 wounded.

On 2 January more Japanese soldiers were seen trying to swim along the coast for safety. They provided target practice for the US troops. As Allied troops closed in on the remnants they came across many hundreds of bodies. Many Japanese troops committed suicide. On a small island post in *Simeni Creek* two Japanese officers emerged and ignored the Australian troops watching them. They casually strolled about and one went to wash. Lieutenant-Colonel Arnold called on them to surrender on a count of ten. One officer draped a sword and flag against his heart and was gunned down. The other one hanged himself. Of the commanders at Buna, it was reported that Captain Yasuda died in a *banzai* charge. Colonel Yamamoto had led his men in three final *banzai* cheers and then committed *seppuku* (ritual suicide by disembowelment).

The fighting at Buna was over. Overcoming the coastal garrison had required the efforts of the entire US 32nd Division as well as the 18th Australian Brigade. Brigadier Wootten, commander of the Australian 18th Brigade at the *Battle of Milne Bay*, drew up the final plans for the destruction of the Japanese at Buna. Hundreds of bombing and strafing raids had been made on Japanese positions. In all there were 2,870 Allied casualties, dead and wounded, of whom 913 were Australian. Over the next few days the soldiers at the front were enraged when they learned that on 1 January 1943 the socialist wharf unions in Australia had gone on strike. It was an event that added to a sorry union legacy, which included pilfering from war supplies, harassment of Allied troops and even sabotage. On occasions Australian and American officers had to restrain their troops from killing the striking stevedores.

MacArthur's Victory Propaganda: By the end of the battle, a humbled Eichelberger, fully aware of the difficulties that had faced his predecessor, Major-General Harding, was equally irritated by the ignorance of his commander. When MacArthur, in a typical piece of propaganda misinformation for the US press, had released a Christmas *communiqué* to the effect that there were now minimal mopping up operations around Buna, Eichelberger was incandescent with rage. Back in America flattering portraits of MacArthur appeared in *Life* magazine and the *Saturday Evening Post* proclaiming his great American victory. Subsequently Republican Senator Arthur Vandenburg from Michigan began to tout MacArthur as a potential Presidential candidate for the 1944 elections. Joseph Medill Patterson of the *New York Daily News*, who had clamored for his rescue from *Corregidor* in January, reported, "the Republicans are talking about running him for President some day."[61] Other supporters in the press were Patterson's sister Cissie at the *Times-Herald* in Washington, Patterson's cousin Colonel Robert

McCormick at the *Chicago Tribune* as well as the newspaper chains of Randolph Hearst and Frank Gannett.

It did not go unnoticed at the White House. Secretary of State Stimson noted in his diary, "MacArthur, who is not an unselfish being and is a good deal of a *prima donna*, has himself lent a little to the story . . . playing into the hands of people who would really like to make him a candidate."[62] A Roper Poll for *Fortune* magazine reported that his popularity at 57.3 percent was almost equal to that of Republicans such as Wendell Wilkie (35.8 percent) and Thomas Dewey (24.7 percent) combined.

Eichelberger, while not averse to seeing his own name in print, was not prepared to dangle for it, on one occasion instructing an Army press officer, "I would rather have you slip a rattlesnake in my pocket than to have you give me any publicity."[63] Nevertheless stories did appear about Eichelberger in *Life* magazine and the *Saturday Evening Post*. MacArthur, furious with envy, summoned Eichelberger to his quarters: "Do you realize I could reduce you to the grade of colonel tomorrow and send you home?"[64] This after Eichelberger had served in the 'field' for four months, sometimes fighting on the front line with his staff and troops at great personal risk. After some delay MacArthur deigned to put forward his name for the award of the US Distinguished Service Cross but Eichelberger found that many on the list were commanders who had not served in forward positions. He later discovered that his own troops had collectively sought for him to be awarded the Congressional Medal of Honor, America's highest award. It was approved in Washington. MacArthur vetoed the award. Eichelberger was not informed. There was only one star in MacArthur's firmament.

Politics of another kind were alive in Australia. On 5 January, Prime Minister Curtin's Australian Labor Party passed a landmark vote to allow Australian Militia troops, the conscripted Army Reserve, to defend their country wherever their generals sent them— albeit even then only south of the equator in the South West Pacific Area. Previously, only volunteers could fight outside of Australia, although that did include Australia's League of Nations mandated areas in New Guinea. Remarkably until then, the Australian Labor Party had called for young Americans to die in Australia's defense but had not required Australians to do likewise. It should be noted that 200,000 militia conscripts did voluntarily transfer to the Australia Imperial Force (AIF) during the course of the war, so that they could fight anywhere.

Victory at Sanananda: On 8 January, Americans were told by MacArthur that the *Battle of Buna-Gona* was won; the Papuan campaign "can now be regarded as accomplished."[65] Yet the Japanese stronghold at Sanananda that Generals Blamey and Herring considered to be the most vital of the Japanese coastal garrisons remained in enemy hands. Because of MacArthur's stance it is a battle that is often expunged from histories of the period. In reality, even though the Japanese defenders at Sanananda ran out of rice altogether by 12 January, they continued their heroic defense for another week. On 12 January a tank attack supported by troops was forced back by anti-tank guns that the Australians did not know the Japanese possessed. Soldiers on both sides suffered equally.

At Killerton Junction one battalion lost ninety-nine men including two company commanders in return for a few yards of territory. Fortunately Colonel Tsukamoto, with supply lines broken, no longer had the resources to continue to hold the position and ordered a pull back. The *Battle of Sanananda* was peculiarly constructed along a road with lush jungle swamps at either side. Japanese bunker positions were constructed on small islands either side of the road—like the beads hanging from a necklace. Nevertheless, Australian troops gradually closed in on the last remaining Japanese positions at Sanananda that Japanese forces were equally determined to hold. Lieutenant-Colonel Allchin of the Australian 2nd Battalion 10th Regiment described it as "nothing but dirty, filthy, typhus ridden jungle and swamp . . . walls of green jungle foliage with its drawling roots reaching out into the stagnant pools infested with mosquitoes. . . ."[66]

At the hospital at Sanananda, Lieutenant Bunji Shigemori, who was forming fighting units from among the patients, received an instruction from Colonel Yokoyama: "We must consider Buna as fallen. It is our duty to hold Sanananda against Australian and American armies. We must display the bravery of the Japanese Army. Even though you are a patient, you should not hesitate to advance."[67] On 15 January the diary entry of a soldier who had previously admitted to cannibalism, read, "Hard to stand on account of beriberi. Good news, but none is certain. Heard our planes had come; all propaganda."[68]

On 16 January, in a double envelopment, Australian troops closed in on Sanananda from the north and American GIs from the south. Lieutenant Riichi Inagaki, a paymaster, mused on the reasons for defeat. He put it down to cumulative casualties. Nevertheless he marveled at his comrades standing up to their armpits in swamp water. They fought on despite suffering from malaria and vitamin B deficiency that made many of them so blind that they could only fire in the direction of attacks on the basis of sound. During the night torrential rain was accompanied by lightning bolts, which sent electric charges through the troops lying in pools of water. The condition of the Australians was not much better. One Australian commander sent back a secret report begging for replacements and complaining that he was keeping men in the field "with hallucinations caused by their fevers" as a result of which they were "unreliable and actually a danger to their sub-units."[69]

Major-General Kensaku Oda, having had no instructions for five days from Lieutenant-General Hatazo Adachi, commander of the Eighteenth Army in Rabaul, sent a desperate message,

> Those not . . . in bed with illness are without food and too weak for hand-to-hand fighting . . . Starvation is taking many lives, and it is weakening our already extended lines. We are doomed. In several days, we are bound to meet the same fate that overtook Basabua [Gona] and Buna . . . Our duty will have been accomplished if we fight and lay down our lives here on the field.[70]

On the same day Sergeant-Major Shimamoto noted in his diary that he had seen "some soldiers fixing a dead enemy to eat because rations have run out in the front line."[71]

Finally the next day, 17 January, Major-General Adachi gave permission for General Oda to begin a withdrawal, if possible, up the coast to Lae or Salamaua. Similarly, Major-General Tsuyuo Yamagata ordered an evacuation on 20 January. Yamagata managed to escape the final Allied advance. Oda stayed with the wounded men, smoked a final cigarette, then placed a cloak on the beach, knelt and bowed in the direction of Japan and put a gun to his head. Many soldiers killed themselves. Others were captured and killed by the Australians. Those who survived were surprised by the kindness that they were shown. The remnants of their forces fled into the jungle mostly suffering unknown fates, though diaries were found of some soldiers who survived for months after the end of formal resistance. Captain Shiro Nishio, a 33-year-old doctor in the 51st Independent Engineers Regiment wrote a last letter to his wife starting, "Beloved Mineko . . . it is with poignant regret that I shall not again see the face of Toshiko [his son]. I have decided to destroy myself on April 18 [1942] at nine o'clock somewhere in New Guinea . . ."[72] In fact Nishio was captured before he could commit suicide and was later described by his captors as a highly intelligent man. Not all Japanese soldiers were the demented fanatics of Hollywood legend.

Of the estimated 7,500-plus Japanese troops used at Buna-Gona-Sanananda, some 1,200 wounded were evacuated during the course of the battle; of the remainder it is thought that more than 6,000 died while the Allies took just 200 prisoners. After the battle it was noted that some Japanese troops had taken their own lives. However, most fought to the end. As Corporal John Prentice told war reporter, George Johnson, in a coconut grove outside Soputa Village, whose junctions led to Gona and Sanananda, "You've got to kill 'em. They won't give in." Prentice had also told Johnson, "My job now is to get back to my wife. After all, I've really only been married 5 days! And I can't see her [Claire] again till we clean up this other little job up here. That means killin' Japs."[73] A few days after this chance meeting, Corporal Prentice was dead—shot while taking out a Japanese machine gun nest.

Albeit at odds with his urgent orders to attack at all costs during the early stages of the battle, MacArthur stated afterwards,

> There was no reason to hurry the attack because the time element was of little importance . . . The utmost care was taken for the conservation of our forces with the result that probably no campaign in history against a thoroughly prepared and trained Army produced such complete and decisive results with so low an expenditure of life and resources.[74]

This was another MacArthur lie. Eichelberger had been told quite categorically by General MacArthur on 30 November that "time was of the essence," and again on

13 December, "time is working desperately against us."[75] Throughout the battle MacArthur had urged speed and had complained about the "lightness" of casualties.

As usual with MacArthur, it was a story of more lies, propaganda and self-serving fantasy. Having failed to land a rapid and decisive victory at Buna, Gona and Sanananda, which MacArthur needed in order to project his desire to command the Allied drive to Tokyo via New Guinea and the Philippines rather than the through the *Pacific*, he now spun the story that the slow pace of the campaign was deliberate and aimed at saving lives. However, the Joint Chiefs of Staff were not fooled. They had sources of information other than MacArthur. The Commander of the Fifth Air Force in the South West Pacific Area, Lieutenant-General Kenney, made a detailed report of the horrors of the *Battle of Buna-Gona* to his ultimate boss, General 'Hap' Arnold, noting, "there are hundreds of Bunas ahead of us" and speculated that the amount of blood and money it would cost to defeat Japan "may run to proportions beyond all conception."[76]

Misinformation About the Cost of the New Guinea Campaign: An analysis of US casualties at the *Battle of Buna-Gona-Sanananda* makes a farce of MacArthur's claims that his mainland campaigns were 'low cost' compared to Admiral Nimitz's 'Central Pacific Strategy.' Allied forces lost some 3,498 troops killed (72 percent of them Australian) out of 20,000 soldiers deployed at Buna, Gona and Sanananda. Of the 9,825 men of the US 32nd Division who started the two-month campaign 686 were killed, and 1,954 were wounded; the chances of an American soldier dying in this major 'field' battle in New Guinea were three times higher than being killed on *Guadalcanal*.

However, victory in terms of total casualties came at fantastic cost. The US 32nd Division's 11,000 troops plus replacements suffered aggregate casualties of 9,688; 7,125 were due to illness and over 3,000 of these troops had to be hospitalized. The 126th Infantry Brigade had effectively ceased to exist, in mid-November out of its 3,040 troops, only thirty-two out of 131 officers remained in charge of just 579 enlisted men when they were shipped back to Australia at the end of March 1943. Australians had similarly suffered from the ravages of illness. By the end of 1942 some 15,575 cases of infectious disease had been reported including 9,249 cases of malaria, 3,643 cases of dysentery, 1,186 cases of dengue fever and 186 cases of scrub typhus.

On 10 January Major Mansfield Gunn, a medical officer on General Eichelberger's staff, wrote that there

> is a growing incidence of scrub typhus here . . . There are some tremendous rats in the area, and no doubt the fleas on same are carrying the infection from the dead Japanese to our soldiers. One medical officer just died of the disease . . . it is the toughest situation any of us have ever been in . . . Sickness of all sorts, particularly of the various tropical fevers is on the increase also, so I expect that almost everyone in the division will come out of here

either wounded or sick. I do not intend to paint a depressing picture, but that is the truth as things stand today. The figures will be appalling to you when you see them.[77]

A post-war US Army history of the East New Guinea campaign concluded, "the victory there, proportionate to the forces engaged, had been one of the costliest of the *Pacific War*."[78]

Japanese casualties from the whole Kokoda Trail Campaign have been estimated at over 10,000 of the 13,500 troops who participated. Of these it is thought that 6,500 died, mainly from malnutrition and disease. However, it is estimated that only 5 percent of the troops who were sent on the Buna-Kokoda mission ever returned to Japan. Masao Naka, a five-foot tall 24-year-old second lieutenant in the 42nd Regiment was captured alive weighing just 115 lbs. He was too weak and confused to kill himself. Naka had fought in China, at Nanking and Shanghai, in Malaya and *Singapore*, in Rabaul and New Guinea. This last campaign he rated as by far the hardest. They had been opposed by 30,000 troops at Port Moresby, which had allowed Blamey's commanders to frequently reinforce or relieve fighting units at regular intervals. It meant that there were never more than 3,500 Allied troops fighting at any given time; a luxury rarely afforded to Japanese soldiers such as Masao Naka. Hirohito and his senior commanders rarely viewed his soldiers as much more than expendable commodities. Moreover, while frequently inadequate, Blamey's supply chain never broke down completely as was the case for Horii's forces.

It has also to be questioned whether MacArthur, if he had been better informed of conditions on the ground, need have pressed for the final destruction of the Japanese forces at Buna-Gona-Sananander with all the losses that the battle incurred for American and Australian troops. When interviewed after the war, the only surviving field officer of the campaign, Major Mitsu Koiwai of the 2nd Battalion 41st Infantry, explained, "We lost at Buna because we could not retain air superiority, because we could not supply our troops, and because our navy and air force could not disrupt the enemy supply line," but he also added, "Tactically the Allied co-ordination of fire power and advance was very skilful. However, we were in such a position at Buna that we wondered whether the Americans would bypass us and leave us to starve."[79] 'Bypass' would indeed have been the sensible strategy. The tactic of isolating Japanese garrisons to let them 'wither-on-the-vine' would eventually be adopted by MacArthur but only after the US Joint Chiefs forced him to isolate, not take, Rabaul. With his usual breath-taking mendacity, MacArthur would later claim the strategy of isolating Japanese garrisons as his own.

At the *Battle of Buna-Gona-Sanananda*, MacArthur and Blamey could claim an important victory, albeit with a 3:1 battlefield advantage against Japanese troops who were literally starving to death. Blamey had little respect for the bravery of the Japanese troops and his comments, even by the standards of the time, displayed an unattractive racist contempt for his enemy: "You are fighting a shrewd, cruel, merciless enemy . . .

Beneath the thin veneer of a few generations of civilization he is a sub-human beast who has brought warfare back to the primeval . . ."[80]

'Fuzzy Wuzzy' Angels: The Role of Papuan Natives: The later stages of the battle showed that atrocities were not always confined to the Japanese. On 10 December, when a stretcher party brought back captured Japanese troops who were too wounded or ill to walk, local road builders went berserk and butchered them. It was payback for what they had suffered under Japanese occupation. It seems that however poorly the Australians and other white men had treated the natives of New Guinea, they were not in the same league as the Japanese. Emboge, a Papuan chief in the Buna area, who was accused of murdering white men for the Japanese explained to ANGAU (Australian New Guinea Administrative Unit) Patrol Officer David Marsh, "What else could we do? The Kiawa [white men] treated us badly before the war and they deserted the people when the Japanese landed at Buna. We tried the Japanese but we did not like them at all."[81] The following day Emboge was asked for help in finding natives to hack down jungle for an Allied airfield at Popondetta and he soon delivered 500 Papuan workers.

Natives could be tricky to handle for both sides. When injured flying officer Ken Dineen approached a village after being shot down he found himself backed against a palisade by a large group of spear-waving natives: "I drew my revolver and picked out one who seemed to be the ringleader."[82] Dineen was saved by two youths who guided him to the village. Further tension ensued when one villager became concerned that he was interested in his woman. The native need not have worried. "He was wasting his time," recalled Dineen, "I was not fit enough, nor did I have the inclination."[83]

However, the contribution made by Papuan natives to the campaign was largely overlooked after the war. Without the astonishing physical effort required by thousands of Papuans to 'sherpa' tons of *matériel* over the Owen Stanley Mountains, the *Battles of Kokoda, Buna, Gona* and *Sanananda* could not have been won. That the Allied logistics chain held up was largely due to the remarkable work done by Captain H. T. 'Bert' Kienzle, an ANGAU officer. A rubber planter in civilian life, Kienzle was one of the rare Australians to have an intimate knowledge of the Owen Stanley area. Along with Captain Dr. G. H. Vernon, who he appointed as the overall medical officer for the Kokoda Trail, Kienzle made sure that the Allied supply lines, often stretched, never broke down. Native porters were recruited, managed, fed and cared for. Under their guidance, soldiers' equipment, munitions, food supplies, weapons and clothing were carried up and down the ridges and trails that traversed ninety-six miles of dense, mountainous jungle. From an initial group of 600 porters, the number grew to a peak of 1,600; in all some 3,000 Papuans were involved in the logistics exercise of the Kokoda Campaign. Although sickness and desertions were sometimes high, the Papuans never flinched from going into combat areas.

Care for the wounded was particularly important for the morale of the men. A medical officer noted of the Papuans: "They carry stretchers over seemingly impassable barriers, with the patient reasonably comfortable. The care, which they show to the patient, is magnificent."[84] Potter's 21st Brigade acknowledged the important role of Papuan carriers: "They cannot be too highly praised. They performed all tasks asked of them, tasks that few white men could have stood up to, if called upon to do so."[85] Kienzle's supply chain management and the Papuan porters gave the Allies a marked advantage over Horii, who largely depended on the Formosan and Korean laborers (effectively indentured) that he had brought from Rabaul. While Horii was sometimes able to pay Papuans to act as guides, in general, there was little love for the Japanese whose treatment of the natives was as brutal as the other Asian peoples that they had conquered. For Australian troops, the Papuans came to be held in such high regard that they became known as the 'Fuzzy Wuzzy Angels,' a term that was used with affection and not as a racial pejorative.

US Forces' Baptism of Fire and the Failure of MacArthur as Commander: It is clear that the senior Australian commanders viewed their Papuan porters more favorably than they regarded their American allies. Blamey's view of American troops was not complimentary. Like most of his senior commanders Blamey believed that a diet of Hollywood movies had led most American GIs to believe that they were almost certain to die in battle. Major-General Vasey used to relate a story of overhearing a US GI remarking about Australian troops hurrying up a track toward the front: "Hell, those guys are in a hurry to die."[86] In general they lacked the aggressiveness that came to be associated with the Australians.

Similarly, Australian Major H. G. Harcourt was a scathing critic of US patroling practice. In New Guinea, US Army patrols were infrequent and, unlike the Australian Army, only done by volunteers. Complaints about US Army standards were not confined to the Australians. Criticism of the cautiousness of US troops was often leveled at the regular US Infantry by the US Marine Corps. Eventually the Australian and US troops would reach a reasonable level of grudging respect during the later campaign along the northwest coast of New Guinea. At Buna-Gona and Sanananda however there was little love lost between them.

Although generals on the ground such as Eichelberger climbed a rapid learning curve from which they later profited, it is clear that they had to relearn many of the lessons that had plagued the Allied efforts in the early months of the *Pacific War*. By way of example the complete disregard for the use of tanks and artillery in jungle warfare showed that they had learnt nothing from Percival's experience in Malaya or Wainwright's experience on *Corregidor*. The astonishingly high levels of disease among Allied troops also revealed that their commanders in Australia, unlike General Slim on the India-Burma border **[see Chapter 26: The Battles of Arakan, Imphal, and Kohima: Slim Boxes Clever]**, had gained little awareness of the importance of training and equipping troops to stay healthy during protracted jungle engagements. MacArthur, relying as he did on the 'field' visits of his deputy, the loathed Major-General Sutherland and his other 'Bataan gang' lackeys, remained remote from the realities of the battles being fought. When MacArthur moved his HQ from Brisbane to Port Moresby in November, he issued a portentous *communiqué* proclaiming, "The Supreme Commander has taken to the field";[87] except he had not. The Governor's elegant white mansion at Port Moresby was not the 'field.' The 'field' was a ten-day hike over the Owen Stanley Mountains, a challenge that a field commander such as General Stilwell would have relished, but not one that would appeal to MacArthur, who was in any case of an older generation; however, even the short hop by airplane was too much trouble for the Allied commander of the South West Pacific Area.

Instead of getting to grips with conditions on the ground, MacArthur preferred to pontificate on strategy as he paced his veranda in a pink silk dressing gown with a black dragon on the back. Eichelberger wrote bitterly to his wife, "the great hero went home without seeing Buna before, during or after the fight while permitting press articles from his GHQ to say he was leading his troops in battle . . ."[88] In spite of the Australian Army's urgent need for supply, six months after MacArthur's arrival at Port Moresby there was only one wharf from which to unload supplies. MacArthur's priorities lay with propaganda, not logistics. MacArthur's luxurious living, his gold encrusted caps and high-falutin' pronouncements did not endear him to the Australian troops in New Guinea any more than it had done to the US soldiers on Bataan. When MacArthur's press officer, the appropriately named Colonel LeGrande Diller, had MacArthur and Eichelberger photographed in a jeep at a training camp at Rockhampton, Australia, he had it lyingly captioned in the US press as "Generals MacArthur and Eichelberger at the front in New Guinea."[89]

The caption might have been forgivable if MacArthur had visited the front line, but during the Kokoda and Buna Campaigns he never did. While in the Burma-China-India Theater, General Stilwell would be criticized for spending too much time with his troops on the ground, the exact opposite criticism could be made of MacArthur. In both the Philippines and thus far in New Guinea, he had shown himself to be an 'armchair' general, and not a very good one at that.

If MacArthur was lazy and duplicitous during the Buna-Gona-Sanananda Campaign, many would argue that his Chief of Staff, Major-General Richard Sutherland was worse. Eichelberger noted that Sutherland "knew how to work on MacArthur like Paderewski playing the piano."[90] Behind his back, however, Sutherland referred to MacArthur somewhat disparagingly as the 'Old Man' and claimed the key decisions in the *Southwest Pacific* Theater as his own. Lieutenant-General Kenney remembered Sutherland as "an arrogant, opinionated, and very ambitious guy . . . I don't think that Sutherland was even loyal to MacArthur."[91] MacArthur's monomania blinded him to the faults of his own staff.

MacArthur also displayed remarkable meanness of spirit. When Major-General Vandegrift and his 1st Marines were finally relieved after their heroic four month defense of Henderson Field on *Guadalcanal*, MacArthur had them encamped in a malaria-ridden area some forty-five miles outside of Brisbane. When Vandegrift found a more suitable location in Melbourne for his Marines' furlough and recuperation, MacArthur refused to supply them with provisions.

Apart from MacArthur's inter-force rivalries, even within his own *South Pacific* Command MacArthur did little to assuage the bitter rivalry that developed between Australian and American troops. Eichelberger would later write: "The Australians didn't think they needed much help from any-one, many of the commanders I met had already been in combat in North Africa and though they were usually too polite to say so, considered the Americans to be at best inexperienced theorists."[92] Americans who had been unfairly patronizing or downright critical of Australian performance on the Kokoda Trail did not take kindly to the Aussie forces giving them back their own medicine in spades after the initial failures of the US 32nd Division at Buna. It did not help that MacArthur refused to incorporate Australians in the senior command structure of the South West Pacific Command Area, relying instead on the American 'Bataan gang' that he had brought from the Philippines. Major-General Rowell described MacArthur's HQ as the "Philippine performing circus."[93]

MacArthur, aware that an America audience would only be interested in the actions of American soldiers, wrote Australians out of the story of the East New Guinea Campaign. This was not too difficult for him to do given that he only ever mentioned himself in dispatches from the 'front.' His control of the 'story' was helped by Australian Prime Minister Curtin, who MacArthur encouraged to effectively stifle Allied press freedom. The end result of MacArthur's propaganda was that neither the full horrors of the East New Guinea Campaign nor the truth about the significant, indeed the larger role of Australian troops, were ever satisfactorily revealed to the outside world. From his initial doubts, inculcated by MacArthur and his acolytes, Eichelberger was completely won over by the quality of Australian troops who he applauded in his memoirs by saying that when the going got tough, the "man from down under"[94] was a great soldier. He needed to be. In a war pockmarked by horrific battles, in many respects the *Battles of the Kokoda Trail*, followed by the *Battle of Buna-Gona-Sanananda* were, in terms of the depth of human suffering of the troops on both sides, perhaps the most ghastly of all.

For the Australians and Americans, they would never again go into an operation that had been so poorly planned and where the organization of supplies, artillery and munitions were so badly managed. The American GIs of the 32nd Division in particular may have performed poorly, a reflection of their inexperience and inadequate training— but it was hardly their fault. Above all the 32nd Division was let down by MacArthur, a remote commander, who, insufficiently apprised of conditions on the ground, failed to provide them with adequate training and logistical support. It was fortunate for MacArthur's reputation that in Eichelberger, he unearthed one of the most courageous and talented field commanders of *World War II,* who restored the 32nd Division historic reputation as a superb fighting unit. Eichelberger's Chief of Staff, Clovis Byers, who later fought in Korea, would later write that his commander's actions at Buna, "constitutes the most inspiring example of leadership I have ever witnessed."[95]

The 32nd Division would later perform with distinction in the northern New Guinea Campaign at the *Battle of Saidor* in April 1944, at the amphibious landing at Aitape on 3 May 1944 and would hold back General Adachi's ferocious counter-attack at the

Battle of Driniumor River. Later they fought one of the hardest engagements in the *Battle of Leyte Island* in the Philippines Campaign, and after fighting in *Luzon*, finally gained the distinction of capturing the great Japanese general, Tomoyuki Yamashita 'The Tiger of Malaya,' on 2 September 1945.

Allied Troops Win 'Superman' Status: In spite of these failings the Allied troops proved at Buna, Gona and Sanananda that they were soldiers to be reckoned with. In the first six months of the war British, American and Dutch troops had been paralyzed by fear of Japan's 'supermen' soldiers; the boot was now firmly on the other foot. Captain Murase sent back the following observations regarding his Australian opponents:

> Each man was skilled in combat, gallant, brave, fought to
> the last man; infiltrated through openings in Japanese
> defenses; he maintains absolute quiet; he was skilled in
> the use of automatic weapons . . . avoided heavy casualties
> from all rushing at once, and found it was best to crawl
> . . . he excelled at sniping . . . he excelled at night warfare
> . . . he was skilled in the use of and acquiring information
> from local people . . .[96]

Albeit astonishingly brave and prepared to die, almost to a man, for their Emperor, Japanese troops displayed a stubborn lack of existential imagination, which was the flipside of their fanatical loyalty that was to characterize their performance throughout the remainder of the war. Although officers were able to organize brilliantly conceived defense emplacements, tactical awareness and attention to logistics was sometimes limited. They expected their troops to compensate for lack of *matériel* with 'will' alone. Against the Australians at the Kokoda Trail and afterwards, they met their match in this department.

Above all, Japanese officers showed a pathological disregard for the lives and well-being of their troops. On 28 December at Sanananda, Kiyoshi Wada noted in his diary, "All officers even though there is a scarcity of food, eat relatively well. The condition is one in which the majority is starving. This is indeed a deplorable state of affairs for the Imperial Army."[97] Remarkably, once they had overrun Japanese positions, the Allied troops found significant stockpiles of rice. Sometimes mouldy bags of rice were found to have been used in the construction of pillboxes. Whatever Japanese officers' prowess in defense construction, it would seem that their logistical abilities were generally poor. It was an observation that would continue to be made throughout the *Pacific War*—a result of both poor training and perhaps more importantly a complete disregard by Japan's senior commanders in Tokyo and by the Emperor for the welfare of their troops. They were not unaware of the conditions in which their troops were fighting. The critical problem of logistics was emphasized by Major Mitsuo Koiwai who concluded, "We lost at Buna because we could not retain air superiority, because we could not supply our troops, and because our navy and air force could not disrupt the enemy supply line."[98]

In addition, Lieutenant-General Kenney was particularly critical of the Japanese Air Force which, in spite of their good planes, "do not seem to have a clear conception of the proper role of the Air Force."[99] He believed that their use of penny packet air raids rather than mass attacks failed to wipe out American air power at a time when they had significant numerical advantage. Furthermore, Kenney noted the decline in Japanese pilot quality. "His [Japan's] original highly trained crews were superb," averred Kenney, "but they are dead."[100]

When he got back to Melbourne, journalist George Johnson complained, "there are remarkably few people who have even the remotest idea of what young Australian and American troops went through to drive the Japanese 100 miles farther away from Port Moresby—and from Australia."[101] The final say on the *Battle of Buna-Gona-Sanananda* can rest with the haunting words of Lieutenant-General Eichelberger, from his autobiographical *Our Jungle Road to Tokyo* [1950]:

> Buna was ... bought at a substantial price in death, wounds, disease, despair, and human suffering. No one who fought there, however hard he tries, will ever forget it ... I am a reasonably unimaginative man, but Buna is still to me, in retrospect, a nightmare. This long after, I can still remember every day and most of the nights.[102]

20 Guadalcanal IV: Battle of Tassafaronga and Final Reckonings

[November 1942–February 1943]

[Maps: 20.1, 20.2]

Imperial Japan's Reluctance to Face Defeat: As the New Year, 1943, was about to arrive, Vice-Admiral Ugaki reflected on the roller coaster of Japanese emotions in 1942; he noted in his diary

> How brilliant was the first stage operation up to April!
> And what miserable setbacks since Midway in June! The
> invasions of Hawaii, Fiji, Samoa, and New Caledonia
> [the] liberation of India and destruction of the British Far
> Eastern Fleet have all scattered like dreams. Meanwhile,
> not to speak of capturing Port Moresby, but the recovery
> of Guadalcanal . . . turned out to be impossible.[1]

For public consumption, Hirohito's New Year's Day message for 1943 was more upbeat, "The Darkness is very deep but dawn is about to break in the Eastern Sky. Today the finest of the Japanese Army, Navy and Air Units are gathering. Sooner or later they will head toward the Solomon Islands where a decisive battle is being waged between Japan and America."[2] In fact the Emperor and his Army had already thrown in the towel in their bid to retake *Guadalcanal.*

With November's sinking of transports at the *First and Second Naval Battles of Guadalcanal,* the Navy's efforts to re-supply the army there with a fresh force of troops capable of retaking Henderson Field effectively came to an end; however, it would take many weeks for the scale of the disaster and the new reality to sink in. The few troops who struggled ashore were no longer a viable fighting unit. Meanwhile on *Guadalcanal* a desperate Lieutenant-General Hyakutake informed Lieutenant-General Hitoshi Imamura, ". . . an average of 100 men starve to death daily."[3] By December over half of his troops had *beri beri* or malaria. The position was clearly hopeless. Imamura retreated into a state of mute indecision. On 12 November the Japanese Navy, having muttered darkly for well over a month, finally proposed that *Guadalcanal* should be abandoned. For a Navy still gorged on expansion it was a bitter blow; by the nature of Japan's regime and its creed of Empire, the decision to retreat was for a long time too painful to contemplate.

However, by early November some senior staff officers at the Imperial General Headquarters were coming to a similar conclusion. On 18 November, Colonel Tanemura wrote in his *Imperial Headquarters (Army) Diary*, ". . . the fake pride of Imperial Headquarters is forcing us to wage the Decisive Battle on Guadalcanal," though he also noted, "If we should be defeated on Guadalcanal, it is certain we will lose the war."[4] However, it was not a unanimous view. The Imperial General Staff was persuaded by Tsuji to send Lieutenant-Colonel Imoto Kumao to supervise a new offensive. Kumao came to the conclusion that withdrawal from *Guadalcanal* was imperative.

In Rabaul frustration within the Army's officer cadre was mounting. During one academic war game based on *Guadalcanal*, a young officer blurted out, "The people [at Army HQ] in Tokyo are insane! Do you honestly think there is the slightest chance of success in another attack?"[5] In fact locally conducted war gaming had showed that Allied aircraft would destroy the reinforcement convoys before another assault on Henderson Field could take place.

At the most elemental level, further campaigns were no longer logistically possible. To supply a credible campaign with an even larger contingent of troops would now absorb over 600,000 tons of shipping which was way beyond Japan's resources. It was Lieutenant-General Kenryo Sato, Chief of the Military Affairs Bureau, who first struck up the courage to tell Prime Minister Tojo that *Guadalcanal* had to be abandoned, "We have no choice. Even now it may be too late. If we go on like this, we have no chance of winning the war."[6] It was pointed out to Tojo, ". . . even if we wanted we couldn't give the General Staff all the ships they demand. If we did, our steel-production quota of over 4 million tons would be cut by more than half and we would be unable to continue the war."[7]

The Battle of Tassafaronga: **[Map: 20.1]** After the failure to supply reinforcements to their troops at the two *Naval Battles of Guadalcanal*, the Japanese were forced to supply their troops by submarine. A roster of sixteen submarines made a trip each night. However, it was a logistical exercise that teetered on the edge of sustainability. Each submarine had a capacity of up to thirty tons of food that was enough to keep the Seventeenth Army fed for one day. Each day these supplies would have to be manhandled through the jungles to the frontline. An attempt was made to supplement the submarine deliveries by the use of quantities of small boats; however, this plan was quickly disrupted by air attacks.

By 26 November the supply situation on *Guadalcanal* had become critical; the Seventeenth Army under the new leadership of Lieutenant-General Hitoshi Imamura demanded help in the face of impending starvation. Complete exhaustion of *Guadalcanal*'s stocks of vegetables, meat and barley was expected on the day that Imamura took command. Front line troops had not been fed for days and in the non-frontline areas rations were reduced by 70 percent. On 21 November, Major Nishimura of the 228th Infantry noted in his diary that a dried plum had been his only food that day. An officer told him, "Rice. I really want rice. I want to give my men as much as they want. That is the only wish I have. Even when mortars are falling like a squall or the land is reshaped by bombs I don't worry. But I can't stand looking at my men become pale and thin."[8]

In addition to submarines, destroyers continued to dash down the 'Slot' at sunset. To overcome the supply problems, while at the same time giving more time protection to the delivering destroyers, a system was devised by which drums filled with food and medical supplies would be towed by destroyers to *Guadalcanal*; here they would be cut loose and be retrieved by small boats or swimmers. Each destroyer would pull up to 240 drums. In this way destroyers would not have to hang around for unloading but would race back up the 'Slot' as quickly as possible, before daylight brought US pilots on the hunt from Henderson Field. The first 'drum' run by destroyers was planned for 30 November. Rear-Admiral Tanaka on the destroyer *Naganami* and a second destroyer, *Takanami*, would act as escorts to six destroyers hauling drums. In order to save weight the haulage destroyers carried just their eight torpedoes in their tubes without spares.

On 29 November, decoding of a Japanese message alerted Vice-Admiral 'Bull' Halsey, Commander of the Allied forces in the *South Pacific*, that Rear-Admiral Tanaka would lead a supply run to *Guadalcanal* on the following day. Rear-Admiral Carleton Wright, who had replaced Rear-Admiral Thomas Kinkaid on the previous day, received an urgent message at 7.40 p.m. with orders to intercept. In a manner that had become a pattern in the *Solomons*, Wright was promoted to this position with little or no experience of surface command. He had never fought a night action nor had he ever even designed a tactical plan for a surface sortie of the type now planned. None of his cruisers had previous experience of the type of close range gun battle that had characterized previous battles in the 'Slot.' What he did have was a detailed plan for night action left by his predecessor, Rear-Admiral Kinkaid.

Leaving at midnight on 29 November, Wright aboard his flagship USS *Minneapolis*, needed to sail at his cruiser's full speed to make the 578 mile journey. Three more heavy cruisers accompanied him: USS *New Orleans*, USS *Pensacola*, and USS *Northampton*. In addition Task Force 67 was assigned six destroyers. At 6.30 a.m. Rear-Admiral Wright sent a message to his colleagues stating: "Information enemy forces estimated eight destroyers, six transports probably attempting land reinforcements Tassafaronga Area 2300 tonight X will proceed through Lengo Channel and destroy enemy."[9]

Tanaka led his force out of *Shortlands* and made his way in a northeasterly detour before turning south and approaching *Guadalcanal* via the *Indispensable Straits* north of *Savo Island*. The Japanese force passed to the south of *Savo Island* and spread out along the coast of *Guadalcanal* to unload their drums. Meanwhile Rear-Admiral Wright was bearing down on the Japanese supply force as he made twenty knots through *Ironbottom Sound*. Some 13 miles away, at 11.06 p.m., the *Minneapolis* picked up SG radar signals indicating the presence of Japanese ships at a distance of 23,000 yards. Wright put his cruisers and lead destroyers into two columns 4,000 yards apart. Some ten minutes later, Commander William Cole on board the USS *Fletcher* confirmed the contacts and radar amplification showed that there was a target group of six ships. At 11.16 p.m. Cole asked for permission to fire torpedoes. Wright refused this on the grounds that they were not close enough; accordingly he messaged: "RANGE ON BOGIES EXCESSIVE AT PRESENT."[10] Wright was correct only if torpedoes were set on fast speed settings rather than intermediate speeds; five minutes later, Cole, seeing his opportunity to fire literally slip by, let fly with his first salvo of five torpedoes. Just as they hit the water, Wright changed his mind and gave the order to commence fire. *Fletcher*'s executive officer, Lieutenant Joseph Wylie described Wright's responses as "the most stupid thing I have ever heard of."[11] Commander Cole fired off his second salvo of torpedoes and then opened fire with his guns. The USS *Perkins* fired off its full salvo of eight torpedoes. USS *Drayton* fired off a couple. Together the *Fletcher, Perkins,* and *Drayton* fired off twenty torpedoes. However, Wright's delay caused his force to pass by their optimum firing position.

When Wright's cruiser forces opened fire with their guns, *Takanami*, being closest to Wright's advancing line, bore the brunt of the shelling and, although she managed to loose off her full complement of torpedoes, within a few minutes she was a burning wreck. Although the Japanese had been taken by surprise, another demonstration of their poor radar, Tanaka and head of the column Captain Torajiro Sato skilfully maneuvered his destroyers in the gloom behind the blazing *Takanami* and abreast of Wright's line and collectively discharged forty-four Long Lance torpedoes. It would prove to be the most successful torpedo attack of *World War II.*

Seven minutes after she had opened fire, USS *Minneapolis* was hit by two torpedoes at the bow, destroying gun turrets and causing the forward aviation tanks to explode. Her bow was blown half off, the wrecked portion of which dragged the cruiser to the right. In addition to killing thirty-seven men, the ship's power and steering were destroyed as well as three out of four stations. USS *New Orleans* was even worse hit. A torpedo hit abreast of the forward turret blew up the munitions store and aviation fuel tanks with such force that the entire bow of the ship sheared off and sank. Everyone working in the forward part of the ship was killed; 183 men in total. On the bridge, Chaplain Howell Forgy remembered, "I opened my eyes to find we were in a cave of fire . . . The great wall of flame all around me actually dried my sopping uniform in seconds."[12]

Less than ten minutes later USS *Pensacola* took a torpedo amidships and lost power and communications. In addition the ship took on a thirteen-degree list; 125 crewmen were killed. In the confused night action, USS *Northampton*'s starboard machine gunners opened up with 'friendly' fire on the USS *Lamson*. Finally, after another ten-minute interval, the *Northampton* took two torpedo hits, which killed fifty men and disabled most of the engine room and the ship's power. The blast ripped through the forward bulkhead as well as blowing upward through the second and main deck compartments. Fire also broke out as the ship listed ten degrees to port. By 2 a.m. the *Northampton* was listing thirty-five degrees and water pressure for the firemen was falling. Captain Kitts ordered the salvage party to join him in the water. At 3.04 a.m. the *Northampton* rolled over and sank stern first with her bow rising sixty degrees in the air.

Less than twenty-three minutes after the engagement had started, Tanaka called off the action and ordered a retreat. *Takanami* sank a few hours later and just forty-eight of her crew of 244 made it to the shores of *Guadalcanal*. Meanwhile the *Northampton*'s fire raged out of control and she had to be abandoned in the early hours of 1 December. She sank just after 3.00 a.m. Destroyer escorts picked up 773 survivors. Somewhat miraculously the three other heavily damaged cruisers survived. With heroic work by the crew and salvage teams, *Minneapolis, New Orleans* and *Pensacola* managed to make their way to *Tulagi* and were eventually repaired and put back to work. They could be thankful that Tanaka's destroyers had had to leave their recharge torpedoes in dock to make way for supplies for the troops on *Guadalcanal*.

In spite of the disastrous nature of the defeat, Rear-Admiral Wright was given a Navy Medal. He wrongly claimed in his report to have sunk four Japanese destroyers and damaged others. He also attributed some of the Japanese torpedo strikes to submarines; "The observed positions of the enemy surface vessels before and during the gun action makes it seem improbable that torpedoes with speed-distance characteristics similar to our own could have reached the cruisers."[13] Meanwhile Halsey's report condemned Cole and the destroyer force for firing off their torpedoes at too great a range and for circling *Savo Island* before returning to the attack. Nimitz's official report concluded, "Destroyers fired torpedoes at an excessive range. Torpedo firing ranges at night of more than 4,000 to 5,000 yards are not acceptable," and went on to suggest of Cole that, "By firing star shells at the moment of launching torpedoes, they removed any chance of surprise."[14] Indeed not one of the twenty torpedoes fired by Wright's destroyer force scored a hit—or at least a hit that exploded. Very likely US destroyers had been sent into battle with malfunctioning torpedoes. The aftermath of the battle produced a gross injustice. In the official documentation of the battle Nimitz and Halsey erroneously heaped blame on the one man, Commander William Cole, who had "handled his ships with both skill and determination, bringing them through the long night unscathed."[15]

In hindsight it seems likely that, in line with the consensus of most US officers of his generation, Rear-Admiral Wright intended to rely heavily on the big guns of his cruisers to win the battle. Torpedoes as a tactical strike weapon clearly figured little in his planning. The *Battle of Tassafaronga* proved beyond doubt that destroyers with torpedoes were more than a match for cruisers with guns. Curiously US naval intelligence, after *Pearl Harbor* and six sea battles at *Guadalcanal*, had failed to work out the existence and capability of Japan's Type-93 Long Lance torpedo. Despite the many photographs of Japanese destroyers with their large deck mountings, their weapons had not been highlighted let alone understood—this in spite of the well-known top-heaviness of Japanese destroyers.

The US Navy's Torpedo Scandal: **[Map: 20.2]** At this point the US Navy still seems to have been completely unaware of the vast technical superiority of Japanese torpedoes to their American counterparts. During the interwar period, the Mark XIV torpedo (for submarines) and Mark XV torpedo (for destroyers) were developed for the US government at the Newport Torpedo Station. Instead of contact exploders, they developed a 'magnetic-influence exploder' designed to explode underneath a ship's keel where steel was thinner compared to the armored sides of warships; the resulting gas bubble would thus destroy the enemy ship's hull. Meanwhile if the depth setting was too shallow and the torpedo collided with the hull, it was designed to still explode. On the orders of the Torpedo Desk at the Bureau of Ordnance, the top secret Mark-6 exploder was kept back from the US Navy and held back in case of war. Pre-war Mark-5 exploders were the standard issue. Even the existence of the Mark-6 exploder was kept top secret. It was only after *Pearl Harbor* that the new Mark-6 exploder was issued.

It was a sophisticated device. The technological concept had been taken from German magnetic mines of *World War I*. Unfortunately the Mark-6 exploder did not work. Newport, which was made the monopoly designer, producer and tester of torpedoes in 1923, never carried out live tests. In practice it became apparent that the magnetic exploders either went off too early or not at all. The torpedoes themselves ran too deep because they were tested with a warhead weight different to the actual armed weapon. At the *Battle of Midway*, officialdom never questioned why half a dozen torpedoes released at close range by Commander John Waldron and his colleagues in their near suicidal attack with antiquated Douglas Devastator bombers, never exploded. The failure of US destroyer attacks also passed unnoticed: USS *Bagley* at the *Battle of Savo Island*, USS *Duncan* at the *Battle of Cape Esperance*, USS *Cushing*'s six shots at the battleship *Hiei* at the *Battle of Santa Cruz*, and USS *Laffey*, USS *Monssen* and USS *O'Bannon* at the last *Naval Battle of Guadalcanal*. The day after this battle, when USS *Benham* had to be scuttled, USS *Gwin* fired four torpedoes at the stricken ship to no effect and had to finish her off with gunfire. A similar 'did-not-work' event occurred at the *Battle of the Santa Cruz Islands* when USS *Shaw* had to scuttle the USS *Porter*. That same evening eight 'fish' fired by USS *Mustin* and USS *Anderson* to scuttle the crippled carrier USS *Hornet* failed to explode. Remarkably this catalogue of failure did not raise a brouhaha within the ranks of senior naval officers.

For the destroyer captains it took longer to work out that they were firing duds. In part this was due to the relative infrequency of surface naval engagements and use of torpedoes than for the submariners for whom the torpedo was their primary weapon. However, the failures of the Mark XV also reflected problems with US Navy guidelines on torpedo use. Navy 'War Instructions' (FTP 143; published in 1934) gave standard practice guidance regarding use of torpedoes; destroyers were ordered to use guns as their initial and main weapon of attack and were advised to reserve torpedoes for the enemy's capital ships. Neither is it surprising that the US Navy was nearly always outfought at night. The 'War Instructions' further advised that cruisers were to avoid night actions. Remarkably throughout the naval actions in the *Solomons*, and almost a year after *Pearl Harbor*, the Navy's key operational manual had not been updated.

For the users, the sea captains and submariners, the solution was self-evident—to switch off the magnetic activator. Still a high percentage of hits failed to explode. The Mark XIV and Mark XV tended not to run true and in some cases ran in a broad circle and came back to hit the sender. In addition Newport produced remarkably few torpedoes. In spite of having three shifts of 3,000 workers the company in 1937 was producing just 1.5 torpedoes per day. The US Navy thus started the war with a desperate shortage.

It was not just the Navy that suffered from dud torpedoes. A USS *Enterprise* pilot who flew an Avenger at the *Battle of Santa Cruz* noted, "Before *Pearl Harbor* nobody thought there was going to be a war so weapons were badly tested. I don't think our training was ideal, either. But those lousy torpedoes were completely inferior. We'll never know how many hits were made that simply did not go off."[16] Similarly a TBF gunner, also flying from the *Enterprise* noted that at the *Battle of Santa Cruz Islands*, "I believe we hit the *Hiei* [Japanese battleship]. Whether or not it exploded I can't tell you. There were all kinds of problems with the torpedoes. They'd hit but didn't go off, a defective weapon. I think that's why we started doing more bomb work than torpedo work . . ."[17]

The Bureau of Ordnance (known as BuOrd) displayed remarkable sloth and incompetence in dealing with the situation. After feedback from submarine skippers doubting the reliability of the Mark XIV torpedo, tests were carried out on 1 August 1942, which showed a 10-foot error in depth of running for the Mark XIV but not the others. Problems with running depth had been known about since 1938, when a division of destroyers reported that their exercise torpedoes were being retrieved with heads covered in mud in water that was ninety feet deep. It seems that rather than using nets to gauge running depths in tests, Newport used a barograph carried in the practice heads of torpedoes. However, the Newport designers forgot Bernoulli's early-eighteenth century theorem relating to *Conservation of Energy* whereby a moving fluid swops kinetic energy for pressure ($1/2pu^2 + P$ = constant). The design and placement of the barograph was flawed. As historian Captain Russell Crenshaw has noted, "The result was that a torpedo had to run deeper than desired for the pressure at the orifice leading to the depth mechanism to equal that measured statically for the depth set. The faster the torpedo moved through the water, the deeper it had to go to satisfy the pressure."[18]

In addition problems with the firing spring mechanism were not addressed. Although the submariners realized quite quickly that their torpedoes did not work, it was not until 1943 that the scale of the problem, indeed the whole scandal of incompetence, started to become clear. It later emerged that the Bureau of Ordnance (BuOrd) orchestrated a cover up of the Mark XIV and Mark XV's defects with their fallback position being the supposed incompetence of the submariners. At the beginning of the war, a US naval officer had showed off the design of the Mark-6 exploder to Professor Albert Einstein, the already legendary physicist, who was handily ensconced at nearby Princeton University. Condescending to consider a subject well below the complexity level of general relativity he told the officer that the Mark-6 would not work. Einstein warned that the rate of deceleration when a torpedo hit its target would prevent the firing pin spring from working. He even sketched a mechanism to put on the nose of a Mark XV torpedo to decrease the rate of deceleration.

In spite of Einstein's advice and the many complaints filtering back to Newport, the Torpedo Station remained stubbornly insistent on the superb quality of their products and continued to blame the slovenliness of the operators. Every torpedo tested had had a dummy run (minus warhead) at the test range at Newport and came with certified documentation and records. On 24 July 1943, some eight months after the *Battle of Tassafaronga*, the submarine, USS *Tinosa*, scored a beam shot on the former whaler, *Tonan Maru*, which had been converted into a tanker. The exploding torpedo brought the *Tonan Maru* to a halt and the *Tinosa* maneuvred to give the stricken tanker a broadside shot to dispatch it to the depths. From a thousand yards, *Tinosa* fired eight torpedoes, one after another from the perfect broadside position. *Tinosa*'s crew was close enough to hear the 'clang' as they bounced off the *Tonan Maru*'s hull; one can only imagine the rising anger and frustration of the *Tinosa*'s captain, Lieutenant-Commander L. R. 'Dan' Daspit. When he got back to *Pearl Harbor* he marched straight into Rear-Admiral Lockwood's office and demanded action. Further experiments showed that a glancing blow, with a lesser deceleration, such as the *Tinosa* achieved when it hit the *Tonan Maru* with its first beam shot, had much better odds of detonating. It became apparent that US submarines could only score with a bad or more difficult glancing shot.

Lockwood, deciding finally to dispense with the services of Newport, devised his own series of tests. Two torpedoes were fired into the steep cliffs on the south side of uninhabited *Kahoolawe Island* (*Hawaii*). One exploded, one failed to detonate. The recovered dud was found to have released the firing pin without setting off the detonator. Lockwood then constructed a tower from which torpedoes were dropped onto a steel plate to replicate the speed of a torpedo hitting the side of a ship. Seven out of ten did not explode; it was found that the firing pin spring failed under extreme deceleration and failed to drive home the detonator pin—just as Einstein had predicted. Lockwood's work produced a solution to the exploder mechanism but it was not until the spring of 1944 that BuOrd got around to testing their torpedoes in wind tunnels and discovered that depth reading by their barographs were widely out of kilter with what they had expected. As a result it was only in the last year of the war that the US Navy was able to produce a reliable torpedo. Even then it did not possess the oxygen-based technology of the Japanese weapon. The use of oxygen had been trialed in the US in the early 1930s but development of the technology was abandoned.

Japanese Torpedoes and Tactics: By contrast with the travails of the US Navy, the Japanese had developed a torpedo, which was not only remarkably advanced in terms of speed and range but was also reliable. In the 1920s, following the Washington Conference, Japanese naval planners had set about finding out how they could overcome the inherent 'numbers' disadvantage of the 5:5:3 formula for capital ships set at the 1921 Washington Conference. Their response was to develop a fast, long range, high impact torpedo; this weapon was designed to make their destroyers prolific capital ship killers. **[See Appendix A: Submarines: America Draws Tight the Noose]**

The Type-93 torpedo (that become known as the Long Lance) was a technological *tour de force*. Whereas the US Navy had concentrated on a magnetic exploder, the Japanese Navy developed a unique oxygen propulsion system to replace the compressed air systems that had formerly propelled most countries' torpedoes. This increased not only the speed but also the range of the Type-93 to as much as 40,000 yards compared with the maximum range of 13,500 yards for the American Mark XIV. The Type-93 carried a warhead explosive almost 25 percent greater in weight than the US torpedo. Such was the Type-93's greater range that for over a year from the start of the war, US commanders hit by torpedoes, such as Rear-Admiral Wright at the *Battle of Tassafaronga*, often ascribed their launch to undetected submarines.

But what is perhaps most surprising is that some senior US officers were already quite aware of Japanese superiority in torpedo technology and night fighting. In October 1942 Rear-Admiral Norman Scott had brought a paper written by Captain Albert Rooks of the USS *Houston* to the attention of Vice-Admiral 'Bull' Halsey; even before *Pearl Harbor*, Rooks had written about how the Japanese had focused on the need to train in night fighting after the experience of the *Russo-Japanese War*. Rooks had also noted their emphasis on development of their 'light' forces' technology as a result of the Washington Naval Conference. Rooks' work did not come from some special new source but from the Office of Naval Intelligence. No better illustration can be found of the sclerotic dysfunction of the US Navy in the year after *Pearl Harbor*.

Against overwhelming odds Rear-Admiral Tanaka won a sensational victory at the *Battle of Tassafaronga*. Even with the advantage of radar and surprise, a much larger and heavily armed US force had been trounced by the superior night tactics and weaponry of Tanka's 'supply' destroyers. After the war, Tanaka was typically modest: "I have heard that US naval experts praised my command in that action. I am not deserving of such honors. It was the superb proficiency and devotion of the men who served me that produced the tactical victory for us."[19] Naval historian Samuel Eliot Morison concluded, "... but despite the brief confusion of his destroyers, Tanaka made no mistakes at *Tassafaronga*."[20] For an American Navy that believed that it was getting to grips with competing with the Imperial Navy, the *Battle of Tassafaronga* was a shocking setback.

However, as before in the numerous naval battles for control of *Guadalcanal*, tactical naval victories did not lead to strategic advantage. Tanaka failed to deliver his supply drums. Furthermore when Tanaka did succeed in dropping 1,500 drums some three days later, US aircraft were able to machine gun the floating barrels and managed to sink over 300. A third 'drum-run' was seen off by aggressive action by US PT boats on 7 December. The Imperial Navy was now at the end of its tether with regard to using more of its destroyer force as speedy food transports. Tanaka's Chief of Staff complained, "we are more a freighter convoy than a fighting squadron these days. The damn Yankees have dubbed us the 'Tokyo Express.' We transport cargo to that cursed island, and our orders are to flee rather than fight. What a stupid thing!"[21] However, the Imperial Navy agreed to a last attempt on 11 December with Tanaka leading a force of eleven destroyers; attacked by five PT boats, Tanaka's flagship destroyer *Teruzuki* was hit by a torpedo and was scuttled. Only 200 of the 1200 drums were recovered.

The final days of the naval conflict also proved the worth of the PT boat. The 'Hooligan Navy' as the PT boats were called had finally been organized into a useful force by Commander Lloyd Mustin. He set up patrol schedules and organized better information coordination with the 'normal' navy. Tactics were also improved. Open water was avoided as was still water because it showed wakes more clearly. Decoy runs by selected units were practiced. On 8 December *PT-59* captained by John Searles sank Japanese submarine *I-3* as it attempted to deliver food to *Guadalcanal*. The episode considerably lifted the morale of the PT forces. As Mustin observed, "This was quite a feather in the cap of those PT boys."[22] After his sinking by a PT boat, in an action in which he was wounded, Tanaka was relieved of his command and one of Japan's most talented naval officers spent the rest of the war at a desk job in *Singapore* and then finally Burma. It was also the end of the attempt to supply the army in *Guadalcanal* with a view to the recapture of Henderson Field. At the end of the month Emperor Hirohito approved a withdrawal from *Guadalcanal* to a new defensive line to be set up at *New Georgia*.

Shipboard Radar Developments in the Pacific War: Radar developed rapidly as the war progressed. Although prototypes had been tested earlier, the first shipboard radar system deployed on US naval ships was the CXAM. The first six units were delivered in 1940 and fitted on the battleship USS *California* and the aircraft carrier USS *Yorktown*, as well as four heavy cruisers. Another fourteen units of an upgraded CXAM-1 were delivered later in the year. The heavy, large-scale equipment only made it suitable for larger ships. It was a huge technological advance in that it enabled detection of planes from seventy-five miles out. (At the *Battle of the Coral Sea*, Lexington's CXAM-1 spotted Japanese aircraft sixty-eight miles away.) For smaller ships SC-Radar was developed at a higher frequency. It needed careful maintenance to work correctly and its reliability was sometimes reduced by rainsqualls or land mass, which tended to introduce clutter. It was designed to detect enemy aircraft at up to sixty miles in range.

Perhaps the greatest leap forward however came with the development of high frequency SG radar that could detect enemy ships at 15,000–75,000 yards when set at long range or up to 15,000 yards at short range. SG radar operated a 3-degree beam, which displayed a blip for an object on a specially coated monitor that remained until the next sweep refreshed it. The whole system was small enough to be deployed on smaller US warships such as destroyers. Although the development of SG radar gave the US a significant advantage because its destroyers, acting as pickets, could pick up enemy Japanese ships long before they could pick up US ships, its use was initially mitigated by poor operation and bad seamanship. Needless to add the advantages of SG radar were significantly diminished by the fact that US destroyers were equipped with torpedoes that did not work. By 1943 however the development and use of SG radar gave the US Navy a significant tactical advantage in combat with Japanese forces that still relied on trained night-sight spotters.

Japan's Defeat at Guadalcanal: Tojo, faced by the armed forces' increasing logistical impasse, called a cabinet meeting at which the Army and Navy were offered just 290,000 tons of shipping. The offer was rejected and Tojo called a special cabinet meeting on the evening of 5 December at which a further 95,000 tons was added to sweeten the deal. A furious Lieutenant-General Shizuichi Tanaka ordered General Kenryo Sato, the Chief Army spokesman and key advisor to Tojo, to come to his house to make his explanations. Having explained Tojo's resource allocations as requested, Sato turned to leave and was assaulted by General Tanaka who had to be restrained from drawing his sword. The next day Tojo himself faced Tanaka's wrath; he screamed at the Prime Minister, "What are you doing about the war? We'll lose it this way. *Kono bakayaro* [you damned fool]!"[23] Although Tanaka was led away and officially reprimanded, Tojo caved in to the request for more shipping.

The deadlock was finally broken when the Imperial General Staff sent Colonel Joichiro Senada to Rabaul to gauge the situation. Arriving on 19 December, Senada met Lieutenant-General Hitoshi Imamura and his senior staff and quickly came to the conclusion that *Guadalcanal* would have to be abandoned. This was the recommendation that Senada took back to Tokyo, though it took another week of bureaucratic obfuscation before the Imperial General HQ ordered its staff to plan a new line of defense in the *Solomons*. Senada also pointed out that the focus on *Guadalcanal* was distracting attention from the collapsing position in New Guinea. At the same time that it was decided to withdraw from *Guadalcanal*, it was decided to refocus resources on countering the gathering momentum of General MacArthur's advance in New Guinea.

Underlining the desperation of the situation, on 23 December Lieutenant-General Hyakutake sent another pleading radiogram: "No food available and we can no longer send out scouts. We can do nothing to withstand the enemy's offensive. Seventeenth Army now requests permission to break into the enemy's positions and die an honorable death rather than die of hunger in our own dugouts."[24] Although General Hajime Sugiyama, Chief of the Imperial Army General Staff, and Admiral Osami Nagano, Chief of the Imperial Navy General Staff, gave their advice to the Emperor regarding the withdrawal from *Guadalcanal* on 28 December, it was not until New Year's Eve that Hirohito formally agreed to withdraw Japanese forces from *Guadalcanal*. Even then it took a two-hour Imperial Conference with the Emperor before a decision was forthcoming. The Emperor berated the Army's failings; a probing Hirohito asked, "Why was it that it took the Americans just a few days to build an airbase and the Japanese more than a month or so?"[25]

Curiously at the moment that Japan's senior command admitted defeat on *Guadalcanal*, Rabaul had never been busier. On 30 December photographs of *Rabaul Harbor* showed that it was occupied by twenty-one warships and seventy merchant vessels. A worried Lieutenant-General Kenney wrote on 1 January 1943, "When the Jap accumulates that much tonnage it means trouble for me."[26] The problem was not getting *matériel* to Rabaul, it was getting it to *Guadalcanal*. With that problem taken off the table, the newly accumulated *matériel* in Rabaul would be aimed at halting MacArthur's advances on New Guinea. Arguably Japan's firepower in troops, aircraft, ships and *matériel* was still greater than that of the Allies at this time.

Meanwhile on *Guadalcanal*, Vandegrift and the 1st Marine Division was finally relieved and shipped to Australia for 'rest and recovery.' It had been a ten-week campaign of almost continuous fighting; an astonishing performance by an American fighting unit, which gave an example for all US infantry of what was possible in the face of an unrelenting foe. On average the 'original' Marines who had landed at *Guadalcanal* lost 20 lbs in body weight. Many were too weak to climb the nets slung over the side of the convoy transports. Up to 30 percent of some units were deemed to be unfit for any future combat. Their position was taken over by the US Army's XIV Corps comprising the 25th Infantry and 23rd Infantry Divisions (normally known as the Americal Division); in addition, the US Army units were supported by the 2nd Marine Division. This 50,000 strong force was put under the command of Major-General Alexander Patch. In spite of this massively increased strength, a three-week offensive against Japanese positions on Mount Austen was forced to a halt on 4 January. Mount Austen was a formidable natural defensive position. The official US Army history described it as "not a single peak, but the apex of a confusing series of steep, rocky, jungled ridges . . . a dense forest covers the summit."[27] It overlooked Henderson Field from about six miles away and might in theory have been capable of supporting Japanese heavy artillery to interdict Allied aircraft.

The Japanese had managed to haul artillery onto some of the ridges and launched attacks at close range from the dense jungle. Perhaps more importantly the valley adjacent to Mount Austen provided superb natural cover for the Japanese who enhanced the quality of the natural defenses with a chain of bunkers, gun emplacements and firing trenches. The positions were held by the remnants of two regiments from Gifu and were commanded by Major Inagaki Takeyoshi. Colonel Stanley Larsen guessed that the so-called 'Gifu Strong Point' was defended by about 400 enemy soldiers; "They had constructed a circular fortified zone about 300 yards in diameter . . . forty-two pillboxes made of dirt. They had built them long enough before so that the weeds had grown over them. You could get to about fifteen feet of them and not see what was there. They were mutually supporting."[28]

Even supporting the US troops with supplies was testing. A jeep road nearby Mount Austen took some supplies that then had to be manhandled up jungle tracks. Other supplies were pulled up the *Mtanikau River* against the current on rafts; this became known to the GIs as the 'Push Push Maru.' B-17s also made drops. However, this tended to damage a high percentage of equipment. Lieutenant William Schumacher complained "even water cans split. Almost all the 0.30 caliber ammo got bent and wasn't usable."[29]

As was usually the case with the jungle engagements in the *South Pacific*, there was no grand tactical plan. Troops simply advanced to a point where they could locate the enemy pillboxes and firing trenches, then used tank, artillery or mortar fire to take out the Japanese defensive positions one by one. Battles consisted of mini battles, organized on site by junior officers, which took out Japanese positions. Ultimately superior US weaponry and weight of firepower told. The conquest of the 'Gifu Strong Point' ended with a *banzai* charge against the company charged with covering the Japanese waterhole.

Stanley Larsen, commanding a unit of the 25th Division, recalled, "It was a steep slope. I've only been involved in two *banzai* charges, and they are terrifying. In this one eighty-five Japanese were killed. Twenty-one were officers and the rest enlisted. F Company did not lose a single man. We had a bulldozer up there and we bulldozed a mass grave and all were buried there."[30]

Renewing the offensive a week later, Major-General Patch's forces took Mount Austen, 'Sea Horse Ridge' and 'Galloping Horse Ridge.' Japanese forces suffered losses of 3,000 killed; it was a ratio of twelve Japanese dead for every American. It was the fag end of Japan's *Guadalcanal* Campaign. On 14 January Lieutenant-General Hyakutake began preparation for withdrawal of his troops from *Guadalcanal* by sending a fresh battalion of troops to cover the now completely bedraggled force. Although Admiral 'Bull' Halsey had received prior intelligence about the operation, it was, perhaps not surprisingly, erroneously interpreted as a build-up of Japanese forces for another crack at Henderson Field. Halsey took action to resupply *Guadalcanal* for the expected action by sending a supply convoy on 29 January. Three nights later, unobserved by the US Navy, Hyakutake began a withdrawal of troops from *Guadalcanal* that was completed on 7 February. A total of 10,652 Japanese soldiers were successfully extracted. The *Guadalcanal* Campaign ended with a whimper that was completely out of character with the four preceding months. Only on 9 February did Major-General Patch realize that US forces had sole possession of *Guadalcanal*.

Guadalcanal's Final Reckoning: Halsey's action report, dated 17 April, noted,

> Until almost the last moment, it appeared that the Japanese were attempting a major reinforcement effort. Only skill in keeping their plans disguised and bold celerity in carrying them out enabled the Japanese to withdraw the remnants of the *Guadalcanal* garrison. Not until after all organized forces had been evacuated on 8 February did we realize the purpose of their air and naval dispositions; otherwise with the strong forces available to us ashore on *Guadalcanal* and our powerful fleet in the *South Pacific*, we might have converted the withdrawal into a disastrous rout.[31]

Nevertheless the most famous land battle of the *Pacific* campaign was over. It was a stunning victory for US forces, particularly the Navy and its Marines.

Japan had lost perhaps the decisive encounter of the *Pacific War*. From the first they had miscalculated. Yamamoto had revealed a catastrophic intellectual feebleness in his evaluation of the situation on *Guadalcanal* after the surprise American attack. Either he needed to use the entire strength of the combined fleet to retake it or he should have decided to fight the Americans closer to Rabaul. The middle course that was followed, the gradual feeding in of forces proved the worst of all. In the end both Japanese air power and sea power were gradually whittled away and sacrificed on the anvil of Henderson Field.

In the course of the six-month battle some 1,592 US troops were killed (1,042 of which were Marines) and 4,283 wounded; about half the casualties were also Marines. Some 5,400 Marines and soldiers were also struck down by malaria. After they were relieved most of the 1st Marine officers were promoted and went out to other units. The sick were hospitalized and usually reassigned to easier billets when they healed. Older men were sent home. Few troops served two campaigns with the same regiment and three was extremely rare. There was a noticeable change in combat relationships as the war progressed. Walter Johnson in the 43rd Division, recalled, "After you're in combat, it's harder to make new friends for some reason. Guess you don't want them to die and hurt you. I think a lot of guys felt that way."[32]

For America, *Guadalcanal* was a heroic victory achieved by soldiers who knew that they were fighting for their lives. Whatever the tactical and *matériel* causes of US victory at *Guadalcanal*, it was the men on the ground and in the air who won the battle. Fighter pilot Roger Haberman asserted, "The men at Cactus [*Guadalcanal*] were absolutely dedicated to what they were doing. There wasn't a single slacker, not one . . . Out of forty pilots we had fourteen killed and four wounded, two broke down, and the rest had malaria. So we were ravaged when we left. We were no longer effective. But we had held on."[33]

Because, halfway through the battle, America was able to relieve its troops, some 60,000 in aggregate were employed on *Guadalcanal*. By comparison the Japanese Army, which was unable to relieve its troops because of losses and logistical constraints, suffered an estimated 32,000 deaths from combat and disease out of 43,000 troops employed—a death toll twenty times higher than the US. At least half of these men would have lived if the Japanese Army had conducted an even slightly normal policy of surrender. Few of the Japanese were buried. *Guadalcanal* became an island of the dead. Ian Page, a New Zealand bomber pilot recalled, "there were partial skeletons and bones laying about everywhere, some covered by parts of uniforms."[34] When a gruesome smell woke the occupants of his tent, Page discovered that "the cause of the smell was found to be the top half of a corpse which the heavy rain had released from the hillside, and it had become lodged in bushes outside our tent."[35] On casualty numbers alone *Guadalcanal* represented a massive defeat for the Japanese.

Other *matériel* statistics are also telling. On paper the naval battles at *Guadalcanal* were won by Japan in a contest that was broadly even. The Japanese Imperial Navy lost just 1 light carrier, an escort carrier, 2 battleships and 3 heavy cruisers, 1 light cruiser and 11 destroyers. An estimated 12,000 Japanese seamen lost their lives. By comparison the US lost 2 fleet carriers, (the key capital weapon of the naval war), 6 heavy cruisers, 2 light cruisers and 14 destroyers. An estimated 3,000 American seamen died during the conflict. Importantly in a war of attrition that Japan could only lose, a small Japanese victory in the naval battles represented a pyrrhic victory. Not only could the US increasingly replace its core naval assets, it could also repair them and, over time, massively increase them. By contrast as the war progressed Japan's overused and under-maintained fleet became increasingly 'clapped-out'; as for replacements the cupboard was virtually bare.

In many respects the same was true of the contest in the air; however, here the victory in material terms belonged more clearly to the US Air Force that lost 715 planes to over 800 lost by the Japanese. It is interesting to note that 264 US aircraft were lost in combat while 451 aircraft were from operational losses; a strong indication of the wear and tear on planes, as well as unreliability of *World War II* aircraft. Mechanical failure, maintenance mistakes, navigation errors, bad weather, landing mistakes by exhausted pilots or low level 'hot-dogging' by over-exuberant pilots, all caused a high level of losses. *World War II* aircraft, particularly in situations of maximum performance in daily combat mode, inevitably had a short shelf life.

Japan's fighter losses during the *Battle of Henderson Field* amounted to 83 land-based fighters and 36 carrier-based fighters; aggregated, these losses were four times more than the major naval *Battle of the Coral Sea*. In general, because most of the air battles took place around Henderson Field, some 400 miles away from the Japanese airbases at Rabaul, most downed US pilots were recovered; this was not the case with the Japanese. For Japan the loss of experienced pilots was much graver than the loss of planes. The 2,362 Japanese pilots and aircrew lost at *Guadalcanal* could never be replaced by men of equivalent training or experience. By comparison the eminent *Guadalcanal* historian Richard B. Frank has estimated that just 420 Allied pilots and aircrew were killed, a better than 5:1 advantage over the Japanese.

The mathematics of Japanese pilot numbers is exemplified by the career of Japanese flying ace, Saburo Sakai. At the time of his application to flying school, there were 1,500 applicants for this non-commissioned category. Only seventy were admitted of whom just twenty-five graduated to become pilots in the Japanese Navy Air Force. Of this number just ten were fighter pilots. If added to the number of Navy officers (6) and Navy cadets (10) who also qualified as fighter pilots, it meant that in 1938 Japan produced only twenty-six fighter pilots for its Navy—less than a quarter of the number of pilots lost at the *Coral Sea, Midway* and *Guadalcanal* in 1942. Not surprisingly attrition losses at *Guadalcanal* were devastating because experienced pilots, such as Sakai, who was shot down and badly wounded in the head, could not be replaced. By the time of the *Battle of the Santa Cruz Islands*, the last carrier battle of 1942, the decline in Japanese aircraft carrier pilot quality was already being remarked upon by US observers.

Rifles, Carbines, Shotguns: **[Chart: C.8]** For the Marines that set out on the *Battle of Guadalcanal*, the rifle was their constant companion. As mortar man Tony Balsa noted, "They gave us an ammo belt with six clips or so . . . But in our pockets we always carried extra clips, six or eight usually . . . I never knew a combat infantryman that didn't carry more than the assigned load of ammunition."[36] The fear of running out of bullets in the jungle, when resupply was uncertain, concentrated minds.

At first the Marines carried the Springfield, a bolt-action rifle introduced in 1903. It had a 5-bullet magazine but each 0.30 caliber bullet had to be put into the breach by manual release of the bolt. Albeit dated, of its type it was a good weapon that was both accurate and reliable. Ranged against it on *Guadalcanal* was the Arisaka Model-38 that came into service in 1905, the thirty-eighth year of the Emperor Meiji's rule. Although its firing mechanism was based on the German Mauser, the Arisaka was a poorly built weapon with substandard assembly and poor sights. Technically outdated Japanese manufacturers were unable to produce a weapon strong enough to take a 0.30 caliber bullet. The typically tiny Japanese infantryman ended up carrying a weapon 50.25-inches long, which was six inches more than the Springfield but only capable of taking a 0.25 caliber bullet. The lengthy barrel was required by Japanese engineers to produce a weapon with sufficient accuracy and muzzle velocity. With bayonet attached the Arisaka often stood higher than the typical infantryman; it was also a pound heavier than the Springfield.

Seemingly the Japanese infantryman was outgunned at *Guadalcanal*. However, the Arisaka Model-38 had one superb advantage. Japanese chemists had produced a bullet that was virtually smokeless and the long barrel of the Arisaka hid the flash of a round being fired. In jungle conditions where the enemy was rarely seen, the Japanese could more easily sight the US soldier by the flash of his gun. Furthermore the Arisaka's smaller recoil made reloading and sighting a second shot much quicker. The bullet fire by the Arisaka also 'wobbled' because Japanese manufacturers could not produce barrels of fine enough tolerance. Although this reduced velocity, the wobble produced a distinctive 'crack' that made it difficult to judge the direction from which it came. Platoon leader Ernest Gerber complained, "We couldn't see where the gun was firing from."[37] Similarly Scott Wilson, an infantryman of the 25th Division noted: "The density of the growth of the jungle absorbed sound, distorted it. It was very hard to tell from which direction the bullets were coming. You would have to see leaves or something move."[38]

The yaw of the Arisaka bullet produced nastier wounds that compensated for its smaller caliber. US military medical analysis reported: "The 0.256 bullet, especially one made with a gliding metal (an alloy of copper and zinc) jacket, when it hit a target had an explosive effect which tended to separate . . . small globules of lead scattered through the wound and embedded themselves elsewhere in the flesh."[39] Another unintended advantage of the Arisaka was its lighter bullets, which were cheaper to manufacture and to transport; an important advantage given Japan's limited manufacturing capacity and logistical frailty.

However, the *Battle of Guadalcanal* was the last action of the war to feature a Springfield versus Arisaka engagement. During the course of the campaign, the Garand M1 replaced the Marines' Springfield rifles. Although the M1 was slightly heavier than the Springfield, compensation came in the form of an eight-round magazine and a recoil mechanism that ejected and reloaded a new bullet automatically. The increased rate of fire, combined with a higher muzzle velocity significantly increased the Marines' stopping power. As Tony Balsa noted, "The Springfield 0.30 was a good rifle for its time. The M1 was better. It was semi-automatic and fired as fast as you pulled the trigger."[40] The M1 was also easy to use with relatively light recoil that made rapid fire easier. Perhaps most importantly, "When you hit someone with it, it knocked them down." As Balsa recalled, "Someone hit with the Springfield might fight back. If the M1 hit you in the arm or leg, that was it, you'd stay down."[41] Perhaps the greatest downside of the M1 was that it tended to emit a large puff of smoke that was visible in daylight while at night a one-inch flame could be seen coming out of the end of the barrel. US soldiers sometimes referred to the M1 as 'old smoke pole.'[42] Japanese soldiers would alter their aim accordingly with the result that US doctors noted an unusually high percentage of head wounds.

A seven or eight man infantry unit would also carry a Thompson sub-machine gun. However, it was a weapon rarely favored by the Marines at *Guadalcanal*. Marshall Chaney echoed the commonly held view, "we didn't like the 0.45 caliber Thompson. In heavy cover it sounded too much like the Japanese 0.25 caliber rifle."[43] The Thompson would be replaced in 1943 by the M1 Carbine (not to be confused with the M1 Garand). It was short, making it lighter to carry and used a fifteen- or thirty-round detachable box; the M1 Carbine weighed just 5.2 lbs versus the 9.5 lbs of the Garand M1. The M1 Carbine was produced by the Winchester Company using a short-stroke gas piston designed by David 'Carbine' Williams. He developed a prototype while he was in prison for murder following the killing of a sheriff during a raid on his illegal still in North Carolina during Prohibition in the 1930s. After his release Williams was employed by Winchester in 1939 to refine the carbine designs of the recently deceased 'Ed' Browning (brother of the legendary gun maker John Browning).

The M1 Carbine, originally produced as a low volume special, became one of the most successful weapons of the war. Although it fired a light 0.30 caliber bullet at a low velocity, it fitted into the trend toward rifles which placed less reliance on accuracy and more emphasis on speed, weight and volume of fire. Given that a high percentage of kills in the *South Pacific*'s jungle conditions came within twenty-five yards of the enemy, it is not surprising that the semi-automatic M1 Carbine became a favorite of the Marines. The Marines were also issued with Winchester 12-gauge shotguns—80,000 of which were purchased by the Marine Corps in *World War II*. In the confines of the jungle, these were especially favored. Against tree top Japanese snipers, a tactic favored by the Japanese, the shotgun was particularly effective. Marine Robert Kennington, who was frequently 'point' on jungle patrols, bluntly described its advantages. "The shotgun would make a hole through the leaves and a hole through the sniper."[44] Even General Vandegrift's successor on *Guadalcanal*, Major-General Alexander Patch, carried a shotgun.

While the Japanese Arisaka rifle had it advantages, by the end of the *Battle of Guadalcanal*, US arms manufacturers had developed weapons that gave their troops on the ground a much heavier weight of fire. Bullets mattered. Although mortars and grenades were the major killers of the *Pacific War*, bullets tended to end the career of a soldier while survivors of a mortar wound generally recovered to fight again. By the end of the *Guadalcanal* Campaign, US light arms development had handed the Marines a significant technological advantage.

Admiral King Attends to Logistics: If the US logistics planning and execution before the *Battle of Guadalcanal* was deficient, it was little better nine months later. At the beginning of the war, Admiral King had delegated logistics planning to Vice-Admiral Frederick Horne and his assistant Rear-Admiral Lynde McCormick. When the war started Horne had been pulled off the retirement list. In spite of his experience he was not up to the job. An aircraft procurement officer on his staff, Captain Paul Pihl recalled that, concerning the job of running logistics, "[Horne] didn't have the faintest idea what the hell he was going to do with it."[45] Horne operated with the lightest of touches and clearly had little understanding of what his subordinates were doing.

Perhaps fortunately for King, Pihl had known the admiral for years and felt free enough to go to King's office in early 1943 to vent his misgivings. King was impressed enough to pull Pihl in to his own staff where he provided logistical plans for the strategies being prepared by COMINCH (Commander in Chief, US Navy). Pihl's presence started to increase King's awareness of logistical issues. In April, Pihl's newly created Logistical Organisation Planning Unit (LOPU) reviewed the situation on the west coast. In a damning report, Pihl concluded, "There is no overall coordinated supervision of logistical operation on the *Pacific Coast*. Coordination is sporadic and extra-curricular . . ."[46]

After dispatching a mission to the *Pacific* to investigate and receiving the findings that chaos on the West Coast was holding up supplies to Nimitz, King decided to act. His conclusion was that the building of warehousing on the *Pacific Coast* was leading to hoarding of supplies in the new facilities. King immediately canceled all new building projects with the logic that if there was no space to stores supplies, they would get shipped out faster.

Horne was not appreciative of Pihl's criticism and King's interference and wrote back to King with more than a little feeling: "It is a matter of fact and record that the degree of efficiency and comfort our advance forces enjoy is beyond anything previously experienced in warfare."[47] Without question King's increasing focus on supply had an effect on improving the flow of *matériel* to the *Pacific*, though problems continued to surface. Perhaps it was inevitable given the massive increase in industrial output, combined with the exponential growth of personnel serving at a distance of 5,000 miles or more from America that there would be strains on logistics. But, however creaky the supply chain, the breathing space enabled by victory at the *Battle of Guadalcanal* allowed the Navy to organize itself for the next push planned for the *Central Pacific*.

Reflections and Consequences of the Guadalcanal Campaign: Japan's military leadership immediately recognized the scale of the reversal at *Guadalcanal*, fought over what was initially seen as an insignificant airfield in the remote *South Pacific*. They, perhaps even more than their US counterparts, realized that *Guadalcanal* represented the decisive turning point of the war in the *Pacific*.

Major-General Kawaguchi, who had come so close to taking 'Edson's Ridge' and with it Henderson Field, wrote to his friend, the journalist Gen Nishino, "We lost the battle. And Japan lost the war." Nishino replied, ". . . the day is bound to come when the truth about Guadalcanal will be known and people realize you were right."[48] Major-General Kawaguchi noted that the Japanese Army was not the only service "buried in the graveyards of Guadalcanal."[49] Japan's air and naval services were as much diminished by the *Battle of Guadalcanal* as the Army.

The short-term ramifications of the *Battle of Guadalcanal* were that the Japanese Combined Fleet's focus on Henderson Field allowed MacArthur to gain a tenuous foothold at Buna on the northeastern shore of New Guinea that would otherwise not have been possible. Much as it would have pained MacArthur to acknowledge the fact, it was the absorption of Japanese naval and air firepower by the Marines on *Guadalcanal* that allowed MacArthur to begin his triumphant advance from New Guinea to the Philippines. *Guadalcanal* made it possible for MacArthur to move from defense to offense. Thus the opening up of northern New Guinea and the Philippines would introduce the possibility of interdicting the supply of oil to Japan from the East Indies. As historian Eric Bergerud, has concluded, "By the fall of 1943 it was all too clear to Tokyo that the door to Southeast Asia had been cracked open; Tokyo also knew its industrial economy would collapse if that door was kicked in."[50]

Senior officers in Tokyo had few doubts that *Guadalcanal* was the turning point of the *Pacific War*. Fleet Admiral Nagano, who served as Naval adviser to the Emperor and then Chief of Naval General Staff, was asked, after the war, what was the key moment of change: "I look upon the Guadalcanal and Tulagi operations as the turning point from offensive to defensive, and the cause of our setback there was our inability to increase our forces at the same speed as you."[51] Similarly Captain Toshikazu Ohmae, a senior staff planner at the Imperial Navy's GHQ, was adamant, "After Guadalcanal, in the latter part of 1942, I felt we could not win."[52] Likewise Lieutenant-General Kawabe, former Deputy Chief of the Japanese Army General Staff, concluded, "As for the turning point . . . it was, I feel, at Guadalcanal."[53]

Part V
Toil and Sweat: The Pacific, India, Burma, and China: January 1943–June 1944

21 Battle of the Bismarck Sea: Tipping Point of US Air Supremacy

[January 1943–March 1943]

[Drawing: 21.1] [Maps: 21.2, 21.3, 21.4, 21.5, 21.6, 21.7]

At the beginning of 1943, as the Japanese campaign on *Guadalcanal* was winding down to defeat and withdrawal, Japanese attention, and more importantly their resources, were switched to New Guinea. Here, after the defeat at the *Battles of Kokoda* and the *Battles of Buna-Gona-Sanananda*, Japan faced a new threat to their control of the southeast corner of New Guinea. They anticipated that MacArthur would advance northwards in a move that would threaten both Rabaul and the northern New Guinea corridor toward the Philippines. In Rabaul, Lieutenant-General Harukichi Hyakutake, commander of the Seventeenth Army in Rabaul, planned to reinforce Lieutenant-General Hatazo Adachii's Eighteenth Army and fight for the control of the areas due north of Port Moresby on the east coast of New Guinea's *Gulf of Huon*. However, unbeknownst to Hyakutake and Adachii, in the latter half of 1942, new US Army Air Force commanders were undertaking a transformation of their forces that would, in combination with Australian forces on the ground, render their attempts to sustain Japanese control of the *Gulf of Huon* untenable. In the first fifteen months of the war, after a disastrous beginning the US Army Air Force, along with the air arms of the Navy and the Marines had achieved a parity with the Imperial Japanese Navy Air Force in the *South Pacific*. This was about to change; arguably from its initial role as the minor service in the *Pacific War*, the US air arms were about to leap forward to take center stage in the war.

MacArthur Ousts US Air Force Lieutenant-General George Brett: Lieutenant-General George Brett had enjoyed a lively *entrée* to war. Starting as Chief of the Air Corps in May 1941, he found himself effectively replaced a month later by General 'Hap' Arnold when General George Marshall's reorganization of the Army moved Arnold to the post of head of the US Army Air Force (USAAF). From Washington, Brett moved to London to advise on the requirements of the Lend-Lease agreement with Winston Churchill. He fell out with British authorities not only in London but also in Egypt where he criticized the military arrangements. From here he was moved to Rangoon and negotiated co-operation agreements for the US with General Sir Archibald Wavell, Britain's Commander in Chief in India, and Chiang Kai-shek. Subsequently Brett became Wavell's deputy at the short-lived America-British-Dutch-Australia (ABDA) Command. He departed Java on 23 February 1942 and washed up in Australia where he took up command of all US Army Forces based there.

The task faced by Lieutenant-General George Brett was an unenviable one. Roosevelt and Marshall had made it clear from the beginning that their priorities in fighting the war on two fronts would lie in Europe. War materials, in desperately short supply at the beginning of 1942 would be allocated to begin with on an 85:15 split toward Europe, later adjusted to 70:30. Brett's leadership of American forces in Australia was cut short when MacArthur was brought back from the Philippines in March 1942. Their relationship had already started at a low level. While MacArthur was surrounded at Bataan and *Corregidor*, Brett was already recommending, quite correctly, that saving the Philippines was a hopeless cause and that throwing more air resources at it would be wasteful and potentially damaging for the defense of other areas including Australia.

Even the issue of getting MacArthur back to Australia brought bad blood. Brett, without any new planes, sent four clapped out B-17 Flying Fortress to *Mindanao* to bring back the new Commander in Chief; only one arrived, minus functioning brakes. A furious MacArthur, seemingly unreflective regarding his good fortune in having been hoiked out of *Corregidor*, complained directly to Marshall who forced Vice-Admiral Herbert Leary to send four brand-new Navy B-17s from the Anzac Area Command. The episode should have highlighted to MacArthur Australia Command's lack of resources. Instead MacArthur made an immediate request for a bombing mission against Japanese forces in the Philippines. It was a futile, theatrical gesture on MacArthur's part and Brett, now commander of Allied Air Forces in the South West Pacific Area, was naturally reluctant. After his own transport experiences at *Mindanao*, MacArthur should have known that Brett's beaten-up old bombers were in no condition to make such a long-range attack. A bombing mission to the Philippines, that could be no more than a token gesture, took place but only after a long-running spat with MacArthur's Chief of Staff, the bullying and thoroughly duplicitous Major-General Richard Sutherland. As a result of this episode MacArthur officially reprimanded Brett and lobbied for him to be replaced.

The whiff of hypocrisy was apparent a year later when MacArthur sent his Deputy Chief of Staff, Major-General Richard Marshall, to the Pacific Military Conference in Washington on 12 March 1943, in part to demand new aircraft. The Casablanca Conference (codenamed SYMBOL) duly called for ". . . adequate forces . . . be allocated to the Pacific and Far Eastern Theaters."[1] Even then the US War Department insisted that it could not provide planes because of the requirement for the strategic bombing of Germany.

Like most of his contemporaries, Brett's opinion of MacArthur was far from flattering: "General MacArthur has a wonderful personality when he desires to turn it on. He is, however, absolutely bound up in himself. I do not believe he has a single thought for anybody who is not useful to him . . ."[2] Remarkably Brett only met MacArthur face to face on seven occasions. Dealing with his subordinates, the 'Bataan gang,' was also exasperating. Brett noted, "Marshall, Willoughby, Marquat and Casey . . . have talked a great deal but accomplished little. They have an exaggerated idea of their own importance . . . [they] are, in fact, 'Yes-men.' They are officious and have no proper sense of the need for cooperation with the forces operating under the Commander in Chief."[3] Something had to give. With MacArthur having made himself indispensable in the US media as America's greatest war hero, there could only be one loser. Marshall, a friend of Brett's, reluctantly recalled him in July 1942. As Brett's replacement, Marshall offered Lieutenant-General Frank Andrews, who, knowing MacArthur by reputation, refused. After being turned down by Andrews, Marshall then offered MacArthur the choice of either Brigadier-General James Doolittle, the famous aviator and hero of the recent bombing raid on Tokyo, or Major-General George Kenney. Not surprisingly MacArthur chose Kenney. Doolittle was a superstar, a darling of the US media; in MacArthur's universe there was only room for one star.

General George Kenney: The son of a carpenter, Kenney was born in Yarmouth, Nova Scotia, Canada, while his parents were vacationing there. He grew up in Brookline, Massachusetts and after graduation from the local high school entered the Massachusetts Institute of Technology to study civil engineering though he was forced to quit when his father ran out on the family. With a former classmate he set up a civil engineering company, Beaver Contracting and Engineering Corporation and undertook various projects including bridge building. However, when the United States entered *World War I*, he joined the aviation section of the US Signal Corp and, after learning to fly, was sent to the Western Front in France. Here he shot down two enemy aircraft and on 10 January 1919 he was awarded the Distinguished Service Cross by Brigadier-General 'Billy' Mitchell, the noted pioneer of naval aviation.

Having been given a coveted captaincy in the post-war regular Army, he served as commander of the 8th Aero Squadron along the Mexican border during the *Mexican Revolution*. After recovering from an accident in Texas, he married a nurse who died two years later in childbirth after bearing him a son. A year later in June 1923 he married the nurse who he had entrusted to bring up his child.

Appointed an Air Service inspector at the Curtis Airplane and Motor Company in Garden City, New York, in 1920, Kenney inspected aircraft and test flew them. Later at McCook Airfield in Dayton Ohio, he worked on the placement of 0.30 caliber machine guns on De Havilland DH-4s. The British designed De Havilland was manufactured by the newly founded Dayton-Wright company set up by former Detroit auto executives with Orville Wright employed as a consultant. Their aim was to bring mass manufacturing techniques to the aviation industry. Kenney retained a strong interest in the technical development of aircraft, an interest that would serve him well in the South West Pacific Command (SWPA). Kenney then attended Air Corps Tactical School (ACTS) at Langley learning the techniques of formation command. He became an instructor there and developed a keen interest in low-level flying and attack at a time when the Air Corps was becoming dominated by the principles of high-level bombardment.

Entering the War College in Washington in 1932, Kenney became acquainted with Richard Sutherland and Stephen Chamberlain, who were to become MacArthur's chief and deputy Chief of Staff respectively in the SWPA. Afterwards Kenney took on staff roles and helped draft legislation that would grant the Air Corps greater autonomy within the Army structure. In 1939 Kenney was made Chief of the Production Engineering Section at Wright Field Ohio. A year later Kenney became assistant Military Air *Attaché* in France. He wrote a controversial report suggesting changes to Air Corps' tactics and equipment; this included the recommendation to upgrade fighter armament from 0.30 to 0.50 caliber machine guns. It was a recommendation that was taken up and eventually became a decisive factor in winning US fighter dominance in the *Pacific War*. Never slow in giving forthright opinions, he gave a withering critique of the US Air Corp by comparison with the Luftwaffe. Promoted to Major-General on 26 March 1942, Kenney became commander of the Fourth Air Force where he was responsible for training pilots.

After being selected by MacArthur, Kenney transferred to Australia, reporting to his Commander in Chief on 28 July 1942. Kenney set about the immediate shake-up of an Air Force he found in disarray, beset by problems of supply and poor leadership. He removed four generals and some forty colonels from command and began a ground-up reorganization of a Fifth Air Force that had started life as the Philippine Department Air Force at Nichols Field in May 1941. The Allied Air Forces (AAF) were also separated into their component command structures, the US Army Air Force (USAAF) and the Royal Australian Air Force (RAAF). In the USAAF younger officers, Brigadier-General Ennis Whitehead and Brigadier-General Kenneth Walker, were promoted to command Fighter Command and Bomber Command respectively.

New Aircraft and New Tactics: Kenney's key strategic priorities were to increase the range of his fighters so as to extend the Fifth Air Force's ability to contest airspace over the *Solomon* and *Bismarck Seas* and to improve his forces' attack success rate in disrupting Japanese supply. Kenney was an energetic leader who *Time* magazine described as "a cocky, enthusiastic little man who can inspire flyers with his own skill for improvisation."[4] It was an apt description. Apart from his evident leadership skills, Kenney was above all an innovator who leapt on any new advance in technology to give his Fifth Air Force an edge in the air war with Japan. Apart from his interest in new weaponry, Kenney also reorganized the logistics of his forward airbases where he found that management, food supply, and medical facilities were in woeful condition. Low morale was widespread. Even more discouraging was the lack of logistical coordination for spare engine parts and equipment. The paper system for requisitioning parts was routed through Townsville and took months. Kenney relieved Major-General Ralph Royce and other poor performing officers. Above all Kenney was able to develop a clear strategic plan for the use of the Fifth Air Force in supporting the Allied ground troops in New Guinea and the *Solomons*. In 1944 Kenney explained:

> The first step in this advancement of the bomber line is to gain and maintain air control as far into enemy territory as our longest range fighters can reach. Then we put an air

blockade around the Jap positions or section of the coast, which we want in order to stop him from getting supplies or reinforcements. The bombers then go to work and pulverize his defensive system, methodically taking out artillery positions, stores, bivouac areas and so on. Finally comes the air cover escorting the amphibious expedition to the landing beach . . . and the maintenance of strafers and fighters overhead, on call from the surface forces until their beachhead is secured. If emergency supplies are needed we drop them by parachute. The ground troops get a transport field ready as fast as possible so that we can supplement boat supply by cargo carrying airplanes . . . The transport field becomes a fighter field, the strafers and finally the heavies arrive and it is time to move forward again.[5]

Kenney set in motion profound changes in bomber tactics. Because of heavy losses from daytime operations, he ordered attacks to be made at night. Secondly he questioned the effectiveness of high altitude bombing, a legacy of the political domination of the US Air Force by the 'bomber faction' in the 1930s. High altitude bombing was the standard mantra of Air Corps tactics for attacking shipping. However, with few bombers available in 1942, it was rarely possible to put up more than a dozen planes at a time; the critical mass was lacking for effective high-level bombing of Japanese supply ships. Kenney began to re-orientate his forces toward low-level attack. From his experience and advocacy of low-level flying, Kenney ordered the use of instantaneous fuses. When he discovered that Brigadier-General Walker had abandoned this system, he ordered trials on SS *Pruth*, a ship sunk off Port Moresby. In low-level attacks it was shown that, even though none of the bombs launched at the SS *Pruth* had hit the target, fragments from near misses ruptured its sides. Kenney had won the argument.

While he became better known for his innovations in bombing, Kenney also took a keen interest in fighter technology and was quick to recognize the importance of the new twin engine, twin boom, Lockheed P-38 Lightning fighter for his theater of the war. After a first flight in 1939, Lightning deliveries to combat units started in 1941. Fitted with extra fuel tanks, it was the ideal long distance fighter that Kenney sought for the extension of the range of his Air Force and thus its ability to disrupt Japanese supply transports. With two engines, it gave added security to pilots who usually had to conduct their long-range mission over the open sea. Although it was initially plagued by technical problems, the P-38 Lightning became Kenney's favorite fighter. Kenney, probably more than any other general in the *Pacific War*, understood the importance of 'range extension' as a critical component of strategic planning in a theater in which armies could not move by land.

The P-38 Lightning had formidable technical specifications. Its armament consisted of four Browning 0.50 caliber machine guns, one Hispano M2 20 mm cannon with 150 rounds, and four M10 three-tube 4.5-inch rocket launchers. The Lightning was also highly versatile, being able to swap its rocket launchers for six 500 lb bombs or, when increased range was required, a combination of drop tanks and bombs.

Even more impressive were its flying characteristics. With a top speed of 443 mph the Lightning outperformed both the Curtis P-39 Airacobra (376mph) and the Grumman Wildcat (331mph). The Lightning also had a higher ceiling, 44,000 feet versus 35,000 and 39,000 for the P-39 and Wildcat respectively. The Lightning's rate of climb at 4,700 foot per minute was also double that of the Wildcat and almost 25 percent better than the Airacobra P-39. Most importantly for Kenney, the P-38 Lightnings' range was 1,300 miles (without extra fuel tanks) against 525 miles for the P-39 and 845 miles for Wildcat. If Kenney was to build and defend advance airfields, increasing the range of his fighters was critical. Hitherto range was the major factor that had favored Japan's aircraft. The P-38 Lightning was the only plane available to Kenney that could negate Japan's range advantage.

At every point of comparison, except maneuverability, the P-38 Lightning outperformed the Zero: apart from heavier armament (four 0.50 mm machine guns versus two 0.30 mm machine guns), the P-38's top speed was 112 mph more than the Zero, it had an 11,000 foot higher ceiling, and could climb 52 percent faster. Perhaps the only major drawback for the P-38 was pilot comfort. Opening the cockpit during flight destabilized the P-38's tail. Pilots had to fly with closed canopies and they broiled in the tropical sun. Typically P-38 pilots flew naked apart from shorts, tennis shoes . . . and a parachute harness. For the pilots it was a price worth paying for the P-38's two engines, which gave them a measure of safety on missions that took them over thousands of miles of sea and inhospitable jungle.

Fighters that did not meet Kenney's requirements were modified with or without the approval of Washington. When the new P-47 Thunderbolt, built by Republic Aviation Corp, was delivered to Australia, Kenney complained that it did not carry enough fuel "to go anywhere."[6] He therefore junked the P-47's drop tanks developed in the United States and had a prototype designed locally, which he then outsourced to Ford of Australia for mass production.

The Marines' Grumman Wildcat F4F and the US Army's Bell P-39 Airacobra, which were heavily armored and had a far superior capacity to survive machine gun bullets than the Japanese Zero, were hampered by limited range, 845 miles for the Wildcat and 525 miles for the P-39; hence the attraction to Kenney of the P-38 Lighting with its 1,300 mile range (without extra fuel tanks). It should be noted that the 'real range' of *World War II* aircraft was usually half the 'brochure' range claimed by the manufacturers; 'warm up' time, assembly and formation time, high intensity flying in combat, wear and tear, and safety margin time, all cut into operating ranges in 'real world' conditions. By comparison the lightly armored Mitsubishi A6M Zero had a 1,930 mile 'brochure' range, but was armed with lighter weapons than their US counterparts, carrying a pair of 0.303 caliber Type-97 machine guns, derived from the British Lewis gun, and a pair of 20 mm Type-99 autocannon based on the Swiss Oerlikon FF. By comparison the Grumman F4F Wildcat was armed with six 0.50 caliber Browning machine guns. The result was that the main Japanese fighter could fly further, stay long on the battlefield and was more maneuverable, but was extremely vulnerable because of its lack of armor.

Above all Kenney demonstrated that whatever America's economic and *matériel* advantage over Japan, it still needed commanders in the field to translate that economic superiority into battlefield advantage. Kenney rapidly achieved this translation and long before American *matériel* superiority became overwhelming; he can be justly credited with one of the most significant achievements of the *Pacific War*.

While Lieutenant-General Claire Chennault in China, through his 'Flying Tigers' fame, and Lieutenant-General Curtis LeMay, who organized the strategic bombing of Tokyo, emerged as much better known Air Force commanders, arguably Kenney's achievements in the *South Pacific* exceeded them both. As Major-General 'Possum' Hansell, 'Hap' Arnold's Chief of Staff, commented, Kenney "did things with air forces that left airmen gasping. MacArthur owed much of his brilliant success in the Southwest Pacific to General Kenney's imaginative performance."[7] Indeed Major-General Hansell even ascribed the origination of MacArthur's 'wither-on-the-vine' strategy to Kenney. While MacArthur was clearly increasingly pleased with his choice of Air Force commander, MacArthur's obsession with self-promotion at the expense of all others clearly impacted the level of plaudits received by Kenney. Public neglect was a fate that would be shared by MacArthur's field commanders, Lieutenant-Generals Krueger and Eichelberger.

Kenney's startlingly innovative and successful command of the Fifth Air Force provided MacArthur with the cutting edge 'new' tactics demanded by the *Pacific War* but it was a contribution that MacArthur largely edited out of contemporary press coverage of campaigns in the *South Pacific*. In reality much of the foundations of MacArthur's self-manufactured legend were built on the strategic and tactic innovations of Lieutenant-General Kenney. As his Air Force colleague 'Possum' Hansell would later assert, "No air strategist or tactician showed greater imagination and inventiveness than Kenney."[8]

Gunn's Gunships: **[Drawing: 21.1]** It is not always generals who bring about military transformations. Another colorful figure who helped transform the potency of the Fifth Air Force was a junior officer, Paul Gunn, a resident of the Philippines, who had got caught up in the fighting at the start of the war.

Gunn was born in Quitman, Arkansas. He had enjoyed a colorful life. Having enlisted with the Army in *World War I* at the age of seventeen, he joined the Navy after the war and became an aviation machinist's mate. A born entrepreneur, he bought an Army surplus seaplane, and learnt to fly in his own time. In 1923 he was invited to join the Navy as a pilot and became one of its most skilled aviators. He was particularly adept at low-level flying. After retiring in 1939, he went to *Hawaii* to start a private air charter business and then on to Manila to do the same thing. In 1941, after the invasion of the

Philippines he had to leave behind his wife and four young children, all of who were interned for the duration of the war. By this time he had been drafted into the Army Air Corps as a captain. His aircraft were commandeered by the military. Thereafter he became a legendary figure as a freewheeling officer who would volunteer for any dangerous rescue or reconnaissance mission. On one occasion, shot down by a Japanese Zero, he managed to land his aircraft in a jungle clearing and made his way to safety.

Though technically a transport officer, the freewheeling Gunn took to 'hanging out' with the 3rd Attack group and made himself useful by commandeering twenty-four brand new North American Aviation B-25 Mitchell bombers belonging to the Royal Netherlands Air Force; the bombers were aircraft originally destined for the Dutch East Indies but were held back after the fall of *Java* in March 1942. Gunn's reward was to fly one of the new B-25s on their first mission to *Mindanao*. On a subsequent mission he landed on a beach and picked up a Japanese double agent. Upon delivery of new A-20 Douglas Havoc bombers, he proceeded to design a strafing-nose with four 0.50 Browning machine guns salvaged from wrecked fighters as well as designing and fitting auxiliary fuel tanks to increase the light bomber's range.

At this point, Lieutenant-General Kenney happened upon him at Townsville Airfield, and, recognizing his unconventional genius for innovation, ordered him to convert the B-25 Mitchell's forward fuselage turret into an 8-gun platform, four in the center fuselage and four each in two side pods attached to the center fuselage. In his self-serving post-war autobiography Kenney, leaving Gunn out of the narrative, wrote that he had "suggested four guns in the nose, two on either side of the fuselage, and three underneath . . . I figured I'd have a skip-bomber that could overwhelm the deck defenses of a Jap vessel as the plane came in for the kill with its bombs."[9] In fact 'Pappy' Gunn had already drafted plans for a B-25 gunship some two months before he met Kenney.

Filching the good ideas of others was not detrimental to the war effort. Even Kenney's skip-bomb was a development of a weapon that the British had already invented and that General 'Hap' Arnold had ordered to be tested at Eglin Army Airfield in Florida. Kenney's aide, Major William Benn, had seen some of the Eglin tests. He brought the idea to Kenney who tested it in *Fiji* while he was on his way to Australia to take over command from Brett. Kenney's skip bomb, successfully trialed on the SS *Pruth* outside Port Moresby, became thereafter a mainstay weapon used by Kenney in low-level attacks on Japanese shipping. As for Gunn's gun-platform for the Mitchell bomber, a pilot of the 38th Bomber Group recalled the development of the new B-25 weapon system:

> Originally we had a nine-man crew which included a bombardier and we attacked from altitude but with poor results. Then they got rid of the bombardier and stuck four 0.50 caliber machine guns in the bombardier's compartment and also two in blisters on each side make a total of eight which could spew out a lot of lead very fast.[10]

Working around the clock, Captain Gunn had a squadron of Mitchell B-25s fitted out by February 1943.

MacArthur and Sugiyama Reorganize after Guadalcanal: The technological, strategic and engineering work done by Kenney, Gunn and other airmen in the last quarter of 1942 was to have a significant impact on the plans of MacArthur and Sugiyama in the following year as they sought to redefine the conflict after the Japanese withdrawal from *Guadalcanal.*

In Japan, Imperial General HQ was figuring out what to do after it was agreed with the Emperor on 31 December 1942, that they should withdraw from *Guadalcanal.* Hirohito only approved the decision with a proviso: "It is unacceptable to just give up on capturing Guadalcanal," he said, "We must launch an offensive elsewhere."[11] In response Army Chief of Staff, General Hajime Sugiyama, promised to "take the offensive in the New Guinea area and restore the morale of the troops."[12] The order to withdraw from *Guadalcanal* was formally issued on 4 January and the exercise was completed on 7 February.

While the Japanese were planning a new offensive in New Guinea, the Allies were conceiving a plan to envelop Rabaul, the lynchpin of Japanese power in the *Southwest Pacific.* In Phase-I, Halsey, the commander of US forces in the *South Pacific* would move north from *Guadalcanal* toward Rabaul via *New Georgia*; MacArthur's Phase-II would follow with a move up the northern coast of New Guinea to seize Lae, Salamau and Finschhafen. In Phase-III, Halsey would take the *Shortland Islands* and *Bougainville Island* while MacArthur would take Cape Gloucester on the western tip of *New Britain Island.* At this point the so-called ELKTON-III Plan, codenamed Operation CARTWHEEL, called for thirteen separate coordinated actions that would converge on the assault and capture of Rabaul at the eastern tip of *New Britain.* The details were signed off during staff meetings between the respective staffs of Nimitz and MacArthur in March 1943.

Fortunately for MacArthur he developed a strong working relationship with Rear-Admiral Daniel Barbey who took command of 7th Amphibious Force in January 1943. Lacking even a single attack transport (APA), Barbey trained his troops in embarking into LSTs (Landing Ship, Tank) and LCIs (Landing Craft, Infantry) (both not yet available) by throwing nets over cliffs. It was not an ideal situation but with war materials still in short supply, Barbey made do with what he had. More important from MacArthur's point of view was the reorganization of US forces in Australia. He created an administrative organization, the US Army Forces in the Far East (USAFFE) that was to act as the administrative headquarters for the Sixth Army. To lead it, Lieutenant-General Walter Krueger, an Army veteran of forty-three years' service was transferred from the Third Army in San Antonio. In addition to the Sixth Army, MacArthur created a new American force to conduct operations against *New Britain Island*; supplied with the same staff officers as the Sixth Army, the New Britain Force (later called the Alamo Force) would be used to take key targets while General Thomas Blamey and his Australian Forces would be responsible for any continuing campaigns.

One of the main objectives of MacArthur's reorganization was to make sure that General Blamey and the Australians were sidelined. While MacArthur publicly supported the appointment of Blamey as South West Pacific Area's ground commander, his new structure obviated the need to have any American forces reporting to Australia's top general. MacArthur was able to get away with these schoolboy political tactics as a result of his oleaginous courtship of Australia's Prime Minister Curtin. "Mr. Prime Minister, you and I will see this through together,"[13] MacArthur patronisingly assured Curtin at their first meeting on 26 March 1942.

Thereafter Curtin appeared to accept the secondary role assigned to him, presumably on the basis that now that British influence in the Far East was *kaput*, Australia's defense against invasion was wholly dependent on America and MacArthur. Lloyd and Hall in their book *Backroom Briefings: John Curtin's War* [1997] go as far as to suggest that MacArthur's fondness for Curtin was because the American general had a prime minister in his pocket; otherwise MacArthur showed little respect for Curtin's subordinates or, more significantly, Australia's armed forces. The relationship with Curtin was thus "colored by his [MacArthur's] own mystique and sense of destiny. In retrospect Curtin had become just another MacArthur factotum, although a cherished one—another strand in the MacArthur legend."[14]

As Lieutenant-General Krueger later confirmed,

> The reasons for creating Alamo Force and having it, rather than the Sixth Army, conduct operations were not divulged to me. But it was plain that the arrangement would obviate placing Sixth Army under the operational control of CG Allied Land Forces [Commanding General, Blamey], although that army formed part of those forces. Since CG Allied land forces, likewise could not exercise administrative command over Sixth Army, it [the Alamo Force] never came under his command at all.[15]

Similarly Krueger's deputy Chief of Staff confirmed that the Alamo Force had been created "to keep control of Sixth Army units away from General Blamey."[16]

In spite of entreaties from General Marshall and President Roosevelt, MacArthur refused to have Australians or Dutch officers on his staff and was quite blatant in his prejudice. Lieutenant-General Richard Eichelberger recalled, "Shortly after I arrived in Australia, General MacArthur ordered me to pay my respects to the Australians and then have nothing further to do with them."[17] Eichelberger also noted that Lieutenant-General Krueger was "conspicuous in his avoidance of the Australians, either militarily or socially."[18] Although he was supportive in public, behind the scenes MacArthur, at every opportunity, went out of his way to undermine General Blamey. Providing scant evidence, MacArthur told Australian Defence Minister Shedden in January 1943 that Blamey did not "command the fullest support of the Australian Army."[19] In spite of MacArthur's maneuverings, Blamey's Australians did the bulk of the fighting done by the forces under MacArthur's command in 1943. The First Australian Corps was led by Lieutenant-General Sir Leslie Morsehead, while the New Guinea Force was led by Lieutenant-General Sir Edmund Herring.

Maneuvering for Control of the Gulf of Huon: **[Map: 21.2]** While the Imperial Japanese Navy planned to concentrate on the defense of *New Georgia* and the northern *Solomon Islands*, the Army planned to reinforce Lae at the southern neck of the Huon Peninsula from where they would launch a fresh offensive against Wau. Lae was just 190 miles due north of Port Moresby but separated by the daunting spine and jungles of the Owen Stanley Mountains as well as the *Gulf of Huon*. To the north, the Huon Peninsula, a rugged mountainous area of dense tropical jungle embracing the Finisterre Range and the Cromwell Range up to 12,000 feet in height, had no particular significance other than that its garrisons at Lae and Madang, on the southern and northern neck respectively of the peninsula, had strategically located airfields from which Rabaul could be threatened.

Indeed it was the air threat to Rabaul that had been the core strategy behind the establishment of strong Japanese airfield garrisons on the southeastern coast of New Guinea as well as *Guadalcanal*. With the loss of Kokoda, followed by Buna, Gona, and Sanananda, the Japanese had lost control of New Guinea's eastern coast south of the *Gulf of Huon*. The importance of Japan's hold on Lae and Salamaua that both lay further north on the *Gulf of Huon*, was thus significantly increased. This became yet more apparent when at the end of January, Lieutenant-General Hitoshi Imamura and Major-General Toru Okabe failed to overcome the Australian defenses at Wau, another strategically important airfield with a 1,100-foot strip, which lay forty miles to the southwest and inland from Lae.

The town of Wau, located in the Wau-Bulolo Valley, was entirely dependent on aerial supply. At an altitude of 3,300 feet, Wau could only be approached by rough tracks, which criss-crossed numerous rivers including the *Watut, Bulolo, Bitoi, Buisaval, Markham* and *Francisco Rivers*. It was a gold-rush town developed in the 1920s. In January 1942, its 250 inhabitants had been completely stranded when Japanese forces had invaded the coastal areas of the *Gulf of Huon*. When the inhabitants escaped by foot over the Owen Stanley Mountains they were replaced by Australian detachments from Port Moresby who joined the New Guinea Volunteer Rifles at Wau. Commandos were subsequently flown in to reinforce the defenders. Like their American counterparts, Japan's commanders realized that the fall of Buna would bring pressure next on Lae. Furthermore they realized that Wau was now in play as a potentially important airbase for the Allies, as well as a possible launch base for a land campaign against Lae. The flip side to Wau's strategic importance for the Allies was that Wau could be used as the conduit for a new Japanese attack on Port Moresby by a route other than the Kokoda Trail, where the Australians had so heavily defeated the Japanese Army.

Thus Wau's year of splendid isolation and uneasy stalemate was over. On 20 October 1942, Major-General George Vasey had flown into Wau to review Australia's Kanga

Force and to assess its role. To his wife, Jessie, he wrote, "I have been away for a couple of days visiting a most delightful part of this place . . . it was reminiscent of the Kashmir Valleys."[20] Looking beyond the looming battles for Buna, Gona and Sanananda, both the Allies and the Japanese, by the last quarter of 1942, had started to look to future horizons. General Blamey planned to build a highway along the Bulldog Track over which Wau's inhabitants had fled. A thousand native laborers were deployed on this ultimately fruitless task. In December 1942 Lieutenant-General Imamura, commander of the Eighth Army at Rabaul, ordered Lieutenant-General Hatazo Adachi's Eighteenth Army to expand its area of control westward from Lae with the main goal being the acquisition of Wau and its airfield. From November Kanga Force widened its patrols as far as Mubo, a village on the track down to Salamaua while the Japanese too were becoming increasingly active in the area. From 11 to 17 January heavy fighting around Mubo ended with Japanese troops claiming control of the area. Two routes, the Buisaval Track and the Black Cat Track, were now open for a Japanese advance on Wau.

Bomber Tactics and the Shooting Down of Brigadier-General Walker: On 5 January 1943, elements of the 51st Division led by Major-General Toru Okabe were assembled for a troop convoy to leave Rabaul. MAGIC intercepts had given the Allies advance warning of the plan to send troops to Lae on the *Gulf of Huon* with the expectation that they would attempt to advance inland to capture the airfield at Wau. In response Blamey immediately ordered the Australian 17th Infantry Brigade to redeploy from *Milne Bay* to Wau. Transported by Douglas C-47 Skytrains (or Dakotas as they were known by the Royal Air Force [RAF]), it was the first known deployment of a large infantry unit by air. In addition Blamey requested a bombing attack on the harbor at Rabaul before the troop convoy set sail.

On the same day, 5 January, Brigadier-General Kenneth Walker personally led an attack on Rabaul with six B-17s and six B-24s. The raid sank just one merchantman, the *Keijuku Maru*, and did little to interrupt the Lae convoy. Although Kenney appreciated the aggressive energy of his new subordinates, Walker, as well as Brigadier-General Ennis Whitehead, had both been reprimanded for taking 'joyrides' with their crews. "I can always hire a 10 dollars a week man to sweep the floor,"[21] Kenney told Walker; he ordered him to take "No more combat missions."[22] As Kenney later wrote, he was worried about security; "We had plenty of evidence that the Nips had tortured their prisoners until they either died or talked . . . After the prisoners talked they were beheaded anyhow, but most of them had broken under the strain."[23]

As well as 'joyriding' on the 5 January raid, Walker went further in defying Kenney by ignoring his commander's 'night bombing' instructions and launching his B-17 raid at dawn. Brigadier-General Walker believed that a tighter defensive formation between the bombers could mitigate the risk inherent in a midday attack. Major 'Bill' Benn warned him that he would lose two planes saying, "You shouldn't try going into Rabaul at high noon. It's best to keep bombing it at night."[24] For ignoring his orders, a furious Kenney vowed to reprimand Walker when he came back. MacArthur was more pragmatic, agreeing with Kenney in principle but suggesting, "If he [Walker] doesn't come back, I'll put him in for a Medal of Honor."[25] Walker was shot down and killed. As MacArthur had promised, Walker was duly awarded the US Army's highest gong with the citation, "For conspicuous leadership above and beyond the call of duty involving personal valor and intrepidity at an extreme hazard to life. As commander of the V-Bomber Command during the period from 5 September 1942, to 5 January 1943, Brigadier-General Walker repeatedly accompanied his units on bombing missions deep into enemy-held territory."[26]

The Battle of Wau: [**Map: 21.3**] In spite of 416 Allied sorties, the Japanese transports landed Major-General Okabe's forces at Lae and, having barged them down the coast to Salamaua, launched his attack on Wau on 16 January 1943. Two battalions from the 102nd Infantry Regiment under Major Kikutaro Shimomura and Lieutenant-Colonel Shosaku, with about 1,500 troops, moved up the Black Cat Track. The horrendous conditions, which allowed an advance of little more than three to four miles per day, led many of the Japanese Army's porters, many of them Chinese, to drop out. The plan to take artillery pieces and their munitions had to be abandoned. The Japanese had hoped to advance to Wau undetected and ordered their troops to tread in existing footmarks so as not to indicate the strength of their forces. However, Australian scouts on 22 January noted that the six-inch deep footprints must have been made by at least 300–400 men and reported back accordingly. For the next two weeks Brigadier Murray Moten at the Australian Kanga Force HQ in Wau would be under the impression that the approaching Japanese forces were little more than a raiding party of 500 troops—just one-third of the actual number.

The battle became a three-cornered fight between the Allies bringing in reinforcements and supplies for the 17th Infantry Brigade at Wau, Japanese fighters trying to stop them and the inclement weather holding all parties to ransom. Extreme heat during the day combined with cold, dank forest at night created a climate of extreme unhealthiness. An Australian commander estimated that only 30 percent of his men were fit to work at any one time. Malaria, gastritis and diarrhea were common. Muddy tracks such as the Black Cat Trail and the Buisaval Trail, that wound their way over mountainous, forested terrain, had to be fought for in head-to-head firefights because flanking movements were often impossible in the dense vegetation.

Both the Japanese and Australians suffered extreme difficulties in supply. At the beginning of the war Australian supplies were brought to Wau by steamer along the south coast to the mouth of the *Lakekamu River*, from there in small boats up to Terapo village, followed by two days of canoe to Bulldog and then split into 50 lb loads to be carried by native porters on a seven day trek. Sick or wounded soldiers would have to be carried back along the vertiginous tracks by Papuan stretcher-bearers who were in short supply. Medical officer Captain B. H. Patterson noted the extraordinary difficulty of moving the sick or wounded: "Anticipating the steepness and difficulty of the track, we used the boat-shaped wire-netting stretchers used by the miners. We could not have evacuated stretcher cases without them as they had to be half slid, half carried down."[27]

Both Japanese and Allied soldiers faced appalling conditions during the Salamaua Campaign. Soldiers would have to hack their way through thick jungle. Tracks, where they existed, were often overgrown and difficult to find. Even in daylight the 200-foot high canopy excluded light; at night it was pitch dark. An Australian soldier noted, "It rains heavily almost every day thus making living conditions uncomfortable. By day it is hot, by night three blankets are necessary."[28]

Infantryman Robert Kennington described a climate in which "Mosquitoes were so thick you could wipe them off your arms in handfuls. You waded through rivers and you'd come out with leeches . . . you'd look down and there was this creature on your leg full of blood."[29] Nighttime was eerie and anything that moved drew fire. It was always feared, "Japs' would infiltrate at night to slit the throats of unwary soldiers. The conditions of life in the jungle may have been appalling but the coastal swampy marshes were even worse. Apart from the annoyances of mosquitoes, mortal dangers came from animals with a bigger bite in the form of freshwater and saltwater crocodiles. Carl Weber, an officer of the 41st Division, remembered that at one stop during the Salamaua Campaign, a fellow "soldier was caught and killed by a crocodile . . . It was over in the blink of an eye. The croc struck, spun, thrashed about and was gone, leaving a bloodstain in the water. No more bathing."[30]

The swamps themselves were awkward to cross because underwater roots trapped soldier's feet or tripped them headfirst into the mouldy water. Along the coast there were plentiful coconut plantations where much of the undergrowth had been cut back. Trekking through plantations was relatively plain sailing except that troops were much more visible to the Japanese, which had disadvantages of another sort. The lowlands that extended between the plantations, swamps and jungle-covered highlands were covered in razor-sharp kunai grass that grew 5–8 feet in height, which made it hard to traverse, though it did have the advantage of hiding troops from the enemy—though that too was an advantage that cut both ways.

The arrival of fifty-two new C-47 transport planes delivered to 374th Troop Carrier Group transformed the supply situation. Up to forty aircraft began to fly daily into Wau bringing supplies and reinforcements. Nevertheless the vagaries of New Guinea's weather meant that even with new planes air supply was never certain. Meanwhile Okabe's 1,500 under-provisioned troops got as far as the edge of the airfield before being beaten back. In spite of the wide-ranging Australian patrols, on 28 January, Japanese troops appeared by an unknown track and came close to reaching the airfield but were beaten back by Captain 'Bill' Sherlock and twenty troops, who he led with a bayonet charge. Sherlock killed four Japanese soldiers himself. The knoll was retaken but the fight had only just begun. In spite of reinforcements by 6.30 p.m., Sherlock reported that only eighteen of his seventy troops were still alive. Sherlock was killed in a firefight at the end of the action but in holding up the Japanese advance at Wandumi Ridge, he gave Brigadier Murray the chance to reorganize Wau's defenses. Critically

814 fresh Australian troops were flown in on 29 January. As they debarked their Dakotas, they came under fire from Japanese snipers around the field. By this time the Allied and Japanese troops were so intermingled that in the dark they often mistook each other.

In the early hours of 30 January a Japanese attack got within 400 yards of the airfield. The attack presaged a day of heavy fighting in which the defenders' 25-pounders played a significant part. Captain Reg Wise, an artillery officer, was amazed to see a column of 900 Japanese troops advancing. Artillery fire spread-eagled the Japanese who fled into the long kunai grass only for the artillerymen to set it on fire with phosphorus rounds. Bombardier Norrie Jones recalled, "You'd see these blokes all caught in a ring of fire and they're all running around in circles dying of smoke inhalation and phosphorus injury."[31]

Royal Australian Air Force (RAAF) Beaufighters strafed Japanese positions. Gradually air dominance over southern New Guinea was passing to the Australians as air attacks on Rabaul from Halsey's forces in the *South Solomons* required the Japanese to use their fighter aircraft to defend the skies over their own *South Pacific* stronghold. The paucity of Japanese air support at Wau severely undermined their offensive. Apart from their advantages of artillery and air support, Australian troops were also better equipped for close quarter fighting. Sub-machine guns were the key weapon in this type of action. One Jap prisoner wrote about the lack of sub-machine guns, "These were very deadly and demoralizing . . . men armed with rifles did not have much chance against them [machine guns] in close jungle fighting."[32] The nature of the jungle combat was shown by relative statistics on casualties for American troops in the *South Pacific* compared to Europe. Whereas in Europe 19 percent of casualties were caused by small arms fire, in the *South Pacific* the equivalent figure was 32 percent. Casualties from artillery were 57 percent in Europe and only 17 percent in the *South Pacific*.

By 31 January 1943, Okabe's force had been significantly weakened by losses and was barely in condition to fight. Compared to the fresh Australians, the Japanese had been trekking and fighting for two weeks. Captain Saito noted, "This was our fifteenth day we had been beaten by rain, gone without food and walked till our boots filled with blood."[33] Brigadier Moten, who had focused air attack on the cutting off of resupply, correctly observed, "His [the Japanese] supply situation must be acute."[34] Colonel Maruoka, seeing the scale of reinforcements arriving at Wau, by now realized that the chance of taking the town had gone. Okabe's much diminished force was in danger itself of being surrounded and overwhelmed and was ordered to withdraw. Over a quarter of Okabe's force, 1,000 troops, had been killed while total Allied casualties were 349. In hindsight it was clear that the availability of US Air Force transports and their ability to supply and reinforce was the key determinant of victory at the *Battle of Wau*.

The Battle of the Bismarck Sea: [Map: 21.4] In spite of the setback at Wau, Lieutenant-General Imamura had not given up on extending control over the Lae area. US Intelligence intercepts in mid-January had suggested that another troop convoy would be sent to the area. A transportation of Japanese troops to Madang on the northern neck of the Huon Peninsula was considered, but the advance to Lae from here would involve a 140-mile trek through the jungles skirting inland through the foothills of the Finisterre Range. With Japanese air superiority over the *Solomon Sea* being increasingly challenged by the Allies, Imamura was aware of the greater risks of shipping his troops to Lae but nevertheless ordered that transport vessels take 51st Division's 6,900 troops. For MacArthur it was an alarming development given that he was planning to utilize the Lae area to develop a counter-offensive against Rabaul, the capture of which, as part of Operation CARTWHEEL, was the US Joint Chiefs of Staff main strategic target in the *South Pacific*.

Lieutenant-General Kenney with his deputy Brigadier-General Ennis Whitehead, who was stationed at Port Moresby, decided that the convoy should be attacked by air in the *Straits of Vitiaz* between the Huon Peninsula and *New Britain* with *Umboi Island* at its tip. With the failure to interdict the January convoy to Lae, Kenney called for new tactics. High-level bombing was considered too inaccurate to be effective and therefore two new types of low-level bombing were developed. Skip bombing that Kenney had successfully trialled with the now deceased Ken Walker now had its opportunity while 'Mast level' bombing began the attack at below 500 feet and released bombs to land directly into the side of ships. In addition, Group Captain Bill Garing developed 'asymmetric' attacks from different heights and directions that could prevent convoys from deploying normal evasion techniques. These tactics would also serve to confuse Japanese air defenses.

By now, 'Pappy' Gunn, promoted to the rank of major by Kenney, had numbers of modified Douglas A-20 Havoc light bombers with four 0.50 caliber machine guns in the nose as well as a squadron of converted B-25 medium bombers. The converted bombers were not without their problems; they had to lose their rear turrets to make way for ballast to counteract the weight of twelve 0.50 caliber machine guns in the front fuselage. Even then the weight of the guns and ammunition made the converted B-25 difficult to fly, while the firing of the machine guns caused so much vibration that rivets sometimes popped out of the aircrafts' steel plating.

The medium bomber groups included Mitchell B-25s of the 38th Bomber Group, albeit a depleted command, and Martin B-26 Marauders of the 22nd Bomber Group. Heavy bombers consisted of 55 Boeing B-17 Flying Fortress from the 43rd Bomber Group and 90th Bomber Group's Consolidated B-24 Liberators. In addition Lieutenant-General Kenney decided to throw the US 3rd Attack Group at the Japanese convoy even though it was desperately short of trained crews. As a result crews were borrowed from the Royal Australian Air Force (RAAF) to man the available Douglas A-20 Havocs as well as the B-25s. Finally light bombers, Bristol Beauforts, stationed at Port Moresby with 30th Squadron, were also available for the attack. Fighter support would be provided by Bell P-400s, export versions of the P-39 Airacobras, Curtiss P-40 Warhawks and Lockheed P-38 Lightnings.

Ranged against them were eight Japanese destroyers providing anti-aircraft cover for the eight troop carriers as well as 100 fighter aircraft, mainly Mitsubishi Zeros. The

Japanese convoy departed from Rabaul's Simpson Harbor on 28 February 1943. Whereas in January, the convoy had hugged the south coast of *New Britain* on its way to Lae, the second convoy, codenamed Operation-81, led by Rear-Admiral Masatomi Kimura, took the longer northern route around *New Britain*, which would keep it further away from Allied air attacks. In the event, storms over the *Solomons* and the *Bismarck Sea* shrouded the convoy and it was not until 1 March that it was spotted by a patrolling B-24 Liberator. Early on 2 March, Lae was bombed to prevent it providing assistance and later that morning the convoy was located and attacked in the *Straits of Vitiaz*. The troop transport *Kyokusei Maru* was sunk with 1,200 troops on board. Over 900 survivors were picked up by destroyers and taken to Lae. Several merchant ships were also sunk. An attack later that evening caused little damage. Over the day, eight Japanese fighters were shot down. By 3 March the convoy was within range of Bristol Beaufort torpedo bombers based at *Milne Bay* but, in an early attack, all but two failed to find the target because of bad weather. Nevertheless, ninety bombers later set off from Port Moresby. As planned, attacks were made from different heights. The first reward of Kenney's new strategies was the sinking of the destroyer *Shirayuki*, which was hit by heavy strafing—killing or wounding most of the bridge crew. When a bomb blew up the *Shirayuki*'s munition's store and broke off her stern, *Shirayuki* was abandoned and scuttled. A similar fate overtook the destroyer *Tokitsukaze*.

In the confusion caused by the Allies' multi-dimensional attack, the destroyer *Arashio* collided with the transport *Nojima*; both had to be abandoned. Reiji Masuda recalled being in the engine rooms when "our bridge was hit by two 500 lb bombs. Nobody could have survived . . ."[35] By the afternoon three of the other transports had been disabled or sunk. Major Gunn's converted B-25 'flying gunships' proved devastatingly effective. Co-pilot Garret Middlebrook reported "watching hundreds of those Japanese just blown off the deck by those machine guns. They just splintered around the air like sticks in a whirlwind and they'd fall in the water."[36] It was later estimated that twenty-eight of the thirty-seven skip bombs dropped found their target. Most of the damage was done in a twenty-minute spell. By the evening of 3 March, all the transports were sunk or disabled. The remaining four destroyers set about rescuing Japanese troops from the water. That night, American PT boats attacked the remainder of the convoy. Two were damaged by debris from the battle but the remainder sank the crippled transport *Oigawa Maru* as well as another destroyer that was picking up the *Arashio* survivors.

The results of Kenney's sweeping reforms of the Allied Air Forces (AAF) in the South West Pacific Area came to their fruition at the *Battle of the Bismarck Sea*. As Kenney later said, "The Battle of the Bismarck Sea was not something that just happened. It was planned and rehearsed. We prepared. We even picked the spot for the engagement."[37] A combination of revised strategic and tactical thinking with new war *matériel* delivered a blow from which Japanese strategy in the *South Pacific* would never recover. Albeit small in scale, and even allowing for the exaggerations propagated by MacArthur and Kenney the *Battle of the Bismarck Sea* was one of the greatest air victories of *World War II*.

The Murder of Japanese Survivors: The surviving Japanese destroyers took an estimated 2,500 survivors back to Rabaul, leaving more than 1,000 troops in the water on rafts or clinging to debris. Apart from thirst, hunger and exposure to the elements for those still in the water, circling tiger sharks took their share of the survivors.

For the next two evenings PT boats and Allied aircraft also gunned down Japanese survivors 'in cold blood.' It was a massacre of defeated troops who were already being subjected to the ravages of the open sea. For those who survived the massacre, horrors continued. Nine men were found dead on a raft. Five days after the battle an American PT boat off Wanigela intercepted a boat full of fifty-one Japanese survivors. The Americans killed forty-three of them and took the remaining eight into captivity. In total it was estimated that 352 Japanese survivors were murdered. It was a number that did not include those who made it to land on *Goodenough Island*. Many of these were later hunted down and killed. On 9 March Lieutenant Joe Pascoe killed one group of survivors and recovered boxes of sealed documents, which revealed Japanese troop deployments. Those Japanese survivors who did manage to land on friendly territory were finished as combatants. Lieutenant Masamichi Kitamoto observed survivors coming ashore at Tuluvu on the west of *New Britain*: "Their eyes were glassy and deeply sunk into their faces. All were jittery . . . as if they were seeing a horrible dream . . . a pitiful scene of a vanquished and defeated army."[38]

The 63rd Bomb Squadron's blood was up after the killing of Lieutenant Woodrow Moore and his B-17 Flying Fortress crew during the battle. According to the post-war memoir of wingman Tsutomo Iwai, Flight CPO Masano Maki rammed Moore's B-17, sheering off the tail: "both planes broke in two and the four pieces fell, jumbled together."[39] Added to the American pilots' fury at this supposed *kamikaze* attack, the 63rd's pilots were also incensed that members of Moore's crew who had escaped by parachute were machine gunned by three Zeros, probably from 204th Air Group based at Kavieng. Sergeant Gordon of 43rd Bomb Group noted that back at Port Moresby, "We ate dinner and nobody said much. We were all burning. We couldn't wait until the next day when we might have another crack at those rats."[40]

The Allied atrocity was thinly justified by the logic that the murdered Japanese troops would otherwise have returned to fight another day—an argument that was similarly used by Japanese soldiers to excuse the butchering of prisoners. The real motive was clearly revenge. As Jim Harcrow, a captain of a B-17 that did three missions during the battle, recalled, "We'd come back and refuel, bomb up, and go back out again . . . when our guys parachuted, the Japanese shot 'em right in their chutes. So after that we did the same thing. It they were hanging onto a piece of debris, we strafed them in the water."[41] According to the 63rd Bomb Squadron's war diary, "Every man in the squadron would have given two months' pay to be in on the strafing."[42]

For the loss of just thirteen aircraft and their crews, Kenney's attack had prevented all but 900 fresh troops out of 6,610 from arriving in Lae. In total 2,890 troops and sailors were killed, while the remainder were taken back to Rabaul. MacArthur, in his *communiqué* of 7 March, claimed twenty-two ships sunk, including 12 transports, 3 cruisers and 7 destroyers. In addition, MacArthur asserted very precisely that 12,792 Japanese troops had been killed. An Army Air Force HQ investigation in Washington a few months later concluded that MacArthur's report was a gross distortion of the facts. The convoy consisted of sixteen ships and it was estimated with reasonable accuracy that between 3,000 and 3,500 Japanese troops and sailors had perished. However, both MacArthur and Kenney refused to accept the findings. The claimed figures may have been incorrect but there was no doubting that Kenney had scored a major victory. Daytime troop convoys to support operations in New Guinea would never again feature in the months of fighting ahead. Allied Intelligence concluded that the Japanese high command had taken the risk to send troops to Lae because of the critical strategic importance of the area: "It is more than evident that the enemy considers Lae-Salamaua as a key position both as his main outpost protecting Rabaul from the Southwest and also as a base from which further attacks can be made on our positions in New Guinea."[43]

Whatever the numbers of enemy destroyed, the findings from the battlefield showed that Kenney's 'multi-dimensional' attacks had been brilliantly successful. 'Mast level' attacks had outperformed expectations. As for Major Gunn's B-25 'flying gunships,' they had proved themselves a devastatingly effective new weapon. An ecstatic MacArthur sent a message for participating units to Lieutenant-General Kenney, who sent it on to Brigadier-General Whitehead, the architect of the *Bismarck Sea* raid: "Congratulations on that stupendous success. Air power has written some important history in the past few days. Tell the whole gang that I am so proud of them I am about to bust a fuse."[44] MacArthur was generous in his praise to his troops and commanders internally, though that rarely extended to briefing the world's press.

It is interesting to note that, a few week earlier in February, at a conference in General 'Hap' Arnold's offices in Washington, a group of senior test engineers told Kenney categorically that nose-fitted machine gun modifications to North American Aviation's B-25 Mitchell could not work for structural and weight reasons. They were stunned to discover that a squadron had already been fitted out as 'flying gunships' in Australia with another sixty due for conversion. 'Pappy' Gunn had been dispatched from Australia back to the United States to help out the embarrassed engineers. Gunn was thus instrumental in getting the modified B-25 gunships factory-fitted at North American Aviation's Fairfax Airport plant in Kansas. Twelve 0.50 caliber machine guns were put in the nose and side pods with the new addition of a 75 mm cannon incorporated into the central fuselage. On returning to Australia, Gunn admitted to Kenney that he had been flying without an Army Air Force pilot rating. The US Air Force bureaucrats insisted that he return to the United States to take his exams. Kenney intervened directly with 'Hap' Arnold to overturn the ruling. Even in war, the dead hand of bureaucratic legalism was difficult to sever.

Hirohito and a Change in Strategy: For Japan, the *Battle of the Bismarck Sea* was an unmitigated disaster. Imamura's chief of staff was ordered back to Tokyo to explain what had happened. It is known from Captain Jiiyo Eiichiro that the Emperor was becoming increasingly anxious about the turn of fortune in New Guinea. Deliberation by the Imperial General HQ brought about a revision of strategy in the *South Pacific*. On 25 March a joint Army-Navy conference agreed to the prioritization of New Guinea rather than to the campaign in the northern *Solomon Islands*. Directive No. 209 promulgated by the Navy General staff ordered, "enemy fleets in advance bases will be raided and destroyed."[45] In an acknowledgement that Kenney had dramatically turned the air war to America's advantage, the re-establishment of Japanese air superiority was made a priority.

Vice-Admiral Baron Tomoshige Samejima, a veteran of the 1932 First Shanghai Incident, who had spent the early part of the war as the Emperor's naval aide, was sent forward from *Truk* to oversee operations at Rabaul. Samejima, Captain Eiichiro's former boss, may well have been pushed forward at Hirohito's initiative. As with all things concerning the Emperor's supposed interference in operational matters, the facts are murky.

Japan's New Guinea priority was soon mirrored by the US Joint Chiefs of Staff's Operation CARTWHEEL. Both Japan and the Allies were becoming aware that the end game of the *South Pacific* Campaign was MacArthur's advance northwest up the coast of New Guinea towards the Philippines. Imperial General HQ in Japan were not unaware that MacArthur was completely fixated on the recovery of the American colony whose loss had been the major humiliation of his life. For the US Joint Chiefs too, the western New Guinea-*Mindanao-Luzon* (Philippines) route towards Japan remained one of the viable options to bring about ultimate victory in the war. Eventually the Joint Chiefs would decide that the taking of Rabaul was unnecessary; it could be bypassed. Rather than risking a bloodbath taking Rabaul, the most heavily fortified Japanese garrison in the South Pacific, the Joint Chiefs decided that MacArthur should advance westwards along the north coast of New Guinea.

In Rabaul, Masatake Okumiya, a senior staff officer, reflected after the war on the scale of the defeat at the *Battle of the Bismarck Sea*. "Our losses for this single battle were fantastic. Not during the entire savage fighting at *Guadalcanal* did we suffer a single comparable blow."[46] It seems clear, that even those Japanese commanders who had hitherto believed that Japan could win the war, must now have known, albeit privately, that the game was up.

The Collapse of Japanese Air Power in the South Pacific: Even before the *Battle of the Bismarck Sea*, Japan's ability to support the logistical requirements of the 'outer perimeter' of its newly acquired empire was tenuous at best. Afterwards it was impossible. Just two months earlier Japan controlled the airspace over the *Solomon Islands* and the *Bismarck Sea*. At the *Battle of Buna-Gona-Sanananda* that ended on 22 January 1943, Allied air support was not the critical component in the victory; yet after the *Battle of the Bismarck Sea* in early March 1943, a little over a month later, it could be argued that the superiority of US air power had become the most important factor in the winning of every battle whether over land or sea.

Up until January 1943, Japanese domination of the air war in the *South Pacific* was challenged but relatively stable. Two months later, it had sheered away. What were the causes of this sudden transition of aerial dominance from Japan to the United States in the *South Pacific*? In the mathematical modeling of 'chaos,' apparently stable systems tend to collapse suddenly; the air war in the *South Pacific* was no different. The *Battle of the Bismarck Sea* began a sudden and catastrophic collapse in air power that was the result of increasing loads on Japan's points of stress in the *South Pacific* conflict.

There had been longer-term trends at work. In 1940 the United States produced aircraft at the rate of just 3,500 per annum. Within a year the industry was transformed. Output of combat aircraft more than doubled to 8,395 in 1941, and then almost tripled to 24,669 in 1942, and doubled again to 53,183 in 1943; a rise of 1,419 percent in aggregate. The split was approximately 50/50 between bombers of all types and fighters. Although Allied forces in the *South Pacific* could count on just 15 percent of all war *matériel* produced by US industry at the start of the war, that ratio was doubled to 30 percent after the Quebec conference in mid-August 1943. Even with just 15 percent of supply, the rising tide of US military output had nevertheless started to bring a startling rise in equipment available in the *South Pacific* by the beginning of that year. Japan's delivery of combat planes grew from approximately 2,500 in 1941 to 4,000 in 1942, while the US delivery to the *Pacific Theater* over the same period, based on a 15 percent allocation of total production, grew from approximately 1,250 to 3,600 over the same time period. Even Britain's annual production of combat aircraft in aggregate was three times greater than that of Japan in 1942, some of which also found its way to the *Pacific Theater*.

This was not the whole story. Japan had more theaters of operation to supply than just the *Pacific*. More than half of the air allocation went to the Imperial Japanese Army and that was heavily skewed toward China, Burma and the Philippines as well as 'homeland' defense. The war in the *South Pacific* was deemed by Imperial General HQ to be primarily 'naval.' Air cover in the *Solomons* and the *Bismarck Sea* was thus the Navy's responsibility. In addition Japan was facing the problem of shipping transport capacity to the *South Pacific*. By the start of 1943 the mounting loss of cargo ship capacity was affecting Japan's ability to supply its outer perimeter defenses with troops and equipment, including aircraft. Therefore it can be deduced that, in spite of MacArthur's constant grumbling about supply, monthly unit deliveries of new combat planes to the Allies in the *South Pacific* were already substantially exceeding that of Japan by the start of 1943. With the arrival of P-38 Lightnings, P-47 Thunderbolts and the prospect of converted B-25 Mitchell gunships, Kenney's supply of new aircraft was about to receive a significant mark-up in quality as well as quantity.

By comparison the shortage of Japanese aircraft in the *South Pacific* at the start of 1943, meant that airfields were having to 'borrow' planes and crew from fleet carriers. It was an appalling waste of Japan's scarcest commodity—experienced and well-trained carrier crews who took much more time and expense to train than land-based crews. Neither did the Japanese flyers get any upgrade in the quality of their aircraft. Although

Kenney's Fifth Air Force was similarly short of experienced crews in March 1943, his manpower problems paled beside those of the Japanese commanders in Rabaul.

The problems of personnel supply were not just aircrews. In the *South Pacific* there was also a scarcity of ground crews to service aircraft. Japan was a relatively poorly mechanized society compared to the United States in the pre-war decade. Using the motor industry as a proxy for the availability of mechanical 'skills,' it should be noted that Japan produced only 220,000 vehicles between 1925 and 1936. Thereafter Japan introduced laws restricting foreign competition, that until then had been dominated by the three major US companies' Japanese-based subsidiaries, Ford, General Motors and Chrysler; the 'big three' produced 90 percent of Japanese vehicle output.

By comparison US auto production in 1936 alone was 3.29 million units. Ford produced 930,000 cars in 1936, which was almost four times the number that Japan had produced over a ten-year period. The United States, by comparison with Japan, had a vast stock of trained mechanics, many of them underemployed because of the 1930s depression. By comparison the Japanese economy, already stretched by the *Second Sino-Japanese War*, was operating at full capacity when the *Pacific War* started. Unlike America, Japan did not have reservoirs of skilled mechanical labor to tap for the supply of airfield engineers and ground crew.

Lastly America was beginning to win the technological arms race. The raft of tactical and technological innovations with regard to bombing, which were introduced by Lieutenant-General Kenney between January and March 1943 have already been outlined. The new aircraft arriving from America, particularly the Grumman Hellcat, and the Lockheed Lightning, were significant technological advances on the Zero in terms of speed, armament, ceiling and rate of climb, the key parameters of a good fighter aircraft. Furthermore, the dissemination of improved air combat tactics by Commander John Thach, after whom the 'Thach Weave' was named, meant that the new waves of flyers from the US were well versed in how to negate the advantages of maneuverability enjoyed by the Zero.

In summary therefore, it was a multifaceted combination of factors—tactical, technological, and logistical, which led to the sudden collapse of Japanese air power in March 1943. The *Battle of the Bismarck Sea* was symptomatic of the deep disparity in the economic strengths of the US economy versus Japan, about which Admirals Yamamoto and Inoue had openly warned their colleagues with regard to going to war against America. It was a disparity that caught up with the Imperial Japanese forces on the battlefield not gradually but with a sudden 'non-linear' collapse. The *Battle of the Bismarck Sea* was the inflection point of Japanese collapse in the air war.

Transformation of the Ground War: It has already been well observed in Chapters 5 to 10 that Japan's initial success in the *Pacific War* was predicated on surprise, rapid movement, and light, even marginal, logistical support for its forward troop movements. This worked for as long as the Allied powers failed to find a way to respond to Japanese tactical strengths on the battlefield. As soon as Allied ground troops worked out a way to hold ground, and to put up a time-consuming defense, Japan's soldiers lost the advantage of speed and momentum that had been the bedrock of their military tactics since the start of the war. Long drawn out engagements would always favor the side with better logistics; that side was always America. Thus, on the ground as well as in the air, by the beginning of 1943 there was an underlying if largely unseen shift in the balance of military power in the *South Pacific*.

First Japan's forces, operating at the margin of operational logistical sustainability at the best of times, began to seriously overreach. This was first evident on land at *Guadalcanal* and in the *Battles of the Kokoda Trail* either side of New Guinea's Owen Stanley Range. In these encounters Japanese forces suffered staggering losses from malnourishment and disease that amounted to multiples of those killed in actual combat. Japan's senior commanders no longer had the wherewithal to feed their soldiers, even before America had won complete air superiority. Eventually Japan had to resort to using its submarine force as underwater supply vessels—a use for which they were not designed and one that undermined the morale of Japanese submariners and deprived Japan of an important strike asset. It was a vicious cycle of decline.

By contrast, although Allied troops fighting in the same jungle conditions suffered egregiously, death rates from disease were typically less than 5 percent of those suffered by their Japanese opponents. Japanese troops' high death rates were not caused by bad commanders on the ground; Japanese officers in 1943 were from the same school of superb Japanese ground commanders who, at the start of the *Pacific War*, had recorded some of the most remarkable military victories in twentieth-century history. Simply put, the grand design of the war strategy embraced by Imperial General HQ at the start of the war in autumn 1941 had grossly failed to take account of the logistics required for ultimate victory. Japanese campaigns designed for armies to 'live-off the land' could work to some degree in Malaya, the Philippines and the Dutch East Indies, but were not suitable for the largely uninhabitable areas of New Guinea and the *Solomon Islands*, where only pockets of jungle-born natives eked out an existence. It was a design flaw that undermined the entire Japanese war strategy in the *South Pacific*.

Secondly, on the ground, Japan's enemies' tactics had not stood still. Major-General Vandegrift's setting up of more sophisticated defense systems, including the use of barbed wire perimeters, combined with the shift toward zonal, mobile defense at the *Battle of Henderson Field* (*Guadalcanal*), anticipated in some measure the brilliantly conceived and executed 'box' system used by General Slim at the *Battle of Imphal* at the beginning of 1944. Similarly sound defense tactics were also used by the Australian commander, Major-General Sir George Wootten, at the *Battle of Milne Bay*, which provided the Allies with their first land victory of the *Pacific War*. MacArthur never grasped, as Vandegrift, Wootten and Slim did, that defense intelligently conducted could be as aggressive and decisive as attack, particularly against an enemy that could not sustain the logistical supply needed to sustain a protracted siege.

Neither was Vandegrift's sophistication replicated by MacArthur on the Kokoda Trail Campaign. MacArthur, showing that he had learnt nothing from his experience in the Philippines, blithely ordered the Australian troops to attack, 'whatever the cost' rather than set up, as the Japanese would later demonstrate, sophisticated systems of defense entrenchments to halt the Japanese advance. It was only thanks to a courageous fighting withdrawal by Australia's unfairly criticized commanders and their troops, over virtually the entire length of the Kokoda Trail, that the loss of Port Moresby was avoided. In the end it was the over-extension of Lieutenant-General Horii's supply chain that defeated him, not MacArthur's generalship.

What mattered was that both at the *Battle of Henderson Field* and at the *Battle of Milne Bay*, Allied commanders set up defenses to hold up rapid Japanese advances and flanking movements. In both cases the interruption to the planned Japanese timeline for their operations threw their logistical planning into meltdown, particularly in operations where the acquisition of enemy food supplies was an important tactical priority. The result for Japanese troops at *Guadalcanal* was disease and starvation *en masse*. It was a human catastrophe exacerbated by the refusal of all but a handful of Japanese to choose surrender over death.

Thirdly, US ground forces equipment had been significantly upgraded by 1943. The Garand M-1 had become the standard issue infantry rifle. As a semi-automatic weapon, it had a significant advantage over Japanese troops equipped with bolt-action rifles, particularly in the frequent firefights that characterized jungle warfare. Increased provision of machine guns and field cannons to infantry units also contributed to the effectiveness of GIs on the battlefield. In offensive action grenades and mortars were probably the two main killing weapons, but the development of flame-throwers became an essential tool of engagement with Japanese pillboxes and entrenchments. In certain terrains, the increasing availability of American tanks further stacked the battlefield odds against Japan. Japan's light tanks were never a match against the medium M4 Sherman.

America Moves to the Offense: After the key 'tipping point' battles at *Guadalcanal* and the *Kokoda Trail*, the nature of the ground war changed. It was now America that was on the attack. There were key differences between the American advance and the 'advance' campaigns fought by Japan in the early phases of the *Pacific War*.

Japanese commanders knew how to defend key points by the construction of highly sophisticated entrenchment systems. Their commanders were as brilliant in defense as they had been in attack. It helped that they often had nowhere to retreat to and were prepared to fight to the death. On the American side, their advances, unlike the Japanese, were never compromised by timeline pressure caused by inadequate resources; in New Guinea from 1942 to 1944 timeline pressure on the US Army only came from the fact that MacArthur was fighting to retrieve his historic reputation by the rapid re-conquest of the Philippines. From time to time, American troops may have gone hungry, as at the *Battle of Buna-Gona-Sanananda* and later at the *Battle of Salamaua*, but there was never a complete breakdown of forward supply. Unlike the Japanese at the *Battles of Henderson Field* and *Milne Bay*, American troops were able to sustain a siege indefinitely because they could sustain logistical support indefinitely.

The keenly contested air battles at the *Battles of Buna-Gona-Sanananda* and *Guadalcanal* also differentiated them from later ground engagements in the *Pacific War*. At *Guadalcanal*, the US controlled Henderson Field, from which it could fly sorties that prevented daytime resupply of the Japanese forces by transport ship, became the key to the long drawn out battle for the island. Yet the 'Cactus' Air Force, at Henderson Field could not prevent the repeated heavy bombing of its airfield nor could the US dare to bring its *South Pacific* carriers close to *Guadalcanal* except for brief periods. The main reason why Japan was not able to extend its air power to achieve complete superiority at *Guadalcanal* was that its planes had to make a 1,280 mile round trip from Rabaul.

At *Guadalcanal* there was stalemate between the US and Japan at distances where Japanese planes were operating at the edge of their 'real world' operating range. A similar stalemate occurred at the *Battle of Buna-Gona-Sanananda* though the circumstances were slightly different. For the Japanese there was a shorter aerial round trip to the battlefield, just 840 miles. On the other hand the US Fifth Air Force, unlike at Henderson Field, was based just eighty miles away at Port Moresby though it had to fly over the hump of the Owen Stanley Range whose weather frequently made flying impossible. Attacks on Buna could also be made from airbases in northern Australia. However, Townsville Airfield, 'Pappy' Gunn's base, was a 1,500 mile round trip to Buna including a passage over the Owen Stanley Range.

The situation in the air up until early 1943 therefore, was that there was a precarious balance that gave neither side overwhelming advantage when it came to supporting their troops on the ground. It was not until after the *Battle of the Bismarck Sea*, that US soldiers would enjoy the support of significant air superiority in any ground action that they fought. The sudden collapse in Japanese air superiority marked by the *Battle of the Bismarck Sea* brought a cascade of self-reinforcing advantages. US airbases could be brought forward closer to Rabaul, thus lessening the range disadvantages of their aircraft. US forces thereby rapidly achieved complete aerial interdiction of Japanese transport supply by sea to contested battlefronts. In turn the more supplies brought to forward airbases, the more also that the US Air Force could supply forward troop positions by air as well as disrupt Japanese defensive positions on the ground. In turn, airpower could be brought forward. It was a virtuous circle; the more the Fifth Air Force could disrupt Rabaul's own supply lines by disrupting transport both on the way to *New Britain* and in the port itself, the more quickly it could forward its own airfields. The very *raison d'être* of Rabaul's existence as Japan's *South Pacific* stronghold began to be put in doubt.

The *Battle of the Bismarck Sea* was therefore a landmark event in the *Pacific War*. Having established air superiority, MacArthur was able to advance his armies forward from the strength provided by one airbase after another. In effect, the *Battle of the Bismarck Sea* not only permanently ended the possibility of Japanese advance but also gave the key impetus for the Allies advance toward Japan. Arguably in the ranks of air battles fought in *World War II*, the *Battle of the Bismarck Sea*, though small in scale, stands only behind the *Battle of Britain* and the *Air Battle of Kursk* in terms of importance.

Envelopment of Salamaua: **[Map: 21.5]** After victories at the *Battle of Wau* and the *Battle of the Bismarck Sea*, General MacArthur outlined his instructions for the next phase of his campaign in New Guinea:

> Forces of the SWPA [South West Pacific Area] supported by South Pacific Forces will seize the Lae-Salamaua-Finschhafen-Markham River Valley area and establish major elements of the Air Force therein to provide from the Markham Valley area general and direct air support of subsequent operations in northern New Guinea and New Britain, and to control Vitiaz Strait and protect the north-Western flank of subsequent operations in Western New Britain.[47]

As a result of these victories, MacArthur was able to advance his plans to capture the naval bases at Lae as well as the important Nadzab Airfield, situated on a plateau twenty-five miles to the west. As General Blamey noted in a report, "Each forward move of airbases meant an increase in the range of our fighters planes and consequently an increase in the area in which transport planes supplying our troops could be operated. To get airfields further and further forward was thus the dominant aim of both land and air forces."[48]

MacArthur's attack started with a siege of Major-General Okabe's forces left at Salamaua, the stronghold across the *Gulf of Huon* from Lae, from where the Japanese attack on Wau had been directed. Having supplied forces by air for the repulse of Lieutenant-General Hatazo Adachi's attack on Wau, further forces were airlifted to Wau to prepare for the assault on Salamaua under the aegis of the Australian 3rd Division led by Major-General Stanley Savige.

By 29 May the 2/7th Battalion of the 6th Australian Division, having advanced from Wau down the Black Cat Trail, began attacking the southern approaches to Salamaua. Although the Australians were brought to a halt at the *Battle of Mubo*, a flanking attack by the Australian 2/3rd Independent Company from the southwest managed to partially clear Japanese defensive positions dug into Bobdubi Ridge and repelled fierce counter-attacks at the beginning of May. Nonetheless the progress of the campaign was slowed by constraints of terrain and supply. Apart from the occasional hill covered in tall, razor sharp kunai grass, soldiers operated in a gloomy green shroud of tall trees, drooping vines and primeval vegetation. Underfoot lay sodden ground that meshed with rotting plant life giving off a perpetual odor of rot and decay. Sunlight barely penetrated the scene. A Japanese company commander of the 115th Regiment complained, "one advances as if in the dark."[49] A barely tolerable humidity clung to everything while mosquitoes and leeches played on the humans who dared to invade a jungle seemingly designed to keep out humans. A report of the Australian 3rd Division concluded, "Such conditions of rain, mud, rottenness, stench, gloom, and above all, the feeling of being shut in by the everlasting jungle and ever ascending mountains, are sufficient to fray the strongest nerves."[50]

For the many urbanites in the Australian Army, the climate and topography of Salamaua was a shock. However, even those familiar with tropical climates found the area difficult to bear. Errol Flynn, the Hollywood actor, a few years before his rise to stardom had owned a tobacco plantation at Laloki near Port Moresby. In 1933, Flynn stayed briefly in Salamaua while he was on the run from the Australian police for the theft of jewels from his *inamorata*, Madge Parks, and became familiar with the walk up to the gold mines at Wau. Although it was just thirty miles inland, the walk took seven to ten days. Errol Flynn viewed the terrain with distaste, noting that the "crawly sound you heard a few feet away might be a snake, a cassowary or maybe only a wild boar razorback . . ."[51] The peripatetic Flynn, recalled that he had "seen Central Africa, but it was never anything like the jungle of New Guinea."[52] Fighting in these jungle conditions was an art unique unto itself. A senior staff officer of the Japanese 51st Division noted,

> One can rarely see more than 100m through the jungle, so, when one is crawling up on the enemy, it is not difficult to come within 20m. Consequently when perceiving the approach of the enemy, it goes without saying, one must be alert for any rustling of foliage, and must make good use of one's ears, just as at night.[53]

In Rabaul, Eighteenth Army commander General Adachi, under orders from Lieutenant-General Hitoshi Imamura, commander of the Eighth Army in Rabaul, sustained a fierce defense of Salamaua and sent the 66th Regiment as reinforcements from Finschhafen. (Finschhafen, the German founded Lutheran missionary town, situated at the tip of the Huon Peninsula, was named after the German scientist and explorer Otto Finsch). A plan was developed for an attack on Lababia Ridge above Mubo. On 19 June, Lieutenant-Colonel Matsui optimistically informed his troops, "tomorrow at dawn we will start mopping up with entire strength and will destroy the enemy . . . The enemy appears not to be aware of our plans. He is sunbathing at Guadagasal."[54]

On 20 June, the 1,600 troops of the 66th Regiment launched an attack on Australian positions dug in on Lababia Ridge. At 2.25 p.m. on the following day a bayonet attack on the north and east sides of the perimeter got to within 20 yards of the Australian positions. To Private Ray Mathers the sound of *Banzai* screams and bugles sounded "like a pommy football match."[55] Well-constructed defensive positions with scrub cleared, open fields of interlocking fire enabled D company of the 1/6th Battalion to hold back the Japanese attack during three days of heavy fighting. It was the first time that the Australians had used this open field system of defense, not dissimilar to the one constructed by Major-General Vandegrift at Henderson Field. Brigadier Moten recorded it as "a classic example of how well-dug-in determined troops can resist heavy attacks from a numerically superior enemy."[56]

At night the Australians could hear the sounds of groaning, wounded Japanese soldiers. They used the cover of nightfall to remove their dead. The occasional Japanese shouts of "come and fight you conscript bastards"[57] would pierce the night. By 21 June ammunition was running short. Lieutenant-Colonel Dexter was forced to warn his platoon commanders to "keep your bloody fingers off the trigger."[58] To supply the exposed weapons pits on the perimeter, Australian soldiers filled socks with ammunition and hurled them to their colleagues. Japanese troops started to climb trees to fire down on the Australians in their dugouts. Climbing at night, Japanese snipers would open fire as dawn broke. They had reckoned without Captain 'Ted' Exton, an Englishman originally from Boston, Lincolnshire, who was a crack shot: Exton's platoon sergeant, speaking on the field telephone to Dexter suddenly gave a running commentary, "Just a minute—there's a Nip getting up a tree about 100 yards away—Exton's going to have a shot—he's got him and he's bouncing."[59] Although probing attacks continued on 22 June, the crisis had passed and on 23 June the Japanese fired mortar and heavy automatic fire at the perimeter only to cover their retreat.

A week later a new assault by the Australian 15th Infantry Brigade began the painstaking job of clearing the remainder of Bobdubi Ridge where 127 Japanese troops held the high ground. At this point there were 1,126 Japanese troops at Mubo, 122 at *Nassau Bay*, 543 at Salamaua, 540 at Malolo, a coastal village to the north, and 43 at Komiatum. At the same time a further flanking of the Japanese positions was made by the amphibious landing of the US 162nd, 163rd and 186th Infantry Regimental Combat Teams at *Nassau Bay* that threatened the Japanese defensive positions from the southeast. The landing force included troops of the 41nd Division comprising National Guard Units from Oregon, Washington, Idaho and Montana. On the evening of 29 June, a platoon of Australians circled round to reach the beach so as to provide guide lights for the Americans. The 26-man platoon had to wade for over a mile through creek and swamps to reach the sea. Corporal John Stevens of the 17th Brigade recalled hacking their way through driving rain: "It was an incredibly evil swamp; the hellish climax to all we had endured in New Guinea."[60] Arriving to the far south, the platoon had to race up the beach and managed to set up their red lights just in time to guide the US landing craft ashore. Submerged rocks tore gashes in the landing craft and heavy breakers overturned others. Twenty-one LCVPs (Landing Craft, Vehicle Personnel: otherwise known as Higgins boats) were lost, which meant that only 770 of the 1,000 troops were landed.

The establishment of a garrison at *Nassau Bay* enabled the Americans and Australians to bring in field artillery that was impossible to carry down from Wau. After beating off the Japanese counter-attack, they advanced with their guns toward Bitoi Ridge. Heavy fighting by Major-General Stanley Savige's Australian 3rd Division's 15th Infantry Brigade ensued in piecemeal actions as they forced the Japanese to retreat from Mubo, which was finally taken on 11 July. The next advance was toward Mount Tambu where the nearby bay was sought-after as a landing point closer to Salamaua. It was painstaking work. Ernie Pike, a mortar sergeant noted, "Our boys needed to be equipped with ploughs as well as Tommy guns to get the Nips out of those funk holes."[61] The Japanese troops may have been degraded, and one of their number described their condition as being "just like beggars,"[62] but they fought to the death.

The American advance on *Tambu Bay* began on 18 July with the primary aim of securing the ridge that overlooked it from the north, without which the beaches could not be used to unload supplies. It became known as 'Roosevelt Ridge.' The ridge ran off 'Scout Ridge,' which tracked parallel to the coast to Salamaua and was named after their commander Major Archibald Roosevelt, fourth child of President Theodore Roosevelt and his second wife Edith Kermit Carow. It took three weeks of fighting to dislodge the Japanese defenders. Supplies, troops and guns could now be landed in the bay and artillery emplacements set up on 'Roosevelt Ridge.' After it was taken on 12 August, Archibald Roosevelt, a fifty-year-old veteran of *World War I*'s Western Front, was wounded by a Japanese grenade, which shattered his knee. By perverse coincidence it was the same shattered knee which had given him a disability discharge from the US 1st Infantry Division in 1917. Roosevelt became the only US soldier ever to be given a full disability discharge twice for the same injury in two different wars.

Over the next two weeks Australian forces took Komiatum Ridge overlooking Salamaua from the west and forced their way across the *Francisco River*. On 23 August, Allied control of the air and sea to the south of the Huon Peninsula was such that the 3rd Division was relieved by the arrival by sea of the Australian 5th Division led by Major-General Edward Milford. A week later further Allied landings at Lae, threatening to cut off any Japanese line of retreat from Salamaua to the north, forced the remaining Japanese force to abandon Salamaua on 11 September. It was not a beautiful prize:

> Not one building in Salamaua had been missed by bombs.
> A few on the isthmus still stood, with walls blown out,
> roofs holed by strafing, but there was nothing to inspire
> pride of possession. Only yards separated the holes where
> bombs had landed and it was a wonder that any of the
> buildings managed to remain upright. Everywhere the
> stink of the "Pongo" [corpses] hung in the air.[63]

An American GI called Salamaua "a filthy, rat-ridden, pestilential hole."[64]

For the Australian units, the Japanese withdrawal came in the nick of time. Poor weather and the harsh terrain combined with paucity of supplies had severely reduced their fighting effectiveness. In spite of the complaints of Australian commanders on the ground, headquarters had decided on a level of rations before the campaign based on the projection of a few days fighting—rather than the reality of a prolonged battle that lasted from 20 June to the beginning of September. The 58th and 59th Battalions were in continuous contact with the enemy for seventy-seven days. Major-General Savige commented, "The way those 18 and 19 year olds . . . kept at Japs was one of [the] outstanding feats of both wars."[65] On 11 September, a medical officer reported that rations were "quite inadequate considering the strenuous effort involved. Symptoms of malaria and vague dyspepsia are frequent and men are constantly complaining of weakness and inability to stand up to work. Unless the quantity of food is increased the men will not be able to carry on under existing conditions."[66]

The Bombing of Wewak: **[Map: 21.6]** Wewak sat on the easternmost corner of the oval of the *Bismarck Sea*. Wewak Airfield, with its satellite fields of Boram, Dagua and But, was the major airfield and military base on the north coast of New Guinea and effectively operated as the ferry point for supply of aircraft to Rabaul from the Philippines. On 30 July there were just thirty Japanese airplanes there. Yet two weeks later the Wewak Airfield was jam-packed with 176 aircraft of which 107 were bombers. Japan's Army Air Force commanders had decided that Wewak Airfield would play a major role in thwarting the expected US advance on Lae. The Fourth Japanese Air Army had moved large numbers of planes to the area during the Salamaua Campaign and by mid-August it was estimated to be home to approximately 250 aircraft of which about 130 were operational. The poor operating ratios reflected a shortage of spare parts, a lack of maintenance crews and high sickness rates among the Japanese aircrews in their jungle billets.

The Japanese aircraft at Wewak, with their longer range capability, had been attacking the Allied fields at Wau and Salamaua and were lulled into believing that at 340 miles away they were out of range of US escort fighters. Kenney desperately needed a means of getting at Wewak by dominating the airspace over the Markham Valley. To be able to interdict Japanese air attacks, he needed to get his fighters closer to Wewak to give cover to his bomber forces and to pose a threat to Japanese bomber formations going back and forth from Wewak. The problem with building a new airfield was that Japanese bombers could interrupt or delay its construction indefinitely. Kenney finally struck on the idea of building an airport covertly at Tsili, near Marilinan, some 40 miles to the west of Lae. At 298 miles it was just within the US operating range to bomb Wewak and not on an axis traversed by Japanese traffic. Not wanting to be a hostage to fortune if the venture failed, Kenney insisted that it be called Marilinan Airfield rather than Tsili Tsili (pronounced 'silly silly'). Kenney predicted, "With minimum losses to ourselves, we ought to be able to clean out his [the Japanese] whole Air Force out of this theater . . . land troops at will anywhere we pleased and really go places in this war."[67]

Native workers cleared Marilinan Airfield in June and the 4,200-foot runway was able to land C-47 transports by early July. No longer dependent on airdrops, rapid progress could be made. C-47s even brought in trucks cut into pieces that could be welded back together. Kenney was ingeniously creative and expected and encouraged it in his troops. Engineering teams worked shifts twenty-four hours a day. American productivity was extraordinary. As Colonel Dr. Thomas Griffith Jr. has pointed out in *MacArthur's Airman* [1998] ". . . the 700 men and 220 pieces of heavy equipment [bulldozers, graders and trucks] in one American aviation engineer battalion could accomplish in 24 hours the same amount as 50,000 men with handtools."[68] It was an advantage that Japan could not match. Only eight bulldozers were manufactured in Japan from 1943 to 1944. In spite of the bad weather Fifth Air Force engineers were able to improve the runway surfaces and extend its operating length to 7,000 foot. A young Australian officer noted,

> Where a week ago had been a sleepy native village, a tent town straggled through the fringes of the jungle, inhabited by American troops and airmen, both white and negro, Australian soldiers and airmen, Papuan infantrymen, native policemen, carriers and laborers. On the rough earth airstrip, hastily cleared, DC-3 [C-47] transports roared in and out, unloading troops, stores, and construction equipment. A major operational base had sprung from the earth just at the back door of Lae, the enemy's main stronghold.[69]

By August the Marilinan Airfield could handle 150 planes a day.

To cover up the construction work at Marilinan Airfield, Kenney organized the construction of a diversionary strip at Garoka, near Bena Bena. Native crews were ordered to stir up a lot of dust to attract attention. By deception Kenney, as he later put it, had built an airfield, "right in their back yard."[70] In addition, Kenney sought to have barges made up as dummy aircraft carriers to be built to draw off Japanese aircraft. This fanciful project eventually had to be abandoned but the fake airport at Bena Bena worked. Remarkably the presence of the real airfield at Marilinan Airfield was not discovered until 14 August. For the Japanese it was too late.

Having discovered the 'secret' airfield and realizing that Wewak would soon be under attack from American bombers, Lieutenant-General Teramoto launched a pre-emptive attack with thirty-four Ki-43 'Oscars' and seven Type-99 Kawasaki Ki-48 'Lily' light bombers. Arriving under cloud cover, they were missed by radar and patrolling P-38s. However, a dozen P-39 Airacobras, which had been escorting twelve C-47 troop transports, swooped to intercept the oncoming Japanese strike force. In the *mêlée*, two of the damaged 'Oscars' attempted *taiatari* (literally: body strike, a *Kendo* move which came to mean suicide dive) with one of them scoring a direct hit on the Chapel, killing the chaplain and six men. A C-47 transport plane was also destroyed killing all six men aboard and delaying airfield operations. On the Japanese side, Captain Shigeki Namba, from his covering flight of fighters, lamented, "one by one the Ki-48s were shot down in flames."[71] Fourteen confirmed 'kills' of Japanese bombers were claimed. Lockheed P-38 Lightnings and the newly introduced P-47 Thunderbolt fighters met a follow up Japanese attack the next day. A further fifteen Japanese fighters were shot down. The new Thunderbolts claimed the shooting of three Japanese fighters.

With the build-up of opposing air forces at Wewak and Marilinan Airfields respectively, the ground was set for a major contest for control of New Guinea's airspace. On the evening of 16 August a night attack by forty bombers from Port Moresby opened the Allied attack on Wewak's airfields with relatively minor damage inflicted. As the B-24 Liberators dived to make their final run on Wewak's Boram Airfield heavy anti-aircraft fire opened up a "literal hell of smoke and flame criss-crossed by searchlights."[72]

Similarly Dusty Swanson of 321st Squadron recalled,

> We were in the lights during the entire bomb run. I saw
> Joe Casale go down. He started his run right in front of
> me and they received a direct hit. He went down in flames.
> It was not easy, going in for our run after that. Joe was a
> heck of a nice guy and it is really hard to realize it was
> him. His navigator lived in our tent, which really hit
> home.[73]

Swanson and his colleagues were also attacked by twin-engine Kawasaki Ki-45 *Toryu* (dragon slayer) fighters that, while uncompetitive against US fighters, were heavily armed with three cannon and two 0.50 mm machine guns and as such proved effective in action against American bombers. In spite of that there were just two US bomber casualties from the night sorties. The following day, 17 August, confusion reigned at Wewak's Boram Airfield. About seventy men had been killed or burned and damaged aircraft littered the runway. Intelligence officer, Captain Yamanaka, was concerned that the night's attack was a harbinger of daylight raids to come. Although he was the senior officer on base, it was a sign of the Japanese Army Air Force's ossified command structure that Yamanaka felt unable to overrule the order that all aircraft should be brought out for inspection by senior staff commanders coming from Rabaul. At 7.00 a.m. the four airfields at Wewak were packed tip-to-tip with planes. Just as importantly the Japanese Army Air Force, having failed to develop adequate radar was highly dependent on 'manual' spotters. However, communications had been badly damaged during the night and in spite of Yamanaka's efforts, Japanese defenses that morning were effectively blind.

Meanwhile US Air Force's 405th Squadron of Mitchell B-25 bombers approached Wewak. The mission was not going well. The accompanying 71st Squadron's B-25s had aborted their mission while the P-38 escorts from Marilinan Airfield had failed to join them. Also there were problems in jettisoning their fuselage fuel tanks. Most pilots, not willing to go into battle with a fume-filled gas tank in the fuselage, turned back. Not so Lieutenant Garrett Middlebrook who ordered his engineer to clip his parachute harness to the fuselage spars above the tank and to jump up and down until it fell away. It did. Middlebrook joked with his engineer, "I hope you're still in!"[74]

With his fuselage fuel tank jettisoned, Middlebrook joined the one pilot who alone appeared to be still heading toward Wewak's Boram Airfield. It was "... Mr. Determination, Bill Gay, my friend from the first day I entered flying school."[75] A third plane pulled alongside. Without fighter cover the three B-25s flew onwards. As they arrived at Dagua Airfield (Wewak), Middlebrook and Gay were astonished to see planes lined up on both sides of the runway with gasoline tanks and ground crews adding to this unexpected vision of juicy targets. "My God, what a sight!"[76] recalled Middlebrook. The Japanese ground forces were caught completely unprepared. The three pilots, equipped with their 'Paul Gunn' designed eight-gun platforms in their B-25 noses, strafed the airfield to devastating effect. Gasoline tanks and planes burst into flames or exploded. Meanwhile the co-pilots were piling on the misery of the Japanese defenders by the release of 'parafrags' from the bomb bay.

In the 1920s Lieutenant-General Kenney had developed 'parafrags,' short for Parachute Fragmentation Bombs, as a means of dropping time-delayed bombs in low-level attacks that enabled the attacker to escape unscathed. The relatively small 23 lb bombs broke into 25 mm fragments that proved devastatingly effective against the aluminum skins of aircraft and also helped circumvent the protection afforded by an airfield's revetment aircraft defenses. Needless to add that any personnel standing in the open were shredded. Kenney was fortunate that this type of bomb was not sought after in any other US theater and he was able to supply the Fifth Air Force in large quantity. In truth Kenney's universal belief in low-level bombing was contradicted by disastrous results in Europe where German anti-aircraft defense was much stronger. General 'Hap' Arnold sharply informed Kenney, "[low-level] attack tactics have definitely not as you state proven sound 'every day all over the world.' "[77] Against Japanese airfields it worked because they were poorly defended.

At Boram Airfield, a shell-shocked Yamanaka recalled, "It was a sea of flames. This was the first full-scale enemy counter-attack I had experienced."[78] The three B-25s expertly led by Gay maneuvered their way to safety in spite of forty-five minutes of attacks by Nakajima Ki-45 'Oscars.' News of their stunning attack filtered back to Port Moresby where Gay and the three crews received a rousing welcome. Correspondents with notebooks rushed to meet them including Alan Dawes from the *Sydney Telegraph* who described Staff Sergeant Victor Hoffacker, a turret gunner, as a man who "was nearly dancing with delight, fresh from the best spectacle he had seen since the Bismarck Sea."[79] According to the 8th Photo Reconnaissance Squadron an estimated seventy to eighty planes had been damaged or destroyed on the ground. Although the photographers had run out of film and were thus unable to fully verify the victory, MacArthur, with a familiar piece of over optimistic extrapolation, communicated to Washington, "Photographs reveal the total destruction of 120 enemy planes and severe damage to at least another 50 . . . it is estimated that 1500 enemy air personnel were killed."[80] More likely around fifty planes were destroyed.

A follow-up attack by forty-seven Liberators and seventeen B-17 Flying Fortress made even more devastating attacks on Wewak's airfields. Some sixty planes being warmed up on the runway were destroyed. At 9.00 a.m. there followed a strafing attack by thirty Mitchell B-25s and eighty Lightning P-38s. Colonel Don Hall who led the 8th and 13th Squadrons over Boram Airfield recalled, "The surprise was complete. Not an AA gun was fired. Not a plane got off the ground to intercept us. A fellow dreams of a situation like that, but never expects to see it."[81] Hall's gung-ho colleague 'Cowboy Brown' was so excited, he opened the window of his B-25 and blazed away with his Colt 0.45 pistol. Similar attacks were made on the following day, 18 August. After a day's lull, two further raids by Lieutenant-General Kenney's Fifth Air Force were made on 20 and 21 August. On the last of these raids, seventy Japanese planes were destroyed, half of them in combat with the escorting Lightning P-38s.

After four days of attacks and with just thirty operating planes remaining, the Fourth Japanese Air Army was effectively wiped out. It was a victory that was overwhelming and decisive. If the *Battle of the Bismarck Sea* was the inflection point of the air war in the *South Pacific*, the *Battle of Wewak* was the event that confirmed the collapse of Japanese air power in the *Pacific*. Thereafter America had complete control of the skies over New Guinea. Staff officer, Colonel Kazuo Tanikawa would later admit,

> At the time of the air attacks on Wewak on 17 and 18 August our defenses were not alert. We lost 100 planes including light bombers, fighters and reconnaissance planes. It was a decisive Allied victory . . . Consequently our air power was rapidly diminishing and was unable to aid our ground forces that effectively, in the end, constituted one of our chief reasons for losing the war.[82]

Not only did the *Battle of Wewak* crush Japan's airpower in northern New Guinea, but it also interdicted the supply of aircraft to Japan's main regional base at Rabaul. US victory in the air thus went a long way to completing the isolation of Rabaul, the major strategic objective of Operation CARTWHEEL.

Colonel Koji Tanaka, one of the negligent staff officers from Rabaul who had been at Wewak on 17 August, revealed during a post-war interrogation that Wewak's small airports gave little opportunity for aircraft dispersal but more importantly he confirmed that senior officers believed that Wewak's airfields were out of US fighter range. Tanaka and his fellow officers believed that the Americans would confine themselves only to night attacks. The result was that at the *Battle of Wewak* Kenney's Fifth Air Force won a decisive victory that provided it with an air supremacy over mainland New Guinea that it was never to lose. The Japanese Army was now incapable of interdicting the Allied advance on Lae and Nadzab. MacArthur's intelligence officer, Colonel Charles Willoughby, concluded, "The Allied air attack against Wewak this week is unquestionably a milestone in the *Pacific War*. This is the first major reversal suffered by the Japanese Army Air Service in the Pacific."[83]

Adachi's Eighteenth Army Escapes the Net: Allied Occupation of Lae and Nadzab:

[Map: 21.7] The Australian 9th Division, backed up by five destroyers, landed to the east of Lae on 4 September. Apart from a bombing attack from Rabaul the landing was unopposed. Six LSTs (Landing Ship, Tank) began to unload. Admiral Barbey noted later, "Unloading of LSTs, each containing 400 men, 35 vehicles and 80 tons of bulk stores was excellent. One LST was unloaded in 1 hour 42 minutes. Unloading of the remainder was completed within 2 hours 15 minutes."[84] By 10.30 a.m. 7,800 troops and 1,500 tons of stores were ashore. Halted at the *Busu River*, the 2/28th Division established a foothold on the far bank in spite of fierce Japanese opposition. On the west side of Lae, the US 503rd Parachute Infantry Regiment landed and quickly took control of Nadzab Airfield. Lieutenant-General Kenney went with them after telling MacArthur, "They're my kids and I want to see them do their stuff";[85] MacArthur hesitated for a moment before saying, "You're right George. We'll both go. They're my kids, too."[86] Kenney was appalled at the consequences of them both being killed by "some five dollar a month Jap aviator,"[87] but MacArthur was more worried about air-sickness and the disgrace of throwing-up in front of colleagues.

Major-General George Vasey flew into Nadzab with the Australian 7th Division soon after the costliest episode of the Salamaua-Lae Campaign. A B-24 Liberator crashed on take-off after clipping a branch and ploughed into five troop trucks full of soldiers waiting to debark; its four 500 lb bombs exploded and threw its 2,800 gallons of fuel in all directions; there were 151 casualties including 59 dead.

In the advance toward Lae, the 7th Division engaged in fierce fighting with Japanese troops at Jensen's Plantation and Heath's Plantation. In total 345 Japanese soldiers were killed. The 25th Brigade of the 7th Division and the 24th Brigade of the 9th Division entered Lae from west and east respectively on 16 September. A week earlier on 8 September, General MacArthur had issued a *communiqué* stating, "elements of four Japanese Divisions aggregating 20,000 at the beginning are now completely enveloped with their supply cut."[88] It was a gross exaggeration. In fact MacArthur inflated by double the number of Japanese troops at Salamaua and Lae. In addition to 11,000 troops of the 51st Division, Lieutenant-General Hidemitsu Nakano had 1,500 Japanese Navy troops giving him aggregate forces of 12,500. MacArthur's claims of a successful envelopment were likewise untrue. Nakano escaped with over 8,000 of his troops intact. Some had been removed by barge, others by submarine, while others took the overland trails to Finschhafen on the north coast of the *Gulf of Huon*.

On entering Lae, it became clear to the Australians that the enemy had gone. Japanese holding forces had delayed the Australians long enough for the bulk of Lae's garrison to escape north through the mountains of the Huon Peninsula. Major-General Sir George Wootten wrote that Lae "was in an indescribably filthy condition and had been very thoroughly wrecked."[89] The town was full of the stench that was recognized as typical of departing Japanese armies. The evident Japanese lack of hygiene and order bespoke an army and a supply system that had broken down. The conditions of squalor and the evident collapse of Japanese logistics were ample testament to the squeeze applied on reinforcement and resupply by Kenney's victory at the *Battle of the Bismarck Sea*.

Salamaua was quickly rejected as a useful Allied garrison but strenuous efforts were made to make Nadzab Airfield useable as a forward airbase for future operations along the New Guinea coast. Lae itself would be useful as a port mainly to supply Nadzab Airfield. However, development of the airbase was slowed by the poor condition of the 25-mile road that wound uphill from Lae; between October and December it was unusable and delayed the build-up of US forces in the region. The three-month Salamaua-Lai Campaign had ended with 8,100 Japanese casualties of whom 2,850 were killed. Over the same period Australia suffered 1,120 casualties, with 470 killed. During just seventy-six days of participation in the campaign, the US 162nd Battalion lost 81 killed and 396 wounded.

Albeit small-scale, the *Battle of Salamaua* and the *Battle of Lae* were completely different in their *modus operandi* from earlier engagements fought by the Allies in New Guinea. Victory in the air, at the *Battle of the Bismarck Sea* and reinforced by the destruction of Japanese airpower at the *Battle of Wewak*, had transformed the balance of power on the ground. At the *Battles of Salamaua and Lae*, the US Air Force had provided the cutting edge of the Army's advance; it was a pattern to be repeated in all subsequent land engagements of the *Pacific War*. After February 1943, US air power was able to support Allied forces in ground action, provide uninterrupted logistical capacity, interdict the re-supply of Japanese troops and give air cover to amphibious flanking actions.

From now on, MacArthur's advance along the coast of New Guinea would display the same multi-service dimension that General Yamashita had shown in his advance down the Malay Peninsula's east coast in 1941. But Japanese officers and their troops, unlike the Allied Forces in the Philippines, Malaya, Burma and the Dutch East Indies, were prepared to fight and die for every inch of ground yielded.

22 Yamamoto Assassinated and the Battle of New Georgia

[March 1943–October 1943]

[Maps: 22.1, 22.2, 22.3, 22.4A, 22.4B, 22.5, 22.6]

The Assassination of Admiral Isoroku Yamamoto: **[Map: 22.1]** At 7.25 a.m. on 18 April 1943, a few weeks after the establishment of American air supremacy at the *Battle of the Bismarck Sea*, eighteen Lockheed P-38 Lightnings, with their distinctive twin-engine, twin-boom frame, set out from *Guadalcanal* toward the *Solomon Islands'* northernmost major island of *Bougainville*. They flew at wave height to avoid detection. The course they took was not direct. Two planes developed engine problems and had to drop out. A wide semi-circular sweep would take them on a 435-mile course toward their planned interception point at 9.35 a.m. with Admiral Isoroku Yamamoto's flight. Major John Mitchell, who planned the operation, arrived with a specially selected flight of sixteen P-38s at precisely the moment that two Japanese Mitsubishi G4M 'Betty' medium bombers accompanied by six Zero escort fighters arrived over the coastal area of Buin in southern *Bougainville Island*. The 'Bettys' broke off and scampered for safety—to no avail. Captain Thomas Lanphier Jr., formerly a journalism graduate from Stanford University, and his group of four designated attack planes hunted them down. The 'Bettys' crashed deep in the jungle. Admiral Isoroku Yamamoto, the architect of Japan's war-opening victory at *Pearl Harbor* had been assassinated.

The success of Operation VENGEANCE was immediately signaled with the pre-arranged message 'POP GOES THE WEASEL.' When the message was transmitted to *South Pacific* command, Rear-Admiral Turner whooped with joy while Halsey demanded, "What's good about it? I'd hoped to lead that scoundrel up Pennsylvania Avenue in chains, with the rest of you kicking him where it would do the most good."[1] Halsey refused to release the news to the press on the grounds that he did not want to compromise US intelligence operations.

The following day, a Japanese search party led by army engineer Lieutenant Hamasuna found their iconic naval leader still strapped to his cabin seat under a tree, head bowed forward but still holding the hilt of his *kitana* (samurai sword). He had been killed by a 0.50 caliber bullet fired by Lanphier's wingman, Lieutenant Rex Barber, an agricultural engineer from Culver, Oregon, from one of his P-38's Browning machine guns; the bullet entered the back of Yamamoto's jaw and exited above his right eye. Admiral Yamamoto, known by US intelligence to be an officer who demanded exacting punctuality of himself and others, had left Rabaul on the 315 mile inspection trip to Ballalae Airfield that was located on a small island adjacent to *Shortland Island* off the southern coast of *Bougainville*. His radio transmission was intercepted by Admiral Nimitz's intelligence unit and decrypted by Commander Layton and his team. It revealed Yamamoto's schedule in detail. Nimitz wondered aloud, "Do we try to get him?"; Layton answered somewhat oleaginously, "it would be just as if they shot you down. There isn't anyone to replace you."[2] Without hesitation, President Roosevelt ordered Yamamoto's assassination. His own feelings apart, and there is no reason to think that he had any qualms, Roosevelt could never have faced the American people had he let slip this chance to kill 'enemy no.2' (Hirohito was no.1) after his 'treacherous' attack on *Pearl Harbor*. However, Secretary of the Navy, Knox, took the precaution of consulting with leading churchmen to sound out the morality of having Yamamoto murdered.

For the Japanese, the sloppiness of sending information about Yamamoto's plans was plain to many. Rear-Admiral Takatsugu Jojima, commander of the 11th Seaplane Tender Division at *Shortland Island*, raged, "What a damn fool thing to do, to send such a long and detailed message about the activities of the C-in-C so near the front . . . this kind of thing must stop."[3] Vice-Admiral Jisaburo Ozawa was similarly concerned and wanted to send more fighters but by bad luck, Vice-Admiral Matome Ugaki, who should have delivered the message, had to enter hospital with dengue fever.

For weeks the assassination was covered up and many of the details whitewashed in the Japanese media. His remains were put in a coffin and burnt at Buin on 21 April 1943. A month later the *Joho Kyoku* (the Bureau of Naval Intelligence) issued a carefully prepared panegyric that omitted most of the details of his death. Brought back to Tokyo, a portion of his ashes was finally laid to rest in a state ceremony at Tama Cemetery on 5 June. At 10.50 a.m. Japan came to a standstill as citizens across the country stood still to offer a prayer to their departed hero. The remainder went to the family burial site at Chuko-ji Temple in Nagaoka City. Yamamoto was posthumously given the title of Marshal. Other state honors were awarded; the Order of the Chrysanthemum (1st Class) was given by Emperor Hirohito while Hitler decorated him with the Knight's Cross. Admiral Koga was appointed as his successor.

Similar obfuscation would take place on the American side. When he returned to *Guadalcanal* after the assassination mission, Tom Lanphier boasted, "I got Yamamoto! I got Yamamoto!"[4] He was given a half credit for the kill but campaigned relentlessly to be given sole credit; another pilot on the mission, Doug Canning, thought that Lanphier "was not telling the truth" and noted, "He wanted to be President of the United States . . . He thought that being famous would help him."[5] It was only in 2003, some sixty years after the event, that Lieutenant Rex Barber (later promoted to Colonel), formerly an agricultural student from Culver, Oregon, was formally acknowledged as Yamamoto's killer, following a scientific evaluation of the evidence.

The Air Battle for the Solomons: Before his death Yamamoto had implemented a new strategy, codenamed Operation I-GO. The *Battles of Guadalcanal* and *Buna-Gona-Sananda* were heavy setbacks to his plans to expand the perimeter of the Japanese Empire to the east of Australia so as to throttle the supply routes to MacArthur's Allied armies. A complete strategic rethink was required. The conclusion that Yamamoto reached was that expansionist new strategies were no longer possible. In the *South Pacific*, as in the *Central Pacific*, the United States would have to be drawn into a war of attrition so difficult and bloody that they would have to sue for peace on terms favorable for Japan. Japan's war of aggressive expansion would now become a war of aggressive defense. In the *South Pacific* the new strategy would be dependent on air defense—using his bombers to try to disrupt Halsey from building airfields. In April Yamamoto had moved his HQ to Rabaul to oversee Operation I-GO. It was a decision that doomed him. When Watanabe complained that the information about Yamamoto's visit to Ballalae Airfield should be done by courier and not by radio, the communications officer replied, "This code only went into effect on 1 April and cannot be broken."[6]

Yamamoto accurately anticipated that the Allied advance in the Solomons and New Guinea would focus on subjugation of the Japanese stronghold at Rabaul. Apart from one small but important twist, namely the eventual decision to isolate rather than destroy Rabaul, Yamamoto's understanding of the Allies' plan proved completely accurate.

Within five days of the *Battle of Guadalcanal* being officially declared as over on 9 February 1942, Lieutenant-General Kenney authorized a plan to "really take Rabaul apart."[7] This started on the night of 14–15 February with a bombing raid by thirteen B-29 Flying-Fortress bombers from the 63rd Bomb Squadron. Munitions and fuel dumps were targeted. A second wave of ten bombers from 65th Bomb Squadron dropped incendiaries on downtown Rabaul. Two more waves consisted of eight B-17s and four Liberators. There were no fighter interceptions. Japan's failure to regain *Guadalcanal* was thus quickly brought home. Petty Officer Igarashi at Vunakanau Airfield noted that after the bombing, he "felt beaten physically and emotionally."[8]

Yamamoto had further predicted the double-pronged Allied advance through New Guinea and the northern *Solomon Islands*. He therefore set up the 'ring of airfields' around Rabaul that would determine the outcome of the battle ahead. His inspection visit to Ballalae Airfield, the cause of his death, was a key indication of the importance he now placed on these 'ring' airfields. The result was, "Most combat took place inside or very close to a triangle with Port Moresby at the western point, *Guadalcanal* at the eastern point, and Rabaul at the northern apex."[9]

He knew that US forces would advance under the cover of air superiority, which in turn depended on their ability to build forward airfields. In anticipation, Yamamoto ordered a massive build-up of bombers and fighters with the aim of preventing US supply of *matériel* for the building and equipping of their advance airfields. The battle for Henderson Field on *Guadalcanal* was the first of these contests and Yamamoto was sure that others would follow. What he hoped was that the shorter lines of supply from airfields closer to Rabaul would give him the advantage over US forces. Contrary to the reports coming back from his pilots indicating that great air victories were being won against US forces in the *Solomon Islands*, his tour of inspection was beginning to reveal the opposite. One of the things that he would surely have noticed on his tour of the new airfields built to defend Rabaul was that by comparison with the US airfields, they were poorly constructed. As early as 25 October 1942, Rear-Admiral Ugaki had noted in his diary, "every time it rained heavily, about ten planes were damaged due to skidding."[10] The arms race to build new, bigger and better airfields would be won 'hands down' by the US Seabees.

Just as Yamamoto used the post-*Guadalcanal* lull to bolster his defenses for the anticipated battle ahead, Halsey prepared his forces for the next stage of the advance in the central and northern *Solomons*. A firm advocate of unity of command, he oversaw the realignment of air command that had inevitably been confused given the presence of the US Army's Thirteenth Air Force led by Major-General Twining, the Marine Air Corps as well as the New Zealanders who had by now arrived with their Curtiss P-40 Warhawk squadrons and Lockheed Hudson search planes. As well as different services and nationalities, there was a profusion of new equipment; in addition to Warhawks, fighters included the Lockheed P-38 Lightning, Chance Vought F4U Corsair, Bell Airacobra as well as the new Grumman F6F Hellcat, an updated replacement for their Wildcats, which were still the US Navy's mainstay. Bombers consisted of Boeing B-17 Flying Fortresses, Consolidated B-24 Liberators, Dauntless Helldivers, General Motors' Grumman Avengers and North American B-25 Mitchells.

For this extraordinarily diverse force's operational control devolved to COMAIRSOL, the lugubrious acronym for Commander of Air Forces in the *Solomons*. A solution to the intricacies of command and responsibility between Lieutenant-General Millard Harmon, Deputy Commander of air forces of the South Pacific Area and Rear-Admiral Aubrey Fitch, who commanded the US Navy and Marine Air Forces in the *Solomons*, was achieved under Vice-Admiral Halsey's directive that there must be a unified command. Broadly it was agreed that combat command should be vested in the respective services with minimal disruption of normal command channels by COMAIRSOL whose role was largely one of strategy and coordination. Surprisingly, the diffuse system of command adopted avoided most of the 'political' pitfalls and worked extremely effectively.

At *Guadalcanal* there was a concomitant build-up of airfield capacity to take the fighter squadrons. Four new airbases were constructed as well as vast storage facilities to cope with a huge build-up of munitions, gasoline, clothing and food that was brought in to prepare for the campaign ahead. During March 1943 Allied bombers made sporadic attacks on Japanese airfields on *Ballalae, Kahili, Shortland Island* and Munda on the northwest coast of *New Georgia*. In addition a reconnaissance picture was built of Japanese movements, airfields and installations. When photographs revealed the development of a Japanese seaplane base off southern *Bougainville*, a dawn fighter attack was ordered on 28 March. Led by Captain Lanphier of 70th Squadron, six P-38s destroyed eight Japanese seaplanes. Rex Barber of 339th Squadron, later Lanphier's confederate in the slaying of Yamamoto, was lucky to survive the attack when he hit the mast of a Japanese ship and lost three feet of wing. At the end of the month however, even with these kills included, only 16 Japanese planes were shot down. As for the Allies, there was not a single loss recorded in the *Solomon Islands*.

It was to be a brief lacuna in the *Solomons* campaign. At the beginning of April the Japanese returned in force as Yamamoto's I-GO campaign started in earnest. The channel between *Tulagi* and *Guadalcanal* hummed with the to-and-fro of US troop transports, merchantmen, tenders and warships. It was an irresistible target. On 1 April, Japanese bombers, escorted by Zeros, were launched in a mass attack on US assets at *Guadalcanal*. They were met with an assortment of forty-two Allied fighters. After a three hour dogfight twenty Zeros had been shot down versus six planes of Fighter Command.

After a week of sporadic bombing attacks by both sides, Allied watchers on the coast of New Guinea indicated that a major attack was imminent. In total 160 Japanese aircraft were headed down the 'Slot.' All seventy-six Allied fighters were put in the air. Thirty-nine Japanese planes were downed against seven scored in return. Only Major Walden Williams of 70th Fighter Squadron was killed as the US had by now developed a sophisticated and rapid pilot rescue service for pilots dunked in the sea. Brigadier-General Nathan Twining, commander of the Thirteenth Air Force had himself been rescued from the sea by the US Navy in early February after six days spent in rafts with fourteen colleagues after their plane had been forced to ditch on its way from *Guadalcanal* to the US Air Force HQ at *Espiritu Santo*.

Yamamoto also launched mass attacks on US airfields on New Guinea. On 12 April 1943, just six days before Yamamoto's assassination, Mitsubishi G4M1 'Bettys' took off from Vunakanau Airfield near Rabaul. They were accompanied by 130 Navy Zeros along with 65 Zeros from the carriers *Zuikaku*, *Hiyo* and *Junyo*. They were headed for *Milne Bay* and all US fighters were scrambled to meet them. US defenses were sold a dummy. The Japanese attack switched course and was only picked up as it was crossing the Owen Stanley Mountains headed for Port Moresby. Kenney was on hand to witness a *mêlée* involving over a hundred aircraft. Kenney noted that the Japanese "came into sight of my headquarters at 10.23 a.m. Forty-five bombers in one beautifully flown mass formation ... while above them between 60 and 70 fighters for protection."[11] Ten Japanese aircraft including two fighters were shot down. It was the 106th air raid on Port Moresby and the largest to date.

The expected raid on *Milne Bay* the following day, 13 April, did not materialize. But on 14 April Yamamoto waved off the last attack of Operation I-GO. Twenty-three 'Val' bombers and 44 'Bettys' were accompanied by 129 Zeros from the 11th Air Fleet and the Third Fleet. Only three ships at *Milne Bay* took hits and none were sunk. Japanese claims were exorbitant: three large and one medium transport sunk, six transport heavily damaged and forty-four Allied aircraft shot down. In reality only one P-40 Warhawk was lost and the defenders claimed nineteen confirmed kills. In the battle Lieutenant Richard Bong, who was described by Kenney as "a little blonde-haired Norwegian boy"[12] started to make a name for himself with the double shooting of 'Betty' bombers. Kenney, who liked heroes and their legends, told his staff to "watch for that boy Bong."[13] In the combined reports coming from I-GO, the Japanese claimed a massive victory in which their bomber units had supposedly sunk a cruiser, two destroyers, six cargo ships, ten medium cargo ships as well as shooting down 134 Allied planes and damaging fifty-six more. Emperor Hirohito was impressed. "Please convey my satisfaction to the Commander in Chief, Combined Fleet, and tell him to enlarge the war result more than ever."[14]

By contrast, Kenney was damning about the use and effectiveness of Japan's Air Force: ". . . the way he [Yamamoto] had failed to take advantage of his superiority in numbers and position since the first couple of months of the war was a disgrace to the airman's profession."[15] Apart from the rare exception of mass attacks, Japanese attacks were marked by their use of aircraft in 'penny-packets.' Kenney was probably not aware that the inability of the Japanese Navy Air Force to launch sustained heavy bombing was in large part due to their logistical weaknesses including lack of experienced aviation engineers, ground crews, adequate airfield facilities and airfield equipment.

By the end of May however, US morale was rising. Apart from killing Admiral Yamamoto, the Allies had been significantly reinforced over the month. Twining was now able to rotate his pilots to allow them time for rest and recuperation (R&R). The contrast with the Japanese Air Force's 'fight-till-you-die' policy could not have been starker. Essentially for Emperor Hirohito and the Japanese high command, serving pilots, as with their ground troops, were expendable commodities—used until they were either wounded or died.

Guadalcanal now served as the US rest and recuperation (R&R) base for the *Solomon Islands* Campaign and here resting pilots could also be put to use instructing fresh arrivals. The main problem facing the US Army Air Force at *Guadalcanal* was the lack of airfield construction to enable satisfactory dispersal of the 300-plus aircraft that had arrived on the island in the early summer of 1943. After 'Hap' Arnold complained to Vice-Admiral 'Bull' Halsey, new areas for dispersal were organized. Through the spring and early summer the build-up in resources at *Guadalcanal* allowed a steady increase in bomber action against *Bougainville* in night attacks. Daylight attacks by Japanese fighters coming down the 'Slot' also became a daily feature. Costs to Japan duly increased. In a dogfight on 13 May, the Japanese lost sixteen fighters. Towards the end of May, it seemed that Japanese attacks were losing strength. By comparison Allied attacks on southern *Bougainville* were increasing as Curtiss SB2C Helldivers, newly equipped with fifty-gallon auxiliary tanks, extended their operational range.

Nonetheless, by the beginning of June it was clear from reconnaissance that with 225 aircraft assembled at their airfields and some fifty ships in the harbor, Japanese forces at Rabaul were building resources for a major new effort. Nevertheless fighter exchanges remained heavily in favor of the Allies. On 7 June, a major Japanese effort ended with twenty-three of their planes downed against nine Allied aircraft. Apart from the disparity in aircraft losses, the key difference was that all the Allied pilots were rescued while all of the Japanese were assumed to have died. The 12 June air battle was even more one-sided; the Allies scoring thirty-one kills to six losses and two pilots killed. Still, in the short term, the Japanese well of resources appeared undiminished.

Degraded Performance of the Japanese Navy Air Force (JNAF): By 16 June photographs showed that aircraft at Rabaul had increased to 245; the subsidiary 'ring' airfields were also full of planes. There followed the single largest air battle of the entire *Solomon Islands* Campaign; 120 Japanese aircraft went up against 104 defenders in a dogfight over *Savo Island, Tulagi* and Cape Esperance. The Allies scored a remarkable one-sided victory with 49 Zeros and 32 dive-bombers, 81 planes in aggregate, downed for the loss of just 6 aircraft. While the Japanese were still able to commit large forces to the battle, the victory on 16 June continued the pattern of an increasingly one-sided battle for air supremacy. From April to early June 1943 the ratio of the Allies' kills-to-losses averaged about 3:1; on 12 June the Allies scored a 5:1 victory and ten days later the win ratio jumped yet again to 13:1. What was happening?

A 3:1 win:loss ratio for the Allies was already a substantial advantage that spoke volumes about the advances made by Allied equipment as well as the quality of their pilots in the first half of 1943. By comparison at the start of the war Japanese Naval and Military Air Forces had overwhelmed the Allies throughout the Asia-Pacific Region, often winning air battles by ratios of 10:1 or more. In the first half of 1943 the Commander of Air Forces in the *Solomons* (COMAIRSOL) had already achieved a startling turnaround in performance. From the middle of June 1943 there was another huge leg up in comparative performance of Allied fighter forces. As with Lieutenant-General Kenney's remarkable victory at the *Battle of the Bismarck S*ea, it seems that a number of disparate factors had led to a tipping point moment. The gradual erosion of the *Guadalcanal* Campaign was putting increasing pressure, not so much on the availability of aircraft, but on the availability of trained pilots. It was systematic of the entire structure of the Imperial Japanese General Staff that war was planned as a short-term project with the emphasis on attack. The Japanese Navy, even more than the Imperial Japanese Army, was particularly unprepared for a war of attrition; their psychology, inherited from their great victory at the *Battle of Tsushima*, was to focus energy and resources on the winning of a single transformative engagement rather than planning for a long war.

The Japanese Navy was not only failing to train enough pilots, it was also failing to protect them. It is instructive to consider that very few US pilots died when their planes were shot down. In part it was because, unlike their Japanese counterparts, US fighters had better armored cockpits. Moreover without self-sealing fuel lines, Japanese Zero frequently blew up when hit by tracer bullets, killing the pilot instantly. When US pilots ditched or parachuted into the sea, the US Navy had a well-organized search and recovery capability. The Japanese Navy did not. Advantageously most of the dogfights in the April–June 1943 period took place closer to US held areas. US pilots were also better conditioned, with rotation and rest and recreation (R&R) built into the whole logistic framework of the various forces operating under COMAIRSOL.

New Japanese fighters also had to face a multiplicity of challenges given the diversity in capability of the six types of Allied fighter planes with which they were likely to engage. By contrast US pilots in the *South Pacific* only had to develop tactics to combat the Zero. On 28 March 1944, the US Flight Test Engineering Branch concluded after testing a captured Mitsubishi Zero, "The airplane is highly maneuverable, has a fair rate of climb, and good visibility; however, its speed in level flight is low, it is lightly armed, has no armor protection for the pilot, and the fuel tanks are not self sealing. The cockpit layout is fair, leg-room is insufficient for an average sized man . . ."[16] The Zero had abundant good qualities; it was reliable, had an extraordinarily long range, and was, above all, maneuverable and easy to fly. Even with the swathe of more advanced US fighters now arriving in the *South Pacific*, it was not wise to get into a prolonged dogfight with a Zero. Nonetheless, Allied pilots learned to exploit the Zero's weaknesses. Allied fighters with a superior 'ceiling' capability would look to swoop down on a Zero and then skedaddle before the enemy fighter could make his better maneuverability count. By shooting and then diving, US pilots realized that their Japanese counterparts could not follow because of poorer diving speeds. Moreover by working in teams US pilots learned to thwart the Zero's superior maneuverability in dogfights.

In Tokyo the developing catastrophe in the air was being hidden from senior commanders. Although losses were heavy, Japanese crews were reporting massively inflated results for transport ships sunk and enemy 'kills'. On 14 April 1943 Yamamoto ordered a two-pronged force, codenamed Y-1 and Y-2, consisting of 75 fighters and 23 dive-bombers from the Third Fleet (Y-1) along with the 11th Air Fleet's 54 fighters and 44 medium bombers (Y-2), to make a major attack on *Milne Bay*, which had become an important logistical center for the Allied advance in New Guinea and the *Solomons*.

Japanese pilots claimed to have shot down forty-four Allied aircraft. In fact Allied losses amounted to a single P-40 and its pilot killed; four others were shot up and a P-38 crash-landed. Similarly exaggerated claims were made for ships sunk. Supposedly four transports had been sunk and six others heavily damaged. The reality was that only one ship was heavily damaged out of the three that received hits. Admiral Ugaki noted happily in his diary, "Today's operations of Y-1 and Y-2 a great success. Congratulations! But at the same time our losses gradually increased too. This was natural."[17] On this occasion the loss of eight Japanese aircraft was far from a disaster but the action reports of Japanese crews were far from 'natural.' Ultimately the gross misinformation provided by both Army and Navy aircrews prevented their commanders from taking realistic action to change tactics, attempt to upgrade equipment and training, or take other measures to improve results.

Japan's senior commanders were not the only ones deluded in the performance of their aircrews. The Naval General Staff, after briefing Emperor Hirohito on the superb performance of Operations Y-1 and Y-2, sent Admiral Ugaki a message from His Majesty with the pleasing words then recorded in his diary, ". . . convey my satisfaction to the Commander in Chief, Combined Fleet, and tell him to enlarge the war result more than ever."[18]

By October 1943 it had become clear that the air battle over the *Solomon Islands* was taking its toll on the Japanese Navy Air Force (JNAF). An American intelligence report written in that month noted that Japanese pilots

> made glaring tactical mistakes, unnecessarily exposed themselves to gunfire, got separated and lost mutual support, and at times seemed to be completely bewildered. Both bomber and fighter pilots ceased to display the aggressiveness that marked their earlier combat. Bombers ceased to penetrate to their targets in the face of heavy fire, as they had formerly done; they jettisoned bombs, attacked outlying destroyers, gave up attempts on massed transports in the center of a formation. Fighters broke off their attacks on Allied heavy and medium bombers before getting within effective range, and often showed a marked distaste for close-in contest with Allied fighters.[19]

Some Japanese officers were also becoming aware of deficiencies in the performance of the JNAF. Commander Ryosuke Nomura, who took over the role of air operations officer at Rabaul in 1943, became acutely aware of a decline in pilots performance. He attributed this to America's better aircraft, an inability to sustain a high level of maintenance of their own equipment, and a decline in the experience and quality of available pilots. By the beginning of 1943 the number of experienced pilots, normally defined as having more than 600 hours flying, had fallen by 25 percent from its peak and in February the tipping point was reached, which saw pilots with between 300 to 600 hours outnumbering experienced pilots for the first time.

Within several months the JNAF would be sending pilots into battle with less than 200 hours flying time. These new pilots were not only disadvantaged in combat but also in the seeming basic task of preserving their equipment. In February 1943, operational losses of aircraft began to significantly exceed combat losses; 161 were lost on take-off, flight or landing mishaps while 104 were shot down by enemy action. The high command of the JNAF either seemed unaware of the need for rotational relief or simply did not have the resources to provide it. Combat flying is an exhausting and high stress activity and many experienced Japanese pilots must have perished because their levels of concentration collapsed. In the JNAF, pilots literally flew until they dropped.

The Sorry Story of Mitsubishi A7M 'Sam,' the Zero Replacement: As Commander Nomura had observed, the Americans were beginning to outstrip the Japanese Navy Air Force (JNAF) in terms of new and better aircraft. Meanwhile Japan was suffering from severe difficulties in developing, testing and producing new models in a war in which aircraft became obsolescent within two years. The sorry story of the development of Mitsubishi A7M 'Sam,' the intended successor to the Zero, is indicative of Japan's problems.

As early as 1940 the JNAF had commissioned Mitsubishi to start work on a replacement for an aircraft carrier fighter to replace the Zero. It soon became clear however, that there was no engine capable of meeting the Navy's requirements for a fighter that could fly at 397 mph. The Navy demanded a higher rate of climb while at the same time retaining the maneuverability of the Zero A6M-2. The replacement project was dropped in January 1941. For the remainder of the year Mitsubishi focused on upgrading the Zero ending with the A6M-3 version that designer Dr. Jiro Horikoshi completed in April 1942. The Zero was further upgraded leading to a final iteration of the A6M-8 though few were produced at the end of the war. The most effective, most heavily produced upgrade was the A6M-5, which added heavy machine guns, 0.51-inch caliber guns based on the American Browning. But for all its development, because of a lack of a more powerful engine and the increased weight of guns and munition, only 10 mph was added to the speed of the original Zero.

Although development of the new A7M 'Sam' fighter got going again under Horishiki's direction, engines remained the key stumbling block. The Nakajima NK9 being developed could provide the speed required by the Navy but only if sacrifices were made on the wing load, which was required to be not less than 4.6 ounces per square yard. Horikoshi, Mitsubishi's chief air frame designer, wanted to use the new Mitsubishi MK9 engine, an eighteen cylinder radial that was under development, because it could meet both speed and wing load requirements. Unfortunately for Horikoshi, development of the MK9 lagged behind the NK9. Much to Mitsubishi's annoyance, the Navy ordered him to proceed using the underpowered Nakajima-9 engine. As Horikoshi had feared, the NK9 powered A7M1 'Sam' was not fast enough, flying no faster than the Zero A6M.

With lack of factory capacity, Mitsubishi thus focused on production of the Zero A6M. When the new Mitsubishi MK9 engine was finally finished and delivered in October 1944, development of the 'Sam' was again jump-started. The MK9 'Sam' was able to fly at 390 mph, had a 35,000 foot ceiling, was as maneuverable as the Zero and was equipped with two 20 mm cannon and two 0.50 caliber machine guns. Saburo Sakai, who went to Nagoya to test it, enthused that it could outfly anything that the Americans could put in the air. However, production was delayed by an earthquake in the Nagoya region in 1944 and by Allied bombing in March 1945. Eventually only nine A7M2 'Sam' fighters were produced and none saw combat.

There were occasional production successes. The twin-engine Nakajima J1N 'Irving' long-range escort fighter and reconnaissance plane was converted into a successful night fighter when Commander Yasuna Kozono of 251st *kokutai* in Rabaul had the bright idea of installing 20 mm cannon at a 30 percent angle from the front fuselage. Ignoring the orders of his senior officers, Kozono persevered with the idea and on 21 May 1943, two American B-17s were shot down over Rabaul. Ensign Kudo Shugetoshi, who shot down the first B-17 with an 'Irving,' scored six more kills over the next few months and was presented with a sword by a delighted Vice-Admiral Kusaka. It was a rare success. Production problems afflicted other new aircraft. The

D4Y 'Judy' was too slow and had to become a scout plane when it was found that carrying bombs damaged structural components. The Mitsubishi J2M *Raiden* 'Jack,' a high-altitude fighter, was accepted for production in October 1942 but only fourteen had been built six months later; it took another year to produce 141 units. Only seventeen units of the Kawanashi N1K1-J 'George' fighter were built; it was considered the best combat plane produced by Japan, superior to the F6F Hellcat, but came too late to have any effect on the air war. The Nakajima B6N2 'Jill,' a replacement for the ageing 'Kate' torpedo bomber, failed its carrier test on the *Zuikaku* in early 1943 because the arresting gear for use on carriers was insufficiently strong. The 'Jill' had to be sent back for redesign.

For Japan at least part of their problem in developing and producing new aircraft was that at the start of the war Japanese manufacturers were already operating at full stretch. Whereas the US manufacturers such as Boeing, or the new entrants such as Ford and General Motors, simply started new greenfield sites that they could supply with labor and materials, Mitsubishi and Nakajima had to juggle the manufacture of existing models against the risk of closing production lines to introduce new aircraft. **[See Appendix C: Economics of the Pacific War: The 'New Deal' Mobilized]**

The Development of Rabaul: [Map: 22.2] Reflecting the new strategic parameters after the defeats of *Midway* and *Guadalcanal*, Yamamoto's plan to turn the *Solomon Islands* into unsinkable aircraft carriers, necessitated above all the development of Rabaul as the hub of this enterprise. Whereas during the *Battle of Guadalcanal* the number of aircraft housed at Rabaul was around 100, afterwards the number was rarely less than double that figure and often significantly more with sometimes as many as 350. In addition, satellite airfields such as the four on *Bougainville* added significantly to 'housing' capacity.

Airfields at Lakunai and Vunakanau were expanded while in December 1942 a new airfield was built at Rapopo, fourteen miles southeast of Rabaul. Here revetments were built for ninety-four bombers and ten fighters. To the southwest another airfield was constructed for the Japanese Army Air Force (JAAF) at Keravat. Vunakanau Airfield remained the largest of the airfields with a paved mile long, 135ft wide runway with accompanying taxi strip. 150 revetments had been built on either side, all interconnected with taxiways. In addition, the airfield included a huge storage complex and cantonments for over 2,000 ground staff. In spite of these endeavors, poor engineering resulting in bad drainage meant that Vunakanau was only used for emergencies. Finally a fighter field was constructed for seventy fighters further south at Tobera; uniquely it used interlocking steel plates rather than concrete for the runway. Subsidiary bases were also developed at Kavieng on the northern tip of *New Ireland*, Gasmata, and at Buin on the southern tip of *Bougainville* and *Buka Island* off its northern coast.

In addition to the new runways, huge new logistical centers were built. Cantonments to accommodate 10,000 engineering and maintenance staff were constructed. In addition warehouse and buildings had to be built for spare parts, munitions, oil, gasoline fuel, hospitals, food supply and general stores. Sophisticated repair shops were needed for the growth and variety of the airfleet. Japan's facilities were far from adequate in this respect. Shortage of repair capacity meant that aircraft were utilized far beyond their recommended operating cycle. In addition to pilot degradation, the deterioration of the theoretical performance of Japan's Zero because of poor maintenance may be one explanation for the sharp decline in their kill/loss ratio during the air battles of the *South Pacific* after June 1943.

At certain points, engines would need to be disassembled and rebuilt or a new engine inserted. Other parts would need to be reconditioned or replaced. The fact that so many aircraft were found at Rabaul's airfields after the war with little battle damage suggests that the Japanese capacity to service, recondition or rebuild aircraft was seriously deficient. During the course of the battles of the *South Pacific* it is estimated that Rabaul went through a cycle of 150 aircraft ten times, not including the sacrifice of several hundred fleet aircraft and pilots in 1943.

Besides the massive build-up of equipment and airfield capacity at Rabaul, numbers of personnel increased from the original 5,000 troops of the Imperial Japanese Army who occupied the town in early 1941, to a garrison of 76,000 troops plus 21,000 Navy personnel. By November 1943, Rabaul had 23 large capacity anti-aircraft guns (of which 15 were 12 cm guns and eight were 12.7 cm guns); in addition there were 95 guns of 7 cm and 8 cm, as well as 250 smaller caliber rapid-fire guns to intercept lower flying aircraft.

Within eighteen months of its capture Rabaul had grown from a tiny outpost of the Australian Empire to a vast Japanese garrison whose name was on the lips of everyone in Japan. In 1942 a popular song was written called *Rabaul My Love*; it became a big hit with its romanticization of the exotic southern seas.

> So long, Rabaul, 'til we return
> Bidding farewell with teary eyes
> Gazing at the island where my love resides
> Forevermore the Southern Cross.[20]

In reality Rabaul was not so romantic. Not even one of the largest concentrations of Korean prostitutes, so-called 'comfort women,' who were shipped out to Rabaul, could turn it into a place of desire.

Meeting at Casablanca: Roosevelt and Churchill met at the Anfer Hotel in Casablanca, Morocco, on 14 January 1943. The leader of the Free French, Charles de Gaulle, was in attendance at the Casablanca Conference (SYMBOL) along with the President's Joint Chiefs of Staff and Churchill's military team including Army Chief of Staff, Lord Alanbrooke; the Combined Chiefs of Staff had delicate negotiations to pursue regarding strategic priorities for the year ahead. Somewhat to the consternation of the Anglo-Saxon partners, Stalin cried off, citing his need to deal with Germany's armies now encircled and stranded in Stalingrad. His absence increased his importance. It fed

Roosevelt's continued fear that Stalin might do a separate peace deal with Hitler, thus liberating Germany's Eastern Front armies to concentrate on their Western Front. Both America and Britain needed to keep the Soviet Union in the war.

At a meeting of the Combined Chiefs of Staff on 17 January, Admiral King shook his British counterparts by suggesting that if they did not agree to 30 percent of all Allied war *matériel* going to the *Pacific* fronts (up from 20 percent), it "would necessitate the United States regretfully withdrawing from the commitments in the European theatre."[21] It was a bluff: Roosevelt, Leahy and Marshall, even King, recognized that a commitment to Europe was essential in order to keep Stalin in the war. The Soviets had changed sides once. Might they do so again? Nevertheless, it was a bluff that worked. King refused to give up on the *Marianas* as an objective for 1943, pointedly telling Britain's head of Army Staff, General Alanbrooke, that the Americans alone would decide on the route and objectives of their *Central Pacific* Campaign.

Lord Alanbrooke, whose diaries show him to have been somewhat disinterested in Britain's role in Asia, and who would have preferred a static, defensive war in the *Pacific* until Hitler was defeated, complained that for King, Europe was "just a nuisance that kept him from waging his Pacific War undisturbed."[22] What Alanbrooke could never understand was that because of *Pearl Harbor*, the defeat of Japan had an importance to the US public that was not yet equaled in Britain. To placate the Americans regarding Britain's commitment to the *Pacific War*, Churchill even offered to devote all its resources to the region once Hitler was defeated; it was an offer that Roosevelt declined. He was much keener to get a similar commitment from Stalin. Unlike Britain, Roosevelt believed that Stalin might have an 'out'—a possible side deal with Hitler and Japan.

A compromise was patched up to put before Roosevelt and Churchill, whereby it was stated: "operations in the *Pacific* shall continue with the object of maintaining pressure on Japan."[23] Alanbrooke was gratified with a proviso inserted saying that operations in the *Pacific* would not excessively drain the European effort. However, the Joint Chiefs would define the word 'excessive.' Roosevelt, perhaps unaware of the extent of the bitterness of the backstairs wrangling, declared, "There never has been, in all the inter-allied conferences I have known, anything like the prolonged professional examination of the whole scene of the world war in its military, its armaments production and its economic aspects."[24]

America's quest for revenge on Japan was proven just over three weeks later. On 24 January 1943, President Roosevelt, borrowing a phrase from Unionist General Ulysses Grant at the siege of Fort Henry in the *American Civil War*, demanded 'unconditional surrender' from Japan: "In our uncompromising policy we mean no harm to the common people of the Axis nations. But we do mean to impose punishment and retribution upon their guilty, barbaric leaders."[25] It was a statement of intent that in hindsight appears commonplace but at the time caused some surprise. Wars can be won without conquest of the enemy; Roosevelt's demand for unconditional surrender was unusual in boxing him into a strategy. Churchill would later admit to military correspondent, Drew Middleton, "I was startled by the [public] announcement [of unconditional surrender]. I tried to hide my surprise. But I was his [Roosevelt's] ardent lieutenant."[26] It was an ultimatum that was not universally welcomed by those diplomats and 'intelligence' operatives who had hoped to remove Hitler by *coup d'état*.

The demand for 'unconditional surrender' firmed up the commitment to come to Stalin's aid by launching an invasion of the European mainland to relieve pressure on his own forces. Roosevelt's demand for Japan's surrender clearly necessitated a plan for its ultimate invasion and conquest; even if Japan capitulated just prior to an invasion, the Joint Chiefs of Staff still had to come up with a real strategy for rolling back Japan's empire to its home shores. Japan would be forced to surrender by naval blockade, air bombardment and invasion if necessary. The threat to invade, even if it never happened, had to be credible. Simply defeating Japan in battle at sea was not going to be enough. Commanders such as Nimitz at first believed that Japan would surrender before any invasion of its home islands, but as time went on Allied commanders, taking note of the fanatic 'fight to the death' attitude of its troops, increasingly came to the conclusion that Japan would never yield. The Combined Chiefs went away from Casablanca to work on their plans for the subjugation of Japan.

MacArthur and the Bypass of Rabaul: At a three-day meeting of the Combined Chiefs in Washington starting on 12 May 1943 (the third Washington Conference, codenamed TRIDENT), a provisional plan for an advance on Japan was agreed for further study and development. The result of the deliberations was that the US Joint Chiefs of Staff had come to the conclusion that a *Central Pacific* strategy was preferable. Although the Chairman of the Joint Chiefs, Admiral Leahy, tended to support MacArthur, scarred by the experience of *Guadalcanal*, he was more than alive to the difficulties of advancing through jungle terrain, and gave his support to King's *Central Pacific* thrust. Even General Marshall, who nearly always backed Army interests and thus favored MacArthur, nevertheless recognized the appalling conditions and terrain through which his army would have to fight.

From off-stage, MacArthur proclaimed: "From the broad strategic viewpoint I am convinced that the best course of offensive action in the Pacific is a movement from Australia through New Guinea to Mindanao."[27] MacArthur's self-serving rhetoric must have been obvious to all. In spite of his pro-MacArthur bias, Marshall supported the *Central Pacific* strategy. Marshall, like General 'Hap' Arnold, wanted to get to the *Marianas* (*Saipan, Guam* and *Tinian*) from where the bombing of Japan could begin; he therefore too favored the *Central Pacific* route.

Not surprisingly, Admiral King also favored the *Central Pacific* route although the emphasis of his reasoning differed from that of Marshall. King believed that the more urgent task was the strangulation of Japanese commerce; the war could be shortened by choking off imports to Japan of raw materials. This was a task that could be speeded up if, by the taking of the *Marianas*, resupply of their military and naval forces in the *South Pacific* could be interdicted allowing MacArthur to apply pressure on the

Japanese-occupied oil-rich East Indies. The *Central Pacific* thrust was also preferred by Nimitz. He argued that, whereas the islands of the *Solomons* and eastern New Guinea had garrisons organized for mutual defense, the islands of the *Central Pacific* were too widely spaced to help each other. An added advantage was that Nimitz's *Central Pacific* thrust was more likely to draw out the Japanese Navy for a final battle at which they could be annihilated.

However, with the possibility that the US would need a land base from which to invade Japan, an army advance toward Japan was required. Significant land bases would be required on one or more of *Luzon* (the Philippines), *Formosa* or Southern China. The Joint Chiefs of Staff therefore decided on a twin-pronged approach; MacArthur would make a drive up from the south through New Guinea in the *Southwest Pacific*, while Halsey would lead a drive northward through the *Solomon Islands* in the *South Pacific*. Together they would isolate and destroy Rabaul. MacArthur would then advance along New Guinea's east coast before making the leap to the Philippines. Meanwhile Nimitz would be thrusting through the *Central Pacific*. Both campaigns would be mutually supporting. To MacArthur, the Joint Chiefs of Staff made it clear that the jump to *Mindanao* in the southern Philippines was dependent on the success of his advance up the coast of New Guinea.

Thus at the TRIDENT meeting held in Washington in May 1943, Admiral King's planned attack on the *Marshall* and *Gilbert Islands* was approved in spite of MacArthur's furious protestations from his lair in Australia. His protestations were somewhat mitigated by the signing off of Operation CARTWHEEL, which approved the two-pronged advance toward Rabaul. Earlier in the year, at the Joint Chiefs of Staff meeting on 12 February, similar plans had been developed for this envelopment by both Admiral King and MacArthur, whose plan was called ELKTON or ELKTON III in its final iteration.

A further bone was tossed in MacArthur's direction with the compromise that 1st Marine Division would remain in MacArthur's southwest area. It was slated to lead the expected assault on Rabaul. 2nd Marine Division would transfer to Nimitz's sphere and would lead the fiercely contested assault on *Tarawa Atoll* in the *Gilbert Islands* in November 1943, a stepping-stone to the *Marianas Islands* of *Saipan* and *Guam*.

However, by 21 July Marshall had come to the conclusion that there should be an adjustment to Operation CARTWHEEL. Staff calculations had shown him that Rabaul could simply be cut off and isolated. There was no need to undertake the assault on the Japanese Empire's most heavily fortified garrison. A furious MacArthur argued that the capture of Rabaul was essential as a naval base to support the planned re-invasion of the Philippines. Admiral King and General 'Hap' Arnold sided with Marshall. The arguments were fiercely fought with final approval for neutralization rather than subjugation of Rabaul confirmed by Roosevelt and Churchill at the Quebec Conference (codenamed QUADRANT) in August 1943. When the strategy of 'wither on the vine' proved to be highly effective, MacArthur would later claim it as his own innovation. This was far from the truth. It was General Marshall who was persuaded that the ability of the Allies to disrupt the Japanese sea-borne supply lines through aerial power meant that not all the enemies' island garrisons needed to be taken.

In the aftermath of *World War II*, Vice-Admiral Theodore 'Ping' Wilkinson was credited with the concept of establishing airbases on empty islands in the *Pacific*, thus leap frogging Japan's strongly held garrisons; he described it as a "hit them where they ain't"[28] strategy. Before he was hanged General Tojo told MacArthur that the US strategy of attacking the 'empty spaces' was one of the key reasons why Japan lost the war. Just as composer Claude Debussy famously remarked, "Music is the space between the notes,"[29] the rhythm of the *Central Pacific* campaign was dictated by the spaces between the garrisoned Japanese Islands.

Operation CARTWHEEL: [Map: 22.3] The northward thrust of CARTWHEEL from the southeast called for the elimination of Japanese power in the central and northern *Solomon Islands*. Operations would be conducted by Admiral Halsey, Commander of the South Pacific Fleet. Halsey's ultimate objective would be the recapture of the major island of *Bougainville*, which lay 250 miles to the southeast of the Japanese stronghold at Rabaul. The attack would be coordinated by Halsey with Marine and US Army resources based on *Guadalcanal* and the supporting supply bases established on the *Ellice Islands*.

CARTWHEEL's thrust from the southwest, with its main supply and operation bases in northern Australia, would continue the advance northwards from Buna toward Lae and Salamaua and would prepare for the invasion of *New Britain*, the large island off the New Guinea coast where Rabaul was located on its eastern tip. Other islands in the region north of Rabaul would also be recaptured including *New Ireland* and the *Admiralty Islands*, in particular *Manus* and *Los Negros*. This western prong of the thrust toward Rabaul would be led by MacArthur and his South West Pacific Area forces.

The opening shots of CARTWHEEL began with the invasion of the *Woodlark* and *Kiriwana* chain of islands off the southeast coast of New Guinea and due south of *New Britain*. The invasions were unopposed and work began immediately on the construction of an airfield by the 60th US Naval Construction Battalion. With the completion of a 5,200-foot coral surfaced runway, the US Army Air Force (USAAF) 67th Fighter Squadron relocated to Woodlark Airfield (formally called Guasopa Airfield). From here the USAAF was able to provide fighter cover for the bombing assault on Rabaul. At *Guasopa Bay*, a PT boat service and repair centre was established in addition to a forward supply base. Similarly an airfield was constructed on *Kiriwana* for the Royal Australian Air Force (RAAF) 79th Squadron with the addition of a supply base and a seaplane base at Losuia.

Landings at Segi Point and Rendova Island: The Battle of New Georgia: [Maps: 22.4A, 22.4B] Operation TOENAIL was the codename given to the American plan to invade the *Central Solomons* island of *New Georgia*. Its strategic position made it the essential next step in the isolation of Rabaul that was the objective of the broad thrust of

Operation CARTWHEEL. As Rear-Admiral Eliot Morison noted in his *Breaking the Bismarck's Barrier: Volume 6: July 1942–1944* [1950] the importance of the town of Munda on *New Georgia*: "As long as Japan held Munda and had planes, she could stop the Allies at the Russells. If, on the other hand, the Allies could base planes at Munda, they could deny everything below Bougainville to the enemy and would have another leg-up to Rabaul."[30] For the Japanese, Munda Airfield had proved an invaluable facility enabling them to stage planes from Rabaul to *Guadalcanal*; from Rabaul airfields it was 166 miles to *Buka* at the northern tip of *Bougainville*, a further 100 miles to southern fields of *Bougainville* and then 120 miles to Munda. The advantage could work both ways. Munda Airfield on *New Georgia* was the pivot from which the US could win the *Solomons Campaign*.

Halsey's eastern wing of CARTWHEEL had begun its thrust north ten days earlier with landings by the 4th Marine Raider Battalion at *Segi Point* on the southern tip of *New Georgia*, in the *Central Solomons*. Segi Point is a "low, spiky land protruding into Pango Bay and only a stone's throw from Vangunu Island."[31] It had the advantage of being unoccupied by Japanese troops. Indeed the point was manned by an exceptional Australian District Officer, Donald Kennedy, who had taken it upon himself to establish a defense zone around the village of Segi with his home-trained native force armed with scavenged weapons, often from Japanese troops who had been ambushed and killed. Ensign John McNeill described Kennedy as "an excellent organizer and disciplinarian, a mechanical genius, a handsome ladies' man and a bloodthirsty killer in a fight."[32] Until the US Army's arrival, Kennedy had made himself more than useful as a watcher looking out for Japanese bombing attacks down the 'Slot' as well as a source of intelligence on Japanese movements. He also organized the recovery of downed pilots, crewmen and shipwrecked sailors.

Guided by Kennedy, LCTs (Landing Craft, Tank) began to arrive with construction equipment for the building of an airfield. The Segi Point landing was unopposed and in the pattern of development in the advance on Japan, for which *Guadalcanal* had become the model, the Marines began construction of an airbase. The amphibious landing at Segi Point was so smoothly accomplished that it became the 'textbook' model for future operations. Rear-Admiral G. K. Fort, Commander Landing Craft Flotillas, reported to Rear-Admiral Turner: "It appears for the first time in modern warfare that supplies have arrived with or immediately behind the assault troops . . . bulldozers were clearing a strip forty minutes after the first echelon LST [Landing Ship, Tank] had beached."[33]

At the same time the Marines landed on the south coast of *Rendova Island* that sits to the southwest of Munda Point where the Japanese had established their main naval and airbase during the *Battle of Guadalcanal*. Halsey's plan was to cut a road north through *Rendova* and to station artillery on its northern coast. From there US artillery, from across the sea channel, could pound the Japanese garrison at Munda. For the Japanese it was a nasty surprise and left them without a plan or a capability to counter-attack except by air.

The landing at *Rendova Island* at 6.35 a.m. on 30 June was accomplished without the protection that had been afforded by Kennedy's natives at Segi Point. Apart from regular Japanese bombing missions that forced the Seabees to organize detailed camouflaging of their equipment, snipers harassed the engineers. The swampy conditions for bringing stores ashore and constructing roads and warehousing were not helped by torrential rain. The Seabees leader, Commander Roy Whittaker, described the primordial conditions in which his men worked: "They ceased to look like men; they looked like slimy frogs working in some prehistoric ooze. As they sank to their knees they discarded their clothes. They slung water out of their eyes, cussed their mud-slickened hands, and somehow kept the stuff rolling ashore."[34] By nighttime six ships had unloaded, creating pandemonium on the beaches. Eventually the Seabees dropped in the mud and slept.

The following day much of their work was undone by a lunchtime raid that exploded the temporary fuel-depot, ignited stashes of dynamite and blew their largest bulldozer to smithereens. Twenty-one soldiers were killed and all the Seabees' personal belongings were destroyed along with their canteen's galley equipment and most of their supplies of food. The Seabees had to start their work from scratch.

Having cut a rough track through the dense rainforests, the Seabees were more than thrilled to hear the roar of the 155 mm MI Howitzers that the Marines had lugged across the island. As Commander Whitaker noted, "It hurts American construction men down deep to have to lie in mud and be strafed by Japs; now those 155s were giving it back to the Japanese with interest. The firing was a tonic to us. The men went back to unloading furiously."[35] The continuous barrage from *Rendova* would become a dispiriting backdrop for the Japanese defenders at Munda; a diary recorded, "The artillery shelling's accuracy has become a real thing. We can never tell when we are to die."[36] The opening of an artillery barrage on Munda was not the end of the hardship for the Seabees. Two days after landing, another Japanese bombing and strafing attack left thirty dead, wounded 200 and again exploded fuel dumps. On 4 July a further attack brought more damage but anti-aircraft guns downed twelve Japanese planes while US fighters accounted for four more. In spite of the Japanese attacks by 5 July almost all the forces for the occupation of *New Georgia* had been assembled on *Rendova Island*.

However, the main initial battle for Munda was not on the ground but in the air. For the *New Georgia* Campaign, Halsey had assembled the largest air force yet assembled for an operation in the *Solomon Islands*. It was a force that was needed as the Japan Naval Air Force (JNAF) in Rabaul threw every bomber that they had available at the US amphibious invasion. At 11 a.m. on 30 June, sixteen Zeros were shot down out of thirty. In the afternoon a flight of fifty Japanese bombers attacked the landing force and scored a hit on Rear-Admiral Turner's flagship, USS *McCawley*, but at the cost of most of their aircraft. *McCawley*'s anti-aircraft guns brought down four Japanese aircraft, while Corsairs and Wildcats picked off the rest. In a dusk attack the Allies scored eighteen more 'kills' against Japanese bombers. In June alone the Japanese lost 254 aircraft compared to the Allies who had lost just 36 fighters and 13 pilots; a 7:1 ratio overall for the whole month.

Although the Allies were scoring a high success ratio and were able to sustain round the clock 32-fighter defense patrols (which needed a total of ninety-six operational aircraft), after ten days over *New Georgia* pilots were increasingly exhausted. Colonel Merrill Twining demanded more P-38 Lightnings, the plane that had now established itself as the fighter of choice in the *South Pacific*. However, back in Washington General 'Hap' Arnold, heavily committed to upcoming Allied operations to support General Patton and General Montgomery's invasion of *Sicily*, turned down the request. As Arnold later explained in answer to a further request for reinforcements, every newly trained unit "must be thrown against the German until he is beaten."[37] Meanwhile at Segi Point Airfield, it took the Seabees just ten days to build a 3,300-foot runway for limited operations, maintenance and refueling. While it never became a major airfield, Segi Point helped to relieve much of the stress of the air operations—particularly as a place of refuge for damaged aircraft in the months ahead.

The Battle of Kula Gulf: With the failure of the June air battles to hold back the Allied invasion, Admiral Koga, Yamamoto's replacement, turned to the Navy to provide new supplies to the defenders at Munda Point. The 'Tokyo Express,' the name given to the almost nightly supply missions to the Japanese Army on *Guadalcanal* in 1942, was resuscitated in foreshortened form for the supply of *New Georgia*. On the night of 5/6 July, a convoy of ten destroyers raced down toward *New Georgia*, led by Rear-Admiral Teruo Akiyama on his flagship, *Niizuki*. They were intercepted by Rear-Admiral Walden Ainsworth with three cruisers and four destroyers in the *Kula Gulf*, located between the northern shores of *New Georgia* and the perfectly circular volcanic island of *Kolombangara*.

Niizuki took the full blast of Ainsworth's attack and was quickly sunk, killing 300 Japanese sailors and Admiral Akiyama in the process. In a confused nighttime *mêlée*, typical of many of the naval battles in the *Solomon Island* campaigns, the light cruiser, USS *Helena*, was struck and damaged by several Long Lance torpedoes. With its bow blown off, virtually up to the 2-Turret, the *Helena* was clearly mortally wounded. Captain Charles Cecil immediately called for his crew to abandon ship. She sank in barely six minutes: 190 crewmen died out of the full complement of 1,177. *Nagatsuki*, badly knocked about by a 6-inch shell, ran aground and had to be abandoned; US bombers finished off the Japanese destroyer on the morning of 6 July. Four days later the US Marines made a nighttime amphibious landing on the northern coast of *New Georgia* from where they advanced toward Munda Point.

On 15 July, in their first mass sortie for a month, Japan threw 27 'Betty' bombers and over 40 Zeros at Allied positions on *New Georgia*. Faced by 44 Allied fighters, the Japanese lost 15 'Bettys' and 30 Zeros. With just three Allied fighters shot down, the win ratio was a remarkable 15:1. In spite of the heavy losses, photos taken of Rabaul showed that stocks of planes were still high. Nevertheless, it was the last major Japanese attack on Allied forces on *Rendover* and *New Georgia*. Within days the Joint Chiefs of Staff took the decision to call off the invasion of Rabaul and isolate the garrison town instead.

The Rescue of Captain J. F. Kennedy: **[Map: 22.5]** In Rabaul the commander of the Southeast Area Fleet, Vice-Admiral Jinichi Kusaka (cousin of Admiral Ryunosuke Kusaka, Chief of Staff to Admiral Nagumo at *Pearl Harbor*) continued to send supply and reinforcements to *New Georgia*; often this involved runs to *Kolombangara* from where barges would make nighttime transits across the straits to Munda Point. On the night of 2 August the Japanese destroyer, *Amagiri*, having dropped off 900 fresh troops at Vila, on the south coast of *Kolombangara*, was passing through the *Blackett Strait* when it accidently rammed and cut in half an American torpedo boat, PT-*109*; it was captained by John F. Kennedy. His PT boat, one of fifteen which had been deployed with others to intercept Japanese destroyers and barges, exploded, killing two crew members and badly wounding two others. Kennedy and his crew made the 3.5 mile swim to *Plum Pudding Island*, one of a myriad of small islands to the southwest of *Kolombangara*, which was unoccupied by Japanese forces. Kennedy, a former swim team member at Harvard University, swam with the lifebelt strap of his injured machinist mate, Patrick McMahon, gritted between his teeth. They were lucky not to be attacked by either sharks or crocodiles.

Plum Pudding Island was without water and Kennedy swam the four miles to the nearby islands of *Naru* and *Olasana* to scout a better refuge. He returned and led his survivors to *Olasana* where there was fresh water. After surviving for six days on coconuts, they were found by two *Solomon Island* natives, Gasa and Kumana. They had been sent by Sub-Lieutenant Arthur Evans, who, typical of the network of lookouts stationed around the *Solomon Islands* by US forces, was watching for Japanese air and naval activity from his hideout on the slopes of Mount Veve, the volcano at the center of *Kolombangara*, when he had fortuitously spotted the explosion of Kennedy's PT boat.

At Gasa's suggestion, Kennedy inscribed a message carved into a coconut shell for the natives to take back; at great personal risk Gasa and Kumana rowed their dugout canoe 35 miles to the nearest US base at *Rendova Island*. A somewhat astonished PT commander, presuming Kennedy and his crew to be dead, sent a boat to rescue the future president and his ten surviving crewmembers. It was a youthful adventure that made a war hero of John Kennedy and helped propel his meteoric post-war political career, making him at 43 years of age the second youngest President of the United States of America (President Theodore Roosevelt was a year younger when he assumed office). The famous 'coconut shell message' was proudly displayed by President Kennedy in the Oval Office of the White House and now resides at the former President's library in Boston.

Griswold's Hard Slog to Take Munda Airfield: **[Map: 22.6]** Meanwhile on the ground in *New Georgia*, on 2 July US forces led by the US 43rd Division, with an overwhelming advantage of 15,000 troops compared to 9,000 Japanese, had landed at Zannana with a view to attacking westwards towards Munda Point. It was a battle that took far longer than the Allies had envisaged. Stubborn Japanese resistance and their ability to infiltrate US lines and cut supplies meant an advance at a snail's pace, despite their control of the air and sea. The conditions bordered on the unbearable. Sergeant Antony Coulis described one advance thus:

> We alternatively crawled up and down greasy ridges. We forded numerous jungle streams and swam three of them. The repeated torture of plunging into icy streams; the chopping away of endless underbrush and foliage; the continuous drizzle of rain; the days without hot food or drink; the mosquitoes tormenting us at night. It was sheer physical torture . . .[38]

At Munda the Japanese commander, Major-General Nabor Sasaki, had constructed a barrage of defensive entrenchments around the airport and halted the US advance. As Halsey later recalled, "Rugged as jungle fighting is by now we should have been within reach of our objective, the airfield. Something was wrong."[39] The now deceased Yamamoto's plan to turn the *Solomons* into a killing machine in order to persuade the United States to parley for a negotiated peace, seemed to be working. With the battle turning into a stalemate, on 15 July Vice-Admiral 'Bull' Halsey sent the famously tough Major-General Oscar Griswold, XV Army Corps Commander, to *New Georgia*. Major-General John Hester, who had turned down help from the Marines, was removed from command of the 43rd Division and replaced by *Guadalcanal* veteran Major-General John Hodge.

An LCT (Landing Craft, Tank) captain, Jack Johnson described the operation as a "screw-up. General Hester was army. I had him aboard one time. He was a little fart. He wore these high lace-up boots and carried a riding crop."[40] However, much of the blame was placed on Rear-Admiral Turner, commander of the amphibious forces who had insisted that Hester retain divisional command as well as overall command of the landing operations. Neither had it helped that the 43rd National Guard Division was untested in battle. Griswold found them in a state of near psychological collapse and realized that they would need to be reinforced by the 37th Division. In the end a further 35,000 Allied troops had to be deployed to break down Japanese resistance. Even with tanks and flame-throwers, ground had to be bought one entrenchment at a time. After ten days of desperate fighting, often hand to hand, American patrols reached the edge of the airfield. Eventually on 3 August General Sasaki gave the order to retreat. Griswold sent a message to Halsey declaring: "Our ground forces today wrested Munda from the Japs and present it to you as sole owner"; Halsey replied, "keep 'em dying."[41] The Japanese order to retreat was too late for some as advance units of the US 43rd and 37th Divisions converged on Munda, while the 148th Regiment cut the line of retreat overland to Bairoko. US troops finally overcame the fierce defense of Munda Point Airbase on 5 August.

Griswold wrote, "The month's fighting had not been the Americans' finest hour in the Solomon Islands Campaign" and Halsey reflected, "the smoke of charred reputations still makes me cough."[42] Operation CARTWHEEL had fallen a month behind schedule.

With *New Georgia* close to being lost, troops were transferred to the port of Vila on the southern coast of *Kolumbangara*. The following day, 6 August, the US Navy scored a small but conclusive victory when six US destroyers sank three Japanese destroyers, *Hagikaze, Arashi* and *Kawakaze* for no losses at the *Naval Battle of Vella Gulf*.

With the principal central *Solomon Islands'* strategic asset of Munda Point Airfield lost, the Japanese abandoned Munda but fighting continued as the Japanese held Bairoko Port some eight miles to the north. US losses at 1,136 soldiers killed were high compared to the 1,500 or so Japanese who died and reflected the strength of the entrenchment systems around Munda Point and the fierceness of the Japanese defense. US air supremacy over *New Georgia* had given little advantage. The denseness of the vegetation made spotting and air attack on enemy positions virtually impossible. At Munda, Rear-Admiral Turner learned that however many transport boats were planned for in an invasion plan, more would always be required. More worrying was the fact that it had taken more than 30,000 troops to overcome just 5,000 Japanese troops at Munda. As a COMINCH (Commander in Chief US Navy) planning memorandum noted, "If we are going to require such overwhelming superiority at every point where we attack the Japanese, it is time for radical change in the estimate of the forces that will be required to defeat the Japanese now in the Southwest and Central Pacific."[43] The alternative would be a radical rethink of strategy.

For the Allies, the capture of Munda Point Airfield was a landmark victory because rapid restoration of the 4,000-foot runway, expanded to 6,000 feet by October, in addition to several taxiways, gave them a base from which all of the *Solomon Islands* could be reached by US fighters and bombers. The invaluable 73rd Seabees aided by the 131st Engineer Regiment managed a nine-day turnaround to make Munda Point Airfield operable. Japan's airbases at *Ballalai Island* and *Kahili Airfield* on southern *Bougainville*, the last remaining major island of the *Solomon* chain were now just 120 miles away—a short hop. By mid-October Munda Point had become the busiest US airfield in the *Solomon Islands* with aircraft movements as high as 564 per day. In November 1943 Vice-Admiral 'Bull' Halsey declared the airfield the finest in the *South Pacific* and the Seabees were awarded with a citation. Commander Doane received special mention: "by virtue of his planning, leadership, industry, and working 'round the clock' to make serviceable the Munda Airfield on August 14th, 1943, a good four days ahead of the original schedule."[44] The ability of the US forces to rapidly construct airfields was a testament not only to the Seabees' morale and organization but also to their better equipment. Neither was the importance of airfield construction ignored by Admiral Nimitz who recorded in a Commander in Chief Pacific (CINCPAC) report, "one of the outstanding features of the war in both the North and South Pacific areas has been the ability of US forces to build and use airfields, on a terrain and with a speed which would have been considered fantastically impossible in our pre-war days."[45]

The *New Georgia* Campaign was an essential component in the strangulation of Rabaul. Nonetheless, *Pacific War* combatant and naval historian Eliot Morison concluded,

> The Central Solomons ranks with Guadalcanal and Buna-
> Gona for intensity of human tribulation. We had Munda
> and we needed it for the next move, toward Rabaul; but
> we certainly took it the hard way. The strategy and tactics
> of the New Georgia campaign were among the least
> successful of any allied campaign in the Pacific.[46]

It is a criticism that underplays the skill of the Japanese defense of *New Georgia*. Halsey's next move proved more successful. *Kolumbangara Island* was bypassed as Nimitz urged him to jump to the almost deserted island of *Vella Lavella*; Halsey noted that it was "thirty-five miles nearer the *Shortlands* and *Kahili*. According to coast-watchers, its garrison numbered not more than 250, and its shoreline would offer at least one airstrip."[47] Major-General Minoru Sasaki, who had fled with his troops to *Kolumbangara* was effectively isolated and his forces rendered useless.

Still Japanese commanders clung by their fingertips to their last remaining islands in the *Central Solomons*. As troops were being withdrawn from *Kolumbangara Island* on the nights of 6, 7 and 8 October, dogfights brought the Allied air forces fifty-six more 'kills.' A fierce battle for control of the airspace above the *Vella Lavella Island* to the northwest of *Kolumbangara* raged until 15 October. In spite of the extraordinarily heavy aircraft casualties suffered by Japan in the central and northern *Solomon Islands*, on 11 October there were still 294 aircraft at Rabaul and a further 71 stationed on *Bougainville*. Although COMAIRSOL (Commander of Air Forces in the *Solomons*) was now taking its toll on the southern airfields of *Bougainville*, it was clear that Japanese air defense, now being fought over shorter lines than previously, was far from being defeated.

23 Battle of Attu and the Battle of the Komandorski Islands

[1 June 1943–16 August 1943

[Maps: 23.1, 23.2, 23.3, 23.4]

Within the context of the *Pacific War*, the episodes that involved *Attu* and *Kiska* were as outlying as their geographic location. This does not mean that the *Battle of Attu* and the *Battle of Komandorski* are without interest. Indeed their oddity is interesting in itself, while the remarkable suffering of combatants on both sides is something that should not be forgotten. The *Battle of Attu* in May 1943 also sheds light on the quality of Japanese leadership and their military and technical accomplishment as well as the fanaticism that characterized the Japanese armed forces in the *Pacific War*. The flip side to these observations is the appalling complacency and lack of professionalism of American commanders at the *Battle of Attu*. It was the bravery and endurance of the American GI that saw them through.

The Geographic Importance of the Aleutians: Thus far *Hirohito's War* may have helped exacerbate a point of misunderstanding about the *Pacific War*. Much emphasis has been placed on the logistical 'Everest' faced by the United States in defeating and conquering a country that was over 5,000 miles distant across the vast expanses of the *Pacific*. Without retracting the logic of these arguments, it should be pointed out that there were places where America and Japan were much closer. The *Aleutians* chain of seventy islands stretching out into the *North Pacific* from Alaska pointed menacingly toward Japan. The threat went both ways. The distance between *Severo-Kurilsk*, the northernmost of Japan's *Kurile Islands*, which extend north eastwards beyond *Hokkaido*, and *Attu*, the westernmost of the *Aleutian Islands* that curl out from Alaska like a skeletal dog's tail, is just 735 miles. They are separated by Russia's Kamchatka Peninsula.

Vitus Bering, the Danish sailor and explorer, who served as an officer in the Russian Navy, and gave his name to the straits dividing Russia from Alaska, discovered *Kiska* in the mid-eighteenth century. *Attu* became a fur-trading outpost of the Alaska Commercial Company, founded by a grant of license given by Catherine the Great. Such trading organizations, including that of the ubiquitous Stroganov family, which brought trade and Russian colonists to the further reaches of Siberia, enabled Russian Imperial expansion in Siberia and Alaska—the latter until its sale to the United States for US$7.2m in a deal arranged by Secretary of State, William Seward, in 1867.

Although in practice the *North Pacific* proved to be a quiet backwater of *World War II*, there had long been fears that it could become a fulcrum of action between the combatants.

The noted military strategist, General Billy Mitchell, went so far as to declare to a US Congressional committee in 1935, "I believe that in the future, whoever holds Alaska will hold the world. I think it is the most important strategic place in the world."[1] It was a far cry from the derogatory name of 'Seward's Icebox' that had previously been given to Alaska. Indeed Japan had taken the strategic value of the *Aleutians* so seriously that in the negotiations resulting in the *Washington Naval Treaty* [1922], the United States had yielded to Japan's insistence that no American naval bases should be developed there. It was an agreement quickly abandoned after *Pearl Harbor*. By the spring of 1942 some 45,000 American troops had been deployed in Alaska with some 13,000 placed on the major *Aleutian Islands* of *Unalaska* and *Umnak*.

It should perhaps be noted that had the Soviet Union not signed a neutrality pact with Japan in 1941, it is very possible that the *Aleutians* and the Kamchatka Peninsula, rather than the *Solomon Islands* and New Guinea in the *South Pacific*, would have become the major battlegrounds of the *Pacific War*. Billy Mitchell's analysis of the strategic importance of the *Aleutians* was not incorrect.

America feared that Japan would establish an airbase from which they could interdict shipping from Seattle to the eastern Soviet Union—remembering that, despite the neutrality pact agreed in April 1941 between the Soviets and Japan some two years after their border war known as the *Battle of Nomonhan*, they remained the deadliest of geopolitical rivals in northeast Asia. At the start of the war it was also considered possible that the *Aleutians* might be the first stepping-stone of Japanese encroachment on to the American mainland. Conversely Japan feared that America would use the *Aleutians* as a base for the long range bombing of Japan. The distance from *Attu* to Tokyo is just 2,000 miles.

Attack on Dutch Harbor and the Invasion of Attu: At the beginning of June 1942 Rear-Admiral Kakuji Kakuta led a force of light carriers *Ryujo* and *Junyo* plus destroyers to 180 miles southwest of *Unalaska*. Linked to *Unalaska* by a bridge is the much smaller island of *Amanak*, which is the location of *Dutch Harbor*, the main HQ for the US's fleet in the *North Pacific*—today it is the largest fishing port in the United States. On 3 June Kakuta launched bombers against *Dutch Harbor*'s naval base and barracks. After two days of attacks they departed having killed 78 American soldiers and destroyed 14 aircraft and a barracks-ship. Remarkably the nearest US Air Force base was over 800 miles away. Although Rear-Admiral Robert Theobald had been instructed to go to *Attu* to intercept Kakuta's carriers after Rochefort's intelligence had tipped Nimitz off about Japanese naval plans, Theobald ignored the intelligence advice and second-guessed the Japanese plan by stationing himself due south of *Dutch Harbor*, assuming that the supposed plan to invade *Attu* and *Kiska* was a decoy. It was a mistake that cost Admiral Theobald his career.

On 6 June, 500 Japanese Marines landed on *Kiska*, 600 miles west of *Unalaska*, where they found a ten-man squad of American troops manning a weather station. An eleventh man, Charlie House, escaped. He hid in the wintery wastes of the mountainous

107 square mile volcanic island before the hostile conditions forced his surrender. The following day the 302nd Independent Infantry Battalion made an unopposed landing on the island of *Attu*, three times larger than *Kiska* and 205 miles to its west. American troops would find it equally mountainous and inhospitable. The Aleuts awoke to find a ship at anchor off Chichagof Harbor. At first it was assumed that it was an American ship sent to evacuate them. But there was no mistaking the Japanese flag when it was raised. Attuan Innokenty Golodoff recalled, "On Sunday morning a little after eleven we were all coming out of church when we saw them [the Japanese] coming out of the hills. So many of them."[2] The young Japanese recruits shot up the village wounding one Aleut in the leg. Another, Foster Jones, was murdered when Japanese troops occupied his home. The invaders announced that the Attuans were now liberated from the American imperialists and promptly forced them onto a transport ship and took them to Japan.

Curiously *Attu* was entirely treeless even though its rich soil provides evidence of an ancient forest in a warmer age. The climate of *Attu* is notoriously bad, affected as it is by an almost permanent weather cycle known as the Aleutian Low. Warm air, the Japanese current, collides with blasts of artic cold producing icy fogs and violent storms. The forty-three Aleut residents of Attu village lived by their ancient art of sea hunting. Kayaks known as *baidarkas* were made from skins and the villagers would surround their prey—sea otters, sea lions and walruses—before dispatching them with harpoons or latterly by rifle. Fish, often salmon, was the staple diet. In the eastern *Aleutians*, whaling was also part of popular culture. On land the Attuans supplemented their fish diet by hunting or with gulls' eggs filched from *Attu*'s craggy cliff faces.

The island of *Aggatu* was also occupied but quickly abandoned. Little did the Japanese soldiers realize as they planted their Japanese flags in the *Aleutians* that, two days earlier, Japan had lost four of its six fleet carriers at the catastrophic defeat of the *Battle of Midway*. Indeed, as if nothing of import had happened, work began on building an airbase on *Kiska* and several on *Attu*.

On *Attu*, Lieutenant-Colonel Hiroshi Yanekawa established a base at *Holtz Bay*, which was reinforced with a contingent that eventually numbered 2,300 troops by March 1943. But, in effect, the pickets deployed by Rear-Admiral Charles 'Soc' McMorris marooned the Japanese soldiers there. For the Japanese troops it was a hard life; "The loneliness in this remote northern base is hard to imagine,"[3] wrote a Japanese war correspondent.

The Battle of Komandorski: **[Map: 23.1] [Map: 23.2]** It has been suggested that the capture of *Attu* and *Kiska* had been simply a diversionary tactic aimed at drawing the US carrier fleet out of their refuge at *Pearl Harbor*. This may partly have been the case but as has been explained, there was a strategic logic to the occupation of the *Aleutians*. The problem was that the catastrophe at *Midway* meant that Japan's ability to reinforce or develop its foothold there was severely constrained. Their troops had to eke out an existence on the most barren of islands, which had previously hosted only the most hardy Russian fur traders and the 880 Aleuts who constituted the entire population of this remote Alaskan island chain. Supply had to be sustained across an ocean that they no longer controlled. At the end of March 1943 a Japanese naval force, comprising 2 heavy cruisers (*Nachi* and *Maya*), 2 light cruisers (*Tama* and *Abukama*) and 4 destroyers (*Wakaba*, *Hatsushimo*, *Ikazuchi* and *Inazuma*), was dispatched to resupply *Attu* and *Kiska* under the command of Vice-Admiral Boshiro Hosogaya.

The breaking of the Japanese Navy's JN-25 code by Station HYPO on *Hawaii* gave advance notice of the resupply attempt and Admiral Nimitz dispatched Admiral McMorris with heavy cruiser (USS *Salt Lake City*), a light cruiser (USS *Richmond*) and 4 destroyers (USS *Bayley*, USS *Coghlan*, USS *Dale*, USS *Monaghan*) to intercept— unaware that Japan had reinforced its squadron with an extra heavy cruiser and light cruiser. At 180 miles west of *Kiska* and south of the *Komandorski Islands*, American pickets intercepted Hosogaya's forces setting off a classic naval gunnery battle.

Although *Nachi* took the first hits, which destroyed its electric systems, it was *Salt Lake City* that eventually came off worst; it took the brunt of *Maya*'s gunnery and came to a dead halt. *Richmond* and *Dale* had to make smoke to protect the American heavy cruiser that, as a 'sitting duck', was fortunate not to take a hit from the Japanese destroyers' Long Lance torpedoes. Meanwhile the remaining American destroyers launched their own torpedo attack—again unsuccessfully. Hosogaya, fearful that the US force was accompanied by an aircraft carrier withdrew his forces, including the supply transports, when his forces were on the cusp of a famous victory. There was no carrier nearby but the *Asaka Maru* transport ship did report the approach of two formations of American bombers from *Adak*. The *Battle of the Komandorski Islands* thus ended with a tactical victory for Japan but a strategic defeat and thereafter their forces in the *Aleutians* could only be supplied by submarine. McMorris's forces took 20 casualties with 7 killed while Hosogaya's forces had 14 killed out of a total of 26 casualties.

The Re-taking of Attu and Kiska: **[Map: 23.3]** In immediate response to Japan's *Aleutian* occupations, the United States had set about occupying *Adak Island* some 210 miles east of *Kiska* and constructed two airfields. Subsequently the island of *Amchitka*, just sixty miles east of *Kiska*, was also occupied by American troops though the construction of an airport proved difficult because of the bitter weather conditions.

By early 1943 America felt strong enough to decide on a plan of assault to retake *Attu* and *Kiska*. When 11,000 troops of the 7th Infantry, some of whom had been patrolling the Mexican borders, were loaded onto transport ships in Seattle on the west coast of America at the end of April, they must have assumed that they were embarked for the warm tropical climes of *Hawaii*. They were surprised to find themselves at *Cold Harbor* at the foot of Alaska without winter clothing; some still had short sleeve shirts. Their commanders had unkindly decided that winter uniforms would slow them down in an operation that was only expected to take a couple of days. American GIs would go into battle wearing summer uniforms fighting Japanese soldiers wearing fur-lined clothes.

The author of this catastrophic mistake is supposed to have been General John DeWitt, commander of the United States Western Defense Force, who had been given the responsibility for supervising the recapture of *Attu* and *Kiska*. DeWitt, who harbored a visceral hatred of all Japanese people after *Pearl Harbor*, was best known for advising President Roosevelt to have all 'undesirables' [Japanese] rounded up and interned. The result was the incarceration of 110,000 men, women and children of Japanese ancestry, many of them born in the United States and fiercely proud of their new nationality. De Witt's attitude to this human tragedy was best summed up by his blithe observation, "a Jap is a Jap."[4]

Although the US transports arrived off *Cold Harbor* on 30 April, storms prevented an immediate advance to *Attu* and the convoy continued north to the *Bering Sea* to avoid enemy detection. The convoy arrived off *Attu* on 11 May. American commanders were so complacently confident of success that they supplied their troops with just a single day's worth of 'K' Rations. [See Chapter 15: **Battles of the Kokoda Trail, subsection** *Asaku Koryu versus 'K' Rations*] The Northern Force, commanded by Lieutenant Colonel Albert Hartl, led the 1st Battalion of the 17th Infantry Regiment against the Japanese troops dug in at *Holtz Bay* and *Chichagof Harbor*. Landing at 4.15 p.m. Hartl advanced inland before coming across the first Japanese resistance.

Private Raymond Braun of the 17th Infantry recalled, "Our landing on that rock was screwy. We had been in boats all day long waiting to come into the island. Then we landed in fog as thick as mashed potatoes, expecting a wild dash across the beach with bullets flying, and there weren't any."[5] However an hour inland they were hit by a Japanese artillery barrage. Delayed by inadequate maps, American troops dug into the muskeg, the soft and spongy wet soil, which covered the low-lying areas of *Attu*. By the time tracked vehicles, used to pull artillery, had moved just seventy-five yards from the beach, it had become clear from the tracks spinning through the thick black mud that the island's topography presented unique logistical challenges. Even foot soldiers could get bogged down. Lieutenant Darwin Kry of the 49th Field Artillery Battalion recalled a soldier carrying a 105 mm shell uphill: "Its 54 pounds pushed his feet almost to the knees in the sticky mud and bent his back."[6]

The following day, 12 May, Colonel Edward Earle led a larger southern force of the 2nd and 3rd battalions, which was tasked with a flanking advance up Massacre Valley, the taking of Clevesy and Jarmin passes and a linking up with the Northern Force. In reserve the 1st and 3rd Battalions of the 32nd Infantry stayed on board the transports. Landing at 3.30 p.m. because of morning fog, Earle's troops advanced without enemy contact into Massacre Valley. Living up to its name, from the valley's ridges Japanese troops opened fire on the now trapped US battalions, forcing them to flee to the cover provided by a hill at its center. Other soldiers took cover behind the banks of streams. Meanwhile rolling icy fogs made artillery or air support impossible. A freezing cold night, albeit just three hours long in the arctic summer, was suffered by both Southern and Northern Forces as they slept in the open in their summer uniforms. Even when GIs were asleep "their bodies trembled violently from the cold. Empty shell cases, ration boxes, anything that would burn, had been torn up and consumed in tiny fires to heat the last packages of coffee and warm stiff fingers for a moment."[7]

The American advance was painstaking. The Japanese defenders could see the advancing Americans but they couldn't see the Japanese. Sergeant William Jones complained, "The Japanese had dug tunnels for strong points that we couldn't see through the fog. They sniped at us every time the fog lifted. As soon as we concentrated our fire back where we thought they were firing from, they pulled back into the tunnels."[8]

Northern Force's advance became similarly bogged down on 12 May by a Japanese ambush. Reinforcements were brought up, including the 4th Infantry Regiment from *Adak*. An advance was finally enabled when the fog cleared and the three accompanying battleships were able to launch a ferocious bombardment of Japanese positions. However the delays in the US advance meant that by 14 June, soldiers had run out of food. Lieutenant Anthony Brannen dropped food from his B-24 but the parachutes were blown into a crevasse. The next day he tried again, but crashed into the mountains and was killed. In the succeeding days heavy fog made food supply difficult and exceedingly dangerous for the pilots. A Japanese counterattack was then driven off a ridge that came to be known as Bloody Point. On reaching the highest point of the ridge, a sword wielding Japanese officer had led a 45-man attack that was quickly dispatched. Artillery was brought up to positions that commanded *Holtz Bay*. By now thousands of troops had trench foot, an excruciating condition that swelled feet and damaged nerves and muscles. Some men were forced to crawl on hands and knees.

Advance on Cold Harbor: From their commanding positions the Americans could clear the ridges that held down the Southern Force in Massacre Valley. Nevertheless, 7th Infantry's slow progress brought about the replacement of General Brown with Major-General Eugene Landrum on the morning of 17 May. For the latter the timing appeared fortunate when the Northern and Southern Forces were able to link up at Jarmin Pass later that day. The 17th and 32nd regiments now began the piecemeal assault of Point Able and the snow covered Cold Mountain; it took them several days to winkle out the Japanese defenders mainly with grenades or bayonets. The difficulties of dealing with Japanese foxholes was well summed up by Corporal Tony Pinnelli:

> I started crawling straight up the hill at the little knoll behind which I had seen the smoke. I made it to the knoll without being seen. The Japs were behind it, like I figured, and they were watching down the hill toward our left flank. I crawled up on the rise of ground and threw a grenade. The first one was short. I tried another, and it fell into the Jap hole, but they threw it out.[9]

Cold Mountain succumbed on 20 May. However, defense on Point Able was to last until 22 May. The last Japanese defender, having killed two American GIs, threw himself off the peak—screaming as he fell.

All the while US forces were taking heavy losses from ambushes, booby traps and snipers. It did not help that poor communication led to significant losses from friendly fire as US bombers hit their own troops. For the US soldiers the fighting conditions were beyond miserable. In their summer uniforms they froze, with many suffering frostbite. In the midst of firefights, American troops would have to take it in turn to huddle in tents around small stoves to warm themselves. Sudden hurricane force williwaws would blow off the mountains hurling "snow, then ice and then dirt that reduced visibility to the length of your arm."[10] Others were so desperate for warmth that they burnt their rifle butts. Some soldiers froze to death, a particular risk when they got lost in the icy fog—soldiers becoming so disorientated that guide ropes were fixed between posts. Furthermore, freezing mud made logistical supply by truck all but impossible.

The Battle of Chichagof Harbor: [**Map: 23.4**] On 22 May, American troops also began the push downhill toward *Chichagof Harbor*. On two ridges in their path, Fish Hook and Buffalo, the Japanese threw up formidable defenses, forcing US troops to take out dug-in positions one by one. Carefully prepared zigzag trenches, 3 feet wide and 4 feet deep, and tunnels that connected firing pits enabled Japanese officers to shift their soldiers from place to place. Machine guns were placed no more than 200 yards apart in positions that enabled them to give crossing enfilades of fire. Apart from these traditional defensive weapons, the Japanese troops also employed barrage mortars that flung shells skywards before they fell to earth with parachutes, exploding and sending shrapnel over a wide area.

Observation posts were skillfully camouflaged. Similarly buildings such as radio shacks, latrines, officer positions, barracks, kitchens and supply buildings were dug into the ground and covered with sods of earth. Few details were overlooked; in case of limited visibility firing pits were provided with sighting posts covering likely lines of enemy incursion. It was later found that Japanese troops had been given sturdier entrenching tools with sharper edges to cut through *Attu*'s tundra. Caps with fur-lined earflaps were found in quantity as well as knitted hats in wool and silk to fit under helmets. Fur-lined boots were also issued. Japan's troops did not suffer from the trench foot and frostbite that turned US soldiers' feet black and gangrenous—sometimes requiring amputation. Short skis suitable for travel over the granular type snow found in the *Aleutians* were supplied to the defenders. Above the snowline Japanese defenders were provided with white parkas. Below the snowline, to match the brown-green tundra, Japanese soldiers were provided with capes colored to match, under which they could shelter all day. Noticeably the only thing Japanese troops were not provided with were routes for withdrawal. It was a sign of things to come six months before Admiral Nimitz's *Central Pacific* campaign began at the *Battle of Tarawa*.

With the Americans running short of food and artillery munitions in positions that made them difficult to supply, the task of taking out the Japanese positions was made doubly awkward. Individual bravery helped get them through. As the 4th Infantry were patiently slugging their way down a particularly muddy hill pock marked with dug-in

Japanese positions, Private Fred Barnett slid down the hill on his back hurling grenades and firing into Japanese trenches. His colleague followed finding that Barnett had seemingly killed forty-seven Japanese soldiers.

At Fish Hook Ridge, the attack was led by 7th Infantry's Private Joe Martinez, who charged the Japanese lines carrying a BAR machine gun (Browning Automatic Rifle) and shooting the defenders in their foxholes. As Sergeant Glenn E. Swearingen and Sergeant Earl L. Marks recalled,

> The farther we went into the pass the worse it got. Once Private First Class Joe P. Martinez got caught in one of those hot spots and it made him mad. He had a BAR and he got to running from hole to hole spraying hot lead into each one until his BAR was empty. Then he grabbed an M 1 from somebody and went on like a wild man with that. He was a tornado that day . . .[11]

In spite of a hail of bullets he cut a swathe through Japanese lines, enabling colleagues to follow his path. From one of the final foxholes he took a bullet to the head and died the following day. Martinez, from Ault, Colorado, was awarded the Medal of Honor, becoming the first Hispanic-American to win the award in *World War II*. As his citation recorded, "His example inspired others to follow."[12] Not counting *Pearl Harbor*, his Medal of Honor was also the first combat award earned on American soil since the *Indian Wars* of the nineteenth century.

On 28 May, a US night patrol infiltrated Japanese lines in order to gauge Japanese defense intentions in the final phases of the battle. They were astonished to see Japanese soldiers crazed with *sake* jumping up and down and screaming at the top of their lungs. It was also seen that wounded Japanese soldiers were being put to death with morphine or simply shot dead. The patrol was lucky to get back alive as sentries mistook them for Japanese; it was shouts of "Brooklyn Dodgers, New York Yankees and Joe DiMaggio"[13] that saved them. The leader of the patrol, Lee J. Bartoletti reported on what he had seen but aroused little interest from his commanding lieutenant. Nevertheless Bartoletti warned adjacent foxholes that an attack could be expected. He was right. At 3.30 a.m. the Japanese commanding officer Colonel Yamazaki led about 1,000 Japanese troops in one of the largest banzai attacks of the war.

Before the attack Dr. Paul Nobuo Tatsuguchi, an American educated Japanese physician wrote in his diary,

> The last assault is to be carried out. All the patients in the hospital were made to commit suicide. Only 33 years of living and I am to die here. I have no regrets. Banzai to the Emperor. I am grateful I have kept the peace of my soul which edict bestowed to me. At 1800 took care of all the patients with grenades. Good-bye Taeko, my beloved

wife, who has loved to the last. Until we meet again, grant
you Godspeed.[14]

Most American troops were caught off guard as they went to eat a hot meal at the
regimental kitchen, before the arctic sun started to light the early morning. They were
overrun and the battle descended into a primordial hand-to-hand brawl with bayonet and
sword.

In the Chichagof Valley the 17th Infantry were charged by intoxicated Japanese
troops screaming, "We'll drink your blood."[15] Many US troops, unable to extricate
themselves in time, were butchered in their sleeping bags. The tent of an aid station was
collapsed and many wounded were trapped under the fallen canvas. Onward Yamazaki
charged toward the reserve positions occupied by engineers, drivers, artillerymen and
medics. They grabbed guns that lay to hand and joined in the pell-mell action managing
to fight off the Japanese charge. One soldier later told his son James LaVerdure that
he was stabbed three times and took a bullet through his helmet before he killed a
sword wielding Japanese officer—later bringing the sword home as a souvenir. "Japs,
lots of them, began appearing through the fog in the strange glow of the red flares," an
American soldier recalled. "They charged through the disorganized company, reducing
it to little pockets of fiercely resisting men who shot down column after column, and
still they came ... They were yelling and shooting, bayoneting, grenading—utterly
destroying everything in their way. For the next hour everything was a blur of shouts
and explosions and screams and running figures."[16]

As Yamazaki's attack petered out some of the surviving Japanese troops blew
themselves up with grenades. Yamazaki was among those who committed suicide. In
the *mêlée* Dr. Paul Tatsuguchi was apparently shot dead by US troops as he tried to
surrender. His diary was found by Dr. J. Lawrence Whitaker, a US battalion surgeon,
who, in one of the stranger coincidences of the *Pacific War*, had studied with Tatsuguchi
at Loma Linda University School of Medicine in California.

American interrogators were surprised to find that the few Japanese soldiers who did
surrender spoke quite freely. Major William Verbeck noted, "The Japanese prisoner ...
has never been told not to talk in event of capture because the possibility of capture is
never considered by the enemy. As a result, this well-disciplined Japanese soldier obeys
orders and answers any questions we direct at him."[17] In Tokyo, on 31 May, the Japanese
government reported, "it is assumed the entire Japanese force has preferred death to
dishonor."[18]

Consequences of the Battle of Attu: As the sun began to emerge a scene of devastation
greeted onlookers with hundreds of bodies littering the battlefield. As one GI noted, it
looked like a dug-up graveyard. Afterwards the frozen GIs looted the Japanese dead of
their much warmer clothes and headed back to the camp kitchens to line up for food. In
the confusion a surviving Japanese soldier infiltrated a food queue hoping to snag a hot
meal. He overrated his English speaking ability when he asked the soldier behind him

how the Brooklyn Dodgers were faring. At the scene of the battle, a chaplain of the 7th Infantry mournfully observed, "I am glad the're [the Japanese] dead, really glad ... [but] How can I go back to my church when I've got it in me to be glad men are dead."[19] After this climatic engagement, isolated pockets of Japanese resistance were cleared over the next three days with the final fire-fights taking place on 31 May—almost three weeks after the first landings.

In spite of the excellent preparations made by Japanese commanders, after the *Battle of Attu* a US platoon leader noted:

> I feel very definitely that if a continual advance is made
> on the Jap, he becomes confused and doesn't quite know
> what to do next. One thing is certain. This business about
> his being a superman is so much tripe. When you start
> giving him the real business, he will run like hell and be
> twice as scared as you are—and when I think how scared
> I was, that's saying a lot.[20]

But what the Americans had thought would be an easy operation had turned into a fiercely fought battle that took over two weeks to yield victory for 14,000 US troops over a force of just 2,300 Japanese diehards. In a victory that presaged the tough battles of the *Central Pacific* ahead, American troops took 3,929 casualties including 549 dead. A US Navy supply clerk, Edward Trebian, recalled, "There were so many [bodies] ... The Army just cut a path with a bulldozer and then shoved 'em in ... What else could they do?"[21] But for most veterans of the *Battle of Attu* the abiding memory was of the freezing cold. Eugene Telgmann of the 18th Engineers Battalion swore, "it was so cold that he never warmed up in four years."[22] Remarkably some soldiers of the 7th Infantry, like John Casey, subsequently made landings in the vastly different terrains of *Kwajalein, Leyte Gulf* and *Okinawa*. At *Attu* the slog across the *Pacific* had just begun.

After the desperate *Battle of Attu*, American commanders anticipated a much harder campaign on *Kiska* where 5,200 Japanese were believed to be stationed, more than twice as many as *Attu*. Some 29,000 American and 5,300 Canadian troops were deployed on *Kiska* on 15–16 August. Three battleships and a heavy cruiser supported them with an offshore bombardment. Cover was provided by 168 aircraft. In the event they found a deserted island—the Japanese having left some two weeks earlier. Apart from twenty GIs killed by Japanese booby-traps and more tragically, friendly fire, it was a bloodless operation. The *Aleutians* role as a possible fulcrum of a significant role in the *Pacific War* was ended.

For the Aleuts themselves the brief war in their homelands was a catastrophe. 'Rescued' by the Americans meant being housed in appalling conditions on the Alaskan mainland; some 20 percent of their population died during their few years of exodus. When they returned they found that their homes had been ransacked by Japanese and American troops of anything of value including guns, fishing tackle, furs, and heirlooms, including Russian Icons. It would take years for the Aleut communities to recover and years for them to receive reparation from the US government. Only on 10 August 1988 did President Ronald Reagan sign the *Civil Liberties Act*, which granted reparations to the Aleuts and Japanese Americans who were interned in *World War II*. The Aleuts received a US$5m trust fund plus US$15m for the loss of *Attu*, US$1.4m for the restoration of churches and US$20,000 per individual who survived the camps. The US government issued a formal apology. In Japan, ceremonies continue to be held annually for the fallen soldiers who lost their lives in what is known as the *Forgotten War*.

The Attuans who were shipped off to Japan by the Japanese troops, who had supposedly freed them from American tyranny, fared even worse. In Japan they were forced to learn Japanese under pain of death. Put to work, men, women and children were whipped or beaten if their efforts were not satisfactory. Food was so deficient that within a year some Aleuts starved to death. Only 25 of the 42 Attuans returned to the *Aleutians* but not to *Attu*, whose community was forever destroyed.

24 The Huon Peninsula: Operation CARTWHEEL Completed

[September 1943–April 1944]

[Maps: 24.1, 24.2, 24.3, 24.4]

The Huon Peninsula Campaign: **[Map: 24.1]** Within a week of the occupation of Lae on 16 September 1943, MacArthur and Halsey set about the next stages of Operation CARTWHEEL's envelopment of Rabaul. MacArthur ordered a rapid deployment to take the minor port of Finschhafen at the tip of the Huon Peninsula. It was a split advance. While the Australian 9th Division took the coastal route to Finschhafen, the Australian 7th Division would cut through the center of the Huon Peninsula to New Guinea's northern coast with a view to cutting off Adachi's coastal retreat toward Madang. While MacArthur was making his northern thrusts in New Guinea on Rabaul's western flank, Halsey, after his occupation of *New Georgia* was preparing to make his northwesterly thrust from Rabaul's eastern flank by a landing at *Empress Augusta Bay* on the east coast of *Bougainville Island*. The twin-pronged advances aimed to bring Rabaul and its eventual isolation closer.

Situated on the eastern tip of the Huon Peninsula, Finschhafen was strategically placed adjacent to the *Straits of Vitiaz* which separated it from the island of *New Britain* on whose eastern tip was situated Rabaul. Finschhafen's main use was as a center for barge traffic, which brought supplies to Japanese troops on New Guinea from Rabaul. While units of the 9th Division were to make an amphibious landing north of Finschhafen, at the same time another of its battalions would advance up the southern coast of the Huon Peninsula toward Finschhafen from the west.

On 22 September 1943, Australian 9th Division veterans of action at the *Battle of Tobruk* in North Africa landed on the beaches north of the Japanese garrison at Finschhafen. In a typically confused amphibious landing the four assault companies missed Scarlett Beach and washed up on an adjacent headland next to Siki Cove. An Australian soldier recalled,

> Ahead and above us, on top of a headland about 100 feet away, a Japanese machine-gun opened fire with tracers. Its first burst went high into the air, the second into the water beside the boat. The third burst crashed over my head and hit two men behind me; I heard them cry out as I jumped on to the coral and splashed through a pool or two to the beach.[1]

After being initially repulsed at Siki Cove, the 9th Division moved inland and after a fierce fight took the heights at Katika. In the late afternoon a force of 70 Japanese aircraft including 40 escort fighters attacked the amphibious landing but, alerted by USS *Reid* acting as picket, 60 fighters from the convoy's escort carriers intercepted the attack. In a crushing defeat some thirty-nine Japanese aircraft were shot down in the ensuing dogfight. American control of the air, and a fear of a repeat of the *Battle of the Bismarck Sea*, prevented Admiral Mineichi Koga using naval forces to re-supply Japanese forces on New Guinea. From now on the troops would have to forage for local food and live without rice—a severe hardship for a Japanese soldier. First-Lieutenant Toshiro Kuroki would later complain,

> Since our arrival on November 11th we have had hardly any rice ... The divisional commander and the staff officers do not seem to realize that the only way the men can drag out their lives from day to day is by the endless hunt for potatoes. How can they complain about slackness and expect miracles when most of our effort goes into looking for something to eat.[2]

Contrary to the intelligence provided by MacArthur's staff that Finschhafen was garrisoned by no more than 350 Japanese soldiers, Lieutenant-General Hatazo Adachi had stationed some 5,000 troops of the Eighteenth Army in the area. Nevertheless eleven days after landing, 20th Brigade entered Finschhafen. Australian troops scrounged for souvenirs.

Although the balance of air power in the *Southwest Pacific* had been shifted toward America after the *Battle of the Bismarck Sea* and the bombing of Wewak, Japanese air power and its potential ability to disrupt operations in New Guinea remained significant. *Truk Atoll*, Japan's main naval and air force garrison in the *Pacific* continued to supply fifty aircraft a month to Rabaul. On 12 October 1943, Kenney's Fifth Air Force launched 349 sorties on Rabaul's airfields and docks; 100 Japanese aircraft were destroyed along with large numbers of merchant ships and three destroyers. MacArthur privately congratulated Kenney, declaring, "George, you broke Rabaul's back yesterday. The attack marks the turning point in the war in the southwest Pacific."[3] As usual with MacArthur's declarations of victory, his pronouncements were premature. Japanese aircraft made attacks on *Oro Bay* and Finschhafen on 15 and 17 October albeit with heavy losses, estimated at 100 aircraft. The Japanese Navy Air Force continued to take prolific losses both in attack and defense. Kenney made another major strike on Rabaul on 29 October when low-level attacks by Mitchel B-25s and Lockheed P-38s shot down sixty-eight aircraft and destroyed a further twenty-six on the ground.

Meanwhile around Finschhafen the battle had only just begun. Attention switched to the three and a half mile track leading uphill from Finschhafen to the former German mission at Sattelberg. The Japanese dug in. "I eat potatoes and live in a hole," wrote one

Japanese infantryman, "and cannot speak in a loud voice. I live the life of a mud rat or similar creature."[4] The problem of logistics for the Japanese Army in New Guinea was now becoming evident to all. First-Lieutenant Uchimura of the 41st Division wrote in his diary,

> In air superiority . . . we are about a century behind America . . . This present war is termed a war of supply. Shipping is the secret victory or defeat in this war of supply in countries thousands of miles across the sea . . . To have regular shipping lanes, air superiority is essential. Ah, if only we had air superiority . . . If only we had planes . . .[5]

Over the next three weeks a stalemate developed around the Sattelberg Track that Adachi sought to relieve by sending 7,500 troops from Madang, where General Adachi was stationed with the bulk of the Eighteenth Army. A Japanese counter-attack was launched on 16 October. Colonel Kaneki Hayashida's 79th Regiment assembled a mile to the west of the heights of Katika; they were ordered to "attack and surprise the enemy in Katika from the rear and annihilate them."[6] The plan was to link with Japanese raiders from the sea and to push back the Australians to their beachhead at Scarlett Beach. The weight of Japan's attacks on the heights at Katika forced the Australian 9th Division to abandon its positions. Numbers of Australian units were surrounded but Major-General Sir George Wootten, in a statement of faith that foreshadowed General Slim's tactics at the *Battle of Imphal* in Burma, had drilled into his platoons the doctrine that Japan's flanking attacks cut their own soldiers off, not only from their line of retreat, but also their line of supply. The trick was for the Australians to stand firm rather than make a panicky retreat.

Australians too had received reinforcements from MacArthur and, with the firepower provided by abundant artillery, held back the Japanese assault causing them heavy casualties. Brigadier Evans who had pulled his troops back to a tight perimeter around Scarlett Beach from which the Japanese 79th Regiment had been beaten back with heavy losses was relieved of command by Brigadier Wootten for yielding ground 'unnecessarily.' It was a controversial decision given that Evans's tactics had eventually worked. In the aftermath, the Australians counted 679 Japanese dead though the actual numbers killed were probably double. For Japan's commanders, the battle was a severe disappointment: "It appeared at one stage that the attack was on the verge of success," stated Lieutenant-General Adachi, "but it ended in a complete failure."[7]

Wootten, born of English migrant parents in Sydney, had enjoyed a distinguish career in *World War I* before leaving the Army to become a solicitor. Famously he became prodigiously fat, weighing over twenty stone even though he was just five foot nine inches tall. His burgeoning girth did not prevent him becoming a member of the Old Guard, a semi-official militia created to ward of the perceived threat of socialist revolution. At the outbreak of *World War II*, Wootten joined the Australia Imperial Force

(AIF) and fought with the 7th Division at Tobruk. Returning to Australia, he took an active part at *Milne Bay*, Buna, Sanananda, Lae and Finschhafen. From his experience in the field he developed new tactics for combatting Japanese flanking techniques. In spite of his comical 'Falstaffian' presence, his skill as a field commander was undoubted. Even MacArthur, not much given to praising even American officers, described Wootten as "the best soldier in the Australian Army."[8]

From 19 October, the Australian 9th Division moved back to the attack supported by Matilda tanks and on 25 October, Major-General Shigeru Katagiri ordered his forces to retreat five miles inland to the German mission at Sattelberg, which at 3,150 feet, overlooked the entire area. For the Australians it was a painstaking advance through narrow jungle tracks full of deep glutinous mud, which had also been heavily mined. Supply was problematic for both sides. For the Japanese troops however, starvation beckoned; there was evidence from corpses that they were reduced to eating ferns and the core of bamboo. Japanese supply could only be made by submarine, airdrops or fishing boats. Allied aerial dominance made the use of barges impossible.

A Japanese diarist from the 79th Regiment wrote, "Everyday just living on potatoes. Divided the section into two groups, one group for fighting and the other to obtain potatoes. Unfortunately none were available. On the way back sighted a horse, killed it and roast a portion of it . . . At present our only wish is just to be able to see even a grain of rice." Meanwhile a happier diarist in the 80th Regiment wrote, "Received rice rations for three days . . . It was like a gift from Heaven and everybody rejoiced." In spite of this unexpected trove, the diarist's emotions were mixed; hearing raucous American voices at night, he noted: "They are probably drinking whisky because they are a rich country and their trucks are able to bring up such desirable things—I certainly envy them."[9] Starvation took its toll on the Japanese ability to fight. After taking 'Feature-2200,' one Australian observer noted that Japanese troops were "Weak from lack of food and the strain of continuous shelling and mortaring, the few Japs that evacuated the position were apparently unable to carry their weapons, other than rifles."[10]

The Sattelberg Campaign developed into an exceptionally fiercely fought encounter. Even the 26th Brigade, in their first continuous battle since serving in North Africa, was shocked by the ferocity of the fighting and the conditions of engagement. A battalion diarist noted: "Many of the lads consider it to have been harder and more nerve-racking than any 10 days at Tobruk or El Alamein."[11] On 22 November Adachi ordered another counter-attack to take Pabu, a hilly area that commanded the supply route to Katagiri's forces at Sattelberg. The Australian 2/32nd Battalion held out at Pabu for ten days. It was a localized battle that Adachi would later pinpoint as the critical moment of the Huon Peninsula Campaign.

The attack on the near-vertical southern slopes saw some of the most difficult fighting with Australian troops having to inch forward without the help of tanks. On 22 November, Sergeant Tom Derrick, born in Adelaide, a vineyard worker of poor Irish descent and a veteran of Tobruk, in one of the most extraordinary individual actions of *World War II*, refused orders to withdraw, telling his company commander, "Bugger the

CO. Just give me twenty more minutes and we'll have this place. Tell him I'm pinned down and can't get out."[12] He grabbed a sack of grenades and climbed up the sheer slope grasping at vines to haul himself upwards. With one hand clinging to a vine, Derrick used the other to lob grenades into enemy machine gun positions, "a man . . . shooting for [a] goal at basketball."[13] Urged on by his colleagues who covered his ascent, Tom Derrick single-handedly took out eight machine gun nests killing fifteen Japanese on the way. Sattelberg was taken on 27 November 1943 and the battalion commander insisted that Derrick have the honor of hauling the Australian flag over the town. He was awarded the Victoria Cross and later, Derrick, an archetypal Australian 'digger' was promoted to Lieutenant.

After his defeat at the *Battle of Sattelberg*, Lieutenant-General Shigeru Katagiri began a long retreat toward Madang. A two-pronged attack forced the Japanese back from Wareo and the coastal village of Gusika: "All that remained of the 20th Division in this area consisted of abandoned foxholes, entrenchments, ammunition and ration dumps, equipment, weapons, camps, medical aid posts and graves."[14]

On 5 December, a fresh 4th Brigade, commanded by Brigadier Cedric Edgar, relieved Australian troops. After completing the capture of Wareo and Gusika, 4th Brigade, covered by the 26th Brigade, moving inland parallel to the coast, started the 50-mile advance toward Sio. The 9th Division, having conducted the largest operation by any Australian unit in the war to date, was relieved by the 5th Division for the final mopping up operations around Sio that extended into early March 1944. During the campaign, the Australians had 1,082 casualties of whom 283 were killed. It was estimated that over 5,500 Japanese troops were killed though many more were thought to have died of starvation. Only 4,300 Japanese soldiers are thought to have arrived in Sio. Most of their supply and heavier equipment was also lost. As usual in the New Guinea campaigns, tropical illnesses took their toll of troops on both sides.

Perhaps the most important result of the occupation of Sio was the discovery of a box containing codebooks with current cipher codes. It was without question the major intelligence coup of the *South Pacific* Campaign and a crucial determinant of the later westward advances along the northern coast of New Guinea. Their discovery and subsequent utilization saved the lives of many thousands of Australian and American infantry.

The Battle of Shaggy Ridge: [**Map: 24.2**] While the 9th Division was taking the coastal route toward Madang, the Australian 7th Division commanded by Major-General George Vasey had struck north from Lae along the Ramu Valley that bisected the Finisterre Range. Grassy, flat and cool it was an area with the most benign climate and terrain in the *South Pacific*. For the Japanese these advantages were limited because the terrain offered little cover from an Allied air force that had become increasingly dominant after the *Battle of the Bismarck Sea*. Fighting therefore mainly took place at the ridges and rocky outcrops that criss-crossed the valley. The fighting resembled *Guadalcanal* but on a larger canvas.

The route would bring 17,000 Australian troops to the northern neck of the Huon Peninsula. Major-General Masutaro with detachments of the 20th Division set up defensive position in the rocky ridges that crossed the Ramu Valley; they became known as 'Shaggy Ridge' after Captain Robert 'Shaggy Bob' Clampett, who was the first to reconnoiter the area. 'Shaggy Ridge' was a narrow razorback with an altitude of 5,000 foot "A thick rain forest covered the crest of the ridge. Heavy mists frequently obscured the position for days at a time . . . Such was the vantage point of the eminence that on clear days observation was possible as far as the sea near Madang."[15]

Series of defensive positions were dug in to key high points in the Ramu Valley. From October onwards there was a profusion of mini-battles for control of the commanding positions; the 'Battles of Palliser's Hill,' 'Pimple,' 'Kankiryo Ridge,' 'Prothero I,' 'Prothero II,' 'Green Sniper's Pimple' and 'Cam's Saddle' became known in aggregate as the *Battle of Shaggy Ridge*. Throughout November Japanese positions on 'Shaggy Ridge' and its surrounding strongholds were bombarded incessantly by US artillery and mortar fire. Nevertheless, Japanese artillery, which was carefully camouflaged, continued to fire from platforms carved into the ridges. The 7th Division fought protracted engagements at 'Shaggy Ridge' through December 1943 as the combatants' swapped attack and counter-attack.

Nevertheless on Christmas Day 1943, Australian fighting units sat down to a rare feast: "Breakfast—porridge, Burdekin ducks [a species of shelduck found in Australia], buns and tea; Dinner—giblet soup, roast turkey and seasoning, green peas, mashed potatoes, shredded carrots, gravy, plum-pudding and sauce, tea and buns."[16] The sharp contrast with Christmas 1942, at the *Battle of Buna-Gona* the previous year, was noted by many. It was a measure of the extent to which Allied logistics had now achieved an overwhelming advantage over their Japanese enemy. On 31 January Japanese resistance was broken and 'Shaggy Ridge' was occupied. The battle had cost the Australians 193 casualties including 46 killed. An estimated 500 Japanese defenders were killed. In support of the offensive through the Huon Peninsula, MacArthur pursued Adachi as he retreated from Sio on the north coast of the Huon Peninsula. The 8th Brigade of the 5th Australian Division trailed Adachi's 4,200 troops along the coastal route. However, hard the trek was for the Australians in monsoon conditions, for the Japanese it was worse. By the wayside bodies of emaciated Japanese were frequently found unburied; death had come to them from exhaustion, illness and starvation.

Acting on a suggestion by staff member Major-General Stephen Chamberlain, MacArthur authorized an amphibious landing at Saidor, a settlement further up the coast towards Madang and blocking the Japanese line of retreat from Sio. For the future Saidor also boasted an airstrip that would provide another point of pressure on Japanese air control of New Guinea's northern coast. On 2nd January 1944 the lightly defended beaches of Saidor were pounded by the guns of dozens of US warships as well as high-level bombing from B-29s. Kenney's B-25 gunships swept the area with a hail of bullets that strafed everything in sight. As US Captain Meredith Huggins noted, "There was very little opposition when we landed. We found a few Japs wandering around in shell shock. What a contrast from the days of Buna and Sanananda, only a year before, when we were fighting with rifles, grenades, and rocks!"[17] What was clear to troops on the ground who came back after periods of rest and recuperation was that there was a perceptible change in the weight of fire that Allied forces could bring to the point of contact with the enemy.

Some 7,500 men and their supplies were speedily landed. The immediate benefit was that Adachi was forced to order his troops to take a circuitous 200-mile march through interior trails to reach Madang. His half-starved forces would have to cross the Finisterre Range with its impenetrable jungle, rivers, gullies and precipitous tracks. On 18 February long-range Australian patrols made their first contact with US forces at Saidor. A week earlier MacArthur had prematurely announced the end of the Huon Peninsula Campaign, claiming the entrapment and destruction of the 79th, 80th and 238th Infantry Regiments, a total of 14,000 Japanese soldiers. In reality the whole region was not finally cleared of Japanese units until April 1944. A month earlier a 6,000-foot runway had been completed at Saidor, as well as infrastructure and supplies for a garrison of 15,000 troops. A stepping-stone had been laid down for MacArthur's planned advance along New Guinea's northern coast.

Recognition for Australian Forces in New Guinea: The success of Australian troops in jungle conditions had not gone unnoticed by senior British officers. From the beginning of 1943 General Wavell, the Commander in Chief in India, had been taking considerable interest in the Australian's jungle war with the Japanese in New Guinea. Apart from written reports, two Australian officers, Major A. A. Buckley and Major W. N. Parry-Okeden, were sent to India and gave lectures to commanders from May to September 1943. Wavell's replacement in June 1943, General Claude Auchinleck went one step further by accepting General Vasey's offer to train up to fifty Indian Army officers at Canungra in Queensland. Nineteen Indian Army officers duly joined the Australian 7th Division. The importance of the Australian contribution to the development of General Slim's jungle tactics prior to the *Battles of Arakan-Imphal-Kohima* in northeast India, at the beginning of 1944, has rarely been highlighted.

Perhaps even more importantly, it should be noted that the greatest victories credited to General MacArthur during the course of the Pacific War, at the *Battles of the Kokoda Trail, Buna-Gona-Sanananda, Wau, Salumaua, Finschhafen, Shaggy Ridge, Sattelberg* and the engagements of the Huon Peninsula Campaign, were won by Australian force of arms. Outside of Australia these battles are barely known. Not only are they less famous than the American actions in the *Pacific War*, but they were fought at a time when there was a poverty of logistical support and a still competitive Japanese aerial threat. It was a background that made these victories even more remarkable. It was only in the Huon Peninsula Campaign that Australian forces would begin to benefit from the overwhelming aerial, naval and logistical power that marked MacArthur's campaigns thereafter. MacArthur's battles in the eighteen months to March 1944 were won by Australian fighting spirit rather than any strategic or tactical deftness on MacArthur's part.

Hardships faced by the Australians were extreme. They were plagued by a variety of skin rashes collectively known as 'jungle rot,' as well as dysentery, scrub typhus and other tropical diseases. Between September 1943 and March 1944, 9,942 men out of 28,059 engaged in New Guinea had to be evacuated because of malaria. The Australian diet was appalling. When fires could not be lit, canned bully beef had to be eaten cold. Fresh vegetables were a rarity. Australian soldiers rarely had the 3,750 calories per day that they needed to maintain their weight. Army doctors reported a chronic shortage of Vitamins B and C. When US soldiers had to share Australian rations they usually found them inedible.

After the Huon Peninsula Campaign, it was the American 'Alamo Force' under Lieutenant-General Walter Krueger that took the lead in advancing the Allies along the north coast of New Guinea towards the Philippines. This was simply a case of putting US soldiers at the forefront as MacArthur neared his date with destiny—or at least his rewriting of history and his desire to erase the memories of his disastrous defense of the Philippines. In August 1943 Labor Prime Minister John Curtin had won re-election in a landslide victory. Like many Australians, Curtin believed that they had borne more than their fair share of the war—indeed they had. Their participation had after all taken in North Africa, Malaya as well as New Guinea. In spite of resistance from General Blamey and MacArthur, who warned that there would be a cost to the war effort, the Australian Defense Committee proposed a reduction in the army from 492,000 to 371,000 by July 1944. In spite of MacArthur complaints, the reduction probably suited MacArthur particularly as by mid-1944 the Allied forces in the Far East began to be swamped with new soldiers and *matériel* from the United States.

By early April MacArthur had 750,000 troops under his command including six US infantry divisions, three regimental combat teams, and three special brigades. Although the Australians still provided five divisions, MacArthur could now afford to assign them a secondary role. Just as importantly Kenney's air force had undergone a transformation over the previous twelve months. Two-hundred plane raids could now be launched with very little interference from Japanese aircraft. From April 1944 onwards, Australian troops began to be used in mopping up operations in the *Southwest Pacific*. The virtual elimination of Australia's role in pushing the Japanese further out of the *Southwest Pacific* can only partly be attributed to Curtin's defense cutbacks. MacArthur was generally dismissive of Australian troops and their abilities and was inclined for reasons of self-interest and publicity in America to extol only the virtues of US troops. It cannot be coincidence that when it came to the hard-won Australian campaigns, MacArthur never appeared in person to wave the flag with his accompanying US press cohort.

As a result, the Australian contribution to the war effort has never received the attention that it deserved in American accounts of the *Pacific War*. Australian troops did more than any other nation to show how Japanese troops could be defeated in jungle terrains. It is an omission from American histories of the period that is only matched by the failure of British historians to sufficiently acknowledge the significant role of Australian troops in the *Pacific War*. Far too much attention has often been given to the poor performance of Australian units during the fall of *Singapore* and Malaya, rather than the remarkable jungle victories won by their forces in New Guinea.

The Battles of Arawe and Cape Gloucester: [Map: 24.3] Earlier on 15 December 1943, the US amphibious task force led by Rear-Admiral Daniel Barbey, aboard his flagship, the destroyer USS *Conyngham*, arrived off the southern coast of *New Britain*'s western tip. Barbey's armada consisted of troop transports, landing ship-dock USS *Carter Hall*, 8 further escort destroyers, 2 submarines, tugboats and tenders. The invasion armada, arriving via the Huon Peninsula shortly before dawn, was sighted by Japanese spotters at 3.30 a.m. At Rabaul, Japan's Eleventh Air Fleet immediately prepared to attack the US invaders.

Although there were 120 Japanese troops defending Arawe, albeit with reinforcements on the way, heavy machine gun fire thwarted the attempt to land 112th Cavalry Regiment's 1st Squadron at Umtingalu. However, the landing at *Pilelo Island* and later at 7.30 a.m. the main landing at House Fireman Beach were successful. The Arawe Peninsula was rapidly secured. By the end of the day some 1,600 troops had disembarked. Japanese air attacks at 9.00 a.m. caused minimal damage to the Allied forces for the loss of several Zeros. Over the course of the next two weeks, Kenney's Fifth Air Force would score 'kills' against 24 Japanese bombers and 32 fighters. Thereafter Japan's air strength appears to have petered out. From 1 January 1944, Japanese air attacks were limited to nighttime raids. In the first fortnight of the US invasion, Barbey was able to unload over 540 artillery pieces and some 6,000 tons of supplies. Over time the 112th Cavalry set up a defensive field of fire while Seabees made good an airstrip for use by spotter planes.

On the ground the commander of the 17th Division, Lieutenant-General Yasushi Sakai, who believed that this was not the main attack on *New Britain*, nevertheless ordered Major Masamitsu Komori to counter the Allied landing with elements including the 141st Infantry Regiment. In response to Komori's first probing attacks, Brigadier-General Julian Cunningham requested and received reinforcements in the form of three infantry companies of the 158th Infantry who arrived early in the New Year, 1944. Lieutenant-General Krueger also dispatched a company of the US Marine Corps 1st Tank Battalion to help Cunningham's counter-attack against Japanese positions on 16 January. Thereafter Japanese attacks on Arawe's defenses were small scale and sporadic. Komori forces, albeit by now sick and starving, were ordered to stay in the field.

Meanwhile on 26 December 1943, Major-General William Rupertus had led the main landings of 1st Marine Division at Cape Gloucester on the north coast of the western tip of *New Britain*. It was their first action after a prolonged period of rest and recuperation in the south of Australia following their heroic efforts on *Guadalcanal*. Lieutenant-General Sakai, appointed by General Hitoshi Imamura in Rabaul on 4 October to take command of Japanese forces in western *New Britain*, had about 4,000 troops in the area. Their new commander ordered his troops to carry out "certain death warfare to the utmost, in such a way that not even the slightest disgrace will adhere to your name."[18] Heavy fighting followed as the Marines moved south through swampy terrain to secure *Borgen Bay* against opposition from Major-General Iwao Matsuda's 17th Division supported by the 65th Infantry and elements of the 51st Division. When the Marines' advance stalled at *Suicide Creek*, Rupertus, brought in Lieutenant-Colonel 'Chesty' Puller, one of the heroes of the *Battle of Henderson Field*. Believing in the strength of their firepower, Puller insisted on a frontal attack, "we have the power to drive and we are going to drive."[19] If the initial fighting was fierce, it was the appalling weather that most concerned the troops. Heavy rain fell for two weeks, in one instance washing away clothes and supplies. Electrical storms were reminiscent of naval bombardments. A Marine veteran of *Guadalcanal* recalled lightning balls "ten feet in diameter setting the kunai grass on fire. We had five men killed in one tent when lightning struck the tent pole and arced to the nails in their shoes and killed them all in place."[20] Major-General Harold Deakin on Rupertus's staff asserted that conditions on Cape Gloucester were worse than *Guadalcanal*.

After costly counter-attacks failed on 16 January, engagement was light as Matsuda withdrew his forces and by 24 February, Imamura had ordered all remaining Japanese forces at Cape Gloucester to withdraw to the east. For the next six weeks the 1st Marines chased the Japanese troops along the coastal tracks.

On 30 March, Colonel Sato who had been given command of the rear-guard by Matsuda was cut down, sword in hand; his band of seventy men all perished. Major Komori was also killed in the retreat. Wracked with malaria he stumbled into a sentry post manned by the 5th Marines and was gunned down with three other soldiers. The diary recovered from Komori's body recorded a last entry that read, "We are very tired and without food."[21] Just three Japanese soldiers were captured. Desultory fighting continued until June by which time the area had long been bypassed. Somewhat unnecessarily the Australian 5th Division, which replaced the US Army 40th Division in November, continued active operations. At Cape Gloucester more than 1,000 Japanese troops died. By comparison, aggregate American losses at Cape Gloucester and Arawe were 382 killed and 1,200 wounded. The utility of the *Battles of Cape Gloucester* and *Arawe* has frequently been questioned. Once it had been decided to isolate Rabaul as the end game of Operation CARTWHEEL, the Cape Gloucester Campaign was largely redundant. A planned PT boat base at Arawe was never built and Lieutenant-General Kenney had openly stated that the Japanese airfield at Cape Gloucester was not needed. The benefits of the engagement were limited even though it has later been argued that US casualties were relatively light.

Colonel Charles Willoughby, MacArthur's devoted intelligence chief, made a more grandiloquent case for the Arawe and Cape Gloucester Campaign:

> To immobilize with a relatively small force the Japanese Eighth Army on the Rabaul flank represents a professional utilization not only of astute staff intelligence but of time and space factors cannily converted into tactical

advantage. It was correctly anticipated that not only would the projected Arawe landing immobilize enemy New Britain reserves in fear of further coast assaults threatening Rabaul, but that the bulk of enemy opposition to be met at Arawe would be reinforcements caught belatedly en route to Lae . . . and through these seemingly scattered actions, there runs a thread of design, the operative 'leitmotif,' the flexible, inexorable advance on the Philippines—somewhere—somehow—some time![22]

In reality Lieutenant-General Kenney's victory at the *Battle of the Bismarck Sea* had already made the transport of Japan's Eighth Army reinforcements to the Huon Peninsula practically impossible. Willoughby's claims of tactical skill on MacArthur's part are surely overrated in his analysis though his observation about the importance of the Philippines, at least to his commander, was obviously completely correct. Perhaps the campaign was most notable for the extensive use of new equipment. The 1st Marines were equipped with Browning light machine guns, Garand semi-automatic rifles, Thompson machine guns, bazookas and flame-throwers. US troops could now employ a weight of fire power in combat that would have been unimaginable in the early days on *Guadalcanal*. If nothing else, the *Battles of Cape Gloucester* and *Arawe* were useful training exercises for tougher battles ahead.

The Admiralty Islands Campaign: **[Map: 24.4]** The *Admiralty Islands* (*Manus* and *Los Negros*) stood at the northeastern exit of the *Bismarck Sea* and commanded an important strategic point some 600 miles from Rabaul, 820 miles from the Japanese forward fleet garrison at *Truk*, and 1,370 miles from Davao City on *Mindanao Island* at the southern tip of the *Philippines*; the Joint Chiefs believed that Seeadler Harbor had the potential to serve as a naval anchorage for the *Pacific* Fleet and the invasion fleet aimed for the conquest of the *Philippine Islands*. It was planned that the Seabees would build two giant floating docks. The *Admiralty Islands* were also the last link in the chain of Operation CARTWHEEL, which would conclude the isolation of Rabaul.

In preparation for the invasion of the *Admiralty Islands* Allied forces took control of the *Green Islands*, situated just 117 miles southeast of Rabaul. On 29 January 1944 Major-General Barrowclough, leading the 3rd New Zealand Division and the 14th New Zealand Brigade, landed on the island of *Nissan* without opposition. Over the next week 120 Japanese soldiers were killed in sporadic firefights in which 10 New Zealanders and 3 Americans also died. The *Green Islands* provided a PT patrol boat base and another airfield with which the noose around Rabaul could be further tightened.

At Rabaul, Lieutenant-General Hitoshi Imamura fully recognized the importance of the *Admiralty Islands* and at the end of 1943 requested a full division for their defense. Troops were not available however, and the existing defense forces were bulked up by 750 men of the 2nd Battalion of the 38th Division and later by 530 troops of the 1st

Battalion. In all there were approximately 4,000 Japanese troops on the island when US amphibious forces landed on the smaller *Los Negros Island* on 29 February.

Originally the invasion of the *Admiralty Islands* had been planned for April 1944 but when Lieutenant-General Kenney's spotter planes noticed that there was no sign of life on the islands, MacArthur decided to bring forward the invasion to the end of February. It was a mistake. MacArthur's chief of intelligence, Colonel Willoughby, was convinced that Kenney's intelligence was incorrect and information from ULTRA intercepts seemed to support him. Kenney had been duped. The Japanese appeared to be absent because Colonel Yoshio Ezaki had ordered his troops not to move about during the day so as to conceal their building of two new airstrips and to conserve anti-aircraft ammunition. In spite of Kenney's assertions regarding the weakness of Japanese defenses, MacArthur's staff officers were still appalled at the high level of risk in the assault. Even Lieutenant-General Kenney noted, "we had already outrun the capabilities of our supply system."[23] Ignoring these limitations, MacArthur was determined to follow his instincts and attack the *Admiralty Islands*. He would later reminisce, "I felt that the situation presented an ideal opportunity for a coup de main which, if successful, could advance the Allied timetable in the Pacific by several months and save thousands of Allied lives."[24] Perhaps more importantly, the capture of the *Admiralty Islands* would advance the timetable in the race to the Philippines.

It could not have escaped MacArthur's attention that his competitor, Admiral Chester Nimitz, was crashing through the *Central Pacific*. In the first week in February Nimitz had taken *Kwajalein* and *Majura Atolls* to gain control of the *Marshall Islands*. Nevertheless MacArthur, fully aware of the risks of forwarding the *Admiralty Islands* operation, covered his tracks by describing the attack as a 'reconnaissance in force.' The misgivings of MacArthur's staff were confirmed when a covert reconnaissance mission by Lieutenant J. R. McGowan and five men of the 158th Infantry reported on 27 February that the place was "lousy with Japs."[25] However, with just two days to landing-day, it was too late to pull back.

A group of nine destroyers had been rapidly assembled and prepared to carry troops for an amphibious invasion. They were joined by the only high-speed transports then available. With just over 1,000 troops it was a risky venture—even if they were unaware that they were outnumbered by 4:1. In addition the light cruiser USS *Phoenix*, lying in Brisbane, was ordered to make speed to join them. The amphibious force was led by Rear-Admiral William Fechteler. Brigadier-General William Chase commanded the 5th US Cavalry Regiment of 1st Cavalry Division which would lead the amphibious landing. MacArthur, in his classic grandiloquent style, told his courtiers that his father had fought with the 5th Cavalry against legendary Apache chief Geronimo in 1884 at the end of the *Apache Wars* (1858–1886) during which the United States had sequestered the ancient Apache tribal lands in Arizona, New Mexico and West Texas. He recalled, "A troop of this same 5th Cavalry . . . rode through to help us. I can still remember how I felt when I watched them clatter into the little post, their tired horses grey with desert dust . . . They'd fight then and they'll fight now."[26]

After the initial heavy machine gun fire, the 5th Cavalry came ashore on *Los Negros* on 29 February and overran the Japanese positions. At 4.00 p.m. MacArthur, who had accompanied the invasion force aboard Vice-Admiral Thomas Kinkaid's flagship, the light cruiser, *Phoenix*, made a rare visit to the front and risked sniper fire to visit his troops. It was an act of distinct bravery for MacArthur to come ashore on *Los Negros*. Nonetheless, one wonders whether he would have been as supportive with his presence if the mission had been conducted by Australian troops rather than the more glamorous US 5th Cavalry, with all its potential for favorable press coverage back in America.

John Gunther, the legendary journalist and author of the bestselling 'Inside' series of books, wrote, "he stalks a battlefront like a man hardly human, not only arrogantly but lazily."[27] Meanwhile a correspondent for the *Saturday Evening Post* who was granted a place in MacArthur's entourage gushed, "With his yellow trench coat swinging out behind and smoke trailing from his pipe, MacArthur paced off the puddled coral runway himself . . ."[28] A carefully choreographed picture was taken of MacArthur standing over a dead Japanese soldier; MacArthur's accompanying quotation, carefully crafted, was, "That's the way I like to see them."[29] The photograph, the main reason one suspects for his visit to *Los Negros*, was duly sent to the US press with panegyric copy about the General's bold strategic stroke. It was vintage MacArthur self-promotion.

By the end of the following day Chase's outnumbered force found itself in a tight spot facing a determined enemy trying to dislodge it from his beachhead perimeter. He would have to hold out for a week without reinforcements; they were scheduled to arrive on 6 March but faced by impending catastrophe their arrival was brought forward to 4 March. Meanwhile, Major-General Yoshio Ezaki, surprised by the US point of attack, planned a counter-attack to wipe out the 5th Cavalry on the night of 3 March. In a series of *banzai* charges, Ezaki's troops hurled themselves at the 5th Cavalry defenses where the defenders' Browning machine guns worked all night killing an estimated 750 Japanese troops.

In one entrenchment Sergeant Troy McGill was one of only two survivors out of an eight-man squad. He ordered back his colleague while holding up the advancing Japanese infantrymen with his rifle; when it jammed he used it as a club until he was killed. For his selfless heroism McGill was posthumously given the Medal of Honor. The 5th Cavalry took 305 casualties in the night action; 61 were killed. The 2nd Squadron and the Seabees 40th Naval Construction Battalion were awarded Presidential Unit Citations.

The 7th Cavalry reinforcements arrived on 4 March and the 12th Cavalry arrived on 6 March with supporting tanks and artillery. By 9 March *Los Negros Island* had been overrun and Seeadler Harbor had been secured. The mountainous and heavily forested *Manus Island*, surrounded by thickly grown swamps was invaded on 15 March. After twelve days of heavy fighting and pounding of Japanese entrenchments the 2,700 troops on the island were all but wiped out. Japanese stragglers continued to fight. The entry of the diary found on the body of a dead Japanese soldier records on 31 March, "Although we are completely out of rations, the march continues . . . will this unit be annihilated in the mountains? As we go along, we throw away our equipment and weapons one by one."[30] His last entry was on 1 April. Outlying islands were gradually cleared of Japanese over the next few months. Out of the estimated 4,000 Japanese troops on the *Admiralty Islands*, just 75 troops were captured alive. US forces lost 330 men killed and suffered 1,189 other casualties.

For launching a risky, indeed reckless, amphibious landing against defending forces that outnumbered him 4 to 1 (compared to a normal requirement of a 3:1 troop superiority for the attackers in an amphibious landing), MacArthur was awarded a Bronze Star. Even Admiral King commended the *Admiralty Islands* Campaign as a "brilliant maneuver."[31] Chase was similarly awarded, though he declared, "They [the Navy] didn't support us; they saved our necks."[32] Rear-Admiral William Fechteler similarly reflected, "Actually we're damn lucky we didn't get run off the island" and questioned whether, "MacArthur ever questioned his own judgment in this matter."[33] Fortunately by this point in the New Guinea Campaign the weight of US naval and air power had indeed become overwhelming; even high-risk gambits, or mistakes, such as the invasion of the *Admiralties*, turned into wins. Victory embellished MacArthur's record, which was every bit as important as the strategic gains won. As a footnote to the victory, Brigadier-General Clyde Eddleman, who had been one of the *Los Negros* planners, made the ruthful observation, "if we had waited a couple of weeks, we could have done it much easier."[34]

Even while the fighting continued, the 40th Seabee Battalion, the 8th Engineering Squadron and members of the 532nd Engineering Boat and Shore Regiment began construction of the air and naval facilities on *Los Negros* and *Manus*. Within a week Momote Airfield was increased to 3,000 foot and by May had been lengthened to 7,000 foot and made 100 foot wide. By 18 April it was accommodating a US bomber group. At the same time a new 8,000-foot airfield was built at Makerang Plantation. New facilities included a 37,000-barrel fuel depot and a floating Liberty Ship dock and an evacuation hospital. The result was that by early summer the Seabees, with the help of 1,230 native workers, had completed a major logistical center available to support operations along the northern coast of New Guinea and the Philippines beyond.

Whatever the risks taken in the *Admiralty Islands*, the net result of the battle was clear. The encirclement and isolation of Rabaul was complete; the strategic objectives of Operation CARTWHEEL had been met. In addition a major new logistics center had been established, providing a crucial stepping-stone in the US advance toward Japan. MacArthur noted, "For all strategic military purposes, this completed the campaign for the *Solomon Islands*."[35]

MacArthur's South Pacific Turf War: The planned occupation of the *Admiralty Islands* led to one of the bitterest of turf wars when General Marshall suggested that the development of *Manus* and *Negros Islands* be delegated to Halsey for the building of a base for Nimitz's *Pacific* Fleet as well as Halsey's Seventh Fleet. Not surprisingly since this was going to be principally a naval operation, Nimitz sent a memo to Admiral King copied to General MacArthur in which he requested that for this operation Halsey be put under his command as Commander in Chief, Pacific (CINCPAC).

MacArthur exploded. In a long letter to Marshall on 27 February MacArthur complained,

> I am in complete disagreement with the recommendation of Admiral Nimitz regarding the Bismarck Archipelago. He thus has proposed to project his own command into the southwest Pacific ... It is quite evident that the ultimate issue in question is the control of the campaign in the Pacific, and immediately, that for the initial major objective, the Philippine Islands, which have always been in my area ... my professional integrity, indeed my personal honor would be so involved that ... I request that I be given early opportunity to present the case personally to the Secretary of War and to the President before finally determining my own personal action in the matter.[36]

In other words he was threatening to resign unless he got his way. MacArthur even petulantly declared that *Seeadler Harbor* was to be closed to all ships other than Halsey's Seventh Fleet, which operated under his strategic control as Commander in Chief of the *Southwest Pacific*. Vice-Admirals Halsey and Kinkaid, along with Captains Johnson and Carney were called to Brisbane to resolve the issue. Late on 3 March they met MacArthur and were greeted by a fifteen minute lecture, even tirade, which ended with him pointing his famous cob pipe at Halsey and demanding, "Am I not right, Bill?" In unison the four naval men chorused, "No, Sir."[37]

Halsey, for whom MacArthur had developed the deepest friendship, went on to assert, "General, I disagree with you entirely. Not only that, but I'm going to go one step further and tell you that by limiting use of the Manus naval base to the Seventh Fleet you'll be hampering the war effort."[38] When MacArthur repeated his feeling of personal insult relating to Nimitz's memo, Halsey said, "General, you're putting your personal honor before the welfare of the United States."[39] With a look of complete devastation, MacArthur exclaimed, "You can't really mean that? We can't have anything like that." Turning to his Chief of Staff, Major-General Sutherland, he lectured him saying, "Dick, there will be nothing like that."[40] Halsey returned to his HQ at *Noumea* thinking that the issue was now resolved. It was not. The Joint Chiefs and Nimitz were forced to bring the issue to Roosevelt on 11 March. The President, always reluctant to 'mix it' with MacArthur, could smell a 'turd' and decided to keep this one at arm's length by handing it back to the Joint Chiefs to resolve. In the end they gave in to MacArthur, though Marshall warned, "there should be a clear understanding that the Pacific Fleet will have unrestricted use of them [the harbors and facilities at *Manus* and *Los Negros*]."[41]

It was an episode that fully displayed not only the peculiar psychology of MacArthur but also the fear in Washington of his political and media clout. *Time* magazine, clearly briefed by MacArthur and his acolytes, had already warned that MacArthur had been pushed into a secondary role in the *Pacific*: "It is plain that this state of affairs is precisely the opposite of what he expected when he was ordered to leave *Corregidor* and the men on Bataan. It is also plain that it is the opposite of what the US people have expected."[42] Had any other commander in the war 'back-channeled' and behaved as badly as MacArthur, they would in all likelihood have been sacked. Indeed the fact that this issue was brought before Roosevelt was clear evidence that, in issuing MacArthur with orders, the Joint Chiefs of Staff had to bear in mind political as well as military issues. At this point the Joint Chiefs would have been all too aware that MacArthur was even being seriously mooted as a Republican candidate to run against Roosevelt. No wonder the Joint Chiefs did not want to take a decision to thwart MacArthur's wish to retain control of the naval base at the *Manus* and *Los Negros Islands*.

It should be noted that while MacArthur was wildly popular in the United States, with his own forces he was less so. Soldiers and Marines resented the misleading *communiqués* from the front from a General who only made sporadic visits there and then only to have his photograph taken. They ridiculed his fastidious and overly ostentatious uniforms, his well-known and much discussed life of pampered luxury, and the excesses of his sycophantic court. Chief of the courtiers was MacArthur's famously obnoxious Chief of Staff, Richard Sutherland. Officers and soldiers alike were scandalized that Sutherland, with a wife back in America, drafted his mistress, a married Australian woman, into the US Army so that he could employ her and keep her in tow. Another member of MacArthur's staff, in a way that was typical of the petty jealousies of his court, complained, "Sutherland was screwing the socks off her every night and we didn't know what else to do with her, so we made her a receptionist."[43]

Nevertheless, in spite of the inter-service rivalries, as historian Douglas Ford has noted the US "Navy and Army managed to place their political battles aside in order to focus on their ultimate task of defeating the enemy."[44] The Army versus Navy rivalry in the *South Pacific* worked largely because by an unlikely quirk of history, MacArthur and his fleet commander, Vice-Admiral 'Bull' Halsey, who had the seemingly unenviable task of reporting to both him and Nimitz, became the unlikeliest of best friends. This was probably because Halsey, like MacArthur, "was a strong advocate of unity of command in the *Pacific*" and also because of Halsey's willingness "to close with the enemy and fight him to death." Halsey's "blunt, outspoken, dynamic"[45] manner also won over the normally aloof, stand-offish MacArthur.

In the event, later in the year, Nimitz would choose *Ulithi Atoll* not the *Los Negros Islands* for his forward anchorage in the *Pacific*, inconvenient because of its lack of land mass but 600 miles closer to Japan. Though never disclosed, one wonders whether the spat with MacArthur over the *Admiralty Islands* had a bearing on his decision—it seems highly likely.

The Occupation of Emirau: Earlier, in response to wider simmering disputes about forward strategy and priorities, the Joint Chiefs of Staff called MacArthur and Nimitz to a strategy meeting in Washington set for 2 March 1944. The Joint Chiefs determined that critical decisions needed to be made. MacArthur, as usual, refused to attend. Sutherland, never popular in Washington, went in his place. The case was made for an advance up through New Guinea to *Luzon* in the Philippines. However, King argued for *Formosa* and southern China as the best take off point for attacking Japan. Perhaps most importantly Nimitz argued that MacArthur's plan to invade *New Ireland* and capture the Japanese base at Kavieng would divert Naval resources and delay his advance in the *Central Pacific*, in particular in the *Marianas*, the all-important base from which bombing attacks could be made.

Much to MacArthur's annoyance, it was made clear the *Central Pacific* campaign was the primary strategic drive; MacArthur's role would be subsidiary. A future Philippines campaign, it was opined, could serve as a useful means of diverting Japanese resources away from the *Central Pacific*. Starting the mass bombing of Japan from the *Marianas* was the Joint Chief of Staff's most urgent priority. To this end, because of the delay that it might cause, the Joint Chiefs ordered MacArthur to bypass and isolate the Japanese garrison at Kavieng on the northern tip of *New Ireland*. For the longer term MacArthur and Nimitz were told to prepare for the invasions of *Luzon* and *Formosa* respectively, almost a year hence, on 15 February 1945.

Second to Rabaul, Kavieng on *New Ireland* was the most important Japanese garrison on the *Bismarck Archipelago*. It was unclear why MacArthur insisted on the taking of the garrison when the commander of the South Pacific Area, Vice-Admiral 'Bull' Halsey, who came under MacArthur's command for the *Solomon Islands* and New Guinea campaigns, made clear, "the geography of the area begged for another pass."[46] Instead the US Joint Chiefs of Staff ordered Vice-Admiral 'Bull' Halsey to occupy the island of *Emirau*, some ninety miles to the northwest of Kavieng. *Emirau*, occupied only by 300 natives, was approximately eight miles long and two miles wide. Accordingly on 15 March Rear-Admiral 'Ping' Wilkinson, commander of the III-Amphibious Force, who was preparing for the invasion of Kavieng at his base in *Guadalcanal*, reorganized his command for the occupation of *Emirau*. It was duly occupied on 20 March.

Nevertheless the accompanying Naval force that comprised four battleships, USS *Mexico*, USS *Idaho*, USS *Tennessee* and USS *Mississippi*, in addition to escort carriers USS *Manila Bay* and USS *Natoma* with fifteen destroyers, decided to pound Kavieng for good measure. Expecting an imminent Allied invasion, Rear-Admiral Ryukichi Tamura, ordered that all western prisoners, mainly Australians and Germans, be put to death. Twenty-three were hung at Kavieng Wharf. The military court in Melbourne recorded that Corporal Horiguchi, whose defense pleaded that he was under orders, took each victim to the wharf: "When each victim arrived at the edge of the wharf he was told to sit down," recalled Horiguchi in court. "Sailors then placed a noose of rope over the victim's head and strangled him. The bodies were then thrown into one of two barges and cement sinkers were secured to the bodies by wire cable."[47] Rear-Admiral Tamura was found guilty and hanged while five others were given lengthy prison sentences as war criminals.

Emirau was occupied by the 4th Marines without incident, as was the much larger *Mussau Island* in the *St. Matthias Group*. The only engagement occurred when a group of Japanese soldiers in a large open canoe, who had been intercepted by an American destroyer about forty miles from *Mussau*, opened fire with their small arms and were duly blown out of the water. On *Emirau*, the Seabees built two bomber runways and storage and support facilities for up to five capital ships in *Hamburg Bay*. In addition a PT boat base was constructed as well as several hospitals. To add to the region's military logistical assets, a port capable of handling 800 tons of cargo per day was built. The Australian 8th Infantry Battalion took over the island from the US 147th Infantry in September 1944. The envelopment of Rabaul was complete. The *Bismarck Archipelago* and the *Solomons* now became a graveyard for Japanese troops dying of hunger and disease. For the US Army and Navy, the islands that it chose to occupy became logistical stepping-stones on the inexorable advance toward Japan.

25 The Isolation of Rabaul and the Starvation of Bougainville

[November 1943–August 1945]

[Maps: 25.1, 25.2, 25.3, 25.4]

The Planning of the Bougainville Campaign: [Map: 25.1] The western hook of Operation CARTWHEEL, which had started with the Huon Peninsula, was completed with the capture of the *Admiralty Islands* in March 1944. While MacArthur was operating in the west, Vice-Admiral 'Bull' Halsey was working the eastern channel of Operation CARTWHEEL. Having secured *New Georgia* and *Kolumbangara* by the first week of October 1943, the next island on the advance toward Rabaul was *Bougainville*, the largest island of the *Solomons* group. As Halsey developed his plans for the subjugation of *Bougainville* in November 1943, he found his strategy very much moulded by the disposition of Japanese forces on the island. Following their original March 1942 invasion, they developed airfields across the island, with the aim of providing cover for their intended advance into the southern *Solomons* and then on to the island chains east of Australia. Their main *Bougainville* airfield was in the north at *Buka Island*; others were in the south at Buin (Kahili) and *Ballalae Island* situated between *Bougainville* and *Shortland Island*, and on the east coast of *Bougainville* at Kieta.

The Japanese occupation barely touched the dense jungle of *Bougainville*'s mountainous terrain. Its climate and topography was arguably the most challenging of any battleground in the entire *Pacific War*. The majority of the estimated 40,000 native population lived on the eastern plains or the southern or northern tips. In general they resented the Japanese invaders and co-operated enthusiastically with the Australian coastal watchers located around the island. As means of communication and supply the interior tracks had been largely neglected and supply to Japanese garrisons and their airfields from Rabaul was largely done by air or barge. Air power was such that Japan's military strategists understood that airfields were the advance guard of military action. This was not so much because of the damage that Japanese aircraft could do to the enemy in the field. Albeit psychologically important, Japanese air power against enemy infantry in the jungle conditions was diminished. However, Japanese planes could disrupt or destroy amphibious landings, and even more importantly air attack on enemy shipping could prevent supply and reinforcement. When roles were reversed and it was MacArthur and his commanders who had the momentum of attack in the *South Pacific*, they did not need to invent a new strategic formula for success. They merely copied the Japanese.

Over the autumn of 1943 Vice-Admiral 'Bull' Halsey and his staff, seeking to close their account with Operation CARTWHEEL, debated a direct attack on Japanese strongholds in southern *Bougainville*. Studies showed that the time and cost of investing these heavily fortified garrisons made it an unattractive proposition; a full-scale invasion furthermore would set back MacArthur's aggressive timetable to reduce Rabaul. Instead, careful reconnaissance showed that airfields could be constructed midway up the west coast of *Bougainville* at Cape Torokina on *Empress Augusta Bay*, which Halsey chose as his invasion site and the location for new airfields. The strongly fortified southern tip of *Bougainville* would thereby be bypassed. After weighing up the ability of the Seabees to construct airfields on *Bougainville*'s swampy western shores, on 22 September Halsey cut the discussion dead: "It's Torokina. Now get on your horses!"[1]

Vandegrift, the hero of *Guadalcanal*, planned and started the *Bougainville* campaign but would not lead the operation to its conclusion. Promoted Commandant of the Marines, the first serving Marine to become a four-star general, Vandegrift departed for Washington. His replacement Major-General Charles Barrett informed the 3rd Marine Division that their mission was to "land in the vicinity of Cape Torokina, seize and occupy and defend a beachhead including *Torata Island* and adjacent island— 3,750 yards west of Cape Torokina—allowing approximately 2,250 yards inland from the beach and 3,600 yards east of Cape Torokina. To prepare and continue the attack in coordination with the 37th Infantry on arrival."[2] It was Barrett's last major contribution to the war. He fell from the third floor of the officers' quarters on *Noumea* and suffered a cerebral haemorrhage—his death was recorded as accidental but was a suspected suicide. Major-General Roy Geiger, who was the Director of Marine Aviation Corp in Washington, took his place.

Vice-Admiral Theodore Wilkinson would command the transports; Major-General Allen Turnage was put in charge of the 3rd Marines as well as the 8th Brigade of the 3rd New Zealand Division who were designated for the invasion of the *Treasury Islands*. As well as bypassing the heavily fortified Japanese garrisons, Halsey may well have considered the possibility of drawing the Japanese fleet into a major engagement by his aggressive advance. As for the bypassing of *Buka* on the southern tip of *Bougainville*, it was no easy task given the paucity of maps inland from the coastal lodgements planned for *Empress Augusta Bay*.

Diversionary raids on *Choiseul Island* to the southeast of *Bougainville* were carried out from 28 October 1943. Lieutenant-Colonel Victor Krulak who led the attack with the elite Marine 1st Parachute Regiment described the island as "the most rugged of all the Solomons. It's home of the giant banyan whose roots cover an acre . . . It's never daylight in most of the island. The jungle cover makes it like late afternoon."[3] An attack on the village of Sangigai was hard fought with the Marines outnumbered. "The outcome appeared to be in question," averred Krulak in his later account of the action, "until the Japs destroyed their chances by an uncoordinated banzai charge which was badly cut up by our machine guns."[4] Seventy-two Japanese dead were counted for the loss of just six Marines. Captured charts included one that showed the sea minefields placed around southern *Bougainville*. Halsey would use these charts to send US minelayers to put sea mines in the clear channels. Two Japanese ships were sunk as a result. After their successful raids, the Marines were taken off the island by three LCIs (Landing Craft, Infantry) sent from *Vella Lavella* on the night of 3 November.

The raids led the Japanese into believing that the south tip of *Bougainville* was the main target of the next full-scale US invasion. The attack certainly added to the confusion at Japanese Army HQ. Krulak, who won the Navy Cross, and would later be promoted to general, argued, "that the strategic effect for the commitment of 750 men in an undertaking where they were bringing in 38,000 men was significant."[5] At the same time, the invasion of the *Treasury Islands* to the southwest by New Zealand 8th Infantry Brigade (3rd Division) also led the Japanese to believe that an assault on the south of *Bougainville* was imminent. The *Treasury Islands* were captured with a handful of deaths and casualties, which mainly occurred when USS *Cony*, a Fletcher Class destroyer, took two hits in a mid-afternoon Japanese bombing raid from Rabaul.

The choice of *Empress Augusta Bay* on the west coast of *Bougainville*, surrounded by five Japanese airfields within a sixty-five miles radius, two each at the southern and northern extremities of the island and one on the east coast, was a risky strategy given that the nearest Allied fighter base was at *Vella Lavella* 140 miles away, with bombers 180 miles away at Munda Point Airfield. However, it was a challenge which Major-General Nathan Twining, now commander of COMAIRSOL (Commander of Air Forces in the *Solomons*), with a force of some 650 combat aircraft, felt capable of meeting.

The Bombing of Bougainville and Rabaul: During October, Major-General Twining's bombers hammered repeatedly at Japanese airfields on *Bougainville* with as many as ninety aircraft used in a single raid. His AIRSOL (Air Solomons) units comprised units of the New Zealand Air Force as well as bombers of the Thirteenth Air Force and 1st and 2nd Marine Air Wings. Japanese airfields were struck particularly hard at *Kahilia* and *Kara*, but attacks were also made on *Balalele*, *Buka*, *Choiseul*, *Kieta* and the *Treasuries*. By the end of the month it was apparent that the enemy had been worn down. The final four missions of the month were undertaken without fighter escort.

In support of the attacks made by Major-General Twining's AIRSOL (Air Solomons) forces, Lieutenant-General George Kenney, Allied air commander in the *Southwest Pacific*, launched an air campaign against Rabaul in mid-October with the aim of reducing its ability to strike at the planned Allied invasion of *Bougainville*. On 11 October a photographic reconnaissance mission showed that there were 128 bombers and 145 fighters stationed at Rabaul. Lieutenant-General Kenney's Fifth Air Force launched 349 aircraft, 213 bombers and 125 P-38s against them on 12 October. It was the largest air raid to date in the *Pacific War*. Three large Japanese merchantmen were sunk as well as many smaller boats. Ammunition dumps were blown up and an estimated 100 aircraft were destroyed. Fortunately for the Japanese, a week of storms and heavy rain prevented any sustained pounding of its port and airfields. Although a raid by fifty B-25 Mitchells was delivered on 18 October, another six days of inclement weather prevented any further attacks on Rabaul until 23 October. Then six fine days allowed continuous bombing. The campaign reached its crescendo on 2 November; 72 B-25 Mitchells and 80 Lightning P-38s made a daring low-level bombing and strafing attack on Simpson Harbor. It was a costly attack. Nine P-38s and eight B-25s were shot down or crashed.

In addition to the air attacks, Halsey's Task Force 38 comprising the veteran USS *Saratoga* and the new light carrier USS *Princeton*, that he had persuaded Nimitz to release to him, joined forces with Rear-Admiral Merrill's Task Force 39 comprising four new light cruisers, USS *Montpelier*, USS *Cleveland*, USS *Denver* and USS *Columbia*. They *rendezvoused* off Buka and Bonis Airfields in the early hours of 1 November and pounded them with 2,700 rounds of five-and six-inch shells. The cruisers then retreated to *Shortland Island* where they shelled Japanese garrisons at Poporang, Ballalo and Faisi. Meanwhile, as dawn broke, Halsey, bringing his aircraft carriers in range of Rabaul for the first time, launched an attack against Buka Airfield with 15 dive-bombers, 11 torpedo bombers and 18 fighters. A second wave of 21 dive-bombers, and 14 fighters again attacked *Buka* and its harbor mid-morning. Most importantly the two airfields nearest the planned landing point at *Empress Augusta Bay* had been rendered unusable.

The losses incurred by Japan in the attacks on its airfields in early and mid-October 1943 forced Admiral Koga to make the most unpalatable of decisions. He was now made to pay dearly for his repeated earlier refusals to provide Vice-Admiral Kusaka with reinforcements. His fleet carriers, *Zuikaku, Shokaku* and *Zuiho* were stripped of 82 fighters, 45 dive-bombers and 40 torpedo bombers that were sent south to reinforce Vice-Admiral Kusaka's dwindling air fleet at Rabaul. In addition a total 250 aircraft from Vice-Admiral Jisaburo Ozawa's air fleet were loaned to Rabaul for ten days to make up what was hoped would be temporary shortages. As Admiral Fukudome later noted, the carrier planes were scheduled only for defensive actions. It was a desperate gamble, particularly as carrier pilots took longer to train than 'land' pilots. Fukudome observed that when in the middle of this loan period the American forces' offensive against *Bougainville* commenced, Kusaka "just couldn't stand by and not employ them."[6] For the time being Japan's most expensive asset, its carrier fleet, was made inoperable; for the longer term, the quality of its carrier crews, already weakened, would be furthered degraded.

Bougainville Invaded: On 1 November 1943 the 3rd US Marine Division and I-Amphibious Corps landed at Cape Torokina at the northern head of *Empress Augusta Bay* on the west coast of *Bougainville* and secured a beachhead so that the Seabees could immediately start construction of an airfield. Intelligence had correctly forecast that there were fewer than 300 Japanese troops in the vicinity of Cape Torokina and nearby *Purata Island*. On landing, the main enemy turned out to be the heavy surf; a Marine platoon sergeant remembered, "the closer we got to the beach the swells became greater and finally we were in a kind of canyon . . . it just pitched our landing craft right up on the beach."[7] He was more fortunate than some. Many of the following LCVPs (Landing Craft, Vehicle Personnel) smashed into some that had already beached, damaging many beyond repair. With the shoreline littered with smashed or broaching boats, some LCVP's had to dump their unfortunate Marines into deep water, forcing them to struggle ashore with their equipment, all the while pounded by crashing waves.

Lieutenant-General Alexander Vandegrift, the Marine Corp's 'Commandant elect' in Washington, who had been urgently recalled to action after Major-General Barrett's death before the start of Operation CHERRYBLOSSOM, had gone ashore from the USS *George Clymer* and was himself lucky to escape being crushed to death when he tried to get back on board. His Chief of Staff who viewed the episode recalled: "He darn near got swamped right on the beach there . . . the surf began to break heavily . . . I was standing on the beach, helpless, and I could see the Commandant of the Marine Corps about to be upended right underneath the broached boat."[8] Vandegrift survived and was soon back in Washington.

At 7.18 a.m. a first Japanese air strike was beaten off by P-38s with the loss of seven out of their thirty Zeros. By the end of the day 21 Zeros had been downed along with a 'Betty' and 4 'Vals'—25 Japanese aircraft in total for the loss of just one Wildcat fighter. The Allied air force pilots were to be kept busy, often being required to fly for eight hours a day. In spite of the complaints of Major-Generals Harmon and Twining, newer generations of fighters such as the Lockheed P-38 Lightning and the Corsair were scarce and they were still forced to rely occasionally on planes such as the P-39 Airacobra, which was unusable over 17,000 feet. Furthermore the Douglas P-70 Nighthawk was ill-equipped to counter skilful Japanese night attacks.

As they moved ashore the 9th Marines discovered that the beaches rose sharply for about ten yards then fell away into a virtually impassable swamp. As one participant recorded, it "was like running across thirty feet of the Sahara and suddenly dropping off into the Everglades."[9] Vice-Admiral 'Bull' Halsey would later note that the terrain was "worse than anything ever encountered before in the South Pacific."[10] The Marines had to use logs to cross to find firmer ground. By nightfall they managed to establish a perimeter that tied into the 3rd Marines on their right. However, because of the chaotic landing quantities of equipment had been dumped far down the coast and much of it was never recovered. Fortunately there was little resistance from the Japanese although two Marines were killed by machine gun fire during the landing.

On *Purata Island* there were minor skirmishes. One Marine engaged in an hour-long shoot-out with a Japanese soldier across the island. Having failed to kill each other, the Japanese soldier, having reached the beach on the other side, threw himself into the water. The Marine recounted the story:

> I don't know where in hell he thought he was going. I was
> too Goddamn mad to shoot him. I threw down my gun
> and helmet, took a good run and dove in after him. The

little bastard was scared to death. I grabbed him by the neck and pulled him toward the beach. That was the hardest part—getting him back on solid ground. I couldn't get him up on the beach but went to work on him in shallow water. Then I dragged him up on the sand and kicked his head apart. The slimy bastard. I'd been chasing him for over an hour.[11]

Inland at Cape Torokina there was one main point of Japanese resistance. Twenty-five log and earthen pillboxes had been constructed around the perimeter of the cape and only three were destroyed by the largely ineffectual naval bombardment that had preceded the landing. After the war, Frederick Henderson, a Navy officer who took part in the operation complained: "it was a disaster, the gunfire plan. I am convinced that if they had taken our plan [to bring the cruisers in to 3,000–4,000 yards from the beach] it would have been a cakewalk to have gone in and taken those beaches."[12] Even Vice-Admiral Wilkinson, who commanded the invasion force, would later admit that the Naval bombardment had been inadequate with a high proportion of shells falling short. The crews of the new warships coming from America were often inexperienced and inadequately trained. He further noted: "Poor anti-aircraft gunnery also characterizes most of our new ships on first arrival in the South Pacific."[13] It was a complaint that was to be repeated in the beach assaults that followed in the *Central Pacific* island groups of the *Carolines, Marshalls* and *Marianas.*

The defense made by a handful of Japanese troops at Cape Torokina was a sign of the problems to come on more heavily defended beach garrisons in the *Central Pacific.* The Japanese network of pillboxes and entrenchments were finally taken in fierce close quarter fighting: "some of the bitterest hand-to-hand fighting of the campaign took place here in the narrow trenches outside the pillboxes," recorded the 3rd Marines official historians Robert Arthur and Kenneth Cohlmia, "Men fought with clubbed weapons, knives and fists."[14] The most stubborn of the pillboxes, and the one that contained a 75 mm field gun, was stormed by Sergeant Robert Owens and four other soldiers. Owens was awarded a Medal of Honor for this action. After the firefight 153 Japanese bodies were counted.

The following day heavy equipment such as bulldozers were disgorged from the LSTs (Landing Ship, Tank). Seabees immediately set about building workshops and storage facilities. As the Seabees began to erect their temporary city, communication teams waded through the swamps or crawled through bush, sometimes under sniper fire, to lay communication wires to the front line troops. As one commentator observed, "Working parties were punching with every last ounce of blood to get ammunition, oil, supplies, vehicles, rations, and water out of the boats and above the high water line."[15]

Inevitably the narrow beach became jammed with supplies until a way could be found to transport *matériel* across the swamps to higher ground. At 5 p.m. on Day-2,

2 November, Vice-Admiral Wilkinson ordered his transports to withdraw even if they had not finished unloading because he feared a Japanese cruiser attack. By dusk a perimeter between 600 and 1,000 yards had been established. The Marines had dug in. As one Marine recalled,

> These were trained men who knew the law of the jungle:
> each man must be in his foxhole at dark and there he must
> stay until dawn. Anyone out of foxhole during the hours
> of darkness was a Jap. Sudden death for the careless . . .
> with only centipedes and lizards and scorpions and
> mosquitoes begging to be acquainted—wet, cold,
> exhausted, but unable to sleep—you lay there and
> shivered and thought and hated and prayed. But you
> stayed there . . . For it was great to be alive.[16]

Strategic Considerations and Other Challenges on Bougainville: Whatever Major-General Twining's technical and medical problems, the Allied air operations worked well enough that the Japanese forces, estimated at 20,000 troops, clustered around the shores of southern *Bougainville*, found themselves outflanked and cut off from supply. Moreover to strike at Cape Torokina overland from the north, Japanese troops would have to trek through mountainous jungle. Vice-Admiral Halsey had no intention of capturing the whole island immediately. The establishment of advance airbases to be able to challenge Japanese air power in Rabaul and to disrupt supply to the 50,000 Japanese army personnel of the Seventeenth Army on *Bougainville* was enough. Halsey could leave *Bougainville*'s jungle and its climate to ravage an increasingly isolated and starving Japanese Army.

In this respect MacArthur's strategies for forward development by the construction of advanced airbases was little different to those of his counterparts. However, whereas the Japanese, at the start of the war, had in most cases swept aside the Allied armies in South East Asia which outnumbered them, capturing large numbers of prisoners along the way—in the Allied advance toward Rabaul and beyond, MacArthur's forces did not try to defeat the enemy in open battle. Japanese armies had destroyed US and British forces by using surprise, speedy advance and the use of rapid flanking movements. Japan's tactics had been helped by the inept defense and poor skills of the western armies. By contrast Japanese commanders proved themselves able to construct highly sophisticated defense systems so that even their outnumbered forces could hold up Allied advances. Allied tactics therefore were to build the beachheads for airbases and then to defend them stoutly. It was a tactic that had worked for Lieutenant-General Vandegrift at *Guadalcanal* and would be re-employed repeatedly in the *Pacific War*.

The Battle of Empress Augusta Bay: [**Map: 25.2**] American deceptions regarding their invasion of *Bougainville* had worked. The fleet of US transports was spotted leaving

Guadalcanal, which had now become the Allies' main logistics base in the *Solomons*, on the morning of 31 October. At 10 a.m. Vice-Admiral Sentaro Omori was ordered to intercept. At 3 p.m. he set sail with two heavy cruisers, *Myoko* and *Haguro* and two light cruisers, *Sendai* and *Nagara*, in the direction of the *Shortland Islands* believing that this would be Halsey's next target. When search planes failed to find the target he gave up, returned and dropped anchor at Rabaul at 9 a.m. on 1 November. No sooner had he done this than he learned that the Americans were already on the beaches of Cape Torokina.

Six hours later Omori set out again, this time supported by a further six destroyers and met up with six destroyer transports carrying troops to set ashore on *Bougainville*. Omori concluded that it was too late to send troops and persuaded Vice-Admiral Kusaka and Admiral Koga that he could win an engagement with Rear-Admiral 'Ping' Wilkinson's covering fleet—leaving the US Marines stranded.

However, in the first major attempt to dislodge the Marines from *Empress Augusta Bay*, he was ill prepared, with his forces never having trained together for night action. Against them was Rear-Admiral Aaron 'Tip' Merrill's Task Force 39, with four light cruisers and eight destroyers, which had accompanied the amphibious landing at Cape Torokina. Merrill with his four new light cruisers was outgunned and was necessarily cautious regarding the Japanese fleet's destroyers equipped with Long Lance torpedoes. Merrill thus planned to 'liberate' his destroyers in the hope that their advance attack would intercept Omori before the Long Lances could be put to use. As for Omori, he was disadvantaged by lack of knowledge as to the whereabouts of Merrill's forces. Moreover he had to rely on spotter aircraft because of the paucity of the Imperial Japanese Navy's radar. After the war Omori would inform his interrogators: "We had some modified aircraft radar sets in action but they were unreliable. I do not know whether the sets or operators were poor, but I did not have confidence in them."[17] By contrast, at 2.30 a.m. on 2 November, USS *Montpellier*'s radar picked up Omori's fleet 35,900 yards out and set about implementing Merrill's battle plan.

In a confusing night action in the early hours, fighting split up into three interconnected engagements. The light cruiser *Sendai* launched eight torpedoes aimed at Merrill's cruisers but only managed a single strike on destroyer USS *Foote*. Burke's 45th Destroyer Division attacked Omori's left flank but missed with all twenty-five torpedoes when the Japanese Admiral coincidentally implemented a hard right turn just as they were fired. Merrill's cruisers opened fire on the *Sendai* and a hit with a 6-inch shell jammed its rudder before explosions ripped through the ship causing it to sink. No fewer than four Japanese ships managed to collide with each other causing considerable damage. The Japanese destroyer *Hatsukaze* was struck by Omori's flagship *Myoko* and was so crippled that she was easily battered to a sad end when Burke's reformed 45th Destroyer Division with five destroyers found her at 5.30 a.m.; *Hatsukaze* sank at 5.40 a.m.

USS *Spence* and USS *Thatcher* had also collided though they were able to continue to fight. Japanese ships' ineffectual radar meant that they found it difficult to locate the enemy while miscommunication and misidentification similarly prevented Merrill's forces from making concerted attacks. When hits were eventually scored on Vice-Admiral Omori's flagship, *Myoko*, four of them were duds and the other two failed to slow the heavy cruiser. At 3.20 a.m. Omori's heavy cruisers were finally able to open fire and landed three shells on USS *Denver*; luckily for its crew all three rounds failed to detonate. Nevertheless the damaged *Denver* slowed down, whereupon the accompanying cruisers correspondingly reduced speed. After the brief gun engagement Vice-Admiral Omori retired in the mistaken belief that his Long Lances had sunk or heavily damaged Merrill's cruisers. Omori had received a false report claiming "one torpedo hit on leading US cruiser, two torpedo hits on second US cruiser, two torpedo hits on third US cruiser. Shell fire also reported on US Force."[18]

As dawn broke Merrill urgently called for all available fighters to come to his aid to see off an expected air attack from Rabaul. Bad weather delayed them and only 8 Hellcats, 1 Marine Corsair, 3 P-38s and 4 New Zealand P-40s managed to take off. They shot down eight of the 98 planes dispatched from Rabaul, mostly recently arrived Zeros as well as 18 'Val' dive-bombers. Rear-Admiral Merrill's forces formed a defensive circular cordon and opened fire on the incoming planes at 14,000 yards. The ensuing wall of fire claimed seventeen Japanese aircraft. Merrill's fleet sustained just two hits; one of these on the USS *Montpelier* caused minor damage and killed one unlucky American sailor.

By daybreak Japan had lost a cruiser and destroyer sunk and several more ships heavily damaged. Apart from heavy damage to one destroyer, by good fortune and the radar and communication deficiencies of his enemies, Merrill's forces escaped from the *Battle of Empress Bay* without serious harm. Halsey would reflect that the Japanese naval assault on his amphibious landing at Cape Torokina "was the most desperate emergency that confronted me in my entire term as COMSOPAC (Commander South Pacific)."[19] Remarkably, faced by superior forces, at the *Battle of Empress Augusta Bay*, Merrill not only survived but also scored a minor victory in what turned out to be the last major naval engagement of the *Solomons* campaign.

US Carrier Raids on Rabaul: Vice-Admiral Omori's force withdrew to Rabaul. It was joined there by four more cruisers and numbers of destroyers that had been sent from *Truk*. The hitherto reluctant Koga had, according to Admiral Fukudome, decided to commit some of the best units from the hitherto undamaged Second Fleet "to cooperate with the carrier-based planes which had been sent from Vice-Admiral Ozawa's fleet in order to check the [US] *Bougainville* operations."[20] The Imperial Japanese fleet, so sure footed in the early days of the war, was now hesitant—mixing decision with indecision. However, it has to be seen that their now diminished forces were hopelessly compromised by the need to sustain operations against MacArthur's advance up the east coast of New Guinea as well as Halsey's rampage up the *Solomons* towards Rabaul. It was a hesitancy compounded by the increasing air superiority being established by the Allied air forces in the *South Pacific*.

Nevertheless, another Japanese attack was now planned on the landing forces at *Empress Augusta Bay*. Halsey realized that the situation for his troops on *Bougainville* was still critical. Unless he was able to ward off the new naval threat that intelligence had informed him was on the way, his forces on *Bougainville* would not receive the planned reinforcement transports bringing the 37th Division from *Guadalcanal*. He was prepared to throw everything at Rabaul to stop their next naval attack, including risking his precious carriers: "perhaps the success of the South Pacific War, hung on it being stopped."[21] Against conventional wisdom that carriers should not be exposed to land-based attack, Halsey was prepared to risk Rear-Admiral Sherman's Task Force including carriers USS *Saratoga* and USS *Princeton* to a force of over 200 Japanese planes assembled at Rabaul.

The risks for Halsey were personal as well as professional. "I sincerely expected both air groups to be cut to pieces and both carriers stricken, if not lost. (I tried not to remember my son Bill was aboard one of them), but we could not let the men at Tokorina be wiped out while we stood by and wrung our hands."[22] Halsey's Chief of Staff, Admiral Carney, recalled that before making the decision to attack with his carriers, his commander "suddenly looked 150 years old."[23]

On 5 November 1943, helped by bad weather, a surprise air raid on Rabaul by a US aircraft carrier force consisting of USS *Saratoga* and USS *Princeton* and led by Rear-Admiral Frederick Sherman caused heavy damage to four cruisers in harbor; *Maya*'s engine room was hit by a bomb killing seventy; heavy damage was caused by a 500 lb bomb on *Mogami; Takao* took a double blow from two 500 lb bombs while three 500 lb bombs that narrowly missed *Atago* nevertheless killed twenty-three seamen and caused severe damage to the ship's plating. Two other cruisers and three destroyers also suffered light damage. Captain George Chandler, a P-38 fighter pilot described how "There were B-24 bombers up high and B-25 bombers attacking right down on the deck dropping 'frag' bombs on the airplanes along the runways . . . we did our best work at high altitude, but we also took part in combat a thousand feet off the ground."[24]

A cautious Admiral Mineichi Koga withdrew his forces back to *Truk*. The Japanese Naval threat to the invasion of *Bougainville* was ended. A Japanese naval officer later admitted that they had given up on *Bougainville* mainly because of "the serious damage received by several Second Fleet cruisers at Rabaul by carrier attack . . ."[25] The success of the raid on Rabaul left Halsey ecstatic. "It is real music to me and opens the stops for a funeral dirge for Tojo's Rabaul."[26]

Given breathing space by the attack on Rabaul, by 8 November some 34,000 troops of the US 37th Division were landed and digging in on *Bougainville*. Before that Nimitz, in the midst of preparing his own thrust through the *Central Pacific* had finally relented and acceded to Halsey's request for reinforcement by sending Rear-Admiral Alfred Montgomery's Task Force 38. The new carriers and their escorts arrived too late to participate in Sherman's first raid. No matter. On 11 November, six days after the spectacularly successful attack on Rabaul, a follow-up attack was launched by Sherman's carriers as well as Montgomery's recently arrived Task Force, comprising new fleet carriers USS *Bunker Hill*, USS *Essex* and USS *Independence*. The cruiser *Agano*, which had remained behind after the 5 November raid was torpedoed and badly damaged while thirty-five Japanese aircraft out of 120 launched in a counter-attack on Montgomery's carriers were shot down with no damage to his ships.

Disastrously for Admiral Koga, the decision to send his carrier pilots to Rabaul had failed spectacularly. Over the course of the 'loan' of his aircraft and crew, Koga's air fleet had lost 43 of its 82 Zeros, 38 of its 45 dive-bombers, 34 of its 40 torpedo planes and all 6 of its 'Judy' spotter planes. Ominously for the future, Koga had lost eighty-six of his 192 experienced pilots and crew. The 'loan' had achieved little to prevent the occupation of *Bougainville* and did minimal damage to Nimitz's fleet; the debt incurred could never be repaid. The reality of the failure of Japan's Navy air arm did not percolate through to Japan. Fantastical reports were constantly relayed by the *Naikaku Johokyoku* (Cabinet Bureau of Information) pointing to a victorious Operation RO-GO; a series of spectacular air battles over *Bougainville* had supposedly been won by the Japanese Navy Air Force. Newspapers reported victories that added up to the destruction of 5 American battleships, 10 aircraft carriers, 19 cruisers, and 7 destroyers. The truth was that for all their efforts only two cruisers, the USS *Birmingham* and USS *Denver* had taken torpedo hits—both repairable.

By mid-November, it was becoming increasing difficult for Vice-Admiral Kusaka to sustain air attacks against the convoys that were feeding supplies into *Empress Augusta Bay*. On 12 November, out of 113 Zeros available at Rabaul, 25 needed major repair while a further 29 were scheduled for maintenance leaving just 59 operational. Only 17 out of 36 Mitsubishi G4M 'Betty' bombers were serviceable. It was a similar story with the assorted 'Vals,' 'Kates,' and 'Judys.' Out of an aggregate of 202 aircraft on that day, perhaps as few as 110 were serviceable. That did not mean they could all fly. At any one time it was estimated that at least a third of available crews were grounded with malaria or other tropical ailments. Maintenance crews, stretched at the best of times, were also debilitated. Given that Japanese crews, unlike their American counterparts, were never granted 'rest and recuperation' respites, the operational quality of pilots and navigators inevitably deteriorated. Death was the only release from an individual pilot's declining spiral of operational performance.

Nevertheless Kusaka persevered with what resources were available. On 17 November, nine 'Betty's' and five 'Kates' launched an early morning attack on a convoy of LSTs (Landing Ship, Tank) and APDs (fast transport destroyers) escorted by destroyers. The USS *McKean*, an APD, took a torpedo hit from Superior-Flight Petty Officer, Gintaro Kobayashi, and sank within fifteen minutes. The *McKean* was a Wickes Class destroyer built in 1918 which was refitted and commissioned as an APD in 1940 In Japan the attack was claimed as a major victory against a carrier force and was optimistically described as the *Fifth Air Battle of Bougainville*. Four Japanese aircraft did not return and several more were damaged. In a raid later that day, 10 'Vals' and 55 Zeros attacked another convoy. No ships were sunk. Ten Japanese planes were shot down. Thereafter raids were largely limited to light nighttime attacks.

Whatever the reports in the press, troops on the ground in Rabaul knew that the battle to sustain Japan's *South Pacific* garrison was drawing to a close. Virtually uninterrupted heavy bombing in October and November persuaded the *Kempeitai* that non-essential personnel should be sent home. Lieutenant Matsuda, who had written so gushingly about Rabaul when he arrived in 1943, later wrote: "Commander Kikuchi visited chief of staff Kato to advise that non-combatants, such as nurses and comfort women, be sent back to the homeland at the earliest opportunity . . . The reason for it was that keeping women on the battlefield in the fight to the finish was not a humane thing . . ."[27]

The Imperial Japanese Navy would take six months to replenish its carrier pilots with less well-trained and inexperienced replacements. In the meantime the carrier fleet itself, Japan's most expensive and precious strategic asset, was forced to remain idle in *Truk* as Nimitz began his island hop through the *Central Pacific*.

The Battle of Cape St. George: A final minor naval engagement of the *Solomon Islands'* campaign took place on 25 November at Cape St. George off *Buka Island* on the northern tip of *Bougainville* where Japan's main airbase was located. Five destroyers had been sent from Rabaul to deliver 900 troop reinforcements to the island while at the same time taking off valuable naval air technicians from an airbase that had been made largely inoperable.

Intercepted by Captain Burke's 45th Destroyer Division, a force of five US destroyers, *Onami* was hit by a spread of fifteen torpedoes and immediately exploded and sank; in the same attack· *Makinami* was torpedoed, broke in two and then was finished off by gunfire, while *Yuguri* was sunk after a long chase back toward Rabaul. Caught by three US destroyers, the *Yuguri* had been pounded by shellfire and suffered a devastating explosion at 3.05 a.m. Some 630 Japanese sailors were killed in the battle.

The minor action at the *Battle of Cape St. George* brought an end to the long running saga of the 'Tokyo Express.' It was the last of the fifteen naval engagements of the *Solomon Islands* Campaign, twelve of them surface battles. Post-war historians have tended to look at the *Battle of Midway* to define the defeat of the Japanese Imperial Navy but in reality it was the long attrition of the *Solomons* Campaign from June 1942 to November 1943 that neutered the fighting capability of Japan's Navy. Halsey may have missed *Midway* through illness but he more than made up for it in the long-running series of naval engagements over the next seventeen months—though without the defining fleet battle victory that his ego demanded. From the beginning of 1944 the remaining Japanese troops on *Bougainville*, some 40,000 in total, were effectively abandoned. Allied air and sea power was such that troops and supplies could no longer be moved even by small craft either by day or night.

The Battles for the Airfield Perimeters: [**Map: 25.3**] By19 November, the remaining elements of the 3rd Marine Division had been landed at *Empress Augusta Bay* in addition to the US Army's 37th Infantry Division. Their advance through the swamps that stretched inland made heavy going. There were days when 300 yards was all that could be achieved; some nights soldiers would have to sleep upright in swampy water with their weapons tied to trees. Jungle patrols became the normal routine of the Marines. Although the sparse Japanese forces were waiting for the arrival of reinforcements and were averse to major engagements, ambushes remained a constant danger. Japanese snipers were a constant source of fear. "Snipers were the worst," according to Adam GiGenaro, squad leader with the 3rd Marine Division on *Bougainville*, "We dreaded them. You didn't know where the fire was coming."[28] Paths were overgrown and the dense undergrowth gave ample cover for troops lying in wait. Marines added dogs, German Shepherds and Dobermans, to their patrols; their senses were much sharper than those of their human handlers. In the *Bougainville* campaign where the Japanese were unable to bring up much artillery, the K9 (dog) companies proved useful though in later island campaigns heavy gunfire would drive the dogs mad.

Expansion of the beachhead eventually brought the 37th Division up against determined Japanese troops that Lieutenant-General Hyakutake had sent overland, hacking their way through the jungle. In addition, on 6 November four Japanese destroyers made a daring run to drop 800 troops at *Koromokina* adjacent to Cape Torokina. It had taken him some time to work out that that the landing at Cape Torokina was not a diversionary raid similar to the one carried out earlier at *Choiseul Island*.

Fierce battles now raged along the coast to the south at Koiari, as well as at 'Piva Trail,' 'Coconut Grove' and 'Piva Forks.' On 9 November heavy fighting along the 'Piva Trails' leading to Piva Village cost the lives of twelve Marines as well as thirty other casualties. The bodies of over 140 Japanese would later be discovered. In the craggy hills and ridges overlooking the beachhead and the planned airstrips, the Japanese forces embedded artillery positions, which rained fire on the key US position below. Nevertheless by 10 November the beachhead perimeter was expanded inland far enough for the Seabees to start the first fighter landing strip. Four weeks later it was ready to take forty Chance Vought F4U Corsair fighters. From Cape Torokina the flight to Rabaul and back was just within the 250-mile fighter radius that was the key measure for any American island 'hop' in the *South Pacific* campaigns. The ability to provide fighter protection to bombers flying to Rabaul effectively rang the death knell on Japan's key *South Pacific* garrison. On 18 November a firefight involving Marine patrols expanded into a week-long *Battle of Piva Forks*. Lieutenant Steve Cibek gave a lurid account of conditions:

> We were a veteran company, with Guadalcanal behind us,
> and we thought we knew jungle. But here on Bougainville
> we were battling a jungle such as we had never dreamed
> of. For nineteen days we struggled in miasmal swamps,
> fought vines that wrapped themselves around our necks
> like whips, birds that dived at us like screaming Stukas,
> bats whose wings whirred like falling artillery shells, and
> snakes and lizards and insects without name or number.

> For nineteen days we attacked this natural enemy with
> our machetes and knives, hacking our way through almost
> solid barricades of vegetation run riot.[29]

Cibek would later have a ridge named in his honor after he managed to take it and then used Japanese dug foxholes to hold his position over the next three days.

'Cibek's Ridge' became an important observation post. Most usefully they spotted a Japanese artillery unit that began pounding Marine battalions as they assembled for a major advance on 24 November. Fourteen Marines were killed and many more wounded. However, fire directed from 'Cibek's Ridge' silenced the battery within minutes and allowed the 2nd and 3rd Marine battalions to advance; as one of them recalled, "For the first hundred yards both battalions advanced abreast through a weird, stinking, ploughed-up jungle of shattered trees and butchered Japs. Some hung out of trees, some lay crumpled and twisted beside their shattered weapons, some were covered by chunks of jagged logs and earth, a blasted bunker, their self made tomb."[30] As had become increasingly frequent in the jungle engagements of the *South Pacific*, it was weight of artillery fire that was the key to US dominance.

During the battle, 'Thanksgiving' was celebrated. Turkeys sent by Major-General Geiger arrived with Marine cooks on 23 November and they were prepared the night before the attack. Frontline troops were not forgotten. Relays of carrying parties dodged snipers to take turkey to the front. A Marine observed,

> Some meat got there, some didn't. But it was a good stunt
> and a necessity; no one would have been forgiven if it had
> been left to rot down at the Division Commissary just
> because we had a battle! The men sat on logs eating
> turkey. Nearby a Jap lay rotting in the swamp. Heads and
> arms of dead Japs floated in the nearby jungle streams.[31]

By the end of Thanksgiving Day the *Battle of Piva Forks* had been won and the Japanese driven off the high ground that overlooked the projected site for the US bomber fields. A total of 1,107 Japanese dead were counted. Marine casualties were 115 dead and wounded. It had been a fierce fight but the back of Japanese resistance at *Empress Augusta Bay* had been broken.

Nonetheless the Marines still had to fight to clear the remaining Japanese units from strong defensive positions on higher ground. Foremost of these was so-called 'Hellzapoppin Ridge' from where it would have been possible to rain down fire on the proposed bomber fields. Three patrol units from the Marine Parachute battalion began the attack on 9 December. A Japanese counter-attack killed twelve Marines and wounded a further twenty-six. From 9 December to 21 December Marine Battalions took over the task of taking 'Hellzapoppin Ridge.' Major-General Roy Geiger called for air attacks to reduce the Japanese resistance; although some US bombers hit their mark on 13 December, another bomb landed on Marine positions north of the ridge and caused two Marine deaths from 'friendly fire.' It was a frequent hazard of war in the *South Pacific*. A further seventeen bomber sorties on 14 December and eighteen sorties on 15 December began to diminish the defenders' resistance and three days later hundred pound bombs were dropped with delayed fuses. Further punishment on Japanese positions was meted out by batteries of American 155 mm howitzers, which rained shells on the enemy.

'Hellzapoppin Ridge' was taken on 18 December after eleven days of fierce fighting. Then 'Hill 600A' was taken during a brief skirmish a week later on Christmas Eve. Just one Marine was killed and the Marines repulsed, but inexplicably the Japanese abandoned their positions and slipped away into the jungle. It was the last offensive engagement by the Marines on *Bougainville*.

By Christmas 1943 a coastal cantonment 11,000 yards long and projecting 8,000 yards inland from the beachhead had been established. The northern line was entrenched on steep hills while the eastern flank was protected by marsh, jungle and kunai grass. Within the perimeter work began on an internal network of roads to allow rapid redeployment of troops. Major-General Robert Beightler, the only officer to command a division, the 37th 'Buckeye' Division from Ohio, for the duration of the war, was an enthusiastic road builder. Infantryman Marshall Chaney of the 37th Division recalled, "On Bougainville they started with basically no roads at all, but doggone, he [Beightler] had some all-weather roads and feeder roads built . . . after the war they kept him happy by putting him in charge of the Ohio Highway Deparment."[32]

With Japanese artillery attacks on the Seabees operations eradicated, preparation for two more airstrips could be more rapidly advanced. Piva Uncle Airfield was prepared to base 126 light bombers and 40 fighters, while Piva Yoke was planned as a fighter field to accommodate 115 aircraft. It was a herculean task of infrastructure building that required the carving out of cantonment areas from the jungle and the building of living accommodation, clerical offices, medical centers, storage warehouses, munitions dumps and gasoline tanks.

One project involved the building of a ration dump for the Quartermaster Corps. Six bulldozers and twenty dump trucks cleared an area the size of four city blocks over a two-month period. Sawmills were set up to make lumber from felled coconut trees. Basic storage sheds and offices were constructed on elevated platforms to protect supplies from hungry rodents and damp. A further 4.5 square mile area was cleared for the setting up of a fuel dump to supply the projected three airfields.

The 'oil tank farm' constructed to supply three airfields would eventually consist of one 10,000-barrel tank and eighteen 1,000-barrel tanks as well as tanker mooring, underwater pipelines, and five miles of overland piping. Seabees worked at night, sometimes interrupted by sniper fire, to clear the jungle and lay down steel matting for the runways. The bomber field was completed by 10 December allowing for the arrival of seventeen F4U Corsairs of Marine Squadron VMF-216 as well as six SDBs Dauntless dive-bombers, and four transport planes. With logistical supply now possible by air, the development of the cantonment at *Empress Augusta Bay* could be even further speeded up. Having completed Piva Uncle Airfield, work now began on Piva Yoke, which was completed by 3 January 1944.

Hospitals and staff quarters were also erected. Buildings were constructed for the Chaplain and the Red Cross. By spring 1944, 'Loewe's *Bougainville*' movie theater had been set up. More usefully the Seabees built bridges and walkways across streams and swamps.

The Seabees' building work was vital but at the perimeter it was the Marines who had to construct their own defensive pillboxes. Usually 12 foot to 15 foot square and 8 foot deep, "the soil was mostly sand and easy to dig," noted one rifleman, "We would then reinforce them with other trees. We left firing ports to the front and we left inclines to the rear to crawl out."[33] Learning from the Japanese, pillboxes were interconnected with trenches. Usually four to six men would occupy each emplacement. The pillboxes were

> wired in behind double-apron or concertina barbed wire. In front of the wire there were minefields . . . flares tied to trees and set off by pull wires, flashlights; thermite grenades; and cans full of gasoline. Grenades with wires attached were set up as booby traps along obvious approach routes. Oil drums, each with scrap metal packed around a Bangalore Torpedo, were wired for electrical detonation.[34]

The Marines prepared for anything that the Japanese could throw at them.

Foot Rot and Ulcers: If the Japanese had temporarily gone quiet, the climate and conditions on *Bougainville* were enemies that did not go away. Chuck Albes, a 3rd Marines intelligence officer, recalled, "The following campaigns we participated in on Guam and Iwo Jima were far more violent than Bougainville. I came a lot closer to being killed during both of those campaigns. But of all the twenty-eight months I spent overseas nothing compared to Bougainville for miserable living conditions."[35]

The climate was foul, alternating between the baking hot and the damp and humid. Albes complained: "The sun was so hot the mud would dry and there would be clouds of dust. In late afternoon, however, the rain clouds would build up over Mount Bagana . . . and by five o'clock in the afternoon it was absolutely pouring. The next day the cycle repeated itself."[36] Daytime temperatures reached 100 degrees; more debilitating was the damp of the swamps that meant that Marines' feet were never dry. Eugene Edwards, a sergeant in an amphibious tractor battalion, moaned, "Your feet began to rot, your clothes were stinking, you would get skin ulcers between your legs . . . and were just downright miserable . . ." To compound the misery there were "Bugs, spiders and ungodly numbers of insects biting on you."[37]

Similarly Colonel Frazer West noted, "Jungle rot was the major problem . . . Got primarily on scalp, under arms, and in genital areas . . . it was miserable—no other word for it." As for jungle ulcers Frazer West described the only cure: "I'd get the corpsman to light a match to a razor blade, split the ulcer open, and squeeze sulfanilamide powder in it. I must have had at one time thirty ulcers on me."[38] It was probably worse for the lower ranks, and, as for the poorly supplied Japanese, conditions must have been abominable. Diarrhea was an everyday occurrence. If it was not treated it could easily turn to dysentery that could be fatal. It did not help that getting troops to observe even basic sanitary rules while fighting was extremely difficult. A Marine sanitary team complained, "Troops in combat are very lax about personal measures."[39] However, even troops behind the lines were typically careless because "men in the rear areas wore very few clothes and did not use bed nets, repellents, nor Freon Pyrethrum dispensers to any appreciable degree."[40] More esoteric diseases were also picked up including lymphatic filariasis—carried by blood-sucking black flies that deposited roundworm parasites into the victims' bloodstream. It caused skin rashes, urticarial papules (fluid-filled red bumps on the skin), abdominal pain and occasionally blindness. In some cases victims suffered from elephantiasis, the most extreme symptom of filariasis, which thickened the skin and swelled legs; attacks on the male genitals could lead to a patient's scrotum swelling to the size of a basketball.

Furthermore the low marshy ground of *Empress Augusta Bay* was a paradise for the malaria-carrying Anopheles mosquitoes. Apart from the *Koromokina* and *Piva Rivers* there were myriads of semi-stagnant streams. Creeks between the rivers were named *Dead Jap Creek, Buir Creek* and *Seabee Creek*. Although each Marine was issued with sixty Atabrine Tablets and four bottles of insect repellent, incidence of malaria was inevitably high. A freon-pyrethrum 'bomb' was also issued per four Marines. The so-called bomb was an aerosol that had been invented in 1941 using CFC-12 gas (later of ozone destroying fame). After it was found at the beginning of the *South Pacific* campaigns in 1942 that malaria was killing five soldiers for every one killed by the Japanese, the production of the US pharmaceutical industry went into overdrive and produced over 40 million units during the course of the war. Later in the war freon bug-bombs were filled with DDT, which one army medical officer would describe as "the atomic bomb of the insect world."[41] In 1945 the *New York Times Sunday* magazine delighted in the chemical advances, "A double delight is dichloro-difluoromethane with its thirteen consonants and ten vowels" because it, "brings death to disease-carrying insects . . ."[42]

Disease did not just affect troops on the ground. The main enemy of the *Solomon Islands* Allied Air Force was also malaria, which, in the month of March 1943, had caused the loss of 72.18 days per 100 flight officers. Only with the introduction of mosquito-screened latrines later in the year did infection rates start to fall significantly. Nevertheless in December 1943, the US Thirteenth Air Force alone lost some 24,232 man-days of which just 219 could be directly linked to combat injuries. Food supply was also problematic. Pilots complained about a diet based on dehydrated eggs, Spam, stew and C-Rations. Despite the unappetizing food, Allied pilots, unlike their Japanese counterparts, did not starve and were occasionally even supplied with a bottle of beer. Furthermore Allied pilots were relieved and rotated after just six weeks of active combat; six weeks on and six weeks off became the norm.

Lieutenant-General Hyakutake's Counter-Attack: [Map: 25.3] After the establishment of a strong perimeter for the *Empress Augusta Bay* cantonment, Halsey began to implement the replacement of all the Marine forces with army troops. On 15 December, the 1st Marine Amphibious Corps was replaced by the Army's XIV Corps and two weeks later, the American Division took over from the 3rd Marine Division—the first units arriving from Fiji on Christmas morning and taking up position on the 3rd Marines left flank. In sync with these changes Major-General Geiger was replaced by Major-General Oswald Griswold.

The last regiment of the American Division arrived under the command of Colonel Joseph Bush and took up positions vacated by the Marines on the right flank. The last of the Marines finally exited *Bougainville* by the end of January. The early weeks of the year occupied the American Division with improvements to the defensive positions and the regular patroling of the perimeter. The new arrivals included the 1st Battalion of the Fiji Infantry Regiment, who were well trained and had exceptional skills as jungle fighters. They reconnoitered the coastal terrains adjacent to *Empress Augusta Bay* and distinguished themselves in a firefight with a Japanese position at Pipipaia where they killed forty-seven Japanese soldiers without incurring a single loss. This contact and others that followed convinced Major-General Griswold that a Japanese counter-attack could be expected. Under interrogation Japanese prisoners revealed that there would be a full-scale assault in early March.

By now, Lieutenant-General Hyakutake was under extreme pressure to reduce the bombing of Rabaul, which was under almost daily attack from aircraft stationed at *Empress Augusta Bay*. Heavy losses were being incurred. On 17 January 1944, 29 dive-bombers and 18 torpedo planes escorted by 70 fighters hit Rabaul, sinking 5 ships and bringing down 17 of the 70 fighters that had been sent up to intercept. Losses in the course of January were such that Admiral Koga at the end of the month sent the 2nd Air Squadron from *Truk* bringing Admiral Kurita's force back up to over 300 aircraft. It was a losing battle however, and the last major dogfight over Rabaul took place on 20 February when an incoming force of 145 aircraft was intercepted by 50 Japanese fighters; 23 Zeros, almost half of the defending fighter planes, were shot down. The end of major aerial interdiction from Rabaul was not unconnected with Vice-Admiral Marc Mitscher's dismantling of their central supply base, *Truk*, in his famous marauding attack of 17–18 February. [See **Chapter 30: Pacific Island Hop: The Gilberts, Marshalls, and Carolines**] US losses over Rabaul were by now relatively light, though on 3 January the leading Marine Corps ace, Major Gregory 'Pappy' Boyington, the charismatic leader of the 'Black Sheep' Squadron was shot down and spent the rest of the war in captivity.

Boyington, born in Coeur d'Arlene, Idaho grew up in a logging town and later in Tacoma, Washington. Starting as a Marine Corps Reserve, Boyington trained at Pensacola, Florida becoming a Marine Corps regular in July 1937. He resigned in August 1941 and signed a contract with CAMCO (Central Aircraft Manufacturing Company) that subsequently became the American Volunteer Group, better known as the 'Flying Tigers,' which served in Burma and China.

Later re-absorbed into the Marines, the scrappy, hard drinking, probably bipolar 'Pappy' Boyington commanded 214th Marine Squadron whose Chance Vought Corsair fighters became known as the 'Black Sheep' Squadron. He became a rare 'Ace in a Day' when, leading his newly formed squadron, he shot down five enemy planes. His flight commander praised his "brilliant combat record, readiness to undertake the most hazardous types of mission, and a superior type of flight leadership."[43] He was duly awarded a Medal of Honor. Overall he was credited with twenty-five kills in the *Georgia-Bougainville* Campaigns before his last action involving a four-plane sweep over Rabaul. His wingman, Captain George Ashmun, was shot down and killed, while Boyington got his twenty-sixth kill before bailing out of his stricken plane.

Boyington was picked up by a Japanese submarine and, after being moved to *Truk*, ended up at Omori Prison Camp near Tokyo. His was a rare example of health being improved in a Japanese prisoner of war camp as a result of enforced sobriety. After the war Boyington finally received his Medal of Honor from President Truman and was also awarded the Navy Cross and promoted to Colonel. A hard-drinking philanderer, he ran through a series of wives and many careers, including stints as a wrestler, and a novelist and a minor Hollywood celebrity. Boyington also appeared in a double act with pilot Masajiro Kawato, who claimed to have shot him down—though it later transpired to be a fraudulent claim. Buried at Arlington National Cemetery not far from the grave of boxing world champion Joe Lewis, a friend noted, "Pappy wouldn't have to go far to find a good fight."[44]

It seems that Hyakutake was operating under the false intelligence that just one division not two were manning the US defense of its airfields. In planning to destroy the airfield cantonment built by Halsey, Hyakutake had the double disadvantage that the Americans now controlled the sea. Any troops taken by destroyer would have to run a risky gauntlet, not only of the US Navy but also of the now dominant Air Solomons (AIRSOL) forces. By the first quarter of 1944 Japanese air attacks from Rabaul were largely confined to small-scale hit and run affairs that did little damage—though a lucky strike on 23 January by two Japanese bombers scored a direct hit on the living quarters of Brigadier-General John Hodge and his senior staff officers.

The 4,300 men of the 45th Infantry Regiment sent overland by Hyakutake were commanded by Colonel Isashi Magata. Considered to be the 'crack' unit on *Bougainville*, Magata's force included artillery, mortar and engineering battalions. They were supported by 4,150 troops of the 23rd Infantry Regiment led by Major-General Shun Iwasa and 1,350 men of the 13th Regiment led by Colonel Toyo Horei Muda. The three units were commanded by Major-General Masatane Kanda. After the arduous jungle trek to reach their jumping off points by the evening of 7 March, Hyakutake sent them off with the resounding if risible message: "time has come to manifest our knighthood with the pure brilliance of the sword. It is our duty to erase the mortification of our brothers at Guadalcanal. Attack! Assault! Destroy everything! Cut, slash, and mow them down. May the color of the red emblem of our arms be deepened with the blood of American rascals."[45] Major-General Kanda had also given his paean to battle: "The cry of our victory at Torokina Bay shall resound to the shores of our beloved Nippon. We are invincible."[46] The Japanese troops had another incentive. With a supply of food adequate only until 1 April, the reward of overrunning the American base was the plentiful and luxurious supply of food to be found in the US commissary.

Hyakutake's forces proved far from invincible, though not for want of effort or blood on their part. The Japanese artillery barrage opened on the morning of 8 March and focused on the destruction of the airfield at Piva Yoke. The destruction of a bomber and three fighters, with one man killed, was a poor return from the attack though it did force a temporary evacuation of aircraft to *New Georgia*. Artilleryman Stan Coleman vividly described the Japanese artillery attack: "All of a sudden we heard a very different kind of 'whoosh.' It was made by a shell at the end of its flight, not the beginning. It was 'incoming mail.' All hell broke loose. In the rear some fuel dumps went up. Every American artillery piece in the perimeter went into action."[47] The US artillery counter-attack was far more accurate; as soon as a Japanese position was spotted, their artillery were kept moving from position to position by the accuracy of US gunnery. Daylight also saw the introduction of a new American weapon. "Four blue Marine Corsairs came in with rockets. Rockets were a new ground-support weapon and I had never seen them . . . The rockets in flight made a fearful display. There was a tremendous concussion when they struck their target."[48]

That night Japanese troops attacked 'Hill 700' during a heavy downpour. The first attacks were beaten off but at 2.30 a.m. on 9 March, Major-General Shun Iwasa launched his main attack sending his troops clambering up the steep 70-degree slopes and screaming maniacally. Confusingly threats were shouted in English. A prolific slaughter followed though one group of Japanese soldiers took out a pillbox and set up a machine gun post on the saddle of the hill. It was dearly bought. The day's assault cost the lives of some 500 or more Japanese soldiers.

A US counter-attack launched by Major-General Beightler and the 145th Reserve managed to regain much of the ground lost and that night they dug in while the Japanese kept them awake with sporadic machine gun fire. Major-General Iwasa launched another assault at 6.45 a.m. on 10 March along with an attack by Muda's force on 'Hill 260.' At 11.15 a.m. an air strike by thirty-six US aircraft dented the Japanese attack and the day ended with a stalemate. Using a loud speaker, an American-Japanese called on Kanda's troops to surrender with honor—a call that was greeted with a blast of mortar fire.

At daybreak on 11 March, Iwasa aimed another attack on a promontory called 'Pat's Nose,' some 150 yards to the west of 'Hill 700.' Flanking 37 mm guns cut the Japanese charge to shreds. After an hour of almost suicidal attack Iwasa's troops receded leaving some eighty-four dead behind them. The following day they were pushed off their positions on 'Hill 700' and Iwasa pulled back his shattered forces to 'Blue Ridge.' During their retreat they were bombed incessantly by plane and pounded by a US destroyer's 5-inch shells. Meanwhile, on the same day, the Americal Division strove to drive Muda's forces off the 'South Knob' of 'Hill 260.' The US troops were beaten back. Major-General Griswold refused their request to pull back and a repeat performance was ordered for the next day. Again the American troops were rebuffed and Major-General Hodge decided that it would be best to isolate the 'South Knob' and simply pound it into irrelevance with artillery and mortar fire. It was estimated that over 10,000 105 mm rounds struck the Japanese positions before they finally retired on 28 March. Ninety-eight Americal Division soldiers were killed and 581 wounded in the three-week battle; 560 Japanese dead were counted on the 'South Knob.'

As for Colonel Magata, his attack on the US 129th Regiment of the 37th Division was advantaged by easier terrain that did not require a vertiginous ascent to engage the defenders. However, the interlocking of American 75 mm howitzers with 40 mm cannon and mortar fire made the job of penetrating the 37th Division a deadly one for unsupported Japanese light infantry. In addition the 37th Division was also able to call up Sherman tanks to repel Japanese troops from any vantage points taken. Despite repeated attacks from 12 to 16 March, Magata made no headway and finally withdrew his forces. As they re-established their defenses one US soldier observed, "Enemy dead were strewn in piles of mutilated bodies, so badly dismembered in most cases a physical count was impossible. Here and there was a leg or an arm or a blown-off hand."[49] The same witness noted: "At one point . . . Five enemy were piled one on top of the other, as each has successively approached the location to use a predecessor as a barricade and then fall on top of him as he in turn was killed."[50]

With a force now whittled down to fewer than 5,000, Kanda re-launched his assault on the lines of the 37th Division on 23 March. It was an attack that Major-General Beightler expected after interrogation of Japanese prisoners. The American GIs had cut a fifty yard swathe in front of their positions to create a deadly killing zone. A Japanese night attack was repulsed by a hitherto unequaled barrage of US artillery fire from seven battalions. Concentrated along a very narrow sector a combination of light and heavy artillery as well as mortars rained down 4,000 shells on Kanda's troops. An infantryman of the 129th Regiment recalled, "I remember what they called a million-dollar barrage and it's something you never forget . . . It was all jungle in front of us . . . they knocked everything down . . . Many, many, many killed!"[51] Artilleryman Stan Coleman participated in the slaughter, ". . . 37th was hit with an all-out *banzai* attack. We swung our guns to maximum elevation . . . we fired all night long and into the day. I loaded shell after shell . . . it sounded like thunder that lasted for hours. When we ceased fire, smoke lay over the land everywhere. I loved the smell of gunpowder. Still do."[52]

In the gullies and ravines in front of their positions lay more than 3,000 dead Japanese; many more were found in the hills. American medical teams on the island, who had been ordered to carry out autopsies on the Japanese bodies to analyse the effectiveness of American weapons found that their bodies had been hit by so many different missiles that their task was made pointless. Bodies had become a jumble of pieces. US artillery had literally cut them to shreds.

Leonard Owczarzak, a 90 mm gunner went forward the next morning to view the scene of the battle. MPs were keeping the souvenir hunters at bay and furthermore they wanted to prevent unnecessary voyeurism, because they "thought it was unhealthy. I can see why. The sight was frightful. I saw Japanese soldiers stacked up four deep like cordwood. There were hundreds of them . . . We smashed them. I never saw anything like it in the rest of the war."[53]

At the end of March 1944 Hyakutake finally requested permission from Imperial GHQ in Tokyo to withdraw his remaining forces. It was estimated that the three weeks of operation had cost the lives of some 8,500 Japanese soldiers with a further 3,000 wounded—a casualty rate of 87 percent of the Japanese forces that set out for *Empress Augusta Bay*. In spite of the fanatical bravery of his troops, Hyakutake's ill coordinated attacks had failed catastrophically. Ultimately it was an assault undone by the massive superiority of firepower available to the 37th and Americal Divisions.

Years later a rifleman of the 129th ruminated,

> The Japanese were very strange . . . There was a little hill outside the perimeter and a man come over the hill and the men in my platoon would just take aim and shoot him. And the next would come over the same way and we'd shoot him. And then the next would come over the same place instead of spreading out. We got the impression that they were either doped up or drunk. They never seemed to think.[54]

Black Soldiers of the 93rd Division: In *World War II* there was a high degree of racism in the organization of the American army. In spite of a historic record of courageous service in the armed forces by Black Americans, many White officers and soldiers asserted that Blacks were inferior, difficult to train and lacked patriotic fervor and bravery. It did not help that Black soldiers were recruited into segregated 'Black-only' units. Generally they were used for service operations, transportation, and stevedoring or construction labor. By the end of 1943 there were fewer than 150,000 Black troops in combat designated outfits. What is more, nobody wanted them. Remarkably resistance was greatest in the *South Pacific*. The *Fiji Times and Herald* warned that the natives would be uncontrollable once they saw how much the Black GIs were paid. The US consul general warned ". . . if these [Negro] troops were accorded European privileges, [native] dissatisfaction would result."[55] Black politicians and liberal Congressmen nevertheless pressed for greater Black participation in the war effort, especially in combat roles. Congressman Hamilton Fish of New York, who extolled the sterling service of Black troops under his command during *World War I*, exerted particular pressure for them to be used at the sharp end of fighting in the *South Pacific*.

Although Secretary of War, Henry Stimson, had personal reservations about the use of Black troops in combat, he felt it was politic to urge commanders in the *Pacific* to take them. On *Hawaii*, Lieutenant-General Delos Emmons had to be ordered to take the Black 93rd Division as a garrison unit. At first there was no intention to put them into a combat situation but again politics intervened and Major-General Harmon was ordered to put them through jungle training with a view to sending them to *Bougainville*.

The Black 24th Infantry was already operating in the *South Pacific*. Originally sent to Etafe in *New Caledonia*, these Black troops were designated for the defense of the island in case of a Japanese invasion attempt. When that threat diminished, the 24th was put on service detail involving the unloading of ships, building of roads, operation of Quartermaster store facilities and ordnance supervision. Some of the 24th's units were sent to *Guadalcanal* to do work details. It was work with which the 24th was tasked throughout the war. However, the first battalion of the 24th was sent to *Bougainville* on 30 January under Colonel John Thomas and was assigned a role in the corps reserve. In addition a Black artillery unit, the 2nd Battalion of the 54th Coastal Artillery was posted from *Espiritu Santo* and joined the XIV Artillery Corps.

The 93rd Division was generally considered to be the better of the two Black divisions. Activated in May 1942, it had been trained hitherto largely in the deserts of Arizona at Fort Huachuca. By the autumn of that year Lieutenant-General Joseph McNarney was reporting, "the 93rd Division appeared to be in fine shape. . . ."[56]

On 11 March 1944 the 1st Battalion of the 24th Infantry Regiment, supported either side by units of the 37th Division helped repulse a perimeter attack. Two Black troops were killed in the action but it was reported that the Black unit acquitted itself well. Reports in the press immediately brought a reaction from the war department, which ordered the deployment of Black combat units as a matter of national policy. By the time that the Black soldiers of the 24th Infantry were relieved and sent to the *Russell Islands* on 25 June, they had lost eleven men in combat and it was considered that their limited combat experience had been a success.

Unfortunately the posting of the Black 25th Regiment of the 93rd Division to *Bougainville* turned into a disaster. After arriving in *Guadalcanal* on 17 February, the Black troops of the 25th Regiment underwent intensive jungle training for three weeks. They were then dispatched to *Bougainville* and arrived at *Empress Augusta Bay* on 29 March, where they were assigned to 'quiet' stations. Major-General Griswold's operations memorandum of 30 March simply stated: "The 25th RCT will receive intense training and patrolling in jungle operations."[57] The 25th's initiation started well in an exercise to pursue the Japanese north along the *Laruma River*. When a machine gun emplacement was discovered F-Company waded across and knocked out the enemy's pillboxes. Twenty Japanese were killed at a cost of five wounded Black GIs. Private Wade Fogge was awarded a Bronze Star for using a rocket launcher to destroy three Japanese pillboxes.

For their next mission on 6 April, K-Company's White officer, Captain James Curran, was ordered to make a two-mile trek from 'Hill 250' to set up a trail block. Artillery observers and Sergeant Brodin of the intelligence section of the 164th Infantry, who acted as guide and adviser to Curran, accompanied K-Company. While they investigated some old Japanese hospital huts, nervous troops of K-Company's 1st and 2nd Platoon as well as the 1st Machine gun section opened fire. Two Black patrolmen were hit by friendly fire and Curran was unable to bring the firing under control. When 1st Platoon was ordered to withdraw, some of its troops dropped their packs and fled. A disorderly withdrawal ensued with troops disobeying orders and firing wildly. Eventually Curran was forced to order a full retreat back to 'Hill 250.'

In spite of the claims of some Black soldiers there was no evidence of the presence of Japanese soldiers. Lieutenant Oscar Davenport and nine other men were killed. Twenty more were wounded. A machine gun, mortar and a radio had been abandoned. In addition the troops in their panic had thrown away two Browning light machine guns, eighteen M-1s and three Winchester carbines. The next day the 25th Regiment L-Company, sent out to retrieve bodies, retreated after a brief firefight in which one of its soldiers was killed. The bodies were not recovered. Another attempt on 8 April ended with the troops of L-Company refusing to handle the bodies. It was only on 9 April that K-Company troops were able to retrieve bodies and equipment.

The panic experienced by 93rd Division troops was not unique to Black troops. There had been similar episodes of panic, friendly fire and wild shooting against a non-existent enemy from White troops—the first few days of action by the 32nd Division at the *Battle of Buna* showed that White boys from Wisconsin and Michigan were just as liable to panic when thrown into the front line with inadequate training and leadership. Blame could be placed on the lack of jungle training and the rawness of the Black troops. Inevitably the incident had unfortunate consequences. A review of the episode concluded that Black troops had a poor ability to absorb information, that the morale of White officers was low and that junior Black officers lacked authority. However, the 25th Regiment's commanding officer, Colonel Everett Yon claimed: "Had this organization been given prior instruction and had been accompanied by an experienced platoon of the 164th Infantry in its initial action, the results would have been far different."[58]

Subsequent good performance by other Black units on *Bougainville* was forgotten and rumors of the K-Company fiasco inevitably began to circulate. Given the institutional racism of the Army senior brass, it was perhaps not surprising that exaggerated and malicious stories began to spread. In an interview after the war General Marshall claimed that the 93rd Division, "wouldn't fight—couldn't get them out of the caves to fight."[59] The result of the *Bougainville* scandal was to severely circumscribe Black participation in future combat deployment in the *Pacific War*. Nevertheless, after impeccable service during the invasion and conquest of *Saipan*, Black soldiers dampened any internal speculation as to their combat ability. "The Negro Marines are no longer on trial," Marine Corp commander, Lieutenant-General Vandegrift, declared, "They are Marines, period . . ."[60]

Racism was not confined to the US Army. The Australian Army had a 'No Blacks' policy and pressured General Douglas MacArthur not to accept Black units and to send back any that had arrived. To his credit, MacArthur refused to bend.

The Starvation of the Japanese on Bougainville: Reinforcement of any kind was not a luxury afforded to the Japanese. After the heavy defeats of March 1944, the Japanese forces thereafter turned to survival including the organization of farms to grow food. They were increasingly cut off as Allied airbases on *Empress Augusta Bay* and elsewhere in the *Solomon Islands* destroyed the logistical chain on which the Seventeenth Army on *Bougainville* depended. The deployment of soldiers as farmers inevitably weakened the forces that were kept in the field without solving the problem of rations. In April 1944 the Japanese Army on *Bougainville* cut its ration of rice per soldier to 250 grams per day from the standard ration of 750 grams. Within six months there was no rice to give. Morale collapsed. Many soldiers simply wandered into the jungle to forage as best they could. Thousands, perhaps tens of thousands would die of starvation and related diseases. As Australian historian Gavin Long noted, "The neglect by the Japanese officers of their own men seems to have been only a little less callous than their neglect of their prisoners of war."[61] To be fair to the Japanese, logistical support from Rabaul had long since broken down. What is perhaps less explicable is that Japanese commanders did not try to lessen the abject suffering of their men by offering to surrender.

With neither side incentivized to seek confrontation, the Japanese because they could not win and the Americans because they no longer needed to fight for total control of the island, the armies of both sides settled into a pattern of co-existence. In the 37th Division area, one infantryman recalled that at a company baseball game,

> Someone noticed a raggedy-assed Jap way out in the shadows of the jungle off right field watching a game . . . He came back for other games and was soon a rather regular fan . . . the 37th GIs figured 'he can't be all bad'; besides, he somehow managed to root for 37th teams, showing his approval of hits and runs for the home team![62]

Similarly one Japanese soldier infiltrated the US camp and watched movies. When a captured Japanese film showed the sinking of the USS *Lexington*, he gave himself away: "there suddenly came shouts of "*Banzai! Banzai!* from the tangled but huge branches of a banyan tree on a near side of the row of seats . . . [he] was overcome with patriotism at the sight of his comrades in the air force sending an enemy ship to the bottom! He was pulled from the tree . . . perhaps the last victim of the carrier *Lexington*."[63] By August the state of calm was such that Hollywood 'headliners' began to make their appearance in *Bougainville* in shows organized by the United Services Organizations (USO). Randolph Scott came first followed by Bob Hope, Frances Langford and Jack Benny.

Of the 65,000 Japanese troops on *Bougainville* at the time of Halsey's investiture of *Empress Augusta Bay*, only 21,000 remained at the time of surrender. 44,000 died in total. Over the course of the year after the US invasion, it has been estimated that over 8,000 Japanese troops were killed in combat while 36,000 died from disease and starvation. Over the same period 1,243 US troops were killed. In terms of numbers *Bougainville* was one of Japan's heaviest defeats in *World War II*; it was a victory won above all by the interdiction of Japan's supply lines to its troops by the building of advance airfields and the day to day grinding down of Japanese air power first at Rabaul and the northern *Solomon Islands*. After *Bougainville*, Rabaul was in effect isolated. Halsey's completion of Operation CARTWHEEL in combination with the taking of the *Green Islands*, the *Admiralty Islands* and *Emirau* by MacArthur, ended the ability of Rabaul, the most important of Japan's 'super-bases' in the *South Pacific* region, to exert an influence on the outcome of MacArthur's westward drive along the north coast of New Guinea toward the Philippines.

After the war senior intelligence officer, Colonel Matsuichi Juio, whose job it was to anticipate MacArthur's moves revealed that his bypass strategy was

> The type of strategy we hated most ... Our strongest points were gradually starved out. The Japanese Army preferred direct assault after the German fashion, but the Americans flowed into our weaker points and submerged us, just as water seeks the weakest entry into a ship. We respected this type of strategy ... because it gained the most while losing the least.[64]

The Battle of Porton Plantation: The Nasty Business of 'Mopping Up': [Map: 25.4]

Later MacArthur replaced the 37th and Americal Divisions with 30,000 men of the Australian II Corps commanded by Lieutenant-General Sir Stanley Savige. It was part of the general scheme adopted by MacArthur to use American troops for forward operations as the Allies pressed toward Japan and to sideline Australian troops into garrison duties and 'non-headline' operations. As he was increasingly sidelined by MacArthur, Blamey and his senior officers became increasingly humiliated and disillusioned.

The result was that given his head on *Bougainville* with Australian soldiers, instead of following MacArthur's 'wither on the vine' strategy, Lieutenant-General Savige, supported by Blamey, adopted a strategy of aggressive deep patrols. After the war there was much criticism of a campaign that appeared to exist only to serve the Generals' peacetime careers. John Hetherington in his biography *Blamey, Controversial Soldier* [1973], concluded that the campaigns launched by Blamey "had no strategic value in the defeat of the Japanese Forces in the South West Pacific or in the defense of Australia."[65] Arguably 1,048 Australians lost their lives unnecessarily in 'mopping-up' operations on New Guinea and *Bougainville*.

By the end of 1944, the Japanese troops had been driven into enclaves in the far north or far south of the island. The plight of Japanese troops was not helped by the marauding activities of native guerrilla forces commanded by Lieutenant P. E. Mason and later by Captain C. W. Seton. In effect they instituted a reign of terror. Operating in conjunction with the Australian Army, it is estimated that irregular native forces killed some 2,000 Japanese soldiers over an eight-month period. Natives were not always friendly and soldiers on both sides might be butchered with impunity if they were unwary. Fighting was often vicious with the *Bougainville* natives being quick to use their knowledge of the terrain to come across Japanese troops unaware and kill them, often with knives or spears. Native forces from New Guinea who had been trained and organized by Australian officers were also effective. Captain Jack Costelloe, an officer with ANGAU (Australian New Guinea Administrative Unit) recalled their rescue mission for Sikh prisoners. They surprised a party of six Japanese soldiers and proceeded to run amok:

> Two were knifed before they realized what had struck them, the third although knifed in the side appeared to possess considerable physical strength, for he commenced to run away, at the same time shouting at the top of his voice. His demise was completed when the native guiding the party hurled a tomahawk at him, cleaving his skull in two.[66]

An attempted counter-attack against Australian forces by Major-General Kanda at the end of March 1944, along the Buin Road, was devastated by machine gun emplacements and the defensive rifle pits set up by the Australians who had received advance warning of the attack. Follow up attacks using tanks put Kanda's forces to flight. Of 2,400 troops used in the attack, some 620 were killed and more than 1,000 wounded. Poor communication and command coordination, inaccurate artillery fire, and unimaginative frontal suicide charges, had again condemned Japanese troops to slaughter and defeat. The Japanese had been outgunned and outthought. After the war a Japanese observer noted that in the face of the increasing use of Sherman tanks by the US, "the fighting spirit of our men dropped considerably due to the lack of anti-tank equipment."[67]

The reputation of the nasty, unloved and somewhat pointless campaign in *Bougainville* was brought to its lowest point by the fiasco of the *Battle of Porton Plantation* on 8–10 June 1945. An attempted amphibious flanking movement by a force of 190 Australian troops found themselves outgunned by an estimated 500 Japanese. As a result of poor reconnaissance and planning, the Australians lost their heavy equipment, including guns, on the reef as well as their reserve supplies of ammunition. A lack of serviceable boats turned the mistaken choice of a landing beach into a fiasco. There were no reserve troops and no aerial supply backup. Captain Blue Shilton observed: "it was a very badly planned operation with no real appreciation of the enemy strength and no thought of the troops' chances of survival. An operation to satisfy higher command and impress General Blamey who was in the area."[68]

Blamey tried to paint the disaster as a stirring episode to equate with Gallipoli and Tobruk. For the troops who had to swim back to the rescue barges stuck on the reef, the experience no doubt seemed less heroic. Apart from coming under fire from the Japanese, the local wildlife was equally unfriendly. Sharks patroled the lagoon while Pilot Jack Hearn recalled seeing Australian soldiers "hit and killed, fallen overboard and grabbed by huge sea-going salt-water crocodiles. Flying low down over the reefs, I have had crocodiles snap at the aircraft like a dog would as you pass low over the top of them."[69]

Unlike the rewards for MacArthur and the higher American and Australian commanders, there would be little glory for the messy business of 'mopping-up' on *Bougainville*.

Reflections on Bougainville and Rabaul: For Halsey, Nimitz and MacArthur the *Battle of Bougainville* had achieved its purpose. The creation of a secure airfield cantonment on *Bougainville* meant that Japan's stronghold at Rabaul and its subsidiary network of airfields could be kept quiescent. Japan's ability to supply its hitherto most important *South Pacific* garrison was almost entirely curtailed. Supply by ship was impossible. In the harbour some "31 sunken ships could be seen from the air."[70] From now on time and lives did not need to be wasted on the further reduction or capture of Rabaul. MacArthur could head off north to reconquer northern New Guinea and edge toward his beloved Philippines. Nimitz could continue his charge for glory across the *Central Pacific* while Halsey was liberated to go seek the naval victory that his illness prior to the *Battle of Midway* had denied him.

As for Rabaul, the feared Japanese fortress for which the *Battle of Bougainville* had been fought, the end was miserable rather than glorious. As Rabaul had come under intense bombing attack the only means of survival for the 60,000 strong garrison was to burrow into the mountains. It ended with a tunnel system that was 150 miles long in which the Japanese were forced to live as troglodytes. Even after MacArthur's seizure of the *Admiralty Islands* in February 1944, General Imamura continued to expect an invasion of the eastern tip of *New Britain* where Rabaul was located. "All the troops," he later wrote, "made up their minds to fight to the end."[71] There was no realistic expectation that they could hold out. In his diary Major-General Masatake Kimihara wrote, "it will be extremely difficult to hold Rabaul."[72] In the end there was no need to fight. It had long been decided to bypass Rabaul. The garrison could be surrounded and bombarded at will. In February and March 1945 heavy US air raids reduced the once powerful garrison to rubble. On 1 March Joe Holguin reported that after the air raid, "we beheld a scene of total devastation. Buildings were toppled and there were fires everywhere. The whole town was burning and in ruins . . . smoke filled the entire area and tended to obscure the sun."[73]

Isolated and abandoned at Rabaul, many Japanese soldiers felt that their moment of glory, the chance to die for their country had been lost. It was an insult to the *Bushido* code to which they had been inured: "They believed that they were entitled to a Nipponese *Götterdämmerung* ('Twilight of the Gods' and effectively the 'End of the World'), and MacArthur was denying them it . . ."[74] Instead, for the remainder of the war the Japanese had to sustain themselves as best they could. At Rabaul's Naval HQ, Lieutenant Okawara, who became Japan's Ambassador in Washington in 1980, later reflected on the food situation in Rabaul: "The rice supply gradually became very scarce. We had to live on 100 grams of rice per day."[75] Daily operations ceased to be military and consisted almost entirely of the search for food. It was a squalid and inglorious end to Japan's *South Pacific* adventure.

26 Battles of Arakan, Imphal, and Kohima: Slim Boxes Clever

[August 1943–July 1944]

[Maps: 26.1, 26.2, 26.3, 26.4, 26.5, 26.6, 26.7, 26.8]

General 'Bill' Slim: While the Americans and Australians were tipping the balance of the *Pacific War* in the *South Pacific*, the balance of power in Burma rested firmly with the Japanese. The British, having lost entire armies in Malaya and Burma in 1942 were patiently rebuilding their forces under the guiding hand of Lieutenant-General 'Bill' Slim. Meanwhile the pressure to supply and relieve Chiang Kai-shek's *Kuomintang* Armies fighting the Japanese in central China was growing. By mid-1943 both Japan and Britain were limbering up for renewed engagement. In Japan, Prime Minister General Hideki Tojo saw the India-Burma frontier as a place to recoup some of the pride and prestige being lost in the *South Pacific* after the loss of the *Solomons* and southeast New Guinea, while in northeastern India, the British Army was ready to push back into Burma. It was a unique moment in the *Pacific War* when facing Allied and Japanese Armies were offensive-minded at the same time. The result, particularly for military historians, would be perhaps the most intriguing land battle of the *Pacific War*.

"The epithet 'The Forgotten Army' was taken up by the troops," recalled Lieutenant-General 'Bill' Slim, "and before it became a statement of pride it reflected the fears and frustrations of soldiers thousands of miles from home whose hardships and deprivations were not widely appreciated."[1] In the post-war era even British historians, Burma specialists apart, have ignored Slim and his great victories at *Imphal* and *Irrawaddy River*. Roy Jenkins's otherwise excellent 900-page biography of *Churchill* [2001] gives due weight to General Montgomery and *El Alamein* but fails to even mention Slim or the great conflicts on the India-Burma front during *World War II*. American historians are similarly blank on the subject. Ronald Spector's well-regarded *Pacific War* history, *Eagle Against the Sun* [1985] makes scant reference to General Slim or his Fourteenth Army. John Toland's *The Rising Sun* [1970] is equally opaque on the subject. Yet the *Battle of Imphal* and the later *Battle of the Irrawaddy River* were the finest land victories of the *Pacific War* achieved by a general who was probably the most talented Allied military commander faced by Japan.

After a fighting retreat from the borders of Malaya, via Rangoon and Mandalay in Burma, Slim's Burma Corps had reached India in April 1942. Albeit bedraggled they were at least intact as a fighting force. What now? They had reached India, the jewel and heart of the British Empire but they were in its nether regions, at its most far-flung corner in the remote states of Assam and Nagaland as well as the farthest reaches of east Bengal.

From Dimapur, the main railhead for India's northeast region, the distance to Calcutta was 682 miles; New Delhi, where Field Marshal Archibald Wavell was Commander in Chief, India, and later Admiral Mountbatten Commander in Chief, South East Asia Command (SEAC), were based, was a further 812 miles down the road. Ledo was 200 miles north of Dimapur, the railhead through which passed all the supplies to be airlifted by the so-called Hump to Chiang Kai-shek's Chinese Armies and to General Clair Chennault's Fourteenth Air Force. The logistical task of simply feeding the British Army let alone supplying Chiang's army by air was immense. In total 750,000 men were spread out over a 700-mile front consisting of mountainous jungle terrain. It was an area the size of Germany.

After a year-long hiatus, the man chosen to lead this army and the campaign planned for the re-conquest of Burma and defeat of the Japanese occupying armies was the unlikely figure of General William 'Bill' Slim. Born near Bristol, but brought up in Birmingham by his ironmonger father, Slim was educated at St. Philip's Grammar School and King Edward's School but his family was unable to afford him a university education. After leaving school he taught at a primary school and worked as a clerk for a metal working company; however, he managed to escape this humdrum existence by joining the Birmingham University Officers' Training Corps in 1912. With *World War I* just two years away the timing for advancement was impeccable . . . if he survived.

Slim was wounded at the *Battle of Gallipoli* (a fact that would later endear him to all Australians) and then again in actions in Mesopotamia where he would earn a Military Cross for bravery. In wartime conditions he rose rapidly in rank. After being evacuated to India he was made an 'acting' Major in the 6th Gurkha Rifles. At the end of the war he was transferred permanently to the Indian Army with the rank of full Captain. His career prospered and in 1934 he was transferred back to England to teach at the Army Staff Training College at Camberley; a job he did for three years until the end of 1937. In 1938 he was promoted to Lieutenant-Colonel and given command of the 2nd Battalion of the 7th Gurkha Rifles before being appointed head of the Senior Officers' School at Begaum in Bombay Province in June 1939. At the outbreak of war Slim was transferred to active command in the Middle East where he fought in Ethiopia against the Italians, was wounded yet again in Eritrea, recovered and led the Indian 10th Infantry in the *Anglo-Iraq War* before going on to see further action in the Syria-Lebanon Campaign and the invasion of Iran. It was the action-packed life of a highly capable field commander but not one perhaps destined for greatness. Square of build with short greying hair and 'bulldog' expression, Slim was not a flamboyant figure but his easy manner and voice of quiet authority made him a hugely popular commander even if he was not possessed of obvious star quality. Major-General Frank Messervy, who served under Slim in 1943–1944 (7th Indian Infantry Division then IV Corps) observed: "I never saw him cross—never. I never saw him edgy."[2]

From a genteel but impoverished family and devoid of any of the usual social connections for career advancement, Slim had even had to make ends meet during his service years by writing adventure stories under the *nom de plume,* Anthony Mills.

When he was plucked out of obscurity by Delhi to become General Alexander's commander for Burma Corps in the middle of the retreat from Rangoon, Slim's career advancement had been due simply to hard work, proven skill in the field and good luck—the latter a prerequisite for all great commanders.

The Burma Railway: [Map: 26.1] While Slim began the task of providing for his defeated troops, Colonel Keiji Suzuki, a staff officer at the Imperial General GHQ in Japan, was already advanced in his plans for the post-war rule of Burma by Japan. The Baho government was set up under the puppet regime of Thakin Tun Oke. In June 1942 however, 300 Japanese officials were sent from Japan to form a military administration (*Gunseikanbu*) under Lieutenant-General Shojiro Iida. Ba Maw, the leading Burmese self-rule activist in the 1930s, who had been freed from prison by the Japanese, was appointed the new government's puppet head.

Prime Minister Tojo, taking advice from the Total War Institute of which he was head, ordered that *Gunseikanbu* (Japanese Military Administration) should take over active management of Burma. 'Co-prosperity' was deferred—supposedly only temporarily in deferment to the exigencies of war. *Gunseikanbu* immediately took over thirteen of the fifteen government departments. Communism was outlawed as was any agitation for self-determination. This was ironic in the sense that before *World War II*, Britain was already moving purposefully toward self-determination in its colonies. The Japanese administration took the children of leading Burmese families as hostages by sending them to 'special' schools for indoctrination. The new regime's Burmese Director of Press and Publicity, Dr. U Hla Pe, would later describe Burma's new government as being nothing more than "an executive commission."[3]

The effect of Japan's imposed military government was brutal on the civilian population. Burmese businesses were expropriated and houses and buildings taken over. Japanese soldiers and administrators were far more racist even than the British who they had replaced. The Japanese sent some 540 *Kempeitai* (secret police) to Burma; using the classic tactics of '*agents provocateurs*', potential dissidents were weeded out. Disobedience was met with summary execution. The *Kempeitai* also managed the army's needs for *jugen ianfo* (comfort women). In practical terms the need of the Japanese Army to 'live off the land' led to a confiscatory requisitioning of food—often paid for at prices well below the market. Cattle numbers in Burma halved within twelve months. In addition, by 1944, the Japanese Army had press-ganged 800,000 Burmese as forced laborers. Tens of thousands of this so-called *chwytagyi* (sweaty army) would die in the building of the Burma Railway.

The building of the railway, linking Rangoon and Bangkok, became one of the main priorities of the new government as Japan sought ways to avoid shipping men and supplies from the *South China Sea* to the *Indian Ocean*. Even by the spring of 1942, Japanese shipping was in short supply. As early as April that year work gangs began to be transported northwards from as far away as *Java* and *Sumatra* as well as *Singapore*. For fourteen months the railway was driven through 260 miles of dense jungle—in conditions far worse than those displayed in the epic *Bridge on the River Kwai* [1957] starring William Holden, Alec Guinness and Jack Hawkins. Ignoring the articles of the Geneva Convention, prisoners of war were used as slave labor in grim jungle work camps. Australian medical officer, Edward Wear recorded in his diary, "The state of health in these camps can only be regarded as an everlasting appalling disgrace."[4] **[See Appendix D: The Japanese Empire: From Co-Prosperity to Tyranny]**

Any notion that Burma had been 'liberated' by Japan was soon dispelled. Bogyoke Aung San's Burma Independence Army (BIA) was assembled in Rangoon under the pretence of re-equipment and was promptly disbanded. In the few weeks in which it had operated with a free hand the BIA had implemented a 'racist' reign of terror against the tribal peoples and their village headmen, who were not sympathetic to the Burmese cause. In some cases BIA officers simply acted as gangster racketeers. Aung San, by his own hand, dispatched one recalcitrant village headman by driving a bayonet through his stomach. In spite of this Bogyoke Aung San and a select cadre of officers were selected to lead a new and more rigorously recruited force of 4,000 men now renamed the Burma Defense Army (BDA). The BDA, a similarly legalized gangster-type entity, was loathed in equal measure.

The First Arakan Campaign: **[Map: 26.2]** After the retreat from Burma, Wavell reorganized the command structure and personnel on the eastern border with Burma. The Eastern Army commander, Lieutenant-General Charles Broad, was retired and the commander of Eastern Army's IV Corps, Lieutenant-General Noel Irwin, was promoted to take his place. Meanwhile the newly formed XV Corps, that included remnants of the recently arrived Burma Corps, was put under the command of Major-General Slim with its HQ based at Barrackpore near Calcutta. Slim's XV Corps also commanded the 14th Indian Division that was stationed at Chittagong, the southernmost Indian city on the *Ganges Delta* that was situated along the coast from the hills and valleys of the Arakan area of Burma. Irwin then moved his HQ to Barrackpore and ordered Slim to relocate to Ranchi in Bihar, several hundred miles to the west, where he was to raise and train new troops for future campaigns in Burma.

Wavell now urged an invasion of the Arakan (Operation NIBBLE AND CANDY) with a view to capturing the strategically important island of *Akyab* (Sittwe) that boasted both a port and an airfield. It was reckoned to be an ideal base for providing air cover for a future reinvasion of Burma. In the event 14th Indian Division's campaign, which started on 17 December 1942, commanded by Major-General Wilfred Lloyd, suffered from the same failings that had characterized the British Army's performance in the Burma retreat. Poorly trained troops, unprepared for jungle operations, were quickly demoralized by their failure to penetrate well-conceived Japanese defenses. The apparent superiority of Japanese troops and their flanking movements caused mayhem. An awestruck Jatt officer noted: "One could stare at the Jap line for hours on end with binoculars and scarcely see a thing move or a leaf displaced."[5] Japanese troops' intricate defenses, consisting of log bunkers and linked firing trenches, served notice that the

Japanese army was as capable in defense as in attack. Furthermore Irwin's foolish mantra that soldiers should hold ground at all costs, without providing a realistic strategy of support or survival, inflicted unnecessary damage on the 14th Indian Division. In addition essential support equipment was either denied or poorly used. Irwin and Wavell had overruled Slim's suggestion that more tanks were needed. Where tanks were used, instead of deploying them in force to drive though enemy position, they were fed in as Slim described it, "in penny packets."[6]

Nevertheless Japan's defenders, for the first time, experienced the horrors of waiting for enemy attacks in the mosquito-infested conditions of jungle life. Thus Corporal Fujida waxed philosophically when he gloomily addressed his diary in anticipation of his likely demise, "What is War? A tragedy—the mutual infliction of human beings, the oppression of peoples—the use of civilization to get at each other's throats . . ." Addressing his girlfriend, Fujida continued, "Should I die—Mizue [his girl] you ought to have chosen another man and been happy—look after mother—goodbye all."[7]

As well as psychological stress, troops on both sides suffered the more mundane problems of jungle life. Private Dick Fiddament of the 2nd Royal Norfolks complained that his "hairy chest would get prickly heat and it could send you on the verge of bloody insanity. You shouldn't scratch, but you did scratch and it would bleed. The itch would become infected and sore. You'd get it on your head, get it round your private parts—any part of your body."[8] However, it was not poor health but poor planning, tactics and morale that did for Operation NIBBLE AND CANDY.

The British assault buckled. Unable to breach the Japanese defensive positions at 'Sugar–4' and 'Sugar–5,' the British forces fell back. Wavell compared it to the fierce battle fought by the Australians and Americans in New Guinea: "It seems quite clear that we are facing a form of 'Buna' and 'Gona.' "[9] Fusilier W. C. Smith noted: "it was like a scene from Dante's Inferno—as screams and yells from the wounded and dying filled the air, even above the bombardment, and all the casualties seemed to be our own."[10] It was an action that cost the life of Lieutenant David Graves, son of the renowned novelist and poet Robert Graves who had written so movingly about trench warfare in *World War I*. David Graves' body was never found. Reviewing the operations planned by Major-General W. L. Lloyd's 47th Indian Brigade, Slim had warned that frontal assaults would fail. Irwin again ignored his advice.

When Major-General Lloyd ordered the 47th Indian Brigade to withdraw on 25 March 1943 before it was completely cut off, Irwin countermanded the order and sacked Lloyd. A week later Japanese forces crossed the supposedly un-crossable Mayu Range and cut the coastal track that was the natural escape route for the advanced British troops. British 6th Brigade HQ was overrun and its commander Brigadier Ronald Cavendish was killed. The 47th Brigade now fled piecemeal as best it could across the Mayu Range. With all equipment and command structure lost, the remnants had ceased to be a fighting unit. Basic mistakes had been made. The troops lacked food, equipment and ordnance. Having been soundly beaten by an enemy on the attack in Malaya and Burma, the British Army now found itself beaten by a Japanese Army in defense. It was a side to their military abilities that Irwin had not anticipated though he could not have been unaware of the Australian and American experience in the *South Pacific* a year earlier. Wavell summed it up in a note written in mid-March: "The Japanese are setting us a rather fresh problem in tactics combining fanaticism and mobility of the savage with modern weapons and training. He is refusing to surrender and fighting to the death with modern weapons very skilfully employed."[11]

Irwin blamed the soldiers of the 14th Division and by implication Slim, who was ultimately the responsible commander. On 9 April 1943 Irwin, after receiving a captured Japanese document, complained that it indicated: "British troops are surrendering readily."[12] He harrumphed, "I'll have courts of inquiry all ready for such cases including loss of equipment when I get the 14th Division troops out."[13] It was an analysis with which Slim would not agree. A Japanese soldier's diary entry of 2 April regarding the fighting in the Arakan succinctly summed up the problem: "The troops opposing us are British and have no will to fight and are just knocked down in the stride of our attack."[14] Naturally Irwin took no responsibility himself for putting his troops in an impossible situation. For Slim too it was an uncomfortable position in which to find himself, responsible but not in charge: "I have rarely been so unhappy on a battlefield. Things had gone wrong, terribly wrong . . . Yet I had no operational control . . ."[15]

Having supposed that Slim might be relieved of command, Lieutenant-General Irwin was in for a shock. It was Irwin, not Slim, who was required to 'carry the can' for the failure of the Arakan campaign. Irwin's incompetence had cost the British Army a year in which it would have to be 'rebooted.' Having signaled to Slim that he would be replaced, Irwin was forced later in the day to send another message: "You're not sacked. I am."[16] Irwin was posted back to England on 'sick leave' and thence to command the Army in Scotland. Slim meanwhile, was put in command of the 14th Army that would now comprise IV Corp, XV Corp and the reserve XXXIII Corp.

Wingate and the Chindits: **[Map: 26.3]** To cover up the scale of the Arakan disaster, the British Army trumpeted the successes of another Burma operation. The Chindits, named after the mythical beasts that guard the entrance to Burmese temples, were a group of specially trained jungle fighters under the leadership of Brigadier-General Orde Wingate. Wingate came to the fore with guerrilla tactics that he developed in the Abyssinian campaign. Thereafter he became maniacally evangelistic about the tactical advantages created by irregular forces operating behind enemy lines and supported by air. As Colonel Bernard Fergusson, one of his closest confederates explained,

> Briefly, his point was that the enemy was most vulnerable
> far behind enemy lines, where his troops, if he had any at
> all, were of inferior quality. Here a small force could
> wreak havoc out of all proportion to its numbers . . .
> Supply should be by air, communication by wireless . . .
> His proposal was to cut the enemy's supply line, destroy
> his dumps, tie up troops unprofitably behind the line . . .'[17]

Both Wavell and Churchill, at least for a while, fell under his charismatic spell. As Fergusson attested, "Nobody seriously believed in him except General Wavell, and everybody regarded him as a bit of a nuisance . . . even I thought the whole thing a bit crazy."[18]

Wingate was indeed an original. Brought up as a member of an evangelist sect, the Plymouth Brethren, he was weaned on 'hell-fire' and the Bible. The fight with the Japanese was not just a war, it was a crusade; in *The Campaign in Burma* [1946] Lieutenant-Colonel Frank Owen noted: "To see Wingate urging action on some hesitant commander was to realize how a medieval baron felt when Peter the Hermit got after him to go crusading."[19] Large chunks of the Old Testament were learnt by heart. Wingate had a brilliant memory. In Palestine he became a noted supporter of the Zionist cause and became known to the Jews as 'The Friend.' A fearless horse rider, he gloried in his own rebellious and unconventional behavior. Wingate had a preening pathological ego and, famously, he would sometimes walk around camp and hold staff meetings stark naked.

Obsessed about health and diet, he would wear an onion or garlic around his neck and occasionally nibble from these treats. Clearly a hypochondriac, Wingate despised or disregarded the illnesses or weakness of others. He was a highly paranoid man who always imagined conspiracies against him. Like Douglas MacArthur, Wingate had a 'Napoleon Complex' about which his closest friends would tease him. Even his wife Lorna, a girl he had met when she was sixteen aboard the P&O liner, *Cathay*, at Port Said, described him as being like 'Clive of India.' Perhaps most bizarrely he would often walk around with an alarm clock strapped to his wrist.

Even his strongest supporters recognized the less than angelic nature of his character. After the war Fergusson wrote, "Wingate would do any evil that good might come. He saw his object very clearly in front of him and to achieve it he would spare no friend or enemy; he would lie; he would intrigue; he would bully, cajole and deceive. He was a hell of a great man and few people liked him."[20] For a British press and British Army in need of a hero, he was a boon. Articulate, charismatic, persuasive, he captivated or repelled in equal measure. Slim, who was hardly a fan, gave a balanced description when he described Wingate as "a strange, excitable, moody creature, but he had fire in him. He could ignite other men . . . you might be angry at his arrogance . . . You could not fail to be stimulated either to thought, protest, action by his somber vehemence and his unrelenting persistence."[21] In the darker years of the war, he played a similar role for British propaganda that MacArthur played for the United States. Churchill, Alanbrooke and other senior commanders realized that Wingate was somewhat 'unhinged' and that he was not suitable for the highest command. Lord Moran, Churchill's doctor recorded: "Wingate seemed to be hardly sane . . . in medical jargon a borderline case."[22] Indeed on one earlier occasion in July 1941, Wingate attempted suicide with a rusty Ethiopian knife in the Continental Hotel in Cairo.

In spite of or possibly because of his idiosyncratic methods, Wingate bullied his troops into the tough physical condition that would be needed for jungle trekking.

Within weeks 70 percent of his troops had reported themselves to sick bay, forcing him to inveigle the medics to get them quickly discharged. Medical absenteeism eventually fell to 3 percent. Sergeant Arthur Willshaw noted: "Flabby flesh had disappeared, chests had filled out, muscles developed where only outlines existed before . . ."[23] Non-swimmers were shown how to swim and literally 'thrown into the deep end.'

As a result of Wingate's proselytising energy, Operation LONGCLOTH was given its head. In early February 1943 Wingate and 3,000 Chindits crossed into Burma and engaged in three months of military activity, mainly the disruption of railway lines. This much-lauded success, albeit very temporary, was shrouded in confusion on both sides. Tilbahadur Thapa, a Gurkha in No.1 column recalled an engagement where "a free for all developed man to man, kukris, bayonets, swords, hand-to-hand. Both sides fired blindly, even killing each other, Gurkhas killing Gurkhas and Japanese killing Japanese by mistake in the confusion."[24]

The Chindits were supplied by air. There were 'micro' successes. Colonel Mike Calvert killed 100 Japanese troops in a particularly successful patrol ambush. He recalled, "We let fly with everything we had and a lot of Japs could never have known what hit them. It was one of the most one-sided actions I have ever fought in."[25] For the most part however, the Chindits spent the latter part of their mission evading Japanese forces, up to three divisions, who sought them out. From Wingate's starting force, 818 were either killed, captured or died of disease. Out of the 2,182 who returned, over 600 men were so incapacitated by their ordeal that they never returned to combat. Although the Chindits had usefully tied up large numbers of Japanese troops, the railways were quickly repaired. Looked at objectively a casualty rate of, effectively, 50 percent was catastrophic. Nick Neill would later complain: "I was 21 years old and untrained in charge of 50 equally inept young Gurkhas . . . We were badly trained, badly led, and the plans were overoptimistic."[26] As the official Gurkha history recorded, "Never have so many marched so far for so little."[27] This was a complimentary conclusion set beside that of the official Indian history that proclaimed: "The strategic value of the operation was nil."[28] Perhaps the only practical benefit of the Chindit operation was demonstrating the possibility of landing supply aircraft on hastily prepared jungle clearings.

Slim and other senior commanders were sceptical of the usefulness of Wingate's 'Long Range Penetration' (LRP) tactics but nobody could gainsay the usefulness of the propaganda lift in the English press. *Reuters* described the Chindits as "The British Ghost Army" while the *Daily Mail* hailed Wingate as "Clive of Burma." An over-enthused journalist, Marsand Gander filing for the *Daily Telegraph* from New Delhi, had his sensationalized account headlined "BRITISH JUNGLE FORCE KEPT JAPANESE ON THE RUN." Perversely a glamorous but hugely costly failed venture was used in the press to cover a much less costly failure in the Arakan in the first half of 1943.

Nevertheless the Chindits had more than a little impact on the Japanese. Increasingly they became aware of the need to plan and coordinate 'interior' defense. As Japanese soldier Yuwaichi Fujiwara noted, "Wingate's Chindits first expedition changed Japanese thinking. We thought that the north Burma jungles were a defense against the British advance into Burma. We now realized that they could be traversed by both sides."[29]

Slim's Rebuilding of the Army in Assam: [**Map: 26.4**] After the *First Arakan Campaign* Slim, with the spotlight elsewhere, was able to spend the remainder of 1943 preparing the army for the struggle ahead. In no small measure he owed a great deal to the support of the new commander of the Eastern Army, General Sir George Giffard, and indeed Admiral Lord Louis Mountbatten, who, in the same month, August 1943, Churchill and Roosevelt had appointed as Supreme Allied Commander, South East Asia Command.

It owes much to Slim's unassuming charm that he was able to command the respect and support of men as varied as soldiers such as Wavell and Giffard, as well as the acerbic 'Vinegar Joe' Stillwell and the crashing snob and military dilettante Louis Mountbatten. Indeed when Stillwell, head of the US-Chinese Northern Combat Area Command, refused to accept the command of Giffard, to whom his forces supposedly reported, Stillwell volunteered to report to Slim who also reported to Giffard. This weird cocktail of reporting relationships in the end worked because Slim and Stillwell, both schooled as corps commanders, had a strong professional respect for each other. Over a nine-month period, Slim not only rebuilt the Fourteenth Army, but also provided the 'glue' that made workable the complex command structures of the India-Burma-China theater.

The key to Slim's work in rebuilding the Fourteenth Army as an effective fighting unit was to restore 'morale.' Slim explained that the importance of 'morale' in a military sense was that it was the ". . . intangible force which will move a whole group of men to give their last ounce to achieve something, without counting the cost to themselves; that makes them feel they are part of something greater than themselves."[30] An essential part of building that morale as Irwin had learnt too late was to learn how "individually to be better soldiers than the Japs."[31] As one officer in the 7th Indian Division, who had observed the Arakan debacle wrote, the British soldiers needed to improve "Skill with all weapons, including grenades, camouflage, digging, bayonet fighting etc. etc . . . leading patrols, ambushes, siting trenches, fire control and so on."[32]

But first Slim set about making sure that the troops were kept healthy, and well supplied. For Slim, the old adage, "an army marches on its stomach" was of paramount importance. As Slim insisted, "Before we could get on with our real job—fighting—we had to feed, clothe, house . . . ."[33] The logistics of food were complicated by the fact that the Fourteenth Army was one of the most racially diverse armies ever assembled; it included British, Americans, Indians, Chinese and Africans; they also differed in religion and caste. Over thirty different types of ration packs had to be prepared. This was no simple task. Supply requisitioning procedures in India were archaic and Slim needed to force through changes. In addition, the railway to Dimapur was not capable of the necessary throughput to provision his 750,000 troops and this necessitated investment and operational changes to more than quadruple line capacity from 600 tons per day to 2,800 tons. This was no easy task given that there was no bridge over the *Brahmaputra River*, which necessitated the moving of train carriages onto ferries. In order to ensure that his troops had fresh food, Slim even set about building and operating duck farms and nursery gardens covering 18,000 acres. Improvisation was essential. "No boats? We'll build them! No vegetables, we'll grow 'em! No Eggs? Duck farms! . . . Malaria, we'll stop it!"[34]

Health was also made a priority. Remarkably 90 percent of the casualties from the *First Battle of Arakan* were from malaria. Officers who did not ensure that at least 95 percent of their men took daily doses of Mecaprin were dismissed. Troops were forbidden to shower after sunset when mosquitoes became more active. Malaria rates fell from over 60 percent to 13 percent. Previously when soldiers fell sick they were sent back for medical treatment to Calcutta or beyond. Slim moved doctors and medical facilities close to the front so that those who fell ill could be treated immediately and return to service within weeks rather than months.

Jungle survival was also taught. "With our training we always felt we were masters of the jungle,"[35] recalled Chindit medical officer, Major Desmond Whyte, during the second of Wingate's LRP (Long Range Penetration) operations. The importance of rapid treatment for tropical and jungle diseases was a great concern to the very practical Slim who noted: "In 1944, for every man evacuated with wounds we have one hundred and twenty evacuated sick."[36] Units were de-wormed. Clothing and shelter were improved. Deliveries of mail were speeded up and camp entertainment was encouraged.

Nevertheless, it was not enough to simply feed and clothe his troops effectively. At heart he knew that the real problem faced by his officers and troops was that, after more than a year of humiliating defeats and retreats including the Arakan Campaign, they did not truly believe that they could compete with the Japanese. Slim needed to counter rumors which "were assiduously spread picturing the Japanese as the super-bogeymen of the jungle, harping on their savagery, their superior equipment and training . . ."[37] In this respect one of Slim's main tasks was to train his troops in jungle living, marching and fighting—to show them that the jungle was not the enemy but simply a 'neutral' canvas. 'Jungle craft' was taught in two-month training courses in southern India. A training pamphlet emphasized the

> ability of a soldier to live and fight in the jungle; to be able to move from point to point and arrive at his objective fit to fight; to use ground and vegetation to the best advantage; and be able to 'melt' into the jungle either by freezing or intelligent use of camouflage; to recognize and be able to use native foods; to possess ability to erect temporary shelters to ward off tropical downpours . . . In short, the jungle is home to the jungle fighter . . .'[38]

Another pamphlet urged the British soldier to "use his sense of smell. It is a curious fact, but the Japanese soldier possesses a peculiar, unpleasant odour which is most persistant."[39] The pamphlet failed to point out that the *bata-kusai* (too close to butter) foreigner was equally odorously distinctive.

As soon as the Japanese proved themselves supreme in the jungles of Malaya, the Delhi printing presses started to churn out military tactical publications faster than the British Army was delivering guns. Colonel Francis Brink's *Japanese Tactical Methods* [1942] gave a detailed account of the Malayan campaign. The Military Intelligence Department in New Delhi also cranked out War Information Circulars, which provided detailed information on the equipment, organization and tactics of the Imperial Japanese Army. However, it was the Army in India Training Memoranda War Series that provided the bulk of new material for officers. The distribution and use of these new manuals was taken seriously. In a memorandum of April 1942, General Gracey's 20th Indian Division's officers were warned: "This is not to be regarded as just 'another piece of bumph.' "[40]

The March–April issue of the Army in India Training Memoranda War Series made the extremely wise observation,

> Certain of the tactics of jungle warfare are specialized and, to employ them successfully, special training is required. This does not mean, however, that there is any black magic about this form of warfare. All the well known principles of war still apply . . . it is evident that almost as many of our mistakes were due to our neglecting the original principles of war, as were due to our not having learnt and practiced . . . those principles necessary for this type of warfare.[41]

Apart from the publication and dissemination of leaflets, officers were taught how to lead units in jungle conditions. Lectures on battle-craft were compulsory. In May 1943 a revised manual entitled *Japanese in Battle Part I: Enemy Methods* was published and distributed. Apart from chapters on patrols and roadblocks etc., the manual also illustrated fifteen different examples of Japanese defensive positions including detailed diagrams of the layout and construction of bunkers, examples of which had been examined and analysed in detail at Buna and Gona in southern New Guinea as well as Arakan. How to overcome these defense systems with flame-throwers, grenades and 'beehives' (shrapnel shells) was also explained in detail.

Indeed the supposed Japanese expertise in jungle warfare was often overdone. Colonel Tsuji, General Yamashita's tactical genius during the Malaya Campaign, was bitter about the lack of jungle training of troops that had come from northern China. In large part the difference between the two armies at the start of the *Pacific War* was in the more mundane aspects; the emphasis on speed and mobility, the concentration of strength at points of enemy weakness, intelligence, patroling, fitness, health, clothing, the correct selection of weaponry, and the provision of reliable logistic support.

Talented British officers, who had performed well in jungle conditions, were also brought back to India to teach. Brigadier Steward, who, almost alone in the British Malayan Army, had taken his own battalion on jungle training exercises, was particularly sought after. General Wavell would later write that he ordered Stewart's return to India, ". . . to impart his knowledge and ideas to units preparing for the return match with the Japanese."[42] In addition, Wavell brought Australians to lecture British officers. Their experience of successfully fighting the Japanese in jungle battles at *Milne Bay*, the *Kokoda Trail* and the *Battles of Buna, Gona*, and *Sanananda* provided essential combat information.

Furthermore Slim emphasized the importance of exercises at night given the Japanese penchant for operations after dark. Valuing all parts of the army equally was also one of Slim's mantras; the roles of cooks, medics, administrators, supply handlers, drivers were fully respected. Slim treated them as 'real' soldiers and insisted that they should be trained as combatants. All personnel were potential front line soldiers. In spite of the new training regimen, there were some things that even Slim believed that his soldiers could not better *vis-à-vis* their Japanese counterparts: "The Japanese could—and did— do many things we could not."[43] Japanese tactical skills such as infiltration and encirclement were copied but never mastered.

Finally Slim had to define a new range of tactics. Japanese strengths were analysed. Their fast-moving flanking movements, often unseen through jungle cover, were difficult to defend against. In the past, as soon as British lines of supply and communication had been cut, headlong retreat or fighting withdrawal had ensued. However, Slim understood that the Japanese jungle flanking movements depended on speed and the carrying of a minimal supply of rations. If fighting engagements could be prolonged, it would be the Japanese who would be cut off from resupply. Slim therefore developed the concept of the 'box'—a defense based on holding an enclosed perimeter when surrounded, which could be supplied by air until the enemy had worn himself out.

In a sense it was a modern interpretation of the legendary British 'square' made so famous by the Duke of Wellington at the *Battle of Waterloo*. Instead of retreating when encircled by the Japanese, Slim trained his commanders to form *ad hoc* defensive garrisons against which Japanese commanders would have to batter away. These garrisons, the so-called 'boxes,' would depend on resupply from the air, Troop Carrier Command (TCC), and air attack support from Royal Air Force (RAF) Tactical Air Force (TAF). If the 'boxes' were the 'anvil' as Slim described them, the rapid supply of reserve forces, sometimes by air, would provide the 'hammer' with which to annihilate the enemy. As *Japanese Tactical Methods* pointed out, "The idea that a force which is surrounded is in a hopeless position must not be permitted . . . troops must realize that the enemy who are behind them are just as much cut off from their comrades as they are themselves."[44] It was a mantra virtually identical to that preached by Major-General Sir George Wootten at the *Battle of Finschhafen* in September 1943.

Neither did Slim forget the importance of 'weight of fire'; the lessons of the walls of lead thrown at the Japanese by Major-General Vandegrift at *Guadalcanal* and the Australians at the *Battle of Milne Bay* were absorbed. A committee of senior officers chaired by Brigadier Ronnie Cameron (48th Indian Infantry Brigade) concluded, 'Blitz Parties,'[45] units armed with automatic weapons, should be used to dislodge Japanese troops. It was the application of the principle of concentration of mass at the point of attack. The ratio of Thompson and Bren machine guns given to British combat units was increased significantly.

In the *17th Indian Division Training Instruction Manual* emphasis was placed on 'jungle-mindedness'; the manual explained, "the new draft will not know the jungle. They will feel lost and confused—if not actually frightened of it."[46] Slim therefore insisted that his troops experienced long periods of jungle living. Under the training command of Brigadier Henry Chambers, Indian troops were moved to jungle training camps fifty miles from Bethamangala in the state of Mysore in southern India. A British officer described the area as "sited and prepared exactly as it might have been in war—complete with round defense, stand-to's, concealment, patrols, bunkers, fox holes, crawl trenches and an adherence to the rules of jungle warfare more rigid than that ever practiced in the Burma Campaign."[47] At night, troops being trained were kept alive to the task by 'jitter parties' that would imitate the Japanese tactics of degrading Allied troops by trying to keep them awake at night. Training was far from pleasant. As one Indian recruit described the training regime, "It was by far the toughest thing I have ever been through. Instead of training for the jungle, it would have been more beneficial to those who were destined to enter hell!"[48]

For this new tactical development integration of TCC (Troop Carrier Command) and TAF (Tactical Air Force) was critical and Slim set up an effective joint HQ with them at locations near Barrackpore. As Slim recorded: "We pooled intelligence resources, our planners worked together and, perhaps most effective of all, the three commanders [Slim, Brigadier-General Old (TCC), and Air Marshal John Baldwin (TAF)] and their principal officers lived in the same mess."[49] The result was that prior to the start of a campaign, logistics for air supply were pre-prepared by the TCC. "The complete maintenance for a division for several days, everything it would require, from pills to projectiles, from bully beef to boots, was laid out, packed for dropping, at air strips."[50]

Above all Slim was a persuader. He understood the need to talk to men of all ranks to cajole, encourage and to teach. On tours of the front he would often hold four or five meetings a day with units, officers at HQ, or simply with groups of men or individuals he bumped into. As Slim recalled in his battle memoirs, *Defeat into Victory* [1956], possibly the best campaign book written by a *World War II* commander, "I was in those first few months more like a parliamentary candidate than a general . . ."[51] It helped that he possessed the 'common touch.' Slim wielded a 'dead-pan,' ironic sense of humor that delighted the troops. "Forgotten Army," he used to begin his speeches, "they've never even heard of us!"[52] To the British troops in Burma, he would become their 'Uncle Bill,' one of the most popular commanders ever to lead a British Army.

The Commonwealth Troops of the 14th Army: It is frequently overlooked that when the British Army is mentioned as having lost and then retaken Burma, it was a Commonwealth force whose largest elements were Indian troops drawn from the Indian Army. These included the Indian IV Corps, XV Indian Corps, XXXIII Indian Corps and

XXXIV Indian Corps. If General Slim's 14th Army was the 'Forgotten Army', its Indian soldiers were its forgotten troops; it comprised 8 divisions of Indian troops versus just 2 divisions of British troops. Thus the great majority of the soldiers who defeated and reconquered Burma were Indian not British. An Indian Army that numbered just 200,000 prior to *World War II* grew to 2.5m troops in 1945.

It was the largest volunteer army in history—a fact that must have galled Mahatma Gandhi and Jawaharial Nehru, the leaders of the Indian National Congress, who, believing that Britain was fighting a losing cause, advocated civil disobedience for taking India to war without the consent of its citizens. However Congress's leaders refrained from outright support of Japan and Indians of all casts and races not only volunteered in numbers but fought with valor and distinction.

It should also be noted that 30,000 of the 40,000 Indian troops who were captured in Singapore were recruited to join the Indian National Army (INA) to fight alongside the Japanese Army under the command of Subhas Chandra Bose, a young radical leader with the Indian National Congress, who was expelled by Gandhi and Nehru in 1939 and placed under house arrest by the British the following year. Bose escaped to Germany and helped form a 3,000-strong Free India Legion, comprised of soldiers captured by General Erwin Rommel's Afrika Korps. Bose married his German secretary and started a family while running a Free India Radio station from Berlin. However, when it became clear that a German invasion of India was unlikely, he embarked on a German submarine to Madagascar and from there in a Japanese submarine to Sumatra. He became the leader of the Indian National Army, eventually moving to the Japanese controlled *Andaman Islands* where he set up the Provisional Government of Free India.

Although Indian troops fought in Ethiopia, Egypt, Libya, Iraq, Persia, Lebanon and Tunisia against the German and Italian Armies, it was in the furthest reaches of North East India and in Burma where they fought their most famous actions. However, Indian troops also fought in Borneo, Malaya, Hong Kong and Singapore. During these early *Pacific War* campaigns more than 36,000 Indians were killed and almost the same number wounded; 67,340 were taken prisoner by the Japanese, who treated Indians with much greater cruelty than Caucasian prisoners. While death rates of British prisoners during the three-and-a-half years of imprisonment was 22 percent, the Indian prisoner death rate over the same period was 50 percent.

Even more forgotten than the Indian troops who served in the 14th Army were their African troops. The 82nd (West Africa) Division comprised units raised on the Gold Coast and Nigeria while the 81st (West Africa) Division additionally drew units from the Gambia and Sierra Leone. The 28th Infantry Brigade, known as the Lushai Brigade, was drawn from East Africa. The African troops became known as some of the most feared by the Japanese.

Lastly, it should be noted that the legendary Gurkha regiments, who menacingly carried their curved kukri knives into battle, were recruited from the independent nation of Nepal. They fought with great distinction at Arakan, Imphal, Fort Dufferin, Meiktila and Irrawaddy as well as alongside Major-General Orde Wingate's Chindits.

Independence for Burma: On 22 January 1942 Tojo announced the Japanese government's intention to grant independence for Burma. Ba Maw made his way to Tokyo on 11 March to understand the terms of this concession only to discover that it was conditional on the Burmese government's declaration of war on Britain and the United States. Burma's leader was also told that Burma would be the base for Japan's invasion of India. Ba Maw accepted Tojo's blandishments. On 1 August the military rule of Burma was abolished and Ba Maw, taking the title *Nainggandaw Adipadi* (*der Führer*: the Leader) declared: "Today, after more than fifty years of British occupation, Burma resumes her rightful place among the free nations of the world."[53]

Bogyoke Aung San's BDA (Burma Defense Army) was again renamed this time as Burma National Army (BNA). Aung San became defense minister with Ne Win nominated as his deputy. The message of Tojo's gift of 'independence' did not seem to reach Japanese soldiers on the ground; they continued to slap Burmese soldiers who failed to salute them.

The Second Arakan Campaign and the Battle of the 'Admin Box': [**Map: 26.5**] The first test of Slim's new army and his tactical innovations was the Second Arakan Campaign at the beginning of 1944. The Arakan was the area of western Burma adjacent to the *Bay of Bengal*. It was the site of the start of a series of battles that were to become the turning point of British fortunes in Burma. While Slim was determined to begin its re-conquest, he was aware that Japanese forces had been significantly reinforced over the winter months and from analysis of their troop movement, predicted that they would attack the important strategic capital town of Imphal in the state of Manipur, some 270 miles to the north of Arakan's border with India.

This knowledge did not stop Slim from pressing forward with the advance of the 5th and 7th Indian Divisions in the Arakan at the end of December 1943. Having been elevated to Army commander, Slim devolved ground command of the campaign to Lieutenant-General Philip Christison, a former colleague of Slim's at Camberley Staff College. The battle did not start well. Major-General Harold Briggs advanced the 5th Division down the coastal plain but was stalled at Razabil where defenses had been cleverly prepared by Lieutenant-General Hanaya Tadashi. Major-General Briggs engaged in a series of completely unproductive frontal assaults. The Japanese trench structures proved largely impervious to British air and artillery attack. Log-covered dugouts were normally constructed for ten soldiers and used as a base for food and munitions. Once bombardment had ceased the soldiers would spread out along a spider's web of shallow 'crawl' trenches at the end of which were deeper foxholes for individual soldiers or machine gun emplacements. Again the Japanese defense displayed a level of tactical sophistication that belies the post-war myths of the Japanese being only capable of the *banzai* charge.

The Japanese counter-plan for the Arakan did not rely only on defense. While the 7th Division under Messervy planned an assault on Buthidaung on 7 February, Slim received notice three days earlier that a column of troops had appeared out of the jungle to the rear of the British force. It was a classic Japanese flanking operation planned by Lieutenant-General Tokutaro Sakurai and codenamed HA-GO (Headlong attack). The surprise was complete. Christison admitted: "I had no inkling that the Japanese plan . . . envisaged the complete surrounding of 15 Corp, the cutting of its communications and an attack on Corps HQ."[54] The Japanese force of 7,000 troops with supporting artillery and engineers, led by Colonel Tanahashi, aimed to cut off the British line of retreat over the Ngakyedauk Pass and to fall upon their base at Sinzweya. Travelling with just seven days of supply of food for his troops Sakurai had planned a campaign based on speed and the expectation that British forces once flanked would fall into the chaotic patterns of retreat that had characterized their defeats in both Malaya and Burma in 1942. There was a hubristic assumption that the British forces at the start of 1944 had learnt nothing from the preceding eighteen months.

In the first test of Slim's new tactics, British forces did not 'cut and run.' Slim ordered his commanders to hold the base at Sinzweya at any cost and the fierce battle that ensued became known as the *Battle of the 'Admin Box.'* Here, support staff—cooks, administrators and mule train personnel—were drafted into defending the key administrative and store areas of XV Corp HQ. Their performance in beating back wave after wave of Japanese attacks fully justified Slim's emphasis on training all army personal as potential combatants. It was a brutal engagement. At the beginning of the siege, Japanese troops broke into the hospital compound where, in a familiar pattern of barbarity, they shot and bayoneted thirty-one patients and doctors. Wounded gunner, Bert Wilkins of the Royal Artillery escaped and hid in bushes where he witnessed "the Japanese bayoneting and killing, and running about."[55] In addition to the battles raging at the 'Admin Box,' 5th and 7th Division dug into their own 'boxes' and defended themselves from Tanahashi's encircling attacks. Meanwhile Slim's long-prepared plans for air supply were dusted off and put into action. Over the twenty-one days of the main action British troops received airdrops of 1,600 tons of supply for the loss of just one aircraft. Within a few days the balance of confidence on the battlefield changed. Successful resistance increased British morale. Four days after Tanahashi's surprise attack, Slim noted: "It was good to see how the attitude had altered from that of 1943. Now confidence and the offensive spirit reigned in everyone."[56]

Air supply was critical. As Slim later observed: "We had often canvassed the possibility [of 'boxes'] during the retreat in 1942 but Jap air superiority and lack of aircraft of course ruled it out."[57] While British confidence was rising, Japanese confidence was plummeting. Sakurai's plan had been predicated on a seven-day schedule that would end with their forces resupplying themselves at British expense when the supply base HQ at Sinzweya was overrun. XV Corps' new stand and fight tactics not only caused high Japanese casualty rates but also led inexorably to the starvation of the Japanese troops. Second Lieutenant Satoru Nazawa recorded: ". . . the men of the Tanahashi regiment, the 112th Regiment, were all like half dead, even the ones who were alive, because we were just so hungry. We didn't eat anything. We didn't have water, and our mouths were dried up."[58] The diary entry for 13 February, found on a dead Japanese officer, recorded the bitter complaint, "Planes are bringing whiskey, beer, butter, cheese, jam, corned beef and eggs in great quantities to the enemy. I am starving."[59]

Slim's emphasis on the importance of a well-fed army clearly paid dividends. Even the importance of 'brewing' tea was not ignored. Troops were required to carry solid fuel burners. Boiling water killed potential diseases and maintained soldiers' water intake. Lieutenant-Colonel Mike Lowry, a 7th Division battalion commander recalled that tea was always "a welcome morale booster . . . within five minutes the water boiled, we drank and became new men again."[60] It was not just better provisions that differentiated the British and Japanese forces. In slugging it out against the British 'boxes,' the Japanese also found themselves outgunned. Lowry noted: "Every day artillery duels took place . . . the Jap was outclassed; to his one shell we put down at least twenty."[61]

As the Japanese forces weakened, Slim's 5th and 7th Divisions gradually moved to the offensive. On 23 February, 123rd Brigade advancing from the west, reopened the Ngakyedauk Pass and the following day saw the end of the siege of the 'Admin Box.' Five hundred casualties were immediately evacuated for treatment. By contrast, the fleeing Japanese troops were bereft of help or support. Some 5,000 bodies were recovered from the battlefields, many of them dead from starvation or from its associated diseases. Of the remaining 2,000 of Tanahashi's force, many more died as they retreated piecemeal back towards their own lines. Slim's 5th Division renewed the offensive against Razabil. Learning from the previous mistakes of Briggs and from Japanese tactics, they encircled the Japanese positions. By using tanks to clear the jungle around Japanese defenders' deeper trench fortifications, they were able to attack trenches from the air or destroy them with delayed action high explosive shells that could wreck the bunker façades. After three days Razabil was taken.

The *Battle of the 'Admin Box,'* although a minor battle in the context of *World War II*, was a crushing defeat for Japan. More importantly it was the morale-lifting victory that Slim needed to re-energize the entire Eastern Army. The myth that only Japanese could fight in jungle conditions was exploded. "It was a victory," Slim noted, "a victory about which there could be no argument and its effect, not only on the troops engaged but the whole Fourteenth Army, was immense . . ."[62] Slim argued: "It was the turning point of the Burma campaign. For the first time a British force had met, held, and decisively defeated a major Japanese attack, and followed this up by driving the enemy out of the strongest possible natural positions it had been preparing for months and were determined to hold at all costs."[63] The *Battle of the 'Admin Box'* may not have been a victory of great magnitude but was, Slim asserted, "one of the historic successes of British arms."[64] For survivors, their reward a few weeks later was a visit by the British force's sweetheart, Vera Lynn. Setting off on her first ever flight, a flying boat took her to Calcutta via Gibraltar, Cairo and Bombay. She sang at every stop up and down the Arakan Road. Performing in torrential rain, she gave encores until the officer in charge of entertainment was forced to intervene. On one day she visited five hospitals. It was an exhausting schedule but as Thomas Hankin testified, he "was not the only one with tears in my eyes, with joy and hope."[65]

Some entertainment was less well received. In Poona, Private G. Coulthard of the 10th Gloucesters saw an Errol Flynn film that portrayed the war in Burma as a largely American affair. "Fucking Hoorah!" shouted an exasperated British soldier, "Now we can all fuck off back home."[66] The cinema audience howled with laughter. The Oscar nominated Hollywood film, *Objective Burma!* [1945], was loosely based on Merrill's Marauders and portrayed Errol Flynn's character, Captain Nelson, parachuting into Burma to blow up a Japanese radio surveillance station.

Wingate and Long Range Penetration, LRP–2: **[Map: 26.6]** Four days after Slim had been alerted to Sakurai's flanking movement, which had temporarily put his Arakan campaign into such disarray, on 8 February 1944, Orde Wingate's second Long Range Penetration (LRP) plan, Operation THURSDAY, went into action. After much preparation and rethinking, Wingate had developed the concept of LRP–2. Nine thousand troops would be inserted into Burma to form semi-permanent garrisons from which short-distance raiding patrols would be mounted. Gliders provided and operated by Colonels Cochrane and Allison of the 1st Commando Air Group would perform the task of transporting troops and supplies to the dropping zones. With typical messianic zeal, Wingate prefaced his training notes with the Bible's *Book of Zechariah*, Chapter 9 Verse 12, "Turn you to the stronghold, ye prisoners of hope."[67]

A garrison was thus set up at 'Broadway' by Brigadier Calvert while another at 'Aberdeen' to the north of Indaw was set up by Colonel Bernard Fergusson's 16th Brigade which entered Burma from Ledo with 400 mules and 4,000 men. They arrived completely exhausted and with a close to mortal thirst. His desperate men drank anything. "We found some waterholes at noon . . . they were stinking but acceptable. That night we found two moderately good holes, one for mules and one for men; but we drank both dry . . ."[68] It was an epic travel adventure, wonderfully illuminated by Fergusson's own account *Beyond the Chindwin* [1945] but not a useful means of delivering troops in a condition to fight a successful military action. Moreover Fergusson felt let down by Wingate who had promised him the backup and the support of 14th Brigade, only to find that his commander had sent them elsewhere.

Mike Calvert's 77th Brigade established a third base at 'White City.' The results were mixed. Calvert's garrison at 'White City,' fed with artillery and heavier equipment by air including anti-tank guns, Bofors 40 mm cannon and Vickers machine guns, fought off a determined Japanese attempt to destroy them. Three weeks of intense, sometimes hand to hand fighting, held off the Japanese attackers. Calvert, who would become the only Brigadier in *World War II* to lead a bayonet charge recalled, "the sequence of attack was the same practically every night and only varied in intensity."[69] If value was to be found in 'White City,' it did at least draw off Japanese forces that might otherwise have been used against Stilwell's simultaneous North Burma Campaign, which had targeted the capture of the strategic crossroad town of Myitkyina. In addition there was some disruption of supply and troops to Mutaguchi's western offensive in northeast India. The Chindits were perhaps fortunate that they were allowed time to establish themselves before the Japanese began to take them seriously. Major-General Nazoe Noburu warned Mutaguchi that LRP–2 was a large-scale operation but the 'know-all' Japanese commander dismissed it as "a mouse in a bag."[70] However, Fergusson's 16th Brigade, already over extended physically in their efforts to establish 'Aberdeen,' were unable to capture Indaw as Wingate had ordered.

It was then, on 24 March 1944, returning from a flying inspection of the LRP–2 bases, that Wingate's B-25 Mitchell bomber crashed and killed all aboard. Command devolved to his deputy, Brigadier Lentaigne, a Gurkha officer imposed on Wingate by Wavell, who loathed his deceased commander and his methods. By Allied agreement Lentaigne's Chindits were then placed under the overall command of General Stilwell who used them to harass and disrupt the Japanese as he besieged Myitkyina. The Chindits' finest hour came at the *Battle of Mogaung* when Brigadier Calvert led the heavily depleted 77th Brigade from 'White City' to Mogaung, which denied the Japanese forces supply from Mandalay. **[See Chapter 27: The ICHI-GO Campaign and the Battle of Myitkyina]** By the end of 1944, the last of the Chindits had left Burma and thereafter Wingate's units were gradually absorbed by Slim into the regular army.

Mutaguchi and the March on Delhi: Meanwhile, at the beginning of March, Slim was fully aware that Sakurai's counter-attack in the Arakan was a diversionary effort designed to draw British forces away from the centerpiece of Japan's main plan, which was an attack on Imphal. This strategically located town at the center of the Imphal Plain was adjacent to Burma on its west central borders. At Imphal, on a 650 square yard campsite, was a bustling complex of army camps in addition to supply dumps, hospitals, vehicle servicing depots and administrative centers.

The area was surrounded by jungle-covered mountains on all sides; the Naga Hills to the northeast were 5,000 feet high while to the south the Chin Hills towered even higher at 6,000–9,000 feet. East and west were guarded by seemingly impenetrable jungle hills. Supply to the area came by air or from the railhead at Dimapur to the north. From there supplies had to be taken by vehicles on a 148-mile long, winding, mountain road. Along the way it passed through the mountain village of Kohima.

Lieutenant-General Geoffrey Scoones, the commander of IV Corps was prepared for a limited offensive across the *Chindwin River* in Burma. The aim was to press the Japanese while General Stilwell was attacking from the north and Wingate was establishing the semi-permanent garrisons that would be the main feature of LRP–2 (Long Range Penetration–2). To the south of Imphal the 17th Indian Division led by General 'Punch' Cowan was situated at Tiddim, 163 miles away. Major-General Douglas Gracey with the 20th Indian Division was located just thirty miles from Imphal and twenty miles from the airport at Patel that stood at the edge of the Imphal Plain.

Japan's new Fifteenth Army field commander, Lieutenant-General Renya Mutaguchi, was appointed to his post in July 1943 and immediately lobbied for a campaign to invade India. Mutaguchi, who had been one of the successful commanders in the Malaya Campaign, was an overtly political commander with a history of intrigue behind him.

He had been a member of the ultra-nationalist Cherry Society when they launched a coup in 1930 but subsequently jumped to the 'Imperial Way' faction and boasted of his role as an instigator of the war with China:

> I started off the Marco Polo Bridge Incident, which broadened out into the China Incident, and then expanded until it turned into the Great East Asia War [*Second Sino-Japanese War*] If I push into India now, by my own efforts, and can exercise a decisive influence on the Great East Asia War, I, who was the remote cause of the outbreak of the war, will have justified myself in the eyes of the nation.[71]

In spite of the misgivings of Field Marshal Count Hisaichi Terauchi, Commander in Chief in Burma, War Minister Tojo and Imperial General HQ, with the agreement of Emperor Hirohito, approved the plan. By taking Imphal and moving northward to the railhead at Dimapur in the Brahmaputra Valley, Mutaguchi would cut off communications and transport to Ledo whose airfields serviced the Hump, the name given to the air route that delivered supplies to Chiang Kai-shek's forces in Eastern China. Ledo was also the start point for the road being constructed to transit northern Burma, with the aim of linking up with the Burma Road to Kunming in Eastern China.

Mutaguchi, suspected of harboring megalomaniac plans to conquer India, was distrusted by his divisional commanders as well as Field Marshal Count Terauchi. In anticipation of a rapid victory, Mutaguchi, a notorious drinker and womanizer, decamped to Motoso Yanagida's HQ with an entourage of twenty *geisha*. Supposedly he believed that he was destined to win the battle that would bring Japan victory in the war. His instructions to his troops for Operation U-GO were nothing if not messianic: "The army has now reached the state of invincibility, and the day when the Rising Sun shall proclaim victory in India is not far off . . . We must sweep aside the paltry opposition we encounter and add luster to army tradition by achieving a victory of annihilation."[72] For Mutaguchi, cutting logistical supply to China was never going to be enough. His invasion of Assam was planned merely as a prelude to his 'March on Delhi.'

Supply and the Opening of the Burma Railway: The possibility of invading India was in theory made possible by the opening of the Burma Railway at a formal ceremony on 25 October 1943. In reality parts were still unfinished as Mutaguchi's campaign began. Some 260 miles long, the railway, with sixty-three bridges more than 100 foot long, was extremely vulnerable to air attack and never achieved anywhere near its intended 3,000 ton per day capacity. For the duration of Operation U-GO, the Burma Railway could barely manage more than 400 tons a day. Although some of the troops deployed to invade India arrived by ship, others had to march along the unfinished railway. An Australian prisoner, watching the marching Japanese troops, observed: "They were exhausted and were driven harder than we were."[73] With a hint of pity, another Australian prisoner noted "the ordeal of this Nippon cannon-fodder struggling to the front in such primitive conditions."[74] Furthermore, Mutaguchi had to deploy his troops in the face of increasingly dominant Allied air power.

Lieutenant-General Katoku Sato, commanding the 31st Infantry Division, had to transport his troops 1,000 miles before the offensive was launched. He was deeply pessimistic about the plans for the campaign, though he was partially mollified by promises of 250 tons of supplies before 25 March and then ten tons per week afterwards. None of these supplies actually arrived. Before leaving the *Chindwin*, Sato toasted his fellow officers with champagne telling them, "I'll take the opportunity, gentlemen, of making something quite clear to you. Miracles apart, everyone is likely to lose his life in this operation. It isn't simply a question of the enemy's bullets. You must be prepared for death by starvation in these mountain fastnesses."[75] They were prophetic words.

Operation U-GO and the Battle of Imphal: **[Map: 26.7]** Mutaguchi's Operation U-GO was planned as a four-part attack. Lieutenant-General Motoso Yanagida's 33rd Division would encircle and destroy the 17th Indian Division, Major-General Tsunoru Yamato's force comprising units from the 33rd and 15th Divisions would attack the 20th Indian Division and then fall on Imphal from the east. Infiltrating from the north, Lieutenant-General Masafumi Yamauchi would circle south to attack Imphal. Meanwhile the 31st Infantry Division led by Lieutenant-General Kotoku Sato would cut the road links to Dimapur by taking the mountain village of Kohima and prevent Slim's army being resupplied or reinforced by road.

Supporting Mutaguchi's forces would be the Indian National Army (INA) led by the former senior Congress Party politician, Subhas Chandra Bose. They would support the left flank of the 33rd Infantry Division while a guerrilla unit, the *Bahadur* Group, would seek to turn Slim's Indian troops against their British commanders. Bose, who came out in open support for the Axis powers after the German invasion of Belgium, had resigned from the Congress Party and set up the 'Forward Bloc' in Bengal, a proto-national socialist party. After an escape to Kabul, his subsequent career took him to Moscow and Berlin where he made daily broadcasts inciting an Indian uprising. Later Bose left from Bordeaux in a Japanese submarine bound for *Singapore*, thence to the *Andaman Islands* where a Japanese army had "caught Britain's command with their gin and tonics half down."[76] Of 60,000 captured Indian troops, Bose persuaded just a third to join him in a new pro-Axis command that formed the backbone of the INA. The troops that joined him were not necessarily ideologically in tune with their new leader. Lieutenant Harbans Singh who joined the INA explained, "I have travelled the world and seen the standard of the German Army, they will win."[77]

Crossing the *Chindwin River* on 8 March, Mutaguchi's campaign began a week before Slim's anticipated date. This was hardly a mistake but Slim had badly underestimated the scale of the Japanese attack. Lieutenant-General Geoffrey Scoones, commander of IV Corps also failed to withdraw Cowan's 17th Division from Tiddim soon enough. Both he and Slim had underestimated the Japanese ability to cross the jungle terrain on the northern borders of Manipur-Burma with a significant force. The result was that unexpectedly large forces appeared to the north of Imphal and at Kohima, an area that was under-resourced in defenders. There opened up the frightening prospect that Japanese forces would march on Dimapur and capture the railhead and the strategically vital airfields of northeastern India and secure control of the Brahmaputra Valley.

The Japanese 33rd Division, reputedly containing the toughest Japanese troops in Burma, rapidly encircled and battered 'Punch' Cowan's 17th Indian Division and forced him to make a fighting retreat northwards toward Imphal. Major Ian Lyall-Grant recalled: "The Japanese thought by blocking the road back to Imphal, we would abandon our vehicles and guns and stream back to Imphal where they would defeat us, as we would have no weapons or equipment."[78] However, this was Slim's '1944' Fourteenth Army not the one that the Japanese had pushed out of Burma in the early months of 1942. At Imphal, Lyall-Grant's "Brigadier was cool and cheerful as a cricket . . . and we sat round the fire as plans were made for the next day."[79] Similarly Gracey's 20th Division was flanked by the Japanese and pushed back. Neither retreat resembled the chaotic pell-mell fallbacks that had characterized the campaigns in Malaya or Burma. From the north the Japanese advance was thwarted. Like spokes from a wheel, the roads out of Imphal formed the strong points of the defense. Slim explained, "it was only along these that guns, tanks, and vehicles could move."[80] The defenses held.

As Slim later acknowledged: "As I struggled hard to redress my errors and to speed by rail and air these reinforcements I knew that all depended on the steadfastness of the troops already meeting the first impetus of the attack. If they could hold until help arrived, all would be well."[81] Indeed as early as 4 April, Slim became convinced that Imphal would not be taken. With Imphal 'secure,' and able to be supplied by air, Slim was "now more interested in destroying Japanese divisions than in 'relieving' Imphal."[82]

Not only were the British forces now better equipped and trained but they also held important tactical advantages. The RAF (Royal Air Force) controlled the air. Secondly the British had tanks. For the sake of speed, Mutaguchi had decided not to take artillery and would therefore have no answer to the British tanks. Lastly, in a manner familiar to most of Japan's *World War II* campaigns, logistical support was threadbare. Speed would make up for poor logistics. In his instructions to his troops Mutaguchi had emphasized, "When we strike we must reach our objectives with the speed of wildfire . . ."[83] Troops carried food for twenty days and, as in the campaigns of 1942, they expected by the speed of their advance to be able to feast on captured stores. It did not help their logistical efforts that Japanese lines of supply through the jungle were being disrupted by Wingate's LRP–2 campaign. Just as importantly a well-managed British defensive retreat from the first encounters had denied Mutaguchi's forces the supplies that they had expected to capture and to live on. For Japanese troops, the lure of British stores was more than just survival, it had become a hungrily anticipated treat. Second Lieutenant Satoru Nazawa noted after the capture of Maungdaw in the *First Battle of Arakan*:

> There was another field storage of the enemy. We saw there were mountains of corn beef, bacon, cheese, cigarettes and rum lying around . . . We had this kind of excitement, or more like comedy. We thought, my goodness, these people are fighting in such a luxurious condition. If they came and took our camp, well, they would just find a bit of dried fish and a bit of rice, nothing else.[84]

When Lieutenant-General Yanagida, who by this time was sick and dying, failed to press his 33rd Division aggressively enough, Mutaguchi replaced him with Lieutenant-General Nobuo Tanaka. "All officers and men fight courageously,"[85] he proclaimed but in private his guard slipped when he noted: "the officers and men look dreadful. They've let their hair and beards grow and look like wild men of the mountains."[86] On 20 May, Tanaka launched a ferocious attack on Bishenpur, the village that guarded the gateway to the Imphal Plain. Wave after wave of the cream of Japanese infantry were dashed against the British defensive positions. After ten days Tanaka pulled back. Slim was astonished by the Japanese 33rd Division perseverance, "There can have been few examples in history of a force as reduced, battered, and exhausted as the 33rd Japanese Division delivering such furious assaults, not with the object of extricating itself, but to achieve its original offensive intention."[87]

Tanaka made a last effort at breaking through to Imphal on 2 June. In exhorting his troops, Tanaka asserted, "The coming battle is the turning point. It will denote the success or failure of the Greater East Asia War . . . regarding death as something light as a feather, you must tackle the task of capturing Imphal. For that reason it must be expected that the division will be annihilated."[88] Having suffered casualty rates of 70 percent, the 33rd Division hobbled away from the battlefield; 12,000 of their number were dead of whom 5,000 had died of disease and starvation. Remarkably it was only on 8 July shortly before the cancellation of Operation U-GO that Mutaguchi ordered the remnants of 33rd Division to retire across the *Chindwin*.

After the *Battle of Imphal*, John Hudson of the Sikh Engineer Platoon complained that the British press was dominated by news of the D-Day landings and that Burma was ignored: "Press reporters never reached our besieged positions and any stories that were printed . . . were bland, late and inaccurate . . . we were important to our kinsfolk and nobody else, but when a bullet struck home we were just as dead as the lads in Europe and we were glad they could not see the conditions we had to endure."[89] It annoyed the troops at Imphal too when they heard that the newly struck Burma Star medal was being awarded to base troops at Calcutta. They bawdily joked that it was being awarded to those who were "standing firm in the Howringhee brothels."[90]

The Battle of Kohima: **[Map: 26.8]** If Japanese forces had been massacred at the *Battle of Imphal*, the *Battle of Kohima* took on an even more 'gothic' horror. Sitting at almost

5,000 feet, the village of Kohima was flanked by steep jungle-covered hills and surrounded by much higher mountains. Lieutenant-General Kotoku Sato's forces reached the village's huts on 6 April. Battles raged for control of hills and promontories. On 9 April the 1,200 British defenders were pushed back to Garrison Ridge and the water supply for the village was taken by Sato's 15,000 troops. From 11 to 14 April the battle raged over 'Bunker Hill'; three days later 'Garrison Hill' became the focus and then the Field Supply Depot: ". . . the Japanese remorselessly began to crawl and bomb and bayonet their way along Kohima Ridge . . . The actions were hand-to-hand combat, fierce and ruthless, by filthy, bedraggled, worn-out men . . . ."[91]

Most famously there was a five-day tussle across the tennis courts belonging to the Deputy Commissioner's bungalow. Soldiers dug in on either side had to live through torrential rain and eat, shit and sleep in their trenches. The courts were covered in the bloated bodies of slain Japanese soldiers. Enormous black flies filled the air. The stench of death was gut wrenching. Major John Nettlefield observed, "The place stank. The ground everywhere was ploughed up with shellfire and human remains lay rotting as the battle raged over them. Flies swarmed everywhere and multiplied with incredible speed. Men retched as they dug in . . ."[92] Hand grenades rather than tennis balls criss-crossed the courts. The resilience of the defenders proved the morale that Slim had instilled in his troops. In one notable engagement, John Harman, son of the millionaire owner of *Lundy Island*, a Lance-Corporal with the Queens Royal West Kent Regiment, singlehandedly charged a Japanese trench, killed its five occupants, before being fatally shot returning to his own lines. Dying in his company commander's arms he gave his last words: "I got the lot. It was worth it."[93] Harman was awarded a posthumous Victoria Cross.

Finally to the astonishment of the Japanese, on 29 April, British tanks managed to get to an elevation above the tennis courts and crashed down on the Japanese attackers, relieving the heroic Royal West Kents and the Assam Regiment. Slim described it as "the nearest thing to a battlefield of the First World War in the whole Burma campaign."[94] The concentration of fire in such a small area, over such an extended period was unique in the Burma Campaign. "There was no jungle vegetation," noted Frank Lowry, "only shattered tree trunks."[95]

Compounding the horrors of the manic slaughter of Japanese troops was their lack of food. Air supply was paltry. On the ground Sergeant-Major Sadashige Imanashi, who had set off with 270 head of cattle, arrived at Division HQ with just fourteen. "The remainder are dead, worn out on the journey or fell down into the valley,"[96] he reported.

'Jail Hill,' 'GPT Ridge' and 'Field Supply Depot' fell to the British by 13 May. With his troops weakened by malaria and dying from dysentery and beriberi, Sato urged Mutaguchi to allow him to retreat. Permission was refused. In spite of the much-diminished strength of Sato's forces, the retaking of 'Kohima Ridge' was difficult work. Slim noted: "Wooded ridges had been improved by the Japanese genius for inter-supporting field works and concealment, until it was as formidable a position as a British Army had ever faced."[97] After taking 'Hospital Spur,' Richard Sharp, a BBC war correspondent, broadcast one of the rare graphic descriptions of the fighting and conditions at Kohima to reach Britain: "Now all that is left is the litter of war—piles of biscuits, dead Japs with flies, heaps of Jap ammunition, broken rifles, silver from the District Commissioner's bungalow. And among it, most incongruous of all, there's a man cleaning a pair of boots, another boiling tea . . ."[98]

By now Lieutenant-General Slim had become highly critical of Lieutenant-General Sato's wasteful 'human battering ram' tactics though he was unaware that his opposite number was under orders. Mutaguchi, much to his fury, was told by General Masakazu Kawabe, Burma Area Commander in Rangoon, that an assault on Dimapur was "not within the strategic objectives of the 15th Army."[99] However, with the road wide open and with Dimapur bereft of defenders, this would have been the logical strategy. Instead Sato's 20,000 strong 31st Infantry Division wasted its strength in dashing itself against the 'rock' of the vastly outnumbered 2,500 British defenders at Kohima. Some Japanese regiments were almost entirely wiped out. Manabu Wada, a transport soldier of Mutaguchi's 31st Division, recalled: "Our losses had been dreadful . . . At the beginning of the operation the regiment was thirty-eight hundred strong . . . [now] we were reduced to just a few hundred."[100] By the end, one lieutenant of the 58th Infantry recorded: "Even the invalids and the wounded were driven to the front to help supply manpower. Even those with broken legs in splints were herded into battle, malaria cases too. I saw one man, whose shoulder had been shattered by a bullet, stagger forward to the front."[101]

In-fighting between the Japanese generals increased as events turned against them. When Sato received a second refusal from Mutaguchi to allow him to retreat, he started to rant: "This is shameful. Mutaguchi should apologize for his own failure to the dead soldiers and the Japanese people."[102] Finally, General Sato, a supporter of the 'Control Faction' who hated Mutaguchi, simply refused to take his orders and withdrew his forces. For many Japanese troops even this was too late. "Many soldiers died on the retreat to the Chindwin [River]," said Yuwaichi Fujiwara. "We called the road to Sittaung the 'death road.' "[103]

Sato was sacked. To silence him Mutaguchi sent him a staff officer, Colonel Shumei Kinoshita, to hand him a sword with which to commit suicide. When this failed, Mutaguchi arranged for him to be stripped of rank, declared mentally ill and removed from the country. Sato would have preferred a court martial so as to expose Mutaguchi, but the wily commander refused to give him this opportunity. It did not save Mutaguchi. By the end of the year he too had been removed from command.

Whatever his thoughts about the capabilities of Japanese commanders, Slim was profuse in his admiration for Japanese troops: ". . . there can be no question of the supreme courage and hardihood of the Japanese soldiers who made the attempts. I know of no army that could have equalled them."[104] Such was the capability of the Japanese infantry that it was just as well that at the peak of the battle the British Army was able to muster a two to one numerical advantage against Mutaguchi's forces. Even soldiers on the front line had to admire the bravery of the Japanese. "The Japanese were magnificent in defense," recalled Lieutenant Trevor Highett of the Dorsetshire Regiment. "Every army in the world talks about holding positions to the last man. Virtually no other army, including the Germans, ever did, but the Japs did . . . We thought they were formidable . . ."[105] Japanese troops were never relieved; British troops were rested in relays. Nevertheless, the British and Indian survivors of the *Battle of Kohima* were in dreadful condition by the time they were relieved; Private Tom Cattle remembered that he

> was filthy, unshaven, covered in impetigo, covered in lice, with boils on my arms. My feet were in terrible condition. We were thin, hungry, thirsty and tired . . . My face was covered in sores, it was difficult to have a shave . . . We were covered in purple gentian violet in our armpits and crotch, put there by the medical staff . . . We were visited by an ENSA [Entertainments National Service Association] party including Vera Lynn . . . We had new clothes and boots, and were soon on the move again.[106]

If the *Battle of Kohima* was tough for the British and Indian troops, it was worse for the Japanese. War correspondent Shizuo Marayana recorded that at Kohima, "we were starved and then crushed . . . we and the enemy were close together for over 50 days and could watch each other's movements, but while they got food, we starved."[107]

Ultimately the mistakes made by Slim in the dispersion of his forces at the start of the campaign were overcome because of the vast improvement in the training, morale and leadership of the Indian and British forces. Coordination of air support was also critical to the transformed performance of the troops on the ground. Day and night, Royal Air Force (RAF) Hurricanes and newly arrived Spitfires strafed Japanese lines as well as their logistical support. As artillery officer, Lieutenant Junichi Misana noted, "The plane was the enemy."[108] In addition airlifted supply was critical as was the timely use of mechanized firepower in the form of artillery, tanks and heavy machine guns.

Because of his management of coordinated action by the Allied air forces, Slim was able to achieve a notable first in modern warfare. Getting Mountbatten's backing to usurp the authority of the US Chief of Staffs in Washington, Slim was able to requisition seventy-nine American transport planes being used in the Hump operations to airlift troop reinforcements from the Arakan. It was an easy decision. If the *Battle of Imphal* had been lost, and the main railhead of Dimapur with it, the Hump would also have been fatally compromised. Thus 5th and 7th Division became the first troops in history to be redeployed by air from one battlefield to the next. By 30 June, Operation STAMINA had flown some 19,000 troops, 14.3 million pounds of rations, 1,303 tons of animal grain, 12,000 bags of mail, 43.5 million cigarettes and 835,000 tons of oil and oil products. Air Marshal Sir John Baldwin delighted in the well-oiled machine of his logistical operation: "Nobody has seen a transport operation until he has stayed at Broadway in the full light of the Burma full moon and watched Dakotas coming in and taking off in opposite directions on a single strip all night long, at the rate of one landing or one taking off every three minutes."[109]

It was an operation that was virtually uninterrupted by Japanese aircraft whose number by the summer of 1944 had be reduced to less than ninety in the whole of Burma. Flight-Lieutenant Owen Parry, reported, "We had very little opposition from enemy fighters, the Spitfires dealt with them pretty easily. The majority of sorties by Jap fighters seemed to be sneak air raids on airfields or ground targets, they were a nuisance only."[110]

Mutaguchi, from Defeat to Catastrophe: While British aerial supply worked like clockwork, Mutaguchi, who had counted on speed to provide him with captured British supplies, did not have the luxury of air supply and increasingly had to rely on land-based logistical support. In this he was not helped by the fact that the oxen and cattle that Mutaguchi had driven behind his troops advance to haul supplies as well as provide food 'on the hoof' started to die from exhaustion as well as disease.

Manabu Wada, complained, "Matches struck at this altitude went out immediately, so we could not light cooking fires or boil water. Our cattle and horses fell down the mountainside, taking our provisions with them; the slopes were so steep we couldn't go down to retrieve anything."[111] By the middle of April Wada complained that they "had no rations left. The British burned all their food and supply depots so that not even a grain of rice . . . was left for us . . ."[112]

Mutaguchi's logistical breakdown not only denuded his troops of food but also denied them munitions. Wada pointed out, "The enemy's heavy and medium artillery opened up on us as a prelude to their infantry attacks. For our part, we were limited to reply with just a few shells a day . . . We watched as enemy reinforcements arrived by truck with more and more ammunition to be thrown immediately against us."[113] For both troops and commanders, the supply situation led to utter despair. In a desperate note to Mutaguchi, Sato, having had two requests for supply to his troops at Kohima ignored, protested bitterly, "Since leaving the Chindwin, we have not received one bullet from you, nor a grain of rice."[114] While Slim had won his tactical battle with Mutaguchi, it was the Japanese commander's failed logistical foresight that turned a defeat into a national catastrophe.

Although Mutaguchi has usually taken the blame for not withdrawing his troops from Imphal and Kohima early enough, it seems clear that he would not have been allowed to retreat by either his superiors in Rangoon or more importantly Imperial General HQ in Tokyo. As Mutaguchi's forces battled to break the stranglehold of Slim's defense of the six roads leading into Imphal, Vice-Chief of the Army General Staff, General Hikosaburo Hata, paid them a visit at the front. Reporting back to Tojo, Hata declared: "There is little probability that the Imphal operation will succeed."[115] Tojo, desperate for a victory to make up for the loss of the *Marshall Islands*, flew into a violently abusive rage and accused Hata of defeatism. Colonel Tanemura, who accompanied Hata, later recorded in his diary, faced by Tojo's tirade, Hata remained silent: "If I'd been Hata I'd have ripped off my staff insignia and fought him."[116]

Mutaguchi also knew the situation was hopeless but later admitted that he could not bring himself to inform the Burma Area Commander, General Masakazu Kawabe, how hopeless the situation had become. "I was hoping that General Kawabe would perceive in silence what was in my heart."[117] There is little question that the obduracy by senior commanders on the ground and in Tokyo turned their defeat at Imphal and Kohima into the most deadly campaign fought by the Japanese in *World War II*. Possibly because the Burma campaigns were a sideshow to the main action of the *Pacific War*, the *Battles of Imphal* and *Kohima* have never been given the prominence that their scale, conclusiveness and pivotal nature deserve. For both Japan and the Allies, Burma was at the margin of their strategic interests, and its importance lay largely in its location as a supply route for Chiang Kai-shek's Chinese Army. Purely in terms of numbers, the armies faced by Slim in Burma were far greater than anything faced by US forces in the *Pacific Island* engagements. Only in MacArthur's re-conquest of the Philippines' main island of *Luzon* did engagements exceed the scale of Burma.

Slim's natural modesty and generosity meant that he would always be subject to the risk that other less moral men would claim credit for what was his victory. Lord Mountbatten, as was his wont, did try to claim the credit for the victory at Imphal and his wife Edwina made the absurd boast: "If the battle of Imphal is won, it will be almost entirely due to Dickie overriding all his generals."[118] Fortunately on this occasion nobody took Mountbatten seriously. In fact any credibility he had as a military commander was fatally undermined by his absurd decision to move his South East Asia Command (SEAC) headquarters from Delhi to Kandy in *Ceylon*. Given that it was already clear that SEAC was never going to be 'navy' orientated, his removal to a distance a further 1,000 miles from the front than Delhi was preposterous. Mountbatten's headquarters at Kandy became legendary for ostentatious luxury. Staffing at SEAC increased from 7,000 to a mind boggling 10,000 people without an operation to plan between them. Having quit Delhi, Mountbatten added to the *Opéra Bouffe* nature of his command by proposing to establish his own embassy there.

Field Marshal Viscount Alanbrooke, Chairman of the Chiefs of Staff Committee, and closest military adviser to Churchill, who proved himself a fair judge of military commanders and had been instrumental in advancing the careers of 'performing' commanders such as Montgomery and Slim, judged Mountbatten thus: "Seldom has a Supreme Commander been more deficient of the main attributes of a Supreme Commander than Dickie Mountbatten . . . I find it very hard to remain pleasant when he turns up! He is the most crashing bore I have met on a committee, is always fiddling about with unimportant matters and wasting other people's time."[119] Nevertheless, in spite of his absurdities, Mountbatten's consistent support of Slim meant that his foolishness never jeopardized British success in Burma.

Slim did not just defeat Mutaguchi's forces, he ground them down until they were annihilated. From the 100,000 Japanese troops who took part in the *Battles of Imphal* and

Kohima, there were, according to Japanese sources, 72,000 casualties of whom it is estimated that more than 30,000 were killed. However, that was not the end of the Japanese massacre. After Field Marshal Terauchi finally approved withdrawal on 9 July 1944, Slim ordered Lieutenant-General Scoones to pursue the retreating Japanese. It was the turn of Mutaguchi's army, which had proudly set out to conquer India to face the bitter tribulations of pell-mell flight from the battlefield. By now, with all Japanese logistical systems completely smashed, Mutaguchi's starving soldiers, harassed by the British in their rear, died in droves. Forced to eat snails, lizards, snakes and monkeys where they could find them, thousands of Japanese were too weak to make the return journey across the *Chindwin River*. Half buried in mud brought about by the monsoon that had arrived, Japanese soldiers discarded their equipment and fled as best they could. Some blew themselves up with grenades. Thousands simply collapsed and expired by the trailside. Many drowned in the *Chindwin*. Not a single piece of artillery was brought back to Burma. Some 17,000 pack animals died. Lieutenant Iwaichi Fujiwara, noted, "Most officers and men were suffering from a vicious circle of malaria, amoebic dysentery, beriberi and skin diseases brought on by fatigue and malnutrition. Clothing and boots were torn and broken, almost all equipment was lost, and the soldiers looked like ghosts."[120]

The sudden collapse took the hitherto hard-pressed British Army by surprise. As Lieutenant John Hudson wrote: "We were unprepared for the state of our enemy. They had seemed so strong up to the last days and now, to our astonishment, we were chasing a sick and dying enemy ..."[121] Up until this point most British soldiers, formerly onvinced of the superhuman fighting ability of the Japanese, had not imagined the conditions under which the enemy was living and fighting. As Hudson pointed out: "Facing them on the ground, we had seen only the ferocity of their aggression, but not the price they were paying."[122] The tipping point, when it came, was dramatic. It was one thing to sustain morale on the attack, quite another during the Japanese Army's first taste of retreat in Burma. "... the change from a long offensive and death-struggle to the path of retreat slackened the fighting-spirit," recalled Lieutenant-General Iwaichi Fujiwara. "Commanders of some units had difficulty in controlling their men."[123]

By some estimates a further 35,000 Japanese troops perished on the retreat. In all the *Battles of Arakan, Imphal* and *Kohima* cost an estimated 65,000 Japanese lives—some 65 percent of Mutaguchi's force and more than double the number who died in the seminal *South Pacific* conflict at the *Battle of Guadalcanal*. Only during the *Battle of Luzon* (the main island of the Philippines), an engagement where US victory against an already strategically defeated and defensive Japanese army was inevitable, were the Japanese casualty rates of Slim's masterpiece battle exceeded. By contrast with Japanese losses, the number of British troops killed was 4,500 with total casualties of 17,857. In the overwhelming brilliance of its strategic and tactical innovations, the collective of the *Battles of Arakan, Imphal* and *Kohima* matched or bettered General Montgomery's more famous victory at the *Battle of El Alamein*, where German casualties amounted to 10,000 (5,000 dead) out of a total of 96,000 troops. Slim had inflicted on Japan the most stunning military defeat in its history.

It seems appropriate to leave the last words, typically modest, with Lieutenant-General Slim:

> My army had indubitably won this battle . . . the plan of the Imphal battle had been sound and we adhered to it. Basically, it had been to meet the Japanese on ground of our own choosing, with a better line of communication behind us than behind them, to concentrate against them superior forces drawn from Arakan and India, to wear them down, and, when they were exhausted, to turn and destroy them. All this we had done in spite of my mistakes in mistiming the withdrawal of the 17th Division from Tiddim and underestimating the strength of the Japanese thrust at Kohima.[124]

27 The ICHI-GO Campaign and the Battle of Myitkyina

[January 1944–August 1945]

[Maps: 27.1, 27.2, 27.3, 27.4, 27.5, 27.6, 27.7, 27.8, 27.9, 27.10]

The Japanese Army, largely because of the diminution of the Japanese Navy and logistical constraints, had been virtually powerless to stop the Allied advance in New Guinea and the *Solomon Islands* in 1943. Further losses were anticipated by Army GHQ in the following year, with General MacArthur expected to sweep up the northern New Guinea coast toward the Philippines. New Guinea was viewed as a holding operation to delay the inexorable American advance. With its shorter lines of supply, the Philippines was seen as the place to block MacArthur's advance toward Japan. A great naval victory in this area was also hoped for. On the Asian continent the Japanese Army, not so dependent on naval supply, was logistically less constrained. Hence the Japanese Army's focus at the beginning of 1944 was the establishment of a position of strength in China, Burma and Northern India. [**Map: 27.1**]

ICHI-GO and Operation KOGO: [**Map: 27.2**] On New Year's day 1944, Chiang Kai-shek sent a cable to President Roosevelt in Washington warning him that the strategy agreed with Stalin at the Tehran Conference at the end of November 1943 [codenamed EUREKA], with its entire emphasis on the European front, would leave China open to attack. "Before long Japan will launch an all-out offensive against China."[1] Western intelligence sources disagreed. Meanwhile Chiang's Chief of Staff, Joseph Stilwell, was more intent on the recapture of Burma from where he had been expelled two years earlier. Chiang would not have to wait long for his fears to be proved correct.

In April 1944, the launch of Operation ICHI-GO, the largest military operation in Japanese history, was part of a belated Japanese Army strategy to vanquish all of mainland Asia and was coordinated with Operation U-GO's invasion of India. Clearly losing the maritime war in the Pacific, the Imperial Japanese Army determined on one last throw of the dice on the Asian mainland. If successful, overland supply lines from Burma to southern Korea could be secured. In addition Japan hoped for a bargaining chip with which to negotiate with America. If the *Kuomintang* government could be annihilated, America would be faced with having to invade and conquer China whose freedom had ostensibly been the *casus belli* of the *Pacific War*. Japan also hoped to interdict Chennault's Tenth Air Force bombing of the Japanese home islands from bases in southern China. As Hirohito recalled in his *Dokuhaku Roku* (post-war testament),

"One shred of hope remained—to bash them at Yunnan in conjunction with operations in Burma. If we did that we could deal a telling blow to Britain and America . . ."[2]

A total of 150,000 Japanese troops were assembled to cross the *Yellow River*; they were the advance guard of a campaign that would eventually involve 500,000 of their soldiers. They were supplied with enough ammunition for two years. To support the troops, the Japanese Army Air Force had amassed 200 bombers with enough fuel for eight months. Over the course of the next nine months battles would be fought over three regions, Henan in central China to the east of Nanking between the *Yellow River* and *Yangtze River*, and Hunan and Guangxi in the south to the east of *Hong Kong* and Guandong Province and to the south of the *Yangtze River*. Running in tandem with the ICHI-GO Campaign, Chiang Kai-shek's best trained and equipped troops, Y-Force, based in Yunan Province, as well as Merrill's Marauders, were fighting alongside Stilwell for the control of northern Burma. Meanwhile on the Burma-India border, Japanese forces led by Lieutenant-General Mutaguchi were already fighting the British Fourteenth Army for the control of Imphal, capital of India's border state of Manipur.

Japan's first phase of the battle, codenamed Operation KOGO [**Map: 27.3**], was aimed at opening the Pinghan Railway that runs from Peking in the north to Wuhan. South of Peking the *Yellow River* runs southwest to east, the second longest in China and the sixth longest in the world. It exits south of Peking into the *Bohai Sea* in the northwesternmost corner of the *East China Sea*. In 1938 Chiang Kai-shek had opened the levees that hold back the river in order to delay the Japanese advance. It worked but at a cost of an estimated 500,000 Chinese lives. The fertile plains of Henan province were destroyed and its people drowned or starved. Although the Japanese army had eventually moved south to take the key strategic city of Wuhan on the *Yangtze River*, afterwards the agricultural hinterland of Henan remained unoccupied and only loosely and partly controlled by the *Kuomintang* (Nationalists) and the Japanese. The latter, although they had 1.5 million soldiers in China, did not have the resources to control the country in depth.

For most of the *Pacific War*, the Japanese were content simply to control the *Yangtze River* from Wuhan, extending along the rich fertile delta that eventually passes through Nanking and Shanghai before exiting into the *East China Sea*. A further 466 miles upstream to the west of Wuhan behind a barricade of mountains, lay Chiang Kai-shek's wartime capital of Chongqing.

In effect there was a form of stalemate between the three sides in the conflict: the Japanese Army, the *Kuomintang* and the Chinese Communist Party (CCP). Mao had secretly come to an arrangement with the Japanese not to fight each other. Less formalized were the discreet trading arrangements that local *Kuomintang* commanders often arranged piecemeal with the occupying Japanese Army. The result was that goods were often traded between the two sides including, on some occasions, *matériel* provided by the American Lend-Lease operation over the Hump; army-appointed middlemen would simply sail down the *Yangtze River* with their illicit goods from Chongqing to Wuhan and on to Shanghai.

For Japan, somewhat occupied elsewhere in the *Pacific* as well as in the *Solomon Islands* and New Guinea, the lacuna in their Chinese operations suited them well. Likewise Chiang Kai-shek realized that he did not have the resources to train and arm even his core divisions let alone the local *Kuomintang* forces led by his provincial commanders. Although Roosevelt had promised in 1943 to arm and modernize the *Kuomintang*'s core ninety divisions (out of a theoretical total of 360), in practice the Hump could only provide enough *matériel* to modernize thirty divisions, X-Force and Y-Force. Stilwell was training these divisions for the retaking of northern Burma, which itself would open up land supply routes to Chongqing along the Ledo–Burma Road. Without resources to equip his armies on the eastern Japanese front, Chiang Kai-shek knew that any head-on engagement with Japanese forces in central China would probably end with 'free China's' complete defeat and destruction. With Japan largely content to remain quiescent between 1942 and 1944 therefore, the majority of fighting in China actually took place at a local level, in struggles for control in agrarian regions, village by village, between *Kuomintang* and Communist forces.

This uneasy balance came to an end at the beginning of 1944. Japan needed to change the balance of power in China. By this point in the war, Japan was facing economic strangulation from the US Navy's incursions along its trade routes from South East Asia. **[Appendix A: Submarines: America Draws Tight the Noose]** Having finally sorted out their 'malfunctioning' torpedo problems, the US Navy's submarine forces were beginning to have a dramatic impact on Japan's merchant navy and its ability to supply Japan with oil and other essential commodities. In the first three months of 1943 US submarines sank 57 Japanese merchantmen. By the last quarter of the year the submarine tally had risen to 106, accounting for 65 percent of Japanese merchant ships sunk in that period. In the following quarter, January to March 1944, US submarines sank 136 merchant ships with an aggregate weight of 500,000 tons. Furthermore with tanker capacity unable to maintain supplies from the Dutch East Indies, domestic Japanese stocks of oil and gasoline products were in steep decline. **[Appendix B: Oil, Raw Materials and Logistics: 'Just Start Swinging']** Indeed, after the half dozen major naval battles and loss of *Guadalcanal* in the *Solomon Islands* at the beginning of 1943, the decision was made to base a large portion of the Japanese fleet in *Singapore*, close to the production sources of oil in *Borneo* and the Dutch East Indies. This in itself further hampered Japan's ability to engage in a submarine war.

The logistical purpose of the ICHI-GO Campaign was therefore to create a supply chain linking Indochina with China. If Japan could conquer south and southwestern China, a rail supply route could be established linking Vietnam with southern Korea. The route would send goods by train from Hanoi to Wuhan, Peking, via Manchuria and down through Korea to Busan from where there was a short hop to Japan across the *Japan Sea*. Thus the Japanese Army first needed to establish control over the *Kuomintang*-held provinces, thereby liberating the Pinghan Railway that connected Wuhan to Peking. A secondary objective of ICHI-GO was to interdict Chennault's strategic bombing of Japan and the Fourteenth Air Force's bombing of Japanese targets in China.

At the end of April 1944, crack units of Japan's *Kwantung* (Manchuria) Army, led by the 3rd Tank Division, crossed the *Yellow River* at Zhengzhou (capital of Henan Province) and moved south and then east in a circling engagement that trapped three divisions of the 380,000 strong *Kuomintang* Army led by Generals Tang Enbo and Jiang Dingwen at the strategically placed city of Luoyang. Cut off from its lines of supply, Luoyang, which was attacked on 13 May, held out for twelve days before succumbing to the vastly better equipped and trained Japanese forces. A million bags of flour were captured by the invaders. Jiang Dingwen noted: "I'd already thought that there were not enough troops . . . we faced the enemy on three sides. The area to defend was huge and the troops were very few."[3] Jiang would also blame the setback on confusing orders sent by Chiang Kai-shek.

Having defeated General Tang Enbo at the *Battles of Henan-Hunan-Guangxi*, capturing thirty-seven towns and cities in thirty days in April–May 1944, General Shinroku Hata, commander of the China Expeditionary Army, was promoted to Field Marshal on 2 June.

Jiang observed that the people of Henan, for years abused by the *Kuomintang*, now took revenge on its Army, killing its officers and stealing stores. As Jiang lamented: "Actually this is painful for me to say; in the end the damages we suffered from the attack by the people were more serious than the losses from battles with the enemy."[4] It was retribution for the Henan famine of the previous years that the *Kuomintang*'s fragile logistics, as well as its corruption and incompetence, had done much to exacerbate. However, both Tang and Jiang were later accused by the *Kuomintang* leadership of being completely unprepared for combat in the First War Zone, having spent the previous two years engaged in personal enrichment. Guo Zhonghuai would later accuse Tang of "running like a rat . . . and completely losing contact with his army . . . he didn't even know where his armies were."[5] Everett F. Dumright on the US Embassy staff in Xian concluded that the Japanese invaders met only token resistance and that the "Chinese suffered heavy losses in men, material, and crops. Loss of wheat crop, best in years, most serious loss."[6]

Mao's Soviet adviser observed: "the CCP leadership rejoices at the news of the defeat suffered by Chiang Kai-shek's troops in Honan [Henan] and Hunan . . . His [Mao's] calculations are simple—whenever Chiang Kai-shek suffers a defeat, [Yanan] benefits from it."[7]

Stilwell's Strategic Priorities: Why was Stilwell content to leave central and southern China to the mercies of Japan? He would later suggest that he knew that the Japanese offensive would blow itself out as the logistics of their advance become unsupportable. It seems likely that this was at least in part an excuse. Stilwell's reputation was vested in the armies of X-Force and Y-Force, whose training he had personally overseen. These units had been trained respectively in India and on the China-Burma border. They had also been supplied with a high percentage of the money, arms and supplies agreed under the terms of the Lend-Lease funding, whose distribution was, in effect, controlled by

Stilwell. Y-Force based to the east of Kunming in Yunnan province could have easily been made available for the defense of central and southern China. Stubbornly, Stilwell's strategic priorities always remained firmly rooted in Burma.

The opening of the Ledo Road and its linkage with the Burma Road that ran from Lashio to Kunming was Stilwell's strategic priority—much of his effort as well as the lives of thousands of soldiers and civilians had been vested in its completion. The realization of this project, Stilwell believed, would open almost limitless flows of *matériel* to China. Everything else was secondary. Perhaps more importantly, unlike the Hump, the air route under the control of his loathed rival Lieutenant-General Claire Chennault, the road was controlled by Stilwell. If he could complete the building of the Ledo–Burma Road by the destruction of the Japanese Army in northern and central Burma, he then believed that he could swing around Y-Force, move back eastwards and not only defeat Japan's China-based armies but capture a port on the south coast of China from where the final US assault on the Japanese home islands could be based.

There would be personal side benefits to this strategy. First, Stilwell could avenge himself on the Japanese Army for the crushing defeat inflicted on him in Burma in the spring of 1942. Second, he could prove Chiang and Chennault wrong in their supposed belief in the supremacy of air power. Chennault had believed that an important means of defeating the Japanese Army was to use air power to destroy its logistical capabilities. He believed that Stilwell showed "a complete lack of conception of the true use of air power or even of basic military power."[8] Chennault compared his own military vision with Scipio Africanus who had defended Rome by attacking Carthage. "I can cause the collapse of Japan," he asserted.[9] However, there is no record of Chennault ever saying, as Stilwell asserted, that the war in China could be won in the air alone. Trying to put the two of them in harness was a match made in hell. It undermined the effectiveness of both. Ultimately Marshall failed to resolve the issue of command in the North Combat Area Command (NCAC) and in hindsight he should be held responsible for not sorting out this conflict of personalities and strategies.

Field Marshal Shinroku Hata: It is an indication of the centrality of China and Manchuria to Japanese political and military strategy that in March 1941, General Shinroku Hata was given command of Japan's China Expedition Army after being Japan's Minister of Defense. Hata was born in Fukushima Prefecture (located in the northwest of Japan's main island of *Honshu*) before moving to Hakodate at the southern tip of *Hokkaido Island* when he was twelve. Two years later he showed his academic credentials when he won a place at the prestigious First Tokyo Middle School but, no longer able to afford his education when his father suddenly died, enrolled instead at the Imperial Japanese Army Academy. As was usual for the brightest military students (Napoleon included) he specialized in artillery and graduated as a Second Lieutenant in 1901. After serving in the *Russo-Japanese War* in 1905, Hata was put in for training at the Imperial Staff College where he graduated twenty-second in 1910. In 1912 he became Japanese military *attaché* in Berlin and served as an observer in the German campaign on the Western Front. He went on to serve as a member of the Japanese delegation at the *Treaty of Versailles* in 1919.

After *World War I*, Hata served on the Imperial Army General Staff and was promoted to Lieutenant-General in 1931 when he was made Inspector-General of Artillery Training. In 1935, Hata became head of the Imperial Army Air Service and the following year was made commander of the Japanese Army in Taiwan. He became a full general in 1937 at the same time as his promotion to the Military Council, responsible as Inspector for all Military Training in the Imperial Japanese Army. After the Rape of Nanking, he was sent to replace the recalled General Iwane Matsui as commander of the Central China Expeditionary Force in February 1938.

In this role Hata, between March 1938 and May 1939, was responsible for the conquest of Jiangxi and Zhejiang Provinces in the central coastal areas of China, including the *Yangtze Delta*, which comprised the country's wealthiest heartland. It was later estimated that up to 5 million Chinese civilians died as a result of the Zhejiang-Jiangxi Campaign and after the war he was prosecuted and found guilty of not doing enough to prevent war atrocities during this period. (He was given life imprisonment but was paroled in 1954.) In May 1939 Hata became *aide-de-camp* to Hirohito, in which role he advised the Emperor on military affairs and strategy. In August that year his career took an even more elevated turn when he became Minster of War, serving in the cabinets of Prime Minister Abe and then Prime Minister Admiral Mitsumasa Yonai. Hata, who strongly opposed the anti-German, anti-*Tripartite Pact* policies of Admiral Yonai, was instrumental in orchestrating his removal from office at the end of July 1941. Two months later on 27 September the *Tripartite Pact* was signed with Hitler and Mussolini.

After the ICHI-GO Campaign, Hata would be transferred to Hiroshima in November 1944 to take charge of the Second General Army. Later, after the dropping of the first atom bomb, perhaps not surprisingly given that he witnessed the nuclear catastrophe, he became one of the key advocates of unconditional Japanese surrender. Field Marshal Hata's career practically defines Japan's entry to and participation in *World War II*. By no means a fanatic by the standards of the time, he was in the middle ground of right-wing military sentiment in the pre-war period.

Operation TOGO-I and the Battles of Changsha and Hengyang: **[Map: 27.4]** On 27 May 1944, Field Marshal Hata, from his base at Wuhan, ordered the Thirteenth Army to advance on Changsha, the capital city of Hunan Province. Later the Twenty-third Army based in Canton, would join them. With a combined force of 360,000 troops, the biggest ever fielded by Japan, General Isamu Yokoyama was able to outflank the National Revolutionary Army's Fourth Corps at Wangyang Mountain near Liuyang (to the east of Changsha) and cut it off from its lines of supply and retreat. In the three previous battles for the city the defenders had managed to counter-march and prevent encirclement but General Zhang Denen not only failed in this respect but fled his command leaving IV Corps to its fate.

Zhang's order to retreat directly contravened the orders to stay and fight issued by Xue Yue, commander of the Ninth Military Front. Three years earlier Xue Yue had heroically held the city but this time, as Theodore White noted, "His units were three years older . . . their weapons three years more worn, the soldiers three years hungrier than when they last won glory."[10] An infuriated Chiang Kai-shek ordered Zhang's arrest on a charge of "incompetence of command and desertion upon combat engagement."[11] He was imprisoned and later executed.

By 18 June America's bomber base at Hengyang Airfield, in Hunan Province south of Changsha, was under siege. China, until then a sleepy backwater of America's interest in *World War II*, suddenly drew the attention of Washington when Chiang and Chennault demanded further supplies over the Hump to enable more air attacks on the advancing Japanese Army. They also requested more arms for the Chinese troops on the ground. Marshall vetoed the requests. He was appalled by the cost of the Hump and its drain on supplies of transport aircraft, a lack of which he believed had delayed the advance of American troops in France and Italy. The Secretary of War, Henry Stimson, complained that the Hump "has been bleeding us white in transport planes."[12] By now General 'Hap' Arnold, supported by Marshall, was eyeing the shift of their B-29 Superfortress bomber force to the *Marianas Islands*, including *Guam, Saipan* and *Tinian*. Stilwell was delighted by this reversal for his rival, Chennault, and noted that he believed that Chennault's request for more supplies was a campaign designed "to duck the consequences of having sold the wrong bill of goods."[13] Stilwell had argued at the third Washington Conference in May 1943 (codename TRIDENT) that air cover was pointless if there was 'nothing' on the ground.

From Changsha, Japanese forces advanced to Hengyang where they were twice repelled by General Fang Xianjue's 10th Corps, which was dug in behind well-constructed barricades. Defensive fortifications with cross fusillades of machine gun fire on open ground wrought heavy casualties on the advancing Japanese infantry. The apparent failure of the assault on Henyang was such that, combined with the fall of *Saipan* on 9 July **[see Chapter 32: The Invasions of Saipan, Tinian, and Guam: General Tojo Upended]**, it caused the fall of Prime Minister Tojo Hideki's cabinet on 18 July 1944.

A renewed assault on Hengyang in August brought heavy casualties to the Japanese 68th and 116th Divisions. When stalemate was threatening to force the Japanese to abort the siege, Japan's 58th Division broke into the northwest of the city and renewed its assaults. Although reinforcements from the Chinese National Revolutionary Army attempted to raise the siege, they were thwarted with heavy casualties on both sides. After seven weeks of fighting, General Fang Xianjue was eventually captured and his 10th Corps forced to surrender on 8 August. Hengyang Airfield and Lingling Airfield were lost to the Japanese.

With better allocation of resources and better strategic prioritization, the Hump could have more than adequately equipped Chinese armies capable of holding the Japanese. As it was, the dribble of modern armaments and supplies that made it to Chiang's western armies was often filched by corrupt commanders and officers. In May 1944, a US intelligence officer sent an excoriating report for the War Department on corruption in the *Kuomintang*'s National Revolutionary Army, which noted, "During the first week of February 1944, Lieutenant Budd, railhead officer at Kunming, dispatched 250 trucks for Kweiyang [in Guizhou Province halfway between Chongqing and Kunming]. Of this number 192 trucks failed to report and were either hijacked or stolen outright by Chinese drivers."[14] The problem of Chiang's armies was not that the Chinese soldiers were poor but that, with the exception of Stilwell's pet projects, X-Force and Y-Force, they were poorly equipped, supplied and led. At the *Battle of Hengyang*, Theodore White noted of China's soldiers that only "one in three had a rifle."[15]

Here, out of 17,000 Chinese troops, only 3,000, mainly wounded casualties, remained alive. Theodore White witnessed the courage of the Chinese defenders: "All that flesh and blood could do, the Chinese soldiers were doing. They were walking up hills and dying in the sun but they had no support, no guns, no direction. They were doomed."[16] Even when the Chinese soldiers did have guns, they were nearly all poor-quality bolt-action rifles rather than semi-automatics. Machine guns, field cannon, mortars, the three biggest killing weapons of the *Pacific War*, were in short supply. More exotic weapons such as flame-throwers were simply not available. Similarly Chinese artillery was sparse and antiquated. Although the Chinese forces usually outnumbered Field Marshal Hata's Japanese forces, they were massively outgunned. Chinese forces in eastern China were not helped by Stilwell's refusal to allow Chennault to divert 200 fighter aircraft to help the ground forces in eastern China. Moreover Chiang and Stilwell's suspicions about the loyalty of Xue Fue, their commander in Hunan, and General Zhang Fakui in Guangdong and Guangxi, made them reluctant to send precious supplies or reinforcements. Neither did it help that Washington vetoed the use of the Fourteenth Air Force's B-29s to bomb the Japanese depots at Wuhan. Stilwell, Chief of Staff of the *Kuomintang* Army, was seemingly delighted at the setbacks to Chiang's forces on the eastern front. He replied to Marshall's negative responses for more supplies by writing, "Instructions understood and exactly what I had hoped for . . . Pressure from the Generalissimo compelled me to send the request."[17]

In spite of Marshall's refusal to provide Chiang's armies with aerial support and their ground forces with modern weaponry and supplies, had the US Joint Chiefs of Staff taken notice, the 51-day siege of Hengyang would have given the lie to the idea circulating in Washington that the *Kuomintang*'s soldiers were incapable and unwilling to fight. As Werner Gruhl, former chief of NASA's (National Aeronautics and Space Agency's) Cost and Economic Analysis Branch, has pointed out regarding the *Battle of Hengyang*, "This little recognized brave defense alone cost the Chinese more lives than US forces lost in the well-chronicled struggle and losses to take Okinawa in the following year."[18]

The Cancellation of ANAKIM and Stilwell's New Plan: **[Map: 27.5]** While Field Marshal Hata's armies were slamming Stilwell's *Kuomintang* forces in the east,

Stilwell's interests remained firmly planted on his western front in Burma. After his famous stomp through the jungles of northern Burma to reach India in 1942, General Stilwell had flown to New Delhi, where he was met by reporters. "I got a hell of a beating. We got out of Burma and it was humiliating as hell. I think we ought to find out what caused it and go back and retake it."[19] It was not a statement quite as famous as General MacArthur's "I will return" after he left his soon-to-be defeated troops at *Corregidor* to go to Australia, but Stilwell's sentiments were clearly similar. Like MacArthur and the Philippines, Stilwell's desire to return to Burma had elements of an obsessive desire to avenge his former defeat and wipe the record clean.

The key element of Stilwell's strategy in the aftermath of the 1942 defeat was first to ensure supply to China—in the short term by means of the airlift over the Hump. Second, plans were made and approved for the construction of the Ledo Road, which would ultimately give a land route to supply China. Third, the Allies laid plans for a re-invasion of Burma in 1943. The ANAKIM plan was conceived as an amphibious landing, which would outflank the bulk of Japanese forces in central Burma and enable the capture of Rangoon. The longer-term objective was to re-open the rail supply route from Rangoon to Kunming. The British would provide the troops and boats, supplemented by the United States, while Chiang's Chinese divisions would divert Japanese resources by invading Burma from the north.

After initial enthusiasm, all the Allies found cause to backslide. Stilwell had great difficulty in persuading Chiang Kai-shek to commit and threatened to withdraw Lend-Lease supplies. Chiang, after the fiasco of 1942, was naturally reluctant to commit himself and demanded a *quid quo pro* in terms of supply and Allied commitment of sufficient naval and air power. "Peanut [Chiang] won't fight,"[20] Stilwell disingenuously wrote to Marshall. Roosevelt dispatched General 'Hap' Arnold and he found that Chiang was not as difficult to deal with as Stilwell made out. After a successful meeting in Chongqing with 'Hap' Arnold, who promised Chiang adequate air support, Chiang gave a clear affirmation of Chinese military support. Chiang backed up his support with a letter to Roosevelt, which guaranteed the *Kuomintang* Army "to perform its assigned task at the specified time without fail."[21] Stilwell's reports managed to put a negative spin on this meeting, with the result that Roosevelt concluded that Stilwell "had exactly the wrong approach in dealing with Chiang Kai-shek."[22]

Similarly, Roosevelt was observant enough to note that Stilwell failed to include any role for air power in his strategy for retaking Burma. Stilwell was as culpable of under-estimating the importance of air power as Chiang and Chennault would sometimes be of overestimating its importance. Chennault had been given command of the Fourteenth Air Force by General Marshall. Chennault's forces, independent of Stilwell, absorbed the 'Flying Tigers' as well as control of the Hump operations. It was another blow to Stilwell's hopes of a unified command and partly explains his lack of interest in the Fourth Air Force's airfields. Thus Stilwell was dismissive of a Japanese advance up the *Yangtze River* basin in April 1943. He had a blazing row with Chiang when the

Generalissimo ordered General Chen Chang to bring 70,000 troops from Y-Force to the *Yangtze* to block a Japanese advance.

Meanwhile, the British and Americans failed to agree on the sourcing of amphibious craft for Operation ANAKIM. They were in short supply and were needed for the planned invasion of Normandy. At the Casablanca Conference [codename SYMBOL] in January 1943, Operation ANAKIM was delayed until November 1943. Churchill was not too concerned. He had doubts about the entire prospect of retaking Burma: "you might as well eat a porcupine one quill at a time,"[23] he famously quipped. The failure of the Arakan Campaign in the winter of 1942–1943 must also have inured him to the prospect of further failure in Burma. On 8 May Field Marshal Alanbrooke noted that Churchill was particularly sharp with General Sir Archibald Wavell about the Arakan Campaign: "Archie [Wavell] was indignant and I had to pacify him."[24] Curiously it was a meeting with Stilwell, whom he liked, that may have persuaded Churchill to kick Wavell upstairs by making him Viceroy and promoting General Sir Claude Auchinleck in his place.

Stilwell was to be bitterly disappointed by the delay to ANAKIM and predictably blamed Chiang. Given the complete disagreement between all the service chiefs in India and Burma, let alone the hostilities between Stilwell and Chiang Kai-shek, and Stilwell against everyone, it was perhaps not surprising that neither Churchill nor Roosevelt felt committed to the China-Burma-India Theater. At the Combined Chiefs of Staff meeting in Washington on 14 May 1943 (TRIDENT), Alanbrooke recorded that the various commanders were asked to give their views:

> . . . Wavell was called upon followed by Somervell [Lieutenant-General Brehon Somervell] who contradicted him! Then Stilwell who disagreed with both and with himself as far as I could see! He is a small man with no conception of strategy. The whole problem seemed to hinge on the necessity of keeping Chiang Kai-shek in the war. Chennault was called upon followed by more Stilwell and more confusion! President and PM had some more to say about it in the end, and by the time we left what is not a very simple problem had become a tangled mass of confusion. [25]

Stilwell's primary strategic concern as Chiang Kai-shek's Chief of Staff was to strike at the key road routes of the Myitkyina-Mogaung area. By taking control of these logistics routes, Stilwell aimed to link the Burma Road with the Ledo Road, which was being constructed through the precipitous, jungle clad hills of the Eastern Himalayas. This new highway would enable the Allies to bring supply overland all the way from Calcutta to Chiang Kai-shek's southeastern Chinese strongholds at Kunming and Chongqing. However, without British support, Chiang refused to risk his troops alone and called off ANAKIM. Given the inter-service and inter-country wrangling, the cancellation of ANAKIM could not have surprised or upset anybody—Stilwell excepted.

In hindsight the cancellation of ANAKIM was a correct decision for a plan, which in 1943 overreached Allied capacity on the Asian mainland. However, an incandescent Stilwell accused Britain and Chiang Kai-shek of backing out of a fight. The setback fed Stilwell's hatred of the British: "The more I see of the Limeys the worse I hate them," he wrote. "The bastardly hypocrites do their best to cut our throats on all occasions. The pig-fuckers."[26]

At the May 1943 TRIDENT meeting in Washington, in spite of protests from 'Hap' Arnold about the logistical difficulties, Roosevelt put his weight behind Chiang and Chennault's plan for a build-up of the Fourteenth Air Force to 500 planes by the end of November 1943, to be supported by an increase in Hump supplies to 7,000 tons per month with the first 4,700 tons per month going to Chennault after 1 July. It was envisaged that Chennault's airbases would have the multiple role of diminishing Japanese aerial power in China, disrupting Japan's logistical infrastructure in China, attacking commercial shipping to Japan, supporting Stilwell's campaign to retake northern Burma and carrying out strategic bombing attacks on Japan itself. But even Roosevelt was aware of the danger of mission creep. He warned that the Hump "would never be able to transport the combat essentials for your army . . . and Chennault's Air Force . . . Accordingly we must keep constantly in mind our first essential, namely that the land route of supply to China must be opened at the earliest opportunity."[27]

Intriguingly, from early 1943 Roosevelt was sceptical about the Navy's plan to defeat Japan through the *Central Pacific* and still viewed China as the likely base from which Japan would be attacked. In February 1943 Roosevelt averred that he had no intention of spending the time "it would take to bring Japan to final defeat merely by inching our way forward from island to island across the vast expansion of the Pacific . . . If we took one island, in the advance from the south, once a month . . . I figured out it would take about fifty years before we got to Japan."[28] For a brief period in 1943, it appeared that the route to Tokyo through China trumped either the *Central Pacific* route favored by Admiral King or the New Guinea-Philippines route advocated by MacArthur. Roosevelt's thinking may also have been colored by his post-war ambitions to welcome China into the club of 'Great Powers,' by dint of its huge population. With Japan defeated, Roosevelt saw China as America's future friend in the East. In essence it was an extension of Roosevelt's pre-war concerns that China's vast markets should remain within America's commercial orbit.

In spite of Roosevelt's preferences for China, the cancellation of Operation ANAKIM and the shift in priorities toward Chennault and Chiang's air strategy remained an 'open sore' in Stilwell's relationship with Roosevelt, Chiang Kai-shek and Mountbatten. From now on Stilwell planned to go it alone. He hid from Admiral Louis Mountbatten, Commander of SEAC (South East Asia Command) and his superior officer, his intention to recapture the strategically located city of Myitkyina. Some 500 miles north of Rangoon, Myitkyina, the Kachin capital, was placed at the focal point of north Burma's road systems as well as being located on the west bank of the *Irrawaddy River*. Stilwell's contempt for Mountbatten and the British can be gathered from his description of Mountbatten arriving at the front in northern Burma on 6 March 1944. Having landed with a sixteen fighter-plane escort, Mountbatten descended from the plane "In knife-edge, impeccable tan tropical uniform with three rows of campaign ribbons and six-inch shoulder bars encrusted with stars, crowns, cross swords and batons and royal initials . . ."[29] Stilwell met him wearing standard issue combat trousers and a field jacket minus insignia. He looked as though he was on a hunting party.

As a *poseur* Mountbatten was well matched by Stilwell. Ironically, although the two men were at the opposite ends of the sartorial spectrum, they were both play-acting in their different roles. Stilwell's orneriness and disregard for the insignia of office were as carefully studied as Mountbatten's pomp and ceremony. Lieutenant-General Slim, certainly no 'peacock,' noted on one visit to Stilwell's HQ:

> I was struck, as I always was when I visited Stilwell's headquarters, how unnecessarily primitive all the arrangements were. There was, compared with my own or other headquarters, no shortage of transport or supplies, yet he delighted in an exhibition of rough living, which like his omission of rank badges and the rest was designed to foster the idea of a tough, hard-bitten, plain, fighting general.[30]

Fortunately for Stilwell, Slim, the one British officer he wholeheartedly respected, and the commander to whom he had agreed to report, had an identical view of the strategies required for the north Burma region. In his memoirs Slim recalled,

> . . . he and I were determined on the same things—to get more Chinese divisions for the Ledo force [Y-Force] to push hard for Myitkyina, and to use Wingate's Chindits to aid that push. After my experience with Sun's 38th Chinese Division in the Retreat, I had always agreed with Stilwell that his Chinese, given a fair chance and a superiority in numbers, could beat the Japanese.[31]

The Training of X-Force: After the beating handed out to his Chinese troops during General Iida's spectacular conquest of Burma, Stilwell went to Chiang Kai-shek and, in his usual blunt way, described the failings of the Chinese units. He recommended: "A few dependable, well-equipped, well supported divisions would be worth far more than double the number . . ."[32] He also suggested a purge of the Chinese officer cadre. The reforms suggested by Stilwell were not implementable. While Chiang is usually described as a dictator, his powers were far from absolute. The byzantine power structure of the army, factional and regional politics, the distribution of favors given and received as well as graft, all meant that Chiang was not the all-powerful figure that has sometimes been supposed.

However, in the aftermath of defeat, there was a single 'silver-lining' on which Stilwell pinned all his future hopes. Sun Li-jen's 38th Division and other elements of the

Fifth Army that had attempted to block Iida's advance through central Burma, had made their way to India. Here Stilwell could arm and train them to his own specifications without interference from Chiang or his court. They would be his troops and with them he planned to re-conquer Burma—the so-called X-Force would be the 'imperial guard' of his grand plan.

The strategy seemed simple enough. To keep China in the war with Japan, Chiang Kai-shek needed supplies. In the short term these would be supplied by an airlift from northern India to Kunming, a route that became known as the Hump; in the long term he planned to build a road from Ledo in northernmost India across the foothills of the Himalayas to connect with the Burma Road to Kunming. When this was completed convoys of trucks would carry supplies along this 1,079-mile route. X-Force would seize northern Burma from the Japanese down to the linkage point between the Ledo Road and the Burma Road, to make this plan possible. To support this strategic plan, Y-Force, comprising Chinese Divisions on the eastern border of China would also invade Burma. Having thus secured overland supply lines to fully equip the *Kuomintang* forces, the last element of Stilwell's plan was to lead the Chinese armies to the south of China where a coast base would be established for the invasion of Japan.

It was a plan that won the support of Washington, in spite of the vast logistic effort of sending supplies across the *Atlantic Ocean*, around Africa's Cape of Good Hope and across the *Indian Ocean* to Bombay. It was a 12,000-mile long ocean journey. Then a 1,500-mile train journey from Bombay to Calcutta was followed by an 800-mile rail journey on narrow gauge to Ledo to link with the 1,079-mile Ledo–Burma Road. At 15,500 miles, the supply line to China became the longest military logistics chain that the world has ever seen or is likely to see again.

In India, Stilwell secured a base for the training of 8,000 X-Force troops at Ramgarh Cantonment in Bihar State in central India. It was not an arrangement that pleased Britain. The use of Chinese soldiers in the retaking of Burma was not welcome but Washington insisted and got its way. X-Force would be housed and fed by Britain while they would be equipped and trained by America, which was intent on not using its own troops in the China-Burma-India Theater. In October the 8,000 troops of X-Force were reinforced by Chinese troops brought by airlift over the Hump. General Luo Zhuoying only half-jokingly said, "Put 50 in a plane naked. It's only three hours."[33] Some 40 percent of the recruits were rejected as being either too thin or too diseased. They were sent back to China and reallocated to Y-Force. Stilwell was characteristically blunt and laid the blame squarely on Chiang: "The Peanut's promise to me of the pick for India is so much wind; last year 68 percent of the men sent were rejected for trachoma or skin disease . . ."[34]

By the end of December 1943 some 32,000 troops were being trained at Ramgarh. In aggregate more than 53,000 Chinese troops were trained there over two years including instructors and troops sent back to Y-Force. Three divisions were formed in India including 22nd Division, 30th Division and Sun Li-jen's 38th Division. Unlike the Indian units of the British Army, the Chinese divisions had Chinese commanding officers with Americans only acting in the capacity of advisers and liaisons. For Stilwell the training of X-Force was the start of a love affair with his Chinese troops. On 21 October 1941, Stilwell noted in his diary: "Our training school for the Chinese troops is going in grand style. The boys are learning fast. They get good chow, medical attention, efficient instruction, AND their pay, as well as movies, athletics etc. They love it . . ."[35] After a reorganization in mid-1944 X-Force, the 30th and 38th Divisions became battle groups in the New Chinese Army led by General Sun Li-jen. The 20th Division was allocated to the New Sixth Army, a mixed force whose battle groups included the Marauders (5307th Composite Unit), the Chindits and the Indian 36th Division.

At Ramgarh, Chinese soldiers were vaccinated against cholera, typhoid and smallpox. They were also fed regularly three times a day—an unknown luxury in the Chinese army. Within three months the average weight gain of the troops was 21 percent. The troops were equally amazed at the quality of their new uniforms, boots, helmets, and packs. New guns and bayonets were expected but the provision of artillery and trucks was an unheard of luxury for soldiers that had always marched to battle. The quality of the Chinese troops quickly impressed the American staff officers.

A surprised artillery commander, Brigadier-General George Sliney reported: "We demonstrate and they copy. They are the greatest mimics in the world and are learning very, very fast."[36] Relationships with American soldiers were not always easy. Chinese officers resented taking orders from US trainers who had no battle experience. In one sudden eruption of anger guns were drawn. As for punishment, Stilwell had given strict orders that Americans were not to interfere in internal discipline. Chinese soldiers were executed for fishing using hand grenades or beaten to a pulp for losing a blanket. It was not always easy to watch. Stilwell, for whom X-Force was his precious 'baby,' closely oversaw the whole training program. For more than a year he commuted between New Delhi and Ramgarh. Slim noted that at the Chinese training camp, "Everywhere was Stilwell, urging, leading, driving."[37] The Chinese troops adored him.

The Building of the Ledo Road: [Map: 27.6] [Map: 27.7] By the summer of 1944 Stilwell's Chinese forces were ready to help him retake northern Burma from where he had been ejected in 1942. Then, Chinese forces had retreated east and west through the jungles of northern Burma—now they would return along a purpose-built road. Whatever the strategic rationale or lack of it, the Ledo Road was an extraordinary feat of engineering passing through 9,000 foot high mountain ranges swathed completely in dense jungle. The average annual rainfall was 150 inches, and 14 inches in 24 hours had been recorded. The winding road reached heights of 4,500 feet often with sheer drops into the jungle below. The entire journey from Ledo (Assam) to Kunming (Yunnan Province, China) would be 1,079 miles along some of the most tortuous terrain over which road building had ever been attempted. Of the more than 15,000 American soldiers who worked on the Ledo Road, 60 percent were Black. The US Army also employed 35,000 local laborers, mostly recruited from British tea plantations in Assam.

Conditions were intolerable with men having to work sometimes knee-deep in a primordial slime caused by constant rain. Leeches and malaria-bearing mosquitoes added to the discomfort. Earth slides could destroy a day's work not to mention the men who could be buried. Scrub typhus, which often led to delirium and death, was rampant. Casualty rates were high with more than 1,133 American soldiers killed: of whom 624 were in combat, 173 in aircraft accidents, 74 from typhus and malaria, 53 by drowning and 44 by road accidents. Furthermore it was estimated that more than 4,000 local laborers died while working on the project.

A regiment of Chinese engineers also worked on the road. Needless to say that the Army engineers, who became known reverentially as the 'Hairy Ears,' had to live in appalling conditions with heat, insects, snakes and particularly leeches being the main enemies. The name 'Hairy Ears' derived from a song, most of it unprintable, which became the engineers' anthem:

> The Engineers have 'Hairy Ears' and live in caves and
> ditches,
> They bang their jocks against the rocks, those hardy
> sons of bitches . . .[38]

It was a rare moment of pleasure when, the road having been completed as far as Shimbwiyang three days ahead of schedule on 27 December 1943, a convoy of vehicles arrived carrying doughnuts and 9,600 cans of beer.

Major Charlton Ogden of Merrill's Marauders described the Ledo Road as "a great broad, raw gash through the forest dipping, rising, winding, cutting back, going on days without end, prevailing uphill for the first half of the march, prevailing down for the second but every mile of it steep."[39] Both the Marauders and X-Force would use the road to reach their assembly point in northern Burma.

Brigadier-General Lewis Pick, a US Army engineer, led the construction operation. Given the monsoon conditions under which he had to work, Pick's background as an engineer on the *Missouri River*, where he had organized a series of dams, reservoirs and irrigation systems to run off flood water, was by no means un-useful to his new task. Pick assured *Life* magazine, "I can keep up with Stilwell as fast as he can drive the Japs out of this area."[40]

Even when the all-weather road was built, constant landslides required high levels of maintenance. Two 4-inch fuel pipelines were laid at the side of the road. In addition Pick built roadside landing strips for cargo planes approximately every thirty miles and between Ledo and Mogaung there were an astonishing 700 bridges (some as long as 1,200 feet) crossing ten major rivers. In total 13.5 million cubic yards of earth were moved—equivalent to a ten-foot tall by three-foot wide wall from New York to San Francisco. Storage depots and encampments also had to be built along the way. As for the equipment—caterpillars, rollers, power shovels, cranes and bulldozers—they had to be brought from 12,000 miles or more by American 'Liberty' cargo ships across two oceans and three continents. **[See Appendix B: Oil, Raw Materials and Logistics: 'Just Start Swinging']**

The cost of building the road was astronomic: an estimated breakdown suggests that the total costs were in the region of US$150m (US $2.5bn in 2015 terms) comprising the following: US troop labor (US$31.7m), Chinese troop labor (US$2.4m), Indian military and civilian labor (US$9.4m), materials and supplies (US$33.9m), equipment, fuel and supplies (US$51.9m) and sundry overheads (US$19.4m).

The Road to Myitkyina: The building of the Ledo Road into northern Burma by summer 1944 enabled Stilwell to launch his bid to retake northern Burma. By retaking Myitkyina and Lashio, Stilwell aimed to bring about the linkage of the Ledo Road with the Burma Road, thereby bringing relief to landlocked China. At the beginning of 1944 Stilwell's plans for the invasion of northern Burma were set. Using some 500 trucks supplied by the British, the Chinese troops were transferred to Ledo with 200 tons of supply. X-Force were thus assembled in northern India and advanced along the Ledo Road that Major-General Pick and his army of 65,000 engineers, troops and plantation workers had carved through the eastern Himalayas that bordered northern Assam and Burma. By January 1944 Pick had reached Shingbwiyang in northern Burma and from here X-Force entered the Hukawng Valley with the intention of fighting their way southeastwards toward Myitkyina.

By late February Stilwell had pushed his Chinese troops just some sixty miles into the Hukawng Valley. Movement was slowed by the early arrival of monsoon rains combined with the caution of Chinese commanders, who followed Chiang's rescript to preserve strength at all costs. The track to Myitkyina ran through valleys of dense jungle hedged by hills and mountains criss-crossed with thousands of gullies, gorges, rivers and streams. Within this terrain rapid advance was difficult. However, with the arrival of Merrill's Marauders, the 5307th Composite Unit (codename GALAHAD), on 24 February, Stilwell now had a force trained in jungle warfare and survival. Stilwell sent them on a flanking operation to get behind the lines of Lieutenant-General Shinichi Tanaka's 18th Division.

The Battle of Myitkyina: [Map: 27.8] The three battalions of 3,000 Merrill's Marauders hacked their passage through dense jungle to appear behind Tanaka's lines. On 3 March 1944, the 3rd Battalion established roadblocks at the Kachin village of Walawbum, while the 2nd Battalion dug in further to the northwest at Kumyan Ga. The 1st Battalion was held in reserve. Fierce fighting ensued involving waves of *banzai* attacks. Eight hundred of Tanaka's troops were killed, though he was eventually able to retreat and bypass the Marauder's roadblocks. Meanwhile on 7 March, the Marauders were relieved by Chinese troops. Tanaka set a new defensive line at Jambu Bum in the low hills at the southern exit of the Hukawng Valley. The prospect appeared of further hard slog to reach Myitkyina against the more-than-able Tanaka.

Elsewhere in Burma the course of events also appeared dicey for the Allies. Rather than launching an invasion of Burma, the British forces were defending a Japanese invasion of Assam and were holding off Mutaguchi's forces at Imphal (8 March to

3 July) and Kohima (4 April to 22 June). The outcome appeared to be in the balance with no sense yet of the eventual outcome.

Stilwell again decided to outflank Tanaka. The Marauders' 2nd and 3rd Battalions were sent east of and then south of Tanaka's new line through the steeply jungled Tanai Valley. They were helped by the Kachin tribes' guerrilla forces, which screened their advance, guided their path and provided logistical support in the form of elephants to carry supplies. Meanwhile the Marauder 1st Battalion outflanked Tanaka to the west by cutting a 20-mile swathe through a dense bamboo forest and jungle before falling on a Japanese encampment at Shaduzup where a roadblock was formed. Stilwell now learned that Tanaka was planning a flanking movement of his own to encircle the left flank of the advancing Chinese army and ordered the 2nd and 3rd Marauder Battalions to block their path at the villages of Nhpum Ga and Janpan respectively. Here the Marauders were helped by the presence of *nisei* (Japanese-Americans) in the unit; Private Kurmit A. Bushur recalled, "Hank Gosho, a *nisei*, who along with his friend, my platoon sergeant Rocky Curtain, went into no man's land [against orders] tapped into a communications line and was able to get the Japanese battle plan."[41] A fierce 11-day battle ensued at Nhpum Ga where the 2nd Marauder Battalion was completely surrounded.

The Japanese captured the only water hole and the conditions suffered by the besieged Marauders were appalling, engulfed as they were with the rotting smell of dead mules and excrement. As one soldier complained, it "would have been utterly unbearable if there had been any alternative to bearing it."[42] As at the *Battle of the 'Admin Box'* air drops of supplies including water enabled the Marauders to hang on until the 1st and 3rd Marauder Battalions broke through to relieve the siege on 9 April. The operation cost the Marauders 59 dead and 314 wounded while a further 379 men were evacuated suffering from the usual variety of jungle diseases. Private Bushur, who was hit by a Japanese machine gun round, was fortunate to be airlifted out after the battle. An effective fighting force of just 1,400 troops remained of the 3,000 who set out. Nonetheless, these surviving troops too, after six weeks of continuous fighting and hacking their way through the jungles of northern Burma, were exhausted.

Thus by the end of April, the remaining Marauders, who had by now been issued with fresh clothes and were catching up with their post from America, fully expected to be shipped back to India for a period of rest and recuperation. Instead Stilwell threw them yet another flanking movement. The Marauders would never forgive him. Stilwell was perhaps fortunate not to be murdered by one of the large number of psychopaths in this most extraordinary military unit.

Mainly recruited from the *Southwest Pacific* and *Trinidad*, the Marauders were the dregs of the Army who signed on for three months training and three months fighting. In India 10 percent of them had gone AWOL and they terrorized locals by their wild drinking and indiscriminate shooting of sacred cows. According to Sergeant Robert Passanisi, "many marauders did not play by the rules; going AWOL was common" but he noted, "When the chips were down, everyone was in the field doing his job."[43] Private Kermit Bushur similarly recalled,

My squad leader was a convicted felon. His name was
Tom Larson. He had been convicted of killing a man in
Tennessee. It was his wife's lover. Tom was always quick
to use a knife . . . And later he killed a man with his knife.
He was sentenced to life in prison . . . And then that one
time in the war . . . they would let them go into combat if
they wouldn't take any training, just take them right from
the prison and go right into combat. Well, Tom took it. He
says, that's better than sitting here in the jail. And he was
the best man I knew. I would follow him into the hubs of
hell. He was really a wonderful fellow.[44]

The Marauders' credo read, "My pack is on my back, my gun is oiled and loaded, and
as I walk in the shadow of death I fear no sonofabitch."[45] Any fears of being 'fragged'
were far from his mind as Stilwell set out to capture Myitkyina with one of the most
audacious plans of *World War II*: he recorded in his diary, "The die is cast and it's sink
or swim."[46] Chiang, to help the liberation of Burma, reluctantly agreed to release 40,000
troops from Yunnan in eastern China. Led by General Huang Weili, the Japanese border
forces were easily overpowered. But, within three days of this assault Japan's Imperial
General Staff ordered the start of the ICHI-GO Campaign in central and southern China.

Stilwell realized that in order to inspire his Chinese troops, he needed to ask more of
the limited American forces and demanded leadership from their example. In spite of a
near mutinous spirit within the Marauders, Stilwell, with two Chinese regiments and
some Kachin guerrillas, led them and their mule trains for sixty-five miles over the
6,000-foot high, and supposedly impassable, Kumon Range. Bitterly cold peaks were
followed by descents into humid, jungle-filled gorges while monsoon rains turned steep
hills into muddy slides.

It was an epic trek to rank with any carried out by fighting units in *World War II*. As
usual Stilwell "looking more like a duck hunter"[47] than a soldier, led the way. On 16
May after almost three weeks of trekking in the most arduous conditions, Stilwell and
his force appeared on the outskirts of Myitkyina Airfield and the following day
completely surprised the Japanese defenders. The Marauders' 1st Battalion also seized
the ferry terminal at Pamati, on the *Irrawaddy River*. Merrill described his Marauders as
being decimated by typhus, foot rot, jungle sores, malaria and dysentery. Accidents
were also a significant cause of casualties, whether caused by faulty munitions or falls.
Sergeant David Quaid, the Marauder photographer, had to be invalided out of Burma
after he was ingloriously injured by a glancing blow from a sack of mule-feed in an
airdrop. When they arrived in Myitkyina they were filthy and bedraggled: what Stilwell
described as "a pitiful but splendid sight."[48]

Stilwell was 'cock-a-hoop'; in his diary he wrote in capitals, "WILL THIS BURN
UP THE LIMEYS!"[49] Admiral Mountbatten, head of South East Asia Command
(SEAC), had been so sceptical about the viability of the northern campaign that Stilwell

had sworn Slim to secrecy about his intention to take Myitkyina. Though it is doubtful whether he 'burnt up,' even Mountbatten must nevertheless have been embarrassed to be congratulated on a campaign that he knew nothing about. Churchill demanded to know how "the Americans by a brilliant feat have landed us in Myitkyina."[50]

Mountbatten had to swallow his pride and write to congratulate Stilwell's success in crossing the Kumon Mountains, "a feat which will live in military history."[51] In private though, Mountbatten could not refrain from trying to bask in reflected glory; to his daughter he wrote, "Isn't the news of the capture of Myitkyina airfield great? It is one of my most interesting fronts, commanded by my deputy General Stilwell."[52] After the war, Mountbatten, the man whose idea for conquering Burma was based on amphibious landings, would try to take credit for the strategic brilliance of the reconquest of Burma. Nevertheless, the British had their own reasons to cheer. By mid-May Major-General Slim, at the *Battles of Imphal* and *Kohima*, had won one of the most crushing large-scale engagements of *World War II*. **[See Chapter 26: Battles of Arakan, Imphal, and Kohima: Slim Boxes Clever]**

Mountbatten himself was not wholly without contribution to the Allied cause. He organized a trip for his dear friend Noel Coward to go to Ledo to entertain the troops. English high society's favorite piano tinkler's camp little ditties did not go down well, particularly with the tough Black troops building the Ledo Road; northern Burma was a long way from the fashionable watering holes of Mayfair in London. Coward was slow handclapped. In his *Middle East Diary* [1944], Noel Coward described the experience when he referred to Black soldiers as "mournful little Brooklyn boys, lying there in tears . . ."[53] Stilwell was not sympathetic to Coward's failure; he cryptically told his friend Lieutenant-General Daniel Sultan, "If any more piano players start this way you know what to do with the piano."[54]

If the surprise capture of Myitkyina Airfield had been a daredevil romp, Stilwell's forces now faced a protracted siege of the town. Myitkyina could have been taken the same afternoon if Stilwell had moved fast enough, but it was soon flooded with reinforcements and Major-General Genzo Mizukami set about organizing a rigorous defense of a town, which stood elevated above the surrounding rice paddies. Stilwell found himself short of troops as it gradually dawned on him that the Japanese had been reinforced and were marshalling their defenses with more than five times the estimated number of 1,000 defenders. To add to his difficulties, Slim, fully engaged fighting General Mutaguchi's forces in Assam, would not be able to resupply him with troops for several months. Although Chinese reinforcements were flown into the newly captured Myitkyina Airfield, Stilwell was still short of troops. Furthermore national pride and anglophobia probably prevented him from flying in the British 36th Division who became available for the final assault at the end of July.

The much put-upon Marauders had to remain in the line to be joined by untrained engineers and raw Marauder replacements, troops who had previously been guarding the *Panama Canal*. It was not a success. Brigadier-General Haydon Boetner, who had been given the field command at Myitkyina, reported back to Stilwell that the American road engineers "are in many cases simply terrified of the Japs—they would not follow their officers, refused to attack, and ran under fire."[55] Boetner, an experienced staff officer with little battle experience, proved to be an inept field commander who squandered his troops in poorly planned attacks on the town.

The original Marauders were now so racked with dysentery that many of them cut holes in the seat of their combat trousers. By May over seventy-five Marauders were falling sick daily to dysentery, malaria and scrub typhus. Officers nevertheless turned out troops from the hospital and forced the sick to fight. The treatment of the Marauders would later become a scandal and *cause célèbre* in America. To add to their woes, Brigadier-General Frank Merrill suffered a second heart attack and had to be airlifted out. Apart from being outnumbered by the defenders, Stilwell lacked artillery, which could not be brought through the jungle. Moreover the besiegers were hampered by full monsoon conditions.

The Battle of Mogaung: [Map: 27.9] In mid June 1944 Myitkyina's supply route to the north via the *Irrawaddy River* was cut off by the Chindits, part of Major-General Slim's Fourteenth Army. The Chindits, part of the second 'Long Range Penetration–2' (LRP–2) force organized by Brigadier-General Orde Wingate, had been dispatched behind enemy lines to draw Japanese forces away from both Mutaguchi's anticipated invasion of India and Stilwell's attempt to reconquer northern Burma.

After holding out for two months against relentless Japanese attacks on their garrison at 'White City,' on Stilwell's orders Calvert's 77th Brigade trekked through jungle for 160 miles to get to Mogaung, which they had been ordered to capture. In appalling monsoon conditions, Calvert's soldiers fought off daily Japanese attacks. By the time they reached Mogaung, the 77th Brigade, including Gurkhas, Lancashire Fusiliers, the King's Regiment and the South Staffords, comprised just 530 fit men out of the 3,500 who had landed behind enemy lines fourteen weeks earlier. Against them were an estimated 4,000 Japanese troops in Moguang. Stilwell sent the 114th Chinese Regiment to support them with 75 mm artillery, although they did not participate in the final attack.

The two-week battle started with the capture of the Pin Hmi Inn Road Bridge. The action to capture this strategic point was led by the Gurkha officer, Captain Michael Allmand, who blew up a Japanese machine gun post as well as killing three Japanese soldiers with his *kukri* (curved hunting knife used by the Nepalese Gurkhas) in hand-to-hand combat. Two days later he led B-Company's assault on a ridge overlooking Mogaung. On 23 June, Calvert's remaining troops launched a final dawn assault that at last secured Moguang, the first major town to be recaptured from the Japanese since the British-Chinese ejection from Burma in 1942. Captain Allmand was killed in the final assault as he charged a machine gun nest, despite being debilitated by trench foot. He was awarded a posthumous Victoria Cross for his exploits.

Gurkha rifleman, Tulbahadur Pun was similarly awarded a Victoria Cross for his single-handed attack with a Bren gun on the focal Japanese defensive position of 'Red

House' on the edge of Mogaung. He killed three Japanese soldiers while the other five fled; he held his position and continued to give covering fire to the rest of his platoon. Pun's Victoria Cross citation in the *London Gazette* on 7 November read: "His outstanding courage and superb gallantry in the face of odds which meant almost certain death were most inspiring to all ranks and beyond praise."[56] In 2007 Pun was refused entrance to the UK on the grounds that he could not demonstrate close enough ties with Great Britain. In the ensuing scandal, the Labour Party's Immigration Minister, Liam Byrne, was forced to overturn the ban on Pun after a populist campaign led by the British actress Joanna Lumley, whose father Major James Lumley had fought at the *Battle of Mogaung*.

An American liaison officer, probably acting sycophantically to the pro-Chinese Stilwell, caused outrage when he informed the BBC that Mogaung had been captured by Chinese-American forces. Even the Chinese commander, Colonel Li, was furious and ordered that an apology should be made. When Calvert was ordered to march to Hopin, he refused. The American liaison, pandering to his commander's anglophobic views, sent a message to Stilwell telling him that the 77th Brigade "were cowards, yellow, deserted, they walked off the field of battle, they should all be arrested."[57] Mountbatten intervened and ordered an immediate medical inspection by officers including Brigadier-General Merrill, which concluded that Calvert's few surviving troops, after 116 days of marching and fighting in jungle conditions, were physically and mentally exhausted. Calvert was brought before Stilwell who disparaged the Chindit's performance, refused to have the wounded flown from the battlefield and launched into the British officer. Stilwell threatened to court-martial Lieutenant-Colonel 'Mad' Mike Calvert for refusing to fight. In a fiery exchange Calvert in return gave 'as good as he got.' No foreigner to insubordination and direct speaking, Stilwell roared with laughter. When Calvert had finished giving his verbal report, an astonished Stilwell, unaware that the Chindits had been fighting unrelieved for four months, awarded Calvert the American Silver Star. Ultimately, Stilwell served the Chindits better than the Marauders whom he despised.

Myitkyina Falls at Last: The capture of Mogaung not only blocked Japanese supply to Myitkyina but also ended any means of escape. On 27 June, Mizukami evacuated Myitkyina's wounded by raft only for them to be picked off by Kachin guerrilla troops as they floated downstream. The previous day, a frustrated Stilwell replaced his field commander Brigadier-General Boetner, who had succumbed to malaria, with Brigadier-General Theodore Wessels. The change in command did not produce instant results though Wessels did raise morale by visiting all his units on the front line. However, in one tragic episode an American battalion, during a flanking movement, came across some Orientals who they wrongly assumed to be Chinese. The American troops were mown down by Japanese machine gunners and only a remnant managed to return. For his heroics in the fighting retreat Private Anthony Firenze received the Distinguished Service Medal.

The 3rd Battalion of the Marauders made an important breakthrough with the capture of Myitkyina's other airfield on the north of the city on 27 July. Four days later General Mizukami committed suicide. The remaining Japanese defenders hung on until 3 August. General Pan Yu-kun of the Chinese 50th Division finally conceived a plan that would break the Japanese defenders. Fifteen heavily armed raiding parties, each carrying eight grenades, two days' rations, 200 rounds of ammunition for rifles and 800 for Thompson sub-machine guns, infiltrated the Japanese defenses at night and remained hidden. When the 50th Division attacked at dawn, the hidden raiders emerged to cause complete confusion among the Japanese. Other American forces joined in the attack around the narrowing Japanese perimeter and Myitkyina was finally taken. Chinese soldiers had proved that, when well led, equipped and supplied, they were more than a match for the Japanese. As Chinese soldier Wen Shan observed, "We had officers who did not steal men's food, as they did in China."[58]

Unlike Stilwell, Lieutenant-General Slim was warm in his praise of his fellow commander after the *Battle of Myitkyina*, writing, "the success of this northern offensive was in the main due to the Ledo Chinese divisions—and that was Stilwell."[59]

The whole campaign to secure northern Burma had cost 6,400 casualties of whom 2,200 (272 killed) were Americans, a high proportion given that the Marauders had comprised just 3,000 troops out of 40,000 deployed. By the time of the fall of Myitkyina, almost none of the original Marauders remained. As Second Lieutenant Herbert Clofine recalled, in the space of five months the Marauders, "fought five major battles and 32 minor engagements . . . when the unit wasn't fighting, we were marching. Not marching, actually. We were hiking through some very treacherous terrain."[60] After the war, when Brigadier-General Frank Merrill met Lieutenant-General Nobuo Tanaka, the Japanese commander was amazed that the Marauders comprised so few troops versus the Division of 18,000 Japanese troops that he had in the field.

For historians used to dealing with the sweeping military campaigns on Germany's Eastern Front, involving millions of troops, emphasizing the importance of units of such miniscule scale as were involved in the fighting in northern Burma may seem misplaced. The issue however, was how difficult it was to transport and sustain even tiny numbers in these hostile terrains where logistics required the extensive use of pack animals, donkey, mule, and horses, even buffalo. Just looking after animals involved considerable work. Marauder Charlton Ogburn Jr. in his autobiographic account *The Marauders* [1959] recalled the difficulties of animal management: "a leader had to be provided for every animal" and advised, "Anyone who thinks a mule is balky should try launching one across a 100 yard river."[61] Ogburn observed quite correctly that even keeping a few thousand men on active operations in jungle conditions was a gargantuan feat. Logistical difficulties meant that large swathes of territory, as in New Guinea and the Solomons could be won or lost by relatively small forces. The strategic importance of these battles was not diminished by the small number of troops involved.

In spite of their success, shortly after the end of the *Battle of Myitkyina*, what remained of Merrill's Marauders was consolidated into the 475th Infantry.

Stilwell: Victory into Defeat: Stilwell earned the bitter hatred of his American troops by briefing the media that the *Battle of Myitkyina* was won by the Chinese. Indeed the Chinese had fought well but by a perverse psychology Stilwell refused to grant promotions and bravery awards to the Marauders. "I had him in my rifle sights," lamented one soldier, "I coulda squeezed one off and no one woulda known it wasn't a Jap that got that sonofabitch."[62]

Neither were the Chindits happy. Operation THURSDAY that ended with Colonel Calvert under Stilwell's command, saw the Chindits suffer 2,572 casualties (1,034 killed). Most of the remaining Chindits were unfit for battle, and many were unable to walk. A medical inspection of Master's brigade on 17 July showed that there were only 118 fit men out of 2,200.

Immediately after the battle, Brigadier-General Lewis Pick's engineers began the task of making good the Ledo Road from Shimbwiyang to Myitkyina and then linking up to the Burma Road into northeastern China. It would be another five months before the first supply convoy would make its way across the entire route from Assam to Kunming.

On 25 January 1945 the completed Ledo–Burma Road was finally opened for traffic. China's land isolation with the west was over. When the first trucks arrived in China in Kunming after a wearisome twenty-four days, Chiang Kai-shek proclaimed, "We have broken the siege of China. Let me name this road after General Stilwell in memory of his distinctive contribution . . ."[63] Burma's Ledo Road, was never popularly known as the Stilwell Road just as the Ledo Road or 'Pick's Pike' "never became the main artery of supply to China."[64] Given the success of the Hump, the completion of the road was something of a pyrrhic victory.

It was planned that when completed the Ledo Road would be able to ship an estimated 65,000 tons of *matériel* per month to China and thereby replace the Hump. It was an estimate that was fiercely opposed by Lieutenant-General Claire Chennault, commander of the US Fourteenth Air Force based in China. He believed that the airlift would prove much more effective. In the event Chennault was proved correct. When Lend-Lease supplies to China ended in July 1945, the Hump was delivering 45,000 tons per month to Kunming versus just 6,000 tons per month from the Ledo–Burma Road. In effect the Ledo Road turned out to be the costly 'White Elephant' that Churchill had predicted.

Furthermore, as a tactical adjunct to the defeat of the main Japanese Army at Imphal on the Burma-India frontier, Stilwell's victory at Myitkyina played almost no role in Slim's victory. Although in hindsight it is therefore clear that Stilwell's famous engagement at the *Battle of Myitkyina* was the climax of a strategic error, it should nevertheless be remembered that the reconquest of northern Burma and its elimination of Japanese fighter bases enabled the shortening of the Hump airlift, which made possible General Tunner's prodigious increase in supply to China.

But in essence the epic efforts of Merrill's Marauders were largely fruitless; the *Battle of Myitkyina* was a pyrrhic victory—particularly when set against the concurrent tragedies on the *Kuomintang*'s eastern front from the Japanese ICHI-GO incursions.

The *Battle of Myitkyina* proved to be Stilwell's last hurrah. Although he was promoted to the rank of four-star general, Stilwell overestimated the strength of his position following his victory at the *Battle of Myitkyina*. For Chiang, Stilwell had won glory in Burma while Chiang Kai-shek's armies in Hunan and Guangxi, for which Stilwell was also responsible, had been crushed with vast loss of life. In hindsight it is clear that Stilwell should have focused much more on the war in China.

Remarkably Stilwell, who through his mistaken strategy and resultant misallocation of resources was in large part responsible for the ICHI-GO debacle, took comfort from the defeats of the Chinese Army. In his diary, Stilwell, who had displayed notable diffidence toward helping out Chiang's armies on the eastern front, wrote that if the ICHI-GO defeats were "just sufficient to get rid of the Peanut [Chiang] without entirely wrecking the ship, it would be worth it."[65] Perversely Stilwell tried to use the failures in central China compared to his success at the *Battle of Myitkyina* to leverage his own position in his personal battle with Chiang Kai-shek. With ICHI-GO now threatening Sichuan and indeed Chongqing itself, Marshall was persuaded by Stilwell to demand from Chiang full authority over the entire *Kuomintang* National Revolutionary Army, as well as the incorporation of Communist forces, which Mao was now offering in return for support in terms of money and equipment. **[See Chapter 28: Battle for China: FDR, Chiang, Mao, and 'Vinegar Joe']**

For the powers in Washington, the incorporation of Mao's forces into an active participation in the war against Japan would release some 500,000 *Kuomintang* troops that were effectively quarantined in the north as a buffer to Communist advance. American logic was perfect. However, Chiang knew better than Washington or the pro-Mao US state department that any alliance with the Communists would simply strengthen their position *vis-à-vis* his own. Whilst Roosevelt's priority was to win the *Pacific War* as quickly as possible, Chiang Kai-shek knew that a war for the future of China would soon follow. Neither Stilwell nor the US State Department, nor Marshall, nor Roosevelt ever understood why Chiang was seemingly so reluctant to fight. The reality was that Chiang Kai-shek wanted to fight the Japanese, but not in Burma. He also wanted to fight the Japanese without yielding large swathes of China to further Communist incursion. Finally, and not unreasonably, Chiang wanted to fight when he had the logistical wherewithal to do so. America would only 'get' Chiang's line of thinking after he had fled to Taiwan and China had fallen to the Communists.

So when Chiang Kai-shek threatened to withdraw Y-Force eastward across the *Salween River*, Stilwell went ballistic. He fired off a report to Marshall, painting the bleakest possible picture of the situation in China. Stilwell's report to Marshall concluded: "To sum up, there is still a faint chance to salvage something in China but action must be quick and radical and the G-Mo [Chiang Kai-shek] must give one commander full powers . . . the chances are definitely not good, but I can see no other solution at the moment."[66] Marshall duly stirred up Roosevelt, who was sitting in Quebec with Churchill, to send an ultimatum letter to Chiang demanding that Chiang hand overall military power and authority to Stilwell. But as it turned out, in the final showdown, it was Stilwell who was sacked from his post on 19 October 1944 when he overplayed his hand by unnecessarily humiliating the Generalissimo. **[See Chapter 28: Battle for China: FDR, Chiang, Mao, and 'Vinegar Joe']**

The Battles of Kweilin and Liuzhou: **[Map: 27.10]** While Stilwell was basking in victory at the *Battle of Myitkyina* and hubristically challenging Chiang Kai-shek's control over the *Kuomintang* armies, ending in his dismissal, fighting on China's eastern front was continuing. A week after Stilwell's removal, the last phase of the ICHI-GO Campaign saw the Japanese 11th and 23rd Armies advance from Changsha toward Kweilin in the northeastern region of Guangxi Province. Chiang's 120,000 strong army, using the delaying tactics that had served it well over eight years of war, fought an intelligent delaying rear-guard action. It was a fighting retreat that absorbed the energy of Japanese attacks while denying them the opportunity for a knock-out battle.

The result was that the 150,000 Japanese troops did not reach Kweilin and Liuzhou until 1 November 1944. Here 20,000 of Chiang's troops, albeit exhausted and dispirited by the action at Changsha, managed to hold on for ten days until they were forced to retreat. When the Japanese Army entered Kweilin (Guilin) mass rape ensued, and the women who survived were forced into service as 'comfort women' by General Yasuji Okamura—the gawky, squinted eyed, bespectacled Japanese officer of caricature legend. Purportedly, as early as 1932 Okamura was the first Japanese general to implement a system of pressganging women into military prostitution units to serve the *Kwantung* Army. He was later accused of having killed as many as 200,000 Chinese civilians in a campaign of brutal reprisal in Guangxi Province. Atrocities in the Tai-Shan district of *Kwantung* (Guangdong) Province were particularly appalling. More than 700 civilians were massacred and 559 shops were torched. After the war Okamura was found guilty of murder at the Nanking War Crimes Trials but was protected by Chiang Kai-shek who employed him as a military advisor in the civil war with Mao's Communists. Later Okamura recruited former Japanese officers to help train and rebuild the *Kuomintang*'s army after its retreat to Taiwan.

By the end of the year the Japanese had established control over two-thirds of Guangxi Province including the capital Nanning, which was set ablaze. The route northward to Sichuan was open but after an advance of almost 1,000 miles the Japanese army was exhausted, its supply lines over-extended. The shortages of food and munitions were becoming critical. Chinese and American forces had been careful to blow up ammunition and supply depots to prevent them falling into Japanese hands. At the major depot at Tusham, Major Frank Gleason organized the destruction of 50,000 tons of supplies, the equivalent of a month's supply over the Hump.

Between August and the end of December the *Kuomintang* armies had suffered 100,000 casualties of whom 70,000 died, approximately two-thirds of US army deaths in the entirety of the four-year *Pacific War*. In addition it is estimated that 110,000 Chinese civilians were killed. Japanese forces too had suffered with 60,000 casualties. Although Chiang and General Albert Wedemeyer, Stilwell's replacement, feared that the Japanese would now advance on Kunming and Chongqing, they did not realize the extent to which the Japanese attack was played out. Their armies, in spite of some of the hardest fought and greatest victories of *World War II*, were exhausted and stretched to their logistical limits. Although they had reached the borders of Indochina, the end game of their campaign, in terms of what ICHI-GO had promised to deliver, it turned out to be an entirely pyrrhic victory.

The threat of B-29 Superfortress strategic bombing attacks on Japan was only briefly lifted. By early 1945, the airfields captured on *Saipan, Tinian* and *Taipan*, more easily supplied direct by ship from America's west coast, had more than replaced the strategic bombing work of Chennault's Fourteenth Air Force from the Chinese mainland. Furthermore, although Chennault had suffered losses in aircraft, crew and equipment as a result of the ICHI-GO Campaign, new airfields were built further inland. With the US Air Force now completely dominant over China, Chennault was able to bomb and severely restrict rail operations, which attempted to move essential commodities from Indochina to Busan in Korea via Wuhan, Peking and Manchuria.

In addition the fight against Chinese guerrilla activity throughout China was stretching their resources as never before. In 1944 alone, fighting Chinese insurgency cost Japan 64 percent of its emergency military budget. Above all at exorbitant cost, ICHI-GO had failed to resolve Japan's impending logistical crisis. In the wake of ICHI-GO Japanese high command realized that in spite of their 'victories,' no matter how pyrrhic, they needed to change their China policy. It was an admission of effective defeat in the war against the US. In spite of their paranoia about the spread of communism in Japan, Tojo and Hirohito decided to adjust their strategy in China; from now on Mao Zedong's Communist regime based in Yanan was effectively fully legitimized. By 'going easy' on Mao, Hirohito hoped that he could gain traction with the Soviet Union who he hoped to use as a peace intermediary with the United States. **[See Chapter 28: Battle for China: FDR, Chiang, Mao, and 'Vinegar Joe']**

For the *Kuomintang* the results of ICHI-GO were also mixed. They had clearly suffered a massive defeat but in reality their Japanese enemy was no longer capable of inflicting further damage. As long as they yielded no further ground, 'free China' could survive and wait for the now seemingly inevitable triumph of American arms against the Japanese. Furthermore, 'Vinegar Joe' Stilwell had shot his bolt. Having tried to use the defeat of Chiang's forces as one of the levers to give himself total command of the *Kuomintang* armies, Stilwell had overreached himself and was sacked. **[See Chapter 28: Battle for China: FDR, Chiang, Mao, and 'Vinegar Joe']** Lieutenant-General Albert Wedemeyer replaced Stilwell as Chief of Staff of US Forces China Theater, while Lieutenant-General Daniel Sultan replaced Stilwell in the continuing campaign to expel the Japanese from Burma.

In spite of his downfall, in America, Stilwell's venomous propaganda continued to degrade Chiang Kai-shek's reputation. In the *New York Times*, war correspondent Brooks Atkinson, formerly a fashion writer, concluded that Chiang ". . . has seen no need to make sincere attempt to arrange at least a truce with them for the duration of the war ... No diplomatic genius could have overcome the Generalissimo's basic unwillingness to risk his armies in battle with the Japanese."[67]

As a result of the machinations of Stilwell and other Mao supporters inside the Roosevelt administration, the narrative that Chiang hoarded war material to fight the Communists after *World War II* and refused to allow his troops to fight the Japanese became the standard version of the war in China. It is a charge and a version of events that has no basis in fact. The ICHI-GO Campaign and its battles, the least written about major engagements of *Pacific War*, were epic encounters that proved the willingness of the Chinese soldier to fight. To suggest otherwise besmirches the memory of millions of Chinese who died in the fourteen-year war to expel the Japanese between 1931 and 1945. As in Europe, where Russia absorbed the major military death count, in Asia, it was Chiang Kai-shek's *Kuomintang* armies that took the big hits in the *Pacific War*'s death toll. Thus, although Chiang may have adopted cautious defensive tactics, well suited to his army's lack of modern equipment and war *matériel*, both the Generalissimo and his troops had repeatedly proved, over a ten-year period, that they were not reluctant to fight.

Stilwell's Strategic Failures: In hindsight Stilwell should have allocated more resources to the Hump rather than the Ledo Road, which was shown to be a 'white elephant' almost as soon as it was built. Furthermore, Chiang Kai-shek's forces in central and southern China should have been modernized rather than Stilwell's Y-Force stationed on the country's remote eastern borders facing Burma. Ultimately the attempt to establish a road link between Assam in northern India and Sichuan Province in China by the retaking of northern Burma was not worthwhile. However brilliant Stilwell's victory at the *Battle of Myitkyina*, the strategic objectives of this campaign were flawed. British Field Marshal Lord Allanbrooke hinted at the irrelevance of Stilwell's campaign, when he said, "It is clear, now that Stilwell has led us down to Myitkyina, we shall have to go on fighting in Burma."[68] For Alanbrooke and Churchill, the possibility of a Chinese army occupying Rangoon could hardly be desirable for Great Britain, Burma's colonial masters. In fact as soon as overwhelming Allied air superiority in Burma had been achieved, thus securing the ability to air supply Kunming over the 'lower Hump', the strategic utility of Burma's reconquest was minimal.

Stilwell's neglect of the Chinese theater of the war and his obsession with the retaking of northern Burma, which he had lost in 1941, came close to losing China altogether—and arguably did eventually lose China to Mao and the Communists. This was not entirely Stilwell's fault. Chiang and Chennault had clearly overestimated the efficacy of bombing to hold back the Japanese Army. Nonetheless, ultimately Stilwell was at fault for failing to manage the tricky relationship with Chiang and Chennault. On 17 May 1944 the director of British Military Intelligence in India reported, "It has been the lowest common denominator of appreciation of China's prospects that, however much conditions depreciated, China would not capitulate ... There is now a distinct possibility of China's collapse ... The Generalissimo, faced with a crumbling structure, has no machinery with which to save it."[69] For America this could have been a disaster—necessitating the invasion of China after the defeat of Japan.

Chiang Kai-shek has usually taken the blame for China's military failure. The near collapse of *Kuomintang*-controlled China has rarely been explained in the context of a country that, after seven years of war, was in a state of complete economic exhaustion and collapse. It had not helped that the Japanese had flooded southern China with US$100m of counterfeit money. Corruption was certainly rampant in 'free China' by 1944 but the real problem was that the Chinese economy had simply imploded. Not surprisingly officials in power, whether civilian or military, inevitably began to operate in a *sauve qui peut* mode.

It is worth noting that the heroic actions of Merrill's Marauders at the *Battle of Myitkyina* and their total of 272 killed, albeit laudable, were a fleabite in the fabric of the war compared to the 90,000-plus Chinese troops who lost their lives in the battles of the ICHI-GO Campaign. It is a sad truth that the state histories of the Chinese Communist Party (CCP) in China, for reasons of state mythology, dare not face the fact that it was the *Kuomintang* and not the CCP that did most of the fighting against the Japanese in the *Pacific War*. CCP propaganda has taken precedence over remembrance of Chinese soldiers who sacrificed their lives to fight Japanese aggression. The historic role of the *Kuomintang* in fighting the war was also undermined by the pervasive corruption of their army, which was increasingly reported by US observers, often sympathetic to the Communists, as the war drew to a close. Of equal importance to the much-neglected record of the history of the *Second Sino-Japanese War* component of the *Pacific War*, was that it was the populations and areas of China controlled by the *Kuomintang* that suffered the heaviest toll from the depredations inflicted by the Japanese Army.

Western historians have been almost as complicit as communist China in hiding the truth of the fourteen-year *Second Sino-Japanese War*. Stilwell's version of events and his view of Chiang became the dominant post-war narrative posited by historians such as Barbara Tuchman who won a Pulitzer Prize for her bestselling history *Stilwell and the American Experience in China, 1911–1945*. That the American-Chinese *Battle of Myitkyina*, Stilwell's great moment, had almost negligible strategic value has been largely overlooked. Meanwhile British historians, obsessed with the Burma campaigns of Slim's Fourteenth Army when they have deigned to look beyond Europe, and American historians, heavily focused on the naval and island engagements of the *Pacific War*, have largely ignored the fact that it was the Chinese on their eastern front who did the heavy lifting before and during the *Pacific War*. As Chiang Kai-shek complained in one of his more bitter moments after receipt of the Marshall-Roosevelt ultimatum, "He [Roosevelt] wants to use Chinese troops to make war, otherwise he'd have to send over a million American troops to East Asia to sacrifice themselves."[70] Chinese soldier Wen Shan observed during the war: "An American considered a Chinese life to be worth a great deal less than an American one."[71] In this respect, it seems that not much has changed with regard to western writing about the *Pacific War*.

The series of battles at Luoyang, Changsha, Hengyang, Gweilin and Liuzhou, that comprise just the major engagements of the ICHI-GO Campaign, barely register in the annals of most western histories of the *Pacific War*; in reality they bear witness to the heavy price paid by the Chinese to recover their country from the Japanese. Like the Soviets in Europe, in Asia, it was not the western powers but China that carried the heaviest burden of suffering in the *Pacific War*.

Furthermore, leaving aside his deleterious effects on the historiography of the period, Stilwell's obsessive desire to restore his pride by retaking Burma and building his 'white elephant' Ledo–Burma Road, at the expense of protecting the arguably much more important eastern front in China, had damaging longer-term consequences. In Henan and Hunan, the great breadbaskets of China, the *Kuomintang* had suffered 200,000 casualties (90,000 dead) in Operation ICHI-GO versus 23,000 Japanese killed. Chinese civilian casualties were probably much higher—perhaps as high as 500,000. In Henan the largely US-controlled United Nations Relief and Rehabilitation Agency (UNRRA) reported that starvation in the region had been made considerably worse by the ravages of the ICHI-GO Campaign. Furthermore the destruction of *Kuomintang* forces and its reputation in these areas undermined Chiang in his upcoming fight with Mao's communists.

Although the anti-Chiang Ambassador Clarence Gauss was replaced by the pro-Chiang Patrick Hurley, while Stilwell's replacement, Albert Wedemeyer, also proved much more accommodating to the *Kuomintang*, much of the damage to post-war relations between the US and China had already been done. The poison left by Stilwell in the US Democrat administration that continued under President Harry Truman after the death of Roosevelt clearly undermined America's commitment to fight the Communist takeover of China.

ICHI-GO Runs out of Steam and the Future of Asia Deliberated at Yalta: In spite of the failures of Stilwell, the Japanese Army's series of epic victories across central and eastern China proved to be pyrrhic in terms of their accomplishment. The main aims of ICHI-GO failed. Although a linkage was made to Indochina, which was nominally under the control of the French Vichy government, the Japanese Army was, by the beginning of 1945, too weak to organize any logistical advantage from this liaison.

Moreover, while the Japanese advance to Kweilin did manage to shut the US airbases in the vicinity, these were removed and opened elsewhere. Although no longer able to bomb Japan from their new locations, they could and did attack Japanese ground forces in China and Burma. Chennault's Fourteenth Air Force did ultimately degrade Japanese supply chains to a degree that helped bring Operation ICHI-GO to a standstill. Meanwhile, the loss of range whereby the Fourteenth Army could bomb Japan from China had little consequence after the capture of the *Marianas Islands* of *Saipan, Tinian* and *Guam* in the autumn of 1944. These islands became the launch pad for the devastating bombing campaign against Japan. Thus Japan's destruction of the *Kuomintang* armies combined with their occupation of large swathes of China ultimately achieved very little—not even the hoped for logistical structure to bring supplies to Japan via Busan. In occupied China the war effort petered out while the Japanese puppet administration of Wang Jingwei lost any remaining strength after he was hospitalized in Nagoya in March 1944. He died from complications from pneumonia on 10 November.

Machinations now began for the post-war settlement of Asia at Yalta (codenamed ARGONAUT, and MAGNETO) Stalin's chosen conference site on the *Black Sea* on 4 February 1945. Chiang Kai-shek, his armies defeated and forgotten, was not invited. In Chiang's absence, Stalin, in return for his own promise to declare war on Japan within ninety days after the end of the European War, demanded military and logistical concessions in Manchuria, maintenance of Outer Mongolia under Soviet control as well as sovereignty over the *Kurile Islands* that stretched from north of Japan to Russia's Kamchatka Peninsula. A suspicious Chiang observed, "The influence of this conference on China will be great. I hope Roosevelt isn't plotting with Churchill and Stalin against me."[72] Chiang's suspicion turned to anger when he discovered that there were secret protocols relating to Manchuria. Ambassador Hurley was equally incensed at the hint of concessions to the Soviets while Mao bathed in the knowledge that the arrival of Stalin's forces could well tilt the military balance in his favor in the impending clash with the *Kuomintang*. What Mao did not know was that one of the secret agreements at Yalta was Stalin's promise not to actively support Mao's Communists versus Chiang Kai-shek—though, as the post-war period would soon show, promises made by Stalin were not worth a great deal.

Nevertheless with the war suddenly brought to an end by the atomic bombing of Hiroshima and Nagasaki, China found itself free of enslavement for the first time in fifteen years. Nominally, it was now one of the four major powers of the world. In reality however, free non-Communist China had been left chronically weakened and friendless. Economically, the war had brought complete devastation to 'free China.' Moreover it was left with two competing claimants, the Communists in the north and the *Kuomintang* in the center, south and east of the country. While on paper Chiang appeared to have the upper hand, his forces, which had taken the brunt of the *Pacific War*, were significantly more battered and war weary than their Communist counterparts.

Indeed it is ironic that the respective military strategies of America and Japan in the last year of the war, two countries implacably opposed to Communism, managed to weaken Chiang's Nationalist cause and at the same time strengthen Mao. Essentially both sides had slugged it out to a military draw in China by the time that the war ended. It is often forgotten that even at the end of the war, China absorbed by far the largest weight of numbers of the Imperial Japanese Army. China may not have provided the thrilling victories and encounters that marked the campaigns in the *South Pacific* but arguably it was the anvil on which a large portion of Japanese military assets and economic resources were crushed. Without the battle for China, the defeat of Japan by the United States and its allies would have been substantially more difficult, and, except for nuclear weapons, arguably impossible.

The war in China exhausted all key parties except the Communists: Japan was defeated, Chiang and the *Kuomintang* areas were exhausted and America was war weary and psychologically not prepared to follow up in China with a strategic plan for the future. As with the defeat of the Soviet Union in the *Afghan War* of the late 1980s, the administration in Washington thought that, after the *Battle of Myitkyina* and the opening of the Ledo–Burma Road, its job was done. Just as America's neglect of post-*Afghan War* [1989] politics led to the rise of the Taliban and Al Qaeda, the neglect of post-war China by the US enabled the rise of Mao Zedong. In terms of the post-war drama of the fall of China to Communism, both America and Japan would pay a heavy price for the military strategies and actions of their commanders in China in 1944.

28 Battle for China: FDR, Chiang, Mao, and 'Vinegar Joe'

[January 1942–August 1945]

[Charts: 28.1, 28.2]

'Vinegar Joe' Stilwell's Sticky Brief in China: The brief given to Lieutenant-General Joseph 'Vinegar Joe' Stilwell to keep China in the war after his appointment as Chiang Kai-shek's Chief of Staff in January 1942 was, seemingly, simple. In reality it was anything but. As Marshall would later comment, of the assignments given to his commanders, General Stilwell's was "one of the most difficult."[1]

Although supportive of his friend Lieutenant-General Stilwell, Marshall's focus and the strategy pursued both by him and his President was to defeat Hitler and secure 'Europe First.' The 'Europe First' policy was deeply hated by General MacArthur, by Admiral King, who loathed the English, and by Stilwell who was also an anglophobe. Whereas the Navy, less required in Europe, was able to commandeer resources for its *Central Pacific* strategy, and MacArthur was able to bully Washington, through the press, to secure sustainable supply for an American-Australian Army, Stilwell was more or less hung out to dry. Although China had been the *casus belli* between Japan and America, with regard to providing military support in the China Theater, Stilwell had to beg, borrow or steal troops.

Apart from the troops building the Ledo Road, the only frontline American troops under Stilwell's command were recruited from the misfits and miscreants taken from the US Army stationed in America. The 3,000 troops of 5307th Composite Unit (codenamed GALAHAD), arrived in India on 31 October 1943 and were loosely modelled on the British Chindits, whose commander, Major-General Orde Wingate, helped train the American recruits in the arts of Long Range Penetration (LRP). 5307th Composite Unit was put under the command of Brigadier-General Frank Merrill, a former military *attaché* in Tokyo and intelligence officer under MacArthur; American journalists famously dubbed them Merrill's Marauders.

As Chiang Kai-shek's Chief of Staff, Stilwell only had nominal control of the Chinese armies. In his first Burma campaign, when the Chinese armies were pushed out of the country, Stilwell had found it almost impossible to exercise personal command over the 80,000 Chinese troops supposedly under his command. At Lashio in 1942, during the retreat from Burma, General Lin Wei effectively vetoed Stilwell's orders or, as Lin Wei put it, he "exerted influence."[2] British Burma commander, Major-General 'Bill' Slim, pointed out, "Such was this 'influence' that no Chinese Army Commander would carry out an Alexander-Stilwell-Lo order unless it had been passed by him [Wei]."[3]

Chiang Kai-shek, appointed by Roosevelt and Churchill as Supreme Allied Commander in China, retained complete authority as both military leader and head of state. Understandably he was loath to give up control; the result was that Stilwell needed to plead, cajole and sometimes bribe his Chinese officers to fight. Stilwell's control of American Lend-Lease assets and supplies was the only leverage that he could use against Chiang. Instead of learning to live with and manipulate the Chinese armies to his advantage through careful diplomacy, 'Vinegar Joe' quickly embarked on aggressive confrontation with Chiang Kai-shek.

Byzantine Allied Command Structures in Asia: **[Chart: 28.1]** If the court of Chiang Kai-shek and his generals was fraught with political complexity, the command structure of the region in which he found himself was positively byzantine. From the summer of 1943, Stilwell reported to British General Giffard, head of the Eleventh Army Group in India. In order to be able to coordinate military campaigns for the retaking of Burma, Giffard had both Stilwell's Northern Combat Area Command (NCAC) and Major-General 'Bill' Slim's Fourteenth Army under his command.

To add further confusion it was decided by Roosevelt and Churchill at the QUADRANT Conference in Quebec in mid-August 1943 that the overall command of the South East Asian Theater should be given to a British officer. In the erroneous expectation that naval operations and amphibious landings would play a large part in the retaking of Burma, Churchill chose Admiral Lord Louis Mountbatten as head of South East Asia Command (SEAC). To balance UK-US interests, Stilwell was made his deputy. Giffard's Eleventh Army Group thus reported to Mountbatten and also to his deputy 'Vinegar Joe' Stilwell. The result of this convoluted structure was that Stilwell reported to Giffard in his NCAC role while within the SEAC structure Giffard reported to Stilwell.

To American wags SEAC became known as 'Save England's Asian Colonies.' They were largely correct; for all his great qualities as a war leader, Churchill was a Victorian at heart who espoused the paternalistic benefits of Empire as well as the 'greatness' that it conferred on Britain, and for whom its recovery was the main goal of the war against Japan. He had strongly opposed the *India Act* [1935] that had furthered Indian progression toward independence and once famously announced: "I have not become the King's first minister in order to preside over the liquidation of the British Empire."[4] For Stilwell, British involvement in the war was less than desirable. Not only did Stilwell view the British as poor fighters, particular after the rout of Burma Corps in 1942, but he also resented the fact that their main aim in Asia seemed to be the re-acquisition of her colonies. Stilwell was certainly correct in this observation but somehow, like Roosevelt and most of his American contemporaries, failed to understand that America's entire involvement in the *Pacific War* was a result of America's own imperial interests in Asia. Indeed Stilwell was in part influenced by the liberal-leaning, anti-imperialist John Paton Davies. Born to missionary parents in China, the 36-year-old US Foreign Service officer at Chongqing displayed a pathological dislike of Great Britain when he stated: "Britain can be a first-class power only as it has the empire to exploit. Imperial role . . . means association with other peoples on a basis of subjugation, exploitation, privilege and force."[5] These were the views, strangely unconscious as to America's own imperialist agenda, which helped feed Stilwell's innate anglophobia.

Stilwell, famous for his hatreds, loathed the 'upper-crust' Giffard and resisted reporting to him. Major-General Slim made the humorous observation, "To watch Stilwell, when hard pressed, shift his opposition from one of the several strong-points he held by virtue of his numerous Allied, American and Chinese offices, to another was a lesson in mobile offensive-defense."[6] It was an absurd situation. The matter was only settled when Stilwell agreed to report to General Slim, the only British soldier for whom he had any respect. Astonishing everyone present at a SEAC meeting, Stilwell declared: "I am prepared to come under General Slim's operational control until I get to Kamaing."[7] The compromise was accepted. In practice this odd arrangement was made to work because Slim and Stilwell liked and respected each other. For all the cantankerous awkwardness displayed to others, Stilwell was a model of decorum to Slim who had the utmost professional respect for a colleague with whom he would always enjoy a harmonious relationship.

The management structure was further complicated by the fact that Stilwell, understandably, also chose to report directly to his mentor, George Marshall, and the US Joint Chiefs of Staff on whose supply of *matériel* he was ultimately dependent. To complicate matters further Roosevelt, who had strong family ties with China would often intervene personally. This was never welcome to Stilwell who thought that Roosevelt was a "flighty fool." [8]

Lines of communication to Washington were further muddied by Roosevelt's authorization of a succession of emissaries sent to China. On Roosevelt's authority, Lauchlin Currie, a Canadian economist and favorite of FDR, Wendell Willkie, the failed Republican presidential candidate in November 1941, Vice President Henry Wallace, Colonel Barrett's Dixie Mission, and Roosevelt's roving trouble-shooter Patrick Hurley, all undertook special information gathering trips to China. Finally, the ultimate decisions about strategic priorities were made at conferences normally attended by Roosevelt and Churchill, sometimes Stalin and just once by Chiang Kai-shek (the 'Cairo Conference,' codenamed SEXTANT) in November 1943.

Chiang Kai-shek's Dilemma: When Stilwell arrived in Chongqing in 1942, he, like many American observers, failed to understand the Chinese perspective of the war. Chiang Kai-shek, since the late 1920s, had been trying to unify China, rid it of a feuding warlord culture, defeat Mao's communist insurgency, as well as hold back Japan's increasing incursion into northern China. In effect from July 1937, following the Marco Polo Bridge Incident, Chiang had been engaged in total war with Japan.

The economic and human cost to China had been staggering. By 1939, China's entire east coast, the fount of its prosperity, as well as the immediate hinterland, had been annexed by Japan. Over half of China, its wealthy half, was under Japanese control. Meanwhile Chiang Kai-shek's government had been forced into exile in Chongqing, in the remote southwest. As for Chiang's former capital, Nanking, it had been infamously ravaged. The Rape of Nanking, where up to 250,000 of its citizens were massacred, was merely the tip of the iceberg in being the most famous example of an attempt to terrorize and subjugate large swathes of the Chinese population. It was a genocidal campaign that killed an estimated 20 to 30 million Chinese people during the course of the *Second Sino-Japanese War.*

There were other costs. Chiang's armies had suffered some four million casualties. Vast swathes of central China had been decimated by crop destruction and starvation. What remained was heavily taxed to sustain the costs of the war effort. By the end of 1941 average prices had risen by 2,000 percent over a five-year period. Moreover the rate of price inflation was on a steep uptrend: 173 percent in 1941 to 235 percent in 1942. Thereafter the need to sustain China's armies and the extra economic stress from an increasing staff of relatively pampered US army personnel, some 27,000 by 1944, pumped further demand and price pressure into the Chinese economy.

There was also rampant corruption inside Chiang's armies with generals frequently selling supplies of munitions and food. It was a commonplace that Chinese generals faked the number of troops they employed to draw extra pay to fill their pockets. Allegedly General Tang Enbo, a former Green Gang bodyguard from Shanghai, who became a favorite of Chiang, even traded Lend-Lease goods with the Japanese Army along the *Yangtze River.* The Green Gang, founded in the early eighteenth century was the most powerful of Shanghai's Triads by the twentieth century, controlling most of the city's criminal activity involving transport, opium, gambling and prostitution. Its *zongshi* (grandmaster), Du Yuesheng, known as 'Big-Eared' Du, was a close pre-war confederate of Chiang Kai-shek. It could not have surprised Chiang that some of his army materiel would end up in Shanghai or that up to 30 percent of his army was fictitious. Even blood donated by the American Red Cross, and delivered over the Hump, found its way into Shanghai's pharmaceutical shops. Meanwhile in the streets of Chongqing, *Kuomintang* soldiers died of starvation.

Chiang's control over his generals was often tenuous at best. The loyalty of his generals was always in doubt, particularly Yu Hanmou, Zhang Fakui, and Xue Yue of the 7th, 4th, and 9th War Zones respectively. Even after Chiang's triumph at the Cairo Conference in 1943, a young generals' plot, aimed at getting rid of corruption, was unearthed. Furthermore it was suspected that commanders of the *Kuomintang* forces in Guangxi and Zhejiang were in secret contact with the Communists. Even so, the *Kuomintang* government, which had been suddenly forced to transplant itself from Nanking to Chongqing in the remote province of Sichuan, with all the concomitant problems of infrastructure and logistics, continued to work. Bank loans were made to farmers, seed was distributed, canals and irrigation were managed and refugees were resettled; it was far from perfect but there was a semblance of order. Against all the odds, the workaholic Chiang had sustained his government.

Even Chiang's then Finance Minister, T. V. Soong, had predicted at the beginning of 1937, that if there was a Japanese invasion of northeast China, "within three months . . . China will be on the verge of bankruptcy and facing revolution."[9] Soong's predictions turned out to be wrong. Neither bankruptcy nor revolution ensued in the immediate aftermath of Japan's full-scale invasion of China in 1937—an outcome that was above all a testament to Chiang's force of will. However, with the constant prospect of war, China's outlook remained tenuous. The country's survival owed much to Chiang's fierce determination. Owen Lattimore, a China expert, who came to work as an adviser to Chiang Kai-shek in July 1942, although frequently critical of Chiang, nevertheless described him as "a genuine patriot," "a great man" who was "sometimes . . . more far sighted than either Roosevelt or Churchill."[10]

Chiang, who rarely received credit for keeping 'free China' operating, never failed to garner criticism for what was often a corrupt and dysfunctional regime. Although Chiang, a renowned ascetic with only a modest interest in money, made attempts to stamp out corruption, he never succeeded. If Chiang ran a government which often appeared brutal, oppressive and byzantine in its operation, it should be remembered that the country that the *Kuomintang* inherited from the Qing Dynasty was backward, and apart from a very few international enclaves, entirely medieval in its social and governmental structures.

In the 1930s Chiang had faced the monumental task of unifying China, unwinding the unequal treaties that had been extorted by the West in the nineteenth century, expelling the so-called foreign enclaves, and fighting an incipient Japanese Empire that had decided to subjugate his country. In the circumstances it was perhaps not surprising that Chiang took China down the often ugly, National Socialist totalitarian path rather than the road of liberal democracy. Chiang's quasi-dictatorial government, for which he has often been criticized, was suitable for a country that needed to fight for its survival. Even Britain had in effect suspended democracy and its self-proclaimed liberal values for the duration of the war.

Chiang, in spite of harboring a deep antipathy toward the West for its carve up of China's wealthy east coast into foreign controlled enclaves and its insistence on legal 'extra-territoriality' for its citizens, was pragmatic enough to understand that, to survive the Japanese onslaught, he needed international help. From 1938 this aid would come from the Soviet Union, but after the *Nazi-Soviet Pact*, he sought help from a United States that was becoming increasingly fearful and opposed to Japanese expansion. Chiang was a patriot who was prepared to make any compromise if it could save his nation.

Chiang's patriotism and his willingness to place pragmatism over ideology were clearly indicated by his appeal to Gandhi not to disrupt the British war effort. In spite of Britain's legacy of abuse of China's sovereignty in the wake of the nineteenth century *Opium Wars*, Chiang, much to Churchill's chagrin, flew to India on 18 February 1942, three days after the fall of *Singapore*, to meet Gandhi in person. They were an unlikely pair. Gandhi and Chiang, if completely different in styles, were both revolutionaries and anti-imperialists. Subsequently Mahatma Gandhi sent Churchill a hand-written note: "I consider the five hours of frank, sincere discussion that we [with Chiang Kai-shek] had in Calcutta as the most satisfying and unforgettable experience in my life."[11] As a result of the meeting, Gandhi pledged that any political actions against the British would be done in a way that would not impede the military effort against the Japanese.

Starvation in Henan Province: After five years of war with Japan, the Chinese economy was severely disrupted. Since the late 1920s Chiang had been trying to unify China and rid it of its warlord structure. By 1936 he was on the verge of wiping out Mao's communists. Complete unification of China, barring Japanese-controlled Manchuria seemed a hair's breadth away. The Xian Incident, in which Chiang Kai-shek was taken hostage, put paid to that dream. The beginning of the modernization of China's medieval economy had been tantalizingly close; Japan's full-scale invasion of China in 1937 put paid to these hopes—until Deng Xiaoping came to power forty-one years later.

In a wrenching dislocation, Chiang was forced to move his capital 900 miles to Chongqing in China's remote western province of Sichuan. The Nationalist (*Kuomintang*) government was thus cut off from its rich east-coast sources of funding and depended for its tax revenue on the agricultural hinterlands of central and western China. The wealthiest and most populous of these was Henan province. During periods of good harvests, such as 1937–1939, onerous taxation on the agrarian sector was just about sustainable, but thereafter it was not, as successive poor harvests plagued central China. After the below average harvest of 1940, the *Kuomintang*'s *Yuan* (executive council) authorized taxes to be collected by the physical handing over of grain. Inevitably the new policy wrought hardship on the landed population whose rice harvest in the south dropped from 753.3 million *shidan* (1 *shidan* = 3.1 bushels =27.93 US liquid gallons) in 1939 to 165.1 million in 1940. A similar collapse was seen in the wheat harvest in the north, which saw production fall from 201 million *shidan* in 1940 to 165 million *shidan* in 1941. In spite of the failing harvest, the *Kuomintang*'s sometimes brutal grain requisition policy had the full backing of Lauchlin Currie, President Roosevelt's special adviser to Chiang's government.

Agrarian difficulties were compounded by the complete failure of the spring 1942 harvest as a result of drought. Yields fell by 80 percent or more. The summer remained dry with the result that the autumn crop withered away. Meanwhile requisitions continued apace. Contemporary accounts of the consequences were gruesome. Zhang Zhonglu, head of Henan's construction ministry, was told of a family in Zheng County that gave their last grain to the tax collectors before jumping in the river to drown. Peasants sold possessions, sometimes their children, to buy grain at grossly inflated prices in order to fill their tax quotas.

On his trip around the province, Zhang Zhonglu reported: "starving people were digging up grass roots, taking leaves, and stripping bark from the trees . . . an unceasing stream of refugees begging for food was so misery-inducing that you couldn't bear to look."[12] Dead bodies littered the roadsides. Cannibalism became widespread. Escapees from the famine piled themselves atop trains going west, only to be crushed to death under railway bridges. "You could exchange a child for a few steamed rolls,"[13] Zhang noted.

Officials were often incompetent or corrupt. Nevertheless, there was little that could have been done even if the *Kuomintang* had possessed a well-drilled bureaucracy. Grain was unavailable from other areas and the potential supply was also prevented by the Japanese blockade. In any case, movement of supply would have been logistically impossible. Feeding Chiang's vast standing army was problematic enough. Bounded by Mao's Communists to the north, the Japanese Army to the east and the Japanese Army in Burma blocking possible supply from Rangoon-Lashio-Kunming (Yunnan province), outside help for China was all but impossible. Meanwhile supplies over the Hump were needed to keep the *Kuomintang* forces in the field. In poor agrarian countries elsewhere at this time, famine remained a hazard of life for which there was no convenient solution; in British-controlled Bengal in 1943, an estimated 2 to 3 million people died of starvation and disease in spite of the absence of the unique wartime problems of logistics faced by Chiang's government.

This did not stop foreign reporters heaping all the blame for the famine onto Chiang and his officials. Roving war journalist Theodore White, who would later become the creator of President John F. Kennedy's Camelot mythology at Jacqueline Kennedy's bidding, wrote a stinging piece in *Time* magazine that was barely diminished by the intervention of owner Henry Luce's, a supporter of Chiang. White noted "dogs eating human bodies by the roads, peasants seeking dead human flesh under cover of darkness, endless deserted villages, beggars swarming at every city gate, babies abandoned to die on every highway."[14] White subsequently resigned from *Time* and vented his full fury against the *Kuomintang* in his end of war book *Thunder out of China* [1946]. It was a book that provided the background to Feng Xiaogang's epic film of the famine, *Back to 1942* [2012].

Chiang Kai-shek was genuinely shocked by the reports from Henan, noting in his diary, "It's unbearable to hear about this dreadful situation."[15] But there was little that Chiang could do. He too was at the end of his tether: "During the six years of the War of Resistance [*Second Sino-Japanese War*]," he wrote in his diary, "my strength has been exhausted and my mind had been dulled . . . We are exhausted . . ."[16]

The Communist-controlled areas of Yanan fared somewhat better. Taxes were high but were better gradated towards those richer farmers who could afford to pay. Moreover Mao had the advantage of having to provision a much smaller standing army compared to the two million troops on the payroll of the *Kuomintang*. Nevertheless it is salutary to note that the death of an estimated four million people, who died in the Henan famine of 1942–1944, constituted what was a minor disaster compared to the 40 to 50 million or more who died in the famine caused by Mao's Great Leap Forward, the collectivization of Chinese agriculture in 1958.

Stilwell's Campaign to Undermine Chiang: Stilwell, unlike Chiang, was by character completely unable to be flexible to the political and cultural nuances that his role required. He was a man who would not bend in a job that, above all, required flexibility. In spite of his ability to speak Mandarin-Chinese, he displayed remarkably little empathy toward his hosts. On one occasion Stilwell told Theodore White of *Time* magazine, "The trouble with China is simple: We are allied to an ignorant, superstitious peasant son of a bitch."[17]

After the denouement of his failed campaign to save northern Burma from the Japanese advance in March 1942, Stilwell stormed into Chiang's offices to berate him for undermining his control of Chinese armies in the field. Stilwell failed to understand that Chiang's caution, his determination to preserve his poorly equipped, outgunned forces, were tactics that had worked to preserve China as an independent nation after some five years of total war. Chiang might also have pointed out that much better equipped British and American armies, facing relatively small invading Japanese armies, had been driven out of Malaya and the Philippines within months of the start of the *Pacific War*. Both General Douglas MacArthur in the Philippines and Lieutenant-General Arthur Percival in Malaya had failed, partly because, in underestimating the talent of Japanese commanders and their troops, they had been too aggressive in the deployment of their forces. Chiang had not made these mistakes. As a result he had survived. Stilwell remained completely oblivious to the strategic and tactical intelligence of Chiang's 'harass and withdraw' approach to a much better equipped and trained Japanese army.

Chiang's opinion of the West's military capabilities continued to fall as British forces were rapidly ejected from Rangoon and then forced to flee back to India. His opinion of Stilwell was little better. No doubt colored by his own experience of fighting the Japanese, Chiang viewed Stilwell as a reckless commander. Not surprisingly, he was not prepared to risk all on such a man. Stilwell, thus thwarted, began to see Chiang as the embodiment of all of China's evils, a man he described in his diary as "a stubborn, prejudiced, conceited, despot."[18] That was the least of his insults. By 1943 Stilwell was referring to Chiang, his Commander in Chief, as "this insect, this stink in the nostrils"[19] and accused him of "corruption, intrigue, obstruction, delay, double crossing, hate, jealousy, skulduggery . . . bigotry and ignorance and black ingratitude."[20]

Stilwell, never reticent in his complaints, poured vitriol in the ears of anyone in Washington who would listen. Generals 'Hap' Arnold and George Marshall, both supporters of Stilwell, were appalled at the tone of his bitter hostility toward Chiang who he dismissively called 'Peanut' in his frequent, often ranting memoranda. Roosevelt, having seen one such missive to Marshall, concluded that Stilwell "has exactly the wrong approach in dealing with Generalissimo Chiang who, after all, cannot be expected, as a Chinese to use the same methods as we do . . ."[21]

Stilwell, a natural corps commander and happiest when cajoling his troops in battle, was rarely able to see the bigger picture. Even if Stilwell had been prepared to sit back and command from a regional HQ, whether New Delhi or Chongqing, it is doubtful that he would have been a capable strategist. The concerns of other commanders were rarely of interest. When in April 1943 Chiang withdrew 70,000 troops from Y-Force on China's western border to face a Japanese offensive in Hubei and Hunan Province, Stilwell launched furiously into Chiang, fuming that the Japanese incursion was a minor operation to seize Chinese river steamers. When the sizeable Japanese offensive was repelled, Stilwell was dismissive; he claimed that it was simply a raid that was withdrawing.

Not surprisingly, Roosevelt and his colleagues in Washington were confused by the differing accounts they were hearing from China. On 12 May 1943, at a pre-Washington Conference (codenamed TRIDENT) briefing meeting, FDR asked General Stilwell and Lieutenant-General Chennault for their opinion of Chiang. Stilwell said, "He's a vacillating, tricky, undependable scoundrel who never keeps his word."[22] To the same question Chennault replied, "Sir, I think the Generalissimo is one of the two or three greatest military and political leaders in the world today. He has never broken a commitment or promise made to me."[23]

At the Anglo-American QUADRANT Conference in Quebec in mid-August 1943, Churchill and Roosevelt decided that China would be used as the base for bombing Japanese shipping and their mainland; Southern China was also considered a possible assembly point for the eventual invasion of the Japanese home islands after the proposed conquest of *Formosa*. Meanwhile the plan for a north Burma campaign was confirmed for February 1944. Stilwell, thinking of his future enhanced status, envisaged a new role for himself as Commander in Chief of all China's armies with a mandate to command without any interference from Chiang. It may not have occurred to Stilwell, but four years earlier he had been a long-serving army colonel with no combat experience while Chiang had twenty years commanding the Chinese Army through civil wars as well as the war with Japan.

While Stilwell was at his most eloquent in denouncing Chiang, he could be diffident at meetings with politicians and fellow commanders. Before the QUADRANT Conference in Quebec in August 1943, where Churchill declared his preference for an attack on *Sumatra* rather Burma, Stilwell was asked to present his strategy for the conduct of the war. He remained silent and uncommunicative. Roosevelt wondered whether he was ill. By contrast Chennault made a slick presentation of a strategy, which required the provisioning of 7,129 tons of supply per month to support the US Fourteenth Air Force in its bid to take control of China's skies.

Before going back to China after QUADRANT, Stilwell found time to dine with a journalist in New York so that he could brief against Chiang. Even Marshall, who was understandably patient with his friend and chosen appointee in China, would on occasions chide Stilwell. At the November 1943 Cairo Conference (code named SEXTANT), Chiang had agreed to Stilwell's demands for 10,000 tons per month over the Hump and had also supported his plan for the invasion of north Burma to open up road links with China. In fact it was a plan for which Chiang had lobbied for 18 months even though Stilwell was claiming it as his own. Yet Stilwell insisted on bending Marshall's ear on Chiang's multiple failings. An exasperated Marshall suggested that if Stilwell was as appallingly treated as he claimed, then he should leave China and be replaced. Stilwell demurred. Having fallen into Marshall's trap, Stilwell was then told to quit his whingeing and to "stop your outrageous talk."[24]

If Stilwell was vitriolic about Chiang behind his back, he was only marginally more polite in his presence. It must be asked why Chiang put up with Stilwell at all. Chiang was forced to beg for supplies from Stilwell for his armies even though the supplies were on Chinese soil and would eventually have to be paid for by China under the terms of the Lend-Lease arrangements. Stilwell ruthlessly used the leverage of supplies and the threat of their withdrawal as a means of keeping Chiang quiescent. In drawing up plans for the re-conquest of Burma, Stilwell even withheld operational military details from Chiang. It was outrageous behavior given that as Supreme Allied Commander in China, Chiang was Stilwell's superior. Though Chinese troops, comprising X-Force based in India and Y-Force based in China, were under Stilwell's direct command, nevertheless they were still Chinese soldiers of the Generalissimo's *Kuomintang* Army. On occasions it was his wife, Meiling, who would have to remind an incandescent Chiang of the big picture, which was to stay on good terms with Roosevelt. It was not just Chiang who bore the brunt of Stilwell's tongue. Joseph Alsop, a young American journalist who was a distant cousin of FDR, described Stilwell as talking to Fourteenth Air Force's General Chennault as if he were "a bluff but not very affectionate uncle toward a hopelessly wayward nephew."[25]

Chiang has often been criticized for his handling of the campaign in China against the Japanese forces stationed there. Much of this criticism represents the long tail of Stilwell's campaign of poison against Chiang during and after his tenure as commander of NCAC (North Combat Area Command). It has usually been a one-sided affair. For obvious reasons, Chiang Kai-shek's successors in Communist China, never keen to shed light on their own treacherous part in the war, were not his natural defenders. Neither were the US Democrats, who have always been on the defensive about their role in the strategic loss of China. From the evidence, it is clear that Chiang was a reasonable and ultimately pragmatic man who was prepared to accept almost any humiliation from Stilwell as long as the supply lines across the Hump remained open. It is notable that in his dealings with Chiang, Stilwell's successor, General Albert Wedemeyer, worked without histrionics and achieved considerable success.

Roosevelt, Chiang and China: As for Roosevelt, he was strongly committed to China for reasons that were personal as well as political. Historically the Roosevelt family, through his maternal grandfather Warren Delano, had made their fortune from the Shanghai opium trade; indeed it is often forgotten that in the nineteenth century, America was almost as complicit as Great Britain in the Chinese drug trade. In fact President Adams had denounced China's refusal to accept British opium "as an enormous outrage upon the rights of human nature, and upon the first principles of the rights of nations."[26] Nevertheless, like many Americans of his background, Roosevelt had developed a rose-tinted view of the Orient. Furthermore he was a committed anti-imperialist—somehow disassociating in his mind America's aggressive expansion in Asia and the *Pacific* and conflating the word 'imperial' solely with the European powers of the old world.

Roosevelt, seemingly oblivious to American imperialism, both in terms of its colonies and its commercial exploitation of Asia, entered the war determined that the European empires, even those of his allies such as Britain, would be dismantled as thoroughly as that of Japan. He affirmed, "When we have won the war, I will work with all my might and main to see to it that the United States is not wheedled into the position of accepting any plan that will . . . abet the British Empire in its imperial ambitions."[27] Roosevelt seemed unaware that in the 1930s, Britain was moving toward self-government in India just as America was moving toward self-determinism in the Philippines. Churchill, the proud imperialist, was by now largely out of step with British consensus.

Whereas for Churchill China was "four hundred and twenty million pigtails,"[28] Roosevelt, reflecting his vision of the post-war world, was determined that China should be one of the great powers. It was a view that reflected the moral optimism of the China lobby in Washington. By contrast Roosevelt admitted to Chiang that there was a problem with Churchill: "Britain does not want to see China become a power."[29] The missionary influence on America's support for China was profound. In general the China lobby was God-fearing, staunchly anti-communist and pro-*Kuomintang*. In addition to powerful Congressional support for the China lobby, influential journalists such as Henry Luce and Walter Lippmann were numbered in its ranks. Luce had been born in Dengzhou in China where his parents had been missionaries; after returning to America, Luce went on to found the iconic and highly influential *Time* magazine in 1922 and bought *Life* magazine in 1936.

On the evening of 23 November 1943, Chiang Kai-shek, who had revered Roosevelt from afar, met his idol at the Cairo summit. Pointedly Stalin, because of his unacknowledged relationships to Mao Zedong and the Chinese Communist Party (CCP) refused to attend. To be pictured next to Churchill and Roosevelt, with his wife Meiling at his side, undoubtedly led Chiang to believe that he had 'hit the big time.' Furthermore, Roosevelt agreed to virtually all his requests: the US occupation of Japan assisted by Chinese troops, Japanese post-war electoral self-determination and support for anti-colonial policies. Chief among these was Roosevelt's pledge to help end the rights of Britain in *Hong Kong* and its other Chinese enclaves. Chiang made clear his distrust of the Soviet Union but agreed to follow Roosevelt's lead on this relationship. Most important from Chiang's point of view, Roosevelt promised to arm and train a full ninety Chinese divisions. The Cairo Declaration, made on 1 December 1943, announced that Manchuria, the *Pescadores Islands* and *Formosa* would be returned to China while Korea would be established as an independent state. In private it was agreed that Japanese assets in China would be handed over to the *Kuomintang* as part of a package of reparations. The declaration rounded up a triumphant week for Chiang. It was the apogee of his relationship with the United States and the West. On 3 December Chiang wrote, "the whole world treated Cairo as a great victory for China."[30]

The sad truth for Chiang was that Stilwell's ill will had already seeped into the general thinking in Washington. Stilwell was quite open in his personal vitriol against

Chiang. Stilwell would freely rage against, "crazy little bastard with that hickory nut he uses for a head" and denounced his, ". . . usual cockeyed reasons and idiotic tactical and strategic conceptions. He is impossible."[31] In particular the perception that Chinese forces would not fight in spite of the vast sums being expended on the Hump caused disillusionment about China's value to the war effort. British Field Marshal Lord Alanbrooke noted in his diary at the Cairo conference that American "hearts are really in the Pacific."[32] While it was important to keep China in the war as a means of tying down Japanese troops and *matériel*, unbeknownst to Chiang, Admiral King had wrought an upgrading of the importance of the *Central Pacific* campaign during the summer of 1943 and the charge to Japan was now in the hands of Nimitz, the Marines and the US *Pacific* Fleet.

Any chance that Chiang could be seen as an equal was undermined by the assessment of the Chinese economic position by the American ambassador to Chongqing, Clarence Gauss. "It must be accepted as a fact that the Chinese cannot solve their desperate economic problems," Gauss reported.[33] He doubted the capacity of Chinese forces to provide further resistance to the Japanese as well as retain the loyalty of the Chinese peasantry, particularly in Henan province. Along with information reported back by Graham Peck, a US Office of War Information official who resided in China throughout the 1940s, the conclusion in Washington was that Chiang's war machine was no longer fit for purpose. It was a cruel reflection on a leader and a country that, over six years of heavy fighting, had sacrificed more than any other ally to hold back Japan. Chiang's exhausted armies had provided a breathing space for US forces in the Philippines and the *Pacific*; ultimately it would be American soldiers who would be the main beneficiaries of the Chinese people's resistance to Japan in the early years of the *Pacific War*.

The constant charges of corruption levelled at Chiang's government, although justified, also took their toll on Washington's confidence in its Chinese ally. Stilwell complained that the *Kuomintang* government was a "cesspool [of] corruption neglect, chaos . . . hoarding, black market, [and] trading with the enemy."[34] It was a damning assessment and one that was made all too often by American observers, but usually without a full understanding of the constrained context within which Chiang was forced to operate.

US Ambassador Gauss further undermined Chiang's credibility by reporting the terror tactics of Dai Li's Gestapo-like Military Investigation and Statistics Bureau (known as the *Juntong*). It was a ruthless organization known for the kidnap and torture of suspects and was fiercely anti-communist in its leanings. Gauss suggested that Chiang's totalitarian methods might be inimical to American interests after the war. It was a curious observation, given the closeness with which Dai Li operated in partnership with US Rear-Admiral Milton Miles's quaintly named Sino-American Co-operation Organization (SACO). SACO became the main intelligence-operating unit for America's alliance with China. In a war in which Chiang was fighting a three-cornered battle against Mao as well as the Japanese, the importance of intelligence was paramount.

Nevertheless, supposedly at Roosevelt's request, Stilwell took it upon himself to plan an assassination of Chiang. His chief of staff, Brigadier-General Frank Dorn, was told to think up something. Dorn suggested that Chiang's plane should develop a problem and that Chiang be issued with a faulty parachute. Colonel Carl Eifler meanwhile suggested the use of the *botulinus* toxin. That Stilwell might have discussed alternatives to Chiang with Roosevelt and administration officials seems quite likely but it stretches credulity to think that Roosevelt ordered Chiang's assassination. Certainly there appears to be no corroboration of the Stilwell derived account. In the event no assassination attempt was ever made.

Whenever Roosevelt felt mystified about what was going on in China, he sent special emissaries. Lauchlin Currie, a Canadian economist who had become the President's main economic adviser in 1939, became an early personal emissary to China. At Harvard, Currie had been a strong critic of monetary tightening at the start of the depression and in a stance that anticipated John Maynard Keynes's advocacy of pump priming, recommended that America should run larger fiscal deficits. After a mission to China in January 1941, Currie, after meeting with both Chiang and Zhou Enlai, by now Mao's representative in Chongqing, strongly recommended that China should be added to the roster of countries served by the Lend-Lease program. Currie told Chiang, "We like their [the Communists'] attitude towards the peasants, towards women and towards Japan."[35] (Later it was strongly suspected by the FBI that Currie was a Soviet spy, providing information to Elisabeth Bentley, the courier for KGB intelligence.)

Again in July 1942, Roosevelt sent Currie to resolve the differences between Stilwell and Chiang. He returned with the conclusion that Stilwell should be replaced, but also reported tittle-tattle regarding Meiling's opposition to Roosevelt's 'Europe First' policy. More damaging were his reports of misallocations of funds and corruption by the Soong family, particularly by T. V. Soong who, for most of the period of the Japanese War, was Chiang's Finance Minister. Roosevelt's emissaries were never helped by the poison placed in their ear by Stilwell. What he never fully understood was that his constant and unbalanced sniping at Chiang not only undermined the Generalissimo's credibility but also his own.

Meiling and the Soong Family: [Chart: 28.2] If there was disharmony behind the scenes, a different scenario was presented to the American public. Aware that Roosevelt would be moved by public support for the Chinese cause, Meiling traveled to the United States in February 1943 with her nephew David Kung and her cross-dressing niece, Jeanette Kung. Here she stayed at Hyde Park, Roosevelt's private home in upstate New York.

As a graduate of Wellesley College, sent there by her Methodist father, Meiling was extraordinarily adept at playing political roles in both Chinese and American cultures. Even the obdurate Stilwell was impressed with her abilities; he described her as "Quick, intelligent. Wants to get things done. Wishes she was a man . . . Very frank and open . . . Direct, forceful energetic, loves power, eats up publicity and flattery, pretty weak on history. No concession to the western viewpoints in all China's foreign relations."[36]

Possessed of an austere elegance, with a slightly manly look, she was not a classical beauty but she made men swoon. She oozed power and worldliness and could deal with powerful men on their own terms. Meiling also possessed an acute intelligence and razor-sharp humor as well as an indefinable aura. The English poet W. H. Auden, who met Meiling on his travels in China with the novelist Christopher Isherwood, described her thus: "She could be terrible, she could be gracious, she could be business-like, she could be ruthless . . . Strangely enough, I have never heard anybody comment on her perfume. It is the most delicious either of us has ever smelt."[37]

In the early stages of China's courtship of America, her skills were invaluable. In 1943 she became the first person without a government position, as well as the first woman, to address the US Congress. A Texas Congressman, Sam Rayburn, introduced her as "one of the most outstanding women of all the earth."[38] She wore a simple black *qipao*, a body hugging dress revealing the arms but with high Mandarin collar, that had been fashionable among Chinese socialites in 1920s Shanghai. It was decorated only with a bejewelled brooch of the Chinese Air Force and revealed a bright-red lining in the side slit that came to her knee. Meiling dazzled Congress with her elegance, beauty and, most importantly, with her speech.

She recalled the historical and friendly links between their countries, and of course asked for American support. "The 160 years of traditional friendship between our two great peoples . . . which has never been marred by misunderstanding, is unsurpassed in the annals of the world."[39] Conveniently Meiling overlooked Commander Andrew Hull Foote, who landed Marines in Guangzhou (Canton) and defeated a 5,000 strong Chinese army in 1848. Somewhat more accurately Meiling reminded Americans, "during the first four and a half years of total aggression, China has borne Japan's sadistic fury unaided and alone."[40] Both US politicians and the American public were mesmerized. In Hollywood she was greeted as a superstar. Her welcoming committee was a Who's Who of the great stars of the period and included Rita Hayworth, Ginger Rogers, Ingrid Bergman, Marlene Dietrich, Judy Garland, Shirley Temple and Mary Pickford. She also met Spencer Tracey and Henry Fonda, who was wearing his naval uniform, and was seated at dinner with David O. Selznick, the powerful Hollywood producer of the recent blockbusters *Gone with the Wind* [1939] and *Rebecca* [1940].

Life magazine on 30 June reported gushingly about Meiling's appearance at the Hollywood Bowl where she made a 45-minute speech to a 30,000 strong crowd:

> To the tinselled home of make-believe last week went a realistic star of the first magnitude. Under the serene blue California skies, Madame Chiang Kai-shek concluded her nationwide tour at a spectacular mass meeting held in the Hollywood bowl. All Hollywood had contributed talent toward making this event a triumph of showmanship. But it was Madame Chiang's gracious charm, her indomitable spirit and her deeply stirring account of

> China's six-year war against Japanese aggression, which
> made the dramatic climax of the afternoon . . .[41]

In fact Meiling was so persuasive on her US trip that it was feared by Washington that she might upset the orthodoxy of Roosevelt's 'Europe First' strategy. He even confided to Treasury Secretary Henry Morgenthau who recalled, "he [Roosevelt] was just crazy to get her out of the country."[42]

Back in Chongqing she courted foreign visitors and made up for Chiang's inability to learn English in spite of his efforts. She softened his seemingly harsh and austere demeanor. Later, her brazen quest for power, and her family's scrambling for position and money, frequently undermined her credibility with Americans on the inside of the goings-on in Chiang's inner circle.

Corruption at the Court of Chiang Kai-shek: With the amount of *matériel* shipment to China and its circuitous delivery route, it was perhaps inevitable that corruption, both on a large and small scale, became rampant. It gradually became apparent that Meiling's relatives, the Soong family, were major beneficiaries of Lend-Lease to China, although innumerable Americans were also later implicated in financial scams, including lobbyists and counsel close to the White House.

T. V. Soong, as a Director of the Southwest Transportation Company that operated trucks carrying Lend-Lease supplies, was widely suspected of selling American vehicles onto the black market. However, the main source of his wealth probably derived from financial manipulation and the currency exchange of the funds that passed through his hands. The British Foreign Office thought, "The Soongs diverted billions of dollars to their own pockets and much of the money never did get out of the US."[43] Such was the scale of the spoils that the Soongs not only seem to have fought within themselves, particularly with Ailing Soong and her banker husband Kung Hsiang-his (often referred to as H. H. Kung), but also with Chiang's most important henchmen the Chen brothers, who controlled the *Kuomintang*'s secret police. Nevertheless, in 1945 it was T. V. Soong who became Chiang's Prime Minister, and *Encyclopaedia Britannica* listed him that year as the world's richest man.

Meiling too, probably had her hand in the honey pot. Famously, Graham Peck at the Office of War Information recalled seeing a crate of Meiling Soong's luxuries dropped and smashed at Kunming Airfield by American GIs, who resented the import of these products while US pilots were dying flying the dangerous route over the Hump; Graham Peck recalled, "The soldiers dropped and broke all the other crates they trans-shipped. When they had kicked every fur coat and trick clock around in the dust as thoroughly as time would permit, they threw the mess into the waiting planes."[44]

Although Chiang, in spite of historic links to Shanghai's Green Gang crime syndicate, made attempts to stamp out corruption, the example of his wife's family's excesses always made it unlikely that he would succeed. Long after his presidency, Harry Truman revealed to writer Merle Miller in an interview that became the bestselling book *Plain*

Speaking [1974], "They're [the Soongs] all thieves, every damn one of them . . . they stole seven hundred and fifty million dollars of the US$3.8bn that we sent to Chiang. They stole it, and it's invested in real estate down in Sao Paulo and some right here in New York."[45]

Gossip about Chiang and Meiling's private life also attracted unfavorable attention. Meiling amazed Gardner Cowles of *Look* magazine when she told him that her husband only believed in sex to produce children, "and since he had already had a son by a previous marriage and was not interested in having any more children, there would be no sex between them."[46] Leaving aside the credulity of Meiling's statement, Chiang certainly indulged in carnal pleasures outside his marriage. An affair was rumored with Miss Chen Ying, a nurse. On one occasion it was reported that a furious Meiling flung a pair of high-heeled shoes out of a window, inadvertently hitting a guard. These were stories that did not fit well with the charade fed to the US press that Chiang was a God-fearing Methodist convert.

As for Meiling, the English press baron Lord Beaverbrook averred to Joseph Kennedy that she was a lesbian. Conversely Gardner Cowles, journalist and owner of a string of regional newspapers such as the *Des Moines Tribune*, the *Minneapolis Star*, the *Jackson Sun* and the *Rapid City Journal*, who toured China with Wendell Wilkie, claimed that Meiling had a romance with the prominent Republican politician. Wilkie, born in Elwood, Indiana, was a corporate lawyer with Firestone Tire and Rubber Company, who had switched from being a Democrat to become an unlikely Republican presidential candidate against Roosevelt in 1941. Roosevelt, drawing Wilkie into his 'big tent,' sent him as an emissary to China in 1942 where he is said to have enjoyed a 'one-night stand' with Meiling. Cowles recorded that the two of them disappeared midway through a banquet causing Chiang to prowl round his house looking for his wife. At 4.00 a.m. "a very buoyant Wilkie appeared, cocky as a young student after a night out with a girl."[47] Supposedly Meiling may even have imagined a future with Wilkie: "If Wendell could be elected, then he and I would rule the world."[48] Cowles's story was never corroborated by other sources. Whatever the truth of the regional newspaper tycoon's story, there was never any doubt about her ability to exert sexual power over powerful men. The reputedly bisexual Admiral Lord Mountbatten found Meiling, "most striking looking and extremely handsome . . . the most lovely legs and feet imaginable."[49]

Not everyone gushed. The State Department's representative in Chongqing, John Service, no fan of the Chiang Kai-shek regime, heard many rumors about the Chiangs' private lives and the corruption of the Soong family. Doubts even spread about the possibility of their separation. Service wrote, "There is so much smoke, it would seem that there must be some fire."[50] In the summer of 1944 the rumors that swirled around Chiang's court became so damaging that he arranged a tea party for foreign correspondents at which he categorically denied stories circulating about his private life. Meiling theatrically declared: "never for a moment did I stoop or demean myself to entertain doubts of his uprightness."[51]

Familiarity with Meiling bred suspicion. Her diva-like behavior while staying as a guest at the White House became legendary. Eleanor Roosevelt, a fan of Meiling, would nonetheless describe her as the most difficult person ever to stay with them. However, there is little doubt that when the Roosevelt Administration got to know more about the Chiangs, they were both fascinated and repelled. When added to the vitriol leached by Stilwell and the State Department about the corruption of the Soong family, rumors about the Chiangs' private life contributed to undermine the credibility of Chiang Kai-shek's *Kuomintang* regime.

Mao's Brilliant Propaganda War: If America's relationship with China was strained by the open hostilities between Stilwell and Chiang Kai-shek, it was the incipient relationship that increasing numbers of American visitors sought with Mao Zedong's Communists that brought the Stilwell-Chiang relationship to its nadir. By mid-1944 the combination of liberal New Deal attitudes among America's Democrat elite and the Chinese Communist Party's brilliant propaganda campaign to disarm the West, contributed to the development of a pro-Mao and anti-Chiang mood within the Roosevelt administration.

In January 1944, John Paton Davies Jr., writing from the State Department, suggested that the Chinese Communist Party (CCP) ran "the most cohesive, disciplined, and aggressively anti-Japanese regime in China."[52] While it was true that the CCP's forces were better disciplined than their *Kuomintang* counterparts, the Communist's military resources were used sparingly against Japan. Ambassador Gauss presented the more balanced view that the CCP's military achievements against Japan "seem to have been exaggerated"[53] and noted: "They appear to have avoided meeting the Japanese in frontal clashes . . . it would seem safe to say that Communist participation has been on a relatively minor scale."[54] The net result of the mixed messages coming from China was that Washington increasingly criticised Chiang's obduracy in not working with Mao's Communists.

On the surface, the formalities of a Chinese Communist Party (CCP)-*Kuomintang* alliance against Japan remained intact to the extent that the CCP was allowed to maintain an office at Chongqing, presided over by Zhou Enlai, an old friend and former colleague of Chiang at the Whampoa Military Academy in the 1920s. In practice, the CCP offered little co-operation with the *Kuomintang*'s war effort against Japan. This did not prevent Zhou Enlai, oozing charm from every pore, from wooing his foreign visitors. The legendary American war correspondent Martha Gellhorn told Jung Chang and Jon Halliday, joint authors of *Mao, The Untold Story* [2005], "She would have followed Zhou to the ends of the world had he beckoned."[55] More prosaically, Gellhorn's husband, the novelist Ernest Hemingway, now on his third wife, said, "he [Zhou] does a fine job of selling the Communist standpoint on anything that comes up."[56]

The presence of Zhou Enlai in Chongqing proved a significant propaganda boon to the Chinese Communist Party (CCP); Zhou, a major figure in the early history of the CCP and at one time the leader of the Long March, who had even briefly outranked

Mao, was a man of exceptional intelligence, charm and diplomatic skill. Visitors to Zhou Enlai in Chongqing, were captivated by this most compelling figure. He became a 'must-see' person for any eminent visitor and always compared favorably with Chiang.

Furthermore, on visits to Mao's enclave in Yanan, American newspapers swallowed lock, stock and barrel Mao's protestations of willingness to work together with the *Kuomintang* to combat Japan. The *New York Times* accepted at face value Mao's assertion that the Chinese Communist Party (CCP) had "never wavered from its policy of supporting Chiang Kai-shek."[57] Mao encouraged journalists to believe that his 'New Democracy' platform aimed to create a mixed economy rather than an orthodox Marxist-Leninist system. "It might be more appropriate to call ourselves a Democratic party,"[58] Mao speculated alluringly to an American audience. In addition he suggested that the US might provide the CCP with aid to modernize China and even asked an American reporter whether Sears Roebuck, at the time the largest US department store business, would be interested in opening a mail order business in China.

It was an entirely disingenuous strategy of misinformation. In reality, in 1939 Mao had ordered the Communist Party to focus aggressively on engaging *Kuomintang* forces with the object of wresting territory from their control. It was a strategy that Mao even hid from Stalin and his preferred Chinese stooge, Wang Ming. In 1925 the CCP sent Wang Ming to Moscow to study at the Sun Yat-sen University in Russia. Four years later he was sent back with the '28 Bolsheviks' as their leader. Stalin's intention was that Wang Ming would take control of the CCP and he duly became a leading member of the Politburo and head of the Secretariat of the Central Committee of the CCP. In reality Mao fed Wang enough rope to hang himself, and a combination of resentment and Mao's successful political maneuvering denied him his chances of leadership.

It was also reported by the *New York Times* that Yanan was "a Chinese wonderland City."[59] Most damaging, however, was the blatant propaganda lie planted by Mao that Chinese Communist Party forces alone were tying down 80 percent of Japanese forces in China. Meanwhile liberal elements of the American press were relentless in their largely one-sided criticism of Chiang's government. In *Life* magazine, Theodore White wrote that Chiang was head of "a corrupt political clique that combines some of the worst features of Tammany Hall and the Spanish Inquisition."[60] As the conservative commentator William F. Buckley Jr. noted in an obituary after Theodore White's death on 15 May, 1986, "Like so many disgusted with Chiang Kai-shek, he [White] imputed to the opposition to Chiang thaumaturgical social and political powers. He overrated the revolutionists' ideals, and underrated their capacity for totalitarian sadism."[61]

Stilwell, normally a staunch Republican right-winger, who detested Roosevelt and the New Deal, allowed his distaste for Chiang to sway him towards the Communists. "Chiang Kai-shek," according to Stillwell, could not "see that the mass of Chinese people welcome the Reds as being the only visible hope of relief from crushing taxation, the abuses of the Army, and Tai Li [Dai Li]'s Gestapo."[62]

Mao's Yanan Rectification Movement: Even people antipathetic to communism often described Yanan as a haven of peace and a tranquil island of camaraderie. It was a myth carefully cultivated by Mao and the Communist leadership. While it was the case that Mao's stronghold at Yanan was never seriously threatened during the course of the *Pacific War*, as the Japanese concentrated their attacks against the *Kuomintang*, the Chinese Communist Party was riven by warring factions, which, after 1942, descended into bloody terror.

Mao was not an all-powerful leader at the start of the *Pacific War*. The Soviet favorite was Wang Ming, who along with other Moscow educated leaders, known as the '28 Bolsheviks,' were referred to by Mao as the 'Dogmatist Faction.' Meanwhile Mao also had to cope with rivalry from the 'empiricist' faction that included former party leader Zhou Enlai as well as several of the Chinese Communist Party's most able military commanders, Peng Dehuai and Chen Yi.

The beginning of the Rectification Movement's (*Zhengfeng*) can be traced to 1 February 1942 when Mao Zedong gave a speech at the opening of the Chinese Communist Party (CCP) Central Committee's Party School in Yanan. *Rectify the Party's Style*, as its publication was entitled, called for a study of the CCP's history and suggested that the "Party not only needs democracy but needs centralization even more."[63] It was a seemingly innocuous suggestion. The roots of *Zhengfeng* seemingly derived from Confucian philosophy with its emphasis on the importance of ethical education: "The cultivation of the person depends on rectifying the mind,"[64] Confucius had instructed his followers.

Subsequently Mao organized the Rectification Meetings at which party members were expected to indulge in self-criticism and confession. Mao and his close allies including Kang Sheng, the Chinese Communist Party's ruthless head of intelligence and security, took charge of the Central General Study Committee. The methods of false confession and psychological torture developed by Kang Sheng would define Mao's grip on authority over the Chinese Communist Party in the coming decades. Later residents of Yanan would recall that in the valleys and caves outside the town, victims of psychological bullying produced "screams and howls like wolves every night."[65] Suicide was frequent. One victim who survived swallowing glass was immediately forced to write self-criticism.

What started out as an internal discussion ended in late 1943 with the Rectification Campaign becoming a system of mass arrest, torture and execution. Contrary to the assertion of some apologists, "there was no actual purge,"[66] executions carried on well into 1944 as false confessions, by prisoners trying to save themselves, multiplied. It is estimated that some 10,000 Chinese Communist Party members, many of them former inhabitants of *Kuomintang*-controlled areas, were executed. Wang Ming, Mao's primary target, was spared but he and the '28 Bolsheviks' were forever sidelined. Meanwhile Zhou Enlai and the 'empiricists' swung into line behind Mao.

The Rectification Movement was not without its critics. In a cycle that was to repeat itself time and again, intellectuals were at first invited to be open, before the party turned against them, destroyed them in self-criticism meetings, paraded them as criminals and tortured them until they revealed confederates real or imagined. It was a trick to be frequently repeated when Mao became China's leader. The gradual progression to torture was a strategy recommended by Mao. "It is not good to correct too early or too late," Mao argued on 15 August 1943. "Too early . . . the campaign cannot unfold properly; and too late . . . the damage [to torture victims] will be too profound."[67]

Wang Shiwei, one of the '28 Bolsheviks,' a journalist for *Liberation Daily*, wrote an article *Wild Lilies* [1942], which criticized Mao for his womanizing as well as the luxuries enjoyed by the senior cadres of the Chinese Communist Party (CCP). It had not gone unnoticed by others that Mao purloined the ambulance sent as a gift by Chinese New York laundry workers to the CCP to carry war wounded. He used it as private transportation for himself and his 23-year-old mistress, the actress Jiang Qing. The 45-year-old Mao would later marry her after he had dumped his third wife, He Zizhen, with whom he had had five children. The ambulance vehicle was the only car in Yanan. On Mao's orders, Wang Shiwei was expelled from the party in October 1942 after being found guilty in a 'struggle session' in June. He survived until July 1947 when Mao ordered his execution. In an irony that presaged the Cultural Revolution, the Lu Xun Art Institute became a center for the torture of deviant party members and it even managed its own labor camps where prisoners were held under appalling conditions.

The reasons for Mao's drive to implement the Rectification Movement have been much debated. Undoubtedly Mao's campaign served to define the ideological path of the party and unify a Chinese Communist Party that contained southern peasants who had comprised the bulk of the Long Marchers as well as tens of thousands of young men—mainly fervent, educated urban refugees from the war with Japan, who saw future hope in the utopian messages emanating from Yanan. As a result of the Rectification Campaign, Mao was also able to develop a different Marxist line from the Soviet model. Mao was a patriot who refused to countenance a future in which China would be reduced to the status of a Soviet vassal state. It is unlikely that the development of arcane, often meaningless, communist dogma—pseudo ideology—was the main reason for Mao's championing of the Rectification Movement. Mao was a totalitarian leader who had a burning desire for power. Rectification was ultimately a tool for his self-advancement and one that he used throughout his subsequent career whenever his own position was threatened; thus in 1956, Mao unleashed the *Let a Hundred Flowers Bloom* campaign, almost a carbon copy of the Rectification Movement, as a result of the failure of his economic policies after the defeat of the *Kuomintang*.

From 1942 onwards 'Maoist thought' became the paramount guiding light of party ideology. Ultimately the Rectification Movement unified the party, not as a result of some cozy camaraderie as Stilwell, US State Department and most of Roosevelt's emissaries came to believe, but because it imposed a reign of totalitarian terror. The discipline thus secured served Mao well as he put himself firmly atop the Chinese Communist Party's power pyramid, while at the same time organizing an army and concomitant political and propaganda campaign to crush the *Kuomintang*.

The Military Strengthening of Mao and his Phoney War Against Japan: Just as Mao's propaganda produced a false image of internal Chinese Communist Party workings, so too the reality of Mao's war effort against the Japanese was that it was negligible. Indeed, a secret directive acquired by the *Kuomintang* neatly captured the truth of Mao's intentions towards the Japanese. In it, Mao explained, "The Sino-Japanese War affords our party an excellent opportunity for expansion. Our fixed policy should be 70 percent expansion, 20 percent dealing with the *Kuomintang* and 10 percent resisting Japan."[68]

The Chinese Communist Party (CCP) grew its Eighth Army from 45,000 in 1937 to 400,000 by 1940. Meanwhile, over the same period the New Fourth Army was increased from 15,000 to 100,000. Most of the CCP's fighting energy was aimed against the *Kuomintang,* not the Japanese. In September 1939, Zhou Enlai, while going to have a broken arm reset at the Kremlin Hospital in Moscow, informed Stalin that the CCP's membership had "increased sevenfold [to] 498,000" since the start of the war.[69] With the CCP trying to expand their region of influence in the north, Chiang had to station a 500,000 strong force to guard against them. This was a war within a war.

It was rarely recognized that the Chinese Communist Party (CCP), whatever their public protestations, were never prepared to work under Chiang's command. As a result of the Xian Incident in 1936 **[see Chapter 3: Japan versus China: From Phoney War to Total War]**, Chiang had been forced to compromise his instinctive distrust of the Communists and had agreed to work with them to fight the Japanese; in practice the relationship had barely worked, and was constantly undermined by CCP forces' attacks on the *Kuomintang* after 1939. The change in the CCP-Kuomintang relationship tracked Mao increasing dominance of his comrades. Co-operation broke down almost completely after the Wannan Incident in January 1941.

This event, whose causes are still much disputed, resulted in the destruction of part of the Communist's Fourth Army and the killing of 7,000 Communist soldiers and its Chief of Staff, Hsiang Ying, by *Kuomintang* (Chinese Nationalist Party) forces. Usually described as a *Kuomintang* atrocity, it now seems that the Wannan Incident was orchestrated by Mao who "deliberately set Hsiang Ying's group to be killed by the Nationalist [*Kuomintang*] Revolutionary Army, in the hope that the massacre would persuade Stalin to let him off the leash against Chiang."[70] Mao not only guided his troops down the wrong track so that they would fall directly into the path of the *Kuomintang* Army, but also failed to notify Zhou in Chongqing what was happening, which would have enabled Zhou to get Chiang to call off the encirclement of his Fourth Army troops. When the massacre was complete, Mao wrote to Zhou Enlai calling on him to crank up a public relations campaign against Chiang: "We will strike all the way to Sichuan [Chiang's base] . . . Now it is a matter of a total split . . . of how to overthrow Chiang."[71]

Nor were *Kuomintang* forces angels in their dealings with the Chinese Communist Party (CCP). Apparently General Gu Zhutong, commander of the *Kuomintang*'s Third War Zone, allowed the rape of captured Communist nurses and other female staff. For a year and a half they were locked up in barracks that the *Kuomintang* then used as an

Army brothel. For his efforts in defeating this unit of the CCP's Fourth Army, Gu was awarded the Grand Cordon of the Blue Star and White Sun, the highest honor for a Chinese commander. Gu went on to enjoy a glittering *Kuomintang* career, becoming Taiwan's defense minister in 1950.

Lu Zhangcao: A Spy in Chiang's Camp: In addition to the secret deals with the Japanese, Mao benefited from information sent by a high-ranking spy within the *Kuomintang*. Lu Zhangcao, who had been the Young Marshal, Zhang Xueliang's chief of staff at the time of the Xian Incident in 1936, became a *Kuomintang* general as well as a spy for Mao. Lu Zhangcao had been born in the Manchurian province of Liaoning. In 1905, as a young boy, he had seen his peasant farmer parents' home torched by the Japanese during the *Russo-Japanese War* of 1905 and grew up with a visceral hatred of Japan. During the Xian Incident negotiations with the Communists, Zhou Enlai, the Chinese Communist Party's most able diplomat, had used his seductive charm to win over Lu Zhangcao to the Communist cause.

Lu stayed within the *Kuomintang* and became one of Chiang's most aggressive and successful commanders in fighting the Japanese. One of his original innovations was the development of a Marine brigade trained to hide underwater using reeds with which to breathe. As a spy he also provided important information to Mao that was used to crucial advantage against Chiang Kai-shek. Of course Lu was not privy to Mao's double game with the Japanese. Only after the war did he formally switch sides and became one of the fifty-seven founding generals of the People's Liberation Army after the formation of the People's Republic of China (PRC).

Lu also became a legendary and much celebrated figure in the Chinese Communist Party's (CCP) historiography of the revolution. No doubt because of Mao's duplicity, Lu was one of the few CCP generals who could genuinely claim significant combat action against the Japanese, even if he actually did this in a *Kuomintang* uniform. Thus Mao, who supposedly never fully trusted Lu, recognized his propaganda usefulness and later lauded his army as a "model of guerrilla warfare and of the fight of common people"[72] Mao's praise did not stop Lu from being purged during the Cultural Revolution and he was forced to spend seven years in a remote gulag. Before that Lu had become Minister of Railways and greatly expanded its network.

Later rehabilitated, he returned to Peking where he was given Deng Xiaoping's former house. After a lifelong addiction to tennis, Lu became Chairman of the China Tennis Association in 1982 and also played well into his nineties. He was a highly intelligent, indeed learned man who spent the latter part of his life embedded in his well-stocked study: "I have not done much my entire life," he confided, "mainly three things, fight the Japs, build the railway and play tennis."[73] He was the last of the 'founder generals' to die in October 2009. His funeral was attended by Chinese President Hu Jintao as well as his predecessor Jiang Zemin. To close associates in private he confided, *sotto voce*, the truth that it was the *Kuomintang* that did most of the fighting to defeat Japan.

Mao Gulls the US Vice-President: Henry Wallace, who was Roosevelt's Vice-President in his second term of office, was yet another personal emissary sent to China to find out what was 'really going on.' During his mission in June 1944, Wallace came to the conclusion that Stilwell should be replaced by Lieutenant-General Albert Wedemeyer, a right-hand man to Mountbatten at South East Asia Command (SEAC) headquarters in Kandy, Ceylon. Wallace also reported that Chiang was "prejudiced against the Communists."[74] Wallace advised FDR that he should "induce the Generalissimo to reform his regime and to establish at least the semblance of a united front." The gullible Henry Wallace also made a tour of Siberia with Owen Lattimore; they were completely taken in by the "Potemkin show" put on by Stalin. A documentary film of the visit, scripted by Lattimore, informed its viewers that a village "in Siberia is a forum for open discussion like a town meeting in New England."[75]

Wallace, having been gulled by the Soviets and by Mao, now duly proclaimed that Chiang was a "short term investment" and that he did not have "the intelligence or political strength to run post-war China."[76] It was a remarkably dismissive conclusion about a man who, for over twenty years, had unified a warlord-riven country, and fought a modern Japanese army for over half of this period. Albeit an ill informed and one-sided analysis, it was inevitable that some mud would stick.

Until now Chiang had resisted American efforts to allow US representatives to meet the Chinese Communist Party. "It's only reasonable that I should strongly refuse," he wrote.[77] After Wallace's visit however, Chiang was forced to give in to American insistence. The way was paved for the Dixie Mission.

The Dixie Mission: The US Army Observation Group, which became known as the Dixie Mission, was originally an idea developed from a memorandum written by Foreign Service officer, John Paton Davies Jr., on 15 January 1944. It proposed the benefits of contact with Mao's Communist groups in Yanan. Stilwell leapt at the idea. It was another means of humiliating Chiang. Although the Generalissimo resisted any Allied parleying with the CCP, Vice-President Wallace managed to exert enough pressure for Chiang to be forced to accept the Dixie Mission, without *Kuomintang* supervision.

Colonel David Barrett led the mission that began its work in July 1944. Barrett was a China expert who developed a perfect command of the Peking dialect after becoming an assistant military *attaché* for language study in 1924. The remainder of his military career was spent almost entirely in China. For the Dixie Mission, Barrett was given responsibility for military analysis while Foreign Service official John Service, the son of missionaries from Sichuan, wrote the political reports. Aside from a few minor criticisms, Service's report was fulsome in its praise of the CCP and its senior leadership at Yanan. Although he found the conformity of thinking somewhat puzzling, he nevertheless praised it. Service noted:

> There is no criticism of party leaders ... there is no
> tension in the local situation ... there is no feeling of

> restraint or oppression ... there is no hesitation in
> admitting failure ... there are ... no beggars, nor signs of
> desperate poverty ... total ... unity of the army and
> people.[78]

The visitors to Mao's utopian hideaway failed to note that, as the purged Wang Shiwei observed, "Yanan is very dreary and lacks amusements" not least of which was that "the ratio of men to women is 18:1 and many young men are unable to find girlfriends."[79]

Disarmingly, Mao assured Colonel Barrett that the Chinese Communist Party (CCP) "would serve with all our heart under an American general with no strings or conditions attached."[80] As a result of their trip, Barrett, the leader of the Dixie Mission, perversely suggested that the US should supply arms to the Communists as a means of preventing their return to a close alliance with the Soviet Union; as if there had been a break in their relationship. Without American support, Barrett suggested, "the chances of civil war would increase and Mao would return to his close alliance with the Soviet Union."[81] Liberal elements within the senior leadership of the Roosevelt administration chose to believe the Dixie Mission rather than the report produced by the US Military Intelligence Division of the War Department. The latter more realistically concluded that CCP discipline and democracy was entirely Soviet in style and stated categorically, "Real opposition groups are summarily repressed as traitors."[82] Their stark conclusion was that although pragmatism might require the US to supply Mao's army, "it is completely unrealistic to deal with them on the assumption that they are not communists."[83]

It was not just the military that was riven by internecine fighting between pro-Communist and anti-Communist factions. John Service sent back a report concluding: "he [Chiang] has achieved and maintained his position in China by his supreme skill in balancing man against man and group against group, by his adroitness as a military politician rather than as a military commander, and by reliance on a gangster secret police."[84] At the US State Department, Stanley Hornbeck, the head of the Far Eastern Division, ignored John Service's pro-Communist reports from Chongqing over which he scribbled, "rash, exaggerated, and immature."[85]Conversely John Paton Davies, who was assigned to Stilwell, wrote: "The Generalissimo is probably the only Chinese who shares the popular American misconception that Chiang is China."[86] Eventually the pro-Mao lobby which had been strongly supported by Stilwell, won out. In 1944, Hornbeck was transferred to The Hague as Ambassador to the Netherlands.

Chiang believed that Stilwell had been taken in by Communist propaganda, which had led Stilwell to believe that Mao was more of an agricultural reformer than a Communist. Stilwell, he believed was under the mistaken belief "that the Chinese Communist Forces, if placed under his command, would obey his orders and fight the Japanese. . . ."[87] Fortunately for Mao, his bluff was never called, and his disruption of Chiang-US relations eventually worked perfectly. Later Chiang would assert that Stilwell's subversion by the Communists, "almost caused the disruption of Sino-American military cooperation in the China-Burma theater of the war."[88]

Further anti-Chiang propaganda was stirred by the influential 'intellectual left' in both America and Europe. American journalist, Harold Isaacs, a Trotskyite who later became a political scientist at the Massachusetts Institute of Technology, had published his seminal pro-Communist work *The Tragedy of the Chinese Revolution* [1938], which described the *Kuomintang*-Chinese Communist Party split in 1928. André Malraux's novel, *La Condition Humain* [1933], set in 1920s Shanghai, was similarly critical of Chiang and the Soongs. Meanwhile the legendary fellow-traveller, Edgar Snow, author of *Red Star over China* [1937], scooped the world by trekking across China to meet Mao Zedong and wrote a highly influential account of his life which portrayed him sympathetically as an 'agricultural reformer.'

On Mao's orders, Communist underground operatives in Shanghai had carefully recruited Snow. An American, Snow was a well-known writer on the *Saturday Evening Post* and the *New York Herald Tribune* and was considered to be politically sympathetic. Detailed instructions from Mao on how to treat Snow were summarized as "Security, secrecy, warmth and red carpet."[89] Mao mixed fact with falsehoods, which the gullible Edgar Snow swallowed completely, writing that the Chinese Communist Party (CCP) leadership was "direct, frank, simple, undevious."[90] There seems little doubt that Snow and other western writers created a background of intellectual respectability for Mao and the CCP. Thus the CCP provided an attractive alternative to Chiang Kai-shek for men of action and basic integrity like Stilwell and others in the Roosevelt administration, who had developed a visceral distaste for Chiang Kai-shek's *modus operandi*.

Little did any of the Chinese Communist Party (CCP) supporters in Washington realize that, after the *Nazi-Soviet Pact* of 23 August 1939, Mao began a long-term collaboration with the Japanese intelligence service. Mao's point man for this operation, Pan Hannian, worked with Japan's Vice-Consul in Shanghai, Eiichi Iwai, on the profitable exchange of information. Iwai even installed a radio at home to enable direct communication with Yanan. Far from fighting the Japanese, Mao sought to supply Japan with information that would help them destroy Chiang. One CCP intelligence officer even boasted: "... I knew personally, the Japanese annihilation of the [*Kuomintang* underground army] south of the *Yangtze* [was one of the] masterpieces of co-operation between the Japanese and our Party."[91] In east central China, Mao and the Japanese agreed a *quid pro quo* whereby the CCP would not interdict Japan's trains while the Japanese Army would not contest the CCP control of the countryside. Not surprisingly the Communists were able to expand their influence in these areas rapidly. From a position of near annihilation in 1936, when Chiang had them virtually surrounded to the north of Xian, the CCP's recovery during the Japan war years was remarkable. By 1944 the CCP had 700,000 troops and controlled areas with a population of ninety million. They were now a force to be reckoned with even though Chiang, with a 1.5 million strong army and 200 million people under his control, still had the upper hand. The war with Japan served the Communists well.

On Japan's side, Prince Mikasa, Hirohito's brother, who was serving in China, would later explain that they viewed the Communists as just a nuisance compared to Chiang, who was the only threat that they took seriously.

Roosevelt Turns the Screws on Chiang: General Marshall, Chief of Staff of the US Army, rejected Wallace's recommendation to axe Stilwell. To the contrary, Marshall recommended that Stilwell after his victory at the *Battle of Myitkyina* **[see Chapter 27: The ICHI-GO Campaign and the Battle of Myitkyina]** be promoted to full general; a rank that was held only by Marshall himself, Eisenhower, MacArthur and 'Hap' Arnold. Furthermore, after several years of misinformation regarding the fighting abilities and the desire to fight of Chiang and his armies, the Joint Chiefs of Staff had come to the conclusion that it was time to exploit their supply of *matériel* by imposing Stilwell on Chiang as the Commander in Chief of all of China's armies.

In effect, Marshall offered Stilwell command of Chiang's armies before Chiang Kai-shek had been informed. Stilwell, high on his promotion and the military victory of his forces at Myitkyina, concluded that the time for taking revenge on Chiang for all his perceived slights was now at hand. Via the Joint Chiefs, Roosevelt sent a message to Chiang demanding that Stilwell be given command of all China's armies. It was a humiliating demand with only a few palliative words. Stilwell, who received a copy of the message from Marshall with an accompanying order that he should 'behave,' was delighted. In his diary Stilwell noted: "The cure for China's trouble is the elimination of Chiang Kai-Shek."[92] Chiang was stunned by the Joint Chiefs' demands. Remarkably they wanted Stilwell to have the same command structure in China as Eisenhower enjoyed in Europe. The fact that the United States in China, unlike Europe, had practically no foot soldiers on the ground, did not seem to trouble the logic of their argument. From an America supposedly committed to the expunging of colonialism in Asia, Roosevelt's attitude to the Chinese displayed remarkable racial superiority and colonial arrogance. Inevitably Chiang saw the request as a threat not only to his own power but also to Chinese independence. Would he simply exchange a China controlled by Japan for a China dominated by the United States? In the depths of his despair Chiang became convinced, "Roosevelt has already determined to overthrow me."[93]

In spite of his fears, Chiang felt that he had little choice but to accept Roosevelt's terms. In exchange though, he asked for the appointment of an American intermediary to deal with Stilwell. Chiang's mood changed as reports from Washington vacillated. A meeting between Roosevelt and Chiang's representative and brother-in-law, H. H. Kung, was positive. Chiang's mood lifted. A letter from the War Department threatened, "Should our common goal of fighting Japan unfortunately be stifled by your decisions, the United States and China would have limited opportunity for further cooperation."[94] Chiang's mood fell.

Then gloom. A letter from FDR, showing the influence of the pro-Mao lobby inside his administration, urged Chiang to work more closely with Mao on joint military activity against Japan. The Roosevelt administration had clearly been given its lead by the report produced for the Dixie Mission by John Service and Colonel David Barrett.

Roosevelt Sends a Cowboy: Drawing strength from trouble stirred in Washington by the Dixie Mission report and the gradual seepage of pro-Chinese Communist Party views expressed by John Service, John Paton Davies and others, Stilwell's confidence grew. Blaming Chiang for the extremely difficult situation in Burma, Stilwell sent a stern message to Roosevelt and Churchill while they were meeting at the Second Quebec Conference (codenamed: OCTAGON) on 16 September 1944, mischievously complaining that the Generalissimo was refusing to provide relief for his troops in Burma. It was an untruthful accusation. In fact Chiang had dispatched the 200th Division and 10,000 fresh troops to Burma—this in spite of the inroads being made in central and southern China by Japan's ICHI-GO Campaign. **[See Chapter 27: The ICHI-GO Campaign and the Battle of Myitkyina]**

Taking advantage of the stirrings of discontent with Chiang in Washington, Stilwell suggested that he should be given immediate direct command of Chinese forces. He wanted absolute control. Fearing a looming disaster in Burma and China, Marshall reacted. His staff drafted a stiff letter for Roosevelt to sign in which he demanded that Y-Force be left in Burma and that additional troops should be made available. It was also further demanded that Stilwell be given full and absolute command of the Chinese Army; the missive ordered Chiang to place "General Stilwell in unrestricted command . . ."[95] The 'Ultimatum Letter' was forwarded to China; its concluding message to Chiang was, "you must be prepared to accept the consequences and assume personal responsibility."[96]

By August 1944, a concerned Roosevelt had already put in place a personal emissary in China. Patrick Hurley, who was given the principle mission "to promote efficient and harmonious relations between the Generalissimo and General Stilwell to facilitate General Stilwell's exercise of command over the Chinese armies placed under his direction."[97] He was also tasked with drawing the Communists into the Chinese Army's command structure. The ageing Hurley, with his tall ramrod stance, mane of white hair and flailing moustache, may have looked like a character from the Old West but he was not an unaccomplished man. Born on an Indian reservation of the Choctaw Nation, Hurley became a lawyer in Oklahoma and then a soldier, rising to the rank of Colonel with the American Expeditionary Force on the Western Front in *World War I.*

Later he became Secretary of State for War in the cabinet of Republican President Herbert Hoover. At the outbreak of the *Pacific War*, Roosevelt sent him on missions as the President's representative to Bataan and elsewhere. Hurley was mildly eccentric with a deep love of the Wild West where he had grown up. Famously when he first met Mao at a dinner held in his honor, much to the consternation of his diplomatic handlers, he hollered "Yahoo!," a traditional Indian war cry. Thereafter he would refer to Mao Zedong as 'Moose Dung.'

Post-war historians have often represented Hurley as some kind of unhinged right-wing fanatic because he came to see through Mao's initially cuddly façade as an agricultural reformer. He also became increasing outspoken in his support for Chiang Kai-shek as a bulwark against communism in China. At first Hurley was as taken in by Soviet and Chinese Communist Party propaganda as were Paton Davies and Service at the State Department. After a conversation with Soviet Foreign Minister, Molotov, in Moscow, Hurley was for a while convinced: "the Chinese Communists are not in fact communists . . ." he averred and went on to insist "that Russia is not supporting the so-called communists in China and . . . that Russia desires closer and more harmonious relations with China."[98] Hurley was not the first or last American visitor to be duped by Mao Zedong and the Soviets but he did later admit to his mistakes and became a staunch supporter of Chiang and the fight against communism. In reality, in spite of his eccentricities, Hurley was a skilled and pragmatic diplomat: qualities that had led Roosevelt to overlook Hurley's Republican roots. On arrival Stilwell had immediately liked Hurley, describing him as a "breath of fresh air, a real American."[99] Ironically, the breath of fresh air was to become Stilwell's nemesis.

Vinegar Joe's 'Ultimatum Letter': *In situ,* Hurley realized that delivery of the Marshall-Roosevelt 'Ultimatum Letter' was not only unnecessary but also potentially destructive. In the continuing negotiations that had involved Patrick Hurley along with Chiang, T.V. Soong, Finance Minister, He 'Lucky' Yingqin, Military Chief of Staff, and Bai Chongxi, commander of Chiang's crack Guangxi troops, most of the points mentioned in the 'Ultimatum Letter' had already been agreed. There was no need to give Chiang the letter. "Joe, you have won this ball game,"[100] Hurley told Stilwell. In Chinese translation, Roosevelt's letter sounded even more aggressive and offensive in its demands.

With the prize of absolute command within his grasp and with the President's letter in his hand, Stilwell could not resist the temptation to humiliate his nemesis, Chiang Kai-shek, once and for all. Hurley, who went with Stilwell to meet Chiang over a cup of tea, pleaded with Stilwell not to deliver the letter: "No chief of state could tolerate such an insult as this letter . . ."[101] Stilwell's moment of glory and revenge was not to be stayed. A visibly shocked Chiang put down the letter and placed his teacup upside down before ushering Stilwell and Hurley out of the room. After the 'tea party,' Chiang broke down and sobbed. He would later describe the episode as "the most severe humiliation I have ever had in my life."[102] It was worse even, he claimed, than his capture by his own generals at Xian in 1936.

If Chiang was downcast, Stilwell was ecstatic. He revelled in Chiang's crushed visage and thought it was funny. Writing to his wife he boasted of his role as avenging angel, "Rejoice with me we have prevailed . . . his head is in the dust. The dope is that after I left, the screaming began and lasted into the night."[103] Furthermore, sheer glee laced his boast that he had "handed this bundle of paprika [the 'Ultimatum Letter'] to the Peanut . . . The harpoon hit the little bugger right in the solar plexus and went right through him."[104]

Hurley wisely decided to let passions settle before approaching Chiang. In fact Chiang soon regained his composure and called for Hurley to meet him alone. By the end of five hours of talking, Hurley realized that Chiang would not be budged at any price on the need to remove Stilwell. Chiang concluded with due fairness, "Stilwell is a professional, works hard, is resolute, and good at his own military doctrine, which is to attack . . . [but] he has no strategic thinking . . . [or] basic political skills . . . [and] is very arrogant."[105] In essence Stilwell's latest performance had expended Chiang's "last drop of confidence."[106] The following day Chiang formally wrote to Hurley to tell him that he would accept any US General as commander of his armies except Stilwell. As a further sweetener Chiang also offered to hand over all of the Chinese Army's logistical apparatus. It finally dawned on Stilwell that he was at extreme risk. His grand display of hubris had led him to massively overplay his hand. Too late Stilwell woke up to what he had done and he scrambled to recover his situation by proposing to suspend plans to work with Mao. It was too late. Hurley, who had previously tried to save Stilwell, wrote to Roosevelt and strongly urged him to have Stilwell recalled. In the letter Hurley explained, "Chiang reacts favorably to logical persuasion and leadership, [but] reacts violently against any form of coercion." Hurley also very accurately concluded that Stilwell "is incapable of understanding or co-operating . . . every act is a move toward complete subjugation of Chiang Kai-shek."[107]

Hurley's letter was a damning indictment of Stilwell's character. Chiang too wrote to Roosevelt telling him: "it seems to me that there can be no question as to my right to request the recall of an officer in whom I can no longer repose confidence."[108] Chiang also assured him, "with a qualified American officer, we can work together to reverse the present trend and achieve a vital contribution to the final victory."[109] Though Stilwell and others had undermined Roosevelt's confidence in Chiang, nonetheless he decided that it would be better not to take any action that could cause the collapse of Chiang's government. Above all Roosevelt was determined to avoid the necessity of an invasion of China to defeat the Japanese after the conquest of Japan's home islands.

Roosevelt decided to lance the boil. Stilwell would be recalled. Marshall, who later believed that he had made a mistake in not recalling Stilwell earlier, concurred. In spite of Marshall's support to this point, dissatisfaction with Stilwell in Washington had also been building. Generally Roosevelt's emissaries had been negative about both Stilwell and Chiang. Furthermore the Generalissimo's acolytes had briefed against Stilwell. T. V. Soong had lobbied assiduously against Stilwell who he described as ". . . completely unfit to be a major military leader."[110]

The US government, thanks to Hurley's patient negotiation, had wrung huge concessions out of Chiang in terms of its ability to control the Chinese Army and Stilwell was now expendable. For Roosevelt and Marshall, it was a deal worth taking. As Slim concluded, Stilwell ". . . overestimated his own indispensability to Chiang and the extent to which the American government would go in his support . . . ."[111] Stilwell was dismissed and replaced by General Albert Wedemeyer, then Chief of Staff at Kandy to South East Asia Command (SEAC) commander, Admiral Lord Mountbatten. Change brought the possibility of rationalizing the byzantine structures of Stilwell's command. With Stilwell gone, Roosevelt no longer insisted on complete control of Chiang's armies. Meanwhile Stilwell's command was bifurcated. While Wedemeyer took the Chief of Staff role in Chongqing, Lieutenant-General Daniel Sultan was appointed as ground commander of American-Chinese forces in Burma. It was a logical division that Stilwell himself should have implemented.

Unprofessional and curmudgeonly to the last, Stilwell departed immediately without waiting to brief his successor or even leaving him a briefing dossier. Stilwell's staff had no plans to hand over to Lieutenant-General Wedemeyer, who was told that Stilwell kept everything in his hip pocket. To his wife Stilwell wrote that he was delighted to be "hanging up my shovel and bidding farewell to as merry a nest of gangsters as you'll meet in a long day's march."[112] Few were unhappy to see him leave. As war correspondent Louis Allen noted, "The universal verdict on Stilwell is not kind . . . [X-Force troops excepting] the Chinese detested him, the British—with the possible exception of Slim—loathed him, his own men hated and feared him."[113]

Why the Kuomintang Armies were so Ineffective during the Pacific War: Chiang's *Kuomintang* regime was indeed far from pretty, but the criticisms against it nearly always lacked context. While it is difficult to argue with the facts of the corruption of Chiang and his court, the American press and indeed the American government failed to grasp the main issues; one such was the actual role of the Communists in fighting for China's survival. Mao not only had no real intention of working with the *Kuomintang,* but was actually working with the Japanese and increasing his own territory with the aim of subjugating China. Chiang's analysis was correct.

During the war the Chinese Communist Party (CCP) greatly increased its military resources, contributed little to the war effort and did everything in its power to sabotage Chiang's military capability. Mao's priority was always to conserve his resources and use the war with Japan as a means of achieving ascendancy over the *Kuomintang—* the very strategy for which Chiang Kai-shek was roundly accused by Stilwell and many others. Meanwhile Mao and Zhou Enlai played a masterful game with the western press, visiting intellectuals, the US State Department and ranking emissaries sent by Roosevelt and of course Stilwell. All these parties failed to see beyond the simple comparisons between Chiang's heavily bombed, corrupt, impoverished and chaotic makeshift capital of Chongqing, whose population increased tenfold during the war, and the seemingly disciplined calm of Mao's mountain hideout in Yanan. Above all, Mao convinced key constituencies in the West of the CCP's goodwill and worth as an ally.

Probably of even greater significance in the breakdown of relations between Chiang and Stilwell were their rarely noted differences in strategic priorities. Chiang's constant complaint was that Stilwell, who had complete control of the Lend-Lease resources, lacked a broad strategic vision, and placed the importance of the retaking of northern Burma above the importance of holding back the Japanese from Eastern China.

Like MacArthur and the Philippines, Stilwell appeared to place his personal interest in revenge for defeat in Burma in 1942 above larger strategic priorities. His championing of the building of the Ledo Road, an immensely wasteful use of resources, was another strategic blunder. On the positive side Stilwell was probably correct in his view that the overreliance on the B-29 bombing campaign against Japan from Southern China was a mistake; its absorption of the Humps' capacity by the need to fly aviation fuel over the Himalayas seriously obstructed America's ability to equip a poorly armed *Kuomintang* Army. However, it was a mark of Stilwell's ineffectual political touch that he failed to sway either Chiang or Washington against the over-reliance on air power which absorbed so much of the Hump's logistical capacity; it was an argument in which the Fourteenth Air Force's General Chennault, the ultimate Washington outsider, outmaneuvered Stilwell, in spite of the latter's close relationship with General Marshall. In hindsight Marshall too seems to have failed. When it became clear that the Hump was proving an effective supply route, the importance of the Ledo Road should have been downgraded. Furthermore US military strategy should have reduced the Hump's supply allocation for Chennault's over-extended air operations. Most importantly Stilwell should have been ordered to focus attention on the equipping and training of the *Kuomintang*'s armies on China's eastern front.

The thirty divisions of Stilwell's Y-Force on the northern Burmese border absorbed the vast majority of the 'non-oil' military resources that made it over the Hump. The issue of corruption and theft by the Soong family and others, of Lend-Lease resources, for which America's lack of controls was probably as much to blame as Chiang's inability to control his wife's family, has tended to obscure the fact that it was Stilwell who had ultimate control of these resources. In spite of the pleadings of Chiang and Chennault, Stilwell deliberately ignored the supply and logistical requirements of the sixty divisions that Chiang needed to combat against the more than one million troops that Japan had stationed in China.

Stilwell's poison warped the Roosevelt administration's perception of the real issues that were at stake in China. It led to the *canard* that, during *World War II*, Chiang was hoarding resources to fight the Communists while doing nothing to fight the Japanese. On 26 September 1943 Stilwell had opined to Marshall, "He [Chiang] believes the war in the *Pacific* is nearly over, and that by delaying tactics, he can throw the entire burden on us."[114] In fact the exact opposite was true. Certainly he was faced by the reality that he needed to keep a watching eye on the Communists, but Chiang nevertheless demonstrated a constant determination to defeat the Japanese in China throughout the *Pacific War*. The charge of being unwilling to fight against the Japanese does not sit squarely with the facts of Chiang's and his *Kuomintang* armies' remarkable resilience during more than a decade of conflict with Japan—a military resistance to Japan that no western power in the region had matched. Indeed Stilwell's successor, Lieutenant-General Wedemeyer, if critical of many aspects of *Kuomintang*'s military capability, nevertheless asserted that the *Kuomintang* forces had displayed "amazing tenacity and endurance in resisting Japan."[115] It is interesting to speculate on how the war would have progressed had China succumbed to Japanese force of arms at the start of the *Pacific War*. With the release of upwards of a million Japanese troops, the course of the conflict with Japan might have been wholly different. As it was, the anti-Chiang poison left by Stilwell and the US State Department was to have a profound effect on America's post-war relations with China, and indeed the development of the *Cold War* in Asia.

What Stilwell and the Roosevelt administration never came to appreciate was that the *Kuomintang* forces were profoundly incapacitated by their exertions in the first four years of the *Second Sino-Japanese War* and the six years of conflict before that. By 1941, Chiang Kai-shek's military effectiveness had been ground down by Japanese success on the battlefield, the expulsion from the political and economic heartland of Shanghai and Nanking, the blanket bombing of Chongqing, and the successful isolation of the *Kuomintang*-held areas from world markets. The economic crisis was such that men could not easily recruited let alone fed. Recruitment fell from a peak of 1.98 million men in 1939 to 1.67 million in 1941. In a war in which attrition rates, often from disease, amounted to up to 40 percent of an infantry unit per annum, continual recruitment was essential. Yet recruitment itself created a spiral of decline. The taking of healthy young men from the land reduced the ability of 'free China' to produce enough grain to feed its armies.

Ray Huang, the noted historian of the Ming Dynasty, who fought in the *Kuomintang* Army, recalled that, having completed his training with the 14th Division stationed in Yunnan Province on the border with Vietnam, he was sent with a team to Hunan to find 1,500 recruits: "The armed soldiers from the escort team accompanied the *baojia* elders to comb through villages to round up men. The conscription law had reached the bottom of the manpower barrel. The purchases of substitutes became increasingly abused and human cargo degenerated in quality."[116] Because of disease and desertion, only 500 of the men from Hunan reached the 14th Division in the summer of 1941. No wonder that Chiang had difficulty in flying over decent recruits to X-Force in India at this time. Like most Americans who viewed China as brim-full of manpower, Stilwell, in his published papers, complained, without ever seeming to reflect on the problems facing Chiang. On arrival at the 14th Division, Ray Huang was shocked to find that

> All battalions and companies were down to half strength. Obviously the division had at one time been lavishly equipped. There were German-style helmets, gas masks, and canvas tenting sheets. But they appeared in a way that you would find in a flea market: one piece here and another there . . . Two or three shared one blanket. They had no toothbrushes and used bamboo sticks for toilet paper. They washed their faces with a common towel, so that if one man's eye became inflamed, the whole platoon caught the infection.[117]

If the condition of Chiang's troops was bad in 1941, by 1945 it had deteriorated further. As a result of inflation, an infantryman's pay of fifty *yuan* per month could purchase a couple of pounds of cabbage. Recruitment collapsed by half from its peak in the last year of the war. X-Force may have been well provisioned and equipped, and Y-Force reasonably so, but for the rest of Chiang's army, men, provisions and equipment were in desperately short supply by 1944. *Kuomintang* arsenals were only operating at 55 percent of capacity. During Operation ICHI-GO, coal production fell by 17 percent and pig iron production by 23 percent. Industry could produce just 510 machine guns and 15,300 rifles in 1944. As for bullets, only 12.8 million were produced—less than five per soldier.

Even with the help of Lend-Lease, the *Kuomintang* forces had little offensive capacity because its armies had by now been forced to live off the land. In 1944 the logistics for mobile offensive operation just did not exist. Against this background of lack of food and a lack of recruits, it was not surprising that Chiang saw the 14th Air Force as almost the only means of exerting attacking pressure on the Japanese forces in China. It is noticeable that when the 'short Hump' directly over Burma from Calcutta, under Major-General Tunner's direction, began to deliver a vastly increased tonnage of supplies to the *Kuomintang* forces from the end of 1944, the offensive capability of Chiang's armies responded accordingly.

In the spring of 1945, a 70,000 Chinese force destroyed a Japanese army in west Hunan Province inflicting 11,000 casualties. The field commander General Ho Ying-Chin was so upbeat that he noted: "The Chinese commanders at the front all wanted to undertake an offensive drive eastward to sever enemy lines of communication."[118] Seven days before the dropping of the atom bomb on Hiroshima, Wedemeyer wrote enthusiastically to General Marshall in Washington, "we now look forward confidently toward a successful advance to the coast."[119] So much for the *Kuomintang*'s supposed lack of desire for offensive action. When well provisioned with food and munitions, Chiang's forces were clearly not only capable, but also very willing to conduct offensive action.

Stilwell should have understood the economic, manpower, provisioning and equipment problems faced by Chiang Kai-shek and should have briefed Washington accordingly. Either he simply did not have the broad intellect and understanding to present Chiang's genuine economic difficulties in China, or he was simply obscuring the situation to try put more power into his own hands. Both explanations ring true. Others too were irresponsible and incompetent in their reporting including the various missions sent by Roosevelt, ambassadors as well as the supposed experts of the State Department. Roosevelt would remain in the dark about why the *Kuomintang* would not fight. It could not. As Hans Van De Ven concludes in *War and Nationalism in China 1925–1945* [2003], the background of economic collapse in 1941, "explains Nationalist strategy better than easy assumptions about a patriotic deficit, an obsession with Communism, or a backward cultural preference for the defence."[120]

Chiang was all too aware of the desperate straits of 'free China' and perhaps he too should take some of the blame for not sharing his country's predicament more effectively with Washington. On 11 April 1943 Chiang wrote in his diary:

The poverty of government employees has reached an unbelievable point. Unable to raise families, many let their wives have abortions . . . What misery! I cannot bear it! Heavens! If the Japanese bandits are not defeated soon, or the war should drag on for another year or two, then China cannot make it, and I must fail in the mission that God commands me to perform.[121]

Stilwell's Bitter Legacy: In the aftermath of Stilwell's fall, attitudes towards 'Vinegar Joe' were as divided as his relationship with Chiang. To Roosevelt, Mountbatten wrote a cringingly camp message, saying, "I was sorry to see Stilwell go not only because I personally liked him, but because it meant that I lost my beloved Al Wedemeyer."[122] However, Stilwell had not made himself popular at Mountbatten's South East Asia Command (SEAC) HQ at Kandy; a film entitled *Background Tokyo* had concentrated exclusively on Stilwell's campaign in Burma as if the British (and Mountbatten) were not involved. A less sensitive Lieutenant-General Slim noted in his autobiography, "In the 14th Army and, I think, throughout the British forces our sympathies were with Stilwell—unlike the American 14th Air Force who demonstratively rejoiced at his downfall . . . We saw him go with regret, and he took with him our admiration of him as a fighting soldier."[123]

Apart from Chennault and US Fourteenth Air Force's distaste for Stilwell, Merrill's Marauders, to whom Stilwell never gave due credit at the *Battle of Myitkyina* in northern Burma, were undoubtedly happy at his dismissal: the pro-Mao elements within the State Department less so. After Stilwell, Wedemeyer proved to be a solid anti-Communist. As ever, General 'Bill' Slim's judgment was balanced. He concluded that Stilwell was ". . . an excellent tactician but a poor administrator. At higher levels he had neither the temperament nor the strategic background or judgment to be effective."[124] As he proved at the *Battle of Myitkyina,* Stilwell was an outstanding corps commander and a great fighter, but he was not a manager of logistics or politics. It was a classic case of a man who had been promoted above the level of his competence.

Chiang, showing himself to be a much greater man than the mean-spirited Stilwell, offered to award him China's highest honor, the Grand Cordon of the Blue Sky and the White Sun: "Told him to stick it up his arse" was Stilwell's predictable response.[125] Nevertheless, in spite of Stilwell's usual vinegary lack of manners, Chiang still insisted on renaming the Ledo Road as the 'Stilwell Road' when it was completed, though to the engineers who built it, the Ledo Road would always be known as 'Pick's Pike.' Ironically, the fact that the Stilwell Road turned out to be the most monumental of all 'white elephants' perhaps reflected the broader strategic fiasco created by 'Vinegar Joe.'

It was Stilwell who was to have the last say in this bitterest of personal conflicts. He gave a blistering account of the whole episode of his relationship with Chiang to two

Mao sympathizers, Brooks Atkinson of the *New York Times,* who was better known as a theater and fashion critic, and Harold Isaacs of *Newsweek.* Without seeking out Hurley or a *Kuomintang* view of 'Vinegar Joe's account, Atkinson, who clearly should have stuck to Broadway reviews, asserted that Stilwell "was more intimately acquainted with the needs and capacities of the Chinese Army than the Generalissimo."[126] The article was an unalloyed paean of praise for Stilwell whose removal from command Atkinson described as representing "the political triumph of a moribund, corrupt regime that is more concerned with maintaining its political supremacy than driving the Japanese out of China."[127]

The conduct of the war in China destroyed lives, careers and indeed nations. Stilwell's career never recovered. Although he was appointed to the command of the US Tenth Army in the last days of the *Battle of Okinawa*, in November 1945 he was put out to grass as head of the War Department Equipment Board. The following year he died after surgery for liver cancer. The Mao-friendly State Department employees, John Service and John Paton Davies, were purged. J. Edgar Hoover, the legendary head of the FBI, had Service arrested and wanted to try him as a spy. Although Service was cleared of all charges, his career remained under a cloud until his resignation in 1962. John Paton Davies was also forced out of the State Department during the McCarthyite communist witch-hunt. Colonel Barrett had a falling out with Roosevelt emissary John Hurley and was denied his promotion to Brigadier-General. He retired from the Army to teach Chinese language and Shakespeare at the University of Colorado.

As for Chiang Kai-shek, he suffered the withdrawal of support from the US administration, partly as a result of which, he lost his country to Mao Zedong and the Communists. Chiang was forced into bitter exile in *Formosa.* The Chinese people would suffer the degradations of Maoist totalitarianism in which tens of millions of people would perish during the forced collectivization of the Great Leap Forward and the purges of the Cultural Revolution. Most damagingly America was drawn into a 45-year war to rid Asia of Soviet expansion and influence. Both the *Korean War* and the *Vietnam War* were in part legacies of US failures in China during the *Pacific War*.

For America and her Allies, the short-term effects of the diplomatic and military setbacks in China were of little consequence; Stilwell's failure in China did not delay America's closing of its account with Japan. By the beginning of October 1944 it had become clear to Stilwell that Washington's interest in China had all but evaporated. Merrill, who had been at the Second Quebec Conference (codenamed OCTAGON) which ended in mid-September 1944, made it clear to Stilwell on his return to Chongqing that the reported statements by Admiral Nimitz on the need for bases in Southern China, were mere window dressing to confuse Japanese intelligence. Brigadier-General Thomas Handy, a shadowy figure at the Operations Division in Washington, whom General Eisenhower had appointed as Chief of the Strategy and Policy Group, had admitted that all along the Stilwell mission "was primarily political and that not much in the way of real action by the Chinese was hoped for."[128] It must have been bitter news for Stilwell. On 4 October 1944, Stillwell noted in his diary that he had received intelligence from Washington, ". . . this theater is written off and nothing expected from us. No troops will be sent."[129]

Ultimately the China-Burma-India Theater became a sideshow in the strategic thrust of the war effort against Japan; its main success had long since been won by Chiang in holding down Japan's 1.5 million troops at the critical early junctures of the war. Moreover, if not as exhausted as Chiang's 'free China', the Japanese economy, was already running at full stretch as a result of the *Second Sino-Japanese War* by the time that it embarked on the *Pacific War*. This in itself was by no means insignificant in America's ultimate victory. The military collapse of the *Kuomintang* in China in the face of Operation ICHI-GO in 1944 did not doom the American war effort or its timetable. That was entirely because of the success of Admiral King's brilliantly conceived and executed 'island-hopping' strategy in the *Pacific*; a strategic and tactical concept for closing out the war far superior to that conceived by Stilwell. Ironically though, America's political and military mistakes in China during the *Pacific War*, meant that, within four years of its end, 'free China', the entity for which the United States had pushed Japan to war, was lost for a generation to the ravages of ultra-leftist Maoism.

29 Jump to Hollandia: MacArthur's Greatest Victory

[March 1944–October 1944]

[Maps: 29.1, 29.2, 29.3, 29.4, 29.5, 29.6]

While Chinese forces were engaged in their long drawn-out war of attrition with Japan on the Asian mainland, the main Allied strategic thrust continued through the *Pacific* and in New Guinea. In the opening months of 1944, while General Shunroku Hata was planning the ICHI-GO Campaign in central China, MacArthur and his staff were planning to roll up Japanese forces garrisoned along the northern coast of New Guinea.

Intelligence, Deception and the Jump to Hollandia (Jayapura): [Map: 29.1] With control of the air and sea virtually complete, MacArthur could afford to bypass the remaining Japanese strongholds on the northwest coast of New Guinea. It was a move supported by extraordinarily detailed intelligence about Lieutenant-General Hatazo Adachi's Eighteenth Army troop dispositions. As a result of obtaining the codes captured at Sio, MacArthur informed Marshall, ". . . the enemy has concentrated the mass of his ground forces in the Madang-Wewak area, leaving relatively weak forces in the Hollandia area. He is attempting to concentrate land-based air forces in the area of western New Guinea and is developing additional fields in order to concentrate this area into a bulwark of air defense."[1] Formerly Army Codes had been impenetrable. Now MacArthur knew that the bulk of Adachi's Eighteenth Army was waiting for him at *Hansa Bay* while Hollandia was lightly defended. The jump to Hollandia was a self-evident strategy.

In hindsight it is clear that Japan was already defeated on New Guinea. Although there remained 350,000 Japanese troops in the *Southwest Pacific* region, because of American dominance of land and air, it was almost impossible to move them or indeed supply them. US air power had forced the Japanese Combined Fleet to flee to the Philippines and ports even further to the west. As a result Japan's expensively constructed submarine fleet became virtually the only means of transport to Lieutenant-General Hatazo Adachi's land-locked forces. The knock-on effect of the use of submarines as little more than cargo vessels severely reduced their effectiveness in interdicting the American naval advance across the *Pacific* as well as fatally undermining the morale of Japanese submariners.

For MacArthur a new strategic direction now offered itself. From 1942 until the beginning of 1944 MacArthur had been a firm advocate of taking enemy strongholds, such as Rabaul, head on. In spite of the example of the *Battle of Buna-Gona-Sananander*,

MacArthur had argued vigorously for a direct attack on Rabaul. He declared that the decision by the Joint Chiefs to bypass Rabaul would "go down in history as one of the times' greatest military mistakes."[2] In hindsight few have agreed with him. As Naval officer and historian Samuel Eliot Morrison concluded, with more than 100,000 soldiers embedded in Rabaul's formidable garrison, "Tarawa, Iwo Jima and Okinawa would have faded to pale pink in comparison with the blood which would have flowed if the Allies had attempted an assault on fortress Rabaul."[3]

Even MacArthur came round to the new orthodoxy. Now he wanted to hit the empty spaces. In his *Reminiscences* [1964] published shortly before his death, MacArthur boasted: "It was the practical application of this system of warfare . . . to bypass Japanese strongpoints and neutralize them by cutting their lines of supply . . . to . . . hit 'em where they ain't'—that from this time forward guided my movements and operations."[4] Conveniently forgetting his previous insistence that the Japanese garrison at Rabaul be assaulted rather than isolated, he declared: "New conditions and new weapons require new and imaginative methods for solution and application. Wars are never won in the past."[5] Pacing the veranda of the governor's mansion at Port Moresby he boomed at his air force commander, Lieutenant-General George Kenney, "Starve Rabaul! The jungle! Starvation! They're my allies."[6] Indeed, when the Allies' 'isolation' policies were implemented, troops located at Japanese garrisons were quickly reduced to squalor, disease and starvation. Implicit in MacArthur's narrative is that he was the progenitor of this strategic innovation. He was not.

Tellingly the 'wither on the vine' strategy eventually adopted by MacArthur was the one most disliked by the Japanese. As one Japanese intelligence officer noted in a post-war interrogation:

> [Isolation] was the type of strategy we hated most. The Americans, with a minimum of losses, attacked and seized a relatively weak area, constructed airfields and proceeded to cut the supply lines to the troops in that area. Without engaging in a large-scale operation, our strongpoints were gradually starved out . . . The Americans flowed into our weaker points and submerged us, just as water seeks the weakest entry to sink a ship.[7]

For Adachi, a skilled general, his problems in defending 1,000 miles of coast were further exacerbated by his inability to supply and reinforce by sea after the debacle of the *Battle of the Bismarck Sea*. Although Imperial General HQ sent 50,000 troops of the Second Army under Lieutenant-General Fusataro Teshima to the easternmost garrisons at *Wakde Island*, Sarmi and *Biak*, the Japanese loss of air and naval control meant that the Second and Eighteenth Army could not act in mutual support. Having lost control of the air, once troops were committed to an area, moving them was almost impossible. Attempts to move troops by land simply exposed them to disease, exhaustion and starvation because of the impossibility of setting up and maintaining logistical support.

MacArthur's westward advance along New Guinea's northern coast had been approved at the Quebec Conference (codenamed QUADRANT) between Roosevelt and Churchill in August 1943. This was not the original plan. The initial plans brought by the Combined Chiefs of Staff (CCS) planners to Quebec had suggested a twin advance through China and the *Central Pacific* to capture the Philippines, *Formosa* and the *Ryuku Islands* (*Okinawa*) in 1945 and 1946. Final operations against Japan were mooted to begin in 1945 and end in 1948. The Allied leaders and their commanders had been appalled at the proposed timescale and sent the plan back to the drawing board. Japan had to be defeated within a year of the planned defeat of Germany.

A revised plan suggested the two-pronged attack with Nimitz through the *Central Pacific* and with MacArthur along the New Guinea coast and the Philippines. Whether MacArthur's advance along the north coast of New Guinea was needed was a moot point. MacArthur's eventual goal, *Luzon*, the main northern island of the Philippines, was too far away as a launch pad for the invasion of Japan. "The idea of rolling up the Japanese along the New Guinea coast, throughout *Halmahera* [in Indonesia] and Mindanao and up through the Philippines to *Luzon*, as our major strategic concept, to the exclusion of clearing our Central Pacific line of communications to the Philippines, is to me absurd,"[8] King wrote to Nimitz. The British also inquired whether MacArthur's advance was necessary and whether resources would be better allocated to Operation OVERLORD (the cross-Channel invasion of France). They suggested that operations in New Guinea could be curtailed in favor of Nimitz's thrust through the *Central Pacific*. The British inquiry, which stepped into the sticky territory of US Army and Navy politics, was quickly brushed aside. American Joint Chiefs of Staff remained adamant that both campaigns should continue. The question of rationality of the two-pronged *Pacific* attack was swept under the carpet and no priority was allocated to either campaign. *De facto* the Combined Chiefs allowed a two horse race between the Army and Navy with MacArthur and Nimitz their chosen jockeys. In mid-1943 Stilwell's China route was still in the running and although it was somewhat favored by Roosevelt, it was a clear outsider with his military chiefs. "The Joint Chiefs' directive was, in effect, a reconciliation among conflicting strategic and tactical concepts."[9]

Rather than choosing a winner between the strategies, with all the 'blood on the floor' that such a political battle as this would entail, the American Joint Chiefs of Staff simply decided that they could afford to do them all. However logical the British suggestion, as they were not doing the fighting, the outcome of this decision was never in doubt; Churchill acquiesced. From his point of view there were bigger political battles to be fought, in particular the timing of the invasion of *Nazi*-controlled Europe. While the *Central Pacific* thrust was certainly the most productive route from a strategic viewpoint, in hindsight it can be seen that a competitive twin-pronged strategy helped to keep the Japanese off balance and stretched their resources. While the twin-pronged advance in the *Pacific* may have been viewed as politically expedient, in hindsight the push-pull twin strategy worked. Needless to add, the twin strategy introduced an element of competition and hence speed that was not unwelcome to either the Joint Chiefs of

Staff or their political masters. MacArthur for one was forced to reappraise his tactics and pursue the 'hit-em-where-they-ain't' methods, previously ignored, that significantly speeded up his advance. Details of tactics and resources would be decided as the advances progressed, with the Quebec Conference broadly expressing the view: "the earlier acquisition of strategic bases closer to the Japanese homeland . . . are more likely to precipitate a decisive engagement with the Japanese fleet."[10]

In spite of the US insistence on the twin-pronged approach, there was no doubting that the *Central Pacific* route had emerged as favorite among the US joint Chiefs of Staff. Nimitz's advance toward the *Marianas* was more likely to draw out the Japanese fleet than an advance along New Guinea's northern coast. In large part, invading the *Marianas* reflected the importance of the US being able to bomb Japan. At the next leaders' conference at Cairo in November 1943 (codenamed SEXTANT), the British and American Chiefs affirmed that where timing issues brought conflicts between the two prongs, the *Central Pacific* would take preference. The Joint Chiefs confirmed that the *Central Pacific* route to Tokyo was "strategically, logistically, and tactically better than the Southwest Pacific Route."[11] Nonetheless after his recklessly high-risk success at *Los Negros* on the *Admiralty Islands* the Joint Chiefs were not prepared to hold MacArthur back from his next project, the leap westward along the north coast of New Guinea. Preparations were now set in train. Intelligence reports and maps were prepared, reconnaissance missions carried out, false information given out to deceive the enemy, stores were prepared and the amphibious fleet assembled.

Hollandia was to be MacArthur's chosen first target. A coastal city 500 miles distant from Sio on the eastern end of New Guinea's northern coastline, it was not the next American objective expected by Lieutenant-General Adachi after the wrapping up of the Huon Peninsula Campaign. The major garrison ports of Madang and Wewak, west from the Huon Peninsula, were the more likely targets though Adachi himself expected it to be *Hansa Bay*, opposite *Manam Island*, that neatly bisected his two major garrisons. However, Hollandia, further to the west, with its numerous airfields and its deep-water bay that would be capable of holding fifty Liberty Ships was seen by MacArthur as the prize that would speed up his gallop toward the Philippines—providing him with an important logistical base for that future campaign. Adachi meanwhile viewed Hollandia as Japan's most important redoubt of last resort: "Hollandia is at the final base and last strategic point of this Army's New Guinea operations," he wrote, "Therefore, it is expected that if we are unable to occupy [Port] Moresby, the Army will withdraw to Hollandia and defend this area to the last man."[12] **[Chart: B.1]**

Before the Hollandia Campaign, Captain G. Harris, a specialist in deep reconnaissance, who had spent a year spying in *New Britain*, was sent by submarine with six Australians, four New Guinea soldiers and an Indonesian interpreter, to reconnoiter the area. However, natives informed on them; Japanese troops caught up with them and engaged in a prolonged firefight. Harris was wounded and stayed behind with two others to give his patrol a chance to escape to the south. The Indonesian who escaped recalled watching Captain Harris's final moments from a safe distance: "The three kept up the action for four hours, until Bunning and Short lay dead and Harris, alone, wounded in three places, faced the enemy with an empty pistol. Then they rushed him."[13] Harris was questioned and when he failed to respond he was bayoneted to death. After weeks in the jungle several of Harris's patrol survived.

General Kenney Makes Good on His Promises of Air Domination: Although Japan's commanders had remained determined to hold their defensive perimeter in western New Guinea after the isolation of Rabaul, they continued to be hampered by basic infrastructure and logistics weaknesses. To defend against the American western thrust along New Guinea's north coast, Japan needed to control the air, which they realized was the key to countering MacArthur's strategy. As well as planning to increase aircraft production to 40,000 planes in 1944, the Japanese air forces aimed to increase the number of airfields from 27 to 120 with 35 new ones planned for completion by April 1944. Only nine were completed on schedule. The lack of airfields enabled Lieutenant-General George Kenney, commander of MacArthur's Allied Air Forces in the *Southwest Pacific*, to plan mass attacks that could overwhelm targeted fields packed with planes with nowhere else to hide. In large part the Japanese construction failure was down to a lack of modern equipment such as bulldozers, rollers and trucks, as well as the use of poorly motivated local labor. Koreans and Formosans, brought from overseas, and provided with even worse provisions and living conditions than Japanese troops were little better. The vast majority of these 'slave laborers' sent to the *South Pacific* were worked to death in dire conditions. **[See Appendix D: The Japanese Empire: From Co-Prosperity to Tyranny]**

Concerningly for MacArthur and his plans, intelligence suggested that Hollandia was teeming with life, particularly around its airfields. The Allies' ULTRA intercepts indicated that the Japanese had held back aircraft at Hollandia believing their airfields there to be out of the reach of American bombers and escort fighters. Such was the resulting concern about the Japanese ability to batter any approaching amphibious force, that MacArthur was forced to call upon Nimitz's carriers for help. That was not a plan that pleased Kenney. Professional jealousy aside, Kenney was concerned that aircraft carriers would only be able to stay on station for a few weeks. What then? "Carrier based aircraft," he declared, "do not have staying power and therefore do not have the dependability of land-based aircraft."[14] At 500 miles distance, Hollandia was thought to be too far away for a land-based air attack. Or was it? On 5 April at a conference in Brisbane, the naturally self-assured George Kenney boasted that he would wipe out all Japanese air opposition before Nimitz's carriers got within distance of the New Guinea coast. MacArthur, always happy to stick one in the Navy's eye, was delighted.

Kenney ordered Major-General Ennis Whitehead, Deputy Commander of the Fifth Air Force "to take out the air from Wewak to Hollandia and keep it beaten down so that aircraft from the carriers escorting the expedition can handle any Japanese attempt to bust up the convoy."[15] On 30 March, Whitehead launched his first air attack on Hollandia's airfields. The Japanese had brought in over 100 new aircraft to add to the

250 aircraft based there, though, as usual, only half or fewer were operational. Later, one former Japanese supply officer at the base admitted that he thought that only 25 percent of their aircraft were airworthy. However, in a recurrence of past problems, the Japanese were not able to clear enough ground around the airfield to disperse their aircraft sufficiently. Against them the Allies had the Fifth Air Force's 803 fighters and 780 bombers operating at a 75 percent utilization rate, and a further 150 aircraft from the Royal Australian Air Force (RAAF). The Japanese were unaware that in February Kenney had received fifty-eight new P-38 Lockheed Lightnings fitted with 300-gallon auxiliary fuel tanks to enable them to escort bombers to their long-range targets. With a 570-mile combat range they could fly to Hollandia and back.

At 10.35 a.m. on 30 March 1944, the P-38s brought seventy-five B-24 Liberator bombers to Hollandia's airfields where 350 Japanese aircraft lay crowded and unprotected by revetments. The Americans dropped 5,900 20-pound and 100-pound fragmentation bombs from 10,000 to 12,000 foot. Allied Air Force Intelligence summarized the mission:

> [it was a] 140-ton attack during the day on Cyclops and Hollandia aerodromes, with photographs showing twenty-five airplanes destroyed and sixty-seven others damaged on the ground. Fuel dumps were hit, and one great column of smoke rose to 10,000 foot and was visible 150 miles away . . . Anti-aircraft was slight, medium, and heavy—inaccurate.[16]

A reported 124 pilots and ground crew were killed with a further 60 wounded. In post-war interrogation, Colonel Kaneko would note, "the use of many small bombs was effective in this sort of operation."[17]

Where fighters were able to take off there were strong indications of a degradation of both technical competence and command capability. American pilots reported that Japanese tactics "seemed to be almost totally lacking in any organized manner. Except in very few cases they seemed to be unwilling to mix with our fighters . . . The enemy fighters contacted were in disorganized bunches, or in pairs, and occasionally alone . . . they seemed to mill around with no apparent purpose."[18] It was apparent that the supply of Japanese pilots to the southern front was not only limited but poor in quality and training.

The next day, 31 March, saw a follow-up attack by sixty-seven B-24s. Although Japanese spotters gave seventy minutes' notice of the American attack, their airfields were still a scene of chaos from the attacks of the previous day. Corporal Fukuda, a 23-year-old air gunner dispassionately recorded that the bombing

> destroyed everything except the campsites in the jungle.
> All our forty serviceable planes and another twenty under
> repair were smashed. I had a high regard for the B-24s
> [Liberators], but I was terrified of B-25s [North American

> Mitchell medium bomber: Kenney's gunship], and regarded highly the P-38 [Lockheed Lightning], which was better than any Japanese fighter.[19]

The airfields were so badly cratered that many returning Japanese fighter pilots had to fly to bases as far distant as *Wakde Island*. For US bomber pilots and their crews it had been an almost entirely perfect mission. One observer noted, "Bombing gorgeous, entire target uncovered" while another commented that Japanese "pilots seemed to be having a great amount of difficulty with the P-38s."[20] Intelligence photos showed that 219 Japanese airplanes had been destroyed over the two days. US losses amounted to just a single P-38 fighter. Heavy American bombing attacks continued for the next three days. In the course of the Hollandia air campaign bombing proficiency reached new levels; the 90th 'Jolly Rogers' Bombardment Group flew 730 sorties with 90 percent reaching their target, while losing just three aircraft and their thirty-three crewmen. Within a few days Hollandia's air defenses had been wiped out, giving MacArthur virtually clear skies for Operation RECKLESS's amphibious landings. Although Japan continued to feed aircraft into New Guinea, Japan's air power in northwest New Guinea never recovered.

When American troops reached Hollandia's airfields, Kenney wrote later that they found "a graveyard of aircraft, anti-aircraft defenses, wrecked and sunken vessels and barges, and smouldering piles of what had once been fuel, aviation stores and food supplies."[21] The bombastic Kenney had made good on his promises to destroy the Japanese Navy Air Force in western New Guinea without the Navy's help. Victory in the air created the preconditions for victory on land.

Landings at Hollandia: Operation RECKLESS, arguably MacArthur's most successful military campaign, which took him 650 miles along the New Guinea coast, began on 22 April when US forces, comprising in total 79,800 troops and personnel carried by an amphibious force made up of 217 ships landed at Hollandia and Aitape. Aitape was targeted as a landing site with the objective of taking the nearby Tadji Airfield that would bypass and supersede the need to take the Japanese garrison and airfields at Wewak. As MacArthur later wrote, "I now planned a maneuver which at one stroke would move us almost 500 miles forward and at the same time render some 40,000 troops ineffective."[22]

The Japanese were dumbfounded. The surprise was complete. Until the day of the landing they had expected the invasion to occur at *Hansa Bay*. "The Allied invasion of Hollandia and Aitape was a complete surprise to us . . ."[23] Major-General Jo Iiumura, a senior Japanese commander, reported to his interrogators after the war. Even the Allied troops believed that Wewak would be the next target; Larry Sims of the United States 96th Service squadron noted:

> We were based at Finschhafen and rumor had it that the next assault was going to be on Wewak . . . the navy

had been shelling Wewak for several weeks ... The
Japanese ... would find empty life jackets and inflatable
rafts washed up on the beach ... It looked so much like
an assault on Wewak was about to take place that General
Adachi, the Japanese commander, moved his troops by
forced march from Hollandia south to Wewak to help in
the defense. It turned out this whole thing was a big
deception and it was successful beyond anything
expected.[24]

MacArthur's flanking movement at Hollandia prevented the Japanese Eighteenth
Army based at Wewak from moving westwards except through the jungle. An aide to
MacArthur noted, "the Japanese whom we had passed at Wewak had to work their very
slow and murderous way through our great ally, the jungle, to attack us many weeks
later—sick and demoralized through dysentery, starvation, and malaria."[25] Having
failed to break through they would then be trapped. As Major-General Jo Iimura
complained, ". . . we were neither able to reinforce nor send war supplies to their
defending units."[26] Attempts to march between garrisons were fraught with danger, not
only from disease but also from Allied strafing attacks. On the march from Madang to
Wewak, Lieutenant-General Shigeru Katagiri who had led the Japanese forces at the
Battles of Finschhafen and *Sattelberg* was killed.

After the Aitape landing on 22 April the 1,000 Japanese troops in the area were
quickly overwhelmed. On the same day landings were also completed at Hollandia in an
operation commanded by Lieutenant-General Eichelberger and I-American Corps
including the 41st and 24th Divisions. The trickiness of the New Guinea coast was
demonstrated by their landing on a Hollandia beach that was made impassable on all
sides by deep swamps; one soldier recalled ". . . if you held your head back and your
rifle high over head you should be able to make it we were assured. A number didn't,
stepping into holes . . . For me, I was miserable with that swamp water streaming down
my front and into my boots; I wondered what kind of animals might be in the
swamp. . . ."[27] Fortunately for Lieutenant-Generals Krueger and Eichelberger, Japanese
resistance was so light that many of the troop landings could move to an alternate beach.
Four hours after the initial assault MacArthur was able to go ashore to make an
inspection. After declaring it one of the best operations he had ever seen MacArthur told
Eichelberger that if a new army was created in the *Southwest Pacific*, he would be
appointed its commander.

Within four days Hollandia's airfields had been taken. A total of 4,478 Japanese
troops were killed in the action. An astonishingly high number of Japanese troops, 611
in total, surrendered; it proved to be an exception in a New Guinea campaign in which
the Japanese troop fought to the death. Hollandia also yielded a rare reward in the form
of rich supply dumps numbering 600 in total. General Eichelberger recalled: "There
were pyramids of canned goods and tarpaulin-covered hills of rice which looked like

Ohio haystacks. There was *sake* and beer. There were tons and tons of quinine and other medical supplies . . . Hollandia was the richest prize—supply wise—taken during the Pacific War."[28]

While US forces were landing at Aitape, 120 miles to the east, at the same time, an amphibious fleet emerged through the mists of Hollandia's enormous natural harbor. The 11,000 Japanese troops, few of them frontline infantry, fled to form *ad hoc* defensive positions in the hills. The 41st Division came ashore while another landing by the 21st Division at Tanahmerah Beach some twenty-two miles to the west completed the 'triple landings' of 22 April. MacArthur triumphantly announced in his *communiqué*: "The operation throws a loop of envelopment around the [Japanese] Eighteenth Army dispersed along the coast of New Guinea."[29]

As for the Japanese troops who fled into the hills, their travails were just beginning. On 29 April, Toshikazi Kudo from the 77th *Sentai*, recorded in his diary: "Even the CO is eating coconut now"; on 3 May he reported, "Only six of us left," and four days later he noted that he had, "Slept in native huts; as we stole from them they got angry."[30] Many troops simply roamed aimlessly looking for food. Kiichi Ishii of the 68th Anti-aircraft Battalion recorded, "It rains three times a day and makes me mad. Caught some red frogs and ate them."[31] Officers suffered the same privations as their men; entries from the diary of Lieutenant-Colonel Okada, commanding officer of 49th Anchorage Unit, recorded that on "23 April. I am in command of reserves in the hills to the west. 13 May. Eating leaves and grass. 17 May. 1,000 men decreased to 700. 2 June. There is no food. 5 June. No food. My body is weak."[32]

Having taken command at Hollandia shortly before the American attack, Major-General Mazazumi Inada now had to organize a retreat eastwards toward Sarmi. Beginning in May, nine groups left at intervals provided with a week's rations at best. There were no maps. The 19th Infantry harassed the rear-guard group and by early June they had killed 405 Japanese soldiers and captured 64. Thousands died on the trails to Sarmi. Of the 7,220 troops estimated to have left Hollandia only about 500 (7 percent) survived the journey. Hollandia was rapidly converted into an immense logistical center. Eichelberger recorded in his memoirs:

> Road construction had proceeded simultaneously [with building runways], and this was a gigantic task. Sides of mountains were carved away, bridges and culverts were thrown across rivers and creeks, gravel and stone "fill" was poured into sago swamps to make highways as tall as Mississippi levees . . . Hollandia became one of the great bases of the war. In the deep water of Humboldt Bay a complete fleet could lie at anchor. Tremendous docks were constructed, and 135 miles of pipeline were led over the hills to feed gasoline to the airfields. Where once I had seen only native villages and an expanse of primeval forest, a city of 140,000 men took occupancy.[33]

The *Battle of Hollandia* represented a great victory for MacArthur and it was undoubtedly the finest of his career until the *Battle of Inchon* in the Korean War. It was audaciously conceived and brilliantly executed, a coastal flanking maneuver that left more than half of Adachi's army stranded and useless. Nevertheless Lieutenant-Colonel Willoughby was sycophantically wide of the mark when, years later, he wrote that Hollandia was on a par with Hannibal's victory against the Romans at the *Battle of Cannae*. At Hollandia, MacArthur's forces outnumbered the Japanese by over two to one in numbers and effectively more when it is understood that many of the Japanese troops were non-combat personnel. Additionally he possessed overwhelming superiority in the air and at sea. While it was a brilliant tactical victory, a textbook example of an amphibious flanking movement, it was a battle that was relatively easily won.

The Battle of Biak Island: [Map: 29.2] [Map: 29.3] At the end of May 1944, the US advance along the coast moved on to *Biak Island*. Shunning beach defense, Colonel Kuzume Naoyuki, commanding 11,400 troops, allowed the US forces to proceed ashore before opening fire from their well-prepared entrenchments. The 41st Division commanded by Major-General Horace Fuller landed on 27 May and by the evening had put some 12,000 troops ashore supported by Sherman tanks, artillery and 2,400 tons of supplies.

However, the ease of the landing turned out to be misleading. Having ignored the reports from ULTRA intercepts that *Biak* was heavily garrisoned, MacArthur believed Willoughby's intelligence sources that suggested that there were between 5,000–7,000 defenders, about half of the actual number. The US forces were completely taken by surprise by the scale and ferocity of the Japanese resistance that started with a tank-led counter-attack on the day after their landing. Colonel Naoyuki Kuzume had sprung a nasty surprise. Remarkably the following day saw the first 'tank-on-tank' battle of the *South Pacific* Campaign. Five Sherman M4s destroyed seven lighter Japanese tanks. Japan's Type-95 Ha-Go light tank and the Type-97 Chi-Ha medium tank, fitted with a 47 mm cannon, were easily outclassed by the Sherman M4's larger caliber 75 mm gun. Although the army rushed through a new tank to compete with the Sherman, only 166 Type-3 Chi-Ni medium tanks had been built by the end of the war. Even before the 'mini' tank battle, in a reminder of past habits, MacArthur had already issued a premature *communiqué* that claimed the "end of the New Guinea campaign."[34] All that was left to do according to MacArthur on 3 June was "mopping up."[35] With Nimitz's forces preparing to deploy for the invasion of *Saipan*, MacArthur no doubt felt the heat of competition.

For a while the Americans were incapable of progress beyond their beachhead. In stark contrast to his public pronouncements, MacArthur complained to his staff, "The situation at *Biak* is unsatisfactory"[36] but unable to acknowledge his mistake in underestimating the size of the Japanese forces on *Biak*, he refused to send reinforcements. On 5 June, MacArthur, from the comfort of his quarters in Brisbane, radioed Krueger to complain, "I am becoming concerned at the failure to secure the *Biak* airfields . . . is the advance being pushed with sufficient determination? Our negligible ground losses would seem to indicate a failure to do so."[37] It must have been a bitter pill for him to take that while MacArthur's invasion of a small island in New Guinea was stalling, his former *protégé*, General Eisenhower, was celebrating the triumphant landings on France's Normandy beaches on 6 June. Fuller caught the thick end of MacArthur's wrath.

In spite of MacArthur's castigations it took ten days of hard fighting just to capture Mokmer Airfield and withering Japanese fire prevented its utilization for a further week. Feeling the heat from MacArthur, on 12 June Krueger radioed Fuller to tell him, "I again must urge you to liquidate hostile resistance with utmost vigor and speed to permit construction on Mokmer and other airdromes to be undertaken. Since you have not reported your losses, it is assumed that they were not so heavy as to prohibit advance."[38] As at Buna, MacArthur was blithely unaware of conditions on the ground. "It was really a terrible operation," recalled one officer who was there, "Men had to fight in extreme heat with only one canteen between them."[39] Soldiers died as they crawled to find water. Under pressure from MacArthur, Krueger was forced to relieve his old friend, Horace Fuller. Eichelberger and his staff, then at Hollandia, were called in to replace him. As at the *Battle of Buna*, Eichelberger revitalized the troops.

After reviewing the situation Eichelberger wrote that poor planning with regard to the number of troops needed had been responsible for the debacle on *Biak*. Instead of enjoying the textbook 3:1 advantage over the Japanese defenders, Fuller's forces had had no more than parity. Eichelberger also noted: "This is the toughest terrain I have seen yet to fight in except at Buna. The interior is a series of coral cliffs with numerous natural caves. It has been and will continue to be a rough fight."[40] In a report that should have provided plenty of concern for those planning the invasion of islands closer to the Japanese homeland, Eichelberger warned, "Japanese defense of *Biak* was based on brilliant appreciation and use of terrain."[41] The *Battle of Biak Island* with its withdrawn, inner island defense strategy would subsequently become the norm in the *Battles of Peleliu, Iwo Jima* and *Okinawa*.

Meanwhile the US Fifth Air Force, seeking more runways, occupied the neighboring *Owi Island* and started the construction of two runways. Bomber and fighter groups would be stationed there along with a garrison of 15,000 soldiers. Air resistance was minimal. Kenney was dismissive of his opponents saying that the Japanese had "left everyone contemptuous of the capabilities of Nip air force."[42] Although his forces later destroyed about 100 Japanese aircraft on *Halmahera*, the largest and second most northerly island in the *Moluccas*, between western New Guinea and the southern Philippines, it was becoming apparent that what resources had remained in New Guinea had flown off to the Philippines.

Control of *Biak* was seen as a critical strategic point and it was thought that a major Japanese effort to relieve the island might lure the US Navy into a decisive encounter. *Biak*'s airfields were seen as crucial to provide air support to Operation A-GO, Vice-Admiral Kusaka's plan to destroy the American fleet in a final determining naval engagement in the *Philippine Sea*. While Imperial high command was shocked by the sudden appearance of US troops on *Biak*, the Imperial Japanese Navy's Chief of Staff, Admiral Ryunosake Kusaka, saw it as a possible opportunity: "If we take it back that will draw the [US] Pacific Fleet in sufficiently close so that we can have the Decisive Battle near Palau."[43] After several failed efforts to bring the US Navy to battle, Kusaka, seized the moment and sent the giant battleships *Yamato* and *Mushashi* steaming toward *Biak*. They were sighted by a B-24 Liberator reconnaissance plane and turned back— probably not because of the aerial threat but mainly because it had become clear that Nimitz's assault on the *Marianas (Saipan, Guam and Tinian)* had brought the full US fleet. A cataclysmic naval battle, long sought, was proffered in the *Philippine Sea*.

On *Biak Island* the well-provisioned and dug-in Japanese forces fought a dogged defensive campaign. By mid-June the remaining Japanese troops were dug into a fortified complex built underground in what became known as the West Caves northeast of Mokmer from where they overlooked the airfields. Eichelberger noted: "The caves obviously had connecting corridors and exits which permitted the Japanese, literally, to disappear from the face of the earth, and reappear at will in our midst."[44] Later it was found that the caves had networks of rooms, even bedrooms for officers, linked by ladders, with light provided by petrol-driven generators. The storming of the caves overlooking Mokmer Airfield came after Eichelberger ordered a switch of the point of attack to a flanking advance from the south rather than from the north as had previously been tried. Having pushed back the Japanese defenders into the caves, the troops dumped hundreds of barrels of gasoline and then lit it with TNT to seal them up. Eventually US engineers managed to flood underground fissures with petrol which, when ignited, blew up the defender's main munitions store.

On 22 June Colonel Kuzume called his surviving officers together and ordered all men who could stand to launch a final *banzai* charge. He then burnt all documents and the regimental flag before committing ritual *seppuku* (suicide by disembowelment). One group of Japanese troops launched a *banzai* charge on a 12-man unit of the 186th Infantry. The Japanese were machine gunned in droves; at the end of the charge 109 Japanese bodies were counted for the loss of a single US infantryman. For his courageous defense of *Biak*, Colonel Kuzume was posthumously given a double promotion to Lieutenant-General.

Nevertheless a few remaining soldiers clung to their positions until 27 June when US troops finally penetrated the underground caverns. Inside Eichelberger found "an almost unimaginable purgatory" and bodies that "littered almost every square foot of ground."[45] Many had been fried by flame-throwers or were decomposed. A butcher's shop was discovered where the meat being prepared was human. The conditions in which the Japanese had fought were appalling, "The chamber in which we found ourselves was large, dark, unbearably hot, fetid, and swarming with flies. All of us were dripping with perspiration . . ."[46]

By now most of the Japanese garrison had perished though pockets of troops fought guerrilla actions into August. Some 4,800 Japanese dead were counted though the estimated number of those who died exceeded 10,000. Some 450 Japanese soldiers were captured, an unusually high number. The US forces lost 474 dead and almost 2,000 wounded, mainly in Fuller's 41st Division. In addition there was the usual high quota of tropical diseases.

Biak was quickly developed into a major logistical garrison. Apart from the heavy bomber airfields on *Biak* and *Owi* that were gained for Kenney, construction crews built jetties, wharfs, storage facilities, and accommodation, even a 400-bed hospital. Eight LST (Landing Ship, Tank) loading berths were constructed as well as two floating docks for Liberty Ships. *Biak* became a logistical center capable of supporting 70,000 air and ground troops; eventually it would support MacArthur's return to the Philippines at *Leyte Island.*

The Battle of Lone Tree Hill: **[Map: 29.4]** From the airbases of Hollandia, the Allies could dominate the entire air space as far as the Vogelkop Peninsula at the western tip of New Guinea. A further existing good airfield, a 5,400-foot strip built by the Japanese, had been added to the roster at the end of May, when US forces overwhelmed the surprised Japanese forces defending *Wakde Island*, killing some 759 troops for the loss of 40 US soldiers. Wakde Airfield would enable Kenney to supply Lieutenant-General Krueger's invasion of *Biak* with close air support. Just four Japanese soldiers were captured. The occupation of *Wakde* was a taster for the much bigger operation to capture the adjacent mainland Maffin Airfield and Sawar Airfield, as well as the anchorage of *Maffin Bay*. Moving further up the coast Krueger's 158th Regimental Combat Team landed at Sarmi on 14 June at the strategically important *Maffin Bay*. Dug into caves on the hill overlooking the coastal plain and its jetty were Lieutenant-General Hachiro Tagami and the 223rd and 224th Infantry Regiments. MacArthur's intelligence head, Colonel Willoughby, had again grossly underestimated the number of Japanese troops defending the garrison at 4,000; in reality the number was double and, including non-combat personnel, amounted to 11,000 troops.

'Lone Tree Hill,' a 160-foot high ridge, was covered in lush tropical jungle that extended 1,200 metres to the coast road. It comprised a series of hills including Mount Saskin, 'Hill 225,' and 'Hill 265.' An estimated 2,000 Japanese troops had dug into caves, crevices and carefully constructed log bunkers. The US attack was led by the 158th 'Bushmaster' Infantry RCT (Regimental Combat Team) that had been formed from the Arizona National Guard. Unusually, it was highly mixed racially with a high proportion of American Indians and Mexicans. Their commander was the flamboyant Brigadier-General Edwin Patrick, an aggressive whisky-drinking soldier who distinguished himself by wearing a bright-green jump suit and a helmet sporting a large red star. He was a conspicuous target who survived the *Battle of Lone Tree Hill* but fell to a Japanese machine gun the following year on *Luzon*.

Two weeks of hard fighting followed in which 500 defenders were killed and 300 wounded. As with *Baik*, the fact that Japanese resistance had been underestimated did not change MacArthur's timetable. Neither was he helped by inadequate maps. When

Colonel Prugh 'Pop' Herndon ordered a tactical withdrawal, Brigadier-General Patrick replaced him with his own Chief of Staff Colonel Earle Sandlin. Although Patrick pressed the attack again, before he could complete the task, Krueger decided to relieve the 158th Regimental Combat Team (RCT) with the fresh 6th Division under Major-General Frank Sibert, recently arrived from *Hawaii*.

His plan to carefully reconnoiter the area before making an attack was scotched by MacArthur's timetable and specifically Krueger's need to use *Maffin Bay* to stage troops and supplies for further westward operations. 'Lone Tree Hill' could not therefore be bypassed. Sibert's 20th Regimental Combat Team (RCT) was sent in blind and were drawn into a trap that left them cut off by 22 June. Sustaining significant losses, Sibert's forces managed to claim 'Lone Tree Hill' on 23 June but fighting continued with other Japanese positions on 'Hill 225,' 'Hill 265' and Mount Saksin. The latter held out till 27 June. When Sibert told Krueger about the heavy losses among his officers, Krueger replied, "Well, I know you've got a fighting unit now."[47] As one Navy captain laconically explained, "Any time the Army wanted to give new troops just in from the states some actual contact with the enemy, they would just march them westward until they met the Japs, and in that way they got some very good jungle training . . ."[48]

The remaining Japanese retreated into the jungle, which would continue to wreak a heavy toll on their numbers in terms of starvation and disease. The American forces were made to pay a high price with some 140 dead (70 of them GIs from the 'Bushmasters' regiment) and over 850 wounded. *The Battle of Lone Tree Hill* accounted for almost half of the casualties at Sarmi. In spite of the heavy costs, *Maffin Bay* would briefly provide a staging post for future operations in *Biak, Noemfloor*, Vogelkop and the Philippines. Subsequently it has been questioned whether the *Wakde*-Sarmi operations were strictly necessary as the area soon became a quiet backwater. Isolation, a tactic that had worked well along New Guinea's coast would probably have been the better option.

MacArthur's rapid advance up the coast of New Guinea owed much to intelligence. By now ULTRA was a well-oiled code-breaking machine which was able to provide the Allies with detailed information about Japanese movements. It allowed strongpoints to be bypassed and isolated. A report on the work of US Army Intelligence concluded: "never has a commander gone into battle as did the Allied Commander South West Pacific, knowing so much about the enemy."[49] [See **Appendix F: ULTRA: American Intelligence in the Pacific War**]

The *Battle of Lone Tree Hill* was followed by General Krueger's invasion of the *Noemfloor Island*. On this elliptical island the Japanese had shipped 3,000 Javanese laborers to construct three airfields and their defenses. Thousands died from malnutrition and disease. Those found stealing Japanese supplies were murdered; only 403 of the Javanese survived the ordeal. They claimed that Japanese soldiers would bury sick workers alive. Forced Formosan laborers, given just half the rations of a Japanese soldier, fared little better; one-third died of malnutrition and disease before the invasion. *Noemfloor* was invaded to interdict infiltration of troops into *Biak* and also for its airfields that by now were unused, as the Japanese Navy Air Force in New Guinea had all but ceased to exist by June 1944. On 2 July the US 158th 'Bushmasters' RCT (Regimental Combat Team) led the assault in what was an 8,000-man infantry force. The attack was preceded by a heavy naval bombardment. Colonel Suesada Shimizu, who had pursued a withdrawn defense nevertheless attempted a counter-attack with his 219th Infantry Regiment on 5 July but was beaten back. Sporadic localized fighting continued until the end of August by which time an estimated 1,700 Japanese troops were dead; just 186 Japanese troops were taken prisoner. Sixty-six Americans lost their lives.

The Battle of Driniumor River (The Battle of Aitape): **[Map: 29.5]** Just over a week after the landing at *Noemfloor*, Lieutenant-General Hatazo Adachi's Eighteenth Army, which had been encircled at Jayapura (Hollandia), was retreating westward toward Aitape with 20,000 troops, when it was blocked by the US 32nd Infantry Division and by the US 112th Cavalry Regiment at the *Driniumor River*.

Based on intercepted radio messages alerting MacArthur of Adachi's plans, the US 43rd Division and 124th Regiment were ordered to join Major-General Charles Hall's forces. On the night of 10 July, Adachi's forces launched a mass attack on US positions across the river. It would be simplistic to assume that this was an example of the brainless leadership of Japanese officers. However, Adachi, like many Japanese before and after him in their long retreat, was left without the tools for tactically sophisticated action. By now Japanese units were massively outgunned, virtually bereft of artillery, unprotected from the air and without the logistical wherewithal to sustain protracted operations. On 6 July he had candidly told his soldiers, "I cannot find any means nor method which will solve this situation strategically or tactically. Therefore, I intend to overcome this by relying on our Japanese *Bushido* . . . This will be our final opportunity to employ our entire strength to annihilate the enemy. Make the supreme sacrifice, display the spirit of the Imperial Army."[50] The outcome of the direct frontal charge had a certain inevitability. Machine gun posts killed so many Japanese troops that their bodies eventually formed walls too high to fire over. Nevertheless the American lines were broken and a retreat was ordered. After a nightlong retreat they managed to regroup.

Dogged fighting continued throughout July with some US troops still clinging to their defensive positions at the *Driniumor River*. Having failed to break the US defenses, on 4 August Adachi ordered a general retreat back east to Wewak. They continued to be harried in their retreat by US forces until the end of August. US troops suffered over 3,000 casualties of whom some 440 were killed. An indication of the brutality of the fighting was that over the twenty-five days of the battle the 112th Cavalry Regiment suffered a 62 percent casualty rate. Second Lieutenant Dale Eldon Christensen from Cameron, Iowa, was awarded a Medal of Honor for singlehandedly taking out Japanese machine gun posts with hand grenades on 16 and 19 July. He would be killed in an action on the day that Adachi withdrew his forces from the battle. Another Medal of Honor was awarded to Second Lieutenant W. G. Boyce, from Cornwall, New York who died on 23 July when he threw himself onto a grenade to save his platoon. Japanese losses subsequent to the American landing on 22 April and including the *Battle of Driniumor River* (sometimes the *Battle of Aitape*) were later estimated at over 8,800.

Having secured the northern coast of New Guinea, MacArthur's last invasion on the New Guinea mainland took place at Sansapor on its easternmost projection, the Vogelkop Peninsula. The Japanese garrison at Manokwari was cut off and attempted to retreat to Sorong. In limited fighting some thirty-four Americans were killed. As with most of the northwest coast of New Guinea, MacArthur bypassed significant Japanese troop concentrations. By the end of the New Guinea Campaign, the Allied Forces had suffered some 24,000 casualties of whom 17,107 were Australian. Even now resentment lingers at MacArthur's claim that Australian troops were poor soldiers who avoided engagement with the Japanese. In part it was a reflection of inter-force rivalry that existed on both sides. Tom King, a commander of the Royal Australian Air Force's Tactical Reconnaissance Squadron, recalled:

> We got on all right with the Americans; they were nice fellows individually, but we had mixed thoughts about them as soldiers. It wasn't that they lacked courage . . . [but] Where the Australians did aggressive attacking and patrolling, the Yanks were very happy to go in and set up a perimeter defense, cut off the Japanese supply lines and just sit there.[51]

At the end of August General George Marshall, Chief of Staff of the US Army, and General MacArthur had their only meeting of the war at *Goodenough Island* off *Milne Bay* at the southeastern tip of New Guinea. Although it was largely due to Marshall's support in Washington that MacArthur's armies had been supported both in *matériel* and in his war plans, MacArthur, with just a short distance to travel, grumbled about making the trip. On MacArthur's behalf Marshall had also fought Admiral King's assertion that the *Pacific Ocean* was the Navy's domain alone: "he seemed to regard the operations there as almost his own private war; he apparently felt that the only way to remove the blot of the navy disaster at *Pearl Harbor* was to have the navy command a great victory over Japan."[52] Curiously King's personalization of the war effort was not so different from MacArthur's obsession with avenging his own humiliation in the Philippines.

However, MacArthur, the beneficiary of Marshall's support, was far from appreciative. In spite of Marshall making the not inconsiderable effort to cross the world to make a tour of inspection in the *South Pacific*, MacArthur greeted him with a certain *froideur*. It cannot have been pleasant for the egotistical MacArthur, once Marshall's boss, now to have to report to him even though they were both four-star generals. It is noticeable that during the course of the *Pacific War*, MacArthur did not once make the trip back to Washington to report to his boss. Marshall, clearly aggrieved at the lack of warmth in MacArthur's reception, turned snappy in return. When MacArthur started a sentence with the words, "My staff . . .," Marshall sniped, "You don't have a staff, General. You have a court."[53]

The Battle of Morotai Island: **[Map: 29.6]** Lying at the northern end of the northern *Moluccas* off the west coast of New Guinea, *Morotai Island* was invaded on 15 September to provide a base for the invasion of the Philippines. In early 1944 the Japanese had started to prepare the defenses of the larger neighboring island of *Halmahera*. The Japanese 32nd Division was sent from China. However, heavy losses were sustained when many of their troop transports were sunk by US submarines. Symptomatic of the chaos that had struck the retreating Japanese Army by this stage, the 32nd Division was withdrawn and the airstrips, that they had started to prepare, were abandoned.

ULTRA intercepts indicated that the islands were now weakly defended. Nevertheless a task force with over 50,000 US troops was prepared to take the island and its 500 defenders. The 155th, 167th and 124th Regimental Combat Teams landed on *Morotai* at 6.30 a.m. and rapidly established a beachhead. Landing conditions were difficult. Even General MacArthur, on a rare visit to the front, was forced to wade through chest-deep water to the shore. Sporadic fighting followed over the week with over 300 Japanese killed and 13 captured in return for 125 US casualties, of whom 30 died. Kenney's powerful air support was not needed. An aide recalled that from *Morotai* MacArthur gazed northwest toward his beloved Philippines: "They are waiting for me there," he said, "It has been a long time."[54] The Messiah was on his way.

Morotai was rapidly developed into a major military base and headquarters for MacArthur's invasion of the Philippines. Plans included accommodation for 60,000 Army and Air Force personnel. In effect a town would be built in short order. By 3 November runways plus hard-standings had been built for over 250 aircraft. Storage, munitions, fuel dumps, ports and hospitals (1,000 beds) were also completed. *Morotai* would become the main staging post for aircraft coming up from Australia to the Philippines. Even after the construction of the airbase on *Leyte Island* in the Philippines, *Morotai* thus remained an important base.

Anticipating the next stage of the conflict MacArthur created the Army Service Command (ASCOM), which he placed under the command of Brigadier-General 'Jack' Sverdrup. This new group took charge of all aspects of logistics and supply. Sverdrup, MacArthur's chief engineer, was required to report directly to General Krueger.

Strategies of the New Guinea Campaign: In effect the battle for the *South Pacific* was over. It ended a battle for control of an area that possessed no strategic value for either side other than its proximity to other areas. Although the US and Australian campaign in New Guinea and the *Solomon Islands* drew military resources from the Japanese defense of the *Central Pacific*, its main *raison d'être* was first to allow General MacArthur to bring force to bear on the recapture of America's colonial possession, the Philippines, and secondly to interdict supplies of oil from the Dutch East Indies to Japan.

New Guinea and the *Solomon Islands*, some of the least inhabited places on the planet, provided resources barely more important than a few coconuts and wild edible root plants, supplemented by stealing from the subsistence farming of native villages. Virtually all food and *matériel* had to be imported into the area to sustain the armies that fought there. Indeed the location of every engagement of the *South Pacific* Campaign was bereft of every basic infrastructure required for the sustenance of life such as roads, shelter, clean drinking water, storage, medical facilities etc.

Almost uniquely in *World War II*, battles were won or lost and casualties were sustained in large numbers, not because of death caused by weapons but death caused by malnutrition, disease and even outright starvation. The *South Pacific* Campaign, fought over a two-year period from mid-1942, was, above all, an island war. Even on the larger landmass of New Guinea, garrisons were in effect islands surrounded by a mountainous terrain of dense tropical vegetation. By land, troops were quickly reduced by climate and disease. Movement by sea or air was the preferred option. Given that at the start of *World War II* technological development in the air had advanced aircraft to the point that aerial firepower massively outweighed naval power, the ability to project air power by the building or acquisition of airfields was of paramount importance. As early as 1936, Admiral Yamamoto had written: "As I see it, naval operations in the future will consist of capturing an island, then building an airfield in as short a time as possible—within a week or so, moving up air units, and using them to gain air and surface control over the next stretch of ocean."[55] In effect MacArthur's campaign up through the *South Pacific* simply reversed the direction of the strategy and tactics that Japan had used so effectively at the start of the war. "Victory," MacArthur informed his staff, "depends on the advancement of the bomber line."[56]

If there were any new developments *vis-à-vis* strategy in the *South Pacific* it was probably in the American ability to construct new airfields at speed. Without question the Seabees, perhaps the single most overlooked troops of the war in terms of importance, became an essential new ingredient in the Allies' armament. It is interesting to note the efficacy of the Seabees versus the 'forced labor' battalions, often sustained on half rations, used by the Japanese for the building of their airfields. Even Emperor Hirohito was startled by the speed at which the Allies could build airfields compared to Japanese efforts—often two or three times quicker. In addition to slow construction of airstrips, Japanese engineering often cut corners with mundane but important aspects of construction. At Vunakau Airfield at Rabaul, 6.5 miles of taxiways, which took planes from the ninety fighter and sixty bomber revetments to the runway, were unpaved. In the frequently damp conditions, Japanese planes, particularly laden bombers that lacked tricycle gear and mainly relied on trail-dragging wheels, would often be slowed or even get stuck in the mud before getting to the take-off point. As Rabaul came under increasing assault the need to get planes up in the air rapidly became ever more important, but airfield design and construction hindered this fundamental task.

America's vastly superior logistical ability from the beginning of 1943 also helped their ability to ship equipment and materials with which to build the advance airfields that the *South Pacific* Campaign required. Thus *Guadalcanal* became a vast air and naval base from which all the *matériel* requirements of the *Solomon Islands* Campaign passed through. The campaign for the recapture of the *South Pacific* started with the fight for control of a half-built airfield at Henderson Field on *Guadalcanal* that could manage fifty aircraft and ended with the capture of *Morotai Island* where the US Seabees immediately set about the building of an airbase capable of holding 250 planes and 60,000 troops.

It had taken Japan three months to capture the *South Pacific* while it took American forces thirty months to recapture it. Given the air dominance that the Allies were able to achieve it has to be questioned why it took the Allies ten times longer to conquer New Guinea and the *Solomon Islands* than it had taken the Imperial Japanese Armed Forces at the start of the war. This was particularly surprising given the immense advantages of the twin-prong advance through the *Central Pacific* as well as the *South Pacific*. As Admiral Nimitz pointed out, "The two Allied forces advancing across the Pacific operated as a team, each relieving the other of a portion of its burden . . . Had there not been a Central Pacific drive to attract and hold Japanese forces elsewhere, the southwest Pacific forces would have met far greater resistance in the New Guinea area."[57] It was a compliment that was never returned. MacArthur never acknowledged any usefulness in the capture of *Saipan* and the other *Marianas* or Nimitz's *Central Pacific* thrust in general. The difference in speed of advance was caused first because the Allies in their initial defense of jungle positions were complacent, poorly equipped and inept. It is noticeable that the US Army's pre-war *Basic Field Manual: Jungle Warfare* (FM 31-20), gave practical information about how to navigate a jungle but not a word about how to fight in one; the idea of jungle defenses and how to overcome them was just never considered before the *Pacific War*.

By contrast, unlike the US, British, Dutch and Australian forces, the Japanese Army had developed sophisticated tactics for jungle defense. Bunkers, pillboxes, foxholes, tunnels, crawl-ways, firing pits and all the paraphernalia of entrenchment had been thought out by the Japanese before the war. As late as the *Battles of Buna-Gona-Sananander* the Allied forces had not worked out that Japanese jungle entrenchments had to be painstakingly scouted one at a time and a plan to disable them devised accordingly. In the final resort, Japanese troops were also prepared to fight to the death.

Only after the arrival of Lieutenant-General Robert Eichelberger did the Americans grope their way, in every sense, towards a solution of how to dismantle jungle defenses. It was a terrain that lent itself to well organized and determined defense: a fact that skilled Allied commanders such as the Marine Major-General Alexander Vandegrift (*Battle of Guadalcanal*), the Australian Major-General Sir George Wootten (*Battle of Finschhafen*) and Lieutenant-General William Slim (*Battle of Imphal*) would come to understand as the war progressed. Unlike MacArthur who, even after the *Battle of Buna-Gona-Sananander*, would blithely order attack whatever the circumstances, these commanders began to realize that, given the Japanese propensity to under-provision their troops with logistical support, if the enemy could be stalled in jungle conditions, they withered and died. Thus defense was attack.

In spite of MacArthur's slowness in getting up to speed on how to conduct modern warfare in jungle conditions, even his harshest critic could not deny him the brilliance of his campaign as he rampaged along the north coast of New Guinea toward his date with destiny in the Philippines. Notwithstanding the naval dominance that had been established by Halsey and others and the transformation of American air capability by Kenney, the speed of MacArthur's advance was impressive. The 500-mile leap to Hollandia, cutting off Adachi's retreat was a masterpiece in strategic thinking and was brilliantly executed by MacArthur's veteran army commander, Lieutenant-General Krueger, head of the Sixth Army. In Eichelberger, Krueger also possessed a highly talented ground commander.

Nevertheless it is a moot point as to whether the level of casualties incurred at the *Battles of Lone Tree Hill, Biak* and the *Driniumor River* were justified. The tactical urgency pressed on the commanders by MacArthur was only justified if his strategy of pressing to the Philippines was the best means to defeat Japan quickly. Among America's high commanders MacArthur found himself in a minority of one, at least until September 1944 when the balance of strategic thinking began to move in his favor. Even then there was broad recognition that Nimitz's thrust through the *Central Pacific* was the key to rapid victory. The Joint Chiefs increasingly saw the New Guinea Campaign and later the Philippines as of secondary importance—a means of tying down large numbers of Japanese troops in the *Southwest Pacific*.

MacArthur's political objectives with regard to strategy meant that he was an appalling manager of his ground commanders. He would bully, whatever the circumstances on the ground, even when delays were caused, as was frequently the case, by failures of intelligence as to Japanese troop dispositions provided by his own staff or by inadequate provision of supplies or aerial support. At the *Battles of Buna, Salumaua, Los Negros, Driniumor River* and *Biak*, MacArthur would ignore the realities of the battlefield when delays threatened his personal timetable. Although he could argue and frequently did, that his aggregate casualties from the *Admiralties* to the *Battle of Morotai* were just 11,300 compared to the 20,000 suffered in Nimitz's *Marianas* Campaign there was no comparison in terms of how much strategic importance both sides attached to these respective conflicts. The *Marianas* could be copiously supplied before their invasion; by and large Adachi's forces could not. MacArthur could simply have relied on the jungle to win his battles had he been prepared to adopt a low-cost war of attrition. At *Biak* and the *Driniumor River* MacArthur chose confrontational battle rather than a strategy of isolation. Given MacArthur's character and his obsession with redeeming himself after the Philippines debacle, it can only be judged that personal pride and ambition were the real motives for his relentless pressing of soldiers to speed up their advances. It is highly unlikely that he understood let alone reflected on his own motives.

Recognition of the leading role of air dominance in the *South Pacific* Campaign is not to discount the importance of the Army. The capture of airfields needed boots on the ground. As Krueger, commander of the Sixth Army in New Guinea, stated, infantry was "the arm of final combat."[58] Naval resources were also needed to transport supplies and troops and to deliver and protect amphibious landings. The air arm of the respective armies may have been the most important service arm in terms of tactical and strategic objectives but in reality the engagements were fought with a careful orchestration of all the service elements of air, sea and land. The failure of one service necessarily interdicted the success of another. Nevertheless it would be fair to describe the air arm in the *South Pacific* as *primus inter pares*.

Ultimately the US and its allies won the war in the *South Pacific* because its Air Force was able to compete with Japan's Air Force from *Guadalcanal* onwards until the *Battle of the Bismarck Sea*; thereafter the US quickly established air superiority over the *Bismarck* and *Solomon Seas*. From this point onwards, with supply by sea doomed, Japanese soldiers could be simply bypassed at will and left to rot. By an estimated multiple of five times, more Japanese troops died of disease and starvation in the *South Pacific*, than by the bullet, shell, bomb or bayonet. In effect the Allies' reversal of Japanese tactics for conquering the *South Pacific*, turned the uniquely hostile terrain of New Guinea and the *Solomon Islands* into a killing machine that destroyed the Japanese armies deployed in the region. MacArthur's new-found belief in 'isolation' tactics did not mean that he had given up the destruction of the Japanese armies that his pride demanded. Speed, the desire to get to the Philippines quickly, made 'isolation' tactics a useful short-term ally, but this did not did mean that he was prepared to spare his troops when the opportunity for self-aggrandizement presented itself. As MacArthur told one of Krueger's staffers, "I'm going to bypass the main Japanese strongholds until I get to the Philippines. Then I'm going to meet the enemy head on and destroy him."[59]

General Adachi's Last Words of Pathos, Love, Death and Redemption: The New Guinea Campaign is strongly identified with the leadership of General MacArthur. Given his ruthless control of the media this is not surprising. A broader historical acknowledgement of his superb generals, Krueger and Eichelberger, has been buried under the weight of MacArthur's monstrous ego. MacArthur's assumption of the plaudits for the New Guinea Campaign would have been the equivalent of General Eisenhower taking credit for the conquest of Sicily instead of Generals George Patton and Bernard Montgomery. Both the American and British generals became highly identified with that campaign while Eisenhower, Supreme Commander of the Allied Expeditionary Force, remained quietly in the background. The role played by Japanese generals is even more overlooked. Lieutenant-General Hatazo Adachi and his forces, virtually bereft of air power or naval support, as well as provisions and equipment, conducted a remarkable 30-month defense of New Guinea in which over 100,000 Japanese soldiers laid down their lives—as many as the US suffered in the entire *Pacific War*.

It is worth recalling some of the final words of General Adachi before he committed suicide after his surrender to Allied forces in 1945 and his subsequent trial and sentencing to life imprisonment—for his responsibility for executions of Allied soldiers by the Japanese Eighteenth Army. Born of an impoverished samurai family in Ishikawa Prefecture, on the northern coast and half way up the main island of *Honshu*, Adachi went through the usual route of Staff College followed by service in the *Kwantung Army* in Manchuria. During the Shanghai Incident in July 1937 he gained a reputation for leading from the front and was indeed wounded by a mortar barrage that gave him a permanent limp. He was a 'soldier's general' who, like the American 'Vinegar Joe' Stilwell, shared the miserable living conditions of his troops. In a final address to his fellow officers Adachi declared:

> I felt it a great honor to have been appointed the C-in-C in November 1942 ... and posted to the point of strategic importance in order to ensure that the tide of war moved in our favor ... However, notwithstanding the fact that my officers and men did their best in the exceptional circumstances, surmounting all difficulties, and that my superiors gave the utmost assistance, the hoped-for end was not attained, because of my inability ... The crime deserves death. During the past three years of operations more than 100,000 youthful and promising officers and men were lost and most of them died of malnutrition. When I think of this, I know not what apologies to make to His Majesty the Emperor and I feel that I myself am overwhelmed with shame ... I have demanded perseverance far exceeding the limit of man's endurance of my officers and men, who were exhausted and emaciated as a result of successive campaigns and for want of supplies. However, my officers and men all followed my orders in silence without grumbling, and, when exhausted, they succumbed to death just like flowers falling in the winds. God knows how I felt when I saw them dying, my bosom being filled with pity for them, though it was solely to their country that they dedicated their lives. At that time I made up my mind not to set foot on my country's soil again but to remain as a clod of earth in the Southern Seas with the 100,000 officers and men, even if a time should come when I would be able to return to my country in triumph.[60]

Albeit demonstrative of the peculiar fanaticism that infused the spirit of the Imperial Japanese Army and which explained the extraordinary feats of endurance that characterized their defense of New Guinea and the *Solomon Islands*, Adachi's words also bespeak a nobility of spirit that brings to mind the chivalric codes of the Arthurian or Teutonic knights. The mixture of pathos, love, death and redemption through self-sacrifice implicit in Adachi's final words are themes that achieve an almost 'Wagnerian' ecstasy. The grandeur and nobility of Adachi's expressions sit in sharp contrast to our knowledge of the bestial brutality often meted out to New Guinea or *Solomon Islands* natives or captured Allied troops by Japanese troops and their officers. It could also be argued however that the existential romanticism of the Japanese military elite was a cause of, rather than a contrast to, the record of their Army's atrocities whose numbers suggest, less the exigencies of war, but an institutionalized pattern of behavior.

While there is no evidence that most of Japan's senior generals actually ordered the murder of Allied prisoners or the intolerable treatment that they suffered, arguably, both the noble and the villainous aspects of military 'romanticism' were so inextricably entwined that it was this fanatical psychological state, imparted to their junior officers and troops, that was the fundamental root cause of the vast catalogue of Japanese atrocities in the *Pacific War*. **[See Appendix D: The Japanese Empire: From Co-Prosperity to Tyranny]**

30 Pacific Island Hop: The Gilberts, Marshalls, and Carolines

[May 1943–June 1944]

[Maps: 30.1, 30.2, 30.3, 30.4, 30.5, 30.6]

Admiral King's Central Pacific Strategy: [**Map: 30.1**] The *Central Pacific* component of America's two-pronged strategic advance toward Japan started to be planned as soon as 'turnaround' victories had been won by the Australians in southeastern New Guinea and by the Marines on *Guadalcanal*. With the Japanese clearly losing their grip on *Guadalcanal*, which had been the focus of the war in the *South Pacific* in the second half of 1942, the question the Navy faced at the beginning of 1943 was, what now? At the Casablanca Conference (codename SYMBOL) in January 1943, attended by Roosevelt, Churchill and Charles de Gaulle, the main decision was to put off the European Theater second front, the invasion of France, for another year—much to Stalin's chagrin. The British had concluded that the Allied invasion of France would have to be delayed until 1944 because the German Army would be able to reinforce troops in France quicker that the Allies. Nevertheless, in the wider picture 'Europe First' was again confirmed as the key strategy to win the war against the Axis powers.

However, Asia was not ignored. King demanded that resources for the *Pacific* should be increased from 15 percent of the total war effort to 30 percent. Both MacArthur and Nimitz would benefit from a promise of a doubling of war *matériel*.

As for strategy in the *Pacific*, MacArthur was convinced that Admiral King's *Pacific* Navy should act only as a supporting role for his drive up through New Guinea, the Philippines, southern China and then on to Japan. In essence MacArthur wanted the Navy, under his command, to deploy as he thought fit in the pursuance of his strategy. His championing of a 'unified command' in the *Pacific* was entirely self-serving. Admiral King's naval strategy, and the one ultimately supported by the Joint Chiefs of Staff, did not assume the passive supporting role for Nimitz's US Navy that MacArthur had counted on. Plan ORANGE, detested by MacArthur [see **Chapter 6: Plan ORANGE and MacArthur's Philippines Debacle**], which had been the master plan to deal with Japanese aggression from the early years of the twentieth century, called for a *Central Pacific* drive starting with the capture of the *Marshall Islands*. King urged action along this line.

At the Joint Chiefs of Staff meetings, chaired by Admiral Leahy, Roosevelt's most relied-on adviser who became increasingly influential as the war progressed, King was strongly supported by General 'Hap' Arnold, Commander of the US Army Air Force. He favored a rapid advance through the *Central Pacific Islands* so that he could get close enough to Japan to set up 'strategic bombing' of Japanese cities. It was 'strategic bombing' and Arnold's support of King that was the key to the defeat of all MacArthur's attempts to thwart Nimitz's *Central Pacific* thrust. Nimitz may have had earlier doubts about the viability of bombing Japan from the *Marianas*, but ultimately that was a judgment call that was made by 'Hap' Arnold and fully backed by Admiral King and General Marshall.

Nimitz however, usually an aggressive commander, at first found himself urging caution. An attack on the *Marshall Islands* posed numbers of problems. First there was very little intelligence available about Japanese dispositions and it was too far from *Hawaii* for air reconnaissance missions. Crucially an attack on the *Marshall Islands* could not be supported by land-based aircraft, either bombers or fighters.

The 'black shoe' Navy commanders like Nimitz and Admiral Raymond Spruance, the appointed commander of Task Force 50, later renamed the Fifth Fleet, believed that the risks of an amphibious assault would increase exponentially if it had to rely just on carrier aircraft support. Although this analysis was not be supported by the 'brown shoe' Navy aviators such as the leading exponent of carrier tactics, Admiral John Towers, who believed that carriers should be allowed considerably more operational freedom than simply to hug close to shore to backup amphibious attacks, the US Navy's dominant 'black shoe' Admirals felt that a first move to the *Marshall Islands* was too risky without land-based aircraft backup.

The outcome of the *Marshall Islands* debate was an adjustment to Plan ORANGE. Lying some 540 miles south of *Kwajalein Atoll* in the *Marshall Islands*, the *Tarawa Atoll* in the *Gilbert and Ellice Islands* (a British colony until the Japanese occupation on 10 December 1941) offered an alternative route into the *Central Pacific. Tarawa Atoll* was within reconnaissance range of the *Marshalls* while *Makin Atoll*'s seaplane base, 100 miles to the north, was even closer. At the same time *Tarawa Atoll* stood within land aircraft range of the US-controlled airfield of *Funafuti Atoll*, site of the capital of the *Ellice Islands (*now *Tuvalu*, the world's fourth smallest country*)*, to the south and from the fighter airstrip on *Baker Island* in the *Phoenix Group of Islands* to the east. An attack on *Tarawa* therefore could uphold the principle of invading garrisoned Japanese islands only when the land-based US Air Forces could support amphibious landings.

For King an additional attraction to *Tarawa Atoll* was that its capture would interdict any attempt made by the Japanese Imperial Navy to use *Tarawa* as a launch pad for an assault on *American Samoa, Samoa* (a New Zealand League of Nations Mandate) and *Fiji* (a British colony); the importance of these islands being their strategic position on the supply route from the west coast of the US to Australia, which served as MacArthur's home base. King need not have worried. After *Guadalcanal*, which the Japanese covertly evacuated on 9 February 1943, Imperial General HQ gave up any further expansionist vision. The loss of three fleet carriers (half of their total) at the *Battle of the Midway* combined with the destruction of naval assets over the course of six major naval encounters at *Guadalcanal* had brought an erosion of Japanese naval power, which was irreversible because of Japan's strained logistical and industrial capacity.

At the Imperial General Headquarters in May 1943 a heated discussion took place between the Army and Navy. As long as the Japanese Navy was dominant, it had the wherewithal to defend its 'island perimeter'; without it Japan seemed doomed. Army Colonel Saburo Hayashi recorded, "the conference acknowledged that island operations without command of the air and sea face no alternative but self-destruction."[1] Between the *Aleutians* and the coast of New Guinea, a distance of 2,500 miles, the Japanese Navy would be stretched too thin even if it did have the logistical support for such a strategy. As a young staff officer attached to Colonel Joichiro Sanada, operations chief, Army General Staff, pointed out, the Japanese Navy ". . . after the sea battle of *Midway* . . . [Japan] may be fighting in too large an arena."[2]

In addition to strategy there was also the question of who would garrison the now increasingly vulnerable islands. The Navy did not have the manpower resources while the Army was stretched and resented having to 'bale out' their inter-service rivals. Indeed when the submarine USS *Pollack*, a Porpoise Class submarine, sank the Army troop transport, *Bangkok Maru*, on its way to *Narawa Atoll*, drowning all on board, the Chief of the General Staff in Tokyo raged, "Let the Navy defend the Gilberts!"[3]

The new strategy envisioned by Yamamoto, and later his replacement, Admiral Koga, was to draw the US Navy into the attack of their perimeter island defenses so as to allow the Japanese fleet to engage and annihilate it. To enable this strategy to work, troops would be dispersed among island garrisons that would have to be defended well enough and long enough for the Japanese Navy to assemble and concentrate its forces. Some had doubts whether the strategy was workable, and in hindsight after the *Battle of Midway*, the 'perimeter' set by the Navy was over ambitious. As Lieutenant-General Tokusaburo Akiyama lamented after the war, "The front lines almost everywhere were stretched too tight, like overblown balloons. We should have retreated to regain reserve elasticity."[4] In reality, by summer 1943, Japan did not have the naval manpower or logistical resources even to sustain the defensive strategy that it had adopted, let alone contemplate aggressive action.

Having decided on the targets for the first amphibious operation and won over King to the *Gilberts* 'first,' *Marshalls* 'second' strategy, Nimitz's final piece of the jigsaw was the appointment of an Admiral to command the amphibious forces. Spruance elected to offer the position to Rear-Admiral 'Terrible' Turner who was currently serving in this capacity for Vice-Admiral 'Bull' Halsey's Third Fleet. Another turf war ensued between 'Terrible' Turner and Marine commander, Major-General 'Howlin' Mad' Holland Smith—perhaps not surprising given their respective nicknames. After much argument it was agreed that Turner would have command of the Marines until they got to the beaches and that Holland Smith would have command thereafter.

TRIDENT Conference 12 May 1943: At a meeting at the White House, British Prime Minister Sir Winston Churchill and President Franklin D. Roosevelt met in the third of their series of Washington strategy conferences. The codenamed TRIDENT meeting had difficult issues to face. General Marshall still wanted to invade Normandy in 1943 but was thwarted, although he was able to force the British to agree to a definite invasion date in 1944. It was also decided to launch bombing campaigns aimed at destroying *Nazi* logistical infrastructure. To take pressure off the European Eastern Front, the British also advocated the invasion of Italy in order to knock them out of the war. In a round of hard bargaining Roosevelt and Marshall agreed to an Allied invasion of Italy only on condition that Britain committed to the establishment of a 'cross-channel' second front in 1944.

Meanwhile in Burma, the British cited logistical constraints for the cancellation of Operation ANAKIM, an amphibious campaign supported by the United States' General 'Vinegar Joe' Stilwell. ANAKIM aimed to complete a landing near Rangoon to outflank Japanese forces in central and western Burma. From Rangoon it was planned to strike north where the advance would meet up with Chinese forces, which would simultaneously invade Burma from western China. The supply blockade of the *Kuomintang* government at Chongqing would be lifted. It had been envisaged that ANAKIM would thus open up the possibility of an advance to southern China, which could then become the launch site for the invasion of Japan. Like Stalin in Europe, the cancellation of an Asian 'second front' would disappoint Chiang Kai-shek. He was only barely mollified by the increased supply of *matériel* over the Hump and an increased bombing campaign. As with Stalin, US strategic concern above all else was to keep the *Kuomintang*'s army in the field and to prevent their doing a 'side' peace deal with Japan. For General MacArthur the delay of Operation ANAKIM, seemingly wiping out the challenge of the 'China-*Formosa*' line toward Japan, gave him increased hope that a 'single line' from the south via New Guinea and the Philippines would win the day. He would again be disappointed.

The *Pacific* was the last major item on the agenda at TRIDENT. Churchill "felt that the time had now come to study the long term plan for the defeat of Japan . . . on the assumption that Germany would be out of the war in 1944 and that we could concentrate on the great campaign against Japan in 1945."[5] This was Admiral Ernest King's moment. He forcefully argued that the direct route toward Japan via the *Central Pacific* was the most efficient. The *Marianas Islands*, hitherto virtually unknown to the Combined Chiefs of Staff, let alone Roosevelt and Churchill, became the focal point of a strategy both to locate a bombing strike force to attack Japan and to draw out the Japanese Combined Fleet from its South East Asian hideaways for the decisive naval engagement of the *Pacific War*. In giving his presentation on the envisaged *Central Pacific* thrust (Operation GALVANIC) to Roosevelt and Churchill, Admiral King was not unpractised. As he later recorded, "It took me three months to educate Marshall about the importance of the *Marianas*."[6]

The British were presented with the US Joint Chiefs of Staff *Strategic Plan for the Defeat of Japan* [19 May 1943]. The plan offered three main points; the blockade of *matériel* going to Japan from South East Asia, particularly oil, secondly the bombardment of Japanese cities and industrial centers, and thirdly the invasion of the Japanese home islands. The *Pacific* strategy would "maintain and extend unremitting pressure against

Japan in the *Pacific* and from China."[7] The force of King's arguments helped persuade the British, though after the TRIDENT Conference's 'battles' with regards to Europe, Italy and Burma, the British were happy to enter the calmer waters of the *Pacific* where in any case, they had not much 'skin in the game.'

The TRIDENT Conference effectively set the seal on American domination of *Pacific* strategy. With the cancellation of ANAKIM and the adoption of Operation GALVANIC, Britain was, to all intents and purposes, relegated to the back seat in the direction of the *Pacific War*. Britain's focus, not surprisingly, was fixed on the war in Europe. Although British Chief of Staff, Field Marshal Alanbrooke had mounted a minor rear-guard action to oppose any build-up of resources in Asia while the war in Europe was in the balance, the Joint Chiefs of Staff, and particularly Admiral King, were adamant that the Allies should press forward in the *Pacific*. In his diaries Field Marshal Lord Alanbrooke simply noted, "the work was easier and there was less controversy. We dealt with the *Pacific* and accepted what was put forward."[8] Admiral King, whose role as the key strategist of the *Pacific War* is often neglected, had won through, first against his US colleagues and now against the British. Nothing, other than the defeat of Japan, could have made the anglophobe King happier.

King left the conference delighted with the outcome. His *Central Pacific* strategy, approved by both Roosevelt and Churchill, was fully on track. Nimitz was now authorised to crash through the *Central Pacific*, to take key islands on which logistical and airfield bases would be constructed before making the next leap forward. The end target would be the *Mariana Islands* of *Saipan, Guam* and *Tinian*. From there King planned to take *Formosa* and link up with Chiang Kai-shek's forces in China, from where the final assault on Japan would begin. The plan to invade *Formosa* was yet to be approved but that would be an argument for another day. TRIDENT ended with a written statement of intent and terminated on 27 May 1943.

It was assumed that the 'triple' Allied thrust, from the delayed China-Burma-India front, from MacArthur's drive through the Philippines and from Nimitz through the *Central Pacific* would eventually converge on *Formosa* and the coast of Southern China as the assembly point for the invasion of Japan. The TRIDENT meeting thus allowed America to take complete control of the *Pacific War*, itself a reflection of its growing military and political power not only in the region but also in the world. However, the thrust of the stated strategic priority, 'the bombardment of Japanese cities' also dealt a crippling blow to MacArthur's hopes to monopolize a 'single line' approach to Japan. *Luzon*, the major northern island of the Philippines, the holy grail of MacArthur's 'single line' to Japan, was too far away for an effective bombing campaign against Japan. Only King's '*Marianas*' line' would enable the mass bombing sought by the US Joint Chiefs of Staff.

QUADRANT Conference 17 August 1943: Eleven weeks later Churchill and Roosevelt met again, this time in Quebec (codename QUADRANT). Having been roundly defeated with regard to Asian strategy last time round at TRIDENT, the British came up with an alternative plan for the defeat of Japan, involving a land campaign through Burma and Southern China from where Japan would be blockaded. It was estimated that Japan could be defeated by 1948—not an acceptable timetable for the Americans.

Roosevelt was not prepared to wait that long and the Americans insisted on the *Central Pacific* plan that Admiral King had outlined at TRIDENT. The British acquiesced. The seizure of the *Gilberts, Marshalls, Carolines, Palaus* and the *Marianas* were again approved by the Combined Chiefs. As a sop to Churchill, Roosevelt agreed to the establishment of a South East Asia Command (SEAC) under Lord Louis Mountbatten for the conduct of operations in the China-Burma-India Theater. As had become the norm at these Allied conferences, King also took the opportunity to push for more resources for the *Pacific* theater *vis-à-vis* Europe.

Operation GALVANIC: Bombardment of Tarawa Atoll: [Map: 30.2] Operation

GALVANIC was now set in motion. In mid-November 1943, Admiral Spruance led out his *Central Pacific* force from *Hawaii* for *Tarawa Atoll* aboard his flagship, the heavy cruiser, USS *Indianapolis*. However, Spruance warned, "If . . . a major portion of the Japanese fleet were to attempt to interfere with Galvanic, it is obvious that the defeat of the enemy fleet would at once become paramount . . . the destruction of a considerable portion of the Japanese naval strength would . . . go far towards winning the war . . ."[9] Even within the Navy there were critics of the planned invasion of *Tarawa Atoll*. With Spruance using the Fifth Fleet and 30,000 Marines, 'brown shoe' Vice-Admiral John Towers grumbled, "Spruance wants a sledgehammer to drive a tack."[10] Both before and after the battle, *Tarawa Atoll* turned out to be one of the most controversial engagements of the *Pacific War*.

At dawn on 20 November, USS *Maryland* and USS *Colorado*, sister dreadnoughts of the *World War I* Colorado Class, laid down a barrage of fire on the defenders of *Betio*, the main island guarding the *Tarawa Atoll*. It provided a measure of revenge for the *Maryland*, which had been damaged at *Pearl Harbor*, that the combined fire power of their sixteen 16-inch guns was able to quickly knock out three of the four 8-inch guns, which were defending *Betio* both from the lagoon-side to the north and the open sea to the south and west. A fortunate hit on one of the Japanese guns' ordnance stores sent up a massive fireball. The US battleships, seemingly rendered instantaneously obsolete by the Japanese aircraft carrier attack on *Pearl Harbor*, had at last found their *raison d'être* as floating gun platforms to support the amphibious landings of Nimitz's *Central Pacific* drive. Rear-Admiral Howard Kingman, responsible for planning the bombardment of *Tarawa*, told the press called aboard Rear-Admiral Turner's flagship, "Gentlemen, it is not our intention to wreck the island. We do not intend to destroy it. Gentlemen . . . we will obliterate it."[11] The air and naval barrage of the island lasted for three hours. Its ferocity fed the US Naval officers present with confidence. One such, secure on the bridge of the docking-landing-ship USS *Ashland*, boasted, "They'll [the Marines] go in standing up. There aren't fifty Japs left alive on the island."[12] Some of the Marines' officers were equally optimistic. Lieutenant-Colonel Herbert Amey, commander of the 2nd Battalion, 2nd Marines, at a briefing of his staff boasted, "As we hit the beach the planes will be strafing very close in front of you to keep the Nips down until you get in there and knock off what's left of them. I think we ought to have every Jap off the island—the live ones—by the night of D-Day."[13] D-Day is often associated with the Normandy Landings in France but was a widely used expression to express the first day of landing for amphibious assaults throughout the *Pacific War*.

In spite of the overwhelming power that the US Navy had brought to the island, some of the soldiers had doubts about the landing plans. Colonel David Shoup, who commanded the assault troops, shared his concerns with Robert Sherrod who was reporting for *Time* as well as *Life* magazine: "What worries me more than anything is that our boats may not be able to get over that coral shelf that sticks out about 500 yards. We may have to wade in."[14] Colonel 'Red Mike' Edson, hero of the *Battle of Edson's Ridge* at *Guadalcanal* was aware of the importance of the battle ahead: "The enemy must endeavor to hold it and make sure its capture is as costly to us as possible. This will be the first attempt to defend an atoll . . . as it is our endeavor at seizing one."[15]

At the highest level it seems likely that Admirals Nimitz, Commander in Chief Pacific (CINPAC) and Spruance, commander of the Fifth Fleet, and General 'Howlin' Mad' Holland Smith underrated the likely level of Japanese defense. Preferring speed and surprise, the naval barrage was much shorter than the two days of 'softening up' expected by 2nd Marine Divisions commander Major-General Julian Smith. He was also shocked to discover that Holland Smith intended to hold back all of the 6th Marines as reserves. Julian Smith concluded that his resources were too thin for the planned full frontal attack and asked that General Holland Smith put his orders in writing. As his wife later recalled, ". . . if the assault proved unsuccessful he didn't want to wind up the scapegoat and become known as the General most responsible for the slaughter."[16]

Before dawn the Marines were roused and fed; a last meal of steak and eggs with fried potatoes and coffee, then a final check of their combat kit—an M-1 Garand semi-automatic rifle, bayonet, three days of rations and water, bedding, grenades and 125 bullets, gas mask, toilet items, three pairs of socks and underpants, an entrenching tool (after a rifle the most essential piece of kit), a first aid kit, and cigarettes. They were then moved toward the debarkation stations. Military chaplains passed through the troops offering last minute homilies. "God Bless you—and go out there and bring glory to our Corps," said one; Father Francis Kelley from Philadelphia and veteran of *Guadalcanal* ended his service with, "God Bless you and God have mercy on the Japanese."[17]

At 6.15 a.m. Hellcat fighters, Avenger bombers and Dauntless dive-bombers roared in from the carriers USS *Essex* and USS *Bunker Hill* lying offshore. For the naval watchers it appeared to be a devastating attack. They were gone in ten minutes and the Navy continued its bombardment storm.

The Rikusentai (Special Japanese Marines) Dig In: It was clear that the naval bombardment had made virtually no impact on the defenses that had been prepared by

Rear-Admiral Tomanari Sichero. Following the August 1943 raid made on *Makin Island*, 62 miles to the north of *Tarawa Atoll*, Japanese high command had become alerted to the vulnerability of *Tarawa* and had set about reinforcing the atoll with the 6th Yokosuka *Rikusentai* (Marine paratroopers or Special Naval Landing Forces: SNLF) and the Sasebo 7th *Rikusentai*, and building up its defenses. The *Rikusentai*, were crack Naval paratroopers modelled on the German Luftwaffe paratroop brigades; the Army equivalent was the *Teishin Shudan* (Army paratroopers).

In all there were 50,000 *Rikusentai* troops during the *Pacific War*, commanded by Naval officers trained at the Imperial Army Infantry School. With their dark-green uniforms, modelled on their German paratrooper equivalents, dark-brown belts and harnesses, and 'white anchor' patches, the *Rikusentai* were the super-elite of the Japanese Imperial forces. Recruits were made to learn by heart Emperor Meiji's 1882, *Imperial rescript to Soldiers*. They also adopted the song *Umi Yukaba* (If I Go Away to Sea: 1937). It contained the prophetic line, "Across the sea, corpses in the water . . . I shall die for the Emperor." It eventually became the standard song sung by *kamikaze* pilots before their 'death' missions: the last line read,

> But if I die for the Emperor,
> It will not be a regret.[18]

As early as autumn 1943 at Imperial General Headquarters (IGH), Major-General Kondo had anticipated that the Americans would attack the *Gilbert Islands* after *Guadalcanal* and urged, "It is very important to start immediately to build the airbase at *Tarawa*."[19] The result was that, with recognition of its potential as an American target some thirteen months in advance, there was a generous amount of time to prepare defenses. As Marine historian, Colonel Joseph Alexander has concluded, in *Utmost Savagery, Three days of Tarawa* [1995], "American expeditionary forces would not encounter a more sophisticated series of defensive positions on any subsequent island until they reached Iwo Jima in 1945. Yard for yard, Betio was the toughest fortified position the Marines would ever face."[20] For the Japanese it was a 'water edge' strategy following a directive assumed to be from the Navy division of IGH that ordered the defenders to "concentrate all fires on the enemy's landing point and destroy him at the water's edge."[21]

Rear-Admiral Keiji Shibazaki, an aggressive young officer, who replaced Sichero before the American assault, famously exhorted his troops to build defenses to "withstand assault by a million men for a hundred years."[22] Shibazaki was the 49-year-old third son of a farmer and fertilizer dealer from Hyogo Prefecture. By all accounts he worked wonders in improving the fighting spirit of the *Rikusentai* units with whom he had previously worked as a staff officer: apparently he "immediately began to strengthen morale."[23] It seems likely that he would have fully understood that it was a suicide mission in all but name.

However, it was the experienced naval engineer, Rear-Admiral Sichero, who had begun the construction of some 500 pillboxes and bunkers across an island that was just

800 yards at its widest point and two miles in length. The bomb shelters, built of logs made from coconut trees reinforced by corrugated iron and sand, were all but impervious except to direct hits from large caliber shells. When the barrage was over, troops filled the firing pits with their well-designed fields of fire over the lagoon and its beaches.

In the shallow approaches to the beaches, Shibazaki planted obstacles as well as 'kettle' mines to impede landing boats or to direct them into the defenders' line of fire. In addition a double line of barbed wire fencing dug into the coral shallows almost completely encircled the island at between 50 to 100 yards from shore. Nevertheless there were weaknesses in the defense structures caused by the lack of materials. According to Warrant Officer Kiyosha Ota, the only officer survivor of the *Battle of Tarawa*, Rear-Admiral Shibazaki searched desperately for a cargo ship to bring cement and steel reinforcing bars to make 4,500 tetrahedrons that he planned to place around the island. Ota also noted, "the weak point in the defensive installations was that all the pillboxes were not yet converted to concrete."[24]

The lack of air cover was a much more serious limitation to Shibazaki's ability to defend *Tarawa Atoll*. In mid-October Admiral Koga, following incorrect intelligence had taken the 'Combined Fleet' to *Entiwok* and *Wake Island* looking for Spruance's Fifth Fleet. Having concluded that American naval activity in the *Central Pacific* was a ruse to distract the Japanese Navy from an attack on the naval and military stronghold of Rabaul in the northern *Solomons*, Koga had sent them 173 naval aircraft from Carrier Division-I.

On 5 November, Rear-Admiral Frederick 'Ted' Sherman's Task Force 38 engaged in a series of dogfights over Rabaul in which over 100 of Koga's skilled Navy pilots were killed. Given the difficulty of replacing Marine pilots the aerial battle was a catastrophe for Japan's carrier capability. Vice-Admiral Shigeru Fukudome was explicit about the strategic consequences of the Rabaul air battle defeat, "Fleet air strength was almost completely lost, and although the *Gilbert Islands* appeared to be a last chance for a decisive battle, the fact that the fleet's air strength had been so badly depleted enabled us to send only very small air support to Tarawa."[25] Moreover, despite the preparations, the Imperial Navy's Fourth Fleet, under the command of Vice-Admiral Masami Kobayashi, had just two days' notice that *Tarawa Atoll* would be the target. It was far too short a time to coordinate a naval intervention.

As Rear-Admiral Turner's amphibious landing developed on *Tarawa*, Vice-Admiral Shibazaki pulled his men back from the southern beaches from where they had originally expected the bulk of the landings and reinforced the troops on the lagoon side. Shibazaki had ordered his troops "to defend to the last man all vital areas and destroy the enemy at the water's edge."[26] The tactical template for the defense came from an October 1942 order from the Yokosuka 6th SNLF (Special Navy Landing Force):

> Wait until the enemy is within effective range [when assembling for landing] and direct your fire on the enemy transport group and destroy it. If the enemy starts a

landing, knock out the landing boats with . . . tank guns
and infantry guns, then concentrate all fires on the
enemy's landing point and destroy him at the water's
edge[27]

DAY-1: *Amphibious Assault on Tarawa:* At 9.00 a.m. on 20 November the US Marines
were launched at the beaches. Immediately problems became apparent. The Navy
planners, having to extrapolate *Tarawa*'s tides from readings elsewhere, had failed to
account for the combination of a neap tide, the twice monthly occurrence when the tide
rises least at the end of the moon's first and last third, and an apogean tide, when the moon
lies at the extreme of its elliptical orbit and thus fails to bring sea levels to their typical
height. The studies of apogean tides with 'harmonic' analysis were not available until the
late 1980s, when Professor Donald Olsen, professor of physics at Southwest Texas State
University, published his essay *The Tide at Tarawa* [1987] in *Sky and Telescope* magazine.
It was simply bad luck that 19 November was one of only two days in which neap and
apogean tides coincided in the whole of 1943. Such are the vagaries of war.

The result was that the Higgins boats (the main troop landing craft) with their four-
foot draft failed to clear the coral reefs that protected the inner lagoon even at high tide.
The Marines were trapped inside. Some Marines would spend hours bobbing up and
down in the *South Pacific* waiting to land. One officer noted, "We were so seasick and
disgusted that we'd have thanked the Nips for shooting us."[28]

As the US amtracs (also known as LVT: Landing Vehicle, Tracked) approached the
beach, Warrant Officer Ota remembered that they had been ordered to open fire when
US troops were just 150 yards away: "All our positions opened on the enemy landing
craft with a tremendous volume of machine gun and rifle fire. The Americans appeared
to be surprised and confused."[29] A Marine recalled the early moments when the
Rikusentai opened fire on the advancing amphibious vehicles:

> The amtrac [LVT] started getting hit and our first reaction
> was that the tractors on our flanks had lost control of their
> guns. The sudden realization that there were Japs still
> alive on the island and capable of resistance snapped
> everyone out of their joviality. I remember a violent,
> turbulent trip shoreward—explosions, detonations,
> bodies slumping and bloody, and finally crunching to a
> stop; somebody screaming, "Get out here fast"—throwing
> equipment out and scrambling over the side onto the
> beach.[30]

Troops inside the unarmored amtracs took heavy casualties and as they reached the
beaches were often unable to get over the logged escarpments. The scenes on the beach
rapidly resembled a massacre.

On Red Beach-1 Major John Schoettel's 3rd Battalion was having considerable difficulties. Casualties were mounting at an alarming rate. Schoettel, directing operations from his boat at the reef, heard a plaintive message on his radio from a Marine on the beach, "Have landed. Unusually heavy opposition. Casualties 70 percent. We've had it. Can't hold. We're licked."[31] Some companies had been all but wiped out. Warrant Officer John Leopold, who viewed the scene on Red-1 recalled, "I don't believe more than three hundred [out of 1,000] came through unscathed. The beach should have been called Annihilation Beach. It was red with blood."[32]

At 9.59 a.m. Schoettel sent a message to Colonel David Shoup: "Receiving heavy fire all along beach. Unable to land all. Issue in doubt"; eight minutes later Shoup received a second message reporting, "Boats held up on reef of right flank Red-1. Troops receiving heavy fire in water."[33] When Shoup recommended that Schoettel land on Red-2, he was disheartened to receive the message, "We have nothing left to land."[34] Incongruously Colonel Shoup, a 39-year-old from Covington Indiana and veteran of *Guadalcanal*, was the ruffian commander of 2nd Marines as well as being an avid poet.

It soon became apparent that there was a shortage of LVTs (Landing Vehicle, Tracked). At 9.58 a.m. when Shoup ordered his reserve combat team, 1st Battalion, 2nd Marines to land on Red-2, it was found that there were only enough LVTs to take Companies A and B. C company had to wait until midday. Although the LVTs were able to get ashore because they were 'tracked,' casualties were heavy. Others simply remained trapped inside their Higgins boats. Private N. M. Baird recalled, "We were 100 yards in now and the enemy fire was awful damn intense and getting worse. They were knocking boats out left and right. A tractor'd [LVT] get hit, stop and burst into flames, with men jumping out like torches . . . The bullets were pouring at us like sheets of rain."[35] At least eight LVTs were hit and failed to reach the beaches.

Simply getting to the beaches was a feat in itself. Some of the LVTs (Landing Vehicle, Tracked) dropped their ramps too early and Marines jumped into the sea only to disappear. Weighed down by their combat kit, some of them drowned. Marines, who disembarked safely, had to wade laboriously to shore carrying waterlogged backpacks and with guns held over their heads; all the while they were under heavy fire from the Japanese beachside trenches. Some Marines had to wade for 400 to 700 yards under constant fire. War correspondent Robert Sherrod, who had embedded himself with the Marines wrote:

> . . . we had seven hundred yards to walk slowly into that
> machine-gun fire, looming into larger targets as we rose
> onto higher ground. I was scared, as I have never been
> scared before . . . bullets were hitting six inches to the left
> or six inches to the right. I could have sworn that I could
> have reached out and touched a hundred bullets.[36]

When they did get ashore, the Marines had to start to fight immediately, clinging to whatever cover they could find at the fringes of the beach. Lieutenant-Colonel Herbert

Amey urged his men forward shouting, "come on men we're going to take the beach. Those bastards can't stop us."[37] These were his last words. Amey, who had earlier boasted how easy the landing would be, fell dead in the sea along with a pile of other bodies and dead fish.

Landing troops in deep water had other unintended consequences. Radios arrived ashore full of salt water or riddled with bullets. The TBY radios supplied to the Marines were in any case cursed for their unreliability. By the time of future operations they would be replaced by SCR 300s (Signal Corps Radio; a light back-mounted radio manufactured by Galvin Manufacturing Company, now Motorola, and the first to be name 'walkie-talkie') and heavier 610s for field operation. Communications were to be a problem in the first days of the battle. Runners had to risk their lives to carry messages. Disruption of communication was so bad that a message to Brigadier-General Leo Hermle, to take over command from Colonel Shoup, never reached him; Hermle, who had gone ashore in the early afternoon, had made a hazardous passage to shore but was bedevilled for the remainder of the day by communications problems. With so many boats unable to reach shore, much of the Marines' munitions and provisions piled up at the end of a pier.

The only relatively safe route to shore proved to be the channel to the west side of the long supply pier that jutted 700 hundred yards out from the shore and beyond the coral ridge that protected the inner lagoon, bisecting Red Beach-2 and Red Beach-3. Lieutenant William Hawkins and a group of specially trained riflemen forming the Scout-Sniper Platoon, had been assigned to clear out enemy positions along the pier with the help of Lieutenant A. G. Leslie and a squad of engineers including a flame-thrower unit. Although the flame-thrower successfully burnt out one group of Japanese soldiers, it had the undesired consequence of burning down 50ft of the pier down to the waterline; the missing pier would later hamper the delivery of supplies.

As for Hawkins, Lieutenant Paine described him as behaving like "a madman. He cleaned out six machine-gun nests, with two to six Japs in each nest. I'll never forget the picture of him standing on that amtrac, riding around with a million bullets a minute whistling by his ears, just shooting Japs. I never saw such a man in my life."[38] Hawkins, an engineer from Tacoma, Washington was mortally wounded the following day after successfully taking out four Japanese pillboxes; he charged a fifth with the aim of putting a grenade through the firing slot; he was cut down and "practically torn in half,"[39] by a heavy machine gun. Gushing blood, the Marines got him back to the beach; he was given twenty-five pints of blood but died of his wounds in the night. He was duly awarded the Medal of Honor.

It was not just Marines who were consumed by blood lust. Tank commander Oonuki recalled a colleague who returned to their shelter after a foray against the Marines: "I've just killed a dozen Americans," the man boasted as he wielded a samurai sword dripping with blood, "I'm going back out to kill more. Who will come with me?"[40] As for Oonuki, he passed out when his shelter was blown open and swept over with a flame-thrower. When Oonuki came to, he escaped to the east and crossed over to *Bairiki*; after making himself sick eating shellfish, he fell asleep and was captured.

On Red Beach-2 soldiers on those amtracs which managed to reach the beach were amazed to see Japanese troops standing and throwing grenades. Amtracs tangled into barbed wire, slewed sideways or crashed into the sea wall of the eastern side of the pier. Semi-professional baseball pitcher, John Spillane, scooped up grenades that landed in his amtrac and hurled them back. He caught one in mid-air. A sixth grenade blew his pitching hand to shreds and he later had it amputated.

Tractors or smaller rubber boats started to transfer troops and supplies from the end of the pier to Red Beach-2. At 10.36 a.m. General Julian Smith radioed V-Amphibious Corps: "Successful landing at Beaches Red-2 and 3. Toe hold on Red-1. Am committing one LVT [Landing Vehicle, Tracked] from division reserve. Still encountering strong resistance throughout."[41] On board USS *Maryland*, urgent calls were being made from the beaches for bombing and strafing missions, as well as demands for plasma, medical supplies and ammunition. For the Marines the supporting bombing missions were not always welcome; as one Marine noted, the bombers were "absolutely impartial; he dropped half his bombs on us and half on the Japs."[42]

On Red Beach-1 two tanks were landed at 11.30 a.m. With infantry in support they moved 300 yards before being held at an anti-tank ditch. Both tanks were disabled though one of them managed to sustain fire from its rear machine gun. On Red Beach-3, tanks of 2nd Tank Platoon advanced over to the west runway of the airfield; they worked on Japanese pillboxes though several of them succumbed, one to a magnetic mine while another became stuck in a shell hole. Third Tank Platoon of Company-C landed intact on Red Beach-3 and attacked south; although enemy positions were knocked out, by the end of the day three of the tanks had been destroyed, one by friendly fire from a US dive-bomber.

At midday Colonel Shoup sent Lieutenant Evans Carlson back to the USS *Maryland* to report first hand the account of the battle so far. Carlson made a hazardous return journey and informed General Smith of the situation with the final comment that no matter how hard the action, Shoup, who had received severe shrapnel wounds in his legs as he came ashore, intended to stick it out. Most importantly Shoup insisted that reserves should be brought into Red Beach-2 from where he would try to link up all the beach landings. At 9.59 a.m. a desperate Colonel Shoup called for help from the reserves only to get the answer, "We have nothing left to land."[43] By midday the battle was still going badly with Colonel Shoup calling frantically for help and reporting: "Still encountering strong resistance . . . issue in doubt."[44] Disembarking troops found themselves pinned down behind logs on the beaches. To make matters worse, many of the amtracs that tried to make their way back to the reefs to pick up more troops were sunk. By the end of the first day, half of them had been destroyed. "It was," wrote veteran combat journalist Robert Sherrod, "the only battle which I ever thought we were going to lose."[45]

The amtrac was originally developed in 1935 to work in swampy areas. However, the Marines requested a more seaworthy version that was built by the Food Machinery Corporation (FMC), based in Dunedin, Florida. It could carry eighteen fully equipped Marines or 4,500 lbs of equipment. Derivatives with 75 mm howitzer turrets were later developed. In total, by the end of the war FMC and other manufacturers delivered over 18,000 units in all its iterations.

In spite of the unpropitious beginnings, a wounded Colonel David Shoup took charge of the 2nd Marines. After getting them ashore he organized their advance to the Japanese first line of defense. He would later be awarded the Medal of Honor. Two Stuart tanks that were able to land at the east end of the island were quickly destroyed by the Japanese, and although the three Sherman tanks that landed on the western end of the island were more effective they too perished. Nevertheless by nightfall the American advance had reached the boundaries of the airfield.

The Japanese defenders too faced problems. The bombardment had destroyed communications lines to the Japanese HQ and prevented control of Rear-Admiral Shibazaki troops. He was, however, able to receive a message of limited usefulness from Emperor Hirohito: "You have all fought gallantly," he commended, "May you continue to fight to the death. *Banzai*."[46] Shibazaki would not have long to wait to die. Later in the afternoon as command and control was becoming even more difficult, Shibazaki and his staff, while moving to take up a new position on the south of the island, were killed by a naval 5-inch 'air-burst' shell after a Marine spotter directed fire from destroyers USS *Ringgold* and USS *Dashiell*. Without leadership the Japanese troops could only act in isolation. Their counter-attack, expected by the Marines, never materialized. By the end of Day-1, the 5,000 troops who had managed to get ashore had suffered over a thousand casualties, including dead and wounded. Coast Guardsman, Karl Albrecht, who arrived in a later wave on Red Beach-3 recalled his surprise as he waded ashore, ". . . the rows of Marines along the beach weren't lying there waiting for orders to move. They were dead. There were dead all over. They appeared to outnumber the living."[47]

As evening fell, the Marines dug in to the precarious enclaves that they had established. Major-General Julian Smith would later reflect that the Japanese should have launched their counter-attack that night while the American position was at its weakest. It may be that Shibazaki's destroyed communication lines prevented coordination of an attack; later, it became apparent from captured Japanese that the lack of message-pads may have shown an overreliance on wire communication. As Captain Eugene Boardman, a Japanese-speaking officer, noted, the failure to find message pads "indicated a lack of training in using runners. The effectiveness of the preliminary naval bombardment in breaking up the Japanese wire communication system was possibly all the more fateful on this account."[48]

DAY-2: Tarawa: As dawn broke on Day-2 of the battle, Colonel Shoup was to be found some thirty yards inland from Red Beach-2 resting against the side of a Japanese air-raid shelter. Some twenty-five of their troops were still inside and sentries had been posted either side to stop the Japanese from escaping. Overnight Japanese troops had infiltrated through the lines and some had swum out to wrecks in the lagoon and hampered the Marines with their machine gun or sniper fire. However, Shoup's main concerns were the supply of water and ammunition and he ordered Lieutenant-Colonel Evans Carlson to get supply from the landing pier to the beach. Eighteen amtracs were rounded up to provide a shuttle service, taking munitions and provisions to the beach in one direction and ferrying wounded Marines in the other. Stocks of equipment, food and water were stored on the pier and would be shipped to the beach as required by Colonel Shoup.

Meanwhile 75 mm M1 Pack Howitzers that had been brought ashore during the night were assembled and targeted at blockhouses from where Japanese machine gunners had targeted Marines as they waded towards the beaches on Day-1. The Japanese blockhouses were put out of action and the movement of troops to shore was thereby considerably de-risked. By 8 a.m. the whole battery of Pack Howitzers was brought ashore by rubber boat or manhandled along the length of the pier. The battery was assembled and faced to the east.

The second day of fighting (21 November) saw expansion and consolidation of the Marines' position on the island from their three landing points at Red Beach-1, Red Beach-2 and Red Beach-3. Having taken the entire west end of the island, reinforcements could be brought in more speedily. Many of the Marines who had been forced to spend most of the previous day and night in their Higgins boats were finally able to come ashore. Tanks and other heavy equipment such as armored bulldozers were also brought to the beaches. The 6th Marines landed and advanced eastwards along the south coast axis between the beach and the airstrip. The mood of the Marines started to change at midday. Lieutenant-Colonel Rixey noted, "I thought up until 1 o'clock today it was touch and go. Then I knew we would win."[49] As they approached some positions, they found no opposition; the Marines noticed that some of the Japanese troops, perhaps having run out of ammunition, were starting to commit suicide together. In one bunker seventeen Japanese soldiers were found to have committed mass suicide. Nevertheless, there was still hard fighting ahead. At 1.45 p.m. Colonel Shoup urgently sent back a message to Major William Jones of 1st Battalion, 6th Marines, who had been designated to land at Green Beach, to "BRING IN FLAMETHROWERS IF POSSIBLE."[50]

Delays in maneuvering the USS *Feland* away from reefs meant that Jones was unable to land on Green Beach until 6.40 p.m. On the way he lost one of his supply tractors to a Japanese 'teapot' mine, the horned 47 lb mines that were used in the shallow water approaches to beaches. The tractor was blown out of the water landing upside down and all but one man aboard was killed. Light tanks were also landed on Green Beach but, after finding terrain difficult, others were diverted to Red Beach-2.

At 4 p.m. Colonel Shoup sent back a message reporting that his troops were "dishing out hell and catching hell. Pack howitzers in position and registered for shooting on tail (of *Betio*). Casualties many; percentage dead not known; combat efficiency; We are winning."[51]

At 4.55 p.m. the 2nd Battalion, 6th Marines, led by Lieutenant-Colonel Murray, landed on *Bairiki*, the small atoll connected to *Betio*. Fifteen Japanese occupied a pillbox with two machine guns and Murray called for aerial bombardments to support his landing. By chance a low strafing run ignited a can of gasoline and ignited the pillbox, burning its occupants to death. As a result, somewhat fortuitously, the Marines came ashore without opposition.

DAY-3 and DAY-4: Tarawa: In the late afternoon of the 22 November, Colonel Merritt Edson, Chief of Staff of the 2nd Marine Division debarked from the USS *Maryland* and made his way to Colonel Shoup's command post on 'Red Beach-2.' He immediately took command of the forces on *Betio*, leaving Shoup to focus on the direction of his seven landing teams. For the next morning the two colonels requested naval gunfire to concentrate on the east end of the main runway and the eastern part of *Betio* with a safety margin of 500 yards set for the nearest Marines.

Attacks were launched by Hays's 1st Battalion, 8th Marines to the west to clean out a remaining pocket on the north coast between Red Beach-1 and Red Beach-2, while the 1st Battalion, 6th Marines were ordered to attack Japanese positions along the south coast. Light tanks led the attack shielding infantry moving in close support. To destroy the strongly constructed pillboxes, the light tanks would have to maneuver in front so that their 75 mm guns pointed directly into their narrow openings. Major W. K. Jones's 1st Battalion of the 6th Marines made short work of the south coast killing an estimated 250 Japanese troops until they reached the positions of the 1st Battalion, 2nd Marines. Hays, who lost one of his light tanks to a magnet mine, gained little ground though several strong defense positions were wiped out. With the exception of this small enemy pocket, the western half of *Betio* was held by 2nd Marine Division.

On the same morning to the northeast of *Betio*, Major 'Jim' Crowe's 2nd Battalion, 8th Marines attacked enemy strongpoints including a steel pillbox and a large bombproof shelter, which all enjoyed interlocking fire (defensive machine gun fire where approaches could be covered by more than one position). A Marine advance was made possible when a mortar scored a direct hit above a long emplacement causing an ammunition dump to explode and destroying the enemy position. Assault engineers with flame-throwers and demolition equipment stormed the top of the bombproof shelter. The Bangalore Torpedo (a long thin projectile) proved invaluable; a mine developed by an English sapper in 1912, the Bangalore Torpedo consisted of linked tubes that could clear a path fifteen yards long and one yard wide through wire or undergrowth. It was also used to clear minefields. A determined Japanese counter-attack was held back by First-Lieutenant Alexander Bonneyman Jr. whose unit blew open the door and incinerated the attackers by pouring diesel oil into the airshafts and drove back the remainder.

Princeton graduate Bonneyman came from Santa Fe, had three children, and was a successful entrepreneur who owned three copper mines. Because of his age the 33-year-old Bonneyman was exempted from call-up but volunteered anyway. He was killed before a Marine charge could rescue him; the charge was filmed by Sergeant Norman Hatch with a 35 mm movie camera while Sergeant Obie Newcomb took snaps—or rather Pulitzer Prize winning photographs. Hatch's movie was used in the award winning documentary film, *With the Marines at Tarawa* [Director: Louis Hayward, 1946]

Bonneyman's determined stand allowed the Marines to keep hold of the shelter; when the occupants decided to make a run for it, racing from the southern and eastern exits, the Japanese troops were mown down by machine gun, rifle fire and lobbed grenades. Bulldozers were brought up to seal in any remaining Japanese while explosives were dropped down the airshafts. The area was then cleared of Japanese, many of whom committed suicide. Robert Sherrod noted four Japanese soldiers in one tin-roofed hole who "had removed the split-toed, rubber soled jungle shoes from their right feet, had placed the barrels of their 0.303 rifles against their foreheads, and then had pulled the trigger with their big toes."[52] Others simply pulled grenades to their chest. Bonneyman was posthumously awarded a Medal of Honor.

A further slow advance was made in the afternoon but General Julian Smith, who had earlier gone ashore to confer with Colonel Edson, was forced to report at 4 p.m., "Situation not favourable for rapid clean-up of *Betio*. Heavy casualties among officers make leadership problem difficult."[53] In particular the Japanese remained strongly entrenched in positions to the east of the airfield. That evening, starting at 7.30 p.m., Japanese troops, in groups of fifty, began counter-attacks against the lines held by the 6th Marines. At 4 a.m. on 23 November the Japanese made their strongest counter-attack; they screamed inanities in English such as "Marine you die!" and "Japanese drink Marines' blood."[54] Out of a force of 300 Japanese troops, some 200 were wiped out within fifty yards of the American lines; the slaughter was helped by accurate artillery gunnery and supporting fire from destroyers offshore, which had killed a further 125 Japanese troops at greater distance from the front. Many of the Japanese were found to be naked, already wounded and wrapped in bandages or wearing only loincloths; many did not have guns and carried only knives, bayonets or swords.

Apart from a few pockets of resistance most of the defenders were now pushed into the far east of the island. At 11.50 a.m. General Smith sent a message to Admiral Harry Hill to report, "Decisive defeat heavy enemy counter-attack last night destroyed bulk of hostile resistance. Expect complete annihilation of enemy on *Betio* this date."[55]

General Julian Smith led the final assault with elements of the 2nd and 8th Marines. Pounding the enemy positions with 75 mm howitzers, the Marines followed up behind armored half-track vehicles and tanks. Dug-in enemy positions were dispatched by flame-throwers. Finally the Navy pounded the sand-spit that led over to *Bairiki*. By the end of this fourth day of fighting it was estimated that fewer than 100 Japanese were left alive. However, hidden snipers continued to be a problem for several days. In this final push 475 Japanese defenders were killed and 14 prisoners taken, mainly Korean laborers.

As for the Marines, some of them had not slept for seventy-six hours: "No time for sleeping," said Private Muhlbach, "no matter how exhausted we were . . . Your thoughts are of the enemy. You want to get at them and kill them. That's all I could think of."[56] The next day, 24 November, the British Union Jack and the Stars and Stripes were raised in a formal ceremony. Somewhat incongruously the British colony had been restored to its rightful owners using a flag that had been found in the kit bag of a Japanese soldier.

For the next few days the Marines cleared up the remainder of the atoll where a few Japanese troops had been stationed or where some survivors of *Betio* had managed to hide. A radio operator sent a last message to Tokyo: "Our weapons have been destroyed and from now on everyone is attempting a final charge. May Japan exist for a thousand years."[57]

Costs and Lessons of Tarawa: For most of the observers of the action at *Tarawa Atoll*, it was a first 'wake-up' call to the ferocity of the war that lay ahead. Correspondents had not been present at Henderson Field at the US Marine *Battle of Guadalcanal* where the Americans had mainly been defenders rather than attackers. In spite of the ferocity of the Marine battles over six months at *Guadalcanal*, casualties were approximately the same as those suffered in three days at the *Battle of Tarawa Atoll*.

First reaction was one of pride. Correspondent Richard Johnston wrote, "It has been a privilege to see the Marines from privates to colonels, every man a hero, go up against Japanese fire with complete disregard for their lives."[58] *Time* magazine headlined a map of *Tarawa* with *Betio: One Square Mile of Hell* [6 December 1943] and reported, "Last week some two to three thousand US Marines, most of them dead and wounded, gave the nation a name to stand beside those of Concord Bridge, the Bonhomme Richard, the Alamo, Little Big Horn and Belleau Wood. The name was Tarawa."[59] Johnston was one of twenty-five war correspondents, five photographers and two artists who were 'embedded' with the US Marines in the *Gilbert Islands* campaign. Never in history had a battle been so fully covered by the press.

It is hard to gainsay the performance of the Marines in this first amphibious assault of the *Pacific War*. Although they were clearly well trained outside San Diego by Lieutenant-General 'Howlin' Mad' Holland Smith, *Tarawa Atoll* was the first island action of the war and because of failings in planning and execution, not to be repeated, it was also the toughest. Amphibious landings drew high casualty rates and during active 'fighting days' in the *Pacific*, the mortality rate per unit of 1,000 soldiers per day was 1.78 compared to 0.36 in Europe—almost five time greater. Overall casualty rates, including wounded troops, were also more than three times greater in the *Pacific* at 5.5 per thousand per day, compared to 1.74 in Europe. With the higher chances of combat death in the *Pacific* it might have been expected that desertion rates would be higher. In the Army they amounted to 1 percent of troops whereas in the Marines desertion rates were as low as 0.1 percent—ten times less. The legend of the Marines' superior *esprit de corps* during the *Pacific War* was not mythical.

If the correspondents had learnt a lot about the fighting qualities of the Marines, they in turn had learned a great deal about the Japanese soldier. Throughout the battle Marines frequently engaged in hand-to-hand fighting. The Marines were shocked to discover that the enemy troops did not live up to the propaganda stereotypes of the short, bespectacled, bucktoothed 'Jap.' Private First-Class Robert Muhlbach recalled that many of the Japanese troops were over six foot tall and

> They were good at defending themselves, and so we had
> to parry and thrust, and they were good! Those guys were
> so much bigger than the average Jap. They were naval
> landing forces [*Rikusentai*], like Japanese Marines, and
> they were larger. They were very accurate with their
> weapons, and good with their bayonets . . . They were
> good and we were pretty good, too. So it was two of
> probably the best military outfits in the war.[60]

Lieutenant Thomas also had a bruising hand-to-hand encounter. "I had the field telephone in my hand when I was rushed by the biggest Jap I've ever seen," he recalled. "We grappled for a few seconds, and I managed to kick him off me and throw him to the ground. Then I picked up a 0.45 and finished him off."[61]

General Holland Smith, the Marines' commander, who after the war, called into question the need to have taken *Tarawa Atoll*, declared:

> I don't see how they ever took Tarawa. It's the most
> completely defended island I ever saw . . . I passed boys
> who had lived yesterday a thousand times and looked
> older than their fathers. Dirty, unshaven, with gaunt
> sightless eyes, they had survived the ordeal, but it had
> chilled their souls. They found it hard to believe they
> were actually alive . . .[62]

He was not the only senior commander to be stunned by the devastation and bloodiness of the battle. Nimitz wrote to his wife, "I have never seen such a desolate spot as *Tarawa*. General Richardson, who saw battlefields in France last year, says it reminded him of the Ypres field, over which the battle raged back and forth for weeks. Not a coconut tree of thousands was left whole . . ."[63] It had been a close run engagement. In spite of the seemingly overwhelming power and superiority in numbers of troops and their equipment, Major Rathvon Tomkins, one of the principal actors in the battle, stated categorically, "Tarawa was the only landing in the *Pacific* the Japs could have defeated us."[64]

"You killed my son on Tarawa,"[65] one distraught mother wrote to Admiral Nimitz after the *Battle of Tarawa*. Little did this mother or the mothers of 1,009 Marines and 687 Naval personnel killed, in addition to 2,101 wounded casualties, realize that the *Battle of Tarawa* was part of a strategic thrust that would bring ultimate victory in the war with Japan. With an attacking force of 35,000 men, it was a fearful loss of life in just three days of fighting on the two square miles of *Tarawa Atoll*; fearful that is, until it is noted that on the other side only seventeen out of 2,619 Japanese troops, including one officer, survived the slaughter. Like the Spartans at the *Battle of Thermopylae*, Japan's elite *Rikusentai* (Special Japanese Marine Forces) had laid down their lives to 'buy' time. Although many Japanese soldiers committed suicide rather than surrender, it was also the case that many US Marines, in the heat of battle, did not 'take prisoners.' In addition, just 129 Japanese and Korean laborers, out of a workforce of 2,200, were left alive. A hundred kilometers to the north the comparatively lightly defended *Makin Atoll* and its seaplane base was taken with some 305 casualties (64 dead).

For future operations, the *Battle of Tarawa* provided invaluable lessons. The Army and Navy had massively overestimated the destructive firepower of naval bombardment. Three hours would not be enough to subdue let alone destroy Japanese defenses. In the future bombardments would be longer and heavier, lasting for days rather than hours, and there would be no expectation of future amphibious landings to be a 'walk on the beach' for the Marines. *Tarawa* taught the Naval commanders the importance of the amtracs to successful operations. With 125 such vehicles, there had been enough to carry only the first three waves. More were needed to allow flexible sequencing of landing of specialist items and reinforcements depending on the requirements of the first waves. In an amphibious landing, amtracs were not simply ferries but part of the flow of tactical deployment. There was also a need for spare amtracs to replace those that were put out of action, destroyed or broken down. In the future more amtracs would also require more LSTs (Landing Ship, Tanks) to carry them. The battle also taught the importance of specialist equipment for dealing with the Japanese Army's defensive structures; flame-throwers, grenades, Bangalore Torpedoes, armored bulldozers and tanks. The importance of better field communication equipment also became clear from the frequency of communications breakdowns and the difficulty of maneuvering messages around a congested and deadly battlefield.

However, in this 'knife edge' encounter, the Marines won through in spite of the *matériel* and tactical deficiencies that became evident after later analysis. Lieutenant-General Vandegrift, the heroic leader of the Marines at *Guadalcanal*, who later became commandant of the Marine Corp would later reflect, "Tarawa was the first example in history of a sea-borne assault against a heavily defended coral atoll . . . In the final analysis . . . success at Tarawa depended upon the discipline, courage, and fighting ability of the individual Marine. Seldom has anyone been called upon to fight a battle under more difficult circumstances."[66] Under such circumstances, the *de facto* practice of taking no prisoners can easily be understood. The propensity of Japanese soldiers to fake death while hiding a grenade or surrendering with a grenade wired to them, effectively suicide bombers, meant that Marines would often shoot first and ask questions later.

General MacArthur and Pacific War Politics: Given the scope of the media coverage of the *Battle of Tarawa*, it was perhaps inevitable that there was a public backlash that was in part whipped up by newspapers. Some journalists questioned whether the *Tarawa Atoll* operation had been needed and whether the high cost in life could be justified. It did not help that General MacArthur among others had been briefing against Admiral Nimitz and the *Central Pacific* strategy. It was a political campaign that MacArthur had been waging since the TRIDENT Conference in May 1943. On 22 September, two months before the assault on *Tarawa*, the *New York Times* was given the benefit of MacArthur's wisdom regarding the foolishness of 'island hopping.'

After the *Battle of Tarawa*, MacArthur went into overdrive in his efforts to kibosh his Naval colleagues' plans, agreed at TRIDENT, for the *Central Pacific* thrust. While on a tour of the *Southwest Pacific*, Brigadier-General Fred Osborn of War Department Staff was handed a statement by General MacArthur to give to Henry Stimson, head of the War Department, in order to lobby the President indirectly, ". . . Mr. Roosevelt is Navy minded. Mr. Stimson must speak to him, must persuade him."[67] The specter of a Washington Naval conspiracy was to haunt MacArthur throughout the war. MacArthur also claimed disingenuously, "I do not want command of the Navy," but immediately contradicted this statement when he asserted, in his typically monomaniacal manner,

> but [I] must control their strategy, be able to call on what
> little the Navy is needed for the trek to the Philippines . . .
> these frontal attacks by the Navy, as at Tarawa, are tragic
> and unnecessary massacres of American lives . . . Don't
> let the Navy's pride of position and ignorance continue
> this great tragedy to our country.[68]

Furthermore MacArthur boasted that he would win the war in a year. MacArthur's stance was a tiresome re-engagement of the argument about *Pacific War* strategy that had been waged between the Army and Navy since the beginning of the year.

A further power struggle ensued in the early months of 1944. At a meeting at *Pearl Harbor* on 27 January, doubts were expressed by Nimitz as to whether, even if they arrived at the *Marianas Islands* (*Guam*, *Saipan*, and *Tinian*), the bombing of Japan from these distances would be feasible. In spite of the importance of the meeting, MacArthur had again refused to attend. Nevertheless, without the presence of Admiral King, MacArthur's Chief of Staff, the recently promoted Lieutenant-General Richard Sutherland, appeared to win the old argument that there should only be 'one line' toward Japan and that it should move via New Guinea toward the Philippines. With Nimitz, Halsey and Sherman now seemingly supportive of MacArthur's 'single line' through the Philippines, MacArthur was led to believe that he had finally won the battle for control of *Pacific* strategy. A 'single line' through New Guinea would mean a 'single command' under MacArthur. He had reckoned without Admiral Ernest King, who was more than a match for MacArthur both in terms of intellect and will power. King quickly whipped his subordinates into line—his line through the *Central Pacific*; in a scathing letter to Nimitz he made it clear, "The idea of rolling up the Japanese along the New Guinea coast, through *Halmahera* and Mindanao, and up through the Philippines to *Luzon*, as our major strategic concept, to the exclusion of clearing our Central Pacific line of communications to the Philippines, is to me absurd."[69] King also made it clear that MacArthur's proposed plans were "not in accordance with the decisions of the Joint Chiefs of Staff."[70]

King may have squashed MacArthur but petty squabbles continued. When Nimitz refused to authorize more Naval forces to be committed to the *South Pacific* until the powerful airbase at Rabaul in the *North Solomons* had been reduced, MacArthur refused to provide heavy bomber support for Vice-Admiral 'Bull' Halsey's Third Fleet. "My own operations envisage the maximum use of my air forces," he told Nimitz, who, in turn, counselled Halsey to remain calm; Halsey confirmed that he would "refuse to get into a controversy with him or any other self-advertising son of a bitch."[71]

Nevertheless, the decision by the Joint Chiefs of Staff in March 1943 to make Halsey's Third Fleet in the *South Pacific* answerable to MacArthur with regard to broad strategic direction, though still operationally answerable to Nimitz, again fed the fires of the General's delusion that he had won the battle for control of strategy. Invited to Brisbane to meet MacArthur, Halsey arrived in some trepidation. Unexpectedly he succumbed immediately to MacArthur's charm offensive. Halsey was met by MacArthur and his staff as his Catalina flying boat landed and he was whisked away for talks. Halsey would later recall, "Five minutes after I reported I felt as if we were lifelong friends. I have seldom seen a man who makes a quicker, stronger, more favorable impression . . . The respect that I conceived for him that afternoon grew steadily during the war . . . I can find no flaw in our relationship."[72] In spite of occasional arguments it was a friendship that endured. Unsurprisingly MacArthur, using his characteristic Olympian rhetoric, also tried to 'turn' Halsey by telling him:

> They're going to send me a big piece of the fleet—put it absolutely at my disposal. And I tell you something else: the British are going to do the same. I want my naval operations to be in the charge of an American . . . How about it Bill? If you come with me, I'll make you a greater man than Nelson ever dreamed of being.[73]

'Brown Shoe' versus 'Black Shoe': Naval aviators wore khaki uniforms and 'brown shoes' while the traditional Navy officers wore blue and white uniforms with 'black shoes.' Vice-Admiral John Towers, who was the leading proponent of making the carrier the lynchpin of naval formations, a concept that only became fully accepted after *Pearl Harbor*, believed, given the shift to the importance of naval aviation, that *Central Pacific* command should go to a 'brown shoe,' preferably to himself. Towers had also been overlooked for Nimitz's job as CINPAC (Commander-in-Chief Pacific). He came to be seen by the 'black shoes' as a bitter, over-ambitious man. For the affable, popular and highly regarded Admiral Spruance, who got on well with even the most difficult people, Towers was the exception. Spruance wrote, "If you were not an admirer of Towers and did not play on his team your path was not made smooth if he could help it . . . Towers was a very ambitious man."[74]

However, Towers' views were strongly supported publicly by Halsey's Third Fleet carrier commander, Rear-Admiral Frederick Sherman, as well as Washington-based Admiral Harry Yarnell. Nimitz sharply upbraided Admiral Towers for his comments about Spruance's appointment as commander of the *Central Pacific* Force and insisted that he was the right man for the job; Towers subsequently wrote to Yarnell, his 'brown shoe' confederate, "To put it bluntly his [Nimitz's] reaction was to the effect that I did not know what I was talking about."[75] Ultimately Nimitz moved toward balancing 'black shoe' and 'brown shoe' commanders with the ruling that a 'black shoe' carrier commander would have to have a 'brown shoe' chief of staff and vice versa. Nimitz's adoption of this structure was not only politic but also reflected the fact that there were few high ranking 'brown shoe' officers in a fleet which had only built its first aircraft carrier, a converted 'oiler,' USS *Langley*, some thirty years earlier.

Vice-Admiral Towers's contribution to victory in the *Pacific War* has often been overlooked in post-war historiography. He managed an expansion of the Fleet Air Arm in the *Pacific* from a force of 2,000 to 39,000 aircraft over the course of the war. Unlike the Japanese, who quickly ran short of naval aviators after *Guadalcanal*, Towers' training programs provided a more than adequate stream of naval aviators who increasingly began to dominate the aerial engagements between Japan and America as the war progressed.

Operation FLINTLOCK: Onwards to the Marshall Islands: In spite of General MacArthur's attempted hijack of strategic control of the *Pacific* campaign by trying to have the US Navy's *Central Pacific* campaign aborted, the short-term furor over the casualty rates suffered at *Tarawa* did not impede Admirals Nimitz and Spruance. Albeit argued by MacArthur that Nimitz's Central Route was "time-consuming and expensive in our naval power and shipping."[76] it was a self-serving argument that flew in the face of the evidence. The Marines had jumped 2,500 miles from New Zealand to *Tarawa Island* at the cost of four days fighting. Australian soldiers and American GIs had taken almost a year and a half of almost continuous fighting to make the 300-mile journey from Port Moresby to Madang on New Guinea's northern coast.

Operation CARTWHEEL, had proved much more laborious, time consuming and costly in equipment and lives—albeit from MacArthur's point of view the lives lost were largely Australian and therefore more 'politically' expendable. It was also self-evident that the lines of supply by ship from the west coast of the United States to Nimitz's *Pacific* fleet and Marines (assuming 5,026 miles: San Diego to *Kwajalein Atoll*) was some 4,082 miles shorter than the roundabout route from the US to New Guinea via Australia (assuming 9,108 miles: San Diego in the US to Jayapura in New Guinea via Brisbane in Queensland, Australia). In mid-1943 the effective supply chain to MacArthur was almost double that of Nimitz's in distance with all the concomitant issues of increased dangers of Japanese submarines, increased cargo capacity requirements, timescale, flexibility of response to changing materials needs, and the Australian dockers' union problem.

In spite of his note given to Brigadier-General Frederick Osborn and MacArthur's sending of his Chief of Staff, Sutherland, to Washington to lobby the Joint Chiefs of Staff (after MacArthur had refused to go himself), they remained firm in their commitment to Nimitz's *Pacific* drive. It was a strategic decision demanded by logistical logic and strategy. The Air Force's objective to reach the *Marianas* in order to start bombing Japanese cities was just too important. Although not the major topic of the December 1943 Cairo Conference (codename SEXTANT) that ended just as *Tarawa Atoll* had been taken, the *Central Pacific* route was again confirmed as the main strategy to defeat Japan with Nimitz confirmed as its commander. A stake was finally driven through the heart of MacArthur's ambitions to take control of the war in the *Pacific*.

The next targets on the way to the *Marianas* were the *Marshall Islands*, which had been annexed from the German Empire during *World War I*. Japan had been rewarded with the mandate for the *Marshalls* at the *Treaty of Versailles* and had subsequently absorbed them into the Japanese Empire. In the intervening years the *Marshalls* had become out of bounds to non-Japanese and after 1938 all foreign ships had been banned. US intelligence had no idea about what was there until immediately before the US's amphibious attack when MAGIC intercepts gave some clues as to Japanese troops dispositions in the various *Marshall Island*s, which allowed them to leave some, such as *Wotje*, to 'wither on the vine.'

It had already been decided that the main target would be *Kwajalein Atoll*; its 380 square mile lagoon made it one of the largest in the world. While some, including Rear-Admiral Turner, questioned the risks of going straight to the 'heart' of the *Marshall Islands*, calling the move too aggressive and "dangerous and reckless," Nimitz and Spruance were adamant. However, lessons had been learnt from *Tarawa*. Spruance determined that *Kwajalein* would be struck with "violent, overwhelming force and swiftly applied."[77]

In fact Japan's defenses in the *Marshall*'s, prepared over ten years, were less well established than those on *Tarawa Atoll*. By January 1944 there were just 28,000 troops available to the regional commander, Vice-Admiral Masami Kobayashi, for the defense of the area. After the continued attacks on Rabaul and *Truk* by the US Navy and MacArthur's air chief Lieutenant-General Kenney, there was also very little air support. Rear-Admiral Monzo Akiyama had only prepared linear beach defenses on *Kwajalein*; the 'in-depth' bunkers and structures that had proved so effective for the defenders at *Tarawa* were entirely absent. In addition the 8,000 troops sent to defend the *Marshalls*, unlike the crack *Rikusentai* who had been sent to *Tarawa*, were mainly low grade, poorly trained soldiers, half of whom were not combat trained. Akiyama had also spread his assets thinly over a number of outlying atolls of the *Marshall* group including *Wotje*, *Mili*, *Jaluit* and *Maloelap*.

As planned, land-based bombers from *Tarawa* were able to inflict severe damage on the defensive assets of the *Marshalls* in preparation for the amphibious landings being prepared by Rear-Admiral Turner. Such was the tonnage of bombs dropped on *Kwajalein* that one observer reported, "The entire island looked as if it had been picked up to 20,000 feet and then dropped."[78] US aircraft carriers also carried out air raids. The airstrips at *Jaluit* and *Mili* were knocked out and during November 1943 and some 71 Japanese aircraft were shot down or destroyed on the ground.

Occupation of Majuro and the Battle of Roi-Namur: [Map: 30.3] The amphibious plans of Operation FLINTLOCK began to unfold at 11 p.m. on 30 January 1944 with the Twenty-seventh Army's capture of the lightly defended *Majuro Atoll* situated 190 miles southeast of *Kwajalein*. A single Imperial Japanese Army warrant officer was taken prisoner. By 9.50 a.m. *Majuro* was completely in US hands and could provide an advance airfield for an assault on *Kwajalein Atoll*. A ship service yard was quickly set up at *Majuro* though because of the destruction of Japan's air capability at *Kwajalein*, no US ships suffered any damage in the attack. Over the next year the hitherto remote backwater of *Majuro Atoll* would become the most active port in the world. A seaplane base on *Darrit Island* was soon made operational and within two weeks Seabees constructed an emergency 5,800-foot runway on *Dalop Island*. A 4,000-yard fighter airfield was also built on *Uliga Island* and a 35-mile causeway was built to link up *Majuro*'s islets. *Majuro* provided a huge natural harbor that became the US Navy's main forward anchorage and logistics base until the occupation and fitting out of *Ulithi Atoll* ten months later.

Majuro's neighbouring islands of *Roi-Namur* were also occupied on 31 January starting with *Enneubing Islet*; landing in amtracs the 4th Marines quickly overran the nineteen defenders. Through the day, the outlying islets of *Mellu, Obella, Ennubirr, Ennumennet* and *Ennugarret* were also occupied. Opposition was light with some 50 Japanese defenders killed in return for 1 Marine and 7 wounded.

On D+1 (Landing Day plus 1), 1 February, the Marines began the assault on the main island of *Roi*. A spotter plane revealed that Japanese troops were not taking the advantage of cover and Colonel Jones opined to Major-General Schmidt, "This is a pip."[79] The opposition was so light that the Marines and their supporting tanks began to run away uncontrolled over the island leaving defenders hidden behind their lines. Major-General Harry Schmidt was forced to call Colonel Jones to bring his troops back, "Can you control your tanks and bring them back to the O-1 Line [operation launch line] for a co-ordinated attack?"[80] The revisited assault only served to confuse the Japanese defenders who were quickly wiped out.

On D+2 Colonel Franklin Hart took on the occupation of *Namur* that lay across a sand-spit from *Roi*. Unlike *Roi*, the defenders on *Namur* provided stiff resistance. At one large concrete structure, unsuspecting Marines threw satchel charges into a building that turned out to be the main munitions dump. An enormous explosion sent black smoke 1,000 foot into the air and rained torpedo heads and debris all over the island. A Marine witness described the scene:

> An ink-black darkness spread over a large part of Namur such that the hand could not be seen in front of the face. Debris continued to fall for a considerable length of time which seemed unending to those in the area who were all unprotected from the huge chunks of concrete and steel thudding on the ground about them. Before the explosion,

the large blockhouse was conspicuously silhouetted against the skyline. After the explosion, nothing remained but a huge water-filled crater. Men were killed and wounded in small boats a considerable distance from the beach by the flying debris.[81]

The blast that left a 100-foot crater killed twenty Marines and left another 100 wounded. The Marine attack, supported by tanks, continued in the afternoon against Japanese troops well dug-in to trenches and protected by pillboxes. In one notable action, Lieutenant John Power flanked round the back of a pillbox and singlehandedly charged its backdoor. In spite of taking a bullet in the stomach he continued to storm the Japanese position firing into the pillbox. The pillbox was quickly taken but Power, pulled out by his colleagues, died a few minutes later. He was posthumously awarded the Medal of Honor.

The battle ended with a Japanese *banzai* charge from a pocket in the northern corner of the island that temporarily forced the Marines to pull back. During the action Private Richard Sorenson, trapped in a foxhole with six colleagues, threw himself on a Japanese grenade. Remarkably, Pharmacist's Mate Second-Class, James Kirby, who was tending to fifteen wounded Marines nearby, managed to tie Sorenson's severed artery and saved his life. Sorenson lived and received a Medal of Honor while Kirby was given a Bronze Star. Another Medal of Honor, the fourth awarded in the battle, was given to Lieutenant-Colonel Aquilla Dyess who was killed by a machine gun as he led an attack on a last Japanese position.

On 12 February a second massive explosion, this time on *Roi*, also caused significant casualties after a Japanese air attack hit on an American munitions dump. War correspondent Bernard Redmond, who was attached with the Seabees, reported, "Tracer ammunition lit up the sky as far as we could see and for a full half hour red-hot fragments rained from the sky like so many hailstones, burning and piercing the flesh when they hit . . . A jeep exploded in our faces a few yards away."[82] Although it was later estimated that the initial heavy bombardment of *Roi-Namur*, showing that lessons had been learnt from *Tarawa*, had killed at least 50 percent of the islands' defenders, the 4th Marines Division nevertheless suffered 172 dead and 547 wounded in this hard fought battle.

The Battle of Kwajalein and the Battle of Eniwetok: **[Map: 30.4]** Having learned their lesson from *Tarawa* where the naval bombardment lasted for just three hours, *Kwajalein* was saturated with naval shells for three days starting on 28 January 1944. This time armor-piercing shells were fired so that they broke into bunker defenses before exploding. After *Tarawa* Nimitz had ordered the creation of different types of Japanese pillbox and troop fortifications to aid the development of 'bunker-busting' shells and improve gunnery practice. By the time that the Army's 7th Division with 41,000 available troops, landed on *Kwajalein*, it was estimated that only 1,500 of the 5,000 defenders were still left alive.

British Royal Navy observer Anthony Kimmins watched the American bombardment with amazement: "Nothing could have lived through that sea and air bombardment," he recalled, "[The bombardment] was the most damaging thing I have ever seen. [Ashore] I have never seen such a shambles in my life. As you got ashore the beach was a mass of highly colored fish that had been thrown up there by nearby explosions."[83]

Other lessons from *Tarawa Atoll* included the need for more amtracs rather than Higgins boats to get the troops ashore; Congress rushed through a bill for the increased building of amtracs. Before Tarawa Rear-Admiral Turner had doubted the need for amtracs; an infuriated Holland Smith had replied, "I'm telling you straight out, Admiral, either produce a 100 amtracs or the deal's off."[84] It was one of their many colorful exchanges during the *Pacific War*. Fifty amtracs were rushed forward from *Samoa* and a further 100 amtracs designated for the Marines lying in San Diego, which could not be brought in time for *Tarawa*, were made available for *Kwajalein*.

Training of backup unit commanders was also improved to enable the passing on of leadership duties when officers were killed or wounded. Many Marines who served at the *Battle of Tarawa* were sent back to the US to become trainers of new or untested units. Moreover it was learned that backpacks were too heavy for Marines to carry into battle; at *Tarawa* they had been discarded. However, carrying an entrenching tool was considered essential. Meanwhile, Major Henry Crowe of the 2nd Marines also suggested in his battle report, "an armored bulldozer would be ideal for closing over small pillboxes."[85] It was an idea that would be taken up later at the *Battle of Iwo Jima*. Waterproofing of radio transmitters was also recommended. On the positive side it was reported, "the men are very enthusiastic about the M-1 [Garand semi-automatic]."[86] Furthermore Lieutenant-Colonel Kenneth McCleod also noted, "I found also that Benzedrine [bennies] tablets came in quite handy."[87] Being able to keep awake for days on end had been essential on *Tarawa*.

Many of the improvements and innovations suggested in the collated reports of the commanders at *Tarawa* were brought to bear at *Kwajalein* and other amphibious landings of the *Pacific War*. Although the Japanese defenders fought bravely over a four-day period, the outcome of the battle was never in doubt. The relatively slow advance of the US Army's 7th Infantry Division against a weakened enemy reflected their more conservative tactics of moving forward only after an artillery barrage. By contrast the Marines would tend to attack on the run to keep the Japanese defenders off-guard.

As at *Roi-Namur*, the attack launched by the Marines started with the smaller atolls of the island adjacent to the main island of *Kwajalein*. Just 2.5 miles long and 800 yards wide, *Kwajalein* was invaded on D+1, by Major-General Holland Smith's V Amphibious Corps, comprising 7th Infantry Division, led by Major-General Charles Corlett. Casualties on D-Day were light with twenty-one killed and eighty-seven wounded. However, heavy fighting erupted for the next three days as US forces cornered more-experienced Japanese troops, the Imperial Japanese Army's 2nd Mobile Division and units from the Japanese Special Naval Landing Forces. The US Army troops were shocked by the occasionally primitive defense of the Japanese defenders. One platoon was assaulted by a hundred Japanese troops carrying six-foot spears. The US commander in his official report laconically observed, "Their appearance suggests that they would be effective if the soldiers using them could get close enough to the enemy."[88]

The 7th Infantry Division's loss of life at *Kwajalein Atoll* was 176 killed and 767 wounded, less than a fifth of that of *Tarawa*. Out of the total Japanese garrison of 8,000 (including 3,000 Korean laborers) there were just 130 survivors. Apart from the rapid and overwhelming victory, an added bonus for the US forces was the capturing of the current hydrographic charts showing details of all of Japan's *Pacific* bases.

A gushing *Newsweek* magazine declared in its 14 February edition, "the US Navy won the most brilliant victory of the *Pacific War*."[89] This time overwhelming US force had worked. As Rear-Admiral Turner concluded, "Maybe we had too many ships for the job, but I prefer to do things that way. It saved a lot of lives."[90] The US could afford such largesse. Before the attacks on the *Marshalls*, Secretary of State for the Navy, Frank Knox, announced that in just eleven months, the United States had built 419 combat ships, thereby doubling the size of the US Navy. Productivity gains had been astonishing; output of naval tonnage had increased 250 percent versus an increase in labor of just 30 percent.

On 17 February Spruance launched another amphibious invasion of the most northeasterly of the *Marshall Islands*' garrisoned atolls at *Eniwetok*. Defended by the 1st Amphibious Brigade led by Major-General Yoshimi Nishida, a fierce defense was put up by the Japanese garrison and it took four days for the 22nd Marine Regiment and the 106th Infantry to subdue the main island of *Engebi*. Shorter work was made of *Parry Island* that took just a day to control. American forces took 879 casualties (275 dead). Again Japanese losses were startling. Out of 3,380 Japanese troops and laborers, just 16 soldiers and 48 laborers survived.

In Tokyo there was shock and incomprehension at the speed and 'low cost' of the US victory in the *Marshall Islands*. The implications for Japan's future were dire. As Ichiro Koyose, permanent Director of Japan's Imperial Rule Association said in an address, "The Marshall Islands are the front-porch entrance to Tokyo . . . The enemy is probably finally thinking of some such thing as bombing Tokyo in deadly earnest . . ."[91]

Operation HAILSTONE: The Destruction of Japan's Main Pacific Garrison at Truk Atoll: **[Map: 30.5]** With the conquest of the *Marshall Islands* complete, Nimitz did indeed turn his thoughts to bombing. However, the immediate target was *Truk Atoll* in the *Caroline Islands* of Micronesia, not Japan. *Truk*, which had become part of the Japanese Empire after the *Treaty of Versailles*, lay some 600 miles to the west of *Kwajalein* and was often described as an equivalent to Britain's *Gibraltar* or America's *Pearl Harbor*. A large atoll with numbers of sizeable islands within its compass, *Truk* served as the forward anchorage of the Japanese combined fleet in the *Pacific Ocean*. With five airfields, cargo terminals, docks, and service yards, the atoll was the heartbeat of Japan's perimeter defense.

It was assumed that *Truk* would remain an impregnable redoubt. However, after the rapid fall of *Kwajalein Atoll* and the *Marshall Islands*, Japanese Imperial Navy GHQ in Tokyo ordered the evacuation of the major capital ships from *Truk* on 12 February. Admiral Koga, commander of the Combined Fleet, duly sent his ships to the *Palau Islands* on the edge of the *Philippine Sea*. Following the death of Yamamoto, Japan's Combined Fleet had gone into its shell. In a whole year since the *Battle of Santa Cruz Islands*, Japanese aircraft carriers had not shown their faces in a combat zone. By comparison a reinforced US Navy, supplied with new carriers and surface vessels from America, was now not afraid to go head to head with an island fortress, even one as well provided with *matériel* as *Truk*. Leaving just a skeletal force of cruisers and destroyers, *Truk*'s defense rested in the hands of Japan's island air force against Vice-Admiral Marc 'Pete' Mitscher's advancing 'Fast Carrier Force,' Task Force 58, which was part of Admiral Raymond Spruance's Fifth Fleet.

Spruance was foiled in the attempt to catch the Japanese fleet at anchor. Nevertheless *Truk* remained a worthwhile target. A week after the Combined Fleet's departure, Nimitz authorised an attack with land-based bombers, surface forces and submarines, combined with dive-bombers and torpedo plane attacks from Vice-Admiral Marc Mitscher's fast carrier fleet, Task Force 58. Mitscher's force alone was able to deploy over 500 aircraft. Task Force 58 contained the cream of America's newly built fleet. It comprised five fleet carriers, USS *Essex*, USS *Yorktown*, USS *Intrepid*, USS *Enterprise*, USS *Bunker Hill*, as well as four light carriers, USS *Belleau Wood*, USS *Cabot*, USS *Monterey* and USS *Cowpens*, plus seven battleships and an armada of cruisers, destroyers and support vessels.

It was a measure of the US Navy's new confidence and a sign of the massive superiority now achieved by US aircraft in the air that they could contemplate an assault against Japan's legendary *South Pacific* fortress. The man put in charge of Task Force 58, Vice-Admiral Marc 'Pete' Mitscher, was the grandson of a German immigrant. Born in Hillsboro, Wisconsin before his family moved to Oklahoma in that state's land boom in 1889, his father was a federal Indian Agent who later became mayor of the city.

Mitscher entered the US Naval Academy at Annapolis in 1903. He was a mediocre student, graduating 113 out of 131. It was an inspired decision that guided him to choose aviation as early as 1915; a year later he became one of the Navy's first aviators. He subsequently became a pioneer in the development of aircraft carriers and was involved in the design of the USS *Saratoga*, the first purpose-built carrier, on which he served for three years. Mitscher landed the first aircraft on *Saratoga*'s decks. In 1941 Mitscher assumed command of the newly commissioned USS *Hornet* and participated in the Doolittle Raid under Vice-Admiral 'Bull' Halsey's command.

In April 1943, Halsey appointed Mitscher as Commander of Air Forces in the *Solomons* (COMAIRSOLS) where he oversaw all air operation in Halsey's advance up the *Solomons*. It was his most testing command. For Halsey however, he was the perfect man for the job: "I knew we'd probably catch hell from the Japs in the air," Halsey admitted. "That's why I sent Pete Mitscher up there. Pete was a fighting fool and I knew it."[92]

Tiny, wizened, taciturn and grumpy, Mitscher, wearing his lobsterman's cap to cover his bald pate, was hardly the likeliest figure to inspire. He shared Vice-Admiral 'Bull' Halsey's dislike of detail and the reading of official reports and preferred to get his information 'first hand.' He was a man who knew his own mind and often seemed oblivious to the advice of others. The Navy's pre-eminent fighter tactician, Commander John Thach, former Arkansas pheasant shooter turned one of the Navy's leading aviators, noted that Mitscher, "had his own convictions and he didn't see the need to hear from anybody else much."[93] Nevertheless the post-war consensus is that Mitscher was probably the most capable carrier fleet commander on either side. Mitscher would sit in a tall chair at the end of the flag-bridge; somewhat eccentrically, he would face the stern because he did not like the wind in his face. In spite of his oddities, Mitscher's successes won the respect of most of those who served under him. He was to become a highly popular commander; in particular to his pilots. He was a 'brown-shoe' Admiral who loved his aviators of whom he said: "You can train a combat pilot for fifty thousand dollars. But never, ever tell a pilot that. We can't buy pilots with money . . . each of these boys is captain of his own ship."[94]

Nevertheless, Operation HAILSTONE, the initiative to raid the legendarily formidable *Truk* in February 1944 was a leap of faith that shook many of his crew. As one seaman recalled, "They announced our destination over the loudspeaker once we were underway. It was *Truk*. I nearly jumped overboard."[95] Approaching *Truk* behind a storm front, Mitscher took *Truk* by surprise with a dawn attack. A total of 127 Japanese aircraft were shot down on 16 February. US carrier aircraft proved that they could now outmatch island airbases, thereby overthrowing the tactical orthodoxies of the early years of the *Pacific War*.

Eventually air and sea actions cost the Japanese 300 planes, *Truk*'s entire air defense. Every vessel in harbor was sunk by Mitscher's Task Force 58 including fourteen naval ships with an aggregate of 191,000 tons; naval vessels sunk included 3 light cruisers (*Agano, Kator* and *Naka*), 6 destroyers (*Oite, Fumizuki, Maikaze, Hagio, Isogu* and *Tachikaze*), 2 submarines, and sundry naval craft. In addition 32 transports and merchant ships were destroyed. Vice-Admiral Masami Kobayashi's still substantial fleet had disappeared beneath the waves. *Truk Lagoon* (*Chuuk*) has subsequently become "one of the world's greatest wreck dives."[96] On land virtually every installation on *Truk* was wrecked including gas and munitions dumps, hangars, barracks, airstrips, revetments and gun emplacements.

A Japanese force of 27,000 troops was left high, dry and useless. As damaging from Japan's viewpoint as the tonnage sunk, little of the cargo and few of the soldiers from troop ships were rescued. Vast quantities of *matériel* for Japan's *Pacific* Island garrisons were sunk and irrecoverable. It was a crushing victory and one for which the US paid a small price with just 40 men killed and 25 planes lost. Damage to Task Force 58 was minimal; USS *Intrepid* sustained some damage and returned to the west coast of America for repair, while the battleship, USS *Iowa* took a bomb hit. In return *Truk*'s once proud garrison, previously considered the rock of Japan's *Pacific* defenses, was reduced to impotence. Nimitz could afford to bypass it and did so.

Raids on the Marianas and Palau: **[Map: 30.6]** With *Truk* in ruins, Admiral Mitscher's Task Force 58 refueled. By 1944, fleet refueling had developed into a slick operation; carriers, battleships, cruisers filed through a designated seventy-five by twenty-five mile area and hooked up with oilers via heavy hoses hoisted between the ships. Steaming side by side, 20–70 foot apart, tankers would replenish accompanying warships. Meanwhile transport carriers, CVEs (designation for Aircraft Carrier, Escort), of which the US built 122 during the course of *World War II*, catapulted planes from their short decks; the replacement aircraft would be flown by pilots to replenish the fleet-carriers with the aircraft, and crews that they had lost at *Truk*.

CVEs (Aircraft Carrier, Escort), typically half the length and one-third the dead weight of fleet carriers were built on cargo vessel hulls and were slow moving, generally making less than twenty knots. They should not to be confused with light-carriers, CVLs (designation for Aircraft Carrier, Light) that were designed for fleet action. Transport carriers were the 'fetch and carry' vessels that enabled the US to sustain its fleet-carrier strikes force at the required vast distances from the United States. It was a logistical capability that the Imperial Japanese Navy could only dream of possessing.

Having replenished his Task Force, Mitscher pressed forward with two fleet-carriers, USS *Enterprise* and USS *Yorktown*, under Rear-Admiral Joseph 'Jocko' Clark, to raid the *Marianas*. Operation CHERRY TREE, named in honor of George Washington, would launch air raids on the airfields of *Saipan, Guam, Tinian* and *Rota*: "I cannot tell a lie," Mitscher announced to his crews, "D-Day is Washington's birthday. Let's chop down a few Nip cherry trees."[97] As Mitscher's USS *Yorktown* approached the *Marianas* on 22 February 1944, a dawn attack was launched by a formation of 'Jills,' 'Judys' and 'Bettys.' Half were shot down without a hit on any of his ships. Vice-Admiral Kakuji Katuta, operating from his HQ on *Tinian*, sent another wave of bombers. The gunners on the light-carrier USS *Belleau Wood* destroyed the Japanese torpedo bombers, which had evaded the covering Hellcats.

In addition to hitting the island's airfield, Mitscher planned to photograph the four main *Marianas Islands* that Nimitz intended to invade later in the year. Airfields and beaches were of particular interest. After the war the Japanese admitted that Mitscher's raid on the *Marianas* destroyed 168 aircraft. However, the photographs taken by Lieutenant Commander Edgar Stebbins in his specially converted Avenger were the greater prize. A jubilant Mitscher sent a message to his crews, "we expected a fight; we had a fight; we won a fight. I am proud to state that I firmly believe that this force can knock Hell out of the Japan anywhere, any time ... I give you a stupendous Well Done!"[98] From here Mitscher drove on to 'knock Hell' out of Hollandia, the major Japanese port and logistical center on New Guinea's northern coast for the benefit of General Douglas MacArthur. **[See Chapter 29: Jump to Hollandia: MacArthur's Greatest Victory]**

The raids brought back useful intelligence for future landings but also showed, for reasons of America's rapid improvement in fighter aircraft and pilot training, that US aircraft carriers now completely outmatched the land-based aircraft put up by the

Japanese. In effect the raid proved that the US could now enjoy unfettered command of the *Pacific Ocean*. Mitscher would later tell Captain Luis de Florez, the noted aeronautics engineer, "We'll go in and take it on the chin. We'll swap punches with them. I know I'll have losses, but I am stronger than they are . . . I don't give a damn now if they do spot me. I can go anywhere and nobody can stop me. If I go in and destroy all their aircraft, their damn island is no good to them anyhow."[99]

At the end of March, Spruance's Fifth Fleet set out from *Majuro Atoll* (*Marshall Islands*) and moved west to raid the island garrisons of *Peleliu* and *Babelthuap* that lay off the southern edge of the *Philippine Sea*. Spruance feinted south to confuse Admiral Koga and then moved rapidly to the west on the evening of 29 March to catch him unawares at dawn the next morning. Although Koga's Second Fleet, with Vice-Admiral Kurita at its head, had vanished, Spruance's aircraft still found plenty of targets to occupy themselves. Sixty ships of an aggregate 104,000 tons were attacked and sunk, including destroyers and oilers. Many other ships were damaged. US flyers reported the shooting down of ninety-three enemy aircraft with many more destroyed on the ground.

Numbers of Japanese ships made their escape in spite of channels being blocked by mines dropped by pilots from USS *Enterprise*. *Musashi* was one of the ships that escaped and although the US submarine, USS *Tullibee*, managed to score two hits, they were brushed off by the behemoth Japanese battleship seemingly with no effect on her speed. The *Tullibee* was less fortunate; one of her own Mark XIV torpedoes circled back in a great arc and sank her. All hands perished apart from a single lookout, Clifford Kuykendall, Gunners Mate 2nd Class, who was picked up by a Japanese destroyer after a night swimming alone in the *Pacific Ocean*. In all the raid cost 25 US airplanes downed; 26 pilots were rescued and 18 were lost. With *Palau*'s defenses thus beaten up, Task Group 58 set out to bombard *Ulithi, Yap* and *Woleai*.

History has tended to underplay the importance of Mitscher's carrier attacks on *Truk, Palau* and the *Marianas*. They were stunning victories and at the time Washington understood their importance. In recognition of his sequence of successes Spruance was given his fourth 'star' and promoted to full Admiral. Mitscher and Turner were promoted to Vice-Admiral and Holland Smith was promoted to Lieutenant-General.

Retreat to Mindanao, the Death of Admiral Koga and an Intelligence Coup: In the face of Mitscher's onslaught, Admiral Koga's Combined Fleet, yet to recover from the losses of its pilots in the northern *Solomons*, had had no choice other than retreat from the *Palau Islands*. Koga ordered the combined fleet to Davao, the main city of *Mindanao Island* in the southern Philippines, which was a further 600 miles to the west. Returning to an oil-starved Japan was not an option. The fuel-guzzling Combined Fleet needed to get close to the source of oil in the Dutch East Indies and *Borneo*. The defining major confrontation that would turn the war in their favor would have to wait. Leaving from *Palau*, Koga turned to his chief of staff, Rear-Admiral Shigeru Fukudome, and said, "Yamamoto died at exactly the right time," and added, "Let us go out and die together."[100] His wish was granted sooner than he might have expected.

On 31 March, on his way to Davao in the southern Philippines, Admiral Koga's plane, caught in a typhoon, crashed and killed all on board. Another plane carrying some of Koga's colleagues, including Vice-Admiral Shigeru Fukudome, went down off the Philippine island of *Cebu*. After a harrowing escape from his crashed flying boat, Fukudome was picked up by Filipino guerrillas while he was trying to swim to safety. He was brought to Lieutenant-Colonel James Cushing, formerly an engineer on the Philippines, who was organizing resistance on the island. Only the plane carrying communications, clerical staff and the secret codes arrived safely in *Cebu*.

However, following the crash of Fukudome's aircraft, Filipino shopkeeper, Pedro Gantuangoko, spotted a box floating offshore on 3 April and picked it up in his fishing boat. It contained a red leather briefcase carrying Z Plan. Fukudome assumed that the plan had sunk with the seaplane. By contrast an anxious Imperial Army HQ ordered *Cebu*'s commander Lieutenant-Colonel Seiiti Ohnisi to send troops to search the area for survivors and for the document box; interrogations resulted in Filipino villages being burnt to the ground. Hundreds of Filipino villagers were killed. Eventually a cornered James Cushing agreed to hand over his prisoners, Fukudome included, if Ohnisi promised to stop the killing of innocent civilians.

Thus, remarkably, Fukudome made it back to his own lines. However, a US submarine sent by General MacArthur picked up the Z Plan briefcase, which shopkeeper Pedro Gantuangoko had passed on to the Filipino guerrillas. As a cover story for the sending of a submarine, which was sure to be reported by the Japanese Army's Filipino informers, the mission picked up forty American men, women and children who were still on the island. Back in Brisbane, *nisei* operatives (second-generation Japanese-Americans) at the Allied Translator and Interpreter Service (ATIS), Yoshikazu 'Yosh' Yamada, a Hawaiian who later received a Legion of Merit award, and George 'Sankey' Yamashiro, translated the text that was then sent to Admiral Nimitz. Developed by Koga, Z Plan outlined the new strategy for the defense of the inner perimeter of islands around Japan as a means for drawing out the US fleet for a 'final showdown.' The plans were of considerable importance in helping Nimitz plan for the major naval engagement at the *Battle of the Philippines Sea*, often referred to as *The Great Marianas 'Turkey Shoot.'*

The importance given to the capture of Z Plan was such that after copies of all the documents were made, the original box and documents were returned from Australia to the Philippines by submarine and placed back in the wreck of the seaplane by American divers. It was probably the greatest intelligence coup of *World War II*.

Admiral King's Central Pacific Strategy Vindicated: If there were doubts, partly stirred by MacArthur, about the wisdom of King's *Central Pacific* campaign after the *Battle of Tarawa Atoll*—after the *Marshalls* campaign there were none. Having learnt the lessons of *Tarawa*, Nimitz's forces steamrollered the Japanese forces out of their outer perimeter island garrisons. It was a breathtaking demonstration of American industrial power and how to use it in its most efficient way through concentration of firepower. The island campaigns from *Tarawa* to *Eniwetok* had demonstrated either the paucity of MacArthur's strategic capabilities or the cynical political calculation of his motives for trying to derail Nimitz's *Central Pacific* thrust. Far from costing lives, Nimitz's island hopping campaign showed that immense 'mobile' firepower could be brought and concentrated rapidly across the *Pacific*'s vast battlefield. Huge gains in strategic 'real estate' were bought at relatively little cost (*Tarawa* excepted) in terms of American life, equipment and indeed time.

The Japanese Navy, without code breaking 'intelligence,' increasingly out-matched in the air by better planes, better-trained pilots and better tactics, and overwhelmed by a brand-new Navy produced in American shipyards since the outbreak of war, was ill equipped to compete. Japan's logistical capabilities, stretched to breaking point by the perimeter defense, originally designed by Admiral Yamamoto, simply broke down under the weight of Nimitz's onslaught. Meanwhile Japanese industry, increasingly strangled by its lack of capacity and raw materials was incapable of making up Japan's material losses, let alone compete with the build-up of US naval assets.

By contrast America's lines of supply, albeit longer than Japan's (5,026 miles: San Diego to *Kwajalein Atoll* versus 2,567 miles: Tokyo to *Kwajalein Atoll*), were increasingly secure because of their control of air and sea. At minimal cost the *Gilbert* and *Marshall*'s Campaign had punched through Japan's out-perimeter. By the time the *Battle of Eniwetok* had been won and the assault on *Truk* carried out by Mitscher's rapid carrier force, the *Gilbert* and *Marshall Islands* Campaign had shattered Japan's outer defensive perimeter and brought 800,000 square miles of the *Pacific* under US control. Japan's inner sanctuaries were now open to assault. The problem for the United States now was the inverse of the early years of the war. Japan's internal lines of supply were getting shorter while America's were getting longer. Were the US Navy and Army up to the challenge?

For Japan the rapid demise of its resistance in the *Central Pacific* was a profound shock that was capped by the death of yet another Commander in Chief of the Combined Fleet. After waiting nearly five weeks, the Imperial Japanese Navy announced the death of Admiral Koga on 3 May 1944. The following day, Admiral Seimu Toyoda assumed command as Chief of the Combined Fleet. Aware that US forces would be making further advances in the *Central Pacific*, he sent out a message (Combined Fleet Ultrasecret Dispatch 041213) to his commanders that was realistic in its historic analysis, over-optimistic in its forecasts, and constant in its call for a 'single event,' *Battle of Tsushima*-like war strategy. The message was bombastic in its tone:

> The war is drawing close to the lines vital to our national defense. The issue of our national existence is unprecedentedly serious, an unprecedented opportunity exists for deciding who shall be victorious and who defeated . . . We must achieve our objectives by crushing with one stroke the nucleus of the great enemy concentration of forces, thereby reversing the war

situation, and, together with our armies, shifting directly to the offensive . . . our entire forces, united in our noble cause, fighting to the death, will destroy the enemy who enjoys the luxury of material resources. Realizing the gravity of responsibility for the fate of our Empire, with its history of more than 2,600 years, full of reverence for the glory of the Imperial Throne and trusting in the help of God, I will endeavor to comply with the Emperor's wishes . . .[101]

Part VI

Japan's Forces of Empire Annihilated: June 1944–February 1945

31 The Great Marianas 'Turkey Shoot' (Battle of the Philippine Sea)

[February 1944–June 1944]

[Maps: 31.1, 31.2, 31.3, 31.4]

The Navy's Strategic Plan for the Marianas: Successes in the *Gilberts, Marshalls* and *Carolines* left Nimitz's forces strung across a long line of islands in the *Central Pacific*. Thus far the advance toward Japan, as a result of America's victory in the air in the *South Pacific* and *Central Pacific* areas, had been unimpeded by Japan's Combined Fleet. That pacificity could not be expected to continue as Nimitz embarked on the next stage of his advance toward Japan. From the start of the war the occupation of the *Marianas Islands* (*Saipan, Guam, Rota* and *Tinian*) had been Admiral King's prime target for Nimitz's sweep through the *Central Pacific*. King saw them as the essential location for naval and airfield bases from which an attack could be launched on *Formosa* and then southern China. From here the Navy would be able to apply the economic strangulation of Japan that King and others believed would force Japan to surrender.

Even within the US Navy, the *Marianas* strategy did not necessarily carry unanimous support. Vice-Admiral Raymond Spruance had, since his victory at *Midway*, become, along with Halsey, the Navy's highest profile combat commander, and preferred to stay silent or neutral on plans of broader strategy. However, his Chief of Staff, Captain Carl Moore, forwarded a strategic paper that advanced the proposal that the capture of *Truk* and the *Marianas* was a potentially costly distraction from the strategic priority of getting to the coast of southern China. Turning Japanese logic on its head, Moore argued that the garrison at *Truk* was a logistical liability rather than an asset to Japan because it would need to be resupplied by sea. Similarly he argued that the *Marianas* were an unnecessary diversion. Spruance, a close friend of Moore, was happy to give his views a hearing. General Marshall, Chairman of the Joint Chiefs of Staff was also firmly opposed to the Navy's *Marianas* strategy. King and Nimitz agreed with the bypass of *Truk* but not the *Marianas*, which they believed were an essential logistical stepping stone to *Formosa*. However, whereas Admirals King, Nimitz and Spruance saw *Formosa* as the natural take-off point for the invasion of Japan, Marshall, in line with MacArthur's wishes, pressed for a military invasion of the Philippines and the use of the northern island of *Luzon* as the launch pad for the conquest of Japan. The Joint Chiefs of Staff did ultimately accept Moore's logic on the matter of bypassing *Truk*, but the contentious issue of whether to take the *Marianas* divided the Army and Navy.

General 'Hap' Arnold broke the strategic stalemate. Although the US Army Air Force was a division of the Army and nominally reported to Marshall, Arnold's long-term plan was to make the Air Force an independent service. He pinned his hopes on the development of the Boeing B-29 Superfortress that was designed specifically for the long-range bombing of Japan. Arnold had championed its development immediately after *Pearl Harbor*. When it was clear that the Superfortress, designed to have a 'there-and-back' range of 6,000 miles, would become available by 1944 as a result of a fast-track development process, Arnold came down strongly in favor of an assault on the *Marianas* from where he would be able to base his bombers. Given the cost of the Superfortress program, at US$2.0bn in 1944 prices, by far the most expensive single weapons system of *World War II*, there was a self-justifying logic to the implementation of a strategy that would enable its use. Albeit for different reasons therefore, both the Navy and Air Force wanted to take the Marianas. While the Air Force wanted them as a base to bomb Japan, the Navy wanted them as stepping stones to Formosa. It was an alliance that Marshall and the Army were powerless to resist.

At the Combined Chiefs of Staff meeting at the Cairo Conference (codename SEXTANT) in December 1943, it was agreed after considerable wrangling that the *Marianas* would be targeted for invasion in October 1944—a date that would be brought forward after the decision to bypass *Truk*. In the meantime MacArthur's advance to the Philippines was also approved. Thus, to placate all sides a twin-pronged advance through the *Southwest Pacific* and *Central Pacific* by MacArthur and Nimitz respectively was planned for 1944—a competitive race to get to *Luzon* and the *Marianas* had been set up.

Japan Prepares for a Naval Showdown: [Maps: A.1, B.3, B.4] For Admiral Koga, before his death, and for Japan's planners on the Imperial Navy's General Staff, the raids by Admiral Spruance and Mitscher had been an alarm call. The raids on Hollandia (New Guinea) and *Palaus* indicated that US strategy would involve a thrust northwards by MacArthur toward the Philippines. However, Spruance's rampage through the *Central Pacific* alerted Japan's commanders that the *Marianas*, the last line of the inner perimeter defense, was also liable to attack. *Saipan* was lightly defended by comparison with *Truk*. Mitscher's raids had highlighted the importance of *Saipan, Guam* and *Tinian* and their lack of preparedness. As Vice-Chief of Staff Admiral Shimada warned Tojo on 18 June 1944, "If we ever lose *Saipan*, repeated air attacks on Tokyo will follow. No matter what it takes, we have to hold there."[1] Admiral Soemu Toyoda, Koga's successor, and the Imperial Navy GHQ had suddenly become aware that Japan's "absolute national defense line"[2] was in peril.

In February 1944, Admiral Koga had flown to Japan for meetings with the Imperial General Staff. Urgent measures were put in place to provide air reinforcements throughout the remaining *Pacific* chain of garrisons. Requests to beef up military and civilian defenses on *Saipan* were also made. Time was short and cargo ships in shorter supply still. Nevertheless 30,000 Japanese troops were transferred from Manchuria.

The cost of supply to the *Marianas* was rising. By autumn 1943, having solved their torpedo problems, US submarines' 'kills' of Japanese merchantmen were increasing rapidly. **[See Appendix A: Submarines: America Draws Tight the Noose]** More and better submarines, as well as more experienced commanders, were starting to wreak havoc on Japanese shipping. Perhaps most importantly the problem of the Mark XIV torpedo's exploder-head malfunction had been solved. The now busy route between the *Ryuku Islands* (*Okinawa*) and *Saipan* soon attracted the attention of American submarines. On 29 February USS *Trout*, subsequently lost, sank a troop transport bound for *Saipan* from *Formosa*; the 7,100 ton *Sakito Maru* went down with 4,000 soldiers. On 21 May, Captain L. N. Blair led out a team of submarines (USS *Pilotfish*, USS *Pintado* and USS *Shark II*) from *Midway Island*; collectively the team was known as 'Blair's Blasters.' Increasingly US submarines patrolled in wolf-pack groups of three or four; other prominent wolf-packs were the 'Fins' and the 'Pirates.' The change in operating procedure reflected a number of factors. The management of submarine strategies and targets was becoming more professional and was moving away from the lone-wolf romanticism of the early submarine commanders. Submarine operations were increasingly synchronized with fleet operations or intelligence reports on Japanese convoy or fleet movements.

In addition to better tactics and operating procedures an increasing number of US submarines were being produced and delivered to the *Pacific* theater. Thus the not inconsiderable tally of 57 Japanese merchant ships sunk by US submarines in the first quarter of 1943 rose to 136 in the first quarter of 1944. To combat this threat, by 1944 Japan was getting better at organizing convoys with protecting escort destroyers. Wolf-packs were a counter-response to these measures, which increased the chances of avoiding destroyers and getting away a spread of torpedoes.

Furthermore, as Japan's defense perimeter receded from the *Central Pacific* and from the *Solomons* and New Guinea, the 'pool' in which US submarines now operated was becoming increasing constricted. Coordination of US submarines into wolf-packs was a logical development. 'Blair's Blasters' began their operations at the beginning of June. On 2 June the USS *Pintado* sank a 4,700 ton cargo ship; USS *Shark* damaged another. Both submarines were homeward bound but caught up with a *Saipan*-headed convoy on 4 June. *Shark* and *Pintado* sank seven vessels with an aggregate of 24,000 tons. The action not only cost Japan precious ships but also the lives of 4,000 out of 10,000 troop reinforcements headed for *Saipan*. The remaining 6,000 troops arrived without arms, munitions or food supplies.

On the southern routes too, Admiral Toyoda's fleet supplies were taking casualties from US submarines. On 5 June, USS *Puffer* sank two of the Combined Fleet's oil tankers. On 6, 7, and 10 June, USS *Harder* logged the sinking of three Japanese destroyers as well as damage to two more. Commander Dealey informed General MacArthur that a force of three battleships supported by cruisers and destroyers, under the overall command of Admiral Ugaki was on its way to relieve *Biak*. Such was the pressure from US submarines that the fleet commander, Vice-Admiral Ozawa, was even forced to admit, ". . . in temporary recognition of need to bow before enemy submarine dispositions . . . decided to move anchorage to Guimaras on 13th."[3] The 6 foot 7 inches tall, moon-faced Vice-Admiral Jisaburo Ozawa was nicknamed *onigawara* (gargoyle) because of his famed ugliness. He had a compensating reputation for high intelligence. Born in Miyazaki Prefecture on *Kyushu Island*, the traditional breeding ground for naval officers, he had graduated forty-fifth (out of 179) in his naval class in 1909, two years after Admiral Spruance. In the interwar years he travelled extensively in Europe and America. In 1937 Ozawa served as Chief of Staff of the Combined Fleet. He was an early promoter of naval air power and in 1940 had innovated the tactic of using warships focused in support of carrier-based strike forces under a single command; it was a model subsequently copied by the US Navy. Both during and after the war he was considered by many to be Japan's finest naval commander. His refusal either to accept promotion to full Admiral or to sit on the Imperial Navy's general staff also indicates that he was far from being the greatest admirer of Japan's wars of aggression.

Admiral Toyoda, in common with the Imperial Navy's staff officers in Tokyo, still believed that the Americans' next main thrust would come in the *South Pacific* along the north coast of New Guinea. (Toyoda, like most of his fellow officers, were genuinely astonished that America had the capacity to conduct simultaneous offensive operations in New Guinea and through the *Central Pacific*). At the beginning of May, Toyoda set his strategy accordingly. On 3 May Toyoda issued secret operational orders from his flagship *Oyodo* in *Tokyo Bay*. "The Combined Fleet will direct its main operations in the area extending south of the Central Pacific to the north coast of New Guinea . . . it will destroy the enemy offensive strength, in particular the enemy task forces."[4]

The goal was for the US fleet to be lured into the *Ulithi-Palau* area. Toyoda suggested that by combining with Japan's land-based garrisons in the area (the *Marianas, Palau* and *Yap*) he could muster 598 land-based aircraft. With the Japanese carriers' ability to use their island bases to 'shuttle bomb' the US fleet, Toyoda expected to be able to deliver the knock-out blow sought by the Japanese Navy since *Pearl Harbor*. ('Shuttle bombing' meant that a Japanese strike squadron could in theory attack the US fleet, fly on to refuel and rearm at *Guam* or another island, and bomb again on the way back to their carriers—a perfect scenario which in theory gave two strikes for the price of one.) Even when a reconnaissance mission over *Majuro Atoll* in the Marshalls showed that Nimitz's fleet had left their anchorage, it was Toyoda's assumption that they were headed south to join up with MacArthur rather than north to attack *Saipan*.

Thus Toyoda confidently expected Nimitz to fall into his 'southern trap.'[5] Whether he truly believed that this could succeed, given the one-sided pasting that Spruance's Task Group 58 had given Japan's island garrisons in the first few months of the year, must be open to question. The major naval engagement had been expected at the end of May. Toyoda's forces gathered at *Taiwi-Taiwi*, an island off the northeastern tip of *Borneo* on 16 May. Any hope of secrecy quickly disappeared when submarine USS *Bonefish*, commanded by Commander Thomas Hogan, sank the destroyer *Inazuma* in the *Sulu Sea* between *Borneo* and the Philippines, and the following day happened across a Japanese carrier and accompanying fleet. Thereafter Toyoda's forces were tracked to *Taiwi-Taiwi*.

Toyoda's problems were not limited to the task of pitching his force against a US carrier fleet that he must have realized was significantly larger than his own. The Combined Fleet was running out of fuel. Although it was stationed outside *Singapore* so as to be close to the crude oil-producing East Indies and *Borneo*, the Combined Fleet had run out of refined oil. As Vice-Admiral Ozawa revealed in his post-war interrogation, "About two or three months before the Marianas Campaign we felt the shortage [of oil] very keenly."[6] Stockpiles had run down and the East Indies refinery capacity was inadequate. Toyoda was forced to order his fleet to take on *Borneo* oil that was pure enough to be taken from wells and light enough to be fed directly into his warships' oil tanks. It was a sweet crude, today known as Tapis, with a low viscosity and just 0.04 percent sulphur. The main disadvantage of taking on *Borneo* crude oil in its unrefined state was the level of highly inflammable gas that it gave off; it was a risk that Admiral Toyoda was forced to take.

The Bombing of the Marianas and Operation A-GO Set in Motion: [Map: 31.1] Toyoda was mistaken in his anticipation of the next American strategic thrust. US air carrier strikes began to beat down on the *Marianas Islands* of *Guam*, *Saipan* and *Tinian* from 12 June, less than a week after the Allies' Normandy landings in France. Nimitz's *Central Pacific* run, Operation FORAGER, had begun. On 12 June 1944, about 200 miles from *Guam*, Mitscher's carriers had turned into the wind and aircraft took off to attack the main airfields of the *Marianas*. Battle commenced with a dogfight over *Guam* in the early afternoon of 12 June. Hellcat fighters sent by the light carrier USS *Belleau Wood* came together with the Zeros stationed on *Guam* as well as incoming fighters and bombers from the other *Marianas Islands*. Eighty-one Zeros were destroyed on the ground and in the air at a cost of eleven Hellcats. The dual lasted for an hour with some thirty-five Japanese fighters shot down before the Hellcats were recalled to their carriers in response to radar contacts at 10.00 a.m., picking up an inward bound Japanese strike some 150 miles to the west. As well as damage to the airfields, the harbors of the *Marianas* were left with five cargo ships sunk, as well as a tanker and four escort destroyers.

In a subsequent mission an escaping Japanese convoy of twenty-one vessels, which had been spied 220 miles northwest of *Saipan*, was attacked with devastating effect. Eleven vessels with an aggregate 26,000 tons were sunk. Admiral Toyoda, commander of the Combined Fleet soon realized that these islands, not the south, would be the next main invasion target. With *Saipan* under bombardment by air and sea, at 5.55 p.m. on 13 June, Vice-Admiral Ozawa, whose Combined Fleet was under way crossing the *Sulu Sea* from *Taiwi-Taiwi* to *Guimaras* in the central Philippines, received Toyoda's message to prepare for Operation A-GO.

Two days later at 8.55 a.m. on 15 June, Admiral Toyoda sent a message to his fleet commander, Vice-Admiral Ozawa, "On the morning of 15th a strong enemy force began landing operations in the Saipan-Tinian area. The Combined Fleet will attack the enemy in the Marianas area and annihilate the invasion force. Activate A-GO Operation for decisive battle."[7]

However, Toyoda's failure to anticipate that the US's next move would be against *Saipan* rather than New Guinea, meant that most of Japan's 500 'inner perimeter' aircraft were stranded too far to the south; it had not helped that on 28 May, Toyoda had transferred 118 fighter planes and forty bombers from the Philippines and the *Central Pacific* to airfields at Vogelkop and the *Moluccas* to support the Japanese garrison at *Biak* (northern New Guinea). Thus the Japanese defenders on *Saipan*, from its 'unsinkable' airfields, had just fifty aircraft to ward off any American bombing attack—the remaining Japanese defense fighters had to be scrambled from airfields far and wide. Meanwhile, there was no possibility of re-supplying the *Marianas* either from Japan or with the forces committed to the *Caroline Islands* or *Palaus*. Of the initial attacks on the airbases on the *Marianas*, Rear-Admiral Alfred Montgomery would later write, ". . . the fact that there was no air opposition for the next three days may be attributed to the success of the initial sweep."[8]

Nevertheless, the Imperial Japanese Navy pressed forward with the plan for Ozawa's Combined Fleet to intercept the US fleet as it was pinned down to supporting its beach landings on *Saipan* on 15 June. At this stage of an island invasion, as supplies were brought ashore and as Seabee engineers raced to construct land-based facilities for the invading US Army, the US Navy's carrier force would be fixed in place; they would not be able to avoid a naval engagement if the Japanese Navy chose to take them on. The opportunity for a decisive encounter with the US Navy seemed to have arrived.

This was not what the US Navy was expecting. If the Japanese were surprised by the choice of the *Marianas* as their next attack, Admirals King, Nimitz and Spruance were surprised that the Japanese fleet came out to fight for them. Even as the Japanese fleet gathered at *Taiwi-Taiwi*, Nimitz and his staff did not believe that Japan would bring its Navy to dispute control of the *Marianas*. Rear-Admiral Turner, who planned the landings for Operation FORAGER had commented, ". . . the Japanese Fleet will not interfere with our operations plan against the *Marianas* . . . but will conserve their strength until a time when they can go into action in waters nearer their main bases."[9] With this presupposition in mind, Nimitz's orders to the main fleet were simply to "capture, occupy, and defend the *Marianas*."[10] Nimitz and Turner were wrong. As his fleet lay at *Taiwi-Taiwi*, Admiral Toyoda's thoughts were entirely aggressive. For the Imperial Navy, still seeking the defining total victory, the *Battle of Tsushima* event of the *Pacific War*, the US invasion of the *Marianas* presented them with their opportunity to annihilate the American carrier fleet and force them to negotiate a peace that would leave Japan's Asian Empire intact. Like his predecessors Toyoda hoped to lure the American Fleet, preferably south of the *Marianas* where a "decisive battle with full strength will be opened."[11]

Throughout the war Japanese officers remained obsessed by the idea of winning the war by destruction of US carriers; it was single-stranded strategy for victory. Indeed, Admiral Paul Wenneker, German naval *attaché* in Tokyo during the war noted, "The Japanese Navy thought always of the US carriers. They talked about how many were building, and how many were in the *Pacific* and that these must be sunk; but it was always the carriers they talked about."[12] By now Japanese fighter response from the islands was negligible. As the US forces began their bombardment of *Saipan* on 13 June, Admiral Toyoda ordered virtually the whole Japanese fleet to prepare for attack and the implementation of Operation A-GO. Toyoda told the departing fleet, "The destiny of our Empire lies in the outcome of this battle. Each member will fight to the end. . ."[13]

By 17 June the cream of the Imperial Japanese Navy was collected in the *Philippine Sea*. Four days earlier US submarine USS *Redfin* reported movement of major capital ships across the *Sulu Sea*. The Japanese fleet consisted of 5 fleet carriers, *Taiho, Shokaku, Zuikaku, Junyo* and *Hiyo* in addition to 4 four light carriers, *Ryuho, Chitose, Chiyoda* and *Zuiho*. The carrier fleet was supported by 5 battleships, *Yamato, Musashi, Kongo, Haruna* and *Nagato*, 19 cruisers and destroyers and 24 submarines. Then on 15 June, USS *Flying Fish*, under Commander R. D. Risser, spotted a carrier fleet off the *San Bernadino Strait* at the southern tip of *Luzon*. It was travelling eastwards about 1,260 miles from *Saipan*. On the same day USS *Seahorse* spotted Admiral Ugaki's force steaming northeast some 300 miles east of the *Surigao Straits*. This detachment, which had been sent to relieve Japan's forces fighting for their lives on *Biak* off the coast of New Guinea, had been recalled to join the Combined Fleet.

Fleet commander Vice-Admiral Ozawa ordered his ships to advance on the *Marianas*. Knowing Spruance, unlike Halsey, to be a cautious commander, he fully expected his American opponent to stay within a hundred miles of the amphibious landings at *Saipan*. However, with memories of the *Battle of Midway* when US carriers suddenly appeared from a surprise direction, Ozawa had concerns that an American carrier force might appear. For this reason he divided his carriers into two forces to allow his second division to lag behind and cover the possibility of being outflanked. Curiously Spruance stayed close to *Saipan* because he shared similar worries to Ozawa.

Late on 18 June, Nimitz's staff, having decoded Japanese communications, were able to inform him and Admiral Spruance, commander of the Fifth Fleet, that Ozawa's force was 600 miles to the southwest of *Saipan*. "The Japs are coming after us,"[14] Spruance told Rear-Admiral Turner whose forces were busily unloading themselves and their supplies on the beaches of *Saipan*. Aboard his flagship, the heavy cruiser USS *Indianapolis*, Spruance could view the vulnerable transports and requested Turner to move what he could further to the east; as for those that had to stay Spruance promised to "join up with Mitscher's Task Force 58 and try to keep the Japanese off your neck."[15] Spruance was quite clear that his primary task was to protect Turner's transports that he believed would be the primary target of the Imperial Japanese Navy's attack. It was a belief that was heightened by Rear-Admiral Turner's report that the Marines were facing heavy going trying to establish an extended beachhead on *Saipan*.

Spruance's battle plan had been simply expressed: "Our aircraft will first knock out enemy carriers as operating carriers . . . then will attack enemy battleships and cruisers to slow or disable them."[16] Vice-Admiral Charles Lockwood, COMSUBPAC (Pacific Area Submarine Commander) radioed his submarines to warn them, "Now that contact with enemy forces has been made, shoot first and report later."[17] Curiously there were no instructions made with regard to the possibility of a Japanese flanking operation to hit the landing transports, which was one of Spruance's main concerns. Spruance believed that Vice-Admiral Ozawa would advance his forces as close to *Saipan* as possible. In the event his assumption of Japanese strategy was misplaced. As ever Japan's primary focus was to destroy American carriers in a defining war-winning battle. Although outnumbered in carriers by 15 to 9 Ozawa believed that Japan's land-based aircrews would make up for the imbalance in carriers. Ozawa also guessed correctly that Spruance would stay close to the invasion forces.

Before the Japanese fleet arrived Admiral Spruance had time to launch a surprise carrier raid led by Rear-Admiral Joseph Clark's Task Group 58.1 against *Iwo Jima* on 16 June. An estimated sixty Japanese planes were destroyed and the airfields bombed, making sure that the *Marianas* could not in the short term be supplied from the north. Just four US planes were lost.

Avalanche of New US Navy Matériel: **[Map: 31.3]** The US Fifth Fleet that faced the advancing Imperial Navy was a vastly different creature than when the two navies had last fought a carrier battle at the *Santa Cruz Islands* in October 1942. In the first four carrier battles, the Japanese Navy's carriers had either matched or outnumbered their American opponents. At the *Battle of the Coral Sea*, the *Battle of Midway*, the *Battle of the Eastern Solomons* and the *Battle of Santa Cruz Islands*, the Imperial Navy had largely fought with America's pre-war *Pacific Ocean* navy. Eighteen months later it was an entirely different navy, a brand new US Navy that faced Ozawa.

Whereas Japan had added just one carrier, the *Taiho*, commissioned in March 1944, the US fleet had been transformed by the new *matériel* that had come on stream after the huge naval building plan planned in the *Two Oceans Act* [1940]. New Essex Class carriers included the USS *Essex* (December 1942), USS *Bunker Hill* (May 1943), USS *Lexington* (February 1943: replacement for the *Lexington* sunk at the *Battle of the Coral Sea*), USS *Yorktown* (April 1943: replacement for USS *Yorktown* sunk at the *Battle of Midway*), USS *Hornet* (November 1943: replacement for USS *Hornet* sunk at the *Battle of Santa Cruz Islands*) and USS *Wasp* (November 1943: replacement for the USS *Wasp* sunk by Japanese submarine September 1942). In addition to the six new Essex Class carriers, Admiral Spruance's fleet also had the battered old warhorse USS *Enterprise* (a Yorktown Class carrier) and eight Independence Class carriers.

Independence Class carriers were light-carriers developed in the immediate aftermath of *Pearl Harbor*. In an attempt to get carrier capacity on stream as quickly as possible it was proposed that existing cruiser hulls be converted into small light-carriers. (Independence Class carriers had 11,000 tons displacement and carried thirty-three aircraft versus the Essex Class, 27,000 tons and 100 aircraft.) Independence Class light-carriers differed significantly from escort carriers, which were little more than aircraft transporters, because their cruising speed allowed them to fight alongside fleet carriers. President Roosevelt intervened to authorize the Independence Class program in one of the few military interventions of his presidency. The Independence Class carriers came on stream at more or less the same time as the Essex Class; together they presented a formidable though untested new navy.

In addition to Spruance's 15 carriers, he was supported by 7 battleships, 79 cruisers/ destroyers, and 28 submarines. The *Great Marianas Turkey Shoot* (the *Battle of the Philippine Sea*), with 193 US and Japanese combatant ships involved, would be the third largest naval engagement of the steel-age after the *Battle of Leyte Gulf* (244 ships some four months later) and the *Battle of Jutland* (250 ships: in the *North Sea* in *World War I*). By comparison the largest naval battle in the European theater in *World War II* involved just thirty-eight ships (Italian and British) at the *Battle of Spartivento* in November 1940 in which no ships were sunk.

In terms of scale the *Great Marianas Turkey Shoot* dwarfed the four carrier battles that preceded it. At the *Battle of the Coral Sea*, the *Battle of Midway*, the *Battle of the Eastern Solomons*, and the *Battle of Santa Cruz Islands*, the largest carrier engagement involved 7 carriers at *Midway*; by comparison there were 24 carriers at the *Great Marianas Turkey Shoot*. It was, by a factor of almost 350 percent, the biggest carrier battle in history.

Spruance could put up 956 aircraft to just 450 Japanese carrier-based aircraft; in addition throughout the course of the battle the Japanese force was able to call on a total of 300 land-based aircraft. If the *Great Marianas Turkey Shoot* was taken simply as an air battle it would rank as by far the largest aerial engagement in US history. On a world scale the *Great Marianas Turkey Shoot* was the fourth largest aerial battle in history after the *Battle of Kursk* (4,800 aircraft), the *Battle of Britain* (4,500 aircraft) and the *Battle of St Mihiel* (2,000 aircraft: *World War I*). Arguably, if the invasion of *Saipan*, involving an amphibious armada of 524 ships carrying 71,000 soldiers, is added to the aerial and naval material engaged, the *Battle of the Philippine Sea* (*aka 'The Great Marianas Turkey Shoot'*) combined with the *Battle of Saipan* was the largest military-naval engagement in history.

Another peculiar feature of the *Great Marianas Turkey Shoot* was that unlike most of the great naval battles of history, it took place in the open sea and not close to land. Indeed it was remarkable that America was deploying its forces 2,500 miles from *Hawaii*, which itself stands 3,500 miles from the west coast of America; 6,000 miles in aggregate. The US Navy's advanced fleet base was at *Majuro* in the *Marshall Islands*, 1,800 miles southeast of *Saipan*. Meanwhile Ozawa had deployed his fleet, not from Japan, 800 miles from Saipan, but from *Taiwi-Taiwi* on *Borneo*, 1,890 miles distant from Saipan, because they needed to be close to their oil supply; in other words the 'home' fleet was deploying from a virtually identical distance to the US fleet. To put the distances in context, it is interesting to note that the entire engagement in Europe in *World War II* took place within a radius of 1,000 miles.

Advances in Radar, Flight Direction Operation, Computer Driven Anti-Aircraft Gun Systems: It was not just weight of forces that differentiated America's new *Pacific* fleet that appeared at the *Battle of the Philippine Sea*. The US Navy had made spectacular advances in radar which meant that Japanese strike forces could be engaged a long distance away from the carriers. Advances in command and control management were clearly evident during the battle and showed a huge upward learning curve compared to the chaotic US carrier performance at the *Battle of Santa Cruz Island* some eighteen months earlier.

By contrast Japanese radar remained poor, and judging by a post-war interrogation of Vice-Admiral Ozawa, their operators lacked training; after the war, when asked about radar on his ships, he responded, "All ships were equipped with radar, but I was very doubtful whether or not our men had mastered the use of radar."[18] To a subsequent question regarding US naval strengths, Ozawa informed his questioners, "The particular strength of your task force is the use of radar, interception of radio messages, and intercepting by radar of Japanese air attacks, which they can catch and destroy ['eat up'] whenever they want to. That is the strength."[19]

In September 1940, before America's entry into the war, Churchill had ordered that Britain's world-leading technology in Range and Direction Finding (RDF) radar should be transferred to the United States. At the end of that year, British scientists John Randall and Harry Boot of Birmingham University developed the cavity magnetron, a small device that produced microwave frequencies operating more efficiently in the 3–30 GHz waveband. Centimetric or microwaveband radar enabled screens to pick up small objects and was, atomic fusion a part, the most significant invention of the war. The radar technology transferred to the US by the Tizard Mission led to the creation of the Radiation Laboratory (RadLab) at Massachusetts Institute of Technology (MIT) in Boston that went on to produce over 100 different radar systems used in *World War II*. By 1944, the United States had a massive technological lead in radar, a technology that, in the form of SC and SK long-wave air search, was put to devastating use in the air battles of the *Great Marianas Turkey Shoot*.

By 1944 the Combat Information Center aboard a flagship had become the essential brain of any US Naval operation. Full of radio sets and glowing green radar screens, the Combat Information Center, a room sometimes called Radar Plot, had become the primary locus of tactical intelligence. In addition to the advanced radar sets produced by RadLab at Massachusetts Institute of Technology (MIT), the Flight Direction Officers also had four-channel VHF radio, a far more advanced system than that available to the Japanese and one that was difficult for the enemy to jam. The development of IFF Responders (Identification Friend or Foe) was also a new technological development that helped differentiate enemy bogeys from US aircraft without the need for visual identification.

It was in the Radar Plot room aboard US warships that the Navy's bright young men would log the ship's positions along with that of the rest of the fleet and coordinate radar and intelligence updates to be able to brief commanding Admirals on all possible data and battlefield scenarios. It was a high-tech world incomparable with the Navy's primitive systems at the outbreak of the war.

Japanese battle tactics never developed from the massed attack format, which worked well at the start of the war but proved too inflexible to deal with the huge improvements made in US radar as well as in command and control capability. The United States Navy and Imperial Japanese Navy both utilized standard analog mechanical ballistic computers during *World War II* for most of their cruiser and battleship applications. Fundamentally, both achieved the same task: calculating future target positions and generating gun orders to hit the target ship utilizing available input from such sources as the director, range-finding equipment, and gyros etc. It was *Aichi Tokei Denki* (Aichi Electric Clock Company) that produced Japan's first low angle analog computer in 1932, the Type-92 *Shagekiban*, which was based on models produced by Barr and Stroud of Glasgow in 1924.

During the war the automated weapons systems were more broadly adopted. The US Navy, with greater resources and backed by an established industrial base operating below capacity, was soon able to produce a more advanced fire control system, which was highly automated. The development of the US Mark-38 Gun Fire Control System (GFCS) reduced the number of operators to just one; by comparison Japan's Type-92 *Shagekiban* needed seven operators and the Type-94 *Sokutekiban* eight operators. Although Japan later developed a more advanced control system, the Type-98 *Hoiban*, which was put on the super-battleship *Yamato*, it still required a seven-man operating crew. The US Mark-38 GFCS was built around the Mark-8 Range-keeper, a stereoscopic rangefinder and radar that computed key data such as targets, gun orders, direction of travel and time of flight. The US Navy utilized the Mark-8 Range-keeper for all Iowa Class battleships as well as fitting the system on pre-war combat ships during refits. The reduction in operatives on the new US anti-aircraft systems made possible by advances in weapon automation was also a factor in allowing designers to put more guns on warships without overloading their ships with gun crews.

The brains of the whole system were provided by the Mark-1A Fire Control Computer, which was an electro-mechanical analogue-ballistic computer. During *World War II*, servomechanisms (power trains) were developed that allowed the guns to automatically steer to the range-keeper's commands with no manual intervention. The Mark-1 and Mark-1A analogue computers contained approximately twenty servomechanisms, mostly position servos, to minimize torque load. It was an integrated command and control automated gun system that provided accurate firing solutions for one or more gun mounts. The target could be static or moving and worked against targets on the surface (ships) or in the air (aircraft). By contrast the Japanese system needed human intervention, a team of seven skilled technicians who still had to make visual correction of shots. By 1944, when the Mark-1A Fire Control Computer system had been implemented on nearly all US combat ships, the American Navy achieved a significant technological advantage against the Imperial Japanese Navy in terms of accuracy of fire.

Work done at the Massachusetts Institute of Technology (MIT) further advanced the accuracy of anti-aircraft fire. Navy Gunner Lloyd Mustin and three Naval colleagues enrolled as graduate students at MIT's Electrical Engineering department where they studied under Dr. Harold Hazan, a pioneer in the development of servomechanisms, a means of amplifying low power signals to control heavy mechanisms. It was the key technology for the invention of automated mechanisms for anti-aircraft weapons.

Then Dr. Charles Draper, a pioneer in servo mechanisms and an adviser to Sperry Corp's gyroscopes and instrumentation division, turned his attention to anti-aircraft guns. Input came from US Navy gunners Mustin and Rivero, who made a compact size 'lead Computer' that hugely simplified 'aim and fire'. "The gunner would then have to make but one alignment, that of front and rear sights on the target, in order to have his gun correctly orientated to produce hits."[20] After graduating from MIT with a Master of Science degree, Mustin became an Assistant Production Officer at the Naval Gun Factory in Washington DC. As many as 80,000 units of Draper's gunsights were produced during the war. After serving as a gunnery officer on the cruiser USS *Atlanta*, Mustin went on to become Commander in Chief of gunnery and radar for Vice-Admiral Willis's Second Battleship Squadron. Mustin would eventually become a vice-admiral himself.

In spite of the advances brought by scientists and naval engineers, anti-aircraft automated fire control system still had limitations. Even with the wall of lead that carriers and the accompanying ring of defensive surface ships could put into the air by the end of 1944, the US Mark-38 system still needed a thousand 5-inch rounds to shoot down one aircraft. However, 'kills' were not the only benefit of anti-aircraft gunnery. As Japanese pilots testified, flying, aiming and releasing bombs or torpedoes was not easy while passing through an inferno of exploding shells. Fortunately for the US Navy, by 1944 America could afford to produce munitions in vast quantity and provide the supporting logistics.

A new cadre of young Flight Direction Officers (FDOs), many of them former Wall Street bankers, skilled in the utilization of the new technologies now pouring from US research laboratories onto the *Pacific* battlefield, had drastically changed the face of US naval performance. The recruitment and training of specialist personnel was one of the unheralded achievements of the wartime US Navy. In a matter of years America's civilian labor force was turned into an effective fighting force. As Ralph Clark, a Grumman Aircraft Engineering Co. field service employee noted, "We had shoe clerks building airplanes, we had shoe clerks repairing airplanes, and we had shoe clerks flying air-planes. That's not taking away from shoe-clerks, but 90 percent of the people involved in aviation had never touched an airplane before the war."[21]

Finding and using talent, sometimes bypassing the formal hierarchies, was critical to success. When Mitscher's Chief of Staff, Commodore Arleigh Burke, the 'black shoe' destroyer commander, who had been forced on Mitscher by Nimitz, noticed that a young reserve lieutenant was bypassing the chain of command to talk privately to the Admiral, he discovered that Charles Sims was a fluent Japanese linguist and cryptanalyst who could listen in to Japanese pilots real time conversations and interpret their tactics and plans. He also translated documents and interrogated Japanese prisoners.

In addition to better command and control technology, by 1944 US combat ships were fitted with the best anti-aircraft guns of *World War II*, including the US 5-inch/38 DP gun, the automatic 40 mm Bofors cannon and the light automatic 20 mm Oerlikon. *Werkzeug Maschinenfabric Oerlikon*, a Swiss company named after the Zurich suburb in which it was based, used a design originated by the German, Reinhold Becker, in 1914. Even the smallest caliber of US anti-aircraft weapons was fitted with computer guidance systems by the autumn of 1944. The 40 mm Bofors auto-cannon designed by AB Bofors in the 1930s was licensed to the United States where the Chrysler Motor Company produced 60,000 units plus 120,000 barrels by the end of 1943.

The US Navy's Bureau of Ordnance purchased a twin-mounted example that arrived for testing in New York in August 1940. The Bofors muzzle could produce a remarkable 19,000 revolutions per minute, enabling the gun to project a shell accurately for 7,500 foot. A year later, Chrysler signed contracts for licensed production at the bargain cost of US$600,000 (US$100,000 of which was never paid because Bofors never provided the two engineers that the contract promised). Consisting of 1,000 parts, Bofors component manufacture was spread over twelve Chrysler factories. In fact the trials of the Bofors had been so successful that America filched UK-specified designs and illegally began to manufacture 40 mm Bofors before licensing was formally agreed. Improvement by Chrysler in manufacturing techniques managed to halve the time it took to manufacture the Bofors; technical changes to the specifications also transformed the weapon and significantly improved its shipboard performance. The fire rate of 120 shells per minute was increased to 140 shells per minute. The 40 mm Bofors was just one example of the awesome competitive industrial edge possessed by America when it ramped up its war effort against Japan.

The US Navy was so enthralled by the weapon that whenever a Bofors shot down a Japanese plane, they posted the serial number of the successful gun direct to Chrysler. Carrier commander Admiral A. C. Davis even wired Chrysler to tell them, "It is not possible to tell you how gratifying it was to see the really wonderful control and performance of the entire installation."[22] In one battle a US battleship reported that its Bofors alone shot down thirty-two aircraft. The 40 mm Bofors anti-aircraft gun, the longest running weapon ever produced, is still in use today.

US Superiority in Aeronautics Technology and Combat Techniques: [Map: 31.4]

Technological changes were also evident in the air. The new Grumman F6F Hellcat was soon to prove itself the master of the Zero. Although it resembled the Wildcat in appearance the Hellcat was an all-new design; soon after *Pearl Harbor*, Roy Grumman and his co-designers worked closely with leading Wildcat fighter pilots and the Navy Bureau of Aeronautics to develop a fighter for the *Pacific* theater that was carrier-friendly and capable of taking on the Mitsubishi Zero.

Fitted with a 2,000 HP Pratt & Whitney engine (compared to the 1,200 HP Wildcat), the Hellcat demonstrated significantly improved performance with maximum speed increased from 320 to 380 mph. Combat range was improved by 115 miles to 945 miles;

the 'ceiling height' was also increased by 8 percent to over 34,000 foot. Perhaps most important was the Hellcat's rate of climb which increased to 3,500 feet per minute compared to 2,200 feet per minute for the Wildcat. In battle with the Zero, the Hellcat's faster speed in the dive and its ability to out-climb and fight from above was a significant advantage. Throughout the war American pilots learnt that it was unwise to stay and dogfight with a Zero. Once a Japanese pilot was on your tail, pilots would shove forward the joystick and dive at a speed of 300 plus mph. US fighters, unlike Zeros, retained aileron integrity at this speed and could make a rolling pull out that the Japanese could not follow.

Once in a position to fire, the Hellcat had six 0.50-inch Browning machine guns firing 400 rounds per minute. It was a weight of lead that the Zero could not match. As the report made after its trial concluded, "When attacking, use your superior power and high-speed performance to engage at the most favorable moment. To evade a Zero-52 on your tail, roll and dive away into a high-speed turn."[23] The importance of the US Navy's new carrier fighter was shown in the ratio of its kills to losses that amounted to 19:1 during the *Pacific War*. It scored some 5,163 kills in all and became by far the most successful Navy plane of the war.

The observations of fighter ace Ensign Edward Wendorf regarding the capability of the Hellcat versus the Zero are illuminating:

> Comparing the performance of the Hellcat versus the Zero, I feel that the Hellcat was by far the more durable of the two aircraft, due mainly to fact that the wing fuel tanks were self-sealing—a bullet or incendiary could pass through the wing tank, which would seal immediately without causing a fire or explosion—and because the pilot had a lead silhouette of armor protecting his backside. On the other hand, the Zero was faster and more maneuverable, thanks to the weight-saving features of not having the self-sealing fuel tanks and the armor plating protecting the pilot. This I think was a net disadvantage. A number of times in later fights I was outmaneuvered—the Zero turned inside me—and my plane was hit, but it was not disabled. By contrast, only a few rounds fired into the Zero usually resulted in the pilot being hit and the Zero crashing into the sea, or a fire starting and the airplane either burning or exploding. As an example of the ruggedness of the Hellcat, the plane that I flew back the day I was shot had three 37 mm holes, about seven 20 mm holes, and more than 250 7.7 mm bullet holes or small fragment holes from anti-aircraft fire. Several of the smaller fragment holes were in the

engine area, but the good old Pratt & Whitney continued
to purr right down to the time that I nosed-up on deck.[24]

The addition of the Vought F4U Corsair fighter-bomber also strengthened the fleet air arm. Although the Corsair, with its long nose, was a more difficult plane to land on carriers, it proved to be even faster than the Hellcat and was also able to out-climb the Zero, which was nearly always the decisive factor in their dogfight encounters. The Corsair achieved an 11:1 kill to loss ratio during the course of the war.

By comparison, the Imperial Japanese Navy was still operating aircraft that were pre-war designs including the Mitsubishi A6M Zero fighter, virtually unchanged since its introduction in July 1940. In the same year the Navy had introduced the Aichi D3A 'Val' dive-bomber, modeled on the German Heinkel He 70; it had large elliptical wings fitted with dive brakes and had a fixed undercarriage. Designed in the same generation as the German Stuka and the Douglas Dauntless, it was the match of both except in bomb load and range. Operationally it was a remarkably successful plane sinking more Allied ships than any other Axis aircraft in *World War II*. However, by 1944 it was outdated. Similarly the Nakajima B5N 'Kate,' with 230-mile speed and 880 kg load, was the world's best torpedo bomber at the start of the war. Moreover it could function in a multi-task role as a high-level bomber and reconnaissance plane. Nevertheless it was, by the standards of technological advance in the *Pacific War*, a vintage 1937 design by the start of Operation A-GO.

Even the replacements often lacked the modern technologies available to US aircraft at the start of the war. The 'Val's' replacement, the Aichi-built 'Judy' had long range but lacked self-sealing fuel tanks and armor plate. As for the Nakajima B6N 'Jill' replacement for the 'Kate,' its short wings and high landing speeds meant that it could only be used on longer fleet carriers. At the *Great Marianas Turkey Shoot* however, two-thirds of Ozawa's aircraft were of pre-war design—in wartime conditions of rapid technological advance, Japan's main attack arm had become obsolete.

Just as important as the improving quality of American equipment was the quality of their training and tactics. As early as mid-1942 Commander John Thach developed a defensive maneuver to combat the more agile Mitsubishi Zero. After it was successfully trialled at *Midway* where he served aboard USS *Yorktown*, by 1944 the 'Thach Weave' had become standard operating practice in the fleet air arm. Saburo Sakai recalled the reaction of Japanese pilots to the new American fighter tactic:

> For the first time Lieutenant-Commander Tadashi Nakajima encountered what was to become a famous double-team maneuver on the part of the enemy. Two Wildcats jumped on the commander's plane. He had no trouble in getting on the tail of an enemy fighter, but never had a chance to fire before the Grumman's teammate roared at him from the side. Nakajima was raging when he got back to Rabaul; he had been forced to dive and run for safety.[25]

Just as important as the 'Thach Weave' was the identification of the Zero's main weakness, which was it poor performance in the dive. The development of the 'Thach Weave' and other tactics by the US Navy air arm was a major factor in turning the balance of aerial battles hugely in their favour after 1943. Veteran pilot of actions in China, *Guadalcanal*, New Guinea, the Philippines and *Iwo Jima*, Lieutenant Kazuo Tsunoda, complained, "The American tactics were very practical and efficient. During the war I thought that the Americans were very sly. Their way of fighting was not fair, but their teamwork was very good."[26] US Navy ace Commander Scott McCuskey repaid the compliment when he noted: "I respect the Japanese pilots . . . They had some marvellous fliers but sometimes they didn't seem to have the team concept that we had."[27]

Lastly American commanders were now battle-seasoned professionals. In command of Operation FORAGER and the Fifth Fleet was Admiral Raymond Spruance, who according to Admiral King had an intellectual ability "unsurpassed among the flag officers of the United States Navy."[28] He was also brave. At the critical juncture at the *Battle of Midway*, it was Spruance who ordered the all-out attack on Nagumo's carriers, which carried the day.

By contrast to their American counterparts, Japanese pilot skill declined markedly after the *Battles of the 'Slot'* at *Guadalcanal*. Diminution in quality was already evident at the *Battle of Santa Cruz Island*. Before the war, naval aviator training lasted for three and a quarter years. By summer of 1944, pilots belonging to 601st Naval Air Group, manning the *Taiho, Shokaku* and *Zuikaku*, had just six months of training; however, this compared well with the pilots of *Chitose, Chiyoda* and *Zuiho* with just three months training, and just two months for the fliers on *Junyo, Hiyo* and *Ryuho*. Inexperience of flight crews was matched in many cases by poorly trained flight engineers and hangar operatives.

Commander Masatake Okumiya, a pilot from 58th Etajima Class in 1930 and an experienced aviator, was able to compare the *Midway* fleet commanders with those available at the *Battle of the Philippine Sea*: "In only the two short years . . . the average age of the senior group leaders had dropped by at least ten years. Unfortunately, too, the skill of the aircrews, which flew in the Marianas conflict, had deteriorated in direct proportion to the average reduced age of their commanding officers."[29]

US pilot Edward Wendorf's views also bear witness to the changing quality of the Japanese pilots that he faced:

> The abilities and caliber of the Japanese pilots I engaged also declined tremendously with the progression of the war. I speak only for our experience in VF-16, but I would expect it to compare with that of other squadrons operating at the same time. Early in the war, around Kwajalein, the Japanese pilots were extremely tough, and our kill ratio was only about 5:1. Later, around Truk, Palau, and Hollandia, our ratio grew to about 12:1. And

around the Marianas, VF-16 shot down an estimated twenty-five to thirty Japanese aircraft during that one-day "Turkey Shoot"—without losing a single plane or pilot to enemy aircraft. I feel sure that this was due to the attrition of first-rate Japanese pilots and Japan's inability to train replacements in an orderly manner.[30]

The Japanese Navy had failed to rotate experienced fliers into the training schools. Furthermore, practice for trainee pilots was constrained by lack of fuel and the inability of carriers to move from their secure anchorages.

US Naval Logistics and Operating Practices: By contrast to the increasing logjams in the Japanese logistics and infrastructure, the US Navy made vast strides in logistics and operations that gave American Navy commanders much more flexibility in movement. Important technological changes in fuelling techniques gave Mitscher's 'Fast Carrier Force' range and flexibility. Mitscher's operations officer, Captain Duke Hedding, while serving as Chief of Staff to Rear-Admiral Charles Pownall in 1943, had noted the inefficiency of 'at sea' fuelling. After the fall of the *Gilbert Islands*, it was decided that in future all refuelling would be done at sea rather than rotating groups 1,000 miles back to the *New Hebrides*. Inevitably the further that the US fleet moved away from its bases, the importance of fuel management increased significantly. Instead of tankers moving to fuel fast-moving warships, Hedding suggested that combat ships should go to the tankers acting effectively as static gas stations. "We all know how to fly formation. Let's set the tanker up there and just run the fuel lines across."[31] By 1945 the US Navy could keep its ships at sea for forty days compared to just twenty-one in the British Royal Navy.

Perhaps of greatest importance, and an area often overlooked, was the Navy's creation of the logistic networks that made major naval operations possible, eventually up to 6,000 miles from the west coast of America. Much of this capability was built by Vice-Admiral William Calhoun; he had graduated twelfth in class at the Annapolis Naval Academy along with officers who would become much better known, such as Bob Ghormley, Frank Fletcher, Jack Towers and John 'Slew' McCain. Calhoun's special skill was logistics. Over the course of the war, 'Uncle Bill' Calhoun's command would eventually grow to 455,000 men aboard 290 ships. Spruance would recall Calhoun's vital importance to the American Navy in the *Pacific* when he stated, "There was nothing the fleet wanted that Uncle Bill couldn't get."[32]

Calhoun managed the Service Squadrons (ServRon) that enabled the Pacific Navy to operate. ServRon-8 managed the transport of *matériel* from the west coast of America to *Majuro* and later *Ulithi*, ServRon-2 managed hospitals and repair ships, ServRon-12 managed harbors and port facilities. ServRon-6 meanwhile was created as a dedicated unit to support Spruance's 5th Fleet. Ammunition ships (AKSes) doubled up as general stores that each carried up to 5,000 inventory items out of the 40,000 items that might be required at any given time. Gasoline tankers were known as AOGs and AFs known as 'reefers' carried dry goods. **[See Appendix B: Oil, Raw Materials and Logistics: 'Just Start Swinging']**

The Great Marianas Turkey Shoot (The Battle of the Philippine Sea): [Map: 31.2] In spite of the US Navy's huge numerical superiority, Ozawa nevertheless had three potential advantages; first, sailing eastward against the prevailing winds, his fleet would be able to launch strike forces without having to reverse course; second, Japanese carrier planes had a 150-mile range advantage for scouting and a 100-mile range advantage for attack. This was the main disadvantage of America's more heavily armed and armored aircraft. Finally the Japanese air fleet, using the airfields in the *Marianas*, would be able to 'shuttle bomb' the Americans. Nevertheless Nimitz and all the US senior command had complete belief in their ability to deliver a crushing victory.

Spruance lined up his forces in five Task Groups in two lines west of *Saipan*. In the north of the most westerly line was placed Rear-Admiral William Harrill's Task Group 58.4 with just three carriers (fleet carrier USS *Essex*, and light carriers USS *Langley* and USS *Cowpens*). To his south lay the surface force Task Group 58.7 comprising seven fast battleships (USS *Washington*, USS *North Carolina*, USS *Indiana*, USS *Iowa*, USS *New Jersey*, USS *South Dakota* and USS *Alabama*). In the more easterly line, three further carrier groups lined up with Task Group 58.1 (fleet carriers, USS *Hornet*, and USS *Yorktown*, and light carriers USS *Belleau Wood* and USS *Bataan*) to the north, Task Group 58.3 (fleet carriers USS *Enterprise*, USS *Lexington*, and light carriers USS *San Jacinto* and USS *Princeton*) in the middle and furthest south Task Group 58.2 (fleet carriers USS *Bunker Hill*, USS *Wasp*, and light carriers USS *Cabot* and USS *Monterey*). Spruance's Task Group commander was Vice-Admiral Marc Mitscher aboard the fleet carrier USS *Lexington*.

Backing up Admiral Spruance's Fifth Fleet carrier force were thirteen escort carriers carrying 301 planes. The carrier fleet was also screened by 7 battleships, 7 heavy and 5 light cruisers, 94 destroyers, 28 destroyer escorts and 2 new command ships carrying the latest communications technology; one of these was the USS *Rocky Mount*. In addition to surface craft, 48 submarines were assigned to cover Operation FORAGER. These included USS *Albacore*, USS *Stingray*, USS *Finback* and USS *Bang*, which acted as screening 'lookouts' for Spruance's carrier force.

On 17 June, Vice-Admiral Kakuta on *Saipan* launched land-based air attacks from *Truk* and *Yap* on Rear-Admiral Turner's landing forces. Although some damage was done to service vessels and one landing craft had to be scuttled, there were just thirty US casualties.

As the two fleets came within range on 18 June, Ozawa's Japanese bogeys, with their much longer range than US aircraft, were seen to have spotted Task Force 58, while US reconnaissance aircraft could not find Ozawa's fleet. For the time being Ozawa knew more than Spruance. Ozawa was within range but, because it was late in the day, would have to risk making a night attack. To the great disappointment of his aircrews, the strike sent out by Rear-Admiral Sueo Obayashi from the carrier *Chiyoda* of the 3rd Carrier Division to hit Spruance's Fifth Fleet that evening was recalled. Ozawa deemed a night attack too risky, and therefore turned south in the night so as to keep the distance advantage enjoyed by his aircraft for the morning. Ozawa had no intention of charging pell-mell toward *Saipan*; he intended to fight Spruance at arm's length, a range at which his aircraft's superior range could be made to count without risking his own ships. He told his subordinates, "I will pound the American fleet with carrier-based planes, land-based bombers, and the guns of my surface vessels. I will give them no time to counter-attack."[33]

The officers of the Japanese carrier force were probably completely unaware of the remarkable technical and training advances, not to mention quantitative additions, made by the American fleet since their last carrier encounter at the *Battle of the Santa Cruz Islands*. The Imperial Japanese Navy had won the tactical duel at that battle and Ozawa's officers were uniformly confident that history would repeat itself. Commander Masatake Okumiya reflected, "We had never assembled in one striking force so much carrier aviation, and our pilots were convinced that they would shatter the attacking American fleet."[34] Similarly, the carrier *Hiyo*'s captain, Toshiyuki Yokoi, recalled, "We were completely undetected, we were sure of it; sure also we would sight the American fleet before it sighted us, and destroy it. Fighting morale was at fever pitch from the supreme commander right down to the lowest mess hand."[35]

Privately some officers had doubts. Lieutenant Zenji Abe was one of the dwindling group of aviators who had fought at *Pearl Harbor*. He later admitted to his nervousness about the air arm's lack of training. Practice had been virtually non-existent in the weeks leading up to the advance on *Saipan*; he complained, "This unbelievable situation was causing various disadvantages in service to our aircraft and capability of the pilots."[36] Reconnaissance pilots were raw recruits and lacked practice in using their radio sets or even to test their reliability. New radar sets were later described as totally unusable.

Later on the evening of 18 June, Nimitz's powerful Huff-Duff radio direction finders picked up radio messages from Ozawa's Combined Fleet; it placed them 300 miles southwest of Spruance's Task Groups. Spruance was notified at 10.00 p.m. However, a garbled message from USS *Stingray* suggested to Spruance that Ozawa was perhaps less than 200 miles distant although this later turned out to be a mistake. At 11.30 p.m. Vice-Admiral Mitscher, commander of Task Force 58, sent Spruance an urgent message asking for permission to advance westward in order to meet Ozawa's fleet that he intended to engage in an aircraft strike to be launched at dawn on 19 June. After an hour's consideration Spruance blocked Mitscher's request and ordered him to stay on station protecting *Saipan*. Mitscher's tactics would have had the added advantage of avoiding 'shuttle-bombing' by the Japanese carrier strike force. However, Spruance could argue in return that by keeping his carriers close to *Guam*, he could keep the Japanese airfield there unusable and unable to sustain 'shuttle-bombing.' As he pointed out, "The use of enemy airfields on *Guam* and *Rota* was available to the enemy except as our carrier-based aircraft were able to keep those fields neutralized."[37]

Ultimately Spruance refused to allow Mitscher's advance because his primary orders were quite clear: "capture, occupy and defend *Saipan, Tinian* and *Guam*."[38] The aggressive Mitscher was shocked by his commanding officer's decision. However, he should have understood from Spruance's battle plan that the landing on *Saipan* was always the strategic priority. It is interesting to note that Vice-Admiral Willis 'Ching' Lee, commander of the battleship group, Task Group 58.7, who would have led any western advance, was averse to Mitscher's proposed aggressive strategy because it risked a night fight for which his personnel were inadequately trained. The Japanese reputation as capable naval night-fighters still lingered from the fierce nighttime naval battles of the *Guadalcanal* Campaign. Most importantly, however, the strengths of Lee's Task Group lay in their speed of maneuver as an anti-aircraft screen for the carrier fleet. It is interesting to note that Lee, known as an aggressive commander, sent a message to Mitscher stating in stark terms, "Do not, repeat not, believe we should seek a night engagement."[39]

Spruance, from his 'picket' submarines, now knew that Ozawa's fleet was approaching in at least two sections. He naturally feared that one of these groups might advance from an unexpected direction in a possible flanking movement and he was loath to leave Rear-Admiral Turner's transports landing forces subject to a surprise attack. Thus Spruance advised, "End run by other carrier groups remains possibility and must not be overlooked."[40] It was a decision that has colored much of the history of the battle. Spruance's main concern was to cover the landings of troops and equipment at *Saipan*. He viewed that as his primary task. Spruance could not be certain that if he moved westward to meet Ozawa that there was not another force awaiting in the flanks to fall unawares on what would now be defenseless Marines and their transports off *Saipan*. Diversionary tactics had after all been a mainstay of Japanese actions in the past. In this battle however Ozawa chose a head-on confrontation. As Ozawa later explained in interview after the war, "It would take too much fuel to take the longer route, which had been considered, but we planned to go in straight and we did not change that plan during the approach."[41]

Spruance, like all fighting admirals, must have been torn between the naturally aggressive desire to destroy the enemy, balanced with the greater strategic considerations. As a great admirer of Japan's Admiral Togo, the hero of the *Battle of Tsushima* [1905] Spruance could understand the virtues of waiting for the right moment. "The way Togo waited at Tsushima for the Russian fleet to come to him has always been on my mind. We had somewhat the same situation, only it was modified by the long-range striking power of the carriers."[42] Rather than close with the enemy to get within range to launch, Spruance decided to stand back and absorb whatever Ozawa threw at him. It was a decision that had the added advantage of reducing risk. As earlier carrier battles had demonstrated, finding an enemy carrier fleet was far from easy. It was far safer to wait for the Japanese to arrive and use Spruance's spanking new fleet with its up-to-date equipment to knock them out of the sky.

However, even among his own staff, Spruance's decision was controversial. As Commodore Arleigh Burke, Spruance's Chief of Staff, bitterly observed, "we knew we were going to have hell slugged out of us in the morning."[43] Burke was so angry that he spent the night drafting bitter messages (never sent) with his new-found confederate Commander Jimmy Thach. Ultimately they realized that the final call had to rest with the Fifth Fleet's admiral. Meanwhile Mitscher was incandescent, furious at what he considered to be a lost opportunity of historic proportions.

Ozawa's forces advanced in two parts; a vanguard led by Vice-Admiral Takeo Kurita consisted of 3 light carriers, 3 battleships, 5 cruisers and 10 destroyers, which was followed by two carrier divisions consisting of 6 carriers, 2 battleships, 8 cruisers and 15 destroyers. Not including 43 seaplanes, Ozawa's force could muster 430 carrier aircraft, 222 Zeros, 113 dive-bombers and 95 torpedo planes. By comparison the Task Groups led by Vice-Admiral Mitscher had 891 aircraft including 475 fighters, 232 dive-bombers and 184 torpedo planes. At dawn on 19 June Vice-Admiral Kurita was placed about 100 miles northeast of Ozawa's main fleet that was 300 miles from Spruance's Task Group. Spruance sent his forces westward at full speed to close to within 200 miles, which was the minimum launch range of his aircraft. On board USS *Enterprise*, the carrier's Air Officer, the booming voice of Commander Thomas Hamilton's announced, "Morning men! Here's some news! We are going to give the Japanese Emperor half of the *Pacific Ocean* ... Yes, boys, we'll give him the bottom half."[44] Laughter and cheers were followed by the order to the pilots to "man your planes."[45]

By contrast Ozawa's planes, as he had planned, could launch at 300 miles and did so at 8.30 a.m. An hour and a half later the SC radar of the battleship USS *Alabama* picked up first contact with enemy bogeys some 140 miles away. The information was relayed to Admiral Mitscher's FDO (Flight Direction Officer), Lieutenant Joseph Eggert, a 31-year-old former Wall Street banker, whose responsibility it was to oversee the air defenses for the more than 100 US warships stationed to the west of *Saipan*. The US navy had identified stockbrokers and bankers as choice picks to work in the fast-moving and spatially complex business of 'flight direction.' Eggert duly worked out the time/distance equations for the hour in which he had to get his aircraft in the air to intercept the Japanese bogeys.

Before Ozawa's carrier aircraft arrived, the Hellcats had time to climb to 25,000 feet and fell on a group of Japanese aircraft launched from *Truk* and *Yap* (half way between *Palau* and *Guam*). Thirty Japanese fighters and five bombers were shot down in the first encounter for the loss of only one US aircraft. At 10.36 a.m. Ozawa's first carrier air strike approached fifty miles from Spruance's Task Groups. Covering US fighters launched by Lieutenant Eggert downed a further twenty-seven aircraft. A group of four bombers got through to Rear-Admiral William Harrill's surface group and a bomb hit and damaged the USS *South Dakota*, killing twenty-seven men, but failed to put the battleship out of action. No Japanese planes reached the US carriers.

Half an hour later a second larger Japanese strike force of 107 aircraft (61 'Judy' and 'Jill' bombers as well as 47 Zeros) appeared on the radar screens. They were met sixty miles out from Spruance's front line. An estimated seventy Japanese planes were shot down. Seven Japanese bombers breached the US aerial defences to attack Rear-Admiral

Alfred Montgomery's Task Group 58.2 carrier group (USS *Bunker Hill*, USS *Wasp*, USS *Cabot* and USS *Monterey*) and Rear-Admiral John Reeves Task Group 58.2 (USS *Enterprise*, USS *Lexington*, USS *San Jacinto* and USS *Princeton*). A torpedo scored a near miss when it exploded in *Enterprise*'s wake. Four of the Japanese bombers were shot down and all three of the torpedo planes that attacked the *Princeton* were also destroyed.

A third strike wave of 57 aircraft moving in from the north, was intercepted by 40 fighters at 1.00 p.m. and 7 were shot down. A few were able to make attacks, all ineffective, and the remainder returned to their carriers.

Ozawa's fourth strike was incorrectly directed and, failing to find the American carriers, broke off in two parts to refuel at either *Guam* or *Rota*. The *Rota* group came across Rear-Admiral Montgomery's Task Group 58.2 by accident and attacked the USS *Wasp* as well as USS *Bunker Hill*. Nine out of eighteen Japanese aircraft were shot down without scoring any hits. Twenty-seven Hellcats intercepted the larger group of forty-nine Japanese planes; they were all shot down or shot up beyond repair. Afterwards, aboard the USS *Lexington* a pilot made the immortal remark, "Why, hell, this is like an old-time turkey shoot down home!"[46] Unknowingly, he had given the *Battle of the Philippines* its most popular name.

Some US groups scored remarkably heavily. Commander C. W. Brewer took off from fleet carrier USS *Essex* with a squadron of 8 Hellcats and scored kills on 11 dive-bombers and 10 fighters. Lieutenant George Carr alone bagged five kills. It took the shine off their performance that later that day Brewer was killed over *Guam*. Carr was not the only star performer. Ensign Wilbur Webb, flying a VF-2 from USS *Hornet*, scored six kills within a few minutes over *Guam*. The most famous fighter ace to emerge from the air battle however was Lieutenant Alex Vraciu, the son of Romanian immigrants from East Chicago, Indiana. Graduating from DePauw University in 1941, he had enrolled immediately as a pilot in the US Navy Reserve. Serving on USS *Independence*, Vraciu scored his first 'kill' in an engagement at *Wake Island* in October 1943 and after accounting for four Japanese aircraft during the attack on *Truk Atoll* on 17 February 1943, he took his tally up to nine, becoming his group's leading ace.

When he returned from his mission at the *Great Marianas Turkey Shoot*, as was the custom when taxiing past the conning tower, he held up his hands to indicate that he had shot down six enemy bandits. By the time he left his cockpit, a photographer had raced to his airplane to take the seminal photograph of the battle showing a grinning Vraciu holding up a full right hand and the first digit of his left hand. Using just 360 bullets, he had managed to shoot down six Yokosuka 'Judy' dive-bombers in a little under eight minutes. The following day he claimed his nineteenth victim, which made him the leading Naval air ace. Awarded a Navy Cross, Vraciu went back to the US to help sell war-bonds for the government and married his childhood sweetheart. He returned to the front and was shot down by anti-aircraft fire over the Philippines. Rescued by Filipino guerrillas, who made him their leader, he conducted operations against the Japanese for six weeks before being returned to the US Navy. After the war Vraciu became a test pilot before retiring in 1964 to become a banker. In his late nineties he continued to travel and lecture from his home in Danville, California.

One of the tips he received for staying alive "was to swivel your neck before starting a strafing run, to make sure enemy fighters were not on your tail."[47] For Vraciu and the other American pilots, the day's events were euphoric and bestirred an increasingly confident bravado. When Ensign Wilbur 'Spider' Webb from USS *Hornet*, the new Essex Class carrier named after the *Hornet* sunk at the *Battle of Santa Cruz Islands*, downed a Japanese and chanced upon a Japanese air group he called out on his air-to-air radio, "Any American fighter pilot, this is Sydney Webb. I've got about forty of 'em cornered over *Orote Point* [*Guam*] and I could use some help."[48] Webb dived in scoring six kills and two probables; he managed to get his F6F Hellcat back to the *Hornet* but it was so full of holes that the maintenance crews decided to scrap it.

On the first day of battle the Japanese had lost 366 aircraft in the air as well as seventeen on the ground. In addition the Task Group's anti-aircraft gunners accounted for nineteen more Japanese aircraft. The cost of the day's fighting to the US Navy was just thirty planes. Of the four strike waves sent by Ozawa against Spruance's fleet, just forty got through to the Task Group. Under withering fire from the US Navy's now highly effective anti-aircraft guns they caused minimal damage. Finally it had dawned on the Japanese carrier commanders that, since the *Battle of Santa Cruz Islands*, the Americans had developed an awesome superiority in naval weapon systems. As Commander Masatake Okumiya recalled, "They [the Japanese pilots] never stood a chance against the determined defense of the Hellcat fighters and the unbelievable accuracy and volume of the ship's anti-aircraft fire."[49]

The Sinking of the Taiho: For Ozawa the tragedy of the day was compounded by the loss of his newest carrier and flagship, the *Taiho*. The radical design of the *Taiho* used steel decks; as a result they could withstand 500 lb bombs. Having a deck impervious to attack would enable the *Taiho* to land and relaunch planes no matter if the deck had been hit. *Taiho*'s new deck system was never tested, falling instead to a US torpedo strike. USS *Albacore*, commanded by Captain J. W. Blanchard, was one of the submarines that had been sent by Admiral Lockwood to intercept Ozawa's advancing fleet. At 8.08 a.m. Lieutenant Commander James Blanchard raised the *Albacore*'s periscope to find himself in the middle of the Japanese force. He picked out the *Taiho*, unaware that it was Ozawa's flagship. Because of a failure of his computer guidance system, Blanchard fired a spread of six torpedoes to increase his chances of a hit. He then dived away as Japanese destroyers sought him out.

Four torpedoes missed. Bomber pilot Sakio Komatsu, in a remarkable act of selfless bravery, spotted a fifth torpedo heading toward his carrier and dived his aircraft to intercept it at the cost of his own life. However, another one of the torpedoes did indeed find its mark on the carrier's forward starboard flank. The strike hit the steel outerplate of the gasoline tank. While it did not explode, a breach in the deck joint enable gasoline fumes to leak into the hangar areas. At first, this did not seem to be a major problem.

With the bow some five feet down as its compartments filled with water, the captain reduced the *Taiho*'s speed by a few knots.

However, the forward elevator had jammed between the landing deck and upper hangar deck. The elevator pit filled with a mixture of seawater and aviation gasoline. A build-up of vapors made the air below decks intolerable; sailors smashed the ships portholes simply to enable them to breathe. Nobody thought to smother the elevator pit with foam. Eventually an inexperienced damage-control officer opened up the carrier's ventilation systems in an attempt to clear the noxious vapors. It was a disastrous mistake. The fumes spread throughout the *Taiho* and at 2.30 p.m. an electric generator on the hangar deck ignited the aviation gas fumes causing a catastrophic explosion that not only lifted the carrier's landing deck but also blew out the *Taiho*'s sides and perforated her hull.

Most of the crew below decks were instantly killed. Ozawa was persuaded to abandon ship by his friend and Chief of Staff, Captain Toshikazu Ohmai, who advised his commander, "The battle is still going on and you should remain in command for the final victory";[50] out of 2,150 crew just 500 survived. At 4.30 p.m. following a second massive explosion which ripped the ship apart, the *Taiho* slipped stern-first beneath the waves.

Some three hours after the *Taiho* was hit, another American submarine, USS *Cavalla*, locked onto the *Shokaku* and launched a spread of six torpedoes of which at least three scored hits on the starboard side. The forward aviation fuel tanks were punctured and exploded in flames; planes that had just landed for refuelling instantly became fireballs. By noon the *Shokaku* was listing to port because of excessive countermeasures for a list to starboard and was also sinking at the bow. It had gone dead in the water. Hangars by now were an uncontrollable inferno in spite of the experienced fire control crews who had saved the carrier after it incurred heavy bomb damage at the *Battle of the Coral Sea*. Like the closed sided *Taiho*, the *Shokaku* was filled with gasoline vapors and when a bomb exploded in the hangars, the ship simply blew apart at the seams. The *Shokaku* then rolled over and took down 1,263 men including 376 air group personnel. Hearing the explosion that sank the *Shokaku*, the USS *Cavalla*'s Captain Herman Kossler radioed Vice-Admiral Charles Lockwood, "Believe that baby sank."[51] An ecstatic Lockwood radioed back, "Beautiful work Cavalla. One carrier down, eight more to go."[52] It was clear that Lockwood's submarine force had finally cured the malfunctions inherent in the Mark XIV's design and manufacture which had previously rendered them ineffective.

As Commander C. L. Moore of USS *San Jacinto*'s commander of Air Group-51 and its fighter squadron observed, "The battle . . . was undoubtedly the greatest carrier action fought to date and the most one-sided." The explanation of the overwhelming victory was clear. "Enemy planes, almost without exception, on receiving 0.50 caliber fire in the vicinity of the engine, burst into flames . . . Japanese pilots were reported to be inexperienced, inferior gunners and were inclined to separate and engage singly."[53]

The Last Hurrah of Japan's Carrier Fleet: Now fully aware of the nature of Ozawa's frontal attack and certain that there would be no flanking movement, Spruance felt free to liberate Mitscher to advance on the enemy's fleet. Thus far not a single US plane had even caught sight of the enemy's carriers. A great victory had been won but the commanding officers, particular Mitscher, were not happy. At 4.30 p.m. the mood in Mitscher's flagship improved when they received a message from Spruance, "Desire to attack the enemy tomorrow if we know his position with sufficient accuracy."[54]

During the night his Task Group sailed west and planned to catch Ozawa's carriers in a dawn attack. Meanwhile Ozawa, believing erroneously that there were still large numbers of aircraft operating from *Guam* and that many of his missing aircraft had landed there, decided to continue the battle even with as few as 150 aircraft now available. Vastly inflated combat reports, a feature of Japan's aircraft crews in the *Pacific War*, led Ozawa to believe that four of Spruance's aircraft carriers had been sunk and that six more were on fire. All of these reports were untrue.

Indeed throughout the battle, Vice-Admiral Kurita on *Guam* sent completely misleading reports on the success of their aerial operations as well as inaccurate numbers on available aircraft. It was only after a fleet-wide inventory was taken by radio that Ozawa accurately gauged the paucity of his remaining resources; the following day, 20 June, he cancelled plans to refuel and steamed at full speed to *Nakagasuku Bay* in *Okinawa*. The reality of the situation on *Guam* was articulated by a Japanese soldier who wrote in his diary,

> The enemy, circling overhead, bombed our airfield the whole day long. When evening came our carrier bombers returned, but the airfield had just been destroyed by the enemy and they could not land. Having neither fuel nor ammunition the fifteen or sixteen planes were unable to land and had to crash . . . It was certainly a shame. I was unable to watch dry-eyed. "The tragedy of war" was never so real.[55]

On 20 June, far from catching Ozawa at dawn, Mitscher's scout planes failed to find the Japanese fleet until 3.40 p.m. and confirmation of the target was not made for another fifteen minutes. It should be noted that the difficulty of finding Ozawa's fleet highlights the risks that would have been run if Spruance had not overruled Mitscher and Burke's proposed advance on 19 June. Now 3.45 p.m. and over 200 miles to the west, Ozawa's fleet was only just within range. Moreover it would take an hour for Mitscher to 'spot' and launch his strike aircraft. Commander Gus Widhelm, who had led USS *Hornet*'s dive-bombers at the last carrier engagement, the *Battle of Santa Cruz* two years before, told Mitscher, "We can make it but it's going to be tight."[56] Mitscher replied immediately, "Launch them"[57] This time Spruance had concurred with his aggressive suggestion; with the invasion of *Saipan* clearly free from danger Spruance was only too happy to comply with his commander's request. On board USS *Lexington* Mitscher exhorted his crews, "Give 'em hell, boys. Wish I were with you."[58]

With just over an hour of daylight left, it meant that his crews would have to return in the dark. Commander Jackson Arnold, of Air Group-2 on USS *Hornet* noted, "the flight to the target was beyond the combat radius of our planes."[59] At 6.30 p.m. 226 aircraft attacked Ozawa's carriers. Mitscher reported, "6 carriers, 6 cruisers, 4 battleships present, carriers without airplanes on deck and only a few airborne."[60] In fading light Dauntless dive-bombers from the USS *Lexington* scored a hit on the carriers *Hiyo* and *Junyo*. The air defenses of the carriers had been severely depleted by the previous day's massacre. As the departing strike forces from the *Lexington, Enterprise* and *San Jacinto* finished their runs, the following *Belleau Wood* strike group were uninterrupted by Zeros.

Four of *Belleau Wood*'s Grumman Avenger torpedo planes scored at least one hit on the *Hiyo*. Lieutenant George Brown, leader of the Avengers, who had vowed to get a hit on a Japanese carrier, was hit by anti-aircraft fire. Brown's crewmen, George Platz and Ellis Babcock, bailed out of the fire stricken plane and watched as Brown's group completed their attack: "We came in at about four hundred feet from the water to get a satisfactory launch of our torpedoes and dropped them on converging courses, which presumably did not allow the enemy carrier to take effective action."[61] Captain Toshiyuki Yokoi was unable to maneuver the *Hiyo* out of their path and took one of the Avengers' fish in the starboard quarter. Brown was hit and wounded in the action and, despite the efforts of his colleagues to guide him, he disappeared on the way back to the *Belleau Wood*. In the same attack Lieutenant Tate may also have scored a hit with a torpedo but managed to find his way home. Strikes by the USS *Bunker Hill*, USS *Cabot* and USS *Monterey* scored three bomb hits on the battleship *Haruna*. However, the *Chiyoda*, in spite of claims by the Avengers that they had scored torpedo hits, managed to take evasive action.

As with *Taiho* and *Shokaku*, fire and devastating explosions from the leakage of aviation fuel sank the *Hiyo* with the loss of 250 lives. Two hours after their torpedo hit, George Brown's crewmen, from their watery vantage point, saw the *Hiyo* sink by the stern in a little over six minutes. Before the end, the wounded Captain Yokoi had time to give a short speech to his crew who responded by cheering "*Banzai!* Ten thousand years' life to the emperor!"[62] Yokoi saluted his officers and watched them jump off the side. Yokoi, determined to go down with his ship, sat in an empty ammunition box and waited. He slid down the deck and went down deep. An underwater explosion rocked the *Hiyo* and hurled Yokoi back to the surface. He was picked up. In later life he reflected, "To an old fashioned sea captain like myself, it was my duty to go down with my ship. But what was I to do when it sent me back up?"[63]

Of the remaining carriers, *Zuikaku, Junyo* and *Chiyoda* all sustained bomb damage, as did the battleship *Haruna*. The *Ryuho* emerged unscathed apart from very minor damage from near misses. The oiler *Genyo Maru* was damaged by attacks from USS *Wasp* and later had to be sunk. *Seiyo Maru*, another oiler, was also sunk. At the end of the second day of fighting Ozawa's fleet had just thirty-five carrier planes still operational. The loss of three fleet carriers was a heavy blow to Ozawa, though he took heart from the reported destruction of 110 of the 140 American strike planes on this second day of the battle. In fact his defenses accounted for just 11 out of 226 American aircraft that took part in the mission. Over the course of three days, Ozawa's carrier force had lost 433 aircraft and a high proportion of its ground crews, engineers and deck staff; 200 land-based aircraft had also been destroyed. The aircraft may have been easily replaceable but the aircrews and engineers were not.

Cuckoos in the Night: For the returning US Navy pilots the nightmare of a dark landing beckoned. For many it would be a first, for some a last, night landing. It was a prospect for many that was more dangerous than a tussle with a Zero. Mitscher ordered his carriers to put on their lights. A startled Lieutenant John Harper exclaimed, "Whoa! This looks like a big city at night."[64]

In spite of illuminating the carriers with searchlights and flares, ninety-nine aircraft were lost; many landed in the sea while others crashed into their carriers' decks. Commander Arnold (later an Admiral) recorded that 7 fighters, 2 torpedo planes and 12 dive-bombers were forced to splash before getting back to the *Hornet*. Avenger pilot, Lieutenant Ralph Cummings, described the scene: ". . . by the time we arrived there was bedlam. It was too pitiful to be disgusting. Planes made passes at everything floating."[65] On USS *Lexington* a damaged Curtiss SB2C Helldiver with a wounded pilot, crashed into several parked but manned aircraft killing a pilot, an air crewman and a chock-man. It was one of many accidents. For the deck crew the night landings were almost as bad for them as for the pilots. To add to the confusion of the return, a Japanese 'Val' bomber, clearly lost, made repeated attempts to land on US carriers, *Wasp* and *San Jacinto*.

Commander Arnold was one of the lucky ones. His Hellcat landed in the dark, and spun over the side of the carrier but was held up by a 40 mm gun mount. A dozen flight deck crewmen managed to hang onto the wing of the aircraft while Arnold scrambled out of his cockpit and up onto the flight deck just as the Hellcat toppled into the *Pacific Ocean*. On USS *Enterprise* the returning Hellcat pilots sat in gloom because of the loss of their Air Group Commander, William 'Killer' Kane. Coming in to land with almost no gas left in his tank, Kane was waved-off at the last minute because a previous plane's heavy landing had fouled the deck. Out of gas, he was forced to ditch: "Everybody else ran out of ideas. I just ran out of altitude."[66] It was the second time in a week that he had got his feet wet. Only late in the afternoon of the next day did a destroyer approach, signalling the question of how many gallons of ice cream they would exchange for 'Killer' Kane who they had picked up. That night there was jubilation aboard the *Enterprise* but no ice cream, which had all been handed over to the destroyer.

A high proportion of US aircraft landed on the wrong US carriers; of nine planes landing on *Cabot*, all but two were 'cuckoos.' For those who ditched, most crews were picked up at first light. For some it was a less than comfortable night. Ensign Edward Wendorf, who had narrowly avoided a mid-air collision while attempting to land, cartwheeled his Hellcat into the sea; after making a fortunate underwater escape from his cockpit, Wendorf had to beat off sharks with a shoe. The chaos was exemplified by the account of the USS *Wasp* VF-14 group: "Five of our fighter pilots made it safely back to the *Wasp*; four landed on the *Bunker Hill*; two each on the *Cabot* and *San*

Jacinto; and one each on the *Enterprise* and *Monterey*. One of our pilots landed aboard the *San Jacinto* without the compass or generator in his plane, and with no signal officer, barrier or landing lights on the ship—and only three gallons of gas left."[67]

Aboard the light carrier, USS *Monterey*, future President Gerald Ford, a fireman, watched the scene and later recalled, "Aircraft landings on a carrier are always exciting, but that night to stand on the bridge, watching pilots bring their planes to the deck in the worst of conditions, was an unforgettable experience."[68]

Remarkably, despite the loss of 99 of the 226 planes that had reached the Japanese Combined Fleet, over the next two days 84 pilots and 76 crewmen were pulled from the water. In all only sixteen pilots were lost. Another twenty-two personnel were killed in the extraordinary night maneuvers. Given the chaos, the night landings, and the need to pick up survivors, by morning the Fifth Fleet was in no condition to launch a vigorous pursuit of the enemy. However, Mitscher would not be afforded the opportunity even if he had wanted it. On the orders of Admiral Toyoda, Ozawa now withdrew his forces. The *Battle of the Philippine Sea* had ended in a crushing defeat for the Imperial Japanese Navy.

Reflections and Recriminations: In spite of the crushing nature of the victory, the reaction of the American victors was lacking in exuberance. In part this may have been explained by the heavy losses incurred by the aircrews on their night return on the evening of 20 June. The extent of the devastation of the Japanese aircrews, and Japan's inability to train and replace their losses, was to a large extent unknown, although the diminution in the fighting capability of their pilots had already been noted.

As for the major scores against Japanese fleet carriers, the somewhat 'looked-down-upon' US submarine force had achieved them. Furthermore, a light-carrier, the *Belleau Wood*, rather than a main fleet carrier, had sunk the *Hiyo*. Perhaps the main reason for the lack of enthusiasm for one of the greatest victories in US naval history was that there was dissension within the ranks between the 'brown shoe' airfleet officers and the 'black shoe' sailors. For Admiral Mitscher and the 'airfleet' officers, Spruance's refusal to countenance a western advance to meet Ozawa head-on was an opportunity missed to completely annihilate the Japanese fleet; Mitscher would end his report of the battle with more than an implied criticism, "The enemy had escaped. He had been badly hurt by one aggressive carrier air strike, at the one time when he was within range. His fleet was not sunk."[69] Rear-Admiral 'Jocko' Clark, commander of the *Hornet*, was more damning, "A chance of a century was missed."[70]

Unbeknownst to Spruance, Turner's warning that things had been going badly on *Saipan* proved to be premature. The situation improved dramatically thereafter and in hindsight Turner could have sent the remaining transports to the east and out of harm's way. Spruance could therefore have advanced as Mitscher had recommended without endangering the invasion of *Saipan*. It was a decision that haunted Spruance after the war. Writing to the naval historian Eliot Morrison, whose 14-volume *History of the United States Naval Operations in World War II* remains the standard reference on the subject, Spruance with great candor concluded, "As a matter of tactics, I think that going after the Japanese and knocking their carriers out would have been much better and more satisfactory than waiting for them to attack us; but we were at the start of a very important and large amphibious operation and we could not afford to gamble and place it in jeopardy."[71]

Dissensions came as no surprise to Spruance and his colleagues. Chief of Staff, Carl Moore, wrote shortly after the battle, "There will be a lot of kibitzing in *Pearl Harbor* and Washington about what we should have done by people who don't know the circumstances and won't wait to find them out."[72] Spruance had indeed lost an opportunity and possibly exposed his carrier fleet to greater damage by allowing Ozawa a first strike; earlier in the war this would have mattered but since autumn 1943 the overwhelming superiority of US naval pilots, aircraft and training meant that 'first strike' was no longer an advantage that Japanese carriers were capable of exploiting. By contrast with the 'brown shoe' aviators, the 'black shoe' sailors were almost entirely in support of Spruance's cautious tactics. There was no need for Spruance to take the risk of being over aggressive.

Nimitz was thereafter unfailingly supportive of Spruance though in the Commander in Chief, Pacific (CINCPAC) summary he did conclude, ". . . it can be proved that our main body of carriers could have pushed to the westward without concern for the expeditionary forces . . . a decisive fleet air action could have been fought, the Japanese fleet destroyed, and the end of the war hastened."[73] However, it seems doubtful, given the nature of Japanese psychology and the obdurate stance of the Emperor, whether the sinking of a few more Japanese carriers would have had any impact on the duration of the war.

In addition, post-war analysis suggests that because of the disposition of Ozawa's forces, the US Navy's strike forces would have had to negotiate a withering barrage of anti-aircraft fire to get to his carriers and that aircraft losses could have been catastrophic. Apart from their failures in tactical reconnaissance, it would be hard to fault the leadership of the US Navy at the *Battle of the Philippine Sea*. In the ultimate reckoning, Spruance's tactics did result in the effective annihilation of Japan's offensive naval capability. In judging Spruance, these facts speak for themselves. As for the view in Washington, Admiral King was adamant that Spruance's course of action was correct, ". . . the *Saipan* amphibious operations had to be protected from enemy interference at all cost. In his plans for what developed at the Battle of the Philippine Sea, Spruance was rightly guided by this basic obligation."[74] In mid-July 1944, when he arrived with Nimitz in *Saipan* for a brief tour of the *Pacific* theater, King immediately told Spruance, when he got off the plane, ". . . you did a damn good job there. No matter what other people tell you, your decision was correct."[75]

Japanese reaction to the battle was testament, if further was needed, to the success of Spruance's tactics. Even though the official report from the First Mobile Fleet asserted that four or five US carriers had been sunk (actually none) and that 160 US aircraft had been shot down (actually just 42 were lost in battle not included the 99 from night landings), it was clear to everyone that they had suffered a major defeat. Ozawa resigned. In Tokyo, Admiral Toyoda responded, "I am more responsible for this defeat than Admiral Ozawa, and I will not accept his resignation."[76] Japan's last realistic chance of stopping the US Naval advance was gone.

In the 'Top Secret' Japanese official post-battle analysis entitled *Impressions and Battle Lessons (Air) in the "A" Operations*, published on 1 November 1944, attention was focused on the poor level of training given to aircrews. The 1st Flying squadron had six months training but the 2nd and 3rd Flying Squadrons only had two months and three months respectively. The 2nd Squadron in particular was delayed by lack of teaching personnel and equipment and "The training could be started only in the first week of April, and in the first week of May when the men went into action, they could barely man monoplanes as far as their training was concerned, and their maneuver was extremely poor."[77] As for the Combined Fleet's reconnaissance squadron, "none of the pilots had more than 100 nautical miles of flying experience."[78]

Radar and communications were also deficient to the extent that the pilots "had not a single practice of transmission . . . and the radars were totally unusable."[79] The result, the report concludes, was that on 19 June, half of the pilots failed to find their targets at all. Deficiencies were also noted in the Japanese forward base at *Tawi*, in reconnaissance, the flank protection of their aircraft carriers, the poor operation of anti-submarine defense and the poor design of carrier gas tanks. By now however, adjustments to carrier policy were too late. As a Japanese official lamented after the fall of *Saipan* and the subsequent naval defeat, "Hell is upon us."[80] The *Battle of the Philippines* was the last hurrah of the once proud carrier fleet that had humbled America just two and a half years earlier. Hindsight has shown that Spruance, the man Admiral King considered to be "the most intelligent officer"[81] in the Navy, by his decision to sit back and wait for the Japanese advance, had won the greatest naval victory in American history. Japan's carrier threat, the spearhead of its quest for Empire in the first year of the war, had been completely broken by the *Great Marianas Turkey Shoot*.

32 The Invasions of Saipan, Tinian, and Guam: General Tojo Upended

[June 1944–August 1945]

[Maps: 32.1, 32.2, 32.3, 32.4, 32.5]

The Mariana Islands: A History: **[Map: 32.1]** The *Marianas* comprise fifteen tropical islands 1,600 miles east of the Philippines, but the end game of Admiral Chester Nimitz's thrust through the *Central Pacific* was to capture the main islands of *Saipan, Tinian* and *Guam* and their airfields. Strategically their airfields, some 1,400 miles southwest of Tokyo, would enable the US Army Air Force to begin its long wished for bombardment of Japan's major industrial cities. For Japan, the island had an importance that went beyond the purely military. *Saipan* in particular was considered to be a home island. The Portugese explorer Magellan had discovered the *Marianas* for Spain in 1521 although they were not formally claimed and taken under Spanish control until 1667. Over the next 100 years the indigenous Chamorro population was largely wiped out and the survivors were mainly Spanish *mestizo* stock. Named after the widow of Philip IV of Spain, Queen Mariana of Austria, the *Marianas* were put under the jurisdiction of Spain's Philippine Empire.

After the American conquest of the Philippines in 1898, a by-product of America's intervention in the *Cuban War of Independence*, Spain was forced to cede *Guam* to the United States. For America it was a useful staging post and telegraph point linking the west coast of America to its newly acquired colony, the Philippines.

Spain, having decided to exit its Asian Empire, put the other islands in the *Marianas* up for sale. America, deciding that the price was too steep, lost out to Germany, which was eagerly playing catch-up in the Asian empire game; they paid US$4m and became the proud new owners of *Saipan* and *Tinian*. German ownership of these islands was short lived however. Japan, an ally of Britain, took advantage of *World War I* by occupying Germany's Asian assets. Although *Saipan* had been awarded to Japan as a League of Nations mandate after *World War I*, it was treated by the Japanese as a possession. Airfields and military assets were enhanced and, more importantly, Japan invested in a Japanization of the island. The Japanese government encouraged colonization from *Okinawa* and other parts of southern Japan while at the same time introducing the Japanese language and culture to the indigenous peoples. In effect *Saipan* became more than an Imperial asset; it became a 'home island.'

The outbreak of the *Pacific War* rapidly changed the importance of *Saipan*. It became a logistic center for the perimeter that formed the heart of Yamamoto's strategy. A garrison of some 30,000 troops was established over time, increasingly consisting of remnants of Army groups from other engagements in the *Pacific*. Until the fall of *Tarawa Atoll* in November 1943, the emphasis on building *Saipan*'s defensive capacity was relatively limited. After this point however, Japan's Imperial HQ was certainly aware that Nimitz's *Central Pacific* thrust was most likely aimed at an approach to Japan via the *Marianas*. It was well understood that *Saipan, Tinian* and *Guam*, America's colony, which had been occupied by Japanese forces on 8 December 1941, would be able to be used as a base for the bombing of Japan's main islands.

However, by the time that Japan got around to making the defense of *Saipan* a priority, the ability to supply the island with troops, building equipment and supplies, was limited. In a sign of Japan's impending strangulation, on 6 March the *Amerika-Maru*, carrying 1,700 of the *Marianas*' more important citizens and families of the South Sea Development Company, was sunk on its way to Japan. Similarly five out of seven troop ships in a convoy sent to *Saipan* were torpedoed in May 1944. Only 5,500 of the designated force of 7,000 arrived; many of them, rescued from the water, were not only traumatized but also left without guns or equipment.

For America's military planners *Guam*'s importance lay in its land mass, not its far from perfect harbor facility. *Saipan*'s attractions were similar, while *Tinian* was selected for its mainly flat lands that could accommodate the large airfields needed for the US Air Force's new long-range bomber, the Boeing B-29 Superfortress. Ushi Point Airfield on *Tinian* was rated as better than Aslito Airfield on *Saipan*.

Preparations for the Marianas Campaign: On 5 June 1944, the same day that US and British forces launched the D-Day landings in Normandy, a mighty armada left *Pearl Harbor*, headed for *Saipan*. Included in the convoy was Vice-Admiral Marc Mitscher's 'Fast Carrier Force.' By the time the landing armada reached the island, its ranks had swollen to some 535 ships carrying some 71,034 troops comprising the 2nd and 4th Marines as well as the US Army's 27th Infantry Division.

The monumental logistical task was the responsibility of Rear-Admiral Richard Turner. Operation FORAGER required 77 transports, 34 cargo ships, 98 auxiliaries including oilers, hospital ships, munitions ships, cold storage vessels, minesweepers and tug boats. The troop transports, often converted from luxury liners, were stripped out and reconfigured by Vice-Admiral William Calhoun. Tiers of bunk beds were constructed from iron piping. The conditions were spartan. The troop transport vessels were little more than floating ovens; even deck space was limited by the use of every available corner for deck cargo. It would have been little comfort to American GIs that their conditions were luxurious compared to Japanese troop ships. The newly introduced attack transports (APA) took fewer troops and were largely filled with stores, munitions and special assault equipment. AK cargo vessels came in the rear carrying Seabees and their construction equipment for repair of bombed airfields and the building of accommodation and storage blocks. To get troops ashore, Turner needed 152 landing craft of various sizes as well as specialist craft for unloading tanks. Docks (LSDs: Landing Ship, Docks) were brought to carry small troop landing craft. In addition the invasion armada included twenty-five LCIs (Landing Craft, Infantry). Turner's force as it approached the *Marianas* comprised 551 ships compared to the 88 that he had commanded at *Guadalcanal* two years earlier. The logistics fleet was manned by a large contingent of US Coast Guards who augmented the ranks of experienced sailors needed to crew the ever-expanding US armada as it moved inexorably toward the Japanese home islands.

In total Operation FORAGER would involve 300,000 Navy, Marine and Army personnel. Simply maintaining this number of troops in the 'field' required vast logistic resources, particularly with regard to the fact that they had to operate at a 5,700-mile distance from the west coast of America. Troops not only had to be fed, watered and clothed, but the 682 vessels (including warships) that brought them to the *Marianas*, as well as 2,125 aircraft had to be provided with fuel and needed constant maintenance.

To make the invasion of the *Marianas Islands* possible, the head of Service Squadron-10, Commodore Nick Carter, turned the safe anchorages of the *Marshall Islands, Majuro Atoll, Kwajalein* and *Entiwok*, each 300 miles apart, into naval bases and logistical centres. Apart from docking facilities, Carter had to build metal workshops, carpenter workshops, munition and food stores. Men were housed on specially constructed floating barracks. Refrigeration vessels and mobile water distillation plants were required to sustain the needs of US forces for food and water. Administrative facilities were needed to process the ordering dispatch chains for fuel, food, medical supplies and mail. It was a logistical exercise of extreme complexity. A typical shipload of munitions could contain seventy-five different types of ammunition, all of which had to be unloaded sorted and forwarded onwards to their point of use. Men who manned these ships to the front line were as at risk of instant death as the troops in the trenches. A hit almost anywhere on any fuel or ammunition carrier was usually instantly fatal to every crewmember. But as Nick Carter testified, "We never hesitated to send ammunition ships forward whenever and wherever they were requested."[1]

Neither could the US 'safe' anchorages feel completely safe from attack; bypassed Japanese island garrisons, occasionally provisioned by specially designed 'cargo' submarines, continued to mount raids even though they were subjected to repeated bombing by US land-based aircraft. On occasions tropical typhoons could hurl deadlier weapons against the US anchorage lagoons than any Japanese attack. It is axiomatic that logistics and support troops rarely receive plaudits; yet in the exacting conditions of the south and central *Pacific* in which they had to operate, the men who served to support the US advance on the *Marianas* were deserving of much greater credit than they ever received.

The US troops, both Marines and Army, were under the overall command of Lieutenant-General Holland 'Howlin' Mad' Smith, a man of legendary ferocious temper. A fellow officer described him as being "of medium height, perhaps five feet nine or ten inches, and somewhat paunchy, His once-black hair had turned grey. His once close-trimmed mustache was somewhat scraggy. He wore steel-rimmed glasses and he smoked cigars incessantly."[2] The US Army's 27th Division meanwhile would be commanded by the 51-year-old Major-General Ralph Smith. By character the quietly spoken Smith was considered an intellectual whose calm demeanor belied an exotic life. Taught to fly by Orville Wright he had received only the thirteenth pilot license ever issued. He was also a graduate of the Sorbonne and the French *Ecole de Guerre*.

The invasion of the southwest coast of *Saipan* was preceded by a two-day bombardment of the island involving some fifteen battleships, four of them resurrected from the shallow graveyard of *Pearl Harbor*. On 13 June, unhampered by a Japanese air defense, already annihilated by Mitscher's fast carriers, the US Navy minesweepers cleared the shorelines of *Saipan*. The following day Rear-Admiral Jesse Oldendorf and Rear-Admiral 'Pug' Ainsworth brought their bombardment groups 1,000 to 3,000 yards offshore and proceeded to pound *Saipan*. Their surface forces could deploy an astonishing 102 major caliber guns alone; these consisted of eighteen 16-inch guns and eighty-four 14-inch guns. Hundreds of smaller caliber guns on cruisers and destroyers also pounded the island. Thus, apart from the sustained air attack on *Saipan*, it was estimated that about 160,000 shells pummelled the Japanese defenders.

There was no response from gun emplacements on the island and where emplacements were observed, they appeared unoccupied. Indeed Admiral Ted Ruddock, an ordnance expert, noted that the main danger to the US surface fleet appeared to come from their own side: "On Saipan . . . ricochets endangered ships [our own] on the other side of the island. I, for one, had a frantic call from another flag officer to quit trying to sink him."[3]

There are questions as to the effectiveness of the bombardment of *Saipan*. AP (armor piercing) shells used special hardened steel alloys containing nickel, chromium and molybdenum. Deep caves and concrete meters thick could be penetrated. However, as a shortcut in development, the Navy's AP shells had been fitted with Army fuses that required a down angle of 15° to explode on impact, otherwise they had a tendency either to be dud or to ricochet wildly. This seems to have been the case at *Saipan* where the fleet fired their guns at an average range of 2,000 yards compared to an optimal range of 8,000 yards to achieve the required 15° angle. Thus, like the submariners earlier in the war, the surface fleet found themselves with a deeply flawed weapon. HC (High Capacity) shells were also widely used; these shells broke up on impact and in theory were devastating against ground troops. However, given that the defenders on *Saipan* dug themselves into caves, the use of HC munitions was of doubtful value. Thus apart from depriving the defenders of sleep and inflicting a psychological blow to the Japanese, it seems that the naval bombardment, despite its large scale, inflicted less damage than might have been expected.

For the defenders the plan was simple; to hold out for as long as possible. However, with a shortage of equipment with which to build strong defenses, Lieutenant-General Yoshitsugu Saito, a pedestrian tactician, relied largely on the natural barriers put in place by Mount Tapotchau in the center of the island. Saito hoped to hold out until the combined Japanese Navy, now assembling to the east of the Philippines, could wipe out the US Navy's forces in one final cataclysmic engagement. As Emperor Hirohito exhorted Tojo's appointee as Naval Minister and Navy Chief of Staff, Admiral Shigtaro Shimada, "Rise to the challenge; make a tremendous effort; achieve a splendid victory like at the time of the Japan Sea naval battle [in the *Russo-Japanese War*]."[4]

For most of the defenders however, death was seen as the most likely outcome. A Japanese soldier's journal noted, "We are waiting with Molotov cocktails and hand grenades ready for the word to forward recklessly into the enemy ranks with our swords in our hands. All that worries me is what will happen to Japan after we die."[5]

The Battle of Saipan: **[Map: 32.2]** At midnight on 14 June cooks aboard the eighty landing ships started to prepare the Marines' traditional send-off breakfast of fried eggs and bacon, steak and black coffee. The first wave Marines were woken and fed at 2.00 a.m. At 7.00 a.m. on 15 June, the bows of thirty-four LSTs (Landing ship, Tanks) opened to disgorge the US landing forces. Some 719 amtracs made their landing on eight beaches on *Saipan*'s southwest coast. On *Saipan*, Sergeant Yamauchi, who had finally fallen asleep after a night of deafening American naval bombardment, woke, parched and hungry, noticing that the Marines "advanced like a swarm of grasshoppers. The American soldiers were all soaked. Their camouflage helmets looked black. They were so tiny wading ashore."[6]

Operations officer, Colonel Robert Hogaboom recalled, "The opposition consisted primarily of artillery and mortar fire from weapons placed in well-deployed positions . . . as well as fire from small arms, automatic weapons and anti-boat guns sited to cover the approaches to . . . the landing beaches."[7] Major-General Harry Schmidt, commander of 4th Marine Division, who established a command post in a foxhole just fifty yards from the beach, later observed, "It was the hottest spot I was in during the war, not even excepting *Iwo Jima*."[8] Nevertheless by 9 a.m., 8,000 Marines had been landed. A beachhead ten miles wide and 600 yards deep was quickly established with 20,000 Marines who easily beat back Saito's counter-attack led by tanks in the early hours of 16 June.

On 18 June, Emperor Hirohito warned Tojo, "If ever we lose *Saipan*, repeated air attacks on Tokyo will follow. No matter what it takes, we have to hold there."[9] Two days later Hirohito's worst fears were realized. For the defenders all hope of fighting off the Americans ended with the destruction of Japan's Combined Fleet at the *Battle of the Philippine Sea*, some 700 miles to the west of *Saipan*, on 19–20 June. **[See Chapter 31: The Great Marianas 'Turkey Shoot' (Battle of the Philippine Sea)]**

Perhaps aware for the first time that his hold on power would be tenuous if the Japanese people were subjected to continuous aerial attack, Hirohito showed rare angst when faced by a military setback. Indeed as the situation on *Saipan* became increasingly hopeless, Hirohito ordered Admiral Shimada to retake the island. The Imperial command led to the futile drawing up of a draft plan that bore no relation to reality. It was never carried out. It was only after he convened a meeting of Field Marshals and Fleet Admirals on 25 June, that Hirohito accepted that *Saipan* could not be recovered. However, his forsaken troops did not surrender.

Hitherto, the Marines had only had to deal with flat, featureless atolls. From *Saipan* onwards a different type of terrain would have to be negotiated. The outside world may have been surprised by the increasing death toll that would now be taken by Nimitz's island hopping but it was no surprise to the Marine's commander, Lieutenant-General Holland Smith who declared at a meeting before the battle, "we are up against mountains and caves where Japs can dig in. A week from now there will be a lot of dead Marines."[10] On *Saipan* US progress was rapid on the coastal plains but the approaches to Mount Tapotchau, inevitably led to a rapid slowdown of momentum. Saipan's rocky defensive outcrops were given colourful nicknames such as 'Hell's Pocket' and 'Death Valley', which nevertheless accurately conveyed the difficulty of the terrain. First-Lieutenant John Chapin of the 3rd Battalion, 24th Marines, recalled that after he came ashore his troops soon came under artillery fire:

> Suddenly, WHAM! A shell hit right on top of us! I was too surprised to think, but instinctively all of us hit the deck and began to spread out. Then the shells really began to pour down on us; behind, on both sides, and right in our midst ... The fire was hitting us with pinpoint accuracy, and it was not hard to see why ... towering 1500 feet above us was Mount Tapotchau, with Jap observation posts honeycombing its crest.[11]

In spite of the difficulties, the Marines were typically bullish in their approach compared to the Army. When 2nd Marine Division stalled fighting its way up Mount Topatchau, Major-General Thomas Watson gave his troops short shrift; he was heard shouting over a field telephone, "There's not a god damn thing up on that hill but some Japs with machine guns and mortars. Now get the hell up there and get them!"[12] His assistant division commander was Brigadier-General Merritt 'Red Mike' Edson, who had been awarded a Medal of Honor for his heroism on *Guadalcanal*. US Marine casualties were high and the difficulty of the fighting, requiring officers to lead from the front, led to many high ranking casualties (Lieutenant-Colonels and Majors), greater than in any other battle in the Marine Corp's history. Difficulties in moving operations forward inevitably brought tension between the rival Marine and Army forces.

The lack of progress of the 27th Infantry was starting to cause problems of infiltration by Japanese troops and also exposed the adjacent Marine divisions to enfilading fire on their flanks. On D+9 (Landing Day plus nine days) Holland Smith sent an excoriating message to Major-General Ralph Smith:

> The failure of the 27th to advance in its zone of action resulted in the halting of attacks by the 4th and 2nd Marine Divisions on the flanks of the 27th in order to prevent dangerous exposure of their interior flanks. It is

directed that immediate steps be taken to cause the 27th
Division to advance and seize the objectives ordered.[13]

Marine Lieutenant-General 'Howlin' Mad' Holland Smith, after winning the agreement of Rear-Rear-Admiral Turner, called on Admiral Spruance aboard the USS *Indianapolis* with a view to having Major-General Ralph Smith sacked. It was explained that the 27th Infantry's commander had shown "that he lacks aggressive spirit and his division is slowing down our advance. He should be relieved."[14] Spruance concurred and signed an order to that effect, "You are authorized and directed to relieve Major-General Ralph Smith from command of the 27th Division, US Army."[15] Eventually, it was 2nd Marine Division on the left flank that fought its way to the summit of Mount Tapotchau. However, the summit of the political battle between the Army and Navy was still some way off.

As usual in the *Pacific* the Marines would normally be much more aggressive in their taking of enemy positions, relying much less on artillery support and detailed preparation than the Army. Inter-service rivalry flared into open warfare; Lieutenant-General Robert Richardson, who commanded all the Army forces in the *Pacific* ordered an inquiry into the *Saipan* campaign, which concluded that Ralph Smith's sacking was "not justified by the facts" and that Holland Smith "was not fully informed regarding conditions in the zone of the 27th Infantry Division."[16] In person Richardson was much ruder. On a visit to *Saipan* he harangued Holland Smith, telling him:

> You had no right to relieve Ralph Smith. The 27th is one
> of the best-trained divisions in the Pacific. I trained it
> myself . . . I want you to know that you can't push the
> army around . . . You and your corps commanders aren't
> as qualified to lead large bodies of troops as general
> officers in the army . . . You marines are nothing but a
> bunch of beach runners anyway. What do you know about
> land warfare?[17]

Remarkably Holland Smith held his tongue but reported the episode to Rear-Admiral Kelly Turner. In addition Richardson outrageously breached Army etiquette by landing on *Saipan* without permission during the battle and handing out commendations to the 27th Infantry. Turner then duly chewed out Lieutenant-General Richardson. Richardson then went to complain about Turner to Admiral Spruance aboard the USS *Indianapolis*. Spruance tried to deflect the situation—as did Nimitz. However, the whole matter eventually ended with reports landing on the desks of Marshall and the Joint Chiefs where another lively encounter between Marshall and King ended inconclusively. The backdrop to the entire dispute was vested in interservice rivalry with the Marines suspecting, not without foundation, that there were plots to have them subsumed into the US Army.

The 'Smith versus Smith' row would eventually backfire on Holland Smith. Although he led the Marines at *Iwo Jima*, Holland Smith was excluded from command of the

Marines at *Okinawa*. Even his superiors questioned the degree of Holland Smith's aggressiveness. After lunching with Admiral Ernest King who visited *Saipan* in mid-July 1944, the Navy's supportive Chief of Staff commented, "The trouble with Holland Smith is that he's like Stilwell in China. All he wants to do is fight."[18] In spite of the support of Admiral Spruance and Vice-Admiral Turner, Nimitz, because of the 'bad blood' between the Army and Holland Smith, stood him down at *Okinawa*. For the remainder of the war, Holland Smith, whose aggression in handling his Marines had been one of the hallmarks of the US thrust through the island groups of the *Central Pacific*, was forced to sit out its concluding phases in bitter contemplation.

In the press opinion was quite evenly divided. Newspapers that supported General Douglas MacArthur tended to support Ralph Smith. The *San Francisco Examiner*, owned by the legendary MacArthur loyalist, William Randolph Hearst, wrote that the "Allegedly excessive loss of life attributed to Marine Corps impetuosity of attack has brought a break between Marine and army commanders in the Pacific."[19] Holland Smith was described as a "butcher." Similarly the *New York Journal* argued, "Americans are shocked at the casualties on Saipan following already heavy losses by Marine commanders on Tarawa and Kwajalein."[20] However, *Time* magazine and those in the circle of its influential owner, Henry Luce, strongly believed that the Marines were much better trained for the conditions of the *Central Pacific* Campaign and were equipped to move at the speed that was demanded. *Time* reporter Robert Sherrod became a close friend of Holland Smith during the *Marianas* Campaign and gave solid support to his actions—claiming that the 27th Infantry had frozen in their 'fox-holes.' After the war, Holland Smith managed to pour gasoline on the smoldering remains of this unseemly episode with his spirited memoir, *Coral and Brass* [1949]. Ralph Smith, happily ensconced as an academic at Stanford University's Hoover Institution, did not respond in kind.

It is worth noting that the official US Army history would later conclude, "No matter what the extenuating circumstances were—and there were several—the conclusion seems inescapable that Holland Smith had good reason to be disappointed with the performance of the 27th Infantry Division . . ."[21] In hindsight however, given the repercussions that materially affected Holland Smith, it is debatable whether his decision to relieve Smith of command was the wisest course of action. Although the affair of 'Smith versus Smith' escalated from a command decision to a national debate, in general inter-service rivalry promoted healthy competition that did not damage the war effort. Even the harm done by the 'Smith versus Smith' affair was quite limited. At the highest levels of command it was a spat that was quickly put aside. In the end the main casualties of the dispute were probably the careers of the two Smiths themselves.

The *Battle of Saipan* reached its zenith on 7 July when the unimaginative Lieutenant-General Saito ordered a *banzai* charge by his remaining troops. In a broad address to his troops Saito announced, "Whether we attack or whether we stay where we are, there is only death. However, in death there is life. We must utilize this opportunity to exalt true Japanese manhood. I will advance with those who remain to deliver still another blow to the American devils, and leave my bones on Saipan as a bulwark of the Pacific."[22] In the event Saito was too sick to join the charge. Getting out of his sick bed, Saito sat down on a rock and according to a captured officer, "Facing the misty East saying *Tenno Heika! Banzai!* [Long live the Emperor] . . . he drew his own blood first with his own sword and then his adjutant shot him in the head with a pistol."[23]

The largest '*Banzai*' suicide attack of the war by Japanese troops drunk on *sake* resulted in the overrunning of the US 105th Infantry's 1st and 2nd Battalions and their almost complete annihilation. Major Ed McCarthy recalled, "It was like the movie stampede staged in the old Wild West movies. . .The Japs just kept coming and coming."[24] Lieutenant George O'Donnell wrote to his parents:

> It had just finished pouring, and we were all soaked, with our teeth chattering . . . And then, from our right and below us, there came thousands of Japs! For two hours they . . . came right at us. It was like a mob at a big football game, all trying to get out at once . . . We had a hard struggle keeping them from overrunning us, and we had a field day, firing, firing, until our ammunition ran low.[25]

They got to within ten yard of his position. Although there were 650 American casualties, headquarters troops managed to hold off this insane action in which some 4,300 Japanese soldiers were slaughtered. The wounded attackers, some walking with crutches, were barely armed. Within days the *Battle of Saipan* was effectively over though numbers of Japanese soldiers would continue to hide out. Remarkably a group of forty-five soldiers commanded by Captain Sakae Oba held out until 1 December 1945, when they were finally persuaded that the Emperor had indeed surrendered.

For their bravery in fighting Saito's *Banzai* charge, three US soldiers were awarded the Medal of Honor; a mortally wounded Lieutenant-Colonel William O'Brian for ignoring his injuries to climb on to a jeep to machine gun charging Japanese troops; a wounded Sergeant Thomas Baker for refusing to be carried back to his lines and insisting on being given a pistol to hold off the Japanese while his colleagues retired; and battle surgeon Captain Ben Salomon who, while defending the wounded under his charge, manned a machine gun post and slaughtered ninety-eight Japanese troops before he was finally overcome. Out of the 70,000 US troops who landed on the island some 2,949 were killed and 10,464 were injured. By contrast virtually all of the 30,000 Japanese garrison perished. Vice-Admiral Nagumo, the former commander of the *Kido Butai* (carrier strike force), the victor of *Pearl Harbor* and defeated commander at the *Battle of Midway*, who had been sent to command the island, shot himself.

As for the civilian population, on 1 July an Imperial Rescript was sent, which encouraged the civilian population to commit suicide; they were promised a status in death equivalent to that of soldiers. On 9 July, American troops watched in astonishment as hundreds of islanders, mainly women and children, threw themselves off Morubi

Cliffs that stood 800 foot above the sea. Although many jumped voluntarily, it was noted that Japanese soldiers herded them towards their doom and shot those who baulked. Others walked into the sea to drown carrying their children with them. An officer on a minesweeper reported on the spectacle,

> Part of the area was so congested with floating bodies we simply can't avoid running them down . . . [one girl] had drowned herself while giving birth to a baby . . . A small boy of four or five had drowned with his arm firmly clenched around the neck of a Jap soldier; the two bodies rocked crazily in the waves.[26]

It was clear that the civilian population had been completely inculcated with belief that "the Americans would rape, torture and murder them, and that it was more honorable to take their own lives."[27]

As many as 20,000 civilians may have perished over the course of the *Saipan* Campaign. It was alleged by some that Hirohito feared the propaganda consequences of it being found out how well the Americans would treat the captured Japanese population. After the war it was claimed by loyalists that the rescript had been sent without the Emperor's knowledge. In any event rescripts were never drafted by the Emperor or his advisors but were presented by the government for him to sign. The fanaticism displayed at *Saipan* had a profound effect on the thinking of the US Joint Chiefs of Staff. Until then it had been imagined that Japan might surrender before it was invaded; afterwards they let it be known to Britain's senior commanders that, "as a result of recent operations in the *Pacific* it was now clear to the United States Chiefs of Staff that, in order to finish the war with the Japanese quickly, it will be necessary to invade the industrial heart of Japan."[28]

For Japan, the fall of *Saipan* clarified all previous assumptions and expunged any remaining hopes. In Tokyo, Danish diplomat, Lars Tillitse, noted that after *Saipan*, "Japanese with insight knew that Japan had to prepare for the worst."[29] Indeed at the end of June 1944, the Japanese cabinet, clearly expecting American bombing of their cities, published an *Outline for Encouraging the Evacuation of Schoolchildren*, which called for the evacuation of 350,000 third to sixth graders from major cities.

The Fall of Tojo: In Japan, the loss of *Saipan* crystallized the increasing discontent with Prime Minister Hideki Tojo's government. In spite of the measures taken to restrict access to information about the course of the war it was an open secret that things were going badly. Since the loss of the *Battle of Midway*, Japan had been forced to retreat from the *Solomon Islands*, New Guinea, as well as the defensive perimeter in the South Pacific; the *Marshall Islands*, the *Carolines*, the *Gilberts* and finally the quasi home-island of *Saipan*. In Japan living standards that had stagnated during the war with China, were now plummeting. Food and consumer goods of any kind were difficult to find. Domestic governance became increasing draconian. Travel beyond 100 kilometers needed a special permit. Trains were becoming increasing dilapidated. A seven-day working week was instituted. Geisha houses were shut along with more popular outlets for entertainment. Japanese comedian Roppa Furukawa complained, "What kind of a Tokyo this turned out to be! Ah, it's no fun being alive any more!"[30] All this before America's B-29 Superfortresses had dropped a single bomb on Japan.

Increasingly blame fell upon Tojo, whose unpopularity had risen as he took more power to himself. From the outset he had combined his role as Prime Minister as well as Army Minister but from February 1944 he had also assumed the job of Chief of Staff of the Imperial Japanese Army. Admiral Shimada, who was both Navy Minister and Navy Chief of Staff, was seen as his compliant cipher. It was a concentration of power unique in the post-Meiji Era and one that was becoming increasingly uncomfortable for the ruling elite and quite likely the Emperor himself. Quiet opposition centered around Prince Konoe as well as another former prime minister, Admiral Keisuke Okada and General Koji Sakai, head of the Imperial General Staff. Sakai warned Konoe that he needed to act to end the war before its ally, Germany was defeated: "Germany still has the defensive power, and while the enemy has to fight in both east and west we should take advantage of the situation and enter into negotiations for peace. It will not be to our advantage to wait until Germany is defeated."[31]

At a meeting of the unofficial group of Hirohito's advisers, the *Jushin*, it was concluded, "a powerful new cabinet must be formed that will surge forward unswervingly."[32] To begin with, Tojo believed that by offering the resignation of Admiral Shigetaro Shimada, he could form a new cabinet that would be acceptable. However, after meeting with Marquis Koichi Kido, the Emperor's Lord Keeper of the Privy Seal, he was told that with regards to his assumption of power there were concerns from among the Emperor's senior advisers "and that the Emperor is extremely annoyed,"[33] Tojo concluded that he had lost Hirohito's support. He resigned on 18 July 1944.

A new cabinet was assembled after much discussion in the *Jushin* (Privy Council). General Kuniaki Koiso, a former Chief of Staff of the *Kwantung* Army, and Governor General of Korea, was brought back to be Prime Minister while Admiral Mitsumasa Yonai was brought into the cabinet as Navy Minister. From the backstage discussions led by Prince Konoe, it was clear that many were as concerned about the domestic threat of communist activity as much as the continuing failure in the war with America. In the end it was considered essential to have a general as prime minister who would be capable of controlling the Army. However, Koiso was little more than a figurehead. The key figure in the Army was General Hisaichi Terauchi who commanded all Japan's forces in the *Pacific* region. Ironically he was considered to be too important to move into the post of prime minister.

The Battle of Guam: On 24 July 1944 General Roy Geiger led the 3rd Marine Division's invasion of *Guam*. With 36,000 troops it took almost three weeks of fighting to secure the *Marianas'* largest island, some thirty miles long and up to nine miles wide. After making amphibious landings either side of the Orote Peninsula, fierce Japanese resistance meant that it took four days for the beachheads to meet up.

Lieutenant-General Hideyoshi Obata, who took command after Lieutenant-General Takeshi Takashina was killed on 28 July, withdrew his forces to the north to make a last stand in the mountains. With his forces running short of food and ammunition, there was little chance of him holding out for long and after his forces were defeated between 2–4 August at Mount Barrigada, which commanded the northern axis of the island. The formal defense of the island largely ended, though it was another week before *Guam* was secured. Obata committed suicide on 11 August. He was one of some 18,000 Japanese troops to die. The Marines took almost 500 prisoners of war.

Lieutenant-Colonel Carlson's Battle Plan for Tinian: [Map: 32.3] Just three miles

south of *Saipan, Tinian Island* had a curiously different climate. *Tinian* with its unusually sandy soil did not favor the dense jungle vegetation so common on other *Pacific Ocean* islands. In its less oppressive climate and with its abundant water, *Tinian* grew oranges, lemons and coconuts. The main export from the island however was sugar cane, produced by *Nanyo Kohatsu K.K.* (South Sea Development Company), which had leased *Tinian* in 1926. In the late summer of 1944, the unharvested sugar cane crops on the flat lands of northern and central *Tinian* had grown above head height.

The elongated 'N' shaped island covers 39 square miles and at it greatest distance north to south is approximately ten miles in length. Two elevations towards the northeastern end, Mount Maga and Mount Lasso, at 390 foot and 540 foot above sea level respectively, were matched by unnamed hills on the south of the island that rose to 580 foot A reef surrounded virtually the entire island. With the economic exploitation of the island came 15,380 Japanese inhabitants who significantly outnumbered the 6,000 locals by the start of the *Pacific War*. Unluckily for the inhabitants, the Japanese Navy decided that an airfield should be built; the result was a 4,750-foot runway constructed at Ushi Point.

By autumn of 1944 the forces defending *Tinian* included a mixture of Imperial Japanese Army and Navy troops with the largest unit being the 50th Infantry Regiment. Commanded by Colonel Keishi Ogata, the regiment had fought in Manchuria throughout the war before being transferred to *Tinian* in March 1944 where it became part of Japan's 29th Infantry Division that also occupied *Guam*. Ogata's regiment, along with three infantry battalions, had a 75 mm artillery unit, an engineering unit, and an anti-tank group with six 37 mm guns. A company of twelve light tanks also accompanied the troops. By chance, the invasion of *Saipan* stranded the 1st Battalion of the 135th Infantry, which had been doing amphibious training on *Tinian*. In total the Army's forces consisted of 6,600 officers and men.

In addition, Captain Goichi Oya commanded 1,400 soldiers of the 56th *Keibitai* (Naval Guard); it was a mark of the nature of inter-force rivalry that Oya obeyed orders from Colonel Ogata only in secret so as not to undermine the morale of his men. Differences in food and the issuance of liquor were a contributory factor in the rivalries. In a captured Japanese diary, a soldier wrote, "The Navy stays in barracks buildings and has liberty every night with liquor to drink and makes a big row. We, on the other hand, bivouac in the rain and never get out on pass. What a difference in discipline!"[34]

Included in the defenders' number were artillerymen responsible for the fixed gun installations that included three 6-inch British-built Armstrong Whitworth guns, as well as ten dual-purpose 120 mm guns and four 76.2 mm guns. In addition the Imperial Naval Special Landing Forces (*Kaigun Tokubetsu Rikusentai*), the crack troops who had wrought such havoc on the Marines' landing at *Tarawa* the previous year, managed the smaller field artillery. In total the Japanese garrison on the island numbered 8,323. Ranged against them were units from the recently formed US 4th Marines Division, who were the first troops to sail from the United States straight into a deployment— *Kwajalein* in the *Marshall Islands*. Having retired to *Hawaii* their next assignment was the assault on *Eniwetok*. Supporting the 4th Marines were the better-known 2nd Marines who could trace their origins back to the famous *Battle of Belleau Wood* in *World War I*. However, it was at *Tarawa Atoll* that the 2nd Marines had earned undying fame. Both the Marine units had fought on *Saipan* and arrived at *Tinian* understrength and less than fresh.

Ogata concentrated his defenses on Mount Lasso while he maintained his HQ further north at the Ushi Point Airfield. Tinian Town, with its wide beaches and break in the coral reef that surrounded the island, was considered by Ogata as the only practicable landing point for the US Marines. Rear-Admiral Turner, in command of the amphibious fleet, was equally certain that this should be the landing site. However, Rear-Admiral Harry Hill, Lieutenant-General Holland Smith and Major-General Harry Schmidt, whose task it would be to take his Marines ashore, were equally determined that Tinian Town should be avoided. By choosing a remote beach and effectively flanking the expected attack on Tinian Town, the plan devised by Major-General Schmidt's planning officer, Lieutenant-Colonel Evans Carlson, would render Ogata's plan of defense completely redundant. Reconnaissance had shown that Tinian Town and its beaches were heavily defended; they feared that any landing here would be a repeat of the bloodbath that consumed the 2nd Marines at *Tarawa*. With this in mind Holland Smith reconnoitered the alternative Yellow Beach at *Asiga Bay* on the northeast coast as well as White Beaches-I and -II on the northeastern tip of the island.

Marine swimmers were sent ashore at night to map the beaches; in spite of difficulties with tides and strong currents, the swimmers managed to get back to their boats with information that ruled out Yellow Beach but indicated that, albeit narrow, the White Beaches were possible if they could get their landing craft across the coral reefs. Lieutenant-Commander Draper Kauffman's underwater team had reported back, "no mines or manmade underwater obstructions were found."[35] Their additional advantage was that artillery based in *Saipan* three miles away was within range; moreover the White Beaches were within easy reach of the prime target, Ushi Point Airfield.

Ferocious arguments followed with Holland Smith, Rear-Admiral Hill and Major-General Schmidt on one side against the implacable and recently promoted Vice-Admiral Raymond Turner on the other. Turner bellowed at Smith, "Holland, you are not going to land on the White Beaches, I won't land you there."[36] Holland Smith's reply was equally rambunctious, "Oh, yes you will, you'll land me any Goddamned place I tell you to. I'm the one who makes the tactical plans around here. All you have to do is tell me whether or not you can put the troops ashore there."[37] Not to be outdone, Turner responded, ". . . if you keep talking about this idea they'll think you're just a stupid old bastard."[38] Eventually Spruance was called in to adjudicate the verbal boxing match. Turner backed down. The White Beach Plan was on.

On 22 July *Tinian* had the distinction of having the first napalm bombs (a mixture of jellied gasoline) dropped on it by a flight from recently captured Isely Field on *Saipan*. The test was inconclusive, though napalm would become an important weapon in the bombing of urban Japan in the last months of the war.

In preparation for the landing, the battleship USS *Colorado* destroyed the gun installations flanking the White Beaches at Faibus San Hilo Point. At the same time, to sustain the deception that Tinian Town would be the main landing site, the battleships USS *California* and USS *Tennessee* blitzed the area around the town. *Asiga Bay* was also bombarded. Firing at *Tinian* from all sides had it problems; an overshoot from the west of the island almost hit the cruiser USS *Montpelier*. Diversionary underwater reconnaissance actions were also taken at Tinian Beach. Meanwhile bombing attacks flattened Tinian Town. By the end of 23 July the town and its facilities were smashed and burned. Meanwhile pontoons were being prepared to use as causeways to get over the coral reef and onto White Beach. As a contingency air supplies were planned in case a typhoon disrupted the first line of ship-bound logistics.

The Battle of Tinian: In the early morning of 24 July an intense bombardment lit up White Beach-I and -II. As well as the battleships USS *California*, USS *Tennessee* and the cruiser USS *Louisville*, the attack was joined by four destroyers and 156 artillery pieces located on the south coast of *Saipan*. At 6 a.m. the landing ships began to disgorge the fifty LCI (Landing Craft, Infantry) gunships that led the assault on the beaches. The LCI, whose manufacture had begun in 1943 enabled a single 158 foot vessel to carry 180 troops to shore. Travelling at sixteen knots the LCIs were armed with four 20 mm Oerlikon Cannon on the bow.

At Tinian Town the battleship USS *Colorado* and supporting warships opened a bombardment. Landing craft were launched to fake an attack on Tinian Town beach. At 2,000 yards from the shore, the landing craft turned around and retreated back to the landing ships. However, Japanese 6-inch coastal guns opened fire and scored six hits on the destroyer USS *Norman Scott*, killing her captain and eighteen crewmen. USS *Colorado* took twenty-two hits killing forty-four crewmen. For keeping his ship on station and fighting back in spite of his wounds, Captain William Granat and numbers of his crew would receive the Navy Cross. The Japanese battery would remain active until the USS *Tennessee*'s 14-inch guns completed the destruction of *Tinian*'s coast guns on 26 July.

Over at White Beach, within an hour of landing beachheads had been established. Although eleven Marines were killed in a sharp firefight, the landing had gone remarkably smoothly. Many of the Japanese 'kettle' mines did not explode; their deterioration was testament to Japanese neglect of the northerly White Beaches. Surprise was complete. Lieutenant Silas 'Moose' Titus, from Company G of the 25th Marines recalled, "getting out of the landing boat and there on the rocks was a shell-shocked Jap staring at me with rifle in hand; he didn't shoot me so I shot him."[39] Unloading of supplies began immediately on White Beach-I. By the end of Day-1, Major-General Schmidt had landed 15,600 troops along with all their essential supplies and support. The Marines now prepared for the expected counter-attack.

A month earlier, Colonel Ogata had instructed his commanders that any establishment of a beachhead would be "destroyed at the water's edge by counter-attack."[40] With news of the American landing to the north, artillery units were moved to *Asiga Bay*, while to the northwest at Marpo Point, Captain Izumi assembled 900 troops and began to march north. Others joined from different points on the compass. Izumi had no idea that he was outnumbered by 15:1. Their attack was nonetheless determined. A Marine correspondent reported that at one US machine gun post, the gunners

> held their fire until the Japanese were 100 yards away, then opened up. The Japanese charged, screaming, "*Banzai*," firing light machine guns and throwing hand grenades. It seemed impossible that the two Marines—far ahead of their own lines—could hold on ... The next morning they were found slumped over their weapons, dead. No less than 251 Japanese bodies were piled in front of them . . .[41]

The Navy Cross and the Silver Star were awarded posthumously to the young Marines, Corporal Alfred Daigle and Private Orville Showers respectively.

Banzai charges were repelled by devastating fire from 37 mm cannon while the Marines also made short work of the Japanese tanks. Lieutenant Jim Lucas of the 4th Marines saw one tank begin "to glow red ... and careened into a ditch. A second, mortally wounded ... stopped dead in its tracks. The third tried frantically to turn and then retreat, but our men closed in, literally blasting it apart. Bazookas knocked out the fourth tank with a direct hit which killed the driver. The rest of the crew piled out of the turret, screaming."[42] The sole surviving Japanese tank made its escape. Their failed tank attacks did not dissuade the Japanese infantry from repeated attacks during the night. As light rose early the next morning the Marines were bemused by a series of explosions: "Jap bodies began to fly ten to fifteen feet in the air in the area in front of our lines."[43] It later transpired that Japanese troops were committing suicide using the landmines that they were carrying into battle. A total of 1,241 Japanese troops were counted dead along with a further estimated 700 wounded. A quarter of *Tinian*'s entire defense force had been wiped out. Ogata's best troops had been destroyed.

On Day-2 the Marines expanded their beachhead to take in all the north of the island including Ushi Point Airfield. Thereafter for the next six days they moved gradually southward taking Tinian Town on Day-6. The flat sugar cane fields of *Tinian* were highly conducive to the advance of the 4th Tank Battalion supported by infantry. Ahead of their movement, P-47s dropped 147 napalm bombs to clear a path during the advance through *Tinian*'s cane fields—ninety-one of them containing a revised mixture devised by technical officer Lieutenant-Colonel Wang. The first attempts on *Tinian* had mixed napalm powder (metallic salt from naphtha used in the manufacture of soap) with captured Japanese aviation fuel. It burnt too quickly. When mixed with motor gas and oil, the napalm powder was much more devastating. Wang had arrived in the *Marianas* just five days before the invasion of *Tinian* armed with a film to show the devastating effect of napalm. Dropped from a low level the napalm bombs proved effective against cane if less so against trees. Major-General Clifton Cates, the 4th Division commander, recalled:

> The first morning they put it down, I went up to the front line and those planes came in over our heads it seemed to me like about a hundred feet in the air . . . [They] let go their napalm bombs right over our heads . . . maybe two or three hundred yards in front of us. It was a very devastating thing and particularly to the morale of the Japanese . . . I didn't feel too comfortable sitting up there . . . I figured that some of them might drop short.[44]

Some Japanese troops were fried alive while others fled in terror at the effects of this new weapon. The Marines' southern march was an onslaught against which the Japanese defenders were heavily outgunned both on the ground and in the air.

At this stage the greater irritant faced by the Marines was their drenching from a heavy tropical storm. Of even more concern was the need to get oil ashore in the squally conditions. It was a problem made more difficult by the fact that the rapid advance of the Marines was consuming 600 drums of oil a day rather than the predicted 400. Fighting became heavier as Major-General Schmidt's forces approached the southern tip of the island. It became increasingly clear that Colonel Ogata would make this area his last stand. On 29 July Ogata gave his last recorded order—to assemble and fight to the last along the wooded ridges at the southern end of the island. Similarly Captain Oya ordered his *Rikusentai* to make their final stand on 'Hills 560' and 'Hill 580' located at *Tinian*'s southeastern tip. On 31 July, the final large-scale attack of the *Battle of Tinian* was opened with a ferocious barrage delivered by battleships, aircraft and artillery. Heavily mined approaches slowed the pace of advance and Japanese counter-attacks became more persistent and more successful. Moreover as the Marines moved forward increasing numbers of civilians emerged waving white flags. As usual in the island battles, Japanese commanders had paid scant regard to the welfare of civilian inhabitants. Young officer, James Underhill, later a Marine Lieutenant-General noted that:

> The state of these people was indescribable. They came in with no possessions except the rags on their backs. They had been under a two-month intense bombardment

and shelling and many were suffering from shell shock
. . . They had existed on very scant rations for six weeks
and for the past week had had practically nothing to
eat. They had been cut off from their own water supply
for a week and had caught what rainwater they could in
bowls and cans. Hundreds of them were wounded and
some of their wounds were gangrenous. Beri, syphilis,
pneumonia, dysentery, and tuberculosis were common.
[They needed] shelter, food, water, clothing, medical
care, and sanitation.[45]

As the Marines reached the cliffs on either flank, they started to work along them to close the pincer. It was here that some of the fiercest fighting of the *Tinian* campaign took place. Although heavy fighting continued until 3 August, the 'mopping up' still had to be done. The 2nd Marines were relieved by 8th Marines on 6 August and two days later 4th Marines were sent back to *Saipan* for 'rest and recuperation.' Over the next five months, 8th Marines killed a further 500 Japanese troops who had held out; the costs to 8th Marines were 38 killed and 125 wounded. As usual in the last months of the war, 'mopping up' was expensive in terms of time, stress and casualties for the troops involved. Mopping up accounted for more than 10 percent of the 328 US soldiers to lose their lives on the island. Just 313 troops out of Japan's 8,323-man garrison allowed themselves to be captured—the rest had been killed.

Overall, *Tinian* had proved to be an exceptional campaign—possibly the most successful US island invasion of the *Pacific War*. Admiral Spruance described the capture of *Tinian* as "The most brilliantly conceived and executed amphibious operation in *World War II*."[46] Many of the lessons of *Tarawa* a year earlier had been absorbed. On *Tinian* a defense force 25 percent larger than *Tarawa* was overwhelmed at one-third the cost in American lives. The key difference was not only the success of Carlson's battle plan with its unanticipated flanking beach landing but the nature of the terrain faced by the Marines. As Major-General Clifton Cates, later appointed Commandant of the Marine Corps in 1948, observed, "The fighting was different from most any that we had experienced because it was good terrain . . . It was a good clean operation and I think the men really enjoyed it."[47] If any US amphibious operation in the *Pacific War* could be described as being 'like-a-picnic' it was *Tinian*. Perhaps it is for that reason that the *Battle of Tinian* has received less attention than it perhaps deserves.

Colonel Nakagawa's Preparations on Peleliu: **[Map: 32.4]** The last island battle of the central *Pacific* campaign took place on the island of *Peleliu* (one of the sixteen islands of the current nation of *Palau*) some 350 miles to the southwest of *Guam* and 700 miles east of the Philippines. *Peleliu* was the second-most southerly of the *Palau* chain, desired for its spacious airfield. For both Japan and the United States it was the airfield that made *Peleliu* the jewel of the *Palaus*.

The landing would be led by Major-General William Rupertus and the 1st Marines Division, whose command he had inherited from Major-General Vandegrift who, after *Guadalcanal*, had become the obvious choice as the new commander of the Marine Corps on 1 January 1944. Under Rupertus's command was 'Chesty' Puller, the hero of the *Battle of Henderson Field* on *Guadalcanal*. Major-General Paul Mueller's 81st Infantry Davison, known as the 'Wildcats,' would support them. The assault was planned by Major-General Roy Gieger, commanding General of the III-Amphibious Corps. Major-General Julian Smith, who had commanded the 2nd Marine Division at *Tarawa Atoll*, was appointed Commanding General, Third Fleet Expeditionary Troops, would lead the landing forces.

Rupertus was a capable, unflamboyant officer with considerable experience. He had served variously in Shanghai and Latin America, where he became Marine Commandant at *Guantanamo Bay* (Cuba). At both *Guadalcanal* and Cape Gloucester, Rupertus had performed with distinction. However, he tended to occasional periods of depression, which followed the loss of his wife and two children to an epidemic of scarlet fever while on a tour to China. In spite of his mistrust of the Army as a result of the 'Smith versus Smith' controversy, the problems of inter-force rivalry that had plagued the *Battle of Saipan* did not re-emerge during the *Peleliu* operation. Perhaps not surprisingly after the recent success on *Tinian*, the 1st Marines commander, Major-General William Rupertus, predicted that it would take a few days to subdue an island that measured just five square miles. It was one of the least accurate forecasts of the war. Against all expectations the *Battle of Peleliu* lasted for two and a half months and involved by some accounts the heaviest fighting for any island in the *Pacific*.

The commander of the 11,000 troops of the 14th Infantry Division defending the island was Lieutenant-Colonel Kunio Nakagawa, an officer with an impeccable record after receiving nine leadership medals for actions in the *Second Sino-Japanese War*. Nakagawa had been appointed to the command of the island by the new commander in the *Palau Islands*, Lieutenant-General Inoue Sadao, who was Tojo's appointment to lead the 12,000 troop reinforcements sent to the island. After the defeats in the *Marshall Islands* and the destruction of *Truk*, Prime Minister Tojo had designated *Peleliu* to be within the Absolute National Defense Zone. It was a controversial appointment. Nakagawa, regarded by many to be the most able defensive tactician in the Imperial Japanese Army, was the logical choice to prepare *Peleliu*'s defenses. However, a storm erupted in Japanese Navy ranks because Vice-Admiral Seichi Ito, supposedly the ranking officer on *Peleliu*, would therefore report to a mere Army Lieutenant-Colonel. Severe difficulties in co-operation between the Army and the Navy ensued. To assuage sensitivities, that were even greater than those inter-force rivalries evident on *Tinian*, Admiral Sadao sent Major-General Murai as window dressing, though it seems likely that Vice-Admiral Seichi Ito was not actually on *Peleliu* when the island was attacked.

Nakagawa adopted new techniques for island defense devised by a research group sent by the Imperial Army HQ in Tokyo; beach defense was abandoned in favor of 'internal' defense based on the building of an interlocking network of bunkers, caves, and tunnels. Hidden gun positions made them almost impregnable to grenade and flame-thrower attack. It was a tactical defensive deployment plan that became the blueprint for the later action at *Iwo Jima*. At the northern end of the island, which Nakagawa correctly anticipated would be the US landing point, man-made caves were blasted into the overlooking coral promontories and filled with a 47 mm gun and six 20 mm cannon. They were then sealed shut leaving narrow firing slits. In addition beaches were heavily mined though their defenses were lightly manned to draw the attackers into the maws of the 'internal' fortifications.

The invasion force pushed off from its base in the southern *Solomon Islands* on 4 September with the intention of forcing a landing on *Peleliu* on the morning of 15 September. The obligatory naval shelling from 5 battleships, 4 heavy cruisers and 4 light cruisers preceded it. Any buildings or aircraft on the island were obliterated and the Navy believed that few Japanese could be left alive. The lack of any response from the island convinced Rear-Admiral Jesse Oldendorf that there were no more targets. Colonel Lewis 'Chesty' Puller, a heroic veteran of both *Guadalcanal* and *Tarawa* was not convinced: "Well Sir, all I can see is dust. I doubt if you've cleaned it out. I know they have underground oil dumps for that airfield. We haven't seen that blow. I've been boning over those maps for weeks and I believe they'll have pillbox stuff, fortifications like we've never seen."[48] Puller was correct. On *Peleliu* the US bombardment had caused almost no casualties and the island's defensive capabilities had been barely impaired. Significantly the US battleships failed to target the coral promontories that flanked the landing beach. Ultimately the main use of the vast expenditure of ordnance at *Peleliu* was probably the clearance of vegetation from the Japanese defense positions.

On board their transport ships, the Marines prepared for action. Sterling Mace of the 3rd Battalion, 5th Marines, described the scene on board:

> Into the ship's hold we descended to find the amphibian tractors with their diesel engines roaring. The sound was deafening. The smell of acrid fumes was sickening . . . men and equipment reverberated off the steel hull. We huddled, thirty-six men and a 37 mm field piece to a tractor, waiting for the bow doors to open. Suddenly, the doors opened wide letting the dawn's light shed on us. Out of the bay doors poured the 'Alligators' [amtracs] . . . One after another they splashed into the sea and, in full throttle, left the LST behind in its wake.[49]

The Battle of Peleliu: The 1st Marines landed at 8.32 a.m. on 15 September on the northernmost of the west coast beaches including White Beach, while 5th and 7th Marines landed on center beach and the southern Orange Beach. On either flank deadly hidden guns, dug into the coral promontories by the Japanese defenders, destroyed over sixty amtracs and 'ducks' (DUKWs; six-wheeled amphibious trucks produced by General Motors) used to transport soldiers and supplies.

Many Marines had to wade ashore in chest-high water after their transports were knocked out. As Sterling Mace recalled, "In the time it took from the amphibian tractor in the surf to the beach everything was a mass of confusion."[50] Raked by machine gun fire, casualties were extremely heavy. Those who survived to the beach frequently scrambled ashore without equipment that they had been forced to abandon either in their vehicles or because it was threatening to drown them as they waded through deep water. The embedded *Life* magazine war artist Tom Lea recorded, "We ground to a stop . . . on the coarse coral . . . and we ran down the ramp and came around the end of the LVT [amtrac] . . . Those Marines flattened in the sand on that beach were dark and huddled like wet rats in death as I threw my body down among them."[51] Only in the center, where the Marines were further from the raking fire of the coral promontories, was rapid progress made.

The 5th Marines raced towards the airfield where they were engaged in a counter-attack by Colonel Nakagawa's light tanks supported by infantry. However, US dive-bombers and the Marines' artillery quickly saw of this offensive. One US M-48A1 Sherman medium tank alone destroyed eleven Japanese tanks that had surrounded it. Brigadier-General O. P. Smith later described it as being "like Indians round a wagon train."[52] By the end of the first day the Marines had suffered 900 casualties including over 200 fatalities. On Day-2, the airfield was captured though there was heavy fighting around Japanese pillboxes. By Day-3 the airport could start to be put to use for aerial reconnaissance and artillery spotting. Heat exhaustion, with temperatures as high as 115 degrees, and lack of drinking water now became the most pressing of problems for the Marines. Journalist Robert 'Pepper' Martin of *Time* magazine reported:

> *Peleliu* is a horrible place. The heat is stifling and rain falls intermittently—the muggy rains that bring no relief, only greater misery. The coral rocks soak up the heat during the day and it is only slightly cooler at night. Marines are in the finest possible physical condition, they wilted on *Peleliu*. By the fourth day there were as many casualties from heat prostration as from wounds . . .[53]

Just eleven days after the landings, Marine F4U Corsairs began to be used for dive-bombing caves and hidden gun emplacements. It was the shortest take-off and bombing run of the war. Napalm, which had been greedily ordered after the experiments on *Tinian*, was used to clear vegetation. Meanwhile Colonel Lewis 'Chesty' Puller, commander of the 1st Marine Regiment, ordered Captain George Hunt, after the war a long-serving editor of *Life* magazine, to clear the 'Point.' By using smoke grenades for cover, a rifle platoon, using M1 rifles with M7 grenade launchers managed to take out the 20 mm cannon as well as the 47 mm gun emplacement. 1st Marines K Company, 3rd Battalion then held out for thirty hours against four major Japanese counter-attacks that ended with hand-to-hand fighting. By the time that they were reinforced only 18 men out of 175 were not wounded.

Having taken the 'Point,' the Marines now moved forward towards the defenses on Mount Umurbrogol. Stripped of its jungle scrub by the weight of American fire, the approaches to the mountain were described by Major Gordon Gale of the 5th Marines as "a complex system of sharply uplifted coral ridges, knobs, valleys, and sinkholes."[54] Hidden in the man-made caves were hospitals, ammunition stores, barracks, kitchens, water supplies as well as command and communication centers. Here they found themselves trapped between fire from two ridges in what became known as 'Bloody Nose Ridge.'

At night Japanese troops infiltrated Marine positions and killed them in their foxholes, forcing them to dig two-man positions in which one Marine could sleep while the other kept guard. Snipers also targeted stretcher-bearers. Ground was hard won. After a week of fighting on their way toward Mount Umurbrogol, Puller's 1st Marines suffered 1,749 casualties out of 3,000 men. Puller's troops had suffered 60 percent casualty rates— more than double the level at which a US fighting unit was considered to be no longer operative. The 1st Marines were subsequently out of action for almost six months. The 81st Infantry Division and the 321st Regiment Combat Team finally relieved them. The 5th and 7th Marines then turned their attention to *Peleliu*'s mountain ridges. By mid-October these units too had suffered 50 percent casualties. In a war of superlative military exploits, the Marines' performance on *Peleliu* was a highpoint. As Major Gayle responded when asked how the fighting men were doing, "Every Marine fighting in those hills is an expert. If he wasn't, he wouldn't be alive."[55]

It was another month before Japanese resistance was broken. Almost all of the 10,900 Japanese troops who garrisoned *Peleliu* were killed. It was later worked out that it took 1,539 rounds of ammunition to kill each Japanese soldier; US troops fired 13.3 million bullets, 1.5 million 0.45 caliber rounds, 693,000 0.50 caliber rounds, 150,000 mortar bombs and used 118,000 grenades. The most useful weapon to destroy enemy positions however was the flame-thrower. Using gasoline trucks and pumps, the Marines were able to improvise a system of throwing napalm hundreds of feet into the Japanese defensive positions. However, the development of a Sherman tank, specially designed as a long-distance flame-thrower, was probably the most important technical advance of the *Peleliu* Campaign.

At the end, having burnt his regimental colors, Lieutenant-General Nakagawa committed suicide. He had achieved his aim of fighting a defensive battle to the end and not wasting his troops' energies on the type of *banzai* charge favored by Major-General Murai. Lieutenant-General Sadao Inoue on *Koror Island*, fifty miles to the north of *Peleliu*, had sided with Nakagawa sending a message to Murai that read, "It is easy to die but difficult to live on. We must select the difficult course and continue to fight because of the influence on the morale of the Japanese people. Saipan was lost in a very short time because of vain *banzai* attacks with the result that the people at home suffered a drop in morale."[56]

Tanks in the Pacific War: On the Asian mainland, light tanks had proved effective in Malaya and had helped General Yamashita to clear British roadblocks and defenses on the route south. Indeed the lack of tanks is often cited as one of the main reasons for the abject failure of the British campaigns in Malaya and Burma. A similar lack of tanks severely hampered Chinese resistance to the Japanese Army in the early stages of the *Second Sino-Japanese War* and later during the battles of Japan's ICHI-GO Campaign. This was not a testimony to the quality of Japanese tanks.

Russian tanks in the *Battles of Nomonhan* had roundly defeated the Type-95 Ha-Go, a light tank, which had been Japan's main field weapon in the 1939 border war with the Soviet Union. Japan's most-produced medium tank was the Type-97 Chi-Ha, which was a scaled-up version of the Type-95. Designed in 1936, the Type-97, of which over 2,000 (including variants) were produced, was already outdated by the start of the *Pacific War*. Fortunately for the Japanese Army, the US Army was even worse prepared in terms of mechanization.

America's heavy tank, the M-6 proved so poor that it never saw action. In effect the US Army started the war with almost no tanks. During war games exercises in Louisiana in September 1941, they painted the word 'tank' on the side of trucks to simulate real tanks. Even after *Pearl Harbor* the 10th Armored Division's tank crews had to practice manoeuvres by marching down streets pretending that they were in a tank. The first tanks to see action were the 192nd and 194th Tank Battalions; their lightweight M3 Stuarts, armed with a 37 mm cannon, were quite evenly matched with Japanese offerings in the early actions on the Philippines but were destroyed by Japanese air attack. However, for the US, redemption finally came with the development of the Sherman medium tank with its 75 mm gun. After the Russian T-34, it became the most produced tank of *World War II*. The Detroit Arsenal Tank Plant set up by Chrysler used the manufacturing line systems employed in the US auto industry and produced over 15,000 M4 Shermans and variants. Along with eight other manufacturers, including Ford Motor Company, 49,234 Shermans were produced during the course of the war.

Well armored, reliable and heavily armed, the Sherman proved highly effective in some actions, such as on *Peleliu*, when it was finally delivered to Asia and the *Pacific* in 1943. Stilwell's X-Force, armed with 100 Shermans, also used them to good effect in the advance through northern Burma to Myitkyina. However, in general in the jungles of the *Solomon Islands* and New Guinea or the paddy fields of China and South East Asia, terrain was highly unfavourable to the use of tanks, although they were used as bunker busters in the island battles of Nimitz's charge through the central *Pacific*. Very often though, bulldozers were more useful in digging out Japanese bunkers or blocking off tunnels and caves.

In essence, in the closed battle conditions of the *Pacific*, the tank was not the crucial weapon that characterized the war in Europe. It is no coincidence that the best tanks of the war, the Russian T-34 and the German Panzer IV were developed for the open plains of the Russian steppes where their speed of maneuver was decisive. Whereas in the *Pacific*, a group of a dozen tanks was significant, at the *Battle of Kursk* more than 8,000 tanks were deployed by the Russians and Germans. **[See Appendix C: Economics of the Pacific War: The 'New Deal' Mobilized]**

Was Peleliu Necessary? After almost ten weeks of battle the island had been taken. By most reckoning the fighting for Umurbrogol Ridge represented the hardest single action of the *Pacific* Campaign. Eight Marines received Medals of Honor of which five were awarded posthumously. *Time*'s 'Pepper' Martin concluded, "For sheer brutality and fatigue, I think it surpasses anything yet seen in the Pacific . . ."[57]

It was estimated that more than 10,000 Japanese troops lay dead. Just 202 of the island's occupants surrendered, of whom 19 were Japanese, with the remainder being Korean and Okinawan laborers. After the battle ended, a handful of Japanese Army and Navy troops still occupied the maze of tunnels in the Umurbrogol Mountains. After failing to persuade them to surrender, the tunnels' entrances were blasted shut. To great amazement, five of the survivors trapped inside managed to dig their way out five months later and were captured. In 1947 the US government, after rumors surfaced of more Japanese survivors on *Peleliu*, sent 120 Marines to search the island; a Japanese lieutenant of the 2nd Infantry with twenty-six bedraggled troops emerged along with eight sailors of the 45th Guard Force. It was the last official surrender of *World War II*.

Tragically, with the benefit of hindsight, it was clear that the taking of *Peleliu* was completely unnecessary. While it had been included as a target in the battle plans of both MacArthur and Nimitz as they plotted their different routes toward Japan, *Peleliu*'s capture became a 'white elephant' project. With *Peleliu*'s airfields devoid of aircraft and too far away to be supplied by an ever-weakening Japanese logistical capability, the island presented no threat either to MacArthur or to the American logistical center being established on *Ulithi Atoll* 500 miles to the northeast. Supposedly *Peleliu* needed to be captured to protect MacArthur's right flank. But protect him from what? Given the inability of Japan to move around its troops in the *Pacific* by 1944, *Peleliu* exercised no external threat whatsoever. As for *Peleliu*'s utility as a base, the proof was in its later use. Having taken *Peleliu* at a cost of an astonishing 9,804 casualties including 1,794 dead (1,252 Marines), the island's airfield and natural harbor were barely used as *Ulithi Atoll*, won at virtually no cost, became the staging post for the later campaigns against *Iwo Jima* and *Okinawa*.

Two days before the assault, on 13 September, Vice-Admiral 'Bull' Halsey, MacArthur's unlikely friend in the Navy, had suggested that the assault on *Peleliu* be cancelled and the troops used instead on *Leyte Island* in the Philippines. Herein perhaps lies the answer to the 'why *Peleliu*' question; it seems hardly likely that Nimitz would have wanted to help his *Pacific War* rival. MacArthur may have been monomaniacally competitive but Nimitz too was a man who fought his corner albeit more quietly. *Peleliu* may simply have been one of these 'corners.' Whatever the reasons for Nimitz's decision to press the attack on *Peleliu*, that he only ever justified on the basis that the invasion force was already at sea, it was clear in hindsight that this was one of the few identifiable missteps in Nimitz's *Central Pacific* Campaign.

Lieutenant-General Rupertus, supposedly angry at the loss of Marine lives in an unnecessary action (or perhaps punished for his poor leadership at *Peleliu*) was awarded a Distinguish Service Medal and sent back to America as Commandant of the Marine

Corps at Quantico, Virginia. Rupertus, who was nearly immobile during the battle because of an ankle injury sustained in a training exercise, has often been criticized for his unimaginative tactics and his reluctance to bring in the Army's 81st Infantry earlier. Colonel Puller, often idolized as the quintessential Marine, was also injured and was unable to survey the battlefield; had he been able to do so he may not have ordered so many costly and fruitless assaults that left numbers of Marines embittered about his leadership at *Peleliu*. Puller's leadership may also have been affected by the killing of his brother Lieutenant-Colonel Sam Puller, a 4th Marine, by a sniper's bullet on *Guam* a few weeks earlier. A Medal of Honor company commander in 1st Marine Battalion, Captain Everett Pope, became an outspoken critic of Puller after the war. However, the criticism of Puller did little to impede a career that saw him perform with undoubted distinction commanding the landing at the *Battle of Inchon* and later leading his troops at the 17-day fighting retreat in freezing conditions at the epic *Battle of Chosin Reservoir* during the *Korean War*. Puller became the most decorated officer in Marine Corp history.

However, it should be emphasized that the reputation of both Rupertus and Puller undoubtedly suffered as a result of the brilliant and inspired defensive leadership of Lieutenant-Colonel Nakagawa, perhaps the true hero of the action at *Peleliu*. As has generally been the case in post-war analysis of the battles of the *Pacific War*, failures have usually been attributed to Allied commanders with little reference to the skills, in some cases exceptional skills, of Japanese officers.

Advance to Ulithi Atoll and the Logistics of the Central Pacific: [Map: 32.5] On 23 September 1944, the week after Nimitz's forces launched their invasion of *Peleliu*, the Army's 81st Division made an unopposed occupation of *Ulithi Atoll*. Perversely, at no cost in US lives, Nimitz's forces acquired an asset that, unlike *Peleliu*, would be of inestimable value in the last year of the war. A reconnoiter of *Ulithi Atoll* by the survey ship USS *Sumner* quickly established that the atoll could provide secure anchorage for up to 700 ships. As such *Ulithi* held a bigger capacity than either *Majuro* (*Marshall Islands*) or *Pearl Harbor*. By comparison with the size of the lagoon, twenty-two miles long by fifteen miles wide, the size of *Ulithi Atoll*'s land area was miniscule. The forty islets in aggregate had a combined landmass of just 1.7 square miles. Usefully however, on *Falalop*, the Japanese had developed a runway. By 17 October, the Seabees had furnished the atoll with two 6,000-foot runways.

Situated 360 miles southwest of *Guam* and half way to *Peleliu, Ulithi Atoll* was perfectly placed to act as a naval logistical center for the projected campaigns against the Japanese home islands. US Service Squadron-10 was quickly dispatched to turn *Ulithi* into a workable naval service yard. Commodore Worrall Carter had developed a mobile service force whose development reached its apogee at *Ulithi*. Pontoon piers were built and sections were filled with sand and sunk and then tethered to the shore. They would prove capable of withstanding the battering of the *Central Pacific*'s extreme weather. In one of the more remarkable logistical operations of the war, an entire service base was constructed in a month. Eventually facilities around the lagoon would include docks, hospitals, workshops, metal fabrication shops, foundries, munitions stores, gasoline depots, storage facilities, administration offices and barracks. An army of technicians—welders, carpenters, electricians, fitters—were constantly being ferried around the lagoon or flown from islet to islet by light aircraft. It was a spectacular sight that greeted new arrivals. For Ensign Norman Stark, an F6F fighter pilot arriving on the USS *Hornet*, the arrival at *Ulithi* was memorable:

> Entering the Lagoon the ships followed, one by one in single file. It took several hours for the whole Fleet to navigate the channel and drop anchor. That was a sight I will never forget. I looked forward and saw at least six ships ahead of the *Hornet*. As I looked back, I saw ships in a line that disappeared in the distance, hidden by the curvature of the earth. Every time we returned to Ulithi the sight of such a mighty Fleet would transfix me.[58]

The Seabees also created a fleet recreation center on *Mog Mog Island* that could cater for 8,000 men and 1,000 officers per day. Facilities included a 1,200-seat theater as well as a 500-seat chapel. On *Asor Island*, the US Navy located a radio station, the port director's office and a cemetery. *Sorlen Island* became the center for the service and repair of smaller ships. The USS *Abatan*, a huge tanker vessel, was permanently in place to distil the vast amount of drinking water needed by a lagoon that was home to tens of thousands of sailors. The *Abatan* also baked bread and pies while a nearby barge tender produced over 1,000 gallons of ice cream per day. Lieutenant-Commander Norman Stark, remembered his 'rest and recreation' visits to *Mog Mog* with relish: "Christmas Dinner 1944 was something I shall never forget. I had no idea anything so delicious was even contemplated considering our location and the conditions under which we were operating. I have never had a better meal in any restaurant, no matter how highly rated."[59]

It was an extraordinary enterprise situated as it was in the middle of the *Pacific Ocean* some 6,700 miles from San Francisco. (To put it in context, the distance from London to San Francisco is 5,350 miles). Oil tankers brought some 6 million tons of oil per month from the west coast of America to *Ulithi* from where a shuttle of forty tankers delivered diesel oil to Nimitz's *Pacific* fleet. At *Ulithi* itself a reserve of 100,000 tons was stored. The capacity of *Ulithi* to hold ships made up for the relatively limited anchorage of the *Marianas Islands*. *Saipan* and *Tinian* had runways but were largely bereft of anchorage. However, Nimitz ordered the dredging of *Guam*'s harbor at Apra and ordered the extension of the breakwater. Though not as big as *Ulithi*'s, by the beginning of 1945 facilities were developed on *Guam* that could nevertheless support about a third of the *Pacific* Fleet. At the same time that the port was ready for operations, Nimitz moved his forward HQ to *Guam* for the remainder of the war. The island became the main administrative hub for the vast logistical task of transporting the American Army to Japan and for sustaining the active *Pacific* operations of the now enormous US fleet.

If *Ulithi Atoll* continued to provide the much needed naval base for the final approaches to Japan, the main purpose of the *Mariana Islands* and the reason for their subjugation was to build airfields for the Boeing B-29 Superfortress heavy bomber. On *Tinian* the existing airdrome near Marpi Point was redeveloped and North Field, as it became known, was ready to use from February 1945. Meanwhile West Field, near Tinian Town, became operational in March. On *Guam*, North Field launched its first flights in January while another field at Pati Points only became operational in June 1945; Harmon Field became headquarters of Twenty-First Bomber Group.

Bombing operations started on a small scale on 24 November 1944 and steadily built up in scale and intensity over the succeeding months. Prince Naruhiko Higashikuni, Commander in Chief of Home Defense would later recall:

> The War was lost when the Marianas were taken away
> from Japan and when we heard the B-29's were coming
> . . . We had nothing in Japan that we could use against the
> weapon. From the point of view of the Home Defense
> Command, we felt that the war was lost and said so. If the
> B-29s could come over Japan, there was nothing that
> could be done.[60]

33 Battle of Leyte Gulf: 'Bull' Halsey's Mad Dash for Glory

[October 1944]

[Maps: 33.1, 33.2, 33.3, 33.4, 33.5, 33.6]

Scale and Historic Importance of the Battle of Leyte Gulf: In terms of scale, the *Battle of Leyte Gulf* deserves to be considered one of the greatest naval battles of history. In effect it was the last fully-fledged fleet battle in history and brought an end to the last vestiges of the 'Dreadnought Era.' The combined forces in the battle comprised over 280 frontline warships and almost 1,000 vessels in all if submarines, escorts, PT boats, and fleet auxiliary ships (both supply and repair) are included. Deployment of the respective Japanese and American navies took place over 450,000 square miles, an area the size of France, while the engagement itself occupied an area the size of Great Britain. Curiously, in spite of the name given to this largest of naval battles, not a single action took place in *Leyte Gulf*, which was simply the landing point for General MacArthur's amphibious forces as he initiated his return with the American Army to the Philippines. [For the *Battle of Leyte Island* see Chapter 34: "I Have Returned": MacArthur Regains the Philippines]

In fact the *Battle of Leyte Gulf* is the name given to a collection of five naval battles that took place over three days: the *Battle of Palawan Passage*, the *Battle of Sibuyan Sea*, the *Battle of Surigao Strait*, the *Battle of Samar Island*, and the *Battle of Cape Engano*. If the *Battle of Leyte Gulf* has not achieved the historical prominence that its scale would indicate, the reason perhaps lies in the fact that even if the Japanese Navy had won, the final outcome of the war already seemed certain. Unlike the battles of *Salamis* [490 BC], *Actium* [31 BC], *Lepanto* [1571], or *Trafalgar* [1805], the *Battle of Leyte Gulf* was never going to change the course of history; it did not decide the outcome of a war, merely its duration. The power of Japan's all-important aircraft carrier force had already been destroyed at the *Battle of the Philippines Sea* (the *Great Marianas Turkey Shoot*).

For the Japanese, the battle was the last throw of the dice by its navy to achieve an overwhelming victory that might force the Americans to the negotiating table. While *Leyte Gulf* could be seen as a final *banzai* charge of the Japanese Navy, its outcome, as a result of serious strategic and tactical mistakes made by Admiral 'Bull' Halsey, was for a time in the balance. In short, it was a 'close-run thing.'

Pacific Theater Turf Wars: MacArthur, Nimitz and FDR in Honolulu: The location of the *Battle of Leyte Gulf* reflected yet another battle: a turf war between General

MacArthur, Supreme Commander of the South West Pacific Area (SWPA) on the one hand and Admiral Nimitz, Commander in Chief Pacific Ocean Areas (POA) on the other. After the *Marianas* Campaign, the endgame of Nimitz's 'island hop' across the *Pacific*, the American Joint Chiefs of Staff faced a choice—to invade the Philippines, or to leave it to 'wither on the vine' by invading *Formosa*. With the exception of General George Marshall who favored bypassing *Luzon* and *Formosa* by going direct to *Kyushu*, Admiral Ernest King and the other Joint Chiefs, Admirals William Leahy (Chairman) and General 'Hap' Arnold, favored invasion of *Formosa* at least until the summer of 1944.

Initially, Admiral Chester Nimitz, Commander in Chief, United States Pacific Fleet, agreed with this plan. Apart from obviating the need for the retaking of the strongly defended Philippines, *Formosa* was a 560 miles shorter stepping-stone to Japan itself and would cut Japan's remaining supply lines to South East Asia. In addition, *Formosa* could act as a base for the invasion of Japanese-held southern China. Some in the US Air Force optimistically argued that a force of just 200 B-29 bombers, based in *Formosa*, could bring about the Japanese defeat in China. However, the key proponent of the Philippines route was MacArthur. Having constantly sniped at the cost of lives involved in Nimitz's *Central Pacific* campaign, MacArthur now asserted that the taking of *Formosa* would be a "massive operation, extremely costly in men and shipping, logistically precarious and time consuming."[1] He was prepared to take his case to Washington.

Presidential election politics now intervened. Roosevelt decided to hold a meeting with MacArthur and Nimitz in *Honolulu* in July 1944. Ostensibly the *raison d'être* was to discuss strategy for the final approaches to the Japanese homeland. For Roosevelt however, it was political posturing prior to his campaign for re-election for an unprecedented fourth term. MacArthur protested bitterly about the "humiliation of forcing me to leave my command to fly to *Honolulu* for a political picture taking junket."[2] It was a bizarrely hypocritical complaint; nobody was more alive to the possibilities of political grandstanding than MacArthur.

Not to be outdone, MacArthur 'showboated' into *Honolulu*. Instead of joining Admirals Leahy and Nimitz and senior generals to greet Roosevelt, their Commander in Chief, aboard the USS *Baltimore*, MacArthur landed early and headed straight to his billet at General Richardson's quarters at Fort Shafter. As FDR was about to disembark MacArthur arrived with the sirens of his escort blaring in a large open top limousine borrowed from a local 'Madam,' to which his staff had quickly added the insignia of a four-star general. With studied informality he wore khaki trousers, a brown leather air force jacket and the cap of a Filipino Field Marshal; ascending the gangway he stopped halfway to wave and soak up the applause of the crowd that had gathered to see the President. Meeting FDR in his cabin, MacArthur, in spite of the stop-over at his *Honolulu* billet where he could easily have changed into more appropriate hot weather attire, explained his strange dress by saying, "you haven't been up there where I came from, and it's cold up there in the sky."[3] Poor chap: the sickly US President had travelled twice the distance to see his Army's commander in the *Pacific*. MacArthur, like his

British counterpart in South East Asia Command (SEAC), Louis Mountbatten, was a theatrical popinjay who loved flags, uniforms and all aspects of military regalia. But whereas Louis Mountbatten mainly strutted peacock-like to satisfy his own vanity, MacArthur always had an eye to the main chance of media coverage and political self-promotion.

However much he complained about the trip to *Honolulu*, and particularly Roosevelt's motivation for the visit, it was an opportunity for self-advancement that MacArthur used to the maximum effect. Treating Admiral Nimitz as if he were not in the room, MacArthur dominated the strategic discussions and attempted to impose his will on an ailing President, on whose physical decline he passed comment. At a private meeting with Roosevelt, MacArthur's behavior was bullying:

> Mr. President, the country has forgiven you for what took place on Bataan. You hope to be re-elected president of the United States, but the nation will never forgive you if you approve a plan which leaves 17 million Christian American subjects to wither in the Philippines under the conqueror's heel until the peace treaty frees them. You might do it for reasons of strategy or tactics, but politically, it would ruin you.[4]

MacArthur's rudeness with regard to his Bataan comments was breathtaking given the general's own heavy responsibility for the loss of the Philippines. His attempt at moral blackmail was equally repugnant. However, it was behavior he could get away with because of the 'heroic' image that he had carefully cultivated for himself in the American press. In essence MacArthur's hold on the American press and the American people was such that his position was almost impregnable. It may even have been a fleeting thought in his mind to consider the possibility of running as the Republican candidate against Roosevelt in the upcoming presidential elections. However, there is no evidence, as some conspiracy theorists have posited, that Roosevelt swung toward the Philippines invasion plan as a means of thwarting the likelihood of a MacArthur candidacy.

For MacArthur, the re-capture of the Philippines was the centerpiece of his plans. In his biographical accounts, *Reminiscences* [1964], MacArthur recalled,

> The Philippine Islands had constituted the main objective of my planning from the time of my departure from Corregidor in March 1942. From the very outset I regarded this strategic archipelago as the keystone of Japan's captured island empire, and, therefore, the ultimate goal of the plan of operations in the Southwest Pacific Area.[5]

After the war, MacArthur supported his arguments by referring to Lieutenant-General Shuichi Miyazaki, Chief of Operations Section, Imperial General Headquarters, who, in post-war interviews stated, "Viewed from the standpoint of political and operational strategy, holding the Philippines was the one essential for the execution of the war against America and Britain."[6] There were some cogent arguments for the choice of *Luzon* in the Philippines over *Formosa*. Filipino guerrillas were already harassing the Japanese occupier, while in *Formosa*, an island that Japan had had possession of for more than half a century, they might expect a greater level of popular support. Further, it was initially estimated that the subjugation of *Formosa* might take twelve divisions, an aggregate number of troops that was not yet available to the US commanders in Asia.

MacArthur assured Roosevelt that losses in retaking *Luzon* would be minimal. He pompously asserted, "Mr. President, my losses would not be heavy, any more than they have been in the past . . . your good commanders do not turn in heavy losses."[7] In spite of this intended slight at Nimitz's expense, given the sometimes heavy losses taken by US forces in the thrust through the *Central Pacific*, MacArthur's arguments were beginning to sway even Nimitz. That evening Roosevelt spoke to his doctor, Ross McIntire: "Give me an aspirin before I go to bed. In fact, give me another aspirin to take in the morning. In all my life nobody ever talked to me the way MacArthur did."[8] For all his harassment of the President, MacArthur was far too optimistic when he assured Roosevelt at their final lunch that he and Nimitz saw eye to eye and "understand each other perfectly."[9] Back on his plane, MacArthur turned to his aide and boasted, "We've sold it."[10] When he returned to his South West Pacific Area Command HQ in Brisbane, MacArthur informed his staff, "the President has accepted my recommendations and approved the Philippines plan."[11]

MacArthur's optimism was misplaced. Roosevelt, although technically Commander in Chief of the US military, was too wise a bird to commit to a strategy without the recommendations of his Joint Chiefs of Staff. Back in Washington, in spite of MacArthur's seeming victory in *Honolulu*, Admiral King stuck to his belief in the *Formosa* strategy. A decision remained stalled. However, the Joint Chiefs of Staff did agree that the taking of the southern Philippines island of *Mindanao* (planned for 5 October) and then *Leyte* (planned for 20 December) in the central Philippines would be advantageous. The go-ahead for these operations was thus given while the question of *Luzon* or *Formosa* was deferred.

In fact the plans for the invasion of *Leyte Island* were fast-forwarded. After Vice-Admiral Marc Mitscher's Task Force 38 launched carrier attacks on *Leyte*, the strategically located island to the south of *Luzon*, they soon found that there were no Japanese planes or ships left to target. Halsey radioed Nimitz on 12 September, and bullishly recommended that *Leyte* be invaded immediately because the "enemy's non-aggressive attitude was unbelievable and fantastic . . . the area is wide open."[12] Much to MacArthur's annoyance, Major-General Richard Sutherland, standing in for his superior who was in transit, reported to the Joint Chiefs, who were attending the second Quebec Conference with Roosevelt and Churchill, that the South West Pacific Area (SWPA) Army would be ready to launch an invasion of *Leyte* on 20 October. The Joint Chiefs quickly approved the new timetable. MacArthur may have been miffed not to have made this decision himself but he was certainly delighted that this turn of events would bring him back to the Philippines even sooner than expected. The *Leyte* decision would have a decisive impact on the eventual conclusion to the *Luzon-Formosa* debate.

Admiral Toyoda's Grand Strategy: [Map: 33.1] Vice-Admiral Kinkaid's Seventh Fleet and accompanying amphibious fleet, under the command of MacArthur and his South West Pacific Army, comprised an astonishing 738 ships including, 18 escort carriers, 12 battleships, 24 cruisers and dozens of destroyers. Accompanying them were hundreds of transports, PT boats and support vessels. The armada included five of the battleships partially sunk or damaged at *Pearl Harbor*. The fleet opened fire at 6.55 a.m. and bombarded the beaches of Dulag on the eastern shores of *Leyte* before landing a first wave of 70,000 men from the 7th and 96th Army Divisions. A further 100,000 men waited in transports in *Leyte Gulf*.

For the Japanese high command the American advance on *Leyte* was not unexpected. But that begged the question of what to do? Logically after its huge setback at the *Battle of the Philippines Sea*, Japan should have sued for peace. The war was lost and most senior commanders knew it. Japan's only point in continuing was to cause as much grief to American forces as could cause American politicians to deflect them from their demand for unconditional surrender. From now on the defense of Japan was characterized by the planning of heroic last actions as if the traditions of *seppuku* (ritual suicide by disembowelment) had become institutionalized within the war rooms of the Japanese Imperial command.

Admiral Soemu Toyoda, who had been promoted to Commander in Chief of the Combined Fleet in May, continued the reckless pattern of *Kaigun* (Navy) leadership in seeking the 'knockout blow' that would win the war; it was a gamble but he pleaded for the "last chance to destroy the enemy, who enjoys the luxury of material resources."[13] Everyone knew that the possibility of a 'knockout' blow was now all but a fantasy. At a joint Army-Navy meeting of high-ranking officers at the luxuriously appointed Navy Club in Tokyo on 19 October, a heated argument broke out between officers of the two services. It was the Army generals who were furious as they realized that the Navy's suicide mission to prevent the American occupation of the Philippines could well leave Japan defenseless. A Japanese admiral spuriously argued, "If the fleet does not take the offensive now, the war will be lost."[14] When the Army Imperial GHQ Liaison questioned the naval strategy to risk all on the relief of *Leyte*, the head of naval operations responded that it was "a fitting place to die . . . [and offered] the chance to bloom as flowers of death. This is the Navy's request."[15] At the end of the raucous Navy Club meeting, Army officers angrily left the room.

After the *Battle of the Philippines Sea* Japan possessed just eighty-one serviceable warships. The rates of depletion had actually speeded up as the war progressed. In the twenty-one months from December 1941 to October 1943 the Japanese navy lost 199 warships (626,893 tons) and 149 naval auxiliaries (790,088 tons) while over the next eight months they lost 196 warships (335,046 tons) and 225 naval auxiliaries (1,115,389 tons). Yet even with what remained of the fleet, it was difficult for the Japanese Navy to keep its ships fueled. At the peak of its power, two-thirds of Japan's warships were kept in the south near the oil supplies of *Sumatra* and *Borneo* in order to conserve remaining oil stocks in Japan. As the naval historian H. P. Willmott has noted, "Japan could supply the nation with oil or it could supply a navy in home waters with oil, but not both and not both at the same time."[16]

Rear-Admiral Koyanagi, after the war, recalled that after the *Battle of Midway* they "were at a loss as to what to do."[17] The situation after the *Battle of the Philippines* was even more desperate. As Admiral Toyoda concluded,

> If we were beaten at the [invasion of the] Philippines and even if the fleet remained to us, the southern sources of [oil] supply would be isolated. When it returned to Japanese waters the fleet could not be refuelled: left in the south it could not be supplied with arms and ammunition. It would be pointless therefore, to lose the Philippines and save the fleet.[18]

Moreover the *Battle of the Philippines Sea* saw the effective end of Japan's offensive capabilities with the sinking of the carriers *Taiho, Shokaku* and *Hiyo*. These were assets that Japan no longer had the capacity to replace. Perhaps even more importantly, the '*Great Marianas Turkey Shoot*' cost virtually an entire generation of aircrews—the third batch since the beginning of the war. Lastly Japan did not have the capacity to retrain carrier aircrews in time to fully man their remaining carriers in their attempt to halt the invasion of the Philippines.

Meanwhile the US Navy had not stood still since the denouement of *Pearl Harbor* and the lucky victory at the *Battle of Midway*. The forces assembled by Nimitz at *Leyte Gulf* benefited from one of the greatest naval building programs in history. Not including the ships handed over to their allies, in the years after *Pearl Harbor*, the United States commissioned 18 Essex Class carriers, 9 Independence Class light carriers, 77 escort carriers, 8 battleships, two battleship/cruisers, 13 heavy cruisers, 33 light cruisers, 349 destroyers, 420 destroyer escorts, and 203 submarines. By contrast, by September 1944 Japan was down to its last twenty-nine destroyers. **[Charts: C.2, C.3]**

Charged with offering a plan of action in these straitened circumstances, Vice-Admiral Takeo Kurita presented SHO-GO ICHI (Operation VICTORY) to Imperial General HQ on 18 August. The plan called for a coordinated attack by the remainders of the Japanese fleet on the naval forces assembled for the invasion of the Philippines. It was a complex plan; indeed an overly complex plan. Pulling together forces as far apart as *Singapore* and Tokyo, a distance of 3,490 nautical miles, Kurita planned an assault on *Leyte Gulf* by three converging naval forces. The division of the navy into three forces originated from the extensive damage to Ozawa's carrier fleet at the *Battle of the Philippine Sea*. As Ozawa admitted under questioning by US Rear-Admiral R. A.

Oftstie, "I had the intention to combine the two fleets, provided your invasion took place sometime in November. While I was reshaping the fleet, your invasion came a little sooner than expected."[19]

A Southern Force under Vice-Admiral Shoji Nishimura with two out-dated battleships, *Fuso* and *Yamashiro*, would approach *Leyte Island* from *Borneo* via the *Sulu Sea*, skirt the north coast of *Mindanao* and approach the southeastern *Straits of Surigao* separating *Leyte* from *Mindanao*. Meanwhile Vice-Admiral Takeo Kurita's Center Force left *Singapore* on 18 October and refueled in Brunei; comprising the cream of Japan's remaining fleet including the leviathan twin super-battleships *Yamato* and *Musashi*, Center Force would approach the Philippines from the west taking a passage north of the *Palawan Islands*, through the straits separating the islands of *Mindoro* from *Panay* and then through *Sibuyan Sea* to the *San Bernadino Straits* separating *Luzon* from *Samar* to its south. Kurita would then fall on the invading US armada at *Leyte Gulf* from the northeast.

The key to the strategy was using Vice-Admiral Jisaburo Ozawa's Northern Force, sailing from Japan with the last remaining fleet carrier and three light carriers, which would act as a decoy. It was intended that Ozawa's force of carriers would draw Halsey north from its position guarding the passage east of the *San Bernadino Straits*. "We expected complete destruction,"[20] Ozawa admitted after the war. Toyoda's plan gambled that Vice-Admiral 'Bull' Halsey, well known to the Japanese as an aggressive hothead, would strike north to destroy Ozawa's Northern Force and thus leave open the *San Bernadino Straits*, giving Kurita's Center Force passage to attack MacArthur's unguarded invasion fleet. Toyoda and the Imperial Japanese Navy staff were sure that Halsey would not want to miss the chance to destroy a carrier fleet that had escaped Admiral Spruance at the *Battle of the Philippine Sea*. As Spruance later wrote to his wife Margaret, "What happened during this whole Leyte action was just what I was expecting off Saipan and was trying to prevent—being drawn off to the westward while part of the Jap fleet came in around our flank and hit the amphibious force at Saipan."[21]

Part of Toyoda's strategy was hobbled even before the Southern and Central forces set off on their doomed voyages. In the strategy to soften up the Philippines prior to invasion, Halsey's US carrier forces began bombing operations on 10 October. The Japanese committed planes drawn from the Philippines as well as *Formosa*, China, the home islands, as well as the carrier forces under Ozawa's command. Within three days some 321 Japanese planes had been lost with the sinking of only two American cruisers to show for it. By 18 October, Japan's 1st Air Fleet had just seventeen planes to repel the US's 685 planes. Three day later Japan's defense forces were reduced to just eight planes. Quite possibly Kurita was never informed of the catastrophic air defeat that meant that his Center Force, comprising only surface ships, would have no air cover.

The truth on the ground was evident to some. Vice-Admiral Shigeru Fukudome, who witnessed an aerial battle on 12 October, captured the sense of devastation increasingly felt by Japanese officers in the field:

Our planes appeared to do so well that I thought I could desire no better performance. In a matter of moments, one after another, planes were seen falling down, enveloped in flames. "Well done! Well done! A tremendous success." I clapped my hands. Alas! To my sudden disappointment, a closer look revealed that all those shot down were our fighters, and all those proudly circling above our heads were enemy planes! Our fighters were nothing but so many eggs thrown at the stone wall of the indomitable enemy formation. In a brief one-sided encounter, the combat terminated in our total defeat.[22]

Kurita had even expended the carrier aircrews being trained at Oita Naval Base. After the war the US Naval War College concluded that America's overwhelming victory in this engagement was the result of "the failure of the Japanese to realize a) the excellence of Allied radar b) the Allied capability of long range interception and c) the method of conducting such long range interceptions."[23]

Again comparisons with US military-industrial output capacity are salutary. During the course of the war the United States produced 279,813 planes to 64,800 produced in Japan. The balance of aircraft engines produced was 728,467 to 104,446. The US Navy alone ended the war with 40,000 aircraft and 60,000 trained pilots. As a Japanese officer lamented in 1944, "Japan's national power . . . will gradually decrease, no matter how much effort Japan may exert, and, although she may be able to engage in a decisive battle before the end of year, it will hardly be possible for her to counter any powerful attack during, and after, next year."[24]

Admiral Halsey Waits off the San Bernadino Straits: With Japanese air defenses annihilated by Vice-Admiral 'Bull' Halsey's Third Fleet, for a 'gung-ho' commander, the job of covering the flanks of MacArthur's *Leyte* invasion was a seemingly dull task made even worse by Nimitz's reminder to his commanders of their operational parameters, with the message: "movements of major units of the Third Fleet through Surigao and San Bernadino Straits will not be initiated without orders from CINCPAC [Commander in Chief, Pacific Area Command]."[25] Nimitz thus closed off the possibility of Halsey being drawn off station to the west but his orders gave no parameters with regards to movements north. Many American officers believed that the Japanese fleet, badly mauled in the *Battle of the Philippines Sea*, would not dare to venture out so soon afterwards.

In contrast to the conservatism of Nimitz's orders, Halsey was clearly determined not to miss any opportunity to use his forces to deliver a final and crushing defeat of Japan's carrier fleet. He clearly believed that his friend and rival Admiral Spruance had missed this opportunity at the *Battle of the Philippine Sea* where Spruance had stuck closely to his brief to protect the invasion force in their occupation of *Saipan*. In similar circumstances it is unlikely that Halsey would have done the same. For reasons of health and unlucky timing, Halsey had missed personal involvement in the great carrier battles that defined the *Pacific War*; he had missed the *Battle of the Coral Sea* by a day and at the *Battle of Midway* ill-health had forced him to pass command to his then cruiser commander, Admiral Spruance; finally at the *Battle of the Philippine Sea*, because of Nimitz's decision to rotate the commanders of the Third Fleet, it was Spruance who had drawn the 'lucky' straw in coming up against the Japanese carrier fleet for the second time in his career and winning another crushing carrier battle.

Halsey, a man of modest intellect, whose rambunctious qualities had been taken up by the American media as a perfect symbol of the US Navy's fight back after *Pearl Harbor*, had grown increasingly vain about his importance and self-image. Fame had been handed to him for conducting the US Navy's first raids after *Pearl Harbor* and then for the *Doolittle Raid* in which he had played only a minor role. In the *Solomons* Campaign, Halsey had been promoted into the position of a desk-jockey to take over from Vice-Admiral Ghormley as Commander of the *South Pacific Area*; he had indeed conducted a brilliant campaign but he had missed the opportunity to experience carrier action at the *Battle of the Santa Cruz Islands* [October 1942] where his carrier commander, Rear-Admiral Kinkaid had been defeated. In spite of this, the able Kinkaid was promoted to Vice-Admiral in June 1943.

Halsey's public image was that of a 'fighting' Admiral but perversely he had never experienced fleet combat. Vice-Admiral 'Bull' Halsey wanted to be remembered as a fighting commander and after Spruance's great victory at the *Battle of the Philippine Sea*, he could see that time was running out for him to achieve the great naval victory that his ego demanded. On 28 September 1944, Halsey had written, "In all my recommended operations I aim to achieve superiority at the point of contact through weight of numbers, surprise, superior performance, stratagem, or some other device, and I am also always prepared to change schedules if I see a situation which permits me to capitalize on a momentary enemy weakness."[26] It was an insight into his beliefs that would have important implications in the ensuing battle. Admiral Nimitz was clearly worried enough about the Third Fleet commander's impetuousness to warn Halsey on 8 October that he should be aware of his responsibilities with regard to the entirety of MacArthur's planned invasion of the Philippines on the southeast coast of *Leyte Island*. Again on 21 October, Nimitz, clearly alarmed that Halsey might give way to his personal agenda, sent Halsey a message on board his flagship, the battleship USS *New Jersey*, reminding him of his responsibility to cover the invasion at *Leyte Gulf*.

On 22 October Halsey ordered his strongest carrier force, Task Group 38.1 under Vice-Admiral John McCain to retire to *Ulithi Atoll* for re-provision, to be followed the next day by Rear-Admiral Ralph Davison's Task Group 38.4. It was unfortunate timing. After midnight on 23 October, American submarines USS *Darter* and USS *Dace* sighted two columns of enemy ships at the southern end of the *Palawan Passage*, 350 miles west of *Leyte Gulf*. An unconcerned Halsey cancelled Davison's retirement but left McCain to continue his eastward passage to *Ulithi*. With his three remaining groups,

Halsey fanned out toward the *San Bernadino Straits*; Rear-Admiral Frederick Sherman's Task Group 38.3 off *Luzon* to the north; Rear-Admiral Gerald Bogan's Task Group 38.2 (including Halsey on the battleship, USS *New Jersey*) off the *San Bernadino Straits* and Davison's Task Group 38.4 off *Leyte Island* to the south.

Closer to shore Vice-Admiral Kinkaid's Seventh Fleet, part of MacArthur's invasion forces, had three task force units of destroyers and destroyer escorts protecting sixteen escort carriers: Taffy-1 (stationed off *Mindanao Island*), Taffy-2 stationed off *Leyte Gulf* and Taffy-3 (stationed off *Samar Island* to the south of the *San Bernadino Straits*). As for the bulk of Kinkaid's surface fleet, they were prepared for an attempt by Japanese forces, via the *Surigao Straits*, to interdict MacArthur's amphibious landing. By the early morning of 23 October search planes from Bogan's Task Group 38.2 had spotted Vice-Admiral Kurita's Center Force and Vice-Admiral Nishimura's Southern Force and Kinkaid and Halsey guessed at their respective routes through the *San Bernadino* and *Surigao Straits* respectively. Finally McCain, who was by now 600 miles away, was called back by Halsey from his passage to *Ulithi Atoll*. At 8.37 a.m. Halsey ordered all his carriers to launch air strikes at the approaching Japanese Center Force led by Admiral Kurita as it traversed the *Sibuyan Sea*.

The Battle of Sibuyan Sea: The Sinking of Musashi and USS Princeton: **[Map: 33.2]**
Before the battle, Vice-Admiral Kurita, fully aware of the likelihood that his fleet would be annihilated, addressed his less than enthusiastic commanders:

> I know that many of you are strongly opposed to this assignment. But the war situation is far more critical than any of you can possibly know. Would it not be shameful to have the fleet remain intact while our nation perishes? I believe that the Imperial General Headquarters is giving us a glorious opportunity. Because I realize how very serious the war situation actually is, I am willing to accept even this ultimate assignment to storm into Leyte Gulf. You must all remember that there are such things as miracles.[27]

Admiral Kurita's battle started badly. In the first of a litany of mistakes Kurita failed to take anti-submarine precautions after a radio operator on board the *Yamato* picked up signals from American submarines. On the morning of 23 October, Kurita's flagship *Atago* was sunk by torpedoes fired from the submarines USS *Darter* and USS *Dace*. So rapidly did his ship go down that Kurita was forced to take an early morning salt-water bath in which he was forced to swim for his life. Less fortunate were 359 of his crew who died. Of *Atago*'s sister ships, the heavy cruiser *Maya* was sunk, while the *Takao* was heavily damaged. The *Takao* was escorted out of the battle taking with it two Japanese destroyers from the battles ahead. In reply, at the so-called *Battle of Palawan Passage*, the Japanese won a fortuitous, albeit token, prize when *Darter* ran aground and her entire crew had to be rescued by the USS *Dace*.

Pressing onward, Kurita's surface force now faced the onslaught of Halsey's carrier attacks. Deprived of McCain's stronger airpower, Bogan's group's carriers concentrated their attacks on the battleships *Nagato, Yamato* and *Musashi. Musashi* became their principal target. The first torpedoes to strike *Musashi* barely registered on its heavily armored hull and it maintained its speed at over twenty knots. This was followed up just after midday by a second wave of VB-15 Helldivers and VF-15 Hellcats from the USS *Essex* (CV-9), USS *Intrepid* (CV-11) and USS *Lexington* (CV-16), the Essex Class replacement for the *Lexington*, (CV-2), that was sunk at the *Battle of the Coral Sea*. Over the next hour and a half *Musashi* was slowed to ten knots and listed five degrees to port and thirteen feet down at the bow; she began to drop off the back of the fleet.

Commissioned in the summer of 1942, *Musashi*, sister ship to *Yamato*, was the last of the behemoth Japanese battleships. They had been built as a result of the Japanese Navy's strategy to build a navy that was qualitatively better than the US Navy—an outcome of the *Washington Naval Limitation Treaty* [1922]. Japan went to extraordinary lengths to conceal the building of the vast new battleships. The chief engineer, Kumao Baba and the director of the steel mill were notified accordingly in 1937. "This project has been classified top secret, and we have been ordered to assign only absolutely trustworthy employees to it. Each of you has been checked out by the secret police. Your political and religious beliefs, family backgrounds, and contacts with foreigners have proven to be acceptable for the project. However, in order to further assure absolute confidentiality from all of you, we would like you to swear an oath of secrecy."[28]

When a blueprint plan of a section of turret was lost, six engineers and two blueprint makers were imprisoned and tortured. Compared to US battleships with their 16-inch guns, the *Yamato* and *Musashi*, each sporting nine 18.1-inch guns, twelve 6.1-inch guns and batteries of smaller caliber armaments, were fearsome weapon systems. Each 18.1-inch gun weighed 162 tons and their turrets, with 26-inch armor weighed 2,774 tons, more than many destroyers. Shells weighing 1.5 tons could be fired every forty seconds to a distance of twenty-six miles. The force of fire of one of these guns was enough to severely injure or kill a man standing nearby. In experiments, guinea pigs were blown apart.

At 72,000 tons displacement, *Yamato* Class battleships were double the displacement of any warships previously built in Japan. In spite of this weight the *Yamato* Class battleships could travel at twenty-seven knots and had a cruising range of 7,200 nautical miles at sixteen knots. In addition to their fearsome weaponry they sported heavily armored hulls to protect them from torpedo strikes. At least, that was the theory. Designed with a broad beam (a design feature not available to US warships because of the width of the *Panama Canal*), the battleships could box their enormous engine rooms with relatively short sides that could be heavily protected by 18-inch steel, enough to resist torpedoes. The deck was also heavily defended with 7.8-inch steel that could withstand 1,000-kilogram (2,204 lbs) armor-piercing bombs. These were formidable defenses but the allocation of armor to these critical areas meant that other areas had to be compromised, notably the under bow and stern sections. To compensate, a watertight compartment system was designed along with flooding and pumping systems. Events would show that the damage control calculations were over-optimistic. Nevertheless engineer Shigeichi Koga proudly reflected, "Looking at it taking shape on the slipway, it seems like this battleship could never be sunk."[29]

In truth *Pearl Harbor* had demonstrated that the battleship, the weapon of choice during the interwar arms race, the subject of thousands of hours of negotiation at naval disarmament conferences in Washington and London, as well as miles of newspaper column inches, was now a dinosaur. For the Americans, battleships had proved mainly useful in the unglamorous role of offshore batteries to wear down defenders prior to beach landings in the *Central Pacific* and New Guinea campaigns. Japanese battleships had played a similar role at *Guadalcanal*. The aircraft carrier now represented a navy's main strike capability—it lay at the heart of new Japanese naval tactical thinking.

In a shoot-out between battleships and aircraft carriers there could only be one winner. When at 3.30 p.m. a third wave of bombers from the USS *Enterprise* (CV-6), USS *Franklin* (CV-13), USS *Intrepid* (CV-11) and USS *Cabot* (CVL-28, a light carrier) hit the struggling *Musashi* with eleven bombs and eight further torpedoes, making a total of nineteen torpedo hits and seventeen bomb hits, her fate was sealed. A Helldiver rear gunner, Russ Dustan, serving on the *Franklin* recalled, "Musashi was huge! I had never seen anything as big in my entire life. It was a magnificent sight."[30] A ten degree list was corrected by pumping and counter-flooding to six degrees but the bow sagged down by 8 yards and sea water began to sweep over the main deck which was littered with dismembered bodies.

Kurita ordered the struggling *Musashi* to be beached and used as a stationary battery. When her engines failed, the great battleship listed twelve degrees to port and an evacuation was ordered. At 7.36 p.m. *Musashi* capsized and sank by the bow taking 1,023 men to their deaths. Many of the young seamen could not swim and refused to jump into the sea. Others went down clinging to the propellers. Destroyers subsequently picked up 1,326 survivors. A further fifty of these died when 420 of their number were being shipped aboard the *Santosu-Maru*. To hide the shame of the sinking, survivors were relocated to a remote island in the *Seto Inland Sea*. Captain Kenkichi Kato, who was prevailed upon not to go down with his ship, wrote in his notebook, ". . . I am pleased that almost no damage was sustained by other vessels in the fleet in this battle. I somehow feel that, as the main target, the *Musashi* managed to save the fleet."[31] A Japanese seaman recalled that at 7.35 p.m. on 24 October, *Musashi*'s stern rose out of the water:

> Crewmen started to jump off . . . the stern, which was sticking up like a tower from the ocean surface. Before they reached the ocean surface below, they were screaming with horror. Most of them hit the battleship's huge screws before they reached the water. Crewmen were running along the battleship, and several men who jumped off the sides were sucked into the huge holes made by the torpedoes.[32]

At a cost of just eighteen planes, Halsey's Third Fleet had sunk the pride of the fleet, Admiral Yamamoto's former flagship, and a ship that its designers and builders had believed unsinkable.

The carrier attacks, which had also inflicted damage on the battleships *Yamato, Nagato* and the heavy cruiser *Myoko*, forced Kurita to turn away and retreat, but in the late afternoon he turned his ships again toward the *San Bernadino Straits*. The 259 sorties flown by Halsey's Third Fleet, denuded of McCain's stronger Task Group 38.1, had not been enough to turn back the Japanese attack. In diverting American carrier aircraft from attacks on the rest of Kurita's Center Force, the sacrifice of the *Musashi* may not have been entirely in vain. US forces also took casualties. It was Rear-Admiral Frederick Sherman's northerly placed Task Group 38.3 that took the brunt of the attack from land-based aircraft that had been sent from *Formosa* to bulk up the defense of the Philippines. As Sherman turned into the wind to allow his airplanes to take off at 8.40 a.m., his radio operators warned that 200 bogies from bases on *Luzon* were approaching. Sherman canceled his strike at Kurita's force in order to organize the defense of his carriers. The Japanese attack was repulsed with heavy losses but not before a Japanese Yokosuka D4Y 'Judy' dive-bomber planted a 250 lb armor-piercing bomb in the center of USS *Princeton*'s (CVL-23) fight deck.

The *Princeton* was a light carrier whose keel had started life as a Cleveland Class light cruiser named USS *Tallahassee*. By order of Roosevelt's decision to push for more carriers, the keel was turned into an Independence Class light carrier that was commissioned on 25 February 1943 as USS *Princeton*.

The bomb that struck the *Princeton* on 24 October penetrated the upper decks and exploded in the galley. On its path through the hangar, the bomb struck a parked TBM bomber (a General Motors variant of the Grumman Avenger torpedo plane) and ignited gasoline. For reasons that would never be explained the *Princeton*'s automatic sprinkler system failed to work. A series of explosions followed, but at 3.24 p.m. a wrenching explosion in an ammunitions compartment tore the heart out of the *Princeton*. In attendance, USS *Birmingham*, a light cruiser and ironically *Princeton*'s 'sister keel,' was also heavily damaged when she came to the aid of the *Princeton*. *Birmingham* suffered 550 casualties (150 killed) when a magazine on the carrier exploded. The USS *Irwin*, a new Fletcher Class destroyer built by Bethlehem Steel, in spite of taking a blast from the multiple explosions, stayed on station to rescue 646 of *Princeton*'s crewmen. By 4.00 p.m. the fires on board the *Princeton* were out of control and the carrier was abandoned. After the last crewmen were evacuated at 5.00 p.m., *Irwin* fired torpedoes to scuttle the *Princeton* but the damage to the firing tubes sent the torpedoes in a loop that came back and almost sank the *Irwin*. The job of scuttling the *Princeton* now fell to the cruiser USS *Reno*. The *Princeton* sank at 5.50 p.m.

On the *Princeton* 233 men were killed and 426 wounded. Captain John Hoskins, who survived the sinking in spite of losing his right foot, would become the new commanding officer of the Essex Class replacement USS *Princeton* (CV-37) when it was commissioned in November 1945 and the carrier would later see extensive action in the *Korean* and

Vietnam Wars. The USS *Princeton* was the last US fleet carrier lost in the *Pacific War*. In spite of the sinking of the *Princeton*, the *Battle of Sibuyan Sea* was clearly a victory for Halsey's carriers, though not the destructive final encounter that he had assumed.

"Where in hell are those goddam Nip carriers?" Admiral Halsey Swallows the Bait: There was something wrong in the picture of the battle that was now emerging. Where were the Japanese carriers? Both Nimitz and Halsey deduced that Japanese naval command would not launch an assault by their capital surface ships without support from their carriers, which were known to have been sheltering in Japan's own *Inland Sea*. Indeed at 1.34 p.m. Halsey had radioed Vice-Admiral Mark Mitscher, "Enemy carrier strength not located. Keep area to north under observation."[33] Curiously the Japanese carrier group, the Northern Force under Ozawa, designated as the decoy, was the only one not yet detected. According to air operations officer, Doug Moulton, Halsey "must have said at least 25 to 50 times that day 'Where in hell are those goddam Nip carriers?' "[34]

In the late afternoon, at 4.40 p.m., just thirty four minutes before Kurita's Center Force was ordering a reverse tack back toward the *San Bernadino Straits*, Rear-Admiral Sherman's search planes from Task Group 38.3 finally spotted the carriers of Vice-Admiral Ozawa's Northern Force 180 miles to the northeast of *Luzon*. This was a red rag to the appropriately name 'Bull' Halsey. Halsey had a number of choices: he could have kept station and waited for Ozawa's carriers to advance; left a task force behind to cover the *San Bernadino Straits*, and then stormed north; or stormed north with all his forces.

At 5.14 p.m. Kurita reversed back toward the *San Bernadino Straits*, sending a message to Toyoda that read: "Braving any loss or damage we may suffer, the First Striking Force will break into and fight to the last man."[35] Halsey made a significant mistake when he failed to send out further planes in the late afternoon to track Kurita's movements. Halsey was thus unaware that the Japanese admiral had changed course and was again threatening passage through the *San Bernadino Straits*.

At 8.00 p.m. on 24 October Vice-Admiral 'Bull' Halsey, ignorant of Kurita's turn in direction, walked into the Flag Plot on USS *New Jersey*, an Iowa Class battleship, and placed his finger on the map that indicated the position of Ozawa's carrier fleet some 300 miles to the north. Halsey told Admiral Carney, his Chief of Staff, "Here's where we're going. Mick, start them north."[36] He had chosen the third of his three options and planned to 'storm north' taking his entire force without leaving a covering guard at the *Philippine Sea* exit to the *San Bernadino Straits*. By now, without expressly stating the fact, Halsey had taken firm tactical control of the battle from Task Force 38's commander, Vice-Admiral Mitscher. Mitscher had been sidelined and was not happy. "Admiral Halsey is in command now,"[37] he commented curtly and retired for the night.

Had Halsey taken the basic precaution of sending out scouts to check the whereabouts of Kurita's Center Force on the late afternoon of 24 October, he would surely have waited and caught the great Japanese surface fleet as it emerged from the *San Bernadino Straits*. A nighttime action, better suited to Japanese skills, might have ensued. What is equally certain is that, over the course of the night and the early morning, when Halsey could have deployed his carrier's dive-bombers and torpedo bombers, Kurita's fleet would have been completely destroyed. As Rear-Admiral Tomiji Koyanagi later wrote, if Halsey had stayed off the *San Bernadino Straits*, "a night engagement against our exhausted force would undoubtedly have been disastrous for us. Thus the enemy missed an opportunity to annihilate the Japanese fleet through his failure to maintain contact in the evening of 24 October."[38]

Did Halsey really believe that his carrier assault on Kurita's forces had done enough to turn back the Japanese Center Force? The more experienced fast carrier commander, Vice-Admiral Mitscher, was sceptical about the reports that Kurita's force had been completely shattered. He was used to the exaggerated claims of carrier pilots. Mitscher, perhaps miffed that Halsey had taken over his combat command of the fleet carriers, stayed silent.

At 8.22 a.m. Halsey sent Kinkaid the message, "proceeding north with three groups to attack carrier force at dawn."[39] Both Bogan's carrier Task Group 38.2 and Davison's carrier Task Group 38.4 were ordered to join Sherman's carrier Task Group 38.3 in the north, while McCain with Task Group 38.1, on its way back from its aborted passage to *Ulithi Atoll*, was also ordered to re-join the main fleet heading north.

Halsey had committed all his forces to chase down Ozawa's carrier force to the north. Following his tenet that forces should be concentrated, he chose not to leave behind a force to cover the eastern exit of the *San Bernadino Straits*. Yet he had clearly failed to inform his colleagues of his decision not to leave a covering force. Indeed Nimitz and Kinkaid were left to believe that a covering force had been left behind. The confusion in this misunderstanding was created by Halsey's message to his commanders at 3.12 p.m. on the afternoon of 24 October:

> BATDIV 7 MIAMI, VINCENNES, BILOXI, DESRON 52 LESS STEVEN POTTER, FROM TG 38.2 AND WASHINGTON, ALABAMA, WICHITA, NEW ORLEANS, DESDIV 100, PATTERSON, BAGLEY FROM TG 38.4 **WILL BE FORMED AS TASK FORCE 34 UNDER VICE ADMIRAL LEE, COMMANDER BATTLE LINE. TF 34 TO ENGAGE DECISIVELY AT LONG RANGES.** CTG 38.4 CONDUCT CARRIERS OF TG 38.2 AND TG 38.4 CLEAR OF SURFACE FIGHTING. INSTRUCTIONS FOR TG 38.3 AND TG 38.1 LATER. HALSEY, OTC IN NEW JERSEY.[40]

Because of this message, both Nimitz and Kinkaid concluded that by the time that Halsey was heading north to intercept Ozawa's carrier force, Task Force (TF) 34 under Vice-Admiral Lee had been formed and was now standing by as cover to the *San Bernadino Straits*.

Arguably both Nimitz and Kinkaid might have concluded that it would have been strange for Halsey to leave behind Task Force 34, comprising a surface fleet of 4 battleships, 5 cruisers and 14 destroyers under Vice-Admiral Willis Lee without a covering carrier group; also given their awareness of Halsey's obsession with Japanese carriers, would it be likely that Halsey, on board USS *New Jersey*, his Sixth Fleet flagship, that was part of Task Force 34, would knowingly miss out on the chance to engage in a carrier battle? It is an inappropriate criticism to make that Nimitz and Kinkaid should perhaps have second-guessed Halsey. Nevertheless, the clear overriding failure was Halsey's for not giving precise relays of information about his deployments.

As far as Nimitz and Kinkaid were concerned, Vice-Admiral Lee appeared to have been requested to provide ships for a covering force. However, neither Nimitz nor Kinkaid could have picked up a message that Halsey later sent by short range TBS radio to his colleagues in which he made it clear that his earlier message was a preparatory message that should not be acted on: "If the enemy sorties," his TBS radio message read, "TF-34 will be formed *when directed by me*."[41] The italics were inserted by Halsey. Thus both Nimitz and Kinkaid, as a result of Halsey's confused communications, assumed that the covering force, Task Force 34, had been formed and was in place. Halsey, well known for his rapid-fire messages and sometimes confusing orders, had clearly failed to make his deployments clear to all concerned.

As Halsey headed through the night toward Ozawa's carriers with all three of his available Task Groups, 38.2, 38.3 and 38.4, but without Admiral McCain's task force 38.1 that was scurrying to join them from *Ulithi*, there were voices of caution. After receiving reports that Kurita had reversed course and was again heading east toward the *San Bernadino Strait*, Lieutenant Mathews tried to inform Halsey of the dangers of not sending back a covering force. Halsey ignored him. The commander of Task Group 38.2, Rear-Admiral Gerald Bogan, was similarly rebuffed with the message "Yes, we have that information."[42] Bogan did not press but let it be known that he thought that Halsey "was making one hell of a mistake."[43]

On board Rear-Admiral Davison's flagship, Chief of Staff, Captain James Russell, claimed, "Halsey's action [in heading north] was such an obvious mistake to Admiral Davison and me."[44] Davison reportedly said to him, "Jim, we're playing a helluva dirty trick on the transports in *Leyte Gulf*."[45] On board Mitscher's flagship, Captain Burke urged the vice-admiral to speak to Halsey about the decision to storm north; Mitscher simply shrugged his shoulders and said, "Well I think you are right . . . but I don't know you are right."[46] Vice-Admiral Lee's 'blinker' message to Halsey warning him that the Japanese Northern Force was a decoy was also disregarded. Later on board USS *Lexington* staff officers were so concerned that they woke Vice-Admiral Marc Mitscher who, aware of Halsey's short temper, told them, "If he wants my advice he'll ask for it"[47] and returned to his slumber. As for Halsey, he would later try to justify his actions claiming, "the Northern force could not be left to operate unmolested . . . destruction of its carriers would mean much to our future operations."[48] He also claimed that the Japanese Center Force had been "too badly impaired to win a decision."[49]

Thus at 12.35 a.m. on 25 October Kurita's Center Force passed through the *San Bernadino Straits* and into the *Philippine Sea* unchallenged. Against all the odds Admiral Toyoda's decoy strategy had worked. At 1.00 a.m. Halsey woke after a short nap and ordered Task Group 38, steaming north, to slow down to less than twelve knots so as to avoid any risk of a night engagement.

The Battle of the Surigao Straits: [Map: 33.3] On the morning of 25 October, as dawn broke over the Philippines, the scale of the impending crisis was not known to America's naval commanders. Indeed there was cause for celebration. In the early hours Vice-Admiral Shoji Nishimura's Southern Force led by *Fuso* and *Yamashiro*, out-dated twin battleships with 14-inch guns and distinguished by their ungainly pagoda style masts, entered the *Surigao Straits*. They were accompanied by the heavy cruiser *Mogami* and four destroyers. At 8.13 p.m. on the previous evening, Nishimura, perhaps aware that Kurita's main force had temporarily reversed course, sent a message declaring, "It is my plan to charge into *Leyte Gulf* to [reach] a point of Dulag at 0400 hours on the 25th."[50] The message indicated a determined frame of mind and was perhaps goading Kurita to action. Kurita replied to the message indicating that he would pass through the *San Bernadino Straits* at 1 a.m. on 25 October. Nishimura clearly hoped that the Japanese skills at night fighting would equalize the odds against a force that he must have known to be much stronger. Timing was thus of the essence.

Nishimura had failed to meet up with an accompanying force of ships commanded by Vice-Admiral Kiyohide Shima, but pressed on anyway. His understrength surface force was ambushed by Kinkaid's Seventh Fleet surface force under the command of Rear-Admiral Jesse Oldendorf. The atmosphere aboard the vessels of the US fleet was jubilant and excited. A PT sailor recalled the upbeat mood: ". . . rather than rough routine patrolling, [they] would be slinging fish at the enemy at close range."[51] Oldendorf planned to soften up Nishimura's advance with PT boats and before attacking with his cruiser's torpedoes. At 10.36 p.m. PT 131 picked up radar signals of the approaching Japanese force. Sixteen minutes later lookouts on the destroyer *Shigure* spotted the bow waves of approaching PT boats. When *Shigure* turned their guns on the advancing PT boats, they turned and fled. Over the next few hours the PT boats, whose primary mission had been scouting, made numbers of unsuccessful attacks.

At 3 a.m. on 25 October, the five US destroyers led by Captain Jesse Coward in USS *Remey* closed on Nishimura's advancing force and commenced launch of twenty-seven torpedoes at 11,500 yards. Seven minutes earlier, *Shigure*'s lookouts had again been first to spot the US forces. It was too late and a few minutes later, at 3.09 a.m., two torpedoes fired by USS *Melvin* struck the battleship *Fuso* to starboard scoring a hit on its boiler room and halving its speed. Ten minutes later four ships were hit almost simultaneously including the destroyer *Yamagumo*. Hit amidships, *Yamagumo* broke in two, the bow and the stern rising in the air. The now V shaped ship disappeared. On the *Shigure*, navigator Serino noted, "*Yamagumo* received a torpedo hit, and sank with a flash and a roaring sound in a matter of three seconds or so!"[52] Within minutes *Asagumo* and

Michishio also took hits. USS *McDermut* and USS *Monssen* had scored the most devastating torpedo attack in US history. By now *Fuso* was sinking. At 3.25 a.m. Yasuo Kato, who had jumped from the *Fuso* and swum for his life, turned around. He recalled, "The stern rose high above the water slantingly, and I clearly saw the rudder against the night sky. On either side of the rudder, the screws were running with slight noise as though regretfully, or lingeringly.'[53] Finally the PT boats got on the US scoreboard when a torpedo fired by PT 137 at *Ushio* (destroyer) missed and hit the *Abukuma* (light cruiser).

Thereafter *Pearl Harbor* survivors, battleships USS *West Virginia* (sunk and refloated), USS *Maryland*, USS *Tennessee*, USS *California* (sunk and refloated) and USS *Pennsylvania* enjoyed their revenge against Nishimura's crippled strike ships in what turned out to be the last battleship versus battleship engagement in history. Of the battleship squadron only the USS *Mississippi* had not been present at *Pearl Harbor*. The US battleship squadron crossed the 'T' of the advancing Japanese ships.

At 3.53 a.m. *West Virginia* opened fire on the *Yamashiro* (battleship) at 22,800 yards with its 16-inch guns using their newly fitted Mark-8 fire control radar. *California* soon joined in the firefight with *Yamashiro* and *Mogumi* (heavy cruiser). *Yamashiro*, which was also struck by torpedoes, stopped dead in the water; shells proceeded to pound the stationary target. Nishimura's flagship listed forty-five degrees to port and the order to abandon ship was given. Vice-Admiral Nishimura did not move from his seat and went down with his ship along with 1,636 officers and crew. Only ten survivors made it back to Japan, the same number that survived from the *Fuso*. The survivors of Nishimura's crippled force, *Mogami* and *Shigure*, turned tail and crossed with Vice-Admiral Shima's late arriving group, which consisted of heavy cruisers *Nachi* (flagship) and *Ashigara*, the light cruiser *Abukuma* and four destroyers. Indeed the fleeing *Mogami* sliced through the stern of Shima's flagship *Nachi*. Just before this episode Shima had already ordered withdrawal. It was not a pain-free retreat. Later in the day *Asagumo, Mogami* and *Abukuma* all succumbed to land-based American air attack.

Much to General MacArthur's annoyance he missed the fun. MacArthur took his flag to the cruiser USS *Nashville* and told Kinkaid, "There is every reason why I should be present during such a crucial engagement. Besides, I have never been in a major naval action, and I am anxious to see one."[54] Knowing that if MacArthur was killed, it was more than his job was worth, Kinkaid wisely ordered Captain Charles Coney to keep the *Nashville* anchored inside *Leyte Gulf* off Tacloban town. MacArthur thus deprived US forces of an additional cruiser. It was not needed.

Remarkably the Southern Force comprising Nishimura and Shima's groups did not communicate. The captain of the *Shigure* would later explain: "The reason I did not communicate directly with Admiral Shima and inform him of the situation was that I had no connection with him and was not under his command. I assumed [he] knew of conditions of the battle . . . by sighting the burning ships *Fuso* and *Mogumi*, and by seeing me on a retiring course."[55] The *Shigure* was the only ship of Nishimura's command to survive, "a miracle"[56] according to its navigator, Serino, though three months later it too succumbed to a torpedo attack from USS *Blackfin* while on convoy duty off Kota Bharu, Malaya. The *Ushio* was the only Japanese ship at the *Battle of Surigao Straits* to survive the war.

Admiral Nimitz described the action "as perhaps the greatest, quickest and most devastating naval gunfire in the history of warfare."[57] Vice-Admiral Oldendorf was later awarded the Navy Cross. On 6 June, Oldendorf was quoted in the *New York Times* as saying that the *Battle of Surigao* was the "kind of battle you dream about."[58]

Halsey Confuses Nimitz and Kinkaid: Nimitz admitted to being very concerned "because nothing I have seen indicates that Admiral Halsey has left San Bernadino guarded against Japanese units coming through there and getting our ships off Leyte."[59] However, Nimitz, sitting in *Honolulu*, and abiding by his self-imposed rule not to interfere with his commanders' tactical dispositions refused to send a message to Halsey asking him for clarification.

If Nimitz was concerned, Vice-Admiral Kinkaid was even more so. At 4.00 a.m. on 25 October, Captain Richard Cruzen suggested to him that it would be a good idea to ask Halsey for confirmation that the battleships of Task Force 34 had been left behind to guard the *San Bernadino Straits*. Because of the divided fleet command, Kinkaid's message went for forward transmission to MacArthur's radio station at *Manus*. Here Kinkaid's urgent message sat in a pile with other messages marked urgent—of which, given MacArthur's amphibious landing at *Leyte Gulf*, there were many. At 6.48 a.m. Halsey received Kinkaid's urgent request for clarification some two and a half hours after it was sent.

At 6.30 a.m. Halsey had ordered the launch of his first strike of 180 aircraft at Ozawa's decoy fleet to the northeast of the Philippines off Cape Engano.

In spite of the loss of the *Musashi*, Kurita's surface force was substantially still intact and powerful and, having successfully passed through the *San Bernadino Straits* in the night, fell upon the three escort carrier forces (Taffy-1, Taffy-2 and Taffy-3) comprising sixteen carriers with their lightly armed destroyer escorts. At 6.45 a.m. Kurita's bombardment focused on the back-markers, notably of Rear-Admiral 'Ziggy' Sprague's Taffy-3.

Finally an answer came for Kinkaid's request for clarification, though not from the source, Halsey, that he had anticipated. Rear-Admiral Clifton Sprague, commander of Taffy-1, 2 and 3, stationed outside of *Leyte Gulf* sent an urgent message to Halsey and Kinkaid, "Enemy battleships and cruisers fifteen miles astern this unit and firing on it."[60] Shortly afterwards Nimitz received an encoded message from Kinkaid to Halsey reporting attacks on his escort carriers.

Just forty-eight hours earlier one of Sprague's pilots had flown over Halsey's fleet and reported back to Rear-Admiral Sprague, who felt comfortable enough to declare that he "felt well protected because this huge group was nearby (Halsey's Task Group 38)."[61] When Sprague learned the dreadful reality of his situation, Lieutenant Vernon Hipchings, the visual flight director officer, located on the USS *Fanshaw Bay*'s upper bridge heard his screaming rant: "It's impossible! It can't be, it can't be! That son of a bitch Halsey has left us bare-assed!"[62]

At 7.05 a.m., Halsey, completely unaware of the confusion caused by his message the previous evening, was mystified by the message sent by Kinkaid, and was puzzled as to why the commander of the Seventh Fleet had not understood that he was taking all of his ships to the north. He sent a message telling Kinkaid that he was attacking Ozawa's fleet.

At 8.02 a.m. Kinkaid sent a message to Nimitz and Halsey that the Seventh Fleet was pursuing the remnants of Vice-Admiral Nishimura's Southern Force that he had ambushed at the *Surigao Straits* some 200 miles south of the *San Bernadino Straits*. Kinkaid was still waiting for an answer to the message that he had sent via MacArthur's command center at *Manus* some four hour earlier.

At 8.22 a.m. Kinkaid sent Halsey an urgent message, this time in plain English: "OUR ESCORT CARRIERS BEING ATTACKED BY FOUR BATTLESHIPS EIGHT CRUISERS PLUS OTHER. REQUEST LEE COVER LEYTE AT TOP SPEED. REQUEST FAST CARRIERS MAKE IMMEDIATE STRIKE."[63] When Halsey replied that he was in no position to help, Kinkaid sent a now pointless message, "WHERE IS LEE? SEND LEE."[64] It was clear to all that there was a disaster in the making. It was now clear to Nimitz, Kinkaid and Sprague that Halsey had chased north with all of Task Group 38 and that Kurita's still formidable Center Force was bearing down on a practically defenseless amphibious force with its armada of supply ships and transports at *Leyte Gulf*.

On board USS *New Jersey*, Halsey, clearly reflecting on the crisis and his own responsibilities, chuntered aloud, "When I get my teeth into something, I hate to let go."[65] Meanwhile Kinkaid was now fully aware of the scale of the predicament faced by Taffy-3 and the invasion force at *Leyte Gulf*: "At this point, the situation appeared very critical."[66] At 8.30 a.m. Halsey received another plain English message, this time from Admiral Sprague, "FAST BATTLESHIPS ARE URGENTLY NEEDED IMMEDIATELY AT LEYTE GULF."[67] As Sprague must have known by now that the battleships were far to the north, one can only assume that the message was sent for posterity or more likely for the inquiry that he must have known would now follow this looming catastrophe.

At 8.50 a.m. Halsey received reports from his fliers that they had sunk one Japanese carrier and that two others were damaged. It must have been a bittersweet moment for Halsey in the knowledge that his colleagues were being massacred down south as a result of his abandonment of his station at the *San Bernadino Straits*.

At 9.00 a.m., Halsey received another desperate message from Kinkaid, "ENEMY FORCE ATTACKED OUR CVEs [Aircraft Carrier, Escort] COMPOSED OF 4BBs [battleships], EIGHT CRUISERS AND OTHER SHIPS. REQUEST LEE PROCEED TOP SPEED TO COVER LEYTE. REQUEST IMMEDIATE STRIKE BY FAST CARRIERS."[68]

Halsey had responded by ordering Admiral McCain to sail at full speed toward *Leyte Gulf* with his Task Force 38.1. In fact McCain, apprised of the seriousness of the situation, had already turned around Task Force 38.1 without awaiting orders. There was no possibility of his arriving in time. However, McCain dispatched a force of Helldivers, Avengers and Hellcats from 330 miles out from carriers USS *Hornet* (CV-12), an Essex Class replacement for the *Hornet* (CV-8), the Yorktown Class carrier sunk at the *Battle of the Santa Cruz Islands*, USS *Wasp* (CV-18) a Wasp Class replacement for the *Wasp* (CV-7) that was sunk by a Japanese submarine *I-19* after supporting the Marines' invasion of *Guadalcanal*, and USS *Hancock* (CV-19) a new Essex Class carrier. Quite possibly McCain's attack at his aircraft's operational limits may have helped Kurita's decision to retire even though the attacks themselves had caused little damage. All concerned must have known that sending back McCain was a futile gesture. It was too little, too late. Rear-Admiral Ralph Davison later recalled that when he heard of Halsey's communication, he felt like radioing Halsey "What the hell, we told you so!"[69] Apart from sending McCain, Halsey ignored the entreaties of Kinkaid and Sprague and speeded onward toward his moment of destiny with the Japanese Northern Force's carrier fleet.

To add to Sprague's problems, Kinkaid's Seventh Fleet battle forces, spent of shells and fuel following the *Battle of Surigao Straits*, lay 400 miles to the south. At 9.22 a.m. Kinkaid had sent yet another message to this effect. Apart from Sprague's escort carriers, MacArthur's entire transport armada, sitting in *Leyte Gulf*, lay at Vice-Admiral Kurita's mercy. Halsey would later write, somewhat lamely, "Here I was on the brink of a critical battle and my kid brother was yelling for help around the corner."[70] Yet protecting his 'kid brother' was exactly the mission that Nimitz had given him with repeated reminders.

At 10.00 a.m. Kinkaid sent yet another desperate plea: "My situation is critical . . . fast battleships and support by air strike may be able to prevent enemy from destroying CVEs [Aircraft Carrier, Escort] and entering Leyte Gulf."[71]

'Small Boys Attack': The Battle of Samar: [Map: 33.4] On board the USS *Johnston*, the destroyer nearest to Kurita's advancing Center Force fleet as it emerged off *Samar Island*, Lieutenant-Commander Ernest Evans, a Cherokee Indian from Oklahoma, immediately ordered his outgunned ship into a flanking attack on the heavy cruiser *Kumano* and forced the larger Japanese ship out of the line by destroying her bow. Meanwhile three 14-inch and 6-inch shells wrecked the *Johnston*; Japanese destroyers finished it off. Evans commanded his ship to the end in spite of having an arm blown off when an explosion destroyed his bridge. Another officer recalled, "It was like a puppy being smacked by a fire truck."[72] Of the 327 crew, 141 were picked up; 50 died on board, 45 succumbed to wounds on life rafts while drowning and sharks took the rest. Lieutenant-Commander Evans was posthumously awarded the Medal of Honor.

The commander of the escort forces, Rear-Admiral Sprague, now gave his famous 'small boys attack' order to Taffy-3's remaining destroyers, USS *Hoel*, USS *Heerman* and destroyer escort USS *Samuel B. Roberts*. It was a suicide mission and both USS *Hoel* and USS *Samuel B. Roberts* were sunk.

Meanwhile Sprague had ordered the slow moving escorts, not designed for fleet combat, to beat a retreat toward a squall and also ordered his covering destroyers to make smoke. At the same time Sprague put up whatever aircraft were at hand on his escort destroyers and armed them with any available bombs and ammunition. An Avenger pilot recalled, "hitting the Japanese ships with everything in the armory—including the doorknobs."[73] US land-based aircraft also harried Kurita's advancing warships. However, Kurita's faster moving surface forces caught up with the escort carrier fleet, and *USS Gambier Bay*; the Casablanca Class escort carrier, built by Kaiser Shipbuilding Company in Washington State, was bringing up the back of the line. She was sunk by gunfire while other escorts were damaged.

It should be noted that the 'escort carriers' of Sprague's Taffy-1, Taffy-2 and Taffy-3 were essentially transport ships not 'fleet carriers.' 'Escort carriers' were part of the support fleet and were used to ferry aircraft from America to support 'fleet carriers' when they needed replacement aircraft and crews. Escort carriers were also used to take planes to stock 'advance' airfields. Essentially they were cheaply built aircraft transport ships. 'Escort carriers' typically carried twenty-eight planes compared to a 'fleet carrier's' 90–100 aircraft. For defensive purposes they were well armed for attack from the air with 1x 130 mm dual-purpose gun, sixteen 40 mm Bofors anti-aircrafts guns and twenty 20 mm Oerlikon anti-aircraft cannons.

An 'escort carrier' had the speed of a transport ship, about fifteen knots, compared to the speed of 'fleet carriers' that could travel at thirty-three knots. 'Escort carriers' could not therefore be used in a normal fast-paced fleet action, though they were capable of sending up aircraft for defense albeit not with the speed and efficiency of a 'fleet carrier.' The problem for Sprague's 'escort carriers' as they attempted to flee *Samar Island* is that Kurita's surface ships, including battleships, could travel twice as fast and would therefore have hauled in the entire fleet of six 'escort carriers' and likely have sunk them all if Kurita had continued his pursuit. It should be noted, 'light carriers' as opposed to 'escort carriers,' carried up to thirty-five aircraft but had the same speed as fleet carriers and were designed to operate in fleet combat alongside 'fleet carriers.'

Seemingly inexplicably however, with MacArthur's invasion force at his mercy, Vice-Admiral Kurita withdrew. Vice-Admiral Sprague, for one, was both astonished and relieved. "I could not believe my eyes," he recalled, "but it looked as if the whole Japanese fleet was indeed retiring . . . At best I had expected to be swimming by this time."[74] Kurita's forces scuttled back through the *San Bernadino Straits* and made their escape before McCain's fastest ships could catch them. In his monumental, fifteen volume *History of United States Naval Operations in World War II*, Morrison concludes, "In no engagement of its entire history has the United States Navy shown more gallantry, guts and gumption than in those two morning hours between 0730 and 0930 off Samar."[75]

A footnote to the battle was the first systematic use of *kamikaze*. Vice-Admiral Takijiro Onishi who had taken control of the Fifth Base Air Force in *Luzon* on 17 October found that he had a mere 100 serviceable aircraft. Given the paucity of his resources, the decreasing quality of his aircrews and the hugely improved quality of enemy equipment, training, tactics and radar, the resort to suicide attacks was indeed logical. Onishi formed the *Kamikaze* Special Attack Corps and told his commanders, "In my opinion there is only one way of channelling our meager strength into maximum efficiency, and that is to organize attack units composed of Zero fighters equipped with 250 kg bombs, with each plane to crash into an enemy carrier."[76] [**See Appendix E:** ***Kamikaze:* Divine Winds]**

Why did Admiral Kurita Retreat? Why did Kurita spurn the chance to sink sixteen unprotected escort carriers carrying a complement of 450 planes? At the same time Kurita could have entered *Leyte Gulf* itself and wrought havoc with lightly protected troop and supply transports, without which MacArthur's invading army would have been left stranded. It was a remarkable opportunity for the Japanese Navy to score its most significant naval victory since *Pearl Harbor*. By itself it could not have won the war but the annihilation of logistical elements of MacArthur's vast Seventh Fleet naval force at *Leyte Gulf* could well have delayed the advance to Japan's home islands by six months or more.

Much criticized after the war, it is perhaps easier to view his decision with the advantage of hindsight. Kurita's force had received a mauling on the previous day by Halsey's Third Fleet carriers and his ships were running short of fuel. Kurita's warships had also been forced to start their attack while they were in a state of disarray, as they moved to a daytime 'anti-aircraft' defensive formation. The result was that Kurita's forces had become chaotically dispersed. In addition, as his attempted move to 'anti-aircraft' formation indicates, Kurita almost certainly feared that Halsey's carriers were in the vicinity. Vice-Admiral Kurita would later admit, "I did not know that Admiral Halsey had taken his fleet north. I moved only with the knowledge that I was able to acquire with my own eyes and did not realize how close I was to victory."[77] One wonders why Kurita had not heard from Ozawa's Northern Force, under attack from Halsey's carriers, that the American admiral had swallowed the bait, which, after all, was the whole point of Toyoda's plan of attack.

Kurita's motives for withdrawal may never be fully understood. In a brief interview with journalist Masanori Ito after the war, Kurita explained, "The destruction of enemy carriers was a kind of obsession with me, and I fell victim to it . . . As I consider it now, my judgment does not seem to have been sound . . . I was drained both physically and mentally."[78] From this it seems that Kurita believed that there was an American carrier force nearby for him to attack. Rear-Admiral Koyonagi, who was on the bridge of the *Yamato* with Kurita at the time of the withdrawal decision commented, "I think now we should have gone into Leyte Gulf . . . so does Admiral Kurita . . . now with a cool head, I realize we were obsessed by enemy task forces. Just because we got the report—and it turned out to be false—that there was a fleet of enemy carriers nearby, we shouldn't have set out after them."[79]

These statements do not seem to add up. In addressing his officers on his flagship *Atago* before the engagement, Admiral Kurita had asked, "Would it not be a shame to have the fleet remain intact while our nation perishes? I believe that Imperial Headquarters is giving us a glorious opportunity. You must remember there are such things as miracles."[80] Remarkably, with Halsey's swallowing of the bait of Ozawa's Northern Carrier Force, Toyoda's complex and unlikely strategy worked. As planned, Halsey's carrier fleet had removed itself from the vicinity of *Leyte Gulf*. It was a miracle. Kurita spurned it. Given that he believed that this was in any case a doomed mission, effectively a suicide mission, why did he not continue?

Kurita and Koyonagi's statements are also difficult to reconcile with the fact that Kurita immediately headed for the *San Bernadino Straits* rather than north toward any US carrier fleet. Perhaps the truth is more prosaic. In his eighties Kurita told biographer and naval academy student, Jiro Ooka, that he withdrew from *Leyte Gulf* because the war was lost, his mission was futile and he wanted to save the lives of his men. This explanation does at least have the virtue of logic. Perhaps Kurita was one of the few 'sane' officers left in a high command that had lost touch with reality. It did not help that, increasingly, fictitious field reports made to Imperial General HQ were fabricated to the point of incredulity. Believing that Kurita had won a great victory at *Leyte Gulf*, Lieutenant-General Suzuki declared, "We must demand the capitulation of MacArthur's entire forces, those in Guinea and other places as well as the troops on Leyte."[81] In Japan the Emperor declared victory celebrations for the claimed sinking of sixteen American carriers.

Had Kurita followed the brief of a 'do and die' mission, there is little doubt that a great success would have been achieved. Judged from this point of view Kurita's withdrawal was a huge mistake. His critics, who accused him of cowardice for not fighting to the death, engineered his removal from command in December 1944 and he was transferred to the role of commandant of the Imperial Naval Academy.

Shortly before the dramas of Kurita's attack on the escort carriers of the Seventh Fleet, Halsey had caught up with Ozawa's decoy force to the northeast of *Luzon*. Task Force 34, comprising six battleships under Vice-Admiral Willis Lee, which both Kinkaid and Nimitz had expected to be guarding the *San Bernadino Straits'* exit into the *Philippines Sea*, had been sent ahead of Halsey's carrier force. Halsey's aim was to cripple Ozawa's carrier force by air attack and to finish it off with Task Force 34's surface force.

The Battle of Cape Engano: Halsey's Hollow Victory: [**Map: 33.5**] Halsey faced a somewhat pathetic Japanese carrier force; a pale shadow of the proud fleet that had dealt America such a devastating blow at *Pearl Harbor*. Only *Zuikaku*, now Vice-Admiral Ozawa's flagship, still survived. The remainder of his force consisted of three light carriers *Zuiho, Chitose* and *Chiyoda* and two converted carriers, *World War I* battleships, *Hyuga* and *Ise*; flight decks had been added to their aft whereby planes could take off but not land. The 'make-do-and-mend' conversions threw into stark relief the bareness of Japan's naval cupboard. In reality the situation was worse than it appeared. It only became known after the war that Ozawa's carrier fleet was in effect a ghost force, bereft of aircraft, designed largely as bait to lure Halsey north.

The real tragedy of the Japanese carrier fleet was that it could only muster 100 aircraft and crews. In part this reflected the losses incurred in the air battles over *Luzon* a few weeks earlier. As Ozawa admitted in his post-war interrogation, he was forced by Admiral Toyoda to send 150 planes to defend *Formosa*. "My force of carrier planes became very much weakened," Ozawa explained to US Rear-Admiral Ofstie, "Only 110 left, so less than half remained."[82] Japan had found it difficult to replace the almost total loss of its carrier aircrews at the *Battle of the Philippines Sea* but after the losses incurred at *Formosa*, there was no time to replenish the carrier fleet with new crews. Back in Japan, there was a dearth of experienced aviators available to teach. Unlike the US Navy the Japanese had singularly failed to bring back experienced crews to teach the next generation of cadets. There was also a shortage of training planes and even fuel. Many new pilots had to learn their craft from watching films. In the future most of the pilots trained would be for *kamikaze* missions.

At dawn on 25 October, Ozawa launched an attack on Halsey's fleet with just seventy-five planes. Their destruction was almost total with the very few survivors managing to find their way to land bases on *Luzon*. Vice-Admiral Mitscher, handed back tactical command of the Third Fleet's carrier strike force, oversaw a total of 527 sorties over the course of the day. By evening, carriers *Zuikaku, Chitose* and *Zuiho* and the destroyer *Akizuki* had been sunk. In addition the light cruiser *Chiyoda* was severely damaged. Taken under tow, the *Chiyoda* had to be abandoned when American surface ships appeared on the horizon. The now stationary *Chiyoda* stood and fired back at the advancing surface fleet led by Rear-Admiral Laurence DuBose—four cruisers, USS *Santa Fe*, USS *Mobile*, USS *Wichita* and USS *New Orleans* along with nine destroyers, poured fire into the *Chiyoda*. Captain Eichiro Jo was killed along with all 1,470 officers and crew. It was the only recorded episode in *World War II* in which a surface warship was lost with 'all hands.' On paper the sinking of four carriers at the *Battle of Cape Engano* should have made it a great naval victory. However, for Task Group 38 it was a hollow and virtually meaningless victory. Halsey had taken the decoy. He had abandoned Rear-Admiral Sprague's escort carriers and MacArthur's amphibious fleet to the possibility of total destruction.

From the point of view of his personal vanity, Halsey had not won the great naval battle that his vanity craved. Halsey described missing the *Battle of Midway* as "the most grievous disappointment of my career"[83] and it would not be too far-fetched to posit the theory that his misjudgements at *Leyte Gulf* were partly driven by this sense of lost opportunity. Having missed out on *Midway*, the *Battle of the Santa Cruz Islands* and the *Battle of the Philippines Sea*, there were to be no more opportunities for glory. Indeed the *Battle of Leyte Gulf* now descended into a war of words between the winning commanders.

Following Kinkaid's desperate calls for help for his stricken escort carrier force, Nimitz had finally lost patience and sent a message demanding to know "WHERE IS 'REPEAT' WHERE IS TASK-FORCE-34? THE WORLD WONDERS"[84] The last phrase, 'The world wonders' was encryption padding that a well-educated signaling ensign on *Honolulu* had taken from Alfred Lord Tennyson's poem *Charge of the Light Brigade* [1854]. 'The world wonders' should have been removed, as was the padding that preceded the message, which read "TURKEY TROTS TO WATER"[85]; by the mistaken inclusion of just the 'end-padding' in the message given to Halsey, it appeared that Nimitz had deliberately insulted his Third Fleet commander. On receiving the message Halsey's rage became uncontrollable. He would later recount, "I was stunned as if I had been struck in the face."[86] In fact Halsey's behavior was so demented that Halsey's Chief of Staff, Rear-Admiral Robert 'Mick' Carney, was forced to shout at him "Stop it! What the hell's the matter with you? Pull yourself together."[87]

However unintended Nimitz's slight, the incident was symptomatic of the bad feeling and fierce debates that occurred in the immediate aftermath of the battle and beyond. Kinkaid clearly felt that it was the Third Fleet's task to defend the *San Bernadino Strait* and thus protect the northern flank of the Seventh Fleet's invasion armada. In a message to Nimitz and King in Washington, Halsey, rather defensively pleaded that he "believed that the Center Force has been so heavily damaged in the *Sibuyan Sea* that it could no longer be considered a serious menace to Seventh Fleet."[88] [Secret Dispatch 251317] Moreover in his dispatch to Nimitz and King on 25 October, Halsey suggested, ". . . to statically guard *San Bernadino Strait* until enemy surface and carrier attacks could be coordinated would have been childish."[89] This was a poor argument given that Halsey could easily have divided his forces and left his surface Task Force 34 under Admiral Lee to cover the exit from the *Straits*. This indeed is what both Kinkaid and Nimitz quite naturally assumed that Halsey had done.

Nimitz's message 'THE WORLD WONDERS' had its effect however. At 11.15 a.m., forty-two miles from Ozawa's crippled fleet, Halsey's conscience yielded. He retreated southwards with his fleet. In his memoirs, Halsey would write, "I turned my back on the opportunity I had dreamed of since my days as a cadet."[90] Attempts to claim the nobility of self-sacrifice must have rung hollow to the survivors of USS *Johnston* and the families of all the men killed at the *Battle of Samar Island*. The claim of self-sacrifice also seems self-serving because his aircraft carriers had in effect annihilated Ozawa's carrier fleet; what opportunity had Halsey turned his back on?

By the time that Task Group 38 had returned to its original station off *San Bernadino Straits*, Kurita's Center Force was long gone. A Japanese destroyer that had lingered to pick up survivors was sunk. It was the only surface action that Halsey ever witnessed. He had caught a sprat. Halsey vented his spleen on the Japanese survivors. In direct contravention of the Geneva Convention, he ordered Japanese sailors to be shot in the water. "See that those who refuse to cooperate do not reach the beach where they would be potential reinforcements to the garrison there."[91] There were only six Japanese survivors. Atrocities in the *Pacific War* were not all committed by the Japanese.

If Halsey had stayed at *San Bernadino Straits* rather than racing northwards toward Ozawa's carrier fleet, he would have been guaranteed the box seat at a glorious shoot-out between surface fleets. Halsey's carelessness, vanity, and *idée fixe* with regard to unity of command, had cost him the moment of glory that had been his childhood ambition. For posterity it also cost him the hard won reputation that his aggressive leadership has brought from the campaigns fought after *Pearl Harbor* and at *Guadalcanal* and the *Northern Solomon Islands*.

Victory and a Cover-up of Halsey's Mistakes: Whatever mistakes Halsey had made, the *Battle of Leyte Gulf* was a stunning victory for the United States, which had brought the virtual annihilation of the Japanese Navy. However undeserved, plaudits showered down. Forrestal, Secretary of the Navy, wrote to Halsey, "My congratulations to you and all hands. The nation and the whole Navy are very proud."[92] Similarly Marshall described *Leyte Gulf* as "a splendid and historic victory. The Army owes you a debt of thanks."[93] As usual it was Halsey who reaped the applause. Somewhat inaccurately, on 27 October the *New York Times* headlined, "MAIN FLEET BROKEN. HALSEY FORCE INFLICTED A STAGGERING DEFEAT ON ENEMY OFF FORMOSA."[94] Kinkaid and Sprague received little mention.

Within the US Navy, scuttlebutt about Halsey's abandonment of MacArthur's invasion fleet was rampant. When MacArthur overheard his staff criticizing Halsey at a dinner held at the *Leyte* HQ, Price House in Tacloban, he sprang angrily to his friend's defense, "That's enough. Leave the Bull alone. He's still a fighting admiral in my book."[95] Spruance, knowing the pressures of command, refused to criticize his friend. Meanwhile in Washington, Admiral King, now apprised of the narrative of the battle, diplomatically suggested to Nimitz that Halsey needed a rest. Quite plausibly fatigue could have been a factor in Halsey's litany of mistakes at *Leyte Gulf*.

Nimitz, in his message to King on 28 October, had left no doubt as to where he believed the balance of blame should lie. "It never occurred to me that Halsey, knowing the composition of the ships in the *Sibuyan Sea*, would leave the *San Bernadino Strait* unguarded, even though the Jap detachments in the *Sibuyan Sea* had been reported seriously damaged. That Halsey feels that his is a defensive position is indicated in his top secret dispatch 251317."[96] Indeed the following January, Halsey admitted to King, "I made a mistake in that battle"[97] and later reflected that it might have been better if he had had command at the *Battle of the Philippines Sea* and Admiral Spruance at *Leyte Gulf*. However, King did not believe that Kinkaid was blameless. He thought that Kinkaid should have had planes patrolling the *San Bernadino Straits*.

King debated the wisdom of keeping Halsey in command of the Task Group 38 (now renamed the Third Fleet) but ultimately decided that his good record gave him a large balance of credit to set against the mistakes made at *Leyte Gulf*. King was also aware, as he told his staff, "He is the greatest leader of men that we have. The men are crazy about him, and they will follow him anywhere."[98] Old loyalties ran deep with Nimitz too; Nimitz recalled Halsey's fearless aggression after *Pearl Harbor*, "Bill Halsey came to my support and offered to lead the attack. I'll not be a party to any enterprise that can hurt a man like that."[99]

King also had service politics to consider. To remove Halsey and expose the *Battle of Leyte Gulf* as something other than a great victory would likely give MacArthur cause to maneuver for command over the *Pacific* Fleet. While the war was being fought it was better not to air the US Navy's dirty washing in public. This was particularly true as the divided command, for which King was partly responsible, was certainly one of the causes of the near catastrophe at *Leyte Gulf.*

Post-War Recriminations between Halsey and Kinkaid: A wise man would have kept quiet about the events that characterized the catastrophic near miss at *Leyte Gulf.* However, Halsey was not wise, and his vanity prevented any public admission of error. After the war the arguments continued to rage. Any contriteness felt by Halsey during the *Pacific War* seems to have evaporated by the time he wrote his memoirs. Kinkaid took a full broadside. Halsey "wondered how Kinkaid had let [his escort carriers] get caught up like this, and why [their] search planes had not given him warning."[100] In an even more pointed rebuke, Halsey protested, "it was not my job to protect the Seventh Fleet."[101] Given Nimitz's repeated commands to the contrary this was patently untrue. By contrast King's autobiography largely blamed Halsey though he reserved some criticism for Kinkaid.

When Vice-Admiral 'Bull' Halsey's self-serving account of the *Battle of Leyte Gulf* appeared in print in the *Saturday Evening Post*, it created a storm of bitterness and recrimination within Navy circles. Admiral Spruance wrote to Kinkaid to say, "I suspect that you had to loosen your collar when reading Bill's account of the battle."[102] Kinkaid refused to let the matter rest. A sharp rebuttal was printed in *Life* magazine in which Halsey was accused of irresponsibly exposing Admiral Sprague and the invasion force to attack.

In 1947 Samuel Eliot Morison's epic fifteen-volume Pulitzer Prize winning history of the US Navy in *World War II* came out decisively in Kinkaid's favor. The volume covering *Leyte Gulf* was even dedicated to Admiral Clifton 'Ziggy' Sprague, the commander of Taffy-3. Naval historian E. B. Potter, who worked with Nimitz on *The Great Sea War: The Story of Naval Action in World II* [1960], also concluded that Halsey was at fault. However, Potter's draft conclusions were watered down after Halsey, to whom he had sent a draft, warned him off publication. The problem of Halsey' personality was well summed up by Admiral Spruance while he was anxiously pacing up and down the deck of his flagship, USS *Indianapolis*, with a friend, during the *Battle of Iwo Jima*. Without mentioning Halsey, though he must have had him in mind, the normally taciturn and circumspect Spruance grew expansive when he explained:

> Personality in war can be a drawback because it may
> affect a man's thinking. A commander may not have
> sought it; it may have been forced upon him by zealous
> subordinates or imaginative war correspondents. Once
> started, it is hard to keep in check. In the early days of the
> war, when little about the various commanders is known
> to the public, and some admiral does a good or spectacular

job, he gets a head start in publicity. Anything he does thereafter tends toward greater headline value than the same things done by others, following the journalistic rule, "names make news." Thus his reputation snowballs; and soon, probably against his will, he has become a colorful figure, credited with fabulous characteristics over and above the competence in war command for which he has been conditioning himself all his life. His fame may not have gone to his head, but there is nevertheless danger in this. Should he get to identifying himself with the figure as publicized, he may subconsciously start thinking in terms of what this reputation calls for, rather than how best to meet the action problem confronting him.[103]

After the war Halsey commented somewhat regretfully, "I wish that Spruance had been with Mitscher at Leyte Gulf and I had been with Mitscher in the Battle of the Philippine Sea."[104] It was the closest that Halsey ever came to admitting his faults at the *Battle of Leyte Gulf*. Of course if Spruance had been commanding the fleet at the *Battle of Leyte Gulf*, the Japanese commanders would have set a different strategy. Halsey was known to be recklessly aggressive and Admiral Toyoda planned accordingly. As Ozawa said after the war, "We always tried to adapt the operation plan according to the characteristic of the United States commander."[105]

Yet perhaps the root cause of the mistakes made at the *Battle of Leyte Gulf* was the division of command. Before the battle Nimitz himself had directed Halsey, "In case opportunity for destruction of a major portion of the enemy fleet offer or can be created, such destruction becomes the primary task."[106] While this was indeed the primary task for the Third Fleet, would Nimitz's instructions have been so slanted if he had also been responsible for the Seventh Fleet that was under the command of General MacArthur and the South West Pacific Army? Logically Nimitz would have been given command of the entire *Pacific* Campaign; with any other commander than MacArthur in Australia, this would almost certainly have been the case. However, by dint of his vast ego and his media power, the *Pacific* command had been divided as a sop to MacArthur.

There is little doubt that much of the cause of the confusion at the *Battle of Leyte Gulf* lay in the structure of the divided command. While this division of command in the early years of the *Pacific War* may have been a merely sub-optimal though actively fought-over structure, which seemed to work as long as MacArthur and Nimitz were following separate lines of advance in the *Pacific*, by the time of *Leyte Gulf* it had ceased to be a rational command system for the conduct of the war. The amphibious operation at *Leyte Gulf* was a joint operation and a single command should have been an essential prerequisite. A bi-polar naval command led, not only to breakdowns of communication, but also to divided objectives and priorities. Had Halsey been directly responsible for shepherding Sprague's escorts and MacArthur's amphibious forces at *Leyte Gulf*, would he have been so recklessly impulsive in his charge north to face Ozawa's carrier fleet?

Ultimately however, The *Battle of Leyte Gulf* was an overwhelming victory for the United States. The American forces suffered 2,800 casualties and the loss of a light carrier, 2 escort carriers, 2 destroyers and an escort destroyer. By comparison the Japanese Navy lost 12,500 men, a fleet carrier, 3 light fleet carriers, 3 battleships, 10 cruisers, and 11 destroyers sunk. In aggregate 28 of Japan's remaining 80 serviceable warships had been lost. Japan also lost over 300 planes. To all intents and purposes, Japan's navy ceased to be operational excepting the training and planning of *kamikaze* attacks. Reputations for US commanders, at least in the short term, were preserved. Even Halsey garnered a reprieve for actions that, but for Kurita's curious withdrawal of his Center Force at the moment when victory seemed assured, would have caused a serious and humiliating reverse for MacArthur's triumphant return to the Philippines.

Perfect Storm: Typhoon Cobra: **[Map: 33.6]** Halsey's run of misfortune or bad judgment did not end with the *Battle of Leyte Gulf*. The Divine Wind of the *kamikaze* was not the only wind to disrupt Halsey and the US *Pacific* fleet. On 11 December, Halsey formed three Task Groups from the ships which had been sent back for 'rest and recuperation' on *Ulithi*. He was one Task Group short because of the number of ships that had to be repaired as a result of *Kamikaze* damage while patroling off the Philippine coast.

From 14 to 16 December, Halsey patroled the Philippines' coast and launched waves of attacks on *Luzon*'s airfield while MacArthur commenced his attack on *Mindoro Island*. One of the attacks on 15 December was against the airfield at Camp Cabanatuan, the largest prisoner of war camp on *Luzon*. Since the defeats at Bataan and *Corregidor* three years earlier, nearly a third of the 9,000 mainly young Allied POWs had died of starvation or been murdered. The remaining living skeletons were suddenly filled with joy. One prisoner recalled, "All of us who were watching through barbed wire when the planes came and turned it into big hole. I can't tell you how ecstatic we were to see our own work go up in smoke."[107] US prisoners on *Palawan Island* in the *Sulu Sea* were less fortunate. The commandant of the small prison camp heard that MacArthur's convoy was heading across the *Sulu Sea* for *Mindoro*. In response 150 American prisoners were shepherded into the covered trenches that served as bomb shelters. The prison warders showered them with gasoline and set them alight. The few who managed to escape were machine-gunned.

Thanks to Halsey's deployment of Vice-Admiral McCain's 'Big Blue Blanket' not a single Japanese aircraft snuck through the air cordon to threaten MacArthur's transports and landing forces. Some 300 Japanese aircraft were destroyed and thirty Japanese ships sunk. In one of the noted tragedies of the war, one of the Japanese ships sunk was transporting hundreds of American prisoners from the Philippines to China. Not realizing that the Japanese transport contained American prisoners, Halsey did not send rescue ships. A grieving mother of one of the soldiers killed wrote to the admiral to tell him "You ought to be hung as a war criminal!"[108] It was a tragedy that left Halsey in utter dejection. Remorse and exhaustion may have influenced America's most famous fleet admiral in his decision-making in the events that followed.

On 17 December 1944, Admiral 'Bull' Halsey led Task Group 38 toward a pre-arranged refueling site in the middle of the *Philippine Sea*. Uniquely the US Navy had developed techniques of mid-ocean refueling that enabled their fleets to stay on station for longer. The Third Fleet service group, commanded by former submariner, Captain Jasper Acuff, comprised 27 oilers (each carrying 7,000 tons of fuel), 7 munitions ships, and escort carriers protected by 40 destroyers and escorts.

Weaknesses in the American Navy's weather forecasting ability were significant; it was a technology that had been left behind in the exigencies of war. Meteorological facilities aboard Halsey's flagship, USS *New Jersey*, were rudimentary. There were not enough airplanes in the *South Pacific* to do 'manual' weather spotting. Although Commander George Kosco had read a Navy weather warning, experience had taught him that most of the thousands of *Pacific* storms peter out. This one did not. It was one of the five to ten cyclones that typically sweep through the *Philippine Sea* every year. Some turn west toward the Philippines, others jag eastward toward the Chinese coast or Japan. Kosco and Halsey would also have believed that the Third Fleet could ride out a tropical cyclone. It had done so three months earlier. On this occasion, Halsey's meteorologist Commander Kosco had predicted that the storm would collide with a cold front moving across Japan and would turn harmlessly toward the northeast. By contrast on *Saipan*, Lieutenant Reid Bryson, having received confirmation from the Army Air Corps pilots that a cyclone had been located, sent a warning to the Fleet Weather Central at *Pearl Harbor*. Bryson's forecast of a storm headed towards the Philippines was greeted with an abrupt reply, "We don't believe you.'[109]

On the morning of 17 December, Halsey referred in his log to a "Force 5 – fresh breeze, 25–31 mile wind."[110] Aware that there was an impending typhoon, Halsey sought to evade the storm but instead led his force into its heart. Typhoon Cobra did more damage to the US Navy than had been accomplished by the Japanese fleet since *Pearl Harbor*.

As the storm began the lightly fuelled destroyers, which could carry little more than four days fuel on board, were in the process of refuelling but were forced by the bad weather to give up. At 12.45 p.m. Halsey called off all attempts to refuel. After being incorrectly advised by Kosco that the storm was 500 miles away, when in fact it was just 200 miles distant, Halsey ordered a new oil tanker *rendezvous* 200 miles to the northeast. Another change of course, this time to the southwest, was given at 3.33 p.m. as Halsey now desperately sought to avoid the gathering storm. As the evening wore on, sea swells and wind speeds rose. It was an uncomfortable night but worse was to come.

At 5.00 a.m. on 18 December, Halsey ordered the fleet southwards. Unbeknownst to him he was heading into the heart of the cyclone. In spite of the conditions, Halsey recommenced re-fueling at 7.00 a.m. though it soon had to be abandoned. As the day wore on, wind speeds increased from 20 to 30 knots to between 50 to 75 knots with gusts of up to 120 knots reported. Barometric pressure fell to as low as 907 mbar; seas became mountainous. Chief Warrant-Officer, Steven Yorden on board the Farragut Class destroyer, USS *Dewey*, recalled "waves that were 50 and 60 feet high. Sometimes you'd see a destroyer, he'd be sitting up on top of a wave and the next time he would be down so low that you couldn't even see the mast. That's how deep the troughs were."[111]

Carnage at Sea: By 9.00 a.m. alarming messages were being received by Halsey's flagship. At 9.07 a.m. the light carrier USS *Independence* (CVL-22) reported a man overboard; they lost two more men over the next thirty minutes. When winds rose to sixty-six knots at 1.00 p.m., Halsey ordered every ship's commander to abandon station and save his ship as best he could. Halsey would later write, "The 70 foot seas smash you from all sides . . . this typhoon tossed our enormous ship as if she were a canoe . . . we could not hear our own voice above the uproar."[112] He could only imagine the scene on his destroyers.

The executive officer of the destroyer, USS *Hancock*, reported, "The wind was howling all through the ship—we were rolling probably 40 degrees—some men were doing their job in a matter of fact way—others were praying or sitting off by themselves, their faces white with fear."[113] On the USS *Dewey*, the sea crashed through the hatch on the main deck and put out the entire ship's electrics leaving it dead in the water. The captain ordered Yorden, who was in charge of fitting and repair, to try to remove their Mark-33 gun and the mast. However, after perilously retrieving oxygen-acetylene bottles and cutting equipment, Jordan found that he could not cut through aluminum fittings. As for the mast, he discovered that the high wind simply put out the flame of his equipment. It was dangerous work. "They tied a line around me you know so I wouldn't get washed overboard," he recalled, "And I got washed over a couple of times and they fished me back up you know."[114] On the biggest roll on the *Dewey*, Yorden said, "the helmsman, the water was under his arms. That's how deep the water was over the ship . . . it took the stack off. That's what really saved us, I think, was when we lost that stack we lost that big sail."[115]

Many of the smaller ships were unable to steer either upwind or downwind and rolled side-on to the incoming waves. The Fletcher Class USS *Spence* sank after recording a wind speed of 125 knots and taking on thousands of gallons of water. Visibility fell to as little as 1,000 yards. Water came into ventilation shafts, blower intakes and every deck opening. Many ship suffered from loss of steering control, power failures and stoppage of the oil fired boilers and their propulsion systems. Two other Farragut Class destroyers USS *Hull* and USS *Monaghan* capsized. After the last generator failed on the *Monaghan*, every sailor, now completely powerless in his fate, recited aloud the *Lord's Prayer*. The *Monaghan* may well have de-ballasted in preparation to take on fuel. After seven mighty rolls, the *Monaghan* slid down the face of a giant wall of water, was entombed and broke apart. The three ships that were lost keeled over to leeward by fifty to eighty degrees, hung momentarily and then turned over. They floated for a short while before sinking.

The USS *Dewey* may well have survived the storm because, unlike the *Monaghan*, it took on water ballast to lower its center of gravity. This was a problem for many destroyers whose new equipment, such as radar and new weaponry had added weight to the upper decks. Similarly the *Spence* sank after hanging at a fifty degree roll while its sister ship the USS *Hickox*, which had been fully ballasted with sea water survived a seventy-degree roll. Ballast did not necessarily guarantee safety. According to her build specifications, the *Hull*, which had taken on fuel as well as 125,000 gallons of ballast, more than the minimum requirement, should have been safe from capsize. She wasn't. Seaman 'Punchy' Parker, the ship's intramural boxing champion, sobbed: "I can't swim. I can't swim."[116] Chief Quartermaster Archie DeRyckere told the sailor not to worry, "Who the hell you think is gonna swim in that mess anyway."[117]

By contrast the similarly ballasted USS *Dewey* had recovered from a 75-degree roll. In this it may also have been helped by the removal of some of its top-weight; a precaution that the USS *Hull* was unable to carry out. On the destroyer USS *Tabberer*, Shop Fitter 3rd Class Leonard Glaser volunteered to be lowered over the side with a blowtorch and acetylene tank in order to sever the radio mast that had toppled over the side. Glaser, a devout Jew, was indebted to Captain Henry Plage because he had gone out of his way to organize *kosher* food for him. Dropped down to water level, Glaser was frequently submerged by water, but managed to get his torch relit and after five minutes managed to cut away the steel mast pole. The *Tabberer*'s roll immediately lessened. Later, the court of inquiry concluded that all three destroyers that were lost had probably tried to stay on station too long. For this Halsey was clearly the man who bore the main responsibility for the tragedy.

The light aircraft carriers, with their heavy cruiser hulls that were less stable than the fleet carriers, also suffered extensive damage. All aircraft carriers, designed to carry a large amount of moving equipment, such as planes, deck tractors, bombs, and torpedoes, also tended to be top heavy and were more prone to damage from storms than surface ships. As planes were flung loose and crashed around the hanger decks, gasoline fires broke out on the USS *Monterey* (CVL-26), the USS *Cowpens* (CVL-25) and USS *San Jacinto* (CVL-30). On this latter ship it was reported that

> The free aircraft smashed into other aircraft likewise moored, and tore them loose, ripping out the deck eyebolts in many instances. Spare engines, propellers, tractors, and other heavy equipment were all scrambled into the violently sliding mass, and smashed free side to side, ripping open and carrying away the unprotected flimsy air intakes and ventilation ducts.[118]

On the USS *Independence* (CVL-22), also a light carrier, it was noted, "At about 8.30 a.m. a heavy roll caused a section of the bomb stowage to carry away, permitting nearly 25 tons of bombs, including nine blockbusters, to roll around the bomb magazine like beer kegs."[119]

The USS *Monterey*, the worst damaged of the carriers was set on fire by a Vought F4U Corsair that broke free, punctured the fuel tanks on another aircraft and exploded. Although the planes had degassed, there was enough vapor and residual air fuel to feed the conflagration. Fire spread through the central section and then to other decks through the ventilation systems. Fire crews, one of which was led by later US President, Gerald Ford, donned breathing apparatus to fight the inflammation. It took over an hour to put out all the fires. In addition to seven aircraft blown off the flight deck, eleven others in the hangar were damaged beyond repair and almost two thirds of the hangar had been gutted by fire.

On the USS *Altamaha*, an escort carrier that had recently come from *Pearl Harbor* with replenishment aircraft and crews, the inclinometer showed rolls to port and starboard of thirty-one degrees and twenty-nine degrees respectively on a ship where it was considered that a maximum safe roll was 27.5 degrees. The first deck parked plane to be carried away by the winds fell into the lowered elevator and jammed it in the down position. Life rafts, 20 mm and 40 mm guns and radio antennas were also swept away. Planes forced free ran amok and destroyed others. "The commanding officer frequently saw wings and tail surfaces of planes still otherwise secured, ripping bodily from their fittings and blown over the side . . ."[120] It was similarly observed, ". . . the propellers of three or four planes . . . parked on the bow began wind milling at about 200 RPM's . . . and a few seconds later these planes were torn from their moorings and flung like chips over the side."[121] As the storm started to subside on the afternoon of 18 December, Halsey would find that his fleet was dispersed over 2,500 square miles.

The Rescue: USS *Tabberer*, a small John C. Butler Class destroyer, having ridden out the peak of the storm that passed just after midday, against orders, stayed behind to rescue survivors. At 9.30 p.m. a crewmember heard a shout and saw a light in the water. It turned out to be Quartermaster 3rd Class, Vernon Lindquist, a survivor from the USS *Hull*. A further fifteen survivors were pulled out during the night and more during the daylight hours of 19 December. On 20 December a raft with ten survivors from the USS *Spence* was picked up in addition to four more men rescued later that morning. In all the USS *Tabberer* saved five officers and thirty-six men from the *Hull* and fourteen men from the *Spence*.

It was difficult work. The captain of the USS *Tabberer* put the ship upwind of the survivors allowing the ship to blow toward the men in the water. Cargo nets were put over the side and rings with long lines thrown out to men in the water. Strong swimmers also went out with lines attached. Riflemen on board warned off the sharks that were seen circling survivors. Almost all the survivors were wearing *kapok* type life jackets. *Kopak* is porous vegetable plant that was a more pliant and comfortable alternative to cork.

Bosun's Mate 1st Class, Louis 'Skip' Purvis, a strong swimmer who volunteered to swim out to rescue unconscious seamen found his lifeline snagged under the *Tabberer* and was dragged under the destroyer. Much to everyone's surprise he popped up on the other side. After he was brought aboard, Purvis joshed that he was the "first sailor to be keelhauled in two hundred years."[122]

The escort destroyer, sent back to look for survivors, picked up the seven crewmembers to be found alive from the USS *Monaghan*. Some of the rescued recalled miraculous survival stories. Ship's Cook 1st Class, Milburn 'Spiz' Hoffman had floated up from the sinking *Hull*'s forward galley and escaped through an air vent. He and another sailor floated together wearing their *kapok* life jackets. In the morning he found that his colleague had died. Hoffman released the man from his *kapok* and watched him sink from view. In despair, Hoffman gave up and threw away his *kapok*. However, on thinking about how his widowed mother would cope without him, Hoffman decided to recover his *kapok* and as he did so found it floating beside a horsehair mattress. He tied himself to the makeshift raft and used his clothes to shield himself from the burning sun that now beat down between squalls. Hoffman was found burnt, delirious and naked on his mattress. His rescuers dubbed him 'Lord Godiva.'[123]

Archie DeRyckere also survived the sinking and his hopes were raised when he sighted the smoke from a ship. His expectations of rescue were soon dashed by a heavy thump in the back. It was a six-foot shark. He screamed out loud, "You know God, first you take my ship. Then you have me swim around in the ocean all night. And now you're going to feed me to the sharks? That ain't right."[124] As the *Tabberer* approached DeRyckere found himself in the midst of a hail of bullets as sharp shooters and machine gunners protected him from the circling sharks. He was pulled in and survived.

Including the aircraft that were ripped from the decks of battle-cruisers and battleships, a total of 146 aircraft were lost or damaged beyond repair. Nineteen ships registered planes destroyed with the heaviest losses reported by the USS *Cape Esperance* (31), the USS *Altamaha* (32) and the USS *Monterey* (18). Apart from the three ships lost, a further twenty-five ships were damaged, some of which required major repair. 775 lives were lost from the ships that capsized and sank, including 202 from the *Hull*, 256 from the *Monaghan* and 317 from the *Spence*. Another fifteen sailors from ten other ships were killed in accidents or washed overboard. Eighty crewmembers were also injured, of which thirty-four came from the badly damaged light carrier *Monterey*. As Admiral Nimitz concluded, the damage caused by the typhoon "represented a more crippling blow to the Third Fleet than it might be expected to suffer in anything less than a major action."[125] Arguably, after *Pearl Harbor* and the *Battle of Savo Island, Typhoon Cobra* was the US fleet's greatest single disaster of the war. Nimitz, in his confidential letter to Admiral King and staff in Washington, reported, "It was the greatest loss that we have taken in the Pacific without compensatory return since the *First Battle of Savo Island*."[126]

In spite of disobeying orders to escape the storm and return to port, the captain, Henry Lee Page, was awarded the Legion of Merit and the entire crew was presented with the Navy's Unit Commendation Ribbon by Vice-Admiral 'Bull' Halsey.

Court of Inquiry at Ulithi Lagoon: In the aftermath of the disaster, Halsey came under intense scrutiny for his actions both in his misreading of the storm information and for his determination to keep the fleet on station rather than running for cover. A naval court of inquiry was convened on USS *Cascade* at *Ulithi*. With Nimitz in attendance, judge advocate Captain Herbert Gates found Halsey guilty of making an error of judgment but did not recommend sanctions.

Witnesses included Rear-Admiral Gerald Bogan, commander of the fleet carrier USS *Saratoga*, who contended that Halsey was remiss in not taking a southerly course sooner—it was a recommendation that Bogan had made to Admiral John McCain on 17 December. Halsey's excuse was that he wished to stay in touch with MacArthur's invasion force. At the inquiry, Halsey also claimed it was only at "4 a.m. on the 18 December . . . that the fleet was confronted with serious storm conditions."[127] Yet it took him eight hours to give the order to scatter. Halsey's claim was clearly false. He also claimed that he had been given insufficient warning: "I did not have timely warning. I'll put it another way. I had no warning."[128]

It was another episode, following his dereliction of duty at the *Battle of Leyte Gulf*, which put a serious blemish on Halsey's war record. Admiral Hooper, who had presided over the Court of Inquiry, let it be known that it was his opinion that Halsey should be court-martialled. Eventually it was recommended that Halsey should be reassigned to other duties. Halsey himself was mortified by the disaster. On 18 December 1944, Nimitz's confidential report *Subject. Damage in Typhoon. Lessons of. Commander in Chief, Pacific Area Command (CINCPAC) File A2-11, L11-1*, gave a measured analysis of the Typhoon Cobra and the causes of the disaster:

> Seamen of the present day should be better at forecasting weather at sea, independently of the radio, than were their predecessors. The general laws of storms and the weather expectancy for all months of the year in all parts of the world are now more thoroughly understood, more completely catalogued, and more readily available in various publications. An intensive study of typhoons and western Pacific weather was made over a period of many years by Father Depperman at the Manila observatory, and his conclusions have been embodied in the material available to all aerologists. What Knight and Bowditch have to say on the subject is exactly as true during this war as it was in time of peace or before the days of the radio. Familiarity with these authorities is something that no captain or navigator can do without. The monthly pilot charts, issued to all ships, give excellent information as to the probable incidence and movements of typhoons. Stress on the foregoing is no belittlement of our aero logical centers and weather broadcasts. But just as a navigator is held culpable if he neglects "Log, Lead, and

Lookout" through blind faith in his radio fixes, so is the seaman culpable who regards personal weather estimates as obsolete and assumes that if no radio storm warning has been received, then all is well, and no local weather signs need cause him concern.[129]

Nimitz also commented:

In the light of hindsight it is easy to see how any of several measures might have prevented this catastrophe, but it was far less easy a problem at a time for the men who were out there under the heaviest of conflicting responsibilities ... possibly, too much reliance was placed on analysis broadcast from the *Fleet Weather Central, Pearl Harbor*. Weather data was lacking from an area some 240 to 300 miles in diameter ...[130]

Nimitz blamed a general lack of seamanship and over-reliance on weather information. In spite of this and the numerous changes made to training methods, new weather stations were quickly put into action in the area where there had been a hole in weather information. In an oblique criticism of Halsey, Nimitz also noted that

it is most definitely part of the senior officer's responsibility to think in terms of the smallest ship and most inexperienced commanding officer under him. He cannot take them for granted ... nothing is more dangerous than for a seaman to be grudging in taking precautions lest they turn out to have been unnecessary. Safety at sea for a thousand years has depended on exactly the opposite philosophy.[131]

Crucially Halsey's status as America's great naval hero made him virtually immune. The furious Navy Secretary, James Forrestal, wanted Halsey to be removed from command but Nimitz, a loyal and forgiving commander refused to abandon his colleague on the grounds that his mistakes "were errors of judgment committed under stress of war operations stemming from a commendable desire to meet military obligations."[132] Back in Washington, Admiral King, always sensitive to any public criticism of the Navy, also agreed to 'turn a blind eye.' Ever aware of political sensibilities in Washington, King was not going to give over the fleet's greatest public relations asset lightly.

Halsey recovered quickly from the setback of Typhoon Cobra. In January 1945 he conducted a series of raids in the *South China Sea*. In a 3,800-mile voyage along the coastlines of China and Indochina, Halsey's aircraft were constantly deployed in bombing attacks. Piqued by criticism at the court of inquiry, he operated at an even higher tempo than usual. One operations officer described Halsey's force as "a pretty razzle-dazzle outfit . . . we were really raiders. We were operating on the spur of the moment, which was certainly good."[133] Re-establishing his reputation was important for a man almost as vain as General MacArthur. The mission results were indeed impressive. On 12 January a raid on the Japanese port of *Cam Ranh Bay* (Vietnam) comprised 1,500 sorties, sank forty-four Japanese ships (including fifteen warships) and downed 100 aircraft. Losses amounted to just twenty-three American planes and most of their crews were rescued. Halsey boasted that this raid "was a strongly worded notice to the Nips that the *South China Sea* had changed ownership from Japan to the United States."[134] *Hong Kong*, Canton, *Amoy, Formosa* and *Okinawa* were then targeted in a romp that finally ended on his return to *Ulithi* on 25 January. Albeit disastrous, the 'Typhoon Cobra' debacle was consigned to the margins of history and post-war debate.

Halsey's Second Typhoon: Again in June 1945, Halsey, who had taken over command of the Third Fleet from Spruance in late May, sailed into the eye of a typhoon. Halsey's fleet was assaulted by 70-foot waves and 127 knots winds. Many of his ships sustained severe damage though he was fortunate on this occasion not to lose any. Six crewmen died, seventy-five planes were destroyed and a further seventy were damaged. At the Naval court of inquiry that followed, headed for a second time by Admiral Hooper, Halsey was again found to be at fault and it was recommended that the Navy consider whether he and McCain should be relieved of command. Halsey's course change at 1.34 a.m. was blamed for most of the damage suffered.

Their removal was duly discussed but Nimitz, aware of Halsey's vast reputation as a fighter and a naval hero in the United States, decided not to implement the recommendation of the court. Halsey was spared for the second time (third if his errors at *Leyte Gulf* are included), while McCain was disciplined; he was reassigned as deputy head of the US Veterans Administration. Taking the fall for Halsey was clearly a blow to a very fine officer who as Commander of the Fast Carrier Task Force in the last year of the war, had not only supported the Navy's most difficult amphibious operations but had done more than anyone to blunt the threat of the *kamikaze* to the US fleet.

A loyal Halsey later insisted that McCain be invited to the Japanese surrender; Vice-Admiral John 'Slew' McCain Snr (grandfather of John McCain, the current Republican US Senator for Arizona) died of a heart attack four days after returning home. Probably in recognition of its harsh treatment of McCain, the Navy posthumously awarded him the rank of full Admiral. He was awarded the Distinguished Service Medal with two Gold Stars in addition to the Navy Cross that he was awarded for gallantry. He was buried at Arlington National Cemetery. Navy Secretary James Forrestal noted, "He was a fighting man all the way through."[135] Admiral McCain's family would achieve the unique distinction of having a father and son pair achieve the rank of four-star Admiral in the US Navy, when his son John McCain Jr. was promoted to full admiral in February 1967.

34 "I Have Returned": MacArthur Regains the Philippines

[October 1944–August 1945]

[Maps: 34.1, 34.2, 34.3, 34.4, 34.5, 34.6]

Guerrilla War: In the dark days of early 1942 the Allied Intelligence Bureau (AIB) was established to begin the task of setting up an intelligence network to track the movements of Japan's troops and ships. Previously US operations had, in effect, been flying blind. Born in Germany as Adolph Karl Scheppe-Weidenback, Colonel Charles Willoughby had become one of MacArthur's key staffers at Bataan and took command of AIB. Under its aegis, Special Operations Australia (SOS) set up and coordinated guerrilla activity throughout the *South Pacific* to carry out murders and other acts of terrorism. Other departments included 'Coast-watchers' and 'Propaganda' that aimed to raise the morale of civilian Asian populations. These operations were so secret that even Filipino President Quezon never knew of their existence.

Colonel Courtney Whitney Snr was placed in command of Philippine operations and worked closely with MacArthur who insisted that he have an adjacent office. As part of the propaganda effort, Whitney suggested the distribution of scarce items such as cigarettes, matches and chewing gum amongst the Filipinos. The so-called 'victory packages' were printed "with the American and Philippine flags on one side, and the phrase 'I shall return!' over General MacArthur's facsimile signature on the other."[1] The suggestion received MacArthur's hearty endorsement; he scrawled over the proposal, "No objections. I shall return! MacA."[2] However, sycophantic Whitney's plan, it proved remarkably effective. By the end of the war Filipinos were daubing 'I shall return' over every vacant wall.

US military intelligence even developed relations with the communist guerrillas, 'Huks' (short for Hukbalahaps), led by Luis Tarloc for the common cause of ejecting the Japanese. In the jungle-clad hills of northern *Luzon* American escapees from the POW camp at Santo Tomas University, including Lieutenant-Colonel Martin Moses and Major Arthur Noble, put together a force of 6,000 Filipino guerrillas. As the war progressed MacArthur managed to smuggle weapons to these troops whom he designated as USFIP (United States Forces in the Philippines). They carried out a steady stream of guerrilla raids. Although Moses and Noble were eventually captured, tortured and shot, their place was immediately taken by another American, Lieutenant-Colonel R. W. Volckmann. In addition to these insurgency forces, significant spy networks were established in the major cities. When MacArthur learned that Field Marshal Hisaichi Terauchi, supreme commander of all Japanese forces in the *Pacific*, had taken over his penthouse suite at the top of the Manila Hotel, he commented, "He should like it. It has a pair of vases given by the [Japanese] Emperor to my father in 1903."[3]

Field Marshal Hisaichi Terauchi, born in 1879, was a relative of Emperor Hirohito. He was the son of Viscount General Masatake Terauchi who had a distinguished military career, fighting with the Imperial forces during the *Boshin War* to overthrow the Tokugawa Shogunate. He lost a hand in the *Satsuma Rebellion* in 1877. He also served as a Governor-General in Japan in 1910 as well as becoming Japan's Ninth Prime Minister in 1916. His son, Hisaichi, graduated twenty-first in his class at the Army Staff College in 1909 and won rapid promotion thereafter. In 1934 he became head of the Taiwan Army and two years later was appointed War Minister in the military cabinet selected after the 26 February Incident. Along with Yamamoto he was the main architect of Japan's war plans and directed the Army's 'strike south' operations in South East Asia. After Tojo's fall, Terauchi was considered for the position of prime minister but was kept in place in South East Asia to save the Philippines from MacArthur's advance.

To combat the Filipino insurgency efforts the Japanese invaders were forced to deploy considerable resources including the *Kempeitai* in cities and towns; the methods used by the security police included the establishment of informant networks. They used the usual staples of terror including bribery, blackmail, summary arrest, torture and exemplary executions. To counter the insurgency, in 1943 the Japanese military administrators financed the establishment of a pro-Japanese Filipino unit, the *Makapaili* who, in addition to their role of domestic pacification, would also be available as troops to fight a returning MacArthur. As was the case throughout Asia, some nationalists preferred the rule of fellow Asians to that of occidental Caucasians. Other Japanese supporters were simply opportunists.

In the meantime the intelligence provided by a young architect disguised as a water boy at Nichols Field enabled detailed plans to be prepared of underground fuel and munitions storage depots. The plans were smuggled out to a waiting submarine and back to US Air Force Intelligence; US bombers were thus able to target their camouflaged storage facilities with unerring accuracy, much to the amazement of Japanese commanders.

In return, military equipment for the guerrillas was smuggled into the Philippines. Ramon Hernandez, another escapee from Bataan Peninsula, smuggled radio parts into Manila inside hollowed out coconuts and pineapples. Taken into Manila on a handcart the transporters would have faced public beheading on the chopping blocks in front of Fort Santiago had they been discovered. Guns and explosives were delivered to partisans by regular convoys of submarines. Logistics were not always perfect. On one occasion a box meant to contain Thompson machine guns was found to contain US cavalry sabers; soon Japanese commanders were reporting that Japanese soldiers were being sliced and diced by partisans wielding long curved swords.

On *Leyte Island*, located on the eastern side of the central Philippines, the bearded Navy Commander Chick Parsons led terrorist operations; famously he went everywhere barefoot wearing tattered trousers and shirt. He set up a chain of hidden radio stations and sent intelligence reports back to Australia, completely unaware that his information was of particular value because his island had been chosen as MacArthur's point of return to the Philippines. Parsons was not unknown to the *Kempeitai* who put an enormous bounty of US$50,000 in gold on his head. Remarkably the Filipino natives on whose shelter and hospitality he lived, never turned him in to the Japanese authorities. Parsons' intelligence information that the town of Tacloban, at the heart of *Leyte Gulf*, was free of Japanese troops, spared it from the American pre-landing bombardment. Previously it had been incorrectly assumed that Tacloban was full of Japanese troops. MacArthur planned to make it his post-invasion HQ. As a young fresh faced Lieutenant straight out of West Point many years earlier, a survey of Tacloban's potentialities had been MacArthur's first military assignment.

Through the efforts of renegade American officers such as Parsons and local insurgency leaders, by 1944 the number of guerrilla forces in the Philippines had grown to 182,000 along with a network of 126 radio stations and 27 weather-reporting sites.

The US Presidential Elections and the Dubious Strategic Value of Luzon: The recapture of *Luzon* and its capital Manila was MacArthur's overriding objective the moment that he left *Corregidor Island* in *Manila Bay* by PT boat on 11 March 1942. He had promised 'I will return' and was determined to do this in battle after his command of the American Army had led to the most humiliating defeat in the history of the United States of America. For MacArthur, egomaniacal pride vastly outweighed any strategic logic with regard to the reconquest of the Philippines. MacArthur could only assuage his damaged dignity by the recapture of Manila and *Luzon*.

At the end of September the Joint Chiefs of Staff had agreed to an invasion of *Leyte* as a staging post to the invasion of either *Luzon* or *Formosa*. In itself *Luzon* was of little strategic value. As a bombing base for Curtis LeMay's B-29 Superfortresses, at some 2,500 miles from Japan, it was too far away. The *Marianas* (*Saipan, Guam* and *Tinian*) were a thousand miles closer. Similarly *Luzon* was too far away to be an assembly base for an invasion of the Japanese home islands. *Formosa* and especially *Okinawa* were much closer. As a base to interdict Japanese shipping in the *East China Sea, Luzon* was undoubtedly useful. However, *Formosa* would have been just as good or better and such was America's command of air and sea by the end of 1944 that neither *Luzon* nor *Formosa* were needed to interdict supply to Japan.

Ultimately it was the Navy that backed down over *Formosa*. Staunchly supported by Admiral Ernest King and initially by Nimitz, the conquest of Japan's colony *Formosa* had also been supported by the Joint Chiefs of Staff after extensive reports compiled on the subject. It was not MacArthur's arguments for *Luzon* as a base for the attack on Japan that won the day but internal dissensions within the Navy. Admiral Spruance had always considered *Formosa* a waste of time from a strategic standpoint. For him, the most direct route, from the *Marianas* via *Iwo Jima* and then *Okinawa*, was the logical choice for the advance on Japan. Moreover, Nimitz Commander in Chief, Pacific Area Command (CINCPAC), in a study on the subject subsequently suggested that a planned invasion of *Formosa* was impracticable. There were not enough troops and logistical support was compromised. In addition the failure of Chiang Kai-shek's army to hold southern China meant that Chinese forces in the south would be unable to support an Allied invasion of *Formosa*. Furthermore, Japanese forces on the mainland would be able to resupply Japanese defenders on *Formosa*. A further complication was that the Allies held the view that the defeat of the Japanese in *Formosa* would be made more difficult by a population that was wrongly assumed to have been completely 'Japanized' and culturally assimilated.

At their meeting on 29 September 1944 Nimitz presented his Commander in Chief, Pacific Area Command (CINCPAC) paper to King. Although the latter mounted a rear-guard action to defend his pet project, he eventually gave way to the arguments of his subordinates. *Okinawa* now replaced *Formosa* as the end game of the US Navy's *Central Pacific* drive toward Japan. One can only fantasize about the outcome of a meeting in which MacArthur's subordinates would have dared to challenge his conviction that *Luzon* should be taken rather than being left to 'wither on the vine.' This strategic option, albeit one that was used time and again in his romp along the northern coast of New Guinea, when major garrisons such as Madang were bypassed, was never considered by MacArthur with regards to *Luzon*. He tenuously argued that the Philippines needed to be retaken as a debt of honor to the Philippines and its people. Yet that debt would have been paid in full by the surrender of Japan; some 50,000 Americans and Filipinos would eventually have to die to repay America's debt, or rather, as most suspect, to buy back MacArthur self-dignity after the dishonor of his defeat in *Luzon* in 1941–1942.

MacArthur was ultimately allowed to invade the Japanese stronghold of *Luzon*, mainly because it made strategic sense given that the forwarding of the invasion of *Leyte* to October meant that MacArthur was able to promise an invasion of *Luzon* in December. It was a timetable that the pro-*Formosa* faction could not match. **[See Chapter 36: Iwo Jima: The Iconic Battle of the Pacific War]**

What will never be known is whether Roosevelt's confidante, naval advisor and Chief of Staff, Admiral William Leahy, made the key intervention in favor of the move to *Luzon* because Roosevelt did not want the staunchly Republican MacArthur flouncing off with a dramatic resignation just before the Presidential elections due to be held on 7 November 1944.

There is more than an element of conspiracy theory in this suggestion. However, the threat of resignation was a trick that MacArthur had tried before. In late August MacArthur had offered to stand down if the Joint Chiefs of Staff wanted to appoint a single supreme commander. It was a masterly move on MacArthur's part. Roosevelt, and perhaps even more his Joint Chiefs of Staff, feared that the wildly popular MacArthur might prove disruptive of his Democrat Presidential; it was known that some Republicans were calling for MacArthur to be drafted to lead the Republican ticket. MacArthur also knew that in a unified structure he could be the only possible choice. Marshall, Chief of Staff of the Army would not have allowed Admiral Nimitz to assume overall command despite the fact that, given the overwhelmingly important role in the *Pacific War* that was played by the Navy, its logistical support and its Marines, Nimitz would have been the logical choice. Ultimately the Joint Chiefs held their nerve. MacArthur was denied sole command of forces in the *Pacific* and the status quo of a divided command was preserved, at least until the planned invasion of Japan. It is an intriguing idea that the invasion of *Luzon* was awarded as a sop to keep MacArthur onside and out of the way of November 1944's US Presidential elections but it is unlikely to be a theory that will ever be proven.

Hirohito's Reaction to Defeat at Saipan: After the crushing defeat of the Imperial Navy at the *Battle of the Philippine Sea* on 19 and 20 June, and the subsequent loss of *Saipan*, it was clear to many within the higher echelons of government and the military that the war was lost. Tojo resigned on 7 July and was replaced by General Kuniaki Koiso. Born in Utsunomiya in Tochigi Prefecture, Koiso was the son a former policeman whose family had belonged to samurai stock. After attending the Army Staff College, Koiso was commissioned as a First Lieutenant in November 1901. He fought in the *Russo-Japanese War* [1904–1905], at the end of which he had become a Captain. In 1910 Koiso graduated from the Army Staff College, which prepared officers for high command and thereafter followed a career typical of his cadre; posts followed as an Army instructor, service in Manchuria's *Kwantung* Army, secondment to the Army Air Force, military *attaché* in Europe and secondments to the Imperial General Staff. He was promoted to Major-General in 1926.

In the 1920s Koiso joined the Control Faction whose members included Generals Ugaki, Sugiyama, Umezu, and Nagata. In 1935 he commanded the 5th Division based at Hiroshima and in 1935 he was transferred to the command of the Chōsen Army in Korea. He was made a full general in 1937 and joined the Army General Staff in July 1938. Retiring from active duty he served several terms as Minister of Colonial Affairs. From May 1942 to July 1944, Koiso acted as Governor General of Korea where he introduced an extremely unpopular universal military conscription.

His selection as Prime Minister was a surprise, not least to Koiso. He was the classic compromise candidate and as Prime Minister he was disliked by virtually all members of the government including Hirohito and by the Army, which refused to allow him any participation in military decisions. Neither did he have the support of the growing faction of people who believed that the war was lost and that it was essential to conduct peace negotiations. Instead on 4 August Koiso decided to arm the entire nation. In work places and schools, military training was made compulsory. Two weeks later at his Imperial Conference, Hirohito declared that the new emphasis would be on air defense and the development of "sure victory weapons."[4] In a pattern that is familiar in his political interventions, one can only suspect that with the Army in disarray, Hirohito's power of influence with regard to strategy grew increasingly expansive. One of the 'sure victory weapons' was the development of a balloon bomb to be aimed at American citizens on the US mainland. More importantly Hirohito's speech gave moral support for the development of *kamikaze* tactics. It was also concluded that defense of territory would be conducted in the 'interior' and not at the 'water's edge.'

A new direction was similarly indicated by tentative steps toward reconciliation with Chiang Kai-shek and the Nationalists (*Kuomintang*) in China, using overtures to the Soviet Union to bridge a settlement. It was hoped that a move in this direction would enable Japan to release resources and focus on holding back the American advance across the *Pacific*. However, Hirohito was still firmly committed to prosecution of the war with America and Great Britain. On 7 September, on the anniversary of the convening of the eighty-fifth Imperial Diet, Hirohito's rescript declared, "Today our imperial state is indeed challenged to reach powerfully for a decisive victory. You who are leaders of our people must now renew your tenacity and, uniting in your resolve, smash our enemies' evil purposes, thereby furthering forever our Imperial destiny."[5]

Halsey's Raid on the Central Philippines and a Change in Strategy: On 24 August 1944 Admiral 'Bull' Halsey sortied from *Pearl Harbor* aboard his brand new battleship, USS *New Jersey*. Accompanied by three destroyers he headed west to pick up the Third Fleet at *Ulithi* and then on toward the Philippines. The Third Fleet's campaign to soften up Japan's defenses on the Philippines started inauspiciously. On 7 September, off the island of *Mindanao* a US submarine sank the unmarked cargo ship, *Shinyo Maru*. Struck broadside by two torpedoes, the *Shinyo Maru* rolled over and plunged to the bottom of the ocean. With it went 675 American prisoners of war who had been captured on Bataan and *Corregidor* and were being taken to Japan. Just eighty prisoners of war survived and were picked up and sheltered by Filipino guerrillas.

Two days later, Halsey, arriving with the Third Fleet off the Philippines' east coast, launched his carrier strike aircraft at *Luzon*'s airfields. Halsey's pilots went to work armed with intelligence about airfields in the Philippines provided by Filipino guerrillas. After three days of bombardment, an ecstatic intelligence officer brought Halsey the good news that 173 Japanese planes had been shot down and a further 305 destroyed on the ground. Even allowing for exaggeration, it was clear that a significant victory had been won. A jubilant Halsey sent off a message to his carriers: "Because of the brilliant performance my group of stars has just given, I am booking you to appear before the best audience in the Asiatic theater."[6] By audience, he meant the people of Manila.

Perhaps more significantly than his success in destroying Japan's air power in the central Philippines was his firm recommendation that MacArthur should now bypass the southern islands of the Philippines, abandon plans to invade *Mindanao* and make his first landing instead, 'his return,' at *Leyte Island*. MacArthur, exceptionally, given his general loathing of the Navy, had supreme faith in Halsey and was prepared to back his judgment. MacArthur sent a message to the Joint Chiefs of Staff assembled at the Second Quebec Conference (codenamed OCTAGON) to the effect that he could be ready to attack *Leyte* as early as 20 October. In record time, just ninety minutes, the Joint Chiefs of Staff agreed this significant change in strategy.

It was a strategy not without risk. The invasion of *Leyte* was the second biggest amphibious landing of the war to the Normandy Landings in France. The Allies had years to prepare from an English base just twenty miles across the *English Channel*— MacArthur and his commanders were 4,000 miles from their home base and had just two months to prepare themselves. Unlike his rapid advance along the north coast of New Guinea, Lieutenant-Colonel George Kenney, commander of the South West Pacific Air Force reminded MacArthur that his American ground forces would be 500 miles beyond fighting cover. His commanders were reminded of the near fiascos at *Los Negros* and *Biak* when MacArthur pushed for invasions without adequate air cover. MacArthur declared "Goddamn it, George, I'm going back there [the Philippines] if I have to paddle a canoe with you flying cover for me with that B-17 of yours"[7]

Fortunately he could rely on Halsey's Third Fleet and its rapidly expanding fleet of spanking new fast carriers to prepare the way for him by degrading Japanese air strength on *Luzon*. Accordingly Halsey planned a daring aerial raid against Manila, the heart of Japan's Philippine Empire. On 21 September Halsey's planes launched an attack on the main Manila Airfields, Clark and Nichols. Just as MacArthur's planes were caught unawares there on 8 December 1941, the Japanese were completely unprepared for the attack. A Japanese colonel surveying the sky, thinking that the incoming planes were Japanese, exuded pride when he noted to a colleague, "See our splendid eagles. How swiftly they fly. How gracefully they maneuver."[8] Seconds later American bombs were exploding around him. In a two-day rampage, Halsey's forces destroyed 405 Japanese airplanes and sank or damaged 103 ships.

General Yamashita and Hirohito's Intervention: On 6 October 1944, Tokyo received a message from their Ambassador in Moscow informing them that a high level Soviet Foreign Office official had let slip, probably intentionally, that the US Army Air Force (USAAF) in China had been instructed to launch attacks to isolate the Philippines. In any case, the increased level of activity by the Third Fleet also pointed at the increasing likelihood that the invasion of the Philippines was America's next target. At a meeting called on 7 October, Admiral Soemu Toyoda reported a build-up of American ships in Hollandia and *Wakde* on the north coast of New Guinea. He concluded that the Americans would strike next at *Leyte* at the end of the month.

Urgent measures were called for. Field Marshal Terauchi recommended that they should abandon the defense of the Philippines' southern islands and concentrate all their ground forces on *Luzon*. It was a strategy considered far too defeatist by the Army's high command in Tokyo. Neither did Emperor Hirohito agree with this approach. On 9 October, General Tokoyuki Yamashita, 'The Tiger of Malaya,' arrived in Manila to replace Lieutenant-General Kuroda. A commission from Tokyo concluded that Kuroda had virtually given up the struggle and was "devoting more time to his golf, reading and personal matters than to the execution of his duties."[9] Kuroda's defeatism was not unrealistic. He noted, "the power of our air force is negligible at this time" and opposed the building of new airfields at Davao (*Mindanao Island*) and Tacloban (*Leyte Island*) on the grounds that there were not enough planes to use them and that building airfields amounted "to construction for the use of the enemy."[10] Yamashita, the veteran general, who had guaranteed his legend by his sensationally rapid conquest of Malaya, the capture of *Singapore*, and the humiliation of the British Empire, was seen as the man to re-energize the Fourteenth Area Army. Banished by Japan's jealous Prime Minister Tojo, Yamashita was suddenly whisked out of his enforced obscurity in Manchuria. After Tojo's fall and disgrace following the fall of *Saipan*, his successor General Kuniaki Koiso, appointed Prime Minister on 22 July 1944, not only needed a hero to restore Japan's spirits, he also needed a great General to fend off an enemy who was advancing remorselessly toward Japan.

Japan's military commanders viewed the island of *Luzon*, at the junction of the *South China Sea, Formosa* and the Chinese mainland, as well as the *East China Sea,* as the pivot of their Empire. It was the key to Japan's ability to sustain their logistical supply of oil and essential materials. As Admiral Toyoda told his colleagues, "What good would our fleet be if it doesn't have any fuel?"[11] American forces had to be denied a foothold in the Philippines at all costs. Lieutenant-General Shuichi Miyasaki viewed the holding of the Philippines as "the one essential."[12] Operation SHO-GO ICHI (Operation VICTORY) developed by the Imperial General HQ in Tokyo would combine all Japan's naval and military resources to prevent MacArthur establishing any kind of foothold on Philippine soil. The plan, that might involve the sacrifice of the Imperial Japanese Fleet as an effective fighting force, was accepted.

Resources to hand consisted of 224,000 troops on *Luzon* with 23,000 more garrisoned at *Leyte*; a further 185,000 troops were spread around the many Philippine Islands. Yamashita, bowing to the wishes of the Emperor, made an early decision to send 40,000 more troops to *Leyte,* making 63,000 defenders in aggregate. These were not any old troops; they were the cream of the Imperial Japanese Army. It was a curious decision that reflected the views of the Emperor rather than military sense. It split and weakened the forces available to Yamashita for the defense of *Luzon*. The troops fed into *Leyte* were difficult to supply and only had a few days in which to prepare their famed defensive entrenchments.

In post-war revelations it became clear that Hirohito was at least one of the driving forces, if not the primary force, behind the last minute decision to defend *Leyte* to the hilt. In a rare admission after the war Hirohito stated, "Contrary to the views of the Army and Navy General Staffs, I agreed to the showdown Battle of Leyte thinking that if we attacked at Leyte and America flinched, then we would probably be able to find room to negotiate."[13] In spite of over almost eighteen months of constant Japanese defeats and retreat in the *Solomons*, New Guinea and the *Central Pacific*, some in the Japanese Army were increasingly upbeat about their chances of defeating the Americans as they approached Japan's Imperial heart. Major-General Yoshiharu Tomochika, Chief of Staff to the Thirty Fifth Army, would later tell US interrogators, "We were determined to take offensive after offensive and clean up American forces on Leyte Island . . . We seriously discussed demanding the surrender of the entire American Army after seizing General MacArthur."[14]

The result of this last minute intervention from Hirohito meant that far from being the deserted island that Halsey had led his superiors to believe, *Leyte* became lousy with Japanese troops. Thus *Leyte Island* was not the walkover that was anticipated. The *Battle of Leyte* became the American Army's most fiercely contested land engagement of the *Pacific War*. In line with now standard Imperial GHQ policy, it was decided to fight a war in the interior rather than on the beaches where defenders would be subject to naval bombardment. Yamashita had little time. On the same day that he had taken charge of military operations in the Philippines, Vice-Admiral Thomas Kinkaid's armada of 738 ships began to leave the logistical garrisons at Hollandia and *Manus* and traveled northwards.

In Tokyo, on 11 October, Emperor Hirohito received a long line of Japan's senior commanders. For weeks he had shuffled around the Palace unshaven and wearing casual clothes. Now he was dressed impeccably as he received his humbled Generals and ministers to listen to their excuses and apologies. He let it be known that he expected better work. *Radio Tokyo* reported, "High officials received by the Emperor have promised supreme efforts to ease His Majesty's august mind."[15]

In Washington there was alarm of another nature. Republican Presidential Candidate, Thomas Dewey, threatened to expose the fact that Japan's 'unbreakable' Code PURPLE had been broken before the war; he intended to indict Roosevelt for ineptitude in not being better prepared in the Philippines and *Pearl Harbor*. For Marshall the danger of this revelation was existential. For the entirety of the war Japanese commanders and ministers had been unaware that their codes had been broken. Alerted to the likelihood that America would lose one of its greatest military advantages over Japan, perhaps causing massive loss of life, Marshall sent urgent pleas to Dewey not to publicly reveal that the Code PURPLE had been broken. Under pressure, Dewey relented. He would be soundly thrashed in the election.

"I Have Returned": [Map: 34.1] MacArthur had put German-born Lieutenant-General Walter Krueger's Sixth Army in charge of the landing at *Leyte Gulf*. Krueger had drilled his troops into an experienced fighting unit during their eighteen months of fighting in *New Britain*, the *Admiralty Islands* and New Guinea. A fighting soldier, he was a perfect fit for MacArthur; unlike his commanding officer, Krueger courted anonymity. By comparison with men with comparable battlefield victories, such as General Omar Bradley and General George Patton, he never appeared on the cover of *Time* magazine. Krueger's father had been an officer in the Prussian Army and it was probably only because of his father's early death and his mother's decision to move with her three children to join her uncle in St. Louis, Missouri, that Krueger became an American army officer rather than following a career that would have seen him fighting in Hitler's *Wehrmacht*.

Krueger, a super-fit 64-year-old veteran, was a fighting general who preferred the challenge of combat command to the heights of generalship. He is reported to have said, "Hell, I'd rather have a regiment . . . I don't do much except think a lot, scold a lot, pat a man on the back now and then—and try to keep a perspective."[16]

Krueger's landing started with the seizure of four small islets by the 500 strong force of the 6th Rangers led by Major Robert Garrett. These advance 'special forces' took their targets with little resistance on 17 October. Two days later, just before midnight on 19 October, MacArthur's invasion armada gathered at its launch location off *Leyte Gulf*. It was a quiet moonless night; a feared typhoon had swept north out of harm's way. At 4.00 a.m. on 20 October troops aboard their ships were woken and given their traditional 'last supper'; as Commander Paul Austin of 34th Infantry remembered he "had the usual pre-landing breakfast, steak and eggs. This was the only time we ever got that kind of food."[17] At 8 a.m. on 20 October the slow moving old battleships, USS *Maryland*, USS *Virginia* and USS *Mississippi*, now little more than superannuated gun platforms, led the fleet barrage that opened on the Philippine coastline.

After a ninety minute bombardment, troops scrambled down the rope ladders flung over the side of their ships and into their flimsy landing craft. In a twin landing, Major-General Franklin Sibert's X Corps (comprising the 24th Infantry and 1st Cavalry) came ashore in the north of *Leyte Gulf*, near Tacloban, while eleven miles to the south Major-General John Hodge landed with XXIV Corps (comprising 7th and 96th Infantry). On the bridge of the cruiser USS *Nashville*, from where he viewed the amphibious landing, MacArthur turned to a reporter and said, "It's the Sixteenth Division we're up against, the outfit that did the dirty work on Bataan . . . We'll get 'em. We'll get 'em."[18]

To the surprise of Sibert and his troops resistance was light. Sal DeGaetano of the 12th Cavalry Regiment recalled that he was "amazed at the little resistance we encountered that first day."[19] It was only after the fifth wave had landed that Japanese mortars, machine guns and snipers opened up an attack. Under fire the 34th Infantry moved rapidly inland through paddy fields, led by a popular big Hawaiian, Captain Francis Wai. Signals Corps wireman Harold Rant recalled:

> he was really ripping and had knocked out three pillboxes.
> With real luck, he was jumping, running, dodging, and
> crawling under machine-gun fire to get hand grenades in
> the fortresses. At about the fifth one they got him, laced
> him with fire and he was hit ten times through the chest.
> He was one who really broke the spell enough for our
> people to start moving in.[20]

Captain Wai was awarded a Medal of Honor. In spite of his death, it was clearly not a fully committed Japanese challenge and the 34th Infantry moved inland and took control of Tacloban Airfield with minimal effort. For Lieutenant-General Shiro Makino, the US attack had caught him by surprise while he was moving his headquarters inland from Tacloban. In the chaos he was unable to sustain communication with his troops to bring reinforcements to bear on the invasion areas. In addition, in the hurried abandonment of Tacloban, Makino lost nearly all of the 16th Division's communication equipment.

Shortly after noon, ignoring the possibility of Japanese snipers still lurking in the jungle fringes, MacArthur waded ashore a sandbank off 'Red Beach' where the fiercest fighting had been reported. Walking in his wake were Chief of Staff, Richard Sutherland, and President Osmeña. MacArthur sent Major Gaetano Faillace ahead with a camera to capture the moment. It was the most famous of the many thousands of photographs that he took of MacArthur. The general was delighted with the image and its projection of a fearless commander. Then strolling toward the gunfire, he noted the bodies of dead Japanese with considerable satisfaction. This was the moment that he had striven for since his humiliating flight from *Corregidor*. As Lieutenant-General Kenney overhead him say, "This is what I have dreamed about!"[21] An hour later the Signal Corps had set up a transmitter at the beach and CBS newsman Bill Dunn introduced General Douglas MacArthur to the listeners of *Voice of Freedom*. MacArthur walked over, composed himself and spoke words that had clearly been carefully crafted and rehearsed:

> This is the Voice of Freedom. People of the Philippines, *I have returned!* By the grace of Almighty God, our forces stand again on Philippine soil—soil consecrated in the blood of our two peoples . . . at my side is your President . . . Manuel Osmeña . . . Rally to me. Let the indomitable spirit of Bataan and Corregidor lead on . . . Let no heart be faint. Let every arm be steeled. The guidance of Divine God points the way. Follow in His name to the Holy Grail of righteous victory.[22]

Whatever MacArthur's faults, he was a brilliant showman. In the United States Faillace's photograph of MacArthur and the General's speech were rapturously received. When he heard of the rave response in America, MacArthur too was in raptures. Ironically MacArthur had arrived to conquer the island of *Leyte*, a feat his father had achieved in 1900 while quelling native rebellions during America's imperial conquest of the Philippines. The difference this time was that the Americans arrived as liberators rather than conquerors.

The Battle of Leyte Gulf: **[See Chapter 33: Battle of Leyte Gulf: 'Bull' Halsey's Mad Dash for Glory]** While MacArthur's forces were securing a beachhead from which they could consolidate their logistics and airfield before fanning out across the island, Halsey and Kinkaid were winning an overwhelming naval encounter in the waters off the Philippine coast. Curiously *Leyte Gulf*, after which the naval action was named, saw nothing of the naval battle at all.

Air Battles over Leyte Island: After the poor performance of the Japanese Air Force at *Halmahera*, the largest and most northern of the *Moluccas*, which lies between western New Guinea and the Philippines' most southerly large island of *Mindanao*, Lieutenant-General George Kenney was relaxed about the speeded up invasion of the Philippines via *Leyte Island*. He dismissed the worries of his subordinate, Major-General Ennis Whitehead, who was concerned about an invasion that only had carrier aircraft for cover. In spite of his previous contention that carriers did not have 'staying power,' Kenney had become convinced that the air war was largely over. "Jap air is shot," he told Whitehead. His attitudes were colored by a growing racial prejudice against his foe. He convinced himself that Japan's new breed of fliers were "peasant class—rice planters, fishermen, rickshaw pullers—who are too dumb, too slow thinking and utterly lacking in mechanical knowledge or adaptability."[23] Kenney complacently came to the conclusion that it was useless to try to train "this class of plodding, thick-headed, half fed, stupid recruits how to fight against the well drilled show we have out here."[24] Kenney even doubted the need for carrier cover.

Kenney's greater concern was to get hold of the new Boeing B-29 Superfortress with which he believed that he could reach the Japanese-controlled oil fields at Balikpapan on the east coast of *Borneo*. On 13 August, B-24 Liberators had already launched attacks from Darwin but had caused only relatively minor damage. It was considered that the seventeen hour 2,400 mile round trip was too dangerous to repeat. When his request for B-29s was refused he decided to go ahead anyway, launching an attack with B-24s from the Thirteenth Air Force on 30 September and 3 October. Out of 104 bombers sent twelve did not return. The rest were so badly shot up by what a report termed "violent air reaction" that 40 percent of the bombers sent were either lost or badly damaged. Submarines, USS *Redfin* and USS *Mingo* picked up some survivors who had managed to ditch their planes but overall the mission was a disaster.

By extending the P-38 Lightnings' range to 2,000 miles and adding three fuel tanks to the P-47 Thunderbolt and by using the newly captured airstrip at *Morotai,* an island on the northwest tip of the Dutch East Indies, Kenney was able to provide air cover for further raids on 10 and 18 October. In spite of Kenney's claims the results were disappointing. US submarines' sinking of tankers and their cutting of the direct supply route to the Philippines had already sharply reduced the ability of Japan to get oil from South East Asia. Indeed a post-war analysis showed that Kenney's raids had "no strategic effect because more oil was always available . . . than could be shipped out."[25]

The Battles of Breakneck Ridge and Dagami: **[Map: 34.2]** By the end of A-Day on 20 October, Krueger's Sixth Army had established itself on *Leyte* with two beachheads ten miles apart. The landings had gone almost exactly to plan. However, much to MacArthur's chagrin, fighting across *Leyte*'s jungle-covered hills and gorges was a tortuous affair. Extreme heat interspersed with heavy rains and swampy conditions that made the operation of tanks except on the roads extremely difficult, proved a significant impediment to rapid advance. The first problems facing Krueger were logistical. Air raids, typhoons, narrow beaches and the need to manhandle supplies 100 to 200 yards over the sand humps created chaos. Also the swamped roads quickly deteriorated as US trucks moved supplies inland. To get around the problem, amphibious, six-wheel 'DUKWs' were used to bring ammunition and supplies direct to the front.

On 21 October, the Japanese launched their counter-attack in the early hours. An attack on G-Company, 34th Infantry Regiment saw Private Harold Moon surrounded and cut off from his colleagues. In a one-man stand holding a Thompson sub-machine gun he was heard to shout at the Japanese, "If you want me come and get me!"[26] As they charged to attack he mowed them down in swathes; eventually he was cut down by a Japanese machine gun as he attempted to throw a grenade. Moon was awarded a Medal of Honor in an action where G-Company lost fourteen men with a further twelve wounded. Japanese dead were counted at over 600. They were heavily punished not only by the weight of fire of the US defensive entrenchments but also by US air support. Nearby the 3rd Battalion, 34th Infantry, killed 100 Japanese attackers and in the 19th Infantry's defense zone the 1st Battalion accounted for a further 162 Japanese troops. As well as the fighting on the ground, there were major air battles above northern *Leyte*. On 24 October American fighters, based at the newly acquired Tacloban Airfield, intercepted 200 incoming Japanese aircraft and claimed 66 'kills.'

Meanwhile Colonel 'Red' Newman's 34th Infantry had to fight against fierce Japanese resistance along the coast road from Tacloban along the wide and fertile Leyte Valley to *Cariga Bay* on the north coast. By 2 November, Cariga had been captured at a cost to the 24th Infantry Division of 210 killed and 859 wounded. Just thirteen Japanese had been captured, with 2,970 estimated killed.

They continued westward, with US X Corps then marching southwards from *Cariga Bay* toward Ormoc City on *Leyte Island*'s southwest coast. The port of Ormoc was the main staging post into which Yamashita had been feeding troops. On 25 October, fast convoys from the southern island of *Mindanao* to Ormoc started to feed in 2,550 troops of the 41st Infantry Regiment. Along the route X Corps would have to dislodge 4,000 crack soldiers of Lieutenant-General Tadeo Kataoka's 1st Infantry Division, who had moved north from Ormoc where he embedded his troops in the elevated craggy ridges that provided formidable natural defenses. The ridges became known to the GIs as 'Breakneck Ridge' and 'Heartbreak Ridge.' 'Breakneck Ridge' consisted of five heavily wooded ridges with spurs running toward Leyte Valley. Much of the area was unmapped and where maps did exist, they were rarely accurate. Kataoka's 1st Infantry constructed pillboxes and foxholes and shelters placed beyond the ridgeline that prevented direct hits from artillery fire.

Each foxhole or cave had to be taken one by one with grenade or flame-thrower. The climbs to reach the Japanese positions were steep and slippery. Fighting was often reduced to bayonets or hand to hand combat. Lieutenant-Colonel Frederick Weber's 21st Infantry led the first attacks on 7 November. They were repelled by heavy machine gun and mortar fire. Sibert, dissatisfied by the progress made by Weber, replaced him with his own intelligence officer, Colonel William Verbeck. On 13 November, after making progress with the help of tanks, the US 24th Infantry was withdrawn having suffered 630 casualties in a week. The 128th Infantry took over the attack. It took ten days to progress just one mile. Kataoka's 1st Division suffered 1,779 casualties (40 percent of his force) in the engagement.

It was not the end of the battle. In a famous engagement, Colonel Spragins led his 2nd Battalion (known by their call sign 'Doughboy White') on a flanking operation around Japanese lines at 'Breakneck Ridge.' After a long march without adequate supplies Spragins found his unit surrounded and starving. It was a reflection of the problems of supply for both sides that airdrops of food by the US Army Air Force were fought over by Americans and Japanese alike. Apart from this and a delivery of chocolate, Spragins' troops were forced to live off palm hearts. Two weeks after setting off, the starving 'Doughboy White' managed to fight their way out of the jungle. Arriving back to their lines on Thanksgiving Day, 23 November, the 'doughboys' were given their first hot meal in weeks—bully beef, peas and carrots washed down with coffee. In America, President Roosevelt was giving thanks "For the harvest that has sustained us and, in its fullness, brought succor to other peoples; for the bounty of our soil, which has produced the sinews of war for the protection of our liberties; and for a multitude of private blessings, known only in our hearts, we should give united thanks to God."[27]

Meanwhile in the south of Leyte Valley, Major-General John Hodge's troops moved to take control of the Dagami area whose passes lead to Ormoc. It was a possible route for Lieutenant-General Sosaku Suzuki, charged with the defense of the southern Philippines, to launch a counter-attack toward Tacloban. Comprising 6,000 troops, the Japanese 16th Infantry, part of Suzuki's Thirty-fifth Army, albeit half-starved and forced to live off the land, was nevertheless a force to be reckoned with. Hodge's attack with the 1st Battalion, 382nd Infantry on 2 November was driven back in the water-sodden paddy fields in front of Dagami Heights. Their unit report noted a chaotic American retreat in which "Men threw away their packs, machine guns, radios and even rifles. Their sole aim was to crawl back through the muck and get on solid ground once more. Some of the wounded gave up the struggle to keep their heads above the water and drowned in the grasping swamp."[28]

It took another four days of intense fighting for the Japanese 16th Infantry to be pushed back but even then it was only 2,000 yards to a new defensive line. After a further attack using tanks and flame-throwers, killing an estimated 474 Japanese, the Japanese 16th Infantry finally withdrew completely on 10 November. Further south the US 2nd Battalion, 32nd Infantry, and 7th Division occupied Baybay City on the southern road linking Tacloban with Ormoc. In effect MacArthur's forces had cut the island in half encircling Suzuki's forces between Baybay City in the south and Carigara in the north.

MacArthur, ensconced at Tacloban, was well away from the fighting on the ground but was not immune from attack. Zeros targeted his HQ, Price House, with strafing attacks. One tree-level attack put a tracer bullet in the wall about a foot above his head. As his soldiers battled to clear *Leyte*, MacArthur and his staff worked on plans to occupy *Mindoro Island* to the south of *Luzon*. In a particularly heated planning session with all his senior officers present, including Admiral Kinkaid, MacArthur slammed Nimitz's demand that he give assurances that the Navy would be given air cover en route to *Mindoro* to protect them from land-based aircraft, particularly the feared *kamikaze* attacks. MacArthur bellowed, "Warships, what are they for? They have to take risks just as my soldiers and tanks have to take risks."[29] It was a spurious argument but one that the quietly spoken Vice-Admiral Kinkaid calmly rebutted.

The Start of the Kamikaze Campaign: After the earlier crushing naval victory inflicted upon Admiral Toyoda's forces at the *Battle of Leyte Gulf* on 23–26 October, it might have been expected that a period of calm would ensue. But Japan, with the use of *kamikazes*, took the attack to Halsey's victorious fleet. On 25 October *kamikazes* attacked and damaged three escort carriers. The following day the USS *Franklin* and USS *Belleau Wood* were similarly hit and were forced to retire to *Ulithi Atoll*; 148 men were killed and seventy injured. Tellingly forty-five airplanes were destroyed by the *kamikaze* attack, significantly more than had been lost in the entire naval battle at *Leyte Gulf*.

After the crushing victory at *Leyte Gulf*, for the crew and aviators of the Third Fleet the emergence of the *kamikaze* was a depressing and nerve wracking denouement to the last major naval engagement of the war. Battle fatigue was also causing accidents. Halsey noted, ". . . a flight surgeon on the *Wasp* reported that only thirty of his 131 pilots were fit for further fighting."[30] Against this background Halsey called for land airbases to take over the job of providing MacArthur's army with air cover. Although the first two squadrons of P-38s were soon landed at Tacloban, a town of 25,000 inhabitants located some thirty miles from Delug on the narrow straits between *Leyte* and the Island of *Samar*, progress in developing this airfield and others on *Leyte* was unexpectedly slow. Rain was incessant. Thirty-five inches fell in the weeks after the *Battle of Leyte Gulf*. Indeed from 28 October there were three typhoons in just ten days. The result was that only 150 planes were able to land and the lack of air support for MacArthur's forces became so critical that Nimitz ordered Halsey's return to *Leyte* to give additional air cover. Planes from Japan, transiting via *Formosa* to the all-weather aerodromes on *Luzon* had temporarily won back control of the air over *Leyte* to the Japanese. More serious for the invasion force, Yamashita was able to feed in his 40,000 troops from *Luzon* to the *Leyte* ground battle with little aerial impediment.

Tacloban shortly became the scene of a notable event when Richard Bong, one of the newly arrived P-38 pilots was awarded the Medal of Honor in a ceremony at the airfield conducted by MacArthur himself. Son of a Swedish immigrant from Poplar, Wisconsin, Bong ended the war with forty confirmed 'kills' and became one of America's most celebrated war aces. Bong, who always flew P-38s in his fighter pilot career returned to the United States to become a test pilot. He died in California while testing the new Lockheed P-80 Shooting Star jet fighter when the main fuel pump failed. The accident killed him just days before Japan's surrender; the day of his death coincided with the dropping of the atom bomb on Hiroshima.

MacArthur's Logistical Problems: The delay in producing serviceable airfields on *Leyte* compounded MacArthur's logistical problems. Poorly draining runway areas, impassable roads and a lack of coral for surfacing landing strips, held up essential equipment and stretched the US front's lines of supply. Simply building and maintaining key arterial roads and building airports took three to four times the usual man hours and left little or no capacity for construction of storage facilities, hospitals, and repair units.

The logistical operations were not helped by November deluges, which dropped thirty-five inches of rain onto *Leyte* in the first forty days of operation. A Sixth Army engineer recalled, "Construction under these conditions became a nightmare."[31]

Although Tacloban Airfield had been captured with ease, it had been so poorly constructed that a complete rebuild was required. A host of problems ensued: the runway had to be extended from 4,300 to 6,000 foot, the soil was too soft to support the heavier American aircraft, steel matting and coral had to be imported and then used to stabilize the runway surfaces. Moreover, contrary to Kenney's earlier predictions at the end of the New Guinea Campaign, the Japanese air war was not finished. New aircraft were fed into *Luzon*. The 7th Air Division flew from the *Celebes* to add weight to *Luzon*'s airpower. By 23 October, with some 250 naval aircraft and 200 army aircraft, mass attacks began the next day. Some 200 aircraft hit Halsey's carriers while 100 concentrated on the landing forces at *Leyte*. In a new development mass *kamikaze* attacks started on 25 October. Work on the Tacloban Airfield and the new strip at Dulag was inevitably slowed. When sixty-five naval aircraft had to make emergency landings because of damage to the escort carrier fleet, twenty-five of them were wrecked and had to be shoved into the water. On 25 October both Kinkaid and Halsey pleaded for relief. The latter complained, "The pilots are exhausted, and the carriers are low in provisions, bombs, and torpedoes. When will land-based air take over at *Leyte*."[32]

Kenney may have been wrong in predicting that Japanese air power was finished but MacArthur's amphibious landing was stark confirmation of Kenney's earlier fears about reliance on more fragile carrier cover for this sort of extended-range amphibious operation. By 30 October Tacloban Airfield was partially usable though the disruption from nightly bombing slowed redevelopment. Despite Kenney's efforts, Halsey was forced to remain on station with his exhausted carrier forces until late November. Halsey petulantly complained about "Kenney's inability to give Leyte effective air support. I had to stand by and attend to his knitting for him."[33] As for airfields at San Pablo and Buri, they had to be abandoned as unusable. To make up the deficit in airfield capacity, a new one was built near Tanauan though it did not become fully available until 16 December. One of the consequences of the failure to establish rapid construction of airfields on *Leyte* was that the US Army Air Force was not able to interdict the arrival of 22,000 fresh Japanese troops at Omroc on *Leyte*'s northeast coast.

In his complacency regarding Japanese air power on *Luzon*, Kenney had ignored the degree to which the air war was subtly different to the one on New Guinea. Even the largest garrison in the New Guinea–*Solomons* area, Rabaul, had only five airfields. The Philippines had 120, of which seventy were on *Luzon*. Furthermore the lines of resupply from Japan were far shorter. Far from diminishing as Kenney had expected, the threat from the air increased as American forces approached Japan. When faced by this new reality, Kenney was forced to draw the conclusion from the *Leyte* invasion that the US should "stick to land-based support whenever we attempt an amphibious expedition against a hostile shore."[34]

As Major-General Hugh Casey, head of Army Service Command (ASCOM), whose task it was to coordinate the largest landing invasion yet attempted by the US Army, pointed out,

> This [lack of adequate airfields on *Leyte*], in turn, greatly affected the supply situation, including construction materials, by lack of access to the depots, lack of storage space into which to discharge ships, and lack of facilities and spare parts to permit repair and servicing of engineers' heavy equipment as well as other critical transportation and combat vehicles.[35]

He neglected to mention that his engineers were not as adept as the Marines' Seabees in the speedy delivery of service facilities. Thus the rate of tonnage that ships were able to unload into the *Leyte Gulf* area remained at an inadequate 4,600 tons per day until 11 November; thereafter, daily tonnage delivered increased markedly and by December daily discharge from transports was some 75 percent higher than a month earlier.

Against this background MacArthur's *communiqué* of 30 October, which duly appeared in the *New York Times*, was unquestionably a lie. "Two-thirds of *Leyte Island*," he claimed, ". . . was already in American hands, and only a few isolated garrisons remained to be cleaned up on *Samar*. The speedy liberation of the Philippines had already set free 1,500,000 Filipinos."[36] In reality the heaviest fighting still lay ahead.

Apart from the US ground forces, Halsey's Third Fleet, which had returned to the Philippines, continued to be in constant action. One Japanese troop convoy alone was sunk with the loss of 10,000 men drowned. In return, Halsey's fleet took a battering. *Kamikazes* damaged seven of the Third Fleet's carriers. Meanwhile the Seventh Fleet suffered strikes on 2 battleships, 2 cruisers, 2 transports and 7 destroyers. Then on 13 December, *Kamikazes* attacked the USS *Nashville* causing 320 casualties of which 130 were fatal. On the same day a destroyer also suffered forty casualties. Halsey's Third Fleet, which was standing off *Leyte* to provide air cover while the construction of the airfields was being completed, was taking a mauling from Japanese *kamikaze* pilots. So severe was the damage that MacArthur and Nimitz ordered a news blackout to prevent the Japanese from ascertaining how effectively their new *kamikaze* tactics were working. Nevertheless, from the end of October to 25 November when Halsey finally returned to *Ulithi Atoll* for refitting after three months of continuous action, his Third Fleet accounted for 700 Japanese planes in addition to sinking three cruisers, ten destroyers and many transports and auxiliaries.

MacArthur's logistical problems were *de minimis* compared to the logistical problems faced by his adversary on *Leyte*, Major-General Sosaku Suzuki. With the insistence of Imperial Army GHQ that the priority battle to defend the Philippines should take place on *Leyte* rather than *Luzon* coming only on 22 September, a month before the American landing, there was precious little time for Suzuki to prepare. Moreover American control of the air, albeit they had to rely on Halsey's carriers, made Japanese supply to *Leyte* extremely difficult and inevitably incurred heavy losses. The supply problem became ever more extreme as the *Battle of Leyte Island* progressed; the paucity of supply logistics would highlight the catastrophic intervention of Army HQ and the Emperor over the last minute change in strategy to defend *Leyte* rather than concentrate on *Luzon*. Ultimately 40,000 crack Japanese troops would be wiped out, not because they were defeated in battle but because they could not be brought back to *Luzon*. They killed themselves in *banzai* charges, or by suicide or duly starved to death.

'Banzai' Paratroopers Counter-Attack on Leyte: [**Map: 34.3**] The importance of the airfields to the Japanese was indicated by the launch of a suicide mission by the 2nd Parachute Brigade that attempted night landings at American airfields on *Leyte* on the night of 27 November. In the first Japanese airborne operation since February 1942, it was planned that they should seize the airfields until an assault by General Suzuki's Thirty-fifth Army's 11th and 26th Divisions could break through from the east. One Japanese transport plane crash-landed at Buri Airstrip killing all the Japanese paratroopers. Two more planes crash-landed on beaches south of Dulag and far off target; the Japanese parachutists disgorged into the jungle.

Nevertheless, the Kaoru Airborne Raiding Detachment did succeed in occupying key positions on an American airfield. In addition, in the early hours of 6 December Japanese soldiers of the hated 16th Division, which had participated in both the Bataan Death March and the Rape of Nanking, managed to slip down from the mountains and infiltrate American lines near Buri Airstrip, killing sleeping soldiers of a US Army construction battalion. Many were bayonetted before they could move. Another Japanese raiding party shot dead nine sleeping construction officers as they slept in their hammocks. In the *mêlée* that broke out men grabbed weapons and fought hand to hand with their Japanese assailants. One angry American cook shot five soldiers trying to loot his kitchen—always a lure for Japan's under-provisioned and hungry troops.

The attack was followed up by another airborne assault by 1,400 men of the Japanese 2nd Parachute Brigade on 6 December. The parachute jump was led off in three waves by Lieutenant-Colonel Tsunhiro Shirai from Lipa Airfield and Angeles Airfield on southern *Luzon*. They were armed with automatic weapons, land mines and TNT. Shirai carried a Japanese flag inscribed by the commander of air operations in the Philippines, Lieutenant-General Kyoji Tominaga: "Exert your most for your country." Japanese paratroopers carried neatly folded cramming notes in their pockets carrying taunts written out in schoolboy English such as "Go to Hell, beast!"[37]

The Japanese transports, not dissimilar in design to the US DC-3, were flown in toward San Pablo Airfield at twilight just as Major-General 'Joe' Swing was finishing a fried chicken dinner. Swing had been a halfback along with Dwight Eisenhower on West Point's football team. The US troops looked up and saw that unusually the planes were lit up and that a man was standing in the doorway of each one. Captain Kenneth Murphy, standing in the 'chow line' heard General Swing call out, "Look at those Jap planes! They've even copied our flight formations."[38] The GIs rushed to their tents to find their weapons. The Japanese paratroops dropped right down on Swing's 11th Airborne Division, a parachute and glider regiment that had arrived on *Leyte* on 18 November; their orders were to push across the island's Central Mountain Range from the southern Leyte Valley to keep Suzuki's forces encircled by X Corp in the south and XXIV Corps in the north.

In other areas, raw US soldiers were less enlightened. Private Mort Ammerman, a trooper in the 188th Glider Regiment (part of the 11th Airborne Division) had been one of the first to see aircraft flying overhead; he guessed they were American C-47s and "thought some unit of the 11th AB [Airborne] was making a night jump . . ."[39] He went back to sleep as best he could in the pouring rain. Waking up to the sound of gunfire he noticed a pain in his leg—he had been hit. Failing to find his rifle, and leaving a dying friend, he hobbled away to find cover armed only with a trench knife; in the darkness he could hear Japanese paratroopers using bells, whistles and horns to assemble their paratroopers. They repeated badly rehearsed phrases such as, "Everything is 'resistless,' surrender, surrender."[40]

On landing many of the Japanese troops, seemingly drunk on the specially prepared liquor handed to them for their flight, flailed randomly about and screaming "*Banzai!*" while others set to work blowing up gasoline dumps at San Pablo and Buri Airfields. The US paratroopers dug in to their positions. At one end of San Pablo Airfield, Lieutenant David Carnahan set up machine gun posts with forty US paratroopers and waited. After night had fallen, Carnahan and his colleagues saw a column of men marching along the airstrip singing *Sweet Adeline*, an old American Army favorite. Confused as to why American soldiers would be singing in the midst of such a tense situation, Carnahan realized that they were Japanese soldiers only twenty yards from his position when an officer with a distinctive Japanese accented voice called out "Is this the machine gun at the west end of the strip?"[41] Carnahan replied "Yes sir!" at the same time that he machine-gunned the imposters. Clearly a planned ruse, the Japanese officer had over-estimated his English speaking abilities.

'Joe' Swing rounded up his paratroopers and the various construction and service troops and coordinated counter-attacks on Japanese positions. It took four days of heavy fighting to clear the airfields. Meanwhile the intended attack by the Japanese 11th and 26th Divisions became bogged down in the near impassable mountainous jungle tracks of the Mahonag Mountains. When they finally emerged, they were pushed back by Swing's 11th Airborne Division. The surprise Japanese paratroop attack, Operation WA, named after the Thirty Fifth Army's Chief of Staff, Lieutenant-General Takaji Wachi, was a desperate gambit and it failed miserably.

By 9 December, almost two weeks after the Japanese paratrooper assault, Swing had seemingly brought Suzuki's surprise attack under control. But the following day saw continued Japanese attacks. Major-General Ennis Whitehead was sitting at his desk when a bullet came through the wall. He ordered his staff officer to call Lieutenant-Colonel Pal Kaessner to complain about "promiscuous shooting" only to learn that the Japanese had got hold of some American machine guns and were attacking: "Tell the general to get down on the floor." Laconically Kaessner added, "Incidentally, that yelling you hear is a banzai raid on our mess hall."[42] The day after Swing's camp was invaded by paratroopers, Major-General Andrew Bruce's 77th Infantry Division, the self-proclaimed 'Old Buzzards,' were landed on beaches three miles south of the key Japanese port of Ormoc. They were brought 225 miles by ship to make their amphibious landing via the *Surigao Straits* and the *Camotes Sea*. It was an audacious flanking movement from the south that aimed to pincer the Japanese troops at 'Heartbreak Ridge' who were being attacked by X Corps from the north. (The long-distance flanking operation was later replicated by MacArthur in his most brilliant military success at the *Battle of Inchon* in the *Korean War*.) The beaches at Ormoc were taken with a single casualty but overhead a day-long dogfight was soon being waged by Japanese Zeros against the Army's P-38 Lightnings and the Marines' Hellcats. One of the casualties of the day was USS *Ward*, an old destroyer that had won fame for firing the first shots of the *Pacific War* when it had sunk a Japanese midget submarine hours before the attack on *Pearl Harbor*. Hit by a *kamikaze* pilot, the *Ward* burst into flames, was abandoned and finally scuttled.

Three days later on 10 December 1944 Ormoc was taken and Major-General Suzuki took his troops off into the mountains to continue their resistance. While the 'Old Buzzards' were landing at Ormoc, Colonel Orin Haugen was launching an assault by the 11th Airborne's 511th Parachute Infantry Regiment from deployment areas in the Mahonag Mountains to the east of Ormoc. They were confronted not only by the usually tenacious Japan defense but also severe jungle and weather conditions. By mid-December, some six weeks after MacArthur had declared victory, the formal *Battle of Leyte Island* was over though 'mopping up' operations would take months.

Suzuki would eventually attempt to escape by boat to *Mindanao* on 19 April 1945 but was killed by a US air attack. Before leaving he learnt that his *aide-de-camp* Major Rijome Kawahara was killed by a sniper when Cebu City on *Cebu Island* in the Central Philippines fell to American forces on 8 April.

Formosa and Strategic Concerns: MacArthur's haste to declare victory on *Leyte* was probably not unconnected with his planning ahead for an invasion of *Luzon*. On 3 October 1944, MacArthur had finally won his political campaign to prioritize the invasion of *Luzon* over *Formosa*, when Admiral King finally capitulated to the growing consensus within his own Navy ranks. Throughout September a series of events had increasingly diminished the attractiveness of *Formosa*. Halsey, an early convert to the '*Luzon* cause,' had made the intervention with regard to the supposedly barely defended *Leyte*, which led to the fast-forwarding of its invasion. This in turn had enabled MacArthur to bring forward to 20 December the date at which *Luzon* (capital Manila), the key prize in the Philippine Archipelago, could be invaded.

On this basis it was argued that the invasion of *Formosa* could still achieve the same March 1945 timetable. However, there were increasing doubts as to whether the war in Europe, which had earlier been expected to end by November 1944, would be ended in time to release troops for an invasion of *Formosa* on the original schedule. More importantly the overrunning of America's B-29 airfield bases in Southern China by Japan's ICHI-GO Campaign during the summer of 1944 significantly reduced the attractiveness of *Formosa* to General Arnold's bomber force. It was unlikely that the Chinese airfields could be quickly recovered. The ICHI-GO setback also extinguished the need to acquire a port on the Chinese coast opposite *Formosa*, which had been deemed necessary to supply the B-29 Superfortress bombing of Japan from China.

In turn, without a port on the Chinese mainland, *Formosa* was deemed too vulnerable to Japanese supply and infiltration. Moreover if Japan's Operation ICHI-GO in southern China had significantly unraveled the attractiveness of taking *Formosa*, the taking of the *Marianas* in July–September 1944, notably *Saipan, Tinian* and *Guam*, opened up the possibility of direct bombing flights to Japan from newly constructed airfields on these islands. Although the 3,000 mile round trip was at the margin of the B-29 Superfortress's range, the islands had the significant advantage of being able to be supplied by ship direct from the United States.

Instead of bypassing *Luzon*, the US Air Force senior staff and notably Chief of Staff 'Hap' Arnold considered it to be more appropriate to bypass *Formosa*. With Admiral Leahy and the Navy commanders in the *Pacific* (Nimitz, Halsey and Spruance) already won over by early September to the viewpoint that only *Luzon* could provide American forces with their strategic domination of the *South China Seas*, the only hold-out was King. His last ditch objection to the invasion of *Luzon*, on the ground that it would tie up the US carrier fleet for six weeks was shown to be unfounded because of the anticipated rapid build-up of Philippines land-based airfields which would provide most of the cover for the invasion force of troop carriers and transports headed to *Luzon*.

Mindoro: Stepping Stone to Luzon: *Manila* and *Luzon* were the target but to get there MacArthur needed a stepping-stone. Time was of the essence. The recapture of Manila would restore his reputation once and for all and then he could take on the task of conquering Japan. But would it be needed? MacArthur argued that Japan would most likely surrender if *Luzon* was reconquered. *Mindoro*, an island whose northern straits, the *Verde Island Passage*, were just seven miles from *Luzon* was his chosen intermediate target. At 260 miles from the US airfields on *Leyte*, it was a stepping-stone too far away from *Leyte* for comfort—150 miles was the preferred range for fighter cover and bombing support. MacArthur would be out of range of the US Army Air Force fighter's ability to stay on station for long enough to provide consistent air cover; (i.e., they might be able to get there but would have to fly straight back). At the Pentagon, planners warned him that it was too far distant and was therefore too risky. Disregarding doubters in Washington, MacArthur ordered that 15 December be set as D-Day for the landing on *Mindoro*. The safer option of taking the closer islands of *Uson, Panay, Isla sang Negros* or *Cebu* was ignored. MacArthur was in a hurry; his ego required him to get to Manila.

The *Mindoro* invasion fleet left *Leyte* on 12 December 1944 to make the circuitous 550-mile passage from *Leyte Gulf* and through the islands around the *Sibuyan Sea*.

Attacks began after the US convoy was spotted in the late afternoon the following day. The USS *Nashville* was struck by a *kamikaze* pilot with the point of impact not far from MacArthur in his cabin. In an explosion that rocked the ship, 131 men were killed including Brigadier-General William Dunckel's chief of staff, Colonel Bruce Hill and Rear-Admiral Arthur Struble's chief of staff, Captain Abdill; 192 other men were wounded, including Brigadier-General William Dunckel who was due to lead the landing. He was patched up, refused evacuation and made it clear that he was "not going to miss this show."[43] Fortunately for MacArthur, *Mindoro* was lightly defended. He had guessed correctly that Yamashita would garner his resources for the defense of *Luzon*. On 15 December Dunckel led a landing force consisting of 11,878 soldiers from the 24th Infantry Division and the 503rd Parachute Infantry Regiment. On *Mindoro*'s southern beaches, Filipinos waving US Flags met the invasion fleet. Not a single shot was fired. Apart from a firefight with Japanese troops at an air raid warning station in the north of *Mindoro* most of the 1,000 Japanese troops had fled into the jungle. By nightfall, all the abandoned airfields had been taken. Dunckel's landing force was quickly followed by 5,901 service troops and 9,578 Army Air Corp men charged with the rapid build of logistic depots and the construction of airfields to use as a base for the attack on *Luzon*. Two days later, Halsey's covering fleet was wrecked by a typhoon. **[See Chapter 33: Battle of Leyte Gulf: 'Bull' Halsey's Mad Dash for Glory]** Fortunately his covering carriers were barely needed. By 19 December MacArthur's service and engineering crews had made two of *Mindoro*'s four airfields operational. Soon MacArthur could begin the bombing of Japanese positions on *Luzon*. Meanwhile heavy fighting continued in the 'mopping up' operations on *Leyte* but at least now the resupply or reinforcement of Japanese force there was completely cut off.

On Boxing Day 1944, MacArthur announced, for the second time, the end of the *Leyte* campaign (having previously done so on 30 October), and boasted, ". . . Yamashita has sustained the greatest defeat in the military annals of the Japanese Army."[44] Furthermore MacArthur claimed, "The *Leyte* campaign can now be regarded as closed except for minor mopping up operations."[45] In jungle conditions the innocuous phrase 'mopping up' covers up what was often the nastiest part of any campaign in the *Pacific War*. Months of boredom in jungle bivouacs, arduous small-scale jungle patrols, treacherous natives, sudden ambushes, an enemy that never surrendered, and instant death were the daily fare of these 'mopping up' operations; bit-part actions to which no glory was ever attached. As the new commander of the 24th Regiment noted with acid humor,

> Most of this fighting is in inconspicuous little actions, which nobody hears about—mopping up. In Europe when we advance we really capture something. Out here we just capture another island, important enough though it may be, that looks much like all other islands. As one doughboy remarked after we had cleaned out a small objective—"Well, there's another half million coconuts."[46]

Contrary to MacArthur's claims that there were just 6,000 Japanese left on *Leyte*, in the five months after the *Battle of Leyte* ended (six and a half months after MacArthur had claimed victory), General Eichelberger's newly formed Eighth Army would later claim to have killed 27,000 Japanese soldiers. That MacArthur was forced to throw in his reserves not only from the 32nd and 77th Infantry Divisions but also from the 112th Cavalry and the 11th Airborne Division, indicates the difficulty of the *Leyte* campaign that proved far from being the cake-walk predicted by Vice-Admiral 'Bull' Halsey. The crack Imperial troops had shown a much greater battle-craft than had been evident in units on New Guinea. When they yielded ground they retained cohesion and set up new lines of defense. But ultimately they were undone by a strategy that virtually guaranteed that they could not be supplied with food and ammunition. For them it was a doomed mission that seriously undermined the future efforts to defend *Luzon*.

In Tokyo Hirohito berated his new prime minister, Kuniaki Koiso. An angry Hirohito reminded him that a promise had been made that the Americans would not only be stopped at *Leyte* but that Japan would win the greatest military victory since the *Battle of Tennozan* in 1582. Koiso shuffled uncomfortably and promised that the government would fulfil its pledge when *Luzon* was invaded. It was another in a succession of meetings, which suggest that Hirohito's influence in the conduct of the war had increased as constant defeat began to undermine the credibility and political power of the Army.

The *Battle of Leyte Island*, completely overshadowed by the naval *Battle of Leyte Gulf* and largely ignored in the history of the *Pacific War*, proved to be perhaps the greatest land campaign fought by the American Army in the *Pacific War*. US casualties amounted to 15,500 (3,500 killed) out of an army that at its peak numbered 257,766. In post-war interrogation, General Tomochika, Chief of Staff of the Thirty-fifth Army, reported that there were between 59,400 and 61,800 Japanese troops on *Leyte*. He estimated that by the time he left the island on 17 March 1945, some 49,790 of his troops had been killed. General Yamashita admitted to the US Military Commission after the war, that the *Battle of Leyte* Island effectively ended hopes of victory in the Philippines: "After the loss of *Leyte* . . . I realized that decisive battle was impossible."[47]

If *Leyte* was the decisive battle of the campaign, it even further calls into question the need for MacArthur's *Luzon* campaign that followed. With regard to the interdiction of Japan cargo traffic through the *South China Sea* this could have been just as easily accomplished from airfields on *Mindoro* as from *Luzon*. Whether this was required at all given the remarkable successes recorded by Vice-Admiral Charles Lockwood's submariners is a moot point.

Kamikaze and the Bombardment of Lingayen Bay: **[Map: 34.4]** At his headquarter in Baguio, 125 miles north of Manila, the imposing six foot two inch tall Yamashita spoke confidently to the Japanese press about their ability to beat off the impending US invasion of *Luzon*.

On 9 January (on a timetable pushed back from 20 December) MacArthur landed his Sixth Army under Lieutenant-General Walter Krueger in the *Gulf of Lingayen* on the northwest coast of *Luzon*. It was not a surprise choice; it was where the Japanese had come ashore three years earlier. *Lingayen Bay*'s 120-mile long, gently sloping beaches and secure anchorage made it an ideal landing point particularly for an amphibious fleet of 1,000 ships. The invading fleet under the command of Vice-Admiral Thomas Kinkaid, was divided into four groups: 'bombardment' under Rear-Admiral Jesse Oldendorf, 'cover group' under Rear-Admiral Russell Berkey, 'San Fabian Attack Force' under Vice-Admiral Daniel Barbey and 'Lingayen Attack Force' under Vice-Admiral Theodore 'Ping' Wilkinson. On its way from *Leyte* the fleet was constantly attacked by *kamikaze*, sinking four ships and causing over 2,000 casualties. In spite of the *kamikaze* attacks the invasion force was unleashed on the beaches at 10.00 a.m.

MacArthur should have been aware that his invasion force might not meet significant initial resistance. The Japanese pattern of ceding the shoreline while creating strong interior defense was now well established. Documents from a crashed plane recovered by American guerrilla leader, Lieutenant-Colonel Volckmann also indicated that Yamashita would adopt this strategy. In spite of this information, Volckmann's radio message, "There will be no, repeat no, opposition on the [Lingayen Gulf] beaches"[48] was completely ignored at MacArthur's HQ. Oldendorf proceeded to bombard a deserted shore. Yamashita meanwhile was ensconced in the mountains where he intended to build a defensive cantonment onto which he hoped that the American Army would fling itself into oblivion. A similar strategy was adopted for the city of Manila, which was turned into another deeply layered defensive fortification that would force the Americans to fight inch by inch for MacArthur's precious prize. Yamashita, realizing that he was without air cover and by now aware that he would be outgunned by the US Army, adopted static zonal defense as the only viable alternative. It could not have been more different from the fast, free flowing, 'advance and flank and advance' strategies that had won him his reputation in Malaya three years earlier. It was a strategy that was forced upon him by his vast inferiority in firepower including tanks, as well as US air superiority.

Having underestimated *Leyte*, Kenney determined not to make the same mistake with the invasion of *Mindoro* and *Luzon*. For the invasion of *Mindoro* he had called for two heavy bomber groups, three medium bomber groups and three fighter groups. For *Luzon* he requested two more fighter groups, four more bomber groups as well as support from Halsey's carriers to neutralize Japanese aircraft based on *Formosa*. To build these forces, which would operate under Ennis Whitehead's Fifth Air Force, it needed time and contributed to the delay in the timetable for the *Luzon* invasion. Kenney's precautions were necessary. On 9 December the Japanese Navy had 133 operational aircraft on *Luzon* and the Army over 100. This compared with the 286 aircraft that Kenney had on *Leyte* on that date. In numbers Kenney only just had the advantage though in skill and training his forces were far superior. By the beginning of January, Japan's air fleet on *Luzon* had been reduced to an estimated 150 serviceable aircraft though new aircraft could always be fed into the system. But like all his colleagues, Kenney had not foreseen that the decline in Japan's pilots' abilities would shift their strategy toward the use of *kamikaze*.

Japanese air commanders on *Luzon*, realizing now that they were heavily outgunned in the air, devoted themselves almost solely to *kamikaze* attacks. From Clark Field alone, 120 planes were specified for this task, while a similar number from Nichols and other airfields were also available for *kamikaze* missions. On 4 January 1945, as the invading armada steamed toward *Luzon* with Oldendorf's 'bombardment' group in the lead, *kamikaze* pilots made their final preparations. Locks of hair or nail clippings were carefully packaged with last letters home. The familiar leather pilot's helmets were carefully placed on heads so as not to disturb the white cotton *hachimaki* (headbands) that had been used throughout history by samurai before going into battle. Used by the samurai to keep hair and sweat out of the eyes during swordplay, the *hachimaki* became one of the distinguishing rituals before a *kamikaze* pilot left on his final mission. First to be hit was the escort carrier USS *Ommaney Bay*; a twin-engine bomber plunged into its deck killing 93 sailors. The ship became an instant fireball and was evacuated minutes before the escort carrier's munitions store blew up and sank it.

On the next day, 5 January, a stream of attacks followed; the Northampton Class heavy cruiser USS *Louisville* (known as *Lady Lou*) was hit in her forward batteries with one man dead and fifty-nine wounded, but managed to continue; similarly HMAS *Australia* lost 25 dead and 30 wounded and USS *Manila Bay*, 22 dead and 56 wounded, but nevertheless continued to *Lingayen Bay*. Three escort destroyers USS *Goss*, USS *Stafford* and USS *Ulvert H. Moore* were also attacked. The latter was commanded by the President's son, Franklin D. Roosevelt II, who was fortunate to survive a near miss while the *Stafford* was struck by another Zero, which killed two sailors and wounded twelve.

As Oldendorf's ships opened fire on the deserted beach front of *Lingayen Bay* on 6 January, a *kamikaze* scored a glancing hit on destroyer, USS *Richard P. Leary*. More damagingly a Zero struck the veteran *Pearl Harbor* battleship USS *New Mexico*, killing its commander, Captain Robert Fleming, as well as the British observer, Lieutenant-General Herbert Lumsden, who was Winston Churchill's liaison officer to MacArthur. Lucky survivors on the port side of the bridge were Rear-Admiral G. L. Weyler and Royal Navy adviser Admiral Bruce Fraser, although the latter's secretary was killed in the conflagration; in addition twenty-five crewmen were killed with eighty-seven wounded.

On the destroyer USS *Walke*, an exploding *kamikaze* drenched its captain, George Davis, with gasoline fuel and set him on fire. Crewmen smothered the flames but not before leaving burns to most of his body. Davis, in spite of the excruciating pain and continued to direct operations to save his ship. When he had extinguished all fires, he agreed to go below to be treated but died some hours later. Commander Davis was posthumously awarded a Medal of Honor. Other casualties of the day's *kamikaze* attacks included the battleship USS *California* which suffered 45 killed and 151 wounded; destroyer USS *Newcombe* damaged by friendly fire from 40 mm bullets and 5-inch shell fragments, reported 2 killed and 15 wounded; and light cruiser USS *Columbia* which had 13 killed and 44 wounded. HMAS *Australia* became the first of the 'two-timers' with another Zero strike claiming 14 dead and 16 wounded. She continued to pound the shores. *Lady Lou* (USS *Louisville*) was also hit for a second time; Rear-Admiral 'Ted' Chandler, in spite of suffering horrendous gasoline burns, personally led the firefighting crews. He refused to jump the queue for medical treatment and died from smoke inhalation the following day, joining the casualty list of 31 dead and 56 wounded.

With one ship sunk, eleven damaged and hundreds killed, the US Navy had taken its heaviest engagement losses since the *Battle of Tassafaronga* at the end of the *Guadalcanal* Campaign. Oldendorf signalled Vice-Admiral Kinkaid with the alarming news, "If transports receive the same treatment, the troops might be slaughtered before they can land."[49] Halsey's carrier fleet, roaming off the east coast of *Luzon* was urgently called in to blast its airfields prior to 'landing day.'

Landings on Luzon: En route for *Luzon* aboard USS *Bose*, which was accompanying the troop transports, MacArthur reflected to *Life* magazine correspondent, Carl Mydens, that he was retracing the route of his escape by PT boat three years earlier. It was a more comfortable trip this time though it was enlivened when the *Bose* had to turn sharply to avoid a Japanese torpedo. MacArthur watched approvingly as the Japanese submarine was forced to the surface by depth charges and was then rammed by the destroyer, USS *Taylor*. There was a crunching impact and the submarine sank to the ocean floor leaving only a residue of bubbles.

The following morning a Zero dived toward the *Bose* but was obliterated by a massive explosion when it was hit by ack-ack fire just 100 yards from its target. The ship was rocked. MacArthur's physician, Dr. Roger Egeberg, went below to check his boss and found him snoozing. He suspected that his boss was faking it; MacArthur was a man who worked hard on his legend. Remarkably not a single soldier died on the way to *Luzon* though a *kamikaze* did manage to slip through and score a hit on the attack transport, USS *Callaway*; twenty-nine sailors were killed and twenty-two wounded but the 1,188 troops aboard were unscathed.

The invasion on 9 January was met with little resistance. "It was apparent that our landing in the Lingayen-Mabilao area had taken the enemy completely by surprise," Krueger would later write, "He [Yamashita] had probably assumed that the rivers, estuaries, swamps and fish ponds in that area, to say nothing of the high surf, would make a landing there impossible, or at least very unlikely."[50] Krueger was mistaken. Yamashita's troops were not on the beaches by design. Yamashita's forces, placed at San Fernando, were dug into the mountains on Krueger's left flank. Krueger was not the only general fooled. MacArthur had confidently asserted, "the Japanese would not attempt to defend Manila but would evacuate it."[51] In fact Yamashita had left two significant armies to defend Manila.

At 2.00 p.m. MacArthur, aiming to repeat the success of his fortuitous *Leyte* photo stunt, refused to land at the pier constructed for him by the Seabees. Again he waded ashore. This time it was *Life* magazine that recorded his heroism for posterity. His 'misleading' *communiqué* from *Luzon* claimed that he was "in personal command at the front and landed with his assault troops."[52] In fact MacArthur's appearance on shore only came after the establishment of a beachhead fifteen miles deep and thirty miles wide. By 17 January, just eight days after the landing, Lingayen Airfield became operational for General Whitehead's Fifth Air Force—a stark contrast to the problems on *Leyte Island*. A second airfield at Mangaldan was completed by 22 January. Whereas the demand for missions on *Leyte* had significantly exceeded Whitehead's ability to deliver, on *Luzon* available capacity vastly exceeded need. Japanese air cover had in effect been wiped out. Lieutenant-General Krueger even had to ask Kenney to stop blowing up roads and railroads, infrastructure that the US Army would soon need. The main threat from the air to his troops now seemed to come from friendly fire, which drew sharp protests from Krueger.

As for Kenney, his main enemies now appeared to be in Washington where a distinct *froideur* had developed toward him on the part of 'Hap' Arnold. It seems that Kenney's closeness to MacArthur and his bitter struggle to get B-29 Superfortresses for his *Borneo* missions had cooled his relationship with Arnold. Arnold had let it be known that Kenney's constant bickering on the subject, even after the decision was made, jeopardized his command. Moreover Arnold was unhappy that Kenney kept 'ace' pilots at the front too long when they could be more use at home. When the two top 'aces' under Kenney's command, Colonel Neel Kearby and Captain Thomas Lynch were shot down within a few days of each other in March 1944, Arnold was furious. On 5 March Kearby, a P-47 Thunderbolt pilot, with twenty-one kills to his name, had attacked a formation of fifteen Japanese planes near Wewak and was shot down by a Japanese Army Nakajima Ki-43 'Oscar.' Three days later Lynch's Lockheed P-38 was hit by small arms fire from boats in *Aitape Harbor* and bailed out too low for his parachute to open. His wingman, another ace, Lieutenant Richard Bong, survived.

Kenney would later reflect, "Every once in a while Arnold would get sore at me about something or other. He thought I was still working for him, but I wasn't. I was working for MacArthur."[53] The root of the problem as ever was 'who reported to who'—a sensitive subject for 'Hap' Arnold who wanted the Air Force to be a service independent from the army. Kenney managed to bury the hatchet on a visit to Florida on 17 March where Arnold was recovering from a heart attack. As for MacArthur, never the most generous of bosses, his private praise of Kenney throughout the war was unstinting: "I believe that, no repeat, no officer suggested for promotion to General has rendered more outstanding and brilliant service than Kenney . . ."[54]

For his zonal defense Yamashita chose three areas offering strong natural protection; Major-General Rikichi Tsukada's 'Kembu' group defended Clark Field and the adjoining Bataan Peninsula; Lieutenant-General Shizuo Yokoyama's *Shimbu* Group occupied the mountain range to the east of Manila; while Yamashita's own *Shobu* Group defended an HQ at Baguio with a perimeter on the west coast above San Fabian. In addition Manila itself was defended by 17,000 troops under Rear-Admiral Sanji Iwaguchi.

POWs Rescued at Cabanatuan and the Race to Santo Tomas: [Charts: D.2, D.3]
Among the first actions of the Americans' *Luzon* campaign was a rescue mission. After

the fall of Bataan and *Corregidor* some 7,000 troops had been penned up inside the prison camp at Cabanatuan, some eighty miles north of Manila. Many had been transferred to other locations, some to *Formosa*, Japan or Manchuria. Large numbers had also died of malnutrition and disease over the previous three years. As they heard the guns blazing many of them worried that the Japanese would kill them before they were liberated.

On 29 January 1945, 6th Ranger C-Company led by Captain Robert Prince along with a platoon of F-Company commanded by Lieutenant John Murphy, guided by locally set up radio stations, met up with 250 Filipino guerrillas. They headed toward Cabanatuan armed with details of the camp provided them by an infiltrated American reconnaissance group known as the Alamo Scouts. The rangers packed light rations, Tommy guns, two pistols each and a large trench knife. Before leaving, the Rangers Colonel Henry Mucci told his hand-picked troops, mostly big farm boys, "Get in quick and knife 'em up! I don't want any of the POWs killed. Bring out every goddamned prisoner! Bring them out if every Ranger has to carry a man or two on his back."[55]

The Rangers crept into position within yards of the main gate by 7.25 p.m. At 7.44 p.m. the Rangers launched their lightning attack taking the prison forces by storm. Within minutes Japanese prison troops had been killed or had fled into the jungle. Astonished and disbelieving inmates, pale shadows of their former soldierly selves were led or carried out by fit young GIs. Meanwhile on the approaches to Cabanatuan, firefights broke out as pickets placed by the Rangers opened fire on Japanese troops rushing to the scene. As they headed for their *rendezvous* point, local villagers fed the prisoners. With Japanese troops nipping at their heels, the Rangers and the camp survivors arrived at Sibul where 531 Bataan veterans were put aboard waiting trucks to take them to the coast. Their rescue cost the lives of two Rangers, including Captain Jim Fisher, who were killed along with twenty-six Filipino guerrillas. Seventy-three Cabanatuan prison guards were killed along with 151 other Japanese soldiers. The adventurous episode, probably the most celebrated raid in modern US history until the killing of Osama Bin Laden, was reprised in the movie *Back to Bataan* [1945] starring John Wayne and Anthony Quinn.

US intelligence had picked up an order from Japanese high command with regard to dealing with Allied prisoners: "Whether they are destroyed individually or in groups, or however it is done, with mass bombing, poisonous smoke, poisons, drowning, decapitation, or what, dispose of them as the situation dictates. In any case, it is the aim to annihilate them all or not to leave any traces."[56] Throughout Asia the order applied to nearly 200,000 Allied prisoners of war and 125,000 interned civilians. It remains open to question whether Hirohito had knowledge of this order, although given its significance it seems unlikely that he would not have been told.

As MacArthur's troops were landing at *Lingayen Bay*, Lieutenant-Colonel Haskett 'Hack' Conner was taken aside by the 1st Cavalry's Major-General Verne Mudge. He had been ordered to organize two flying columns to make a dash to Manila with the aim of getting to the campus of Santo Tomas University before its prisoner of war inmates could be massacred. Conner's sixty-mile dash was accomplished with firefights with local Japanese troops at regular intervals. There was constant US aircraft support from 32nd Marine Air Group, taking off from an airstrip rapidly built on a paddy field; in effect the airborne Marines rode shotgun as Conner blitzed his way through the *Luzon* countryside.

In his jeep 'Hack' Conner told an accompanying newsman, "It's almost impossible to avoid an ambush in country like this. It's like following a train in the jungle; the first guys are bound to get knocked off."[57] Setting off in the early hours of 1 February, Conner's columns advanced blasting everything that stood in its way. He did not stop to hold ground.

On 3 February as they approached the important Navaliches Bridge, they found it still standing but came under raking fire from hidden Japanese soldiers. Conner's tanks blasted into the undergrowth while his troops engaged in firefights with Japanese infantry. As they fought, Major James Gerhart spotted that that there was a fuse burning on the bridge. He and a Navy bomb disposal officer, Lieutenant James Sutton, ran after it, somehow dodged a hail of bullets and cut the fuse just before it blew up 400 lbs of TNT and 3,000 lbs of picric acid. Later that afternoon US planes swooped low over Santo Tomas and dropped notes to say that help was on its way.

Conner's column slowed down as it reached Manila and wound through its streets. As they approached Santo Tomas, a Chinese boy emerged to tell them that Japanese troops were hiding in the cemetery; sure enough they opened fire as the convoy of tanks and troop carriers sped through and the mechanized column returned fire in kind. Hearing the fighting the prisoners at Santo Tomas waited anxiously. Suddenly a Sherman tank, named 'Battling Basic,' crashed through the front gates followed by the Cavalry troops. Here the hated chief guard rushed onto the Santo Tomas Plaza with his hands in the air. When he suddenly reached for a hand grenade he was felled by a hail of bullets. The remaining prison guards were massacred by Filipino guerrillas. The cavalry fanned out and fought briefly with those Japanese troops who remained to fight. *Life* journalist, Carl Mydens, who accompanied the cavalry, had been interned at Santo Tomas at the start of the war before being exchanged for Japanese journalists during December 1943, and took pictures of the scene.

'Hack' Conner's 1st Cavalry liberated 3,500 inmates. The drama was not over. Colonel Toshio Hayashi, reportedly the most brutal of the prison commandants over the three and a half years of confinement, and sixty of his troops had taken 267 hostages, mostly women and children, and were holding them on the third floor of the Education Building. Despite their best efforts the Rangers were unable to penetrate the buildings' defenses without risking the lives of the hostages. In an incident virtually unique in the *Pacific War*, the two sides began to parley.

At dawn on 4 February, Lieutenant-Colonel Charles Brady, executive officer of the 1st Cavalry Brigade, entered the Education Building unarmed for talks with Hayashi. The impeccably dressed Hayashi, sporting shiny boots, medals and a pair of hip pistols entered the room with six armed soldiers. It was agreed that the Japanese troops could leave with their arms and would be escorted to safety in return for the lives of the hostages. Brady insisted that his men were not to shoot but that they should have a bullet ready in the breach. "Each man is to cover a Jap," Brady insisted. "At a certain point agreed between the Japs and me, we will halt and they will continue. Under no conditions is any man to get trigger-happy. But if they shoot first, let the bastards have it."[58]

At dawn on 5 February Hayashi, carrying his samurai sword, led out his men three abreast while the GIs of E-Troop, 5th Cavalry, marched in single file either side of them. Brady joined Hayashi at the head of this bizarre spectacle as they marched out of the front gate. The respective commanders then argued about how far out the American would march before letting them go, a difficult problem because there was no front line as such. Hayashi wanted protection to continue but at a certain point Brady refused to go any further. The Japanese column marched forward with each of their soldiers bowing or saluting to Brady as they passed. While this comedy was being played out, other prisoners had been liberated from the old Bilibid Prison. Colonel Lawrence 'Red' White, commander of the 148th Infantry, ordered his troops to break in. They found a scene of appalling squalor in which the 600 starved civilian men, women and children had been living. In the military wing where survivors of *Corregidor* and Bataan were kept the conditions were similarly disgusting. Young men in the prime of life in 1941 had been reduced to skeletal old men: 'Red' White's soldiers wept tears of sorrow, the liberated prisoners, tears of joy.

The Battle of Manila: **[Map: 34.5]** On 7 February the area had been cleared enough for MacArthur to drive to the outskirts of Manila, flanked by a team of bodyguards carrying Tommy guns. He visited the prison where, for the time being, the prisoners were still kept for their safety. He must have felt vindicated for his efforts to get back to Manila whatever the strategic logic. Nevertheless the heroic actions of his special forces also proved to be another publicity coup for MacArthur. MacArthur sent out a *communiqué* announcing, "Our forces are rapidly clearing the enemy from Manila."[59] As usual it was a statement of pure invention; the hard fighting for Manila had barely begun. It was a typical MacArthur lie. A misinformed American public glowed in warm appreciation.

The Japanese were not being rapidly cleared from Manila but were settling down for a long siege. Krueger's Sixth Army took several weeks to fight its way through Yamashita's defensive zones to get to Manila. While two divisions had fought their way into the suburbs of north Manila to relieve the prison camps, from the south, General 'Joe' Swing's 11th Airborne Division approached the Tagatay Ridge guarding the *Parañaque River*. Casualties were high and included popular senior ranking officers, Colonel Irving Schimmelpfenning and Colonel Orin Haugen. They were both cut down by machine gun fire in separate incidents on 4 and 11 February respectively as they tried to force through the Japanese defensive Genko Line—a system of bunkers, entrenchment, machine-gun pits and artillery stretching between Fort McKinley and Nichols Field. By that evening however, MacArthur's twin forces from north and south were able to hook up leaving many Japanese troops stranded behind American lines.

Meanwhile the 188th Glider Infantry Division swung to the right of the Genko Line to secure Nichols Airfield. Here the Japanese had prepared fearsome machine gun entrenchments supported by fire from 5-inch guns salvaged from Japanese ships damaged beyond repair in *Manila Harbor*. A field commander radioed back to his field HQ: "Tell [Vice-Admiral 'Bull' Halsey] to stop looking for the Jap fleet. It's dug in here at Nichols Field."[60] On 12 February US Artillery was brought up to pound the Japanese positions while the Marine Air Corps did likewise from the air.

At Fort McKinley eleven pillboxes protected the Japanese outer positions. On 13 February, Private Manny Perez Jr., of the 511th Parachute Infantry, operating as scout, not a job designed for longevity, led a paratrooper platoon in the destruction of all the Japanese defensive positions. Backed by supporting fire Perez weaved his way toward the first pillbox and dropped grenades through the slot. Loading up with more grenades, Perez attacked the next pillbox. This time he fired into the bunker and when eight Japanese soldiers poured out, he killed them all, the last he bayoneted after a hand-to-hand fight. That day they took out nine more pillboxes in similar fashion. The 21-year-old Perez's premonition that morning that he would be killed or wounded did not come to fruition in spite of his astonishing bravery. But thirty days later he was shot dead by a sniper while again taking on the role of lead scout.

By 17 February, the final fortifications of Fort McKinley had been overcome. But the most brutal fighting was still ahead. Rear-Admiral Sanji Iwaguchi's defending Japanese Naval forces had also pillaged guns from the now redundant warships remaining in *Manila Harbor* and constructed heavily dug-in defense positions within the *Intramuros* (literally between the walls) area of old Manila. This centuries-old fortified Spanish walled city ran for several miles with walls 20 foot high and 40 foot wide. It was an imposing barrier. Griswold, the Sixth Army commander, asked for dive-bomber support but MacArthur refused to contemplate the bombing of the old city, dismissing the idea as "unthinkable."[61]

Bizarrely MacArthur nevertheless approved the use of artillery. A six-day barrage levelled the old city. In the end he had no choice because of the appalling cost in terms of GI casualties. Finally American troops penetrated the *Intramuros* area on 23 February and there followed a week of close quarter fighting, one house at a time. Japanese casualties amounted to 12,000 men (more than two-thirds of their defenders). For the civilians conditions were appalling. *Time* correspondent W. P. Grey reported, "Day and night the shelling goes on. How many hundreds or thousands of civilians have already died by fire or shellfire outside *Intramuros*, nobody knows. Hundreds of city blocks are burned or flattened. Many unburned buildings are pocked or shattered by gunfire."[62] The last action took place atop the Finance Building on 3 March when a final redoubt of Japanese diehards were finally killed on the top floor. Bataan had been overrun a week earlier ending with Japanese holdouts detonating an underground arsenal in which they were holed-up; 2,000 Japanese troops were blown to smithereens taking 55 American troops with them. A medic who dealt with the survivors recalled being appalled by the blood and gore, "As soon as I got the casualties off I sat down on a rock and burst out crying."[63]

MacArthur, keen to return to his family home in the penthouse atop the Manila Hotel, rushed up the stairs close behind his troops. The upper floors were strewn with bodies and MacArthur was disappointed to find that his apartment was half burnt out. It was some compensation that a young cavalry officer, seeing MacArthur next to the dead body of a Japanese colonel in the doorway, called out, "Nice going chief!"[64]

The result was that Manila, the 'Pearl of the Orient,' the city that MacArthur had sworn to protect, was devastated, its population decimated. MacArthur did not record the slaughter of Manila's population in his *Reminiscences* [2010]. The fight for Manila cost 8,310 American lives with a further 30,000 wounded. At his desk in Washington, Admiral King, who had warned against the Philippines campaign, muttered, "I tried to tell them, I tried to tell them . . . MacArthur's liberation has destroyed a city and has cost an innocent population one hundred thousand dead."[65] In all, the liberation of the Philippines that MacArthur had sworn would be 'low cost' accounted for 60,628 American troops killed, wounded or missing in action. It was a testament to the appalling fighting and living conditions that the Sixth Army alone suffered 93,400 non-battle casualties. As for the Filipinos, the people that MacArthur swore would never forgive America if it chose to bypass the archipelago, it is estimated that some 200,000 died.

As the final battles for Manila's citadel were being fought, 'Joe' Swing pulled Major Henry Burgess and his 1st Battalion of the 511th Parachute Infantry out of the battle for Fort McKinlay. Burgess, a Wyoming rancher, thought they were due for a rest. He was to be disappointed. He was ordered to take his 412 paratroops inside Japanese-held territory to rescue over 2,000 men, women and children from Los Baños prison camp. After improvising a daring raid comprising a ground force, an amphibious amtrac landing as well as a paratrooper drop, Burgess's forces engaged in firefights with the prison guards while Burgess's amtracs crashed through the front gates. Nuns led their young charges into the fifty-four waiting amtracs and they were shipped across *Laguna Bay*. By chance one amtrac, to the great amusement of the party of priests and nuns that they were carrying, was named *The Impatient Virgin*—probably not the Holy Virgin of their prayers. Although the paratroopers had to fight off detachments of Japan's 8th Division coming from the south, all 2,147 internees were brought out while the paratroops suffered no casualties.

The surrender of Japan that MacArthur had predicted after the fall of *Luzon* did not materialize. Indeed MacArthur, no doubt anxious to be called to lead the invasion of Japan itself, proclaimed the termination of the Philippines campaign on 5 July. It was yet another lie. When Hirohito surrendered on 15 August, fighting was continuing in the south while in the north of *Luzon* three US divisions were still pinned down by fierce battles. Yamashita had dug in his forces well. As he reported before the battle, "The Philippines have an extensive area and we can fight to our heart's content."[66]

Mopping-Up: The Battle of Luzon and Operation VICTOR: [**Map: 34.6**] MacArthur had by now embarked on Operation VICTOR which started on *Mindanao* on 15 March and continued until 15 August 1945 when Hirohito's surrendered. Rather than allowing rest for his troops by simply allowing Japan's outlying posts to 'wither on the vine,' MacArthur set about a triumphal conquest of outlying territories across the Philippines, at the expense of the lives of his troops, with no seeming justification. *Palawan, Zamboangaon, Mindanao, Panay-Northern Negros, Cebu-Southern Negros-Bohol*, and central *Mindanao* were fought for and won. Strategic military justification was to provide air cover to prevent Japanese resupply through the *South China Sea*. It was a specious argument. This work had already been done by Halsey's Third Fleet and even more importantly by the America's underappreciated submarine service.

Most remarkably the VICTOR Campaign was carried out without directive. In effect the Joint Chiefs, probably reluctant to face down a histrionic MacArthur, left him to his own devices. Even when the Joint Chiefs did authorize his actions, such as the invasion of *Borneo* on 1st May 1945, it was questioned by the British what the point of this action was given that Brunei's oil was not required for supply of forces preparing for the invasion of Japan. As his biographer D. Clayton James has noted, "The unauthorized initiation of his Victor Plan was surely MacArthur's most audacious challenge to the Joint Chiefs during the war . . . It is little wonder that the same commander less than six years later would act with insolence toward his superiors in Washington."[67] American troops suffered over 1,000 deaths and 4,000 other casualties in this, MacArthur's pointless campaign.

Judgment on MacArthur's Quest for Manila: In hindsight it is difficult to argue the case that the invasion of *Luzon* was the correct strategic leap toward Japan. The Japanese air force was largely destroyed before MacArthur's invasion of *Luzon* and the airfields there were never to become a factor with regard to the bombing of Japan. Neither was *Luzon* important for cutting off supply to Japan, a job that the US submarine force, with help from Halsey's Third Fleet, had done quite brilliantly and effectively.

Attacks on *Iwo Jima* and *Okinawa*, which were authorized by the Joint Chiefs of staff at the same time as *Luzon*, were much more important stepping-stones in the US advance toward Tokyo. Indeed Admiral Spruance, had argued quite cogently that the best way forward from *Leyte* was to isolate and bypass both *Luzon* and *Formosa* and go direct to *Iwo Jima* and *Okinawa*. Leaving Yamashita's army to rot in the Philippines may not have been the glamorous or politically expedient option favored by MacArthur, but it would undoubtedly have saved hundreds of thousands of Filipino and American lives.

The subtext of personal ambitions interwove with the US commanders' desire to defeat Japan. The invasion of *Luzon* was one of the end goals of MacArthur's three-year campaign for personal redemption. It was a quest that was barely distinguishable with MacArthur's simultaneous bid for control of the final advance on Japan. Ultimately Admiral King won this latter battle for the US Navy, albeit not by his preferred *Formosa* route. The story of internecine disputes is not an attractive story but in the post-war glow of victory, the narrative of US inter-service rivalry in the *Pacific War* has inevitably fallen into the background.

35 Battle of the Irrawaddy River: Slim's 'Mandalay Feint'

[January 1945–May 1945]

[Maps: 35.1, 35.2, 35.2B]

While MacArthur was trying to finish off Japanese resistance in *Luzon*, General 'Bill' Slim was embarking on the destruction of Japanese forces in Burma. Though never a race, it would be a contest that Slim would win with aplomb. It was a speedy victory that not only reflected Slim's special skills as a commander but, in terms of the air power provided, also showed that Burma was strategically much less important to Japan's senior officers than the Philippines.

After the Battle of Imphal, What Next? The *Battle of the Irrawaddy River* (otherwise known as the *Battle of Mandalay*, the *Battle of Pakkoku* or the *Battle of Meiktila*) was unique in the history of land engagements in the *Pacific War* for being the only full-scale offensive conducted by the British Army—albeit an army that was mainly comprised of Indian soldiers. By the end of April 1944, it had become clear to Major-General Slim that the attempted invasion of the Indian province of Assam by the Japanese had been brought to a halt at the *Battles of Imphal* and *Kohima* **[see Chapter 26: Battles of Arakan, Imphal, and Kohima: Slim Boxes Clever]**, where the Fourteenth Army had destroyed the Japanese Army in a defensive engagement. The scale of the British victory was not immediately apparent. It was only as Slim's troops, mainly Indians mixed with sundry British and African forces, pursued the fleeing Japanese forces that the scale of their victory became apparent. The grotesque discovery of vast numbers of corpses left by the wayside and villages full of dead and dying spoke of a vanquished, retreating army that was actually starving to death. An estimated 70,000 troops of General Mutaguchi's approximately 100,000-strong army perished in Japan's attempted invasion of northern India; it was a death rate almost unique in modern history. Nevertheless as late as summer 1944 some British commanders still feared that Japan might make further attempts to invade India.

Mountbatten's Machinations: As for Slim, at the end of what turned out to have been a spectacular victory at the *Battle of Imphal*, he contracted malaria after he broke his own rules by taking a shower after sunset. In spite of his illness he began to plan the next phase in his campaign to retake Burma. He was not alone. Admiral Lord Mountbatten, head of SEAC (South East Asia Command) plotted to recapture the country by a spectacular amphibious campaign aimed at retaking Rangoon. Bolstered by victory at the *Battles of Imphal* and *Kohima*, for which, incredibly, he claimed credit, Mountbatten convinced Churchill of the merits of Operation DRACULA, in spite of the Prime Minister's own preference for an invasion of Japanese-controlled *Sumatra*, which supplied most of Japan's oil.

American support was needed for Mountbatten's proposed amphibious operation. For the American Chiefs of Staff the only point of the Burma Campaign was to open up a land supply route to China in order to supplement or replace 'the Hump.' Although the campaigns in New Guinea and the *Pacific* were progressing well, keeping China in the war with its ability to tie down 1 million Japanese troops was still seen as an imperative strategic objective. Roosevelt and his senior staff, with much rolling of eyes, correctly observed that Britain's main priority was to recapture its former empire. But American criticisms of this were rank hypocrisy. Britain's aims were no more or less overt than America's desire to recapture the Philippines and its own *Pacific* territories. Indeed General MacArthur was far more obsessed with this task than any British commander. In spite of these misgivings, at the Second Quebec Conference (codenamed OCTAGON) in September 1944 the British and American Combined Chiefs, with the necessary support of Roosevelt, approved Operation DRACULA. It was an operation that could satisfy both US and British strategic requirements.

During the intervening months, British military success at the *Battle of Imphal* had enabled Mountbatten to politic his way to further power in the region. General Sir George Giffard, who loathed Mountbatten, had been sacked in May 1944 but remained in place from where he worked effectively with Slim until October. Logically, Giffard, Slim's nominal senior during this period, should have been replaced by Lieutenant-General Slim, who had developed a good working relationship with Mountbatten. While it was argued that Slim was too important in the field to be removed, the suspicion remained that Mountbatten refused to promote him out of jealousy. Mountbatten was not backward in his political machinations. In an act of notable hypocrisy given Mountbatten's own peccadilloes, Air Chief Marshal Sir Richard Peirse, another thorn in Mountbatten's side, was removed on the grounds of adultery with Lady Jessie Auchinleck. Lieutenant-General Sir Henry Pownall and Admiral Sir James Sommerville, who loathed the upstart Mountbatten, were also replaced.

Mountbatten's maneuvering against perceived enemies ultimately backfired. Lieutenant-General Sir Oliver Leese, a protégé of General Montgomery, who had commanded XXX Corp at the *Battle of El Alamein* and then the Eighth Army in Italy, arrived in Delhi with little knowledge of jungle warfare but an inbuilt belief in the superiority of the British troops and officers who had fought in Africa and Italy. Appointed Commander in Chief, Allied Land Forces in South East Asia, in place of Giffard, Leese quickly packed his staff with Eighth Army veterans.

He quickly came to detest the louche behavior of Mountbatten and his staff at Kandy. Invited to Mountbatten's birthday, Lieutenant-General Leese received a rude shock. "Most girls were U's [Mountbatten's] . . .," Leese wrote to his wife, "and they seemed to spend their time sitting on the arms of U and others' chairs. It all seemed a pity somehow, as it gives the playboy atmosphere, in terrible contrast to those from the battle."[1] A band played 'Happy Birthday' while a pretty young wren (members of the Women's Royal Navy Service – WRNS – were called 'wrens') engaged Mountbatten in a passionate embrace. Meanwhile Leese's dealings with Slim, famous for his ability to establish a good working relationship with difficult men, were prickly. In a rare, albeit muted, criticism of a colleague in his autobiography, Slim recalled, "His [Leese's] staff . . . had a good deal of desert sand in their shoes and were rather inclined to thrust Eighth Army down our throats."[2]

Operation CAPITAL and EXTENDED CAPITAL: [Map: 35.1] Slim, passed over for promotion, merely continued with his plans to crush the Japanese army in Burma with Operation CAPITAL. In spite of the scepticism of Churchill, Chief of Staff General Alanbrooke and senior British commanders in London, Slim believed that with his existing forces, he could re-conquer Burma. He realized that once he could engage the Japanese Army in the central plains of Burma, his superiority in tanks and aircraft would enable him to destroy the enemy. The cover of jungle would no longer protect Japanese inadequacies.

Operation CAPITAL was almost lost before it began. After the fall of Kweilin and Liuchow, a desperate Lieutenant-General Albert Wedemeyer, who had replaced Stilwell as Chiang Kai-shek's Chief of Staff, ratted on his former colleagues by peremptorily withdrawing seventy-five Dakota aircraft on which Slim relied to supply his armies. As he made clear at a post-war Press Club lecture in 1946, having to feed an army of 750,000 troops in difficult jungle terrain over an area the size of Poland was a vast logistical exercise. He and his staff had to scramble fast to make up the hole in his supply chain. "Before we could get on with our real business—fighting—we had to feed, clothe, house, and all the time we were doing it, equip, doctor, police, pay and transport by road, ship rail air all of those men. All that and the jungle too!"[3]

The problem of air supply was as much political as logistical. As Field Marshal Lord Alanbrooke noted in a diary entry on 17 January 1945:

> We had a specially long COS [chain of supply] as we had boy Browning back from Kandy, having been sent by Dickie to plead his case for more transport aircraft for the Burma operations ... One of our difficulties arises through the fact that the transport aircraft belong to the Americans, and that the reconquest of lower Burma does not interest them at all. All they want is North Burma and the air route and pipeline and Ledo Road into China. They have now practically got all of these, and the rest of Burma is of small interest to them.[4]

Initially Operation CAPITAL was devised on the assumption that, after the *Battle of Imphal*, the Japanese Army would reform and defend the delta between the *Chindwin* and *Irrawaddy Rivers*. Here Slim believed that he could corral the Japanese forces on the Shwebo Plain and destroy them. However, the Japanese too had undergone significant personnel changes in senior command. Lieutenant-General Heitaro Kimura had replaced Lieutenant-General Masakazu Kawabe as commander of the Burma Area Army. Kimura, an artillery specialist, had spent the 1930s at the War Ministry and served as Vice-Minister of War in General Tojo's cabinet from 1941 to 1943. Lieutenant-General Mutaguchi, who had led the disastrous foray into Assam, was also replaced. Thus Lieutenant-General Shihachi Katamura who had been fighting on the Arakan front since January 1941 was promoted to command of the Fifteenth Army in September 1944. Meanwhile an infantry commander and former Manchurian veteran, Lieutenant-General Masaki Honda had been given command of Thirty-third Army in April 1944. At the beginning of 1945, he was charged with defending northern Burma from the advancing Chinese Forces, which, following the sacking of General 'Vinegar Joe' Stilwell, was now under the command of Lieutenant-General Daniel Sultan who had become Commander of the South East Asia Command (SEAC) on 24 October 1944.

Kimura threw Slim's Operation CAPITAL into disarray when it became clear that he had no intention of fighting Slim's Fourteenth Army on the Shwebo Plain. Against the normal Japanese preference to hold ground at all cost, Kimura, who had been told in November 1944 that he could expect no more reinforcements or supply from Japan, decided to save his depleted forces and yield the *Chindwin-Irrawaddy Delta*. Apart from delaying forces, which sought to ambush the advancing British Army in guerrilla-type raids after the British advance commenced at the beginning of January 1945, Kimura yielded ground and planned his defenses on the east bank of the *Irrawaddy River* to the north and south of Mandalay, Burma's second city and ancient capital. Kimura hoped to draw Slim into a difficult opposed landing across the *Irrawaddy*, stretch his lines of communication and then push him back toward Assam. In other words, he planned a reverse working of the strategy that had destroyed Mutaguchi's army at the *Battles of Imphal* and *Kohima*.

Kimura's strategy was an intelligent and coherent plan. But in his assumption that Slim's primary target would be the recapture of Mandalay, he was completely wrong. Slim believed that wars were won by defeating armies, not by capturing towns or cities. In his hastily revised strategy, renamed Operation EXTENDED CAPITAL, Slim's key aim was not to capture Mandalay but to destroy the Japanese Armies in Burma. Points on the map would then take care of themselves. As Slim outlined in his autobiography, *Defeat into Victory* [1956], "My new plan, the details of which were worked out in record time by my devoted staff . . . had as its intention the destruction of the main Japanese forces in the area of Mandalay."[5]

The Mandalay Feint: Slim devised a plan that would let Kimura believe that the Fifteenth Army's main objective was the capture of Mandalay while concealing a strike force that would thrust south of Mandalay to Meiktila, a town astride the railways that supplied the Japanese forces on the central and northern plains. "Crush that wrist," observed Slim. "No blood would flow through the fingers and the whole hand would be paralyzed, and the Japanese armies on the arc from the Salween to the Irrawaddy would begin to wither."[6] Slim not only understood the importance of his own lines of supply but carefully studied those of his opponents. Kimura would have to react. Slim would thus force the Japanese armies into the open and destroy them. From here he planned to thrust south and capture Rangoon before the beginning of the monsoons in May.

Crossing back into Burma from India, Slim used the *Chindwin River* to transport tanks and supplies southeast for the traverse of the Shwebo Plain. Sappers were sent forward to construct simple boats using local timber. "They were not graceful craft," noted Slim, "but they floated and carried ten tons apiece."[7] The sappers even constructed two escort vessels armed with 40 mm Bofors and 20 mm Oerlikon guns. Named after Mountbatten's two daughters, *Pamela* and *Una*, the army-made patrol boats soon saw their first action, seeing off a Japanese patrol. Lieutenant-General Slim, delighted with his 'homemade' navy, sent off a message to Commander of the Eastern Fleet, Admiral Sir Arthur Power, "Our Chindwin girls have at last reached glorious womanhood."[8]

The key task of thrusting south was given to the aggressively minded Lieutenant-General Frank Messervy's IV Corps, which comprised the 17th Indian Infantry Division and the 255th Indian Tank Brigade as well as the East African Brigade and Lushai Brigade. After receiving his briefing from Slim on 18 December, Messervy immediately began to prepare the complex logistics of his advance. The route from Tamu to Kalemayo could carry tanks and heavy trucks, but from there the roads to Pakkoku, where a crossing of the *Irrawaddy River* was planned, were little more than dirt tracks that wound through steep hills. Where there were bridges across the frequent streams, these were usually inadequate for heavy loads. Messervy's troops, strung out over the 300 miles of the Myittha Valley, would have to be concentrated at Pakkoku and their advance would need to be supported almost entirely from the air. The Fourteenth Army's Chief Engineer, Major-General 'Bill' Hasted, had to build a 100-mile road in little over a month using Bithess, fifty-yard-long hessian rolls treated with bitumen—a technique which was frequently used to build 'instant' airfields. At the same time, Slim required Hasted to be able to supply 500 tons a month of supplies down the *Chindwin River*. When asked to achieve this, Hasted replied, "The difficult we will do at once; the impossible will take a little longer . . . For these miracles we like a month's notice."[9] "You're lucky. You've got two [months],"[10] Slim replied. Using elephants to haul logs, his engineers managed to construct some 541 rafts by May. It is no exaggeration to suggest that the *Battle of Irrawaddy* would be won as much by Hasted's logistics as by force of arms.

Delayed by weather, the Lushai Brigade took the town of Gangaw on 10 January 1945 after a bombardment by four squadrons of B-25 Mitchell bombers sent by the US Army Air Force. Thereafter on 12 January the 28th East African Brigade took over the lead advance toward Pakkoku. Meanwhile Lieutenant-General Sir Montague Stopford's XXXIII Corps, lying east of the *Chindwin*, advanced on Messervy's left flank toward Shwebo with the 19th Division. Stopford's 20th Division simultaneously advanced down the east bank of the *Chindwin River* toward Monywa. From here they moved southwest of Mandalay where they intended to make their crossings of the *Irrawaddy* at Sagaing. Heavy artillery barrages, combined with the dropping of 500 lb bombs by a force of thirteen Mosquito fighter-bombers, weakened the Japanese bunker defenses enough to enable Stopford's 20th Division to take Monywa on 22 January. By this time Stopford's 19th Division had taken Swabo and established a bridgehead across the *Irrawaddy* north of Mandalay at Thabeikkyin on 7 January and further south at Kyaukmyaung on 11 January. The crossings were achieved with minimal resistance as a result of numerous feints concocted by Slim's commanders that deceived the Japanese about which crossing points the Fourteenth Army would take.

Within a week a full brigade had been established in a double bridgehead north of Singu on the east bank of the *Irrawaddy River*. Kimura, whose forces were only recently established on the east bank of the *Irrawaddy*, ordered Katamura's Fifteenth Army to contain the bridgehead at Thabeikkyin while a full-scale attack was launched to destroy Lieutenant-General Stopford's bridgehead at Kyaukmyaung. Katamura's 15th and 53th Divisions launched ferocious attacks but were unable to dislodge Stopford's 19th Division. Slim visited the bridgehead and noted, "The fighting had been severe, the casualties to our men considerable, and the strain of fighting in these restricted places, with their backs to the river no light one."[11] In some of the most intense fighting of the entire Burma campaign, an already understrength 15th Division lost a third of its forces in a week of fighting. As Slim intended, Kimura's attention was diverted from IV Corp's southeasterly advance toward Pakkoku.

Here, although the retreating Japanese forces had cut trees to barricade the track with tree trunks, the East African Brigade cleared the path using elephants and quad-gun trucks. Arriving at the *Irrawaddy*, Messervy chose to cross toward the village of Nyaungu, a few miles south of Pagan. Here the river narrowed to just three-quarters of a mile, although the slanted approach that was needed made the length of the crossing over a mile; it turned out to be the longest opposed crossing attempted in *World War II*. It was a remarkable feat. As the usually understated Slim observed, "I do not think any modern army has attempted the opposed crossing of a great river with so little."[12]

Messervy's crossing of the *Irrawaddy River* on 14 February started badly. At dawn, the 2nd Battalion of the South Lancashire's boats suffered engine failures that drifted their craft beyond the planned landing point or left them stuck on sandbanks. Two company commanders and numbers of troops were killed by Japanese machine gun positions located on the bluffs commanding the river from the east bank. Although one unit made it to the other side, many others returned to the take-off point. Seventeen boats were sunk along with many unlucky troops. Arthur Helliwell of the *Daily Herald* reported that boats were in a poor state of repair and in the river "One youngster threw up his hands and shouted, 'For God's sake save me' as we drifted past, but we were helpless."[13] Fortunately the Japanese abandoned their positions on the eastern bank, thus saving the South Lancashires, who landed there, from being massacred.

In the afternoon the 4th battalion of the 1st Gurkha Rifles and the 1st Burma Regiment managed to establish a bridgehead on the east bank. The deception that Slim's plan was still aimed on the capture of Mandalay, was maintained by Messervy's 'Operation CLOAK,' which involved the capture of Pakkoku further north on the west bank of the *Irrawaddy*. The intention was to fool the Japanese into thinking that a crossing was planned at this strategic point south of Mandalay.

The feints at Pakkoku had worked. The surprise of the Japanese was complete. It took two days for the Japanese to bring forces to attack the bridgehead at Nyaungu. Slim's forces were helped by the surrender of Bose's feckless pro-Japanese INA (Indian National Army) at Pagan. Remarkably Slim had managed to put five divisions across a 200-mile front of the *Irrawaddy River* to the north and south of Mandalay. It was the city that Kimura still believed was Slim's main target. In reality the main thrust was made by Messervy's 17th Indian Division, whose 48th and 63rd Brigades were made to give up their mule trains for motorized transport that enabled them to speed toward Meiktila, Slim's prime objective in the campaign. The 255th Indian Tank Brigade, commanded by Major-General C. E. Pert, accompanied them. Meanwhile Stopford's XXXIII Corps consolidated his position to the north of Mandalay and advanced south. Meanwhile Major-General D. D. Gracey's 20th Indian Division crossed the *Irrawaddy* at Myinmu and approached Mandalay from the southwest. To the astonishment of his men, when the Japanese troops, who had fought the advancing Indian soldiers with their backs to the river, ran out of ammunition, they formed ranks and marched into the river and drowned themselves.

The Siege of Meiktila: In the south, Messervy's 17th Indian Division began their rapid thrust toward Meiktila on 17 February. Ferocious resistance was met at the village of Oyin, where snipers and well-hidden bunkers delayed the advance. Tanks moved into the village and had to deal with teams of 'tank killers.' Lacking anti-tank equipment Japanese infantry teams tackled British tanks by approaching them with mines or converted artillery shells, which they placed under their tracks. These were, in effect, suicide squads. Lieutenant-Colonel Miles Smeeton noted that the Japanese troops' "desperate courage was something . . . we saw with amazement, admiration, and pity too."[14] Failing everything else, Japanese units would try to board the tanks and enter their hatches to disable their crews with hand grenades or small arms. It took a day to clear the village in which some fifty Japanese troops were killed. At one crossroads, Jaharman Sunwar of the 1st Battalion 7th Gurkha Regiment recalled that they "had machine-guns at fixed lines and the Japanese came in crowds. We slaughtered them and their corpses were like grains of rice spread out to dry. A dozer buried them."[15]

Taungtha was reached on 24 February. Still Kimura believed that these were small-scale British operations, which would be quickly dealt with by local Japanese forces. It was only with the capture of Thabutkon Airfield, a few miles from Meiktila, two days later, that Kimura finally awoke to the full threat to his strategic supply base. It was too late. He had been fully duped. At Meiktila Major-General Kasuya Tomekichi commanded just 2,500 transport and administrative staff plus 700 sundry other soldiers. Even hospitals were emptied to man the hastily constructed defensive bunkers. Slim's tanks easily overran the approaches to the town. As he had forecast, "The Japanese had no experience of these massed armored attacks and seemed quite incapable of dealing with them."[16] Nevertheless by the time that Messervy's 17th Indian Division arrived, Kasuya's troops were well dug into the town, where the operation of tanks was less effective. Slim, having failed to persuade the Royal Air Force (RAF) to fly him in to witness the assault, persuaded the US Air Force to fly him there in a B-25 Mitchell bomber.

The 28 February to 1 March saw a determined three-day battle for the town in which the attackers had to winkle out the Japanese defenders position by position. Both houses and pagodas were used as defensive positions by Japanese defenders who were well provisioned with munitions and supplies. The eastern area of the town took another three days to subdue. In places there was hand-to-hand fighting. Acting *Naik* (Corporal) Fazal Din of the 7th Battalion of the 10th Baluch Regiment was 'run-through' by the sword of a Japanese officer as he led his men against a Japanese bunker; Din wrenched the sword from the officer's hand and killed him and another two Japanese soldiers besides. He urged his men forward before he staggered back for treatment, dying as soon as he reached the medical post. He was awarded a posthumous Victoria Cross.

Another Victoria Cross was awarded to Lieutenant W. B. Weston on the last day of the battle on 3 March, when he was wounded at the entrance of a bunker and killed himself and all its occupants with a grenade. The end of the battle was marked by the suicide of fifty Japanese troops who rushed into the lake and drowned themselves. Some 2,000 Japanese were found after the attack though many more were buried in the rubble, bunkers and underground tunnels. The lake continued to disgorge bodies for weeks. Over forty-seven artillery pieces were captured or destroyed. Even more importantly an invaluable Japanese arms dump was captured and blown up.

Few Japanese surrendered. Brigade HQ complained at the lack of 'intelligence.' Notebooks and diaries were taken in abundance but there were few Japanese soldiers to interrogate. Not only did the Japanese not tend to surrender but also the Gurkhas generally refused to take prisoners. Lieutenant John Randle tried to restrain his men but his *Subedar* (junior Gurkha officer) told him, "it's no good, you're wasting your breath."[17] Outside one bunker at Meiktila, a Gurkha NCO hung the gruesome head of a Japanese officer that he had removed from its owner. It proved a popular and much visited trophy.

Kimura now had to give up any plans to counter Slim's attacks with a counter-thrust across the *Irrawaddy* aimed at encircling the British forces. Instead he charged his commanders to retake Meiktila with thrusts from the west and the north. Major-General 'Punch' Cowan, whose 17th Division had taken Meiktila, prepared its defense. Mobile attack units were organized to waylay the advancing Japanese forces. His mobile units, including tanks, took Kimura's advance troops by surprise and exacted heavy casualties. The Japanese advance was hampered by their need to advance only by night because of the Allies' total command of the air. Hurricane and Thunderbolt squadrons flew constant missions over Japanese lines. General Honda was further hindered by the inability to establish working lines of communication between the 18th and 49th Divisions under his control. The key battle took place at Kyigon Airfield to the east of Meiktila where 'Punch' Cowan relied on supplies flown in by C-47 Skytrains. Without enough troops to let Cowan establish a continuous perimeter defense, Japanese troops infiltrated the airfield during the night and had to be cleared by patrols of tanks and aircraft at dawn before supply flights could begin to operate. By 18 March Japanese positions were so entrenched and their artillery so disruptive that Allied flights into the airport had to be abandoned in favour of supply drops.

Nevertheless, the evident superiority of the Allies in the air did wonders for the morale of the troops on the ground. As George MacDonald Fraser noted in his recollections of the war in Burma, *Quartered Safe Out Here* [1993], air supply,

> was an uplifting sight . . . Fourteenth Army . . . feeding and arming its spearhead deep inside enemy territory, demonstrating that this was a siege [Meiktila] which the Japanese, for all their superior numbers, could not hope to win; those leisurely wheeling American planes were symbolic, and the sight of them droning unhindered overhead must have been a bitter one to the withdrawing Japanese armies: not a Zero in the sky, and food and ammunition in massive quantities pouring down on their opponents.[18]

Heavy fighting around the airfield and nearby villages continued for several days but eventually sweeps by British armored forces managed to destroy the remaining artillery pieces. By now Honda realized that his forces were not strong enough to retake Meiktila; his 18th Division had lost a third of their troops and half their guns, while the 49th Division suffered almost 70 percent casualties.

Slim's March into Mandalay: **[Map: 35.2B]** Meanwhile to the north, the Japanese Fifteenth Army was in full retreat. Mandalay had fallen to Stopford's XXXIII Corps on 20 March 1945 after more than three weeks of fighting. Having carefully refused to shell the Japanese stronghold on Mandalay Hill because of the wish to preserve the city's famous temples and pagodas, 19th Division had to advance one machine gun post at a time.

Thereafter Fort Dufferin, a rectangular fortress surrounded by 30-foot thick and 23-foot high stonewalls, was the next major strongpoint. After heavy losses suffered in a medieval-style siege Slim was on the verge of bypassing the Japanese stronghold when their officers suddenly appeared with white flags; an almost unprecedented surrender. Other Japanese troops had escaped through the fort's drains. Slim organized a formal celebration march into Mandalay in which 2nd, 19th and 20th Divisions took part. Mountbatten and Leese were furious not to be asked to participate. As one of Slim's colleagues observed with heavy irony, "It was apparently resented that those who were actually responsible had taken the credit."[19]

Stopford now moved south, clearing up Japanese troops caught in the loop of the *Irrawaddy River*. IV Corps, moving from northwest, started to reopen the road from the river to Meiktila. On 28 March, Kimura, realizing that his forces had been routed, ordered the remnants of his Fifteenth Army to make their way to Toungoo in the western Karen hills. Slim was typically lavish in his praise of his field commanders, particularly 'Punch' Cowan, commander of the 17th Indian Division, of whom he said, "To watch a highly skilled, experienced and resolute commander controlling a hard-fought battle is to see, not only a man triumphing over the highest mental and physical stress, but an artist producing his effects in the most complicated and difficult of all the arts."[20] Noticeably Slim also acknowledged the importance of air power in his victory—particularly that of the Americans. The Allied air forces flew 7,000 sorties during the battle and delivered 1,200 tons of supplies per day, some 90 percent of their total requirement.

The Race to Rangoon: **[Map: 35.2]** Gracey's 20th Indian Division moved south and fell on the already depleted Japanese Thirty-third Army. His corps artillery pounded Japanese troops caught in the open. Captain William Pennington, watching the scene from a forward observation position, recalled, "through my binoculars I could see our enemies' bodies being flayed and flung into the air by the tremendous power of the bombardment, limbs torn apart and scattered as if to the four corners of the earth."[21]

General Kimura's Thirty-third Army was forced to retreat southwards with the intention of making a last stand in front of Rangoon. Japanese troops hid from the Royal Air Force (RAF) by day but at night Gracey's flying columns "would settle down at the crossroads to ambush any Japanese vehicles that might come along. Japanese supply lorries would drive unsuspectingly towards us, often using full headlights, until all hell broke loose."[22] For both sides the race was now on to beat the monsoon. Kimura hoped to hold out in front of Rangoon before the monsoon broke. Slim was equally determined to take Rangoon before the rains came. His supply line, which now stretched the breadth of Burma, Assam and back to Calcutta, was already at breaking point. The monsoon might make his position untenable. Speed was therefore of the essence. Slim was aided by the fact that Japanese units were severely under-strength and almost devoid of tanks and artillery. Also the Japanese Air Force, the 64th *Sentai*, made its last contribution to the war in Burma at the end of April. Subsequently the remnants were withdrawn to Thailand. Thereafter Japanese forces were bereft of air cover.

While XXXIII Corps was charging south, in the west of Burma, Lieutenant-General Philip Christison and the Twelfth Army had been charged by Slim to conquer the Arakan Peninsula. First *Akyab* was taken. From its airfield the Royal Air Force and the US Army Air Force were able to support operations against Shwebo, Mandalay and Pagan to the south. Then amphibious assaults were made on the offshore islands of *Cheduba* and *Ramree* in the *Bay of Bengal*. *Cheduba* was unoccupied but the Japanese defenders on *Ramree* put up a courageous defense. Only twenty Japanese soldiers out of 1,000 troops surrendered. The offensive, which opened on 12 December 1945, took six weeks of heavy fighting to deliver the airfields that could give cover to the final push on Rangoon.

Allied air power was by now overwhelming. By the middle of 1945 the Imperial Japanese Air Force in Burma was down to 200 aircraft. A high percentage of these were not 'goers' because of a shortage of parts and mechanics and there was little prospect of significant supply given Japan's now chronic losses in shipping. By comparison, the US Army Air Force alone could put up over 500 aircraft of all types. Moreover the new aircraft such as the P-47 Republic Thunderbolt could significantly outperform its counterpart, the Nakajima Ki-43 'Oscar,' which had dominated the skies over Malaya and Burma in the early months of the war. The Thunderbolt could carry up to eight 0.50-inch machine guns as well as a 2,000 lb bomb load.

Improved Allied logistics and plentiful supply of aviation fuel also enabled more missions. In the four months of the 1944 monsoon, 24,000 sorties were made, some six times more than the corresponding period a year earlier. In March 1945 aerial supply would reach its peak, with 78,250 tons of supplies delivered and 27,000 military personnel transported. Bombing of railways and bridges crumbled whatever logistical infrastructure remained to the Japanese Army. The Royal Air Force (RAF), flying US-built Consolidated B-24 Liberators, could fly 2,100 miles with a normal bomb load of 5,000 lbs. Commander Lucian Ercolani of the RAF's 159-Squadron

> evolved a new method for low-level bombing to knock bridges down. Bridges are in fact, quite difficult to hit. Amongst many successes, our squadron led the flight that knocked down the famous bridge over the River Kwai. Great annoyance was caused later amongst the crews by the film [*Bridge on the River Kwai*, 1957] when it was said that the bridge was too far away for the air force to reach![23]

The Allied air forces also developed their methods of airdrops. This was a fine art particularly during the monsoon—on one occasion during a storm, a Dakota was seen to come out of a cloud upside down. An accurate drop might require up to eight passes over the dropping zone with all the risk from small arms fire that this might involve. Planes, often the Dakota, would have to have been kept in level trim to prevent supply parachutes snagging on the rudder. If daytime operations were difficult, Lieutenant-Colonel Frank Owen noted, "When the drop took place at night, with the enemy using counterfeit signals to decoy you off course, the fun really began."[24]

Meanwhile on Burma's eastern border, General Sultan, who had taken command of Y-Force after the sacking of Stilwell, drove the Japanese back from Yunnan to the Chinese, where he joined forces with General Sun's X-Force that had advanced eastwards from Assam. Together they pressed southwards. Lashio duly fell to Sun on 7 March and Sultan occupied Hsipaw, thirty-five miles to the southwest. With the Ledo Road now open the first convoy left India on 12 January 1945 and arrived some sixteen days later at the Chinese border before making the last 566 miles of the journey to Kunming. Mountbatten was again quick to claim credit, writing to Churchill and

Roosevelt, "The first part of the orders I received at Quebec has been carried out. The land route to China is open."[25]

On 23 February, any hopes that Slim had that Sultan and Sun would help in the subjugation of Japanese forces in central Burma were dashed when Lieutenant-General Albert Wedemeyer again disappointed his erstwhile colleagues when he insisted on the repatriation of X and Y-Force to fight the Japanese on the *Kuomintang's* eastern front. This was not a disappointment to Lieutenant-General Daniel Sultan, who had erroneously forecast that America's alliance with Britain would collapse if the British insisted on the re-conquest of Burma and Malaya. Sultan was another officer in a long line of senior American commanders who seemed blinkered to the fact that it was America, not Britain, which was now the great Imperial power in South East Asia. Mountbatten flew to Chongqing to try to persuade Chiang Kai-shek to change his mind. However, the Generalissimo was adamant that Chinese troops would not serve south of Mandalay.

Fortunately Slim was able to persuade Leese to retain the British 36th Division that was fighting in the north with the Northern Combat Area Command (NCAC) forces. If the withdrawal of Chinese forces was bad news, the defection of Bogyoke Aung San's Burmese National Army (BNA) was welcomed. Although Slim correctly guessed that Aung San's defection was less an apostasy and more of an opportunistic realization that it would be better for him to end up the war on the winning side, he decided that it was better at least to have him on the side of the Allies. On 17 March, Aung San, whose BNA had largely been restricted to training and communications duties, assembled his forces near Rangoon with the ostensible aim of marching to the front to fight the oncoming British forces at Toungoo. Aung San ratted on erstwhile Japanese allies and attacked his former friends. It was a desultory half-hearted assault, though after the war Aung San would claim a virtual monopoly of the bragging rights to the defeat of the Japanese Army in Burma.

Some of the majority Burmese population was less accommodating to the changing circumstances. Ba Maw set up a Supreme Defence Council to mobilize his people against the onrushing British forces. "We must now fight and win this fourth and final round with the help of Japan," he declared, "for if we lose again we shall be slaves for a very long time more."[26]

XXXIII Corps, after clearing the area to the west of Meiktila thrust southwards down the western flank of the *Irrawaddy* toward Rangoon. Chauk was captured on 18 April while the oilfields at Yenangyaung, one of the main reasons for Japan's invasion of Burma, were retaken on 26 April. Slim's 'blitzkrieg' tactics constantly surprised an enemy who had never encountered motorized forces in open battle; Slim noted, "The Japanese were bewildered by the speed, strength and direction of 20th Division's thrust. Their whole plan for the defense of the oilfields had collapsed; even their retreat was cut off."[27] Karen tribesmen joined in the rout of Kimura's forces after a general uprising against the Japanese was declared in mid-April.

Meanwhile on the eastern flank adjacent to the Karen Hills, Messervy's IV Corps advanced southwards. Heavy fighting, including having to cope with numbers of

Japanese suicide squads, held up the British forces at Pyawbwe and Yamethin. In one *banzai* charge by two companies of Japanese against a platoon of Gurkhas, fighting continued until all that remained was a pile of Japanese bodies around them. George MacDonald Fraser noted, "When the Gurkhas were finally withdrawn it was discovered that they hadn't a single round of ammunition among them."[28] The *Battle of Pyawbe* was General Honda's last 'hurrah.' It ended with a decisive victory for Slim. The battle "shattered Honda's army, but it did more—it settled the fate of Rangoon. The way to the coast was now open."[29]

Honda's army, now reduced to the size of a division, fought bravely but could not hold up the enemy for long. Surrounded on numbers of occasions, Honda even left a message at one location saying, "General Honda was here. Try harder next time."[30] Having written his will, Honda and Colonel Masanobu Tsuji slipped on *longyis* and escaped, disguised as Burmese villagers. IV Corps then raced to Toungoo to capture the airfield before the Japanese could 'dig-in.' The retreating Japanese were hammered by the Karens on the ground and by the Royal Air Force from the air. Toungoo was captured without a fight after a fifty-mile advance in just three days. Thirty miles south of Toungoo, the 1st Division of Bose's Indian National Army (INA) offered their surrender. From here the 17th Division advanced to Pegu, just 50 miles from Rangoon, occupying the town on 29 April. Japanese commanders blew up the bridge and although engineers managed to establish a Bailey bridge, the early arrival of the monsoon that night prevented a crossing.

The Japanese defended the south bank of the river in strength and even launched a counter-attack that temporarily cut off the road back to Toungoo. With his supply lines stretched, Slim had to put his troops on half rations. However, it was clear on his arrival at the front that spirits were high. After apologizing for the lack of supplies, a gunner told Slim to "Put us on quarter rations, but give us the ammo and we'll get you into Rangoon."[31] However, the race to be first into Rangoon was lost. Mountbatten beat him to it with a sly amphibious landing that won him the prize after Slim and his troops had done all the hard slog. Slim was just forty-one miles short. Slim shared the disappointment of his troops who felt robbed of an entrance into the capital of Burma, which they understandably felt was theirs. As George MacDonald Fraser observed, "soldiers have a strong primitive sense of fairness: no one promised them Rangoon, but they felt there had been an understanding, and it had been broken."[32]

Mountbatten, no doubt gratified by his own capture of Rangoon, could afford to be magnanimous and with unusual good grace and due acknowledgement would later write, "Lieutenant-General Slim's plan, of which Lieutenant-General Leese and I entirely approved, was as brilliant in its conception as in its successful execution; for it laid the foundation for the complete destruction of the Japanese Army in Burma."[33]

EXTRACT DIGIT: The early arrival of the monsoon did not result in a fierce fight for Rangoon. Kimura chose not to defend the city and Mountbatten, able at last to launch a mini-version of his beloved Operation DRACULA, landed paratroopers at the mouth of the *Irrawaddy River* on 1 May and a Marine force south of Rangoon early on 2 May. Allied planes flying over the city the next morning observed that the British prisoners at Rangoon Jail had painted signs on the roof that succinctly stated "BRITISH HERE," "JAPS GONE" and "EXTRACT DIGIT"; a clear exhortation to the British Army to 'take its finger out' and occupy the city.

The urgency of the prisoners was understandable. Before the evacuation of Rangoon, prisoners, such as Major Hugh Seagrim, a British officer who had led Karen tribesmen against the Japanese, were executed. Arthur Sharpe, a Bristol Beaufighter pilot, described how Seagrim, later awarded the George Cross, "refused to call the Japs 'master' and persisted in making cheeky remarks to them. He had us laughing all the time."[34] Seagrim earned his family the unique distinction of having siblings with posthumous George and Victoria Crosses; his brother Lieutenant-Colonel Dereck Seagrim was killed in North Africa in 1943 while leading an assault on two machine gun nests in the *Battle of Wadi Akarit*. Other unfortunates murdered towards the end of the Burma Campaign were the crewmembers of a Royal Air Force Liberator who were tortured and beheaded by the *Kempeitai*.

On 3 May 1945 British forces entered an almost deserted city. The battle for Burma was won. At Rangoon's ice-factory, Lieutenant Sydney Pickford of 1st Battalion, 8th Gurkha Regiment, took the surrender of the Indian National Army (INA) troops. As he moved up the jetty, he found his path blocked by an old Chinaman with a beard to his waist; he was "kneeling with his hands clasped in the attitude of prayer. Tears were running down his face. 'Oh, thank God you are back Sir. Thank God the British are back. Now we can live again.' "[35]

Fighting continued after the surrender of Rangoon against the 'flotsam and jetsam' of 70,000 Japanese troops dispersed around Burma. Through Burma's eastern hills, 27,000 Japanese troops, the remnants of Kimura's armies, set out to make the arduous attempt to escape eastwards. The 54th Division was now reduced to just 400 grams of rice per day and troops foraged for bamboo shoots and edible grasses. Protein came in the form of snakes and lizards. In the hills, Japanese troops, in a state of complete despair, pulled pins on grenades to end their misery. Ambushing them between the *Sittang* and *Salween Rivers*, some 12,000 of Kimura's troops were killed and 740 were taken prisoner. The *Battle of the Breakout* reversed the result of the tragic events at the *River Sittang* three years earlier. British and Indian losses were just ninety-five men killed and 322 wounded. The Royal Air Force (RAF) joined in the hunt with Air Chief Marshal Keith Hunt encouraging "a Jap killing competition between squadron."[36] In July alone it was estimated that the Twelfth Army killed 11,500 Japanese men for the loss of just ninety-six killed. During the day, 200 bodies a day drifted down the *Sittang*. Those prisoners that were taken were in such poor condition as to arouse pity from British troops. Ernest Gordon wrote, "They were in a shocking state. I have never seen men filthier. The uniforms were encrusted with mud, blood and excrement. Their wounds, sorely inflamed and full of pus, crawled with maggots."[37] In the subsequent months up until the surrender on 15 August, Kimura's armies, now starving and devoid of weapons and supplies, lost as many men as he had done at the *Battle of the Irrawaddy River*. In aggregate it is thought that of the 153,000 Japanese troops estimated to have opposed the Fourteenth Army at the start of the *Battle of the Irrawaddy River*, some 93,000 died by the time that Japan surrendered in August 1945.

A delighted Churchill radioed his congratulations to Mountbatten in Kandy: "In spite of diminution and disappointment you and your men have done all and more than your directive required."[38] The victory was also a remarkable feat of arms by Indian troops who comprised some 80 percent of the British Fourteenth Army. Some would undoubtedly have observed that when the war was over Britain had a debt of honor to give independence to India.

The Attempted Sacking of Slim: Slim's immediate reward for his great victory was to be sacked from the Fourteenth Army. The haughty and no doubt jealous Lieutenant-General Leese planned a Malayan Campaign without him. Seemingly Mountbatten, perhaps also jealous and with a disposition to take other men's credit, supported the decision. Slim was quietly furious and declined to take command of the smaller Twelfth Army charged with taking over mopping-up operations in Burma and its civilian administration. Though Slim was prepared to slip into retirement if necessary, when Brigadier 'Tubby' Lethbridge went to commiserate with him, Slim threatened, "This happened to me once before, and I bloody well took the job of the man that sacked me. I'll bloody well do it again."[39] Slim may have been a quietly spoken unhistrionic officer but he was no 'pussycat.'

The backlash against Leese and Mountbatten was ferocious. Churchill and Alanbrooke were furious. In his diary of 17 May, Alanbrooke noted, "Leese is going quite wild and doing mad things, prepare a fair rap on the knuckles for him!"[40] Mountbatten backed down and blamed Leese. In the end it was Leese, the foppish guardsman, who was sacked by Mountbatten on Alanbrooke's orders. "Drafted a letter to Mountbatten advising him to get rid of Oliver Leese who has proved to be a failure in South East Asia command. It is very disappointing."[41] He was replaced by Slim, who was promoted to full General rank and made Commander in Chief, Allied Forces, South-East Asia. It was a re-run of Lieutenant-General Irwin's attempt to sack Slim in 1943.

The Battle of the Irrawaddy was an extraordinary feat of arms that has rarely received due attention. At the same time that Slim was forging his bridgeheads across the *Irrawaddy*, General Montgomery in Europe was crossing the relatively narrow *River Rhine*. Backed by the logistical infrastructure of railways and the West's mighty industrial provisions, it was a far easier operation than that accomplished by Slim.

The 'Mandalay Feint,' used to disguise the attack on Meiktila, was one of the most daring and tactically brilliant actions of the entire war. It showed that Slim was not just a superb defensive tactician as he had shown in the largely immobile action at the *Battle of Imphal,* but was capable of planning and organizing expansive and fluid campaigns of great complexity and tactical subtlety against a Japanese commander, Kimura, who was far from unskilful. Slim's ability as a strategist and tactician was backed up by a supreme command of logistics. In the course of his Burma career, Slim had fought a courageous fighting retreat from Burma, reorganized, trained and galvanised his Fourteenth Army, had rebutted the Japanese invasion of India with the decisive defensive encounter with the Japanese army at the *Battle of Imphal* and had re-conquered Burma in a single campaign with his spectacular victory at the *Battle of the Irrawaddy River*.

By any criteria General Slim deserves to be considered the equal or better of any general of *World War II*. In the *Pacific War* only Generals Yamashita, Iida, Vandegrift, Wootten, Krueger and Eichelberger stand comparison, though none of them faced the range of challenges presented to Slim. Without question Slim's reputation was diminished by comparison with others by the fact that he operated in an area that was secondary to Britain's main interests in Europe and only marginal to America's strategic thrust in the *Pacific War*, particularly after China ceased to be seen as useful as a possible jump-off point for an invasion of Japan.

Remarkably, in their neglect of Slim's achievements, British commanders, the men he reported to, were even more culpable than the Americans. It is noticeable in his edited *War Diaries* [2002] Lord Alanbrooke, Chief of Staff of the British Army, Slim is only mentioned half a dozen occasions, less than half the number of entries for society painter Oswald Birley and his wife Rhoda. As for the Irrawaddy Campaign, he mentions with faint surprise in January that in Burma, "operations there have taken quite a different turn, and there is now just a possibility of taking Rangoon from the North!"[42] Alanbrooke's lack of knowledge or apparent interest in what was happening on the ground in Burma was compounded by his ignorance of the difficulties of terrain and enemy that Slim's forces had to overcome; he merely surmises that victory is possible "due to the Japanese forces beginning to crumple up and to be demoralized."[43] This was certainly not how it seemed on the ground.

In some histories of the *Pacific War* the entire British campaign in Burma in 1945 rates little more than a paragraph. Indeed, truth be told, while a great achievement in its own right, the *Battle of the Irrawaddy River* had little impact on the outcome of the war in the *Pacific*. Slim's self-effacing manner, by contrast to the bombastic Montgomery and Patton, as well as the egomaniacal MacArthur, also served to leave him undeservedly lagging behind the reputation of his contemporaries.

The popular writer George MacDonald Fraser, known for his novel *Flashman* [1969], who served under General Slim in the Border Regiment in Burma, summed him up in a brilliant vignette:

> His delivery was blunt, matter-of-fact, without gestures
> or mannerisms ... there was no nonsense of "gather
> round" or jumping on boxes; he just stood with his thumb
> hooked in his carbine sling and talked about how we had
> caught Jap off-balance and were going to annihilate him
> in the open; there was no exhortation or ringing clichés,

no jokes or self-conscious barrack room slang . . . You knew, when he talked of smashing the Jap, that to him it meant not only arrows on a map but clearing of bunkers and going in under shell fire; that he had the head of a general with the heart of a private soldier.[44]

Part VII

Destruction of Japan's Homeland:
February 1945–August 1945

36 Iwo Jima: The Iconic Battle of the Pacific War

[February 1945–March 1945]

[Maps: 36.1, 36.2, 36.3]

Luzon or Formosa? **[Map: 36.1]** In September 1944, after Admiral Spruance's return to *Pearl Harbor* from his successful conclusion to the *Marianas* Campaign, his thoughts turned to the next step in the Navy's drive toward Japan's home islands. Admiral Nimitz told him to go back to California for a holiday. He was ordered to report back in two weeks: "the next operation is going to be *Formosa* and *Amoy*"[1] Nimitz told him. Spruance responded "I would prefer taking *Iwo Jima* and *Okinawa*." Nimitz insisted, "Well, it's going to be *Formosa*."[2] The real debate however, which had plagued the US Joint Chiefs of Staff for the best part of a year, was whether it would be better to take *Luzon* or *Formosa*.

As many others had done before him, Spruance had studied the maps and believed that an invasion of *Iwo Jima* and *Okinawa* would provide the airfields that the United States needed to dominate the *East China Sea* and complete the economic strangulation of Japan. Unlike *Formosa* a thousand miles to the west, *Iwo Jima* lay on the direct route to Tokyo from the *Marianas*. Interior lines of communication and supply from *Saipan, Guam* and *Tinian* seemed to make the advance to *Iwo Jima* and then *Okinawa* the logical path. In spite of Admiral King's seeming cast iron support for the invasion of *Formosa* from the US Joint Chiefs of Staff's and the two volume study that supported it, Spruance was adamant that it was a plan that would never be adopted and ordered his staff not to waste their time working on it.

Spruance returned to California to see his wife and daughter in the small town of Monrovia. His grump at being told that he would have to invade *Formosa* was compounded by the loss of his friend and Chief of Staff, Captain Carl Moore, who at Admiral King's insistence was replaced by Rear-Admiral Cayley Davis. King and Nimitz had insisted that all four-star admirals should have a three-star chief of staff; furthermore 'sailor' ('black shoe') admirals were required to have 'aviator' ('brown shoe') chiefs of staff while 'aviator' ('brown shoe') admirals were required to have 'sailor' ('black shoe') chiefs of staff. For Moore, promotion to Rear-Admiral, which would have enabled him to stay on in the role of Chief of Staff to Spruance, was repeatedly turned down by King. Spruance thus harbored a double grievance toward the head of the Navy in Washington.

Realising that the operational team built by Moore was superb in every respect, Rear-Admiral Davis made no attempt to change it and concentrated instead on making sure that Spruance was liberated from trivia. Davis later wrote, "Spruance was a genuine super-ability [officer] to be guarded against minor distractions. I made up my mind that I would do all in my power to keep his mind free of all deadening inconsequentialities that can waste time. . ."[3]

As it turned out Spruance was correct in his predictions about the likelihood of the invasion of *Formosa* going ahead. Shortly before his scheduled leave in California was ended, he was shown a paper prepared by Commander in Chief, Pacific Area Command (CINCPAC) in which Nimitz recommended that the planned invasion of *Formosa* should be abandoned because he did not have enough troops for the task. Furthermore the Joint Chiefs of Staff could not provide reinforcements or supplies to sustain the invasion of *Formosa*. The loss of airfields in southern China as a result of General Shinroku Hata's Operation ICHI-GO also reduced the attractiveness of taking *Formosa*; its conquest was now seen as being likely to be overly expensive in terms of casualties. Moreover without control of southern China, Japanese infiltration from the nearby mainland made *Formosa*'s conquest doubly difficult.

Otherwise, before these developments, 1,258 miles from Tokyo, *Formosa* could have been an ideal stepping-stone toward the Japanese home islands. American occupation of *Formosa* could have cut off supply to Japan from either the *South China Sea* or mainland China. Japanese airpower on *Luzon* could also have been neutralised. Furthermore *Formosa* was close enough to Japan to base B-29 Superfortresses for the continued pounding of Japanese cities. Indeed it is easy to see why, for so long, it was the preferred invasion destination over *Luzon* for Naval Chief of Staff, Admiral King and indeed the Joint Chiefs of staff.

By comparison northern *Luzon*, favored by some factions within the Army and Navy, was 1,750 miles away from Tokyo, just within the 'brochure' range of a fully loaded B-29 Superfortress, whose notoriously unreliable engines left little margin for error. *Luzon* posed not only the problem of range but also the question of supply, both of bombs and aviation fuel, as well as the logistics of maintaining crews and their aircraft. MacArthur believed, or at least used it as an argument to justify his invasion, that the fall of *Luzon*, the main island of the Philippines, was required to sustain American prestige in the Philippines and Asia. It was a spurious argument but one with which he berated Roosevelt at their famous meeting in *Honolulu* in the summer of 1944.

However, the main reason for the abandonment of the *Formosa* invasion in favour of *Luzon*, finally settled in a Joint Chiefs of Staff directive on 3 October 1944, was the schedule that MacArthur laid out for the reconquest of the Philippines. His plan to make the jump from New Guinea to *Leyte* in October, which had been triggered by Halsey's incorrect summer intelligence that the island was barely defended, moved up the time schedule for a possible invasion of *Luzon* to 20 December 1944. It was a time schedule with which the pro-*Formosa* commanders, led by Admiral King (Chief of Naval Operations), Admiral Nimitz (Commander in Chief, Pacific) and supported by General 'Hap' Arnold (head of US Army Air Force) and Army Deputy Chief of Staff, Lieutenant-General Joseph McNarney, could not complete. With *Luzon* taken, with its ability to control the *South China Sea*, the need for *Formosa* would become redundant. The pro-*Luzon* camp included General MacArthur, Vice-Admiral 'Bull' Halsey, Vice-Admiral Kinkaid and the Army's Chief Logistician Lieutenant Brehon Somervell. Unusually in the turf wars of the *Pacific* campaigns, both the Navy and Army were split on the subject.

Interestingly, Army Chief of Staff General George Marshall favored *Formosa* but thought that both *Luzon* and *Formosa* could be bypassed by going direct to *Kyushu*— probably via *Okinawa*. It was also the strategy seemingly favored by Spruance. Critically however, over the summer and early autumn, Admiral William Leahy, Roosevelt's close confidante that he had brought out of retirement to become his own Chief of Staff as well as the Chairman of the Joint Chiefs of Staff, changed sides to become a supporter of the *Luzon* invasion. It should be noted that MacArthur's persistent lying about the *Leyte* campaign being completed at the end of October, extreme even by his own mendacious standards, was almost certainly driven by his commitment to the Joint Chiefs of Staff to get to *Luzon* by 20 December—though ultimately the invasion would have to be put back to 9 January.

The choice of *Luzon* had knock-on effects. With a campaign to invade Japan from *Luzon* being unsuitable and *Formosa* off the menu, Admiral King naturally turned to the more direct route to Japan's southern island of *Okinawa* via *Iwo Jima*. After opting for *Luzon* the route to Japan would have to take in these two islands. *Okinawa* was close enough to mainland Japan and large enough to provide the airports and harbour necessary for the assault on the mainland later envisaged by Operation OLYMPIC. Airfields on *Okinawa*, needed for the tactical bombing support that would be required by any invasion of Japan, would lop 500 miles off the 1,460-mile distance from *Saipan* to Tokyo. Meanwhile the distance from the city of Naha on *Okinawa* to Kagoshima City on the southern island of *Kyushu* was just 411 miles.

Furthermore the American bomber commanders strongly favored an *Iwo Jima* invasion. For the US Army Air Force and officers such as Spruance, *Iwo Jima* was simply the most direct stepping-stone to *Okinawa*, an island whose proximity to Japan as well as it harbors and airfields were sufficient to sustain both a bombing campaign as well as preparations for the invasion of Japan itself. Indeed *Okinawa*'s unlikely importance lay in the increasing role of strategic bombing as the perceived 'low-cost' way to defeat Japan. Hope remained that strategic bombing aimed at the economic reduction Japan would force it to surrender. *Iwo Jima* was situated 762 miles from Tokyo, half way from the *Marianas* and in an almost direct line.

Herein lay the logic to the capture of *Iwo Jima*. When asked by Spruance about the value of *Iwo Jima* aboard the USS *Indianapolis* at *Ulithi Atoll* on 28 January 1945, Major-General Curtis LeMay responded categorically, "Without Iwo Jima, I couldn't bomb Japan effectively."[4] For LeMay Japanese control of *Iwo Jima* presented two problems: first its radar stations could alert Japan of impending bomber raids enabling it to put up its fighter defenses: secondly fighters based at *Iwo Jima* could attack both outgoing and returning bombers. By acquiring *Iwo Jima*, these problems could be nullified. As for the advantages of *Iwo Jima* coming into American hands, the US Army Air Force could station long-range P-51 Mustang escort fighters there to accompany the B-29 raids; an accompaniment that, from the *Marianas*, was out of the Mustang's range. Moreover, although *Iwo Jima* did not have the land mass or deep water ports needed to accommodate a B-29 Superfortress infrastructure, the island could provide an emergency airfield for Superfortresses either damaged or mechanically sick after their bombing missions to Japan. Ultimately, these were the crucial arguments that determined that *Iwo Jima* had to be acquired before the invasion of *Okinawa* in the southerly *Ryuku* chain of Japanese islands. The Joint Chiefs of Staff directive of 3 October thus gave the go-ahead for the attacks on *Iwo Jima* and then *Okinawa* to run concurrently with MacArthur's campaign on *Luzon*.

Lieutenant-General Tadamichi Kuribayashi: Kuribayashi arrived at Chidori Airfield No.1 on *Iwo Jima Island* on 19 June 1944. It was a suicide mission, a fact that Kuribayashi understood so well that he told his wife Yoshii not to expect the return of his ashes. When Japan was defending its outer perimeter, there were thousands of possible invasion targets for Commander-in-Chief, Pacific Area Command (CINCPAC) to choose from, but as the noose tightened around Japan, the list of targets became short and quite obvious. *Iwo Jima* was one such. For Japan's Imperial General HQ strategy forecasters, an American invasion of *Iwo Jima* was a racing certainty. Kuribayashi's task, on orders signed by Prime Minister Tojo, was to defend *Iwo Jima*, the main island of the *Bonin Island Chain* that lies due south of Tokyo. Tojo told him, "The entire Army and the nation will depend on you for the defense of that key island."[5] In recognition of the arduous nature of his task, he was even accorded an audience with Emperor Hirohito.

Kuribayashi was not a typical product of the Japanese Army. Born to a minor samurai family in Nagano prefecture, Kuribayashi possessed a natural talent for writing both prose and poetry and aspired to be a journalist. Nevertheless he chose to enter the Imperial Japanese Army Academy where he became a cavalry officer, graduating thirty-fifth in his class at the Army War College in 1923. After attaining the rank of captain he was appointed as Deputy Military *attaché* to Washington in 1928. Kuribayashi soon became acquainted with the culture and power of the United States. He studied at Harvard but more importantly travelled widely with eyes open. Later he recalled, "I was taught how to drive by some American officers, and I bought a car. I went around the States, and I knew the close connections between the military and industry. I saw the plant area of Detroit, too. By one button push, all the industries will be mobilized for military business."[6] A prescient observation.

His American experience combined with his natural intelligence made him one of the few high-ranking officers with a realistic view of American power. As he wrote to his wife, "The United States is the last country in the world that Japan should fight. Its industrial potentiality is huge and fabulous and the people are energetic and versatile."[7] Kuribayashi did not just make his opinions known in private letters; he became well known for his outspoken views on the need to reach a negotiated settlement with the

United States. From the earliest stages he considered the war to be unwinnable. Indeed in *Letters from Iwo Jima* [2007], Kumiko Kakehashi's account of the battle as seen through the letters of the participants, she concludes that Kuribayashi's reputation as a defeatist yet patriotic soldier was the reason for his appointment to lead the suicide defense of the island.

Yet there were more logical reasons for his appointment. After his experience as chief of staff of the Twenty Third Army under General Sakai, Kuribayashi was transferred to the 2nd Imperial Guards Division, where he commanded a mixed Army and Navy garrison including veterans of the Special Naval Landing Force (SNLF). It was at least relevant experience, even if the eventual outcome was inevitably going to be defeat. Kuribayashi determined to make the taking of *Iwo Jima* as expensive a campaign as was possible; as the historian James Bradley has noted, "Kuribayashi had lived in America. He knew our national character. That's why he deliberately chose to fight in a way that would relentlessly drive up the number of casualties. I think he hoped American public opinion would shift toward wanting to bring war with Japan to a rapid end."[8] In this respect his thinking was entirely in line with Imperial General HQ's strategy at this stage of the war.

Building the Killing Machine: **[Map: 36.2]** Thus on arrival at *Iwo Jima*, Kuribayashi, this most cultured of men, set about turning the island into a killing machine. He had eight months to prepare. Civilians were ordered off the island except for Korean labourers who were kept to build a network of tunnels and caves from the soft volcanic rock of which the island was made. Kuribayashi's plan was to rely entirely on 'inner' defense. In spite of his command, he had to battle to convince his subordinates. Colonel Kiyoshi Uribe, believing that the beaches around Chidori Airfield offered the only landing ground, argued vigorously for a traditional pillbox defense of the beaches. Though, as Major Yoshitaka Horie pointed out, "How long did our guns last along the beaches at Saipan and Guam? Will you please show me just how effective the beach pillboxes at Tarawa were? Frontal defense against hundreds of naval guns and aircraft is futile."[9]

Although Kuribayashi eventually made a few concessions to the obstinate Colonel Urabe, the main defensive plan was to cede Chidori Airfield No.1 and the central plain of the island to the invaders. Two unlinked defense zones were therefore created. Volcanic Mount Suribachi (literally 'Mount Grinder'), 169 meters high, that towers over the island from its pointed southern tip was constructed as a stand-alone defensive zone with defenders dug into caves and tunnels. North of Chidori Airfield No.1 and in front of Chidori Airfield No.2 a first outer defense perimeter was constructed coast-to-coast consisting of blockhouses and pillboxes. These were built to withstand the heavy bombing and naval artillery pounding that was fully expected.

A second major line of defense was constructed coast-to-coast about 300 yards to the north but still bisecting the end of Chidori No.2's runway; a final defensive line was constructed a further 300 yards back. In all some 750 pillboxes were constructed along with 1,500 man-made caves and sixteen miles of tunnels linking the entire edifice. Throughout the defense system, mortars (mainly 12.6-inch spigot mortars) and artillery (including Colonel Baron Takeichi Nishi's dug-in tanks) were hidden and camouflaged and converging fields of fire were arranged with the installation of heavy machine guns. The preparations were immaculate and brilliantly conceived for the task ahead. During the battle Lieutenant-General Holland M. Smith, Commander, Fleet Marine Force Pacific, would exclaim, "I don't know who he is, but the Japanese General running this show is one smart bastard."[10]

In addition to the constructed defenses the island's northern zone offered formidable natural defenses with volcanic hills, gullies, jagged rocky outcrops and gorges. Kuribayashi's instructions to his men were clear: "Once the enemy invades the island every man will resist until the end, making his position his tomb. Every man will do his best to kill ten enemy soldiers."[11]

Nimitz was not unaware of the challenges presented by the taking of *Iwo Jima* in spite of its diminutive size. This volcanic outcrop of a defunct volcano covered a mere twenty-one square miles, a third of the size of *Manhattan*. On a map *Iwo Jima* looks like a diamond-shaped jagged shark's tooth with Mount Suribachi at the sharp end looking like a misshaped knob of mouldy putty placed as an afterthought; from the ground it was "like a sea monster with the little dead volcano for the head, and the beach area for the neck and all the rest of its scrubby, brown cliffs for the body."[12] John Lardner of the *New Yorker* described *Iwo Jima* as "a miserable piece of real estate . . . no water, no bird, no butterflies, no discernible animal life, nothing but sands and clay, hump-backed hills, stunted trees, knife edge kunai grass in which mites who carry scrub typhus live, and a stead, dry, dusty wind."[13]

Spruance's Plans for the Invasion of Iwo Jima: If Spruance was delighted that King had been forced to abandon the *Formosa* strategy, he was quickly disabused about how easy it would be to take *Iwo Jima*. Marine Commander Lieutenant-General Holland Smith told Spruance quite bluntly, "It will be the toughest place we have had to take. I don't know what anybody wants it for, but I'll take it."[14] He was not the only doomster. At an earlier conference on *Hawaii* with President Roosevelt and Nimitz, MacArthur, who was pitching the invasion of the Philippines as the low cost route to Tokyo, had warned "against the Naval concept of frontal assault against the strongly held island positions of Iwo Jima and Okinawa."[15] In the event, campaigns to liberate *Leyte Island* and *Luzon* cost 48,000 American casualties—hardly cost free, particularly as *Luzon* was too far away from Japan to be used as an assembly and staging point for an invasion of Japan.

The first moves to degrade *Iwo Jima* by heavy bombing and naval shelling proved disappointing. In spite of the now overwhelming superiority of American firepower, *Iwo Jima* continued to be able to send fighters to intercept the B-29 bombing missions over Japan. Holland Smith asked for ten days of bombardment of *Iwo Jima* at the beginning of February 1945 before the landing of Marines. However, Vice-Admiral Turner pointed out that the necessary US battleships were tied up with the support of MacArthur's operations on *Luzon*. In the event the prolonged engagement in *Luzon* meant that only two of the seven battleships identified for use in the bombardment of *Iwo Jima* were made available. If the surface forces came straight from *Luzon* there was every chance that they would have run out of ordnance long before ten days were up. Resupply of battleships and heavy cruisers at sea was at little more than an experimental stage and would therefore require bombardment groups to make the 1,800 mile round trip to *Ulithi Atoll* in order to rearm themselves.

Turner proposed an intensive three-day bombardment that would retain an element of surprise in the timing of the invasion. The Marines countered with a request of four days. Spruance agreed with Turner's more limited offering. His main reasoning was that he doubted whether the simultaneous three-day carrier attack on Tokyo's airfields and other targets could be sustained for more than three days. It was felt that these raids were needed to supress the number of attacks that Japan could launch at the Marines' amphibious landings. Spruance was no doubt concerned that his capital ships would become the main target for Japan-based aircraft and particularly its *kamikaze*.

Availability of ordnance was also an issue and Spruance argued, "There is a limit to the quantity of ammunition which can be made available for pre-D-Day bombardment and no advantage is seen in delivering that quantity in four days rather than in three."[16] Meanwhile the US Navy was concerned that in spite of the seemingly crushing weight of Major-General Curtis LeMay's B-29 bombardment of Japan, their aircraft manufacturing output seemed to be increasing. He blamed the lack of accuracy of high altitude bombing for the problem and wondered whether Spruance's carrier forces might be able to direct more accurate fire on Japan's aircraft factories. Spruance thus directed Mitscher's Task Force 58 to attack factories as well as airfields, "We would use our accuracy to attack military targets and would leave attacks on the civilian population to the Army Air Force."[17] It was an interesting comment in light of the post-war debate relating to the morality of urban bombing. It was not until the beginning of March that LeMay worked out how to use his B-29s to degrade Japanese Industry. [See **Chapter 38: LeMay's B-29 Superfortresses over Japan: Cities in Ashes**]

In the first week of February 1945 Spruance made final preparations for his fleet assembled at *Ulithi Atoll* and, after a brief visit with Nimitz, set off on 8 February for *Saipan* where he would join up with Turner and Holland Smith and their Joint Expeditionary Force. Here final rehearsals were made for the amphibious landing on *Iwo Jima*. Meanwhile Spruance left behind Vice-Admiral 'Pete' Mitscher at *Ulithi Atoll* where he was making final preparations for the raid on Tokyo with his five carrier Task Groups that comprised 16 carriers, 8 fast battleships, 1 battle-cruiser, 16 cruisers, 81 destroyers and 1,200 planes.

On 13 and 14 February Spruance, aboard the *Indianapolis*, made a *rendezvous* with Mitscher's Task Force 58 some 500 miles east of *Iwo Jima*. They completed a final refueling before their advance to Tokyo or "Indian country" as some of Mitscher's staff called it.[18] In strict radio silence Spruance and Mitscher charged at full speed toward

Tokyo in stormy seas hoping to spring a surprise attack. Destroyer pickets sank a Japanese fishing boat and a single plane. At dawn on 16 February aircraft took off from Mitscher's carriers through what Spruance described as the "the damndest, rottenest weather I could think of."[19] Japanese radio stations gave no indication of anything untoward. Complete surprise was achieved. The bomber pilots found that Tokyo was lightly defended and they destroyed an estimated 350 aircraft on the ground. Airfields and their installations were degraded. Thirty-three ships were sunk or damaged. The planned attacks on Tokyo's aircraft factories were less successful. Contrary to the predictions of his team of weathermen, southern Tokyo where the aircraft factories were located, was in Mitscher's words "weathered out."[20] Thirty-two American aircraft were lost during the day. At sea there were no losses apart from damage to two destroyers that collided during the night.

Spruance decided to resume the attacks on 17 February, this time hoping for better weather. But by noon the weather was worsening and further strikes were cancelled. Those already on their way did manage hits on two aircraft engine factories and a Japanese light carrier was sunk at anchorage. *Iwo Jima*, whose amphibious assault was less than forty-eight hours away, now beckoned. By mid-afternoon Spruance's fleet was underway back toward *Iwo Jima* with Spruance promising "to return and finish what we had started."[21]

Bombardment and Landing at Iwo Jima: **[Map: 36.3]** The invasion of *Iwo Jima*, which had been authorized on 3 October 1944, began with an intensive three-day barrage by naval artillery and B-29 bombers on 15 February 1945. Each ship was allocated a target zone on *Iwo Jima* to ensure an even blanketing of the island. Although the bombardment was considerably less than the ten days requested by Major-General Harry Schmidt of the Marine Corps, it is doubtful whether it would have achieved more than a limited success given the nature of the defense works prepared by Kuribayashi. Reporter Robert Sherrod reported, "On Iwo Jima the Japanese dug themselves in so deeply that all the explosives in the world could hardly have reached them."[22]

The US naval fleet comprised 116 ships including 16 carriers with 1,200 planes, 8 newly built battleships, 15 cruisers, 77 destroyers and 100,000 sailors and Marines. John Marquand of *Harper's Magazine* described the scene as looking "like a Hollywood production, except that it was a three billion, not a three million dollar extravagance."[23] At 8.59 a.m. precisely, members of 3rd, 4th and 5th Marine divisions disgorged from their amphibious assault craft on the southeastern beaches of *Iwo Jima*. With their broad beaches of dark grey volcanic sand and low escarpments (compared to the narrower beaches and high escarpments of the western approaches), it was the obvious landing place for Holland Smith's Marines. First-Lieutenant Barber Conable of the 13th Marine Artillery recalled, "The beach was soft, black volcanic ash and very steep. Bulldozers had to pull the DUKWs [six-wheeled amphibious transports] and the guns up the beach."[24] At first, under instructions from Kuribayashi, there was no Japanese response; no machine gun tracer bullets raking the gloomy grey beaches. The plan was to let the

US Marines land large numbers of troops and equipment before letting loose a firestorm from artillery, mortars and machine guns.

US Marines, somewhat surprised by the absence of Japanese defenders advanced across the western beaches and over the modest escarpment covered in wild grass without a tree in sight. More experienced soldiers were not surprised; Warrant-Officer Norman Hatch recalled,

> I went ashore on Iwo Jima right after the first wave. Once I knew the philosophy of the Japanese, I promised myself I'd always go in the first wave, I wanted to get on the beach and dig in before things hit the fan, and sure enough, that's what happened. They let them get on the beach and gave them hell after that.[25]

Advancing toward Chidori Airport, the leading Marines were suddenly cut down by concealed underground positions. Kuribayashi's death machine roared into action. It turned into a battle like no other in *World War II*. Japan's defenders had the advantage over attackers. Mobility, which characterized the advantage usually afforded the attacker in this *époque*, was entirely nullified in a fight that had to be won hole by hole, pillbox by pillbox and cave by cave. By the end of the first day of fighting, 600 Americans lay dead and a further 2,000 more had been wounded. Unusually, some of the highest casualties were engineers of the 133rd Seabees. The western beaches were strewn with wrecked machines, body parts and mangled bodies. At 5.00 p.m. a sickened Keith Wheeler told Robert Sherrod of *Life* magazine, "There's more hell in there than I've seen in the rest of the war put together."[26] The noise was almost unbearable. Sherrod noted,

> As the shells burst, as they crashed and shrieked . . . one of the wounded rose from his stretcher. He rose slowly, bending at the waist. His head was bare and his arms were straight and rigid at his side . . . He sat mouth open . . . and screamed. "Oh my God! My God . . . Good God Almighty!" The corporal sobbed into the dirt.[27]

In addition to standard mortars, *Iwo Jima*'s defenders also used a 'spigot' mortar that was unique to the Japanese army. Consisting of a steel tube resting on a steel base-plate fixed to a wooden base, the mortar could hold a massive 675 lb shell 13-inches wide which was fitted around the top of the steel tube. Range was adjusted by the amount of gunpowder used at the base of the round. When used in unison as planned by *Iwo Jima*'s defenders, the spigot mortars produced a fearsome sound which came to be known as 'screaming Jesus' by the Marines. It was probably better known for its noise rather than for its kill rate though Gunnery-Sergeant John Basilone, the best-known Marine hero of *Guadalcanal* was killed with four others by a Japanese mortar round on the first day on *Iwo Jima*. Basilone, who, on the approaches to Chidori Airport No. 1 took out a blockhouse with grenades, was posthumously awarded a Navy Cross to add to the Medal of Honor that he had previously won.

A Flag on Mount Suribachi: Apart from the battle for the airfields, Marines from the 5th Division took on the fight for Mount Suribachi whose heights commanded the airfields. Here guns would fire from holes dug into the mountain; these would immediately be covered to prevent American artillery getting bearings on their positions. As Corporal Glen Buzzard noted, "Most of the guns were in caves, and they slide right up to the opening, fire, then slide back. They'd put camouflage over them, brush, netting, whatever they had."[28] Progress on Suribachi by 28th Regiment, 5th Marine Division was painstaking. Led by the recently appointed Colonel Harry Liversedge, a former Olympic athlete who had won a bronze medal in the shot put at the 1920 Antwerp Olympics, his Marines moved inland before maneuvring south to take on the defenders of Mount Suribachi; for his personal leadership and bravery Liversedge was later awarded a second Navy Cross citation (having already won a Navy Cross in the *Solomons* Campaign).

By end of the second day of fighting, the Marines fighting their way up Suribachi had taken 3,500 casualties. Progress was slow, just 400 yards day. "At dawn we climb," noted Colonel Liversedge, "We keep on climbing till we reach the top of that stinking mountain."[29] If it was tough for the US Marines, life was even worse for the Japanese soldiers who had no chance of winning this ultimately uneven contest. A Japanese soldier noted in his diary, "Today we annihilate those who have landed," but he later noted on 23 June, the day of his death, "There are no reinforcements for us—are we not losing the battle?"[30]

For the Japanese soldiers, cooped up in their underground burrows, bereft of almost any food or water, the last days and hours of their lives must have been intolerable. Yet under strict orders from Kuribayashi, they had to hold tight and sell their lives dear— and certainly not commit themselves to the death and glory *banzai* charges which had become such a culminating feature of the Japanese Army's defeats in the *Pacific War*. On *Iwo Jima*, Japanese troops earned the respect of the Marines. One soldier noted that if he had to fight in another war, he would want to have the Japanese on his side. Lieutenant-Colonel Joseph Sayers observed, "the terrain was most favourable to the defense . . . The uncanny accuracy of enemy rifle fire caused many casualties."[31]

On 24 February a patrol of forty Marines battled their way to the summit of Mount Suribachi and Platoon Sergeant Ernest Thomas of Tallahassee, Florida raised the Stars and Stripes at 10.30 a.m. with the help of a length of pipe left in the debris. Spotting this, a Japanese officer charged them with his sword but was gunned down. Observing the flag-raising from the bridge of USS *Rocky Mount*, Secretary of the Navy, James Forrestal observed, "the raising of the flag on Suribachi means a Marine Corps for the next 500 years."[32] Half an hour later a group of six Marines put up a larger flag, an event that was recorded by Associated Press photographer Joe Rosenthal. It became the iconic photograph of the *Pacific War*. On the battlefield the sight of the flag flying was uplifting for the Americans and outraged the Japanese who saw this as the first occupation of the Japanese homeland. Barber Conable recalled, "When she heard about it, Tokyo Rose said the flag on the mountain would be thrown into the sea. I hadn't had any sleep for more than sixty hours, so I didn't see them raise it, and it was wonderful to wake up to. I must say I got a little weepy when I saw it."[33]

'Tokyo Rose' was the name given by US soldiers to the Japanese propaganda broadcasts that were given by an assortment of English-speaking females. The most famous of these, Iva Toguri, who had been raised in San Diego and Los Angeles, was convicted and imprisoned at the Federal Reformatory for Women in West Virginia after the war. In fact she had been coerced by the Japanese into making broadcasts and even under duress had refused to renounce her US citizenship. She was released in 1956 after six years in prison. After an investigation in 1976 by the *Chicago Tribune*, which proved that two of the witnesses against her had been threatened by the FBI to give false testimony, she was given a full pardon by President Gerald Ford, who also restored her US citizenship.

On board USS *Indianapolis*, Admiral Spruance wrote to his wife enclosing a copy of the famous photograph of the flag-raising on Mount Suribachi, and described it as the "finest photograph this war has given us to date. When we settle down, I want to have this picture framed. Some first class sculptor should do this in bronze, it is so perfect."[34]

Into the 'Meatgrinder': Overall the first five days of fighting cost the Americans 1,600 dead and a further 4,500 wounded. The beaches were so heavily enfiladed by rifle fire, machine guns and artillery that it was later said, "bullets and artillery were so thick it was like trying to run through the rain without getting wet."[35] If the taking of the beaches and Mount Suribachi was costly, the push northwards from Chidori Airfield No.1 was worse. Hidden in their foxholes, Japanese troops were able to surprise advancing Marines from the rear and then disappear down a rabbit warren of tunnels. Enemy pillboxes, which had been cleared, became active again as tunnels funnelled fresh Japanese troops back into them. Mines made every step treacherous. In this 'hide and seek' battle US troops' guns proved of little use. The enemy had to be winkled out by hand grenade and flame-thrower. These became the weapons of choice.

First invented by the German Army at the turn of the century, the flame-thrower was only adopted by the US in 1940 and was not widely used until the development of the M-2 in 1943. Using four gallons of a mixture of napalm and gasoline, with nitrogen used as a propulsion medium, the M-2 could project five bursts of flame up to forty yards in length. In the conditions of *Iwo Jima* it proved to be a highly effective weapon, though because of the proximity required, Marines equipped with this weapon suffered proportionally higher casualties. The high casualty rates incurred by flame-thrower units spurred the more rapid development of flame-thrower tanks after *Iwo Jima*.

Far from the ten days that Major-General Schmidt, Commander of the 5th Amphibious Corps, estimated that it would take to subdue *Iwo Jima*, the duration of the battle after the fall of Mount Suribachi was a further four weeks. Engagements for small parcels of ground with obtuse names such as 'Motoyama Plateau,' 'Hill 382,' 'Turkey Knob,' 'Nishi Ridge,' 'Baker,' the 'Quarry,' 'Cushman's Pocket' and 'The Amphitheatre' took on the aspect of major battles. Marine historian Colonel John Ripley has pointed out that it took "nine full days for an entire Division, the 5th Marine Division, to seize a piece of ground so narrow you could throw a baseball across it."[36] Operations on the right flank of the island became known collectively as the 'Meatgrinder.' Fighting on *Iwo Jima*'s left flank was almost as severe. 'Hill 362,' an important tactical location, was taken after Major-General Graves Erskine's 9th Marine Regiment (3rd Marine Division) used a quiet nighttime attack to take the sleeping Japanese soldiers by surprise. Members of his division won Presidential unit citations for heroism while he was awarded the Navy Distinguished Service Medal to add to his two Legion of Merit awards won at *Kwajalein, Saipan* and *Tinian*.

An attempted counter-attack by 1,000 Japanese troops led by Captain Inouye Samaji on the evening of 8 March cost 90 Marine lives and 347 casualties in all while Japanese dead numbered 784. By 16 March the Marines had fought themselves to the last enclave of Japanese troops, which centered on a 650-yard long gorge located in the northeast of the island. Taking a leaf out of MacArthur's playbook, General Holland Smith declared that *Iwo Jima* was secure. It was not. On 21 March, Kuribayashi wrote to the Emperor explaining, "We have not eaten or drunk for five days. But our fighting spirit is still high."[37] In spite of the grimness of the battle for *Iwo Jima*, Marine morale remained high and journalists were amazed to find jovial notices posted at caves and foxholes such as 'Suribachi Heights Property Company,' 'Ocean View,' 'Cool Breezes' and 'Cook Wanted.'

Heavy fighting continued up to the northern caves, which were blown up—entombing the Japanese soldiers within. As the final days arrived Kuribayashi's dispatches apologized to his superiors "for not being strong enough to stop the enemy invasion" and noted, "Although my own death approaches, I calmly pray to God for a good future for my motherland . . ."[38] On 24 March Kuribayashi, the suave 53-year-old general, bid "All officers and men on *Chichi Jima* farewell."[39] (*Chichi Jima* was the small island adjacent to *Iwo Jima*.) The General's body was never found and his final end remains uncertain, though it has been speculated that he led a final *banzai* charge. Remarkably just 216 out of over 20,000 Japanese troops were taken alive. American deaths may have been lower at 6,000 but casualties amounted to 25,000. It was the only major battle in the *Pacific War* in which the casualties of the American attackers exceeded those of defenders—a testament to Kuribayashi's skills as a commander. At the end of the dreadful battle for *Iwo Jima*, a wounded Marine complained, "I hope to God that we don't have to go on any more of those screwy islands."[40] He would be disappointed. There was one more.

In fact the fighting on *Iwo Jima* carried on for some years after the war was finished. Over this time, some 867 further Japanese soldiers were captured and 1,602 were killed. The final soldier to surrender was a Navy Lieutenant on 8 January 1949, who only figured out that Japan had lost the war when he found a copy of *Stars and Stripes* showing a photograph of General MacArthur and Hirohito standing together.

Public Criticism in America: In America the mounting horror of the battle soon brought criticism. On 27 February, some three weeks before *Iwo Jima* was beaten into submission, the *San Francisco Examiner* published an editorial implying heavy criticism of the *Iwo Jima* expedition. "General MacArthur is our best strategist," it asserted, ". . . he wins all objectives . . . he saves the lives of his own men, not only for the future and vital operations that must be fought before Japan is defeated, but for their own safe return to their families and loved ones . . ."[41] About 100 Marines stormed the *San Francisco Examiner*'s building only to learn that it was William Randolph Hearst himself who had penned the editorial. His support for MacArthur was consistent; he had been an outspoken backer of MacArthur's father Arthur during the conquest of the Philippines in 1898. The episode nevertheless indicates the inordinate influence that MacArthur carried with large sections of the US press. MacArthur's criticisms grated even further with those who understood his culpability for the high cost of his own campaigns, some of which were vainglorious and of dubious strategic value. Throughout the Pacific War, MacArthur cast a long shadow over the operations of his colleagues as he bid to rein in power for himself.

As for the justifications for the *Iwo Jima* Campaign, about which some commanders, MacArthur included, had earlier expressed some doubts, debate has continued to rage. As it turned out, the use of Mustangs as fighter escorts for the B-29 raids on Japan turned out not to be practical and only ten such missions from *Iwo Jima* were ever launched. Furthermore, while the island may have received 2,251 B-29 landings, very few of them were emergencies. Radar from the island of *Rota*, which was never attacked, continued to transmit warnings to Japanese urbanites of impending attacks. Indeed Marine Captain Robert Burrell, a historian at the US Naval Academy, has argued, "As the myths about the flag raising on Mount Suribachi reached legendary proportions, so did the emergency landing theory in order to justify the need to raise that flag."[42]

It is difficult to challenge the conclusion that it was the action of *Iwo Jima* that embedded American 'reverence for the Marine Corps.' However, with hindsight it might be questioned whether it would not have been better to bypass *Iwo Jima* altogether and to have focused all resources on the taking of *Okinawa*, which could supply the United States' armed forces with the combination of multiple airports and deep harbor facilities that were not available on *Iwo Jima*. It is evident that *Iwo Jima* did not have to be taken. It posed no threat to the US advance to the Japanese home islands and furthermore it was unsuitable as a bombing base because of its small size and lack of a harbor. A second argument has also been tested in the passage of time. After the battle Spruance went ashore to inspect the scene. He noted, "seeing our badly wounded, especially the men who will suffer some permanent disability, takes a lot of the pleasure out of a successful operation."[43] In particular he looked at the nature of Japan's defenses and concluded that even the ten days of bombardment requested by the Marines would not have broken them down. Only rifles, grenades and flame-throwers could achieve that task. Nevertheless, the argument over the shortness of the bombardment allowed by Spruance has simmered ever since.

In the end Kuribayashi did not just lose his battle. That was expected. His skillful defense though, also failed to force the United States to the negotiating table, which had been his primary aim. Indeed American losses and Japan's unique savagery and traditions of glorious self-sacrifice highlighted at *Iwo Jima*, merely confirmed in American minds the barbarity of the Japanese system of government and made its unconditional surrender even more imperative. The heavy losses suffered by the Marines were not without consequence. *Iwo Jima*'s casualty statistics were factored into the US Army's expected losses for the invasion and conquest of Japan. With 350,000 Japanese defenders on *Kyushu*, it was forecast by General Marshall that US casualties could be 280,000 on that island alone—a figure that, on the basis of the usual 3:1 ratio of wounded to killed, would usually translate to 70,000 dead. It was a figure that did not include naval losses, which because of *kamikaze* attacks were escalating as the Japanese mainland neared. Eventually it would make Harry Truman's decision to drop the atom bomb on Hiroshima an easy choice to make.

37 Battle of Okinawa: Slaughter of the Innocents

[April 1945–August 1945]

[Maps: 37.1, 37.2, 37.3]

The 'Fag End' Battle for Okinawa: The battle for *Okinawa* was the bloodiest battle fought by the US Army in *World War II*. American casualties, though small by the standards of the battles of the war on the Chinese mainland, were the highest of any engagement in which they were involved in the *Pacific War*; they were double the more famous *Battle of Iwo Jima*. But compared to other battles in Europe and much smaller engagements in the *Pacific*, the *Battle of Okinawa* has tended to be ignored. By 1 April 1945, when US soldiers waded ashore on the flat lower western flanks of the island, it was known that America would win the war, but not when it would win the war.

After the decision to support MacArthur's campaign to take the main Philippine island of *Luzon* and the country's capital, Manila, rather than leapfrog the island as many had recommended, it was decided to isolate *Formosa* and advance instead on *Okinawa*. It was the largest of the *Ryukyu Islands* that formed a necklace stringing together Japan's major southern island of *Kyushu* with its colony *Formosa*. *Okinawa* offered significant advantages as a stepping-stone to the invasion of Japan's main home islands. It was just 400 miles from the coast of *Kyushu*, which was less than half the distance from *Formosa*. At between two and eighteen miles wide, *Okinawa* was a long, thin island sixty miles in length with prominent protrusions. Covering a not insubstantial 877 square miles, *Okinawa* had space for seven airfields from which the American Air Force could pound Japanese cities and defense capabilities. Moreover *Okinawa* boasted harbors and a safe anchorage capable of housing the now vast American fleet. Perhaps most importantly however, in spite of the Navy's Chief of Staff, Admiral King's preference for *Formosa*, neither Nimitz nor General Buckner believed that the US possessed the resources to land and defeat what was in effect a full-scale Japanese field army that was based there. By contrast *Okinawa* was a more manageable target.

Whatever the now overwhelming odds in the Allies' favor, achieved by their force of arms in earlier engagements, battles still had to be won on the ground. *Okinawa* was no different. Japan had not given up the fight. Imperial Japanese Command, although it was thoroughly aware that the war was lost, nevertheless believed that there was a lot still to fight for; losses could be exacted from the invading US Army in *Okinawa*, which would make US politicians believe that a peace agreement on negotiated terms was preferable to an attempted invasion and conquest of the big four islands of *Kyushu, Honshu,*

Shikoku and *Hokkaido*. Japan's highly ideologically trained and motivated soldiers on the ground may even have convinced themselves that the US could still be defeated.

For many US soldiers, it was a 'fag end' battle, made seemingly pointless by Hitler's suicide on 30 April 1945 and the unconditional surrender of the Germany Army on 7 May. For American troops who, for the next two months, had to endure some of the hardest battles of the entire war, the news of Germany's defeat was sorry comfort. Neither had the mood in the American Army been leavened earlier in the battle by the death of President Franklin D. Roosevelt on 12 April, within the first fortnight of the *Okinawa* Campaign. By contrast this news may have gladdened the hearts of some of Japan's now bitter soldiers. In Japan, government propagandists changed Roosevelt's last words from the actual, "I have a terrible headache" to "I have made a terrible mistake."[1] Set against this, Germany's surrender could not have been anything other than disheartening to the Japanese. Colonel Yahara recalled, "We now realised that we were doomed. It was nonsense to continue the war in this corner of the *Pacific* after our only real ally had collapsed."[2]

Spruance's Raid on Kyushu and the Invasion Plans: **[Map: 37.1]** The main issue confronting Spruance in the invasion of *Okinawa* was how to gain control of the air and thwart the expected avalanche of *kamikaze* attacks. *Okinawa* presented unique problems. Hitherto, in their advance across the *Pacific*, the carrier forces had been able to crush air power over Japanese garrisoned islands far from the homeland. With *Okinawa* the situation would be very different. *Okinawa* was close enough to *Kyushu*, that it could be supplied with a virtually constant stream of new aircraft that the Japanese government had been storing for the defense of the homeland. In addition *Formosa* could act as a base for Japanese aircraft to intercept any US invasion fleet off *Okinawa*.

With the threat of *Kyushu* in mind, in mid-March Spruance ordered Mitscher to carry out another aircraft raid on Japan's southern island. As Task Force 58 prepared for the coming mission, in *Ulithi*'s *Atoll* now highly crowded anchorage, an attack by *kamikaze* was a portent of things to come. On 11 March Operation TAN-NO.2 was a nighttime *kamikaze* attack. USS *Randolph* (CV-15), an Essex Class Carrier commissioned in October 1944 at Newport News, Virginia, had inadvertently left on a light and was struck on its stern quarters by a Yokosuka P1Y1 'Frances' bomber, killing twenty-seven and wounding 105. It was a testament to *Ulithi*'s rapidly developed sophistication as a naval harbour that the carrier was repaired and re-joined the fleet within three weeks. In spite of the attack, Spruance on his flagship USS *Indianapolis* weighed anchor on 14 March and headed northeast with Task Force 58 toward *Kyushu*. Apart from disabling *Kyushu*'s airfields, Spruance aimed to deliver blows to the remainder of the Japanese fleet, much of which was holed up in the port of Kure.

Kyushu's airfields were bombed on 17 March. The giant battleship *Yamato* was spotted in Kure but by the time Mitscher set out to get her on the following day, she was gone. Unlike the raids on Tokyo, this time the raid on *Kyushu* was not without cost. Four major carriers were damaged and a huge explosion ripped through one of the new Essex

Class carriers, USS *Franklin* (CV-13). Burnt out, listing and without power, the *Franklin* was towed back to *Ulithi Atoll* along with the badly damaged USS *Enterprise* (CV-6) and USS *Wasp* (CV-18; the replacement for USS *Wasp* [CV-7] which was torpedoed and sunk on 15 September 1942 as it guided troop convoys to Guadalcanal). The *Franklin* would eventually be towed back to the United States to be rebuilt. Spruance, who had never suffered serious damage to any carrier in any of his campaigns, had temporarily lost three of his eleven fleet carriers in the first week of his Okinawan Campaign. It was a high price to pay even though his raid accounted for 550 Japanese planes destroyed and a further 175 damaged. In addition his carriers had sunk or damaged 17 naval vessels and over 40 merchantmen.

Spruance remained upbeat and sent a message commending "an auspicious beginning for the operations . . . I am proud to have operated with you again."[3] Mitscher regrouped his remaining seven fleet carriers and six light carriers into three Task Groups and headed to *Okinawa* to begin the preparatory bombardments. Meanwhile at *Ulithi Atoll*, the anchorage was packed to overflowing with 617 naval ships and transports. There was a party atmosphere. On what was known as *Mog Mog Island*, Commodore 'Scrappy' Kessing ran the bars and entertainment facilities for sailors lucky enough to get a ride ashore. As many as 20,000 sailors might be catered for in a single day. There were plenty of fights as sailors and supply crews clashed. Bizarrely the latter were better paid. A cruiser captain was appalled to hear a supply crewman shout out, "Suckers! Suckers! I get twenty dollars a day. What do youse guys get?"[4]

At the officer's club boat loads of off-duty nurses would be brought from the hospital ships, USS *Solace*, USS *Relief* and USS *Comfort*. They were pounced upon to dance with sex-starved Navy men to the boogie-woogie sound of an impromptu Black Seabees band. Partygoers included Rear-Admirals 'Mort' Deyo, 'Spike' Fahrion, 'Turner' Joy and 'Babe' Brown as well as a host of destroyer commanders. One of the revellers was Franklin Delano 'Frank' Roosevelt Jr., the President's son and a destroyer officer who had been decorated for valor at the *Battle of Casablanca* against France's Vichy Navy in November 1942. Also in the social *mêlée* gathered on *Mog Mog Island* was Gene Tunney, the great former undefeated heavyweight-boxing champion and two times conqueror of Jack Dempsey. Tunney, who was married to the Carnegie heiress Polly Lauder, was charged with the management of fleet recreation. Jack Dempsey, the iconic boxer of the inter-war period, may also have been there before shipping out to *Okinawa* on the attack transport USS *Arthur Middleton*. Wildest of all the partygoers were the glamorous, swashbuckling young Navy pilots. As Commodore Jim Lamade of the USS *Hancock* noted, "These young pilots . . . are not naval officers as we know a naval officer. They're just flying because it's their job . . . Discipline . . . means nothing to them."[5] It was a wild four days as sailors crammed in the good times before the arduous task ahead.

On 28 March, four days before the planned invasion day, Spruance received a report that the remnants of the Japanese fleet were leaving the *Inland Sea* and headed toward *Okinawa*. Mitscher immediately headed north to meet them. It was a false alarm but while he was there he made further attacks on Japan's airfields and facilities.

Spruance aboard USS *Indianapolis* had to withdraw from the invasion fleet that consisted of over 1,500 ships, the largest in the history of warfare. On 31 March a *kamikaze* attack on USS *Indianapolis* caused heavy damage to the ship's propellers and propeller shaft. Spruance's flagship limped into the recently acquired anchorage at *Kerama Retto*, one of the group of islands that lay fifteen miles to the west of *Okinawa*. On 5 April he transferred his flag to the venerable USS *New Mexico*, a slow out-dated battleship that served at best as a gun platform to pound Japanese positions. Spruance's Flag Secretary, Lieutenant 'Chuck' Barber recalled, "For an old ship, it was a very pleasant place to serve."[6] Meanwhile *Indianapolis* was sent back to the west coast of America for repairs; Spruance intended that she should return and become his flagship once more but fate would deliver her both an exceptional task and a much greater misadventure than any suffered at *Okinawa*.

Lieutenant-General Simon Bolivar Buckner and the Invasion Plans: With the experience of *Iwo Jima* behind them, US commanders did not underestimate the task ahead. Marines, who had performed the major task of Nimitz's drive through the *Central Pacific* would not be enough. For the first time in the *Central Pacific* Campaign the US Army would take the lead.

Its commander, Lieutenant-General Simon Bolivar Buckner Jr., came from a prominent military family. His father, also given the unlikely names Simon Bolivar, fought in the wars of Mexican conquest, commanded a Confederate army at Dover, Tennessee where he was forced to surrender to General Ulysses Grant, became Governor of Kentucky and a Vice-Presidential candidate in 1896. After a relatively quiet war in command of forces defending Alaska, with little action apart from the Japanese invasion of the *Aleutian Islands* of *Attu* and *Kiska*, Buckner, promoted to Lieutenant-General, was appointed commander of the Tenth Army in June 1944. Here Buckner, a renowned martinet, trained them for the planned invasion of *Formosa* before its cancellation in favour of *Okinawa*.

The plans for the invasion of *Okinawa* were meticulous. However, US intelligence, garnered from captured troops as well as aerial photography, had grossly underestimated the strength of the defense forces that had been gauged at 55,000 troops. In fact, strengthened by Okinawans forced into service, the Japanese had more than doubled this number of soldiers to 116,000. Moreover, compared to the estimates that the defenders would have some 150 planes for defense, there were well over 700 aircraft on the island; like much of *Okinawa*'s defenses they were well hidden or camouflaged.

The Japanese Army Deployment on Okinawa: The Japanese had had nine months to prepare for the attack on *Okinawa*. Until June 1944, Japan's Imperial Headquarters had been relatively relaxed about the defense of the island. The loss of *Saipan* changed perspectives. As Colonel Hiromichi Yahara, senior staff officer in charge of operations of the Thirty-Second Army on *Okinawa* observed, "The Marianas line, also known as the Tojo line, had been considered impregnable . . ."[7] Such was the low priority placed on *Okinawa* that, up until May 1944, the Thirty-Second Army reported directly to Lieutenant-General Sadamu Shimomura's Western District Army in *Kyushu* rather than to Imperial General HQ in Tokyo.

Defeat in the *Battle of the Philippine Sea* changed everything. Afterwards, at the end of June, a carrier and twenty ships had put into the harbor at *Okinawa*. Lieutenant-Colonel Hiromichi Yahara was disturbed to see that there was "Not a single soul could be seen on their decks. There was no aircraft in sight. There was not a trace of the buoyant gallantry of men going to battle; the fleet appeared speechless and forlorn."[8] It was only a week later at a meeting at Imperial Headquarter that the Navy informed the Army of the crushing naval defeat in the *Marianas* and the loss of *Saipan*. At first Imperial General HQ believed that the Americans would seize the island of *Daito Jima*, which lay some 200 miles to the east of *Okinawa*. However, like the Americans, the Japanese soon came to realize that *Daito Jima*, a small isolated rock, could not sustain the launch of an American army on the Japanese home islands. By contrast *Okinawa* would be ideal.

Awaking to the danger, immediate plans were made to airlift the 15th Independent Mixed Regiment from Tokyo to *Okinawa* from Manchukuo. They would be supported by Field Marshal Shunroku Hata's 9th Infantry Division which was moved to *Okinawa*. Meanwhile the Military Affairs Section of the War Office promised to give *Okinawa* priority for military supplies. General Atomiya outlined the defense tactics that were to be pursued: ". . . we cannot hope to match the enemy's strength on the ground, at sea, or in the air. Therefore we should attack the enemy from 'underground.' "[9]

Lieutenant-Colonel Yahara, senior staff officer and planning officer for the 32nd Army at Okinawa, correctly forecast that enemy landings would be made on the west coast of the southern part of the island. Here at Kadena were located *Okinawa*'s major assets including the airfields, harbor and the majority of the population. By contrast the northern part of the island was mountainous and of no strategic use or importance. The plan was to hide troops underground to avoid the inevitable US bombardment and then to train artillery fire on the expected American beachhead. In essence it was a plan similar to the one adopted at *Iwo Jima*. Interlocking systems of tunnels, caves, hidden gun emplacements, pillboxes and dugouts would present formidable problems for Buckner's forces. When the enemy had been "lured into a position where he cannot receive cover and support from naval gunfire and aerial bombardment, we must patiently and prudently hold our fire. Then leaping into action we shall destroy the enemy."[10]

Some of Yahara's colleagues were optimistic to the extent of believing that Japanese forces could destroy the invading American army in *Okinawa*. A night before a devastating air raid by American carrier forces on 10 October 1944, Lieutenant-General Isamu Cho, an ultra-nationalist originally from Fukuoka prefecture on *Kyushu*, speaking at a banquet, boasted about the forthcoming annihilation of the enemy. Meanwhile Lieutenant-General Mitsuru Ushijima, a native of Kagoshima on *Kyushu*, averred that the fleet standing off *Okinawa* would provide prime targets for the heroic *kamikaze* pilots: "The brave, ruddy faced warriors with white silken scarves tied about their heads, at peace in their favourite planes, would dash spiritedly out to the attack."[11] It was still believed that Japan's aircraft from the mainland would be able to destroy the American army if they could keep it pinned to the beachhead. Army officers anticipated help from the Japanese Navy. But the degree to which Japanese naval power had been depleted after a series of major engagements, including the *Battle of the Philippines Sea* and the *Battle of Leyte Gulf,* as well as by on-going US carrier and submarine operations, was largely hidden from field officers.

As ever, Japanese soldiers and sailors tended to believe that deficiencies in *matériel* could be compensated for by spirit. Lieutenant-General Cho and Colonel Hiromichi Yahara were no different. Colonel Yahara argued that the American invasion could be thwarted because, "Against steel, the product of American industry, we would pit our earthen fortifications, the product of the sweat of our troops and the Okinawan people."[12] As spring 1945 approached, much of the previous autumn's optimism had been dispelled. *Okinawa*'s capital, Naha, was all but destroyed by American bombing. Furthermore Imperial HQ ordered the 9th Division to be shipped off the island to bolster the defense of the Philippines; these 25,000 soldiers were the best on *Okinawa* and had been at the center of Yahara's plans.

Revised plans called for lines of defense toward the southern tip of the island and in front of the totemic Shuri Castle where Japan's HQ was based. By April Yahara was under no illusions about the nature of the battle ahead. It would be lost, but a long battle of attrition would give time for the build-up of the mainland's defenses: ". . . our proper strategy was to hold the enemy as long as possible, drain off his troops and supplies, and thus contribute our utmost to the final decisive battle for Japan proper."[13] They would sacrifice themselves to Hirohito's greater cause. In spite of the transfer of troops to the Philippines, the Japanese army was still able to muster 116,000 troops, some 56,000 more than had been anticipated by the American planners; this force included 77,000 regular Thirty-Second Army troops plus 39,000 locally drafted soldiers. In addition senior school students were organized into auxiliary support groups.

Bombardment and Landing: **[Map: 37.2]** Admiral Spruance's Task Force 58 provided the usual pre-invasion naval bombardment. *Okinawa* received six days of bombardment compared to the three days given to *Iwo Jima; Okinawa* was hit with some 700,000 shells of every caliber. On *Okinawa*, Colonel Yahara described the bombardment as a sight "of unsurpassed grandeur."[14] Famously, Vice-Admiral Richmond Turner, in command of the amphibious forces, told Nimitz, "I may be crazy, but it looks like the Japanese have quit the war, at least in this sector." Even more famously Nimitz replied, "Delete all after 'crazy.' "[15] By now Nimitz, with his *Central Pacific* Campaign behind him, was experienced enough to know that first impressions of an amphibious landing could be misleading. Nimitz was right to be sceptical. "We poured quite a lot of metal in on those positions," one Marine commander recalled, ". . . it seemed nothing could possibly be living in that churning mass where the shells were falling and roaring but when we next advanced, Japs would still be there, even madder than they were before."[16]

Spruance's Task Force included 7 fleet carriers (soon to be joined by the repaired USS *Randolph*) in addition to 6 light carriers and 8 destroyers acting as pickets. For the first time during *Pacific Ocean* operations against Japan, the US was reinforced by British Task Force 57; including ships from Australia, Canada, South Africa and New Zealand, the combined British and colonies' forces boasted 4 fleet carriers and 6 escort carriers. In all they could muster 450 aircraft, the most powerful fleet assembled in British history. They were designated the task of destroying Japanese airbases in the *Sakishima Islands* starting their bombardment on 26 March.

At the same time troops from the US 77th Infantry Division landed on the small *Kerema Island* group fifteen miles to the west of *Okinawa*. Service Squadron-10 was sent from *Ulithi Atoll* to occupy the island to build a base for light repairs. Having secured a sheltered anchorage and the capture of 600 Japanese troops, the main landing forces led by 24th Corps and the 3rd Amphibious Corps stormed Hagushi Beach on the west coast of *Okinawa* on 1 April (L-Day) 1945. 16,000 troops landed in the first hour and attacked and captured the lightly defended airfields of Kadena and Yomitan. Edward T. Higgins recalled,

> Over our heads the fire support drummed a thunderous tattoo. The little LCI [Landing Craft, Infantry] lay close behind us, their 20 and 40 mm quads and 0.50 mm machine guns pumping in perfect rhythm as they fired scant feet above our heads at the beach. Behind them the destroyers worked back and forth across their grid patterns, slamming three and five inch shells in arithmetic patterns into the jungle above the shore line.[17]

Meanwhile a diversionary force of amtracs aimed at Minatoga Beach on the east coast turned heel and returned to their ships. General Ushijima reported quite incorrectly, "an enemy landing attempt on the Eastern coast of *Okinawa* on Sunday morning was completely foiled, with heavy losses to the enemy."[18] In fact the invasion of the Hagushi Beach was exceeding all expectations. Within two hours the main airports had been overrun and Vice-Admiral Turner reported to Nimitz that there was "Practically no fire against the boats, none against the ships, considerable number of tanks and artillery landed . . . troops advancing inland standing up."[19] Buckner brought forward the second phase of his plan and at the end of the first week of fighting the 6th Marines had occupied central *Okinawa* and sealed off the heavily defended Motobu Peninsula. On the fifth day of the invasion Admiral Spruance wrote to his wife to tell her, "Our landings on *Okinawa* have gone better than our wildest dreams could have led us to expect."[20]

A vast armada of ships, in all some 1,439 ships, was the largest fleet ever assembled— at the Normandy D-Day landings there were 1,213 ships. Spruance's armada brought four full divisions of the Tenth Army (7th, 27th, 77th and 96th Infantry Divisions).

Including non-divisional artillery units, the *Okinawa* landings used 90,000 soldiers in addition to 88,000 Marines (the 1st, 2nd and 6th Divisions). In all 183,000 soldiers (not including Seabees and support staff) were brought to the beaches of *Okinawa* under the command of Lieutenant-General Simon Bolivar Buckner Jr. In addition to artillery, the invasion force also brought 245 tanks, outnumbering Japan by almost ten to one.

A prodigious effort of logistics ensued. Over the first two weeks the American armada spread a five-mile arc around the Hagushi Beachhead and landed some 577,000 tons of supplies; it had to be quickly organized and hauled to the rapidly expanding frontlines to the north. Muddy tracks, not capable of carrying US trucks and vehicles, had to be rapidly converted into usable roads by army engineers and Seabees. The scale of the logistical exercise made Operation ICEBERG the largest amphibious landing in history. By comparison the Normandy landings brought 156,000 troops to France. Supplies landed on *Okinawa* were 750,000 tons compared to 250,000 tons in Normandy—the difference reflecting the much shorter supply lines to Great Britain, 117 miles (Portsmouth to Caen) versus 6,109 miles (San Francisco to *Okinawa*).

Successful conquest by sea has been rare in history (Julius Caesar and Scipio Africanus come to mind) but the distances faced by the US armed forces, over 6,000 miles, were unique in the annals of military invasion. Just keeping a naval task force afloat and operating for two months off the coast of *Okinawa* was a herculean task. In the first two months of the engagement alone, some nine million (forty-two gallon) barrels of oil were consumed as well as 21 million gallons of aviation fuel; it was almost as much oil as Japan's entire remaining strategic reserve. Less obvious items consumed in bulk over the initial months included 2.7 million packs of cigarettes and 1.2 million chocolate bars. Twenty four million items of mail were delivered.

Air Battle over Okinawa: **[Charts: C.14, C.15, E.1]** While the great naval battles had won America control of the *Pacific Ocean*, as American forces approached Japan new threats to their naval supremacy had emerged. Their fleet carriers may have been destroyed but Japanese planes could now fly from land-based airfields. Moreover, although by the second quarter of 1946 Japan's industrial base had been heavily interrupted by acute shortages caused by annihilation of their merchant fleet, the planners had been able to prioritise an increase aircraft production from 8,861 planes in 1942 to 28,180 in 1944. High levels of aircraft production continued to the end though a high percentage of these were simple, low cost *kamikaze* planes. **[Charts: C.14, C.15]**

However, the problem for the Japanese air force was that new breeds of American fighters could out-manoeuvre and outgun the Mitsubishi Zero that had been so dominant in the first year of the war. In February 1943 the somewhat 'dumpy' profiled Grumman F6F Hellcat came into operation on USS *Essex* (CV-9) (the first of twenty-four Essex class carriers). Powered by a 2,000 bhp Pratt & Whitney R-2800 engine, the Hellcat was faster than the Zero at all altitudes. While the Zero remained more agile at low speed, making dogfighting inadvisable, the Hellcat could easily evade them by turning in a high-speed turn or dive. With a hydraulically powered undercarriage, heavier armament for cockpit and fuel tanks, six Browning machine guns (0.50 inch M2/AN Browning air-cooled machine guns with 400 rounds per gun) and the capability to carry bombs or rockets, the Hellcat proved a versatile and hardwearing carrier aircraft. The US Navy's leading ace pilot, Captain David McCampbell who recorded 34 'kills' in the Hellcat described it as ". . . an outstanding fighter plane. It performed well, was easy to fly and was a stable gun platform. But what I really remember most was that it was rugged and easy to maintain."[21] In spite of its late introduction the Hellcat produced more kills (5,271) than any other plane during the *Pacific War*.

The Vought F4U Corsair was also introduced in 1943. The distinctive bent-winged, long nosed Corsair was introduced to the US carrier fleet in 1943 after a long drawn out certification process because of the plane's tendency to 'bounce' while landing on carrier decks. Nevertheless, it was much faster than the Zero and quickly achieved ascendancy. The first Corsair ace, Lieutenant Kenneth A. Walsh, who racked up twenty-one 'kills' during the war, noted that

> I learned quickly that altitude was paramount. Whoever had altitude dictated the terms of the battle, and there was nothing a Zero pilot could do to change that—we had him. The F4U could outperform a Zero in every aspect except slow speed maneuverability and slow speed rate of climb. Therefore you avoided getting slow when combating a Zero . . . There were times, however, that I tangled with a Zero at slow speed, one on one . . . [when] I considered myself fortunate to survive . . . Of my 21 victories, 17 were against Zero, and I lost five aircraft in combat. I was shot down three times . . .[22]

While the Americans now had definitive air superiority in terms of its fighter aircraft and better trained pilots, Japan's new *kamikaze* tactics were difficult to counter for conventional US fighter tactics. Anti-aircraft batteries also found the *kamikaze* difficult to sight. While air attack was relatively light in the first week of the invasion, Japan planned to destroy the American's Fifth Fleet by a mass attack of 400 planes (conventional and *Kamikaze*) flying from *Kyushu*. The suicide attacks were an astonishing sight. Vice-Admiral Carl Brown recalled, "There was a hypnotic fascination to the sight so alien to our western philosophy. We watched each plunging *kamikaze* with the detached horror of one witnessing a terrible spectacle rather than as the intended victim."[23]

Imperial General Staff planners hoped to sink enough ships to destroy the invasion's logistics and to leave American ground forces stranded and helpless against *Okinawa's* Thirty-second Army. Over the course of the Okinawan Campaign some 1,465 *kamikaze* attacks were made. Thirty US Navy ships were sunk and some 157 ships damaged. There were some notable strikes. Vice-Admiral 'Pete' Mitscher's flagship carrier USS *Bunker Hill* (CV-17) sustained a hit which cost 400 lives and 264 wounded; in casualty terms it was the second most costly attack on an American ship in *World War II*. Neither did Spruance's new flagship USS *New Mexico* escape unscathed. At sunset on 12 May, two *kamikaze* aircraft raced toward the *New Mexico*. One was shot down by anti-aircraft fire while the other slammed in the side of the ship not far from the bridge. Fifty men were killed and over 100 injured. Frantic Flag Staffers could not find Admiral Spruance who was feared killed. He was eventually found manning a fire hose. Later a well-practised repair barge pulled alongside to conduct repairs.

Overall Navy losses in personnel were not insignificant. During a campaign planned for three-weeks that lasted three months, more than 4,900 sailors were killed and 4,800 were wounded. Spruance tried multiple strategies to obviate the damage of the attacks including trying to persuade the army to seize several islands to the north of *Okinawa*, on which radar stations and fighter directors could have been placed. Similarly Spruance wanted to seize the large island of *Kumei* to the west to help pick up the approach of *kamikaze* from *Formosa*. Spruance later lamented, "The Army always had some reason why they could not do this."[24]

Spruance turned to the Army Air Force for help, asking MacArthur to bomb Japanese airfields on *Formosa* and General LeMay B-29s on *Saipan* to bomb airfields on *Kyushu*. It proved to be a largely futile effort. Japanese airplanes were kept off-site and camouflaged and LeMay's bombers simply created large craters, which were quickly repaired. When the failure of this campaign became apparent Spruance released them to go back to fire-bombing cities and mining sea channels. The Fifth Air Force flying out of *Luzon* was similarly ineffective against *Formosa*. Japanese losses were staggering. In April alone some 1,100 Japanese planes were shot down. In addition the Japanese Navy resorted to motorboat suicide attacks. As usual it massively overestimated the effectiveness of its aerial attacks with Japanese pilots mythically claiming the sinking of US carriers. The army was somewhat more realistic. Lieutenant-General Michio Sugihara, commander of the Sixth Air Army reported, "Despite many attacks, the Navy cannot block the enemy's carrier force, which is still operating east of Okinawa."[25]

To try to improve the effectiveness of *kamikaze*, Sugihara developed new tactics. This included the use of conventional fighters to act as decoys to Task Force 58's Hellcat and Corsair fighters, so that *kamikaze* could sneak in unchallenged. Results were patchy however, and although numbers of destroyers were sunk, no US capital ships suffered complete loss though some had to return to *Ulithi* or *Hawaii* for repair. The costs to the US invasion force of the *kamikaze* ended up more psychological than material. As one reporter noted, "The strain of waiting, the anticipated terror, made vivid by past experience, sent some men into hysteria, insanity, breakdown."[26]

Another change had taken place in the nature of *kamikaze* attacks; whereas application to join *kamikaze* squads had started off as voluntary, midway through the *Battle of Okinawa* pilots were dragooned into 'volunteering.' By this stage, given the technological advance of US planes as well as battle-craft, in addition to Japan's decreasing capability to train new pilots, even conventional Japanese air operations were in effect suicidal. Nevertheless, by the end of May Spruance and his command team were spent with exhaustion and Nimitz decided to relieve them as the battle drew to a close. In a now familiar takeover, Halsey and his team took charge. Nimitz planned that Spruance should return to the states for a vacation before commencing the planning for Operation OLYMPIC, the invasion of the Japanese mainland island of *Kyushu*.

Marine and Army Dissension: Although the *kamikaze* campaign ultimately failed, it caused moments of high stress within the American Task Force. Nimitz, perhaps more used to the more dashing tactics of Holland Smith and the Marines, was less than happy with what he perceived as General Buckner's cautiousness, forcing his naval forces to be the subject of target practice for the 'Floating Chrysanthemums' for weeks on end. In addition to material losses, Nimitz feared for the morale of his sailors. When Nimitz complained at the slow pace of advance, a tetchy Buckner told him that 'ground' tactics were no business of the Navy. An icy Nimitz retorted, "Yes, but ground though it may be I'm losing a ship and a half per day. So if this line isn't moving within five days, we'll get someone here to move it so we can all get out from under these stupid air attacks."[27]

In a further indication of the increase in inter-service rivalry, the Marines also queried Buckner's tactics. Lieutenant-General Vandegrift, the head of the Marine Corps, wondered why the 2nd Marines Division, sitting in *Saipan*, could not be brought to bear on the situation by means of an amphibious flanking attack against the static Japanese lines. Buckner and his Tenth Army staff, citing the near disaster at Anzio, decided that this was too risky. Again Spruance was sceptical: "There are times when I get impatient for some of [Marine commander] Holland Smith's drive," he complained, "but there is nothing I can do about it."[28] Having seen the speed at which the Marines had worked in the *South Pacific* campaign, Spruance was unimpressed by the Army's methods. "I doubt if the Army's slow, methodical method of fighting really saves any lives in the long run," he complained to his former Chief of Staff, "It merely spreads the casualties over a longer period."[29]

After the war the US Army faced considerable criticism for the slow pace of construction of airfields on *Okinawa*. The famed Marine Seabees, who had built hundreds of airfields across the *Pacific*, were excluded from the construction of new fields on *Okinawa*. In July 1946 Mitscher testified to the Senate Naval Affairs Committee that,

> The sea and air battles off *Okinawa* could have been shortened considerably if the Army had established airfields and put them into operation as rapidly as the Seabees had done in other places. The Army could not. As a result the Navy supported the landing force long after the Army should have been able to supply its own air cover. The Navy suffered losses and damage to which it should never have been subjected.[30]

The reasons for the Seabees exclusion were very likely political. Some suspected that the Army, having missed the American press plaudits, which had been heaped on the

Marines throughout their *Central Pacific* drive, wanted their own chance for glory. Vandegrift, encouraged by Admiral King in Washington, told *New York Herald Tribune* columnist David Lawrence, "Certain high Navy officers here feel that a major mistake was made in the *Okinawa campaign* . . . Why were the Marine Corp Generals who had had far greater experience in handling amphibious operations not given the opportunity to carry on . . ."[31] Lawrence would later characterize the *Okinawa* campaign as a fiasco and ". . . a worse example of military incompetence than *Pearl Harbor*."[32]

Nimitz, unlike his colleagues and in complete contrast to General MacArthur, was no fan of backchannels to the press, and tried to squash the criticism of the Army whatever his private feelings may have been. As the war moved toward its successful and yet 'more costly in lives' conclusion, the spirit of cooperation, that had existed between the services at the start of the war, when America was in crisis, started to dissipate. Nimitz wrote to his wife to complain, ". . . pressure these days does not originate with the Japs"[33] and "The publicity side of the war is getting so large it almost overshadows the fighting side."[34]

Hirohito's Displeasure and New Kamikaze Weapons: It was not only the US Navy and the American press that was unhappy with the tactics at *Okinawa*. In Japan too there were rumblings of discontent. As early as the second day of the invasion, Emperor Hirohito queried, "Why doesn't the field army go on the offensive? If there are insufficient troops, why don't you do a counter-landing?"[35] Hirohito still refused to countenance defeat let alone surrender.

In renewed mass attacks on 12 April a new weapon, the *Oka* (Cherry Blossom) nicknamed by the Japanese as *baka* (foolish) scored a first victim with the sinking of the picket destroyer USS *Manert L. Abele*. The *baka* was a human-guided rocket packing 2,645 lbs of Trinitroanisol that was launched from the underside of a 'Peggy' or 'Betty' bomber some ten miles from the intended target. Travelling at 500 knots it was almost impossible to shoot down; piloting the rocket proved tricky however and for obvious reasons it was impossible to get feedback on how to improve handling and accuracy. By the end of the *Okinawa* campaign, *kamikaze* attacks decreased in intensity. The last *kamikaze* attack on 21 June comprised just 45 aircraft compared to 355 in the first attack. Eventually resource exhaustion and the effects of heavy bombing of airfields on *Formosa* and *Kyushu* had started to impact the weight of *kamikaze* attack. It was not a satisfactory result for Curtis LeMay who complained, "The B-29 is not a tactical bomber and never pretended to be. No matter how we socked at those airdromes, we could not reduce the kamikaze threat to zero."[36] **[See Appendix E: *Kamikaze*: Divine Winds]**

The British Pacific Navy: Only the British remained relatively immune to the impact of *kamikaze* attacks because unlike American or Japanese fleet carriers, they were built with steel plate decks—a design feature copied by the *Taiho*, Japan's last purpose built carrier. While the all-steel design limited the number of planes that they could carry, forty-five to the Americans' eighty, in defensive action at *Okinawa*, their worth was considerably enhanced.

At the Second Quebec Conference (codenamed OCTAGON) on 13 September 1944, Winston Churchill had grandly offered to send a British battle fleet to support the American operations against Japan. In his memoirs Churchill wrote that with regard to the liberation of Asia,

> I was determined that we should play our full and equal part in it. What I feared most at this stage of the war was that the United States would say in after-years, "We came to your help in Europe and you left us alone to finish off Japan." We had to regain on the field our rightful possessions in the Far East, and not have them handed back to us at the peace table.[37]

Roosevelt, without consulting his naval colleagues, immediately accepted the offer. Admiral King glowered furiously. He remained non-committal when Churchill asked how the Royal Navy forces would be used and realizing King's vacillation, asked him point blank, "The offer has been made. Is it accepted?"[38] Roosevelt intervened and answered, "It is."[39] At the Combined Chiefs of Staff meeting the following day, King continued to vent his fury. In one of their most acrimonious meetings of the war, King made it clear that he did not want the British muscling in on the US Navy's glory and that any British force would be a hindrance rather than a help. King was eventually hauled into line by Roosevelt's Chief of Staff, Admiral William Leahy, with the remark, "I don't think we want to wash our linen in public."[40] Admiral Sir Andrew Cunningham wrote, "King with the other American Chiefs of Staff against him, eventually gave way, but with very bad grace."[41]

The British force was led by Vice-Admiral Sir Bernard Rawlings. Born in the Cornish village of St. Erth, four miles from the coastal town of St. Ives, Rawlings had served in *World War I* as a torpedo boat commander. Modest and publicity shy, Rawlings's career progressed rapidly by dint of his industry and quiet ability. Having spent the majority of the war in command of Royal Navy Squadrons in the *Mediterranean Sea*, Rawlings was promoted to second in command of the British *Pacific* Fleet in 1944 and then given command of a powerful British Task Force that was attached to Spruance's invasion of *Okinawa*. It consisted of 2 battleships, 4 fleet carriers, 4 cruisers plus HMNZS *Gambia* provided by New Zealand. In addition, Rawlings' fleet was protected by fifteen modern destroyers.

The size and importance of the British *Pacific* Fleet in aggregate has rarely been given due attention. It comprised ten fleet carriers; HMS *Colossus*, HMS *Formidable*, HMS *Glory*, HMS *Illustrious*, HMS *Implacable*, HMS *Indefatigable*, HMS *Indomitable*, HMS *Venerable*, HMS *Victorious* and HMS *Unicorn*. Together they carried an aggregate of 526 aircraft. A high proportion of them were American planes, including 198 Vought Corsairs, 105 Grumman Avengers and 39 Grumman Hellcats. In addition there were eighty-eight Supermarine Aviation Works Seafires, aircraft carrier cousins of the Spitfire fighters of *Battle of Britain* fame.

As well as the fleet carriers, the British *Pacific* Fleet could boast 2 dedicated repair and maintenance carriers, 9 escort carriers, 4 battleships, 11 cruisers, 35 destroyers, 31 submarines, plus 149 support ships including mine-layers, frigates, sloops, corvettes, landing ships, supply ships and store ships. It was by far the largest fleet ever assembled by the British Navy. While Rawlings's Task Force served creditably at *Okinawa*, the British *Pacific* Fleet would have proved invaluable to any full-scale invasion of the big four Japanese islands. Sadly perhaps for the British Navy, it would never fully get revenge or restitution of its dignity for the ignominious sinking of the *Prince of Wales* by the Japanese in the first days of the *Pacific War*. Nevertheless the British *Pacific* Fleet in 1945 was a mighty show—a crescendo that brought the curtain down on British power in the *Pacific*.

For the embattled Spruance, the British fleet proved an unlikely godsend, which was ironic in view of Admiral King's earlier reluctance to accept their involvement. The British Royal Navy, labeled Task Force 57, put out of action the Japanese airfields based on the *Sakishima Gunto Islands* located 250 miles southwest of *Okinawa*. Moreover the British Task Force served as a bulwark to protect Spruance's fleet from *kamikaze* attack from this direction. Copying the tactics originally devised by Admiral McCain at *Leyte Gulf*, Rawlings stationed anti-aircraft pickets, cruisers and destroyer, some thirty miles ahead of the fleet, which also enabled '*kamikaze* cuckoos' to be weeded out from returning British bombing missions. In addition to protecting Spruance's southwestern flank, Task Force 57 raided the Japanese airfields on *Formosa* with some success.

Admiral Sir Bernard Rawlings was rewarded with generous praise from Spruance and after the war, at a speech in London, he affirmed, "In spite of the fact that Admiral Rawlings and I had no chance for personal conference before the operation, Task Force 57 did its work to my complete satisfaction and fully lived up to the traditions of the Royal Navy."[42] Admiral Sir Bruce Fraser was only too happy to relish the turnaround in American perception of the British fleet. In a delicate but pointed remark in his dispatch to the Lords of the Admiralty 9 May 1945, Fraser noted, "Doubt as to our ability to operate in the Pacific manner was somewhat naturally in American minds. This, however, was soon changed. The toll taken by the suicide bombers on the more lightly armored American carriers led to an increase in the proportionate effort provided by our carriers . . ."[43] However, even Fraser had to admit that the British Forces were highly reliant on American logistical backup that had developed the technology and systems to resupply ships at sea, thus enabling them to stay on station far longer.

Battleship Yamato's Suicide Mission: Not to be outdone by the air force, the Imperial Japanese Navy planned an even more grandiose suicide attack. The *Yamato*, sister battleship to the *Musashi* that had been sunk at *Leyte Gulf*, was marooned in Japan's *Inland Sea*—a behemoth without a purpose. Its 18.1-inch guns could launch a 3,200 lb shell 45,000 yards compared to the 2,700 lb shells of American battleships with their range of 42,000 yards; but without carriers to protect it or even enough diesel oil to use it, *Yamato*, the most imperious, the most elegant and most powerful battleship in the world, had become a useless 'white elephant.' If pilots could give up their lives for the Emperor, why not sailors and admirals?

Thus Operation TEN-GO was born as the Imperial Navy GHQ planned a final sacrifice. Admiral Soemu Toyoda, Commander in Chief of the Combined Fleet, displaying the characteristic fanaticism of the elite officer cadre, described Operation TEN-GO as an opportunity, ". . . to fight gloriously to the death to completely destroy the enemy fleet, thereby establishing firmly an eternal foundation for the Empire."[44]

4,000 tons of precious oil were scraped together from a reserve that was now little more than 50,000 tons in the whole of Japan. Rear-Admiral Seichi Ito, commanding the 'Special Attack Force' must have known that there was little chance of getting to *Okinawa* but in the unlikely event of his succeeding he was ordered to beach the *Yamato* and use its guns to disrupt the American invasion. At 6.00 a.m. on the morning of 6 April, the crew, all 3,332 of them, were called on deck and informed of their mission; in effect Imperial General HQ had volunteered them for a suicide mission. As they sang the national anthem, *Umi Yukaba* (If I go away to the sea), never can the lines have been sung so poignantly,

> If I go away to the sea,
> I shall be a corpse washed up.
> If I go away to the mountain,
> I shall be a corpse in the grass
> But if I die for the Emperor,
> It will not be a regret.[45]

Leaving port at 10.00 a.m., the *Yamato* sailed down the east coast of *Kyushu* and then swung west into the *East China Sea*. The plan was for the *Yamato* to get to *Okinawa* by dusk the following day. Its departure was soon discovered when the submarine picket USS *Hackleback* spotted the Japanese task force and alerted Admiral Spruance. Rear-Admiral Deyo moved his 6 battleships, 7 cruisers and 21 destroyers between the American transports and the *Yamato* that was bearing down from 400 miles away. Although the *Yamato*'s 18.1-inch guns and 28 knot speed outbid anything that any single American ship could muster, Spruance was confident that Japan's last great capital ship could be overwhelmed by superior numbers.

However, as they sped toward their target, *Yamato* turned course and disappeared. When Mitscher's spotter planes again picked up the *Yamato*'s track, he telegraphed to Spruance, "WILL YOU TAKE THEM OR SHALL I?" Spruance, who feared that the *Yamato* might make a run back to a safe haven in *Kyushu*, sent back the message, "YOU TAKE THEM."[46] Vice-Admiral Mitscher, leading Task Force 58's carrier fleet, now had the opportunity to win the glory of sinking Japan's greatest battleship; for Mitscher, one of the earliest trained aviators in the US Navy, who had graduated as pilot No.33 from Pensacola, the sortie of the *Yamato* "provided a clean cut chance to prove, if proof was needed, aircraft superiority."[47] Mitscher's spotter planes from USS *Essex* (CV-9) tracked *Yamato*'s progress. Mitscher shared Halsey's visceral hatred of the Japanese, and was equally eloquent in spouting his racist views in public. At a press conference in San Diego in early January 1945, he stated that the Japanese "are the poorest specimen of man on earth today, and I've had the opportunity to compare them with the so-called head-hunters of the *Solomons*."[48]

At 12.41 p.m. on 7 April, a first wave of carrier dive-bombers hit the *Yamato* with two bombs, blowing away two triple 25 mm aircraft mounts, while four minutes later a torpedo attack landed a strike in her port flank. Within a minute two more bombs struck an aft turret. Shortly thereafter three more torpedoes struck the *Yamato* near her engine room and boiler. A five-degree list to port ensued. The poor weather, with low cloud cover, meant that the attack was far from textbook. Pilot Thaddeus T. Coleman recalled:

> Our training instructions, to dive deeply from 10,000 feet
> or higher, proved useless. Here the ceiling was only 3,000
> feet with rainsqualls all around. Bomber pilots pushed
> over in all sorts of crazy dives, fighter pilots used every
> maneuver in the book, torpedo pilots stuck their necks out
> all the way, dropped right down on the surface and
> delivered their parcels so near the ships that many of them
> [aircraft] missed the ships' superstructures by inches.[49]

A quarter of an hour later a second wave planted four more torpedoes into her port side and one into her starboard. Counter-flooding on *Yamato*'s starboard side, which drowned all the engineers in the boiler rooms, could not prevent listing to port—now at fifteen degrees. Their sacrifice was for naught. Meanwhile the decks were a shambling mess of twisted metal. Worse was to come. A final US carrier onslaught began at 1.40 p.m. with *Yamato* skewered by at least four more bombs and four more torpedoes, causing flooding to boiler and steering rooms. *Yamato* began to turn onto her side. Her speed had dropped to ten knots and she began to turn in a circle to starboard. Fires were raging out of control. Hundreds of Japanese seamen were trapped below decks. The order to abandon ship was given at 2.02 p.m. Vice-Admiral Seiichi Ito shook hands with his senior officers and went to his cabin to die. He was posthumously promoted to full Admiral.

In the meantime young officers tied themselves to the *Yamato*'s bridge. Kosaku Aruga, the *Yamato*'s captain, ordered them to swim for it though he himself was determined to go down with his ship. Aruga tied himself to the compass binnacle. Aruga's last act was to order Lieutenant Hattori to rescue Emperor Hirohito's portrait from the boardroom. Instead of retrieving the portrait, Hattori simply locked the door. Aruga was posthumously promoted to Vice-Admiral. Escorting ships, *Yahagi, Isokaze, Hamakaze, Asashimo* and *Kasumo* were all fatally stricken. At 2.05 p.m. the *Yamato* rolled over on its beam-ends and slipped under the water taking thousands of men down with her. Just 277 members of her crew are thought to have survived. Ensign Mitsuru

Yoshida, the senior radio operator on the Captain's bridge and the senior surviving officer was sucked under water and in spite of being wounded by underwater shrapnel, bobbed to the surface. He had witnessed the last moments on *Yamato*'s bridge and would later write *Senkan Yamato-no Saigo* (The Last Days of Battleship *Yamato*) [1952].

Of Mitscher's performance at *Okinawa*, Admiral Nimitz was highly complementary and would testify, "He is the most experienced and most able officer in the handling of fast carrier task forces who has yet been developed. It is doubtful if any officer has made more important contributions than he toward extinction of the enemy fleet."[50]

Roosevelt Dies as the Marines Advance: By 8 April just the outposts of the Shuri Line, the defensive barrier which incorporated Mount Shuri, had been captured, at a cost of over 1,000 American casualties with four times that number of Japanese killed or captured. The hard slog now began through wooded, hilly terrain honeycombed with caves and dugouts fashioned from the soft coral rock. Jagged ridges and escarpments added to the natural defenses of the few miles north of Mount Shuri. Advance was bought position by position. Eventually the advance held up at 'Kakazu Ridge,' where in some of the most heroic actions of the *Battle of Okinawa*, American soldiers were repeatedly repulsed. Forced back from the ridge into the gorge below, the Japanese bombarded them with their spigot mortar's 320 mm shells. One such round buried and killed thirteen American troops sheltering in a cave. Casualties in the 7th and 96th Divisions from these actions amounted to 451 dead, 241 missing and 2,198 wounded.

To add to Major-General John Hodge's problems, he faced a shortage of shells caused by the loss of two supply ships to *kamikaze*. [See Appendix E: *Kamikaze*: Divine Winds] On 12 April, units of the 22nd Marine Division reached the northern tip of *Okinawa*. Franklin Delano Roosevelt died the same day. The mourning of American GIs on the battlefield was heartfelt. There were celebrations on the streets of Tokyo. Shortly afterwards Japanese planes showered American troops on *Okinawa* with a crass propaganda leaflet entitled *The American Tragedy*, "The dreadful loss that led your late leader to death will make orphans on this island. The Japanese Special Assault Corps (*Kamikaze*) will sink your vessels to the last destroyer."[51] Not surprisingly, American fighting spirit, that Japanese officers continued to doubt, was not diminished. The main battle had barely started. While the Marines had charged north, the Tenth Army's 96th and 7th Division wheeled south and had to overcome fierce Japanese defenses dug into 'Cactus Ridge' and another rocky summit which came to be known as the 'Pinnacle.'

While the American difficulties in gaining ground delighted Yahara because they justified his defensive strategies, Lieutenant-General Cho saw them as a moment for counter-offensive. Prompted by Imperial General HQ's urging of the recapture Kadena and Yontan Airfields to prevent the arrival of ground-based Corsair fighters, Lieutenant-General Cho managed to overturn the attritional defensive mantra of Lieutenant-Colonel Yahara. In spite of Yahara's protests General Ushijima authorized night counter-attacks on 12 and 13 April. Ushijima radioed to Imperial General HQ, "All of our troops will attempt to rush forward and wipe out the ugly enemy."[52] The Japanese counter-offensive, even if it lacked the typical *banzai* element that had characterized much of the *Pacific* Campaign, was nevertheless devoid of coherence, clear objectives and realism. Cho, like many ideological Japanese army officers, believed, 'soft' Americans spoilt by their country's wealth would collapse when faced by Japan's *bushido* spirit. It was a dangerous fantasy that colored the thinking of many of the Japanese Armies less able officers. Cho's counter-attacks were an unmitigated disaster; unsurprisingly, after suffering 5,000 casualties, Ushijima reverted to the defensive strategies advocated by the cerebral, pragmatic Yahara.

The American line, under the command of Major-General Hodge, which had been strengthened by the landing of the 27th Infantry Division on 9 April, now stretched to just four and a half miles; the 27th held the right flank, the 96th the middle and the 7th Division covered the east coast. American forces consolidated their positions until 19 April when Hodge launched the largest artillery barrage seen in the *Pacific War*; it was supported by the battleships and cruisers of Spruance's Fifth Fleet in addition to bombing and rocket attacks by 650 planes of the carrier fleet. In spite of this pounding, by digging their defensive positions into the reverse side of hills and ridges, the Japanese defenders had made most of this American firepower go to waste. Although the US Tenth Army infantry managed to penetrate the Machinato defensive line by the end of April, it was deemed necessary to relieve them. With the arrival of the Marines of the 1st and 6th Division, the Tenth Army began to take control of the battle.

However, Hodge had to deal with another offensive action on 4 May when Ushijima launched an amphibious flanking movement behind American lines. To support this attack Japanese artillery was moved into the open and began a barrage of fire. Again Japanese offensive action failed.

A week later on 11 May Buckner launched another offensive, which was followed by two weeks of intense fighting for 'Conical Hill' on the eastern flank of Shuri and 'Hill 52' (renamed 'Sugar Loaf Hill' by the Marines), which protected its western side. By the end of the month monsoon rains had turned the narrow battlefield into a quagmire of mud, bodies, excreta, garbage and maggots. Even Marine morale took a pounding; Marine 'Bill' Leyden, later a game-show host who was given a star on the Hollywood Walk of Fame, remembered that Marines "just kept scratching at the ground, trying to get in deeper in the mud."[53] A *History of the Sixth Marine Division* [1948] described the fight for 'Sugar Loaf Hill' as "the most bitter, costly, and decisive action on *Okinawa*."[54]

Finally Mount Shuri, which had been expertly tunnelled for defense by Lieutenant-General Cho, needed to be breeched. From 26 May the USS *Missouri* pounded the mountain's castle to destruction. Nonetheless the ground had to be taken and Major-General Pedro del Valle won a Distinguished Service Medal for leading the 1st Marines against Shuri Castle, which was finally secured when the Japanese Thirty-Second Army decided to make a tactical night withdrawal with 40,000 troops to the Kiyan Peninsula. Artillery pounded down on them as they tramped south to new defensive lines. "The nips were caught on the road with kimonos down,"[55] noted Major-General del Valle with suitable relish. The retreat, albeit well conceived and executed, could not compensate for the loss of Mount Shuri, so long a totem to the Thirty-Second Army; its loss caused a decline in morale as the inevitability of defeat loomed. Yahara was told by Police Chief Arai, "Army morale was high at the Shuri battle, but since the retreat it has plummeted."[56] However, it must have been difficult to remain optimistic when arms and munitions were almost exhausted. At Kiyan, 6,000 troops were thrown into the front line with mainly small arms and bamboo spears.

The Japanese Army's Last Stand: [Map: 37.3] The last two weeks of fighting proved the most deadly of all with Japanese defenders pushed back into ever smaller pockets. The Thirty-Second Army's final resistance moved to the southeast of Itoman. Meanwhile 9,000 Imperial Navy troops and sailors supported by 1,000 militia fought from positions dug into the hills above their naval base on the Oroku Peninsula. Rear-Admiral Minoru Ota, a veteran commander of Japanese Special Landing Forces with whom he had fought in the First Shanghai Incident in 1932 and later at the *Battle of New Georgia* [1944], refused to retreat. In a last telegram to his superiors on 6 June, Ota sent a deeply human and heart moving plea on behalf of the natives of Okinawa.

> Since the enemy attack began, our Army and Navy have been fighting defensive battles and have not been able to tend to the people of the Prefecture. Consequently, due to our negligence, these innocent people have lost their homes and property to enemy assault. Every man has been conscripted to partake in the defense, while women, children and elders are forced into hiding in the small underground shelters which are not tactically important or are exposed to shelling, air raids or the harsh elements of nature. Moreover, girls have devoted themselves to nursing and cooking for the soldiers and have gone as far as to volunteer in carrying ammunition, or join in attacking the enemy.
>
> This leaves the village people vulnerable to enemy attacks where they will surely be killed. In desperation, some parents have asked the military to protect their daughters against rape by the enemy, prepared that they may never see them again. Nurses, with wounded soldiers, wander aimlessly because the medical team had moved and left them behind. The military has changed its operation, ordering people to move to far residential areas, however, those without means of transportation trudge along on foot in the dark and rain, all the while looking for food to stay alive.

> Ever since our Army and Navy occupied Okinawa, the inhabitants of the Prefecture have been forced into military service and hard labor, while sacrificing everything they own as well as the lives of their loved ones. They have served with loyalty. Now we are nearing the end of the battle, but they will go unrecognized, unrewarded. Seeing this, I feel deeply depressed and lament a loss of words for them. Every tree, every plant life is gone. Even the weeds are burnt. By the end of June, there will be no more food. This is how the Okinawan people have fought the war. And for this reason, I ask that you give the Okinawan people special consideration, this day forward.[57]

On 13 June, nine days after the 6th Marines made an amphibious landing on the heavily defended Oroku Peninsula, the 4,000 surviving troops, including Ota who put a gun to his head, committed suicide inside the tunnels and caves of the Navy's underground headquarters.

On 18 June, during the final push on Japanese positions on the Kiyan Peninsula, in spite of the best efforts of the Marines to hide his identity, the defenders spotted the three-star insignia of Lieutenant-General Buckner, and launched an artillery attack; a coral splinter from a Japanese artillery rounds pierced his chest and he died ten minutes later as field surgeons tried to save him. He was the highest-ranking American general to be killed in action during *World War II*. He was posthumously awarded a promotion to four-star general by a unanimous act of Congress. The day before his death Buckner's pleas to Ushijima to surrender for the sake of the lives of his troops fell on deaf ears. Colonel Yahara would later reflect in his account of the battle, "The decision to surrender should have been made as quickly as possible, at least before Okinawa was lost."[58] On 21 June organized resistance collapsed. At dawn General Ushijima and Lieutenant-General Cho went to the mouth of their cave in 'Hill 89' refuge and sat in their death seats. In a last word Cho turned to Yahara and commanded, "Yahara! For future generations, you will bear witness as to how I died."[59] Ushijima and Cho committed *seppuku*, ritual suicide by disembowelment with the short, double-bladed *tanto* sword followed by decapitation by *katana* (samurai sword) by staff officer, Captain Sakaguchi. Ushijima penned a last poem,

> We spend arrows and bullets to stain heaven and earth,
> Defending our homeland forever.[60]

Meanwhile Colonel Yahara, who was refused permission to commit *seppuku*, surrendered to American forces after he was found hiding on 15 July; Ushijima had told him, "If you die there will be no one left who knows the truth about the Battle of Okinawa. Bear the temporary shame but endure it. This is an order from your army Commander."[61] Yahara was one of the few survivors. Out of the 116,000 Japanese soldiers who started the defense of *Okinawa* just 7,400 surrendered.

Atrocities on Okinawa: If the Japanese military paid a heavy toll for their participation in the battle, civilian losses were far higher; an estimated 150,000 Okinawans died during the battle, a sacrifice that is still reflected in hostility toward the Japanese mainland. In part, Okinawan civilians were simply incidental victims of fighting that was brutal and relentless. One American GI confessed: "It was a terrible thing not to distinguish between the enemy and women and children ... Now we fired indiscriminately."[62] American soldiers in the *Pacific War* did not always behave with the grace, which history has usually bestowed on them; for many GIs, the Okinawans were simply the Japanese enemy and revenge was uppermost in their thoughts.

Post-war investigation by the journalist George Feifer concluded that cases of rape by American soldiers were widespread. However, Japanese atrocities towards the racially different and culturally and linguistically unique Okinawan natives, were reputedly far greater. Marine-Sergeant Romus Burgin noted that the Okinawans "were happy that we were there. They wanted us to liberate them from the Japs. They didn't like them."[63] In all likelihood the majority of Okinawans, who had been unwillingly absorbed into Japan in 1872, having been formerly a vassal state to China, would have preferred neither nation to occupy let alone fight over their island.

There is ample testament from *Okinawa* survivors that islanders were used as human shields and that the Japanese army urged the citizens of *Okinawa* to commit suicide; many were persuaded that the American invaders would inflict appalling atrocities on their families. Hand grenades were even distributed to civilians for the purpose of blowing themselves up. At the southern end of the island, whole families would leap from the cliffs onto the rocks below. Kenzaburo Ōe, a Nobel Prize winning novelist and noted pacifist, testified that the military organized civilian suicide and in 2008 an Osaka Prefecture court ruled, "It can be said the military was deeply involved in the mass suicides."[64] Indeed when later Japanese history textbooks issued by the Ministry of Education removed reference to the Japanese military's role in mass suicides, there were waves of protest on *Okinawa* involving hundreds of thousands of demonstrators.

For General Marshall and the US Army the *Battle of Okinawa* was a shocking wake-up call as to what they faced with Operation OLYMPIC, the planned invasion of Japan's main southern island of *Kyushu*, a first stage in the planned Operation DOWNFALL to overthrow the Japanese government. Out of the US 154,000 troops that participated in the *Okinawa* Campaign there were 62,000 casualties of which 12,500 were killed or missing in action. If the war on land was brutal, arguably it was almost as bad at sea. Although the Japanese Navy had been effectively annihilated at *Leyte Gulf*, at *Okinawa* the US Navy suffered more deaths than at *Pearl Harbor, Coral Sea, Midway* and the *Philippine Sea* combined. Some 4,907 Navy personnel were killed by *kamikaze* pilots, the *kikusui* (Floating Chrysanthemums) as the Japanese referred to them. Including the dead there were 9,781 Navy casualties. American material losses were also significant.

The United States lost 768 aircraft and 225 tanks. Meanwhile 368 ships (including the British fleet) were damaged. Twelve destroyers were sunk and important capital ships were damaged beyond repair. Although it is estimated that Japan lost 7,830 aircraft, including an astonishing 34 percent to operational accidents and failures, the US Army Air Force well understood that a much greater aerial threat would await them on *Kyushu*.

The net result of the battle did indeed affect US military thinking, though perhaps not in the way that the officers who organized the defense of *Okinawa* and *Iwo Jima*, had previously imagined. US commanders were appalled both at the scale of casualties on Okinawa and at the mounting estimates for casualties if Operation OLYMPIC went ahead. By now, having seen the scale of mass suicide both on the ground and in the air, America's commanders had lost any faith that Emperor Hirohito's government would surrender without a bloodbath of an invasion of Japan's main islands. American troops on the ground were equally fatalistic. A US Marine at *Okinawa* noted that their next battle would be in *Tokyo Bay*: "No one is going to survive. No Marines, no Japs."[65] Ultimately the horrors of more ground war and the expected toll on American soldiers would make the decision to use not only the newly developed napalm firebombs, but also the atomic bomb, an easy one for America's leaders.

38 LeMay's B-29 Superfortresses over Japan: Cities in Ashes

[April 1944–August 1945]

[Maps: 38.1, 38.2, 38.3, 38.4]

The Boeing B-29 Superfortress: The Boeing B-29 known as the Superfortress was originally conceived as a design study requested by the US Army Air Corps in 1938. They wanted a high altitude bomber that would be out of range of enemy fighters and thus capable of daytime attacks. In order to enable high altitude, the cabin would need to be pressurized, a first for an aircraft of this type. Formal specification was issued by the Air Corps in December 1939 for a 'super-bomber' and Boeing, in competition with Consolidated Aircraft and Lockheed, succeeded in producing a prototype, which won orders for 250 planes.

The design of the B-29, with its requirements for a large pressured fuselage to enable high altitude flying, made it an unusually technologically advanced plane for the period. In addition to the pressurized cabin, the B-29 had the first computer controlled armament system. Designed by Sperry Corporation, the gun turrets, sighted by periscopes, were operated by a complex and weighty control system; they were served by five General Electric analogue computers that were able to calculate airspeed, gravity, temperature and humidity to correct the aiming of the four gun turrets, each fitted with two (later three) 0.50 Browning M2 machine guns. The complexity of the design was increased by the need to connect the pressurized front and back cockpits with a pressurized 'crawl' tunnel, above the unpressurized bomb bay, which connected the two. Produced by Garrett AiResearch in Phoenix Arizona, it was by far the largest pressurized aircraft cabin that had hitherto been attempted. In time the technologies developed for the B-29 formed the bedrock of US technological advance in the post-war period. Boeing in particularly benefitted from a development program that would enable it to become the dominant civil aviation company after the war.

The first run of B-29s each took 150,000 man-hours to build and brought a rush of recruitment by Boeing and their host of sub-contractors. Eventually, improved training and productivity gains brought the build time down to a still not inconsiderable 20,000 man-hours. The cost of the program was prodigious, estimated at US$3.0bn, exceeding even the famed MANHATTAN Project that cost US$2.0bn. In fact the MANHATTAN Project would not have been possible without the B-29, which was the only plane large enough to carry and deliver the atom bomb.

Manufacturing time apart, the principal difficulty with the B-29 lay with the Wright R-3350 Duplex Cyclone radial engine. It had been developed in 1937 but the management of the failing Curtis-Wright Corporation decided to put resources into its bread and butter engines. Lack of development resulted in the 18-cylinder engine being rushed into production. A five-year development time was concertinaed into two years. The first B-29 test flight on 30 December 1942 was ended by an engine fire. Six weeks later, on 18 February 1943, a second flight ended with a crash when engines again caught fire. As an interim fix, cuffs were put on the propeller blades, baffling put around the cylinders and nacelle cowl flaps were enlarged to divert more air into the intakes so as to keep the engines cool. Flight Engineer Fred Gardner noted, "these changes didn't do a lot of good during hot summertime operations at Roswell, New Mexico AAF [Army Airfield]."[1] The need to rush the production of aircraft while modifications and redesigns were constantly being introduced meant that few aircraft coming off the production line were serviceable. Only fifteen out of 100 B-29s produced in 1943 were certifiable.

The result was that planes in early 1944 were immediately flown to rectification facilities; it was a chaotic process hampered by lack of hangar facilities and skilled personnel. Engines continued to be the major bugbear. After take-off, B-29s would have to make a shallow climb at minimum safe power in order not to overheat the engines. Flying with these engines required a delicate balancing act. Gardner recalled:

> if an engine started backfiring, it was SOP [standard operating procedure] to feather it . . . B-29s of the vintage we were flying had magnesium supercharger sections. This reduced weight, but the magnesium was prone to start burning if backfire occurred. Therefore, we feathered at the first indication of a backfire. Moreover oil loss caused problems and maintenance to replace cylinders had to be completed after every 25 hours of flight time, often little more than every two missions. Every 75 hours a B-29's four engines would have to be entirely reconditioned. In combat, particularly with the strain put on engines in reaching their maximum altitude, reliability proved to be a major problem and up 10 to 15 percent of aircraft that took off for a mission had to abort. Losses from crashes and combustion often exceeded losses from Japanese fighters or anti-aircraft batteries.[2]

The Wright engine would become known by the pilots as the 'wrong' engine, but it was not until the end of the *Pacific War* that it was replaced. Perhaps not surprisingly bomber attrition rates were high. Over the course of the war, B-29s suffered 40 wrecks per 100,000 flight hours, some 30 percent worse than the B-17. By comparison over the last 30 years bomber wrecks amount to just 2 wrecks per 100,000 flight hours.

Pilots were so disenchanted with the B-29 that Lieutenant-Colonel Paul W. Tibbets, who would later drop the first atom bomb on Hiroshima in the *Enola Gay*, had extreme difficulty in persuading them to fly the new bomber. It was normal to make standard power checks before take-off but the overheating of the engines at standstill was liable to cause combustion. Tibbets therefore required take-off without these procedures to get airflow into the engines as quickly as possible. To shame his pilots into compliance he secretly trained two women to fly the B-29s and then got them to demonstrate to pilots the new take-off procedures. Tibbets declared that the women, Dorothea Moorman and Dora Dougherty, were "putting the big football players to shame."[3]

The B-29 program required a rapid expansion of crews. Fred Gardner, an aircraft maintenance engineer and first-lieutenant, suddenly found himself transferred with forty others to MacClellan Airfield in California where they were trained to be pilots. They were then transferred to Maxwell Army Airfield in Montgomery, Alabama to train as B-29 Flight Engineers. Gardner noted, "The co-pilot trainees were a 'mixed-bag.' They had less flying time than the pilot trainees and in many cases were not rated in four-engine airplanes. The flight engineer trainees were even more of a 'mixed bag.'"[4] It was a hastily planned and bodged program that would inevitably have an effect on the early performance of the B-29 in the field. Nevertheless, the planes and their crews that emerged from the necessarily truncated test and training programs were, on paper, a supremely powerful weapon. The futuristic looking B-29, whose tubular design stood out from other bombers of its era, could fly at almost 32,000 feet at speeds of 350 mph. Few Japanese fighters could reach that height, let alone match its speed. Heavy calibre anti-aircraft artillery shells could reach that altitude but the Japanese defenders, without proximity fuses for their shells, had little chance of hitting their targets except with statistically improbable direct hits.

Twentieth Bomber Command in India and China: Having called for a program to build the B-29 at prodigious expense, the arrival of the new weapon was eagerly awaited by America's field commanders. Both MacArthur and Nimitz were eager to get their hands on the new 'behemoth' bomber. General Henry 'Hap' Arnold, commander of the US Army Air Forces, had other ideas. Although he was a member of the Joint Chiefs of Staff, the US Air Force was a wing of the Army and he thus reported directly to General Marshall.

However, Arnold and his senior commanders had developed a 'bomber-centric' philosophy in the 1930s that suggested that high altitude daytime bombing could win wars. 'Hap' Arnold wanted the B-29 to provide the war-winning strategy that would force the Japanese to surrender and obviate the need to launch an amphibious invasion and conquest of Japan. Arnold's ulterior motive was to establish the Air Force as a fully independent service ranking *pari passu* with the Army and Navy. Up until the end of 1943, the consensus view was that the war against Japan could only be won by an invasion on the ground. Indeed the plan on basic strategy prepared by the Far East War Plans Group stated, "It has been clearly demonstrated in the war in Europe that strategic air forces are incapable of decisive action and hence the war against Japan must rely upon victory through surface forces, supported appropriately by air forces. Final victory must come through invasion of the Japanese home islands."[5] Although the strategic bombing of Germany had yet to prove decisive, it was felt by Major-General Haywood Hansell, who had returned from the Eighth Air Force in Europe to lead Arnold's planning staff in Washington, that the US Army Air Force (USAAF) had yet to be given its chance to fully prove its worth. In addition the impending arrival of the Superfortress would give the US Air Force an unprecedented offensive weapon.

By the time of the Cairo Meetings (codenamed SEXTANT) in November 1943, attended by Roosevelt, Churchill and Chiang Kai-shek, the US Army Air Force was able to force through a much more robust role for itself in terms of the strategy to be adopted for the subjugation of Japan. Thus when the Combined Staff Planners presented their '*Overall Plan for the defeat of Japan*' on 2 December 1943, it stated that the "invasion of the principal Japanese Islands may not be necessary and the defeat of Japan may be accomplished by sea and air blockade and intensive air bombardment from progressively advanced bases. The plan must, however, be capable of expansion to meet the contingency of an invasion."[6] In effect the US Air Force had engineered the prime position for itself with regard to the ultimate defeat of Japan. It was an internal victory that Major-General Hansell, 'Hap' Arnold's Chief of Staff, followed up by getting Admiral Ernest King's agreement in March 1944 that there should be a unified command of all B-29 bombing operations. In other words theater commanders, notably in the areas controlled by the Navy, would not be able to divert bombers located in their areas to their own strategic and tactical concerns. *De facto*, Hansell had achieved 'Hap' Arnold's dream of creating an independent service, paving the way for the *National Security Act* [1947], which authorized the creation of an independent US Department of the Air Force and a name change from the United States Army Air Forces to the United States Air Force.

The Twentieth Air Force was thus formed on 4 April 1944. A separate new command structure that reported directly to Arnold in Washington was created with its own proprietary global communications system. The route to the creation of an independent air arm was well on its way. Nimitz's *Central Pacific* thrust was now the handmaiden to Arnold's grand design to win the war by bombing Japan into submission. It was envisioned that there would eventually be four bomber commands located in China, *Okinawa*, the *Marianas* and the *Aleutians* comprising a force of up to 1,500 B-29s plus a similar force of escort fighters. Cairo's pronouncements made the acquisition of the *Marianas Islands* of *Guam, Tinian* and *Saipan* central to *Pacific* strategy.

In the meantime the initial deployment of the B-29, designated Twentieth Bomber Command, was planned for India with forward bases to be established in Chengdu. Operation MATTERHORN, part of a series of promises to Chiang Kai-shek, was planned to start in the summer of 1944. The choice of deployment was not uncontroversial. Because of logistical constraints and the limited choice of targets because of range, the Joint War Plans Committee felt that the best choice of operation would be the bombing of shipping and oil facilities from bases in Australia until the *Marianas* could be brought on stream. It was a strategy relentlessly urged by Lieutenant-General George Kenney, the Australian-based commander of Allied Air Forces (AAF) in the South West Pacific Area

(SWPA). However, geopolitical arrangements with Chiang Kai-shek trumped the US Army Air Force's (USAAF) strategic preferences.

The crews of Twentieth Air Force were put through a punishing training schedule at Elgin Field in Florida, where in high secrecy a bombing run was set up over the *Gulf of Mexico* to mimic the trip from the *Marianas*. The simulation included the carrying of 8,000 lb loads as well as the setting up of loose formation for climbing to the 30,000 foot bombing height followed by the tight formation that would be required to bat off Japanese fighter attacks.

Ground crews began to relocate to India in December 1943 and between April and May 1944 the 58th Bombardment Wing was transferred to India where it became Twentieth Bomber Command's main combat unit under the direct command of 'Hap' Arnold in Washington. It was planned that ten groups of B-29s (28 per group) would be made ready for deployment by October 1944. It was an important first step toward US Air Force independence. Although the Twentieth Bomber Command mission was extended to include support of troop action on the ground in both China and Burma, the main target was the bombing of targets in Japan. Twentieth Bomber Command was based in Chengdu where Chiang Kai-shek organized 100,000 workers, with virtually no equipment, to build airfields to accommodate the B-29s. Only targets in *Kyushu* were viable because of range.

As a result of work done by the Committee of Operations Analysis it had become apparent that "in Japan the steel production was uniquely vulnerable, because of the heavy concentration of coke ovens upon which steel production depended."[7] Of the six coking plants on which Japan depended for 73 percent of its coke, three were located in *Kyushu* and were thus in range of the US airfields in southern China. Twentieth Bomber Command at Hengyang Airfield, the largest US airfield in China, would also target the coking plants based in Manchuria. In addition to coking plants, the other main targets for Twentieth Bomber Command were Japanese merchant shipping, aircraft factories, ball-bearing plants, electronic industries and petroleum production and storage. Furthermore "Urban industrial areas vulnerable to incendiary attack"[8] were included on the list of preferred targets.

On 15 to 16 June 75 B-29s launched their first operational attack against northern *Kyushu*; the main target was the Imperial Iron and Steel Works at Yawata, which produced 20.1 percent of Japan's coke. Seven aircraft were lost and there was little damage done. Nevertheless the US press was cock-a-hoop. The attack on Japan's home islands had begun. When Japanese intelligence reported that B-29 bases were being built in both India and China at the beginning of 1944, home defenses started to be prepared for mass bombing. Houses were cleared to create firebreaks. By the end of the war some 614,000 houses were destroyed in this process. Indeed the Japanese firebreak program itself accounted for 20 percent of all housing losses during the war and displaced some 3.5 million people. Beginning in December 1943 a planned evacuation of school children was begun. Some 330,000 were evacuated in school groups by August 1944. A further 459,000 were evacuated with their parents. Air raid shelters were also built though it proved to be a spasmodic effort. When urban bombing arrived in earnest only 2 percent of the population had access to shelters. Those that were built were makeshift and consisted of little more than covered trenches. Only key facilities boasted more sophisticated structures. Civilian fire fighting crews were also organized though there was a chronic lack of equipment and training was perforce rudimentary.

More importantly, logistical difficulties prevented the dispersal of industrial facilities. With subcontractors for components often distributed to tiny home workshops spread throughout residential neighbourhoods, industrial relocation was all but impossible. The *kyoryokukai* (subcontractor organizations) system had been developed during the war with the encouragement of the Ministry of Commerce and Industry. It was a means of expanding particularly munitions capacity by the subcontracting of simple machine and drilling jobs to 'mom and pop' lathes set up in the homes of former craft workers.

After the attack on Yawata, the Japanese government deployed 375 fighters to the three air divisions deployed to defend against enemy bombers. To begin with, the defensive actions prepared by the Japanese government were adequate to deal with spasmodic American attacks. Twentieth Bomber Command, led by Brigadier-General Kenneth Wolfe, was unable to instigate a follow-up to the Yawata raid.

In essence the operation of the B-29 was hampered by virtually impossible logistical constraints. All the fuel for their raids had to be transported over the Hump from India to China. This had to be done either by the Humps' transporters or by specially stripped out B-29s. Thousands of mechanics, grounds crews and support staff had to be transferred and stationed in southern China and provided with housing and food, which could not be supplied locally—they could not have lived on the rations of Chiang Kai-shek's forces. The requirements even for one raid were prodigious. Spare parts, maintenance difficulties and continued teething problems with the aircraft itself risked turning the B-29 into the greatest 'white elephant' project of the war. Hansell, who served in Washington as Twentieth Bomber Command's Chief of Staff, later described Project MATTERHORN as "sound. But the logistic requirements were staggering and the logistic plan was horrendous."[9]

For Arnold the apparent failure of the hugely expensive B-29 program to deliver raids was alarming. Leaving aside the war, his career and the future of what he hoped would be a US Air Force, operating as an independent service, was on the line. As Hansell would later reflect, "The Twentieth Air Force was under extreme pressure to perform. One major slip . . . the Twentieth would have been dismembered and parcelled out to the various theatre commanders."[10] Wolfe was relieved of command and replaced by Major-General Curtis LeMay who had previously been operating bombing missions in Europe against Germany. Nevertheless it was not until July that a second raid, comprising just seventeen B-29s was able to launch an attack on Sasebo, Omura and Tobata. Again little damage was reported. August saw just two more bomber raids. Twenty-four B-29s attacked Nagasaki on 10 and 11 August while sixty-one aircraft were again launched at Yawata on 20 August. Twelve of these aircraft were shot down, including one that was rammed in a suicide attack by one fighter aircraft in a force of over 100 fighters. Damage to industrial plant on the ground was again minimal while the losses, at some 20 percent of those who managed to reach the target, were unsustainable.

In spite of the reorganization of his force and its logistical support, in addition to increased training for crews, LeMay's attacks continued to be disappointing both in numbers and results. Of the remaining five China-based raids on Japan up until the last on 6 January, only the 25 October attack on Omura, which destroyed the city's small aircraft factory, proved decisively successful. Although Twentieth Bomber Command also flew missions against targets in Japanese-controlled South East Asia, including Manchuria, *Formosa* and *Singapore*, it was clear that overall the primary mission had failed. The final China-based mission flew from India on 29 March and attacked *Singapore*. Thereafter Twentieth Bomber Command was transferred to the recently captured *Marianas* Islands.

In six months of operations Twentieth Bomber Command lost 125 B-29s. Japanese enemy aircraft or anti-aircraft batteries accounted for just 20 percent of these losses. An astonishing 80 percent of losses were caused by accidents or malfunctions. Given that some 80 percent of the cargo transported over the Hump was fuel it can be easily concluded that the huge logistical exercise carried out over the Himalayas would have been much better served by re-equipping Chiang Kai-shek's armies as had been promised by Roosevelt. In the post-war analysis, even the US Army Air Force deemed Operation MATTERHORN to have been a resounding failure, with fault laid at the insuperable logistical problems, the poor training and inexperience of crews, and the technical problems inherent in the B-29 itself.

The Failure of High Altitude Precision Bombing: It was not until March 1945 that 'Hap' Arnold took the decision to cut his losses in India and China and focus all his B-29 resources on the six new airfields being restored or built on the *Mariana Islands* of *Saipan, Tinian* and *Guam*. Operations began from these island fields on 24 November. A total of 111 B-29s of Twenty-First Bomber Command attacked Tokyo. While twenty-four planes were targeted at the Nakajima Aircraft Company's Musashino aircraft plant in the suburbs of Tokyo, the remainder attacked port and sundry industrial facilities.

The first large-scale B-29 attack on Tokyo caused some damage to industrial plant though its primary success lay in the fact that although they were attacked by 125 enemy fighters, only one B-29 was downed. At least the defensive capabilities of the new bomber were improving. In response to this attack, Japanese bombing sorties against the *Marianas* also increased. In the following month some eleven Superfortresses were destroyed on the ground and a further forty-three were damaged. By contrast the Japanese lost thirty-seven aircraft. In another somewhat futile response to the raids on Japan, some 9,000 balloons carrying bombs were released and prevailing winds carried them towards the United States. Only 285 were ever reported to have reached the US and caused little if any damage.

Major-General Haywood Hansell, formerly Chief of Staff in Washington to Twentieth Bomber Command, had become commander of Twenty-First Bomber Command on

28 August. From the *Marianas* he persisted with the strategy of high altitude daytime bombing that was failing so abjectly in India and China. It was the orthodoxy of the US Air Army Force since the 1930s that planes could be built that would fly high enough to avoid both fighter and ground defenses and that, deployed in sufficient numbers, they could knock out industrial targets. Indeed it was the purpose for which the Superfortress had been designed and built. Hansell was a fierce advocate of precision bombing believing that it was not only morally acceptable but would also be more effective in reducing the enemy's industrial capacity. It was a strategy ardently opposed by fighter pilots such as Chennault who believed that technologies would develop to enable fighters to fly high enough to attack combat bombers. In reality the so-called precision bombing that Hansell and others thought they were doing was not technologically possible. High altitude bombing was very far from precise and less than 5 percent of bombs dropped from 30,000 feet or more would ever land within 500m of the target. The remainder would land usually in the residential areas that surrounded urban factories. Bomb siting was still relatively primitive, air streams and the aeronautical dynamics of bombs were little understood and crews needed time to learn their craft— time that the high death rate of crews did not allow them. So-called precision bombing was a misnomer; in reality it was 'carpet bombing.' The *Marianas* would be the ultimate test of the bomber-centric orthodoxies of the US Air Force.

More important than the scepticism of fighter pilots was the scepticism of other senior commanders about the viability of high altitude bombing. Hansell's replacement on Arnold's Washington Air Staff was Brigadier-General Lauris Norstad who believed that wooden-built Japanese cities would be very susceptible to incendiary bombing. It was a tactical concept that had been in circulation in Air Force strategy circles since the end of 1943. Given Arnold's legendary impatience it was doubted by many, including Arnold's deputy, General Barney Giles, whether Hansell, a superb staff officer but an unproven combat commander, would survive. Hansell believed that high altitude precision bombing could be made to work. However, he also found the concept of firebombing civilian cities morally repugnant. Arriving at Saipan on 12 October 1944, Hansell was greeted with all the familiar logistical difficulties of setting up operations for Twenty-First Bomber Command, which had beset the operations in India and China.

Hansell's second raid on 27 November, which again targeted the Musashino aircraft factory, was disrupted by cloud and high winds, while an incendiary raid two days later burnt out just a tenth of a square mile of the city. Another high altitude precision attack on 3 December against the Musashino Works also failed due to bad weather. Twenty-First Bomber Command's next five raids targeted Nagoya. Some damage was caused to aircraft plants in the city. Though Hansell was encouraged by the results, he was ordered to trial a large-scale incendiary attack using the new M-19 bomb. The 220 lb M-19 incendiary, invented by the Standard Oil Developments Co., had been trialled on mock-up Japanese and German villages at Dugway Proving Ground in Utah in 1943 where it was proved that the incendiary impact of napalm-filled canisters was greater than earlier magnesium fillers, which burnt more intensely but had an inferior energy to weight efficiency. At 900 feet the M-19 broke into clusters of thirty-six individual M-69 bombs which weighed 6.2 lbs each and exploded on impact. They became known as 'Tokyo calling cards.' The M-69s' ballistic qualities meant that precise targeting of incendiaries was impossible. They could only be used effectively as a tool for the mass burnout of Japanese cities with all the concomitant effects on the civilian population. The fact that these bombs were used on Japan and not on Germany led to many post-war assertions, still unproven, that this was the result of racial prejudice—the most likely explanation being that Japan's tightly packed wooden houses were much more susceptible to burning.

Assured that the use of incendiaries did not reflect a shift in tactics, Hansell used the M-19s on the Mitsubishi Aircraft Works in Nagoya on 22 December but again caused little damage. This was followed by a further failed attack on the Musashino aircraft plant in Tokyo on 27 December. A follow-up attack launched against Nagoya was carried out on 3 January 1945. Although this was planned as an area-bombing raid, fires were quickly controlled by Japan's civilian firefighters.

Further unsuccessful bombing raids were carried out on the Musashino plant in Tokyo on 9 January 1945 and the Mitsubishi plant in Nagoya five days later. Again the results were lacklustre. High altitude precision bombing had been defeated by a number of factors, both technical and natural. First, the B-29s had been defeated by cloud and high winds, which made the identification and accuracy of targets and accuracy of strikes highly problematic. As yet there were no good target guidance systems. Second, the B-29's pilots, navigators and bombardiers were perforce scratch-crews who lacked extended training and battle experience. In particular bombardiers needed much longer training than could be gained on practice missions in the US. In effect bombardiers had to learn on the job. Developments in radar had thus far also proved to be disappointing in helping to improve accuracy. Third, precision bombing, which was in reality carpet-bombing, needed greater numbers of B-29s to achieve full effectiveness.

Perversely Hansell's last precision attack on the Kawasaki Aircraft Industries Akashi plant with seventy-seven Superfortresses on 19 January proved highly effective in bringing production to a halt. The factory never reopened. Hansell was therefore shocked to receive a directive to mount an incendiary attack on Nagoya: "We were just beginning to show some improvement in bombing accuracy, both visual and radar. Now we were directed to reverse our painfully achieved progress in accuracy and turn to area bombing."[11] The results of the B-29 program so far were extremely poor relative to the vast resources that had been put into the aircraft's development; 4 percent overall losses were also considered to be heavy and unacceptable. The loss of a single superfortress usually cost the lives of its entire crew of eleven.

The Committee of Operations Analysis (COA) in Washington had already produced a detailed report in October 1944 that outlined the benefits of the use of incendiaries in terms of their psychological impact on urban populations. As for the technical aspects of dropping M-69 incendiary bombs, at the mocked-up Japanese houses at Dugway Proving Grounds in Utah, even Japanese furniture and *tatami* mats were acquired to demonstrate the incendiary qualities of the newly developed M-19 canisters filled with a gelatinous mixture of naphthenic and palmitic acids that became known as napalm.

Despite the success of Hansell's 19 January raid, Arnold had already decided to replace Hansell with Major-General Curtis LeMay, who had been successful in turning around the performance of Twentieth Bomber Command. Brigadier-General Lauris Norstad was despatched to *Saipan*, where on 9 January he relieved Hansell from his post as head of Twenty-First Bomber Command. Norstad suggested that Hansell could become the deputy to LeMay, who was in the process of relocating Twentieth Bomber Command from India to the *Marianas*. Hansell, who had been LeMay's commanding officer in Europe, declined. Norstad would later justify the decision to replace Hansell when he said, "LeMay is an operator, the rest of us are planners."[12] In the post-war period Hansell continued to be an advocate of precision bombing and became a frequent lecturer on the subject at the US Air Force Academy and the Air War College. It can be argued that the world moved in his favor since the development of optical-electronic technology enabled the building of accurate 'fire and forget' guided missiles.

LeMay's early results fared little better than his predecessor. Twenty-First Bomber Command's six large-scale missions from 23 January to 19 February produced only one notable success; an incendiary attack on Kobe on 4 February burnt a significant area of the city and destroyed some major factories. The introduction of new maintenance procedures by LeMay also reduced the numbers of planes that were forced to turn back to base before reaching their target.

For the next two weeks, attacks were made on aircraft factories that aimed to slow down the supply of Japanese planes, particularly *kamikaze* planes, for the battle raging at *Iwo Jima*. But on 25 February LeMay assembled 172 B-29s for Twenty-First Bomber Command's largest incendiary raid yet launched; the resulting attack on Tokyo burned out one square mile of the city. Thick smoke blew over the capital and discolored the falling snow. It became known in Tokyo as the 'Day of the Black Snow.' The attack pointed the way to the use of incendiaries in larger scale bomber raids. Although the targeting of urban areas with incendiaries was designated by Arnold to be a secondary target compared with aircraft factories, the success of the 25 February incendiary raid led LeMay to consider much wider use of this tactic. US Army Air Force planners had estimated that a concerted incendiary campaign against Japan's largest cities could damage or destroy as much as 40 percent of its industrial capacity.

LeMay, with the support of Brigadier-General Norstad, thoroughly rethought bombing tactics. He concluded that precise targeting in daytime attacks at high altitude was impossible. LeMay noted that bombs released at high altitude were often blown off course by the jet stream over Japan. So although the B-29 armadas that he was now capable of launching at Japan were relatively safe from fighter attack, their bombing effectiveness was severely compromised.

LeMay thus came to his most radical innovation, that low-level nighttime bombing with incendiaries could be more productive. B-29s would fly in at between 5,000–7,000 feet, below cloud cover, where accuracy of bomb sighting would be much greater. His analysis showed that Japanese nighttime fighter ability was limited and that their city anti-aircraft defenses were geared to a much higher flight path. A further benefit could accrue in this type of low-level attack. Getting a B-29 to 30,000 feet massively increased fuel demand. A heavier bomb load could therefore replace extra fuel. LeMay further resolved that in view of Japan's limited nighttime defense abilities, he could strip out a large portion of the weighty machine gun turrets as well as their command and control analog computer systems. Again more weight could be added to the bomb loads.

It was a radical rethink that drew muttering dissent from the B-29 crews. Not surprisingly perhaps, they believed that stripping them of their machine gun defenses as well as flying at low altitude would be suicidal. Even LeMay's 'flak' experts predicted that a low altitude attack would incur losses of up to 70 percent.

Major-General Curtis LeMay: Born in Columbus, Ohio on 15 November 1906, LeMay was the son of an ironworker. In spite of his impoverished background he managed to get a place at Ohio State University and, working his way through college, graduated with a degree in civil engineering. In 1929 he joined the Air Corps Reserve and received a full-time commission in January 1930. First a pursuit pilot and then a navigator, he became known as a hard driving perfectionist who believed in incessant training. Throughout his career he was respected and liked by his fellow aviators who always referred to him as the 'Big Cigar.' His promotion to major just before the start of the *Pacific War* was the beginning of a meteoric career progression. He earned plaudits for leading dangerous missions over Germany including deep penetration flights as far as Regensberg from where they had to fly on to North Africa.

He confronted the high level of 'abort' rates in his Flying Fortress commands with brutal simplicity. Robert McNamara reported that LeMay told his pilots, "I will be in the lead plane on every mission. Any plane that takes off will go over the target, or the crew will be court-martialled."[13] The abort rate collapsed. Indeed McNamara described him as "the finest commander of any service I came across in war. But he was extraordinarily belligerent, many thought brutal."[14] LeMay, with his considerable first-hand experience of leading bombers, was a master of the technical briefs of his aircraft. When two Superfortresses of Brigadier-General John Davies's 313th Wing collided, he explained to LeMay that the crash was probably due to the frosting up of windows. LeMay rattled off all the techniques that could be used to prevent defrosting and concluded that as a last resort "depressurize the aircraft and open the windows . . . You can fly along at 40 degrees below zero with the windows open and the crew will be fairly comfortable."[15]

In August 1944 LeMay was transferred to China where he took charge of Twentieth Bomber Command before being appointed to replace Hansell as Commander of Twenty-First Bomber Command in the *Pacific*. By then he had become a convinced sceptic about the efficacy of high altitude daytime bombing where his B-29s were only able to land 5 percent of their bombs in the vicinity of the target.

LeMay was both a formidable and politically astute leader. 'Hap' Arnold had a legendary short fuse and was not a man to give an officer much time to achieve success.

As he was recovering from his fourth heart attack, Arnold was carefully noting the disappointing early results of LeMay's leadership of Twenty-First Bomber Command. Arnold wrote despondently to his deputy General Barney Giles, "I would not be surprised any day to see the control of the Twentieth Air Force pass either to Nimitz or MacArthur."[16] Arnold was under pressure. A critical assessment of the bombing campaign to date, circulated to the Joint Chiefs of Staff, came to the conclusion: "Japan's production capacity has not yet been fundamentally weakened."[17] LeMay knew the gist of Arnold's concerns and sensed that political pressure was building. Furthermore he was familiar with Arnold's character and his habit of giving short shrift to failure. LeMay needed to make a success of the B-29 programme, but he needed to make a success quickly.

After seven weeks in charge, LeMay had sent 1,065 sorties to Japan in eight missions. Only 36.2 percent had bombed their primary targets. Thirty-six B-29s had been lost—an improving but still high 3.4 percent loss ratio. LeMay faced the awkward truth, "I hadn't gotten anything much done any better than Possum Hansell had."[18] Radical action was needed.

The Great Tokyo Air Raid: **[Map: 38.1]** It is generally assumed that the killing of some 65,000 civilians with the dropping of an atom bomb at Hiroshima on 8 August 1945 was the largest single 'killing event' of the *Pacific War*. It was not.

On 6 March 1945, LeMay complained to his public relations officer, Lieutenant-Colonel St. Clair McKelway, "This outfit has been getting a lot of publicity without having really accomplished a hell of a lot in bombing results."[19] Three days later, at 5.34 p.m. on 9 March 1945, 346 Boeing B-29 Superfortresses began to taxi down the airstrips known as the 'Hirohito Highway' on *Guam, Saipan* and *Tinian* (the main *Mariana Islands*) and headed for Tokyo. Not only had the heavy bombers' defensive guns been removed, except for their tail cannon, but also they had been ordered to fly at the seemingly suicidal altitude of 5,000 feet. By obviating the need to carry fuel to take the B-29 to 30,000 feet, LeMay was also able to increase the bomb payload by 65 percent from 6,000 lbs to 9,900 lbs. From a study of photographic intelligence, LeMay would later reveal that he had come to the conclusion, "Japan was poorly prepared for a low altitude night attack. She had little in the way of radar equipment or anti-aircraft guns. I wanted take advantage of her weakness and exploit it for all it was worth."[20]

His enthusiasm for a low-level attack was not universal. Although Lieutenant-General George Kenney, MacArthur's airman, was a known supporter, 'Hap' Arnold had tried it in Europe where it produced very poor results and high casualties. Crews were far from convinced—particularly when they were warned to expect that they would be brutally treated by Japanese civilians if they were shot down. If possible they were advised to ditch their planes in the sea and hope to be picked up by US rescue submarines. The message was clear. They were likely to be killed by an enraged populace. The pilots were stunned and furious when they were told to fly at 5,000 feet with their machine guns removed and many senior officers were equally concerned about the advisability of the mission. Even Curtis LeMay had his doubts. Indeed he sent notification of the attack and its specifications to US Air Force Commander, General 'Hap' Arnold, on a day when he knew that his boss was out of his Washington office.

LeMay would later suggest that he wanted to protect Arnold if his revolutionary new approach to bombing ended in humiliating failure. He may also have feared having his plans countermanded. It was a risk. LeMay himself would have liked to accompany his fliers but his knowledge of developments in the atomic programme ruled him out because of the possibility that he might be shot down and captured. LeMay was understandably nervous about a raid that many of his colleagues considered to be a huge gamble. "I walked the floor because I couldn't go on it [the mission] . . . I'll admit I was nervous about it," Le May later recalled, "I made the decision. I weighed the odds. I knew the odds were in my favor. But still, it was something new. I could have lost a lot of people, appeared to be an idiot."[21]

The target area of Tokyo was the downtown district around the *Sumida River*, tributary of the *Arakawa River* that fed into *Tokyo Bay*. In the sixteenth century this area was a huge marshy estuary. However, after the unification of Japan, which followed the baronial wars that had ended with the supremacy of Tokegawa Ieyasu, it was declared that Edo (Tokyo) would be the new military headquarters of his Shogunate. After the completion in 1603 of Edo Castle (since the Meiji Restoration, the Imperial Palace), the city grew rapidly. Expansion came principally toward the northeast of Edo Castle as the rivers were developed to serve the commercial activity needed to supply the Tokugawa's military garrison.

By 1800 Edo was the most populous city in the world with a population of well over one million citizens. During this time the flat estuary area of the *Sumida River* was filled in and became a built-up maze of canals, stores, factories, and small wood and paper houses that often doubled as workshops. The streets were little more than bustling narrow alleyways. By the twentieth century the area around the *Sumida River* comprised the factory districts of Honjo and Mukojima as well as the densely populated poor residential districts of Asakusa, Shintaya, Kanda and Nihonbashi.

Historically the city was a well-known fire hazard. Frequent earthquakes combined with the use of primitive oil lamps (later kerosene), caused fires that could rapidly escalate into citywide conflagrations. In 1657 the Great Fire of Meireki had killed over 100,000 people. In more recent times, the Great Kanto Earthquake of 1923 killed an estimated 200,000 people in Tokyo and perhaps double that number if the towns and cities in the span of the Great Plains are included. In Tokyo the loss of life, from fire and tsunami was estimated at 150,000. In addition, Japanese citizens, blaming foreigners for the fires and subsequent poisoning of the water wells, murdered some 10,000 Koreans residing in Tokyo.

The first wave of the 334 B-29s launched reached their target at 2.00 a.m. (Guam time) on 10 March. Flying low at 5,000 feet and at night aroused the curiosity of Tokyo's inhabitants. A Danish diplomat, Lars Tillitse, recalled a 'terrific noise' while Robert Guillain, a journalist working for *Agence France-Presse* (then *Agence Havas*), author of *I Saw Tokyo Burning: An Eyewitness Narrative from Pearl Harbor to Hiroshima* [1982], remembered "an odd rhythmic buzzing that filled the night with deep, powerful pulsation and made my whole house vibrate."[22] Crowds gathered in the street and cheered when a B-29 burst into flames, exploded and crashed to the ground. There were few such successes in a raid that lasted just over two and a half hours.

The first of 8,519 canisters of incendiary bombs were released. The M-19 'cluster' bombs burst open, each releasing thirty-eight 6.2 lb hexagonal cylinders, 496,000 in total, which wobbled their way to earth trailed by flapping strips of cloth; Father S. J. Bitter of Sophia University in Tokyo who saw the bombs falling described them as being like 'silver streamers.'[23] Mrs. Sekimura, who had experienced the horrors of the 1923 earthquake, ran for safety with her children. She described the sight of bombs bursting overhead as being "like bunches of bananas."[24] When the cylinders hit the roofs, petroleum jelly would be broadly scattered and ignite producing a seemingly instantaneous combustion. Wind would quickly blow the flames to neighboring properties that would glow, combust and implode. Guillain described "a crackling like the sound of bonfires—the noise it seemed, of houses collapsing."[25] The fire services were overwhelmed. Ninety-six fire engines were lost in the night as well as 128 firemen.

The American attack was helped by strong winds that swept the flames northwest. The air became heated to 1,800 degrees causing buildings and people to ignite spontaneously. Metal twisted and deformed or melted. Ultimately fire obliterated all but the odd stone-built building for some sixteen square miles. Fire spread much faster than people could run. In the narrow passageways a thick black smoke reduced visibility to a few feet. Asphyxiation overcame many. The Japanese government had urged residents to stand fast and protect their properties in the event of attack. Those who stayed as instructed died. Most of those who ran fared little better. Barricades of fire blocked exits in all directions. Some gave up, knelt, faced the Imperial Palace and waited for fire to consume them.

Others jumped into the canals where they were boiled to death. Thousands leapt into the *Sumida River* itself but were incinerated by a fireball. In the morning the river bank was jammed with people looking like formless blackened logs; Captain Kubota described the bodies "as all nude, the clothes had been burned away, and there was a dreadful sameness about them, no telling men from women or even children. All that remained were pieces of charred meat."[26] The tide had already swept thousands of these mutant corpses out to sea.

Some sought survival in the more substantial buildings. Hidezo Tsuchikura took his two children to Futaba School; hiding first in the basement fire shelter, then in the gym and finally clambering to the roof. Here he found a water tower and was able to douse his daughter when she caught fire. Their clothes were steaming from the heat within minutes. Miraculously the Tsuchikura family survived along with a handful of others.

When they descended the three-storey building a few hours later they found every floor packed with people who had been boiled or baked to death. "But the swimming pool," Tsuchikura recalled, "was the most horrible sight of all. It was hideous. More than a thousand people, we estimated, had jammed into the pool. The pool had been filled to its brim when we first arrived. Now there wasn't a drop of water, only the bodies of the adults and children who had died."[27]

At Asakusa Shrine, where, during the Great Tokyo Earthquake in 1923 thousands had successfully sought refuge at the feet of the Buddhist temple dedicated to Kannon, goddess of mercy, a huge throng gathered. This time the seventeenth century temple caught fire along with the people who had sheltered there. Sumie Mishima observed that from the opposite site of the city, "The red glow that spread over the southeastern horizon quickly bulged up and filled the entire sky . . . an eerie pink light settled on the earth and clearly lit up the deep-lined faces of the awestruck people. The burning seemed to go on all night."[28] Several months later Sumie Mishima's own house would be burnt down by another raid. Her collection of Chinese Sung and Ming dynasty books were burnt into glistening white powder. She put the ashes into a broken jar and used it as "the cleanest possible tooth powder."[29]

For three hours wave after wave of bombers dropped their deadly cargoes. For the late arriving B-29 crews the view of the burning city amazed them. Amazement turned to disgust when they picked up the stench of burning flesh. Many crewmen vomited. Updrafts from the fire below tossed the B-29s about like sail boats in a storm. "Gusts from the inferno were so powerful that men were rattled around inside the ships like dice in a cup"[30] reported a US Army Air Force sergeant. Brigadier-General Thomas Powers, LeMay's Chief of Staff, photographed the inferno below and flew back to report the astonishing sight.

A few people miraculously survived. Kinosuke Wakabayashi sheltered behind the concrete walls of the Asahi Brewery warehouse on the *Sumida River* from where he watched as people raced through the flames to dive into the river or shelter on the riverbanks, already clogged with people. Here the flame sucked away the oxygen and left thousands dead like fish "on the bottom of a lake that has been drained."[31] Young housewife Miwa Koshiba, her husband and children abandoned the hole that they had dug in their garden when it became too hot and fled to the river where they viewed the horrific scenes unfolding. She led her family to the large sewer pipe that drained into the river and hid there all night, caking her children in excrement to keep them cool.

Masatake Obata, typical of the many thousands whose household workshop produced aircraft components, was knocked unconscious by a bomb and woke up to find himself on fire. His shoes had been burnt off and so had his toes. He staggered to a trench and chanted Buddhist prayers with his fellow occupants. Brought to a makeshift medical center later that morning, the doctor commanded the orderlies to "Take him downstairs to the morgue in the basement. Let him join the other dead. There is no hope."[32] Obata was left to die on a mat. Three days later he was found by his mother and nursed back to health. His wife, four children and two sisters, who he had urged to seek refuge in Sumida Park while he tried to protect his home and business, all perished.

As morning broke people emerged to find a city of smouldering ash littered with the distorted metal skeletons of cars, bikes, trams and buildings. At Kubota Bridge, people standing shoulder to shoulder had been carbonized. They crumbled at a touch. Survivors were afflicted by eye infections and bronchial complaints. Thousands died in agony over the succeeding days. Medical facilities were simply overwhelmed. The fire had burnt some 261,000 houses leaving 1.15 million people homeless. Twenty-two industrial targets had been completely destroyed and many other unidentified manufactories also wiped out. 82 percent of the main target area of ten square miles had been destroyed. Of the 79,466 dead who were counted and identified, 69,100 were buried in pits. The actual number who were incinerated to ash or washed out to sea was clearly far greater. The contemporary Japanese Naval estimate of about 100,000 dead is generally considered about right.

A week after the Great Tokyo Air Raid the Emperor donned a general's uniform and was driven in his 1935 American maroon-colored 8-cylinder Packard 1202 to see the destruction for himself. It is not clear whether it was explained to him that the 2 to 4 foot high mounds of 'rice plants' were actually bodies that had been fused together in the heat. Hirohito stopped to talk to a few bedraggled survivors. His thoughts on the firebombing of Tokyo were never revealed.

For Major-General Curtis LeMay, the fire-bombing of Tokyo (Operation MEETINGHOUSE) was a stunning success. Some 1,665 tons of incendiaries carried by 334 B-29s had laid waste Japan's capital in a single night. By comparison the largest raid of the war on Germany, at Hamburg, used 3,000 aircraft of all types with 9,000 tons of bombs used over the course of a week and killed 42,000 people. The building of the B-29 bomber force had finally paid off. Losses of fourteen aircraft (4 percent) with five crews picked up and rescued were no higher than a conventional high altitude mission. It was an attack that not only made LeMay's reputation but saved Arnold from the humiliation that he would have suffered from the continued failure of the B-29 to deliver results. Arnold was ecstatic and sent a message: "Congratulations. This mission shows your crews have the guts for anything."[33] Later the import of the Great Tokyo Air Raid became evident to Arnold. In a message to LeMay he concluded, "Under favourable conditions you should then have the ability to destroy whole industrial cities should that be required."[34]

The Firebombing of Japan's Major Cities: **[Map: 38.2]** The dramatically successful firebombing of Tokyo on 9/10 March pointed the way forward. The attack on Tokyo was followed the next day by another mass raid against Nagoya by 310 B-29s. Two square miles were burnt out but remarkably there were no loss of aircraft to the Japanese defenses. Two days later it was the turn of Osaka. For the loss of just two aircraft, 274 B-29s burnt out eight square miles of the city. The attack on Kobe on 16/17 March killed 8,000 people and made 650,000 homeless. Nagoya was revisited two days later and another three square miles of the city was destroyed. In the ten days after 9 March, LeMay had delivered a devastating blow to the industrial infrastructure of Japan's urban centers. He achieved significantly more in these few days than the entirety of the B-29 campaigns of the preceding four months.

There was now a break in the firebombing of Japan simply because the stocks of incendiary bombs in the *Marianas* had been depleted. LeMay reverted to precision bombing on 23/24 March. The night attack on the Mitsubishi aircraft engine factory failed and five of the 251 B-29s were shot down. The failure of another precision attack as well as the high price in men and aircraft merely confirmed the importance of the incendiary campaign. LeMay also began a leaflet campaign urging the Japanese to overthrow their government or face destruction. By the end of March the US Air Force had come to the firm conclusion that the firebombing campaign had proved spectacularly successful. In Washington, the Joint Target Group (JTG), which was responsible for developing the broad strategies based on detailed statistical analysis of targets and operational success/failure, outlined a policy for strikes against twenty-two Japanese cities. It would be a two-fold operation, using incendiaries to raze cities and precision bombing to target key industrial targets. The campaign was intended to be preparatory for the invasion of Japan although numbers of senior commanders in Washington argued that the civil and industrial devastation would be so great that the Japanese would be bound to surrender before the invasion began.

The campaign by which the JTG planned to reduce Japan to rubble was put on hold from the end of March for the next six weeks, as the Twenty-First Bomber Command was required to support the invasion of *Okinawa*. On 27 March, airfields were bombed at Oita and Tachiarai in *Kyushu* as well as an aircraft plant at Omura. LeMay's forces suffered no casualties. A second attack on these targets was made four days later. Airfields were also targeted on 8 and 16 April. Although after 17 May the B-29s were released for other targets, LeMay continued to concentrate his efforts for the next three weeks against targets in *Kyushu* in support of the Okinawa operations. A total of 2,235 sorties were flown against airfields in *Kyushu*. Although just twenty-two aircraft were lost, a loss rate of just 0.01 percent, *kamikaze* attacks on the US fleet stationed off *Okinawa* were barely impeded.

Precision bombing continued to target Japanese aircraft production. On the night of 1 April 121 B-29s attacked the Nakajima engine factory in Tokyo and further attacks were made on engine factories in Shizuoka, Koizumi and Tachikawa. However, LeMay concluded that night attacks were not capable of producing results and reverted to daytime operations. On 7 April long-range P-51 Mustang fighters based in *Iwo Jima* accompanied a B-29 mission for the first time. The large-scale attacks on aircraft factories in Tokyo were mostly successful. Although seven Superfortresses were shot down, VII-Fighter Command claimed to have shot down 101 Japanese aircraft for the loss of just two Mustangs. Another attack on the Musashino aircraft plant on 12 April finally inflicted heavy damage on this facility. In a reflection of JTG's new 'mix and match' strategy, the following night LeMay launched another nighttime incendiary attack that destroyed 10.7 square miles of Tokyo. The key target was the largest arsenal in the Japanese Empire. Just two aircraft were lost. The effect on production was significant. Only half the employees returned to work. Other benefits were brought by incendiary bombing—even if they were only discovered by later interviews with the subjugated Japanese populace after the war. A post-war report noted, "The people of Tokyo were fully cognizant of the great loss of life in the fire of 10 March and consequently were reluctant to stay in the target area to perform fire fighting duties."[35]

A similar large-scale firebombing of Tokyo, Kawasaki and Yokohama with 303 Superfortresses brought similar mass destruction on 15 April with a reported 9.6 square miles destroyed. Over the next two weeks, precision attacks were made on the Tachikawa aircraft factory at Yamato, the Hiro Naval Aircraft Factory at Kure, the airframe factory at Konan, and the oil storage facilities at Iwakuni, Oshima and Toyama. It was clear that side by side with the success of firebombing, the increasing experience of the B-29 crews had begun to improve their proficiency in conventional bombing. It also helped that B-29 raids were now being carried out with larger and larger numbers of aircraft.

With the arrival from China of the 58th and 315th Bombardment Wings in the *Marianas* at the end of April, LeMay's forces could muster five wings with an aggregate of 1,002 planes. By the standards of the era, the B-29 forces now assembled on *Saipan, Tinian* and *Guam* represented a formidable offensive weapon. The release of his bombing support for the *Okinawa* Campaign enabled LeMay to launch his newly enlarged force aimed at the further reduction of Japanese industrial power. By the end of May, Tokyo was so reduced, with some 50 percent of the city completely destroyed, that it was temporarily removed from the list of targets. Tokyo's Imperial Palace was spared because of the risk of killing the Emperor. Nagoya and Yokohama came in for particularly harsh treatment. Two raids on Nagoya by over 450 B-29s on 13 and 16 May burnt out seven square miles of the city, killed nearly 4,000 civilians and left some 470,000 people homeless. It had been one of the more difficult cities to burn because of the "numerous fire breaks and the high percentage of fire resistant structures."[36]

By the end of May about 15 percent of Japan's urban housing stock or some ninety-four square miles of buildings had been destroyed. As for the defense of Japanese cities, Iwao Yamaziki, Minister of Home Affairs, described the government's provisions as "futile."[37] In spite of the ban on bombing the Imperial Palace, either because of inaccuracy or the wilful disobedience of the B-29 aircrews, a raid on Tokyo on 25 May saw the twenty-seven buildings in the Imperial Palace grounds burnt to the ground, with just one reception chamber surviving. Twenty-eight members of the Imperial staff were killed. More importantly from the US point of view, the myth that the Palace had so far survived due to celestial intervention was destroyed; it had a profoundly shocking effect on Japanese diehards. In the same raid sixty-two captured US airmen were incinerated in the Tokyo Army Prison. For Tokyo's citizens, a spirit of resignation and defeat set in: "Not burned out yet?"[38] became a familiar greeting.

June saw a switch in the attack to Osaka and Kobe. On 1 June, a force of 521 Superfortresses escorted by 148 Mustang fighters, was launched at Osaka: 3,960 Japanese died and 3.15 square miles of largely residential housing was burnt out. Remarkably the American fighters' escorts, which found themselves in thick cloud, lost twenty-seven planes from collisions. A further attack on the city on 7 June destroyed a further 2.2 square miles. Two further firebomb attacks on the city, the last on 15 June, added another 5.5 square miles to the toll of urban misery: 300,000 houses in Osaka had been burnt out. Kobe also lost 4.35 square miles to firebombing. The campaign against six of Japan's seven largest cities, Tokyo, Osaka, Nagoya, Yokohama, Kobe and Kawasaki, had resulted in the aggregate destruction of 105.3 square miles.

The May–June 1945 bombing of Japan produced a destruction of civilian housing of 1.44 million units—on a scale that was unprecedented in the history of warfare. In spite of the mass exodus of urban citizens to the countryside some 126,000 people were killed out of total casualties of 442,000 and 13 million more were made homeless at a cost of just 136 B-29s. In terms of planning and execution it was a campaign that was hard to fault. The B-29, after its troubled start, had turned into the war's most feared weapon of mass destruction. It was a campaign whose morality became much debated in the post-war period.

The EMPIRE Plan and the Expansion of Firebombing: **[Chart: C.12]** At the end of June 1945 the bombing strategy toward Japan underwent a series of refinements. Arnold visited LeMay's HQ at *Saipan* in mid-June and after strategic discussions, he signed off on what was known as the EMPIRE Plan. It was decided to focus firebombing attacks on twenty-five second-tier cities (later expanded to fifty-eight cities) with populations of between 60,000 and 325,000 people.

These targets were drawn from a possible list of 171 smaller cities. Niigata and Kokura were excluded for the same reason as the larger city of Hiroshima because they were on the list of potential atom bomb targets. Kyoto had also been excluded from any lists for cultural reasons. Seventeen cities were out of range, which left 137 to be evaluated on the criteria of population density and flammability. The aim was to seek out industrial targets and cities most at risk of incendiary conflagration. Size of transportation infrastructure was a distant third criterion. Typical of such cities was Kagoshima with a population of 190,000 in southern *Kyushu*, which was a major port and rail terminus with large oil storage facilities and four electric power plants. Hammamatsu south of Tokyo had a population of 165,000 people squashed into 4.4 square miles; later famous in the post-war period as the world center of piano manufacture, boasting both Yamaha and Kawai, Hamamatsu was an important railway repair centre as well as producing propellers, ordnance and machinery. Omuta in *Kyushu*, with 177,000 people, produced chemicals, coke, synthetic oil and explosives as well as being the biggest coal shipping port. Yokkaichi, the fourth smaller city targeted on 17/18 June, with 102,000 citizens pressed into just 1.5 square miles, had the largest oil refinery in Japan.

However, LeMay decided to use incendiary attacks only on cloudy days while high altitude precision bombing on 'high value' targets would be preferred on clear days. It was convincing testimony to the increasing effectiveness of precision bombing, which, while remaining imprecise in terms of the number of bombs that hit the target, was nevertheless increasingly effective in destroying large industrial plants. Improved performance had come with increased experience of crews and bombardiers and the doubling of 'numbers' of the typical B-29 raid. As the size of targets reduced, LeMay would frequently mount multi-city attacks on the same day. The number of aircraft that he could deploy was by now massive compared to the start of the bombing campaign. On 22 June, 383 Superfortresses attacked industrial targets in six cities including, Kure, Kakamigahara, Himeji, Mizushima, and Akashi, all in southern *Honshu*. 26 June saw factories in the same region as well as neighboring *Shikoku Island* targeted by 510 B-29s with 148 escort fighters.

The use of incendiaries was further extended. In addition to precision bombing, LeMay, in accordance with the EMPIRE Plan attack, ordered an average of two incendiary attacks a week; targets included Hamamatsu, Kagoshima, Omuta, Yokkaichi, Fukuoka, Shizuoka, Toyohashi, Moji, Nobeoka, Okayama, Sasebo, Kumamoto, Kure, Shimonoseki, Ube, Kochi, Takematsu, Tokushima, Akashi, Chiba, Kofu, Shimizu, Gifu, Sakai, Sendai, Wakayama, Ichinomiya, Tsuruga, Utsunomiya, Uwajima, Hiratsuka, Kuwana, Namazu, Oita, Choshi, Fukui, Hitachi, Okazaki, Matsuyama, Aomori, Ichinomiya, and Tokuyama. Defenses for the civilians in these cities were perfunctory. Although some cities were warned in advance that attacks would take place, it was a slaughter of the innocents designed not only to wipe out localized industrial production but also to reduce the Japanese will to fight and to put pressure on Hirohito to surrender. The success of the operation in terms of reducing morale was confirmed by Yukata Akabane, a civil servant and senior executive officer at the Air Raid Precautions headquarters in Tokyo, who observed, "It was the raids on the medium and smaller cities which had the worst effects and really brought home to the people the experience of bombing and a demoralization of faith in the outcome of the war ... It was bad enough in so large a city as Tokyo, but worse in the smaller cities, where most of the city was wiped out."[39]

In addition to the bombs, LeMay's B-29s dropped 60 million propaganda leaflets between May and July. Produced by Nimitz's Psychological Warfare Office, the objective was to persuade the Japanese people "to take action to terminate the war."[40] Harsh penalties were exacted on Japanese citizens who kept them. However, unlike Germany, there were no Japanese resistance movements to activate. Even communists volunteered to die as *kamikaze* pilots.

In a new tactic designed to convince average citizens that it was the Japanese government, not the Japanese people, which was the target of US enmity, on 27/28 July leaflets were dropped on eleven cities and warned that they were going to be bombed by incendiaries. It was the first time that the US Army Air Force had taken action to minimize civilian casualties. As Japanese air resistance had all but collapsed, radio broadcasts were made from *Saipan* to warn of impending raids. The first week of August saw no let-up in the bombing campaign. The first day of the month, just a week before the dropping of the atom bomb on Hiroshima, LeMay launched 836 B-29s against Hachiojima, Mito, Nagaoka and Toyama. Improvements in technology continued to the end. From the end of June, B-29s began to be fitted with AN/APQ-7 radar that enabled significantly more accurate night bombing. Subsequently precision attacks on oil refineries achieved notable success at Utsube, Kudamatsu, Minoshima and the Maruzen refinery outside Osaka.

The Mining of Japanese Shipping: **[Map: 38.3] [Chart: C.6]** In addition to the bombing of the Japanese mainland, Arnold reluctantly yielded to requests from the Navy to mine the Japanese coastline. As Hansell recalled after the war, "It looked like one more diversion to the local needs of a ground commander, and away from primary industrial targets leading to defeat of the enemy air force."[41] Arnold as ever was only too aware of the political difficulties of keeping a unified command. In his memoirs he noted that at this point in the war, "MacArthur yelled for the B-29's; Nimitz wanted the B-29's; Stilwell and Mountbatten wanted the B-29's—all for tactical purposes."[42]

LeMay was accommodating. At the end of March 313th Bombardment Wing, which had been specially trained for mine laying, began operations in the *Shimonoseki Strait*, which divided the largest Japanese island of *Honshu* from the second most important island of *Kyushu*. The operation was timed to prevent the possible disruption of the *Okinawa* invasion by the Japanese Navy.

The secondary and perhaps more important role of the mining of the *Shimonoseki Strait* was to prevent the supply of *matériel* from Korea across the *Sea of Japan* to the major ports on the southern coast of *Honshu*. The other straits separating Japan's 'fourth island' of *Shikoku* from the main island of *Honshu* were particularly targeted as they guarded the entrances to Japan's last lacuna of safety, the *Inland Sea* with its major ports of Osaka, Kobe and Hiroshima. Mining veteran Lieutenant Commander Ellis Johnson enthusiastically reported on the success of these early missions and concluded, "It can be stated that the continuation of this mine-laying will achieve for the first time by strategic air power, a sea blockade, which previously has been possible only by sea power."[43] The *Shimonoseki Strait* was completely closed for two weeks. Nimitz sent an effusive message to LeMay concluding, "This project, like all your operations to date, has been executed with precision and determination which arouses our admiration. It is a definite contribution toward winning of the war."[44] Subsequently mining was expanded to other key shipping points around *Kyushu* and *Honshu* in Operation STARVATION— aimed less at preventing the import of food (the Japanese government had long since put 'guns before butter') and more at stopping essential war *matériel*, particular oil, from reaching Japan.

Although Japan made a tardy response to the mining operations with an increased allocation of naval resources to clear shipping lanes, both the number of US mines and their sophistication overwhelmed them. Between March 1945 and August in excess of

10,000 mines were laid. The mines weighed either 1,000 or 2,000 pounds. The M-26 thousand pound mine was as powerful as the US Army Air Force's M-13 torpedo that carried 600 lb of explosive. The two thousand pound M-25 mine carried 1,250 lb of explosive. Both were ship killers. Dropped at any height over 200 feet, parachutes broke their fall and slowed entry speed into the water. Workable in relatively shallow depths of 16 to 150 feet, the M-25 could be activated, depending on the model specification, by magnetic, acoustic or pressure activated trigger mechanisms. The post-war Strategic Bombing Survey concluded that Japanese countermeasures were "neither extensive, efficient, nor adequate for the purpose."[45]

It was a flexible and deadly weapon. As Major John Chilstrom has noted in *The Significance of US Army Air Forces Minelaying in World War II* [1992], "The minefield planner could select the Mark-25 (or a smaller mine, such as the 1,000 pound Mark-26) with modifications tailored to the specific water depth, type of vessels, traffic frequency, and minesweeping capability."[46]

At the cost of just 16 B-29s, the 313th Bombardment Wing's mines accounted for the sinking of 293 ships, some 9.3 percent of all merchant ships lost during the *Pacific War*. In spite of Arnold's misgivings, the post-war US Strategic Bombing Survey (*Pacific War*) concluded that the effectiveness of mining the sea approaches to Japanese ports had been underestimated. A Naval Ordnance Laboratory report similarly reported that in the last six months of the war, mines dropped by B-29s accounted for 60 percent of all Japanese shipping losses. In May 1945 mines even overtook submarines in terms of the number of 'ship-kills' achieved. Although Air Force commanders would always prefer bombing to the seeming more passive laying of mines, the statistics speak for themselves. For every thirty-four mines dropped, a Japanese ship was sunk. In the shallow waters of coastal Japan, the mine was a deadly weapon. The Strategic Bombing Survey concluded, "mine laying has been the most economical in both men and material of all types of warfare against shipping."[47] As well as disrupting supplies from its dwindling empire, Japan's inter-coastal commerce was reduced to a trickle.

That is not to say that the bombing of Japanese cities was ineffective in reducing industrial capacity but Prince Fumimaro Konoe admitted that the sinking of Japan's merchant fleet combined with the mining campaign were as effective as the B-29 campaign on the Japanese mainland. After the war, the US Strategic Bombing Survey concluded that the mine laying campaign, Operation STARVATION, was second only to the American submarine in the destruction of Japan's merchant fleet.

In mid-July a further escalation of the bombing of Japan was planned. 'Hap' Arnold reorganized Twenty-First Bomber Command, which was renamed the Twentieth Air Force under Le May. However, with the arrival of General Doolittle's Eighth Air Force that was relocating from Europe, a new overall command structure, the United States Strategic Air Forces in the *Pacific*, was established in *Guam* under General Carl Spatz. In addition to the Twentieth and Eighth Air Forces it was planned that the arriving Allied bomber forces, the Commonwealth Tiger Force, compromising squadrons from Britain, Australia, Canada and New Zealand, would also report to this new entity.

The bombing campaign finally brought home to the Japanese the catastrophe of their rulers' military adventures. Shielded from the truth by incessant propaganda about Japan's supposed victories, the harsh reality of the Japanese war situation only became clear to its citizens as a result of LeMay's aerial campaign. Civil servant Akebane organized the civilian relocation of five million Tokyo residents alone to the countryside between 1944 and the end of the war. In the countryside the rising price of rice was blamed on the new arrivals. By now "the food situation affected all classes,"[48] noted Akebane. He observed, "The chief trouble was not so much in rice but in secondary articles of diet—vegetables, fish, particularly in the cities."[49]

The collapse in morale manifested itself in growing absenteeism, go-slows and even strikes, which were officially forbidden. Increasingly the feared *Kempeitai* were ignored and indeed overwhelmed by disgruntled civilians who had become highly disaffected toward Hirohito's regime—evidence that contradicted MacArthur's mistaken belief that social stability was dependent on the retention of the Emperor as head of state. Albeit successful in reducing Japan's economic capacity and demoralizing its citizens, it did little to prevent the Army's plans for the deployment of 3.15 million men plus 1.5 million naval personnel for the defense of Japan's four main home islands.

Japan's Desperate Last Aerial Weapons: [Map: 38.4] As Germany's defeat crept ever closer, Hitler's generals banked on numbers of secret weapons to turn around their fortunes—including the Tiger II Tank and the V-1 and V-2 rocket bombs. Japan too pinned their hopes on new weapons. Apart from numbers of suicide boats, and submarines, the Japanese Army and Navy built new types of *kamikaze* aircraft and rockets. These were aimed directly at US forces as they approached Japan.

Less well known however, were the weapons developed to attack the United States. Starting in November 1944, the Japanese Army launched balloon bombs toward America. They made use of the jet stream to deliver either anti-personnel bombs or incendiaries. The first were devised to cause indiscriminate death to civilians; the second was devised to set fire to forests, farmland or cities. Of the over 9,300 launched, only 300 reached America, killing six people and causing minimal damage. They were found as far apart as Alaska in the northwest and California in the southwest. Inland, balloons were found in Kansas and Texas. The *Fusen Bakudan* (fire balloon) campaign was not a success. By extraordinary chance however, on 10 March 1945, one of them landed in the vicinity of the secret Hanford nuclear site in Washington State.

The resulting explosion cut power to the plutonium reactor's cooling systems and it was only because precautions had been taken to have a backup system that America did not suffer its first nuclear disaster. The plutonium manufactured at Hanford would be used in the first nuclear detonation in New Mexico, the TRINITY test, as well as the implosion type atom bomb used at Nagasaki. Without Hanford's plutonium it is unlikely that Los Alamos's atom bomb would have been delivered before the planned invasion of the Japanese mainland on 1 November 1945. **[See Chapter 40: Potsdam, Hirohito, and the Atom Bomb]**

An even more bizarre plan to interdict the US advance was the plan to use three behemoth *Sen Toku* 1–400 Class submarine-aircraft carriers to launch a bombing attack on the Gatun Locks of the *Panama Canal*. The spiritual predecessors of America's post-war ballistic submarine force, the I-400 were designed to travel around the world. The Imperial Japanese Navy hoped that by rendering it inoperable, the United States would face significant logistical difficulties in supplying its burgeoning armed forces in the Pacific, some 1.5 million men in the spring of 1945. **[See Appendix A: Submarines: America Draws Tight the Noose]** The vulnerability of the *Panama Canal* was well understood and key locations were protected by barrage balloons as well as a coast battery located at Fort Sherman on Panama's *Atlantic* Coast and Fort Amador facing the *Pacific Ocean*. Ultimately however, the war drew to an end before the plan could be realized.

The Results and Morality of the Bombing of Japan: The firebombing of Japan, (culminating with the dropping of the atom bomb on Hiroshima and Nagasaki, which are dealt with in Chapter 37), has been one the touchstones of post-war debate concerning the morality and legality of mass urban bombing. However, with regard to Japan the debate on the morality of firebombing has tended to be obscured by the moral storm around the issue of atom bombs. Discussions about bombing have tended to center around the destruction of German cities by Marshall of the Royal Air Force, Sir Arthur Harris, better known as 'Bomber Harris.' Professor Anthony Grayling's *Among the Dead Cities* [2006] focuses on the bombing of Hamburg to expound his views on the immorality of mass urban bombing of *World War II*, but makes the sweeping statement that the reason for "the fire bombing of Tokyo and other Japanese cities . . . [was] for no better reason than that they were unbombed, and that there were many bombers and bombs waiting to be used."[50] It is a casual remark that has no basis in fact. Similarly Peter Hitchens in the *Mailonline* opined, "The Americans, by the way, did bomb civilians in Japan, another dubious episode."[51] Some contemporary commentators were similarly swayed by the arguments of American immorality. During the war a group of twenty-eight well-known clergymen and educators such as Baptist Minister Harry Emerson Fosdick and Professor Oswald Garrison Villard published a pamphlet entitled *Massacre of Death*.

However, America, in March 1945, did not have a surplus of planes 'waiting to be used.' LeMay was not happy about having to switch his bomber forces to attack airfields on *Kyushu* to prevent *kamikaze* attacks because he did not have enough planes to both prevent *kamikaze* attacks and degrade Japanese industry. Furthermore LeMay was unhappy because the B-29 was not suitable for the tactical bombing that was required on *Kyushu* and felt that his strategic weapon was being inappropriately deployed. There is no evidence to suggest that LeMay bombed residential cities simply to fill-out time until Japan surrendered. In spite of increasing logistical and economic difficulties, Japan was producing significant quantities of war *matériel* until the last few months of the war, particularly *kamikaze* aircraft that became the main focus of military-industrial output.

Japanese aircraft production—a large proportion of which were *kamikaze* aircraft—reached its peak in the last year of the war. There is ample evidence to show that America's strategic objective was to force Japan's unconditional surrender by economic strangulation—by destruction of its merchant fleet and by aerial bombardment of economic capacity in the form of factories, chemical and industrials plants, ports, power plants and railways.

Another of the implications of the moral arguments against mass bombing was that it was cost free. That was far from the case. Mortality rates for bomber crews were much higher than for foot soldiers or active Navy personnel. A Flying Fortress crewman noted, "we flew day in day out and nobody expected to live through it. I know that the completion of a tour of duty was a surprise to me. It was akin to being born again."[52] In *World War II*, where the tour of duty for heavy bombers was twenty-five missions, the ratio of crewmen killed or missing in action was an extraordinary 71 percent. It is often forgotten that each Superfortress carried an eleven-man crew. Thus the operation of 100 Superfortresses over twenty-five missions could be expected to result in the loss of 1,100 men, its entire initial complement. Statistically it was almost impossible to survive a complete tour of duty as the member of a bomber crew. Bombing was a deadly business. The costs to the US Army Air Force were more than life and death; crews were highly skilled and expensively trained pilots and technicians. Moreover each B-29 Superfortress cost US$605,360 (in 1945 prices), triple the cost of the B-17 Flying Fortress. There even came a point where losses of crewmen threatened the continuation of bombing operations over Japan.

The idea that precision bombing was somehow 'moral' compared to normal bombing was a myth propagated after the war by a Hollywood that indulged in *faux* moral self-indulgence. Thus the movie *Twelve O'Clock High* [1949] starring Gregory Peck was "humbly dedicated to those Americans both living and dead, whose gallant efforts made possible daylight precision bombing."[53] *Bombardier* [1943] starring Randolph Scott, Anne Shirley and Pat O'Brian similarly preached the moral virtues of precision bombing and the courage of those who risked their lives to deliver it. Yet Curtis LeMay's analysis of so-called precision bombing in 1943 noted, "sixty percent of the bombs dropped are not accounted for and about 3 percent land within 5,000 feet"[54] of the target; from high altitude, precision bombing was more random than precise and could more accurately be described as 'carpet bombing.' As Professor Richard Overy points out in *The Bombing War* [2013], ". . . most bombs did not hit the intended target, even when that target was the size of a city centre."[55] Given that, in Japan, residential areas lived cheek by jowl with manufacturing plants, so-called precision bombing inevitably brought high levels of collateral damage. Neither was precision bombing without cost to the US Air Force. American commanders began to reflect on how moral it was to persevere with a tactic for which US crews paid a high price with their lives, while doing little to mitigate the dangers to Japanese civilians. As journalist and historian Harrison Salisbury stated, to attempt daylight precision bombing was "to hold a ticket to a funeral. Your own."[56] Given that a general has an implicit moral duty to prosecute and win war with the least deaths to his own troops, it might perhaps be easier to charge America's air commanders with immorality in sticking too long with precision bombing, a strategy that was alarmingly dangerous for their own aircrews.

Nevertheless American leaders and the US Army Air Force were very much alive to the moral issues of mass bombing and debated the issues themselves—inevitably, given America's criticism of urban bombing by the Japanese against Chinese cities earlier in the war there was considerable moral equivocation on the subject. In spite of the known dangers for US crews, Richard Overy points out, "The American emphasis on the precision bombing tactic, though its results were known to be exaggerated, was publicly promoted to create the illusion of good bombing versus bad."[57] In other words the whole concept of precision bombing was in effect a fraud to salve the consciences of the morally squeamish. Notably, even after the failure of both Hansell and LeMay to achieve success with precision bombing, Washington insisted that Twenty-First Command persevere with this mode of attack.

Ultimately the problem was that precision bombing, at least in the early days of B-29 operation, did not work; this was partly because of the lack of accuracy in dropping bombs, either from high or low altitude, and partly because, with particular relevance to Japan, component supply manufacture (*kyoryokukai*) was widely distributed in household operations housed within densely populated areas. As Curtis LeMay noted in his memoirs,

> We were going after military targets. No point in slaughtering civilians for the mere sake of slaughter . . . It was their system of dispersal of industry . . . I'll never forget Yokohama. That was what impressed me: drill presses. There they were, like a forest of scorched trees and stumps, growing up throughout that residential area. Flimsy construction all gone . . . everything burned down, or up, and drill presses standing like skeletons.[58]

It is clear that at no point did American forces set out to kill Japanese civilians as an aim of US Strategy. For that reason LeMay, before incendiary attacks began, at significant personal risk to their crews, to drop leaflets over intended targets to warn the Japanese populace of impending attacks. American radio also broadcast warnings. For reasons that others will have to explain, Japan's Air Force commanders, who set out to exterminate large swathes of their enemies' populations, particularly in China, are not held to the same standards as the US Army Air Force, which at least took steps to limit civilian casualties. In spite its repugnance, the phrase 'collateral damage,' was nevertheless an accurate description of Japanese civilian deaths as result of US mass bombing aimed at degrading Japan's manufacturing capability. Generals Hansell and LeMay were acutely aware that Japanese civilian deaths would be substantial.

The US Joint Chiefs of Staff wishfully believed that the B-29 attacks on Japan, both precision and firebombing, might precipitate a Japanese surrender that would obviate the need for Operation OLYMPIC, the planned invasion of the main islands. They were not entirely wrong. Prime Minister Baron Kantaro Suzuki would later tell his interrogators, "it seemed to me unavoidable that in the long run Japan would be almost destroyed by air attack so that merely on the basis of the B-29s alone I was convinced that Japan should sue for peace."[59] Even without the intervention of the atom bomb, it seems possible but not certain that Japan, given enough time, would have surrendered. However, this question rests within the realm of 'what ifs' and in this regard it is notable that even after the dropping of two atom bombs it remained in the balance whether or not Japan would surrender. Even Suzuki, a supposed 'dove' within Japan's final wartime cabinet, seems to have flip-flopped on whether to accept unconditional surrender at this point. His post-war answers may have been designed simply to save his own neck. [See Chapter 40: Potsdam, Hirohito, and the Atom Bomb]

Pinpointing the effect of the bombing of Japan on industrial production is difficult because shipping losses, lack of raw materials, and clapped out infrastructure were also taking their toll. However, by the summer of 1945 output from Japan's factories was in free-fall across all sectors. Aluminum production fell to 9 percent of peak output while steel and oil refining fell to 15 percent. Monthly aircraft (mainly *kamikaze*) production, whose output the Japanese government sought to sustain at the cost of everything else, still fell by over 40 percent between 1944 and 1945. [See Appendix C: Economics of the Pacific War: The 'New Deal' Mobilized] The bombing of Japan worked, bringing the country to the point of economic collapse, even though in hindsight a post-war analysis by the United States Strategic Bombing Survey showed that the mining of Japan's seaways by B-29s, which cut off the import of raw materials and involved no loss of civilian life, was just as effective as urban bombing in reducing Japan's industrial output.

About the overall effectiveness of the American bombing of Japan there is little doubt. Apart from a collapse in industrial output, after the war, in an opinion poll conducted by the US Army, 47 percent of Japanese, when asked about the main reason for certainty that Japan could not win the war, answered that it was bombing. When asked what was the hardest thing to endure, 91 percent cited bombing. As Richard Overy concludes in *Why the Allies Won* [1995], "Though there should be necessary arguments over the morality or operational effectiveness of the bombing campaign, the air offensive appears in fact as one of the decisive elements in explaining Allied victory."[60] It is an argument for bombing that is much more applicable to Japan than to Germany, where the returns from strategic bombing were comparatively poor. However, if effectiveness is one of the criteria for the moral judgment on bombing, it is probably more appropriate to look at the then expected military rewards from bombing rather than at the outcome. The Allies clearly hoped that strategic bombing would degrade the industrial power of the Axis powers but there was no historic evidence to show whether this would be effective. In *World War II* strategic bombing was an entirely recent concept, enabled by unproven new technologies, whose effectiveness in war at the time could only be guessed at.

Morality is one issue; legality is another. Professor Grayling points to the Geneva Protocol-1 of 1977 (an addition to the Geneva Conventions of 12 August 1949) that forbids attacks on civilians and civilian targets. Article 52.1 defines civilian objects as "all objects that are not military targets."[61] However, Article 52.2 defines justifiable military objectives as "those objects which by their nature, location, purpose or use make an effective contribution to military action and whose total or partial destruction, capture or neutralization, in the circumstances ruling at the time, offers a definite military advantage."[62] In effect Article 52.2 seems to be a catch-all by which almost any attack on economic installation is legal virtually without regard to human cost. In circumstances of total war this allowed almost everything to be bombed unless it was targeted at civilian starvation (Article 54.2), cultural objects (Article 53) or schools or places of worship (Article 53.3) By definition LeMay's conduct in the bombing of Japan, in its aim to degrade Japanese military industrial capacity, fell within the bounds of legality in war as defined by Articles 52.2 of the Geneva Protocol-I issued in 1977, though lawyers of course could be found who would argue otherwise. By the definitions of Article 52.2 LeMay's so-called precision bombing attacks, aimed at the degradation of economic assets, however imperfect in practice, were legal, although arguably judged by today's conventions the bombing of Japan would fail on the grounds of 'proportionality'—a concept introduced in 1977.

Of course *World War II* was not fought under the 1977 Geneva Protocol-1 or even under the 1949 ones, and the validity of the *ex post facto* moral judgments of post-war critics is questionable enough to undermine the moral judgments made of LeMay and his US Army Air Force operations in 1945 Japan. *Ex post facto* laws are prohibited in Article-1, Section-9 of the US Constitution. In Great Britain, without an explicit prohibition in a bill of rights, *ex post facto* law is technically possible because a sovereign parliament can pass any law that it wants. Nevertheless, *ex post facto* law is by convention avoided in Great Britain. Meanwhile in Europe most governments are constrained from this possibility by the principle of *Nullum crimen, nulla poena sine praevia lege poenali* (No crime and no punishment with a pre-existing penal law), which explains why Article-7 of the *European Convention on Human Rights*, to which Great Britain is a signatory, protects individuals from the injustice of *ex post facto* judgment. Ironically, human rights law therefore judges *ex post facto* judgments, such as those made by commentators such as Professor Grayling, to be immoral.

If the legality and indeed morality of *ex post facto* judgments are discounted, it would seem appropriate to consider the Geneva and Hague Conventions as they stood during *World War II*. Henri Dunant, the founder of the Red Cross, was instrumental in bringing the Geneva Convention into being in 1864. It related entirely to the treatment of combatants. At this time, neither the Geneva Convention nor the Hague Convention expressly dealt with the issue of civilians, confining themselves almost entirely to the fighting between combatants and the treatment of prisoners of war. Wars were still between armies; civilians did not come into the equation. Between 1864 and 1939, the articles related to bombing from the air and civilian targeting were limited to just two.

In 1899 Article IV of the Hague Convention was a *Declaration Prohibiting the Discharge of Projectiles from Balloons* which stated, "The contracting Powers agree to prohibit, for a term of five years, the launching of projectiles and explosives from balloons, or by other new methods of a similar nature. The Present declaration is only binding on the Contracting Powers in case of war between two or more of them."[63] The Article therefore expired on 4 September 1905 and only applied to contracting powers. In 1907 the article was extended to the time of a third conference, which never took place. It might also be noted that the time-lapsed Article XIV (based on Article IV of 1899) was only ever ratified by China, United Kingdom and the United States—neither Germany nor Japan were contracting powers. It was therefore a moot point whether Article XIV was ever binding on the United States with regard to the bombing of Japan.

At the 1899 Hague Convention and Annex to the Hague Convention entitled *Regulations Respecting the Laws and Customs of War on Land*, Article-25 notes, "The attack or bombardment, by whatever means, of towns, villages, dwellings, or buildings which are undefended is prohibited."[64] However, the participants in the follow-up convention in 1899, aware of the possible development of air power, began to back away from the restrictions on the launching of projectiles from the air. The 1898 and 1907 Hague Conventions formed the founding documents of the Permanent Court of Arbitration. However, for the purposes of combatants, the only meaningful legal restrictions with regards to non-combatants were that they were theoretically protected from attack unless they were defended—in which case they were a legitimate target. Given these parameters, in Japan during the *Pacific War*, virtually all towns and cities were legitimate military targets first because of the total interweave of industry and residence and secondly because every town and city was defended, albeit poorly, by anti-aircraft guns and fighter aircraft. The 1907 Hague Convention restrictions were in effect moot with regard to Allied bombing during the *Pacific War*.

Another attempt was made to give legal definition to the subject of bombing at the Washington Disarmament Conference in 1922. It was agreed that an international panel of legal experts would be set up at The Hague and by February 1923 they presented *The Hague Rules for Air Warfare*. Article-22 of the proposed rules stated that bombing should not deliberately target civilians or their property; Article-24 limited bombing to specific military targets and suggested that this should only be allowed in the vicinity of land force operations. In spite of the work of the lawyers, not a single country ratified their proposals. Desultory attempts to find an internationally acceptable solution to the issue of bombing continued for the next fifteen years. In 1932 the so-called Tardieu Plan, named after French Prime Minister André Tardieu, called for the abolition of all bombers and for global regulation to be enforced by the League of Nations. Predictably perhaps the plan did not fly. Nevertheless proposals and discussions continued. The Labour Party Member of Parliament, Philip Noel Baker and a Liberal peer, Lord David Davies, proposed an international air police. However, no government took such impractical ideas seriously. Incongruously, among international statesmen, it was only Hitler who took up the baton of aerial disarmament, proposing to Britain and France at the end of March 1936 that bomber aircraft should be outlawed. Shortly before the Munich Agreement, at a meeting in his apartment on 30 September 1938, Hitler told British Prime Minister Neville Chamberlain that the idea of bombing women and children was abhorrent—even though it was Hitler's German Condor Legion, commanded by Colonel Wolfram von Richthofen, that bombed the ancient Basque town of Guernica on General Franco's behalf on 26 April 1937 during the Spanish Civil War.

On the same day they met, the League of Nations Assembly in Geneva passed a resolution that confirmed *The Hague Rules of Air Warfare*. But as a non-binding resolution, it carried no weight in international law. *World War II* would therefore begin with no binding legal obligations in place regarding bombing and civilian protection. This did not mean that broad international opinion did not find the bombing of civilians repellent or that internationally lawyers would not try to use all these legal snippets to argue that there was legally binding restriction on the bombing of civilians. A year earlier, the destruction of Guernica and the bombing of Spain and indeed the bombing of Chinese cities by Japan, had brought global outrage and condemnation. Picasso responded immediately by painting a huge Cubist work depicting the Spanish event. The result, *Guernica*, would become the world's most famous anti-war painting after it was displayed in the Spanish Pavilion at the 1937 Paris World's Fair. The Guernica episode was brought to the attention of the American public when South African George Steer's article of condemnation was published in *The New York Times*. Moral outrage swept the western world. At this stage the moral standpoint on civilian bombing was more consistent than the legal standpoint.

In spite of this, and a broad understanding by world leaders that there was an unresolved problem with regard to bombing and civilians, *World War II* started with a highly confused legal maze of lapsed agreements, non-binding resolutions and unratified agreements. Inevitably, given the depression of the 1930s and then looming geopolitical crises, the issue of the morality of civilian bombing was not uppermost in their minds.

The problem very simply was that countries before *World War I* had not envisaged the moral implications of total war and what that might mean in terms of conduct. *World Wars I* and *II* were the first in which countries engaged in total war—in other words the mobilization of a country's entire economic capacity as a means for propagating and attempting to win a war. As such, all civilian activity in developed economies was by definition harmful to the enemy and certainly not innocent. This was undoubtedly true in countries such as Germany and Japan where civilians had voted governments into power and had, in vast majority, supported their rulers' expansionist policies and their political structures until faced with defeat.

The difference between *World War II* (and to a limited degree *World War I*) compared to wars of an earlier epoch, was that formerly a country's armed forces had minimal ability to inhibit the harmful military activity of their enemies' civilian population—unless ground forces occupied an enemy's country. The range extension of new weaponry in the 1930s changed all that. In *World War II*, because of the rapid development of aircraft and bomb technology during the 1930s and the even faster progress during the war itself, the ability of countries to attack the civilian-military-industrial complex of an enemy nation had changed markedly. The destructive power of a weapon such as the Boeing B-29 Superfortress would have been almost unimaginable even in the 1930s. In *World War II*, Germany, Britain, the Soviet Union, and Japan were equipped to bomb civilian populations and interdict their harmful civilian-military-economic activity in the conduct of total war. By definition in total war virtually every citizen becomes a combatant of sorts and a potential target. By this definition of harmful activity, the bombing of Japan would have been legal even if the Geneva Protocol-I of 1977 had been in place during *World War II*. Inevitably the technology of war runs ahead of the defined moral and legal conventions, which inevitably trail behind—the same is true currently with the war against global *Jihad* involving the development of drones, whose use has increased exponentially during the presidency of Barack Obama. As the awarding of the Nobel Peace Prize to Obama demonstrates, when it comes to the morality of war, ironies abound.

Anthony Grayling pads out his book with a forty-five page index of the Royal Air Force's (RAF) attacks on Germany. This analysis was clearly made to emphasize his argument that the bombing of German cities was an immoral atrocity. It is evident that there is no equivalent account of the Luftwaffe's earlier attacks on Britain with their notable destruction of cities such as London, Coventry and Plymouth, let alone listing of Japanese attacks on the undefended cities of Asia.

Pertinently the Imperial Japanese Army and Navy Air Forces attacked the civilian populations of major cities such as Shanghai, Soochow, Nanking, Hsuchow, Chongqing and Changsha in China, as well as Manila (the Philippines), Myitkyina (Burma) and Dili (*Timor*). Most of these cities were completely undefended. In the absence of manufacturing capacity in these cities, it can only be assumed that Japanese air raids were aimed at the disruption of civilian life and terrorization.

It should be noted that these cities, unlike Japan, did not contain an industrial infrastructure dispersed amidst its urban housing, and were generally not protected by anti-aircraft guns or fighter planes. Even at the time these bombing attacks by Japan were possibly war crimes even by the limited definition of the existing Geneva and Hague Conventions—although it should be noted that Japan was not a signatory to Article IV of the 1899 Hague Convention relating to the discharge of projectiles from balloons. Disregard of these attacks on Asian civilians by western writers in their discussion of the morality of *World War II* bombing suggests an implicit racism, given that any thorough study of the subject of mass bombing must have revealed the horrors of Japan's bombing of Asian cities. A similar ignorance, or at worst a contempt for Asian life, was revealed by the contention of Ian Buruma, a Dutch human rights journalist and academic, who argued that the bombing of Japan was unjustified because it "had no Holocaust to answer for."[65] Leaving aside the issue of whether revenge, even for a Holocaust, is morally justifiable, Buruma's views imply is a curious denial of the

'Chinese Holocaust' in which some 20 million Chinese citizens or more were murdered by the occupying Japanese Army. It was a holocaust, in which the infamous Rape of Nanking, where an estimated 250,000 people were murdered in Nanking and the *Yangtze River Delta*, was just the tip of the iceberg.

Critics of mass urban bombing have made much play on the words of Winston Churchill's chief scientific adviser, Frederick Lindemann, later Lord Cherwell, who famously described the urban bombing of Germany as 'de-housing.' However, it would be a mistake to conflate LeMay's bombing of Japan with the Allied bombing campaign in Europe where one of the explicit aims, and perhaps the main one, was terrorization of citizens and the psychological and political destabilization of the *Nazi* regime.

Leaving aside any discussion of whether a bombing strategy of 'de-housing' and terrorization in Germany was morally compromised on the grounds of ineffectiveness as argued by Richard Overy in *The Bombing War* [2014],[66] it should be pointed out, terrorization was not the main component of American bombing strategy in Japan. Although tests of napalm were done on specially constructed Japanese houses including the installation of sliding wooden doors, paper screens and *tatami* mats, the purposes of the incendiary attacks themselves were much more focused on the degradation of Japan's productive capacity. This is not to say that the US Army Air Force was unaware of the use of bombing as a weapon of terrorization or altogether unhopeful of generating anti-government sentiment. The psychological war against Japan was evidenced by the significant number of leaflets dropped trying to turn civilians against their own government. Terrorization was undoubtedly a by-product of both precision bombing and firebombing. However, by comparison with Germany, America's urban bombing of Japan was highly successful in reducing Japan's industrial output—an outcome which had been the primary purpose of its strategic bombing strategy.

As for the civilians of the Allied countries that had been attacked by German and Japanese bombers, or had been brutalized on land by the Imperial Japanese Army, it is clear that the moral majority saw mass bombing in retaliation as morally acceptable. Not to have bombed Japan would have simply seemed perverse. While some American humanists and clergymen had railed against the mass bombing of Japan, the majority of Americans welcomed it as righteous revenge. For *Time* magazine the firebombing of Tokyo was unequivocally "a dream come true"; it proved, "properly kindled, Japanese cities will burn like autumn leaves."[67] With sentiment in America accumulating into a crescendo of anger in the US press over the Bataan Death March and other atrocities, there was little sympathy for Tokyo's massacred citizens. "God has given us the weapons," thundered a clergyman's letter in the *New York Times*, "Let us use them."[68] Regardless of these sentiments expressed by some in America, there is no evidence that the senior commanders of the US Army Air Force ever justified their missions as acts of revenge, let alone acts of terror against defenseless civilians. America's bomber commanders seem to have been significantly less racist and bloodthirsty than Navy types such as Admiral 'Bull' Halsey. Professional military logic, aimed at the degradation of Japan's industrial capacity, not racist revenge or the desire to 'de-house' or terrorize civilians, underwrote the actions and decisions of US Army Air Force Generals Arnold, Hansell and LeMay.

Another factor must also be considered. The facts will be more fully laid bare in the final chapter **[see Chapter 40: Potsdam, Hirohito, and the Atom Bomb]** but suffice it to say here that the US War Department estimated that an invasion and defeat of Japan would bring total deaths of American and Japanese soldiers, in addition to Japanese civilians, to more than five million people, possibly as high as ten million—figures that exceeded by twenty to forty times the numbers killed in the bombing of Japan. Given these estimates it must surely have been immoral not to bomb Japan in an attempt to persuade Emperor Hirohito and his government to surrender. Many US commanders believed, incorrectly as it turned out, that Hirohito was sure to surrender when he saw the destruction of Japan's cities by LeMay's Superfortresses.

Moreover, given that anticipated American casualties of Operation DOWNFALL (for the invasion and defeat of Japan) were estimated to be over a million, would it have been moral for the President of the United States not to have used every weapon at his command to prevent the unnecessary deaths of so many US citizens who he was sworn to serve? Most American bomber commanders, admirals and generals, reflecting values learned from their own Christian backgrounds, invariably looked on the killing of civilians with repugnance and, almost as one, detested the atom bomb when it came into being. However, thinking of bombing as repugnant is not necessarily the same as thinking it immoral.

The moral issues relating to the use of bombs in wartime are complex and made more so by the post-war introduction of the concept of 'proportionality.' Nevertheless, by avoiding the absurd and self-indulgent trap of *ex post facto* moralization, the issues relating to the legality and morality of bombing can be put into a historic perspective. First, while there are moral concepts which seem to be universally applicable (for example murder), it should be accepted that what is perceived as morality is for the most part a moving feast and is very much dependent on time and place. The moral compass can move rapidly. Civilian bombing that was broadly regarded as immoral in the west immediately before *World War II* began became broadly acceptable soon afterwards, particularly in those countries that had been on the receiving end earlier in the war. Similarly Americans who were appalled at the bombing of Chinese cities at the beginning of the *Second Sino-Japanese War* in 1936 were 85 percent in favor of the atom bomb at the end. As a result of this moral shift, probably as a result of the desire for revenge as well as the desensitizing nature of *World War II*, the planned charges of *Nazi* war crimes relating to the urban bombing of Allied cities were quietly dropped when the extent of British and American bombing of Germany became clear.

Although morality is a moving target, for anyone who does want to establish a framework for determining the morality of America's bombing of Japan in 1945 a number of elementary questions can be asked: Was the urban area bombing of Japan necessary for the successful prosecution of the war? Was the primary motivation for strategic bombing the degradation of Japan's military-industrial capacity? Did it help foreshorten the war and save lives? Did American commanders make efforts to avoid Japanese civilian casualties? Was it acceptable within the moral framework that existed in society (Allied and Axis) between 1939 and 1945? Was the bombing of Japanese cities legal under the Geneva and Hague Conventions as they stood in 1944? This author, albeit reluctant to pass judgment on what is moral, would argue that the answer to all these questions is yes.

39 Japanese–Soviet Conflict in Siberia, Mongolia and Manchuria

[April 1945–5 September 1945]

[Maps: 39.1, 39.2, 39.3, 39.4, 39.5, 39.6]

The final major military actions of the *Pacific War*, indeed *World War II*, did not take place in the *Pacific*, Southern China or the plains and jungles of southern and eastern Burma, but in the remote, mountain and desert borders that separate Northern Manchuria from Siberia and the even more remote *Kuril Islands* that separate Japan from the Kamchatka Peninsula. These would not be small-scale engagements—in terms of numbers, the battles fought in Manchuria from 9 August to 26 August, particularly the *Battle of Mutanchiang*, were some of the largest of the *Pacific War*. Given that on the day of the invasion, a second atom bomb was dropped on Nagasaki, the impact of this late stage military engagement on the course of history is debatable. Indeed it is the post-war argument about the importance of the Soviet Manchurian campaign in bringing about Japan's surrender *vis-à-vis* the atom bomb, wherein lies the main significance of the Soviet invasion of Manchuria.

Russo-Japanese Relations from the Late Nineteenth Century: At the start of 1941 both Japan and the Soviet Union faced critical issues that superseded their long-term rivalry for dominance in Northeast Asia. It was a rivalry that had emerged with Imperial Russia's nineteenth century expansion into the vast, sparsely populated territories of Siberia, Mongolia and Kazakhstan. Although Russians had started to occupy Siberia as far back as the sixteenth and seventeenth centuries, in ways that can be compared with the later occupation of America by European colonists, it was trade and industrialization that prompted the later more aggressive eastward expansion by the Russian state. Miners, accountants, lawyers and corporations increasingly took the place of Cossack hunters, fur traders and land hungry peasants.

The newcomers created wealth and brought with them the familiar social institutions and culture of civil society in their wake. Peter Semenov-Tyan-Shansky, a leading Russian academic in the fields of botany, zoology and geology, who stayed in Barnaul in 1856–1857, wrote:

> The richness of the mining engineers of Barnaul was expressed not merely in their households and clothes, but more in their educational level, knowledge of science and literature. Barnaul was undoubtedly the most cultured place in Siberia, and I've called it Siberian Athens . . .[1]

Leading intellectuals such as playwright Anton Chekhov, who travelled through Siberia on his way to *Sakhalin Island* in 1890, explored the Wild East in the same way that writers such as Mark Twain explored the Wild West (*Roughing It*, 1872). Not all travels to the east were voluntary. Novelist Fyodor Dostoevsky, along with many dissident intellectuals, was exiled to a *katorga* (penal camp) near Omsk, and pressed into military service in Semey in Eastern Khazakhstan. He married his first wife in the mining and ironworking city of Novokuznetzk (literally: the new-smiths).

A cash strapped Russian state, faced by the repayment of a £15m Rothschild loan and seemingly indifferent to the East, and which had sold Alaska and the *Aleutian Islands* to the United States for US$7.2m in 1867, had by the end of the century woken up to the economic and geopolitical potential of their far flung Siberian Empire. Like the United States and the other Imperial powers embedded in China and South East Asia, Imperial Russia also looked to the emerging potential of Chinese markets.

The Trans-Siberian Railway Transforms the Geopolitics of Northeast Asia: [**Map: 39.1**] The new commitment to the Far East was most clearly expressed by the building of the Trans-Siberian Railway. Mirroring the experience of the United States, where the completion of *Erie Canal* in 1825 opened up the west to trade and to settlers, the completion of the *Ob River* system in 1857 served the same economic and social function. But growth merely brought increased pressure for more infrastructure.

While a 1,680-mile rail link from Moscow to Omsk, in Southwestern Siberia had been built earlier, the construction of a 4,000-mile route from Omsk to Vladivostok in the far east of Siberia, beginning late in the nineteenth century, was on a different order of magnitude. The geopolitical importance of this vast enterprise was indicated by the visit of Russia's crown prince, later Tsar Nicholas II, to Vladivostok in March 1890, where he inaugurated the Far East section of the Trans-Siberian Railway. As with the First Transcontinental Railroad built in the United States, work started at both ends.

Ironically Prince Nicholas's stop in Vladivostok was preceded by a visit to Japan, part of a grand round-the-world tour; no country was more radically affected by the building of a Trans-Siberian Railway than Japan. A railway that could transport troops and heavy weapons was not just an economic threat. While in Japan, Prince Nicholas was threatened; indeed he was fortunate to survive an assassination attempt by a policeman assigned to protect him.

China was equally concerned but with its economic and military power in precipitate decline, which became evident with its crushing defeat by Japan in the *Sino-Japanese War* in 1905, it was Japan that stood as the bulwark to the expansion of Russian power in the East. Diplomatic jostling between Russia and Japan now ensued for suzerainty over Manchuria and Korea. With the completion of the last section of the Trans-Siberian Railway in 1904—the Circum-Baikal Railway—goods and troops could reach Vladivostok without needing to unload onto ships on Siberia's vast *Lake Baikal*. Regional rivalry in the Far East led to the *Russo-Japanese War* of 1904–5, which ended with the almost complete annihilation of the Russian Fleet at the *Battle of Tsushima* in 1905.

The *First World War* and the Russian Revolution presented further opportunity for Japan to diminish Russian, now Soviet, influence in the Far East. Winston Churchill, who had declared that Bolshevism should be "strangled in its cradle,"[2] was not alone in his view. In Russia's eastern empire White Russians overthrew the Bolsheviks in Omsk and Petropavlovsk (Khazakhstan) and moved westwards, capturing Yekaterinburg in the Ural Mountains on 17 July 1918 with the help of the Czech Legions. They liberated the city shortly after the murder there of Tsar Nicholas II and his family. In Siberia the new Provisional All-Russian Government was established in Omsk and soon came to be dominated by its war minister, Rear-Admiral Alexander Kolchak, who established a dictatorship in Siberia after a *coup d'état* in October 1918. Meanwhile in Russian Central Asia, British-led forces managed to push back Red Army units. In addition, British and American forces seized Murmansk and Archangel in Northern Russia.

In the spring of 1919 a White Russian Army advance was forced back by the brilliant Red Army commander, General Mikhail Tukhachevsky. In October Omsk, the capital of the Provisional All-Russian Government, fell to the Red Army, starting a retreat to the Far East. In mid-February 1920 the few remaining White Army combatants made their escape across Lake Baikal and joined General Grigory Semyonov, the new leader of the White Russian Army in Siberia. Here they were supported by a joint international force comprising a 70,000-strong Japanese Army, plus 50,000 Czechs, 8,000 Americans, 4,000 Canadians, 2,500 Italians, 2,500 Chinese, 2,000 Poles, 1,500 British and 1,000 French—almost 140,000 troops in aggregate.

It was a difficult alliance. With the largest force, Japan assumed command in Vladivostok and General Otani issued the order:

> I have the honor to inform you that I have been appointed
> Commander of the Japanese Army at Vladivostok, by His
> Majesty, the Emperor of Japan, and that I am entrusted,
> unanimously, by the Allied Powers, with the command of
> their armies in the Russian Territory of the Far East.[3]

However there was mismatch in expectations. General William Graves, the commander of the American Expeditionary Force to Siberia, was under orders not to engage with the Bolshevik forces other than in the defense of US interests. The commitment of the Western forces was short-lived. In June 1920 Britain, America, France and Italy withdrew from Vladivostok leaving only the Japanese. Fearful of the arrival of communism within their sphere of geopolitical interest, the Japanese Siberian Expeditionary Force remained in Siberia until October 1922 when Prime Minister Tomosaburo Kato, facing increasing criticism of the cost of the expedition, ordered a withdrawal.

The Battle of Lake Khasan and Amur River Clashes: Japan's exit from Siberia did not mean that their fears of communism and the Soviet Union had receded. The annexation of Manchuria and its absorption into the Japanese Empire in 1931, apart from increasing

Japan's economic power and access to natural resources, was in part inspired by the need to thwart the perceived Soviet threat. Facing down the threat of communism was one of the common threads in the rival ultranationalist factions in the Japanese Army—though it was the more anti-Soviet Imperial Way Faction (*Kodoha*) which ultimately crushed the Control Faction (*Toseiha*) after the former's attempted *coup d'état* in February 1936.

As the Soviet Union consolidated its power and strengthened its armed forces in the Far East, clashes with Japan's *Kwantung* Army increased along the disputed borders of the *Amur River*. Some 152 border incidents between 1932 and 1934 led to Japan being described in 1935 as "fascist enemies" at the Seventh Comintern Congress. Faced by this threat from the East, Stalin increasingly looked toward the Nationalist Government in China to help deflect Japan from the Soviet Union's borders. Thus, in the two years from the autumn of 1937, Chiang Kai-shek's armies were supplied with 82 tanks, 1,300 artillery pieces, 1,550 trucks, 14,000 machine guns and 50,000 rifles.

In 1935 armed clashes took place at Halhamiao on the border of Mongolia, a Soviet puppet state, in January, at *Lake Khanka* and Suifenho in Eastern Manchuria in June, and at *Lake Buir* in December. The following year similar border clashes took place in February, March and April. In 1937 Japanese artillery shelled Soviet gunboats when they unloaded troops on the unoccupied island of *Kanchazu* on the *River Amur*. Crewmen on the sunken gunboats were gunned in the water. Some 37 Soviet troops were killed.

The following year a two-week battle was fought at *Lake Khasan* when Japanese troops attempted to occupy territory, which they believed had been ceded to them by the *Convention of Peking* [1860]. The commander of the Soviet Far Eastern Armies, General Vasily Blücher, led a force of 23,000 troops against General Kamezo Suetaka's occupying force of 7,000 troops. In spite of throwing 250 tanks into an attack supported by over 150 bombers, the Soviets were repulsed with heavy losses calculated at over 4,000 casualties. It was a pyrrhic victory. In spite of its success on the battlefield, Japan felt unable to sustain the occupation of Changkufeng and on 10 August, the Japanese Ambassador in Moscow requested a peaceful resolution in return for a withdrawal of Japanese troops.

For his losses at the *Battle of Lake Khasan*, General Blücher was arrested, tortured and killed. His death was part of an extensive purge of 'enemies of the state' within the Red Army that saw eight top commanders executed, including the great Marshal Tukhachevsky. In total some 35,000 Soviet officers were purged. Those sent to *gulags* or executed included 3 of 5 marshals, 13 of 15 generals (of 3-star and 4-star), 8 of 9 admirals, 50 of 57 corps commanders and all Military Commissars. The seeming disarray in the Soviet Army misled Japan's generals into believing that the Red Army had lost its fighting potency. Reflecting this complacency, they were drawn into an extended border war on the Mongolian-Manchurian border in May 1939. The *Battles of Nomonhan*, sometimes called the *Battles of Khalkhin Gol*, are described in more detail in **Chapter 3: Japan versus China: From Phoney War to Total War**. The most serious of the interwar border engagements between Japan and the Soviet Union ended in August 1939 with a severe thrashing of Japan by General Zhukov's Far Eastern Red Army.

The Japanese-Soviet Neutrality Pact: But as the Japanese-Soviet border war dribbled to a close a more pressing matter was taking Stalin's attention. On 24 August his foreign minister, Molotov, was authorized to sign the *Nazi-Soviet Non Aggression Pact* as a prelude to Hitler's invasion of Poland on 1 September 1939. Japanese-Soviet border tensions subsided as both parties addressed other priorities. The Soviets invaded Finland, engaging in the bitterly fought *Winter War*, which was only brought to an end by the *Treaty of Moscow* in March 1940. Furthermore, under the auspices of the *Molotov-Ribbentrop Pact*, Stalin also annexed the Baltic states of Lithuania, Latvia and Estonia. Japan meanwhile was fully occupied in a total war for the subjugation of China.

A mutual interest in neutrality, favored by both Japan and the Soviets because it obviated the need to fight on multiple fronts, came to fruition with the signing by foreign ministers Molotov and Matsuoka of the *Japan-Soviet Neutrality Pact* on 13 April 1941—slated to last for five years.

In practice it lasted for almost the duration of the war. Their long-term geopolitical rivalries may not have been extinguished but the pact continued to serve both nations whose military focus was elsewhere engaged. With the Soviets fighting for survival after Hitler's treacherous invasion of Russia (Operation BARBAROSSA) on 22 June 1941, and Japan's ongoing war in China and its attack on British and American interests on 8 December 1941, neutrality suited both sides. In spite of Stalin's alliance with Britain and America, the Soviets, albeit incongruously given their long-term enmity toward Japan, nevertheless maintained a position of studied neutrality—even insisting on the internment of American combatants, such as a crew from the Doolittle Raid, who strayed onto Soviet soil. For the time being the fiercest of geopolitical rivals turned their backs on each other.

However, by 1945 the situation was clearly changing. Germany was close to defeat with Marshal Georgy Zhukov's armies closing in on Berlin. Meanwhile in the summer and autumn of 1944, Japan had suffered naval defeats at the *Battle of the Philippine Sea* and the *Battle of Leyte Gulf*, which effectively annihilated the Imperial Japanese Navy, heralding its defeat to the Western Allies. From the start of 1945, Japanese attention turned to negotiating with the Soviets for an extension of the *Japanese-Soviet Neutrality Pact*, due to expire in April 1946.

The ongoing negotiations, which Stalin was only too happy to string along, took a crucial turn on 11 July 1945, when Japan's foreign minister, Shigenori Togo, sent an urgent telegram to Ambassador Naotake Sato in Moscow. It stated,

> The foreign and domestic situation for the Empire is very serious, and even the termination of the war is now being considered privately. Therefore the conversations mentioned in my telegram No. 852 are not being limited

> solely to the objective of closer relations between Japan
> and the U.S.S.R., but we are also sounding out the extent
> to which we might employ the U.S.S.R. in connection
> with the termination of the war.[4]

The dove faction within the war council now began a frantic attempt to sue for peace through the good offices of neutral Soviet Union. It was duly suggested that Prince Fumimaro Konoe, the former Japanese prime minister and relative of Emperor Hirohito, would travel to Moscow to discuss terms with Stalin. Konoe later claimed, "he had received direct and secret instructions from the Emperor to secure peace at any price not withstanding its severity."[5] It was an interesting account, though one of doubtful veracity. As ever with Japan's internal politics, the facts are murky; Togo later disputed Konoe's version.

In Moscow the Soviets spun out the discussions and asked for details. For Ambassador Sato, the information as to Tokyo's suggested terms of surrender, were annoyingly vague—reflecting the disagreement and paralysis within the War Council. By 27 July, Sato was becoming increasingly frustrated by his colleagues' apparent vacillation in Tokyo: "It is absolutely impossible to cause the Soviet government to make a move with such a non-committal attitude on our part."[6] In spite of Sato's entreaties and the ultimatum presented by the Allies in the Potsdam Declaration, Foreign Minister Togo, with no clear mandate from the War Council, continued to fob him off—leading Sato to make an even more desperate plea for clarity on 3 August: "So long as we propose sending a Special Envoy [to Moscow] without at the same time having a concrete plan for ending the war . . . the Russians will politely refuse to receive [him and we are wasting valuable time while Japan is being destroyed]."[7] It seems that only Japanese representatives outside of Japan could see the futility of fighting on.

The real problem faced by Togo was that he was a dove in a war council effectively controlled by ultranationalist generals and admirals. Prime Minister Baron Kantaro Suzuki, a retired Admiral, also wavered in his quest for peace, even after the dropping of an atom bomb on Hiroshima changed the nature of the internal debate in Japan's councils of war. **[See Chapter 40: Potsdam, Hirohito, and the Atom Bomb]**

The Yalta Conference: Held just outside the Black Sea resort of Yalta on 4–11 February 1945, the conference, at the Livadia Palace, the summer residence of Tsar Nicholas II, was the second and last meeting of the big three Allied leaders, Roosevelt, Stalin and Churchill. By the time of the next meeting at Potsdam, Roosevelt was dead (replaced by Harry Truman), a not unexpected event to those who observed the dying President at Yalta, while Churchill, less expectedly, lost the British election mid-conference and was replaced by the Labour Party leader and new Prime Minister, Clement Attlee. By the end of the Potsdam Conference, of the original big three, Stalin was the last man standing.

At Yalta the Allies sat down to deal with the fraught issue of how to divide the world after the war ended. Victory was now in sight in both Europe and the *Pacific*. All the leaders arrived in Yalta with an agenda. Stalin's priority was to carve out an area of influence in Central Europe—an essential buffer as he saw it for the Soviet Union's security. The future of Poland became the main fulcrum of debate. Churchill, whose nation was by now seen as the weakest of the three, modestly pressed for free elections and, as ever, Churchill, aside from the issue of Poland, was most preoccupied by Britain's retention of its empire.

Roosevelt's pet project meanwhile was 'international trusteeships' and the concept of collective security provided by a United Nations organization. Meanwhile he wanted Stalin, above all else, to turn his military attentions to help finish off Japan in Manchuria and northern China and to attack Japan in support of the planned US offensive. Roosevelt did not want US troops to carry the burden of casualties in the Far East alone; he did not need the example of *Iwo Jima*, whose invasion by US Marines followed a week after the Yalta Conference ended, to remind him of the ferocity of battle with Japanese troops, who, in the island campaigns of the *Pacific War*, had suffered average death rates of more than 97 percent.

It was already clear to America's commander in chief that the conquest of Japan, if it came to that, would be a bloody affair with a level of casualties that would potentially be unacceptable to the American people. "Russia's entry at an early a date as possible consistent with her ability to engage in offensive operations,"[8] the US joint Chiefs of Staff advised Roosevelt in January 1945, "is necessary to provide maximum assistance to our Pacific Operations."[9] The atom bomb at this point was still an uncertain project.

As a *quid pro quo* for his promising to declare war on Japan within three months of defeating Germany, Stalin demanded that Mongolia should be autonomous and permanently separated from China—in effect a Soviet satellite state. He also demanded control of Manchuria's railways and Port Arthur (*Lushunkou*) as well as the return of *Sakhalin Island* and the *Kurils*, which had been lost to Japan at the *Treaty of Portsmouth* in 1906.

Roosevelt was happy to accede to these requests and even suggested that Port Arthur be turned into an international free port, hoping that this would be a model that Churchill would follow in Hong Kong. However, with regards to Stalin's claims in China, Roosevelt added a proviso, "that the agreement concerning Outer Mongolia and the ports and railroads . . . will require concurrence of General Chiang Kai-shek."[10] To help sell the deal to Chiang, Roosevelt dispatched Ambassador Patrick Hurley to Chongqing to assure Chiang that the US had sought and achieved Stalin's support for a unified China under *Kuomintang* control.

Overall Roosevelt was happy with the deal, particularly with obtaining Stalin's agreement to attack Japan. "This makes the trip worthwhile,"[11] Roosevelt told his Chief of Staff, Admiral Leahy.

Japanese Preparations for the Defense of Manchuria: With Japan engaged, as they thought, in peace discussions with the Soviet Union, the last thing that the leaders in Tokyo expected was a Soviet invasion of Manchuria. Foreign Minister Togo knew that the Soviets were aware that Japan was already seriously discussing acceptance of the Potsdam Declaration in the wake of Hiroshima. So when he was roused from his sleep at 3.00 a.m. on 9 August and given the news, he was astonished.

On the ground Japanese commanders had not been so sanguine. In the preceding months there had been a noticeable increase in Soviet activity in terms of patrols and military exercises—particularly on Manchuria's Eastern Front. The local reports were at odds with the upbeat assessments from high command about Soviet intentions. As Japanese officers later reported, "during July and August, the division received information from subordinate and lateral units indicating the gravity of the situation with regard to the USSR. This information was utterly inconsistent with the optimistic information received from high command."[12] Lieutenant-Colonel Genichiro Arinuma and Major Kyoji Takasugi, staff officers at the *Kwantung* Army HQ, noted after the war, "during May 1945 the Intelligence Section of the *Kwantung* Army Headquarters, reporting on the Soviet build-up along the border, estimated that war with the Soviets during 1945 was unlikely."[13] As for the increasing volume of border incidents, the *Kwantung* Army HQ Intelligence Section put this down to simply an increase in Soviet reconnaissance—an example of either idiocy or wishful thinking.

It was further noted that it was the rainy season and hardly a propitious time to launch an invasion. If an invasion was to come the approaching dry season in September was considered more likely. As Colonel Hiroshi Matsumoto reported after the war, "during the summer, the high water and flood season occurs."[14] Whatever the expectations on the frontlines, the leadership of Japanese forces in Manchuria had been revising their defense operations since April 1945. At this date, Tokyo had recalled most of the elite units back to Japan in preparation for the defense of the motherland. The defense of Manchuria was not only depleted of experienced units but was divested of a high percentage of its equipment—including some 50 percent of its anti-tank guns.

Given these actions by Japan's Army commanders in Tokyo, after April there was a desperate scramble to recruit new troops to make up for the shortfalls. Some 6 out of 10 of the First Area Army's divisions were forced to draw on Japanese residents in Manchuria whose economic importance had previously caused their recruitment to be deferred. As General Kita noted, "none of the First Area Army's major tactical units had been in existence more than seven months, except the 112th Division and the 1st Mobile Division . . ."[15] In addition, almost none of the commanders of Japan's Manchurian defense forces had been in command of their units for more than a year. Kita concluded "in almost every respect the First Area Army was below standards."[16] Internally it was reported that "the recruits brought into the new units had had no prior military training, and the ability and morale of officers left much to be desired."[17] The combat effectiveness of its divisions, a seemingly impressive tally of 700,000 troops, was estimated at 35 percent or less.

What equipment was left to the border forces was in a parlous state. Rifles and artillery were the most antiquated models. Heavy and light machine guns and grenade dischargers were less than half the authorized number. There was even a shortage of bayonets and swords. Ordnance departments set about "forging them out of springs of scrapped motor cars."[18] Other improvised weapons included metal-tipped bamboo spears and explosive packs to be carried by suicide bombers to place underneath tanks—a crude replacement for the anti-tank guns. Rifle rounds per infantryman were limited to 100 and field artillery shells to 500. As well as munitions, fuel was also in short supply. The *Kwantung* Army's only plentiful supplies, in sharp contrast to the Japanese armies in the *Pacific* in 1944, were food.

Furthermore, with the culling of Japan's Manchurian workforce to man new divisions, there was an acute shortage of manual labor and many of the fortifications, planned in the new defense plan drawn up on 19 April, were only half completed. In addition, the failing railway network had only been able to transport some 70 percent of military stores from forward areas to safer positions further back. Most of the underground storage facilities, which were needed because of Soviet air and artillery superiority, were left un-built because of shortages of materials and labor.

After April 1945 all pretense that the Manchurian Army had offensive capability was scrapped. A revised defense plan called for lightly manned border garrisons, whose role in event of attack would be to hold up a Soviet invasion. The main bodies of troops would be pulled back some 50–100 miles from the border for a defense in depth. On the Northeastern Front, where Japanese and Soviet soldiers faced each other in close proximity across the *Ussuri River*, two fallback Japanese defensive lines were in the process of being constructed, one 50 miles from the border and the other around Mutanchiang some 100 miles distant. Defense would be in depth. As Colonel Akiji Kawada, operations officer of the 5th Army Headquarters noted, the forward projection of the 5th Army was unsatisfactory "because it was too extensive a line to be defended by three divisions and, furthermore, from the viewpoint of terrain and positions was unsuitable for prolonged resistance."[19]

In August 1945, as the Japanese commanders in Manchuria were bracing themselves for the possibility of a Soviet invasion, its capability to sustain a competent defensive action was severely constrained. As Colonel Kawada complained, "The shortage of ammunition, explosives, and automotive fuel was particularly acute in the Fifth Army, and led to the belief that it was quite impossible for the Army to fight an extended war of resistance."[20] At best, senior commanders believed that they would be able to hold out for little more than a month.

Deployment of Soviet Forces: [**Map: 39.2**] Unknown to Imperial Japan's generals in Tokyo the Russian Army had been preparing for the launch of an invasion of Manchuria since the agreements made at Yalta. Although one Japanese spy alone "counted 195 military trains, which he estimated were laden with 64,000 troops, 120 tanks, about 2,800 trucks, 500 fighter aircraft, and over 1,000 guns of various calibers,"[21] Imperial Army HQ in Tokyo did not believe that the Soviet Union was preparing for war.

The strategic plan was simple enough. Some 1.5 million troops were assembled on the northern borders of Manchuria. While a minor thrust would come from the north

(2nd Far East Army Group), on the northeastern border adjacent to Vladivostok a major attack would be launched by the 1st Far East Army Group at the same time that Soviet-Mongolian forces from the Trans-Baikal Military District would race across the desert wastes of Inner Mongolia to attack Japanese positions from the west. All three axes would converge on the central plains of Manchuria around the northern city of Harbin and then drive south toward Mukden.

The invasion was planned by a Stalin favorite, Marshal Aleksandr Vasilevsky, an officer who had come to the fore at the *Battle of Moscow*. By the summer of 1945 Vasilevsky had the advantage of a virtually unlimited supply of troops, which could be released from the west. Maintaining a cloak of secrecy, 800,000 troops were transferred by rail to the Soviet's Far East Front. A further advantage was that war matériel was plentiful. With 692 tanks and self-propelled guns, 2,945 mortars and 432 rocket launchers the Soviet forces were heavily armed for a devastating attack. In support they could count on the use of almost 1,000 aircraft. In all areas of aircraft and heavy armament, the *Kwantung* Army in Manchuria was outnumbered by 5 to 1.

If the strategic plan was relatively straightforward, the logistical and tactical elements were not. Logistics had been carefully prepared for the task ahead with due regard to the extreme variables in weather and terrain expected along the lines of attack. Pontoon bridges, A-3 boats and self-crafted rafts were prepared for river crossings on the northeast front. Roads through the swamps on the Russian side of the border were covertly constructed at night and camouflaged in daylight hours. In the northwest the problem of water in the Mongolian deserts was addressed by the creation of water supply units. The 90th Water Supply Company was charged with collection and distribution. To overcome Japanese positions, infantrymen, in spite of the searing summer heat of the desert, were charged with carrying overcoats and cloak tents that could be thrown over barbed wire defenses. Teams of sappers were sent in advance to prepare roads made of logs and brush to cut through the Grand Khingan Mountains. Tactical planning was meticulous.

Infantry assault groups were carefully organized with a range of equipment. 'Blockading subgroups' contained two sapper groups while 'security subgroups' comprised two rifle platoons, a T-34 tank and artillery. Each subgroup also carried high explosives for demolishing bunkers. The crushing success of the Soviet invasion of Manchuria was in large part the result of the detailed logistical planning by Marshal Vasilevsky and his senior commanders.

Soviet Invasion of Northwest Manchuria from Mongolia: On the western borders of Manchuria with Mongolia, the Soviet invasion began with a charge over the barren wastes and gentle hills of the Inner Mongolian plains, toward the Grand Khinghan Mountains 190 miles away, where the Japanese 107th Infantry were garrisoned within elaborate fortifications. As they set off, General Ivan Lyudnikov noted,

> Soldiers, tanks and guns passed through the hills hidden
> in the thick and high grass, again appearing on the slopes.

> And then the sun rose. Figures of people, military
> machines, and the contours of the hills opened before us
> as if on morning maneuvers.[22]

On the first day Soviet forces led by the 205th Tank Brigade of the 36th Army under the command of Lieutenant-General A.A. Luchinsky, brushed aside the limited opposition of small Japanese garrisons placed in isolated desert towns. The first sixty-five miles were covered in a single day. The only obstacles were the swamps along the *Argun River* and the sandy areas toward Khalkin Gol, the scene of Zhukov's crushing victory against the Japanese at the *Battle of Nomonhan* [1939]. Luchinsky's tracked vehicles sped so far ahead of the advancing forces—almost 20 miles at one point—that he was forced to order them to slow down. While the 94th Rifle Corps took the northern route to the Khinghan Mountains, the main body of the 39th Army headed toward the southern reaches.

There were two viable passes through the mountains and the Japanese focused their defenses on these points. When Luchinsky's forces arrived on 12 August however, the Soviets did not use the Japanese playbook. Instead they forced their way through the mountains, which the Japanese commanders had deemed impassable. The double envelopment left the Japanese 107th Infantry pincered, neither able to advance or retreat. The largest Japanese border force at Qiqihar, where the Japanese Army had developed Unit 516, a chemical warfare defense unit, was duly battered into submission. By 14 August, both Solun and and Wangyeiao, the pillars of the Japanese Fortified Region had been captured. A Soviet force, which had underestimated the 50 percent increase in fuel needed to traverse the mountainous passes that their sappers carved through the mountains, thankfully requisitioned the fuel depot at Solun.

Invasion of Northeast Manchuria from Far Eastern Siberia: Unlike the advance in the west, the action in the east was immediate. Soldiers of the Soviet 5th Army crossed the border in darkness at 1.00 a.m on 9 August. At first it was unclear to the Japanese whether they were being attacked. Many believed that the artillery fire was merely night maneuvers to which the Japanese had become inured in previous months. At 3.00 a.m. General Shiina told his officers at the Yeho Officers Club that "an element of their [Soviet] infantry seems to have broken through the borders"[23] and ordered that the border garrison resist until the main force could "destroy the enemy's fighting power by putting up stubborn resistance in depth in our main defensive positions."[24]

Still it was not clear whether it was only a minor incursion as some Japanese commanders believed. There was no clarification as to whether the Soviets were formally at war with Japan until a Tass Agency report was received at 4.00 a.m. on 9 August, three hours after hostilities had been initiated. Tass relayed the information that the Soviet Union had declared war on Japan at 5.00 p.m. on the previous day, 8 August. It provoked a '*Pearl Harbor* Moment' among the Japanese leadership, who realized that it had been duped by the Soviets who had led them to believe that they were helping Japan's peace negotiations in good faith. As the Japanese had done at *Pearl Harbor*, the Soviets launched a surprise attack before an official declaration of war. Foreign Ministry official, Kase Toshikazu, complained that the Soviet invasion of Manchuria was "the most unkind cut of all . . . we had asked for an olive branch and received a dagger thrust instead."[25] Still the *communiqué* sent in Hirohito's name was dismissive of the threat: "However the scale of these attacks is not large."[26]

By evening of 9 August elements of the 5th Army had penetrated some 12–28 miles into Manchuria along a 30-mile front. Already Soviet armor was threatening to cut rail, road and telegraph connections to Mutanchiang. A three-day target had been achieved in one. Fleeing Japanese troops arrived at the *Muleng River* only to find that their colleagues had already blown the bridge and, unable to ford the channels, they were forced to abandon their trucks and heavy equipment and skedaddle downstream of the advancing Soviet forces.

The Soviet progress was so rapid that the Japanese advance garrisons were unable to offer any delay and prevented the 135th, 126th and 124th Divisions from establishing a solid second defensive line. By nightfall of 10 August the Soviets had advanced 55 miles and by the following day they had achieved their eight-day targets in three. Behind them Japanese fortified regions at Pamientung and Linkou were enveloped. By day eight they had succumbed along with the northeastern coastal town of Chongjin situated inside the North Korean border. The fortified garrison of Hutou, north of the confluence of the *Muleng River* and *Ussuri River* (tributaries that fed into the *Amur River*) was also invested. Again the garrison was cut off, leaving just a few soldiers able to make their escape westward toward Mishan and Poli. The remainder settled in for a prolonged siege. As on the Western Front, Marshal Kirill Meretskov's forces penetrated through terrain that had been deemed impassable. This time it was the 1st Red Banner Army, which penetrated the mountainous border region.[26]

The Battle of Mutanchiang: With their border forces overwhelmed, General Shiina determined that the Japanese Army's main forces would make their stand at the mountains that curved in a semi-circle some 40 miles in front of the city of Mutanchiang. Situated on the *Muleng River* and on the main railroad to Harbin in central Manchuria, Mutanchiang was the city through which all Japanese eastern border forces, and indeed the enemy, would have to pass.

The first phase of the battle took place on the ridges overlooking Mutanchiang on 12–14 August. It was some of the bitterest fighting of the war. A Soviet officer described the scene:

> On the heights; among the tangle of trenches, pillboxes, dugouts, and artillery positions; over the precipices; and before the inaccessible grades bellowed tank motors; Japanese guns often struck, and the grass huts and grass blazed. The battle lasted to and fro more than an hour,

perhaps the bloodiest since the beginning of the combat. Finally, the enemy faltered, hundreds of retreating soldiers littered the slopes of the hills and valley of marshy streams. The tanks [257th Tank Brigade] pursued the fugitives. The victory was achieved at a heavy price.[27]

Having broken through the heights, the Soviet 257th Tank Brigade pursued the enemy to the *Mutan River* in front of Mutanchiang. Japanese troops had dug in around the main bridge, which was close to Hualin Station. Just as the Soviet tanks reached the bridge it was blown up, bringing their column to a halt. At this moment

from camouflaged foxholes rose up [*Japanese*] soldiers in greenish tunics, stooping under the heavy loads of mines and explosives, running toward the tanks. Soviet soldiers struck them with point blank fire from automatic weapons, and flung hand grenades. Bursts of tank machine guns mowed down the smertniks [*Kamikaze*]."[28]

Often when Japanese soldiers managed to reach the Soviet tanks their charges failed to penetrate the armor, leaving them little damaged. Only a squad of Japanese firemen from a transport unit, each armed with 33 pounds of explosive, managed to knock out numbers of Soviet tanks as they approached the headquarters of the Japanese 126th Division in Mutanchiang. Emperor Hirohito had already surrendered that day, 15 August, but the fighting continued. At 10.00 a.m. on 16 August Major-General Perekrestov's 65th Rifle Corps completed the destruction of Japanese forces east and southeast of Yehho.

Elsewhere fighting drew to a close but, in some instances, long after Japan's surrender. At Hutou, the fortresses' bunker constructions, risibly called the 'Japanese Maginot Line' by some Japanese officers, were reduced one by one. The war was over but that was probably not known to the Japanese troops hiding in their underground tombs. Gamii Zhefu, one of the few survivors, recalled, "In the tunnels beneath the fort, it was incredibly hot. We were desperate for water."[29] Two weeks later the conditions were indescribable with the starved survivors surrounded by putrid, decaying bodies. Pockets of underground Japanese resistance held out until 26 August when the Soviets brought up poison gas to finish off the holdouts.

For the Japanese civilian survivors worse was to come. Rape and pillage, hitherto a prerequisite of the all-conquering Japanese Armies, was now visited on Japanese and Manchurian civilians alike by elements of the Red Army. Herded into internment camps and provided with minimal amounts of shelter, food or medicines, disease spread rapidly among the civilian population—killing thousands.

The Battle of Sakhalin Island: [Map: 39.3] [Map: 39.4] Situated off the remote northeast *Pacific* Coast of Russia, at its northern tip some 900 miles north of Vladivostok, *Sakhalin* is a large elongated island, 560 miles long and up to 174 miles wide, that also abuts due north from *Hokkaido*, from which it is separated by the 30-mile-wide *La Perouse Straits*. After 1905 it was occupied up to the 50th parallel by Japan—booty from the *Russo-Japanese War.* Heavily forested, often swampy, *Sakhalin* is also mountainous with a central spine, from which rivers take their short course to the sea.

Faced by these unpropitious terrains, the advance southwards, starting on 11 August, by elements of Marshal Vasilevsky's 16th Army, including the 79th Rifles, 2nd Rifle Brigade, 5th Rifle Brigade and 214th Armored Brigade, made heavy weather. Some 19,000 Japanese troops of the 88th Infantry Division in addition to 10,000 reservists, outnumbered by 3 to 1, mounted a staunch defense. Russian superiority in tanks was greatly diminished by the nature of the terrain; as one Soviet officer reported, "when the tank subunits were assigned their missions, [the command] failed to take into account sufficiently the movement capabilities of various tank systems when being employed in forested, swampy, and road-less terrain."[30]

In classic Japanese style, fortified defense areas were made up of entrenchments with machine gun pits and bunkers. Soviet progress was painstaking. It was an amphibious flanking, landing at the port of Toro on the west coast of *Sakhalin* on 16 August, which finally broke their resistance. A 140-man reconnaissance detachment quickly captured the barely defended port and 1,500 troops of the 365th Naval Infantry Battalion and 2nd Battalion of the 113th Rifle Brigade were brought ashore. Japanese forces along the west coast were cut off and the rapid march eastward threatened their line of retreat. Thereafter the Soviet advance southward moved rapidly. The conquest of *Sakhalin* was completed on 25 August when the capital city of Toyohara was taken.

The Occupation of the Kuril Islands: **[Map: 39.5] [Map: 39.6]** The sparsely populated tendrils of the *Kuril Islands* chain stretch out in a gentle curve from northern *Hokkaido* to the tip of the Kamchatka Peninsula. They comprise 56 mostly uninhabited islands. Historically their greatest claim to fame in the *Pacific War* was their covert hosting of the Japanese carrier fleet at *Hitokappu Bay* off the island of *Iturup* before its deployment to attack *Pearl Harbor* in December 1941. Starting with US bombing attacks on Japanese garrisons on the main islands of *Shumshu* and *Paramushiro* on 10 July 1943, the *Kurils* were the subject of periodic US raids until the end of the war. However, at Yalta it was agreed that the Soviets would occupy the *Kurils* along with *Sakhalin Island*, which had been Japanese possessions since the *Treaty of Portsmouth* after the *Russo-Japanese War* of 1904–5.

Even as Hirohito was surrendering, Soviet troops were preparing to make amphibious landings on the *Kuril Islands*. At 2.35 a.m. on 18 August, as a Soviet amphibious force approached *Shumshu Island,* their batteries on Cape Lopataka (Kamchatka Peninsula), just an 8-mile stretch across the sea, opened fire on the intended landing areas. Thus warned Japanese coastal batteries opened fire on the Soviet invasion forces at 5.30 a.m.—sinking thirteen troop boats.

In spite of the chaotic amphibious action, a rare experience for the Red Army in *World War II*, Soviet troops established a beachhead and moved inland to attack Japan's main naval base at Kataoka. After two days of heavy fighting, including tank battles, in which 614 Japanese troops lost their lives, at 5.00 p.m. on 19 August, Lieutenant-General Aleksei Gnechko met his counterpart Major-General Suzino Iwao and accepted his surrender. By 29 August, the central and northern Kurils had been occupied by forward detachments of the Kamchatka Defensive Region. The day before, the Soviet Pacific Fleet, under Vice-Admiral Alexander Andreev, with the support of the 113rd Rifle Brigade, began the seizure of the southern half of the *Kuril* chain. The 13,500-strong Japanese garrison on *Iturup* surrendered without a fight. The *Lesser Kurils*, in the final action of the Pacific War, were occupied on 3–5 September.

The Soviet annexation of the *Kurils* ensured a long running dispute as to ownership of the islands that continues to this day. Although Japan renounced its claims to *Sakhalin* and the *Kuril Islands* in the *Treaty of San Francisco* [1951], it maintains that the four islands immediately adjacent to *Hokkaido* were not included. As a result, there is as yet no formal peace treaty to the *Pacific War* between Russia and Japan.

The Significance of the Soviet Invasions: In itself the Soviet invasion of Manchuria was of little military importance or consequence even though some 674,000 Japanese troops were killed or captured. The cost for the Red Army may have been seemingly low at 12,000 dead and 24,000 sick and wounded but in reality, if Stalin had waited but a few days for Japan's surrender, which must have been expected after the atom bombing of Hiroshima, Manchuria could have been acquired cost-free. But Stalin was not one to quibble over the lives of his own soldiers. Even if Japan had surrendered on 6 August, the day of the Hiroshima bombing, three days before the commencement of the Soviet invasion, Stalin would still have occupied Manchuria and the northern half of Korea. He was determined to reclaim the territories that had been ceded to Japan after the humiliating defeat of Imperial Russia at the *Battle of Tsushima* [1905] and the succeeding *Treaty of Portsmouth*. If that could be achieved with a crushing defeat of Japanese forces, all the better.

As it was, the Soviet invasion brought about the post-war conspiracy theory that America dropped the atom bomb when it did, to stop the Soviets in their tracks—this, it was argued, was the main reason for using an atom bomb on an already defeated enemy. If this was the US government's theory, which it was not, it would have failed. The Soviets would have occupied former Japanese territories anyway. Stalin had agreed, indeed had allowed himself to be persuaded by Roosevelt at Yalta, to invade Japanese controlled territories. Roosevelt need not have concerned himself—Stalin, once Hitler had been disposed of, was only too happy to exact retribution on Japan and take advantage of its weakened state. He envisioned a post-war world in which China would be a buffer vassal nation to the Soviet Union in the Far East, just as the Eastern European nations would act as a buffer to Western Europe.

Stalin could have pushed further into China, South Korea and the northern main Japanese island of *Hokkaido* but chose not to—though he did make the suggestion to Truman, quickly rejected, that the Soviet Army could land in *Hokkaido* and take the formal Japanese surrender there. As great a villain as he was, Stalin, a cautious man, abided by the letter if not the spirit of Yalta. He occupied the territories that had been agreed but no more. At Yalta Roosevelt, and after his death, Truman, still saw Stalin as an ally and a future partner in global peace and security.

As for the 'atomic diplomacy' theory proposed by Gar Alperovitz, Ward Wilson and others, that the Japanese surrendered largely because of the shock of the Soviet invasion of Manchuria—a critical point in their case that the dropping of the atom bomb was unnecessary—their logic is askew. The Imperial Army HQ was already inured to the idea of losing Manchuria. The filleting of the Manchurian Army of nearly all their good troops and equipment in April 1945 meant that Japan's leaders had already given up on keeping hold of their empire. Togo and other Japanese leaders may have been shocked as to the timing of the Soviet invasion on 9 August, but they were not so naïve as to believe that it was altogether unlikely that Stalin would exact revenge on a country that had been its main geopolitical enemy for more than half a century. Stalin's vacillation on any extension of the *Japan-Soviet Neutrality Pact* must have given the clue to all but the diplomatically blind—a characteristic that was evident in the conduct of much Japanese diplomacy, both before the *Pacific War* and at its end.

Although a cabal of Japanese officers based in Switzerland had, in June 1945, tried to initiate a peace deal based on Japan keeping Korea and *Formosa* as part of the Japanese Empire, the plan was barely dignified with a response—even from Tokyo. Manchuria was not even mentioned. The Empire was long lost by the spring of 1945 and the Japanese leaders knew it; hence the appropriation by Imperial Army GHQ of experienced army units based in Manchuria. For Hirohito and his army commanders, their last chance rested solely on the defense of Japan; by making its defense too painful to the US invaders they believed that the allies would agree to a surrender that fell short of unconditional.

Noticeably after the Potsdam Declaration, Japan's tentative offers to make a conditional surrender through Ambassador Sato in Moscow did not include the 'redline' retention of Manchuria or any other possession of Empire. Nevertheless the invasion of Manchuria was arguably a "psychological jolt comparable to that of the atom bomb."[31] This was not because Japan's leaders feared the loss of Manchuria—that was already a given—but because it must have been feared that the Soviets might beat the Americans to the beaches of mainland Japan.

It was the dropping of the atom bomb on Hiroshima that first propelled Japan's military leadership along the path that led to surrender. The atom bombing of Nagasaki and the invasion of Manchuria, both of which followed three days later, merely underlined the futility of further resistance. Ultimately it was the atom bomb, not the Soviet invasion of Manchuria, which persuaded Emperor Hirohito, the doves and even the majority of the ultranationalist military leaders that their last throw of the dice, the last ditch suicidal defense of Japan's main islands, was a pointless and untenable strategy.

40 Potsdam, Hirohito, and the Atom Bomb

[July 1945–August 1945]

[Drawings: 40.1, 40.2] [Maps: 40.3, 40.4, 40.5, 40.6]

Enola Gay and the Dropping of Little Boy: [Drawing: 40.1] [Drawing: 40.2] At 8.15 a.m. on 6 August 1945, a lone B-29 bomber piloted by Colonel Paul Tibbets, which had been hastily named the *Enola Gay* after his mother, dropped a single bomb over Hiroshima and headed out to sea. The bomb, nicknamed Little Boy, 10.5 feet long, 29 inches in diameter, weighing 9,700 pounds and, according to one of its crew, looking like 'an elongated trash can with fins,' fell toward its target, the Aioi Bridge, in the heart of Hiroshima. Surrounded by steep hills, the city sat in a basin fashioned from the fingers of land created by the delta of the *Motoyasu River*.

Hiroshima was just awakening to a warm and sunny morning. The temperature was already 27 degrees centigrade; the trams just north of Aioi Bridge at the Fukuya department store were packed; the streets were full of cyclists on their way to work; at the parade grounds to the west of the Aioi Bridge, bare-chested soldiers, some of the 43,000 stationed in the city, were doing morning exercises. Further from the center, school children were being coaxed into classrooms. A junior college student recalled looking up at the sky after hearing her teacher exclaim, "Oh there's a B . . .!"[1] At that moment, the bomb, inappropriately name Little Boy, which had drifted to a point some 550 feet southeast of its target to 1,900 feet above the Shima Hospital, exploded in a tremendous flash of lightning. "In an instant we were blinded and everything was just a frenzy of delirium."[2] At the center of the explosion site, the temperature reached 5,400 degrees. Even metal at proximity to the explosion was vaporized. People simply disappeared, sometimes leaving their shadows imprinted on stone or tarmac. Those Japanese within 600 yards of the explosion had their internal organs melted within a millisecond; over 90 percent of them died. Birds ignited in mid-air. At two miles away poles burst into flames. At three-quarters of a mile away 70 percent of people died; at one mile away 30 percent were killed. Some 62,000 buildings, two-thirds of the city, were destroyed. Within an instant Little Boy killed 50,000 of the 340,000 inhabitants of Hiroshima.

By the end of the year a further 20,000 had died of radiation sickness and eventually the total number of dead from the attack rose to 150,000. The well-constructed Fukuya Department Store, which had been completed in 1938, was 776 yards from Little Boy's hypocenter and was completely burnt out but remained intact and was used as an isolation unit for the sick for a month after the atom bomb until the symptoms of radiation sickness became better understood. Seeing patients vomiting and suffering from diarrhea, a Dr. Michihiko Hachiya, a director of Hiroshima Communications Hospital, who was treating the sick, suspected at first that the American bomb must have released poisonous bacilli. It is sometimes forgotten that much of the post-war shibboleth about atom bombs developed as a result of the later developed knowledge of the short and long-term effects of radiation poisoning. At the time the atom bomb was thought of by most people as just a very powerful bomb. Indeed a few months after the dropping of Little Boy, a young British officer, Sub-Lieutenant Peter Daniel, whose ship, the battleship HMS *Duke of York*, docked at Kure along the coast from Hiroshima, took a train and blithely ambled around the devastated city unaware of the risks of radiation.

Within a week Hachiya's patients began to suffer subcutaneous hemorrhages and began to vomit blood. Victims hair fell out and their skin turned black while their bodies gave off an intolerable odor. Death was a formality. Gamma rays attacked reproducing cells in the body's bone marrow. When fully formed cells died off. They were not replaced. Hiroshima's suffering did not end with radiation sickness. The *hibakusha* (explosion-affected people) experienced large numbers of deaths by cancer and other illnesses, and to this day they and their progeny, about 250,000 people, suffer from social discrimination, alienation and exclusion—their position in society mirrors that of Japan's two million outcasts, the *Burakumin* (literally: hamlet people).

For some American captives retribution came quickly. One pilot, who had been forced to ditch near Hiroshima in late July and was subsequently interned, was dumped at Aioi Bridge where he was stoned to death. In addition the atom bomb itself killed as many as twenty-three American prisoners. On 8 August Martin Zapf, one of the crew of a B-29, which had ditched off Hiroshima, was taken prisoner and later reported coming across two Americans in prison; a US Navy aviator and an Air Force sergeant were suffering from extreme nausea with green liquid dripping from their mouths and ears. Screaming in pain, the two airmen died that night.

The Japanese Army had suffered a much greater blow. Some 10,000 of their troops are estimated to have died including Lieutenant-General Yoji Fujii, head of the Fifty-Ninth Army, whose charred body was recognized from the sword found next to him. Field Marshal Shunroku Hata, having returned from overseeing Operation ICHI-GO in China to take command of the Second General Army in preparation for the expected American invasion, was also in Hiroshima. He survived.

Meanwhile on the *Enola Gay*, tail gunner Robert Carron remembered, "the mushroom itself was a spectacular sight, a bubbling mass of purple-grey smoke and you could see it had a red core in it and everything was burning inside."[3] Two hours later, a message from Washington was decoded on board the battle-cruiser USS *Augusta* on which President Truman was returning from the three-week Potsdam Conference with Stalin, Churchill and, following Churchill's defeat in British elections, Clement Attlee. Truman immediately set about informing the crew. He said that he had never been happier about any announcement he had ever made. Major Donald Regan, a veteran of five campaigns from *Guadalcanal* to *Okinawa*, who was later to become President Ronald Reagan's Treasury Secretary, recalled that he "understood the horror of the bombing. Nevertheless, these events filled me with joy when they were announced, and I will not pretend otherwise today."[4]

The MANHATTAN Project: [Map: 40.3] [Map: 40.4] On 9 October 1941 Roosevelt sat down with his Vice-President Henry Wallace and Vannevar Bush, the Director of the US Office of Scientific Research and Development (OSRD). Bush was also Chairman of the National Defense Research Committee (NDRC), which coordinated the military-related research activity of some 6,000 US scientists. Having earlier brought to the attention of the President the possibility of building a super-bomb as a result of breakthroughs made in the understanding of uranium, the formal go-ahead was given to build an atom bomb; a project on which the Army had already been doing preparatory work for some months. As well as Wallace and Bush, the Top Policy Group established to monitor the work of building the bomb included Henry Stimson, Secretary of War, General George Marshall and James Conant, a Harvard chemist and President of the University who succeeded Bush as Chairman of the NDRC.

The Army was given the mandate to direct the atom bomb project—codenamed MANHATTAN—and in August 1941 Major-General Leslie 'Dick' Groves Jr. had been given the role of executive management. A former student at the Massachusetts Institute of Technology before becoming an Army engineer, Groves made his reputation in July 1940 as an assistant for construction to the Quartermaster General, Major-General Edmund Gregory, just as the US was embarking on its unprecedented military mobilization. In recognition of his phenomenal energy and hard work, he was also given responsibility for the management of the War Department's 40,000 staff as well as the construction of their war offices, which become known as the Pentagon. Groves was a quietly spoken, intimidating, tyrannical brute of a man; what he lacked in charm he made up for in administrative ability and force of will. He controled his secret empire with an iron fist. Secrecy was a priority and key scientists were tracked by the FBI. In Groves' office at the War Department in Foggy Bottom, Washington, a sign on his desk read, "O Lord! Help me keep my big mouth shut!"[5]

It worked. Remarkably Groves kept MANHATTAN secret from the State Department until 1945. Admirals King and Nimitz were not let in on the secret until 27 January 1945 and the less trustworthy General MacArthur only in June. Groves was a determined anti-communist and later wrote that he believed that while Japan was the immediate target, "There was never . . . any illusion on my part but that Russia was our enemy, and the [MANHATTAN Project] was conducted on that basis."[6] His staunch anti-communism did not preclude his selection of theoretical physicist, Robert Oppenheimer as project leader for the scientific aspects of the project, which was to be located at Los Alamos, New Mexico. Oppenheimer's Communist leanings were well known. Oppenheimer's brother was a Communist, as was his former girlfriend, Jean Tatlock, another physicist who later committed suicide in 1944. Oppenheimer's intellect as a scientist and his administrative talents meant that he was, in Grove's words, "absolutely essential to the project."[7]

The United States started behind in the nuclear arms race. In January 1939, within months of the discovery of nuclear fission, Germany had started its own nuclear program. The following year, Russian scientists began theoretical work on nuclear fission although a bomb-building program did not start until 1942 when intelligence revealed to Stalin that the West was working on a bomb. In Japan, Dr. Yoshio Nishina, who had worked with Niels Bohr in Denmark on theoretical physics, established a nuclear research facility at the Riken Institute in 1931. Nishina had constructed its first cyclotron in 1936 and three years later bought a larger one from the University of California, Berkeley. By 1939 Nishina was pushing for a military program. Although Army Minster Hideki Tojo did not authorize the go-ahead until April 1941, it still gave Japan a six-month head start over the United States. Ultimately Nishina never had the resources to compete with America. In 1943 Nishina reported that a new 250-ton 1.5 meter accelerator was ready for operation except for certain components which were unavailable as they were being used in the construction of munitions.

Acquisition of uranium was problematic. Bringing ore from Czechoslovakia failed when Japanese cargo submarines were intercepted. A German submarine, loaded with 1,200 tons of uranium oxide, was also captured on 19 May 1945. Workable designs for a Japanese atom bomb have recently been discovered at Kyoto University in the Radioisotope Research Laboratory. The notebooks were the work of Professor Bunsaku Arakastu, the leader of Project F—the Navy's competitor to the army-backed work of Nishina. Somehow they had survived the burning of sensitive papers that followed Japan's surrender on 15 August 1945. What is clear is that the Japanese armed forces engaged in a race to produce the first atom bomb and lost. Chieko Takeuchi, widow of the atomic scientist, later recalled her husband saying, "If we'd built the bomb first, of course we would have used it. I'm glad, in some ways, that our facilities were destroyed."[8]

The most critical pre-war scientific breakthrough was made before the start of *World War II* by Otto Frish, a Jewish Viennese-born scientist who, after spells at Birkbeck, London and Copenhagen with Professor Niels Bohr, ended up at the University of Birmingham. In June 1939 he and Rudolph Peierls, a Jew of German origin, produced a memorandum outlining a key development in the race to produce an atom bomb—a calculation showing that just a kilogram of uranium-235, whose isotope could be separated from uranium-238, would be needed to build a bomb. (Previously it had been assumed that tons of uranium would be required, making it militarily impractical.) Alarmingly they warned, "It is quite conceivable that Germany is, in fact, developing this weapon."[9] Peierls had as distinguished a pedigree as Frisch, having worked under Werner Heisenberg and Wolfgang Pauli in Zurich before winning a Rockefeller Scholarship to Cambridge University (UK) and then becoming Professor of Mathematical Physics at Birmingham University. His work with Frisch heralded the possibility of producing a nuclear weapon small enough to be carried by a bomber, which would have the destructive capacity of 1,000 conventional bombs.

Within months the work of Frisch and Peierls was taken up by the British government. Work on the development of an atom bomb, overseen by the MAUD Committee (Military Application of Uranium Detonation), began in March 1940. Their work preceded the formation of the British atomic project, codenamed TUBE ALLOYS, which was brought to the attention of American scientists at Berkeley by Australian physicist Mark Oliphant, who was working for the British government. Churchill, without hesitation, transferred British theoretical and technical know-how to America and TUBE ALLOYS was in effect rolled into the MANHATTAN Project. Otto Frisch moved to the United States. Churchill's generosity was not all it seemed. At a cost of £5m per kilogram of uranium 235 (US$20m at the fixed wartime exchange rate of US$4.03 to the British pound), Britain could not have afforded to go it alone.

Having apprised himself of the key determinants of the project, Groves' first significant move was to acquire a secure supply of uranium from the Belgian Congo. Negotiations were quickly concluded with Edgar Senier, Managing Director of mining conglomerate Union Minière du Haut Katanga, for the supply of 1,250 tons of yellow cake (uranium ore). The cake was shipped to the US where it was stored in a Staten Island warehouse.

From early 1943 various options developed in terms of what type of atom bomb to construct. While Oppenheimer gave priority to the gun-type weapon used at Hiroshima (code name THIN MAN), he also authorized the building of a backup implosion type atom bomb which was considered to be much more efficient in terms of explosive yield from the same amount of nuclear material. The main obstacle to building this weapon was obtaining fissile material at the higher levels of purity required by the implosion design. The design itself was based on the mathematical modeling of John von Neumann, who showed that by using simultaneous explosions of two different explosives, their differentiated shockwaves would compress fissile materials inwards acting as a trigger to a nuclear explosion. The resulting bomb, which was used at Nagasaki, used plutonium at its core and because of its bulbous shape was codenamed FAT MAN. (Unlike THIN MAN that was nicknamed Little Boy, FAT MAN continued to be called Fat Man, supposedly because of Sydney Greenstreet's character in the classic John Huston film *The Maltese Falcon* [1941]).

In term of explosive power, Little Boy was rated at between 13–18 kt TNT while Fat Man was rated at 20–22 kt TNT (1 kt = approximately 1,000 tons of TNT or Trinitrotoluene). Given that the typical heavyweight 1,000 lb bomb used by the US Air Force consisted of approximately 30 percent of charge by weight—usually a mixture of TNT and ammonium nitrate—it took about seven bombs to carry 1 ton of explosive. Fat Man alone was approximately equivalent in explosive power to 2,500 thousand-pound bombs. To give a modern comparison, the largest nuclear device ever tested by the US Army, CASTLE BRAVO, was 15,000 kt, some 750 times more powerful than Fat Man.

At US$2 billion (US$35 billion in 2014 terms) the cost of the MANHATTAN Project was significant but not outlandish. First, it was only the second most expensive project of the war. The development and building of the extraordinarily complex Boeing B-29

Superfortress cost US$3 billion. **[See Chapter 38: LeMay's B-29 Superfortresses over Japan: Cities in Ashes]** Ultimately the atom bomb would be carried by the B-29, the only bomber capable of taking the load. Arguably the bomb and its delivery mechanism cost a combined US$5 billion, but that would be to miss the point. The B-29 program had its origins in 1938, long before the atom bomb was conceived as a project, and was justified by its capabilities as a conventional long-range bomber. Second, the combined cost of the atom bomb and the B-29 program represented just 1.5 percent of the estimated aggregate US$350 billion cost of the war.

This is not to underestimate the scale of the project. It started small with just a handful of scientists. In the first year of the project, MANHATTAN employed hundreds of scientists and take-off only began at the end of 1942 when production was envisaged. In the next two years vast construction works were undertaken at Oak Ridge and Hanford as well as Los Alamos. Oak Ridge, sometimes called Atomic City, was a new-built town in remote east Tennessee, forty miles to the west of Knoxville. The Army purchased 60,000 acres in an area that had access to water and electricity from the recently completed Norris Dam—the first major project of the Tennessee Valley Authority, a component of Roosevelt's New Deal legislation. It was here that separators were built to isolate the fissile uranium-235 isotope from the uranium-238 isotope. A pilot plant was also built for the production of plutonium. From a population of just 3,000 in 1942, the military-controlled city grew to 75,000 by 1945 (now just 29,000). Homes were built at the rate of 1,000 per month. Meanwhile Hanford, a site that covers 590,000 square miles, and sits on a bend of the *Columbia River* in Benton County, Washington, was developed in 1943 to produce plutonium in the world's first full-scale reactor. The main criterion for choosing the site was again easy access to water and electricity. The Yakama tribes were relocated from the region along with the thousand or so residents of White Bluffs. By the end of the war, the blandly named Hanford Engineer Works had built three nuclear reactors.

Los Alamos was selected by Philip Oppenheimer in a remote location on a semi-desert *mesa* in New Mexico to house the MANHATTAN Project's key scientists a long way from other populations. Fortuitously Robert Oppenheimer had spent much of his youth in the area and owned a ranch nearby. The location was kept a strict secret with addresses for its thousands of scientists given only as PO Box 1663, Santa Fe. Los Alamos National Laboratory conducted both theoretical work and design and assembly of the first atom bombs. Gathered here or at the University of Chicago's Metallurgical Laboratory were the cream of the world's nuclear physicists including Nobel laureates Arthur Compton (development of X-Ray technology), Harold Urey (discoverer of deuterium who pioneered isotope separation) and Ernest Lawrence, who had won his Nobel Prize for Physics in 1939 for the invention of the cyclotron—an accelerator used to separate charged particles. Other noted inmates of Los Alamos included the brilliant mathematician John von Neumann. German Jewish *émigrés* working on the project abounded and included Peierls, Hans Bethe, Edward Teller, Leo Szilard and James Franck. Perhaps the most important of the *emigrés* was Italian Physicist, Enrico Fermi who left Europe for Chicago in 1938 on account of his Jewish wife. Fermi, who had won the Nobel Prize for Physics in that year for his work on radioactive elements, constructed the first nuclear reaction. Football fans may have been alarmed to know that the first successful test took place in a squash court below the West Stand of Stagg Field Stadium, Chicago. In September 1944 Fermi moved to Los Alamos to work at the apex of the MANHATTAN Project in its final stages.

Incongruously the German-Jewish *émigrés* donned western clothes—jeans and boots—for Saturday night square dancing. In the wilds of New Mexico, younger physicist partook of other pleasures—causing a baby boom at the same time that they were building the most destructive weapon ever built. Poker schools abounded. The Ukrainian chemist George Kistiakowsky admitted that he "played a lot of poker with important people like Johnny von Neumann, Stan Ulam etc."[10] (Stanislaw Ulam was a Polish-American mathematician, who invented the appropriately named Monte Carlo computation method using random sampling and computational algorithms.) Kistiakowsky admitted to being a card sharp:

> When I came to Los Alamos I discovered that these people didn't know how to play poker and offered to teach them. At the end of the evening they got annoyed occasionally when we added up the chips . . . Unfortunately, before the end of the war, these great theoretical minds caught on to poker and the evenings' accounts became less attractive from my point of view.[11]

At its peak the MANHATTAN Project employed 125,000 people. However, employment turnover in the remote locations of Oak Ridge and Hanford was often as high as 20 percent per month. In all it is estimated that as many as 500,000 people were employed by the MANHATTAN Project over the course of the four years to 1945.

By 31 May 1945 Hanford had delivered enough plutonium to begin critical mass experiments and for the final details of design to be ironed out. Deadlines for the various groups came and went. Frisch's group finalized the core configuration on 24 June; Kistiakowsky's group worked all hours to produce sufficient lens segments for the implosion device; on 27 June Groves met Oppenheimer to discuss shipment of the atom bomb to the *Pacific*. On 4 July, Independence Day, at the Combined Policy Committee, the British government gave its formal approval for the use of atom bombs against Japan. The pressure on the scientists at Los Alamos was intense. Elsie McMillan recalled: "That last week in many ways dragged . . . in many ways it flew on wings. It was hard to behave normally. It was hard not to think. It was hard not to let off steam. We also found it hard not to overindulge in all the natural activities of life."[12] In a letter to Eleanor Roosevelt after the war, Oppenheimer wrote, "people at Los Alamos were naturally in a state of some tension"[13] and recounted a story about their group delusion when a UFO turned out to be the planet Venus.

Gauging the weather forecasts and aware that the Potsdam Conference was about to take place, Groves chose 16 July for the TRINITY test. Oppenheimer chose the codename TRINITY from a poem by the sixteenth-century Elizabethan metaphysical poet, John Donne, to whose poetry he had been introduced by the now deceased Jean Tatlock; it was a plea for redemption from a 'three person'd God':

> Batter my heart, three person'd God: for you
> As yet but knocke, breathe, shine, and seek to mend;
> That I may rise, and stand, o'erthrow me, and bend
> Your force to break, blowe, burn and make me new . . .[14]

The site selected for the TRINITY atom bomb, or The Gadget as the scientists called it, was in the Jornada de Muerto desert some thirty miles southeast of Socorro in New Mexico. Final preparations for the bomb were made at the MacDonald Ranch on Friday 13 July, where a ranch house room was converted into a vacuum-sealed clean room. The University of California, Berkeley, under whose auspices Los Alamos was officially attached, required the Army to sign off a receipt for the millions of dollars' worth of plutonium that they were about to dispose of in spectacular style. On 16 July, the bomb was raised to its platform. At the last minute experimental tests by the Creutz group at Los Alamos warned, The Gadget was likely to be a dud; depression hung over Oppenheimer and his group as they traveled to the Hilton Hotel in Albuquerque for a VIP reception with Army generals. Oppenheimer calmed himself by reading the *Bhagavad-Gita*, the Hindu scripture at the heart of the *Mahabharata*. On Sunday evening, 15 July, much to Groves' annoyance, Fermi offered bets on

> . . . whether or not the bomb would ignite the atmosphere, and if so, whether it would merely destroy New Mexico or destroy the world. He had also said that after all it wouldn't make any difference whether the bomb went off or not because it would still have been a worthwhile experiment. For if it did fail to go off, we would have proved that an atomic explosion was not possible.[15]

Countdown began at 5.25 a.m. on 16 July. A siren wailed at base camp. The observers made for their viewing positions; some lay down in shallow trenches lined up like corpses and fixed their sunglasses. The one minute warning rocket was fired at 5.29 a.m. As countdown to zero arrived The Gadget exploded. At base camp, Isidor Rabi, a Polish-American physicist who was the Nobel Laureate in 1944 for the discovery of nuclear magnetic resonance, wrote,

> Suddenly, there was an enormous flash of light, the brightest light I have ever seen or that I think anyone has ever seen. It blasted; it pounced; it bored its way right through you. It was vision, which was seen with more than the eye. It was seen to last forever. You would wish

it would stop . . . altogether it lasted about two seconds
. . . we looked toward where the bomb had been: there
was an enormous ball of fire which grew and grew and it
rolled as it grew; it went up in the air, in yellow flashes
and into scarlet and green. It looked menacing. It seemed
to come toward one. A new thing had been born; a new
control; a new understanding of man, which man had
acquired over nature.[16]

More pragmatically Fermi waited for the air blast to drop some pieces of paper from head height. They landed 2.5 yards away, from which he calculated the size of the blast as somewhere in the region of 10,000 tons of TNT—Fermi was off by 8,600 tons. Kistiakowsky was blown over by the blast but jumped to his feet, and ever the gambler claimed a ten-dollar bet from Oppenheimer. Los Alamos's Director fished for his wallet but it was empty. Oppenheimer jumped in a jeep and drove back to base camp where Rabi detected a 'High-noon' style strut in his gait. Four hours later, USS *Indianapolis*, carrying Little Boy, exited *San Francisco Bay* and headed for *Tinian*.

Harry Truman and the Potsdam Conference: Some four months earlier, while working on his paper in 'The Little Whitehouse' in Warm Springs, Georgia, the sickly President Roosevelt suffered a cerebral haemorrhage and crashed to the floor, dead. The same evening, 12 April 1945, Vice-President Harry Truman, the obscure and plain-speaking former senator from Kansas, Missouri was sworn into office in the Cabinet Room in the west wing of the White House. After a cabinet meeting eleven days later, Secretary of War, Henry Stimson, lingered and begged a confidential word; he informed Truman that the US Army Corps of Engineers was in the advanced stages of developing a bomb of immense power. Indeed Admiral Yamamoto's doom laden prophesies of American industrial might were about to be realized. By contrast with the extensive research and industrial facilities and the almost half a million people involved in the MANHATTAN Project, Japan's effort to develop a nuclear weapon at the Japanese Nuclear Research Laboratory, established at Riken, employed just 110 scientists.

A mere twelve weeks after becoming President, Truman headed off with some trepidation to Potsdam, the elegant town twenty miles southwest of Berlin, where Frederick the Great had built his exquisite petite rococo palace, *Sans Souci*, and where also, on the adjacent *Lake Wannsee, Nazi* officers and clerks had planned in great detail the liquidation of the Jews at a holiday villa bought by the *Nazi* SS (*Schutzstaffel*: Protection Squadron) from the German industrialist, Friedrich Minoux. This was to be the last of the major wartime leader conferences, and was to have a dramatic impact on the shape of post-war Asia. Truman knew neither Churchill nor Stalin. Churchill he came to like and respect, in spite of his verbosity and grandiloquence, which was absolutely not the style of the farmer's son from Independence, Missouri. For his part, Churchill immediately took to Truman declaring, ". . . he is a man of immense determination. He takes no notice of delicate ground, he just plants his foot firmly upon it."[17] As for 'Uncle Joe' Stalin, Truman, like most other international statesmen before him, was soon charmed in spite of his pallid Kremlin complexion and runt-like stature. The same warm feeling did not flow for Prime Minister Clement Attlee, accompanied by Foreign Minister, Ernest Bevan, who replaced Churchill mid-conference, when much to Stalin's shock, he lost the General Election to the Labour Party; these two Labour politicians Truman described as "sourpusses."[18]

This was not the grand triumphal conference that had been expected. Churchill appeared tired. The exertions of war had depleted his energies. No doubt also the death of his close friend Roosevelt affected him deeply. Before coming to Potsdam, he had visited what remained of Hitler's bunkers in Berlin and noted that if the *Nazis* had won, "we would have been in the bunker."[19] Moreover the British government was close to bankruptcy. The war in Europe may have been won but the cost was 25 percent of Britain's gross domestic product. Britain was a spent force and both Stalin and Truman knew it. There was just Japan to deal with. The future of Asia would not be decided by Great Britain. As for Stalin, he arrived late at the conference as a tactic to magnify the importance of the Soviet Union. He felt that with the loss of more dead than all the other combatant nations put together, it was his country that had done the 'heavy lifting. What America had done in industrial output, the Soviet Union had done in blood.

However, it was Truman, conscious of his 'new boy' status, who became the decisive figure at Potsdam. In part this was due to meticulous preparations of his briefs and his direct no-nonsense approach to negotiation. However, his confidence must, in part, have come from the trump card delivered to him on the afternoon of the second day of the conference. In New Mexico Oppenheimer and his team had successfully detonated the first atom bomb.

Did They Have To Use It? **[Map: 40.5]** The US government did not have to use the atom bomb. The Allies were planning to invade *Kyushu* (Operation OLYMPIC) on 1 November and they could have continued with this plan, keeping the atomic bomb in the locker. Conceivably Japan would have surrendered in the ten weeks before the planned invasion. As General Arnold indicated, "The Japanese position was hopeless even before the first atomic bomb fell, because the Japanese had lost control of their own air."[20] Already by June, it was becoming increasingly difficult for the Air Force to find targets. On the USS *Yorktown* Admiral Radford confided to Henry Luce, owner-editor of *Time-Life*, during his tour of the *Pacific* theater in June 1945, that there were few revetments or rural bridges to find in *Kyushu*. Meanwhile Admiral Frank Wagner in the Philippines told Luce, "in all those millions of square miles there was literally not a single target worth the powder to blow it up; there were only junks and mostly small ones at that."[21]

In the *Pacific*, many of the senior commanders opposed the use of the atom bomb. Admiral Halsey, not known for kindly words about the Japanese, stated in 1946: "The first atomic bomb was an unnecessary experiment . . . It was a mistake ever to drop it . . . [the scientists] had this toy and they wanted to try it out, so they dropped it . . . It killed a lot of Japs, but the Japs had put out a lot of peace feelers through Russia long before."[22] Similarly, Nimitz, in a speech at the Washington Monument on 5 October 1945 noted, "The Atomic bomb played no decisive part, from a purely military standpoint, in the defeat of Japan . . ." and asserted, "The Japanese had, in fact, already sued for peace . . ."[23]

General Dwight 'Ike' Eisenhower, perhaps less aware than soldiers on the ground in *Okinawa* about the unyielding qualities of Japanese soldiers, thought that Japan was defeated and that the bomb should not be used. He told Secretary of War, Henry Stimson, that it was his belief "that Japan was, at that very moment, seeking some way to surrender with a minimum loss of face."[24] Even Admiral William Leahy, Chairman of the Joint Chiefs of Staff, commented, "It is my opinion that the use of this barbarous weapon at Hiroshima and Nagasaki was of no material assistance in our war with against Japan. The Japanese were already defeated and ready to surrender . . ."[25]

The military view of the use of the atom bomb is worth considering but it is not necessarily convincing. In spite of the judgments of the US admirals and generals, the Japanese government in August was still a long way from accepting surrender even though they had been militarily crushed. From intelligence intercepts it was clear that Admirals Leahy, Nimitz and Halsey were simply wrong to believe that Japan was close to surrender on terms that were even close to what was required by the Allies.

First, America's senior officers, both during and even after the war, were largely unaware of the internal political dynamics that drove decision making inside Hirohito's government and within the military. At various times, such as when MacArthur believed that the reconquest of *Luzon* would force a Japanese surrender, military commanders erroneously believed that defeat in battle would force them to capitulate. They nearly all thought that the destruction of Japan by General LeMay's bombing campaign would obviate the need for invasion. Time and again they were proved wrong. The western military logic of understanding when a lost battle is a lost war was not a Japanese logic. Contrary to all US military expectations, there were many Japanese admirals and generals who continued to believe that America could be defeated in battle on the beaches of Japan.

Second, the highest-level US military commanders, all old-fashioned warriors, found the atom bomb, a weapon of mass-destruction, wholly alien to their philosophy of war. And last, it was difficult for these American military leaders to accept any form of diminution of their efforts and those of their troops in bringing Japan to defeat. For them the atom bomb was an abomination, not just because of its vast killing potential, but because it took away their pride in a profession and diminished the importance of a job well done during the course of the *Pacific War*.

Right up to 7 August, the day after the bomb was dropped on Hiroshima, it was clear that Japan's government was not prepared to accept 'unconditional surrender.' ULTRA and MAGIC intercepts gave America a very accurate running commentary on attitudes within Hirohito's administration. In mid-July 1945 a telegram from the Emperor to the Soviet Union asked for peace without offering any specific terms. The wording of the telegram does not speak of any strenuous effort to sue for peace or surrender.

Furthermore, the Japanese Foreign Ministry had indicated to its ambassador in Moscow that the government's minimum terms would include the preservation of Hirohito and the Imperial family, no occupation of Japan and Japanese control of any war crimes tribunals. Explicit terms were not forthcoming, however. In Moscow, an exasperated Ambassador Naotake Sato requested that Foreign Minister Shinegori Togo should provide him with 'concrete terms'—something that he was never able to do because of deep divisions between the 'hawks' and 'doves' within the cabinet. Hirohito, in his post-war account of the war *Showa Tenno Dokuhakuroku*, fails to mention any terms on which he would have been prepared to surrender at this earlier stage. Doubts were not confined to the Japanese side. American credulity with regard to Japanese good faith in diplomacy had been somewhat stretched by the events leading up to *Pearl Harbor*. Even after the destruction of Hiroshima, the military leaders still rejected military occupation, disarmament, war crimes trials conducted by the victors and any threat to the continuity of the Chrysanthemum Throne.

If America had been prepared to accept a limited victory, it too could have offered peace some time earlier. Arguably, since the crushing naval defeat at the *Battle of the Philippine Sea* in June 1944, Japan's last realistic chance of victory, Japan had been a defeated nation. Its ability to wage war had effectively been annihilated. America might realistically have claimed that its military war aims had been achieved and could have suggested to Hirohito's government that Japan yield its Empire in the Philippines, Burma, China and Korea. On this view, the campaigns on *Luzon*, the bombing campaign of Japan, *Iwo Jima* and *Okinawa* were all superfluous to America's victory in the war.

However, the Allies were not prepared to accept anything short of total victory and 'unconditional surrender'—this much had been promised by Roosevelt and supported by Churchill at the Casablanca Conference (codenamed SYMBOL) in January 1943. In the absence of Japan's acceptance of defeat in the summer of 1944, which would have been the logical course for Hirohito's government, the United States and to a lesser extent Great Britain were presented with a dilemma. The Allies had to go on fighting a war, which, to all intents and purposes, had been won—and with an increasingly high rate of casualties. Indeed this is what the Japanese government was counting on with regard to their demands for a limited surrender—that war weariness and the Allied death toll would force them to back off from their demand for unconditional surrender.

However, the *Atlantic Charter* had already formalized a pact that agreed that the Allies would not conclude a separate peace agreement. Given this commitment to force Japan's unconditional surrender could an American government, and more importantly its people, have accepted anything less? In a June 1945 Gallup Poll on the future of the Japanese Emperor, 70 percent of Americans were in favor of Emperor Hirohito either being executed, tried for war crimes, being given life imprisonment, or exiled. Just 7 percent were in favor of him retaining a position as a figurehead leader of Japan. The problem for Truman in July 1945 was that he had a weapon that could be used to end the war and force Japan's surrender. It was less a question of whether he would use the atom bomb, but rather, how could he not have used the atom bomb?

Having suffered over 400,000 deaths in *World War II*, of which 111,000 were in the *Pacific War*, it seems unlikely that the American people would have accepted anything less than complete surrender. In his memoirs President Truman recalled that after his assumption of the Presidential office, when he addressed Congress, and "affirmed the policy of unconditional surrender, the Chamber rose to its feet."[26] One only has to think of the brouhaha that erupted after President George Bush's refusal to press for the conquest of Iraq and the toppling of Saddam Hussein in the *Gulf War* [1990–1991] when just 294 Americans died, to realize that there would have been a tidal wave of protest if Truman had publicly accepted anything less than Japan's unconditional surrender. It had been forced on Germany, why not on Japan?

Leaving aside the issue of politics, there was also the issue of justice. A catalog of war crimes, which had appalled Allied commanders, politicians and civilians alike, meant that popular opinion would not have sat happily with a settlement that would have allowed war criminals to go unpunished. Although less discussed than other aspects of the reasons for sticking to the Casablanca terms of unconditional surrender, the issues of legal restitution were not unimportant.

Within the White House different factions emerged regarding the issue of unconditional surrender. Moderates such as Joseph Grew (formerly Ambassador to Tokyo and now Under Secretary of State) favored some amelioration of the terms and seems to have persuaded Secretary for War Stimson, General Marshall and Secretary of the Navy James Forrestal to his cause. On the other side, however, the so-called 'Abolitionists' (who believed in the abolition of Japan's imperial system), such as Assistant Secretary of State, Dean Acheson, Assistant Secretary of State for Public Affairs, Archibald Macleish, former Secretary of State Cordell Hull, and most importantly the new Secretary of State, James Byrnes were adamant that Japan should surrender unconditionally. In the context of this internal dispute it is interesting to note the conclusions of a US Naval intelligence report that was based on intercepts of Japanese diplomatic traffic by MAGIC and ULTRA. The report, circulated on 27 July 1945, concluded,

> An analysis of Japan's situation, as revealed through Ultra sources, suggests her unwillingness to surrender stems primarily from the failure of her otherwise capable and all-powerful Army leaders to perceive that the defenses they are so assiduously fashioning actually are utterly inadequate. There is nothing in the Japanese mind to prevent capitulation per se, as demonstrated by the advocacy of virtual unconditional surrender by an increasing number of highly placed Japanese abroad. However, until the Japanese leaders realize that an invasion cannot be repelled, there is little likelihood that they will accept any peace terms satisfactory to the Allies.[27]

Whether Japan would have surrendered in the ten weeks before the start of Operation OLYMPIC is an interesting debating point but not one that would have much affected the thinking of President Truman and his closest advisors. If the United States wanted to be sure of Japan's surrender, the dropping of an atom bomb was the easiest way to accomplish the task. The result of the debates internally within the US and at Potsdam was a hard-line stance on the subject of 'unconditional surrender.'

With the utter conviction that they now had the means to impose a crushing and immediate defeat on the Japanese, Truman's administration drew up the terms to be offered to the Japanese. Joseph Grew scripted what came to be known as the Potsdam Declaration. With some confidence the declaration promised the "prompt and utter destruction"[28] of Japan. Most importantly the declaration demanded Japan's unconditional surrender. In an argument that came to dominate thinking about the future of Japan both in Tokyo and Washington, Grew argued that the Declaration should guarantee the future of Japan's Imperial system. Byrnes, however, fought for the issue to be left open.

The Potsdam Declaration, issued on 26 July 1945, called for the elimination "for all time [of] the authority and influence of those who have deceived and misled the people of Japan into embarking on world conquest";[29] the occupation of "points in Japanese territory to be designated by the Allies . . . Japanese sovereignty shall be limited to the islands of *Honshu, Hokkaido, Kyushu* and *Shikoku*, and such minor islands as we determine."[30] Furthermore, repeating the Cairo Declaration [1943] Potsdam called for 'stern justice' for war criminals, not a welcome reminder either to the Emperor or to Japan's military leaders as to the precarious future of their own necks:

> Japanese military forces, after being completely disarmed, shall be permitted to return to their homes with the opportunity to lead peaceful and productive lives . . . [we] do not intend that the Japanese shall be enslaved as a race or destroyed as a nation, but stern justice shall be meted out to all war criminals, including those who have visited cruelties upon our prisoners.[31]

Even the inducements to surrender gave strong notice to Hirohito's government that their freedom of action would be severely constrained when it required:

> The Japanese Government shall remove all obstacles to the revival and strengthening of democratic tendencies among the Japanese people. Freedom of speech, of religion, and of thought, as well as respect for the fundamental human rights shall be established . . . Japan shall be permitted to maintain such industries as will sustain her economy and permit the exaction of just reparations in kind, but not those, which would enable her

to rearm for war. To this end, access to, as distinguished from control of, raw materials shall be permitted. Eventual Japanese participation in world trade relations shall be permitted . . . The occupying forces of the Allies shall be withdrawn from Japan as soon as these objectives have been accomplished and there has been established, in accordance with the freely expressed will of the Japanese people, a peacefully inclined and responsible government.[32]

Finally the Potsdam Declaration reasserted Roosevelt's earlier call for the unconditional surrender that he had made at Casablanca in 1943: "We call upon the government of Japan to proclaim now the unconditional surrender of all Japanese armed forces, and to provide proper and adequate assurances of their good faith in such action. The alternative for Japan is prompt and utter destruction."[33] This last sentence was clearly imbued with the Allies' knowledge of the atom bomb. That very day, USS *Indianapolis* had arrived with Little Boy on *Tinian*. (The Potsdam Declaration was issued on behalf of the Allies who fought Japan—the United States, Great Britain, Australia and China—but did not include the Soviet Union, which did not declare war on Japan until 8 August.)

Prime Minister Suzuki, unable to unify his cabinet, responded to the Potsdam Declaration with *mokusatsu* (to kill with silence or no comment). This was no mere stalling for time. ULTRA intelligence clearly showed that in spite of a 'peace telegram' having been sent to Moscow, the Japanese military, after the Potsdam Declaration, was actively preparing its defenses for the continuation of the war on the Japanese mainland.

Did the Atom Bomb Save Lives? **[Map: 40.6]** Historians such as Alperovitz, the leading exponent of the view that the atom bomb should not have been used, have dismissed the casualty estimates produced in advance of the invasion of *Kyushu* (Operation OLYMPIC), claiming that they were exaggerated.

Yet American casualties had been rising exponentially as the war approached Japanese shores. The tiny island of *Iwo Jima* had cost 6,821 American lives while out of the 154,000 US troops that participated in the *Okinawa* Campaign there were 62,000 casualties of which 12,500 were killed or missing in action. This figure was in addition to the Navy's 9,781 casualties including 4,907 dead. Thus 15 percent of all American casualties in the *Pacific War* took place on *Okinawa*. Together with *Iwo Jima*, the last two actions of the war cost 22 percent of all US war dead in the *Pacific War*, after Japan, in the views of America's admirals and generals, had already been defeated.

Neither were America's material losses insignificant. The United States lost 768 aircraft and 225 tanks. Meanwhile 368 ships (including the British fleet) were damaged. Not surprisingly the State Department and the planners at the Joint Chiefs of Staff took a pessimistic view of any landing on Japan's mainland. It was taken into consideration that Okinawan civilians and militias, still treated as a racial minority by Japanese, had nevertheless fought against the American invaders. US military planners could only assume that the Japanese civilian population would be considerably more motivated to fight to the death. Inevitably, after *Iwo Jima* and *Okinawa*, the use of the atom bomb against Japan became ever more attractive.

In anticipation of the American invasion Japan planned to launch their defensive plan Operation KETSUGO (Decisive). A large part of this plan was to defeat the US Navy before it came ashore: CINCPAC (Commander in Chief, Pacific Area Command) estimated from photographs and ULTRA intelligence that there were 8,010 planes available for defense on the mainland, and commented:

> It is interest[ing] to note that, of this figure [8,010], 40% were combat types, and 45% were trainer-type aircraft which must be considered as available for combat use as suicide planes in the KETSU Operations. MIS, War Department, estimates Japanese production of trainer-type aircraft as at least 550 per month and with the current plane hoarding policy, the number of Japanese trainer planes available for KETSU Operations can be expected to increase unless large numbers can be destroyed on the fields where they are dispersed.[34]

Later estimates by Commander in Chief, Pacific Area Command (CINCPAC) increased this number to 11,190 by 16 July. It is clear that nearly all flights were planned as one-way *kamikaze* attacks. In part this was made necessary by the shortage of fuel, whose allocation, according to intelligence was reduced by 31 percent between June and August. At *Okinawa*, Japan's 2,000 *kamikaze* planes had scored approximately one hit for every nine attacks, but using overwhelming numbers they hoped to improve that ratio on *Kyushu* to 1:6, which would roughly translate into 400 Allied ships being sunk or severely damaged. In addition to airborne *kamikaze*, the Navy had prepared an assortment of naval suicide craft including: 100 *Koryu* Class midget submarines, 250 *Kairyu* Class submarines, 400 *Kaiten* manned torpedoes, and 800 *Shinyo* suicide boats.

Once on the beaches the US Army would have faced a formidable army. By withdrawing troops from China, Manchuria, Korea and northern Japan in the months after March 1945, the Imperial Japanese Army had assembled fourteen Divisions and three Tank Brigades with over 900,000 troops. Large numbers of new divisions were also raised, fifty-one in total, bringing the final number to sixty-five Divisions, although it was estimated that there were only enough guns and ammunition for thirty. On *Kyushu* alone the number of troops swelled from 175,000 at the start of 1945 to 545,000 by August with 75 percent of them concentrated in the south. In aggregate Japan's total number of defenders numbered 2.5 million troops. Added to this number were 28 million Japanese civilians who were armed with everything from muzzle-loaded muskets, bows and arrows, even bamboo spears. Anyone doubting their intention to fight would have been well advised to look at the efforts of the Okinawans. In spite of the intelligence presented by ULTRA, MacArthur was raring to invade, and, with typical duplicity, dismissed the accuracy of the intelligence and doubted Japan's ability to defend *Kyushu* in strength.

Post-war intellectuals may have debated whether or not the atom bomb should have been dropped, and whether US government forecasts of expected casualties were unrealistic or inflated, but there was no mistaking the contemporaneous view of the common man, and, more importantly, the ordinary GI. In France, the news of the atom bombing of Hiroshima was heard by Paul Fussell, a 21-year-old officer, who was due to be part of the invasion force on *Honshu*, the main island of Japan; he recalled, "we cried with relief and joy. We were going to live. We were going to grow up to adulthood after all."[35] Even George Housego, a Royal Artillery gunner from London's East End, who was a prisoner of war in Nagasaki and survived the atom bomb strongly supported the dropping of atom bombs: "I am so pleased they did," recalled Mr. Housego. "We never thought the war would end. The Japanese soldiers were ruthless; they were quite prepared to fight forever and die doing so. Millions more would have died if the government wasn't forced to surrender."[36] Indeed, as historian Alonzo Hamby concluded, "soldiers on the ground often commented, 'The Atomic bomb saved my life.' Such beliefs, reflecting the sentiments of men who lived and breathed a desperate situation that we can scarcely comprehend, were also part of the historical reality of 1945."[37]

Each day that passed after the revelation of the atom bomb brought fresh horrors of war. At midnight on 29 July the American heavy cruiser USS *Indianapolis*, having just delivered nuclear material for Little Boy on *Tinian Island*, was sunk by Japanese submarine *I-58* in a torpedo attack; of the full complement of 1,196 some 300 crew were killed; the remainder survived in the warm waters of the *Philippine Sea*, only to be picked off by sharks. Drowning and madness did for most of the others. After three days and nights in the water only 318 were picked up. This episode was fresh in the minds of Truman's advisers as they planned the dropping of the bomb. As Charles Bohlen, the State Department's Russian expert, succinctly put it, "the spirit of mercy was not throbbing in the breast of any Allied official."[38] Truman could never have faced an electorate with the knowledge that he had failed to use a weapon that could almost instantly have relieved the sufferings of American GIs and their families.

The piecemeal conquest of Japan would have been a daunting task. US military planners did not just plan for the invasion of *Kyushu*. Operation OLYMPIC was a component part of Operation DOWNFALL, the plan to invade and conquer all Japan; the other main component was Operation CORONET, planned for Spring 1946, which was for an amphibious landing on the Kanto Plains south of Tokyo. The US Joint Chiefs of Staff estimated that their thirty divisions of infantry, fleet and air arm would suffer 456,000 casualties (109,000 dead) in the estimated ninety-day OLYPMIC Campaign and 744,000 casualties (158,000 dead) for the CORNET Campaign: an aggregate of 1.2 million casualties (267,000 dead). A study done by William Shockley, later a Nobel Prize winning physicist, for Secretary of War, Henry Stimson, estimated much higher casualties—between 1.7 million to 4 million casualties (400,00–800,000 dead).

It is clear with hindsight that American forebodings were not illusory. Civilians of all ages were being taught to fight with bamboo spears if necessary. Women were instructed how to wrap themselves in explosives before throwing themselves under tanks as human mines. Even after the dropping of the second atom bomb, Fat Man, on Nagasaki on 9 August, at the Imperial Conference that night, Baron Kiichiro Hiranuma argued, "Even if the entire nation is sacrificed to war, we must preserve the *kokutai* [national polity] and the security of the Imperial Household."[39]

Leaving aside the numbers of American soldiers who were spared the assault on Japan's beaches, it was also estimated by the US State Department that upwards of one million Japanese soldiers would lose their lives. Furthermore, Shockley's study for the War Department estimated that Japanese civilian dead would be in the range of 5 million to 10 million. Conceivably Hirohito's government would have surrendered before this eventuality. However, it would be pointless to dwell too long on the 'what ifs' of Operation DOWNFALL; fortunately the dropping of Little Boy prevented any exploration of the US government's scenario of wholesale slaughter. If some of America's senior officers believed that the invasion of Japan would never take place, it may have been in part because the consequences in terms of the loss of life were simply too appalling to imagine.

The Conspiracy Theories: According to his deputy, Lieutenant-General Ira Eaker, Arnold thought, "There were political implications in the decision [to drop the bomb]."[40] As with many momentous events in history, conspiracy theories have followed hard behind. The dropping of the atom bomb is no exception. Leaving aside the patently absurd suggestion that America had to use the atom bomb because of the US$2bn spent on the MANHATTAN Project, the main conspiracy theory sees the atom bomb as a Machiavellian plot led by President Truman and his *éminence grise*, Secretary of State James Byrnes to prevent the Soviet Union from entering the *Pacific War*. Byrnes, who as Roosevelt's Director of the Office of War Mobilization had finally sorted out the management of US economic mobilization for war, had become Truman's Secretary of State on 3 July 1945. **[See Appendix C: Economics of the Pacific War: The 'New Deal' Mobilized]** In the revisionist post-war histories of the dropping of the atom bomb, Alperovitz is the leading exponent of the view that Japanese lives were unnecessarily expended at Hiroshima and Nagasaki as an opening shot in the *Cold War*. It has been argued that the atom bomb was used by Truman as a cynical ploy to prevent Soviet militarily occupation of more territory after Stalin's Potsdam assertion that he would open hostilities on the Asian front in mid-August. Thus British physicist P. M. S. Blackett protested that the dropping of the bomb was "the first major operation of the cold diplomatic war with Russia."[41]

The charge appears largely without foundation even though the MANHATTAN Project scientist Leo Szilard, who met Byrnes on 28 May 1945 reported,

> Byrnes was concerned about Russia's post-war behavior.
> Russian troops had moved into Hungary and Rumania,

and Byrnes thought it would be very difficult to persuade Russia to withdraw her troops from these countries, that Russia might be more manageable if impressed by American military might, and that a bomb might impress Russia.[42]

A similar fragment of evidence is grabbed at by the conspiracy theorists from an entry in the diary of Walter Brown, Byrnes' assistant, who wrote that Byrnes forecast that after the atomic bomb was dropped, "Japan will surrender and Russia will not get in so much on the kill."[43] Reportedly Truman also said, "If this explodes as I think it will, I'll certainly have a hammer on those boys."[44] However, evidence such as this is thin gruel to sustain the argument that the main reasons for using the atom bomb were geopolitical. Perhaps not surprisingly the Soviets saw it otherwise. In his memoirs [1971], Field Marshal George Zhukov, who was at the Potsdam Conference, recorded:

> It was already then [at Potsdam] that the US Government intended to use the atomic weapon for the purpose of achieving its Imperialist goals from a position of strength in "the cold war". This was amply corroborated on August 6 and 8. Without any military need whatsoever, the Americans dropped two atomic bombs on the peaceful and densely populated Japanese cities of Hiroshima and Nagasaki.[45]

However, Zhukov had a different perspective to the lives of his Soviet soldiers than did a democratically elected US President. As historian Antony Beevor records in *Stalingrad* [2007], one of Zhukov's division commanders exhorted his men to fight by walking down his line of troops and emptying his pistol in the face of every tenth soldier—a practice known to the Roman infantry as decimation. More substantively however, no serious policy conversations or memoranda have ever been recovered relating to President Truman that indicate that the decision to drop the bomb was made for any other reason than to end the war and save the lives of Allied troops.

Truman was clearly well aware of the implications that the atom bomb had for international relations but from the records of internal meetings of his administration, it was never a factor in the decision to use the new weapon. Truman and Churchill may have been suspicious of Stalin but he was an ally nonetheless; indeed, America's sponsoring of the United Nations in the spring of 1945, as an organization that would embrace the Soviet Union in a federated global protectorate, was clear evidence of their expectation of a positive post-war relationship with their wartime Allies. This is what Truman fervently wished for. Even America's post-war economic forecasts were predicated on Russia becoming a major trading partner. At the Potsdam Conference, when Stalin announced that he would honor his Yalta pledge to declare war on Japan by mid-August 1945, Truman expressed his extreme pleasure. In his conversations with colleagues and Churchill afterwards there is no evidence to suggest that Truman's expressions of pleasure at Russia's entry into the war were insincere. Indeed American policy under Roosevelt was consistent in that America wanted her Allies to share the burden of the military conquest of Japan and its satrapies in Manchuria and China.

Inconveniently for the conspiracy theorists, the beginning of the *Cold War* was still some way off. The serious first major blow to Truman's hopes of a post-war alliance with the Soviet Union came on 9 February 1946 when Stalin was quoted in a speech in Moscow avowing that communism and capitalism were incompatible and that another war was inevitable. Kennan's famous 'Long Telegram' warning of the Soviets' long-term intentions would arrive on the State Department's desk in February 1946. Meanwhile Churchill's warning of Communist intentions in his 'Iron Curtain' speech in Fulton, Missouri, warmly applauded by Truman, came a month after that, although he had first used the term in a telegram to Truman on 12 May 1945, when he had expressed concern that the movement of US forces out of Europe toward Asia was leaving a power vacuum in Europe: "An iron curtain is drawn down upon their [Soviet] front. We do not know what is going on behind."[46] Nevertheless, Churchill at this point was mainly concerned that they should meet Stalin to finalize European arrangements.

As for Truman, he wrote privately, "To have a reasonable lasting peace the three great powers must be able to trust each other and they must themselves honestly want it. They must also have the confidence of the smaller nations. Russia hasn't the confidence of the smaller nations, nor has Britain. We have. I want peace and I'm willing to fight for it."[47] There seems no reason to doubt Truman's sincerity. Averell Harriman later wrote, "The idea of using the bomb as a form of pressure on the Russians never entered the discussions at Potsdam. That wasn't the President's mood at all. The mood was to treat Stalin as an ally—a difficult ally, admittedly—in the hope that he would behave like one."[48]

Furthermore, Secretary of State James Byrnes and some of Truman's advisers felt that knowledge of the atom bomb would need to be shared with the rest of the world. Dean Acheson, then Under Secretary of State, was instructed to come up with a proposal for the United Nations Atomic Energy Commission of which the Soviets would be a part. Acheson, a Washington hawk with regard to Japan, affirmed, "what we know is not a secret which we can keep to ourselves . . ."[49] Moreover, why, if the atom bomb was used as a means to exert leverage on a then friendly Soviet Union, did Truman never used atomic diplomacy when relations with the Soviets turned hostile in 1946?

Another avenue of criticism in the dropping of the atom bomb has come in the guise of an argument that it was unnecessary because a warning shot could and should have been given. Rear-Admiral Lewis Strauss, assistant to the Secretary of the Navy in 1945 subsequently argued that the use of the atomic bomb "was not necessary to bring the war to a successful conclusion . . ." and he recalled, "I proposed to Secretary Forrestal at that time that the weapon should be demonstrated . . . suggesting that a good place— satisfactory place for such a demonstration would be a large forest of cryptomaria (redwoods) trees not far from Tokyo . . ."[50] However, it is doubtful whether the military would have been happy to show its hand in this way and a demonstration of this kind may have indicated to the Japanese a lack of determination to continue the war on America's part. In the event a committee of the leading MANHATTAN Project scientists led by Oppenheimer decided that mounting a demonstration was not practicable.

There was a more prosaic reason for not giving Japan a warning shot. As Dean Acheson points out in his biographical account of his years at the State Department *Present at the Creation* [1969], "What was not known was that those two bombs comprised our whole stock."[51] In 1945 the production of the uranium-235 isotope was not only expensive but laboriously slow. It would be the end of August before another atom bomb would be available. The US had limited capacity to produce atom bombs before the projected start of the invasion of *Kyushu* (Operation OLYMPIC) on 1 November; as Major-General Groves' assistant Colonel L. E. Seeman told Brigadier-General John Hull, a planner in the *Pacific* theater, "You have a possibility of seven, with a good chance of using them prior to the 31 October."[52] It was perhaps instrumental in persuading Japan to surrender that Japan's Army Minister, General Anami, believed that America had over 100 atom bombs.

Most significant, the belief that America should have demonstrated the power of the atom bomb comes to some extent from the *ex post facto* judgment that the atom bomb was evil and monstrous—a destructive weapon that could be kept in the closet but never used. This was not the view at the time although some of the main scientists of the MANHATTAN Project were already moving in this direction. To Truman the bomb was just another weapon, albeit one of horrifying potency. Also, Hiroshima was a genuine military target as one of the main logistic centers of Japan's military operations, as well as home to some 43,000 soldiers and the headquarters of General Hata's Second General Army.

Even the scientists who had built the bomb believed that its use against Japan was necessary to bring the war to an end. On 11 June, Oppenheimer met with Compton, Fermi and Lawrence in Los Alamos to deliberate on the subject. They reported their conclusions to Washington five days later. Although they were appalled that nuclear fusion would have its first outing as a weapon of mass destruction, with regard to the war they concluded, "We see no acceptable alternative to direct military use."[53] The so-called Target Committee, headed by Secretary of War, Henry Stimson, had already confirmed that the bomb should be used on a live target, but Truman gave significant credit to his scientific committee in directing his decision:

> It was their recommendation that the bomb be used against the enemy as soon as it could be done [and] that it should be used without specific warning . . . against a target that would clearly show its devastating strength. I had realised of course that an atomic bomb explosion would inflict damage and casualties beyond imagination . . . It was their conclusion that no technical demonstration they might propose, such as over a deserted island, would

be likely to bring the war to an end. It had to be used
against an enemy target.[54]

Whatever the attractions of the conspiracy theories surrounding the use of the atom
bomb at Hiroshima and Nagasaki, it is the obvious reason that has the most credence.
Truman's overwhelming duty as President was to the people he served. Any refusal to
use a weapon that was capable of bringing the war to an end, saving whatever number
of American lives, would have been greeted by incomprehension by the vast majority of
American people. While Truman and his advisors were keenly aware of the geopolitical
implications of the atom bomb, the overwhelming reason for using it was summed up
by Secretary of War, Henry Stimson, in *Harper's* magazine in 1947, when he simply
stated, "the purpose [of the atom bomb] was to end the war in victory with the
least possible cost in the lives of the men in the armies which I had helped to raise.
I believe that no man . . . could have failed to use it and afterwards looked his countrymen
in the face."[55]

The Moral Issues of Using the Atom Bomb: Churchill welcomed the news of the
development of the atom bomb as a "miracle of deliverance."[56] He had received news of
the successful Los Alamos detonation on 17 July when the Secretary of War, Henry
Stimson, came to his room and laid a piece of paper in front of him: "Babies are
satisfactorily born . . . It means," he said, "that the experiment in the New Mexican
desert has come off. The atomic bomb is a reality."[57] Churchill's thoughts soon turned to
the American GIs fighting their way across *Okinawa*. He never appears to have harbored
any doubts as to whether the atom bomb should be used.

As for Stalin, to whom Truman gave the news of a devastating new weapon at the
end of Potsdam meetings on 24 July, he sounded relaxed: "good, use it against the
Japanese." His apparent nonchalance was a show. When he returned to his quarters
afterwards, Stalin told Foreign Minister Molotov and Field Marshal George Zhukov
about America's new secret weapon, which he guessed was an atom bomb. Stalin was
furious that his spies had not found out. Molotov responded, "We'll have to talk it over
with Kurchatov and get him to speed things up."[58]

That Truman and his cabinet were aware of the special horrific nature of the weapon,
which they had created, was clear from the outset. On 25 July Truman wrote in his diary,
"We have discovered the most terrible bomb in the history of the world."[59] In truth,
however, there was little doubt that the bomb would be used. It was a 'war-ending'
weapon.

The US military was far from unanimous in whether the atom bomb should be used.
Army Chief of Staff General Marshall gave the opinion that the decision regarding the
bomb was not a military decision and only one that the President could make. MacArthur
regarded the atom bomb as a 'Frankenstein monster,' though in the memoirs he wrote
later in life he did not mention any revulsion. Given his monstrous ego MacArthur
undoubtedly felt robbed of the glorious opportunity to lead the conquest of Japan.

General Eisenhower believed that the dropping of the bomb would prejudice world opinion against the United States. Eisenhower was right with regard to the damage done to America's image over succeeding decades. As the only country ever to have used a nuclear weapon, America cops more than its fair share of opprobrium.

Admiral King "didn't like the bomb or any part of it."[60] Admiral William Leahy, Chairman of the Joint Chiefs of Staff, was even more adamant in his opposition to the use of the atom bomb: "My own feeling was that in being the first to use it, we had adopted an ethical standard common to the barbarians of the Dark Ages. I was not taught to make war in that fashion, and wars cannot be won by destroying women and children."[61]

In America, news of the dropping of an atom bomb on Hiroshima brought euphoria that they had a weapon that would likely bring the war to a rapid end. Mixed with this sentiment were notes of alarm from some newspaper columnists. "Yesterday we clinched victory in the Pacific, but we sowed the whirlwind,"[62] wrote Hanson Baldwin in *The New York Times* on 7 August. While the editor of the Kansas City *Star* observed, "We are dealing with an invention that could overwhelm civilization"[63] and the *St. Louis Post-Dispatch* gloomily observed that science had conceivably "signed the mammalian world's death warrant and deeded an earth in ruin to the ants."[64] These reactions were straws in the wind to the revulsion that would build toward the atom bomb in succeeding decades. In the post-war era, as memories of the horrors of *Iwo Jima* and *Okinawa* faded, the use of the atom bomb started to be questioned. Subsequently the decision would be much criticized. In 1957, the Oxford philosopher Elizabeth Anscombe spoke for many liberal intellectuals when she opposed the award of an honorary degree to Truman on the ground, "For men to choose to kill the innocent as a means to their ends is always murder, and murder is one of the worst of human actions . . . in the bombing of [Japanese cities] it was certainly decided to kill the innocent as a means to an end."[65] By the early 1960s the British, who had supported the use of the atom bomb, were in the throes of an anti-nuclear movement in the form of the Campaign for Nuclear Disarmament (CND) that called for unilateral abandonment of nuclear weapons.

However, there were overwhelming political, military and even humanitarian reasons why the bomb had to be used. By 1945, American leaders were being increasingly apprised of the horrors of war. Stories of Japanese atrocities were circulating throughout America. At sea, *kamikaze* attacks and the hazards of submarines (viz. USS *Indianapolis*) were also taking their toll on Washington's patience.

The degree to which the ultra-nationalists were prepared to continue the fight even after the dropping of the atom bomb shows how impossible it would have been for the Japanese leadership to have surrendered to conventional force of arms. Fortunately, some Japanese leaders had a clearer insight. For Navy Minister Mitsumasa Yonai, the nuclear weapons were a blessing in disguise: "the atomic bombs and the Soviet entry into the war are, in a sense, gifts from God" because they gave Japan an excuse to surrender.[66] The dropping of the atom bomb saved millions of Japanese lives in the slaughter that would inevitably have ensued from a land war with Japan.

From the outset it was apparent that the atom bomb was designed, unavoidably, to kill civilians. In their formative memorandum on the subject, Frisch and Peierls made it clear, "the bomb could probably not be used without killing large numbers of civilians . . ."[67] As has been explained in some detail in Chapter 38, it was a problem that was not at odds with the Geneva and Hague Conventions at the time. In reality the bombing capability of the Boeing B-29 Superfortress, as General LeMay was always keen to emphasize, was also a strategic not a tactical weapon. If used against military targets, as was the case in Hiroshima, both the B-29 and the atom bomb were weapons that would inevitably produce high levels of civilian casualties. It should be noted that the degree to which the atom bomb was seen as a weapon in a different category of morality was largely a post-war phenomenon—in large part led by the gaggle of MANHATTAN Project scientists such as Leo Szilard and James Franck. As historian Bernstein has argued, "avoiding the use of the bomb was never a real concern for the policymakers."[68] For them it was another bomb, albeit remarkably powerful—not a weapon with a unique moral dilemma attached.

As for the issues of whether the atom bombing of a city, however important military, was moral or immoral, the issues have already been covered earlier in this book and need not be repeated. It should be noted that at the time there were no special 'moral' issues regarding the use of the atom bomb compared to more conventional means of bombing cities to destruction. They were both horrific. Differentiation only came later with the rise of movements such as the Campaign for Nuclear Disarmament (CND).

[See Chapter 38: LeMay's B-29 Superfortresses over Japan: Cities in Ashes]

It is interesting to note that internal arguments within Truman's administration were much more concerned with where rather than whether to drop the atom bomb. The philistine Major-General Groves favored the bombing of Kyoto, Japan's ancient capital, as the city most likely to show the atom bomb to best effect. But Henry Stimson, who had tasted the cultural delights of Kyoto on vacation with his wife in 1926, overruled him. In the end Hiroshima was selected as a priority target, along with Kokura, Niigata and Nagasaki, on 31 July. As an important military cantonment and arsenal, Hiroshima was hitherto largely undamaged and, because of its geographical features, would show off the devastating power of the bomb to best effect. Dropping the bomb in daylight hours was considered essential to provide a visual show that would persuade Japan to resign. Oppenheimer recorded in a memorandum on the subject, "we should seek to make a profound psychological impression on as many Japanese as possible."[69]

It is largely in hindsight that people assume that the dropping of the atom bomb was a difficult decision to make. Indeed having studied the ghastly consequences of napalm bombing in the Great Tokyo Air Raid, which killed more people than Hiroshima and Nagasaki combined, it is hard to argue that the atom bomb was any worse. As US *Civil War* Union General William Tecumseh Sherman famously said, "War is Hell," and the grim deaths suffered by many millions of soldiers, sailor and civilians alike during the course of the *Pacific War*, which this book has described in detail, were qualitatively and sometimes quantitatively no different than those at Hiroshima.

Final Negotiations for Japan's Surrender: Truman, whose first speech to Congress as President had endorsed the Roosevelt line on demanding unconditional surrender from Japan, had little room for maneuver on this issue. This fact was clearly understood by those Japanese who stood at a certain distance from Tokyo. Ambassador Sato in Moscow, who was being used as the main conduit for dialogue with the western powers, pleaded with Tokyo, "In the final analysis if our country truly desires to terminate the war, we have no alternative but to accept unconditional surrender or something very close to it."[70] However, Emperor Hirohito's court, and the military cabal that surrounded it, were locked in a fatal embrace that precluded them from facing the stark realities of defeat and its consequences.

The destruction of Hiroshima changed the Japanese government's position far more slowly than was expected in Washington. Perhaps the most remarkable aspect of the dropping of the atom bomb on Hiroshima was that Japan did not surrender immediately. Possibly the leadership had become inured to destruction. Although the incendiary bombing of Tokyo on 8 March had killed over 100,000 people as great fireballs swept through the city, it had still failed to bring Japanese surrender. However, Hiroshima's destruction was the result of a single plane carrying a single bomb. Although communication in the city was paralyzed, it was almost immediately apparent to the Japanese military that a terrible new weapon had been deployed against them. A nuclear device was certainly suspected and Japan's own nuclear scientists were sent to Hiroshima for confirmation. Within days, all of Japan knew of the catastrophe, not only because of fast-spreading war rumors, but also because the Americans themselves informed the Japanese of the Hiroshima events by dropping 6 million leaflets over forty-seven cities. General Marshall was probably not alone in being shocked that the government in Tokyo had not immediately sued for peace.

According to Foreign Minister Togo, after news of Hiroshima reached him, Hirohito made it clear to him that the new weapon made it imperative that the Japanese government should "make such arrangements as will end the war as soon as possible."[71] It is a statement of clarity that does not appear to be supported by Marquis Kido's diaries. It seems highly unlikely at this stage that Hirohito accepted the point-by-point terms of the unconditional surrender demanded by the Potsdam Declaration.

Although the Emperor, locked in his war room bunker, had become resigned to defeat by early 1945, he was reluctant to press his government to surrender, in spite of Prince Konoe, a former prime minister and one of Hirohito's closest confidantes, who was urging peace on almost any terms. To Konoe, surrender was a preferable alternative to the looming threat of communism. However, Hirohito was concerned above all about what the enemy would do to him, suspecting as General Umezu had told him that the Americans would massacre his entire family. In addition to worrying about a bloody end to his own life, Hirohito must have also reckoned it likely that the Japanese Imperial system itself would be abolished. This indeed was probably the major sticking point on which so many American and Japanese lives were lost in the final months of the war.

Some forty-eight hours after the dropping of a bomb on Hiroshima, the Japanese government had still not met formally to discuss the new developments. As last, the hitherto paralyzed Hirohito reacted and informed his Lord Chamberlain, Marquis Kido, that the war must be brought to an end. Yet the supreme council of war, at which Hirohito urged surrender, was not convened until 9 August, some three days after the nuclear devastation of Hiroshima.

In the early hours of 9 August, Japan's woes were compounded by the Soviet invasion of Manchuria. The outlook was bleak. When Prime Minister Sato asked an officer, recently returned from Manchuria, whether the Kwantung Army could repel the Soviets, he responded, "The Kwantung Army is hopeless."[72]

The War Council's dilatory progress is all the more remarkable in light of its knowledge of the power of atomic devices from their own scientists' work. Japan's path toward building an atom bomb was more advanced than is often supposed. Blueprints recently found at Kyoto University's Radioisotope Research Laboratory show that a workable atom bomb design had been developed. Another blueprint found at *Tokyo Keiki Inc.*, revealed the blueprint of a design for a uranium centrifuge that was due to be completed on 19 August 1945. It seems barely worth asking whether Hirohito's government would have used an atom bomb had it become available in time. The answer is obvious. It is therefore clear that by the 9 August the War Council was fully apprised of the impending nuclear holocaust.

In spite of the impending nuclear and Manchuria disasters most of the military members of the cabinet led by General Korechika Anami, Minister of War, believed that better terms could be negotiated. To add to the surreal drama of these discussions, it should be remembered that a plutonium implosion bomb, Fat Man, had been dropped on Nagasaki that morning. The original target had been Kokura but the B-29 had circled for 50 minutes in the hope that mist and haze would clear before moving on to Nagasaki. Here the main target was the Mitsubishi shipyard but Fat Man fell more than a mile off target exploding above the Urakami Catholic Cathedral, the largest center of Christianity in Japan. More than half of Nagasaki's 14,000 Catholics died in the explosion—as did a number of Dutch prisoners of war, though a US *Navajo* soldier from New Mexico survived. British POWs were spared by the fact that they were working underground in the mines. The city's steep hills protected much of the city from the deadly nuclear blast, which was as much as 30 percent more powerful than the one that had obliterated Hiroshima. Nevertheless, US Strategic Bombing Survey (USSBS) later calculated that 35,000 were killed, with more dying later from radiation sickness. In total the USSBS estimated that the two atom bombs eventually killed 125,000 Japanese people—though figures as high as 200,000 have been claimed by other sources.

Still the cabinet dithered. The 'doves' led by Prime Minister Baron Kantaro Suzuki, the 77-year-old admiral who had been appointed prime minister after the fall of *Okinawa*, urged acceptance of the Potsdam Declaration. However, even he insisted on the condition that the Emperor had to be preserved. Foreign Minister Togo and the 65-year-old Navy Minister, Admiral Mitsumasa Yonai, supported him. Against them were the 'hawks' including Army Minister, General Korechika Anami, Chief of the Army General Staff, General Yoshijiro Umezu and Chief of the Navy General Staff Admiral Soemu

Toyoda. They insisted that the Potsdam Declaration would only be acceptable if, in addition to the preservation of the Chrysanthemum Throne, Japan was given the right to self-disarmament, control of war-crimes trials and above all no Allied occupation.

Alternatively Anami suggested, "Would it not be wondrous for the whole nation to be destroyed like a beautiful flower?"[73] The meeting dragged on into the evening, with Hirohito appearing in person to persuade a divided council to accept the Potsdam Declaration.

In the aftermath of the war and leading up to the Tokyo War Crimes Trials, Hirohito's position on surrender was largely obscured, though his concern for his own position is known. His closest adviser, Prince Konoe, thought that a qualified acceptance of the Potsdam Declaration, with a list of conditions, would be a disaster, deducing correctly that the Allies would have viewed it as the same as a refusal to surrender. Nevertheless, from Marquis Kido's diaries, it seems likely that by late afternoon on 9 August, Hirohito had instructed Kido that he supported the one condition stance of the 'doves'—in other words Japan's retention of the Chrysanthemum Throne. At ten minutes to midnight, an emergency Imperial Conference was called at which Prime Minister Suzuki presented the four conditions to the acceptance of the Potsdam Declaration as being the agreement of the Supreme Council. Each councillor argued his position while the meeting was summed up by Baron Hiranuma, President of the Privy Council, who appeared to lean toward the 'doves' camp. At this point Hirohito intervened and in a decisive conclusion sided with the 'doves': "I swallow my own tears and give my sanction to the proposal to accept the Allied proclamation on the basis outlined by the Foreign Minister"[74]—in other words Hirohito accepted the Potsdam Declaration with the one condition being the preservation of his throne.

The next morning, 10 August, Hirohito's decision to surrender profoundly shocked the Imperial Army's General Staff when it was made known. Meanwhile the Allies launched further bombing raids on Tokyo's main arsenal and on targets on *Kyushu* including Kumamoto City. In the afternoon Hirohito met seven former prime ministers, including General Tojo. Both he and General Koiso made clear their opposition to the acceptance of surrender. A rear-guard action within the Army to thwart surrender continued. General Anami released a fighting statement: "Even though we may have to eat grass, swallow dirt, and lie in the fields, we shall fight on to the bitter end, ever firm in our faith that we shall find life in death."[75] Meanwhile, at court the Allied response to Japan's conditional acceptance of the Potsdam Declaration was anxiously awaited.

Eventually, a cable was transmitted to the Japanese embassies in neutral Bern and Stockholm to the effect that the Potsdam ultimatum would be accepted, but with the proviso, "the said declaration does not compromise any demand, which prejudices the prerogatives of his majesty as a Sovereign ruler."[76] In the White House, a meeting was convened by Roosevelt to discuss the Japanese response. He was joined by Secretary of State Byrnes, Chairman of the Joint Chiefs of Staff Leahy, Secretary of War Stimson and Secretary of the Navy Forrestal.

In London Field Marshal Alanbrooke noted in his diary on 10 August:

> Just before lunch BBC intercepts of Japanese peace offers were received in the shape of an acceptance of the Potsdam offer. There was however one rather obscure clause concerning the prerogatives of the Emperor being retained. PM [Attlee] convened a Cabinet for 3 p.m. when the message was examined. Stafford Cripps and Jowitt [former Attorney-General] expressed their legal opinions. Cabinet was unanimous that Americans must assume the major share, but that if they were of the opinion that the clause affecting the Emperor was acceptable, we should agree.[77]

Everywhere opinion was finely divided. In the House of Commons the newly elected member of parliament, James Callaghan, later to become British Prime Minister, devoted his maiden speech to argue the need to "get rid of him [Hirohito]."[78] Notwithstanding British hostility toward the Emperor, Prime Minister Clement Attlee fell into line behind Stimson and Grew.

In Washington, Secretary of War Stimson wanted to accept the Japanese offer, reiterating his established view that Hirohito be retained as Emperor. Secretary of State Byrnes argued vehemently against this condition. After the arguments were made, Truman sided with Stimson on the grounds that the institutions of the Imperial Household could be molded as America saw fit. However, in drafting a reply Byrnes left the issue of retention of the Emperor deliberately vague, merely referring to a future government of Japan being established by "the freely expressed will of the Japanese people."[79] Byrnes' reply concluded, "The armed forces of the Allied powers will remain in Japan until the purposes set forth in the Potsdam Declaration are achieved."[80] In light of Japan's conditional surrender, Truman gave orders to halt the atomic bombing; according to his Secretary of Commerce, Henry Wallace, the president was appalled at the thought of killing another 100,000 at a stroke, particularly "all those kids."[81] Conventional bombing was also halted, at least temporarily. LeMay's 11 August directives regarding a new campaign to carry out "the progressive destruction and dislocation of Japan's military, industrial and economic systems," were put on ice.[82] Yet Washington remained nervous that the Japanese armed forces might not accept surrender. MAGIC intercepts seemed to indicate that acceptance was in doubt. Indeed it was.

Byrnes's message was received in Tokyo after midnight on 12 August. Hirohito now accepted surrender though the military remained horrified at the threat to Japan's *kokutai* (national polity) implicit in the American response. Accordingly the War Council remained deadlocked throughout 13 August. In Tokyo, novelist Yukio Mishima noted that in expectation of surrender, "everywhere there was an air of cheerful excitement."[83] In Washington, the silence of the Japanese government, turned the mood to one of irritation. "The days of negotiation with a prostrate and despised enemy strained public patience," reported the Earl of Halifax, the British Ambassador in Washington.[84] Even

Stimson was tired of the Japanese prevarication and his thoughts turned to the possibility of getting the next atom bomb delivered to a Japanese target by 17 August.

In Tokyo, on the morning of 13 August, Byrnes' reply had been treated with outrage by the Japanese Army, particularly by middle-ranking officers in Tokyo. Generals Anami and Umezu urged outright rejection. Surprisingly perhaps, Prime Minister Suzuki joined the 'hawks' in calling for rejection of America's reply and argued for a continuation of war. Foreign Minister Togo was furious with what he regarded as Suzuki's betrayal of the 'dove' cause. Because of the Army's veto over the appointment of a war minister, Anami could have collapsed Suzuki's cabinet by resigning but he refrained from doing so. Indeed together Anami and Umezu could have continued the war, though it would have meant defying the Emperor—something that they were ultimately not prepared to do. Meetings continued into the evening without resolution. At 9 p.m. Vice-Chief of Naval General Staff Admiral Takijiro Onishi burst into yet another conference between Togo, Umezu and Anami. Onishi, the main architect of the *kamikaze* campaign, told them "Let us formulate a plan for certain victory, obtain the Emperor's sanction, and throw ourselves into bringing the plan to realization. If we are prepared to sacrifice 20,000,000 Japanese lives in a special attack [kamikaze] effort, victory will be ours."[85]

With no reply forthcoming, on 14 August Truman authorized conventional bombing to continue. Mass B-29 attacks hit targets in Tokoyama, Iwakuni, Osaka, Kumagaya, and Isekai. Overnight Tokyo, which was spared bombs, was deluged with leaflets instead; they contained the text of Hirohito's message to Washington on 10 August and Secretary of State Byrnes' reply. In Tokyo the Emperor met his senior military and naval commanders at 10.20 a.m. Present was General Shinroku Hata, who had survived the atom bomb in Hiroshima, and had just arrived in Tokyo that morning. Apart from giving personal testament regarding the power of the atom bomb, Hata stated unequivocally that he had no hope of being able to defeat the expected US invasion of *Kyushu*. In a blow to the 'hawks', he supported the Emperor's decision to surrender. Shortly thereafter Hirohito met the first Imperial Conference since 9 August. Hirohito's orders were made clear:

> I have surveyed the conditions prevailing in Japan and in the world at large, and it is my belief that a continuation of the war promises nothing but additional destruction. I have studied the terms of the Allied reply and have concluded that they constitute a virtually complete acknowledgment of the position we maintained in the note dispatched several days ago. I consider the [US] reply to be acceptable. In order that the people may know my decision, I request you to prepare at once an imperial rescript so that I may broadcast to the nation. Finally, I call upon each of you to exert himself to the utmost so that we may meet the trying days which lie ahead.[86]

Washington heard of the Japanese government's acceptance of the surrender terms at 2.49 a.m. on August 14 from a news report broadcast by *Domei Tsushin*, the official Japanese government news agency.

Hirohito's Radio Announcement: After a day of wrangling over the nature of the script, Hirohito recorded a message to be delivered by radio; it would be the first time that an Emperor had ever been heard by the Japanese people. The Emperor's surrender recording was broadcast to the nation at 12.00 noon on 15 August, Japan standard time. Formal signing of the Instrument of Surrender did not take place until 2 September on board USS *Missouri*, the last battleship ever built by the United States. General MacArthur took the surrender signed by Mamoru Shigemitsu, Minister of Greater East Asia, on behalf of Japan's civilian government and General Yoshijiro Umezu, Chief of the Imperial Japanese Army General Staff, for the military. The surrender was enhanced by the USS *Missouri*'s flying the same flag that was flown on Commodore Perry's USS *Powhatan* on his first expedition to Japan in 1853. It was a symbol that showed that the United States had won an almost century-long struggle for dominance in the *Pacific*.

In Tokyo, on 15 August the drama continued to the last. The senior Army officers including Field Marshals Sugiyama and Hata, as well as Anami, Umezu and Kawabe pledged to support the Emperor's decision. However, when Anami later met a group of coup plotters, he remained ambivalent. In the early hours of 15 August, a group of fanatical younger officers including Major Kenji Hatanaka along with Lieutenant-Colonels Masataka Ida and Jiro Shiizaki went to meet Lieutenant-General Takeshi Mori, commander of the 1st Imperial Guards Division. When Mori refused to join the plotters, Major Kenji Hatanaka drew his pistol and shot him dead. The plotters used Mori's seal on a false set of orders in order to take control of the Palace and hijack the Emperor's recording. They failed to find it and hearing of the plot, General Shizuichi Tanaka, who had commanded the Fourteenth Army in the Philippines at the start of the war, rushed to the Palace with units of the Eastern District Army and restored control.

The plotters escaped and once more approached General Anami, who they found determined to commit suicide. After some discussion and drinking of *sake*, General Anami wrote a *tanka* (short poem) on a scroll and, facing the Imperial Palace, committed *seppuku* (ritual suicide by disembowelment). On another scroll he wrote his final words including the statement, "Believing firmly that our sacred land shall never perish, I— with my death—humbly apologise to the Emperor for the great crime"[87] The nature of 'the great crime' was not explained. Of the plotters, Hatanaka and Shiizaki, along with other officers, committed suicide in the grounds in front of the Imperial Palace. Lieutenant-Colonel Ida survived and was court-martialed, but later became head of general affairs at Dentsu, Japan's largest advertising agency.

Finally the Emperor's broadcast was heard at noon on 15 August:

> After pondering deeply the general trends of the world,
> and the actual conditions obtaining to our Empire today,

we have decided to effect a settlement of the present situation by resorting to an extraordinary measure. We have ordered our government to communicate to the governments of the United States, Great Britain, China and the Soviet Union that our Empire accepts the provisions of their Joint Declaration . . . Despite the best that has been done by everyone . . . the war situation has developed not necessarily to Japan's advantage, while the general trends of the world have turned against her interest . . . The Enemy has begun to employ a new and most cruel bomb, the power of which to do damage is indeed incalculable, taking the toll of many innocent lives. Should we continue to fight, it would result in an ultimate collapse and obliteration of the Japanese nation, but it also would lead to the total extinction of human civilization.[88]

In spite of the curmudgeonly acceptance of defeat and the peculiarities of the Emperor's court language, the Japanese, huddled in groups over their radios in every village and town in Japan, understood the enormity of the message. Some wept, others collapsed to the ground, but movie director Akira Kurosawa noted that in the streets of Tokyo, "The people in the shopping streets were bustling about with cheerful faces as if preparing for a festival the next day."[89] Japan's military adventures were ended; peacetime life was about to resume.

*   *   *

As the destruction of Hiroshima and Nagasaki, as well as the Soviet invasion of Japan's northern empire, brought the *Pacific War* to an end, the world was unaware that a new clash of empires in Asia was about to begin. Stalin's invasion of Manchuria was an augury of his intent to dominate Asia. This was a foreign policy that had its roots in the expansionism of Tsar Nicholas II. But, after the United States had fought at great cost to resist Japan's autarkic hegemony in Asia, it was logical that President Harry Truman would seek to combat similar Soviet encroachment, particularly after the fall of China to communism in 1949—the very country for which America had gone to war in the *Pacific*. The result was that the *Pacific War*'s ending did not produce a clear settlement in an Asia facing up to a post-colonial future. Instead it led to a long drawn-out contest for control. The *Cold War* that ensued was anything but cold in Asia. The post-*Pacific War* settlement, covering a 60-year period, is explained in depth in Francis Pike's *Empires at War, A Short History of Modern Asia since World War II* [IB Tauris, 2010].

Index